InStep
STUDENT BIBLE

NEW TESTAMENT EDITION

InStep is designed to challenge and encourage you to seek a better understanding of yourself, how you relate to others and how to apply the truths of scripture to your life. It offers a guide that will connect you with discovering the real Source for achieving a successful and significant life. As you grow, may you truly experience God's richest blessings in all ways.

Dr. Ron L. Braund

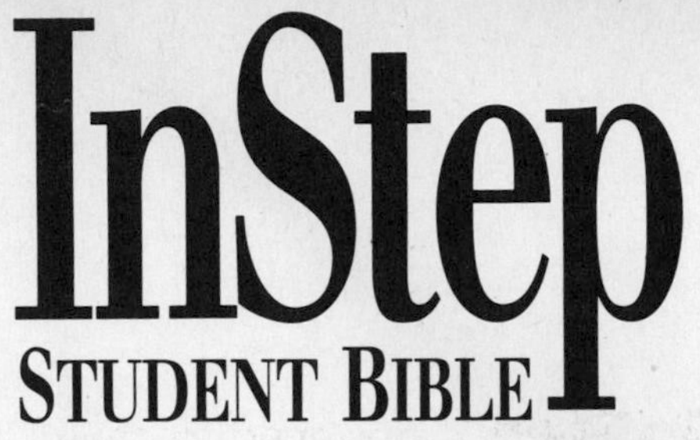

NEW TESTAMENT EDITION

Contemporary English Version

THOMAS NELSON PUBLISHERS
Nashville

InStep: Student Bible, New Testament Edition

Printed in the United States of America

1 2 3 4 5 6 7 8 9 10 11 12 13 14 15 16 17 18 19 20 — 95 94 93 92

About the Author

Dr. Ron L. Braund is a licensed marriage and family therapist from Atlanta, Georgia, who specializes in working with couples and adolescents. He is the president and founder of AlphaCare Therapy Services, Inc., which is a network of outpatient counseling and inpatient treatment centers serving churches and communities in the Southeast. Dr. Braund is married, and he and his wife, Ginger, have two children, Rich and Adam.

Acknowledgments

I want to express my deepest appreciation for those who had a personal commitment to *InStep*'s publication. Their encouragement and expertise helped to bring it to pass. I am particularly indebted to Dr. Ralph Hunt and Denise Wright.

Dr. Hunt provided a wealth of ideas and served as a writer for the meditations and profiles. He has the talent to take a blank page and make it come alive with character.

Denise Wright served as a writer for the meditations. She is a youth worker, mother, and wife who has a heart for God and the ability to tell stories about life in a way that we can all identify with.

THE TWELVE STEPS OF ALCOHOLICS ANONYMOUS*

1. We admitted we were powerless over alcohol—that our lives had become unmanageable.
2. Came to believe that a Power greater than ourselves could restore us to sanity.
3. Made a decision to turn our will and our lives over to the care of God *as we understood* Him.
4. Made a searching and fearless moral inventory of ourselves.
5. Admitted to God, to ourselves, and to another human being the exact nature of our wrongs.
6. Were entirely ready to have God remove all these defects of character.
7. Humbly asked Him to remove our shortcomings.
8. Made a list of all persons we had harmed, and became willing to make amends to them all.
9. Made direct amends to such people wherever possible, except when to do so would injure them or others.
10. Continued to take personal inventory and when we were wrong promptly admitted it.
11. Sought through prayer and meditation to improve our conscious contact with God *as we understood* Him, praying only for knowledge of His will for us and the power to carry that out.
12. Having had a spiritual awakening as the result of these steps, we tried to carry this message to alcoholics, and to practice these principles in all our affairs.

CONTENTS

Welcome to InStep

When we accept Jesus Christ, something new and wonderful is born in our lives. The Holy Spirit of God moves in and begins a transformation that never really ends. Personal wants and desires take new directions. Attitudes get a serious overhaul. Takers become givers, and dirty hearts are scrubbed clean. Getting to know the Bible—God's love letter to Christians—and spending time with other people who are in a right relationship with God become important. We begin to think and live responsibly, and basically, our lives stay on track.

InStep is designed to help you understand the Word of God and discover its power to change thinking. It provides inspiration and motivation to positive action. This Bible enhances three different perspectives to the central theme of following Jesus Christ. It begins with using a Twelve-Step guide (called "Look Inside") for developing a consistent walk as a Christian. It continues with "Look Ahead"—character-building insights essential for developing an attitude that honors God and leads to serving others. Finally, "Look Back" profiles twelve men and women of the Bible who not only had a positive impact on their own world, but who provide strong role models for us too.

This Bible can be very useful in a group setting: you may want to introduce it to your Sunday School or youth group. It will also work within a recovery group that offers some individual accountability.

We think you'll find *InStep*'s devotionals inviting—really a different way to look at starting a "quiet time." The Scriptures are great too: the Contemporary English Version is one of the most readable, easy-to-understand Bible translations ever. And the book introductions, notes at the bottoms of the pages, and helpful subject index and word list give you even more insight into what God's Word says.

LOOK INSIDE

What Are the Twelve Steps, and How Can They Help Me?

Have you ever heard of Twelve-Step "recovery" programs? Today there are lots of them—most of them similar to a program made popular by Alcoholics Anonymous. Now there are recovery groups for chemically dependent people, for those who have food addictions, for those in codependent relationships: you name the problem, and there is probably a support group meeting somewhere.

But what you may not know about the Twelve-Step process is that it traces its roots to a European Christian movement, known as the Oxford

Group. The people who were part of that group weren't necessarily recovering from anything, although some of them were caught in unhealthy lifestyles. They originally established a series of steps through which they sought to stay healthy and to grow spiritually. Members of the group knew that they ran the risk of going the other way of growing cold and indifferent.

InStep has at its heart a special student version of the Twelve Steps. The steps are revised for this generation and emphasize the benefits of establishing a better understanding of yourself and developing a consistent walk with Christ and others. Here are the Twelve Steps as they appear in *InStep*:

1. I admit I cannot be successful on my own . . . I need help, daily.
2. I believe God is there to help me.
3. I will put my life in God's hands and trust Jesus Christ to lead me.
4. I will take a hard look at myself, the way I live and my moral standards.
5. I will admit to God, to myself, and to someone I trust what I do wrong.
6. I want God to take control of my life and make me a complete person.
7. I need God to remove my shortcomings.
8. I will make a list of those I wrong and be willing to make things right.
9. I will make things right with people I wrong, except when to do so would hurt them or others.
10. I need to continue looking inside—admitting when I am wrong.
11. I will pray to God on a regular basis, asking him to direct me and give me the power to live for him.
12. Because God is changing my life through following these steps, I will tell others about them and daily practice what I have learned.

You don't have to be in a program of recovery for physical or emotional problems to get a lot out of the Twelve-Step process. You can be in a course of discovery too—discovering how to live more effectively. But for those of you who *have* found life to be "out of balance" because of substance abuse or some other addiction, *InStep*'s "Look Inside" meditations will offer daily help in getting back on track.

LOOK AHEAD

Becoming the Best I Can Be

Have you thought much about your future—what you are eventually going to be in life? A doctor? A lawyer? A teacher? A politician? A minister? A professional athlete? It's natural to dream about the future. Because you are important to God, because he loves you, he has an interest in your dreams. But for dreams to become reality they need to take the shape of goals and objectives. In the Christian life, no matter what you finally choose to *do*, you need to consider what you are to *be*. This has to do with character—that measurement of who you are when nobody is looking. Character is who you are on the inside, beneath the hair and skin. It is more than just what you look like, how you talk, if you are short or tall, black or white, fat or skinny. Character is what really matters.

How do you build Christian character or reputation? Spending time with and learning from other Christians is one way. And getting to know God better through the Bible and prayer is very important to growing the best you possible. The "Look Ahead" meditations in *InStep* focus on twelve character qualities—each one related to one of the Twelve Steps:

Step 1—**Honesty**
Admitting the truth about myself to myself

Step 2—**Loyalty**
Because God is there for me, I will be there for others.

Step 3—**Courage**
Facing challenges with trust in God and in myself

Step 4—**Purity**
Obeying God in sexual matters

Step 5—**Truthfulness**
Winning trust by admitting my mistakes

Step 6—**Joyfulness**
Enjoying the inward results of right living

Step 7—**Humility**
Becoming more aware of God's greatness and my need for him

Step 8—**Determination**
Being willing to make things right at all costs

Step 9—**Compassion**
Considering how our actions may create reactions in others

Step 10—**Patience**
Learning how to endure and growing in the process

Step 11—**Endurance**
Developing inward strength through daily dependence on God

Step 12—**Gratefulness**
Giving God the credit that is due him

Developing these qualities will make you strong for facing hard times and temptations.

That doesn't mean that the world, the flesh, or the devil won't win a battle once in awhile. They will and do. A trusted friend may introduce you to something or someone that damages you. When that happens, you need to walk the Twelve Steps to effective living once again and get back on the right path.

LOOK BACK

People Just Like Me

Sometimes it's hard to imagine that the people we read about in the Bible actually lived. They combed their hair, took real baths, even had bad breath. For the most part, they were very ordinary people. They had mothers and fathers, and they fought with their brothers and sisters about clothes, who got to sit where, and who got to go first. They had hopes and dreams and made mistakes along the way to accomplishing them. Yet many of them stand out because they were willing to learn how to trust God and be used to make an impact on others. Because of what they did, we can classify them as role models to be followed!

Welcome to *InStep*

What happened to those people we read about in the Bible to cause them to do extraordinary things? On close examination we find a few things that they all had in common. First, they all came to believe that they weren't the beginning and the end of the universe. They knew that there was a God and that each was accountable to him. Second, they were people with character that caused them to stand firm when faced with a challenge. Third, they trusted God when all the odds were against them. That is a part of belief—to trust in and to rely upon God to come through when he says he will.

"**L**ook Back" profiles twelve men and women of the Bible. You will read about how each of them made a personal impact on their world. It will be fun, and hopefully, in the process you will discover that God can use a seemingly ordinary person like you to accomplish extraordinary things for him.

Now read on for a quick introduction to each one of the Twelve Steps of I*nStep*.

Step 1

I admit I cannot be successful on my own . . . I need help, daily.

It is difficult to take an honest look at ourselves. But when we get to the place where we admit we cannot be successful on our own, we get in step and on track. Then we begin to realize that we can make a difference. God wants to use us, but it all begins with owning up to the fact that we need help. See if you recognize yourself or someone you know in the story below.

"I got to where I couldn't stand myself anymore. The games I had been playing between who I really was and who everyone else thought I was got to be more than I could handle. They weren't really the kind of friends I wanted. They were the only ones I could get. They didn't care what I looked like, or if I got straight A's or if I was popular. They just wanted to have a good time. That meant taking chances. Fake I.D.'s, drinking, some drugs, casual sex—whatever it took to fit in. At the time, the high was worth it.

Being successful on our own is a hard thing to do in a generation that tells us, "If you want it, take it!" "Be in control of your life."

It got rough at home though. My parents would ride me about where I was going, what I was doing, and who I was with. Lying was the only way to keep them off track and off my back. At first I felt guilty about it, but the more I lied the easier it got. It seemed to satisfy them, and I got to do what I wanted to. Everyone seemed happy. Everyone but me.

I guess I was kind of relieved when I got caught drinking and driving. Going to those DUI classes for a few nights was better than going to the cemetery permanently. It got my parents' attention anyway. They saw the real me for the first time. And they didn't like what they saw any more than I did, but at least we were looking at the same person. The real me. Someone who needs help."

STEP 1 LOOK INSIDE

Being successful on our own is a hard thing to do in a generation that tells us, "If you want it, take it!" "Be in control of your life." That kind of message, along with the false high from addictive agents like alcohol, drugs, and phony relationships, can make us think we are in control, that we can handle it. But it is really a vicious downward cycle that takes us round and round until we bottom out.

In the story above, the person felt the pain of being rejected. So he looked for relief in other hurting people, in alcohol, sex, fast living. That brought about conflict with parents which caused more pain. Lying and leading a double life became second nature. Until he hit bottom.

HITTING BOTTOM

When we or someone we know "hits bottom," we have the chance to get back in step with God and others. Strange how it works. To get control of life, we have to give up control. Admitting that we can't make it on our own is the first step of the journey to a successful life.

See the chart at the end of this introduction for more reading on this Step.

HONESTY—Admitting the truth about myself to myself

If we are to become people who have good reputations, Step 1 requires that we admit the truth about ourselves to ourselves. This involves guarding against playing games and trying to con ourselves and those around us into thinking that we are what we are not: it's time to get honest. In the chart below you will find the locations of three readings related to this theme.

THOMAS—an honest man who admitted that he did not have all the answers

Step 1 in the discovery process deals with the need to be honest about where we are and who we are. It is important to realize that we are not alone in our struggles, our fears, and our doubts. To help bring this fact into focus, let's begin by taking a look back at Thomas—a man who was filled with questions as he faced an uncertain future. Thomas is a role model for us—especially as we struggle to be honest with ourselves and with others. To learn more about Thomas, see John 20.24–29 and its related reading.

Where to Find

The first page number given tells you where to find a Bible reference related to this step. If a second page number is given, it refers to the location of an InStep meditation.

SCRIPTURE	STEP	STEP LOOK INSIDE	STEP LOOK AHEAD	STEP LOOK BACK	PAGE(S)
MATTHEW 8.23–25	•	•			18, **19**
MARK 4.35–41	•				80
LUKE 15.17	•	•			158, **159**
JOHN 20.24–29	•			•	235, **236**
ROMANS 3.23	•				303
ROMANS 7.18–20	•				310
ROMANS 8.5–8	•	•			311, **312**
1 CORINTHIANS 8.2	•				339
2 CORINTHIANS 3.5, 6	•				356
2 CORINTHIANS 12.8–10	•	•			368, **369**
GALATIANS 4.8	•				377
EPHESIANS 2.1–3	•				386
JAMES 4.6	•		•		477, 478
PSALM 5.1–3	•				555
PSALM 6.4–7	•				557
PSALM 14.1–3	•				562
PSALM 18.6	•				566
PSALM 18.27	•				568
PSALM 22.1, 2	•				571
PSALM 25.16–18	•				574
PSALM 28.1, 2	•				576
PSALM 31.9, 10	•				578
PSALM 39.12, 13	•				589
PSALM 40.12, 13	•				589
PSALM 49.5–9	•				596
PSALM 53.1, 2	•				599
PSALM 55.1–5	•				600
PSALM 62.3, 4	•				605
PSALM 69.1–3	•				611
PSALM 77.1–3	•				619
PSALM 88.1–9	•		•		629, **631**
PSALM 102.1–7	•				643
PSALM 109.22–24	•				652
PROVERBS 6.16–19	•				691
PROVERBS 9.10, 11	•				695
PROVERBS 14.12	•				701
PROVERBS 17.25	•				708
PROVERBS 18.12	•		•		710, **711**
PROVERBS 19.21–23	•				712
PROVERBS 23.19–21	•				717
PROVERBS 26.12	•				721
PROVERBS 28.26	•	•			724, **725**
PROVERBS 29.1	•				724
PROVERBS 29.23	•				726

Step 2

I believe God is there to help me.

I had always taken care of things myself. If I had a problem, I handled it. If there was something in my way, I went over it, around it, and, if necessary, through it to reach my goal. But after all the stuff I had been through at the beginning of my senior year, I hit bottom. I didn't have a single friend I could trust—not one.

"That is when I decided to give God a try.

"I had grown up around the church. My parents were faithful members, and I went to church with them until I got my license. Then I made excuses—said I would meet them there, but would go out to breakfast with some other kids I knew. Our church was big enough that nobody really caught on to what I was doing.

STEP LOOK INSIDE 2

When friends and even family members give up on us, God never does.

"Well, when I wound up feeling so down, I started going to this Sunday night Bible study I'd heard about. I was surprised to see some of my old friends there. The lady who taught the study was great. She was funny, and she dressed cool, too! We were studying the book of John. Did you know that it was written by one of Jesus' closest followers? I didn't. We came to the tenth chapter, and we were learning about the character of Jesus—what he was really like. She said that Jesus was the opposite of a thief—that he wanted to give instead of take. She said that he was a good shepherd—not an uncaring hired hand. She explained that we could be a part of God's family—that he would adopt us and give us everything he had.

"Strange how you get things so twisted. I had always thought that God was like a 'spy in the sky' who was just waiting for the best time to zap me. But what I am learning is that he seems to be someone who cares a lot about the things and the people he has made. My teacher says that God is always ready to help. When friends and even family members give up on us, God never does. He is there to meet us and to help us take the next step. I still have some questions about God, but that is what the Bible is for. I'm going to spend more time reading about him—and I've heard, too, that I'm off to a good start with the book of John!"

In Step 1 we admit that we can't be successful on our own. If we are to continue our personal growth, the next step is to find a new source of strength or power to take charge and guide us. See the chart at the end of this introduction for more reading on this Step.

LOYALTY—Because God is there for me, I will be there for others.

Step 2 focuses on loyalty—God's to us and, looking ahead, ours to him and to others. In the chart below you will find the locations of three readings related to this theme.

MOSES—a man who listened to, was led by, and had lasting loyalty to God

Many men and women of the Bible exhibited loyalty to God and others. Moses is an outstanding example of a man who allowed his life to be touched by God and who remained loyal to God in all circumstances of life. To learn more about Moses, see Acts 7.20–39 and its related reading.

Where to Find

The first page number given tells you where to find a Bible reference related to this step. If a second page number is given, it refers to the location of an InStep meditation.

SCRIPTURE	STEP 2	STEP 2 LOOK INSIDE	STEP 2 LOOK AHEAD	STEP 2 LOOK BACK	PAGE(S)
MATTHEW 14.22–33	•	•			35, **36**
MATTHEW 17.20, 21	•				41
MARK 9.23, 24	•	•			90, **91**
LUKE 13.10–13	•				153
JOHN 3.16, 17	•	•			191, **192**
JOHN 7.37–39	•				203
JOHN 10.7–16	•				210
JOHN 12.44–46	•				217
JOHN 15.12–14	•		•		223, **224**
JOHN 19.16–30	•				231
ACTS 7.20–39	•			•	253, **254**
ROMANS 1.16, 17	•				300
ROMANS 8.37–49	•				314
EPHESIANS 3.16–19	•				388
HEBREWS 2.14–18	•				452
PSALM 4.1	•				553
PSALM 9.7–10	•				559
PSALM 10.17	•		•		560, **561**
PSALM 13.3, 4	•				562
PSALM 17.6–8	•				565
PSALM 18.1, 2	•	•			566, 567
PSALM 20.1–3	•				570
PSALM 23.1–6	•				572
PSALM 34.18–22	•	•			581, **584**
PSALM 36.5–8	•				585
PSALM 46.1–3	•				594
PSALM 55.16, 17	•				601
PSALM 56.8	•				601
PSALM 68.19, 20	•				610
PSALM 71.1–3	•				614
PSALM 77.11–15	•				620
PSALM 79.8, 9	•				623
PSALM 111.7–9	•				653
PSALM 116.1–4	•				655
PSALM 121.1–8	•				664
PSALM 139.1–16	•				674
PSALM 142.1–7	•				677
PSALM 146.5–9	•				679
PROVERBS 17.17	•		•		708, **709**

Step 3

I will put my life in God's hands and trust Jesus Christ to lead me.

Step 2 brings us to the place of really believing God is there to help and that he wants us to establish a personal relationship with him. Now Step 3 asks that we daily put ourselves in God's hands and let Christ become our Lord. Here are a few thoughts as we consider this Step:

What does it really mean to let God call the shots in your life—to put yourself in his hands? Did you ever go on vacation with your family? Chances are your father or mother drove the family car, making the decisions as to how to go, when to eat and where to spend the night. Most of the time everything worked out okay, but on occasion your mom or dad would take a wrong turn and get lost. In short, your parents were controlling of the path you would take. God is more trustworthy than our parents—he won't take any wrong turns.

> ***Until we decide to let God take control on a daily basis, nothing much is going to change.***

Remember when you were little and you would go swimming at the lake? You probably never gave much thought to whether or not you were out too deep or whether you needed to put on more sunscreen to protect your skin. You just went and had a good time because you knew your folks were going to take care of you. They might be talking or reading but you were never out of their sight. They looked out for your safety. It wasn't that you were careless: you still had to swim on your own and look out for yourself. But you knew your parents were always watching, and you could trust them to be there.

STEP 3 LOOK INSIDE

It's a big step to realize we can't make it on our own—that God is there to help and Jesus will guide us. But until we decide to let God take control on a daily basis, nothing much is going to change. We have to be willing to say, "Jesus, take over today." Once we crack the door open, God will keep his eye always on us. That is real security!

See the chart at the end of this introduction for more reading on this Step.

COURAGE—Facing challenges with confidence in God and myself

Step 3 takes courage. To acknowledge that God is there to help is one thing. To put our trust and faith in him is something else. That really does take courage. In the chart below you will find the locations of three readings related to this theme.

JOSEPH OF ARIMATHEA—a man who showed tremendous courage and risked it all for Christ

Step 3 offers a careful look at what gives us the courage to face unique challenges in life and to do so with confidence in God! Let's take a look back at a man in the Bible known only as Joseph of Arimathea. He was a man who risked his social reputation, his job, and everything he had in order to do a courageous thing for his Lord. To learn more about Joseph, see John 19.38–42 and its related reading.

Where to Find

The first page number given tells you where to find a Bible reference related to this step. If a second page number is given, it refers to the location of an InStep meditation.

SCRIPTURE	STEP 3	STEP 3 LOOK INSIDE	STEP 3 LOOK AHEAD	STEP 3 LOOK BACK	PAGE(S)
MATTHEW 6.27–34	•				12
MATTHEW 11.28–30	•	•			26, **27**
MATTHEW 16.24–26	•				40
MARK 15.42–47	•				109
LUKE 1.26–38	•				114
LUKE 9.57–62	•				142
LUKE 11.2–4	•				146
LUKE 12.22–31	•				150
LUKE 18.15–17	•				165
JOHN 1.9–13	•				186
JOHN 5.22–24	•				196
JOHN 6.35–40	•	•			199, **200**
JOHN 8.31–38	•				207
JOHN 14.12–14	•				220
JOHN 19.38–42	•			•	233, **234**
ACTS 2.21	•				244
ROMANS 3.21, 22	•				303
ROMANS 5.1, 2	•				305
ROMANS 8.1, 2	•				311
ROMANS 10.8–10	•				316
ROMANS 12.1	•	•			319, **320**
1 CORINTHIANS 1.18–25	•				331
2 CORINTHIANS 1.3–7	•				353
GALATIANS 3.10–14	•				375
EPHESIANS 1.3–10	•				385
EPHESIANS 2.8–10	•				386
COLOSSIANS 3.1, 2	•		•		410, **409**
HEBREWS 4.1–3	•				454
HEBREWS 6.18–20	•		•		457, **458**
1 PETER 1.3–7	•		•		483, **484**
PSALM 2.10–12	•				553
PSALM 3.3–6	•	•			553, **554**
PSALM 13.5, 6	•				562
PSALM 16.5–9	•				565
PSALM 37.5, 6	•				586
PSALM 61.4, 5	•				605
PSALM 62.5–7	•				605
PSALM 85.8, 9	•				628
PSALM 111.10	•				653
PSALM 116.8–11	•				656
PSALM 118.8, 9	•				656
PSALM 131.2, 3	•				668
PSALM 143.10, 11	•				677
PROVERBS 3.5, 6	•	•			686, **687**
PROVERBS 14.26, 27	•				702
PROVERBS 16.9	•				706
PROVERBS 21.30, 31	•				715

Step 4

I will take a hard look at myself, the way I live and my moral standards.

Step 3 focused on having confidence in God and the courage to put our lives in his hands once and for all. Now it is time to take a look at the way we live and the moral standards we are guided by. We won't get very far in life unless we confront the following attitude:

"IT'S MY LIFE. I'M GOING TO LIVE IT MY WAY!"

"I was so sure when I said those words that I knew what was best for me. My parents tried to offer me 'their experience' but, come on—

God is ready and waiting to restore fellowship with us.

when they were young it was an entirely different world. What do their experiences have to do with my life now?

"So I have been living my life on my own terms. That means I go where I want with whomever I want.

STEP 4 LOOK INSIDE

Sounds good, huh? That's what I thought. But if I take an honest look at my life, I guess I have to admit I don't exactly have control. I have let other people—people who don't know me or really care about me—decide who I am."

Taking a personal inventory of my life—past and present—is the only way to prepare for a successful future. What don't I like about myself? Who do I resent and why? What have I done that makes me feel guilty? Am I ashamed of what I do, where I go, or the people I know?

By taking a long, hard look at ourselves, we can begin to understand what makes us tick. Knowing the *past* helps us to evaluate the *present* honestly and begin to prepare for the *future*.

PURITY—Obeying God with my moral choices

A good reputation always comes wrapped up in strong moral character. Our motives, our actions, our sexual conduct all add up to who we are. God's desire is that we live a pure and blameless life. But how is that possible with all the pressures being put on us today?

One essential for spiritual growth is moral purity. Sexual sin creates heavy baggage for the follower of Christ. It creates a deep tie to the partner that confuses us and helps us to rationalize the behavior while avoiding anyone who may make us accountable for our actions. We are likely to start hanging out with people who are sexually active, stop going to church because of the guilt, or begin building walls around the subject.

GOOD NEWS! THERE IS HOPE!

For those who have given in to temptation on this one, there is hope! First John 1.9 was written to Christians who had failed to live by God's standard. It explains how we can rebound and be cleansed from sin. "But if we confess our sins to God, he can always be trusted to forgive us and take our sins away." This means that even though we are forgiven from our condition of SIN and are no longer separated from God for eternity, our day-to-day sins can separate us from the presence of God. In a manner of speaking, we run away from God when we don't confess our sins daily, just as we avoid our parents when we feel guilty about something we have done.

The good news is that even sexual sin can be forgiven, and God is ready and waiting to restore fellowship with us. If we need to talk to God about some things, let's do it right now and get things moving again in our walk with Christ.

Remember: the only opinion that really counts is the Lord's. In the chart below you will find the locations of three readings related to this theme.

A WOMAN CAUGHT IN SIN—a woman given the opportunity to start all over

Step 4 deals with moral standards. It points to the future and says that we need to get a grip on our values before they are compromised. This is a must if we want to take on the character of Jesus Christ. Looking back through the Bible for people who were "pure" in God's eyes leads to an unusual example of an unnamed WOMAN CAUGHT IN SIN—a woman who was given the opportunity to start all over. To learn more about her, see John 7.53—8.11 and its related reading.

Where to Find

The first page number given tells you where to find a Bible reference related to this step. If a second page number is given, it refers to the location of an InStep meditation.

SCRIPTURE	STEP 4	STEP 4 LOOK INSIDE	STEP 4 LOOK AHEAD	STEP 4 LOOK BACK	PAGE(S)
MATTHEW 23.23–33	•				54
MARK 14.66–72	•				107
LUKE 11.33–36	•				147
LUKE 14.25–30	•	•			156, **157**
JOHN 7.53—8.11	•			•	204, **205**
ROMANS 7.21–25	•				311
ROMANS 13.11–14	•				322
ROMANS 14.13–19	•				324
1 CORINTHIANS 3.1–3	•				332
1 CORINTHIANS 6.18–20	•		•		336, **337**
2 CORINTHIANS 13.5–7	•	•			370, **371**
GALATIANS 6.3, 4	•				380
EPHESIANS 5.3–5	•	•			391, **392**
EPHESIANS 6.1–3	•				393
COLOSSIANS 2.20–23	•				410
2 THESSALONIANS 2.16, 17	•		•		424, **423**
JAMES 2.1–4	•	•			473, **474**
PSALM 51.5, 6	•				598
PSALM 73.21, 22	•				617
PROVERBS 1.8–19	•				684
PROVERBS 2.16–19	•				685
PROVERBS 5.7–14	•				690
PROVERBS 7.6–27	•		•		692, **693**
PROVERBS 10.17	•				696
PROVERBS 11.12, 13	•				697
PROVERBS 13.1	•				699
PROVERBS 15.5	•				702
PROVERBS 15.31–33	•	•			704, **705**
PROVERBS 16.2, 3	•				704
PROVERBS 19.26	•				712
PROVERBS 20.1	•				713
PROVERBS 20.20	•				713
PROVERBS 21.16, 17	•				714
PROVERBS 22.1	•				715
PROVERBS 23.29–35	•				717
PROVERBS 25.17–20	•				720
PROVERBS 25.28	•				720
PROVERBS 26.20–22	•				721
PROVERBS 28.24	•				724
PROVERBS 29.3	•				726
PROVERBS 30.11–14	•				727

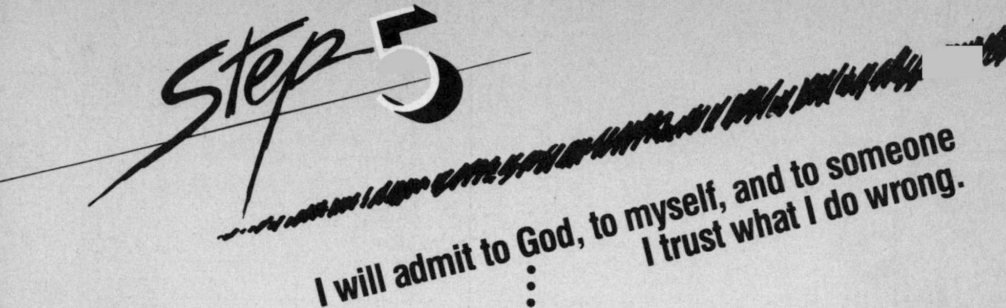

Step 4 was tough. Sometimes it is difficult to look at our moral standards from God's point of view. But we need to get honest if we really want to grow. Step 5 adds an important dimension to keeping life on track. It will take us a step further than we normally go. It involves telling God and someone else the mistakes we have made.

GUILTY AS CHARGED

It's always the same dream. Even though I'm in a different place with different people, I can't get away from them. I run and run, but there they are in front of me, pointing an accusing finger and saying, "You should be ashamed of yourself!" I wake up feeling terribly afraid. I want them to go away and leave me alone. I want this nightmare to stop.

Have you ever heard the expression, "Your sins will find you out?"

> ***Guilt over sin can be like an alarm clock in our lives.***

Maybe you didn't understand it, but it's true. When we try to cover up sins and deny they exist, eventually we lose our inner peace. It can even cause some physical pain. Emotions don't bother us without good reason. Guilt over sin can be like an alarm clock in our lives. It lets us know when we need to "come clean" so we can move on.

The Bible refers to this as conviction. The Holy Spirit uses conviction to help us turn away from sinful actions and turn back to God. Conviction is an inner struggle designed to help us admit to God how we have failed. It's tempting to make excuses or blame someone else for what we have done. But until we settle the wrongs in our lives by admitting them, our conscience will confirm that we are guilty as charged.

STEP LOOK INSIDE 5

In James 5.16 we read, "If you have sinned, you should tell each other what you have done. Then you can pray for one another and be healed." We are going to sin. That is no surprise. It is when we are willing to admit our wrongs to God and then tell someone we trust how we have failed that we restore inner peace and become emotionally free.

See the chart at the end of this introduction for more reading on this Step.

TRUTHFULNESS—Earning trust by admitting my mistakes

If we want to gain a good reputation, we have to develop a commitment to tell the truth consistently. If we don't, people won't trust us. How important is it? How far should we go? What price is there to be paid? In the chart below you will find the locations of three readings related to this theme.

PETER—a man who discovered the importance of telling the truth regardless of the outcome

Step 5 focuses on truthfulness—one of the measurements of real character. When we tell the truth, we have integrity. When we lie, we become difficult to trust. In connection with this Step, we will take a look back at the life of PETER—a man who discovered the importance of telling the truth regardless of the outcome. To learn more about Peter, see Luke 22.54–62 and its related reading.

Where to Find

The first page number given tells you where to find a Bible reference related to this step. If a second page number is given, it refers to the location of an InStep meditation.

SCRIPTURE	STEP 5	STEP LOOK INSIDE 5	STEP LOOK AHEAD 5	STEP LOOK BACK 5	PAGE(S)
LUKE 15.18, 19	•				158
LUKE 22.54–62	•			•	177, **178**
ACTS 4.1–22	•				246
ACTS 5.1–11	•				248
ROMANS 14.20–23	•				324
EPHESIANS 4.14–16	•	•			388, **389**
EPHESIANS 4.25	•		•		391, **390**
EPHESIANS 5.14	•	•			391, **394**
HEBREWS 4.11–13	•		•		454, **453**
JAMES 4.7–10	•				477
JAMES 5.16	•	•			480, **481**
1 JOHN 1.6–10	•	•			501, **502**
PSALM 32.3–5	•				579
PSALM 38.17, 18	•				588
PSALM 51.4	•				598
PSALM 62.8	•				605
PSALM 69.5	•	•			611, **612**
PSALM 103.8–12	•				644
PROVERBS 21.2, 3	•				714
PROVERBS 24.26	•				718
PROVERBS 28.13	•		•		724, **723**

Step 6

I want God to take control of my life and make me a complete person.

Step 5 brought us to the point that we are willing to admit to God, to ourselves, and to someone we trust what we do wrong. Now comes the point at which God desires to take complete control of us so he can make us complete. He becomes the source for our security. And speaking of security, remember this?

Letting go of the past is hard.

WHO NEEDS IT?

"This time I mean it! I don't need that old, stupid blanket anymore! I'm going to leave it here on this shelf and never pick it up again . . . starting tomorrow."

We laugh at these words of poor Linus in the *Peanuts* comic strip. Embarrassed by his dependency on a dirty, old blanket, Linus is determined to get rid of it from his life. But when the going gets tough and Linus must face an uncomfortable moment, he grabs hold of the comfort and security his blanket offers.

STEP LOOK INSIDE 6

We're a lot like Linus. When we try to let go of our past and break the pattern of negative behavior, it is hard. It seems easier to go back than to move ahead. Moving ahead can be a fearful thing. But when we focus once again on how much God loves us, we can let go and let him take away our dirty blankets and make us complete.

See the chart at the end of this introduction for more reading on this Step.

JOYFULNESS—Enjoying the inward results of right living

How do we become truly happy? If we look to friends and circumstances as the sources of our happiness, we will be disappointed every time. Inner happiness (what the Bible calls "joy") is the result of knowing Jesus Christ and daily making responsible choices in life. In the chart below you will find the locations of three readings related to this theme.

DAVID—a man who had a heart for God that resulted in a joy-filled life with God

Step 6 brings us to the place that we give ourselves to God in such a way that we ask him to fill in the empty places of our lives. When that happens, joy fills our hearts. Seeking joy in life is different from seeking happiness. One depends upon a relationship, while the other depends on circumstances. King David is an example of a man who had a heart for God that resulted in a joyful life. To learn more about David, see Psalm 16.10, 11 and its related reading.

Where to Find

The first page number given tells you where to find a Bible reference related to this step. If a second page number is given, it refers to the location of an InStep meditation.

SCRIPTURE	STEP 6	STEP 6 LOOK INSIDE	STEP 6 LOOK AHEAD	STEP 6 LOOK BACK	PAGE(S)
MATTHEW 22.34–39	•				52
MARK 12.28–31	•				101
LUKE 10.25–28	•				144
ROMANS 6.12–14	•		•		308, **309**
ROMANS 12.2	•				319
1 CORINTHIANS 12.1–3	•				344
1 CORINTHIANS 13.4–8	•				346
2 CORINTHIANS 5.16, 17	•	•			360, **359**
GALATIANS 2.20	•				375
GALATIANS 5.22–26	•				380
GALATIANS 6.7, 8	•		•		380, **381**
EPHESIANS 1.15–18	•				385
EPHESIANS 4.17–24	•				391
EPHESIANS 6.10–17	•				395
2 THESSALONIANS 3.3–5	•	•			424, **425**
TITUS 2.11–14	•				445
HEBREWS 4.14–16	•	•			454, **455**
JAMES 1.5–8	•				471
1 PETER 2.1–3	•				485
1 JOHN 4.13–18	•		•		508, **509**
REVELATION 3.19, 20	•				524
PSALM 4.3–5	•	•			553, **556**
PSALM 16.10, 11	•			•	564, **565**
PSALM 19.11–13	•				569
PSALM 34.4–6	•	•			581, **582**
PSALM 91.1–4	•				634
PSALM 95.3–7	•				638
PSALM 119.9–11	•				657
PSALM 119.99, 100	•				660
PSALM 139.23, 24	•				674
PROVERBS 13.18	•				699

Step 7

I need God to remove my shortcomings.

Step 6 encouraged us to turn over control of our lives to God so he can begin making us complete. That is a big step! Now we are ready to move on and learn to allow God to remove from our lives those shortcomings that can bring us down. This process involves taking a step of faith. Here is something to think about as we begin:

THE TRUST FACTOR

A "trust fall." You stand on a six-foot platform, cross your arms over your chest, and fall backwards into the waiting arms of eight people below. The whole idea is to trust them to catch you.

By realizing our limitations and God's power to overcome them, we can let go with confidence.

When I climbed to the top of the platform, I still felt pretty confident. They would catch me. I could trust them. They were my friends. I crossed my arms over my chest as they chanted, "Go, go, go." What seemed so easy to do was now very scary. The realization that when I leaned backwards I would lose complete control was frightening. Shouts of "Come on! . . . Fall! . . . We'll catch you!" echoed around me.

STEP LOOK INSIDE 7

But could I really trust them? Were they strong enough to hold me? Would I be injured? These were natural questions that flooded my mind. But they could never be settled. I did have to trust, so I just leaned back. Wow! What an experience!

Step 6 focused on our willingness to let God move into our lives, take control, and help us correct the mistakes of our past. Step 7 centers on the day-to-day trust in God's leadership and the power he will give to keep us from wanting to take back that control. By realizing our limitations and God's power to overcome them, we can let go with confidence.

Only God can remove our shortcomings and old ways of doing things. We can fall into a new life as we trust him to bring about changes in our lives and repair damage from the past. Much like the chant of the waiting friends, God is saying, "Let go, and let me help you. Choose to trust me."

See the chart at the end of this introduction for more reading on this Step.

HUMILITY—Becoming aware of God's greatness and my need for him

As Christians, it is important that we remind ourselves of just how much we need God in our lives. He saves by grace without any works, but that is only the beginning. The Bible says in 1 Peter 5.6, "Be humble in the presence of God's mighty power, and he will honor you when the time comes." Instead of trying to change ourselves on our own, we must constantly be mindful of our dependence on God to give the power to live for him! God loves us unconditionally. This means we don't have to prove anything to him or perform for him. He loves and accepts us just the way we are, . . . but too much to keep us that way. That means there are changes to be made in our actions and attitude, but God is the One who will make those changes. In the chart below you will find the locations of three readings related to this theme.

MARY—a woman whose greatness is measured by a humble spirit toward God and others

Humility is one character trait that has few models. Yet the Bible does give a few excellent examples of ordinary people who exhibited the trait of humility. Mary (the mother of Jesus) is one prime example. As we take a closer look at who we are becoming, let us consider Mary. She was a humble woman who quietly obeyed God. To learn more about Mary, see Luke 1.46–56 and its related reading.

Where to Find

The first page number given tells you where to find a Bible reference related to this step. If a second page number is given, it refers to the location of an InStep meditation.

SCRIPTURE	STEP 7	LOOK INSIDE 7	LOOK AHEAD 7	LOOK BACK 7	PAGE(S)
MATTHEW 18.3–5	•				42
MARK 9.42–50	•				93
LUKE 1.46–56	•			•	115, **116**
LUKE 9.46–48	•	•			140, **141**
1 CORINTHIANS 10.12, 13	•		•		341, **342**
2 CORINTHIANS 5.18	•		•		360, **361**
1 JOHN 3.4–6	•	•			504, **505**
PSALM 25.6–10	•	•			573, **575**
PSALM 51.1, 2	•				598
PSALM 51.9–11	•				598
PSALM 62.1, 2	•		•		605, **606**
PSALM 103.3–5	•				644
PSALM 119.33–39	•				658
PSALM 119.129–136	•				661
PSALM 141.3, 4	•	•			675, **676**
PROVERBS 3.11, 12	•	•			686, **688**
PROVERBS 12.1	•				698

Step 8

I will make a list of those I wrong and be willing to make things right.

Step 7 reminded us that it is God who actually changes our lives as we cooperate with him. Step 8 teaches us that once we have been changed, we have a responsibility to others. We come to the place that we make a list of any people we have wronged and become willing to set it straight. As we work through this important Step, making things right with those we have hurt will make life right for us.

It is good to go through the exercise of making a list of those we know we've hurt.

NO TALKING

I will not talk in class.
I will not talk in class.
I will not talk in class.
I will not talk in class.

This is so dumb. It's Ms. Brock's fault. If she weren't so boring we wouldn't have to talk during class to stay awake.

96 to go.

She's making me write on the board because I broke a rule, when in fact I broke someone's heart. I'm in trouble for talking and she doesn't even know what I said. If I really were making things right, I would apologize to Christy for what I said about her. It wasn't true. I was just trying to have some fun, but not at her expense.

95 to go.

MAKING THINGS RIGHT

It is good to go through the exercise of making a list of those we know we've hurt. Family members. Friends. Other classmates. God will bring them to our minds if we ask him to. Then we can set the record straight. Even if it's hard. The results will be a new attitude *for* us as well as a new attitude *about* us by others.

See the chart at the end of this introduction for more reading on this Step.

DETERMINATION—Being willing to make things right at all costs

Would people describe us as quitters? Not a real good handle to carry through life, is it? There are times when we feel like throwing in the towel, walking off the court, or turning in the keys and never coming back. Yet if we hang in there and don't let go, we can be known as people who are out of the ordinary—people who can be trusted, who are loyal and hardworking. In the chart below you will find the locations of three readings related to this theme.

ZACCHAEUS—a man who was determined to make things right with others at all costs

Zacchaeus offers a great example of determination. He was willing to make things right with those he had cheated as a tax collector. The determination you need to make things right in your life is the same kind of character seen in the life of Zacchaeus—a man who was determined to make things right with others at all costs. To learn more about Zacchaeus, see Luke 19.1–10 and its related reading.

Where to Find

The first page number given tells you where to find a Bible reference related to this step. If a second page number is given, it refers to the location of an InStep meditation.

SCRIPTURE	STEP 8	STEP LOOK INSIDE 8	STEP LOOK AHEAD 8	STEP LOOK BACK 8	PAGE(S)
MATTHEW 5.43–48	•				10
MATTHEW 6.14, 15	•				11
MATTHEW 7.1–5	•		•		14, **13**
MARK 4.24	•	•			78, **79**
MARK 11.25	•				98
LUKE 6.37, 38	•	•			128, **130**
LUKE 17.3, 4	•				162
LUKE 19.1–10	•			•	166, **167**
JOHN 14.26	•		•		220, **222**
ACTS 9.26–30	•				259
ROMANS 2.1	•				300
ROMANS 12.14–18	•				321
ROMANS 13.8–10	•	•			322, 323
1 CORINTHIANS 4.4, 5	•				333
2 CORINTHIANS 7.8–10	•				362
PHILIPPIANS 2.1–4	•				399
COLOSSIANS 3.12–14	•	•			412, **411**
1 PETER 3.8–12	•				488
1 JOHN 2.9–11	•				503
PSALM 91.14–16	•		•		634, **635**
PROVERBS 17.9, 10	•	•			708, **707**

Step 9

I will make things right with people I wrong, except when to do so would hurt them or others.

Step 8 helped us to take the time to evaluate and make a list of possible broken relationships. Not much fun. But because God is building the character trait of determination in us, we have the renewed strength to take the next step and make things right with those we have wronged.

FOURTH PERIOD HISTORY

Christy was great! She is one of my closest friends. When I told her I was sorry she just said, "Hey, forget it. No big deal." We're going to the movies Saturday.

It's weird. Apologizing to Christy was one of the hardest things I ever had to do. But I feel so much better.

I worked through the list of other people I've hurt. But I decided not to tell Ms. Brock how much I used to talk about her behind her back. I think it would just have hurt her feelings.

STEP 9 LOOK INSIDE

SAYING WE'RE SORRY

Sometimes things are better left unsaid. If a person has no idea of our bad thoughts, or of our actions regarding them, why bring it up? It only hurts them.

We need to keep these things in mind as we think about making things right with people we have wronged:

- Give fresh hurts a little time to heal. This will help us avoid causing unnecessary pain.
- Don't go to people if they are unaware of what happened and if it risks creating new wounds and more misunderstanding.
- Only talk with those who can be a part of solutions rather than those who might cause more problems.
- Be careful in telling someone not involved about problems with others.

See the chart at the end of this introduction for more reading on this Step.

COMPASSION—Considering how our actions may create reactions in others

To make things right with people we have hurt takes a big dose of "compassion." We may not have the gift of mercy, but God can give us compassion for others when we really need it. Compassion is a character trait that softens our view of others. Who needs this? Those we have wronged need it. We may be surrounded by a sea of others who need our compassion and who are going under emotionally because it seems no one really cares. In the chart below you will find the locations of three readings related to this theme.

GOOD SAMARITAN—a man whose compassionate action caused a positive reaction in another

There are many biblical characters who were compassionate people. But the one that stands out above all others is the Good Samaritan. As you look back at his example, you see a man who had little to gain by helping a man in need. However, he did it because it was the right thing to do! To learn more about the Good Samaritan, see Luke 10.29–37 and its related reading.

Where to Find

The first page number given tells you where to find a Bible reference related to this step. If a second page number is given, it refers to the location of an InStep meditation.

SCRIPTURE	STEP 9	LOOK INSIDE 9	LOOK AHEAD 9	LOOK BACK 9	PAGE(S)
MATTHEW 5.23, 24	•				9
MATTHEW 6.12	•				11
MATTHEW 18.15–17	•				43
MATTHEW 18.21–35	•				43
LUKE 6.27–36	•		•		128, **129**
LUKE 10.29–37	•			•	144, **145**
ROMANS 12.19–21	•				321
ROMANS 15.1–6	•	•			324, **325**
2 CORINTHIANS 2.5–8	•		•		354, **355**
PHILIPPIANS 1.9–11	•	•			397, **398**
PHILEMON 8–20	•				448
JAMES 2.14–17	•		•		475, **476**
1 JOHN 3.15–18	•	•			506, **507**
PSALM 133.1–3	•	•			669, **670**
PROVERBS 12.18–20	•	•			699, **700**
PROVERBS 15.1–4	•				702
PROVERBS 16.7, 8	•				706
PROVERBS 18.19–21	•				710
PROVERBS 19.11	•				712
PROVERBS 21.23, 24	•				714
PROVERBS 25.11	•				720

Step 10

I need to continue looking inside—admitting when I am wrong.

Getting honest with ourselves and working through each of the first nine steps will humble us. This is especially true if we have spent years ignoring the way that our words and actions affect others. Step 10 encourages us to stay in step and continue on the path of getting real!

Dealing with our shortcomings on a daily basis helps us stay ahead.

WHAT'S ONE BEER?

They're right. What's one beer? When you blow it, you blow it. One or ten, it doesn't really matter. Getting past my past is really tough. Old habits often die hard. But I am learning—to not let my mistakes beat me down. I have found that if I deal with shortcomings on a daily basis, I can stay ahead. Once I ignore problems they build up again. It becomes too hard to dig my way out.

KEEPING A SHORT LIST

The best way to keep on track is to take a daily inventory of ourselves and how we are living. Keeping relationships open and honest is to keep a short list of people we have problems with. Checking in with ourselves and others needs to be done on a daily basis.

Do we have unfinished business today? Did something happen that put a wedge between us and friends or family members? They may have started it, but we can be part of solving it. In Ephesians 4.25–27, Paul wrote about not going to bed angry. He said, "We are part of the same body. Stop lying and start telling each other the truth. Don't get so angry that you sin. Don't go to bed angry and don't give the devil a chance." That's good advice.

STEP LOOK INSIDE 10

See the chart at the end of this introduction for more reading on this Step.

PATIENCE—Learning how to endure and grow in the process

We need to be patient with our own shortcomings and with the shortcomings of others. Spiritual maturity does not happen overnight. It takes time. Sometimes it's three steps forward two steps back. Remember, God is not finished with us yet. He sees what we can and will become. In the chart below you will find the locations of three readings related to this theme.

PAUL—a servant who learned patience through his trials and remained faithful until the end

Patience may not be one of our strengths—for most of us it isn't. Society teaches us to expect instant gratification and instant success. That's not the real world. To help focus our thoughts on working a little patience into our hectic lives, let's look at the life of the apostle Paul. He learned patience through various trials in his life and yet remained faithful till the end of his ministry. To learn more about Paul, see 2 Timothy 4.9–18 and its related reading.

Where to Find

The first page number given tells you where to find a Bible reference related to this step. If a second page number is given, it refers to the location of an *InStep meditation.*

SCRIPTURE	STEP 10	STEP 10 LOOK INSIDE	STEP 10 LOOK AHEAD	STEP 10 LOOK BACK	PAGE(S)
LUKE 6.43–45	•				131
ACTS 15.36–41	•				272
ROMANS 5.4, 5	•		•		305, **306**
ROMANS 6.1–4	•				307
ROMANS 12.3–5	•				319
1 CORINTHIANS 6.12–17	•				335
2 CORINTHIANS 1.12	•				353
GALATIANS 5.1	•				378
EPHESIANS 4.26–32	•				391
EPHESIANS 5.15, 16	•				393
PHILIPPIANS 2.14–16	•	•			400, **401**
PHILIPPIANS 4.4–9	•				404
COLOSSIANS 3.15–17	•		•		412, **413**
1 THESSALONIANS 4.2–10	•				419
2 TIMOTHY 2.20–25	•				438
2 TIMOTHY 4.9–18	•			•	440, **441**
HEBREWS 6.1–3	•				456
HEBREWS 13.1–5	•				468
JAMES 1.13–15	•	•			471, **472**
JAMES 1.19–26	•				471
1 PETER 1.13–16	•		•		483, **486**
1 PETER 2.13–17	•				487
2 PETER 3.17, 18	•	•			498, **499**
1 JOHN 2.15–17	•				503
PSALM 15.1–3	•				563
PSALM 34.11–14	•				581
PSALM 101.2–4	•				642
PROVERBS 2.20–22	•				685
PROVERBS 10.31, 32	•				696
PROVERBS 15.18–21	•	•			704, **703**
PROVERBS 24.16	•	•			718, **719**

Step 11

I will pray to God on a regular basis, asking him to direct me and give me the power to live for him.

Step 10 encouraged us to continue taking an honest look at who we really are. Step 11 gives us the power source to go on and keep growing in our walk with God.

MOST LIKELY TO SUCCEED

Most Likely to Succeed
Donald J. Thurman
Kathy S. Timmons

It looks pretty good on paper. "Most likely to succeed" . . . like I have some idea of where I'm headed. If they only knew. I have no idea where I am going or how I am going to get there.

"Pray about everything."

I worry all the time. About the past. About the present. About the future. Sometimes I suffer from the "if only" syndrome. "If only" I had, "if only" I hadn't. Then there's the "what ifs." "What if" I do? "What if" I don't?

WHAT, ME WORRY?

The Bible says in Philippians 4.6, 7, "Don't worry about anything, but pray about everything. With thankful hearts offer up your prayers and requests to God. Then, because you belong to Christ Jesus, God will bless you with peace that no one can completely understand. And this peace will control the way you think and feel."

Most of us would rather not worry. The fact is, worry shows that we don't really trust God with our lives. We can say we don't worry; but if our actions say something else, we need to find a solution and tap into our source for strength. The benefit will be living with extraordinary peace about ordinary events in our lives.

STEP 11 LOOK INSIDE

See the chart at the end of this introduction for more reading on this Step.

ENDURANCE—Developing inward strength by daily dependence

It takes much endurance to experience lasting change in our lives. Strong character results when we make it a high priority to stay plugged in to our source of power. It is through daily dependence that we develop the strength to live a consistent life in Christ. In the chart below you will find the locations of three readings related to this theme.

TIMOTHY—a young man who learned endurance and became strong through daily dependence

As we face the future with God on our side, we can be confident that things are going to work out for the best if we develop the right kind of balance in life. Learning how to keep priorities in place will help us cope with any problems we face. Becoming Christians doesn't isolate us from problems. However, it does teach us how to cope with peer pressure and prepares us to become leaders. Timothy was a young man who learned endurance and became strong through his daily dependence upon Christ. To learn more about Timothy, see 1 Timothy 4.6–16 and its related reading.

Where to Find

The first page number given tells you where to find a Bible reference related to this step. If a second page number is given, it refers to the location of an InStep *meditation.*

SCRIPTURE	STEP 11	STEP 11 LOOK INSIDE	STEP 11 LOOK AHEAD	STEP 11 LOOK BACK	PAGE(S)
MATTHEW 6.6	•				11
MATTHEW 7.7–11	•	•			14, **15**
MATTHEW 21.22	•				49
MATTHEW 26.36–46	•				62
MARK 11.22–24	•				98
LUKE 6.46–49	•				131
LUKE 17.7–10	•				162
JOHN 14.15–21	•		•		220, **221**
ROMANS 8.26–30	•				313
1 CORINTHIANS 15.58	•				350
2 CORINTHIANS 9.7–15	•				365
GALATIANS 5.16–18	•	•			378, **379**
GALATIANS 6.9	•		•		380, **382**
EPHESIANS 5.17–20	•				393
PHILIPPIANS 3.12–16	•	•			402, **403**
COLOSSIANS 2.6–8	•				408
1 TIMOTHY 4.6–16	•			•	431, **432**
2 TIMOTHY 2.3–7	•				438
2 TIMOTHY 3.14–17	•				440
1 PETER 4.10, 11	•		•		490, **491**
1 JOHN 5.1–5	•				508
PSALM 1.1–3	•				552
PSALM 37.23, 24	•				586
PSALM 40.1–5	•	•			589, **590**
PSALM 51.12–14	•				598
PSALM 63.2–8	•				607
PSALM 84.4–12	•				627
PSALM 86.11–13	•				628
PSALM 119.140–144	•	•			662, **663**
PROVERBS 4.10–27	•				689
PROVERBS 6.20–23	•				691
PROVERBS 8.32–36	•				694

Step 12

Because God is changing my life through following these steps, I will tell others about them and daily practice what I have learned.

When something wonderful happens to us, we can't wait to tell someone the good news. A best friend, a close family member—it will usually be someone we trust. See if this story sounds familiar . . .

GOOD NEWS TRAVELS FAST

Hi, this is Lisa. I'm not home right now. But if you leave a message, your number, and the time you called, I'll get back to you. Here you go!

BEEP

Lisa, I can't believe you're not home! Where are you? This is one of the most important days in my life and you're not there! I can't call anybody else because you'll get mad I didn't tell you first. So what am I supposed to do now? Okay, I'll just talk to your machine.

I got the job! The lady told me she interviewed twenty-three people, and I was the most qualified. Can you believe it? I'm going to be making twice as much as I did last summer. Does that mean I can work half as much and make the same amount of money? Then I will have more time to talk to you on this dumb . . .

BEEP

These twelve steps are designed to help us stay in step with God and others. Our choosing to live a fulfilling life brings us to the point where we can start helping others on the path.

Becoming a Christian is the most important decision anyone can make. Growing, taking the steps toward maturity, is part of the equation that many people leave out. It's sad, but today we tend to measure success based on what we do, not who we are becoming. We rate people on how they perform when we should check out how well they finish.

STEP LOOK INSIDE 12

As we look inside our hearts and read *InStep*'s meditations for this twelfth and final step, we should think about the different things God has done for us through this process. The feeling we have inside is probably one of gratefulness. Will we be willing to show that we are grateful by telling someone else about our experience?

See the chart at the end of this introduction for more reading on this Step.

GRATEFULNESS—Giving God the credit that is due him

The character quality of gratefulness is demonstrated by showing others what God has done for us. God teaches us how to really live, so it's time to pass the word. It doesn't have to be complicated. In reality, the message of trusting Christ needs to be made so simple that anyone can respond. In the chart below, you will find the locations of three readings related to this theme.

BARTIMAEUS—a man who showed he was grateful by telling others about the good news of Jesus Christ

Step 12 brings us to the end—and to the beginning—of living life as devoted followers of Jesus Christ. Being grateful is a by-product of realizing what the Lord has done in us. As we start to walk with Jesus in a consistent manner, telling others about how to get in step with God is essential. Bartimaeus is a great example of a person who showed his gratitude to God by telling others about the good news of Jesus Christ. To learn more about Bartimaeus, see Mark 10.46–52 and its related reading.

Where to Find

The first page number given tells you where to find a Bible reference related to this step. If a second page number is given, it refers to the location of an InStep meditation.

SCRIPTURE	STEP 12	LOOK INSIDE	LOOK AHEAD	LOOK BACK	PAGE(S)
MATTHEW 5.14–16	•				8
MATTHEW 20.29–34	•				47
MATTHEW 28.18–20	•		•		68, **69**
MARK 5.18–20	•				81
MARK 10.46–52	•			•	96, **97**
LUKE 8.16–18	•				135
JOHN 4.34–38	•				194
JOHN 21.15–19	•	•			238, **239**
ACTS 28.30, 31	•				297
ROMANS 10.14, 15	•				316
1 CORINTHIANS 9.24–27	•				340
2 CORINTHIANS 2.14–17	•				354
2 CORINTHIANS 4.1, 2	•		•		356, **357**
2 CORINTHIANS 5.19–21	•				360
EPHESIANS 3.7–10	•				387
COLOSSIANS 1.9–11	•				407
COLOSSIANS 4.5, 6	•				414
1 THESSALONIANS 1.7–10	•	•			416, **417**
TITUS 2.7, 8	•				445
1 PETER 2.9, 10	•				485
1 PETER 3.15–17	•	•			488, **489**
2 PETER 1.5–9	•	•			494, **495**
PSALM 33.1–8	•				580
PSALM 50.14, 15	•				597
PSALM 51.15	•				599
PSALM 68.32–35	•				611
PSALM 71.17–19	•				615
PSALM 78.1–4	•				620
PSALM 92.1–4	•	•			634, **637**
PSALM 96.1–6	•		•		639, **640**
PSALM 105.1–5	•				646
PSALM 138.1–3	•				673
PSALM 145.4–21	•				678
PROVERBS 18.24	•				710
PROVERBS 19.17	•				712
PROVERBS 22.4	•				715
PROVERBS 23.24, 25	•				717
PROVERBS 25.21, 22	•				720
PROVERBS 27.17	•				722

Index to Topics

Use this handy index to look up subjects that are of particular interest to you. You'll find listings that lead you to insights from scripture, from the footnotes, and from *InStep*'s meditations. Specially set apart in this material are entries for each of the twelve character qualities found in *InStep*. See, for example, the listing titled **COMPASSION.**

Bible Reading Plan

(The New Testament, Psalms, and Proverbs in One Year)

DAY	READING
1	*Matthew* 1.1—2.23
2	*Matthew* 3.1—4.11
3	*Matthew* 4.12–25
4	*Matthew* 5.1–37
5	*Matthew* 5.38—6.23
6	*Matthew* 6.24—7.29
7	*Matthew* 8.1—9.17
8	*Matthew* 9.18—10.42
9	*Matthew* 11.1–30
10	*Matthew* 12.1–50
11	*Matthew* 13.1–58
12	*Matthew* 14.1–36
13	*Matthew* 15.1–28
14	*Matthew* 15.29—16.4
15	*Matthew* 16.5–28
16	*Matthew* 17.1—18.9
17	*Matthew* 18.10–35
18	*Matthew* 19.1–30
19	*Matthew* 20.1–19
20	*Matthew* 20.20—21.46
21	*Matthew* 22.1–46
22	*Matthew* 23.1–39
23	*Matthew* 24.1–51
24	*Matthew* 25.1–46
25	*Matthew* 26.1–30
26	*Matthew* 26.31–46
27	*Matthew* 26.47—27.56
28	*Matthew* 27.57—28.20
29	*Mark* 1.1–28
30	*Mark* 1.29–45
31	*Mark* 2.1–28
32	*Mark* 3.1–30
33	*Mark* 3.31—4.25
34	*Mark* 4.26–41
35	*Mark* 5.1–43
36	*Mark* 6.1–29
37	*Mark* 6.30—7.23
38	*Mark* 7.24—8.26
39	*Mark* 8.27—9.13
40	*Mark* 9.14–37
41	*Mark* 9.38—10.12
42	*Mark* 10.13–45
43	*Mark* 10.46—11.11
44	*Mark* 11.12–33
45	*Mark* 12.1–34
46	*Mark* 12.35—13.37
47	*Mark* 14.1–11
48	*Mark* 14.12–31
49	*Mark* 14.32–52
50	*Mark* 14.53—15.21
51	*Mark* 15.22–47
52	*Mark* 16.1–20
53	*Luke* 1.1–25
54	*Luke* 1.26–56
55	*Luke* 1.57–80
56	*Luke* 2.1–21
57	*Luke* 2.22–3.22
58	*Luke* 3.23—4.37
59	*Luke* 4.38—5.16
60	*Luke* 5.17—6.5
61	*Luke* 6.6–26
62	*Luke* 6.27–49
63	*Luke* 7.1–35
64	*Luke* 7.36—8.3
65	*Luke* 8.4–56
66	*Luke* 9.1–36
67	*Luke* 9.37–62
68	*Luke* 10.1–42
69	*Luke* 11.1–13
70	*Luke* 11.14–36
71	*Luke* 11.37—12.12
72	*Luke* 12.13–34
73	*Luke* 12.35–59
74	*Luke* 13.1–21
75	*Luke* 13.22—14.14
76	*Luke* 14.15—15.10
77	*Luke* 15.11–32
78	*Luke* 16.1–31
79	*Luke* 17.1–19
80	*Luke* 17.20—18.14
81	*Luke* 18.15–43
82	*Luke* 19.1–48
83	*Luke* 20.1—21.38
84	*Luke* 22.1—23.49
85	*Luke* 23.50—24.35
86	*Luke* 24.36–53
87	*John* 1.1—2.25
88	*John* 3.1–36
89	*John* 4.1–42
90	*John* 4.43–54
91	*John* 5.1–47
92	*John* 6.1–21
93	*John* 6.22–59
94	*John* 6.60–71
95	*John* 7.1–31
96	*John* 7.32—8.11
97	*John* 8.12—9.41
98	*John* 10.1–21
99	*John* 10.22–42
100	*John* 11.1–44
101	*John* 11.45—12.11
102	*John* 12.12–43
103	*John* 12.44–50
104	*John* 13.1–35
105	*John* 13.36—14.31
106	*John* 15.1–27
107	*John* 16.1–33
108	*John* 17.1–26
109	*John* 18.1—19.37
110	*John* 19.38—21.25
111	*Acts* 1.1–11
112	*Acts* 1.12—2.13
113	*Acts* 2.14–47
114	*Acts* 3.1–10
115	*Acts* 3.11—4.37
116	*Acts* 5.1—6.7
117	*Acts* 6.8—8.3
118	*Acts* 8.4—9.31
119	*Acts* 9.32—11.30
120	*Acts* 12.1—13.52
121	*Acts* 14.1–28
122	*Acts* 15.1—16.10
123	*Acts* 16.11—17.15
124	*Acts* 17.16—19.10
125	*Acts* 19.11–41
126	*Acts* 20.1–16

Bible Reading Plan

(The New Testament, Psalms, and Proverbs in One Year)

DAY	READING
127	*Acts* 20.17—21.16
128	*Acts* 21.17—23.35
129	*Acts* 24.1—26.32
130	*Acts* 27.1—28.31
131	*Romans* 1.1-32
132	*Romans* 2.1-16
133	*Romans* 2.17—3.20
134	*Romans* 3.21—4.12
135	*Romans* 4.13—5.11
136	*Romans* 5.12—6.14
137	*Romans* 6.15—7.6
138	*Romans* 7.7—8.17
139	*Romans* 8.18-30
140	*Romans* 8.31—9.29
141	*Romans* 9.30—10.21
142	*Romans* 11.1-10
143	*Romans* 11.11-36
144	*Romans* 12.1-21
145	*Romans* 13.1—14.12
146	*Romans* 14.13—15.13
147	*Romans* 15.14-33
148	*Romans* 16.1-27
149	*I Corinthians* 1.1-31
150	*I Corinthians* 2.1—3.23
151	*I Corinthians* 4.1-21
152	*I Corinthians* 5.1—6.20
153	*I Corinthians* 7.1-24
154	*I Corinthians* 7.25—8.13
155	*I Corinthians* 9.1-23
156	*I Corinthians* 9.24—10.22
157	*I Corinthians* 10.23—11.1
158	*I Corinthians* 11.2-34
159	*I Corinthians* 12.1—14.40
160	*I Corinthians* 15.1-58
161	*I Corinthians* 16.1-24
162	*2 Corinthians* 1.1-24
163	*2 Corinthians* 2.1-17
164	*2 Corinthians* 3.1—4.15
165	*2 Corinthians* 4.16—5.10
166	*2 Corinthians* 5.11—6.13
167	*2 Corinthians* 6.14—7.16
168	*2 Corinthians* 8.1-24
169	*2 Corinthians* 9.1—10.18
170	*2 Corinthians* 11.1-15
171	*2 Corinthians* 11.16—12.10
172	*2 Corinthians* 12.11—13.13
173	*Galatians* 1.1-24
174	*Galatians* 2.1-21
175	*Galatians* 3.1-29
176	*Galatians* 4.1-20
177	*Galatians* 4.21—5.26
178	*Galatians* 6.1-18
179	*Ephesians* 1.1—2.10
180	*Ephesians* 2.11—3.21
181	*Ephesians* 4.1-32
182	*Ephesians* 5.1-33
183	*Ephesians* 6.1-24
184	*Philippians* 1.1-30
185	*Philippians* 2.1-30
186	*Philippians* 3.1—4.1
187	*Philippians* 4.2-23
188	*Colossians* 1.1-23
189	*Colossians* 1.24—2.23
190	*Colossians* 3.1-25
191	*Colossians* 4.1-18
192	*I Thessalonians* 1.1—2.16
193	*I Thessalonians* 2.17—4.18
194	*I Thessalonians* 5.1-28
195	*2 Thessalonians* 1.1—2.17
196	*2 Thessalonians* 3.1-18
197	*I Timothy* 1.1—3.16
198	*I Timothy* 4.1—6.21
199	*2 Timothy* 1.1-18
200	*2 Timothy* 2.1—4.22
201	*Titus* 1.1—3.15
202	*Philemon* 1-25
203	*Hebrews* 1.1-14
204	*Hebrews* 2.1-18
205	*Hebrews* 3.1—4.13
206	*Hebrews* 4.14—5.14
207	*Hebrews* 6.1-20
208	*Hebrews* 7.1-28
209	*Hebrews* 8.1—10.18
210	*Hebrews* 10.19—11.40
211	*Hebrews* 12.1-13
212	*Hebrews* 12.14-29
213	*Hebrews* 13.1-25
214	*James* 1.1-27
215	*James* 2.1-26
216	*James* 3.1—4.17
217	*James* 5.1-20
218	*I Peter* 1.1-25
219	*I Peter* 2.1-25
220	*I Peter* 3.1-22
221	*I Peter* 4.1-19
222	*I Peter* 5.1-14
223	*2 Peter* 1.1-21
224	*2 Peter* 2.1—3.18
225	*I John* 1.1—2.6
226	*I John* 2.7-27
227	*I John* 2.28—3.24
228	*I John* 4.1-21
229	*I John* 5.1-21
230	*2 John—3 John*
231	*Jude*
232	*Revelation* 1.1-20
233	*Revelation* 2.1—3.22
234	*Revelation* 4.1—6.17
235	*Revelation* 7.1—11.19
236	*Revelation* 12.1—16.21
237	*Revelation* 17.1—18.24
238	*Revelation* 19.1—21.27
239	*Revelation* 22.1-21
240	*Psalms* 1.1—2.12
241	*Psalms* 3.1—4.8
242	*Psalms* 5.1—6.10
243	*Psalms* 7.1—8.9
244	*Psalm* 9.1-20
245	*Psalms* 10.1—11.7
246	*Psalms* 12.1—13.6
247	*Psalms* 14.1—16.11
248	*Psalm* 17.1-15
249	*Psalm* 18.1-24
250	*Psalm* 18.25-50
251	*Psalm* 19.1-14
252	*Psalms* 20.1—21.13

Bible Reading Plan

(The New Testament, Psalms, and Proverbs in One Year)

DAY	READING
253	*Psalm* 22.1–31
254	*Psalms* 23.1—24.10
255	*Psalms* 25.1—28.9
256	*Psalms* 29.1—30.12
257	*Psalm* 31.1–24
258	*Psalm* 32.1–11
259	*Psalms* 33.1—34.6
260	*Psalms* 34.7—36.12
261	*Psalm* 37.1–40
262	*Psalm* 38.1–16
263	*Psalms* 38.17—39.13
264	*Psalm* 40.1–17
265	*Psalm* 41.1–13
266	*Psalms* 42.1—43.5
267	*Psalm* 44.1–26
268	*Psalms* 45.1—46.11
269	*Psalms* 47.1—48.14
270	*Psalm* 49.1–20
271	*Psalm* 50.1–23
272	*Psalm* 51.1–11
273	*Psalms* 51.12—53.6
274	*Psalms* 54.1—55.8
275	*Psalms* 55.9—57.11
276	*Psalms* 58.1—61.8
277	*Psalms* 62.1—64.10
278	*Psalms* 65.1—67.7
279	*Psalm* 68.1–35
280	*Psalm* 69.1–18
281	*Psalms* 69.19—70.5
282	*Psalm* 71.1–24
283	*Psalm* 72.1–20
284	*Psalm* 73.1–15
285	*Psalms* 73.16—75.10
286	*Psalms* 76.1—78.4
287	*Psalm* 78.5–39
288	*Psalm* 78.40–72
289	*Psalm* 79.1–13
290	*Psalm* 80.1–19
291	*Psalms* 81.1—82.8
292	*Psalms* 83.1—84.12
293	*Psalm* 85.1–13
294	*Psalms* 86.1—87.7

DAY	READING
295	*Psalms* 88.1—89.52
296	*Psalms* 90.1—91.16
297	*Psalms* 92.1—93.5
298	*Psalm* 94.1–23
299	*Psalms* 95.1—96.13
300	*Psalms* 97.1—98.9
301	*Psalms* 99.1—101.8
302	*Psalm* 102.1–28
303	*Psalm* 103.1–22
304	*Psalm* 104.1–35
305	*Psalm* 105.1–15
306	*Psalm* 105.16–45
307	*Psalm* 106.1–12
308	*Psalm* 106.13–48
309	*Psalm* 107.1–16
310	*Psalm* 107.17–32
311	*Psalms* 107.33—108.13
312	*Psalm* 109.1–31
313	*Psalms* 110.1—111.10
314	*Psalms* 112.1—114.8
315	*Psalms* 115.1—118.29
316	*Psalm* 119.1–40
317	*Psalm* 119.41–64
318	*Psalm* 119.65–88
319	*Psalm* 119.89–120
320	*Psalm* 119.121–152
321	*Psalm* 119.153–176
322	*Psalms* 120.1—121.8
323	*Psalms* 122.1—124.8
324	*Psalms* 125.1—127.5
325	*Psalms* 128.1—130.8
326	*Psalms* 131.1—134.3
327	*Psalms* 135.1—139.16
328	*Psalms* 139.17—140.13
329	*Psalm* 141.1–10
330	*Psalms* 142.1—144.15
331	*Psalms* 145.1—147.20
332	*Psalms* 148.1—150.6
333	*Proverbs* 1.1—2.15
334	*Proverbs* 2.16—3.12
335	*Proverbs* 3.13—4.27
336	*Proverbs* 5.1—7.27

DAY	READING
337	*Proverbs* 8.1—9.18
338	*Proverbs* 10.1—11.8
339	*Proverbs* 11.9–31
340	*Proverbs* 12.1–28
341	*Proverbs* 13.1–25
342	*Proverbs* 14.1–18
343	*Proverbs* 14.19–34
344	*Proverbs* 15.1–33
345	*Proverbs* 16.1–15
346	*Proverbs* 16.16—17.6
347	*Proverbs* 17.7–28
348	*Proverbs* 18.1–24
349	*Proverbs* 19.1–29
350	*Proverbs* 20.1–22
351	*Proverbs* 20.23—21.5
352	*Proverbs* 21.6–31
353	*Proverbs* 22.1–21
354	*Proverbs* 22.22—23.18
355	*Proverbs* 23.19–35
356	*Proverbs* 24.1–34
357	*Proverbs* 25.1–15
358	*Proverbs* 25.16—26.16
359	*Proverbs* 26.17—27.10
360	*Proverbs* 27.11–27
361	*Proverbs* 28.1–22
362	*Proverbs* 28.23—29.17
363	*Proverbs* 29.18—30.9
364	*Proverbs* 30.10–33
365	*Proverbs* 31.1–31

Plan for Reading Step Meditations and Their Related Bible Passages

Step	Scripture	Meditation
1	Matthew 8.23–25	Look Inside: *Running on Empty*
	Luke 15.17	Look Inside: *Anything Is Better Than This*
	Romans 8.5–8	Look Inside: *Dear Diary*
	2 Corinthians 12.8–10	Look Inside: *Bodybuilding*
	Proverbs 28.26	Look Inside: *Wise Up*
	James 4.6	Look Ahead: *On My Own*
	Psalm 88.1–9	Look Ahead: *"Listen Up!"*
	Proverbs 18.12	Look Ahead: *Hard of Hearing*
	John 20.24–29	Look Back: *Thomas*
2	Matthew 14.22–33	Look Inside: *Risk Inventory*
	Mark 9.23, 24	Look Inside: *Everyday Faith*
	John 3.16, 17	Look Inside: *People Matter to God*
	Psalm 18.1, 2	Look Inside: *The Crossroad*
	Psalm 34.18–22	Look Inside: *Safe Places*
	John 15.12–14	Look Ahead: *Mutt and Jeff*
	Psalm 10.17	Look Ahead: *See Past the Words*
	Proverbs 17.17	Look Ahead: *Through Tough Times*
	Acts 7.20–39	Look Back: *Moses*
3	Matthew 11.28–30	Look Inside: *The Substitute*
	John 6.35–40	Look Inside: *The Rest Is Easy*
	Romans 12.1	Look Inside: *Living Sacrifices*
	Psalm 3.3–6	Look Inside: *God Is There*
	Proverbs 3.5, 6	Look Inside: *Me, Myself, and I*
	Colossians 3.1, 2	Look Ahead: *Playing on a New Team*
	Hebrews 6.18–20	Look Ahead: *Take a Look*
	1 Peter 1.3–7	Look Ahead: *It's Okay*
	John 19.38–42	Look Back: *Joseph of Arimathea*
4	Luke 14.25–30	Look Inside: *First Things First*
	2 Corinthians 13.5–7	Look Inside: *Pop Quiz*
	Ephesians 5.3–5	Look Inside: *Words Speak Louder Than Actions*
	James 2.1–4	Look Inside: *Out of Focus*
	Proverbs 15.31–33	Look Inside: *Fourth Quarter Foul-Up*
	1 Corinthians 6.18–20	Look Ahead: *Looking Good*
	2 Thessalonians 2.16, 17	Look Ahead: *The Great Umpire*
	Proverbs 7.6–27	Look Ahead: *Trash the Trash*
	John 7.53—8.11	Look Back: *A Woman Caught in Sin*

Plan for Reading Step Meditations and Their Related Bible Passages

Step	Scripture	Meditation
	Ephesians 4.14–16	Look Inside: *Buying a Lie*
	Ephesians 5.8–14	Look Inside: *Dark to Light*
	James 5.16	Look Inside: *Keeping Short Accounts*
	I John 1.6–10	Look Inside: *Going Barefoot*
	Psalm 69.5	Look Inside: *Eyes in the Back of Their Heads*
	Ephesians 4.25	Look Ahead: *"Don't Forget What You're Made Of"*
	Hebrews 4.11–13	Look Ahead: *Roses*
	Proverbs 28.13	Look Ahead: *Internal Control*
	Luke 22.54–62	Look Back: *Peter*
6	2 Corinthians 5.16, 17	Look Inside: *Paid in Full*
	2 Thessalonians 3.3–5	Look Inside: *The Eyes of Love*
	Hebrews 4.14–16	Look Inside: *Picking Up the Tab*
	Psalm 4.3–5	Look Inside: *Tossing and Turning*
	Psalm 34.4–6	Look Inside: *Keep Looking Up*
	Romans 6.12–14	Look Ahead: *"No!"*
	Galatians 6.7, 8	Look Ahead: *Those Cheating Eyes*
	I John 4.13–18	Look Ahead: *Rejected*
	Psalm 16.10, 11	Look Back: *David*
	Luke 9.46–48	Look Inside: *And the Winner Is . . .*
	I John 3.4–6	Look Inside: *Three Strikes and You're Out*
	Psalm 25.6–10	Look Inside: *The Coach Knows*
	Psalm 141.3, 4	Look Inside: *Guardrails*
	Proverbs 3.11, 12	Look Inside: *Play by the Rules*
	I Corinthians 10.12, 13	Look Ahead: *Kick the Habit*
	2 Corinthians 5.18	Look Ahead: *Taking Time*
	Psalm 62.1, 2	Look Ahead: *God Is There for You*
	Luke 1.46–48	Look Back: *Mary*
	Mark 4.24	Look Inside: *Screaming Match*
	Luke 6.37, 38	Look Inside: *Bad Guys Wear White Hats*
	Romans 13.8–10	Look Inside: *Sneaking Out*
	Colossians 3.12–14	Look Inside: *Rude Awakenings*
	Proverbs 17.9, 10	Look Inside: *Let Go*
	Matthew 7.1–5	Look Ahead: *The Know-It-All*
	John 14.26	Look Ahead: *Creating a Scene*
	Psalm 91.14–16	Look Ahead: *Flaps Down*
	Luke 19.1–10	Look Back: *Zacchaeus*

Plan for Reading Step Meditations and Their Related Bible Passages

Step	Scripture	Meditation
	Romans 15.1–6	Look Inside: *A Sitting Duck*
	Philippians 1.9–11	Look Inside: *A Helping Hand*
	1 John 3.15–18	Look Inside: *I'm Sorry*
	Psalm 133.1–3	Look Inside: *Home Sweet Home*
	Proverbs 12.18–20	Look Inside: *Spring Break*
	Luke 6.27–36	Look Ahead: *First Place*
	2 Corinthians 2.5–8	Look Ahead: *Half a Chance*
	James 2.14–17	Look Ahead: *We Have Them Surrounded*
	Luke 10.29–37	Look Back: *Good Samaritan*
STEP 10	Philippians 2.14–16	Look Inside: *Skeletons in the Closet*
	James 1.13–15	Look Inside: *Setting a Trap*
	2 Peter 3.17, 18	Look Inside: *A Bad Mix*
	Proverbs 15.18–21	Look Inside: *Silence Is Golden*
	Proverbs 24.16	Look Inside: *The Good Guy*
	Romans 5.4, 5	Look Ahead: *Be Patient*
	Colossians 3.15–17	Look Ahead: *Guilty by Association*
	1 Peter 1.13–16	Look Ahead: *Disappointments*
	2 Timothy 4.9–18	Look Back: *Paul*
	Matthew 7.7–11	Look Inside: *It Takes a Genius*
	Galatians 5.16–18	Look Inside: *The Constant Battle*
	Philippians 3.12–16	Look Inside: *Press On*
	Psalm 40.1–5	Look Inside: *Checking Out*
	Psalm 119.140–144	Look Inside: *Sticks and Stones*
	John 14.15–21	Look Ahead: *Look Before You Leap*
	Galatians 6.9	Look Ahead: *Power Reserves*
	1 Peter 4.10, 11	Look Ahead: *Getting It Together*
	1 Timothy 4.6–16	Look Back: *Timothy*
	John 21.15–19	Look Inside: *Love That Shows*
	1 Thessalonians 1.7–10	Look Inside: *Everyone Is Watching*
	1 Peter 3.15–17	Look Inside: *Speak Up!*
	2 Peter 1.5–9	Look Inside: *Stay Focused*
	Psalm 92.1–4	Look Inside: *Making It Through the Night*
	Matthew 28.18–20	Look Ahead: *Coming Full Circle*
	2 Corinthians 4.1, 2	Look Ahead: *Admiration Society*
	Psalm 96.1–6	Look Ahead: *Chip on the Shoulder*
	Mark 10.46–52	Look Back: *Bartimaeus*

The Contemporary English Version

Translating the Contemporary English Version

Translation it is that opens the window, to let in the light; that breaks the shell, that we may eat the kernel; that puts aside the curtain, that we may look into the most holy place; that removes the cover of the well, that we may come by the water ("The Translators to the Reader," King James Version, 1611).

The Bible was written to be read! This means that a faithful translation of the Bible must be both *reliable* and *readable*. It must be a text that can be trusted and one that is suitable for both public and private reading, and also for memorizing.

The Contemporary English Version was translated with these goals in mind. Every attempt has been made to produce a text that is faithful to the *meaning* of the original and that can be read with ease and understanding by readers of all ages.

The translators of the King James Version had similar aims. According to the introduction that was published in the earliest editions of the KJV, the translators realized that a Hebrew or Greek word could not always be translated in the same way. They also knew that in order to make the *meaning* clear for their readers, they must often use a *form* that was very different from that of the original languages, but still true to the sacred text. That same translation principle has been followed in the CEV.

Like all reliable translations, the Contemporary English Version is made directly from the original languages of the Scriptures and is not an adaptation of any existing translation or translations. But not everyone who knows the biblical languages can do for today's readers what the KJV translators hoped to do for their own generation. Almost any scholar can produce a literal rendering of the original languages. But this is only the *first* step in the translation process. Two important questions must still be asked: "What do the words mean?" and "What is the most accurate and natural way to express this meaning in contemporary English?"

Not only was the Bible written to be read. It was written to be *understood*. But many readers fail to understand the meaning of a passage, because the translation itself keeps them from doing so. For example, "a kind of firstfruits of all he created" (James 1.18) may faithfully represent the *form* of the Greek text, but the *meaning* is certainly not clear, except for the reader who has special training in biblical backgrounds.

Traditional translations use words such as *justification, righteousness, redemption, reconciliation, propitiation, atonement, salvation, sanctification*, and *repentance*. All of these words are absent from the Contemporary English Version. One reason for this absence is that they are not used in everyday English. But there is an even more important reason: these are nouns, but they describe *actions* that God or people do. For example, the word *salvation* means "God saves people." *Repentance* is more difficult, because it refers to more than one event: Someone sinned and then turned from sin. In the CEV, each of these words may be translated in several different ways, depending on the special meaning they may have in a particular verse.

Many people are surprised to learn that one of the hardest words to translate is *grace*! The word is simple enough to pronounce, but it must always be explained. This is because in the New Testament *grace* means something far different from what it does in ordinary speech. The main problem is that the phrase "the grace of God" describes God in action, treating us much better than we deserve.

Acts 20:32 will show the difference between the way *grace* appears in traditional translations and how it is restructured by the Contemporary English Version. By following the form of the Greek text and using traditional language, the verse may be translated: "Now I commit you to God and to the word of his grace, which can build you up and give you an inheritance among all those who are sanctified."

"**T**he word of his grace" is difficult for several reasons: (1) "word" means "message"; (2) "of" merely shows that there is some relation between "word" and "grace," but it does not tell what the actual relation is; and (3) "grace" is an event, not an object.

There are also other problems in the verse: (1) "build you up" is not contemporary English usage; (2) "inheritance" is used in the special biblical sense of "what belongs to God's people"; (3) "those who are sanctified" is a New Testament way of referring to God's people; and (4) in the Greek text the pronoun "which" refers to "word," rather than to "grace."

In the Contemporary English Version every word, phrase, and clause of the original was carefully studied by the translators. Then, with equal care, they tried to find the best way to translate the verse so it could be easily read and understood. As a result, the form is very different, but the meaning is both *accurate* and *clear*: "Now I place you in God's care. Remember the message about his great kindness! This message can help you and give you what belongs to you as God's people."

The poetic sections of the Contemporary English Version, including the Psalms and Proverbs, are significantly different from those of any existing translation. This is because the translators are concerned with matters of visual attractiveness and the appearance of the text on the page. It is expected of poetry, not only that it *sound* good, but that it *look* good! Moreover, the choice of line breaks in poetry is as important to the translation as the choosing of words. And to alter the lines may result in a *mis*translation, especially for those who are hearing it read.

For this reason, poetic lines have been carefully measured in order to avoid awkwardly divided phrases and words that run over to the next line in clumsy ways. For example, "The lines have fallen to me in pleasant places" appears as follows in two separate publications of the Psalms:

"The lines have fallen to me in pleasant
places."

and

"The lines have fallen to me in ·
pleasant places."

Translating This Version

This is not the CEV translation of the verse. But if it were, the translators would require either that the text appear on the page as only one line or that it be divided as follows:

"The lines have fallen to me
 in pleasant places."

This format looks better and is easier to read and understand, because the text is divided according to "sense units." The goal of the translators is not only to produce an accurate translation that people can understand, but also to present it in a format that is appealing. This is what the psalm composers and others did when they wrote the poetic sections of the Bible, and it is their example that the CEV translators are seeking to follow.

The Contemporary English Version New Testament has been translated directly from the Greek text published by the United Bible Societies (third edition, corrected, 1983). The Contemporary English Version Psalms and Proverbs have been translated directly from the Masoretic Hebrew text printed in the *Biblia Hebraica Stuttgartensia* (4th edition, 1990), published by the German Bible Society. Drafts of the Contemporary English Version New Testament, and of the Psalms and Proverbs, were sent in their early stages for review and comment to a number of biblical scholars, theologians, and educators representing a wide variety of denominations. In addition, drafts were sent for response to all English-speaking Bible Societies and more than forty UBS translation consultants around the world. Final approval of the text was given by the American Bible Society's Board of Trustees upon recommendation of its Translations Subcommittee.

At the back of this book is a Word List which explains a number of terms and phrases. The New Testament books and the Old Testament books of Psalms and Proverbs are each preceded by an introduction (About This Book) and an outline of contents (A Quick Look At This Book). To help the reader, three kinds of notes are included: (1) notes that explain important differences in the Greek or Hebrew manuscripts, (2) notes that give another translation of the source text, and (3) notes that provide helpful information about Bible history and customs.

Books of the New Testament, Psalms, and Proverbs

The New Testament

About the New Testament

In the first century A.D., Christians and Jews used the same Scriptures, which Christians later called the Old Testament. Both of these communities of faith usually used these Scriptures in a Greek translation (called the Septuagint) instead of in the original languages of Hebrew and Aramaic. This collection of sacred writings in Greek was the Bible of the early Christians. They found proof in these writings that Jesus is the Messiah and the Son of God, and they also found there how God wanted them to live.

Later in the first century, Christians started writing the books that would become the New Testament. These were the books about the life and teaching of Jesus (called Gospels), the letters of Paul and others, and the books of the Acts of the Apostles and Revelation. All of these were written in Greek, which was a language that people all over the Roman empire could understand. By the second century, these books were widely used by Christians for preaching, teaching, worshiping, and telling about their faith.

The writings of the New Testament are arranged in an order that gives the greatest value to the four books (Gospels) about Jesus, since they tell about his life and teaching, his miracles, his saving death on a cross, and his rising to life. These four Gospels (Matthew, Mark, Luke, and John) take up almost half of the New Testament, which is another reason why they are placed first.

The Acts of the Apostles follows the four Gospels. It actually continues the Gospel of Luke and shows the connection between the ministry of Jesus and the mission of the early church. Acts shows how the followers of Jesus answered the question of whether Gentiles could also become Christians.

The letters of Paul follow next, and they are arranged roughly in order of their length (from Romans to Philemon). Most of these letters were written to churches Paul had started, and in them he deals with problems that had come up. Paul's letters are then followed by a group of writings known as the "general letters," because they are mostly addressed to a general audience and were to be circulated to other followers. These letters are also arranged roughly in order of their length (from Hebrews to 3 John and Jude).

Revelation is the last book in the New Testament, and it was written to give hope and encouragement to Christians who were suffering because of their faith. It is also a prophecy and contains visions of how God will punish evil people and reward his faithful followers.

The New Testament is the world's most widely read book! More than 70 million copies are printed throughout the world each year, and the complete New Testament has

About the New Testament

been translated into more than seven hundred languages.

How can a book that is almost two thousand years old be in such demand and influence so many lives today? Why are people so interested in a young Jewish carpenter named Jesus, who lived his short life without going more than seventy miles from the small village where he was born? The New Testament is in demand because it tells the good news about Jesus Christ! And this good news is God's powerful way of saving *everyone* who has faith in Jesus. In the New Testament we learn that God is kind and that he loved the people of this world so much that he sent Jesus Christ into the world to save us all.

For these reasons, and many more, people keep coming to the New Testament for the light and power it gives for daily living. Jesus promised his followers that God's Spirit would always guide them to understand the message of the Scriptures. And so, in the New Testament we are not reading dead words from the past. Here we meet Jesus Christ, the living Word of God.

ABOUT THIS BOOK

The Sermon on the Mount (5.1—7.28), the Lord's Prayer (6.9–13), and the Golden Rule (7.12: "Treat others as you want them to treat you") are all in this book. It is perhaps the best known and the most quoted of all the books that have ever been written about Jesus. That is one reason why Matthew was placed first among the four books about Jesus called Gospels.

One of the most important ideas found here is that God expects his people to obey him, and this is what is meant by the Greek word that appears in many translations as *righteousness*. It is used seven times by Matthew, but only once by Luke, and not at all by Mark. So it is an important clue to much of what Matthew wants his readers to understand about the teaching of Jesus.

Jesus first uses this word at his own baptism, when he tells John the Baptist, "We must do all that God wants us to do" (3.15). Then, during his Sermon on the Mount, he speaks five more times of what God's people must do to obey him (5.6,10,20; 6.1,33). And finally, he reminds the chief priests and leaders of the people, "John the Baptist showed you how to do right" (21.32).

Matthew wanted to provide for the people of his time a record of Jesus' message and ministry. It is clear that the Old Testament Scriptures were very important to these people. And Matthew never fails to show when these texts point to the coming of Jesus as the Messiah sent from God. Matthew wrote this book to make sure Christians knew that their faith in Jesus as the Messiah was well anchored in the Old Testament Scriptures, and to help them grow in faith.

Matthew ends his story with the words of Jesus to his followers, which tell what they are to do after he leaves them:

> I *have been given all authority in heaven and on earth*! *Go to the people of all nations and make them my disciples. Baptize them in the name of the* Father, *the* Son, *and the* Holy Spirit, *and teach them to do everything* I *have told you.* I *will be with you always, even until the end of the world.* (28.18*b*–20)

A QUICK LOOK AT THIS BOOK

1. The Ancestors and Birth of Jesus (1.1—2.23)
2. The Message of John the Baptist (3.1–12)
3. The Baptism and Temptation of Jesus (3.13–4.11)
4. Jesus in Galilee (4.12—18.35)
5. Jesus Goes from Galilee to Jerusalem (19.1—20.34)
6. Jesus' Last Week: His Trial and Death (21.1—27.66)
7. Jesus Is Alive (28.1–20)

The Ancestors of Jesus
(Luke 3.23–38)

1 Jesus Christ came from the family of King David and also from
the family of Abraham. And this is
a list of his ancestors.* 2-6a From
Abraham to King David, his ancestors were:
Abraham, Isaac, Jacob, Judah and
his brothers (Judah's sons were
Perez and Zerah, and their mother
was Tamar), Hezron;
Ram, Amminadab, Nahshon,
Salmon, Boaz (his mother was Rahab), Obed (his mother was Ruth),
Jesse, and King David.
6b-11 From David to the time of the
exile in Babylonia, the ancestors of
Jesus were:
David, Solomon (his mother had
been Uriah's wife), Rehoboam, Abijah, Asa, Jehoshaphat, Jehoram;
Uzziah, Jotham, Ahaz, Hezekiah,
Manasseh, Amon, Josiah, and Jehoiachin and his brothers.
12-16 From the exile to the birth of
Jesus, his ancestors were:
Jehoiachin, Shealtiel, Zerubbabel,
Abiud, Eliakim, Azor, Zadok, Achim;
Eliud, Eleazer, Matthan, Jacob,
and Joseph, the husband of Mary, the
mother of Jesus, who is called the
Messiah.
17 There were fourteen generations
from Abraham to David. There were
also fourteen from David to the exile
in Babylonia and fourteen more to
the birth of the Messiah.

The Birth of Jesus
(Luke 2.1–7)

18 This is how Jesus Christ was
born. A young woman named Mary
was engaged to Joseph from King
David's family. But before they were
married, she learned that she was going to have a baby by God's Holy
Spirit.* 19 Joseph was a good man[a]
and did not want to embarrass Mary
in front of everyone. So he decided
to quietly call off the wedding.
20 While Joseph was thinking about
this, an angel from the Lord came
to him in a dream. The angel said,
"Joseph, the baby that Mary will
have is from the Holy Spirit. Go
ahead and marry her. 21 Then after
her baby is born, name him Jesus,[b]
because he will save his people from
their sins."*
22 So God's promise came true, just
as the prophet had said, 23 "A virgin
will have a baby boy, and he will be

---

[a] *good man*: Or "kind man," or "man who always did the right thing." [b] *name him Jesus*: In Hebrew the name "Jesus" means "the Lord saves."

1.1 **JESUS HAD A FAMILY** Jesus is the real Son of God from heaven. But he is also a real man who had an earthly family. Matthew lists many people who had been in Jesus' ancient family for 2,000 years. Jesus needed the help of his parents and other family members to grow up in the world in a way that pleased God. Matthew's long list also helps us to see that the birth of Jesus had been in the mind of God for a very long time.

1.18 **JOSEPH AND MARY BELIEVED GOD** Mary and Joseph were a young couple who trusted God. Even though they didn't understand all that God was going to do, they knew they must believe that their Son from heaven would do a great work. In our own lives we don't always understand what God is doing. But it is more important to trust God than to think we have to understand everything.

1.21 **WHAT DID THEY NAME MARY'S SON?** They named him Jesus, meaning "The Lord Saves." It was a well-known name—the name Joshua is just a different spelling of it. The second part of Jesus' name is Christ (or Messiah), meaning "Anointed One." This meant that God himself filled the life of Jesus in a very special way that made him able to do all the works God sent him to do. But Matthew also reminds us that Jesus was called Immanuel—"God with us."

NOTES

called Immanuel," which means
"God is with us."
24After Joseph woke up, he and
Mary were soon married, just as the
Lord's angel had told him to do.
25But they did not live together before
her baby was born. Then Joseph
named him Jesus.

The Wise Men

2 When Jesus was born in the village of Bethlehem in Judea,
Herod was king. During this time
some wise men[c] from the east came
to Jerusalem* 2and said, "Where is
the child born to be king of the Jews?
We saw his star in the east[d] and have
come to worship him."
3When King Herod heard about
this, he was worried, and so was everyone else in Jerusalem. 4Herod
brought together all the chief priests
and the teachers of the Law of Moses
and asked them, "Where will the
Messiah be born?"
5They told him, "He will be born
in Bethlehem, just as the prophet
wrote,

6'Bethlehem in the land
  of Judea,
you are very important
  among the towns of Judea.
From your town
  will come a leader,
who will be like a shepherd
  for my people Israel.' "

7Herod secretly called in the wise
men and asked them when they had
first seen the star. 8He told them, "Go
to Bethlehem and search carefully
for the child. As soon as you find him,
let me know. I want to go and worship
him too."
9The wise men listened to what the
king said and then left. And the star
they had seen in the east went on
ahead of them until it stopped over
the place where the child was.*
10They were thrilled and excited to
see the star.
11When the men went into the
house and saw the child with Mary,
his mother, they kneeled down and
worshiped him. They took out their
gifts of gold, frankincense, and
myrrh[e] and gave them to him.
12Later they were warned in a dream
not to return to Herod, and they went
back home by another road.

The Escape to Egypt

13After the wise men had gone, an
angel from the Lord appeared to Joseph in a dream. The angel said, "Get
up! Hurry and take the child and his
mother to Egypt! Stay there until I
tell you to return, because Herod is
looking for the child and wants to
kill him."*

---

[c]*wise men*: People famous for studying the stars. [d]*his star in the east*: Or "his star rise." [e]*frankincense, and myrrh*: Frankincense was a valuable powder that was burned to make a sweet smell. Myrrh was a valuable sweet-smelling powder often used in perfume.

2.1 **WHERE WAS JESUS BORN?** Jesus was born in the town of Bethlehem in Judea. Bethlehem had a great history. There King David was born a thousand years earlier to a family begun by a couple named Boaz and Ruth. Boaz was a wealthy Hebrew farmer, but Ruth was from a hated Gentile race who came to true faith in the God of the Bible. Jesus descended from that great family.

2.9 **WISE MEN WORSHIPED JESUS** Even thinkers in faraway Persia—called Iran today—had been expecting a great King to be born in Palestine. Jewish ancestors of Jesus had told the Persians about the coming Savior. So when Persian scholars, called magi (pronounced MAJ-eye), saw a special star in their sky they believed that the King's birth was near. They traveled hundreds of miles across the desert to worship Jesus.

2.13 **GOD PROTECTED HIS SON** Wicked people envy and fear the good. King Herod was such an evil person. He was not the lawful king or even a Jew. He had been given the Jewish (*continued*)

NOTES

14That night Joseph got up and
took his wife and the child to Egypt,
15where they stayed until Herod died.
So the Lord's promise came true, just
as the prophet had said, "I called my
son out of Egypt."

The Killing of the Children

16When Herod found out that the
wise men from the east had tricked
him, he was very angry. He gave orders for his men to kill all the boys
who lived in or near Bethlehem and
were two years old and younger.
17So the Lord's promise came true,
just as the prophet Jeremiah had
said,

18"In Ramah a voice was heard
crying and weeping loudly.
Rachel was mourning
for her children,
and she refused
to be comforted,
because they were dead."

The Return from Egypt

19After King Herod died, an angel
from the Lord appeared in a dream
to Joseph while he was still in Egypt.
20The angel said, "Get up and take
the child and his mother back to Israel. The people who wanted to kill
him are now dead."*
21Joseph got up and left with them
for Israel. 22But when he heard that
Herod's son Archelaus was now ruler
of Judea, he was afraid to go there.
Then in a dream he was told to go
to Galilee, 23and they went to live
there in the town of Nazareth. So the
Lord's promise came true, just as the
prophet had said, "He will be called
a Nazarene."[f]

The Preaching of John the Baptist
(Mark 1.1–8; Luke 3.1–18; John 1.19–28)

3 Years later John the Baptist
started preaching in the desert of
Judea.* 2He said, "Turn back to God!
The kingdom of heaven[g] will soon
be here."[h]
3John was the one the prophet
Isaiah was talking about, when he
said,

"In the desert someone
is shouting,
'Get the road ready
for the Lord!
Make a straight path
for him.' "

---

[f]*He will be called a Nazarene*: The prophet who said this is not known. [g]*kingdom of heaven*: In the Gospel of Matthew "kingdom of heaven" is used with the same meaning as "God's kingdom" in Mark and Luke. [h]*will soon be here*: Or "is already here."

(*continued*) throne by the Roman conquerors for political reasons, so he was afraid when he heard that the true King was being born. Then Herod tried to kill Jesus by murdering a lot of boy babies in Bethlehem. But God had a plan for Jesus' life, so his parents took him away to Egypt. God is a hiding place for all who love him.

2.20 **BLOOM WHERE YOU'RE PLANTED** Jesus' family didn't return to Bethlehem when they came back from Egypt. They went to live far away in the northern farming and fishing district of Galilee. Growing up in the town of Nazareth like other boys, Jesus became a helper in the carpenter shop of Joseph, his earthly father. God usually gives us families so we can learn together. But if you're all alone in the world God cares about you in a very special way.

3.1 **LET YOUR LIFE COUNT FOR JESUS** John baptized people in the Jordan River when they told of their sorrow for their sins. By baptizing people John showed that God must wash away their sins. John was not afraid to stand alone and tell the world that Jesus is the Son of God who takes away people's sins. Be prepared always to show by the way you act that Jesus loves those around you and will take away their sins if they ask him.

NOTES

4John wore clothes made of camel's hair. He had a leather strap around his waist and ate grasshoppers and wild honey.
5From Jerusalem and all Judea and from the Jordan River Valley crowds of people went to John.* 6They told how sorry they were for their sins, and he baptized them in the river.
7Many Pharisees and Sadducees also came to be baptized. But John said to them:

You bunch of snakes! Who warned you to run from the coming judgment? 8Do something to show that you have really given up your sins. 9And don't start telling yourselves that you belong to Abraham's family. I tell you that God can turn these stones into children for Abraham. 10An ax is ready to cut the trees down at their roots. Any tree that does not produce good fruit will be chopped down and thrown into a fire.

11I baptize you with water so that you will give up your sins.[i] But someone more powerful is going to come, and I am not good enough even to carry his sandals.[j] He will baptize you with the Holy Spirit and with fire. 12His threshing fork is in his hand, and he is ready to separate the wheat from the husks.[k] He will store the wheat in a barn and burn the husks in a fire that never goes out.

The Baptism of Jesus
(Mark 1.9–11; Luke 3.21, 22)

13Jesus left Galilee and went to the Jordan River to be baptized by John.*
14But John kept objecting and said, "I ought to be baptized by you. Why have you come to me?"
15Jesus answered, "For now this is how it should be, because we must do all that God wants us to do." Then John agreed.
16So Jesus was baptized. And as soon as he came out of the water, the sky opened, and he saw the Spirit of God coming down on him like a dove. 17Then a voice from heaven said, "This is my own dear Son, and I am pleased with him."

Jesus and the Devil
(Mark 1.12, 13; Luke 4.1–13)

4 The Holy Spirit led Jesus into the desert, so that the devil could test him.* 2After Jesus went without eating[l] for forty days and nights, he was

---

[i] *so that you will give up your sins*: Or "because you have given up your sins." [j] *carry his sandals*: This was one of the duties of a slave. [k] *His threshing fork is in his hand, and he is ready to separate the wheat from the husks*: After Jewish farmers had trampled out the grain, they used a large fork to pitch the grain and the husks into the air. Wind would blow away the light husks, and the grain would fall back to the ground, where it could be gathered up. [l] *went without eating*: The Jewish people sometimes went without eating (also called "fasting") to show their love for God and to become better followers.

3.5 **WHERE IS THE JORDAN RIVER?** This river runs 70 miles to the Dead Sea from Lake Galilee. It was across this river that the ancient Jews miraculously passed into their promised land many hundreds of years before Jesus was born.

3.13 **THE KING WAS A SERVANT** John was surprised when Jesus himself came to the Jordan River to be baptized. But Jesus told John to baptize him anyway. That was how Jesus showed everybody he didn't come to lord it over people. Jesus the king made himself a servant of servants. People often try to be "number one." But Jesus warns us that the first will be last in his new kingdom.

4.1 **ARE YOU TESTED?** Jesus was tested so that he could help us when we're "put to the test" by things that tempt us to sin. He fought the devil's temptations and won. Jesus knows and cares when someone asks us to do something wrong—or when we just feel like doing wrong. We can't fight our battles with sin all alone, but we lean on our great Savior—and he always helps us when we ask him to.

NOTES

very hungry. 3Then the devil came
to him and said, "If you are God's
Son, tell these stones to turn into
bread."
4Jesus answered, "The Scriptures
say:

'No one can live only on food.
People need every word
that God has spoken.' "

5Next, the devil took Jesus to the
holy city and had him stand on the
highest part of the temple. 6The devil
said, "If you are God's Son, jump off.
The Scriptures say:

'God will give his angels
orders about you.
They will catch you
in their arms,
and you will not hurt
your feet on the stones.' "

7Jesus answered, "The Scriptures
also say, 'Don't try to test the Lord
your God!' "
8Finally, the devil took Jesus up on
a very high mountain and showed
him all the kingdoms on earth
and their power. 9The devil said
to him, "I will give all this to you, if
you will bow down and worship
me."
10Jesus answered, "Go away Satan! The Scriptures say:

'Worship the Lord your God
and serve only him.' "

11Then the devil left Jesus, and angels came to help him.

Jesus Begins His Work
(Mark 1.14, 15; Luke 4.14, 15)

12When Jesus heard that John had
been put in prison, he went to Galilee.* 13But instead of staying in Nazareth, Jesus moved to Capernaum.
This town was beside Lake Galilee
in the territory of Zebulun and
Naphtali.[m] 14So God's promise came
true, just as the prophet Isaiah had
said,

15"Listen, lands of Zebulun
and Naphtali,
lands along the road
to the sea and west
of the Jordan!
Listen Galilee,
land of the Gentiles!
16Although your people
live in darkness,
they will see
a bright light.
Although they live
in the shadow of death,
a light will shine
on them."

17Then Jesus started preaching,
"Turn back to God! The kingdom of
heaven will soon be here."[n]*

---

[m] *Zebulun and Naphtali*: In Old Testament times these tribes were in northern Palestine, and in New Testament times many Gentiles lived where these tribes had once been. [n] *The kingdom of heaven will soon be here*: See the two notes at 3.2.

4.12 **STAY OUT OF UNNECESSARY TROUBLE** Jesus had gone to the country of Judea, where he had been baptized by John the Baptist. But John was in prison because he preached the word of God. It was a bad time to be in Judea, and Jesus had much work to do before his death. So Jesus went back up to Galilee where he had grown up. Christians don't look for trouble. The time may well come to stand up and be counted for Jesus. Until then, we should ask God to give us the wisdom to avoid useless arguments.

4.17 **WE MUST TURN BACK TO GOD** God sees us as sheep who have strayed away from their shepherd. Sheep aren't very smart, so they sometimes wander off and get caught in bushes, or fall into holes, or get bitten by wolves. Jesus is our great Shepherd, and he wants to bring us back to where he can feed us and care for us. That means staying close to the other sheep, too. We all need to be part of a Christian church where God's word is taught and where we can learn to be strong members of the family of God.

NOTES

Jesus Chooses Four Fishermen
(Mark 1.16–20; Luke 5.1–11)

18While Jesus was walking along
the shore of Lake Galilee, he saw two
brothers. One was Simon, also
known as Peter, and the other was
Andrew. They were fishermen, and
they were casting their net into the
lake. 19Jesus said to them, "Come
with me! I will teach you how to bring
in people instead of fish." 20Right
then the two brothers dropped their
nets and went with him.*
21Jesus walked on until he saw
James and John, the sons of Zebedee.
They were in a boat with their father,
mending their nets. Jesus asked them
to come with him too. 22Right away
they left the boat and their father and
went with Jesus.

Jesus Teaches, Preaches, and Heals
(Luke 6.17–19)

23Jesus went all over Galilee,
teaching in the Jewish meeting
places and preaching the good news
about God's kingdom. He also healed
every kind of disease and sickness.
24News about him spread all over
Syria, and people with every kind of
sickness or disease were brought to
him. Some of them had a lot of demons in them, others were thought
to be crazy,[o] and still others could
not walk. But Jesus healed them
all.
25Large crowds followed Jesus
from Galilee and the region around
the ten cities known as Decapolis.[p]
They also came from Jerusalem, Judea, and from across the Jordan
River.

The Sermon on the Mount

5 When Jesus saw the crowds, he went up on the side of a mountain and sat down.[q]

Blessings
(Luke 6.20–23)

Jesus' disciples gathered around
him,* 2and he taught them:

3God blesses those people
who depend only on him.
They belong to the kingdom
of heaven![r]
4God blesses those people
who grieve.
They will find comfort!
5God blesses those people
who are humble.
The earth will belong
to them!
6God blesses those people
who want to obey him[s]
more than to eat or drink.
They will be given
what they want!

---

[o] *thought to be crazy*: In ancient times people with epilepsy were thought to be crazy. [p] *the ten cities known as Decapolis*: A group of ten cities east of Samaria and Galilee, where the people followed the Greek way of life. [q] *sat down*: Teachers in the ancient world, including Jewish teachers, usually sat down when they taught. [r] *They belong to the kingdom of heaven*: Or "The kingdom of heaven belongs to them." [s] *who want to obey him*: Or "who want to do right" or "who want everyone to be treated right."

4.20 **THE BROTHERS DROPPED THEIR NETS** Simon and Andrew dropped their nets to follow Jesus. James and John left their boat "right away." When Jesus called them, these men didn't try to hold on to their old way of life. Following Jesus was the one thing on their minds.

5.1 **BE A DISCIPLE** Sometimes we think "disciples" were only the people that Jesus invited to be his special followers when he lived on earth. But Jesus is always looking for disciples. A disciple is a pupil in the school of Jesus. We are Jesus' disciples when we promise to follow and obey him for the rest of our lives. As we read about the disciples of Jesus' time we see that they had a lot to learn, and sometimes the lessons they learned were very hard ones. We too have much to learn, and we must spend time with Jesus in prayer and study if we are to be useful to him.

NOTES

7God blesses those people
who are merciful.
They will be treated
with mercy!
8God blesses those people
whose hearts are pure.
They will see him!*
9God blesses those people
who make peace.
They will be called
his children!
10God blesses those people
who are treated badly
for doing right.
They belong to the kingdom
of heaven.[t]

11God will bless you when
people insult you, mistreat you,
and tell all kinds of evil lies about
you because of me. 12Be happy
and excited! You will have a
great reward in heaven. People
did these same things to the
prophets who lived long ago.

Salt and Light
(Mark 9.50; Luke 14.34, 35)

13You are like salt for
everyone on earth. But if salt no
longer tastes like salt, how can
it make food salty? All it is good
for is to be thrown out and
walked on.*

14You are like light for the
whole world. A city built on top
of a hill cannot be hidden, 15and
no one would light a lamp and
put it under a clay pot. A lamp
is placed on a lamp stand, where
it can give light to everyone in
the house. 16Make your light
shine, so that others will see the
good that you do and will praise
your Father in heaven.

The Law of Moses

17Don't suppose that I came to
do away with the Law and the
Prophets.[u] I did not come to do
away with them, but to give them
their full meaning.* 18Heaven
and earth may disappear. But I
promise you that not even a
period or comma will ever
disappear from the Law.
Everything written in it must
happen.

19If you reject even the least
important command in the Law
and teach others to do the same,
you will be the least important
person in the kingdom of
heaven. But if you obey and
teach others its commands, you

---

[t] *They belong to the kingdom of heaven*: See the note at 5.3. [u] *the Law and the Prophets*: The Jewish Scriptures, that is, the Old Testament.

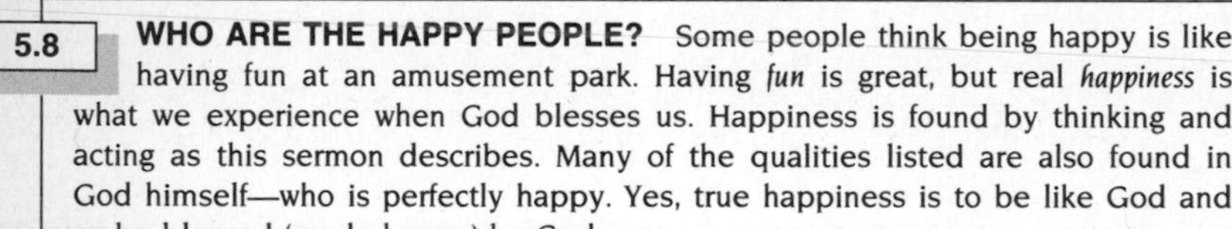

5.8 **WHO ARE THE HAPPY PEOPLE?** Some people think being happy is like having fun at an amusement park. Having *fun* is great, but real *happiness* is what we experience when God blesses us. Happiness is found by thinking and acting as this sermon describes. Many of the qualities listed are also found in God himself—who is perfectly happy. Yes, true happiness is to be like God and so be blessed (made happy) by God.

5.13 **LOOK AND ACT LIKE A CHRISTIAN** You are a Christian, you say. But does anyone else know it? Jesus doesn't employ secret agents. Christians "wear their hearts on their sleeves"—where everybody can see they really do love Jesus Christ. How? By what they say and what they do. Christians use their tongues to bless people, and their actions help people in trouble. If the world can't recognize a Christian on sight, maybe our Christianity isn't very real.

5.17 **WHAT GOOD ARE LAWS?** The *Lex Romana* (Law of the Romans) taught the world that a well-governed nation has fair laws. When respect for law breaks down, the nation itself fails. Some people believe they ought to be completely free to do whatever seems right—*to them*. We call the practice of that theory "anarchy." When anarchy rules, life and property are no longer sacred.

NOTES

will have an important place in
the kingdom. 20You must obey
God's commands better than the
Pharisees and the teachers of the
Law obey them. If you don't, I
promise you that you will never
get into the kingdom of heaven.

Anger

21You know that our ancestors
were told, "Do not murder" and
"A murderer must be brought to
trial."* 22But I promise you that
if you are angry with someone,[v]
you will have to stand trial. If
you call someone a fool, you will
be taken to court. And if you say
that someone is worthless, you
will be in danger of the fires of
hell.

23So if you are about to place
your gift on the altar and
remember that someone is angry
with you, 24leave your gift there
in front of the altar. Make peace
with that person, then come back
and offer your gift to God.

25Before you are dragged into
court, make friends with the
person who has accused you of
doing wrong. If you don't, you
will be handed over to the judge
and then to the officer who will
put you in jail. 26I promise you
that you will not get out until you
have paid the last cent you owe.

Marriage

27You know the command-
ment which says, "Be faithful in
marriage."* 28But I tell you that
if you look at another woman
and want her, you are already
unfaithful in your thoughts.
29If your right eye causes you to
sin, poke it out and throw it
away. It is better to lose one part
of your body, than for your
whole body to end up in hell.
30If your right hand causes you
to sin, chop it off and throw it
away! It is better to lose one part
of your body, than for your
whole body to be thrown into
hell.

Divorce
(Matthew 19.9; Mark 10.11, 12; Luke 16.18)

31You have been taught that
a man who divorces his wife
must write out divorce papers for
her.[w] 32But I tell you not to
divorce your wife unless she has
committed some terrible sexual
sin.[x] If you divorce her, you will
cause her to be unfaithful, just
as any man who marries her is

---

[v] *someone*: In verses 22-24 the Greek text has "brother," which may refer to people in general or to other followers. [w] *write out divorce papers for her*: Jewish men could divorce their wives, but the women could not divorce their husbands. The purpose of writing these papers was to make it harder for a man to divorce his wife. Before this law was made, all a man had to do was to send his wife away and say that she was no longer his wife. [x] *some terrible sexual sin*: This probably refers to the laws about the wrong kinds of marriages that are forbidden in Leviticus or to some serious sexual sin.

5.21 **ANGER IS THE BEGINNING OF MURDER** "Oh, I could just kill you" are not idle words. Anger and murder go together. If we really hate someone enough, we even want to kill that person. But there's another side to the double edge of anger. Our angry thoughts eat *us* up. People have become very sick as the effect of anger and hatred are allowed to build up in the mind. Could this be a warning that God himself will judge hateful attitudes?

5.27 **MARRIAGE IS SACRED** God created marriage. So, like everything else God created, marriage is holy. All our promises are serious, but there is no promise on earth more serious than the promises we make when we marry. When we break our promises to be faithful to our wives or husbands, we are breaking a vow we made before God. God cares about the people we hurt, and he will judge us for hurting those closest loved ones who trusted us.

NOTES

guilty of taking another man's
wife.

Promises

33You know that our ancestors
were told, "Don't use the Lord's
name to make a promise unless
you are going to keep it."* 34But
I tell you not to swear by
anything when you make a
promise! Heaven is God's
throne, so don't swear by
heaven. 35The earth is God's
footstool, so don't swear by the
earth. Jerusalem is the city of the
great king, so don't swear by it.
36Don't swear by your own head.
You cannot make one hair white
or black. 37When you make a
promise, say only "Yes" or
"No." Anything else comes from
the devil.

Revenge
(Luke 6.29, 30)

38You know that you have
been taught, "An eye for an eye
and a tooth for a tooth."* 39But
I tell you not to try to get even
with a person who has done
something to you. When
someone slaps your right
cheek,[y] turn and let that person
slap your other cheek. 40If
someone sues you for your shirt,
give up your coat as well. 41If a
soldier forces you to carry his
pack one mile, carry it two
miles.[z] 42When people ask you
for something, give it to them.
When they want to borrow
money, loan it to them.

Love
(Luke 6.27, 28, 32–36)

43You have heard people say,
"Love your neighbors and hate
your enemies."* 44But I tell you
to love your enemies and pray
for anyone who mistreats you.
45Then you will be acting like
your Father in heaven. He makes
the sun rise on both good and
bad people. And he sends rain
for the ones who do right and
for the ones who do wrong.
46If you love only those people
who love you, will God reward
you for that? Even tax
collectors[a] love their friends.
47If you greet only your friends,
what's so great about that? Don't
even unbelievers do that? 48But
you must always act like your
Father in heaven.

---

[y]*right cheek*: A slap on the right cheek was a bad insult. [z]*two miles*: A Roman soldier had the right to force a person to carry his pack as far as one mile. [a]*tax collectors*: These were usually Jewish people who paid the Romans for the right to collect taxes. They were hated by other Jews who thought of them as traitors to their country and to their religion.

5.33 **OUR PROMISE SHOULD BE ENOUGH** God really rules the world, so we can never be sure we will be allowed to do all we wish. That's why we say, "Till death do us part" when we marry. So we should be careful not to take vows to God we may not be able to keep. But our own "yes" or "no" should be the trustworthy answer of one honest person to another. Otherwise we ought to keep quiet.

5.38 **NOT FIGHTING BACK** Jesus teaches us not to pay back one hurt with another one. We ought to take it when we are harmed, and know that God will see that justice is done in the end. This has always been a very hard teaching for people to live by.

5.43 **LOVE OTHERS AS GOD LOVED YOU** God gave us life itself, and, as if that weren't enough, he even gave his own Son to die for us before we loved him. So then, can we not afford the small trouble of doing kind things for people around us? By loving even our enemies we show the world what God is like. Isn't that how he loved us?

NOTES

Giving

6 When you do good deeds, don't
try to show off. If you do, you
won't get a reward from your
Father in heaven.*
2When you give to the poor,
don't blow a loud horn. That's
what showoffs do in the meeting
places and on the street corners,
because they are always looking
for praise. I promise you that
they already have their reward.
3When you give to the poor,
don't let anyone know about it.[b]
4Then your gift will be given in
secret. Your Father knows what
is done in secret, and he will
reward you.

Prayer
(Luke 11.2–4)

5When you pray, don't be like
those showoffs who love to stand
up and pray in the meeting
places and on the street corners.
They do this just to look good.
I promise you that they already
have their reward.*

6When you pray, go into a
room alone and close the door.
Pray to your Father in private.
He knows what is done in
private, and he will reward you.
7When you pray, don't talk on
and on as people do who don't
know God. They think God likes
to hear long prayers. 8Don't be
like them. Your Father knows
what you need before you ask.
9You should pray like this:
Our Father in heaven,
help us to honor
your name.
10Come and set up
your kingdom,
so that everyone on earth
will obey you,
as you are obeyed
in heaven.
11Give us our food for today.[c]

12Forgive our sins,
as we forgive others.[d]
13Keep us from being tempted
and protect us from evil.[e]

14If you forgive others for the
wrongs they do to you, your
Father in heaven will forgive
you. 15But if you don't forgive
others, your Father will not
forgive your sins.

Worshiping God by Going without Eating

16When you go without
eating,[f] don't try to look gloomy
as those showoffs do when they
go without eating. I promise you
that they already have their
reward. 17Instead, comb your
hair and wash your face. 18Then
others won't know that you are
going without eating. But your
Father sees what is done in
private, and he will reward you.

---

[b]*don't let anyone know about it*: The Greek text has, "Don't let your left hand know what your right hand is doing." [c]*our food for today*: Or "the food that we need" or "our food for the coming day." [d]*sins . . . others*: Or "what we owe . . . what others owe." [e]*evil*: Or "the evil one," that is, the devil. Some manuscripts add, "The kingdom, the power, and the glory are yours forever. Amen." [f]*without eating*: See the note at 4.2.

6.1 **WHY DO WE GIVE?** Giving just to be seen by others doesn't impress God, and in the long run it doesn't impress people either. If we give just so the world can see what good people we are, those observing us soon realize that we're "all show" and no reality. Let's give for the right reason: that we want to help others because God first helped us.

6.5 **HOW SHOULD WE PRAY?** God doesn't want beautiful speeches. He looks for sincere hearts. And this is the first thing to remember about prayer. God already knows our hearts, and our well-formed sentences aren't what count. Jesus shows that truthfulness in prayer is the important thing, not appearances. But he also reminds us that we have to care about the things God cares about. Otherwise our prayers will be selfish.

NOTES

Treasures in Heaven
(Luke 12.33, 34)

19Don't store up treasures on
earth! Moths and rust can
destroy them, and thieves can
break in and steal them.*
20Instead, store up your
treasures in heaven, where
moths and rust cannot destroy
them, and thieves cannot break
in and steal them. 21Your heart
will always be where your
treasure is.

Light
(Luke 11.34–36)

22Your eyes are like a window
for your body. When they are
good, you have all the light you
need. 23But when your eyes are
bad, everything is dark. If the
light inside you is dark, you
surely are in the dark.

Money
(Luke 16.13)

24You cannot be the slave of
two masters! You will like one
more than the other or be more
loyal to one than the other. You
cannot serve both God and
money.*

Worry
(Luke 12.22–31)

25I tell you not to worry about
your life. Don't worry about
having something to eat, drink,
or wear. Isn't life more than food
or clothing? 26Look at the birds
in the sky! They don't plant or
harvest. They don't even store
grain in barns. Yet your Father
in heaven takes care of them.
Aren't you worth more than
birds?

27Can worry make you live
longer?[g]* 28Why worry about
clothes? Look how the wild
flowers grow. They don't work
hard to make their clothes.
29But I tell you that Solomon
with all his wealth[h] was not as
well clothed as one of them.
30God gives such beauty to
everything that grows in the
fields, even though it is here
today and thrown into a fire
tomorrow. He will surely do
even more for you! Why do you
have such little faith?
31Don't worry and ask
yourselves, "Will we have

---

[g] *live longer*: Or "grow taller." [h] *Solomon with all his wealth*: The Jewish people thought that Solomon was the richest person who had ever lived.

6.19 **THIS WORLD IS PASSING AWAY** Yes, scientists tell us that the earth will one day just die. There is a natural law that says everything in this world is going to wear out. So let us pay attention to the things that cannot die. God cannot die, and he has given us souls—an inner life—that can never die. He has prepared an eternal home for those who love him and who love the things he loves. It just makes sense to value the things that will last forever.

6.24 **MONEY IS A HARD MASTER** People who have money for their master are never happy. No matter how long and how hard they struggle, they never get to the point where they feel they have enough. But those who have God for their master are able to be truly satisfied.

6.27 **WORRY IS A DESTROYER** Worry doesn't help us improve our lives. A doctor will tell you that worry ruins your health and shortens your life. God is in charge of everything you see around you and everything you can't see. So isn't it reasonable to trust God in all things? Let's do our duty, and God will take care of the rest. This is the secret of a happy life.

NOTES

Step 8

DETERMINATION—Being willing to make things right at all costs

MATTHEW 7.1–5

THE KNOW-IT-ALL

For once I kept my mouth shut. Do you know how hard that is? I still consider my brother a "know-it-all," but I accept that he has the right to say what he thinks. And he usually does.

Before, I would go crazy. If he even opened his mouth, I would jump in with both feet. I ran him down because I wanted him to be on my level. I was the type who did the least I could just to get by. I always thought it was my brother who was wasting his time studying and being Mr. Good Guy.

Now I see that I was the one wasting time. I was always trying to find the easy way out. My brother warned me that in the long run, my so-called easy way would be a much harder route to take. He was right. Give credit where credit is due.

Don't get me wrong, he still annoys me at times, but I'm learning that if I give him half a chance he has something worthwhile to say.

STEP LOOK AHEAD 8

UP AND DOWN

It is hard to admit we don't have all the answers, particularly when we are around people who seem to. It's important to remember that God thinks we're smart when we are willing to admit we don't know it all. It especially pays good dividends when we admit when we are wrong, let our defenses down, and lift someone else up.

For another "Look Ahead," turn to page 222.

anything to eat? Will we have
anything to drink? Will we have
any clothes to wear?" 32 Only
people who don't know God are
always worrying about such
things. Your Father in heaven
knows that you need all of these.
33 But more than anything else,
put God's work first and do what
he wants. Then all the other
things will be yours as well.
34 Don't worry about
tomorrow. It will take care of
itself. You have enough to worry
about today.

Judging Others
(Luke 6.37, 38, 41, 42)

STEP LOOK AHEAD 8

7 Don't condemn others, and God
will not condemn you. 2 God will
be as hard on you as you are on
others! He will treat you exactly
as you treat them.
3 You can see the speck in your
friend's eye, but you don't notice
the log in your own eye.* 4 How
can you say, "My friend, let me
take the speck out of your eye,"
when you don't see the log in
your own eye? 5 You're nothing
but showoffs! First, take the log
out of your own eye. Then you
can see how to take the speck
out of your friend's eye.
6 Don't give to dogs what
belongs to God. They will only
turn and attack you. Don't throw
pearls down in front of pigs.
They will trample all over them.

Ask, Search, Knock
(Luke 11.9–13)

7 Ask, and you will receive.
Search, and you will find. Knock,
and the door will be opened for
you.* 8 Everyone who asks will
receive. Everyone who searches
will find. And the door will be
opened for everyone who
knocks. 9 Would any of you give
your hungry child a stone, if the
child asked for some bread?
10 Would you give your child a
snake if the child asked for a
fish? 11 As bad as you are, you
still know how to give good gifts
to your children. But your
heavenly Father is even more
ready to give good things to
people who ask.
12 Treat others as you want
them to treat you. This is what
the Law and the Prophets[i] are
all about.

The Narrow Gate
(Luke 13.24)

13 Go in through the narrow
gate. The gate to destruction is
wide, and the road that leads
there is easy to follow. A lot of
people go through that gate.*

---

[i] *the Law and the Prophets*: See the note at 5.17.

7.3 **MIND YOUR OWN BUSINESS** This is often stern but good advice. Nobody likes people who meddle in the concerns of others. God did not appoint us to do his work of judging the worth of people. It is enough that we ourselves measure up to his standards of behavior. Anyway, we usually don't know enough about other people's business to judge them. But God knows and judges the hearts of all.

7.7 **LOOK TO THE LORD FOR YOUR ANSWER** Jesus means for us to *keep on* asking, searching, knocking—and the answer will come at last. God cares about our needs. Like a wise father, he doesn't spoil his children by giving them all they want when they want it. He supplies their needs and answers their wishes in the right ways and at the right times. In the meantime, let's keep talking to God about the things that concern us. God isn't deaf, and he will prove his love to us.

7.13 **GOD'S WAY IS THE BEST WAY** Jesus said the godly way is truly the hard way to follow. That's because we easily prize the wrong things. Some people imagine such things as (*continued*)

NOTES

Step 11

I will pray to God on a regular basis, asking him to direct me and give me the power to live for him.

MATTHEW 7.7–11

IT TAKES A GENIUS

Did you ever play one of those trivia games? No matter how much you think you know, you never know enough? It almost takes a genius to win those games. That's pretty much the way it is in life. We think as we get older and have more experience, we will know all the right answers, but that never really happens. The more we know, the more we need to know, particularly now that we are trying to lead lives that are pleasing to God and others. How are we going to get it all straight?

STEP LOOK INSIDE 11

Our first smart move is to realize we can't. The Lord says to stay in close contact with him, and he will give us the answers we need. But how do we do that? Here's our second smart move. We need to learn to pray. It doesn't take great theological words, and there is no right or wrong way to do it.

WE KNOW ONE

When we talk to the Lord like we would to a friend—when we let him know what is going on in our lives—where we are having trouble or hurting—he promises he'll give us the right response. It took a Genius to get our lives straight, and it's going to take a Genius to keep them that way. Good thing we know One.

For another "Look Inside," turn to page 379.

14But the gate to life is very
narrow. The road that leads
there is so hard to follow that
only a few people find it.

A Tree and Its Fruit
(Luke 6.43–45)

15Watch out for false prophets!
They dress up like sheep, but
inside they are wolves who have
come to attack you.* 16You can
tell what they are by what they
do. No one picks grapes or figs
from thorn bushes. 17A good tree
produces good fruit, and a bad
tree produces bad fruit. 18A good
tree cannot produce bad fruit,
and a bad tree cannot produce
good fruit. 19Every tree that
produces bad fruit will be
chopped down and burned.
20You can tell who the false
prophets are by their deeds.

A Warning
(Luke 13.26, 27)

21Not everyone who calls me
their Lord will get into the
kingdom of heaven. Only the
ones who obey my Father in
heaven will get in. 22On the day
of judgment many will call me
their Lord. They will say, "We
preached in your name, and in
your name we forced out
demons and worked many
miracles." 23But I will tell them,
"I will have nothing to do with
you! Get out of my sight, you evil
people!"

Two Builders
(Luke 6.47–49)

24Anyone who hears and
obeys these teachings of mine is
like a wise person who built a
house on solid rock.* 25Rain
poured down, rivers flooded,
and winds beat against that
house. But it did not fall, because
it was built on solid rock.
26Anyone who hears my
teachings and does not obey
them is like a foolish person who
built a house on sand. 27The rain
poured down, the rivers flooded,
and the winds blew and beat
against that house. Finally, it fell
with a crash.
28When Jesus finished speaking,
the crowds were surprised at his
teaching. 29He taught them like
someone with authority, and not like
their teachers of the Law of Moses.

(*continued*) drugs, alcohol, and immoral living will bring them happiness. But do we need to be told that these things always lead to misery in the end? We make God's way hard for ourselves. God's way really is the road to the gate of everlasting joy and peace. If we miss that way, it is perhaps just because we follow the crowd instead of Jesus.

7.15 **ACTIONS SPEAK LOUDER THAN WORDS** There have always been a lot of talkers who claim to have new answers to life's questions that are better than God's answers. Many people went around preaching "new thought" in early times. They even wormed their way into the Christian church. But their empty words were like vapor that soon vanished. Many similar false prophets are around today. Let's just be patient. In good time we will see that all such claims to superior wisdom will come to an end. We know God's truth by its godly results.

7.24 **SAYING IT DOESN'T MAKE IT TRUE** Those who make outward religious claims sometimes display a religion that is only skin-deep. Such people may deceive those around them with their words—and may even make a good try at deceiving themselves, but God cannot be deceived. What counts in the end is simple, daily obedience. Real faith produces people who do good and lovely things. What they build stands forever, because they build on the foundation of Jesus' words.

NOTES

Jesus Heals a Man
(Mark 1.40–45; Luke 5.12–16)

8 As Jesus came down the mountain, he was followed by large
crowds. 2Suddenly a man with leprosy[j] came and kneeled in front of
Jesus. He said, "Lord, you have the
power to make me well, if only you
wanted to."*
3Jesus put his hand on the man and
said, "I do want to! Now you are
well." At once the man's leprosy disappeared. 4Jesus told him, "Don't tell
anyone about this, but go and show
the priest that you are well. Then take
a gift to the temple just as Moses commanded, and everyone will know
that you have been healed."[k]

Jesus Heals an Army Officer's Servant
(Luke 7.1–10; John 4.43–54)

5When Jesus was going into the
town of Capernaum, an army officer
came up to him and said, 6"Lord, my
servant is at home in such terrible
pain that he can't even move."
7"I will go and heal him," Jesus
replied.
8But the officer said, "Lord, I'm not
good enough for you to come into
my house. Just give the order, and
my servant will get well.* 9I have officers who give orders to me, and I
have soldiers who take orders from
me. I can say to one of them, 'Go!'
and he goes. I can say to another,
'Come!' and he comes. I can say to
my servant, 'Do this!' and he will do
it."
10When Jesus heard this, he was
so surprised that he turned and said
to the crowd following him, "I tell
you that in all of Israel I've never
found anyone with this much faith!
11Many people will come from everywhere to enjoy the feast in the kingdom of heaven with Abraham, Isaac,
and Jacob. 12But the ones who should
have been in the kingdom will be
thrown out into the dark. They will
cry and grit their teeth in pain."
13Then Jesus said to the officer,
"You may go home now. Your faith
has made it happen."
Right then his servant was healed.

Jesus Heals Many People
(Mark 1.29–34; Luke 4.38–41)

14Jesus went to the home of Peter,
where he found that Peter's mother-
in-law was sick in bed with fever.
15He took her by the hand, and the
fever left her. Then she got up and
served Jesus a meal.*
16That evening many people with
demons in them were brought to
Jesus. And with only a word he
forced out the evil spirits and healed
everyone who was sick. 17So God's
promise came true, just as the
prophet Isaiah had said,

"He healed our diseases
and made us well."

---

[j] *leprosy*: In biblical times the word "leprosy" was used for many different kinds of skin diseases.
[k] *everyone will know that you have been healed*: People with leprosy had to be examined by a priest and told that they were well (that is "clean") before they could once again live a normal life in the Jewish community. The gift that Moses commanded was the sacrifice of some lambs together with flour mixed with olive oil.

8.2 **JESUS HAS THE POWER** The man with leprosy came to Jesus with the right idea: his getting healed depended only on Jesus' power and Jesus' wishes—not on what the man did to arrange for his healing. His eyes were on Jesus.

8.8 **WHO IS GOOD ENOUGH FOR JESUS?** The army officer was right. He was *not* good enough for Jesus. But we also should get the message—Jesus didn't come to us because we are good, but because we are sinners who need him. Nobody in church is good enough to be there. But we come to Jesus and become part of his family because he invites us to share his love and receive his forgiveness.

8.15 **SERVING JESUS** Peter's mother-in-law was grateful to Jesus for healing her, and she got up and served him. Do we serve the Lord who has done so many kind things for us?

NOTES

Some Who Wanted to Go with Jesus
(Luke 9.57–62)

18When Jesus saw the crowd,[l] he
went across Lake Galilee. 19A
teacher of the Law of Moses came
up to him and said, "Teacher, I'll go
anywhere with you!"
20Jesus replied, "Foxes have dens,
and birds have nests. But the Son of
Man does not have a place to call
his own."*
21Another disciple said to Jesus,
"Lord, let me wait till I bury my
father."
22Jesus answered, "Come with me,
and let the dead bury their dead." [m]

A Storm
(Mark 4.35–41; Luke 8.22–25)

23After Jesus left in a boat with his
disciples,* 24a terrible storm suddenly struck the lake, and waves
started splashing into their boat.
Jesus was sound asleep, 25so the
disciples went over to him and woke
him up. They said, "Lord, save us!
We're going to drown!"
26But Jesus replied, "Why are you
so afraid? You surely don't have
much faith." Then he got up and ordered the wind and the waves to calm
down. And everything was calm.
27The men in the boat were amazed
and said, "Who is this? Even the wind
and the waves obey him."

Two Men with Demons in Them
(Mark 5.1–20; Luke 8.26–39)

28After Jesus had crossed the lake,
he came to shore near the town of
Gadara[n] and started down the road.
Two men with demons in them came
to him from the tombs.[o] They were
so fierce that no one could travel that
way. 29Suddenly they shouted,
"Jesus, Son of God, what do you want
with us? Have you come to punish
us before our time?"*
30Not far from there a large herd
of pigs was feeding. 31So the demons
begged Jesus, "If you force us out,
please send us into those pigs!"
32Jesus told them to go, and they
went out of the men and into the pigs.
All at once the pigs rushed down the
steep bank into the lake and
drowned.

---

[l] *saw the crowd*: Some manuscripts have "large crowd." Others have "large crowds." [m] *let the dead bury their dead*: For the Jewish people a proper burial of their dead was a very important duty. But Jesus teaches that following him is even more important. [n] *Gadara*: Some manuscripts have "Gergasa." Others have "Gerasa." [o] *tombs*: It was thought that demons and evil spirits lived in tombs and in caves that were used for burying the dead.

8.20 **HAVE YOU TRADED IN YOUR OLD LIFE?** Jesus made himself poor so he could give us the riches of a new life to be spent forever with him. But in order to receive that *new* life, we have to leave the *old* life behind. That frightens some people until they see what Jesus is giving them to replace it. He will supply all our needs and assure us of a heavenly home as well.

8.23 **DON'T BE AFRAID OF STORMS** The world we grow up in is a frightening place sometimes, with its storms of poverty, crime, sickness, and death. The disciples feared the wind and the waves. They had to learn that Jesus is Lord of all, including storms. He is Lord over whatever frightens us. Our fears go away when we learn that Jesus is really in charge of all that happens.

8.29 **SIN MAKES PEOPLE AFRAID OF JESUS** What strange behavior. These two men actually thought Jesus had come to punish them. The evil spirits who lived in the men had confused their thinking. But Jesus had come to save the men from the spirits that tormented them. Even the townspeople were confused. They weren't glad that the demon-possessed men were saved; rather, they were upset because the pigs had drowned. Their thinking was upside-down.

NOTES

Step 1

I admit I cannot be successful on my own . . . I need help, daily.

MATTHEW 8.23–25

RUNNING ON EMPTY

My Dad is going to kill me.
The last thing he said was, "The first thing you need to do is put gas in the car—here's a ten." Can I help it if my share of the pizza was eight bucks? It cost two dollars to get in the game!

Mom always drives it on *E*. She had the car all day; why didn't she put gas in it?

It's not my fault!

But's it's me out here in the middle of nowhere. No gas.
No money. And, okay,
Dad, no excuses.

STEP 1 LOOK INSIDE

RUNNING OUT OF GAS

When we run out of gas spiritually, it is always the result of being out of touch with our source of power. The problem is we tend to keep pushing, never admitting that we're drying up inside. Owning up to the fact that we cannot be successful on our own is just the beginning of full and meaningful life.

For another "Look Inside," turn to page 159.

33The people taking care of the pigs
ran to the town and told everything,
especially what had happened to the
two men. 34Everyone in town came
out to meet Jesus. When they saw
him, they begged him to leave their
part of the country.

Jesus Heals a Crippled Man
(Mark 2.1–12; Luke 5.17–26)

9 Jesus got into a boat and crossed
back over to the town where he
lived.[p] 2Some people soon brought
to him a crippled man lying on a mat.
When Jesus saw how much faith they
had, he said to the crippled man, "My
friend, don't worry! Your sins are
forgiven."*
3Some teachers of the Law of Moses said to themselves, "Jesus must
think he is God!"
4But Jesus knew what was in their
minds, and he said, "Why are you
thinking such evil things? 5Is it easier
for me to tell this crippled man that
his sins are forgiven or to tell him
to get up and walk?* 6But I will show
you that the Son of Man has the right
to forgive sins here on earth." So
Jesus said to the man, "Get up! Pick
up your mat and go on home."
7The man got up and went home.
8When the crowds saw this, they
were afraid[q] and praised God for giving such authority to people.

Jesus Chooses Matthew
(Mark 2.13–17; Luke 5.27–32)

9As Jesus was leaving, he saw a
tax collector[r] named Matthew sitting
at the place for paying taxes. Jesus
said to him, "Come with me." Matthew got up and went with him.
10Later, Jesus and his disciples
were having dinner at Matthew's
house.[s] Many tax collectors and
other sinners were also there.
11Some Pharisees asked Jesus' disciples, "Why does your teacher eat
with tax collectors and other sinners?"*
12Jesus heard them and answered,
"Healthy people don't need a doctor,
but sick people do. 13Go and learn
what the Scriptures mean when they
say, 'Instead of offering sacrifices to
me, I want you to be merciful to others.' I didn't come to invite good people to be my followers. I came to invite sinners."

---

[p]*where he lived*: Capernaum. See 4.13. [q]*afraid*: Some manuscripts have "amazed." [r]*tax collector*: See the note at 5.46. [s]*Matthew's house*: Or "Jesus' house."

9.2 **WHAT WAS JESUS' REAL WORK?** Jesus always put first things first. It's our way to put first things *last*. Our real problem is not our aches and pains. Our real problem is our sins. Some people may laugh at this, but they never ask themselves what caused human suffering in the days of Adam and Eve. Jesus knew sin was the cause. So he forgave the crippled man's sins, and then went on to illustrate his point by healing the man. Jesus is the Savior of both our souls and bodies. But even the bystanders missed his meaning.

9.5 **OUR BODIES ARE IMPORTANT** Our bodies are what we live in. This includes all the experiences we take for granted, like smelling a rose, tasting a good steak, hearing beautiful music, or viewing a lovely mountain scene. God gave us our bodies, so they're worth taking care of.

9.11 **JESUS KEPT STRANGE COMPANY** Jesus never changed his lifestyle to suit his surroundings. He was always the same. Yet, if we can imagine it, Jesus was *the friend of sinners*. This was a fact that disgusted the religious leaders. They had completely misunderstood God's plan in sending his Son into the world—to seek and to save lost people. Not only that, but Jesus even made apostles of such hated people as Matthew the tax collector. This sinner became the writer of the book about Jesus you are reading now.

NOTES

People Ask about Going without Eating
(Mark 2.18–22; Luke 5.33–39)

14 One day some followers of John
the Baptist came and asked Jesus,
"Why do we and the Pharisees often
go without eating,[t] while your disciples never do?"
15 Jesus answered:
The friends of a bridegroom
don't go without eating while he
is still with them. But the time
will come when he will be taken
from them. Then they will go
without eating.
16 No one uses a new piece of
cloth to patch old clothes. The
patch would shrink and tear a
bigger hole.*
17 No one pours new wine into
old wineskins. The wine would
swell and burst the old skins.[u]
Then the wine would be lost, and
the skins would be ruined. New
wine must be put into new
wineskins. Both the skins and
the wine will then be safe.

A Dead Girl and a Sick Woman
(Mark 5.21–43; Luke 8.40–56)

18 While Jesus was still speaking,
a Jewish official came and kneeled
in front of him. The man said, "My
daughter has just now died! Please
come and place your hand on her.
Then she will live again."
19 Jesus and his disciples got up and
went with the man.
20 A woman who had been bleeding
for twelve years came up behind
Jesus and barely touched his clothes.
21 She had said to herself, "If I can
just touch his clothes, I will get
well."*
22 Jesus turned. He saw the woman
and said, "Don't worry! You are now
well because of your faith." At that
moment she was healed.
23 When Jesus went into the home
of the Jewish official and saw the musicians and the crowd of mourners,[v]
24 he said, "Get out of here! The little
girl is not dead. She is just asleep."
Everyone started laughing at Jesus.
25 But after the crowd had been sent
out of the house, Jesus went to the
girl's bedside. He took her by the
hand and helped her up.
26 News about this spread all over
that part of the country.

Jesus Heals Two Blind Men

27 As Jesus was walking along, two
blind men began following him and
shouting, "Son of David,[w] have pity
on us!"*
28 After Jesus had gone indoors, the

---

[t] *without eating*: See the note at 4.2. [u] *swell and burst the old skins*: While the juice from grapes was becoming wine, it would swell and stretch the skins in which it had been stored. If the skins were old and stiff, they would burst. [v] *the crowd of mourners*: The Jewish people often hired mourners for funerals. [w] *Son of David*: The Jewish people expected the Messiah to be from the family of King David, and for this reason the Messiah was often called the "Son of David."

9.16 **NEW AND OLD** New and old cloth don't go together, and neither do new wine and old wineskins. Why did Jesus say this? He was showing his followers that now that he was here, something new was happening, and the old religious customs of the Jews would not be needed.

9.21 **HOW MUCH CAN WE TRUST JESUS?** A man had a dead daughter. A woman had a bleeding sickness. Both of them acted simply as if Jesus could and would immediately help them. Were they right to have such faith? Jesus says our blessings are the results of our faith in him. Have we really tested his ability to the utmost? Are there any limits to what he can do for our good if we trust him?

9.27 **FAITH IS IMPORTANT** Here's another example. The blind men had faith in Jesus, and he said they could be healed because of their faith. The two men came to him confidently, with their hearts full of trust. It meant a lot to Jesus.

NOTES

two blind men came up to him. He
asked them, "Do you believe I can
make you well?"
"Yes, Lord," they answered.
29Jesus touched their eyes and
said, "Because of your faith, you will
be healed." 30They were able to see,
and Jesus strictly warned them not
to tell anyone about him. 31But they
left and talked about him to everyone
in that part of the country.

Jesus Heals a Man Who Could Not Talk

32As Jesus and his disciples were
on their way, some people brought
to him a man who could not talk because a demon was in him. 33After
Jesus had forced the demon out, the
man started talking. The crowds
were so amazed that they began saying, "Nothing like this has ever happened in Israel!"
34But the Pharisees said, "The
leader of the demons gives him the
power to force out demons."*

Jesus Has Pity on People

35Jesus went to every town and village. He taught in their meeting
places and preached the good news
about God's kingdom. Jesus also
healed every kind of disease and
sickness. 36When he saw the crowds,
he felt sorry for them. They were confused and helpless, like sheep without a shepherd.* 37He said to his disciples, "A large crop is in the fields,
but there are only a few workers.
38Ask the Lord in charge of the harvest to send out workers to bring it
in."

Jesus Chooses His Twelve Apostles
(Mark 3.13–19; Luke 6.12–16)

10 Jesus called together his
twelve disciples. He gave them
the power to force out evil spirits and
to heal every kind of disease and
sickness. 2The first of the twelve
apostles was Simon, better known as
Peter. His brother Andrew was an
apostle, and so were James and John,
the two sons of Zebedee. 3Philip, Bartholomew, Thomas, Matthew the tax
collector,[x] James the son of Alphaeus, and Thaddaeus were also
apostles. 4The others were Simon,
known as the Eager One,[y] and Judas
Iscariot,[z] who later betrayed Jesus.

Instructions for the Twelve Apostles
(Mark 6.7–13; Luke 9.1–6)

5Jesus sent out the twelve apostles
with these instructions:
Stay away from the Gentiles
and don't go to any Samaritan

---

[x] *tax collector*: See the note at 5.46. [y] *known as the Eager One*: The Greek text has "Cananaean," which probably comes from a Hebrew word meaning "zealous" (see Luke 6.15). "Zealot" was the name later given to the members of a Jewish group which resisted and fought against the Romans. [z] *Iscariot*: This may mean "a man from Kerioth" (a place in Judea). But more probably it means "a man who was a liar" or "a man who was a betrayer."

9.34 **BEWARE OF A HARD HEART** Jesus had just freed a man from the power of a demon. Demons are evil spirits that can actually live inside people. Nearly everybody was glad for what Jesus had done. But the Pharisees resented Jesus because the crowds were following him instead of them. They should have been glad along with the crowds. But they loved their social position more than they loved God.

9.36 **HOW MUCH DOES JESUS CARE?** Jesus saw the people as though they were sheep without a shepherd. Jesus, as he traveled through the towns of Galilee, was not just another kind man. He was the Lord from heaven. In heaven he and his Father had looked out on a needy, dying world. Then the Lord—the Son of God—said he would come and show his love for us. As the hymn says, Jesus came "out of the ivory palaces into a world of woe." He didn't blind us with his glory, but showed us a kind of love we had never seen before.

NOTES

town.* 6Go only to the people of Israel, because they are like a flock of lost sheep. 7As you go, announce that the kingdom of heaven will soon be here.[a] 8Heal the sick, raise the dead to life, heal people who have leprosy,[b] and force out demons. You received without paying, now give without being paid. 9Don't take along any gold, silver, or copper coins. 10And don't carry[c] a traveling bag or an extra shirt or sandals or a walking stick.

Workers deserve their food. 11So when you go to a town or a village, find someone worthy enough to have you as their guest and stay with them until you leave. 12When you go to a home, give it your blessing of peace. 13If the home is deserving, let your blessing remain with them. But if the home is not deserving, take back your blessing of peace. 14If someone won't welcome you or listen to your message, leave their home or town. And shake the dust from your feet at them.[d] 15I promise you that the day of judgment will be easier for the towns of Sodom and Gomorrah[e] than for that town.

Warning about Trouble
(Mark 13.9–13; Luke 21.12–17)

16I am sending you like lambs into a pack of wolves. So be as wise as snakes and as innocent as doves.* 17Watch out for people who will take you to court and have you beaten in their meeting places. 18Because of me, you will be dragged before rulers and kings to tell them and the Gentiles about your faith. 19But when someone arrests you, don't worry about what you will say or how you will say it. At that time you will be given the words to say. 20But you will not really be the one speaking. The Spirit from your Father will tell you what to say.

21Brothers and sisters will betray one another and have each other put to death. Parents will betray their own children, and children will turn against their parents and have them killed. 22Everyone will hate you because of me. But if you remain faithful until the end, you will be saved. 23When people mistreat you in one town, hurry to another one. I promise you that before you have gone to all the towns of Israel, the Son of Man will come.

24Disciples are not better than

---

[a] *will soon be here*: Or "is already here." [b] *leprosy*: See the note at 8.2. [c] *Don't take along . . . don't carry*: Or "Don't accept . . . don't accept." [d] *shake the dust from your feet at them*: This was a way of showing rejection. See Acts 13.51. [e] *Sodom and Gomorrah*: During the time of Abraham the Lord destroyed these towns because the people there were so evil.

10.5 **JESUS NEEDED ONLY A FEW** A well-known advertisement announces, "The Marines are looking for a few good men." Many times an army's success depends more on its discipline than its numbers. A riotous mob is not an army. Jesus knew he could accomplish his goal with a handful of earnest people. So he chose twelve and instructed them. Yes, one of them would be a traitor, but that didn't hinder Jesus' plan. The apostle who cried out, "Christ gives me strength to face anything" (Philippians 4.13), speaks for all of us. As Jesus strengthens us, we conquer evil with the power of the good news.

10.16 **AN APOSTLE MAKES HARD CHOICES** The world is not always a comfortable place for those whom Jesus sends here. Often being an apostle (or "sent one") means prison, torture, hatred by one's own family, and hatred by the whole world. Such a servant of Christ must decide beforehand that he or she is willing to pay such a price for the privilege of being sent. We are not better than our Master from heaven who suffered all these things for us.

NOTES

their teacher, and slaves are not
better than their master. 25It is
enough for disciples to be like
their teacher and for slaves to
be like their master. If people call
the head of the family Satan,
what will they say about the rest
of the family?

The One to Fear
(Luke 12.2–7)

26Don't be afraid of anyone!
Everything that is hidden will be
found out, and every secret will
be known.* 27Whatever I say to
you in the dark, you must tell
in the light. And you must
announce from the housetops
whatever I have whispered to
you. 28Don't be afraid of people.
They can kill you, but they
cannot harm your soul. Instead,
you should fear God who can
destroy both your body and your
soul in hell. 29Aren't two
sparrows sold for only a penny?
But your Father knows when
any one of them falls to the
ground. 30Even the hairs on your
head are counted. 31So don't be
afraid! You are worth much
more than many sparrows.

Telling Others about Christ
(Luke 12.8, 9)

32If you tell others that you
belong to me, I will tell my Father
in heaven that you are my
followers. 33But if you reject me,
I will tell my Father in heaven
that you don't belong to me.

Not Peace, but Trouble
(Luke 12.51–53; 14.26, 27)

34Don't think that I came to
bring peace to the earth! I came
to bring trouble, not peace.*
35I came to turn sons against
their fathers, daughters against
their mothers, and daughters-in-
law against their mothers-in-
law. 36Your worst enemies will
be in your own family.
37If you love your father or
mother or even your sons and
daughters more than me, you are
not fit to be my disciples. 38And
unless you are willing to take up
your cross and come with me,
you are not fit to be my disciples.
39If you try to save your life, you
will lose it. But if you give it up
for me, you will surely find it.

Rewards
(Mark 9.41)

40Anyone who welcomes you
welcomes me. And anyone who
welcomes me also welcomes the
one who sent me.* 41Anyone
who welcomes a prophet, just
because that person is a prophet,
will be given the same reward

10.26 **FEAR GOD, NOT OTHER PEOPLE** Remember, everyone on earth is doomed to die. If we die in the service of Christ, that is a better death than living to a sick old age. People can destroy only our bodies; God is the Judge of our souls. But he cares very much for us. No servant of his ever died alone—Jesus himself stands near to give us a joyful death that is not an end but a beginning.

10.34 **YOUR TROUBLES ARE CHRIST'S TROUBLES** Sometimes we are tempted to think something is wrong with us, because telling about Jesus very often results in conflict. We call Jesus the "Prince of peace," but often his message brings trouble. Jesus didn't bring peace to everyone in his time. His generation hated him and put him to death. In spite of this, the miracle of God's kingdom was born in many hearts. We also can expect these different kinds of results in our own times.

10.40 **BE KIND TO GOD'S PEOPLE** When we meet a follower of the Lord Jesus, we ought to treat that person as well as we would treat Jesus himself. What acts of kindness have we done to a Christian lately for Jesus' sake?

NOTES

as a prophet. Anyone who
welcomes a good person, just
because that person is good, will
be given the same reward as a
good person. 42And anyone who
gives one of my most humble
followers a cup of cool water,
just because that person is my
follower, will surely be
rewarded.

John the Baptist
(Luke 7.18–35)

11 After Jesus had finished in-
structing his twelve disciples,
he left and began teaching and
preaching in the towns.[f]
2John was in prison when he heard
what Christ was doing. So John sent
some of his followers 3to ask Jesus,
"Are you the one we should be looking for? Or must we wait for someone
else?"
4Jesus answered, "Go and tell John
what you have heard and seen.
5The blind are now able to see, and
the lame can walk. People with leprosy[g] are being healed, and the deaf
can hear. The dead are raised to life,
and the poor are hearing the good
news. 6God will bless everyone who
does not reject me because of what
I do."
7As John's followers were going
away, Jesus spoke to the crowds
about John:
What sort of person did you
go out into the desert to see? Was
he like tall grass blown about by
the wind?* 8What kind of man
did you go out to see? Was he
someone dressed in fine clothes?
People who dress like that live
in the king's palace. 9What did
you really go out to see? Was
he a prophet? He certainly was.
I tell you that he was more than
a prophet. 10In the Scriptures
God says about him, "I am
sending my messenger ahead of
you to get things ready for you."
11I tell you that no one ever born
on this earth is greater than John
the Baptist. But whoever is least
in the kingdom of heaven is
greater than John.
12From the time of John the
Baptist until now, violent people
have been trying to take over the
kingdom of heaven by force.
13All the Books of the Prophets
and the Law of Moses[h] told what
was going to happen up to the
time of John. 14And if you
believe them, John is Elijah, the
prophet you are waiting for.
15If you have ears, pay attention!
16You people are like children
sitting in the market and
17shouting to each other,
"We played the flute,
but you would not dance!
We sang a funeral song,
but you would not mourn!"
18John the Baptist did not go
around eating and drinking, and
you said, "That man has a
demon in him!" 19But the Son
of Man goes around eating and
drinking, and you say, "That
man eats and drinks too much!
He is even a friend of tax
collectors[i] and sinners." Yet
Wisdom is shown to be right by
what it does.

---

[f] *the towns*: The Greek text has "their towns," which may refer to the towns of Galilee or to the towns where Jesus' disciples had lived. [g] *leprosy*: See the note at 8.2. [h] *the Books of the Prophets and the Law of Moses*: The Jewish Scriptures, that is, the Old Testament. [i] *tax collectors*: See the note at 5.46.

11.7 **JOHN ANNOUNCED JESUS' COMING** John the Baptist's ministry signaled the end of the Old Testament period. That is why Jesus said, "But whoever is least in the kingdom of heaven is greater than John" (verse 11). Jesus was announcing the kingdom of heaven. He himself is the King, and wherever he and his message come, his kingdom is in view. John was typical of an earlier time, a time that prepared the way for the King. John prepared the way, though even he did not fully understand the meaning of Jesus' coming (verse 3).

NOTES

The Unbelieving Towns
(Luke 10.13–15)

20 In the towns where Jesus had
worked most of his miracles, the people refused to turn to God. So Jesus
was upset with them and said:*
21 You people of Chorazin are
in for trouble! You people of
Bethsaida are in for trouble too!
If the miracles that took place
in your towns had happened in
Tyre and Sidon, the people there
would have turned to God long
ago. They would have dressed
in sackcloth and put ashes on
their heads.[j]
22 I tell you that on
the day of judgment the people
of Tyre and Sidon will get off
easier than you will.*
23 People of Capernaum, do
you think you will be honored
in heaven? You will go down to
hell! If the miracles that took
place in your town had
happened in Sodom, that town
would still be standing.
24 So I tell
you that on the day of judgment
the people of Sodom will get off
easier than you.

Come to Me and Rest
(Luke 10.21, 22)

25 At that moment Jesus said:
My Father, Lord of heaven and
earth, I am grateful that you hid
all this from wise and educated
people and showed it to ordinary
people.*
26 Yes, Father, that is
what pleased you.
27 My Father has given me
everything, and he is the only
one who knows the Son. The
only one who truly knows the
Father is the Son. But the Son
wants to tell others about the
Father, so that they can know
him too.
28 If you are tired from carrying
heavy burdens, come to me and
I will give you rest.*
29 Take the
yoke[k] I give you. Put it on your
shoulders and learn from me. I

---

[j]*sackcloth . . . ashes on their heads*: This was one way that people showed how sorry they were for their sins. [k]*yoke*: Yokes were put on the necks of animals, so that they could pull a plow or wagon. A yoke was a symbol of obedience and hard work.

11.20 **LOOK OUT FOR PRIDE** The Jewish towns Jesus spoke to "had heard it all before." They were tired of hearing "divine messages." So they ignored Jesus' words and works. They thought they didn't need him because they had the religion of their ancestors. Tyre and Sidon, in the country of Phoenicia, had never heard the prophets or known God's Law. But, strange to say, the wicked cities of Tyre and Sidon were more open to Jesus.

11.22 **JUDGMENT IS COMING** Most people don't like to hear about judgment. "Stories about Jesus and his love are all right," many seem to say, "but don't speak to us of judgment." Nevertheless the gracious, gentle Christ speaks more vividly about divine judgment than anyone in the Bible. So the world should take God's warnings seriously.

11.25 **GOD LOVES ORDINARY PEOPLE** Abraham Lincoln is said to have commented, "God must have loved the common people, he made so many of them." The truth is, we are all quite ordinary if only we admit it. What makes us special is that God created us *all* in his likeness. Too often, what sets us apart is our pride. But Jesus blesses all who are willing to be ordinary for his sake.

11.28 **JESUS INVITES US TO REST** After a while, everybody gets tired of life, at least sometimes. This should remind us that God never intended us to travel this road by ourselves. Jesus wants to walk beside us and share our burdens. He took our greatest burden onto himself—our sins. Compared to that, the "burdens" he gives us are easy to carry.

NOTES

Step 3

I will put my life in God's hands and trust Jesus Christ to lead me.

MATTHEW 11.28–30

THE SUBSTITUTE

The buzzer goes off. Rich Wallace runs onto the court substituting for an exhausted Adam Loyd. Whether Adam has played his best or his worst, it's time for a substitute to come in and relieve him.

While these verses aren't talking specifically about basketball, it's the same idea. Whether or not we've done well or blown it in life, there comes a point when we need to take a rest. We are tired.

STEP
LOOK INSIDE
3

TIME FOR A REST

Sometimes life is a struggle as we carry around guilt, shame, bitterness, fear, disappointments—whatever has discouraged us. We need relief. God has provided the perfect substitute. His name is Jesus.

For another "Look Inside," turn to page 200.

am gentle and humble, and you will find rest. 30This yoke is easy to bear, and this burden is light.

A Question about the Sabbath
(Mark 2.23–28; Luke 6.1–5)

12 One Sabbath Jesus and his disciples were walking through some wheat fields.[l] His disciples were hungry and began picking and eating grains of wheat. 2Some Pharisees said to Jesus, "Why are your disciples picking grain on the Sabbath? They are not supposed to do that!"*

3Jesus answered:

You surely must have read what David did when he and his followers were hungry. 4He went into the house of God, and then they ate the sacred loaves of bread that only priests are supposed to eat. 5Haven't you read in the Law of Moses that the priests are allowed to work in the temple on the Sabbath? But no one says that they are guilty of breaking the law of the Sabbath. 6I tell you that there is something here greater than the temple. 7Don't you know what the Scriptures mean when they say, "Instead of offering sacrifices to me, I want you to be merciful to others?" If you knew what this means, you would not condemn these innocent disciples of mine.*

8So the Son of Man is Lord over the Sabbath.

A Man with a Crippled Hand
(Mark 3.1–6; Luke 6.6–11)

9Jesus left and went into one of the Jewish meeting places, 10where there was a man whose hand was crippled. Some Pharisees wanted to accuse Jesus of doing something wrong, and they asked him, "Is it right to heal someone on the Sabbath?"

11Jesus answered, "If you had a sheep that fell into a ditch on the Sabbath, wouldn't you lift it out? 12People are worth much more than sheep, and so it is right to do good on the Sabbath." 13Then Jesus told the man, "Hold out your hand." The man did, and it became as healthy as the other one.

14The Pharisees left and started making plans to kill Jesus.

God's Chosen Servant

15When Jesus found out what was happening, he left there and large crowds followed him. He healed all of their sick, 16but warned them not to tell anyone about him. 17So God's promise came true, just as Isaiah the prophet had said,*

---

[l]*walking through some wheat fields*: It was the custom to let hungry travelers pick grains of wheat.

12.2 **THE PHARISEES WERE FAULTFINDERS** The Pharisees were hard to please. All they could think about was their precious customs. They were proud because their ancestors had done great things for God. But the Pharisees themselves only seemed to spend their time finding fault with others. We must pray to be rescued from the kind of "religion" whose greatest strength is its ability to find fault.

12.7 **THE SABBATH IS FOR DOING GOOD** For most of us our "day of rest" is Sunday. We have lots of free time when we don't have to work. How do we use it—just for our own relaxation? If so, we're missing a chance to help others.

12.17 **THE PROPHETS DESCRIBED JESUS** Jesus was not just an ordinary person who grew up to be great. His divine life and work were planned by God long beforehand in eternity past. This is why the prophet Isaiah was able to describe Jesus so clearly. God was in charge of history and of Isaiah, and God planned every word and deed of the life of Jesus.

NOTES

18"Here is my chosen servant!
I love him,
and he pleases me.
I will give him my Spirit,
and he will judge
the nations.
19He will not argue or shout
or be heard speaking
in the streets.
20He will not break off
a bent twig
or put out
a faintly burning flame
until he makes justice
win the victory.
21All nations will place
their hope in him."

Jesus and the Ruler of the Demons
(Mark 3.20–30; Luke 11.14–23;12.10)

22Some people brought to Jesus a
man who was blind and could not
talk because he had a demon in him.
Jesus cured the man, and then he was
able to talk and see. 23The crowds
were so amazed that they asked,
"Could Jesus be the Son of David?"[m]
24When the Pharisees heard this,
they said, "He forces out demons by
the power of Beelzebul, the ruler of
the demons!"*
25Jesus knew what they were
thinking, and he said to them:
Any kingdom where people
fight each other will end up
ruined. And a town or family that
fights will soon destroy itself.
26So if Satan fights against
himself, how can his kingdom
last? 27If I use the power of
Beelzebul to force out demons,
whose power do your own
followers use to force them out?
Your followers are the ones who
will judge you. 28But when I
force out demons by the power
of God's Spirit, it proves that
God's kingdom has already
come to you. 29How can anyone
break into a strong man's house
and steal his things, unless he
first ties up the strong man?
Then he can take everything.
30If you are not on my side,
you are against me. If you don't
gather in the harvest with me,
you scatter it. 31-32I tell you that
any sinful thing you do or say
can be forgiven. Even if you
speak against the Son of Man,
you can be forgiven. But if you
speak against the Holy Spirit,
you can never be forgiven, either
in this life or in the life to come.

A Tree and Its Fruit
(Luke 6.43–45)

33A good tree produces only
good fruit, and a bad tree
produces bad fruit. You can tell
what a tree is like by the fruit
it produces.* 34You are a bunch
of evil snakes, so how can you
say anything good? Your words
show what is in your hearts.
35Good people bring good things
out of their hearts, but evil
people bring evil things out of
their hearts. 36I promise you that
on the day of judgment,
everyone will have to account
for every careless word they
have spoken. 37On that day they

---

[m]*Could Jesus be the Son of David*: Or "Does Jesus think he is the Son of David?" See the note at 9.27.

12.24 **WHOSE SIDE ARE WE ON?** The Pharisees said Jesus was a servant of Satan. But Jesus showed them he couldn't be serving Satan and destroying Satan's works at the same time. The truth was that the Pharisees hated Jesus, but he showed them they were really denying the work of God's own Spirit. They were enemies of God and therefore enemies of Christ.

12.33 **WHAT YOU SAY CAN DESTROY YOU** Jesus compared right speech to good fruit, and he compared evil speech to bad fruit. We don't take what we say seriously enough. It is just not true that "sticks and stones will break my bones, but names will never hurt me." Words do hurt and destroy the lives of others as well as ourselves.

NOTES

will be told that they are either
innocent or guilty because of the
things they have said.

A Sign from Heaven
(Mark 8.11, 12; Luke 11.29–32)

38Some Pharisees and teachers of
the Law of Moses said, "Teacher, we
want you to show us a sign from
heaven."
39But Jesus replied:
You want a sign because you
are evil and won't believe! But
the only sign you will get is the
sign of the prophet Jonah.*
40He was in the stomach of a big
fish for three days and nights,
just as the Son of Man will be
deep in the earth for three days
and nights. 41On the day of
judgment the people of Nineveh[n]
will stand there with you and
condemn you. They turned to
God when Jonah preached, and
yet here is something far greater
than Jonah. 42The Queen of the
South[o] will also stand there with
you and condemn you. She
traveled a long way to hear
Solomon's wisdom, and yet here
is something much greater than
Solomon.

Return of an Evil Spirit
(Luke 11.24–26)

43When an evil spirit leaves a
person, it travels through the
desert, looking for a place to rest.
But when the demon doesn't find
a place,* 44it says, "I will go back
to the home I left." When it gets
there and finds the place empty,
clean, and fixed up, 45it goes off
and finds seven other evil spirits
even worse than itself. They all
come and make their home
there, and the person ends up
in worse shape than before.
That's how it will be with you
evil people of today.

Jesus' Mother and Brothers
(Mark 3.31–35; Luke 8.19–21)

46While Jesus was still speaking to
the crowds, his mother and brothers
came and stood outside because they
wanted to talk with him.* 47Someone
told Jesus, "Your mother and brothers are standing outside and want to
talk with you."[p]
48Jesus answered, "Who is my
mother and who are my brothers?"
49Then he pointed to his disciples and
said, "These are my mother and my
brothers! 50Anyone who obeys my
Father in heaven is my brother or
sister or mother."

---

[n] *Nineveh*: During the time of Jonah this city was the capital of the Assyrian Empire, which was Israel's worst enemy. But Jonah was sent there to preach, so that the people would turn to the Lord and be saved. [o] *Queen of the South*: Sheba, probably a country in southern Arabia. [p] *with you*: Some manuscripts do not have verse 47.

12.39 **SIGNS FROM THE SCRIPTURES** The Jewish Scriptures are full of wonderful stories, but they are more than stories—they are signs that point to Jesus. Jonah, Solomon, and many other great people from Israel's history show us things about what God planned to do when he sent his Son Jesus to save us.

12.43 **EMPTINESS IS NOT GOOD** It's one thing to "clean up" our lives by giving up sin. But we need to replace the bad things with good things. Learning from God's word, doing good to others, being more like Jesus—these are the things that should fill up a clean life.

12.46 **WHO ARE YOUR REAL RELATIVES?** Family ties are usually close, and we may imagine there are no relationships closer than the ones within our families. But Jesus makes it clear that the family of God—of God's people—is on a higher level than any earthly ties. Our connection with our earthly family, if we have a family at all, may be only for a time. But our link to God's family is forever.

NOTES

A Story about a Farmer
(Mark 4.1–9; Luke 8.4–8)

13 That same day Jesus left the
house and went out beside
Lake Galilee, where he sat down to
teach.[q] 2Such large crowds gathered
around him that he had to sit in a
boat, while the people stood on the
shore. 3Then he taught them many
things by using stories. He said:
A farmer went out to scatter
seed in a field.* 4While the
farmer was scattering the seed,
some of it fell along the road and
was eaten by birds. 5Other seeds
fell on thin, rocky ground and
quickly started growing because
the soil was not very deep.
6But when the sun came up, the
plants were scorched and dried
up, because they did not have
enough roots. 7Some other seeds
fell where thorn bushes grew up
and choked the plants. 8But a
few seeds did fall on good
ground where the plants
produced a hundred or sixty or
thirty times as much as was
scattered. 9If you have ears, pay
attention!

Why Jesus Used Stories
(Mark 4.10–12; Luke 8.9, 10)

10Jesus' disciples came to him and
asked, "Why do you use nothing but
stories when you speak to the
people?"
11Jesus answered:
I have explained the secrets
about the kingdom of heaven to
you, but not to others.*
12Everyone who has something
will be given more. But people
who don't have anything will
lose even what little they have.
13I use stories when I speak to
them because when they look,
they cannot see, and when they
listen, they cannot hear or
understand. 14So God's promise
came true, just as the prophet
Isaiah had said,

"These people will listen
and listen,
but never understand.
They will look and look,
but never see.
15All of them have
stubborn minds!
Their ears are stopped up,
and their eyes are covered.
They cannot see or hear
or understand.
If they could,
they would turn to me,
and I would heal them."

16But God has blessed you,
because your eyes can see and
your ears can hear! 17Many
prophets and good people were
eager to see what you see and
to hear what you hear. But I tell
you that they did not see or hear.

Jesus Explains the Story about the Farmer
(Mark 4.13–20; Luke 8.11–15)

18Now listen to the meaning of the
story about the farmer:
19The seeds that fell along the

---

[q]*sat down to teach*: Teachers in the ancient world, including Jewish teachers, usually sat down when they taught.

13.3 **SPREAD THE GOOD NEWS** The saying is that "bad news travels fast." What is the best way to make sure the good news about Jesus is heard? Our kind deeds will be a great help. Jesus says we just have to keep on showing and telling everyone what a wonderful Savior we have. This story shows that some people will believe us and others will not. People are different in the way they hear what we say. But God guarantees that the good news we tell about Jesus will multiply itself in the lives of many.

13.11 **STORIES WERE JESUS' WAY OF TEACHING** By telling stories, Jesus offered truth to people in a form that would be understood by those whose hearts God had prepared to receive it. Those whose hearts were not ready for the truth would just be puzzled.

NOTES

road are the people who hear the
message about the kingdom, but
don't understand it. Then the evil
one comes and snatches the
message from their hearts. 20The
seeds that fell on rocky ground
are the people who gladly hear
the message and accept it right
away. 21But they don't have deep
roots, and they don't last very
long. As soon as life gets hard
or the message gets them in
trouble, they give up.
22The seeds that fell among the
thorn bushes are also people
who hear the message. But they
start worrying about the needs
of this life and are fooled by the
desire to get rich. So the message
gets choked out, and they never
produce anything. 23The seeds
that fell on good ground are the
people who hear and understand
the message. They produce as
much as a hundred or sixty or
thirty times what was planted.

Weeds among the Wheat

24Jesus then told them this story:
The kingdom of heaven is like
what happened when a farmer
scattered good seed in a field.
25But while everyone was
sleeping, an enemy came and
scattered weed seeds in the field
and then left.
26When the plants came up
and began to ripen, the farmer's
servants could see the weeds.
27The servants came and asked,
"Sir, didn't you scatter good seed
in your field? Where did these
weeds come from?"
28"An enemy did this," he
replied.
His servants then asked, "Do
you want us to go out and pull
up the weeds?"
29"No!" he answered. "You
might also pull up the wheat.
30Leave the weeds alone until
harvest time. Then I'll tell my
workers to gather the weeds and
tie them up and burn them. But
I'll have them store the wheat
in my barn."

Stories about a Mustard Seed and Yeast

(Mark 4.30–32; Luke 13.18–21)

31Jesus told them another story:
The kingdom of heaven is like
what happens when a farmer
plants a mustard seed in a field.*
32Although it is the smallest of
all seeds, it grows larger than
any garden plant and becomes
a tree. Birds even come and nest
on its branches.
33Jesus also said:
The kingdom of heaven is like
what happens when a woman
mixes a little yeast into three big
batches of flour. Finally, all the
dough rises.

The Reason for Teaching with Stories

(Mark 4.33, 34)

34Jesus used stories when he spoke
to the people. In fact, he did not tell
them anything without using stories.
35So God's promise came true, just
as the prophet[r] had said,

"I will use stories
to speak my message
and to explain things
that have been hidden
since the creation
of the world."

Jesus Explains the Story about the Weeds

36After Jesus left the crowd and
went inside,[s] his disciples came to
him and said, "Explain to us the story
about the weeds in the wheat field."

---

[r] *the prophet*: Some manuscripts have "the prophet Isaiah." [s] *went inside*: Or "went home."

13.31 **WHAT CAN A SEED DO?** The tiny mustard seed grows and spreads its branches. Likewise, the Christian faith has grown from its little beginnings to fill the whole world with the good news about Jesus.

NOTES

37 Jesus answered:
The one who scattered the
good seed is the Son of Man.*
38 The field is the world, and the
good seeds are the people who
belong to the kingdom. The
weed seeds are those who belong
to the evil one, 39 and the one who
scattered them is the devil. The
harvest is the end of time, and
angels are the ones who bring
in the harvest.
40 Weeds are gathered and
burned. That's how it will be at
the end of time. 41 The Son of
Man will send out his angels, and
they will gather from his
kingdom everyone who does
wrong or causes others to sin.
42 Then he will throw them into
a flaming furnace, where people
will cry and grit their teeth in
pain. 43 But everyone who has
done right will shine like the sun
in their Father's kingdom. If you
have ears, pay attention!

A Hidden Treasure

44 The kingdom of heaven is
like what happens when
someone finds treasure hidden
in a field and buries it again. A
person like that is happy and
goes and sells everything in
order to buy that field.

A Valuable Pearl

45 The kingdom of heaven is
like what happens when a shop
owner is looking for fine pearls.*
46 After finding a very valuable
one, the owner goes and sells
everything in order to buy that
pearl.

A Fish Net

47 The kingdom of heaven is
like what happens when a net
is thrown into a lake and catches
all kinds of fish. 48 When the net
is full, it is dragged to the shore,
and the fishermen sit down to
separate the fish. They keep the
good ones, but throw the bad
ones away. 49 That's how it will
be at the end of time. Angels will
come and separate the evil
people from the ones who have
done right.* 50 Then those evil
people will be thrown into a
flaming furnace, where they will
cry and grit their teeth in pain.

New and Old Treasures

51 Jesus asked his disciples if they
understood all these things. They
said, "Yes, we do."
52 So he told them, "Every student
of the Scriptures who becomes a disciple in the kingdom of heaven is like

13.37 **WHAT ABOUT THE WEEDS?** A good farmer tries to keep his fields free from weeds. God is like a farmer in planting the seed that one day results in many faithful believers. But in spite of all the good planting that God does, evil grows along with the good. But we shouldn't worry too much. We just keep on spreading the great news about Jesus. God, the greatest of all farmers, will weed out the evil at last.

13.45 **HOW MUCH IS JESUS WORTH?** It is likely that the pearl in Jesus' story refers to himself. He is the King in the kingdom of God. The idea is that being in the kingdom is worth the very best of our lives. So let us be willing to exchange all that we value in life for Jesus' friendship. Whatever we treasure most comes second after him.

13.49 **GOOD AND BAD TOGETHER** Just as a fish net draws in all kinds of things—good fish, bad fish, seaweed, driftwood—so the Lord will make sure that his "good fish," believers, are finally separated from the evil that surrounds them now in the world. That should be a comfort to us.

NOTES

someone who brings out new and old
treasures from the storeroom."

The People of Nazareth Turn against Jesus
(Mark 6.1–6; Luke 4.16–30)

53When Jesus had finished telling
these stories, he left 54and went to
his hometown. He taught in their
meeting place, and the people were
so amazed that they asked, "Where
does he get all this wisdom and the
power to work these miracles?
55Isn't he the son of the carpenter?
Isn't Mary his mother, and aren't
James, Joseph, Simon, and Judas his
brothers? 56Don't his sisters still live
here in our town? How can he do
all this?" 57So the people were very
unhappy because of what he was
doing.
But Jesus said, "Prophets are honored by everyone, except the people
of their hometown and their own
family."* 58And because the people
did not have any faith, Jesus did not
work many miracles there.

The Death of John the Baptist
(Mark 6.14–29; Luke 9.7–9)

14 About this time Herod the
ruler[t] heard the news about
Jesus 2and told his officials, "This is
John the Baptist! He has come back
from death, and that's why he has
the power to work these miracles."
3-4Herod had earlier arrested John
and had him chained and put in
prison. He did this because John had
told him, "It isn't right for you to take
Herodias, the wife of your brother
Philip."* 5Herod wanted to kill John.
But the people thought John was a
prophet, and Herod was afraid of
what they might do.
6When Herod's birthday came, the
daughter of Herodias danced for the
guests. She pleased Herod 7so much
that he swore to give her whatever
she wanted. 8But the girl's mother
told her to say, "Here on a platter I
want the head of John the Baptist!"
9The king was sorry for what he
had said. But he did not want to break
the promise he had made in front of
his guests. So he ordered a guard
10to go to the prison and cut off John's
head. 11It was taken on a platter to
the girl, and she gave it to her mother.
12John's followers took his body and
buried it. Then they told Jesus what
had happened.

Jesus Feeds Five Thousand
(Mark 6.30–44; Luke 9.10–17; John 6.1–14)

13After Jesus heard about John, he
crossed Lake Galilee[u] to go to some
place where he could be alone. But
the crowds found out and followed
him on foot from the towns. 14When
Jesus got out of the boat, he saw the
large crowd. He felt sorry for them
and healed everyone who was sick.
15That evening the disciples came
to Jesus and said, "This place is like
a desert, and it is already late. Let
the crowds leave, so they can go to
the villages and buy some food."
16Jesus replied, "They don't have

---

[t] *Herod the ruler*: Herod Antipas, the son of Herod the Great (2.1). [u] *crossed Lake Galilee*: To the east side.

13.57 **BEING POPULAR IS NOT THE GOAL OF LIFE** If we're popular we may be pleasing too many people. Jesus knew that most people would not appreciate him. Even though many heard him gladly, in the end he had only a handful of friends. But he reached his goal: he opened a way back to God for us. Doing the will of God, not pleasing people, is what life is about.

14.3 **EVIL OFTEN WINS—FOR NOW** Most of the great novels and stories of fiction are about the triumph of goodness. These stories show that people long for what they really don't see very much of—justice. John the Baptist was the victim of an awful injustice: he died at the mere wish of a young girl. Is there any justice? Yes. In the end God is the rewarder of those who love him. He will set all things right.

NOTES

to leave. Why don't you give them
something to eat?"
17But they said, "We have only five
small loaves of bread[v] and two fish."
18Jesus asked his disciples to bring
the food to him, 19and he told the
crowd to sit down on the grass. Jesus
took the five loaves and the two fish.
He looked up toward heaven and
blessed the food. Then he broke the
bread and handed it to his disciples,
and they gave it to the people.*
20After everyone had eaten all they
wanted, Jesus' disciples picked up
twelve large baskets of leftovers.
21There were about five thousand
men who ate, not counting the
women and children.

Jesus Walks on the Water
(Mark 6.45–52; John 6.15–21)

22Right away Jesus made his disciples get into a boat and start back
across the lake.[w] But he stayed until
he had sent the crowds away.
23Then he went up on a mountain
where he could be alone and pray.
Later that evening, he was still there.
24By this time the boat was a long
way from the shore. It was going
against the wind and was being
tossed around by the waves.* 25A little while before morning, Jesus came
walking on the water toward his disciples. 26When they saw him, they
thought he was a ghost. They were
terrified and started screaming.
27At once Jesus said to them,
"Don't worry! I am Jesus. Don't be
afraid."
28Peter replied, "Lord, if it is really
you, tell me to come to you on the
water."
29"Come on!" Jesus said. Peter
then got out of the boat and started
walking on the water toward him.
30But when Peter saw how strong
the wind was, he was afraid and
started sinking. "Lord, save me!" he
shouted.
31Right away Jesus reached out his
hand. He helped Peter up and said,
"You surely don't have much faith.
Why do you doubt?"
32When Jesus and Peter got into
the boat, the wind died down.
33The men in the boat worshiped
Jesus and said, "You really are the
Son of God!"

Jesus Heals Sick People in Gennesaret
(Mark 6.53–56)

34Jesus and his disciples crossed
the lake and came to shore near the
town of Gennesaret. 35The people
found out that he was there, and they
sent word to everyone who lived in
that part of the country. So they
brought all the sick people to Jesus.*
36They begged him just to let them

---

[v]*small loaves of bread*: These would have been flat and round or in the shape of a bun. [w]*back across the lake*: To the west side.

14.19 **DOES GOD CARE ABOUT OUR NEEDS?** Have you talked to God about the needs of your life? Jesus knew the needs of the crowd who followed him. The disciples spoke to Jesus about the need for food, so he used the small amount they had to feed many. Like a wise investor, God uses the little we have and multiplies it. So we prosper under God's care.

14.24 **JESUS IS LORD OF NATURE** God, not "Mother Nature," is in charge of the weather. On this occasion the wind blew and the waves rose high, but Jesus was Lord of the storm. Why do we fear the powers of nature? God made them all, and he'll help us to stand. The disappointments and sorrows of life are like storms. With Jesus beside us we can walk above those too.

14.35 **CAN JESUS HEAL OUR DISEASES?** Many are living today who have been healed by Jesus' touch. But *we* have to touch *him* too. When the people touched Jesus' clothes, they didn't believe his clothes would heal them. They were showing their complete trust in him. Touching Jesus means believing he lives and that he always gives us what is best.

NOTES

Step 2

I believe God is there to help me.

MATTHEW 14.22–33

RISK INVENTORY

The biggest risk I have ever taken . . .

- a. *Driven over 90 MPH on the highway*
- b. *Had premarital sex*
- c. *Lied to my parents*
- d. *Told someone I was a Christian*
- e. *Believed God is there for me*
- f. *Other*

Some people think that trusting God is a risky thing to do. After all, we can't see him in the same way we can see the people around us. But as we learn more about him, we will find that he is as real for us as Jesus was for Peter on that day when Peter stepped out of the boat and onto a stormy sea to walk to his Lord. And he can be trusted to be as loyal to us as Jesus was to Peter when he reached out his hand to rescue his sinking friend. Even when we slip up and take our eyes off him, he is faithful to reach out to us when we call on him for help.

STEP LOOK INSIDE 2

God encourages us, he welcomes us, but he will never force us to come to him. Instead, he waits for us to take the first step of faith. God is there for us, and that is a sure thing!

For another "Look Inside," turn to page 91.

touch his clothes, and everyone who did was healed.

The Teaching of the Ancestors
(Mark 7.1–13)

15 About this time some Pharisees and teachers of the Law of Moses came from Jerusalem. They asked Jesus, 2"Why don't your disciples obey what our ancestors taught us to do? They don't even wash their hands[x] before they eat."
3Jesus answered:

Why do you disobey God and follow your own teaching?
4Didn't God command you to respect your father and mother? Didn't he tell you to put to death all who curse their parents?
5But you let people get by without helping their parents when they should. You let them say that what they have has been offered to God.[y]* 6Is this any way to show respect to your parents? You ignore God's commands in order to follow your own teaching. 7And you are nothing but showoffs! Isaiah the prophet was right when he wrote that God had said,

8"All of you praise me
with your words,
but you never really
think about me.
9It is useless for you
to worship me,
when you teach rules
made up by humans."

What Really Makes People Unclean
(Mark 7.14–23)

10Jesus called the crowd together
and said, "Pay attention and try to
understand what I mean. 11The food
that you put into your mouth doesn't
make you unclean and unfit to worship God. The bad words that come
out of your mouth are what make
you unclean." 12Then his disciples
came over to him and asked, "Do you
know that you insulted the Pharisees
by what you said?"
13Jesus answered, "Every plant
that my Father in heaven did not
plant will be pulled up by the roots.
14Stay away from those Pharisees!
They are like blind people leading
other blind people, and all of them
will fall into a ditch."
15Peter replied, "What did you
mean when you talked about the
things that make people unclean?"
16Jesus then said:

Don't any of you know what
I am talking about by now?*
17Don't you know that the food
you put into your mouth goes
into your stomach and then out
of your body? 18But the words
that come out of your mouth
come from your heart. And they
are what make you unfit to

---

[x]*wash their hands*: The Jewish people had strict laws about washing their hands before eating, especially if they had been out in public. [y]*has been offered to God*: According to Jewish custom, when people said something was offered to God, it belonged to him and could not be used for anyone else, not even for their own parents.

15.5 **WE MUST FOLLOW GOD, NOT OUR CUSTOMS** Some believe that the custom described in this passage let people say that their belongings were devoted to God, and then keep them—but they could not give them to someone else. Jesus told sons and daughters who did this that they were only avoiding their duty to honor their parents, which was among the most important of God's laws about our duty to people. Such sons and daughters were hiding their sin under false religion.

15.16 **WHAT DO YOU STORE UP IN YOUR HEART?** We are more often concerned about what we put in our stomachs than how we fill our minds or hearts. It is too often what comes out of the mind or heart that hurts us and hurts those around us. Evil thoughts in the heart lead to sinful words and actions, and we become as bad for others as our thoughts are for us.

NOTES

worship God. 19Out of your heart
come evil thoughts, murder,
unfaithfulness in marriage,
vulgar deeds, stealing, telling
lies, and insulting others.
20These are what make you
unclean. Eating without
washing your hands will not
make you unfit to worship
God.

A Woman's Faith
(Mark 7.24–30)

21Jesus left and went to the territory near the cities of Tyre and Sidon.
22Suddenly a Canaanite woman[z] from there came out shouting, "Lord and Son of David,[a] have pity on me! My daughter is full of demons."
23Jesus did not say a word. But the woman kept following along and shouting, so his disciples came up and asked him to send her away.*
24Jesus said, "I was sent only to the people of Israel! They are like a flock of lost sheep."
25The woman came closer. Then she kneeled down and begged, "Lord, please help me!"
26Jesus replied, "It isn't right to take food away from children and feed it to dogs."[b]
27"Lord, that's true," the woman said, "but even dogs get the crumbs that fall from their owner's table."
28Jesus answered, "Dear woman, you really do have a lot of faith, and you will be given what you want." At that moment her daughter was healed.

Jesus Heals Many People

29From there Jesus went along Lake Galilee. Then he climbed a hill and sat down.
30Large crowds came and brought many people who were crippled or blind or lame or unable to talk. They placed them, and many others, in front of Jesus, and he healed them all.*
31Everyone was amazed at what they saw and heard. People who had never spoken could now speak. The lame were healed. The crippled could walk, and the blind were able to see. Everyone was praising the God of Israel.

Jesus Feeds Four Thousand
(Mark 8.1–10)

32Jesus called his disciples together and told them, "I feel sorry for these people. They have been with me for three days, and they don't have anything to eat. I don't want to send them away hungry. They might faint on their way home."
33His disciples said, "This place is like a desert. Where can we find enough food to feed such a crowd?"
34Jesus asked them how much food they had. They replied, "Seven small loaves of bread[c] and a few little fish."
35After Jesus had told the people to sit down,
36he took the seven loaves of bread and the fish and gave thanks. He then broke them and handed them to his disciples, who

---

[z] *Canaanite woman*: This woman was not Jewish. [a] *Son of David*: See the note at 9.27. [b] *feed it to dogs*: The Jewish people sometimes referred to Gentiles as dogs. [c] *small loaves of bread*: See the note at 14.17.

15.23 **GOD HEARS THE CRY OF FAITH** Some people might say Jesus was not very kind to the Canaanite woman because he didn't grant her request right away. Jesus was teaching her and us that earnestness and sincerity matter to God. It is also important for us to find out for ourselves that we really mean what we pray for. When Jesus saw the woman's single-minded trust, he responded at once.

15.30 **GOD WANTS US TO BE HEALED** In this world, we all get sick at times—and some day we'll die. Is this God's best for us? Not at all. Jesus made this point throughout his ministry. In God's kingdom there will be no more suffering because of disobedience. Those things will all be in the past, and we will have the glorious health that God planned for us.

NOTES

passed them around to the crowds.*
37Everyone ate all they wanted, and the leftovers filled seven large baskets.
38There were four thousand men who ate, not counting the women and children.
39After Jesus had sent the crowds away, he got into a boat and sailed across the lake. He came to shore near the town of Magadan.[d]

A Demand for a Sign from Heaven
(Mark 8.11–13; Luke 12.54–56)

16 The Pharisees and Sadducees came to Jesus and tried to test him by asking for a sign from heaven.
2He told them:

If the sky is red in the evening, you say the weather will be good.* 3But if the sky is red and gloomy in the morning, you say it is going to rain. You can tell what the weather will be like by looking at the sky. But you don't understand what is happening now.[e] 4You want a sign because you are evil and won't believe! But the only sign you will be given is what happened to Jonah.[f]

Then Jesus left.

The Yeast of the Pharisees and Sadducees
(Mark 8.14–21)

5The disciples had forgotten to bring any bread when they crossed the lake.[g] 6Jesus then warned them, "Watch out! Guard against the yeast of the Pharisees and Sadducees."*
7The disciples talked this over and said to each other, "He must be saying this because we didn't bring along any bread."
8Jesus knew what they were thinking and said:

You surely don't have much faith! Why are you talking about not having any bread? 9Don't you understand? Have you forgotten about the five thousand people and all those baskets of leftovers from just five loaves of bread? 10And what about the four thousand people and all those baskets of leftovers from only seven loaves of bread? 11Don't you know by now that I am not talking to you about bread? Watch out for the yeast of the Pharisees and Sadducees!

12Finally, the disciples understood that Jesus was not talking about the yeast used to make bread, but about the teaching of the Pharisees and Sadducees.

Who Is Jesus?
(Mark 8.27–30; Luke 9.18–21)

13When Jesus and his disciples were near the town of Caesarea

---

[d]*Magadan*: The location is unknown. [e]*If the sky is red . . . what is happening now*: The words of Jesus in verses 2 and 3 are not in some manuscripts. [f]*what happened to Jonah*: Jonah was in the stomach of a big fish for three days and nights. See 12.40. [g]*crossed the lake*: To the east side.

15.36 **ANOTHER FEEDING MIRACLE** This is not the same as the feeding of the five thousand people told of in chapter 14. See chapter 16, where Jesus speaks of the two feedings separately.

16.2 **MIRACLES DON'T CREATE FAITH** Jesus once said that even if someone rose from the dead, many people still would not believe him. So, sure enough, when Jesus arose from the dead, they didn't believe. That's what Jesus was talking about when he mentioned what happened to Jonah: Jesus' resurrection would be like Jonah's rescue from the belly of the great fish. Faith is trust in God *himself*, not for what we want him to do for us.

16.6 **FALSE TEACHING SPREADS EASILY** Like yeast that makes bread rise, false teaching gradually seems to take over whole societies. We hear all the time about unbiblical religious movements that become popular. Know why you believe in Jesus. Someone has said, "If you don't stand for something you'll fall for anything."

NOTES

Philippi, he asked them, "What do people say about the Son of Man?"

14The disciples answered, "Some people say you are John the Baptist or maybe Elijah[h] or Jeremiah or some other prophet."

15Then Jesus asked them, "But who do you say I am?"

16Simon Peter spoke up, "You are the Messiah, the Son of the living God."*

17Jesus told him:

Simon, son of Jonah, you are blessed! You didn't discover this on your own. It was shown to you by my Father in heaven. 18So I will call you Peter, which means "a rock." On this rock I will build my church, and death itself will not have any power over it. 19I will give you the keys to the kingdom of heaven, and God in heaven will allow whatever you allow on earth. But he will not allow anything that you don't allow.

20Jesus told his disciples not to tell anyone that he was the Messiah.

Jesus Speaks about His Suffering and Death

(Mark 8.31—9.1; Luke 9.22–27)

21From then on, Jesus began telling his disciples what would happen to him. He said, "I must go to Jerusalem. There the nation's leaders, the chief priests, and the teachers of the Law of Moses will make me suffer terribly. I will be killed, but three days later I will rise to life."*

22Peter took Jesus aside and told him to stop talking like that. He said, "Lord, surely God won't let this happen to you!"

23Jesus turned to Peter and said, "Satan, get away from me! You're in my way because you think like everyone else and not like God."

24Then Jesus said to his disciples:

If any of you want to be my followers, you must forget about yourself. You must take up your cross and follow me. 25If you want to save your life,[i] you will destroy it. But if you give up your life for me, you will find it. 26What will you gain, if you own the whole world but destroy yourself? What would you give to get back your soul?

27The Son of Man will soon come in the glory of his Father and with his angels to reward all people for what they have done. 28I promise you that some of those standing here will not die before they see the Son of Man coming with his kingdom.

The True Glory of Jesus

(Mark 9.2–13; Luke 9.28–36)

17 Six days later Jesus took Peter and the brothers James and John with him. They went up on a very high mountain where they could be alone. 2There in front of the disciples Jesus was completely changed. His face was shining like the sun, and

---

[h]*Elijah*: Many of the Jewish people expected the prophet Elijah to come and prepare the way for the Messiah. [i]*life*: In verses 25 and 26 the same Greek word is translated "life," "yourself," and "soul."

16.16 **JESUS IS THE SON OF GOD** But isn't every believer a child of God? Yes, but not in the way Jesus is. He had lived in eternity with his Father and the Holy Spirit. Together the three are one God. Jesus the Messiah (or Christ) was born as a child in this world, and so became the God-Man. He is God in human form—this is how he became our Savior.

16.21 **JESUS CAME TO DIE** Our idea of winning is living. Jesus' idea of winning was dying. That was Jesus' reason for coming into the world. It was his way of exposing Satan's lie that we are the hopeless prisoners of sin and death. Death would not be the end of the life of Jesus on earth. After three days he would rise to live again in even greater glory and power than before his death.

NOTES

his clothes became white as light.*
3All at once Moses and Elijah were
there talking with Jesus. 4So Peter
said to him, "Lord, it is good for us
to be here! Let us make three shelters,
one for you, one for Moses, and one
for Elijah."
5While Peter was still speaking, the
shadow of a bright cloud passed over
them. From the cloud a voice said,
"This is my own dear Son, and I am
pleased with him. Listen to what he
says!" 6When the disciples heard the
voice, they were so afraid that they
fell flat on the ground. 7But Jesus
came over and touched them. He
said, "Get up and don't be afraid!"
8When they opened their eyes, they
saw only Jesus.
9On their way down from the
mountain, Jesus warned his disciples
not to tell anyone what they had seen
until after the Son of Man had been
raised from death.
10The disciples asked Jesus, "Don't
the teachers of the Law of Moses say
that Elijah must come before the
Messiah does?"
11Jesus told them, "Elijah certainly
will come and get everything ready.
12In fact, he has already come. But
the people did not recognize him and
treated him just as they wanted to.
They will soon make the Son of Man
suffer in the same way." 13Then the
disciples understood that Jesus was
talking to them about John the
Baptist.

Jesus Heals a Boy
(Mark 9.14–29; Luke 9.37–43a)

14Jesus and his disciples returned
to the crowd. A man kneeled in front
of him 15and said, "Lord, have pity
on my son! He has a bad case of epilepsy and often falls into a fire or
into water. 16I brought him to your
disciples, but none of them could heal
him."
17Jesus said, "You people are too
stubborn to have any faith! How
much longer must I be with you? Why
do I have to put up with you? Bring
the boy here."* 18Then Jesus spoke
sternly to the demon. It went out of
the boy, and right then he was healed.
19Later the disciples went to Jesus
in private and asked him, "Why
couldn't we force out the demon?"
20-21Jesus replied:

It is because you don't have
enough faith! But I can promise
you this. If you had faith no
larger than a mustard seed, you
could tell this mountain to move
from here to there. And it would.
Everything would be possible for
you.[j]

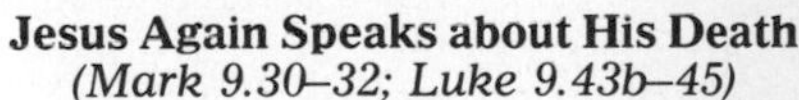

Jesus Again Speaks about His Death
(Mark 9.30–32; Luke 9.43b–45)

22While Jesus and his disciples
were going from place to place in
Galilee, he told them, "The Son of
Man will be handed over to people
23who will kill him. But three days
later he will rise to life." All of this
made the disciples very sad.

Paying the Temple Tax

24When Jesus and the others arrived in Capernaum, the collectors
for the temple tax came to Peter and

---

[j] *for you*: Some manuscripts add, "But the only way to force out that kind of demon is by praying and going without eating."

17.2 **SEE JESUS AS HE IS** The Son of God hid his glory by coming into this world as a man. He took upon himself the form of a servant. But on the mountain he showed himself to his disciples as he really is. Jesus is no longer the meek and lowly servant today. He is the King of Glory. We should realize he is no longer the suffering one, but the risen Christ who lives to share his life with us forever.

17.17 **OUR FAITH MUST BE GREATER** We forgive ourselves too easily for our weak faith. We feel the rightness of Jesus' remark here. We say great words about our mighty God, but we often live as though he were weak. Let's put away our unbelief and show by our lives that our God lives.

NOTES

asked, "Does your teacher pay the
temple tax?"*
25"Yes, he does," Peter answered.
After they had returned home, Jesus went up to Peter and asked him,
"Simon, what do you think? Do the
kings of this earth collect taxes and
fees from their own people or from
foreigners?"[k]
26Peter answered, "From foreigners."
Jesus replied, "Then their own people[l] don't have to pay. 27But we don't
want to cause trouble. So go cast a
line into the lake and pull out the
first fish you hook. Open its mouth,
and you will find a coin. Use it to
pay your taxes and mine."

Who Is the Greatest?
(Mark 9.33–37; Luke 9.46–48)

18 About this time, the disciples
came to Jesus and asked him
who would be the greatest in the
kingdom of heaven.* 2Jesus called a
child over and had the child stand
near him. 3Then he said:
I promise you this. If you don't
change and become like this
child, you will never get into the
kingdom of heaven. 4But if you
are as humble as this child, you
are the greatest in the kingdom
of heaven. 5And when you
welcome one of these children
because of me, you welcome me.

Temptations to Sin
(Mark 9.42–48; Luke 17.1, 2)

6It will be terrible for people
who cause even one of my little
followers to sin. Those people
would be better off thrown into
the deepest part of the ocean
with a heavy stone tied around
the neck!* 7The world is in for
trouble because of the way it
causes people to sin. There will
always be something to cause
people to sin, but anyone who
does this will be in for trouble.
8If your hand or foot causes
you to sin, chop it off and throw
it away! You would be better off
to go into life crippled or lame
than to have two hands or two
feet and be thrown into the fire
that never goes out. 9If your eye
causes you to sin, poke it out and
get rid of it. You would be better
off to go into life with only one
eye than to have two eyes and
be thrown into the fires of hell.

The Lost Sheep
(Luke 15.3–7)

10-11Don't be cruel to any of
these little ones! I promise you

---

[k]*from their own people or from foreigners*: Or "from their children or from others." [l]*From foreigners . . . their own people*: Or "From other people . . . their children."

17.24 **OBEY THE LAW** Jesus agreed that the temple tax was not a good law. But he told Peter to pay it anyway. It was a small price to pay to avoid a foolish quarrel. If we are always demanding our rights, we just seem to be quarrelsome. Let's be willing sometimes to accept wrong for Jesus' sake. God supplies our needs somehow, as he supplied Jesus' and Peter's needs here in this passage.

18.1 **YOU'RE IMPORTANT TO GOD** Self-importance is a pitiful sin. By pushing ourselves forward we really show how frightened we are. We're afraid of being forgotten, that people will ignore us, that we'll be lost in the crowd. So we try to be ahead of others. Christians can afford not to be "big shots"—we have a kingdom that will last forever. Our God won't forget us.

18.6 **DON'T BE A STUMBLING STONE** We don't always see the things in our path that will trip us up. Temptation is like that. We aren't expecting it, but if we aren't careful we trip and fall into sin. It's also very important not to be a stumbling stone of temptation for others. By thoughtless things we do, we may cause others to sin.

NOTES

that their angels are always with
my Father in heaven.[m] 12Let me
ask you this. What would you
do if you had a hundred sheep
and one of them wandered off?
Wouldn't you leave the ninety-
nine on the hillside and go look
for the one that had wandered
away?* 13I am sure that finding
it would make you happier than
having the ninety-nine that
never wandered off. 14That's
how it is with your Father in
heaven. He doesn't want any of
these little ones to be lost.

When Someone Sins
(Luke 17.3)

15If one of my followers[n] sins
against you, go and point out
what was wrong. But do it in
private, just between the two of
you. If that person listens, you
have won back a follower.*
16But if that one refuses to listen,
take along one or two others.
The Scriptures teach that every
complaint must be proven true
by two or more witnesses. 17If
the follower refuses to listen to
them, report the matter to the
church. Anyone who refuses to
listen to the church must be
treated like an unbeliever or a
tax collector.[o]

Allowing and Not Allowing

18I promise you that God in
heaven will allow whatever you
allow on earth, but he will not
allow anything you don't allow.
19I promise that when any two
of you on earth agree about
something you are praying for,
my Father in heaven will do it
for you. 20Whenever two or three
of you come together in my
name,[p] I am there with you.

An Official Who Refused to Forgive

21Peter came up to the Lord and
asked, "How many times should I
forgive someone[q] who does something wrong to me? Is seven times
enough?"
22Jesus answered:
Not just seven times, but
seventy-seven times![r] 23This
story will show you what the
kingdom of heaven is like:
One day a king decided to call
in his officials and ask them to
give an account of what they
owed him. 24As he was doing
this, one official was brought in
who owed him fifty million silver
coins. 25But he didn't have any
money to pay what he owed. The
king ordered him to be sold,
along with his wife and children
and all he owned, in order to pay
the debt.
26The official got down on his
knees and began begging, "Have
pity on me, and I will pay you
every cent I owe!" 27The king felt

---

[m]*in heaven*: Some manuscripts add, "The Son of Man came to save people who are lost." [n]*followers*: The Greek text has "brother," which is used here and elsewhere in this chapter to refer to a follower of Christ. [o]*tax collector*: See the note at 5.46. [p]*in my name*: Or "as my followers." [q]*someone*: Or "a follower." See the note at 18.15. [r]*seventy-seven times*: Or "seventy times seven." The large number means that one follower should never stop forgiving another.

18.12 **GOD WON'T LOSE US** We saw earlier how important we are to God. Jesus showed this very well in the story about the lost sheep. The shepherd valued that one sheep more than all the others. So he went and found it, wherever it was lost. That's the way God cares about each one of us—he never gives up till he finds the one who has wandered.

18.15 **SIN MUST BE CONFESSED** "If I ignore it, maybe it will go away." Too often we think that way about something unpleasant—or even about something sinful. Sin breaks our relationship with God and others. We should confess our sins, not just to please others, but to please God. The kingdom of God cannot be the kingdom of God if sin is permitted. So let us help one another to do away with all things that offend God.

NOTES

sorry for him and let him go free.
He even told the official that he
did not have to pay back the
money.*
28As the official was leaving,
he happened to meet another
official, who owed him a
hundred silver coins. So he
grabbed the man by the throat.
He started choking him and said,
"Pay me what you owe!"
29The man got down on his
knees and began begging, "Have
pity on me, and I will pay you
back." 30But the first official
refused to have pity. Instead, he
went and had the other official
put in jail until he could pay what
he owed.
31When some other officials
found out what had happened,
they felt sorry for the man who
had been put in jail. Then they
told the king what had
happened. 32The king called the
first official back in and said,
"You're an evil man! When you
begged for mercy, I said you did
not have to pay back a cent.
33Don't you think you should
show pity to someone else, as I
did to you?" 34The king was so
angry that he ordered the official
to be tortured until he could pay
back everything he owed. 35That
is how my Father in heaven will
treat you, if you don't forgive
each of my followers with all
your heart.

Teaching about Divorce
(Mark 10.1–12)

19 When Jesus finished teaching,
he left Galilee and went to the
part of Judea that is east of the Jordan
River. 2Large crowds followed him,
and he healed their sick people.
3Some Pharisees wanted to test
Jesus. They came up to him and
asked, "Is it right for a man to divorce
his wife for just any reason?"
4Jesus answered, "Don't you know
that in the beginning the Creator
made a man and a woman?* 5That's
why a man leaves his father and
mother and gets married. He becomes like one person with his wife.
6Then they are no longer two people,
but one. And no one should separate
a couple that God has joined
together."
7The Pharisees asked Jesus, "Why
did Moses say that a man could write
out divorce papers and send his wife
away?"
8Jesus replied, "You are so heartless! That's why Moses allowed you
to divorce your wife. But from the
beginning God did not intend it to
be that way. 9I say that if your wife
has not committed some terrible sexual sin,[s] you must not divorce her
to marry someone else. If you do, you
are unfaithful."
10The disciples said, "If that's how
it is between a man and a woman,
it's better not to get married."
11Jesus told them, "Only those people who have been given the gift of
staying single can accept this teaching. 12Some people are unable to
marry because of birth defects or because of what someone has done to
their bodies. Others stay single for
the sake of the kingdom of heaven.
Anyone who can accept this teaching
should do so."

---

[s]*some terrible sexual sin*: See the note at 5.32.

18.27 **BE QUICK TO FORGIVE** Christians are forgiven people. There can be no greater joy than to know God has forgiven our sins because of Jesus' death on the cross. Surely, then, forgiven people can afford to be great forgivers. Holding grudges isn't worthy of us who are children of a forgiving God. But if we can't forgive others, how can we expect to be forgiven?

19.4 **BE FAITHFUL IN MARRIAGE** Family unity is very important for the purity of Christ's church. We prove our inability to love when we break our marriage promises. How can we say we love others if we don't even have Christian love for our spouses? Let's realize the importance of this and be sure to love our marriage partners until death.

NOTES

Jesus Blesses Little Children
(Mark 10.13–16; Luke 18.15–17)

13 Some people brought their children to Jesus, so that he could place
his hands on them and pray for them.
His disciples told the people to stop
bothering him.* 14 But Jesus said,
"Let the children come to me, and
don't try to stop them! People who
are like these children belong to
God's kingdom."[t] 15 After Jesus had
placed his hands on the children, he
left.

A Rich Young Man
(Mark 10.17–31; Luke 18.18–30)

16 A man came to Jesus and asked,
"Teacher, what good thing must I do
to have eternal life?"
17 Jesus said to him, "Why do you
ask me about what is good? Only God
is good. If you want to have eternal
life, you must obey his commandments."
18 "Which ones?" the man asked.
Jesus answered, "Do not murder.
Be faithful in marriage. Do not steal.
Do not tell lies about others.
19 Respect your father and mother.
And love others as much as you love
yourself." 20 The young man said, "I
have obeyed all of these. What else
must I do?"
21 Jesus replied, "If you want to be
perfect, go sell everything you own!
Give the money to the poor, and you
will have riches in heaven. Then
come and be my follower." 22 When
the young man heard this, he was
sad, because he was very rich.*
23 Jesus said to his disciples, "It's
terribly hard for rich people to get
into the kingdom of heaven! 24 In fact,
it's easier for a camel to go through
the eye of a needle than for a rich
person to get into God's kingdom."
25 When the disciples heard this,
they were greatly surprised and
asked, "How can anyone ever be
saved?"
26 Jesus looked straight at them and
said, "There are some things that
people cannot do, but God can do
anything."
27 Peter replied, "Remember, we
have left everything to be your followers! What will we get?"
28 Jesus answered:

> Yes, all of you have become
> my followers. And so in the
> future world, when the Son of
> Man sits on his glorious throne,
> I promise that you will sit on
> twelve thrones to judge the
> twelve tribes of Israel.* 29 All who
> have given up home or brothers
> and sisters or father and mother

---

[t] *People who are like these children belong to God's kingdom*: Or "God's kingdom belongs to people who are like these children."

19.13 **JESUS CARES ABOUT YOUNG PEOPLE** We make a big mistake if we think Jesus is only for adults. He asked children to come to him, and he prayed for them. Young people, just like older people, need to learn about Jesus. Parents should teach the Bible to their children at home, and take them to church. This is an important way by which God brings us to himself—by our parents' teaching and example.

19.22 **WHAT IS GOODNESS?** The young man thought he had obeyed all the rules. But he was breaking God's very first commandment. He loved something more than God. The young man was a slave to his wealth. Each one of us must settle the question: what do I love most of all? Is anything more important than doing what God wants me to do?

19.28 **IT PAYS TO FOLLOW JESUS** Cash will not be your reward for following Jesus. It will be something much better than that. The friendship of Jesus is the greatest reward anyone can know. You can have his friendship simply by giving yourself to him. That isn't asking very much when you consider that you receive Christ himself in return. Besides, you belong to God anyway. What would you amount to without him?

NOTES

or children or land for me will
be given a hundred times as
much. They will also have
eternal life. 30But many who are
now first will be last, and many
who are last will be first.

Workers in a Vineyard

20 As Jesus was telling what the
kingdom of heaven would be
like, he said:
Early one morning a man went
out to hire some workers for his
vineyard. 2After he had agreed
to pay them the usual amount
for a day's work, he sent them
off to his vineyard.
3About nine that morning, the
man saw some other people
standing in the market with
nothing to do. 4He said he would
pay them what was fair, if they
would work in his vineyard.
5So they went.
At noon and again about three
in the afternoon he returned to
the market. And each time he
made the same agreement with
others who were loafing around
with nothing to do.
6Finally, about five in the
afternoon the man went back
and found some others standing
there. He asked them, "Why
have you been standing here all
day long doing nothing?"
7"Because no one has hired
us," they answered. Then he told
them to go work in his vineyard.
8That evening the owner of the
vineyard told the man in charge
of the workers to call them in
and give them their money. He
also told the man to begin with
the ones who were hired last.
9When the workers arrived, the
ones who had been hired at five
in the afternoon were given a full
day's pay.
10The workers who had been
hired first thought they would be
given more than the others. But
when they were given the same,
11they began complaining to the
owner of the vineyard. 12They
said, "The ones who were hired
last worked for only one hour.
But you paid them the same that
you did us. And we worked in
the hot sun all day long!"
13The owner answered one of
them, "Friend, I didn't cheat you.
I paid you exactly what we
agreed on.* 14Take your money
now and go! What business is
it of yours if I want to pay them
the same that I paid you? 15Don't
I have the right to do what I want
with my own money? Why
should you be jealous, if I want
to be generous?"
16Jesus then said, "So it is. Everyone who is now first will be last, and
everyone who is last will be first."

Jesus Again Tells about His Death
(Mark 10.32–34; Luke 18.31–34)

17As Jesus was on his way to Jerusalem, he took his twelve disciples
aside and told them in private:
18We are now on our way to
Jerusalem, where the Son of
Man will be handed over to the
chief priests and the teachers of
the Law of Moses. They will
sentence him to death,* 19and

20.13 **GOD KEEPS HIS PROMISES** The five groups of workers in Jesus' story were paid what they were promised. Jesus teaches us here that we owe God our service, and he owes us only what he promised. He never had to ask us to share in his work at all. But our opportunity to serve him is itself a gift from him. So our reward is also his gift at the end of our life on earth.

20.18 **JESUS REMINDS US OF HIS MAIN PURPOSE** Yet another time Jesus spoke plainly of his coming death. God would allow wicked men to nail our Lord to a cross. But their evil work would be undone when he arose from the grave. Jesus wants us to know that without his death and resurrection his work would mean nothing. His great purpose was to die in our place for our sins, and so give us everlasting life with him.

NOTES

then they will hand him over to
foreigners[u] who will make fun
of him. They will beat him and
nail him to a cross. But on the
third day he will rise from death.

A Mother's Request
(Mark 10.35–45)

20The mother of James and John[v]
came to Jesus with her two sons. She
kneeled down and started begging
him to do something for her. 21Jesus
asked her what she wanted, and she
said, "When you come into your
kingdom, please let one of my sons
sit at your right side and the other
at your left."[w]*
22Jesus answered, "Not one of you
knows what you are asking. Are you
able to drink from the cup[x] that I
must soon drink from?"
James and John said, "Yes, we
are!"
23Jesus replied, "You certainly will
drink from my cup! But it is not for
me to say who will sit at my right
side and at my left. That is for my
Father to say."
24When the ten other disciples
heard this, they were angry with the
two brothers. 25But Jesus called the
disciples together and said:
You know that foreign rulers
like to order their people around.
And their great leaders have full
power over everyone they rule.
26But don't act like them. If you
want to be great, you must be
the servant of all the others.
27And if you want to be first, you
must be the slave of the rest.
28The Son of Man did not come
to be a slave master, but a slave
who will give his life to rescue[y]
many people.

Jesus Heals Two Blind Men
(Mark 10.46–52; Luke 18.35–43)

29Jesus was followed by a large
crowd as he and his disciples were
leaving Jericho. 30Two blind men
were sitting beside the road. And
when they heard that Jesus was coming their way, they shouted, "Lord
and Son of David,[z] have pity on us!"
31The crowd told them to be quiet,
but they shouted even louder, "Lord
and Son of David, have pity on us!"
32When Jesus heard them, he
stopped and asked, "What do you
want me to do for you?"
33They answered, "Lord, we want
to see!"
34Jesus felt sorry for them and
touched their eyes. Right away they
could see, and they became his
followers.*

Jesus Enters Jerusalem
(Mark 11.1–11; Luke 19.28–38; John 12.12–19)

21 When Jesus and his disciples
came near to Jerusalem, he

---

[u]*foreigners*: The Romans, who ruled Judea at this time. [v]*mother of James and John*: The Greek text has "mother of the sons of Zebedee." See 26.37. [w]*right side . . . left*: The most powerful people in a kingdom sat at the right and left side of the king. [x]*drink from the cup*: In the Scriptures a cup is sometimes used as a symbol of suffering. To "drink from the cup" is to suffer. [y]*rescue*: The Greek word often, though not always, means the payment of a price to free a slave or a prisoner. [z]*Son of David*: See the note at 9.27.

20.21 **WHO WILL BE FIRST?** The mother's request seems selfish and petty. But this only shows how poorly Jesus' followers understood him at that time. They still thought their Messiah had come to give them earthly power. But Jesus' answer may have disappointed them. Greatness will be measured by unselfish service, not by being in control.

20.34 **THE BLIND SEE** Several times we find Jesus giving people back their sight. We might ask, "Why didn't he give back *every* blind person's sight?" Someday he will, if only they will trust him now as their Lord and Savior. He was showing at that time that, as Lord, he has power to do this if we believe. When we have faith in Jesus we see him and his greatness with open eyes.

NOTES

went to Bethphage on the Mount of
Olives and sent two of them on
ahead. 2He told them, "Go into the
next village, where you will at once
find a donkey and her colt. Untie the
two donkeys and bring them to me.
3If anyone asks why you are doing
that, just say, 'The Lord[a] needs
them.' Right away he will let you
have the donkeys."
4So God's promise came true, just
as the prophet had said,

5"Announce to the people
of Jerusalem:
'Your king is coming to you!
He is humble
and rides on a donkey.
He comes on the colt
of a donkey.' "*

6The disciples left and did what
Jesus had told them to do. 7They
brought the donkey and its colt and
laid some clothes on their backs.
Then Jesus got on.
8Many people spread clothes in the
road, while others put down
branches[b] which they had cut from
trees. 9Some people walked ahead of
Jesus and others followed behind.
They were all shouting,

"Hooray[c] for the Son
of David![d]
God bless the one who comes
in the name of the Lord.
Hooray for God
in heaven above!"

10When Jesus came to Jerusalem,
everyone in the city was excited and
asked, "Who can this be?"
11The crowd answered, "This is
Jesus, the prophet from Nazareth in
Galilee."

Jesus in the Temple
(Mark 11.15–19; Luke 19.45–48; John 2.13–22)

12Jesus went into the temple and
chased out everyone who was selling
or buying. He turned over the tables
of the moneychangers and the
benches of the ones who were selling
doves.* 13He told them, "The Scriptures say, 'My house should be called
a place of worship.' But you have
turned it into a place where robbers
hide."
14Blind and lame people came to
Jesus in the temple, and he healed
them. 15But the chief priests and the
teachers of the Law of Moses were
angry when they saw his miracles
and heard the children shouting
praises to the Son of David.[d] 16The
men said to Jesus, "Don't you hear
what those children are saying?"
"Yes, I do!" Jesus answered.
"Don't you know that the Scriptures
say, 'Children and infants will sing
praises'?" 17Then Jesus left the city
and went out to the village of Bethany, where he spent the night.

Jesus Puts a Curse on a Fig Tree
(Mark 11.12–14, 20–24)

18When Jesus got up the next
morning, he was hungry. He started

[a]*The Lord*: Or "the master of the donkeys." [b]*spread clothes . . . put down branches*: This was one way that the Jewish people welcomed a famous person. [c]*Hooray*: This translates a word that can mean "please save us." But it is most often used as a shout of praise to God. [d]*Son of David*: See the note at 9.27.

21.5 **THE KING RODE A DONKEY** We would expect a king to ride into town on a white horse, with trumpets blaring and lots of official ceremony. But the King of kings himself was content to ride a donkey. Jesus didn't need and didn't want earthly glory in order to be King. He was King long before the world was even created. But Jesus showed that he was willing to look unimportant in order to conquer people's hearts.

21.12 **JESUS APPRECIATES TRUE VALUE** The merchants in the temple thought their money was the greatest value. But Jesus set them straight about that. They were in God's house, and they must behave as they should or else get out. Then Jesus healed the blind and the lame in the temple. Churches today are also places for healing broken hearts with the good news about Jesus.

NOTES

out for the city, 19and along the way he saw a fig tree. But when he came to it, he found only leaves and no figs. So he told the tree, "You will never again grow any fruit!" Right then the fig tree dried up.*

20The disciples were shocked when they saw how quickly the tree had dried up. 21But Jesus said to them, "If you have faith and don't doubt, I promise that you can do what I did to this tree. And you will be able to do even more. You can tell this mountain to get up and jump into the sea, and it will. 22If you have faith when you pray, you will be given whatever you ask for."

A Question about Jesus' Authority
(Mark 11.27–33; Luke 20.1–8)

23Jesus had gone into the temple and was teaching when the chief priests and the leaders of the people came up to him. They asked, "What right do you have to do these things? Who gave you this authority?"*

24Jesus answered, "I have just one question to ask you. If you answer it, I will tell you where I got the right to do these things. 25Who gave John the right to baptize? Was it God in heaven or merely some human being?"

They thought it over and said to each other, "We can't say that God gave John this right. Jesus will ask us why we didn't believe John. 26On the other hand, these people think that John was a prophet, and we are afraid of what they might do to us. That's why we can't say that it was merely some human who gave John the right to baptize." 27So they told Jesus, "We don't know."

Jesus said, "Then I won't tell you who gave me the right to do what I do."

A Story about Two Sons

28Jesus said:

I will tell you a story about a man who had two sons. Then you can tell me what you think. The father went to the older son and said, "Go work in the vineyard today!" 29His son told him that he would not do it, but later he changed his mind and went. 30The man then told his younger son to go work in the vineyard. The boy said he would, but he didn't go. 31Which one of the sons obeyed his father?

"The older one," the chief priests and leaders answered.

Then Jesus told them:

You can be sure that tax collectors[e] and bad women will get into the kingdom of God before you ever will!* 32When John the Baptist showed you how to do right, you would not

[e] *tax collectors*: See the note at 5.46.

21.19 **GOD HAS NO LIMIT** Jesus used a fig tree to show his followers that he is Lord of all creation. If what we are asking God for is according to his will, there is no limit to what he can do for us when we have faith in him.

21.23 **A QUESTION FOR AN ANSWER** The religious leaders thought they had trapped Jesus with their question. But he replied with a question they were afraid to answer. Whatever they answered would get them into trouble. So they gave what they hoped was a safe reply—"We don't know." So Jesus told them he wouldn't answer them either. Jesus turned the religious leaders' cleverness back on them.

21.31 **SAYING IS NOT DOING** Some people are experts in talking about religion—they are even very correct in everything they say. But they don't practice what they say. We must be careful that we're not put to shame by those who can't *speak* well, but they *do* the will of God. We ought to learn and *know* God's word, but we must be even more careful to *obey* what God says.

NOTES

believe him. But these evil
people did believe. And even
when you saw what they did, you
still would not change your
minds and believe.

Renters of a Vineyard
(Mark 12.1–12; Luke 20.9–19)

33Jesus told the chief priests and
leaders to listen to this story:
A land owner once planted a
vineyard. He built a wall around
it and dug a pit to crush the
grapes in. He also built a lookout
tower. Then he rented out his
vineyard and left the country.
34When it was harvest time,
the owner sent some servants to
get his share of the grapes.
35But the renters grabbed those
servants. They beat up one,
killed one, and stoned one of
them to death. 36He then sent
more servants than he did the
first time. But the renters treated
them in the same way.
37Finally, the owner sent his
own son to the renters, because
he thought they would respect
him. 38But when they saw the
man's son, they said, "Someday
he will own the vineyard. Let's
kill him! Then we can have it all
for ourselves." 39So they
grabbed him, threw him out of
the vineyard, and killed him.
40Jesus asked, "When the owner
of that vineyard comes, what do you
suppose he will do to those renters?"
41The chief priests and leaders answered, "He will kill them in some
horrible way. Then he will rent out
his vineyard to people who will give
him his share of grapes at harvest
time."
42Jesus replied, "Surely you know
that the Scriptures say,

'The stone that the builders
tossed aside
is now the most important
stone of all.
This is something
the Lord has done,
and it is amazing to us.'

43I tell you that God's kingdom will
be taken from you and given to people who will do what he demands.*
44Anyone who stumbles over this
stone will be crushed, and anyone
it falls on will be smashed to pieces."[f]
45When the chief priests and the
Pharisees heard these stories, they
knew that Jesus was talking about
them. 46They looked for a way to kill
him. But they were afraid to arrest
Jesus, because the people thought he
was a prophet.

The Great Banquet
(Luke 14.15–24)

22 Once again Jesus used stories
to teach the people:
2The kingdom of heaven is like
what happened when a king
gave a wedding banquet for his
son.* 3The king sent some

[f]*pieces*: Verse 44 is not in some manuscripts.

21.43 GOD BLESSES THE ONES WHO HONOR HIM This story is about the history of what happened during the time of the Bible. The owner of the world is God. He made the world and left it to be kept by his chosen people, Israel. But they mistreated God's messengers, the prophets. Then when the Jewish leaders killed their Messiah, God's son, God gave his blessing to his church, made up of Jews and Gentiles, mostly Gentiles. God will bless those who accept his son Jesus.

22.2 ARE YOUR SINS COVERED? Jesus told the story of the banquet to show that not everybody is a citizen of God's eternal kingdom. Some people prove by their actions that their claims to be God's people are false. Others who may look good are only self-righteous. Their sins aren't covered—the way some of the guests weren't covered by the special wedding clothes that people were given to wear at wedding celebrations in those days. Those clothes were like the gift of Christ's own goodness that changes our hearts.

NOTES

servants to tell the invited guests
to come to the banquet, but the
guests refused. 4He sent other
servants to say to the guests,
"The banquet is ready! My cattle
and prize calves have all been
prepared. Everything is ready.
Come to the banquet!"
5But the guests did not pay any
attention. Some of them left for
their farms, and some went to
their places of business. 6Others
grabbed the servants, beat them
up, and killed them.
7This made the king so furious
that he sent an army to kill those
murderers and burn down their
city. 8Then he said to the
servants, "It is time for the
wedding banquet, and the
invited guests don't deserve to
come. 9Go out to the street
corners and tell everyone you
meet to come to the banquet."
10They went out on the streets
and brought in everyone they
could find, good and bad alike.
And the banquet room was filled
with guests.
11When the king went in to
meet the guests, he found that
one of them was not wearing the
right kind of clothes for the
wedding. 12The king asked,
"Friend, why didn't you wear
proper clothes for the wedding?"
But the guest had no excuse.
13So the king gave orders for that
person to be tied hand and foot
and to be thrown outside into the
dark. That's where people will
cry and grit their teeth in pain.
14Many are invited, but only a
few are chosen.

Paying Taxes

(Mark 12.13–17; Luke 20.20–26)

15The Pharisees got together and
planned how they could trick Jesus
into saying something wrong.
16They sent some of their followers
and some of Herod's followers[g] to
say to him, "Teacher, we know that
you are honest. You teach the truth
about what God wants people to do.
And you treat everyone with the
same respect, no matter who they
are. 17Tell us what you think! Should
we pay taxes to the Emperor or
not?"*
18Jesus knew their evil thoughts
and said, "Why are you trying to test
me? You showoffs! 19Let me see one
of the coins used for paying taxes."
They brought him a silver coin,
20and he asked, "Whose picture and
name are on it?"
21"The Emperor's," they answered.
Then Jesus told them, "Give the
Emperor what belongs to him and
give God what belongs to God."
22His answer surprised them so much
that they walked away.

Life in the Future World

(Mark 12.18–27; Luke 20.27–40)

23The Sadducees did not believe
that people would rise to life after
death. So that same day some of the
Sadducees came to Jesus and said:
24Teacher, Moses wrote that if
a married man dies and has no
children, his brother should
marry the widow. Their first son
would then be thought of as the
son of the dead brother.
25Once there were seven
brothers who lived here. The
first one married, but died
without having any children. So
his wife was left to his brother.
26The same thing happened to
the second and third brothers
and finally to all seven of them.

[g]*Herod's followers*: People who were political followers of the family of Herod the Great (2.1) and his son Herod Antipas (14.1), and who wanted Herod to be king in Jerusalem.

22.17 **LET'S DO OUR CIVIC DUTY** The Pharisees thought Jesus might be a political troublemaker who taught people to resist the Roman government. Some Jews, called Zealots, hoped to overthrow the Romans. Was Jesus one of them? No—he surprised the Pharisees by telling them they should pay their taxes but keep their souls for God.

NOTES

27At last the woman died.
28When God raises people from
death, whose wife will this
woman be? She had been
married to all seven brothers.*
29Jesus answered:
You are completely wrong!
You don't know what the
Scriptures teach. And you don't
know anything about the power
of God. 30When God raises
people to life, they won't marry.
They will be like the angels in
heaven. 31And as for people
being raised to life, God was
speaking to you when he said,
32"I am the God worshiped by
Abraham, Isaac, and Jacob."[h]
He is not the God of the dead,
but of the living.
33The crowds were surprised to
hear what Jesus was teaching.

The Most Important Commandment
(Mark 12.28–34; Luke 10.25–28)

34After Jesus had made the Sadducees look foolish, the Pharisees heard
about it and got together. 35One of
them was an expert in the Jewish
Law. So he tried to test Jesus by asking, 36"Teacher, what is the most important commandment in the Law?"
37Jesus answered:
Love the Lord your God with
all your heart, soul, and mind.*
38This is the first and most
important commandment. 39The
second most important
commandment is like this one.
And it is, "Love others as much
as you love yourself." 40All the
Law of Moses and the Books of
the Prophets[i] are based on these
two commandments.

About David's Son
(Mark 12.35–37; Luke 20.41–44)

41While the Pharisees were still
there, Jesus asked them,* 42"What do
you think about the Messiah? Whose
family will he come from?"
They answered, "He will be a son
of King David."[j]
43Jesus replied, "How then could
the Spirit have David call the Messiah his Lord? David said,
44'The Lord said to my Lord:
Sit at my right side[k]

---

[h]*I am the God worshiped by Abraham, Isaac, and Jacob*: Jesus argues that if God is worshiped by these three, they must still be alive, because he is the God of the living. [i]*the Law of Moses and the Books of the Prophets*: The Jewish Scriptures, that is, the Old Testament. [j]*son of King David*: See the note at 9.27. [k]*right side*: The place of power and honor.

22.28 **LIFE IN HEAVEN IS DIFFERENT** The Sadducees were trying to trick Jesus with their words. How could he ever answer such a question? But Jesus turned the tables on them by telling them they had the wrong idea about the life to come. There will be no marrying in heaven. They didn't believe in a resurrection. But in the Old Testament God said that he *is* worshiped by Abraham—years after Abraham had died. God cannot be worshiped by dead people. Abraham, Isaac, and Jacob are alive in heaven.

22.37 **THE LAW SUMMED UP** Here are the Ten Commandments in brief. The most important of all the commandments is the first one: Love God. But people are made in God's likeness. So the second commandment is like the first. We can't say truly that we love God if we don't love people for the sake of God who made them.

22.41 **WHO IS THE MESSIAH?** It was Jesus' turn to test the Pharisees. He asked them what seems like an easy question. Everybody knew the Messiah would come from the family of King David who lived a thousand years before. But Jesus confused the Pharisees by reminding them that David did not call the Messiah his descendant. David called the Messiah "my Lord." So how could David's descendant also be David's Lord? That really gave the Pharisees something to scratch their heads about.

NOTES

until I make your enemies
into a footstool for you.'
45If David called the Messiah his
Lord, how can the Messiah be a son
of King David?" 46No one was able
to give Jesus an answer, and from
that day on no one dared ask him
any more questions.

Jesus Condemns the Pharisees and the Teachers of the Law of Moses
(Mark 12.38–40; Luke 11.37–52; 20.45–47)

23 Jesus said to the crowds and
to his disciples:
2The Pharisees and the
teachers of the Law are experts
in the Law of Moses. 3So obey
everything they teach you, but
don't do as they do. After all,
they say one thing and do
something else.*
4They pile heavy burdens on
people's shoulders and won't lift
a finger to help them.
5Everything they do is just to
show off in front of others. They
even make a big show of wearing
Scripture verses on their
foreheads and arms, and they
wear big tassels[l] for everyone
to see. 6They love the best seats
at banquets and the front seats
in the meeting places. 7And
when they are in the market,
they like to have people greet
them as their teachers.
8But none of you should be
called a teacher. You have only
one teacher, and all of you are
like brothers and sisters. 9Don't
call anyone on earth your father.
All of you have the same Father
in heaven. 10None of you should
be called the leader. The Messiah
is your only leader. 11Whoever
is the greatest should be the
servant of the others. 12If you put
yourself above others, you will
be put down. But if you humble
yourself, you will be honored.
13-14You Pharisees and
teachers of the Law of Moses are
in for trouble! You're nothing
but showoffs. You lock people
out of the kingdom of heaven.
You won't go in yourselves, and
you keep others from going in.[m]*
15You Pharisees and teachers
of the Law of Moses are in for
trouble! You're nothing but
showoffs. You travel over land
and sea to win one follower. And
when you have done so, you
make that person twice as fit for
hell as you are.
16You are in for trouble! You
are supposed to lead others, but
you are blind. You teach that it
doesn't matter if a person swears

---

[l]*wearing Scripture verses on their foreheads and arms . . . tassels*: As a sign of their love for the Lord and his teachings, the Jewish people had started wearing Scripture verses in small leather boxes. But the Pharisees tried to show off by making the boxes bigger than necessary. The Jewish people were also taught to wear tassels on the four corners of their robes to show their love for God.
[m]*from going in*: Some manuscripts add, "You Pharisees and teachers are in for trouble! And you're nothing but showoffs! You cheat widows out of their homes and then pray long prayers just to show off. So you will be punished most of all."

23.3 **A GOOD TEACHER IS A GOOD DOER** Teachers or preachers might think they have done what God expects when others obey what they say. It may seem safe, but it's really very dangerous for teachers to teach others to obey what they themselves do not. It's easy for some leaders to think they're special just because they're leaders. They imagine they don't have to obey God themselves, just get others to.

23.13 **LET'S NOT BE SHOWOFFS** Jesus called the leaders of his day by the right name—"showoffs." And they were worse than show-offs because they really had nothing to show off. Inside themselves they were morally rotten. What they were showing off wasn't real. The message is, beware of pretending to be something you're not. We may deceive ourselves, but we can't fool God.

NOTES

by the temple. But you say that
it does matter if someone swears
by the gold in the temple. 17You
blind fools! Which is greater, the
gold or the temple that makes
the gold sacred?
18You also teach that it doesn't
matter if a person swears by the
altar. But you say that it does
matter if someone swears by the
gift on the altar. 19Are you blind?
Which is more important, the
gift or the altar that makes the
gift sacred? 20Anyone who
swears by the altar also swears
by everything on it. 21And
anyone who swears by the
temple also swears by God, who
lives there. 22To swear by
heaven is the same as swearing
by God's throne and by the one
who sits on that throne.

23You Pharisees and teachers
are showoffs, and you're in for
trouble! You give God a tenth
of the spices from your garden,
such as mint, dill, and cumin. Yet
you neglect the more important
matters of the Law, such as
justice, mercy, and faithfulness.
These are the important things
you should have done, though
you should not have left the
others undone either.* 24You
blind leaders! You strain out a
small fly but swallow a camel.
25You Pharisees and teachers
are showoffs, and you're in for
trouble! You wash the outside of
your cups and dishes, while
inside there is nothing but greed
and selfishness. 26You blind
Pharisee! First clean the inside
of a cup, and then the outside
will also be clean.
27You Pharisees and teachers
are in for trouble! You're
nothing but showoffs. You're
like tombs that have been
whitewashed.[n] On the outside
they are beautiful, but inside
they are full of bones and filth.
28That's what you are like.
Outside you look good, but
inside you are evil and only
pretend to be good.
29You Pharisees and teachers
are nothing but showoffs, and
you're in for trouble! You build
monuments for the prophets and
decorate the tombs of good
people.* 30And you claim that
you would not have taken part
with your ancestors in killing the
prophets. 31But you prove that
you really are the relatives of the
ones who killed the prophets.
32So keep on doing everything
they did. 33You are nothing but
snakes and the children of
snakes! How can you escape
going to hell?
34I will send prophets and wise
people and experts in the Law
of Moses to you. But you will kill
them or nail them to a cross or
beat them in your meeting places
or chase them from town to
town. 35That's why you will be
held guilty for the murder of
every good person, beginning
with the good man Abel. This
also includes Barachiah's son

[n]*whitewashed*: Tombs were whitewashed to keep anyone from accidentally touching them. A person who touched a dead body or a tomb was considered unclean and could not worship with the rest of the Jewish people.

23.23 **REAL GODLINESS IS COSTLY** A cheap religion is one that doesn't cost us very much. The leaders of Jesus' time made sure they could look very religious while at the same time living only for themselves. They paid their little tithes, but they were unjust, merciless, and unfaithful in their real duty.

23.29 **LET'S HAVE TENDER HEARTS** The leaders would praise great people of the past, but Jesus reminded them that they would kill the people God sent in their own time. This applies to us today, too. It's not good enough to be proud of the great stories about Christians of the past. That's easy. But our hard hearts are shown if we don't love God's people who are living today.

NOTES

Zechariah,[o] the man you
murdered between the temple
and the altar. 36I can promise
that you people living today will
be punished for all these things!

Jesus Loves Jerusalem
(Luke 13.34, 35)

37Jerusalem, Jerusalem! Your
people have killed the prophets
and have stoned the messengers
who were sent to you. I have
often wanted to gather your
people, as a hen gathers her
chicks under her wings. But you
wouldn't let me.* 38And now
your temple will be deserted.
39You will not see me again until
you say,

"Blessed is the one who comes
in the name of the Lord."

The Temple Will Be Destroyed
(Mark 13.1, 2; Luke 21.5, 6)

24 After Jesus left the temple, his
disciples came over and said,
"Look at all these buildings!"*
2Jesus replied, "Do you see these
buildings? They will certainly all be
torn down! Not one stone will be left
in place."

Warning about Trouble
(Mark 13.3–13; Luke 21.7–19)

3Later, as Jesus was sitting on the
Mount of Olives, his disciples came
to him in private and asked, "When
will this happen? What will be the
sign of your coming and of the end
of the world?"
4Jesus answered:

Don't let anyone fool you.
5Many will come and claim to
be me. They will say that they
are the Messiah, and they will
fool many people.
6You will soon hear about
wars and threats of wars, but
don't be afraid. These things will
have to happen first, but that is
not the end. 7Nations and
kingdoms will go to war against
each other. People will starve to
death, and in some places there
will be earthquakes. 8But this is
just the beginning of troubles.
9You will be arrested,
punished, and even killed.
Because of me, you will be hated
by people of all nations.* 10Many
will give up and will betray and
hate each other. 11Many false

---

[o] *Zechariah*: Genesis is the first book in the Jewish Scriptures, and it tells that Abel was the first person to be murdered. Second Chronicles is the last book in the Jewish Scriptures, and the last murder that it tells about is that of Zechariah.

23.37 **JERUSALEM'S SIN** The city of Jerusalem had a special place in the heart of Jesus. But his heart was broken—the city would not have him. There would be great pain for them: they would soon be taken over by a cruel invading army. Can we learn from this and welcome Jesus better than Jerusalem did?

24.1 **OUR POSSESSIONS ARE ONLY FOR A TIME** Old Scrooge in Charles Dickens' story A *Christmas Carol* woke up to realize he couldn't take his wealth to the grave. The Jews of Jesus' day greatly prized their temple. In fact the temple had almost come to take the place of God in their minds. For them, the worst thing Jesus could say was that the temple would be destroyed. But years later, that was exactly what God let happen. We need to have greater "life insurance" than buildings or cash.

24.9 **TROUBLE IS COMING** Ever since Jesus went back to heaven the world has had continual trouble. Christians have not escaped. In fact Christians have suffered harshly for believing in Jesus, and untold numbers have died and are dying horribly. What can we say to this? Evil will have its day, but our safety is in God's presence where none of these things can trouble us.

NOTES

prophets will come and fool a
lot of people. 12Evil will spread
and cause many people to stop
loving others. 13But if you keep
on being faithful right to the end,
you will be saved. 14When the
good news about the kingdom
has been preached all over the
world and told to all nations, the
end will come.

The Horrible Thing
(Mark 13.14–23; Luke 21.20–24)

15Someday you will see that
"Horrible Thing" in the holy
place, just as the prophet Daniel
said. Everyone who reads this
must try to understand! 16If you
are living in Judea at that time,
run to the mountains. 17If you
are on the roof[p] of your house,
don't go inside to get anything.
18If you are out in the field, don't
go back for your coat. 19It will
be a terrible time for women who
are expecting babies or nursing
young children. 20And pray that
you won't have to escape in
winter or on a Sabbath.[q] 21This
will be the worst time of
suffering since the beginning of
the world, and nothing this
terrible will ever happen again.
22If God doesn't make the time
shorter, no one will be left alive.
But because of God's chosen
ones, he will make the time
shorter.

23Someone may say, "Here is
the Messiah!" or "There he is!"
But don't believe it.* 24False
messiahs and false prophets will
come and work great miracles
and signs. They will even try to
fool God's chosen ones. 25But I
have warned you ahead of time.
26If you are told that the Messiah
is out in the desert, don't go
there! And if you are told that
he is in some secret place, don't
believe it! 27The coming of the
Son of Man will be like lightning
that can be seen from east to
west. 28Where there is a corpse,
there will always be buzzards.[r]

When the Son of Man Appears
(Mark 13.24–27; Luke 21.25–28)

29Right after those days of
suffering,

"The sun will become dark,
and the moon
will no longer shine.
The stars will fall,
and the powers in the sky[s]
will be shaken."

30Then a sign will appear in
the sky. And there will be the
Son of Man.[t] All nations on earth
will weep when they see the Son
of Man coming on the clouds of
heaven with power and great
glory. 31At the sound of a loud
trumpet he will send his angels
to bring his chosen ones together
from all over the earth.

A Lesson from a Fig Tree
(Mark 13.28–31; Luke 21.29–33)

32Learn a lesson from a fig
tree. When its branches sprout

---

[p] *roof*: In Palestine the houses usually had a flat roof. Stairs on the outside led up to the roof, which was made of beams and boards covered with packed earth. [q] *in winter or on a Sabbath*: In Palestine the winters are cold and rainy and make travel difficult. The Jewish people were not allowed to travel much more than half a mile on the Sabbath. For these reasons it was hard for them to escape from their enemies in the winter or on a Sabbath. [r] *Where there is a corpse, there will always be buzzards*: This saying may mean that when anything important happens, people soon know about it. Or the saying may mean that whenever something bad happens, curious people gather around and stare. But the word translated "buzzard" also means "eagle" and may refer to the Roman army, which had an eagle as its symbol. [s] *the powers in the sky*: In ancient times people thought that the stars were spiritual powers. [t] *And there will be the Son of Man*: Or "And it will be the Son of Man."

24.23 **JESUS WILL RETURN** Every now and then we hear of some new cult or some new messiah. Jesus warns us not to be disturbed by these things that must come. We don't have to run after every religious fad. We know whom we have believed, and we have proved he can be trusted with our lives. We wait for his return when we shall be with him forever.

NOTES

and start putting out leaves, you
know that summer is near.
33So when you see all these
things happening, you will know
that the time has almost come.[u]
34I can promise you that some
of the people living today will
still be alive when all this
happens. 35The sky and the earth
won't last forever, but my words
will.

No One Knows the Day or Time
(Mark 13.32–37;
Luke 17.26–30, 34–36)

36No one knows the day or
hour. The angels in heaven don't
know, and the Son himself
doesn't know.[v] Only the Father
knows.* 37When the Son of Man
appears, things will be just as
they were when Noah lived.
38People were eating, drinking,
and getting married right up to
the day that the flood came and
Noah went into the big boat.
39They didn't know anything
was happening until the flood
came and swept them all away.
That is how it will be when the
Son of Man appears.

40Two men will be in the same
field, but only one will be taken.
The other will be left. 41Two
women will be together grinding
grain, but only one will be taken.
The other will be left. 42So be
on your guard! You don't know
when your Lord will come.
43Homeowners never know
when a thief is coming, and they
are always on guard to keep one
from breaking in. 44Always be
ready! You don't know when the
Son of Man will come.

Faithful and Unfaithful Servants
(Luke 12.35–48)

45Who are faithful and wise
servants? Who are the ones the
master will put in charge of
giving the other servants their
food supplies at the proper
time?* 46Servants are fortunate
if their master comes and finds
them doing their job. 47You may
be sure that a servant who is
always faithful will be put in
charge of everything the master
owns. 48But suppose one of the
servants thinks that the master
will not return until late.
49Suppose that evil servant
starts beating all the other
servants and eats and drinks
with people who are drunk.
50If that happens, the master will
surely come on a day and at a
time when the servant least
expects him. 51That servant will
then be punished and thrown out
with the ones who only
pretended to serve their master.
There they will cry and grit their
teeth in pain.

A Story about Ten Girls

25 The kingdom of heaven is like
what happened one night when
ten girls took their oil lamps and

---

[u] *the time has almost come*: Or "he (that is, the Son of Man) will soon be here." [v] *and the Son himself doesn't know*: These words are not in some manuscripts.

24.36 **WHEN WILL JESUS RETURN?** No one knows exactly when Jesus will come back according to the calendar and clock. But as the world becomes more violent, and disturbances increase, we are shown that the time is nearer. The main thing is to be ready and not be caught by surprise. We don't know when Jesus will return. Today's task is for us to be faithful in what God has given us to do.

24.45 **DON'T FORGET ABOUT THE MASTER** It has been a long time since Jesus spoke these words, almost two thousand years. It would be easy for us to be like the unfaithful servant, to live as though Jesus will never come back. But he has promised he will. It could be today. Let's be ready.

NOTES

went to a wedding to meet the
groom.[w]* 2 Five of the girls were
foolish and five were wise. 3 The
foolish ones took their lamps,
but no extra oil. 4 The ones who
were wise took along extra oil
for their lamps.
5 The groom was late arriving,
and the girls became drowsy and
fell asleep. 6 Then in the middle
of the night someone shouted,
"Here's the groom! Come to
meet him!"
7 When the girls got up and
started getting their lamps
ready, 8 the foolish ones said to
the others, "Let us have some
of your oil! Our lamps are going
out."
9 The girls who were wise
answered, "There's not enough
oil for all of us! Go and buy some
for yourselves."
10 While the foolish girls were
on their way to get some oil, the
groom arrived. The girls who
were ready went into the
wedding, and the doors were
closed. 11 Later the other girls
returned and shouted, "Sir, sir!
Open the door for us!"
12 But the groom replied, "I
don't even know you!"
13 So, my disciples, always be
ready! You don't know the day
or the time when all this will
happen.

A Story about Three Servants
(Luke 19.11–27)

14 The kingdom is also like
what happened when a man
went away and put his three
servants in charge of all he
owned. 15 The man knew what
each servant could do. So he
handed five thousand coins to
the first servant, two thousand
to the second, and one thousand
to the third. Then he left the
country.
16 As soon as the man had
gone, the servant with the five
thousand coins used them to
earn five thousand more. 17 The
servant who had two thousand
coins did the same with his
money and earned two thousand
more. 18 But the servant with one
thousand coins dug a hole and
hid his master's money in the
ground.
19 Some time later the master
of those servants returned. He
called them in and asked what
they had done with his money.*
20 The servant who had been
given five thousand coins
brought them in with the five
thousand that he had earned. He
said, "Sir, you gave me five
thousand coins, and I have
earned five thousand more."
21 "Wonderful!" his master
replied. "You are a good and
faithful servant. I left you in
charge of only a little, but now
I will put you in charge of much
more. Come and share in my
happiness!"

---

[w]*to meet the groom*: Some manuscripts add "and the bride." It was the custom for the groom to go to the home of the bride's parents to get his bride. Young girls and other guests would then go with them to the home of the groom's parents, where the wedding feast would take place.

25.1 **BE PREPARED AT JESUS' COMING** Jesus' story is based on the marriage custom of his time. The girls were wedding attendants. All were waiting for the groom to arrive, but they fell asleep. Five wise girls had extra oil, but five foolish did not. Jesus teaches that we must be sure our commitment to him, the bridegroom, is great enough that we continue to be faithful until his coming.

25.19 **USE YOUR GIFTS EFFECTIVELY** People who are wise in business try to invest their money where it earns more money. We think about that when we're about to put our savings in a bank, as we find out which one pays the most interest. Jesus expects us to be wise in the use of his gifts. The question for us is: How much has God been served by the way we spent our lives?

NOTES

22Next, the servant who had
been given two thousand coins
came in and said, "Sir, you gave
me two thousand coins, and I
have earned two thousand
more."
23"Wonderful!" his master
replied. "You are a good and
faithful servant. I left you in
charge of only a little, but now
I will put you in charge of much
more. Come and share in my
happiness!"
24The servant who had been
given one thousand coins then
came in and said, "Sir, I know
that you are hard to get along
with. You harvest what you don't
plant and gather crops where
you have not scattered seed.
25I was frightened and went out
and hid your money in the
ground. Here is every single
coin!"
26The master of the servant
told him, "You are lazy and
good-for-nothing! You know
that I harvest what I don't plant
and gather crops where I have
not scattered seed. 27You could
have at least put my money in
the bank, so that I could have
earned interest on it."
28Then the master said, "Now
your money will be taken away
and given to the servant with ten
thousand coins! 29Everyone who
has something will be given
more, and they will have more
than enough. But everything will
be taken from those who don't
have anything. 30You are a
worthless servant, and you will
be thrown out into the dark
where people will cry and grit
their teeth in pain."

The Final Judgment

31When the Son of Man comes
in his glory with all of his angels,
he will sit on his royal throne.*
32The people of all nations will
be brought before him, and he
will separate them, as shepherds
separate their sheep from their
goats.
33He will place the sheep on
his right and the goats on his left.
34Then the king will say to those
on his right, "My father has
blessed you! Come and receive
the kingdom that was prepared
for you before the world was
created. 35When I was hungry,
you gave me something to eat,
and when I was thirsty, you gave
me something to drink. When I
was a stranger, you welcomed
me, 36and when I was naked, you
gave me clothes to wear. When
I was sick, you took care of me,
and when I was in jail, you
visited me."
37Then the ones who pleased
the Lord will ask, "When did we
give you something to eat or
drink? 38When did we welcome
you as a stranger or give you
clothes to wear 39or visit you
while you were sick or in jail?"
40The king will answer,
"Whenever you did it for any of
my people, no matter how
unimportant they seemed, you
did it for me."*
41Then the king will say to
those on his left, "Get away from
me! You are under God's curse.

25.31 **JESUS WILL JUDGE THE WORLD** Lots of people may laugh and make a joke about Christ's coming. That's very tragic. Judgment is as certain as the sunrise. The nations of the world often ignore Jesus today. Have they thought about how they will answer the Lord when he sits on his judgment throne?

25.40 **HOW WILL JESUS JUDGE?** What will Jesus care about when he sits as judge of the nations? He will want to know how someone treated his people. No matter how unimportant a person may seem in the eyes of the world, if that person is a child of God by faith in Jesus, then what someone does to that person is at the same time done to Jesus. It will be awful for those who are cruel to the ones who belong to him.

NOTES

Go into the everlasting fire
prepared for the devil and his
angels! 42I was hungry, but you
did not give me anything to eat,
and I was thirsty, but you did
not give me anything to drink.
43I was a stranger, but you did
not welcome me, and I was
naked, but you did not give me
any clothes to wear. I was sick
and in jail, but you did not take
care of me."
44Then the people will ask,
"Lord, when did we fail to help
you when you were hungry or
thirsty or a stranger or naked or
sick or in jail?"
45The king will say to them,
"Whenever you failed to help
any of my people, no matter how
unimportant they seemed, you
failed to do it for me."
46Then Jesus said, "Those people
will be punished forever. But the ones
who pleased God will have eternal
life."

The Plot to Kill Jesus

(Mark 14.1, 2; Luke 22.1, 2; John 11.45–53)

26 When Jesus had finished
teaching, he told his disciples,
2"You know that two days from now
will be Passover. That is when the
Son of Man will be handed over to
his enemies and nailed to a cross."*
3At that time the chief priests and
the nation's leaders were meeting at
the home of Caiaphas the high priest.
4They planned how they could sneak
around and have Jesus arrested and
put to death. 5But they said, "We
must not do it during Passover, because the people will riot."

At Bethany

(Mark 14.3–9; John 12.1–8)

6Jesus was in the town of Bethany,
eating at the home of Simon, who
had leprosy.[x] 7A woman came in with
a bottle of expensive perfume and
poured it on Jesus' head. 8But when
his disciples saw this, they became
angry. They said, "Why such a
waste? 9We could have sold this perfume for a lot of money and given
it to the poor."
10Jesus knew what they were
thinking, and he said:
Why are you bothering this
woman? She has done a
beautiful thing for me.* 11You
will always have the poor with
you, but you will not always have
me. 12She has poured perfume
on my body to prepare it for
burial.[y] 13You may be sure that
wherever the good news is told
all over the world, people will
remember what she has done.
And they will tell others.

Judas and the Chief Priests

(Mark 14.10, 11; Luke 22.3–6)

14Judas Iscariot[z] was one of the
twelve disciples. He went to the chief

---

[x]*leprosy*: See the note at 8.2. [y]*poured perfume on my body to prepare it for burial*: The Jewish people taught that giving someone a proper burial was even more important than helping the poor. [z]*Iscariot*: See the note at 10.4.

26.2 **JESUS FACED THE CROSS** Once again Jesus reminded his followers that he would have to die the death of being nailed to a cross. But they didn't understand. It didn't seem possible that their Messiah would be put to death. Even Muslims today admit that someone was nailed to the cross, but "Jesus the prophet," they say, "could not have been put to death like that. God wouldn't have permitted it." Do we understand that without the death of God's Son we would have no hope of being saved from our sins? He took our punishment himself.

26.10 **GIVE YOUR BEST TO JESUS** The woman at Bethany was a puzzle to Jesus' disciples. They didn't understand what this woman did. Jesus was going to die, so she wanted to express her love and gratitude to him in a special act of sacrifice. The perfume was costly, but nothing was too good for Jesus. Can we not gladly pour out our lives for him?

NOTES

priests 15and asked, "How much will
you give me if I help you arrest Jesus?" They paid Judas thirty silver
coins, 16and from then on he started
looking for a good chance to betray
Jesus.*

Jesus Eats the Passover Meal with His Disciples

(Mark 14.12–21; Luke 22.7–13; John 13.21–30)

17On the first day of the Feast of
Thin Bread, Jesus' disciples came to
him and asked, "Where do you want
us to prepare the Passover meal?"
18Jesus told them to go to a certain
man in the city and tell him, "Our
teacher says, 'My time has come! I
want to eat the Passover meal with
my disciples in your home.' " 19They
did as Jesus told them and prepared
the meal.
20-21When Jesus was eating with
his twelve disciples that evening, he
said, "One of you will surely hand
me over to my enemies."
22The disciples were very sad, and
each one said to Jesus, "Surely, Lord,
you don't mean me!"
23He answered, "One of you men
who has eaten with me from this dish
will betray me. 24The Son of Man will
die, as the Scriptures say. But it's going to be terrible for the one who betrays me! That man would be better
off if he had never been born."
25Judas said, "Teacher, surely you
don't mean me!"
"That's what you say!" Jesus replied. But later, Judas did betray him.

The Lord's Supper

(Mark 14.22–26; Luke 22.14–23; 1 Corinthians 11.23–25)

26During the meal Jesus took some
bread in his hands. He blessed the
bread and broke it. Then he gave it
to his disciples and said, "Take this
and eat it. This is my body."*
27Jesus picked up a cup of wine
and gave thanks to God. He then gave
it to his disciples and said, "Take this
and drink it. 28This is my blood, and
with it God makes his agreement
with you. It will be poured out, so
that many people will have their sins
forgiven. 29From now on I am not
going to drink any wine, until I drink
new wine with you in my Father's
kingdom." 30Then they sang a hymn
and went out to the Mount of Olives.

Peter's Promise

(Mark 14.27–31; Luke 22.31–34; John 13.36–38)

31Jesus said to his disciples, "During this very night, all of you will
reject me, as the Scriptures say,
'I will strike down
the shepherd,
and the sheep
will be scattered.'
32But after I am raised to life, I will
go to Galilee ahead of you."
33Peter spoke up, "Even if all the
others reject you, I never will!"*

NOTES

26.16 **A DISCIPLE GONE BAD** It's hard to imagine how one of the twelve disciples could have done such a terrible thing. Judas, who had lived with Jesus day after day, betrayed him to die. But let's not be too quick to judge. The evil that was in Judas is in the heart of every person. Even sincere Christians who truly love Jesus betray him daily by a variety of ungodly thoughts, words, and actions.

26.26 **THE LAST MEAL TOGETHER** Taking a meal together is often a celebration of close friendship. The bond between Jesus and his disciples was even closer than they knew, for they still didn't understand what was going to happen to Jesus. In fact one of them, Judas, would even sell him out. At this time Jesus did something they would understand later. He invited them to eat and drink what stood for his very body and blood.

26.33 **BOASTING IS DANGEROUS** Jesus made it clear that he would be arrested and the disciples would all leave him. Peter quickly announced his undying loyalty to his Master. He *(continued)*

34Jesus replied, "I promise you that
before a rooster crows tonight, you
will say three times that you don't
know me." 35But Peter said, "Even
if I have to die with you, I will never
say I don't know you."
All the others said the same thing.

Jesus Prays
(Mark 14.32–42; Luke 22.39–46)

36Jesus went with his disciples to
a place called Gethsemane. When
they got there, he told them, "Sit here
while I go over there and pray."
37Jesus took along Peter and the
two brothers, James and John.[a] He
was very sad and troubled, 38and he
said to them, "I am so sad that I feel
as if I am dying. Stay here and keep
awake with me."
39Jesus walked on a little way.
Then he kneeled with his face to the
ground and prayed, "My Father, if
it is possible, don't make me suffer
by having me drink from this cup.[b]
But do what you want, and not what
I want."*
40He came back and found his disciples sleeping. So he said to Peter,
"Can't any of you stay awake with
me for just one hour? 41Stay awake
and pray that you will not be tested.
You want to do what is right, but you
are weak."
42Again Jesus went to pray and
said, "My Father, if there is no other
way, and I must suffer, I will still do
what you want."
43Jesus came back and found them
sleeping again. They simply could
not keep their eyes open. 44He left
them and prayed the same prayer
once more.
45Finally, Jesus returned to his disciples and said, "Are you still sleeping and resting?[c] The time has come
for the Son of Man to be handed over
to sinners. 46Get up! Let's go. The
one who will betray me is already
here."

Jesus Is Arrested
(Mark 14.43–50; Luke 22.47–53; John 18.3–12)

47Jesus was still speaking, when
Judas the betrayer came up. He was
one of the twelve disciples, and a
large mob armed with swords and
clubs was with him. They had been
sent by the chief priests and the nation's leaders. 48Judas had told them
ahead of time, "Arrest the man I greet
with a kiss."[d]
49Judas walked right up to Jesus
and said, "Hello, teacher." Then Judas kissed him.
50Jesus replied, "My friend, why
are you here?"[e]
The men grabbed Jesus and arrested him. 51One of Jesus' followers
pulled out a sword. He struck the servant of the high priest and cut off
his ear.
52But Jesus told him, "Put your
sword away. Anyone who lives by

---

[a]*the two brothers, James and John*: The Greek text has "the two sons of Zebedee." See 27.56. [b]*having me drink from this cup*: In the Scriptures "to drink from a cup" sometimes means to suffer. See the note at 20.22. [c]*Are you still sleeping and resting?*: Or "You may as well keep on sleeping and resting." [d]*the man I greet with a kiss*: It was the custom for people to greet each other with a kiss on the cheek. [e]*why are you here?*: Or "do what you came for."

(*continued*) meant well, but he didn't know what he was promising. Later, he would learn how weak he was. Jesus knew how everybody would act, and Peter had to learn a lesson. We ought not to boast, but we should ask God to help us in the hard places.

26.39 **JESUS DIDN'T WANT TO DIE** What? But dying is what Jesus came to earth for. Yes, but it was the most grim assignment ever given to anyone. It was not only bodily pain that he faced, but he would actually bear the punishment for the sins of the whole world. Jesus was a man, too, and as a man he hated the thought of such an awful death.

NOTES

fighting will die by fighting.* 53Don't you know that I could ask my Father, and right away he would send me more than twelve armies of angels? 54But then, how could the words of the Scriptures come true, which say that this must happen?"

55Jesus said to the mob, "Why do you come with swords and clubs to arrest me like a criminal? Day after day I sat and taught in the temple, and you didn't arrest me. 56But all this happened, so that what the prophets wrote would come true."

All of Jesus' disciples left him and ran away.

Jesus Is Questioned by the Jewish Council
(Mark 14.53–65; Luke 22.54, 55, 63–71; John 18.13, 14, 19–24)

57After Jesus had been arrested, he was led off to the house of Caiaphas the high priest. The nation's leaders and the teachers of the Law of Moses were meeting there. 58But Peter followed along at a distance and came to the courtyard of the high priest's palace. He went in and sat down with the guards to see what was going to happen.

59The chief priests and the whole council wanted to put Jesus to death. So they tried to find some people who would tell lies about him in court.[f] 60But they could not find any, even though many did come and tell lies. At last two men came forward* 61and said, "This man claimed that he would tear down God's temple and build it again in three days."

62The high priest stood up and asked Jesus, "Why don't you say something in your own defense? Don't you hear the charges they are making against you?" 63But Jesus did not answer. So the high priest said, "With the living God looking on, you must tell the truth. Tell us, are you the Messiah, the Son of God?"[g]

64"That is what you say!" Jesus answered. "But I tell all of you,

'Soon you will see
the Son of Man
sitting at the right side[h]
of God All-Powerful
and coming on the clouds
of heaven.' "

65The high priest then tore his robe and said, "This man claims to be God! We don't need any more witnesses! You have heard what he said. 66What do you think?"

They answered, "He is guilty and deserves to die!" 67Then they spit in his face and hit him with their fists. Others slapped him 68and said, "You think you are the Messiah! So tell us who hit you!"

Peter Says He Does Not Know Jesus
(Mark 14.66–72; Luke 22.56–62; John 18.15–18, 25–27)

69While Peter was sitting out in the courtyard, a servant girl came up to

---

[f] *some people who would tell lies about him in court*: The Law of Moses taught that two witnesses were necessary before a person could be put to death. See verse 60. [g] *Son of God*: One of the titles used for the kings of Israel. [h] *right side*: See the note at 22.44.

26.52 **THIS HAD TO HAPPEN** Jesus didn't want his followers to resist his arrest. He could have stopped it by calling the armies of heaven to defend him. But he didn't. Jesus had to let his blood be shed on a cross, so that we sinners could have a way back to God.

26.60 **WHAT SHALL WE DO WITH JESUS?** Here is one who went about doing good, arrested at a signal from his own former friend. They finally got two witnesses to speak against Jesus. The witnesses were needed to satisfy the law in this false trial. Of course the court had already decided what they would do. So Jesus confessed to his divine sonship. Then the leaders had their excuse to accuse him of insulting God. Think about this: What would the world do with Jesus if he were here like this today? Who would stand with him?

NOTES

him and said, "You were with Jesus
from Galilee."
70But in front of everyone Peter
said, "That's not so! I don't know
what you are talking about!"*
71When Peter had gone out to the
gate, another servant girl saw him
and said to some people there, "This
man was with Jesus from Nazareth."
72Again Peter denied it, and this
time he swore, "I don't even know
that man!"
73A little while later some people
standing there walked over to Peter
and said, "We know that you are one
of them. We can tell it because you
talk like someone from Galilee."
74Peter began to curse and swear,
"I don't know that man!"
Right then a rooster crowed,
75and Peter remembered that Jesus
had said, "Before a rooster crows,
you will say three times that you
don't know me." Then Peter went out
and cried hard.

Jesus Is Taken to Pilate
(Mark 15.1; Luke 23.1, 2; John 18.28–32)

27 Early the next morning all the
chief priests and the nation's
leaders met and decided that Jesus
should be put to death. 2They tied
him up and led him away to Pilate
the governor.

The Death of Judas
(Acts 1.18, 19)

3When Judas learned that Jesus
had been sentenced to death, he was
sorry for what he had done. He returned the thirty silver coins to the
chief priests and leaders 4and said,
"I have sinned by betraying a man
who has never done anything
wrong."
"So what? That's your problem,"
they replied. 5Judas threw the money
into the temple and then went out
and hanged himself.*
6The chief priests picked up the
money and said, "This money was
paid to have a man killed. We can't
put it in the temple treasury."
7Then they had a meeting and decided to buy a field that belonged to
someone who made clay pots. They
wanted to use it as a graveyard for
foreigners. 8That is why people still
call that place "Field of Blood."
9So the words of the prophet Jeremiah came true,
"They took
the thirty silver coins,
the price of a person
among the people of Israel.
10They paid it
for a potter's field,[i]
as the Lord
had commanded me."

Pilate Questions Jesus
(Mark 15.2–5; Luke 23.3–5; John 18.33–38)

11Jesus was brought before Pilate
the governor, who asked him, "Are
you the King of the Jews?"
"Those are your words!" Jesus answered. 12And when the chief priests

[i] *a potter's field*: Perhaps a field owned by someone who made clay pots. But it may have been a field where potters came to get clay or to make pots or to throw away their broken pieces of pottery.

26.70 **IT'S EASY TO "NOT KNOW" JESUS** Peter had boasted about his loyalty to Jesus. But later, with enemies all around, Peter found it easier to keep quiet and even say he didn't know Jesus. Are you a disciple of Jesus? Who knows that you are? Or do you hide your faith so as not to offend people?

27.5 **A TRAGIC MAN'S END** Judas will always be a puzzle. Why did he sell Jesus out? Some people think he sincerely believed Jesus was bad for his country. Others say he wanted to make Jesus be more forceful in self-defense. But remember Judas was a thief, too. Great evil was at work deep in the life of this man. Judas would not even ask to be forgiven, choosing to kill himself instead.

NOTES

and leaders brought their charges
against him, he did not say a thing.
13Pilate asked him, "Don't you hear
what crimes they say you have
done?" 14But Jesus did not say anything, and the governor was greatly
amazed.

The Death Sentence

(Mark 15.6–15; Luke 23.13–26; John 18.39—19.16)

15During Passover the governor always freed a prisoner chosen by the
people.* 16At that time a well-known
terrorist named Jesus Barabbas[j] was
in jail. 17So when the crowd came
together, Pilate asked them, "Which
prisoner do you want me to set free?
Do you want Jesus Barabbas or Jesus
who is called the Messiah?" 18Pilate
knew that the leaders had brought
Jesus to him because they were
jealous.
19While Pilate was judging the
case, his wife sent him a message.
It said, "Don't have anything to do
with that innocent man. I have had
nightmares because of him."
20But the chief priests and the leaders convinced the crowds to ask for
Barabbas to be set free and for Jesus
to be killed. 21Pilate asked the crowd
again, "Which of these two men do
you want me to set free?"
"Barabbas!" they replied.
22Pilate asked them, "What am I
to do with Jesus, who is called the
Messiah?"
They all yelled, "Nail him to a
cross!"
23Pilate answered, "But what crime
has he done?"
"Nail him to a cross!" they yelled
even louder.
24Pilate saw that there was nothing
he could do and that the people were
starting to riot. So he took some water and washed his hands[k] in front
of them and said, "I won't have anything to do with killing this man. You
are the ones doing it!"
25Everyone answered, "We and
our descendants will take the blame
for his death!"
26Pilate set Barabbas free. Then he
ordered his soldiers to beat Jesus
with a whip and nail him to a cross.

Soldiers Make Fun of Jesus

(Mark 15.16–21; John 19.2, 3)

27The governor's soldiers led Jesus
into the fortress[l] and brought together the rest of the troops.* 28They
stripped off Jesus' clothes and put a
scarlet robe[m] on him. 29They made
a crown out of thorn branches and
placed it on his head, and they put
a stick in his right hand. The soldiers
kneeled down and pretended to worship him. They made fun of him and
shouted, "Hey, you king of the Jews!"
30Then they spit on him. They took
the stick from him and beat him on
the head with it.

---

[j] *Jesus Barabbas*: Here and in verse 17 many manuscripts have "Barabbas." [k] *washed his hands*: To show that he was innocent. [l] *fortress*: The place where the Roman governor stayed. It was probably at Herod's palace west of Jerusalem, though it may have been Fortress Antonio north of the temple, where the Roman troops were stationed. [m] *scarlet robe*: This was probably a Roman soldier's robe.

27.15 **A CROWD LOVES A CRIMINAL** The crowd had a choice. They could set either Jesus or Barabbas free. What could we expect of this mob? Of course they chose Barabbas. Crowds often love a crook. They're angry if the law robs them of their daring hero. Jesus was only a misunderstood stranger. "So hang him on a cross," they yelled, "and let the criminal Barabbas go."

27.27 **JESUS BECAME A JOKE** Who was this fool, they wondered—this man that Pilate called a king? They said he was a fanatic, good for an hour's fun. So the soldiers tormented him. Have you never heard the mob say it? "Oh, he's just one of those religious nuts." Many a lonely disciple has been pelted with garbage and foul language over the years. But Jesus stood in that place first.

NOTES

Jesus Is Nailed to a Cross
(Mark 15.22–32; Luke 23.27–43; John 19.17–27)

31When the soldiers had finished
making fun of Jesus, they took off
the robe. They put his own clothes
back on him and led him off to be
nailed to a cross. 32On the way they
met a man from Cyrene named Simon, and they forced him to carry
Jesus' cross.
33They came to a place named Golgotha, which means "Place of the
Skull."[n] 34There they gave Jesus
some wine mixed with a drug to ease
the pain. But when Jesus tasted what
it was, he refused to drink it.
35The soldiers nailed Jesus to a
cross and gambled to see who would
get his clothes. 36Then they sat down
to guard him. 37Above his head they
put a sign that told why he was nailed
there. It read, "This is Jesus, the King
of the Jews." 38The soldiers also
nailed two criminals on crosses, one
to the right of Jesus and the other
to his left.
39People who passed by said terrible things about Jesus. They shook
their heads and* 40shouted, "So
you're the one who claimed you
could tear down the temple and build
it again in three days! If you are God's
Son, save yourself and come down
from the cross!"
41The chief priests, the leaders, and
the teachers of the Law of Moses also
made fun of Jesus. They said,
42"He saved others, but he can't save
himself. If he is the king of Israel,
he should come down from the cross!
Then we will believe him. 43He
trusted God, so let God save him, if
he wants to. He even said he was
God's Son." 44The two criminals also
said cruel things to Jesus.

The Death of Jesus
(Mark 15.33–41; Luke 23.44–49; John 19.28–30)

45At noon the sky turned dark and
stayed that way until three o'clock.
46Then about that time Jesus
shouted, "Eli, Eli, lema sabachthani?"[o] which means, "My God, my
God, why have you deserted me?"
47Some of the people standing
there heard Jesus and said, "He's
calling for Elijah."[p] 48One of them
at once ran and grabbed a sponge.
He soaked it in wine, then put it on
a stick and held it up to Jesus.
49Others said, "Wait! Let's see if
Elijah will come[q] and save him."
50Once again Jesus shouted, and then
he died.
51At once the curtain in the temple[r]
was torn in two from top to bottom.
The earth shook, and rocks split
apart.* 52Graves opened, and many
of God's people were raised to life.
53Then after Jesus had risen to life,
they came out of their graves and

---

[n]*Place of the Skull*: The place was probably given this name because it was near a large rock in the shape of a human skull. [o]*Eli . . . sabachthani*: These words are in Aramaic, a language spoken in Palestine during the time of Jesus. [p]*Elijah*: In Aramaic the name "Elijah" sounds like "Eli," which means "my God." [q]*Elijah will come*: Many of the Jewish people expected the prophet Elijah to come and prepare the way for the Messiah. [r]*curtain in the temple*: There were two curtains in the temple. One was at the entrance, and the other separated the holy place from the most holy place that the Jewish people thought of as God's home on earth. The second curtain is probably the one that is meant.

27.39 **THE KING WAS NAILED TO A CROSS** What a strange place for a king—on a cross. Even the people's leaders couldn't miss their chance to laugh at the idea. "Jesus saved others, so let's see him get himself down from that cross," they were saying. Then they laughed. The world is still laughing. What about ourselves? Are we different from that crowd? Has the King's death changed our lives?

27.51 **THE WORLD SHOOK AS GOD'S SON DIED** The death of Jesus was, along with his rising again to life, the central event of all history. As Jesus hung on the cross and the time of his death neared, the sky darkened and the earth shook. The world had been created through the Son of God (see John 1.3), and it was as if his creation was mourning his death.

NOTES

went into the holy city, where many
people saw them.
54The officer and the soldiers
guarding Jesus felt the earthquake
and saw everything else that happened. They were frightened and
said, "This man really was God's
Son!"
55Many women were looking on
from a distance. They had come with
Jesus from Galilee to be of help to
him. 56Mary Magdalene, Mary the
mother of James and Joseph, and the
mother of James and John[s] were
some of these women.

Jesus Is Buried

(Mark 15.42–47; Luke 23.50–56; John 19.38–42)

57That evening a rich disciple
named Joseph from the town of Arimathea 58went and asked for Jesus'
body. Pilate gave orders for it to be
given to Joseph, 59who took the body
and wrapped it in a clean linen cloth.
60Then Joseph put the body in his
own tomb that had been cut into solid
rock[t] and had never been used. He
rolled a big stone against the entrance to the tomb and went away.
61All this time Mary Magdalene
and the other Mary were sitting
across from the tomb.
62On the next day, which was a
Sabbath, the chief priests and the
Pharisees went together to Pilate.*
63They said, "Sir, we remember what
that liar said while he was still alive.
He claimed that in three days he
would come back from death.
64So please order the tomb to be carefully guarded for three days. If you
don't, his disciples may come and
steal his body. They will tell the people that he has been raised to life,
and this last lie will be worse than
the first one."[u]
65Pilate said to them, "All right,
take some of your soldiers and guard
the tomb as well as you know how."
66So they sealed it tight and placed
soldiers there to guard it.

Jesus Is Alive

(Mark 16.1–8; Luke 24.1–12; John 20.1–10)

28 The Sabbath was over, and it
was almost daybreak on Sunday when Mary Magdalene and the
other Mary went to see the tomb.
2Suddenly a strong earthquake
struck, and the Lord's angel came
down from heaven. He rolled away
the stone and sat on it. 3The angel
looked as bright as lightning, and his
clothes were white as snow. 4The
guards shook from fear and fell
down, as though they were dead.
5The angel said to the women,
"Don't be afraid! I know you are
looking for Jesus, who was nailed to
a cross. 6He is not here! God has
raised him to life, just as Jesus said
he would. Come, see the place where
his body was lying.* 7Now hurry! Tell

---

[s] *of James and John*: The Greek text has "of Zebedee's sons." See 26.37. [t] *tomb . . . solid rock*: Some of the Jewish people buried their dead in rooms carved into solid rock. A heavy stone was rolled against the entrance. [u] *the first one*: Probably the belief that Jesus is the Messiah.

27.62 **AFRAID OF A DEAD MAN** The chief priests and Pharisees weren't believers in Jesus, were they? They didn't expect him to rise again, did they? They weren't concerned about what the grieving disciples might do, were they? But see how fearful the Jewish leaders were, asking Pilate for guards and having the tomb officially sealed. Fear often comes from a guilty conscience.

28.6 **THE TOMB WAS EMPTY** Nobody has ever been able to "explain away" how the tomb of Jesus became empty. He lay dead there, wrapped in special grave cloths—then he was gone. The soldiers told everyone the disciples stole the body of Jesus while they were sleeping. But the soldiers couldn't have known what happened when they were asleep. The Jewish authorities could not find the body of Jesus, but his disciples saw him alive.

NOTES

his disciples that he has been raised
to life and is on his way to Galilee.
Go there, and you will see him. That
is what I came to tell you."
8The women were frightened and
yet very happy, as they hurried from
the tomb and ran to tell his disciples.
9Suddenly Jesus met them and
greeted them. They went near to him,
held on to his feet, and worshiped
him. 10Jesus said to them, "Don't be
afraid! Tell my followers to go to
Galilee. They will see me there."

Report of the Guard

11While the women were on their
way, some soldiers who had been
guarding the tomb went into the city.
They told the chief priests everything
that had happened. 12So the chief
priests met with the leaders and decided to bribe the soldiers with a lot
of money. 13They said to the soldiers,
"Tell everyone that Jesus' disciples
came during the night and stole his
body while you were asleep.* 14If the
governor[v] hears about this, we will
talk to him. You won't have anything
to worry about." 15The soldiers took
the money and did what they were
told. The Jewish people still tell each
other this story.

What Jesus' Followers Must Do
(Mark 16.14–18; Luke 24.36–49; John 20.19–23; Acts 1.6–8)

16Jesus' eleven disciples went to a
mountain in Galilee, where Jesus had
told them to meet him. 17They saw
him and worshiped him, but some
of them doubted.
18Jesus came to them and said:
I have been given all authority
in heaven and on earth! 19Go to
the people of all nations and
make them my disciples. Baptize
them in the name of the Father,
the Son, and the Holy Spirit,*
20and teach them to do
everything I have told you. I will
be with you always, even until
the end of the world.

[v]*governor*: Pontius Pilate.

28.13 **A "TALL TALE"** Imagine the Jewish leaders, expecting people to believe that the disciples actually smuggled the body of Jesus out of a guarded, sealed tomb with a heavy stone door. But that was their story—and a lot of people believed it because they wanted to. They needed a story and that was it.

28.19 **BE SOUL WINNERS** Wherever we can, we must tell the great news that Jesus is alive. The Holy Spirit himself will convince people that this good news is true, and many will become Christians. Our lives also must show that Jesus is alive and living in us. That's a fact no one can deny when they really see it.

NOTES

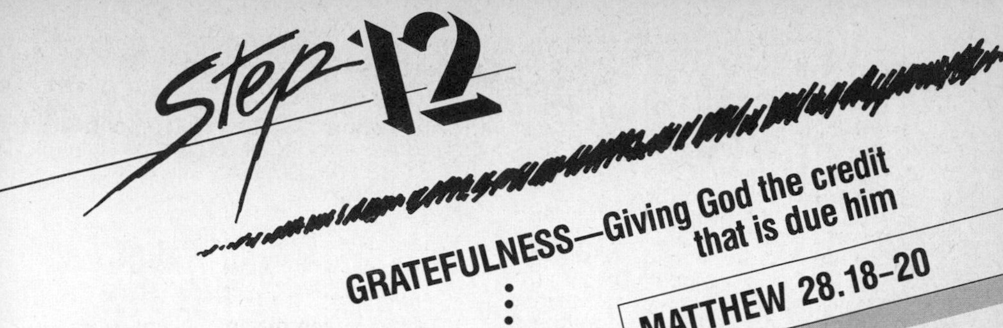

COMING FULL CIRCLE

Following the Twelve Steps as they are illustrated in this Bible helps us to be at peace with God, with ourselves, and with others. They offer key principles for living a healthy, dynamic life. We will come full circle in our journey of discipleship by showing gratefulness to God as we tell others what he has done for us.

When we give proper credit to God, others may be spurred to explore trusting Christ with their future. There is a world waiting to hear this message. We need to use the opportunities God gives us each day to tell someone how our lives are being changed. Practicing this and the other steps every day protects our reputation and the Lord's.

Matthew 28.18–20 says, "Jesus came to them and said: 'I have been given all authority in heaven and on earth! Go to the people of all nations and make them my disciples. Baptize them in the name of the Father, the Son, and the Holy Spirit, and teach them to do everything I have told you. I will be with you always, even until the end of the world.'" That just about says it all.

For another "Look Ahead," turn to page 357.

ABOUT THIS BOOK

This is the shortest of the four New Testament books that tell about the life and teachings of Jesus, but it is also the most action-packed. From the very beginning of his ministry, Jesus worked mighty wonders. After choosing four followers (1.16–20), he immediately performed many miracles of healing. Among those healed were a man with an evil spirit in him (1.21–28), Simon's mother-in-law (1.30,31), crowds of sick people (1.32–34), and a man with leprosy (1.40–45). Over and over Mark tells how Jesus healed people, but always in such a way as to show that he did these miracles by the power of God.

The religious leaders refused to accept Jesus. This led to conflicts (2.2—3.6) that finally made them start looking for a way to kill him (11.18). But the demons saw the power of Jesus, and they knew that he was the Son of God, although Jesus would not let them tell anyone.

This book is full of miracles that amazed the crowds and Jesus' followers. But, according to Mark, the most powerful miracle of Jesus is his suffering and death. The first person to understand this miracle was the Roman soldier who saw Jesus die on the cross and said, "This man really was the Son of God!" (15.39).

This Gospel is widely thought to be the first one written. The many explanations of Aramaic words and Jewish customs in Mark suggest that Mark wrote to Gentile or non-Jewish Christians. He wants to tell about Jesus and to encourage readers to believe in the power of Jesus to rescue them from sickness, demons, and death. He also wants to remind them that the new life of faith is not an easy life, and that they must follow Jesus by serving others and being ready to suffer as he did.

The first followers of Jesus to discover the empty tomb were three women, and the angel told them:

> *Don't be alarmed! You are looking for Jesus from Nazareth, who was nailed to a cross. God has raised him to life, and he is not here.* (16.6)

A QUICK LOOK AT THIS BOOK

1. The Message of John the Baptist (1.1–8)
2. The Baptism and Temptation of Jesus (1.9–13)
3. Jesus in Galilee (1.14—9.50)
4. Jesus Goes from Galilee to Jerusalem (10.1–52)
5. Jesus' Last Week: His Trial and Death (11.1—15.47)
6. Jesus Is Alive (16.1–8)
7. Jesus Appears to His Followers (16.9–20)

The Preaching of John the Baptist
(Matthew 3.1–12; Luke 3.1–18; John 1.19–28)

1 This is the good news about Jesus
Christ, the Son of God.[a]* 2It began just as God had said in the book
written by Isaiah the prophet,

"I am sending my messenger
to get the way ready
for you.
3In the desert
someone is shouting,
'Get the road ready
for the Lord!
Make a straight path
for him.' "

4So John the Baptist showed up in
the desert and told everyone, "Turn
back to God and be baptized! Then
your sins will be forgiven."
5From all Judea and Jerusalem
crowds of people went to John. They
told how sorry they were for their
sins, and he baptized them in the Jordan River.
6John wore clothes made of camel's hair. He had a leather strap
around his waist and ate grasshoppers and wild honey.
7John also told the people, "Someone more powerful is going to come.
And I am not good enough even to
stoop down and untie his sandals.[b]
8I baptize you with water, but he
will baptize you with the Holy
Spirit!"

The Baptism of Jesus
(Matthew 3.13–17; Luke 3.21, 22)

9About that time Jesus came from
Nazareth in Galilee, and John baptized him in the Jordan River.
10As soon as Jesus came out of the
water, he saw the sky open and the
Holy Spirit coming down to him like
a dove. 11A voice from heaven said,
"You are my own dear Son, and I
am pleased with you."

Jesus and Satan
(Matthew 4.1–11; Luke 4.1–13)

12Right away God's Spirit made
Jesus go into the desert. 13He stayed
there for forty days while Satan
tested him. Jesus was with the wild
animals, but angels took care of him.*

Jesus Begins His Work
(Matthew 4.12–17; Luke 4.14, 15)

14After John was arrested, Jesus
went to Galilee and told the good
news that comes from God.[c] 15He
said, "The time has come! God's
kingdom will soon be here.[d] Turn
back to God and believe the good
news!"*

---

[a] *the Son of God*: These words are not in some manuscripts. [b] *untie his sandals*: This was the duty of a slave. [c] *that comes from God*: Or "that is about God." [d] *will soon be here*: Or "is already here."

1.1 **A GOSPEL IS GOOD NEWS** As we read the stories about Jesus' life we may wonder why Matthew, Mark, Luke, and John wrote these things. These writers wanted everyone to know that God has made a way of release from the actions and attitudes that prevent us from knowing him. Jesus is that way of release. He sets us free from the power and blindness of sin.

1.13 **THE DEVIL IS A REAL PERSON** It suits the devil, or Satan, very well to know that most people don't believe in him. Then he can more easily undo the work of God in our lives. Jesus knew all about Satan. He knew he would have to defeat Satan and show everyone that God's work cannot be stopped by the king of evil and his kingdom. That's part of the good news about Jesus.

1.15 **GOD'S KINGDOM IS COMING** More surely than the rising of the sun, the kingdom of God is coming. The King himself has come and has established his claims in the world. Neither devils nor men can now hold back the oncoming kingdom of God. There may be dark nights of waiting, but the sunrise of Jesus' return is always just at hand.

NOTES

Jesus Chooses Four Fishermen
(Matthew 4.18–22; Luke 5.1–11)

16As Jesus was walking along the shore of Lake Galilee, he saw Simon and his brother Andrew. They were fishermen and were casting their nets into the lake. 17Jesus said to them, "Come with me! I will teach you how to bring in people instead of fish."* 18Right then the two brothers dropped their nets and went with him.

19Jesus walked on and soon saw James and John, the sons of Zebedee. They were in a boat, mending their nets. 20At once Jesus asked them to come with him. They left their father in the boat with the hired workers and went with him.

A Man with an Evil Spirit
(Luke 4.31–37)

21Jesus and his disciples went to the town of Capernaum. Then on the next Sabbath he went into the Jewish meeting place and started teaching. 22Everyone was amazed at his teaching. He taught with authority, and not like the teachers of the Law of Moses. 23Suddenly a man with an evil spirit[e] in him entered the meeting place and yelled,* 24"Jesus from Nazareth, what do you want with us? Have you come to destroy us? I know who you are! You are God's Holy One."

25Jesus told the evil spirit, "Be quiet and come out of the man!" 26The spirit shook him. Then it gave a loud shout and left.

27Everyone was completely surprised and kept saying to each other, "What is this? It must be some new kind of powerful teaching! Even the evil spirits obey him." 28News about Jesus quickly spread all over that part of Galilee.

Jesus Heals Many People
(Matthew 8.14–17; Luke 4.38–41)

29As soon as Jesus left the meeting place with James and John, they went home with Simon and Andrew. 30When they got there, Jesus was told that Simon's mother-in-law was sick in bed with fever. 31Jesus went to her. He took hold of her hand and helped her up. The fever left her, and she served them a meal.

32That evening after sunset,[f] all who were sick or had demons in them were brought to Jesus.* 33In fact, the whole town gathered around the door of the house. 34Jesus healed all kinds of terrible diseases and forced out a lot of demons. But the demons knew who he was, and he did not let them speak.

---

[e] *evil spirit*: A Jewish person who had an evil spirit was considered "unclean" and was not allowed to eat or worship with other Jewish people.
[f] *after sunset*: The Sabbath was over, and a new day began at sunset.

1.17 **ARE YOU A FISHERMAN?** Have you ever gone fishing? Then you'll know the work and patience needed to catch fish. But Jesus' disciples, like you, need to work and have patience to catch people for Jesus. Of course we don't actually catch people with real nets. Our net is the good news about Jesus the Savior. If we keep putting out that net we will bring people to know Jesus.

1.23 **EVIL SPIRITS OBEY JESUS** Not all problems in the world have natural causes. Sometimes problems are caused by invisible, spiritual enemies of God. But we must never imagine that God lacks the ability to put an end to these enemies. A word from Jesus, and the evil spirits are gone. Jesus is Lord of all creation, and all things must obey his commands.

1.32 **JESUS IS THE GREAT HEALER** Jesus is Lord of our bodies as well as our minds and spirits. One day we will join the crowd of those who have felt his healing touch. In that day our bodies will be renewed like his. Never again will we know sickness, or pain, or death. That was what God had in mind all along when he created us for himself.

NOTES

35Very early the next morning
Jesus got up and went to a place
where he could be alone and pray.
36Simon and the others started looking for him. 37And when they found
him, they said, "Everyone is looking
for you!"
38Jesus replied, "We must go to the
nearby towns, so that I can tell the
good news to those people. This is
why I have come." 39Then Jesus went
to Jewish meeting places everywhere
in Galilee, where he preached and
forced out demons.

Jesus Heals a Man
(Matthew 8.1–4; Luke 5.12–16)

40A man with leprosy[g] came to
Jesus and kneeled down.[h] He
begged, "You have the power to
make me well, if only you wanted
to."
41Jesus felt sorry for[i] the man. So
he put his hand on him and said, "I
want to! Now you are well." 42At once
the man's leprosy disappeared, and
he was well.
43After Jesus strictly warned the
man, he sent him on his way. 44He
said, "Don't tell anyone about this.
Just go and show the priest that you
are well. Then take a gift to the temple as Moses commanded, and everyone will know that you have been
healed."[j]*
45The man talked about it so much
and told so many people, that Jesus
could no longer go openly into a
town. He had to stay away from the
towns, but people still came to him
from everywhere.

Jesus Heals a Crippled Man
(Matthew 9.1–8; Luke 5.17–26)

2 Jesus went back to Capernaum,
and a few days later people heard
that he was at home.[k] 2Then so many
of them came to the house that there
was not even standing room left in
front of the door.
Jesus was still teaching 3when four
people came up, carrying a crippled
man on a mat. 4But because of the
crowd, they could not get him to
Jesus. So they made a hole in the
roof[l] above him and let the man down
in front of everyone.
5When Jesus saw how much faith
they had, he said to the crippled man,
"My friend, your sins are forgiven."*
6Some of the teachers of the Law
of Moses were sitting there. They
started wondering, 7"Why would he
say such a thing? He must think he
is God! Only God can forgive sins."
8Right away Jesus knew what they
were thinking, and he said to them,
"Why are you thinking such things?
9Is it easier for me to tell this crippled
man that his sins are forgiven or to
tell him to get up and pick up his
mat and go on home? 10I will show
you that the Son of Man has the right
to forgive sins here on earth." So
Jesus said to the man, 11"Get up! Pick
up your mat and go on home."
12The man got right up. He picked
up his mat and went out while everyone watched in amazement. They
praised God and said, "We have
never seen anything like this!"

---

[g]*leprosy*: In biblical times the word "leprosy" was used for many different kinds of skin diseases. [h]*and kneeled down*: These words are not in some manuscripts. [i]*felt sorry for*: Some manuscripts have "was angry with." [j]*everyone will know that you have been healed*: People with leprosy had to be examined by a priest and told that they were well (that is "clean") before they could once again live a normal life in the Jewish community. The gift that Moses commanded was the sacrifice of some lambs together with flour mixed with olive oil. [k]*at home*: Or "in the house" (perhaps Simon Peter's home). [l]*roof*: In Palestine the houses usually had a flat roof. Stairs on the outside led up to the roof that was made of beams and boards covered with packed earth.

1.44 **"DON'T TELL ANYONE"** Jesus didn't want to become known just as a miracle worker, because there was a lot more to it than just that. He wanted to keep his fame as a healer from spreading too fast. But people talked anyway.

2.5 **ONE PERSON'S FAITH BLESSED ANOTHER** Notice here that Jesus rewarded the faith of the ones who *carried* the crippled man. We can bring the needs of others to the Lord in prayer, and he will answer because of our own faith.

NOTES

Jesus Chooses Levi
(Matthew 9.9–13; Luke 5.27–32)

13Once again Jesus went to the shore of Lake Galilee. A large crowd gathered around him, and he taught them. 14As he walked along, he saw Levi, the son of Alphaeus. Levi was sitting at the place for paying taxes, and Jesus said to him, "Come with me!" So he got up and went with Jesus.*

15Later, Jesus and his disciples were having dinner at Levi's house.[m] Many tax collectors[n] and other sinners had become followers of Jesus, and they were also guests at the dinner.

16Some of the teachers of the Law of Moses were Pharisees, and they saw that Jesus was eating with sinners and tax collectors. So they asked his disciples, "Why does he eat with tax collectors and sinners?"

17Jesus heard them and answered, "Healthy people don't need a doctor, but sick people do. I didn't come to invite good people to be my followers. I came to invite sinners."

People Ask about Going without Eating
(Matthew 9.14–17; Luke 5.33–39)

18The followers of John the Baptist and the Pharisees often went without eating.[o] Some people came and asked Jesus, "Why do the followers of John and those of the Pharisees often go without eating, while your disciples never do?"*

19Jesus answered:
The friends of a bridegroom don't go without eating while he is still with them. 20But the time will come when he will be taken from them. Then they will go without eating.

21No one patches old clothes by sewing on a piece of new cloth. The new piece would shrink and tear a bigger hole.

22No one pours new wine into old wineskins. The wine would swell and burst the old skins.[p] Then the wine would be lost, and the skins would be ruined. New wine must be put into new wineskins.

A Question about the Sabbath
(Matthew 12.1–8; Luke 6.1–5)

23One Sabbath Jesus and his disciples were walking through some wheat fields. His disciples were picking grains of wheat as they went along.[q] 24Some Pharisees asked Jesus, "Why are your disciples pick-

---

[m]*Levi's house*: Or "Jesus' house." [n]*tax collectors*: These were usually Jewish people who paid the Romans for the right to collect taxes. They were hated by other Jews who thought of them as traitors to their country and to their religion. [o]*without eating*: The Jewish people sometimes went without eating (also called "fasting") to show their love for God and to become better followers. [p]*swell and burst the old skins*: While the juice from grapes was becoming wine, it would swell and stretch the skins in which it had been stored. If the skins were old and stiff, they would burst. [q]*went along*: It was the custom to let hungry travelers pick grains of wheat.

2.14 **JESUS LOVED SINNERS** Levi was another name for Matthew, who was a tax collector. Tax collectors were hated by everybody because they served the government of the Roman tyrants, and their pay was based on how much they collected. But Jesus loved this tax collector. In fact Jesus loved a lot of unpopular people, and he even ate dinner with them. Thinking we're better than other people is very dangerous. God may decide we're not as wonderful as we like to think we are.

2.18 **WHY DID PEOPLE GO WITHOUT EATING?** Jesus told his disciples that the Pharisees went without eating to show off their religion. This practice is called "fasting" when it is done for religious reasons. It wasn't so much that Jesus was against fasting, since he sometimes advised it (see Matthew 6.17). But he was against worshiping in any way that would be meant to show off to others.

NOTES

ing grain on the Sabbath? They are
not supposed to do that!"*
25Jesus answered, "Haven't you
read what David did when he and
his followers were hungry and in
need? 26It was during the time of Abi-
athar the high priest. David went into
the house of God and ate the sacred
loaves of bread that only priests are
allowed to eat. He also gave some
to his followers."
27Jesus finished by saying, "People
were not made for the good of the
Sabbath. The Sabbath was made for
the good of people. 28So the Son of
Man is Lord over the Sabbath."

A Man with a Crippled Hand
(Matthew 12.9–14; Luke 6.6–11)

3 The next time that Jesus went into
the meeting place, a man with a
crippled hand was there. 2The Pharisees[r] wanted to accuse Jesus of doing
something wrong, and they kept
watching to see if Jesus would heal
him on the Sabbath.*
3Jesus told the man to stand up
where everyone could see him.
4Then he asked, "On the Sabbath
should we do good deeds or evil
deeds? Should we save someone's
life or destroy it?" But no one said
a word.
5Jesus was angry as he looked
around at the people. Yet he felt sorry
for them because they were so stubborn. Then he told the man, "Stretch
out your hand." He did, and his bad
hand was healed.
6The Pharisees left. And right away
they started making plans with Herod's followers[s] to kill Jesus.

Large Crowds Come to Jesus

7Jesus led his disciples down to the
shore of the lake. Large crowds followed him from Galilee, Judea,
8and Jerusalem. People came from
Idumea, as well as other places east
of the Jordan River. They also came
from the region around the cities of
Tyre and Sidon. All of these crowds
came because they had heard what
Jesus was doing.* 9He even had to
tell his disciples to get a boat ready
to keep him from being crushed by
the crowds.
10After Jesus had healed many
people, all the other sick people

[r]*Pharisees*: The Greek text has "they," but see verse 6. [s]*Herod's followers*: People who were political followers of the family of Herod the Great and his son Herod Antipas.

2.24 **DON'T BE A FAULTFINDER** The Pharisees didn't have much use for Jesus because he didn't seem to respect their special customs. So when they saw Jesus' disciples picking and eating grain on the Sabbath, they found fault. But Jesus used their remarks as an occasion to teach. God created the Sabbath as a day for blessing people. The disciples weren't working for profit. They were doing a harmless thing on their day off. It's sad when someone's religion becomes a means of finding fault with others.

3.2 **OLD OPINIONS DIE HARD** Again, Jesus got in trouble for healing someone on the Sabbath. The Jewish leaders had set up detailed rules about the Sabbath, making sure no one did the least work on that day of the week. They were very angry at Jesus for questioning them. They weren't about to change their opinions. They took Jesus' actions as a personal insult, even though he was only trying to help someone.

3.8 **WHAT DOES IT COST TO BE POPULAR?** Popularity means a lot to some people. How about you? Jesus was popular during the early part of his three-and-a-half-year ministry. But he always knew his popularity wouldn't last. The people were glad when he healed their sicknesses. Then he told them they would have to follow him and give up their old ways. So Jesus lost his popularity. We must not give up the truth to be popular.

NOTES

begged him to let them touch him. 11And whenever any evil spirits saw Jesus, they would fall to the ground and shout, "You are the Son of God!" 12But Jesus warned the spirits not to tell who he was.

Jesus Chooses His Twelve Apostles
(Matthew 10.1–4; Luke 6.12–16)

13Jesus decided to ask some of his disciples to go up on a mountain with him, and they went. 14Then he chose twelve of them to be his apostles,[t] so that they could be with him. He also wanted to send them out to preach* 15and to force out demons. 16Simon was one of the twelve, and Jesus named him Peter. 17There were also James and John, the two sons of Zebedee. Jesus called them Boanerges, which means "Thunderbolts." 18Andrew, Philip, Bartholomew, Matthew, Thomas, James son of Alphaeus, and Thaddaeus were also apostles. The others were Simon, known as the Eager One,[u] 19and Judas Iscariot,[v] who later betrayed Jesus.

Jesus and the Ruler of Demons
(Matthew 12.22–32; Luke 11.14–23; 12.10)

20Jesus went back home,[w] and once again such a large crowd gathered that there was no chance even to eat. 21When Jesus' family heard what he was doing, they thought he was crazy and went to get him under control.

22Some teachers of the Law of Moses came from Jerusalem and said, "This man is under the power of Beelzebul, the ruler of demons! He is even forcing out demons with the help of Beelzebul."*

23Jesus told the people to gather around him. Then he spoke to them in riddles and said:

How can Satan force himself
out? 24A nation whose people
fight each other won't last very
long. 25And a family that fights
won't last long either. 26So if
Satan fights against himself, that
will be the end of him.

27How can anyone break into
the house of a strong man and
steal his things, unless he first
ties up the strong man? Then he
can take everything.

28I promise you that any of the
sinful things you say or do can
be forgiven, no matter how
terrible those things are. 29But
if you speak against the Holy
Spirit, you can never be
forgiven. That sin will be held
against you forever.

30Jesus said this because the people were saying that he had an evil spirit in him.

Jesus' Mother and Brothers
(Matthew 12.46–50; Luke 8.19–21)

31Jesus' mother and brothers came and stood outside. Then they sent

---

[t]*to be his apostles*: These words are not in some manuscripts. [u]*known as the Eager One*: The Greek text has "Cananaean," which probably comes from a Hebrew word meaning "zealous" (see Luke 6.15). "Zealot" was the name later given to the members of a Jewish group which resisted and fought against the Romans. [v]*Iscariot*: This may mean "a man from Kerioth" (a place in Judea). But more probably it means "a man who was a liar" or "a man who was a betrayer." [w]*went back home*: Or "entered a house" (perhaps the home of Simon Peter).

3.14 **TWELVE SPECIAL STUDENTS** Jesus chose twelve men to be with him day by day, special students who could learn by sharing Jesus' life with him—eating, sleeping, and traveling where he did. He wanted them to be able to go out and tell the good news on their own. Today, too, a major purpose for our learning about Jesus is to go tell others about him.

3.22 **THE TEACHERS OF THE LAW MADE A BAD MISTAKE** Those jealous teachers of the Law who called the Spirit of God an evil spirit were doing an awful thing. Opposing the Holy Spirit would keep them from having faith in Jesus, and that would keep them lost.

NOTES

someone with a message for him to
come out to them.* 32The crowd that
was sitting around Jesus told him,
"Your mother and your brothers and
sisters[x] are outside and want to see
you."
33Jesus asked, "Who is my mother
and who are my brothers?" 34Then
he looked at the people sitting around
him and said, "Here are my mother
and my brothers. 35Anyone who
obeys God is my brother or sister or
mother."

A Story about a Farmer
(Matthew 13.1–9; Luke 8.4–8)

4 The next time Jesus taught beside
Lake Galilee, a big crowd gathered. It was so large that he had to
sit in a boat out on the lake, while
the people stood on the shore.
2He used stories to teach them many
things, and this is part of what he
taught:
3Now listen! A farmer went
out to scatter seed in a field.
4While the farmer was scattering
the seed, some of it fell along
the road and was eaten by birds.
5Other seeds fell on thin, rocky
ground and quickly started
growing because the soil was not
very deep. 6But when the sun
came up, the plants were
scorched and dried up, because
they did not have enough roots.
7Some other seeds fell where
thorn bushes grew up and
choked out the plants. So they
did not produce any grain. 8But
a few seeds did fall on good
ground where the plants grew
and produced thirty or sixty or
even a hundred times as much
as was scattered.
9Then Jesus said, "If you have ears,
pay attention."

Why Jesus Used Stories
(Matthew 13.10–17; Luke 8.9, 10)

10When Jesus was alone with the
twelve apostles and some others,
they asked him about these stories.
11He answered:
I have explained the secrets
about God's kingdom to you, but
for others I can use only stories.*
12The reason is,
"These people will look
and look, but never see.
They will listen and listen,
but never understand.
If they did,
they would turn to God,
and he would forgive them."

Jesus Explains the Story about the Farmer
(Matthew 13.18–23; Luke 8.11–15)

13Jesus told them:
If you don't understand this
story, you won't understand any
others. 14What the farmer is
spreading is really the message

---

[x]*and sisters*: These words are not in some manuscripts.

3.31 **WHAT ABOUT OUR FAMILIES?** Jesus had always obeyed and respected his parents. But a time came when he had to leave home and carry out the work his heavenly Father gave him to do. We should not neglect those who are closest to us, but God also calls us to serve in a world that needs us.

4.11 **KEEP A GOOD ATTITUDE ABOUT JESUS' TEACHING** Even though Jesus used simple stories to explain his message, still people did not understand. But the reason was that they had the wrong attitude. They never wanted Jesus to say things that made them feel uncomfortable. But sometimes he told the people their lives had to change toward God. So many of them didn't listen to Jesus. They didn't want to change.

NOTES

about the kingdom.* 15The seeds
that fell along the road are the
people who hear the message.
But Satan soon comes and
snatches it away from them.
16The seeds that fell on rocky
ground are the people who
gladly hear the message and
accept it right away. 17But they
don't have any roots, and they
don't last very long. As soon as
life gets hard or the message gets
them in trouble, they give up.
18The seeds that fell among the
thorn bushes are also people
who hear the message. 19But
they start worrying about the
needs of this life. They are fooled
by the desire to get rich and to
have all kinds of other things.
So the message gets choked out,
and they never produce
anything. 20The seeds that fell
on good ground are the people
who hear and welcome the
message. They produce thirty or
sixty or even a hundred times
as much as was planted.

Light
(Luke 8.16–18)

21Jesus also said:
You don't light a lamp and put
it under a clay pot or under a
bed. Don't you put a lamp on a
lampstand?* 22There is nothing
hidden that will not be made
public. There is no secret that
will not be well known. 23If you
have ears, pay attention!
24Listen carefully to what you
hear! The way you treat others
will be the way you will be
treated. 25Everyone who has
something will be given more.
But people who don't have
anything will lose what little
they have.

Another Story about Seeds

26Again Jesus said:
God's kingdom is like what
happens when a farmer scatters
seed in a field.* 27The farmer
sleeps at night and is up and
around during the day. Yet the
seeds keep sprouting and
growing, and he doesn't
understand how. 28It is the
ground that makes the seeds
sprout and grow into plants that
produce grain. 29Then when
harvest season comes and the
grain is ripe, the farmer cuts it
with a sickle.[y]

A Mustard Seed
(Matthew 13.31, 32; Luke 13.18, 19)

30Finally, Jesus said:
What is God's kingdom like?
What story can I use to explain

[y]*sickle*: A knife with a long curved blade, used to cut grain and other crops.

4.14 **WHAT KIND OF GROUND ARE YOU?** Attitude is very important. It can keep the truth of God from taking root in our hearts. If we are slow to believe, or quick to give up, or if we are worriers, these are all poor attitudes. Like poor ground, they cause faith to fail. A good attitude is like rich, moist ground that is good for growing.

4.21 **LET YOUR LIGHT SHINE** In God's sight the world is a dark place because so many people have turned their backs on the light of his truth. Jesus tells us that we must let the truth shine in the world. If we know God's word and live by it, then the world can see our light and be helped by it.

4.26 **HARVEST TIME IS COMING** After the growing season, when the grain is all ripe, the crop is gathered in. If we have done a good job of planting God's truth in the world, our work will multiply and grow. Then God will come to all in whom the seed of his truth has grown, and he will gather them into his everlasting kingdom.

NOTES

Step 8

I will make a list of those I wrong and be willing to make things right.

MARK 4.24

SCREAMING MATCH

I wasn't bothering anyone. After school I came home, kicked off my shoes, grabbed a soft drink, and plopped down on the sofa to unwind in front of the TV. In she comes, screaming about how I leave my clothes everywhere. "You don't care about anything. You're lazy, and I'm tired of waiting on you. I've worked long and hard, and I expect some help." Having heard this speech a million times, I tuned it out. But when she came over and slapped me across the face, I lost it. That's when I grabbed her arm and began shaking her while screaming profanity in her face. The last thing I remember was my mother crying on the floor as I stormed out of the door.

STEP LOOK INSIDE 8

We all wish incidents like this didn't happen, but they do. Parents and teens just don't always get along. Much of the time communication comes in the form of a screaming match. Teenagers usually think it is all their parents' fault—that they just don't understand. As we mature, we see that maybe *we* don't always understand.

After a screaming match, after the silence of being misunderstood, sooner or later the damage of a quarrel has to be repaired.

GENTLE WORDS

To move ahead in life we have to deal with the damage of the past. We need to ask God to help heal the hurts we feel. Then we need to go to the parents we've been arguing with and ask forgiveness. Maybe we can give each other a second chance. We can start today to make things better.

For another "Look Inside," turn to page 130.

it?* 31It is like what happens
when a mustard seed is planted
in the ground. It is the smallest
seed in all the world. 32But once
it is planted, it grows larger than
any garden plant. It even puts
out branches that are big enough
for birds to nest in its shade.

The Reason for Teaching with Stories

(Matthew 13.34, 35)

33Jesus used many other stories
when he spoke to the people, and he
taught them as much as they could
understand. 34He did not tell them
anything without using stories. But
when he was alone with his disciples,
he explained everything to them.

A Storm

(Matthew 8.23–27; Luke 8.22–25)

35That evening Jesus said to his disciples, "Let's cross to the east side."*
36So they left the crowd, and his disciples started across the lake with him
in the boat. Some other boats followed along. 37Suddenly a windstorm struck the lake. Waves started
splashing into the boat, and it was
about to sink.

38Jesus was in the back of the boat
with his head on a pillow, and he
was asleep. His disciples woke him
and said, "Teacher, don't you care
that we're about to drown?"

39Jesus got up and ordered the
wind and the waves to be quiet. The
wind stopped, and everything was
calm.

40Jesus asked his disciples, "Why
were you afraid? Don't you have any
faith?"

41Now they were more afraid than
ever and said to each other, "Who
is this? Even the wind and the waves
obey him!"

A Man with Evil Spirits

(Matthew 8.28–34; Luke 8.26–39)

5 Jesus and his disciples crossed
Lake Galilee and came to shore
near the town of Gerasa.[z] 2When he
was getting out of the boat, a man
with an evil spirit quickly ran to him
3from the graveyard[a] where he had
been living. No one was able to tie
the man up anymore, not even with
a chain. 4He had often been put in
chains and leg irons, but he broke
the chains and smashed the leg irons.
No one could control him. 5Night and
day he was in the graveyard or on
the hills, yelling and cutting himself
with stones.

6When the man saw Jesus in the
distance, he ran up to him and
kneeled down. 7He shouted, "Jesus,
Son of God in heaven, what do you
want with me? Promise me in God's
name that you won't torture me!"
8The man said this because Jesus had
already told the evil spirit to come
out of him.

9Jesus asked him, "What is your
name?"

The man answered, "My name is

---

[z]*Gerasa*: Some manuscripts have "Gadara," and others have "Gergesa." [a]*graveyard*: It was thought that demons and evil spirits lived in graveyards.

4.30 **THE NEWS OF GOD'S KINGDOM SPREADS** Jesus didn't begin his great work in a big way. He chose one of the smallest countries in the world and called a few ordinary men to be his teachers. From their small work the whole world has been hearing the good news about the kingdom of God.

4.35 **CAN YOU SLEEP IN STORMS OF LIFE?** A man was flying from Chicago to Philadelphia. The plane was being bounced around the sky by a violent thunderstorm, but the man lay asleep across his seat and the one next to him. Later the stewardess came by and asked him how he could sleep. He told her that the God of storms was in charge of the plane. He was right—no matter how rough life gets, the God of storms is in control.

NOTES

Lots, because I have 'lots' of evil spirits." 10He then begged Jesus not to
send them away.
11Over on the hillside a large herd
of pigs was feeding. 12So the evil spirits begged Jesus, "Send us into those
pigs! Let us go into them." 13Jesus
let them go, and they went out of the
man and into the pigs. The whole
herd of about two thousand pigs
rushed down the steep bank into the
lake and drowned.*
14The men taking care of the pigs
ran to the town and the farms to
spread the news. Then the people
came out to see what had happened.
15When they came to Jesus, they saw
the man who had once been full of
demons. He was sitting there with
his clothes on and in his right mind,
and they were terrified.
16Everyone who had seen what had
happened told about the man and the
pigs. 17Then the people started begging Jesus to leave their part of the
country.

18When Jesus was getting into the
boat, the man begged to go with him.
19But Jesus would not let him. Instead, he said, "Go home to your family and tell them how much the Lord
has done for you and how good he
has been to you."
20The man went away into the region near the ten cities known as Decapolis[b] and began telling everyone
how much Jesus had done for him.
Everyone who heard what happened
was amazed.*

A Dying Girl and a Sick Woman
(Matthew 9.18–26; Luke 8.40–56)

21Once again Jesus got into the
boat and crossed Lake Galilee.[c] Then
as he stood on the shore, a large
crowd gathered around him. 22The
person in charge of the Jewish meeting place was also there. His name
was Jairus, and when he saw Jesus,
he went over to him. He kneeled at
Jesus' feet 23and started begging him
for help. He said, "My daughter is
about to die! Please come and touch
her, so she will get well and live."
24Jesus went with Jairus. Many people followed along and kept crowding around.
25In the crowd was a woman who
had been bleeding for twelve years.
26She had gone to many doctors, and
they had not done anything except
cause her a lot of pain. She had paid
them all the money she had. But instead of getting better, she only got
worse.
27The woman had heard about
Jesus, so she came up behind him
in the crowd and barely touched his
clothes. 28She had said to herself, "If
I can just touch his clothes, I will get
well."* 29As soon as she touched
them, her bleeding stopped, and she
knew she was well.

---

[b] *the ten cities known as Decapolis*: A group of ten cities east of Samaria and Galilee, where the people followed the Greek way of life. [c] *crossed Lake Galilee*: To the west side.

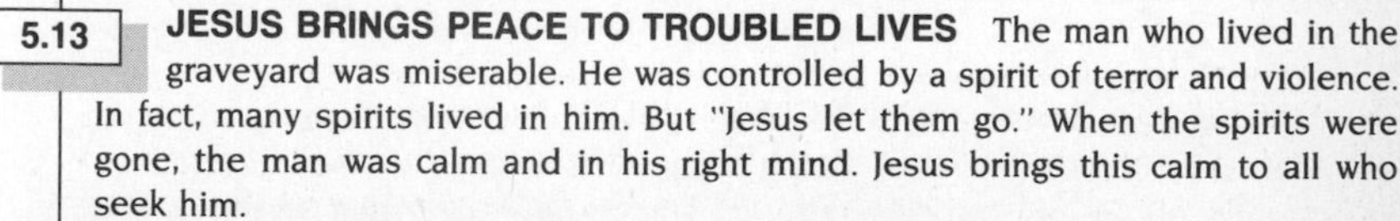

5.13 **JESUS BRINGS PEACE TO TROUBLED LIVES** The man who lived in the graveyard was miserable. He was controlled by a spirit of terror and violence. In fact, many spirits lived in him. But "Jesus let them go." When the spirits were gone, the man was calm and in his right mind. Jesus brings this calm to all who seek him.

5.20 **TELL OTHERS WHAT THE LORD HAS DONE FOR YOU** It's no surprise that the man who had the spirits in him couldn't keep quiet after what Jesus did for him. He was telling everybody he could find. Of course all were amazed at him, because they had known what kind of man he was, but he was in his right mind. Let's never get tired of telling people how much Jesus has done for us.

5.28 **TRUSTING JESUS IS A REWARDING ADVENTURE** The sick woman knew one thing clearly. If she could just touch Jesus she would be well. It was worth standing in the crowd (*continued*)

NOTES

30At that moment Jesus felt power
go out from him. He turned to the
crowd and asked, "Who touched my
clothes?"
31His disciples said to him, "Look
at all these people crowding around
you! How can you ask who touched
you?" 32But Jesus turned to see who
had touched him.
33The woman knew what had happened to her. She came shaking with
fear and kneeled down in front of
Jesus. Then she told him the whole
story.
34Jesus said to the woman, "You
are now well because of your faith.
May God give you peace! You are
healed, and you will no longer be in
pain."
35While Jesus was still speaking,
some men came from Jairus' home
and said, "Your daughter has died!
Why bother the teacher anymore?"
36Jesus heard[d] what they said, and
he said to Jairus, "Don't worry. Just
have faith!"
37Jesus did not let anyone go with
him except Peter and the two brothers, James and John. 38They went
home with Jairus and saw the people
crying and making a lot of noise.[e]
39Then Jesus went inside and said
to them, "Why are you crying and
carrying on like this? The child is not
dead. She is just asleep."* 40But the
people laughed at him.
After Jesus had sent them all out
of the house, he took the girl's father
and mother and his three disciples
and went to where she was. 41-42He
took the twelve-year-old girl by the
hand and said, "Talitha, koum!"[f]
which means, "Little girl, get up!"
The girl got right up and started
walking around.
Everyone was greatly surprised.
43But Jesus ordered them not to tell
anyone what had happened. Then he
said, "Give her something to eat."

The People of Nazareth Turn against Jesus

(Matthew 13.53–58; Luke 4.16–30)

6 Jesus left and returned to his
hometown[g] with his disciples.
2The next Sabbath he taught in the
Jewish meeting place. Many of the
people who heard him were amazed
and asked, "How can he do all this?
Where did he get such wisdom and
the power to work these miracles?
3Isn't he the carpenter,[h] the son of
Mary? Aren't James, Joseph, Judas,
and Simon his brothers? Don't his
sisters still live here in our town?"
The people were very unhappy because of what he was doing.*
4But Jesus said, "Prophets are honored by everyone, except the people
of their hometown and their relatives
and their own family." 5Jesus could

---

[d]*heard*: Or "ignored." [e]*crying and making a lot of noise*: The Jewish people often hired mourners for funerals. [f]*Talitha, koum*: These words are in Aramaic, a language spoken in Palestine during the time of Jesus. [g]*hometown*: Nazareth. [h]*carpenter*: The Greek word may also mean someone who builds or works with stone or brick.

(continued) just for the chance to touch his clothes. The woman spoke of her faith in Jesus and her need was met instantly. Like the woman, we have to care enough to come to Jesus. Our prayer of faith brings us near to him.

5.39 **GOD RULES OVER LIFE AND DEATH** We often think death is the end, and that's final. But to God, death is no more final than sleep. That's why Jesus said the little girl was "just asleep." God is far greater than anything that can happen to us—yes, even greater than death and the grave.

6.3 **JESUS' FAMILIAR FRIENDS REJECTED HIM** We only have to look around our world to see that Jesus isn't loved everywhere. Many people resent him, just as he was resented in his hometown years ago. The world hasn't changed much since then. Sometimes the people who know the most about Jesus love him the least. Some of the Lord's worst enemies live in places like North America and Europe, where the name of Jesus has been very well known for centuries.

NOTES

not work any miracles there, except to heal a few sick people by placing his hands on them. 6He was surprised that the people did not have any faith.

Instructions for the Twelve Apostles
(Matthew 10.5–15; Luke 9.1–6)

Jesus taught in every town and village. 7Then he called together his twelve apostles and sent them out two by two with power over evil spirits.* 8He told them, "You may take along a walking stick. But don't carry food or a traveling bag or any money. 9It's all right to wear sandals, but don't take along a change of clothes. 10When you are welcomed into a home, stay there until you leave that town. 11If any place won't welcome you or listen to your message, leave and shake the dust from your feet[i] as a warning to them."

12The apostles left and started telling everyone to turn to God. 13They forced out many demons and healed a lot of sick people by putting olive oil[j] on them.

The Death of John the Baptist
(Matthew 14.1–12; Luke 9.7–9)

14Jesus became so well-known that Herod the ruler[k] heard about him. Some people thought he was John the Baptist, who had come back to life with the power to work miracles. 15Others thought he was Elijah[l] or some other prophet who had lived long ago. 16But when Herod heard about Jesus, he said, "This must be John! I had his head cut off, and now he has come back to life."*

17-18Herod had earlier married Herodias, the wife of his brother Philip. But John had told him, "It isn't right for you to take your brother's wife!" So, in order to please Herodias, Herod arrested John and put him in prison.

19Herodias had a grudge against John and wanted to kill him. But she could not do it 20because Herod was afraid of John and protected him. He knew that John was a good and holy man. Even though Herod was confused by what John said,[m] he was glad to listen to him. And he often did.

21Finally, Herodias got her chance when Herod gave a great birthday celebration for himself and invited his officials, his army officers, and the leaders of Galilee. 22The daughter of Herodias[n] came in and danced for Herod and his guests. She pleased them so much that Herod said, "Ask for anything, and it's yours!* 23I

---

[i] *shake the dust from your feet*: This was a way of showing rejection. [j] *olive oil*: The Jewish people used olive oil as a way of healing people. Sometimes olive oil is a symbol for healing by means of a miracle (see James 5.14). [k] *Herod the ruler*: Herod Antipas, the son of Herod the Great. [l] *Elijah*: Many of the Jewish people expected the prophet Elijah to come and prepare the way for the Messiah. [m] *was confused by what John said*: Some manuscripts have "did many things because of what John said." [n] *Herodias*: Some manuscripts have "Herod."

6.7 **LET US CONTINUE THE WORK OF JESUS** The twelve apostles may have been surprised when Jesus sent them out to do his work without him. This was just a "trial run," because the day would come when he would not be with the apostles and they would have to continue alone. Jesus expects us to do his work by winning people to faith all over the world. But let's remember that although in one way Jesus isn't here, in another way he is very much with us at all times.

6.16 **OBEYING GOD WILL COST YOUR LIFE** You might not be put to death like John the Baptist, but being a Christian will mean devoting your life to Jesus. In fact, you won't even *want* to live for yourself anymore when you give your life to him. Whether believers live or die, they are the Lord's to use in any way he wants.

6.22 **LUST BRINGS MORE EVIL** Not only was the lust of Herod for his dancing stepdaughter evil, but as lust often does, it brought about more evil—the murder of an innocent (*continued*)

NOTES

swear that I will give you as much
as half of my kingdom, if you want
it."
24The girl left and asked her
mother, "What do you think I should
ask for?"
Her mother answered, "The head
of John the Baptist!"
25The girl hurried back and told
Herod, "Right now on a platter I want
the head of John the Baptist!"
26The king was very sorry for what
he had said. But he did not want to
break the promise he had made in
front of his guests. 27At once he ordered a guard to cut off John's head
there in prison. 28The guard put
the head on a platter and took it
to the girl. Then she gave it to her
mother.
29When John's followers learned
that he had been killed, they took
his body and put it in a tomb.

Jesus Feeds Five Thousand
(Matthew 14.13–21; Luke 9.10–17; John 6.1–14)

30After the apostles returned to
Jesus,[o] they told him everything they
had done and taught. 31But so many
people were coming and going that
Jesus and the apostles did not even
have a chance to eat. Then Jesus said,
"Let's go to a place[p] where we can
be alone and get some rest." 32They
left in a boat for a place where they
could be alone. 33But many people
saw them leave and figured out
where they were going. So people
from every town ran on ahead and
got there first.
34When Jesus got out of the boat,
he saw the large crowd that was like
sheep without a shepherd. He felt
sorry for the people and started
teaching them many things.
35That evening the disciples came
to Jesus and said, "This place is like
a desert, and it is already late.
36Let the crowds leave, so they can
go to the farms and villages near here
and buy something to eat."*
37Jesus replied, "You give them
something to eat."
But they asked him, "Don't you
know that it would take almost a
year's wages[q] to buy all of these people something to eat?"
38Then Jesus said, "How much
bread do you have? Go and see!"
They found out and answered, "We
have five small loaves of bread[r] and
two fish." 39Jesus told his disciples
to have the people sit down on the
green grass. 40They sat down in
groups of a hundred and groups of
fifty.
41Jesus took the five loaves and the
two fish. He looked up toward heaven
and blessed the food. Then he broke
the bread and handed it to his disciples to give to the people. He also
divided the two fish, so that everyone
could have some.
42After everyone had eaten all they
wanted, 43Jesus' disciples picked up
twelve large baskets of leftover bread
and fish.
44There were five thousand men
who ate the food.

---

[o] *the apostles returned to Jesus*: From the mission on which he had sent them (see 6.7,12,13). [p] *a place*: This was probably northeast of Lake Galilee (see verse 45). [q] *almost a year's wages*: The Greek text has "two hundred silver coins." Each coin was the average day's wage for a worker. [r] *small loaves of bread*: These would have been flat and round or in the shape of a bun.

(*continued*) man, a prophet sent from God. It's like what James writes about in his letter (James 1.14): "We are tempted by our own desires that drag us off and trap us." Herod's lust trapped him into committing an awful crime against God.

6.36 **JESUS MAKES MUCH FROM OUR LITTLE** The disciples were anxious about the hungry crowds who followed Jesus. They proposed an ordinary solution: sending the crowds away to buy food. But Jesus solved the problem himself. Sometimes, in ways we may not notice, God uses our few things to do great works. As Lord of heaven and earth, he can use little for much. He made the universe from nothing at all.

NOTES

Jesus Walks on the Water
(Matthew 14.22–33; John 6.15–21)

45 Right away Jesus made his disciples get into the boat and start back
across to Bethsaida. But he stayed
until he had sent the crowds away.
46 Then he told them good-by and
went up on the side of a mountain
to pray.
47 Later that evening he was still
there by himself, and the boat was
somewhere in the middle of the lake.*
48 He could see that the disciples were
struggling hard, because they were
rowing against the wind. Not long
before morning, Jesus came toward
them. He was walking on the water
and was about to pass the boat.
49 When the disciples saw Jesus
walking on the water, they thought
he was a ghost, and they started
screaming. 50 All of them saw him and
were terrified. But at that same time
he said, "Don't worry! I am Jesus.
Don't be afraid." 51 He then got into
the boat with them, and the wind died
down. The disciples were completely
confused. 52 Their minds were closed,
and they could not understand
the true meaning of the loaves of
bread.

Jesus Heals Sick People in Gennesaret
(Matthew 14.34–36)

53 Jesus and his disciples crossed
the lake and brought the boat to
shore near the town of Gennesaret.
54 As soon as they got out of the boat,
the people recognized Jesus. 55 So
they ran all over that part of the country to bring their sick people to him
on mats. They brought them to him
each time they heard where he was.*
56 In every village or farm or market
place where Jesus went, the people
brought their sick to him. They
begged him to let them just touch his
clothes, and everyone who did was
healed.

The Teaching of the Ancestors
(Matthew 15.1–9)

7 Some Pharisees and several
teachers of the Law of Moses
from Jerusalem came and gathered
around Jesus. 2 They noticed that
some of his disciples ate without first
washing their hands.[s]
3 The Pharisees and all other Jewish people obey the teachings of their
ancestors. They always wash their
hands in the proper way[t] before eating. 4 None of them will eat anything
they buy in the market until it is
washed. They also follow a lot of

---

[s] *without first washing their hands*: The Jewish people had strict laws about washing their hands before eating, especially if they had been out in public.
[t] *in the proper way*: The Greek text has "with the fist," but the exact meaning is not clear. It could mean "to the wrist" or "to the elbow."

6.47 **"THE BOAT WAS IN THE MIDDLE OF THE LAKE"** This was Lake Galilee, about 70 miles north of Jerusalem. It is most often called "the *Sea* of Galilee," but it is smaller than many lakes, so "lake" is probably more accurate for a name. Its water is clear and drinkable, and people still fish there. The Jordan River flows through it. It was also called "Gennesaret" in Jesus' day, and many years earlier it had been called "Chinnereth." One of the Herod kings named it "the Sea of Tiberias" to honor a Roman emperor. That's a lot of names for one lake—but it was an important lake.

6.55 **THE POWER OF GOD NEVER RUNS OUT** All who touched Jesus' clothes were healed. By touching his clothing, people showed their faith. The real power was not in the clothing, but in the wearer of the clothing. *All* were healed, not just some. There is no limit to what God can do to bless those who reach out to him.

NOTES

other teachings, such as washing cups, pitchers, and bowls.[u]*

5The Pharisees and teachers asked Jesus, "Why don't your disciples obey what our ancestors taught us to do? Why do they eat without washing their hands?"

6Jesus replied:

You are nothing but showoffs!
The prophet Isaiah was right
when he wrote that God had
said,
"All of you praise me
with your words,
but you never really
think about me.
7It is useless for you
to worship me,
when you teach rules
made up by humans."
8You disobey God's
commands in order to obey what
humans have taught. 9You are
good at rejecting God's
commands so that you can
follow your own teachings!
10Didn't Moses command you to
respect your father and mother?
Didn't he tell you to put to death
all who curse their parents?
11But you let people get by
without helping their parents
when they should. You let them
say that what they own has been
offered to God.[v] 12You won't let
those people help their parents.
13And you ignore God's
commands in order to follow
your own teaching. You do a lot
of other things that are just as
bad.

What Really Makes People Unclean
(Matthew 15.10–20)

14Jesus called the crowd together again and said, "Pay attention and try to understand what I mean. 15-16The food that you put into your mouth does not make you unclean and unfit to worship God. The bad words that come out of your mouth are what make you unclean."[w]*

17After Jesus and his disciples had left the crowd and had gone into the house, they asked him what these sayings meant. 18He answered, "Don't you know what I am talking about by now? Surely you know that the food you put into your mouth cannot make you unclean. 19It does not go into your heart, but into your stomach, and then out of your body." By saying this, Jesus meant that all foods were fit to eat.

20Then Jesus said:

What comes from your heart
is what makes you unclean.
21Out of your heart come evil
thoughts, vulgar deeds, stealing,
murder, 22unfaithfulness in
marriage, greed, meanness,
deceit, indecency, envy, insults,
pride, and foolishness. 23All of
these come from your heart, and
they are what make you unfit to
worship God.

A Woman's Faith
(Matthew 15.21–28)

24Jesus left and went to the region near the city of Tyre, where he stayed in someone's home. He did not want people to know he was there, but they found out anyway. 25A woman whose daughter had an evil spirit in her

---

[u] *bowls*: Some manuscripts add "and sleeping mats." [v] *has been offered to God*: According to Jewish custom, when anything was offered to God, it could not be used for anyone else, not even for a person's parents. [w] *unclean*: Some manuscripts add, "If you have ears, pay attention."

7.4 **FIRST THINGS FIRST** The Pharisees and teachers were "majoring on minors," observing strict rules about washing bowls and other fussy matters. They were forgetting about the really important parts of God's Law—the parts that had to do with how we treat other people. Love is the main point. Let's not lose sight of it.

7.15 **WHAT IS REALLY UNCLEAN** We are kept from being "clean" by what we do more than by what we eat or touch. Let's make sure there is no "dirt" coming out of our hearts, but that the world is a cleaner place because we are in it.

NOTES

heard where Jesus was. And right
away she came and kneeled down
at his feet. 26The woman was Greek
and had been born in the part of Syria
known as Phoenicia. She begged
Jesus to force the demon out of her
daughter. 27But Jesus said, "The children must first be fed! It isn't right
to take away their food and feed it
to dogs."[x]*

28The woman replied, "Lord, even
dogs eat the crumbs that children
drop from the table."

29Jesus answered, "That's true!
You may go now. The demon has left
your daughter." 30When the woman
got back home, she found her child
lying on the bed. The demon had
gone.

Jesus Heals a Man Who Was Deaf and Could Hardly Talk

31Jesus left the region around Tyre
and went by way of Sidon toward
Lake Galilee. He went through the
land near the ten cities known as Decapolis.[y] 32Some people brought to
him a man who was deaf and could
hardly talk. They begged Jesus just
to touch him.*

33After Jesus had taken him aside
from the crowd, he stuck his fingers
in the man's ears. Then he spit and
put it on the man's tongue. 34Jesus
looked up toward heaven, and with
a groan he said, "Effatha!"[z] which
means "Open up!" 35At once the man
could hear, and he had no more trouble talking clearly.

36Jesus told the people not to say
anything about what he had done.
But the more he told them, the more
they talked about it. 37They were
completely amazed and said, "Everything he does is good! He even heals
people who cannot hear or talk."

Jesus Feeds Four Thousand
(Matthew 15.32–39)

8 One day another large crowd
gathered around Jesus. They had
not brought along anything to eat.
So Jesus called his disciples together
and said, 2"I feel sorry for these people. They have been with me for three
days, and they don't have anything
to eat. 3Some of them live a long way
from here. If I send them away hungry, they might faint on their way
home."

4The disciples said, "This place is
like a desert. Where can we find
enough food to feed such a crowd?"

5Jesus asked them how much food
they had. They replied, "Seven small
loaves of bread."[a]

6After Jesus told the crowd to sit
down, he took the seven loaves and
blessed them. He then broke the
loaves and handed them to his disciples, who passed them out to the
crowd.* 7They also had a few little
fish, and after Jesus had blessed

---

[x]*feed it to dogs*: The Jewish people often referred to Gentiles as dogs. [y]*the ten cities known as Decapolis*: See the note at 5.20. [z]*Effatha*: This word is in Aramaic, a language spoken in Palestine during the time of Jesus. [a]*small loaves of bread*: See the note at 6.38.

7.27 **BLESSING CAME TO A GENTILE** The Greek woman from Syria would have been considered "unclean" by the strict Jews of Jesus' time. Jesus referred to this opinion in his remark about "dogs." But he rewarded the woman's faith by healing her daughter. Jesus had come to bless more than just one race of people.

7.32 **HEARING AND SPEAKING ARE ALSO GOD'S GIFTS** Animals can hear and be taught to answer certain sounds. But they can't speak. This is a special gift for those created in God's likeness. We are also given the ability to hear and understand. It was no trouble for Christ, the Creator of these gifts, to give them back to a man who had lost them.

8.6 **THE HUNGRY WERE FED** The four thousand people were fed all they wanted, and there was more left over. No matter what we lack, God has that and more. Through this miracle and the feeding of the five thousand told of in chapter 6, Jesus showed that he is the master of creation and that he has the power to supply all of our needs.

NOTES

these, he told the disciples to pass
them around.
8-9The crowd of about four thousand people ate all they wanted, and
the leftovers filled seven large
baskets.
As soon as Jesus had sent the people away, 10he got into the boat with
the disciples and crossed to the territory near Dalmanutha.[b]

A Sign from Heaven
(Matthew 16.1–4)

11The Pharisees came out and
started an argument with Jesus. They
wanted to test him by asking for a
sign from heaven.* 12Jesus groaned
and said, "Why are you always looking for a sign? I can promise you that
you will not be given one!" 13Then
he left them. He again got into a boat
and crossed over to the other side
of the lake.

The Yeast of the Pharisees and of Herod
(Matthew 16.5–12)

14The disciples had forgotten to
bring any bread, and they had only
one loaf with them in the boat.
15Jesus warned them, "Watch out!
Guard against the yeast of the Pharisees and of Herod."[c]
16The disciples talked this over and
said to each other, "He must be saying this because we don't have any
bread."
17Jesus knew what they were
thinking and asked, "Why are you
talking about not having any bread?
Don't you understand? Are your
minds still closed? 18Are your eyes
blind and your ears deaf? Don't you
remember* 19how many baskets of
leftovers you picked up when I fed
those five thousand people with only
five small loaves of bread?"
"Yes," the disciples answered.
"There were twelve baskets."
20Jesus then asked, "And how
many baskets of leftovers did you
pick up when I broke seven small
loaves of bread for those four thousand people?"
"Seven," they answered.
21"Don't you know what I am talking about by now?" Jesus asked.

Jesus Heals a Blind Man at Bethsaida

22As Jesus and his disciples were
going into Bethsaida, some people
brought a blind man to him and
begged him to touch the man.
23Jesus took him by the hand and
led him out of the village, where he
spit into the man's eyes. He placed
his hands on the blind man and asked
him if he could see anything. 24The
man looked up and said, "I see people, but they look like trees walking
around."
25Once again Jesus placed his
hands on the man's eyes, and this
time the man stared. His eyes were
healed, and he saw everything
clearly. 26Jesus said to the man, "You
may return home now, but don't go
into the village."

---

[b]*Dalmanutha*: The place is unknown. [c]*Herod*: Herod Antipas, the son of Herod the Great.

8.11 **SIGNS FROM HEAVEN DON'T CREATE FAITH** Many people think that if they could just see a miracle they would believe in God. But you need to believe in God first before you can see his miracles. God has done many miracles, but our problem is that we close our eyes to them. Even if someone came back from the dead, many would not believe. In fact, Jesus did come back to life, but many still didn't trust him.

8.18 **UNBELIEF CAUSES BLINDNESS** Lack of faith brings about not physical blindness, but blindness to God's work. The disciples hadn't fully realized how Jesus fed the crowds. He had done it so simply and easily that they missed the lesson about the mighty power of God. Just like the Pharisees who wanted a sign, the disciples had not understood what their own eyes should have told them.

NOTES

Who Is Jesus?
(Matthew 16.13–20; Luke 9.18–21)

27Jesus and his disciples went to
the villages near the town of Caesarea Philippi. As they were walking
along, he asked them, "What do people say about me?"
28The disciples answered, "Some
say you are John the Baptist or
maybe Elijah.[d] Others say you are
one of the prophets."
29Then Jesus asked them, "But
who do you say I am?"
"You are the Messiah!" Peter
replied.*
30Jesus warned the disciples not to
tell anyone about him.

Jesus Speaks about His Suffering and Death
(Matthew 16.21–28; Luke 9.22–27)

31Jesus began telling his disciples
what would happen to him. He said,
"The nation's leaders, the chief
priests, and the teachers of the Law
of Moses will make the Son of Man
suffer terribly. He will be rejected
and killed, but three days later he
will rise to life." 32Then Jesus explained clearly what he meant.
Peter took Jesus aside and told him
to stop talking like that. 33But when
Jesus turned and saw the disciples,
he corrected Peter. He said to him,
"Satan, get away from me! You are
thinking like everyone else and not
like God."
34Jesus then told the crowd and the
disciples to come closer, and he said:

If any of you want to be my
followers, you must forget about
yourself. You must take up your
cross and follow me.* 35If you
want to save your life,[e] you will
destroy it. But if you give up your
life for me and for the good news,
you will save it. 36What will you
gain, if you own the whole world
but destroy yourself? 37What
could you give to get back your
soul?
38Don't be ashamed of me and
my message among these
unfaithful and sinful people! If
you are, the Son of Man will be
ashamed of you when he comes
in the glory of his Father with
the holy angels.
9 I promise you that some of the
people standing here will not
die before they see God's
kingdom come with power.*

---

[d]*Elijah*: See the note at 6.15. [e]*life*: In verses 35-37 the same Greek word is translated "life," "yourself," and "soul."

8.29 **DO WE REALLY UNDERSTAND?** Remember that puzzle you just couldn't solve no matter how hard you tried, then it suddenly came together? The disciples finally understood what their eyes and their ears had been telling them about Jesus. He really was the Messiah, the One sent from God. But they still did not understand his reason for coming.

8.34 **WHAT IS A DISCIPLE?** Is a disciple only someone two thousand years ago who walked around the Holy Land in a robe with a long walking stick? No, a disciple is anyone who follows Jesus in any place or time. To follow Jesus we must leave our old cares behind and begin to care about the things Jesus cares about. Let's not be ashamed to be Christians. Let's be glad we have found Jesus, the greatest treasure of life. Then we can be his disciples too.

9.1 **HAS GOD'S KINGDOM COME?** When you first set foot on some land you bought to build a house on, you say "this is my land," even though you need to go away for a while before you are ready to return there to live. When Jesus came to earth he showed in many ways that the ground he walked on was his own, and that he is the King of kings. The church is here as "the body of Christ," and in that sense the kingdom is here now. Then when Jesus returns, his kingdom will be set up fully, with the King here for all to see.

NOTES

The True Glory of Jesus
(Matthew 17.1–13; Luke 9.28–36)

2Six days later Jesus took Peter,
James, and John with him. They went
up on a high mountain, where they
could be alone. There in front of the
disciples, Jesus was completely
changed. 3And his clothes became
much whiter than any bleach on
earth could make them. 4Then Moses
and Elijah were there talking with
Jesus.

5Peter said to Jesus, "Teacher, it
is good for us to be here! Let us make
three shelters, one for you, one for
Moses, and one for Elijah." 6But Peter and the others were terribly
frightened, and he did not know what
he was talking about.

7The shadow of a cloud passed over
and covered them. From the cloud
a voice said, "This is my Son, and I
love him. Listen to what he says!"
8At once the disciples looked around,
but they saw only Jesus.*

9As Jesus and his disciples were
coming down the mountain, he told
them not to say a word about what
they had seen, until the Son of Man
had been raised from death. 10So they
kept it to themselves. But they wondered what he meant by the words
"raised from death."

11The disciples asked Jesus, "Don't
the teachers of the Law of Moses say
that Elijah must come before the
Messiah does?"

12Jesus answered:

> Elijah certainly will come[f] to get everything ready. But don't the Scriptures also say that the Son of Man must suffer terribly and be rejected?
> 13I promise you that Elijah has already come. And people treated him just as they wanted to, as the Scriptures say they would.

Jesus Heals a Boy
(Matthew 17.14–20; Luke 9.37–43a)

14When Jesus and his three disciples came back down, they saw a
large crowd around the other disciples. The teachers of the Law of Moses were arguing with them.

15The crowd was really surprised
to see Jesus, and everyone hurried
over to greet him.

16Jesus asked, "What are you arguing about?"

17Someone from the crowd answered, "Teacher, I brought my son
to you. A demon keeps him from talking. 18Whenever the demon attacks
my son, it throws him to the ground
and makes him foam at the mouth
and grit his teeth in pain. Then he
becomes stiff. I asked your disciples
to force out the demon, but they
couldn't do it."

19Jesus said, "You people don't
have any faith! How much longer
must I be with you? Why do I have
to put up with you? Bring the boy
to me."

20They brought the boy, and as
soon as the demon saw Jesus, it made
the boy shake all over. He fell down
and began rolling on the ground and
foaming at the mouth.

21Jesus asked the boy's father,
"How long has he been like this?"

The man answered, "Ever since he
was a child. 22The demon has often
tried to kill him by throwing him into
a fire or into water. Please have pity
and help us if you can!"

23Jesus replied, "Why do you say
'if you can'? Anything is possible for
someone who has faith!"*

24Right away the boy's father

STEP LOOK INSIDE 2

---

[f] *Elijah certainly will come*: See the note at 6.15.

9.8 **WHAT DOES JESUS LOOK LIKE?** When Jesus came in a human body he kept hidden most of what he is really like. On the mountain Jesus showed some of his real glory. In that moment the disciples saw the King in his beauty, and they began to see something of the kingdom of God that Jesus had spoken about in verse 1.

9.23 **PRAYER DRIVES OUT DEMONS** Not everyone can cope with demons, and science doesn't have the answer to all such problems. Jesus said that our greatest problem is that *(continued)*

NOTES

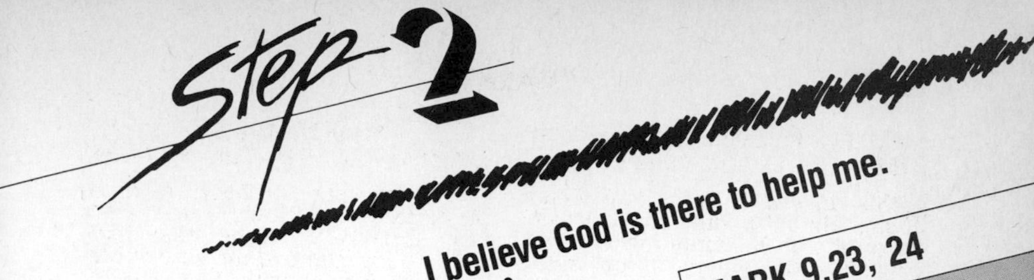

MARK 9.23, 24

EVERYDAY FAITH

Dear Mom and Dad,

Camp is great. The food is gross, but everything else is cool. My cabin is the farthest one from the dining room, so we all have to get up early to make sure we aren't the last ones to breakfast. Breakfast is at 6:30 A.M.! If you are late they make you clear all the tables and stuff. And they sing songs about you. It's kind of embarrassing.

Last night we made this huge fire down by the lake. Mr. Gordon got up and talked about trusting God with our lives. I did it.

Camp is different this year. Everybody seems more grown-up. I talked with my counselor until 2:00 A.M. It was awesome. But they sang about us at breakfast!

Don't be late on Saturday. I am kind of homesick.

Love,
Lonnie

HIGHS AND LOWS

STEP LOOK INSIDE 2

Everyday faith is what we need to live every day with. Spiritual highs are usually followed by spiritual lows. Sort of like a roller coaster. But everyday faith will get us through the lows and temper the highs. It is constant. It is a growing thing. Do we have everyday faith? Faith that will get us through a tough test, a broken relationship, a disappointment?

For another "Look Inside," turn to page 192.

shouted, "I do have faith! Please help
me to have even more."
25When Jesus saw that a crowd
was gathering fast, he spoke sternly
to the evil spirit that had kept the
boy from speaking or hearing. He
said, "I order you to come out of the
boy! Don't ever bother him again."
26The spirit screamed and made
the boy shake all over. Then it went
out of him. The boy looked dead, and
almost everyone said he was. 27But
Jesus took hold of his hand and
helped him stand up.
28After Jesus and the disciples had
gone back home and were alone, they
asked him, "Why couldn't we force
out that demon?"
29Jesus answered, "Only prayer
can force out that kind of demon."

Jesus Again Speaks about His Death
(Matthew 17.22, 23; Luke 9.43b–45)

30Jesus left with his disciples and
started through Galilee. He did not
want anyone to know about it,
31because he was teaching the disciples that the Son of Man would be
handed over to people who would kill
him. But three days later he would
rise to life.* 32The disciples did not
understand what Jesus meant, and
they were afraid to ask.

Who Is the Greatest?
(Matthew 18.1–5; Luke 9.46–48)

33Jesus and his disciples went to
his home in Capernaum. After they
were inside the house, Jesus asked
them, "What were you arguing about
along the way?" 34They had been arguing about which one of them was
the greatest, and so they did not
answer.
35After Jesus sat down and told the
twelve disciples to gather around
him, he said, "If you want the place
of honor, you must become a slave
and serve others!"*
36Then Jesus had a child stand near
him. He put his arm around the child
and said, 37"When you welcome even
a child because of me, you welcome
me. And when you welcome me, you
welcome the one who sent me."

For or against Jesus
(Luke 9.49, 50)

38John said, "Teacher, we saw a
man using your name to force demons out of people. But he was not
one of us, and we told him to stop."*
39Jesus said to his disciples:
Don't stop him! No one who
works miracles in my name will
soon turn and say something bad
about me. 40Anyone who is not

(*continued*) we don't have the faith we should. People of faith have proven that Jesus' promise doesn't fail. The steady prayer of faith will even drive out demons.

9.31 **SLOW TO UNDERSTAND** Jesus warned his disciples several times that he would be killed and then would rise again. But they would not understand until much later when they actually saw the risen Jesus. We wonder how the disciples could have been so slow to catch on. But we, too, are slow to really believe what the Bible tells us about Jesus.

9.35 **WHAT IS REAL GREATNESS?** Some of the disciples were concerned about which of them would be the greatest when Jesus came to his throne as King. They missed the whole point. Jesus spoke of slaves and children—humble people. He was trying to show us how to be humble. That's what real greatness is.

9.38 **"NOT ONE OF US"** Over the years, Christians have often sinned by dividing the church. Although we probably can't start over with one church for all, we can pray not to be separated from one another in spirit. Jesus had other disciples who were working for him. He told his followers to be thankful for them also. We ought to do the same today, thanking God for all who truly seek to follow Jesus.

NOTES

against us is for us. 41And
anyone who gives you a cup of
water in my name, just because
you belong to me, will surely be
rewarded.

Temptations to Sin
(Matthew 18.6–9; Luke 17.1, 2)

STEP 7

42It will be terrible for people
who cause even one of my little
followers to sin. Those people
would be better off thrown into
the ocean with a heavy stone tied
around the neck.* 43-44So if your
hand causes you to sin, cut it off!
You would be better off to go
into life crippled than to have
two hands and be thrown into
the fires of hell that never go
out.[g] 45-46If your foot causes you
to sin, chop it off. You would be
better off to go into life lame than
to have two feet and be thrown
into hell.[h] 47If your eye causes
you to sin, get rid of it. You would
be better off to go into God's
kingdom with only one eye than
to have two eyes and be thrown
into hell. 48The worms there
never die, and the fire never
stops burning.

49Everyone must be salted
with fire.[i]

50Salt is good. But if it no
longer tastes like salt, how can
it be made salty again? Have salt
among you and live at peace with
each other.[j]*

Teaching about Divorce
(Matthew 19.1–12; Luke 16.18)

10 After Jesus left, he went to Judea and then on to the other
side of the Jordan River. Once again
large crowds came to him, and as
usual, he taught them.

2Some Pharisees wanted to test
Jesus. So they came up to him and
asked if it was right for a man to
divorce his wife. 3Jesus asked them,
"What does the Law of Moses say
about that?"

4They answered, "Moses allows a
man to write out divorce papers and
send his wife away."

5Jesus replied, "Moses gave you
this law because you are so heartless.
6But in the beginning God made a
man and a woman. 7That's why a
man leaves his father and mother and
gets married. 8He becomes like one
person with his wife. Then they are
no longer two people, but one.*
9And no one should separate a couple
that God has joined together."

10When Jesus and his disciples

---

[g] *never go out*: Some manuscripts add, "The worms there never die, and the fire never stops burning." [h] *thrown into hell*: Some manuscripts add, "The worms there never die, and the fire never stops burning." [i] *salted with fire*: Some manuscripts add "and every sacrifice will be seasoned with salt." The verse may mean that Christ's followers must suffer because of their faith. [j] *Have salt among you and live at peace with each other*: This may mean that when Christ's followers have to suffer because of their faith, they must still try to live at peace with each other.

9.42 **BE A GOOD EXAMPLE TO OTHERS** If we aren't good examples, we're probably bad ones. That is the way we tempt people to do wrong. We always have to be aware of how others around us see our actions. If anything we do sends a message that sin is "okay," we're in danger of causing a lot of sorrow to others.

9.50 **DO YOU TASTE LIKE A CHRISTIAN?** When Jesus tells us to "have salt," we are reminded that some foods without salt are not very tasty. A sad Christian with a long face isn't a very good advertisement for Jesus. We all get "down in the dumps" sometimes, but let's remember our blessings. Then we'll have a smile and an encouraging word for others.

10.8 **OUR MARRIAGE PROMISES ARE SACRED** Sometimes people enter marriage with a wrong attitude. We easily think only of the fun side of married life. There are also sickness, pain, suffering, and sorrow, and often these experiences in marriage are lifelong. Then the reality of Christian love is tested, and love either blossoms or dies.

NOTES

were back in the house, they asked
him about what he had said. 11He told
them, "A man who divorces his wife
and marries someone else is unfaithful to his wife. 12A woman who divorces her husband[k] and marries
again is also unfaithful."

Jesus Blesses Little Children
(Matthew 19.13–15; Luke 18.15–17)

13Some people brought their children to Jesus so that he could bless
them by placing his hands on them.
But his disciples told the people to
stop bothering him.*
14When Jesus saw this, he became
angry and said, "Let the children
come to me! Don't try to stop them.
People who are like these little children belong to the kingdom of God.[l]
15I promise you that you cannot get
into God's kingdom, unless you accept it the way a child does." 16Then
Jesus took the children in his arms
and blessed them by placing his
hands on them.

A Rich Man
(Matthew 19.16–30; Luke 18.18–30)

17As Jesus was walking down a
road, a man ran up to him. He
kneeled down, and asked, "Good
teacher, what can I do to have eternal
life?"
18Jesus replied, "Why do you call
me good? Only God is good. 19You
know the commandments. 'Do not
murder. Be faithful in marriage. Do
not steal. Do not tell lies about others.
Do not cheat. Respect your father
and mother.' "
20The man answered, "Teacher, I
have obeyed all these commandments since I was a young man."
21Jesus looked closely at the man.
He liked him and said, "There's one
thing you still need to do. Go sell everything you own. Give the money
to the poor, and you will have riches
in heaven. Then come with me."
22When the man heard Jesus say
this, he went away gloomy and sad
because he was very rich.
23Jesus looked around and said to
his disciples, "It's hard for rich people to get into God's kingdom!"
24The disciples were shocked to hear
this. So Jesus told them again, "It's
terribly hard[m] to get into God's kingdom! 25In fact, it's easier for a camel
to go through the eye of a needle than
for a rich person to get into God's
kingdom."
26Jesus' disciples were even more
amazed. They asked each other,
"How can anyone ever be saved?"
27Jesus looked at them and said,
"There are some things that people
cannot do, but God can do anything."*
28Peter replied, "Remember, we
left everything to be your followers!"
29Jesus told him:

You can be sure that anyone
who gives up home or brothers
or sisters or mother or father or
children or land for me and for
the good news 30will be

---

[k]*A woman who divorces her husband*: Roman law let a woman divorce her husband, but Jewish law did not let a woman do this. [l]*People who are like these little children belong to the kingdom of God*: Or "The kingdom of God belongs to people who are like these little children." [m]*hard*: Some manuscripts add "for people who trust in their wealth." Others add "for the rich."

10.13 **CHILDREN CAN COME TO JESUS** We live too much in an adult world. Children belong to God, too, and this fact makes children important. Today's children are tomorrow's adults. Jesus wants them to come early to him. And then we need to keep a simple, trusting, childlike faith in God no matter how old we get.

10.27 **GOD DOES IMPOSSIBLE THINGS** We often meet people who we say are "creative." They're very good at thinking of better ways to make or do things. But God is the great Creator who does "impossible" things. In the beginning he created the universe from just nothing at all. The same God can also remake a sinner into a new person who loves and obeys him.

NOTES

rewarded. In this world they will
be given a hundred times as
many houses and brothers and
sisters and mothers and children
and pieces of land, though they
will also be mistreated. And in
the world to come, they will have
eternal life. 31But many who are
now first will be last, and many
who are now last will be first.

Jesus Again Tells about His Death
(Matthew 20.17–19; Luke 18.31–34)

32The disciples were confused as
Jesus led them toward Jerusalem,
and his other followers were afraid.
Once again Jesus took the twelve disciples aside and told them what was
going to happen to him. He said:

33We are now on our way to
Jerusalem where the Son of Man
will be handed over to the chief
priests and the teachers of the
Law of Moses. They will
sentence him to death and hand
him over to foreigners,[n]* 34who
will make fun of him and spit
on him. They will beat him and
kill him. But three days later he
will rise to life.

The Request of James and John
(Matthew 20.20–28)

35James and John, the sons of Zebedee, came up to Jesus and asked,
"Teacher, will you do us a favor?"
36Jesus asked them what they
wanted, 37and they answered,
"When you come into your glory,
please let one of us sit at your right
side and the other at your left."[o]
38Jesus told them, "You don't really know what you're asking! Are
you able to drink from the cup[p] that
I must soon drink from or be baptized
as I must be baptized?"[q]
39"Yes, we are!" James and John
answered.
Then Jesus replied, "You certainly
will drink from the cup from which
I must drink. And you will be baptized just as I must! 40But it is not
for me to say who will sit at my right
side and at my left. That is for God
to decide."
41When the ten other disciples
heard this, they were angry with
James and John. 42But Jesus called
the disciples together and said:

You know that those
foreigners who call themselves
kings like to order their people
around. And their great leaders
have full power over the people
they rule.* 43But don't act like
them. If you want to be great,
you must be the servant of all
the others. 44And if you want to
be first, you must be everyone's
slave. 45The Son of Man did not
come to be a slave master, but
a slave who will give his life to
rescue[r] many people.

---

[n]*foreigners*: The Romans who ruled Judea at this time. [o]*right side . . . left*: The most powerful people in a kingdom sat at the right and left side of the king. [p]*drink from the cup*: In the Scriptures a "cup" is sometimes used as a symbol of suffering. To "drink from the cup" would be to suffer. [q]*as I must be baptized*: Baptism is used with the same meaning that "cup" has in this verse. [r]*rescue*: The Greek word often, though not always, means the payment of a price to free a slave or a prisoner.

10.33 **STAYING ALIVE IS NOT OUR MAIN PURPOSE** "The will to live" is one of our strongest instincts. Jesus also enjoyed living, but he knew that living was not his main purpose. There was something important to *die* for and he alone could do it. Our lives belong to God who gave them. It is our highest good to give back our lives when he asks us to.

10.42 **WHAT DOES IT MEAN TO BE IMPORTANT?** The most important man in Jesus' time was the emperor at Rome. He thought he had more power than anybody in the world. He ruled most of Europe and parts of western Asia and northern Africa. Who could resist his authority? But Jesus said it is more important to serve than to rule, and the outcome of the Savior's life on earth showed us that.

NOTES

Jesus Heals Blind Bartimaeus
(Matthew 20.29–34; Luke 18.35–43)

46Jesus and his disciples went to
Jericho. And as they were leaving,
they were followed by a large crowd.
A blind beggar by the name of Bartimaeus son of Timaeus was sitting beside the road. 47When he heard that
it was Jesus from Nazareth, he
shouted, "Jesus, Son of David,[s] have
pity on me!" 48Many people told the
man to stop, but he shouted even
louder, "Son of David, have pity on
me!"
49Jesus stopped and said, "Call him
over!"
They called out to the blind man
and said, "Don't be afraid! Come on!
He is calling for you."* 50The man
threw off his coat as he jumped up
and ran to Jesus.
51Jesus asked, "What do you want
me to do for you?"
The blind man answered, "Master,[t] I want to see!"
52Jesus told him, "You may go.
Your eyes are healed because of your
faith."
Right away the man could see, and
he went down the road with Jesus.

Jesus Enters Jerusalem
(Matthew 21.1–11; Luke 19.28–40; John 12.12–19)

11 Jesus and his disciples reached
Bethphage and Bethany near
the Mount of Olives. When they were
getting close to Jerusalem, Jesus sent
two of them on ahead. 2He told them,
"Go into the next village. As soon
as you enter it, you will find a young
donkey that has never been ridden.
Untie the donkey and bring it here.
3If anyone asks why you are doing
that, say, 'The Lord[u] needs it and will
soon bring it back.' "
4The disciples left and found the
donkey tied near a door that faced
the street. While they were untying
it, 5some of the people standing there
asked, "Why are you untying the
donkey?" 6They told them what
Jesus had said, and the people let
them take it.
7The disciples led the donkey to
Jesus. They put some of their clothes
on its back, and Jesus got on. 8Many
people spread clothes on the road,
while others went to cut branches
from the fields.[v]
9In front of Jesus and behind him,
people went along shouting,

"Hooray![w]
God bless the one who comes
in the name of the Lord!*
10God bless the coming kingdom
of our ancestor David.
Hooray for God
in heaven above!"

11After Jesus had gone to Jerusalem, he went into the temple and
looked around at everything. But
since it was already late in the day,
he went back to Bethany with the
twelve disciples.

---

[s] *Son of David*: The Jewish people expected the Messiah to be from the family of King David, and for this reason the Messiah was often called the "Son of David." [t] *Master*: A Hebrew word that may also mean "Teacher." [u] *The Lord*: Or "The master of the donkey." [v] *spread . . . branches from the fields*: This was one way that the Jewish people welcomed a famous person. [w] *Hooray*: This translates a word that can mean "please save us." But it is most often used as a shout of praise to God.

10.49 **LITTLE PEOPLE ARE IMPORTANT** Jesus showed the truth of what he had just been saying by the way he treated a poor blind man. The man was pleading for Jesus to help him. But everybody tried to shut the man up. It was then that Jesus proved his point about who is important. The others must have been ashamed when they saw Jesus stop to heal the blind man.

11.9 **A LOT OF NOISE PROVES NOTHING** A loud car may not mean a powerful engine. More often it means the car needs a new muffler. The noise of the crowd that met Jesus coming into Jerusalem didn't mean they really loved Jesus at all. Later the same crowd would cry out, "Nail him to a cross."

NOTES

Step 12

BARTIMAEUS—a man who showed his gratitude to God by telling others about the good news of Jesus Christ

MARK 10.46–52; MATTHEW 20.29–34; LUKE 18.35–43

Gratefulness is a wonderful thing to see in the life of a growing Christian. It says to all who observe that "God is good to me." Being grateful is usually the response when a real and pressing need is met in our lives. There is a tremendous example of gratefulness demonstrated in the healing of the blind beggar named Bartimaeus. Bartimaeus thought his greatest need was to regain his eyesight. What he later discovered was that regaining his eyesight was his second greatest need.

We don't know how long Bartimaeus had been blind or how he happened to lose his sight, but we know he heard Jesus had the power to cure his blindness. As Jesus was walking by, Bartimaeus cried out to him for help. The people around Bartimaeus tried to get him to be quiet, but he persisted. He shouted even louder until Jesus stopped and called him over. There was no hesitation when Jesus asked him what he wanted. Bartimaeus said, "I want to see!" He knew Jesus was the person to meet his need for new eyes.

Imagine what it was like. As Jesus touched Bartimaeus's eyes, the shapes and colors slowly came into focus, and he could see! Surely, the first thing he saw was the smiling face of Jesus. What joy! What elation! What gratitude! From that day on Bartimaeus never looked back. The Bible says that he got up and followed Jesus.

STEP LOOK BACK 12

While Bartimaeus was grateful for his new eyesight, he later discovered that gaining physical sight had not been his greatest need. His spiritual eyes also had to be opened. We can be sure that Jesus wants to meet our physical needs, but, more importantly, he wants to meet our spiritual needs. One offers temporary relief; the other offers eternal belief.

Look at what God is doing in our lives! Thinking back to what our lives were like as we began this discovery process, we remember that we realized we needed help. Now we are in a position to help others. And this is just the beginning. We can take the opportunity to introduce someone else to Christ. We can tell them about this twelve-step journey we are on and help them discover this as well. There is no better way for us to express our gratitude. Grateful people pass on great news.

This is your last* InStep *meditation.

Jesus Puts a Curse on a Fig Tree
(Matthew 21.18, 19)

12When Jesus and his disciples left Bethany the next morning, he was hungry. 13From a distance Jesus saw a fig tree covered with leaves, and he went to see if there were any figs on the tree. But there were not any, because it was not the season for figs.* 14So Jesus said to the tree, "Never again will anyone eat fruit from this tree!" The disciples heard him say this.

Jesus in the Temple
(Matthew 21.12–17; Luke 19.45–48; John 2.13–22)

15After Jesus and his disciples reached Jerusalem, he went into the temple and began chasing out everyone who was selling and buying. He turned over the tables of the moneychangers and the benches of those who were selling doves.* 16Jesus would not let anyone carry things through the temple. 17Then he taught the people and said, "The Scriptures say, 'My house should be called a place of worship for all nations.' But you have made it a place where robbers hide!"

18The chief priests and the teachers of the Law of Moses heard what Jesus said, and they started looking for a way to kill him. They were afraid of him, because the crowds were completely amazed at his teaching.

19That evening Jesus and the disciples went outside the city.

A Lesson from the Fig Tree
(Matthew 21.20–22)

20As the disciples walked past the fig tree the next morning, they noticed that it was completely dried up, roots and all. 21Peter remembered what Jesus had said to the tree. Then Peter said, "Teacher, look! The tree you put a curse on has dried up."

22Jesus told his disciples:

Have faith in God! 23If you have faith in God and don't doubt, you can tell this mountain to get up and jump into the sea, and it will.* 24Everything you ask for in prayer will be yours, if you only have faith.

25-26Whenever you stand up to pray, you must forgive what others have done to you. Then your Father in heaven will forgive your sins.[x]

---

[x]*your sins*: Some manuscripts add, "But if you do not forgive others, God will not forgive you."

11.13 THE FIG TREE STOOD FOR SOMETHING We wonder why Jesus would curse a fig tree. It was to teach a lesson. The tree stood for something else: Israel. Jesus was showing that the Jewish people of his time—because of bad leaders—were not bearing the fruit that someone would expect from people who had been chosen, blessed, and guided by God. Are we bearing the right fruit today?

11.15 WHAT HAPPENED IN THE TEMPLE? Did Jesus have the right to act the way he did? Maybe we think he should have been more polite, saying, "Would you please take your shops out of the temple?" But Jesus was Lord of the temple, and the merchants had no business there—except to meet God. They were using the house of God for their own selfish purposes, so Jesus chased them out.

11.23 JESUS SOMETIMES USED PICTURES TO TEACH A LESSON Often Jesus used a kind of speech called hyperbole (pronounced hy-PUR-bo-lee), which is a clear overstatement—like when we say, "I could eat a horse," meaning we're very hungry. So, when Jesus wanted to teach the power of prayer, he could say, "You can tell this mountain to jump into the sea." Jesus was a master at using figures of speech like these to teach spiritual lessons.

NOTES

A Question about Jesus' Authority
(Matthew 21.23–27; Luke 20.1–8)

27Jesus and his disciples returned
to Jerusalem. And as he was walking
through the temple, the chief priests,
the nation's leaders, and the teachers
of the Law of Moses came over to
him. 28They asked, "What right do
you have to do these things? Who
gave you this authority?"
29Jesus answered, "I have just one
question to ask you. If you answer
it, I will tell you where I got the right
to do these things.* 30Who gave John
the right to baptize? Was it God in
heaven or merely some human
being?"
31They thought it over and said to
each other, "We can't say that God
gave John this right. Jesus will ask
us why we didn't believe John.
32On the other hand, these people
think that John was a prophet. So
we can't say that it was merely some
human who gave John the right to
baptize."
They were afraid of the crowd
33and told Jesus, "We don't know."
Jesus replied, "Then I won't tell
you who gave me the right to do what
I do."

Renters of a Vineyard
(Matthew 21.33–46; Luke 20.9–19)

12 This is one of the stories Jesus
used when he spoke to the
people:

A farmer once planted a
vineyard. He built a wall around
it and dug a pit to crush the
grapes in. He also built a lookout
tower. Then he rented out his
vineyard and left the country.*
2When it was harvest time, he
sent a servant to get his share
of the grapes. 3The renters
grabbed the servant. They beat
him up and sent him away
without a thing.
4The owner sent another
servant, but the renters beat him
on the head and insulted him
terribly. 5Then the man sent
another servant, and they killed
him. He kept sending servant
after servant. They beat some of
them and killed others.
6The owner had a son he loved
very much. Finally, he sent his
son to the renters because he
thought they would respect him.
7But they said to themselves,
"Someday he will own this
vineyard. Let's kill him! That
way we can have it all for
ourselves." 8So they grabbed the
owner's son and killed him. Then
they threw his body out of the
vineyard.

9Jesus asked, "What do you think
the owner of the vineyard will do?
I'll tell you what he will do. He will
come and kill those renters and let
someone else have his vineyard.
10Surely you know that the Scriptures say,

'The stone that the builders
tossed aside
is now the most important
stone of all.*

NOTES

11.29 **THEY WERE AFRAID OF THE CROWD** Jesus knew that his question would make the leaders fearful. Those who don't care about God live in fear of people. That was the state of the temple leaders in Jesus' time. They had their power only as long as the people supported them. But Jesus' authority came from his Father in heaven. Where do we get our feeling of security—from God or from people?

12.1 **ANOTHER STORY ABOUT ISRAEL** Again, Jesus taught about Israel with a story. The farmer is God. The servants are the prophets. The son is Jesus. The Jewish leaders had often mistreated the people God sent to them. Soon they would lose their country to Roman invaders.

12.10 **JESUS IS THE GREATEST STONE IN GOD'S TEMPLE** God has a "building" not made of stones—it's made of people who trust Jesus as their Lord and Savior. In a stone building, *(continued)*

[11]This is something
the Lord has done,
and it is amazing to us.' "
[12]The leaders knew that Jesus was
really talking about them, and they
wanted to arrest him. But because
they were afraid of the crowd, they
let him alone and left.

Paying Taxes
(Matthew 22.15–22; Luke 20.20–26)

[13]The Pharisees got together with
Herod's followers.[y] Then they sent
some men to trick Jesus into saying
something wrong. [14]They went to
him and said, "Teacher, we know
that you are honest. You treat everyone with the same respect, no matter
who they are. And you teach the truth
about what God wants people to do.
Tell us, should we pay taxes to the
Emperor or not?"*
[15]Jesus knew what they were up
to, and he said, "Why are you trying
to test me? Show me a coin!"
[16]They brought him a silver coin,
and he asked, "Whose picture and
name are on it?"
"The Emperor's," they answered.
[17]Then Jesus told them, "Give the
Emperor what belongs to him and
give God what belongs to God." The
men were amazed at Jesus.

Life in the Future World
(Matthew 22.23–33; Luke 20.27–40)

[18]The Sadducees did not believe
that people would rise to life after
death. So some of them came to Jesus
and said:*
[19]Teacher, Moses wrote that if
a married man dies and has no
children, his brother should
marry the widow. Their first son
would then be thought of as the
son of the dead brother. [20]There
were once seven brothers. The
first one married, but died
without having any children.
[21]The second brother married
his brother's widow, and he also
died without having children.
The same thing happened to the
third brother, [22]and finally to all
seven brothers. At last the
woman died. [23]When God raises
people from death, whose wife
will this woman be? After all, she
had been married to all seven
brothers.
[24]Jesus answered:
You are completely wrong!
You don't know what the
Scriptures teach. And you don't
know anything about the power
of God. [25]When God raises
people to life, they won't marry.
They will be like the angels in
heaven. [26]You surely know
about people being raised to life.
You know that in the story about
Moses and the burning bush,
God said, "I am the God
worshiped by Abraham, Isaac,
and Jacob."[z] [27]He is not the God
of the dead, but of the living. You
Sadducees are all wrong.

---

[y]*Herod's followers*: People who were political followers of the family of Herod the Great and his son Herod Antipas. [z]*"I am the God worshiped by Abraham, Isaac, and Jacob"*: Jesus argues that if God is worshiped by these three, they must still be alive, because he is the God of the living.

(*continued*) the most important stone is called the "cornerstone." All the other stones are anchored to that stone, and its position determines the way the whole building sits. Christians are anchored to Jesus, like a living cornerstone.

12.14 **GIVING TO THE EMPEROR** A follower of Jesus still needs to respect the government. It is one of the gifts God has given to us. If we owe taxes we should pay them. Good Christians are good citizens. We pay God what he has a right to ask for, and the government what it has a right to ask for.

12.18 **THE WORST LIES ARE THE ONES WE TELL TO OURSELVES** The Sadducees were not men of truth. They even deceived themselves. They thought they were true believers in God, but they ignored God's word. Jesus showed them their lie. Let's be honest with God. Then we'll be honest with ourselves and others.

NOTES

The Most Important Commandment
(Matthew 22.34–40; Luke 10.25–28)

28 One of the teachers of the Law
of Moses came up while Jesus and
the Sadducees were arguing. When
he heard Jesus give a good answer,
he asked him, "What is the most important commandment?"
29 Jesus answered, "The most important one says: 'People of Israel,
you have only one Lord and God.*
30 You must love him with all your
heart, soul, mind, and strength.'
31 The second most important commandment says: 'Love others as
much as you love yourself.' No other
commandment is more important
than these."
32 The man replied, "Teacher, you
are certainly right to say there is only
one God. 33 It is also true that we must
love God with all our heart, mind,
and strength, and that we must love
others as much as we love ourselves.
These commandments are more important than all the sacrifices and offerings that we could possibly
make."
34 When Jesus saw that the man had
given a sensible answer, he told him,
"You are not far from God's kingdom." After this, no one dared ask
Jesus any more questions.

About David's Son
(Matthew 22.41–46; Luke 20.41–44)

35 As Jesus was teaching in the temple, he said, "How can the teachers
of the Law of Moses say that the Messiah will come from the family of
King David? 36 The Holy Spirit had
David say,

'The Lord said to my Lord:
Sit at my right side[a]
until I make your enemies
into a footstool for you.'

37 If David called the Messiah his
Lord, how can the Messiah be his
son?"[b]
The large crowd enjoyed listening
to Jesus teach.

Jesus Condemns the Pharisees and the Teachers of the Law of Moses
(Matthew 23.1–36; Luke 20.45–47)

38 As Jesus was teaching, he said:
Guard against the teachers of
the Law of Moses! They love to
walk around in long robes and
be greeted in the market.*
39 They like the front seats in the
meeting places and the best seats
at banquets. 40 But they cheat
widows out of their homes and
pray long prayers just to show
off. They will be punished most
of all.

A Widow's Offering
(Luke 21.1–4)

41 Jesus was sitting in the temple
near the offering box and watching
people put in their gifts. He noticed
that many rich people were giving
a lot of money.* 42 Finally, a poor

---

[a] *right side*: The place of power and honor.
[b] *David . . . his son*: See the note at 10.47.

12.29 **LOVE IS THE GREATEST** If we know God we will love him and all that he loves. Right from the start, this has been the main rule. Religion that is worth the name is really love that comes from God and lives in us. Love is God's greatest gift and the first thing he expects to see in his worshipers—love toward him and toward all people.

12.38 **DON'T BE FOOLED BY SHOWOFFS** A building may be beautiful and admired by everybody. Then one day that building falls into rubbish in a moment: the building was infested with termites that ate out its insides. The teachers of Jesus' time were like that—all they had was an outward show. When they came before God they would fall into ruin.

12.41 **GIVE YOUR BEST TO JESUS** It's a cheap religion that allows us to give only a "tip" to God. By doing so we may tell ourselves we're good people. But God knows our hearts. *(continued)*

NOTES

widow came up and put in two coins
that were worth only a few pennies.
43Jesus told his disciples to gather
around him. Then he said:

I tell you that this poor widow
has put in more than all the
others. 44Everyone else gave
what they didn't need. But she
is very poor and gave everything
she had. Now she doesn't have
a cent to live on.

The Temple Will Be Destroyed
(Matthew 24.1, 2; Luke 21.5, 6)

13 As Jesus was leaving the temple, one of his disciples said to
him, "Teacher, look at these beautiful
stones and wonderful buildings!"*
2Jesus replied, "Do you see these
huge buildings? They will certainly
be torn down! Not one stone will be
left in place."

Warning about Trouble
(Matthew 24.3–14; Luke 21.7–19)

3Later, as Jesus was sitting on the
Mount of Olives across from the temple, Peter, James, John, and Andrew
came to him in private. 4They asked,
"When will these things happen?
What will be the sign that they are
about to take place?"
5Jesus answered:

Watch out and don't let
anyone fool you!* 6Many will
come and claim to be me. They
will use my name and fool many
people.
7When you hear about wars
and threats of wars, don't be
afraid. These things will have to
happen first, but that is not the
end. 8Nations and kingdoms will
go to war against each other.
There will be earthquakes in
many places, and people will
starve to death. But this is just
the beginning of troubles.
9Be on your guard! You will
be taken to courts and beaten
with whips in their meeting
places. And because of me, you
will have to stand before rulers
and kings to tell about your faith.
10But before the end comes, the
good news must be preached to
all nations.
11When you are arrested, don't
worry about what you will say.
You will be given the right words
when the time comes. But you
will not really be the ones
speaking. Your words will come
from the Holy Spirit.
12Brothers and sisters will
betray each other and have each
other put to death. Parents will
betray their own children, and
children will turn against their
parents and have them killed.
13Everyone will hate you
because of me. But if you keep
on being faithful right to the end,
you will be saved.

The Horrible Thing
(Matthew 24.15–21; Luke 21.20–24)

14Someday you will see that
"Horrible Thing" where it

(continued) Everything we have comes from him, and we owe it all to him. Our very lives belong to him. So let's not try to hold back what God has lent to us for only a short while anyway.

13.1 **PLACE YOUR HOPE IN THINGS THAT LAST** Many in Jesus' day placed their hope in the temple. To serve in the temple was the greatest good they could think of. But Jesus pointed out what they should have known—the temple wouldn't last. Nothing that people build will last forever. But the things that God builds can never be destroyed.

13.5 **DON'T BE FOOLED** Some people believe everything they're told. They even believe that all the fun of this world will never end, and so they live without thinking about God. We can believe God when he says that all the treasures of this world will come to an end. When we're in our right mind we must know that. Let's seek what will last forever.

NOTES

should not be.[c] Everyone who
reads this must try to
understand! If you are living in
Judea at that time, run to the
mountains.* 15If you are on the
roof[d] of your house, don't go
inside to get anything. 16If you
are out in the field, don't go back
for your coat. 17It will be an
awful time for women who are
expecting babies or nursing
young children. 18Pray that it
won't happen in winter.[e] 19This
will be the worst time of
suffering since God created the
world, and nothing this terrible
will ever happen again. 20If the
Lord doesn't make the time
shorter, no one will be left alive.
But because of his chosen and
special ones, he will make the
time shorter.
21If someone should say,
"Here is the Messiah!" or "There
he is!" don't believe it. 22False
messiahs and false prophets will
come and work miracles and
signs. They will even try to fool
God's chosen ones. 23But be on
your guard! That's why I am
telling you these things now.

When the Son of Man Appears
(Matthew 24.29–31; Luke 21.25–28)

24In those days, right after that
time of suffering,

"The sun will become dark,
and the moon
will no longer shine.*
25The stars will fall,
and the powers in the sky[f]
will be shaken."

26Then the Son of Man will be
seen coming in the clouds with
great power and glory. 27He will
send his angels to gather his
chosen ones from all over the
earth.

A Lesson from a Fig Tree
(Matthew 24.32–35; Luke 21.29–33)

28Learn a lesson from a fig
tree. When its branches sprout
and start putting out leaves, you
know summer is near. 29So when
you see all these things
happening, you will know that
the time has almost come.[g]
30You can be sure that some of
the people living today will still
be alive when all this happens.
31The sky and the earth will not
last forever, but my words will.

No One Knows the Day or Time
(Matthew 24.36–44)

32No one knows the day or the
time. The angels in heaven don't
know, and the Son himself
doesn't know. Only the Father
knows.* 33So watch out and be

[c] *where it should not be*: Probably the holy place in the temple. [d] *roof*: See the note at 2.4. [e] *in winter*: In Palestine the winters are cold and rainy and make travel difficult. [f] *the powers in the sky*: In ancient times people thought that the stars were spiritual powers. [g] *the time has almost come*: Or "he (that is, the Son of Man) will soon be here."

13.14 **HARD TIMES ARE COMING** Several times in history foreign conquerors destroyed the temple at Jerusalem and even worshiped false gods that they set up there. The Romans took over Jerusalem in the year 70. But Jesus was pointing to a time when false christs will come and deceive many at the end of the age we are living in.

13.24 **THIS WORLD WILL PASS AWAY** We are used to seeing the sun rise every day and the moon at night. The stars all keep their special places in the skies. But God says even these things will fail at the end of this time we are living in. This should make us think about the things that cannot fail. The promises of God about life everlasting with him are absolutely sure.

13.32 **BE READY ALWAYS** Some people try to forecast the date Jesus will return. But Jesus himself warned us not to. The important thing is for us to be watchful and ready *whenever* Jesus might return for us.

NOTES

ready! You don't know when the time will come. [34]It is like what happens when a man goes away for a while and places his servants in charge of everything. He tells each of them what to do, and he orders the watchmen to be on their guard. [35]So be on your guard! You don't know when the master of the house will come back. It could be in the evening or at midnight or before dawn or in the morning. [36]But if he comes suddenly, don't let him find you asleep. [37]I tell everyone just what I have told you. Be on your guard!

A Plot to Kill Jesus

(Matthew 26.1–5; Luke 22.1, 2; John 11.45–53)

14 It was now two days before Passover and the Feast of Thin Bread. The chief priests and the teachers of the Law of Moses were planning how they could sneak around and have Jesus arrested and put to death. [2]They were saying, "We must not do it during the feast, because the people will riot."

At Bethany

(Matthew 26.6–13; John 12.1–8)

[3]Jesus was eating in Bethany at the home of Simon, who once had leprosy,[h] when a woman came in with a very expensive bottle of sweet-smelling perfume.[i] After breaking it open, she poured the perfume on Jesus' head. [4]This made some of the guests angry, and they said, "Why such a waste? [5]We could have sold this perfume for more than three hundred silver coins and given the money to the poor!" So they started saying cruel things to the woman.

[6]But Jesus said:

Leave her alone! Why are you bothering her? She has done a beautiful thing for me.* [7]You will always have the poor with you. And whenever you want to, you can give to them. But you will not always have me here with you. [8]She has done all she could by pouring perfume on my body to prepare it for burial. [9]You may be sure that wherever the good news is told all over the world, people will remember what she has done. And they will tell others.

Judas and the Chief Priests

(Matthew 26.14–16; Luke 22.3–6)

[10]Judas Iscariot[j] was one of the twelve disciples. He went to the chief priests and offered to help them arrest Jesus. [11]They were glad to hear this, and they promised to pay him. So Judas started looking for a good chance to betray Jesus.

Jesus Eats with His Disciples

(Matthew 26.17–25; Luke 22.7–14, 21–23; John 13.21–30)

[12]It was the first day of the Feast of Thin Bread, and the Passover lambs were being killed. Jesus' disciples asked him, "Where do you want us to prepare the Passover meal?"

[13]Jesus said to two of the disciples, "Go into the city, where you will meet a man carrying a jar of water.[k] Follow him, [14]and when he goes into a house, say to the owner, 'Our teacher wants to know if you have a room where he can eat the Passover meal with his disciples.' [15]The owner will take you upstairs and show you a large room furnished and ready for

---

[h]*leprosy*: In biblical times the word "leprosy" was used for many different skin diseases. [i]*sweet-smelling perfume*: The Greek text has "perfume made of pure spikenard," a plant used to make perfume. [j]*Iscariot*: See the note at 3.19. [k]*a man carrying a jar of water*: A male slave carrying water could mean that the family was rich.

14.6 **DO BEAUTIFUL THINGS FOR JESUS** We should love our neighbors. That's a good rule and God himself said so. But he also said we should love him *first*. In a simple way the woman at Bethany was doing just that when she poured the expensive perfume on Jesus. Her love for him was greater than anything else in her life.

NOTES

you to use. Prepare the meal there."
16The two disciples went into the city and found everything just as Jesus had told them. So they prepared the Passover meal.
17-18While Jesus and the twelve disciples were eating together that evening, he said, "The one who will betray me is now eating with me."*
19This made the disciples sad, and one after another they said to Jesus, "Surely you don't mean me!"
20He answered, "It is one of you twelve men who is eating from this
dish with me. 21The Son of Man will die, just as the Scriptures say. But it is going to be terrible for the one who betrays me. That man would be better off if he had never been born."

The Lord's Supper

(Matthew 26.26–30; Luke 22.14–23; 1 Corinthians 11.23–25)

22During the meal Jesus took some bread in his hands. He blessed the bread and broke it. Then he gave it to his disciples and said, "Take this. It is my body."
23Jesus picked up a cup of wine and gave thanks to God. He then gave it to his disciples and said, "Drink
it!" So they all drank some. 24Then
he said, "This is my blood, which is poured out for many people, and with
it God makes his agreement. 25From
now on I will not drink any wine, until I drink new wine in God's kingdom."
dom." 26Then they sang a hymn and
went out to the Mount of Olives.*

Peter's Promise

(Matthew 26.31–35; Luke 22.31–34; John 13.36–38)

27Jesus said to his disciples, "All of you will reject me, as the Scriptures say,

'I will strike down
the shepherd,
and the sheep
will be scattered.'

28But after I am raised to life, I will go ahead of you to Galilee."
29Peter spoke up, "Even if all the others reject you, I never will!"
30Jesus replied, "This very night before a rooster crows twice, you will say three times that you don't know me."
31But Peter was so sure of himself that he said, "Even if I have to die with you, I will never say that I don't know you!"
All the others said the same thing.*

Jesus Prays

(Matthew 26.36–46; Luke 22.39–46)

32Jesus went with his disciples to a place called Gethsemane, and he told them, "Sit here while I pray."
33Jesus took along Peter, James,
and John. He was sad and troubled
and 34told them, "I am so sad that I feel as if I am dying. Stay here and keep awake with me."
35-36Jesus walked on a little way. Then he kneeled down on the ground and prayed, "Father,[l] if it is possible,

[l]*Father*: The Greek text has "Abba," which is an Aramaic word meaning "father."

14.17 **"THE ONE WHO WILL BETRAY ME"** Imagine: one of the twelve disciples—the followers who were closest to Jesus—would betray him to his killers. How could anyone do such a thing? But believers today betray Jesus all the time. Many times we treat him as if he were unimportant, and we sin as if we didn't care about him. In many ways we aren't much better than Judas was.

14.26 **THEY SANG A HYMN** On their last night together before Jesus' death, he and his disciples sang a hymn. Religious singing isn't just something people have "added on" in recent years. It has always been important.

14.31 **PETER WAS HUMAN** Peter had good intentions. He promised Jesus he would never let him down, but he did. Still, Peter was forgiven. It's good to know that we can be forgiven too. When we're human and we slip up, Jesus is ready to take us back when we ask him to.

NOTES

don't let this happen to me! Father, you can do anything. Don't make me suffer by having me drink from this cup.[m] But do what you want, and not what I want."*

37When Jesus came back and found the disciples sleeping, he said to Simon Peter, "Are you asleep? Can't you stay awake for just one hour? 38Stay awake and pray that you will not be tested. You want to do what is right, but you are weak."

39Jesus went back and prayed the same prayer. 40But when he returned to the disciples, he found them sleeping again. They simply could not keep their eyes open, and they did not know what to say.

41When Jesus returned to the disciples the third time, he said, "Are you still sleeping and resting?[n] Enough of that! The time has come for the Son of Man to be handed over to sinners. 42Get up! Let's go. The one who will betray me is already here."

Jesus Is Arrested
(Matthew 26.47–56; Luke 22.47–53; John 18.3–12)

43Jesus was still speaking, when Judas the betrayer came up. He was one of the twelve disciples, and a mob of men armed with swords and clubs were with him. They had been sent by the chief priests, the nation's leaders, and the teachers of the Law of Moses. 44Judas had told them ahead of time, "Arrest the man I greet with a kiss.[o] Tie him up tight and lead him away."

45Judas walked right up to Jesus and said, "Teacher!" Then Judas kissed him, 46and the men grabbed Jesus and arrested him.*

47Someone standing there pulled out a sword. He struck the servant of the high priest and cut off his ear.

48Jesus said to the mob, "Why do you come with swords and clubs to arrest me like a criminal? 49Day after day I was with you and taught in the temple, and you didn't arrest me. But what the Scriptures say must come true."

50All of Jesus' disciples ran off and left him. 51One of them was a young man who was wearing only a linen cloth. And when the men grabbed him, 52he left the cloth behind and ran away naked.

Jesus Is Questioned by the Jewish Council
(Matthew 26.57–68; Luke 22.54, 55, 63–71; John 18.13, 14, 19–24)

53Jesus was led off to the high priest. Then the chief priests, the nation's leaders, and the teachers of the Law of Moses all met together. 54Peter had followed at a distance. And when he reached the courtyard of the high priest's house, he sat down with the guards to warm himself beside a fire.

55The chief priests and the whole council tried to find someone to accuse Jesus of a crime, so they could put him to death. But they could not find anyone to accuse him. 56Many people did tell lies against Jesus, but they did not agree on what they said.

---

[m]*by having me drink from this cup*: See the note at 10.38. [n]*Are you still sleeping and resting?*: Or "You may as well keep on sleeping and resting." [o]*greet with a kiss*: It was the custom for people to greet each other with a kiss on the cheek.

14.35 **DEATH IS NOT NICE** Sometimes we try to make death look beautiful. Jesus didn't think it is. He knew that death is the penalty for sin. He was a young man, and he didn't want to die. But he knew it was the only way to finish the work he came to do so we could be saved. For that reason he accepted a cruel death on a cross, taking the punishment for our sins onto himself.

14.46 **WHY WAS JESUS ARRESTED?** The religious leaders and the mob had convinced themselves that Jesus was a criminal. That was their excuse. The leaders, of course, felt threatened by him. But Jesus said he was arrested so that what the Scriptures say could come true. Long years before this the Hebrew prophets had predicted Jesus' arrest.

NOTES

57Finally, some men stood up and lied
about him. They said, 58"We heard
him say he would tear down this temple that we built. He also claimed that
in three days he would build another
one without any help." 59But even
then they did not agree on what they
said.
60The high priest stood up in the
council and asked Jesus, "Why don't
you say something in your own defense? Don't you hear the charges
they are making against you?"
61But Jesus kept quiet and did not
say a word. The high priest asked
him another question, "Are you the
Messiah, the Son of the glorious
God?"[p]*
62"Yes, I am!" Jesus answered.

"Soon you will see
the Son of Man
sitting at the right side[q]
of God All-Powerful,
and coming with the clouds
of heaven."

63At once the high priest ripped his
robe apart and shouted, "Why do we
need more witnesses? 64You heard
him claim to be God! What is your
decision?" They all agreed that he
should be put to death.
65Some of the people started spit-
ting on Jesus. They blindfolded him,
hit him with their fists, and said, "Tell
us who hit you!" Then the guards
took charge of Jesus and beat him.

Peter Says He Does Not Know Jesus
(Matthew 26.69–75; Luke 22.56–62; John 18.15–18, 25–27)

66While Peter was still in the courtyard, a servant girl of the high priest
came up 67and saw Peter warming
himself by the fire. She stared at him
and said, "You were with Jesus from
Nazareth!"
68Peter replied, "That's not true! I
don't know what you're talking
about. I don't have any idea what you
mean." He went out to the gate, and
a rooster crowed.[r]
69The servant girl saw Peter again
and said to the people standing there,
"This man is one of them!"
70"No, I'm not!" Peter replied.
A little while later some of the people said to Peter, "You certainly are
one of them. You're a Galilean!"
71This time Peter began to curse
and swear, "I don't even know the
man you're talking about!"
72Right away the rooster crowed
a second time. Then Peter remembered that Jesus had told him, "Before a rooster crows twice, you will
say three times that you don't know
me." So Peter started crying.*

Pilate Questions Jesus
(Matthew 27.1, 2, 11–14; Luke 23.1–5; John 18.28–38)

15 Early the next morning the
chief priests, the nation's leaders, and the teachers of the Law of
Moses met together with the whole
Jewish council. They tied up Jesus
and led him off to Pilate.
2He asked Jesus, "Are you the king
of the Jews?"
"Those are your words," Jesus
answered.
3The chief priests brought many

---

[p]*Son of the glorious God*: "Son of God" was one of the titles used for the kings of Israel. [q]*right side*: See the note at 12.36. [r]*a rooster crowed*: These words are not in some manuscripts.

14.61 **JESUS IS THE MESSIAH** Who is "the Messiah"? Jesus, the eternal Son of God who had always lived in heaven with his Father, came to earth. He came to save us from our sins, our disobedience toward God. But when Jesus said that he is the Son of God, the Messiah, the authorities hated him even more. They couldn't get over their pride, like many people today who reject the Messiah and find that putting their faith in Jesus is hard for them to do.

14.72 **PETER WAS SORRY** Poor Peter did exactly what he promised Jesus he would never do. He realized it right away and he was heartbroken. That's the key. Peter was sorry he sinned. It would not be hard for Jesus to forgive him.

NOTES

charges against Jesus. 4Then Pilate
questioned him again, "Don't you
have anything to say? Don't you hear
what crimes they say you have
done?" 5But Jesus did not answer,
and Pilate was amazed.

The Death Sentence
(Matthew 27.15–26; Luke 23.13–25; John 18.39—19.16)

6During Passover, Pilate always
freed one prisoner chosen by the people. 7And at that time there was a
prisoner named Barabbas. He and
some others had been arrested for
murder during a riot. 8The Jewish
people now came and asked Pilate
to set a prisoner free, just as he usually did.
9Pilate asked them, "Do you want
me to free the king of the Jews?"
10Pilate knew that the chief priests
had brought Jesus to him because
they were jealous.
11But the chief priests told the
crowd to ask Pilate to free Barabbas.
12Then Pilate asked the crowd,
"What do you want me to do with
this man you say is[s] the king of the
Jews?"
13They yelled, "Nail him to a
cross!"
14Pilate asked, "But what crime has
he done?"
"Nail him to a cross!" they yelled
even louder.
15Pilate wanted to please the
crowd. So he set Barabbas free. Then
he ordered his soldiers to beat Jesus
with a whip and nail him to a cross.*

Soldiers Make Fun of Jesus
(Matthew 27.27–30; John 19.2, 3)

16The soldiers led Jesus inside the
courtyard of the fortress[t] and called
together the rest of the troops.
17They put a purple robe[u] on him,
and on his head they placed a crown
that they had made out of thorn
branches. 18They made fun of Jesus
and shouted, "Hey, you king of the
Jews!" 19Then they beat him on the
head with a stick. They spit on him
and kneeled down and pretended to
worship him.
20When the soldiers had finished
making fun of Jesus, they took off
the purple robe. They put his own
clothes back on him and led him off
to be nailed to a cross. 21Simon from
Cyrene happened to be coming in
from a farm, and they forced him to
carry Jesus' cross. Simon was the father of Alexander and Rufus.

Jesus Is Nailed to a Cross
(Matthew 27.31–44; Luke 23.27–43; John 19.17–27)

22The soldiers took Jesus to Golgotha, which means "Place of a Skull."[v]
23There they gave him some wine
mixed with a drug to ease the pain,
but he refused to drink it.
24They nailed Jesus to a cross and
gambled to see who would get his
clothes.* 25It was about nine o'clock
in the morning when they nailed him
to the cross. 26On it was a sign that
told why he was nailed there. It read,
"This is the King of the Jews."

---

[s] *this man you say is*: These words are not in some manuscripts. [t] *fortress*: The place where the Roman governor stayed. It was probably at Herod's palace west of Jerusalem, though it may have been Fortress Antonio, north of the temple, where the Roman troops were stationed. [u] *purple robe*: This was probably a Roman soldier's robe. [v] *"Place of a Skull"*: The place was probably given this name because it was near a large rock in the shape of a human skull.

15.15 **OBEY YOUR CONSCIENCE** Pilate didn't do what his conscience told him to. He suspected that Jesus was telling the truth about himself. But Pilate was afraid to go against the will of the mob. Besides, he was afraid that the authorities at Rome might think he was allowing disloyalty against the emperor. We need to pray that we will always he guided by the truth, whether or not it pleases someone else.

15.24 **THE SON OF GOD NAILED TO A CROSS** They nailed Jesus to a cross, the way criminals were put to death. It's called *crucifixion*, a painful death in which nails were driven (*continued*)

NOTES

27-28The soldiers also nailed two
criminals on crosses, one to the right
of Jesus and the other to his left.[w]
29People who passed by said terrible things about Jesus. They shook
their heads and shouted, "Ha! So
you're the one who claimed you
could tear down the temple and build
it again in three days. 30Save yourself
and come down from the cross!"
31The chief priests and the teachers
of the Law of Moses also made fun
of Jesus. They said to each other, "He
saved others, but he can't save himself. 32If he is the Messiah, the king
of Israel, let him come down from
the cross! Then we will see and believe." The two criminals also said
cruel things to Jesus.

The Death of Jesus

(Matthew 27.45–56; Luke 23.44–49; John 19.28–30)

33About noon the sky turned dark
and stayed that way until around
three o'clock. 34Then about that time
Jesus shouted, "Eloi, Eloi, lema sabachthani?"[x] which means, "My
God, my God, why have you deserted
me?"
35Some of the people standing
there heard Jesus and said, "He is
calling for Elijah."[y] 36One of them
ran and grabbed a sponge. After he
had soaked it in wine, he put it on
a stick and held it up to Jesus. He
said, "Let's wait and see if Elijah will
come[z] and take him down!" 37Jesus
shouted and then died.
38At once the curtain in the temple[a]* tore in two from top to bottom.*
39A Roman army officer was standing in front of Jesus. When the officer
saw how Jesus died, he said, "This
man really was the Son of God!"
40-41Some women were looking on
from a distance. They had come with
Jesus to Jerusalem. But even before
this they had been his followers and
had helped him while he was in Galilee. Mary Magdalene and Mary the
mother of the younger James and of
Joseph were two of these women. Salome was also one of them.

Jesus Is Buried

(Matthew 27.57–61; Luke 23.50–56; John 19.38–42)

42It was now the evening before the
Sabbath, and the Jewish people were
getting ready for that sacred day.
43A man named Joseph from Arimathea was brave enough to ask Pilate
for the body of Jesus. Joseph was a
highly respected member of the Jewish council, and he was also waiting
for God's kingdom to come.*
44Pilate was surprised to hear that
Jesus was already dead, and he
called in the army officer to find out

---

[w]*left*: Some manuscripts add, "So the Scriptures came true which say, 'He was accused of being a criminal.' " [x]*Eloi . . . sabachthani*: These words are in Aramaic, a language spoken in Palestine during the time of Jesus. [y]*Elijah*: The name "Elijah" sounds something like "Eloi," which means "my God." [z]*see if Elijah will come*: See the note at 6.15. [a]*curtain in the temple*: There were two curtains in the temple. One was at the entrance, and the other separated the holy place from the most holy place that the Jewish people thought of as God's home on earth. The second curtain is probably the one which is meant.

(*continued*) through the hands and into a plank. The plank was then placed across an upright beam. When the victim's feet were nailed to the beam, the cross was lifted up with the criminal nailed to it. Then the foot of the cross was dropped into a hole to keep the cross upright. They did this to the Son of God.

15.38 **WHY WAS THE CURTAIN TORN?** That seems like an unimportant event for Mark to mention during such dreadful happenings. But the torn curtain was very important. The curtain in the temple separated the holiest place of all from everyone but the high priest. The torn curtain meant that everyone could come to God because Jesus had opened the way for us by his death.

15.43 **JOSEPH FROM ARIMATHEA** Joseph from Arimathea was an important man, but he loved Jesus too. It took courage for him to go and ask for the body of Jesus and take charge of its (*continued*)

NOTES

if Jesus had been dead very long. 45After the officer told him, Pilate let Joseph have Jesus' body.

46Joseph bought a linen cloth and took the body down from the cross. He had it wrapped in the cloth, and he put it in a tomb that had been cut into solid rock. Then he rolled a big stone against the entrance to the tomb.

47Mary Magdalene and Mary the mother of Joseph were watching and saw where the body was placed.

Jesus Is Alive
(Matthew 28.1–8; Luke 24.1–12; John 20.1–10)

16 After the Sabbath, Mary Magdalene, Salome, and Mary the mother of James bought some spices to put on Jesus' body. 2Very early on Sunday morning, just as the sun was coming up, they went to the tomb. 3On their way, they were asking one another, "Who will roll the stone away from the entrance for us?" 4But when they looked, they saw that the stone had already been rolled away. And it was a huge stone!*

5The women went into the tomb, and on the right side they saw a young man in a white robe sitting there. They were alarmed.

6The man said, "Don't be alarmed! You are looking for Jesus from Nazareth, who was nailed to a cross. God has raised him to life, and he is not here. You can see the place where they put his body. 7Now go and tell his disciples, and especially Peter, that he will go ahead of you to Galilee. You will see him there, just as he told you."

8When the women ran from the tomb, they were confused and shaking all over. They were too afraid to tell anyone what had happened.

Jesus Appears to Mary Magdalene[b]
(Matthew 28.9, 10; John 20.11–18)

9Very early on the first day of the week, after Jesus had risen to life, he appeared to Mary Magdalene. Earlier he had forced seven demons out of her. 10She left and told his friends, who were crying and mourning. 11Even though they heard that Jesus was alive and that Mary had seen him, they would not believe it.

Jesus Appears to Two Disciples
(Luke 24.13–35)

12Later, Jesus appeared in another form to two disciples, as they were on their way out of the city. 13But when these disciples told what had happened, the others would not believe.

What Jesus' Followers Must Do
(Matthew 28.16–20; Luke 24.36–49; John 20.19–23; Acts 1.6–8)

14Afterwards, Jesus appeared to his eleven disciples as they were eating. He scolded them because they were too stubborn to believe the ones who had seen him after he had been raised to life.* 15Then he told them:

Go and preach the good news
to everyone in the world.

---

[b]*Jesus Appears to Mary Magdalene*: Mark 16.9-20 is not in some manuscripts.

(continued) burial. Most men in his position would not have wanted to risk their reputation. What about us? Are we afraid to be associated with Jesus because of what our unbelieving friends might think?

16.4 **THE STONE WAS ROLLED AWAY** Can you imagine the noise of that heavy stone being rolled back from the door of Jesus' tomb? If anybody had tried to steal Jesus' body, the guards at the tomb would have caught them at once. But no one was taken prisoner because God himself rolled back the stone, the guards ran away, and Jesus walked out of the tomb alive.

16.14 **THE EARLY DISCIPLES WERE NOT EASY BELIEVERS** The disciples were not ready to believe that Jesus was risen from death. To them, as to us, death seemed very final. They *(continued)*

NOTES

16Anyone who believes me and
is baptized will be saved. But
anyone who refuses to believe
me will be condemned.
17Everyone who believes me will
be able to do wonderful things.
By using my name they will force
out demons, and they will speak
new languages. 18They will
handle snakes and will drink
poison and not be hurt. They will
also heal sick people by placing
their hands on them.

Jesus Returns to Heaven
(Luke 24.50–53; Acts 1.9–11)

19After the Lord Jesus had said
these things to the disciples, he was
taken back up to heaven where he
sat down at the right side[c] of God.*
20Then the disciples left and
preached everywhere. The Lord was
with them, and the miracles they
worked proved that their message
was true.

ANOTHER OLD ENDING TO MARK'S GOSPEL[d]

9-10The women quickly told Peter
and his friends what had happened.
Later, Jesus sent the disciples to the
east and to the west with his sacred
and everlasting message of how people can be saved forever.

---

[c]*right side*: See the note at 12.36. [d]*Another Old Ending to Mark's Gospel*: Some manuscripts and early translations have both this shorter ending and the longer one (verses 9-20).

(continued) were discouraged and downhearted. But they couldn't deny what their own eyes told them at last. They saw Jesus alive, and only then were they ready to spend their whole lives telling others about Jesus.

16.19 **WHERE IS JESUS NOW?** Jesus had come from heaven in the beginning. He was the eternal Son of God, who was born with a human body and lived and died among us. Now he is alive forevermore. Jesus is our living Savior in heaven, from which he will return.

NOTES

ABOUT THIS BOOK

God's love is for everyone! Jesus came into the world to be the Savior of all people! These are two of the main thoughts in this book. Several of the best known stories that Jesus used for teaching about God's love are found only in Luke's Gospel: The Good Samaritan (10.25–37), A Lost Sheep (15.1–7), and A Lost Son (15.11–32). Only Luke tells how Jesus visited in the home of a hated tax collector (19.1–10) and promised life in paradise to a dying criminal (23.39–43).

Luke mentions God's Spirit more than any of the other New Testament writers. For example, the power of the Spirit was with John the Baptist from the time he was born (1.15). And the angel promised Mary, "The Holy Spirit will come down to you . . . So your child will be called the holy Son of God" (1.35). Jesus followed the Spirit (4.1,14,18; 10.21) and taught that the Spirit is God's greatest gift (11.13).

Luke shows how important prayer was to Jesus. Jesus prayed often: after being baptized (3.21), before choosing the disciples (6.12), before asking his disciples who they thought he was (9.18), and before giving up his life on the cross (23.34,46). From Luke we learn of three stories that Jesus told to teach about prayer (11.5–9; 18.1–8, 9–14).

An important part of Luke's story is the way in which he shows the concern of Jesus for the poor: the good news is preached to them (4.18; 7.22), they receive God's blessings (6.20), they are invited to the great feast (14.13,21), the poor man Lazarus is taken to heaven by angels (16.20,22), and Jesus commands his disciples to sell what they have and give the money to the poor (12.33).

To make sure that readers would understand that Jesus was raised physically from death, Luke reports that the risen Jesus ate a piece of fish (24.42,43). There could be no mistake about the risen Jesus: he was not a ghost. His being raised from death was real and not someone's imagination. Luke also wrote another book—the Acts of the Apostles—to show what happened to Jesus' followers after he was raised from death and taken up to heaven. No other Gospel has a second volume that continues the story.

Luke closes this first book that he wrote by telling that Jesus returned to heaven. But right before Jesus leaves, he tells his disciples:

> *The Scriptures say that the Messiah must suffer, then three days later he will rise from death. They also say that all people of every nation must be told in my name to turn to God, in order to be forgiven. So beginning in Jerusalem, you must tell everything that has happened.* (24.46–48)

A QUICK LOOK AT THIS BOOK

1. Why Luke Wrote This Book (1.1–4)
2. The Births of John the Baptist and Jesus (1.5—2.52)
3. The Message of John the Baptist (3.1–20)
4. The Baptism and Temptation of Jesus (3.21—4.13)
5. Jesus' Ministry in Galilee (4.14—9.50)
6. Jesus Goes from Galilee to Jerusalem (9.51—19.27)
7. Jesus' Last Week: His Trial and Death (19.28—23.56)
8. Jesus Is Alive (24.1–12)
9. Jesus Appears. He Is Taken to Heaven (24.13–53)

1 Many people have tried to tell the
story of what God has done
among us. 2They wrote what we had
been told by the ones who were there
in the beginning and saw what happened. 3So I made a careful study[a]
of everything and then decided to
write and tell you exactly what took
place. Honorable Theophilus,*
4I have done this to let you know if
what you have heard is true.

An Angel Tells about the Birth of John

5When Herod was king of Judea,
there was a priest by the name of
Zechariah from the priestly group of
Abijah. His wife Elizabeth was from
the family of Aaron.[b] 6Both of them
were good people and pleased the
Lord God by obeying all that he had
commanded. 7But they did not have
children. Elizabeth could not have
any, and both Zechariah and Elizabeth were already old.
8One day Zechariah's group of
priests were on duty, and he was
serving God as a priest. 9According
to the custom of the priests, he had
been chosen to go into the Lord's
temple that day and to burn incense,[c]
10while the people stood outside
praying.
11All at once an angel from the
Lord came and appeared to Zechariah at the right side of the altar.*
12Zechariah was confused and afraid
when he saw the angel. 13But the angel told him:

---

[a] *a careful study*: Or "a study from the beginning." [b] *Abijah . . . Aaron*: The Jewish priests were divided into two groups, and one of these groups was named after Abijah. Each group served in the temple once a year for two weeks at a time. Aaron, the brother of Moses, was the first priest. [c] *burn incense*: This was done twice a day, once in the morning and again in the late afternoon.

1.3 **LUKE WAS A CAREFUL STUDENT** Luke writes that he "made a careful study." He was different from other biblical writers because he was a Gentile, a non-Jew. He was also a medical doctor. Like a good doctor, Luke paid a lot of attention to details in his writings (this book and the Acts of the Apostles). Notice his detailed interest in the events surrounding the birth of Jesus.

1.11 **WHAT ARE ANGELS?** The word "angel" means messenger, and is usually a messenger from heaven. Angels were especially created by God, and they are not the same as humans. The angel who spoke to Zechariah was Gabriel, whose name means "God is great." Gabriel is a special messenger whom we see doing important tasks for God all through the Bible.

NOTES

Don't be afraid, Zechariah!
God has heard your prayers.
Your wife Elizabeth will have a
son, and you must name him
John. 14His birth will make you
very happy, and many people
will be glad. 15Your son will be
a great servant of the Lord. He
must never drink wine or beer,
and the power of the Holy Spirit
will be with him from the time
he is born.
16John will lead many people
in Israel to turn back to the Lord
their God. 17He will go ahead of
the Lord with the same power
and spirit that Elijah[d] had. And
because of John, parents will be
more thoughtful of their
children. And people who now
disobey God will begin to think
as they ought to. That is how
John will get people ready for
the Lord.

18Zechariah said to the angel,
"How will I know this is going to happen? My wife and I are both very
old."

19The angel answered, "I am Gabriel, God's servant, and I was sent
to tell you this good news. 20You have
not believed what I have said. So you
will not be able to say a thing until
all this happens. But everything will
take place when it is supposed
to."*

21The crowd was waiting for Zechariah and kept wondering why he
was staying so long in the temple.
22When he did come out, he could
not speak, and they knew he had seen
a vision. He motioned to them with
his hands, but did not say a thing.
23When Zechariah's time of service
in the temple was over, he went
home. 24Soon after that, his wife was
expecting a baby, and for five months
she did not leave the house. She said
to herself, 25"What the Lord has done
for me will keep people from looking
down on me."[e]

An Angel Tells about the Birth of Jesus

26One month later God sent the angel Gabriel to the town of Nazareth
in Galilee 27with a message for a virgin named Mary. She was engaged
to Joseph from the family of King
David. 28The angel greeted Mary and
said, "You are truly blessed! The
Lord is with you."

29Mary was confused by the angel's words and wondered what they
meant. 30Then the angel told Mary,
"Don't be afraid! God is pleased with
you, 31and you will have a son. His
name will be Jesus. 32He will be great
and will be called the Son of God
Most High. The Lord God will make
him king, as his ancestor David was.
33He will rule the people of Israel forever, and his kingdom will never
end."

34Mary asked the angel, "How can
this happen? I am not married!"*

35The angel answered, "The Holy
Spirit will come down to you, and
God's power will come over you. So

---

[d]*Elijah*: The prophet Elijah was known for his power to work miracles. [e]*keep people from looking down on me*: When a married woman could not have children, it was thought that the Lord was punishing her.

1.20 **BELIEVING GOD'S MESSAGE IS OUR GREATEST NEED** Zechariah, the father of John the Baptist, couldn't believe the angel's message. He was thinking about his and his wife's lack of natural ability to have children. Our most important need is to believe God for all of life. He is the God of nature, and nature obeys his commands.

1.34 **WHY WAS JESUS BORN TO A VIRGIN?** God might have chosen to let his Son be born in a natural way. But he didn't. Over and over again in the Bible we come across happenings that are not "natural"—they're *supernatural*. God wants us to understand that he is in charge of this world, and our being saved depends on his divine work, not on what we do for ourselves.

NOTES

your child will be called the holy Son
of God. 36Your relative Elizabeth is
also going to have a son, even though
she is old. No one thought she could
ever have a baby, but in three months
she will have a son. 37Nothing is impossible for God!"

38Mary said, "I am the Lord's servant! Let it happen as you have said."
And the angel left her.

Mary Visits Elizabeth

39A short time later Mary hurried
to a town in the hill country of Judea.
40She went into Zechariah's home,
where she greeted Elizabeth. 41When
Elizabeth heard Mary's greeting, her
baby moved within her.

The Holy Spirit came upon Elizabeth.* 42Then in a loud voice she said
to Mary:

God has blessed you more
than any other woman! He has
also blessed the child you will
have. 43Why should the mother
of my Lord come to me? 44As
soon as I heard your greeting,
my baby became happy and
moved within me. 45The Lord
has blessed you because you
believed that he will keep his
promise.

Mary's Song of Praise

46Mary said:
47With all my heart
I praise the Lord,
and I am glad
because of God my Savior.*
48He cares for me,
his humble servant.
From now on,
all people will say
God has blessed me.
49God All-Powerful has done
great things for me,
and his name is holy.
50He always shows mercy
to everyone
who worships him.
51The Lord has used
his powerful arm
to scatter those
who are proud.
52He drags strong rulers
from their thrones
and puts humble people
in places of power.
53He gives the hungry
good things to eat,
and he sends the rich away
with nothing in their hands.
54He helps his servant Israel
and is always merciful
to his people.
55He made this promise
to our ancestors,
to Abraham and his family
forever!

56Mary stayed with Elizabeth
about three months. Then she went
back home.

The Birth of John the Baptist

57When Elizabeth's son was born,
58her neighbors and relatives heard
how kind the Lord had been to her,
and they too were glad.

59Eight days later they did for the
child what the Law of Moses commands.[f] They were going to name

[f] *what the Law of Moses commands*: This refers to circumcision. It is the cutting off of skin from the private part of Jewish boys eight days after birth to show that they belong to the Lord. See Word List: **Circumcise.**

1.41 **CAN UNBORN BABIES BE HAPPY?** The unborn John the Baptist was happy. The word translated "moved" also means "leaped." The unborn baby John was joyful in the presence of his unborn cousin Jesus. This passage shows us that unborn babies are people even when they are still inside their mothers.

1.47 **LET'S SING TO GOD** God's people have always been a singing people. We sing with joy, just as Mary sang, because God has saved us from our sins. If we have something to sing about we will sing, and such singing will usually be happy. But sometimes our songs are rightly sad because our sins caused our Savior's suffering on the cross. We also sing because of our thanksgiving for what God has done for us.

NOTES

Step 7

MARY—a woman whose greatness is measured by a humble spirit toward God and others

LUKE 1.46–56

The character trait of humility can be seen in the life of Mary, the mother of Jesus. Just think about Mary's situation during her early teenage years. She was pregnant, unmarried, and uncertain of her future! That would be a humbling set of circumstances for anyone. However, humility is more than being in a humiliating situation. Real humility is the attitude of a person's heart toward God. It shows its true self by not being self-centered.

When the angel Gabriel told Mary that she was going to have a baby, she reacted with natural surprise! When the angel then said it would be the Messiah, she was humbled. Her response to all this news? "I am the Lord's servant." Basically her attitude was, "I'm here to serve God in whatever way possible. If that means getting pregnant without ever being with a man and trying to explain that to my fiancé Joseph, to my parents, and to all the neighbors, that's fine, because I am a servant."

Fast-forward to a scene in Jesus' childhood when Mary found him teaching in the temple at age twelve. Mary didn't nudge the person next to her and say, "That's my boy!" She knew that all the glory should go to the God she served. Jesus taught thousands, and did many miracles, but Mary never spoke out and said, "Give me a little credit, I brought him into the world." Mary remained humble, always giving credit where credit was due.

STEP LOOK BACK 7

Perhaps the best example of Mary's humble spirit is found in her song of praise on the occasion of visiting her cousin Elizabeth's home. She said,

"With all my heart I praise the Lord, and I am glad because of God my Savior. He cares for me, his humble servant."

True humility always directs praise away from ourselves and toward God and others. How would we rate ourselves on the humility scale today?

Ready for Step 8? Turn to page 29 of* InStep's *introduction.

him Zechariah, after his father.
60But Elizabeth said, "No! His name
is John."*
61The people argued, "No one in
your family has ever been named
John." 62So they motioned to Zechariah to find out what he wanted to
name his son.
63Zechariah asked for a writing
tablet. Then he wrote, "His name is
John." Everyone was amazed.
64Right away Zechariah started
speaking and praising God.
65All the neighbors were frightened because of what had happened,
and everywhere in the hill country
people kept talking about these
things. 66Everyone who heard about
this wondered what this child would
grow up to be. They knew that the
Lord was with him.

Zechariah Praises the Lord

67The Holy Spirit came upon Zechariah, and he began to speak:

68Praise the Lord,
the God of Israel!
He has come
to save his people.
69Our God has given us
a mighty Savior[g]
from the family
of David his servant.
70Long ago the Lord promised
by the words
of his holy prophets*
71to save us from our enemies
and from everyone
who hates us.
72God said he would be kind
to our people and keep
his sacred promise.
73He told our ancestor Abraham
74that he would rescue us
from our enemies.
Then we could serve him
without fear,
75by being holy and good
as long as we live.

76You, my son, will be called
a prophet of God
in heaven above.
You will go ahead of the Lord
to get everything ready
for him.
77You will tell his people
that they can be saved
when their sins
are forgiven.
78God's love and kindness
will shine upon us
like the sun that rises
in the sky.[h]
79On us who live
in the dark shadow
of death
this light will shine
to guide us
into a life of peace.

80As John grew up, God's Spirit
gave him great power. John lived in
the desert until the time he was sent
to the people of Israel.

The Birth of Jesus
(Matthew 1.18–25)

2 About that time Emperor Augustus gave orders for the names of
all the people to be listed in record

---

[g]*a mighty Savior*: The Greek text has "a horn of salvation." In the Scriptures animal horns are often a symbol of great strength. [h]*like the sun that rises in the sky*: Or "like the Messiah coming from heaven."

1.60 **"HIS NAME IS JOHN"** The name John means "God has been kind." It would be John the Baptist's job to announce the coming of the Messiah. Even John's name announces God's kindness in sending his Son to save us from our sins.

1.70 **GOD'S PLAN TO SAVE US IS VERY OLD** Zechariah praised God for his saving work. He said that God long ago planned to send a Savior and that John the Baptist would tell of the Savior's coming. It is important to realize that our being saved was not just a wonderful, unplanned happening in history. It has been God's great plan since ages past.

NOTES

books.[i]* 2These first records were
made when Quirinius was governor
of Syria.[j]

3Everyone had to go to their own
hometown to be listed. 4So Joseph
had to leave Nazareth in Galilee and
go to Bethlehem in Judea. Long ago
Bethlehem had been King David's
hometown, and Joseph went there
because he was from David's family.*

5Mary was engaged to Joseph and
traveled with him to Bethlehem. She
was soon going to have a baby,
6and while they were there, 7she gave
birth to her first-born[k] son. She
dressed him in baby clothes[l] and laid
him in a feed box, because there was
no room for them in the inn.

The Shepherds

8That night in the fields near Bethlehem some shepherds were guarding their sheep. 9All at once an angel
came down to them from the Lord,
and the brightness of the Lord's glory
flashed around them. The shepherds
were frightened.* 10But the angel
said, "Don't be afraid! I have good
news for you, which will make everyone happy. 11This very day in King
David's hometown a Savior was born
for you. He is Christ the Lord.
12You will know who he is, because
you will find him dressed in baby
clothes and lying in a feed box."

13Suddenly many other angels
came down from heaven and joined
in praising God. They said:

14"Praise God in heaven!
Peace on earth to everyone
who pleases God."

15After the angels had left and gone
back to heaven, the shepherds said
to each other, "Let's go to Bethlehem
and see what the Lord has told us
about." 16They hurried off and found
Mary and Joseph, and they saw the
baby lying in the feed box.

17When the shepherds saw Jesus,
they told his parents what the angel
had said about him. 18Everyone listened and was surprised. 19But Mary
kept thinking about all this and wondering what it meant.

20As the shepherds returned to
their sheep, they were praising God
and saying wonderful things about
him. Everything they had seen and
heard was just as the angel had said.

21Eight days later Jesus' parents
did for him what the Law of Moses
commands.[m] And they named him
Jesus, just as the angel had told Mary
when he promised she would have
a baby.

Simeon Praises the Lord

22The time came for Mary and Joseph to do what the Law of Moses

---

[i]*names . . . listed in record books*: This was done so that everyone could be made to pay taxes to the Emperor. [j]*Quirinius was governor of Syria*: It is known that Quirinius made a record of the people in A.D. 6 or 7. But the exact date of the record taking that Luke mentions is not known. [k]*first-born*: The Jewish people said that the first-born son in each of their families belonged to the Lord. [l]*dressed him in baby clothes*: The Greek text has "wrapped him in wide strips of cloth," which was how young babies were dressed. [m]*what the Law of Moses commands*: See note at 1.59.

2.1 **WHO WAS EMPEROR AUGUSTUS?** Augustus was the ruler of the Roman empire, of which Palestine was a small part. He reigned for 45 years, from before the birth of Jesus until several years after. "Augustus" was a title meaning "sacred."

2.4 **JOSEPH WAS FROM DAVID'S FAMILY** Bethlehem was the town where David was born. Its name means "house of bread." This was an interesting name because Jesus called himself "the bread of life." The town of Bethlehem is still there today.

2.9 **WHY THE SHEPHERDS?** Wouldn't the Messiah's birth be announced first to the emperor at Rome, or at least to the high priest of the temple in Jerusalem? No—the humble shepherds were told first. It makes us wonder about what people think is important—and what God thinks.

NOTES

says a mother is supposed to do after
her baby is born.[n]
They took Jesus to the temple in
Jerusalem and presented him to the
Lord, 23just as the Law of the Lord
says, "Each first-born[o] baby boy belongs to the Lord." 24The Law of the
Lord also says that parents have to
offer a sacrifice, giving at least a pair
of doves or two young pigeons. So
that is what Mary and Joseph did.
25At this time a man named Simeon
was living in Jerusalem. Simeon was
a good man. He loved God and was
waiting for God to save the people
of Israel. God's Spirit came to him*
26and told him that he would not die
until he had seen Christ the Lord.
27When Mary and Joseph brought
Jesus to the temple to do what the
Law of Moses says should be done
for a new baby, the Spirit told Simeon
to go into the temple. 28Simeon took
the baby Jesus in his arms and
praised God,

29"Lord, I am your servant,
and now I can die in peace,
because you have kept
your promise to me.
30With my own eyes I have seen
what you have done
to save your people,
31and foreign nations
will also see this.
32Your mighty power is a light
for all nations,
and it will bring honor
to your people Israel."

33Jesus' parents were surprised at
what Simeon had said. 34Then he
blessed them and told Mary, "This
child of yours will cause many people
in Israel to fall and others to stand.
The child will be like a warning sign.
Many people will reject him, 35and
you, Mary, will suffer as though you
had been stabbed by a dagger. But
all this will show what people are
really thinking."

Anna Speaks about the Child Jesus

36The prophet Anna was also there
in the temple. She was the daughter
of Phanuel from the tribe of Asher,
and she was very old. In her youth
she had been married for seven
years, but her husband died.* 37And
now she was eighty-four years old.[p]
Night and day she served God in the
temple by praying and often going
without eating.[q]
38At that time Anna came in and
praised God. She spoke about the
child Jesus to everyone who hoped
for Jerusalem to be set free.

The Return to Nazareth

39After Joseph and Mary had done
everything that the Law of the Lord
commands, they returned home to
Nazareth in Galilee. 40The child Jesus grew. He became strong and
wise, and God blessed him.*

---

[n]*after her baby is born*: After a Jewish mother gave birth to a son, she was considered "unclean" and had to stay home until he was circumcised (see the note at 1.59). Then she had to stay home for another 33 days, before offering a sacrifice to the Lord. [o]*first-born*: See the note at 2.7. [p]*And now she was eighty-four years old*: Or "And now she had been a widow for eighty-four years." [q]*without eating*: The Jewish people sometimes went without eating (also called "fasting") to show their love for God and to become better followers.

2.25 **SIMEON SAW HIS LORD** Once again God picked an ordinary man. Simeon recognized the baby Jesus as the Savior who he knew was to come. Simeon said that God had kept his promise, and that Jews and non-Jews would be blessed by the Messiah's coming. Even Mary and Joseph were surprised by Simeon's words.

2.36 **ANNA TOLD THE PEOPLE ABOUT JESUS** Anna was a prophetess, someone who told others the word of God. She did what we should always be seeking to do—telling others about Jesus. All true believers in Jesus are prophets in this way.

2.40 **JESUS GREW UP LIKE OTHER CHILDREN** During his life on earth, Jesus was God in human form. But being truly human, he had to grow up in the same way we all do. So Jesus *(continued)*

NOTES

The Boy Jesus in the Temple

41Every year Jesus' parents went
to Jerusalem for Passover. 42And
when Jesus was twelve years old,
they all went there as usual for the
celebration. 43After Passover his parents left, but they did not know that
Jesus had stayed on in the city.
44They thought he was traveling with
some other people, and they went a
whole day before they started looking for him. 45When they could not
find him with their relatives and
friends, they went back to Jerusalem
and started looking for him there.
46Three days later they found Jesus
sitting in the temple, listening to the
teachers and asking them questions.
47Everyone who heard him was surprised at how much he knew and at
the answers he gave.
48When his parents found him,
they were amazed. His mother said,
"Son, why have you done this to us?
Your father and I have been very
worried, and we have been searching
for you!"
49Jesus answered, "Why did you
have to look for me? Didn't you
know that I would be in my Father's
house?"[r] 50But they did not understand what he meant.
51Jesus went back to Nazareth with
his parents and obeyed them. His
mother kept on thinking about all
that had happened.
52Jesus became wise, and he grew
strong. God was pleased with him
and so were the people.

The Preaching of John the Baptist
(Matthew 3.1–12; Mark 1.1–8; John 1.19–28)

3 For fifteen years[s] Emperor Tiberius had ruled that part of the
world. Pontius Pilate was governor
of Judea, and Herod[t] was the ruler
of Galilee. Herod's brother, Philip,
was the ruler in the countries of Itu-
rea and Trachonitis, and Lysanias
was the ruler of Abilene.* 2Annas and
Caiaphas were the Jewish high
priests.[u]
At that time God spoke to Zechariah's son John, who was living in the
desert. 3So John went along the Jordan Valley, telling the people, "Turn
back to God and be baptized! Then
your sins will be forgiven." 4Isaiah
the prophet wrote about John when
he said,

"In the desert
someone is shouting,
'Get the road ready
for the Lord!
Make a straight path
for him.
5Fill up every valley
and level every mountain
and hill.
Straighten the crooked paths
and smooth out
the rough roads.
6Then everyone will see
the saving power of God.' "

7Crowds of people came out to be
baptized, but John said to them, "You
bunch of snakes! Who warned you
to run from the coming judgment?
8Do something to show that you really have given up your sins. Don't
start saying that you belong to Abraham's family. God can turn these

---

[r] *in my Father's house*: Or "doing my Father's work."
[s] *For fifteen years*: This was either A.D. 28 or 29, and Jesus was about thirty years old (see 3.23).
[t] *Herod*: Herod Antipas, the son of Herod the Great.
[u] *Annas and Caiaphas . . . high priests*: Annas was high priest from A.D. 6 until 15. His son-in-law Caiaphas was high priest from A.D. 18 until 37.

(*continued*) had the experience of growing and learning. But his unusual ability to grow in wisdom surprised everyone. He understood a lot more about the things of God than any twelve-year-old they had ever met.

3.1 **WHO RULED THE ROMAN WORLD IN JESUS' DAY?** Tiberius, the adopted son of Augustus, was emperor of Rome at the time of Jesus' ministry and death. He reigned during the years 14 through 37. The Herod brothers ruled in Palestine with the permission of Tiberius. Strange to say, the Herods were not even Jews, but Idumeans. The Idumeans were longtime enemies of the Jews. The high priests, not kings, had been the true rulers of the Jews for over five hundred years before the time of Christ.

NOTES

stones into children for Abraham.[v] 9An ax is ready to cut the trees down at their roots. Any tree that does not produce good fruit will be cut down and thrown into a fire."

10The crowds asked John, "What should we do?"

11John told them, "If you have two coats, give one to someone who doesn't have any. If you have food, share it with someone else."

12When tax collectors[w] came to be baptized, they asked John, "Teacher, what should we do?"

13John told them, "Don't make people pay more than they owe."

14Some soldiers asked him, "And what about us? What do we have to do?"

John told them, "Don't force people to pay money to make you leave them alone. Be satisfied with your pay."

15Everyone became excited and wondered, "Could John be the Messiah?"

16John said, "I am just baptizing with water. But someone more powerful is going to come, and I am not good enough even to untie his sandals.[x] He will baptize you with the Holy Spirit and with fire.* 17His threshing fork[y] is in his hand, and he is ready to separate the wheat from the husks. He will store the wheat in his barn and burn the husks with a fire that never goes out."

18In many different ways John preached the good news to the people. 19But to Herod the ruler, he said, "It was wrong for you to take Herodias, your brother's wife." John also said that Herod had done many other bad things.* 20Finally, Herod put John in jail, and this was the worst thing he had done.

The Baptism of Jesus

(Matthew 3.13–17; Mark 1.9–11)

21After everyone else had been baptized, Jesus himself was baptized. Then as he prayed, the sky opened up, 22and the Holy Spirit came down upon him in the form of a dove. A voice from heaven said, "You are my own dear Son, and I am pleased with you."

The Ancestors of Jesus

(Matthew 1.1–17)

23When Jesus began to preach, he was about thirty years old. Everyone thought he was the son of Joseph. But his family went back through Heli,* 24Matthat, Levi, Melchi, Jannai, Joseph, 25Mattathias, Amos, Nahum, Esli, Naggai, 26Maath, Mattathias, Semein, Josech, Joda;

27Joanan, Rhesa, Zerubbabel, Shealtiel, Neri, 28Melchi, Addi,

---

[v] *children for Abraham*: The Jewish people thought they were God's chosen people because of God's promises to their ancestor Abraham. [w] *tax collectors*: These were usually Jewish people who paid the Romans for the right to collect taxes. They were hated by other Jews who thought of them as traitors to their country and to their religion. [x] *untie his sandals*: This was the duty of a slave. [y] *threshing fork*: After Jewish farmers had trampled out the grain, they used a large fork to pitch the grain and the husks into the air. Wind would blow away the light husks, and the grain would fall back to the ground, where it could be gathered up.

3.16 **JOHN BAPTIZED WITH WATER** John was telling the people that being baptized with water was not the main thing. John was showing by water baptism that baptism by the Spirit of God is the important thing. Water baptism is only a sign of baptism by the Spirit.

3.19 **JOHN WASN'T ALWAYS NICE** Sometimes it's hard to tell people the truth they need to hear. When we do, we can get into trouble. Some think we should never say things that make people angry or upset. Do you think John should have told Herod he was wrong to marry his brother's wife?

3.23 **TWO LISTS OF ANCESTORS** This list is quite different from the one in Matthew's Gospel. A lot of scholars think the reason is that this list traces the ancestors of Jesus through his mother Mary. Notice that it doesn't actually call Heli the father of Joseph.

NOTES

Cosam, Elmadam, Er, 29 Joshua,
Eliezer, Jorim, Matthat, Levi;
30 Simeon, Judah, Joseph, Jonam,
Eliakim, 31 Melea, Menna, Mattatha,
Nathan, David, 32 Jesse, Obed, Boaz,
Salmon, Nahshon;
33 Amminadab, Admin, Arni,
Hezron, Perez, Judah, 34 Jacob, Isaac,
Abraham, Terah, Nahor, 35 Serug,
Reu, Peleg, Eber, Shelah;
36 Cainan, Arphaxad, Shem, Noah,
Lamech, 37 Methuselah, Enoch,
Jared, Mahalaleel, Kenan, 38 Enosh,
and Seth.

The family of Jesus went all the way back to Adam and then to God.

Jesus and the Devil

(Matthew 4.1–11; Mark 1.12, 13)

4 When Jesus returned from the
Jordan River, the power of the
Holy Spirit was with him, and the
Spirit led him into the desert. 2 For
forty days Jesus was tested by the
devil, and during that time he went
without eating.[z] When it was all over,
he was hungry.*
3 The devil said to Jesus, "If you
are God's Son, tell this stone to turn
into bread."
4 Jesus answered, "The Scriptures
say, 'No one can live only on food.' "
5 Then the devil led Jesus up to a
high place and quickly showed him
all the nations on earth. 6 The devil
said, "I will give all this power and
glory to you. It has been given to me,
and I can give it to anyone I want
to. 7 Just worship me, and you can
have it all."
8 Jesus answered, "The Scriptures
say:

'Worship the Lord your God
and serve only him!' "

9 Finally, the devil took Jesus to Jerusalem and had him stand on top
of the temple. The devil said, "If you
are God's Son, jump off. 10-11 The
Scriptures say:

'God will tell his angels
to take care of you.
They will catch you
in their arms,
and you will not hurt
your feet on the stones.' "

12 Jesus answered, "The Scriptures
also say, 'Don't try to test the Lord
your God!' "
13 After the devil had finished testing Jesus in every way possible, he
left him for a while.

Jesus Begins His Work

(Matthew 4.12–17; Mark 1.14, 15)

14 Jesus returned to Galilee with the
power of the Spirit. News about him
spread everywhere. 15 He taught in
the Jewish meeting places, and
everyone praised him.

The People of Nazareth Turn against Jesus

(Matthew 13.53–58; Mark 6.1–6)

16 Jesus went back to Nazareth,
where he had been brought up, and
as usual he went to the meeting place
on the Sabbath. When he stood up
to read from the Scriptures,* 17 he was
given the book of Isaiah the prophet.
He opened it and read,

---

[z] *went without eating*: See the note at 2.37.

4.2 **WHAT IS THE DEVIL'S WORK?** The devil's personal name is Satan. "Devil" means accuser or deceiver, and "Satan" means enemy. From his names we can see that the devil's work is to deceive and attack. He began by attacking God's authority, and he tries to deceive people with clever lies. His effort to deceive Jesus failed. All lies have their beginning with Satan, whom Jesus called "the father of lies."

4.16 **JESUS WENT TO THE MEETING PLACE** The temple was in Jerusalem, many miles away from places like Nazareth. So the people met in their little halls for worship. Be careful to notice that Jesus was not against this custom of the people. He was Lord of the Jewish meeting places, too, and he attended them on the Sabbath day along with everyone else.

NOTES

18"The Lord's Spirit
has come to me,
because he has chosen me
to tell the good news
to the poor.
The Lord has sent me
to announce freedom
for prisoners,
to give sight to the blind,
to free everyone
who suffers,
19and to say, 'This is the year
the Lord has chosen.'"
20Jesus closed the book, then
handed it back to the man in charge
and sat down. Everyone in the meeting place looked straight at Jesus.
21Then Jesus said to them, "What
you have just heard me read has
come true today."
22All the people started talking
about Jesus and were amazed at the
wonderful things he said. They kept
on asking, "Isn't he Joseph's son?"
23Jesus answered:
You will certainly want to tell
me this saying, "Doctor, first
make yourself well." You will
tell me to do the same things here
in my own hometown that you
heard I did in Capernaum. 24But
you can be sure that no prophets
are liked by the people of their
own hometown.
25Once during the time of
Elijah there was no rain for three
and a half years, and people
everywhere were starving.
There were many widows in
Israel,* 26but Elijah was sent
only to a widow in the town of
Zarephath near the city of Sidon.
27During the time of the prophet
Elisha, many men in Israel had
leprosy.[a] But no one was healed,
except Naaman who lived in
Syria.
28When the people in the meeting
place heard Jesus say this, they became so angry 29that they got up and
threw him out of town. They dragged
him to the edge of the cliff on which
the town was built, because they
wanted to throw him down from
there. 30But Jesus slipped through the
crowd and got away.

A Man with an Evil Spirit
(Mark 1.21–28)

31Jesus went to the town of Capernaum in Galilee and taught the people on the Sabbath. 32His teaching
amazed them because he spoke with
power.* 33There in the Jewish meeting place was a man with an evil
spirit. He yelled out, 34"Hey, Jesus
of Nazareth, what do you want with
us? Are you here to get rid of us? I
know who you are! You are God's
Holy One."
35Jesus ordered the evil spirit to be
quiet and come out. The demon threw
the man to the ground in front of
everyone and left without harming
him.
36They all were amazed and kept
saying to each other, "What kind of
teaching is this? He has power to order evil spirits out of people!"
37News about Jesus spread all over
that part of the country.

---

[a]*leprosy*: In biblical times the word "leprosy" was used for many different kinds of skin diseases.

4.25 **JESUS TOLD THE TRUTH** The people in Nazareth were slow to believe that this young man who had grown up among them was the one who would make Isaiah's prophecies come true. But Jesus told them that people outside of Israel would be blessed by having faith in him. The people were so angry they wanted to throw him off a cliff. It wasn't what they wanted to hear, but Jesus told them the truth.

4.32 **THERE WAS POWER IN JESUS** Jesus spoke with power, and he had power over evil spirits. He was an amazing teacher. Usually, Jewish religious teachers would depend on the opinions of experts, who depended on experts before them. Jesus, the Son of God, got his power to teach and to heal directly from God.

NOTES

Jesus Heals Many People
(Matthew 8.14–17; Mark 1.29–34)

38 Jesus left the meeting place and
went to Simon's home. When Jesus
got there, he was told that Simon's
mother-in-law was sick with a high
fever. 39 So Jesus went over to her
and ordered the fever to go away.
Right then she was able to get up
and serve them.
40 After the sun had set, people with
all kinds of diseases were brought
to Jesus. He put his hands on each
one of them and healed them.*
41 Demons went out of many people
and shouted, "You are the Son of
God!" But Jesus ordered the demons
not to speak because they knew he
was the Messiah.
42 The next morning Jesus went out
to a place where he could be alone,
and crowds came looking for him.
When they found him, they tried to
stop him from leaving. 43 But Jesus
said, "People in other towns must
hear the good news about God's kingdom. That's why I was sent."* 44 So
he kept on preaching in the Jewish
meeting places in Judea.[b]

Jesus Chooses His First Disciples
(Matthew 4.18–22; Mark 1.16–20)

5 Jesus was standing on the shore
of Lake Gennesaret,[c] teaching
the people as they crowded around
him to hear God's message. 2 Near
the shore he saw two boats left there
by some fishermen who had gone to
wash their nets. 3 Jesus got into the
boat that belonged to Simon and
asked him to row it out a little way
from the shore. Then Jesus sat down[d]
in the boat to teach the crowd.
4 When Jesus had finished speaking, he told Simon, "Row the boat
out into the deep water and let your
nets down to catch some fish."
5 "Master," Simon answered, "we
have worked hard all night long and
have not caught a thing. But if you
tell me to, I will let the nets down."*
6 They did it and caught so many fish
that their nets began ripping apart.
7 Then they signaled for their partners in the other boat to come and
help them. The men came, and together they filled the two boats so
full that they both began to sink.
8 When Simon Peter saw this happen, he kneeled down in front of Jesus and said, "Lord, don't come near
me! I am a sinner." 9 Peter and everyone with him were completely surprised at all the fish they had caught.
10 His partners James and John, the
sons of Zebedee, were surprised too.
Jesus told Simon, "Don't be afraid!
From now on you will bring in people
instead of fish." 11 The men pulled
their boats up on the shore. Then they
left everything and went with Jesus.

---

[b] *Judea*: Some manuscripts have "Galilee."
[c] *Lake Gennesaret:* Another name for Lake Galilee.
[d] *sat down*: Teachers in the ancient world, including Jewish teachers, usually sat down when they taught.

4.40 **JESUS LOVED HIS ENEMIES** Jesus went around healing the very people who would turn against him at last. He knew they would hate him, but he loved them and cared for their needs anyway. As we think about this, we should be glad to receive Jesus as our own Lord. The Son of God was kind to us when we didn't deserve it. He loved us before we loved him.

4.43 **JESUS SHARED THE GOOD NEWS** As we read about his life and work, we realize that Jesus was a man of action. He seems to be always on the move. He intended for everyone to hear the good news about the kingdom of God. So Jesus became our example in this way. He not only did kind things, but he shared the truth about his kingdom with everyone he met.

5.5 **OBEDIENCE BRINGS SUCCESS** Simon could have laughed at Jesus' idea to let the fishing nets down once again. But Simon did as Jesus commanded him, and the nets were overloaded with fish. Too often we follow our own ideas and end up disappointed. But listening to Jesus will result in greater success than we dreamed.

NOTES

Jesus Heals a Man
(Matthew 8.1–4; Mark 1.40–45)

12Jesus came to a town where there
was a man who had leprosy.[e] When
the man saw Jesus, he kneeled down
to the ground in front of Jesus and
begged, "Lord, you have the power
to make me well, if only you wanted
to."*
13Jesus put his hand on him and
said, "I do want to! Now you are
well." At once the man's leprosy disappeared. 14Jesus told him, "Don't
tell anyone about this, but go and
show yourself to the priest. Then take
a gift to the temple, just as Moses
commanded, and everyone will know
that you have been healed."[f]
15News about Jesus kept spreading. Large crowds came to listen to
him teach and to be healed of their
diseases. 16But Jesus would often go
to some place where he could be
alone and pray.

Jesus Heals a Crippled Man
(Matthew 9.1–8; Mark 2.1–12)

17One day some Pharisees and experts in the Law of Moses sat listening to Jesus teach. They had come
from every village in Galilee and Judea and from Jerusalem.
God had given Jesus the power to
heal the sick, 18and some people
came carrying a crippled man on a
mat. They tried to take him inside
the house and put him in front of Jesus. 19But because of the crowd, they
could not get him to Jesus. So they
went up on the roof,[g] where they removed some tiles and let the mat
down in the middle of the room.
20When Jesus saw how much faith
they had, he said to the crippled man,
"My friend, your sins are forgiven."*
21The Pharisees and the experts began arguing, "Jesus must think he
is God! Only God can forgive sins."
22Jesus knew what they were
thinking, and he said, "Why are you
thinking that? 23Is it easier for me
to tell this crippled man that his sins
are forgiven or to tell him to get up
and walk? 24But now you will see that
the Son of Man has the right to forgive sins here on earth." Jesus then
said to the man, "Get up! Pick up
your mat and walk home."
25At once the man stood up in front
of everyone. He picked up his mat
and went home, giving thanks to
God. 26Everyone was amazed and
praised God. What they saw surprised them, and they said, "We have
seen a great miracle today!"

Jesus Chooses Levi
(Matthew 9.9–13; Mark 2.13–17)

27Later, Jesus went out and saw a
tax collector[h] named Levi sitting at
the place for paying taxes. Jesus said
to him, "Come with me." 28Levi left
everything and went with Jesus.
29In his home Levi gave a big

---

[e] *leprosy*: See the note at 4.27. [f] *everyone will know that you have been healed*: People with leprosy had to be examined by a priest and told that they were well (that is, "clean") before they could once again live a normal life in the Jewish community. The gift that Moses commanded was the sacrifice of some lambs together with flour mixed with olive oil. [g] *roof*: In Palestine the houses usually had a flat roof. Stairs on the outside led up to the roof, which was made of beams and boards covered with packed earth. Luke says that the roof was made of (clay) tiles, which were also used for making roofs in New Testament times. [h] *tax collector*: See the note at 3.12.

5.12 **DOES JESUS WANT TO HELP US?** The man with leprosy may have been unsure of Jesus. He believed Jesus *could* heal him, but he had to learn that Jesus really *wanted* to heal him. How happy is the day when we find out that Jesus really wants the very best for us, and he will give what is best when we ask him.

5.20 **HOW DOES FAITH WORK?** Jesus knew that the people who brought the crippled man had faith. How did he know that? They were *determined* to come to him. They even went up on the roof and tore it open so they could let their crippled friend down at Jesus' feet. Real faith will not be discouraged.

NOTES

dinner for Jesus. Many tax collectors
and other guests were also there.
30The Pharisees and some of their
teachers of the Law of Moses grumbled to Jesus' disciples, "Why do you
eat and drink with those tax collectors and other sinners?"*
31Jesus answered, "Healthy people
don't need a doctor, but sick people
do. 32I didn't come to invite good people to turn to God. I came to invite
sinners."

People Ask about Going without Eating

(Matthew 9.14–17; Mark 2.18–22)

33Some people said to Jesus,
"John's followers often pray and go
without eating,[i] and so do the followers of the Pharisees. But your disciples never go without eating or
drinking."
34Jesus told them, "The friends of
a bridegroom don't go without eating
while he is still with them. 35But the
time will come when he will be taken
from them. Then they will go without
eating."
36Jesus then told them these
sayings:

No one uses a new piece of
cloth to patch old clothes. The
patch would shrink and make
the hole even bigger.*
37No one pours new wine into
old wineskins. The new wine
would swell and burst the old
skins.[j] Then the wine would be
lost, and the skins would be
ruined. 38New wine must be put
only into new wineskins.
39No one wants new wine after
drinking old wine. They say,
"The old wine is better."

A Question about the Sabbath

(Matthew 12.1–8; Mark 2.23–28)

6 One Sabbath when Jesus and his
disciples were walking through
some wheat fields,[k] the disciples
picked some wheat. They rubbed the
husks off with their hands and
started eating the grain.
2Some Pharisees said, "Why are
you picking grain on the Sabbath?
You're not supposed to do that!"
3Jesus answered, "You surely have
read what David did when he and
his followers were hungry. 4He went
into the house of God and took the
sacred loaves of bread that only
priests were supposed to eat. He not
only ate some himself, but even gave
some to his followers."
5Jesus finished by saying, "The
Son of Man is Lord over the Sabbath."*

---

[i]*without eating*: See the note at 2.37. [j]*swell and burst the old skins*: While the juice from grapes was becoming wine, it would swell and stretch the skins in which it had been stored. If the skins were old and stiff, they would burst. [k]*walking through some wheat fields*: It was the custom to let hungry travelers pick grains of wheat.

5.30 **WHO ARE THE SINNERS?** Jesus says he came to invite sinners to turn to God. Does that mean some of us aren't sinners and don't need God? Not at all. Jesus was saying that people who *confess* their sins are welcome. People who think they're already good enough cannot come into God's kingdom.

5.36 **OLD AND NEW DON'T MIX WELL** Some people try to "tack Jesus on," thinking that faith can be mixed with unbelieving ways. But you can't build a Christian life on old habits any more than you can put new wine in old wineskins without bursting them, or put a new patch on old cloth without tearing it. We begin life all over again when we become followers of Jesus.

6.5 **THE SABBATH WAS A DAY FOR DOING GOOD** A lot of what Jesus wanted the Jews to know about the Sabbath (Saturday) can be applied to the Lord's day (Sunday) for Christians. It's a special day on which most of us have the privilege of serving God in greater ways than we can on other days. There are people in need everywhere. Many have not known the love and mercy of Jesus. We can take his love to them on the Lord's day.

NOTES

A Man with a Crippled Hand
(Matthew 12.9–14; Mark 3.1–6)

6 On another Sabbath[l] Jesus was
teaching in a Jewish meeting place,
and a man with a crippled right hand
was there. 7 Some Pharisees and
teachers of the Law of Moses kept
watching Jesus to see if he would
heal the man. They did this because
they wanted to accuse Jesus of doing
something wrong.

8 Jesus knew what they were thinking. So he told the man to stand up
where everyone could see him. And
the man stood up. 9 Then Jesus asked
the people, "On the Sabbath should
we do good deeds or evil deeds?
Should we save someone's life or destroy it?"

10 After he had looked around at
everyone, he told the man, "Stretch
out your hand." He did, and his bad
hand became completely well.

11 The teachers and the Pharisees
were furious and started saying to
each other, "What can we do about
Jesus?"

Jesus Chooses His Twelve Apostles
(Matthew 10.1–4; Mark 3.13–19)

12 About that time Jesus went off
to a mountain to pray, and he spent
the whole night there. 13 The next
morning he called his disciples together and chose twelve of them to
be his apostles.* 14 One was Simon,
and Jesus named him Peter. Another
was Andrew, Peter's brother. There
were also James, John, Philip, Bartholomew, 15 Matthew, Thomas, and
James the son of Alphaeus. The rest
of the apostles were Simon, known
as the Eager One,[m] 16 Jude, who was
the son of James, and Judas Iscariot,[n]
who later betrayed Jesus.

Jesus Teaches, Preaches, and Heals
(Matthew 4.23–25)

17 Jesus and his apostles went down
from the mountain and came to some
flat, level ground. Many other disciples were there to meet him. Large
crowds of people from all over Judea,
Jerusalem, and the coastal cities of
Tyre and Sidon were there too.
18 These people had come to listen to
Jesus and to be healed of their diseases. All who were troubled by evil
spirits were also healed.* 19 Everyone
was trying to touch Jesus, because
power was going out from him and
healing them all.

Blessings and Troubles
(Matthew 5.1–12)

20 Jesus looked at his disciples and
said:

God will bless you people
who are poor.
His kingdom belongs to you!*
21 God will bless
you hungry people.

---

[l] *On another Sabbath*: Some manuscripts have a reading which may mean "the Sabbath after the next." [m] *known as the Eager One*: The word "eager" translates the Greek word "zealot," which was a name later given to the members of a Jewish group that resisted and fought against the Romans. [n] *Iscariot*: This may mean "a man from Kerioth" (a place in Judea). But more probably it means "a man who was a liar" or "a man who was a betrayer."

6.13 **WHAT KIND OF DISCIPLE ARE YOU?** Jesus called twelve close disciples (apostles) and most of them remained faithful until the day of their death. But one—Judas—was unfaithful. The Bible shows us that we don't live in a perfect world. Even among those who are called Christians there are those who are not true to Jesus, who betray him by their actions and thoughts. This is a warning to each of us, to be honest with God every day.

6.18 **HOW COULD JESUS HEAL PEOPLE?** Jesus was not a magician. We cannot "learn the art" of healing people in the way Jesus did. Jesus is the Lord from heaven, and he has God's power over nature. He used this power to do good to people and to reveal his heavenly Father's glory.

6.20 **JESUS MADE GREAT PROMISES** God's kingdom will belong to poor people. Hungry people will be fed. Sad people will be happy. Jesus was not promising things the *(continued)*

NOTES

You will have plenty
to eat!
God will bless you people
who are crying.
You will laugh!
22God will bless you when
others hate you and won't have
anything to do with you. God will
bless you when people insult you
and say cruel things about you,
all because you are a follower
of the Son of Man! 23Long ago
your own people did these same
things to the prophets. So when
this happens to you, be happy
and jump for joy! You will have
a great reward in heaven.
24But you rich people
are in for trouble.
You have already had
an easy life!
25You well-fed people
are in for trouble.
You will go hungry!
You people
who are laughing now
are in for trouble.
You are going to cry
and weep!
26You are in for trouble when
everyone says good things about
you. That is what your own
people said about those prophets
who told lies.

Love for Enemies
(Matthew 5.38–48; 7.12a)

27This is what I say to all who will
listen to me:
Love your enemies, and be
good to everyone who hates
you.* 28Ask God to bless anyone
who curses you, and pray for
everyone who is cruel to you.
29If someone slaps you on one
cheek, don't stop that person
from slapping you on the other
cheek. If someone wants to take
your coat, don't try to keep back
your shirt. 30Give to everyone
who asks and don't ask people
to return what they have taken
from you. 31Treat others just as
you want to be treated.
32If you love only someone
who loves you, will God praise
you for that? Even sinners love
people who love them. 33If you
are kind only to someone who
is kind to you, will God be
pleased with you for that? Even
sinners are kind to people who
are kind to them. 34If you lend
money only to someone you
think will pay you back, will God
be pleased with you for that?
Even sinners lend to sinners
because they think they will get
it all back.
35But love your enemies and
be good to them. Lend without
expecting to be paid back.[o] Then
you will get a great reward, and
you will be the true children of
God in heaven. He is good even
to people who are unthankful
and cruel. 36Have pity on others,
just as your Father has pity on
you.

Judging Others
(Matthew 7.1–5)

37Jesus said:
Don't judge others, and God
will not judge you. Don't be hard
on others, and God will not be
hard on you. Forgive others,

---

[o]*without expecting to be paid back*: Some manuscripts have "without giving up on anyone."

(*continued*) people would have *right now*. For instance, in Matthew 5, verse 6, Jesus speaks about being hungry for *righteousness*. When we desire the *right things*, God will finally supply all of our other needs too.

6.27 **WHOM SHOULD YOU LOVE?** Everybody loves his or her friends. But Jesus tells us to love our enemies too. How is that possible? First, it doesn't mean we approve of what our enemies may be doing. It does mean that we see all people as God's special creations. Because our enemies are created by God they are to be treated with respect and kindness whenever we have the chance to do so.

NOTES

Step 9

COMPASSION—Considering how our actions may create reactions in others

LUKE 6.27–36

FIRST PLACE

There are a lot of "firsts" in our friendship; that's what makes it so special. We bought our first tube of lipstick together—"Magenta Madness"! We doubled on our first date. We had each other for moral support the first time we drove a car without supervision. The list goes on and on. But the most memorable first for Vickie and me was experimenting with drugs together. Memorable because it almost killed me.

That part of my life is over now. I'm not part of the drug and drinking scene anymore. I couldn't handle it. It was taking a lot more from me than it was giving. I had to get help.

STEP LOOK AHEAD 9

Vickie's not there yet. I mean, she desperately needs help, but she refuses to get it. She is still denying that anything is wrong. According to her, the problem is with me, not with the drugs. It's been really hard on our friendship.

If I did what I felt like, I would drop Vickie from my life. It would be easier for me, but that wouldn't help her. In fact, it would probably make things worse. I will continue to care about her and give her time to come around. After all, I am learning what should take first place in my life now.

WORTH WAITING FOR

It is good to understand that while our lives are changing, our friends' lives may be staying the same. That means we have to be sensitive and look for ways to encourage them with our successes, not discourage them with their failures. Love and patience may bring them around.

For another "Look Ahead," turn to page 355.

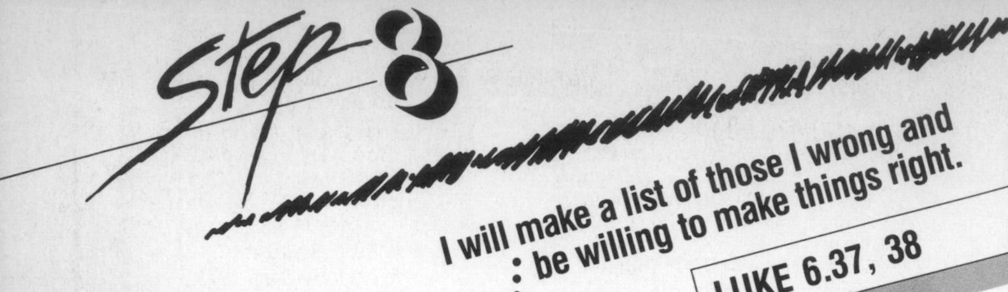

LUKE 6.37, 38

BAD GUYS WEAR WHITE HATS

"Vote for Steve Dobson as Class President"

I can't believe they let Dobson run for an office, let alone win! He is the greatest con artist of all time. The whole school thinks he is bigger than life. After all, he led our team to the state finals. He gets all *A*'s and *B*'s. He dates the head cheerleader. What better choice than Mr. Perfect? If they only knew what I know.

He plays most games spaced out. His girlfriend writes all his papers. And he has perfected cheating on tests, or else the teachers look the other way. He never gets caught—not in school, not on the football field, not in life. I hate him and everyone like him. You used to be able to spot the bad guys; they wore the black hats. Not anymore.

STEP 8 LOOK INSIDE

Jealousy and resentment, although sometimes well founded, are very harmful. The bitterness that results builds up in our lives and cripples us emotionally. We have trouble trusting people because we assume that they are going to take advantage of us—that they are "out to get us." No one is honest. No one is trustworthy. No one cares.

OPEN UP

It is important to open up and talk to people we think have harmed us. We should ask the Lord to help us let go of our feelings of distrust. We may discover that the harm we felt wasn't coming from these people after all; it may have been coming from us.

For another "Look Inside," turn to page 323.

and God will forgive you.* 38If
you give to others, you will be
given a full amount in return. It
will be packed down, shaken
together, and spilling over into
your lap. The way you treat
others is the way you will be
treated.
39Jesus also used some sayings as
he spoke to the people. He said:
Can one blind person lead
another blind person? Won't
they both fall into a ditch? 40Are
students better than their
teacher? But when they are fully
trained, they will be like their
teacher.
41You can see the speck in
your friend's eye. But you don't
notice the log in your own eye.
42How can you say, "My friend,
let me take the speck out of your
eye," when you don't see the log
in your own eye? You showoffs!
First, get the log out of your own
eye. Then you can see how to
take the speck out of your
friend's eye.

A Tree and Its Fruit

(Matthew 7.17–20; 12.34b, 35)

43A good tree cannot produce
bad fruit, and a bad tree cannot
produce good fruit.* 44You can
tell what a tree is like by the fruit
it produces. You cannot pick figs
or grapes from thorn bushes.
45Good people do good things
because of the good in their
hearts. Bad people do bad things
because of the evil in their
hearts. Your words show what
is in your hearts.

Two Builders

(Matthew 7.24–27)

46Why do you keep on saying
that I am your Lord, when you
refuse to do what I say?*
47Anyone who comes and listens
to me and obeys me 48is like
someone who dug down deep
and built a house on solid rock.
When the flood came and the
river rushed against the house,
it was built so well that it didn't
even shake. 49But anyone who
hears what I say and doesn't
obey me is like someone whose
house was not built on solid
rock. As soon as the river rushed
against that house, it was
smashed to pieces!

Jesus Heals an Army Officer's Servant

(Matthew 8.5–13; John 4.43–54)

7 After Jesus had finished teaching
the people, he went to Capernaum. 2In that town an army officer's
servant was sick and about to die.
The officer liked this servant very
much. 3And when he heard about Jesus, he sent some Jewish leaders to
ask him to come and heal the servant.
4The leaders went to Jesus and

6.37 **GOD DOESN'T ASK US TO BE JUDGES** We can't know all about another person the way God does. So we have to be careful what we think about people. God "sees the heart." This means that God understands everything about all of us. What we see is only a small part of another person's life. We ought to be glad we aren't called to be judges. A judge has a terrible responsibility, and most of us don't do a very good job of judging.

6.43 **LET'S INSPECT OUR FRUIT** All believers should be "fruit inspectors." That is to say, we ought to inspect our own lives to make sure that the "fruit" we bear is good because it comes from the right kind of "tree."

6.46 **BUILD ON SOLID ROCK** No one with any sense would build a house on a swamp. And sand is no better—even though it might seem solid enough before the rain comes. But as you look around your world, where do you find a true foundation to build your life on? Ideas come and go, and they turn out to be poor foundations for many unhappy people. Jesus is like a rock that can never fail us. He's the one to build on.

NOTES

begged him to do something. They said, "This man deserves your help! 5He loves our nation and even built us a meeting place." 6So Jesus went with them.

When Jesus was not far from the house, the officer sent some friends to tell him, "Lord, don't go to any trouble for me! I am not good enough for you to come into my house. 7And I am certainly not worthy to come to you. Just say the word, and my servant will get well. 8I have officers who give orders to me, and I have soldiers who take orders from me. I can say to one of them, 'Go!' and he goes. I can say to another, 'Come!' and he comes. I can say to my servant, 'Do this!' and he will do it."*

9When Jesus heard this, he was so surprised that he turned and said to the crowd following him, "In all of Israel I've never found anyone with this much faith!"

10The officer's friends returned and found the servant well.

A Widow's Son

11Soon Jesus and his disciples were on their way to the town of Nain, and a big crowd was going along with them. 12As they came near the gate of the town, they saw people carrying out the body of a widow's only son. Many people from the town were walking along with her.

13When the Lord saw the woman, he felt sorry for her and said, "Don't cry!"

14Jesus went over and touched the stretcher on which the people were carrying the dead boy. They stopped, and Jesus said, "Young man, get up!" 15The boy sat up and began to speak. Jesus then gave him back to his mother.

16Everyone was frightened and praised God. They said, "A great prophet is here with us! God has come to his people."*

17News about Jesus spread all over Judea and everywhere else in that part of the country.

John the Baptist
(Matthew 11.1–19)

18-19John's followers told John everything that was being said about Jesus. So he sent two of them to ask the Lord, "Are you the one we should be looking for? Or must we wait for someone else?"

20When these messengers came to Jesus, they said, "John the Baptist sent us to ask, 'Are you the one we should be looking for? Or are we supposed to wait for someone else?' "

21At that time Jesus was healing many people who were sick or in pain or were troubled by evil spirits, and he was giving sight to a lot of blind people. 22Jesus said to the messengers sent by John, "Go and tell John what you have seen and heard. Blind people are now able to see, and the lame can walk. People who have leprosy[p] are being healed, and the deaf can now hear. The dead are raised to life, and the poor are hearing the good news. 23God will bless everyone

[p]*leprosy*: See the note at 4.27.

7.8 **KNOW WHERE YOU STAND WITH JESUS** The army officer in this passage knew where he stood with Jesus. The officer understood the meaning of authority because he lived by giving and taking orders. He recognized Jesus as his great "commanding officer"—the one who could give an order and it would be done. Jesus honored that man's faith. Do we have faith like this, or do we doubt Jesus' authority?

7.16 **WHO CAN RAISE THE DEAD?** The crowd that saw the widow's son raised to life by a simple command said that Jesus was a prophet. That was true as far as it went. But Jesus was much more than a prophet. He is the Lord of life and death. When we realize this, we also trust him with our own lives—and our own death.

NOTES

who does not reject me because of
what I do."
24After John's messengers had
gone, Jesus began speaking to the
crowds about John:

What kind of person did you
go out to the desert to see? Was
he like tall grass blown about by
the wind?* 25What kind of man
did you really go out to see? Was
he someone dressed in fine
clothes? People who wear
expensive clothes and live in
luxury are in the king's palace.
26What then did you go out to
see? Was he a prophet? He
certainly was! I tell you that he
was more than a prophet. 27In
the Scriptures, God calls John
his messenger and says, "I am
sending my messenger ahead of
you to get things ready for you."
28No one ever born on this earth
is greater than John. But
whoever is least important in
God's kingdom is greater than
John.

29Everyone had been listening to
John. Even the tax collectors[q] had
obeyed God and had done what was
right by letting John baptize them.
30But the Pharisees and the experts
in the Law of Moses refused to obey
God and be baptized by John.
31Jesus went on to say:

What are you people like?
What kind of people are you?*
32You are like children sitting in
the market and shouting to each
other,

"We played the flute,
but you would not dance!
We sang a funeral song,
but you would not cry!"

33John the Baptist did not go
around eating and drinking, and
you said, "John has a demon in
him!" 34But because the Son of
Man goes around eating and
drinking, you say, "Jesus eats
and drinks too much! He is even
a friend of tax collectors and
sinners." 35Yet Wisdom is
shown to be right by what its
followers do.

Simon the Pharisee

36A Pharisee invited Jesus to have
dinner with him. So Jesus went to
the Pharisee's home and got ready
to eat.[r]
37When a sinful woman in that
town found out that Jesus was there,
she bought an expensive bottle of
perfume. 38Then she came and stood
behind Jesus. She cried and started
washing his feet with her tears and
drying them with her hair. The
woman kissed his feet and poured
the perfume on them.
39The Pharisee who had invited Jesus saw this and said to himself, "If
this man really were a prophet, he
would know what kind of woman is
touching him! He would know that
she is a sinner."
40Jesus said to the Pharisee, "Simon, I have something to say to you."
"Teacher, what is it?" Simon replied.

---

[q] *tax collectors*: See the note at 3.12. [r] *got ready to eat*: On special occasions the Jewish people often followed the Greek and Roman custom of lying down on their left side and leaning on their left elbow, while eating with their right hand. This is how the woman could come up behind Jesus and wash his feet (see verse 38).

7.24 **WHO WAS JOHN THE BAPTIST?** We know from what we have read so far that he was the son of Zechariah and Elizabeth, and that he was the man who baptized Jesus. But he was also the living link between the Old Testament and the New Testament. He was a faithful Old Testament kind of prophet. But there were things about God's plan that John did not yet understand. There were things that Jesus came to reveal about God's kingdom that John did not know.

7.31 **LET'S NOT BE TOO HARD TO PLEASE** Elsewhere we read that Jesus said believers should come to him like children. Here's a way *not* to be like children. Sometimes a child is hard to satisfy, like the people who criticized John the Baptist and Jesus for opposite things. We ought to be *childlike*, but not *childish*.

NOTES

41Jesus told him, "Two people were
in debt to a moneylender. One of
them owed him five hundred silver
coins, and the other owed him fifty.*
42Since neither of them could pay
him back, the moneylender said that
they didn't have to pay him anything.
Which one of them will like him
more?"
43Simon answered, "I suppose it
would be the one who had owed more
and didn't have to pay it back."
"You are right," Jesus said.
44He turned toward the woman and
said to Simon, "Have you noticed this
woman? When I came into your
home, you didn't give me any water
so I could wash my feet. But she has
washed my feet with her tears and
dried them with her hair. 45You didn't
greet me with a kiss, but from the
time I came in, she has not stopped
kissing my feet. 46You didn't even
pour olive oil on my head,[s] but she
has poured expensive perfume on my
feet. 47So I tell you that all her sins
are forgiven, and that is why she has
shown great love. But anyone who
has been forgiven only a little will
show only a little love."
48Then Jesus said to the woman,
"Your sins are forgiven."
49Some other guests started saying
to one another, "Who is this who
dares to forgive sins?"
50But Jesus told the woman, "Because of your faith, you are now
saved.[t] May God give you peace!"

Women Who Helped Jesus

8 Soon after this, Jesus was going
through towns and villages, telling the good news about God's kingdom. His twelve apostles were with
him, 2and so were some women who
had been healed of evil spirits and
all sorts of diseases. One of the
women was Mary Magdalene,[u] who
once had seven demons in her.*
3Joanna, Susanna, and many others
had also used what they owned to
help Jesus[v] and his disciples. Joanna's husband Chuza was one of
Herod's officials.[w]

A Story about a Farmer

(Matthew 13.1–9; Mark 4.1–9)

4When a large crowd from several
towns had gathered around Jesus, he
told them this story:
5A farmer went out to scatter
seed in a field. While the farmer
was doing it, some of the seeds
fell along the road and were
stepped on or eaten by birds.
6Other seeds fell on rocky
ground and started growing. But
the plants did not have enough
water and soon dried up. 7Some
other seeds fell where thorn
bushes grew up and choked the

[s]*washed my feet . . . greet me with a kiss . . . pour olive oil on my head*: Guests in a home were usually offered water so they could wash their feet, because most people either went barefoot or wore sandals and would come in the house with very dusty feet. Guests were also greeted with a kiss on the cheek, and special ones often had sweet-smelling olive oil poured on their head. [t]*saved*: Or "healed." The Greek word may have either meaning. [u]*Magdalene*: Meaning "from Magdala," a small town on the western shore of Lake Galilee. There is no hint that she is the sinful woman in 7.36-50. [v]*used what they owned to help Jesus*: Women often helped Jewish teachers by giving them money. [w]*Herod's officials*: Herod Antipas, the son of Herod the Great.

7.41 **HOW MUCH DO WE OWE GOD?** The story about forgiveness was aimed at Simon, Jesus' host at dinner. Simon the Pharisee thought he was better than the woman that Jesus forgave. If only Simon could have known how much he also needed forgiveness, then he would have loved Jesus as much as the woman did. But Simon didn't seem to understand how much he really needed Jesus' forgiveness.

8.2 **EVERYONE CAN BE A SERVANT** Many of us want to be bosses, but Jesus honors us just by letting us be his servants. This was the way it was with the men and women who traveled with Jesus. Notice also that Chuza, one of Herod's officials, is mentioned in the list. The greatest of us can also be great servants.

NOTES

plants. 8The rest of the seeds fell
on good ground where they grew
and produced a hundred times
as many seeds.

When Jesus had finished speaking,
he said, "If you have ears, pay
attention!"

Why Jesus Used Stories
(Matthew 13.10–17; Mark 4.10–12)

9Jesus' disciples asked him what
the story meant.* 10So he answered:

I have explained the secrets
about God's kingdom to you, but
for others I can only use stories.
These people look, but they don't
see, and they hear, but they don't
understand.

Jesus Explains the Story about the Farmer
(Matthew 13.18–23; Mark 4.13–20)

11This is what the story means:
The seed is God's message,
12and the seeds that fell along
the road are the people who hear
the message. But the devil comes
and snatches the message out of
their hearts, so that they will not
believe and be saved. 13The
seeds that fell on rocky ground
are the people who gladly hear
the message and accept it. But
they don't have deep roots, and
they believe only for a little
while. As soon as life gets hard,
they give up. 14The seeds that
fell among the thorn bushes are
also people who hear the
message. But they are so eager
for riches and pleasures that
they never produce anything.
15Those seeds that fell on good
ground are the people who listen
to the message and keep it in
good and honest hearts. They
last and produce a harvest.

Light
(Mark 4.21–25)

16No one lights a lamp and
puts it under a bowl or under a
bed. A lamp is always put on a
lampstand, so that people who
come into a house will see the
light.* 17There is nothing hidden
that will not be found. There is
no secret that will not be well
known. 18Pay attention to how
you listen! Everyone who has
something will be given more,
but people who have nothing
will lose what little they think
they have.

Jesus' Mother and Brothers
(Matthew 12.46–50; Mark 3.31–35)

19Jesus' mother and brothers went
to see him, but because of the crowd
they could not get near him.
20Someone told Jesus, "Your mother
and brothers are standing outside
and want to see you."

21Jesus answered, "My mother and
my brothers are those people who
hear and obey God's message."

A Storm
(Matthew 8.23–27; Mark 4.35–41)

22One day Jesus and his disciples
got into a boat, and he said, "Let's
cross the lake."[x] They started out,

---

[x] *cross the lake*: To the eastern shore of Lake Galilee, where most of the people were not Jewish.

8.9 **WHICH KIND OF SOIL ARE YOU?** Crops can't grow just anywhere. They must have good soil. The seeds of God's great message can't grow just anywhere either. Those seeds grow in people who have an attitude of obedience to Jesus. In such people, the secrets of God's kingdom grow and blossom, and they also touch other lives and help them to grow in the knowledge of God.

8.16 **WHAT YOU ARE WILL SHINE** A light can't be hidden. So, when all is said and done, what we truly are will be seen at last. It makes a great deal of sense to make sure our light is the truth of Jesus. This is the light that God and everyone can see when we live for Jesus in the world.

NOTES

23and while they were sailing across,
he went to sleep.
Suddenly a windstorm struck the
lake, and the boat started sinking.
They were in danger. 24So they went
to Jesus and woke him up, "Master,
Master! We are about to drown!"
Jesus got up and ordered the wind
and waves to stop. They obeyed, and
everything was calm.* 25Then Jesus
asked the disciples, "Don't you have
any faith?"
But they were frightened and
amazed. They said to each other,
"Who is this? He can give orders to
the wind and the waves, and they
obey him!"

A Man with Demons in Him
(Matthew 8.28–34; Mark 5.1–20)

26Jesus and his disciples sailed
across Lake Galilee and came to
shore near the town of Gerasa.[y]
27As Jesus was getting out of the
boat, he was met by a man from that
town. The man had demons in him.
He had gone naked for a long time
and no longer lived in a house, but
in the graveyard.[z]
28The man saw Jesus and
screamed. He kneeled down in front
of him and shouted, "Jesus, Son of
God in heaven, what do you want
with me? I beg you not to torture me!"
29He said this because Jesus had already told the evil spirit to go out
of him.
The man had often been attacked
by the demon. And even though he
had been bound with chains and leg
irons and kept under guard, he
smashed whatever bound him. Then
the demon would force him out into
lonely places.
30Jesus asked the man, "What is
your name?"
He answered, "My name is Lots."
He said this because there were 'lots'
of demons in him. 31They begged Jesus not to send them to the deep pit,[a]
where they would be punished.
32On a hillside not far from there
a large herd of pigs was feeding. So
the demons begged Jesus to let them
go into the pigs, and Jesus let them
go. 33Then the demons left the man
and went into the pigs. The whole
herd rushed down the steep bank into
the lake and drowned.
34When the men taking care of the
pigs saw this, they ran to spread the
news in the town and on the farms.
35The people went out to see what
had happened, and when they came
to Jesus, they also found the man.
The demons had gone out of him, and
he was sitting there at the feet of Jesus. He had clothes on and was in
his right mind. But the people were
terrified.
36Then all who had seen the man
healed told about it. 37Everyone from
around Gerasa[b] begged Jesus to
leave, because they were so
frightened.
When Jesus got into the boat to
start back, 38the man who had been
healed begged to go with him. But
Jesus sent him off and said,* 39"Go
back home and tell everyone how
much God has done for you." The
man then went all over town, telling
everything that Jesus had done for
him.

---

[y]*Gerasa*: Some manuscripts have "Gergesa." [z]*graveyard*: It was thought that demons and evil spirits lived in graveyards. [a]*deep pit*: The place where evil spirits are kept and punished. [b]*Gerasa*: See the note at 8.26.

8.24 **WHO IS THIS LORD OF STORMS?** It almost seems comical that the disciples had such a hard time believing in Jesus. After all, he was right there with them, and they had seen his other miracles. We have a great advantage: we know the whole of Jesus' life, while they didn't. But many times we are just as slow to believe as the first disciples were. Getting to really know Jesus takes time.

8.38 **WHO MAKES THE BEST WITNESS FOR JESUS?** The man who had the demons sent out of him had a lot to tell—and he did. If you met a great doctor who could treat your serious disease, you would tell everyone. But Jesus is the greatest of doctors who heals our disease of sin. That should give us a lot to tell others about.

NOTES

A Dying Girl and a Sick Woman
(Matthew 9.18–26; Mark 5.21–43)

40Everyone had been waiting for Jesus, and when he came back, a crowd was there to welcome him. 41Just then the man in charge of the Jewish meeting place came and kneeled down in front of Jesus. His name was Jairus, and he begged Jesus to come to his home 42because his twelve-year-old child was dying. She was his only daughter.

While Jesus was on his way, people were crowding all around him. 43In the crowd was a woman who had been bleeding for twelve years. She had spent everything she had on doctors,[c] but none of them could make her well.

44As soon as she came up behind Jesus and barely touched his clothes, her bleeding stopped.

45"Who touched me?" Jesus asked.

While everyone was denying it, Peter said, "Master, people are crowding all around and pushing you from every side."[d]

46But Jesus answered, "Someone touched me, because I felt power going out from me." 47The woman knew that she could not hide, so she came trembling and kneeled down in front of Jesus. She told everyone why she had touched him and that she had been healed right away.

48Jesus said to the woman, "You are now well because of your faith. May God give you peace!"*

49While Jesus was speaking, someone came from Jairus' home and said, "Your daughter has died! Why bother the teacher anymore?"

50When Jesus heard this, he told Jairus, "Don't worry! Have faith, and your daughter will get well."

51Jesus went into the house, but he did not let anyone else go with him, except Peter, John, James, and the girl's father and mother. 52Everyone was crying and weeping for the girl. But Jesus said, "The child is not dead. She is just asleep." 53The people laughed at him because they knew she was dead.

54Jesus took hold of the girl's hand and said, "Child, get up!" 55She came back to life and got right up. Jesus told them to give her something to eat. 56Her parents were surprised, but Jesus ordered them not to tell anyone what had happened.

Instructions for the Twelve Apostles
(Matthew 10.5–15; Mark 6.7–13)

9 Jesus called together his twelve apostles and gave them complete power over all demons and diseases. 2Then he sent them to tell about God's kingdom and to heal the sick. 3He told them, "Don't take anything with you! Don't take a walking stick or a traveling bag or food or money or even a change of clothes.* 4When you are welcomed into a home, stay there until you leave that town. 5If people won't welcome you, leave the town and shake the dust from your feet[e] as a warning to them."

6The apostles left and went from

---

[c] *She had spent everything she had on doctors*: Some manuscripts do not have these words. [d] *from every side*: Some manuscripts add "and you ask, 'Who touched me?' " [e] *shake the dust from your feet*: This was a way of showing rejection.

8.48 **JESUS NOTICES ALL WHO SEEK HIM** The Lord was on his way to the house of Jairus, whose little daughter was dying. Just then a sick woman reached out and touched him. We might think Jesus would have been too busy just then to be bothered with her problem. But Jesus cared about her and healed her. We can be sure that Jesus cares about everyone who comes to him.

9.3 **THE APOSTLES TRAVELED LIGHT** The twelve apostles didn't have much to carry as they went from village to village. That may sound bad, but it's good not to have a lot to haul around. How about us? Are we carrying any "baggage" that keeps us from serving Jesus the way we should?

NOTES

village to village, telling the good news and healing people everywhere.

Herod Is Worried
(Matthew 14.1–12; Mark 6.14–29)

7Herod[f] the ruler heard about all that was happening, and he was worried. Some people were saying that John the Baptist had come back to life.* 8Others were saying that Elijah had come[g] or that one of the prophets from long ago had come back to life. 9But Herod said, "I had John's head cut off! Who is this I hear so much about?" Herod was eager to meet Jesus.

Jesus Feeds Five Thousand
(Matthew 14.13–21; Mark 6.30–44; John 6.1–14)

10The apostles came back and told Jesus everything they had done. He then took them with him to the village of Bethsaida, where they could be alone. 11But a lot of people found out about this and followed him. Jesus welcomed them. He spoke to them about God's kingdom and healed everyone who was sick.

12Late in the afternoon the twelve apostles came to Jesus and said, "Send the crowd to the villages and farms around here. They need to find a place to stay and something to eat. There is nothing in this place. It is like a desert!"*

13Jesus answered, "You give them something to eat."

But they replied, "We have only five small loaves of bread[h] and two fish. If we are going to feed all these people, we will have to go and buy food." 14There were about five thousand men in the crowd.

Jesus said to his disciples, "Have the people sit in groups of fifty." 15They did this, and all the people sat down. 16Jesus took the five loaves and the two fish. He looked up toward heaven and blessed the food. Then he broke the bread and fish and handed them to his disciples to give to the people.

17Everyone ate all they wanted. What was left over filled twelve baskets.

Who Is Jesus?
(Matthew 16.13–19; Mark 8.27–29)

18When Jesus was alone praying, his disciples came to him, and he asked them, "What do people say about me?"*

19They answered, "Some say that

---

[f] *Herod*: Herod Antipas, the son of Herod the Great. [g] *Elijah had come*: Many of the Jewish people expected the prophet Elijah to come and prepare the way for the Messiah. [h] *small loaves of bread*: These would have been flat and round or in the shape of a bun.

9.7 **SIN CAUSES FEAR** This is Herod Antipas, son of King Herod the Great who had tried to murder the baby Jesus (see Matthew 2). The Herod family were not the lawful rulers of the Jews, but the Roman government made them kings anyway. Herod Antipas was afraid because his own sins and the sins of his father were on his conscience. He wanted to learn about Jesus, but it was like someone wanting to learn about a threat. It's too bad he couldn't trust Jesus to take his sins away. Let's not make the same mistake Herod did.

9.12 **WHERE DO WE LOOK?** When the five thousand needed feeding, the apostles looked for a natural way to get the job done. Jesus looked to the power of God, who can do things there is no natural way to do. Do we remember to give God a chance to help us?

9.18 **WHO DO YOU SAY JESUS IS?** This was the question Jesus asked his disciples. But each of us needs to answer that question. If we each can say sincerely that Jesus is the Son of God and our Savior, then we are truly Christians. For Peter, saying Jesus is the Messiah was a first great step of faith.

NOTES

you are John the Baptist or Elijah[i]
or a prophet from long ago who has
come back to life."

20Jesus then asked them, "But who
do you say I am?"

Peter answered, "You are the Messiah sent from God."

21Jesus strictly warned his disciples not to tell anyone what had happened.

Jesus Speaks about His Suffering and Death

(Matthew 16.20–28; Mark 8.30—9.1)

22Jesus told his disciples, "The nation's leaders, the chief priests, and the teachers of the Law of Moses will make the Son of Man suffer terribly. They will reject him and kill him, but three days later he will rise to life."

23Then Jesus said to all the people:

If any of you want to be my
followers, you must forget about
yourself. You must take up your
cross each day and follow me.*
24If you want to save your life,[j]
you will destroy it. But if you give
up your life for me, you will save
it. 25What will you gain, if you
own the whole world but destroy
yourself or waste your life?
26If you are ashamed of me and
my message, the Son of Man will
be ashamed of you when he
comes in his glory and in the
glory of his Father and the holy
angels. 27You can be sure that
some of the people standing here
will not die before they see God's
kingdom.

The True Glory of Jesus

(Matthew 17.1–8; Mark 9.2–8)

28About eight days later Jesus took
Peter, John, and James with him and
went up on a mountain to pray.
29While he was praying, his face
changed, and his clothes became
shining white. 30Suddenly Moses and
Elijah were there speaking with him.
31They appeared in heavenly glory
and talked about all that Jesus'
death[k] in Jerusalem would mean.

32Peter and the other two disciples
had been sound asleep. All at once
they woke up and saw how glorious
Jesus was. They also saw the two
men who were with him.

33Moses and Elijah were about to
leave, when Peter said to Jesus,
"Master, it is good for us to be here!
Let us make three shelters, one for
you, one for Moses, and one for Elijah." But Peter did not know what
he was talking about.*

34While Peter was still speaking,
a shadow from a cloud passed over
them, and they were frightened as
the cloud covered them. 35From the
cloud a voice spoke, "This is my chosen Son. Listen to what he says!"

36After the voice had spoken, Peter,
John, and James saw only Jesus. For
some time they kept quiet and did
not say anything about what they had
seen.

---

[i]*Elijah*: See the note at 9.8. [j]*life*: In verses 24,25 a Greek word which often means "soul" is translated "life" and "yourself." [k]*Jesus' death*: In Greek this is "his departure," which probably includes his rising to life and his return to heaven.

9.23 **WE, TOO, HAVE A CROSS** We can't carry the cross that Jesus carried. Only he could die for our sins. But we have our own crosses that he asks us to carry for him. These crosses are the daily decisions we make to live for Jesus, which include loving and caring for those around us. But sometimes when we follow Jesus others won't like it. Sometimes others will say and do mean things to us, just because we want to be like Jesus. But we should remember that Jesus suffered greatly for us, and certainly we can suffer a little for him.

9.33 **THERE IS A TIME TO BE QUIET** Peter liked to talk. But this time God made him be quiet. The reason? Peter should be listening to Jesus. Our first duty to Jesus is to *listen* to him speaking in his Word. We learn as we listen to Jesus, and then we can obey by having faith in him, doing his works and speaking his words.

NOTES

Jesus Heals a Boy
(Matthew 17.14–18; Mark 9.14–27)

37 The next day Jesus and his three
disciples came down from the mountain and were met by a large crowd.
38 Just then someone in the crowd
shouted, "Teacher, please do something for my son! He is my only child!
39 A demon often attacks him and
makes him scream. It shakes him until he foams at the mouth, and it won't
leave him until it has completely
worn the boy out. 40 I begged your
disciples to force out the demon, but
they couldn't do it."
41 Jesus said to them, "You people
are stubborn and don't have any
faith! How much longer must I be
with you? Why do I have to put up
with you?"
Then Jesus said to the man, "Bring
your son to me."* 42 While the boy
was being brought, the demon attacked him and made him shake all
over. Jesus ordered the demon to
stop. Then he healed the boy and
gave him back to his father. 43 Everyone was amazed at God's great
power.

Jesus Again Speaks about His Death
(Matthew 17.22, 23; Mark 9.30–32)

While everyone was still amazed
at what Jesus was doing, he said to
his disciples, 44 "Pay close attention
to what I am telling you! The Son
of Man will be handed over to his
enemies." 45 But the disciples did not
know what he meant. The meaning
was hidden from them. They could
not understand it, and they were
afraid to ask.

Who Is the Greatest?
(Matthew 18.1–5; Mark 9.33–37)

46 Jesus' disciples were arguing
about which one of them was the
greatest.* 47 Jesus knew what they
were thinking, and he had a child
stand there beside him. 48 Then he
said to his disciples, "When you welcome even a child because of me, you
welcome me. And when you welcome
me, you welcome the one who sent
me. Whichever one of you is the most
humble is the greatest."

For or against Jesus
(Mark 9.38–40)

49 John said, "Master, we saw a
man using your name to force demons out of people. But we told him
to stop, because he is not one of us."
50 "Don't stop him!" Jesus said.
"Anyone who is not against you is
for you."

A Samaritan Village Refuses to Receive Jesus

51 Not long before it was time for
Jesus to be taken up to heaven, he
made up his mind to go to Jerusalem.
52 He sent some messengers on ahead
to a Samaritan village to get things
ready for him. 53 But he was on his
way to Jerusalem, so the people there
refused to welcome him. 54 When the
disciples James and John saw what
was happening, they asked, "Lord,
do you want us to call down fire from
heaven to destroy these people?"[l]

---

[l] *to destroy these people*: Some manuscripts add "as Elijah did."

9.41 **STUBBORNNESS GETS IN FAITH'S WAY** Here we see Jesus scolding people who were stubborn and didn't have faith in God's great power. Do we stubbornly cling to ways of thinking that don't give God enough credit?

9.46 **YOU CAN BE A GREAT PERSON** Everybody should want to count for something in the world. But sometimes we make the mistake of thinking we have to push ahead of other people in order to be noticed. Have you heard about Mother Teresa of India? She didn't want fame, but she became famous by being a servant of others. Pleasing God is what makes us count for something.

NOTES

AND THE WINNER IS . . .

Everything in life is geared to "Who is the best?" "Who came in first?" That is why it is so hard to understand when Jesus says, "Whoever wants to be first has to be last." "Whoever would be great has to be the least." That doesn't make sense. Or does it?

When we honestly come to God and admit we have failed and need his help, then we are on our way to becoming great, God's way. Doesn't it make sense that if God created us he would know what is best for us? But we have to step aside and allow God to take over.

DEAD LAST

We have to give up the false pride that tells us "it's my life; I will live it the way I want to. No one is going to tell me what to do." With this kind of attitude we may be a winner for a while, but eventually we will come in last . . . dead last.

For another "Look Inside," turn to page 505.

55But Jesus turned and corrected
them for what they had said.[m]*
56Then they all went on to another
village.

Three People Who Wanted To Be Followers

(Matthew 8.19–22)

57Along the way someone said to
Jesus, "I'll go anywhere with you!"
58Jesus said, "Foxes have dens, and
birds have nests, but the Son of Man
doesn't have a place to call his own."
59Jesus told someone else to come
with him. But the man said, "Lord,
let me wait until I bury my father."[n]
60Jesus answered, "Let the dead
take care of the dead, while you go
and tell about God's kingdom."
61Then someone said to Jesus, "I
want to go with you, Lord, but first
let me go back and take care of things
at home."*
62Jesus answered, "Anyone who
starts plowing and keeps looking
back isn't worth a thing in God's
kingdom!"

The Work of the Seventy-two Followers

10 Later the Lord chose seventy-
two[o] other followers and sent
them out two by two to every town
and village where he was about to
go. 2He said to them:

A large crop is in the fields,
but there are only a few workers.
Ask the Lord in charge of the
harvest to send out workers to
bring it in. 3Now go, but
remember, I am sending you like
lambs into a pack of wolves.
4Don't take along a moneybag
or a traveling bag or sandals.
And don't waste time greeting
people on the road.[p] 5As soon
as you enter a home, say, "God
bless this home with peace."
6If the people living there are
peace-loving, your prayer for
peace will bless them. But if they
are not peace-loving, your
prayer will return to you. 7Stay
with the same family, eating and
drinking whatever they give
you, because workers are worth
what they earn. Don't move
around from house to house.
8If the people of a town
welcome you, eat whatever they
offer you. 9Heal their sick and
say, "God's kingdom will soon
be here!"[q]
10But if the people of a town
refuse to welcome you, go out
into the street and say,* 11"We

---

[m] *what they had said*: Some manuscripts add, "and said, 'Don't you know what spirit you belong to? The Son of Man did not come to destroy people's lives, but to save them.' " [n] *bury my father*: The Jewish people taught that giving someone a proper burial was even more important than helping the poor. [o] *seventy-two*: Some manuscripts have "seventy." According to the book of Genesis, there were seventy nations on earth. But the ancient Greek translation of the Old Testament has "seventy-two" in place of "seventy." Jesus probably chose this number of followers to show that his message was for everyone in the world. [p] *waste time greeting people on the road*: In those days a polite greeting could take a long time. [q] *will soon be here*: Or "is already here."

9.55 **PUNISHMENT ISN'T GOD'S FIRST CHOICE** Sometimes we want to see people punished for not doing what we want them to do. But in the Bible we notice that God often waits a very long time before he punishes people. God's way is to teach by example and word so that people will trust and obey him. He gives us every chance to follow him. We need to learn God's kind of patience.

9.61 **LET'S DECIDE WHAT IS IMPORTANT** The three people Jesus spoke to each had an excuse for not following him. As we think about them, the excuses seem pretty good. But they weren't good enough. *Nothing* is as important as doing what Jesus commands us to do.

10.10 **NOT EVERYONE IS GOD'S FRIEND** Jesus told the seventy-two followers they would meet some in their journey who would be friendly to God's message. But others would *(continued)*

NOTES

are shaking the dust from our feet[r] as a warning to you. You can be sure that God's kingdom will soon be here!"[s] 12I tell you that on the day of judgment the people of Sodom will get off easier than the people of that town!

The Unbelieving Towns
(Matthew 11.20–24)

13You people of Chorazin are in for trouble! You people of Bethsaida are also in for trouble! If the miracles that took place in your towns had happened in Tyre and Sidon, the people there would have turned to God long ago. They would have dressed in sackcloth and put ashes on their heads.[t] 14On the day of judgment the people of Tyre and Sidon will get off easier than you will.* 15People of Capernaum, do you think you will be honored in heaven? Well, you will go down to hell!

16My followers, whoever listens to you is listening to me. Anyone who says "No" to you is saying "No" to me. And anyone who says "No" to me is really saying "No" to the one who sent me.

The Return of the Seventy-two

17When the seventy-two[u] followers returned, they were excited and said, "Lord, even the demons obeyed when we spoke in your name!"

18Jesus told them:

I saw Satan fall from heaven like a flash of lightning.* 19I have given you the power to trample on snakes and scorpions and to defeat the power of your enemy Satan. Nothing can harm you. 20But don't be happy because evil spirits obey you. Be happy that your names are written in heaven!

Jesus Thanks His Father
(Matthew 11.25–27; 13.16, 17)

21At that same time Jesus felt the joy that comes from the Holy Spirit,[v] and he said:

My Father, Lord of heaven and earth, I am grateful that you hid all this from wise and educated people and showed it to ordinary people. Yes, Father, that is what pleased you.*

---

[r]*shaking the dust from our feet*: This was a way of showing rejection. [s]*will soon be here*: Or "is already here." [t]*dressed in sackcloth . . . ashes on their heads*: This was one way that people showed how sorry they were for their sins. [u]*seventy-two*: See the note at 10.1. [v]*the Holy Spirit*: Some manuscripts have "his spirit."

(*continued*) not be so friendly. So we should not be disappointed when everybody isn't friendly to us. Not everyone was friendly to Jesus and his earliest followers, either. In fact, if we're popular with *everyone*, maybe something is wrong.

10.14 **WHERE DOES YOUR TOWN STAND?** Notice here that Jesus spoke to whole towns. What kind of town is yours? What would Jesus have to say to it? We ought to pray for our towns, and try to share the good news in them. At times whole towns have been known to come to faith in Jesus.

10.18 **SATAN IS A REAL PERSON** Satan would rather we didn't believe he is real. Then he could more easily do his evil and deceitful work. Jesus believed Satan was real. But he also saw that Satan was his defeated enemy. If we have trusted our lives to Jesus, then God will keep us from Satan's harm.

10.21 **WHO ARE GOD'S PEOPLE?** Jesus says that his people aren't necessarily the smartest people in the world. In fact, an overactive brain can keep people from realizing the plainest facts of life. It's not what we *know* that helps us to live; it's how we *use* what we know. That's wisdom. Sometimes it's the ordinary people who have the most wisdom to believe the good news about Jesus.

NOTES

22My Father has given me
everything, and he is the only
one who knows the Son. The
only one who really knows the
Father is the Son. But the Son
wants to tell others about the
Father, so that they can know
him too.
23Jesus then turned to his disciples
and said to them in private, "You are
really blessed to see what you see!
24Many prophets and kings were eager to see what you see and to hear
what you hear. But I tell you that they
did not see or hear."

The Good Samaritan

25An expert in the Law of Moses
stood up and asked Jesus a question
to see what he would say. "Teacher,"
he asked, "What must I do to have
eternal life?"
26Jesus answered, "What is written
in the Scriptures? How do you understand them?"
27The man replied, "The Scriptures
say, 'Love the Lord your God with
all your heart, soul, strength, and
mind.' They also say, 'Love your
neighbors as much as you love
yourself.' "
28Jesus said, "You have given the
right answer. If you do this, you will
have eternal life."
29But the man wanted to show that
he knew what he was talking about.
So he asked Jesus, "Who are my
neighbors?"
30Jesus replied:
As a man was going down
from Jerusalem to Jericho,
robbers attacked him and
grabbed everything he had.
They beat him up and ran off,
leaving him half dead.*
31A priest happened to be
going down the same road. But
when he saw the man, he walked
by on the other side. 32Later a
temple helper[w] came to the same
place. But when he saw the man
who had been beaten up, he also
went by on the other side.
33A man from Samaria then
came traveling along that road.
When he saw the man, he felt
sorry for him 34and went over
to him. He treated his wounds
with olive oil and wine[x] and
bandaged them. Then he put him
on his own donkey and took him
to an inn, where he took care
of him. 35The next morning he
gave the innkeeper two silver
coins and said, "Please take care
of the man. If you spend more
than this on him, I will pay you
when I return."
36Then Jesus asked, "Which one
of these three people was a real
neighbor to the man who was beaten
up by robbers?"
37The teacher answered, "The one
who showed pity."
Jesus said, "Go and do the same!"

Martha and Mary

38The Lord and his disciples were
traveling along and came to a village.
When they got there, a woman
named Martha welcomed him into
her home.* 39She had a sister named
Mary, who sat down in front of the

[w] *temple helper*: A man from the tribe of Levi, whose job it was to work around the temple. [x] *olive oil and wine*: In New Testament times these were used as medicine. Sometimes olive oil is a symbol for healing by means of a miracle (James 5.14).

10.30 **WHO IS YOUR NEIGHBOR?** The story of the good Samaritan was hard for the legal expert to take. Most Jews didn't believe there were any "good" Samaritans. But that's why Jesus told the legal expert this story—so that the man could see he needed to love even his Samaritan neighbors.

10.38 **WHAT COMES FIRST—HEARING OR DOING?** Martha was a great doer, and that was fine. But Mary was a great listener, and that was better. Of course, listening without learning and doing is useless. But before we can know what really pleases God, we must first pay close attention to what he says. Then we will know what to do.

NOTES

Step 9

GOOD SAMARITAN—a man who exhibited compassion

LUKE 10.29–37

A sure mark of maturity for any Christian is showing compassion. In many ways, our genuineness is measured by our compassion quotient—how we respond to our friends and neighbors when they have a need. It is easy to come to the aid of a friend and even a neighbor who lives close by. But what about neighbors who are really strangers or people who might be considered outsiders? That becomes a challenge.

One of the best role models of compassion was given by Jesus in response to a question about who our neighbors are. A man from a foreign country, Samaria, stopped to help a stranger in need along the roadside. This "Good Samaritan" helped a man who had been beaten and robbed and then ignored by two religious leaders. He was willing to get involved—to get his hands dirty and even pay the expenses for the care of the wounded man.

True compassion doesn't have social or religious boundaries. To make this point, Jesus illustrated compassion through the thoughtfulness of this Samaritan man, considered by the Jews to be a social and religious outcast. Compassionate people take action without considering social class, color, or the financial condition.

STEP LOOK BACK 9

Are we compassionate? It is easy to ignore people when we are preoccupied with our own problems. We have people to meet, schedules to keep, and money to be made. But when we come upon people in need, will we consider putting our own agenda aside to do what we can to help?

Stories about "Good Samaritans" rarely make the news. That is probably why Jesus told this story—and why we need to see this example as a worthy goal. If we take the time to get involved, it will make a difference in us and in those whose lives we touch. It's the thing to do if we are serious about growing in our walk with God.

Ready for Step 10?
Turn to page 33 of* InStep's *introduction.

Lord and was listening to what he said. 40Martha was worried about all that had to be done. Finally, she went to Jesus and said, "Lord, doesn't it bother you that my sister has left me to do all the work by myself? Tell her to come and help me!"

41The Lord answered, "Martha, Martha! You are worried and upset about so many things, 42but only one thing is necessary. Mary has chosen what is best, and it will not be taken away from her."

Prayer
(Matthew 6.9–13; 7.7–11)

11 When Jesus had finished praying, one of his disciples said to him, "Lord, teach us to pray, just as John taught his followers to pray."

2So Jesus told them, "Pray in this way:

'Father, help us
to honor your name.
Come and set up
your kingdom.*
3Give us each day
the food we need.[y]
4Forgive our sins,
as we forgive everyone
who has done wrong to us.
And keep us
from being tempted.' "

5Then Jesus went on to say:

Suppose one of you goes to a friend in the middle of the night and says, "Let me borrow three loaves of bread. 6A friend of mine has dropped in, and I don't have a thing for him to eat." 7And suppose your friend answers, "Don't bother me! The door is bolted, and my children and I are in bed. I cannot get up to give you something."

8He may not get up and give you the bread, just because you are his friend. But he will get up and give you as much as you need, simply because you are not ashamed to keep on asking.

9So I tell you to ask and you will receive, search and you will find, knock and the door will be opened for you.* 10Everyone who asks will receive, everyone who searches will find, and the door will be opened for everyone who knocks. 11Which one of you fathers would give your hungry child a snake if the child asked for a fish? 12Which one of you would give your child a scorpion if the child asked for an egg? 13As bad as you are, you still know how to give good gifts to your children. But your heavenly Father is even more ready to give the Holy Spirit to anyone who asks.

Jesus and the Ruler of Demons
(Matthew 12.22–30; Mark 3.20–27)

14Jesus forced a demon out of a man who could not talk. After the demon had gone out, the man started speaking, and the crowds were amazed. 15But some people said, "He forces out demons by the power of Beelzebul, the ruler of the demons!"

16Others wanted to put Jesus to the test. So they asked him to show them a sign from God. 17Jesus knew what they were thinking, and he said:

A kingdom where people fight each other will end up in ruin. And a family that fights will break up. 18If Satan fights against himself, how can his kingdom last? Yet you say that I force out demons by the power

---

[y] *the food we need*: Or "food for today" or "food for the coming day."

11.2 **JESUS TEACHES US TO PRAY** We shouldn't just ramble on when we pray. But also, let's not just ask God for things that please us in a selfish way. God knows and cares about our needs, and we should bring them to him. But we ought to study Jesus' prayer so we can learn to ask for those things that please God.

11.9 **KEEP ON ASKING** Don't give up if your prayers aren't all answered right away. Keep on asking. God is much more generous than people. If our requests aren't right, he'll show us how to change them.

NOTES

of Beelzebul. 19If I use his power
to force out demons, whose
power do your own followers use
to force them out? They are the
ones who will judge you. 20But
if I use God's power to force out
demons, it proves that God's
kingdom has already come to
you.
21When a strong man arms
himself and guards his home,
everything he owns is safe.
22But if a stronger man comes
and defeats him, he will carry
off the weapons in which the
strong man trusted. Then he will
divide with others what he has
taken. 23If you are not on my
side, you are against me. If you
don't gather in the crop with me,
you scatter it.

Return of an Evil Spirit
(Matthew 12.43–45)

24When an evil spirit leaves a
person, it travels through the
desert, looking for a place to rest.
But when it doesn't find a place,
it says, "I will go back to the
home I left."* 25When it gets
there and finds the place clean
and fixed up, 26it goes off and
finds seven other evil spirits
even worse than itself. They all
come and make their home
there, and that person ends up
in worse shape than before.

Being Really Blessed

27While Jesus was still talking, a
woman in the crowd spoke up, "The
woman who gave birth to you and
nursed you is blessed!"
28Jesus replied, "That's true, but
the people who are really blessed are
the ones who hear and obey God's
message!"[z]

A Sign from God
(Matthew 12.38–42; Mark 8.12)

29As crowds were gathering
around Jesus, he said:
You people of today are evil!
You keep looking for a sign from
God. But what happened to
Jonah[a] is the only sign you will
be given.* 30Just as Jonah was
a sign to the people of Nineveh,
the Son of Man will be a sign
to the people of today. 31When
the judgment comes, the Queen
of the South[b] will stand there
with you and condemn you. She
traveled a long way to hear
Solomon's wisdom, and yet here
is something far greater than
Solomon. 32The people of
Nineveh will also stand there
with you and condemn you.
They turned to God when Jonah
preached, and yet here is
something far greater than
Jonah.

Light
(Matthew 5.15; 6.22, 23)

33No one lights a lamp and
then hides it or puts it under a

[z]*That's true, but the people who are really blessed . . . message*: Or " 'That's not true, the people who are blessed . . . message.' " [a]*what happened to Jonah*: Jonah was in the stomach of a big fish for three days and nights. See Matthew 12.40. [b]*Queen of the South*: Sheba, probably a country in southern Arabia.

11.24 **FILL YOUR LIFE WITH GOOD THINGS** Like the man who got rid of his evil spirit, we're sometimes satisfied just to get rid of our sins. Being forgiven is great, but God also wants us to be filled with the Holy Spirit. By doing so, we will also replace our old bad habits with new good ones. Then there will be no room for the evil habits to return.

11.29 **SEEING JESUS** Today we wish we could have been there when Jesus walked among the people. We long for a chance to see him. But the people of his day saw Jesus, and most still didn't appreciate who he was. The Son of God was right there in front of them, but they missed it. It is better for us who believe without seeing, than for those who saw and did not believe.

NOTES

clay pot. A lamp is put on a
lampstand, so that everyone who
comes into the house can see the
light. 34Your eyes are the lamp
for your body. When your eyes
are good, you have all the light
you need. But when your eyes
are bad, everything is dark.
35So be sure that your light is
not darkness. 36If you have light,
and nothing is dark, then light
will be everywhere, as when a
lamp shines brightly on you.

Jesus Condemns the Pharisees and Teachers of the Law of Moses

(Matthew 23.1–36; Mark 12.38–40; Luke 20.45–47)

37When Jesus finished speaking, a
Pharisee invited him home for a
meal. Jesus went and sat down to
eat.[c] 38The Pharisee was surprised
that he did not wash his hands[d] before eating. 39So the Lord said to
him:

You Pharisees clean the
outside of cups and dishes, but
on the inside you are greedy and
evil.* 40You fools! Didn't God
make both the outside and the
inside?[e] 41If you would only give
what you have to the poor,
everything you do would please
God.

42You Pharisees are in for
trouble! You give God a tenth
of the spices from your gardens,
such as mint and rue. But you
cheat people, and you don't love
God. You should be fair and kind
to others and still give a tenth
to God.

43You Pharisees are in for
trouble! You love the front seats
in the meeting places, and you
like to be greeted with honor in
the market. 44But you are in for
trouble! You are like unmarked
graves[f] that people walk on
without even knowing it.

45A teacher of the Law of Moses
spoke up, "Teacher, you said cruel
things about us."

46Jesus replied:

You teachers are also in for
trouble! You load people down
with heavy burdens, but you
won't lift a finger to help them
carry the loads. 47Yes, you are
really in for trouble. You build
monuments to honor the
prophets your own people
murdered long ago. 48You must
think that was the right thing for
your people to do, or else you
would not have built monuments
for the prophets they murdered.

49Because of your evil deeds,
the Wisdom of God said, "I will
send prophets and apostles to
you. But you will murder some
and mistreat others." 50You
people living today will be
punished for all the prophets
who have been murdered since
the beginning of the world.
51This includes every prophet
from the time of Abel to the time
of Zechariah,[g] who was
murdered between the altar and

---

[c] *sat down to eat*: See the note at 7.36. [d] *did not wash his hands*: The Jewish people had strict laws about washing their hands before eating, especially if they had been out in public. [e] *Didn't God make both the outside and the inside?*: Or "Doesn't the person who washes the outside always wash the inside too?" [f] *unmarked graves*: Tombs were whitewashed to keep anyone from accidentally touching them. A person who touched a dead body or a tomb was considered unclean and could not worship with other Jewish people. [g] *from the time of Abel . . . Zechariah*: Genesis is the first book in the Jewish Scriptures, and it tells that Abel was the first person to be murdered. Second Chronicles is the last book in the Jewish Scriptures, and the last murder that it tells about is that of Zechariah.

11.39 **LET'S NOT FOOL OURSELVES** Have you heard the tale about "The Emperor Who Had No Clothes"? A certain emperor fooled himself by believing he was dressed in beautiful clothes. The truth was that he was wearing no clothes at all. Even though nearly everyone bowed before the emperor, a small boy spoke up and said, "Look—the emperor has no clothes." That was like the Pharisees who pretended to be holy. Jesus said they were really unholy in their inner lives. Let's not just pretend to be Christians.

NOTES

the temple. You people will
certainly be punished for all of
this.
52You teachers of the Law of
Moses are really in for trouble!
You carry the keys to the door
of knowledge about God. But
you never go in, and you keep
others from going in.*
53Jesus was about to leave, but the
teachers and the Pharisees wanted
to get even with him. They tried
to make him say what he thought
about other things, 54so that they
could catch him saying something
wrong.

Warnings

12 As thousands of people
crowded around Jesus and
were stepping on each other, he told
his disciples:
Be sure to guard against the
dishonest teaching[h] of the
Pharisees! It is their way of
fooling people.* 2Everything
that is hidden will be found out,
and every secret will be known.
3Whatever you say in the dark
will be heard when it is day.
Whatever you whisper in a
closed room will be shouted
from the housetops.

The One to Fear
(Matthew 10.28–31)

4My friends, don't be afraid of
people. They can kill you, but
after that, there is nothing else
they can do.* 5God is the one you
must fear. Not only can he take
your life, but he can throw you
into hell. God is certainly the one
you should fear!
6Five sparrows are sold for just
two pennies, but God does not
forget a one of them. 7Even the
hairs on your head are counted.
So don't be afraid! You are worth
much more than many sparrows.

Telling Others about Christ
(Matthew 10.32, 33; 12.32; 10.19, 20)

8If you tell others that you
belong to me, the Son of Man
will tell God's angels that you
are my followers. 9But if you
reject me, you will be rejected
in front of them. 10If you speak
against the Son of Man, you can
be forgiven, but if you speak
against the Holy Spirit, you
cannot be forgiven.

---

[h]*dishonest teaching*: The Greek text has "yeast," which is used here of a teaching that is not true. See Matthew 16.6,12.

11.52 **KEYS ARE FOR OPENING** Jesus was unhappy with teachers who kept others from the truth. Their "keys to the door of knowledge" were supposed to be for opening the door, not closing it. It was bad enough that they turned away from God's truth, but it was worse that they stood in the way of others. Are we doing everything we can to encourage those who want to know more about Jesus?

12.1 **JESUS WARNED ABOUT QUACKS** "Quacks" are what we call people who pretend to be doctors but really aren't. There are religious quacks, too. Sometimes these people make themselves very rich by peddling their false teaching. Jesus also had to deal with quacks. They cheated people in his time, too. But he warned that their lies would be found out. They can't keep secrets from God.

12.4 **FEAR IS A GREAT ENEMY** President Franklin Roosevelt said, "The only thing we have to fear is fear itself." In this passage we see bad fear and good fear. Bad fear is the kind Roosevelt was talking about, the kind that is always afraid of things that can harm us in this world. Good fear is the fear that comes from respect for the power of God. Let's be sure we're on his side.

NOTES

11When you are brought to
trial in the Jewish meeting
places or before rulers or
officials, don't worry about how
you will defend yourselves or
what you will say.* 12At that time
the Holy Spirit will tell you what
to say.

A Rich Fool

13A man in a crowd said to Jesus,
"Teacher, tell my brother to give me
my share of what our father left us
when he died."
14Jesus answered, "Who gave me
the right to settle arguments between
you and your brother?"
15Then he said to the crowd, "Don't
be greedy! Owning a lot of things
won't make your life safe."
16So Jesus told them this story:
A rich man's farm produced
a big crop, 17and he said to
himself, "What can I do? I don't
have a place large enough to
store everything."
18Later, he said, "Now I know
what I'll do. I'll tear down my
barns and build bigger ones,
where I can store all my grain
and other goods.* 19Then I'll say
to myself, 'You have stored up
enough good things to last for
years to come. Live it up! Eat,
drink, and enjoy yourself.' "
20But God said to him, "You
fool! Tonight you will die. Then
who will get what you have
stored up?"

21"This is what happens to people
who store up everything for themselves, but are poor in the sight of
God."

Worry
(Matthew 6.25–34)

22Jesus said to his disciples:
I tell you not to worry about
your life! Don't worry about
having something to eat or
wear.* 23Life is more than food
or clothing. 24Look at the crows!
They don't plant or harvest, and
they don't have storehouses or
barns. But God takes care of
them. You are much more
important than any birds. 25Can
worry make you live longer?[i]
26If you don't have power over
small things, why worry about
everything else?
27Look how the wild flowers
grow! They don't work hard to
make their clothes. But I tell you
that Solomon with all his wealth[j]
was not as well clothed as one
of these flowers. 28God gives
such beauty to everything that
grows in the fields, even though
it is here today and thrown into
a fire tomorrow. Won't he do
even more for you? You have
such little faith!
29Don't keep worrying about

---

[i] *live longer*: Or "grow taller." [j] *Solomon with all his wealth*: The Jewish people thought that Solomon was the richest person who had ever lived.

12.11 **THE HOLY SPIRIT HELPS US** God never leaves us completely alone. He is always there when we need him. This is especially true when we have to answer people about our faith. The Spirit of God himself makes us able to show others that the good news about Jesus is true. In Acts 7, for example, you can read about how the Holy Spirit helped Stephen speak for Christ.

12.18 **"YOU CAN'T TAKE IT WITH YOU"** Rich and poor alike have to die some day. How foolish it is to hoard money as if we could take it with us when we die. God blesses us with goods in this world so we can use them to benefit others.

12.22 **HOW MUCH ARE YOU WORTH?** Jesus said we are worth more than birds. And we are certainly worth more than flowers in a field. But are we worth more than all the things we can ever own? Yes—it is a great shame when we value our lives by money or property. Those things pass away, but our souls last forever. The lasting things are important to God, and they should be important to us.

NOTES

having something to eat or
drink. 30Only people who don't
know God are always worrying
about such things. Your Father
knows what you need. 31But put
God's work first, and these
things will be yours as well.

Treasures in Heaven
(Matthew 6.19–21)

32My little group of disciples,
don't be afraid! Your Father
wants to give you the kingdom.*
33Sell what you have and give
the money to the poor. Make
yourselves moneybags that
never wear out. Make your
treasure safe in heaven, where
thieves cannot steal it and moths
cannot destroy it. 34Your heart
will always be where your
treasure is.

Faithful and Unfaithful Servants
(Matthew 24.45–51)

35Be ready and keep your
lamps burning just 36like those
servants who wait up for their
master to return from a wedding
feast. As soon as he comes and
knocks, they open the door for
him. 37Servants are fortunate if
their master finds them awake
and ready when he comes! I
promise you that he will get
ready and have his servants sit
down so he can serve them.
38Those servants are really
fortunate if their master finds
them ready, even though he
comes late at night or early in
the morning. 39You would surely
not let a thief break into your
home, if you knew when the thief
was coming. 40So always be
ready! You don't know when the
Son of Man will come.
41Peter asked Jesus, "Did you say
this just for us or for everyone?"
42The Lord answered:
Who are faithful and wise
servants? Who are the ones the
master will put in charge of
giving the other servants their
food supplies at the proper
time?* 43Servants are fortunate
if their master comes and finds
them doing their job. 44A servant
who is always faithful will surely
be put in charge of everything
the master owns.
45But suppose one of the
servants thinks that the master
will not return until late.
Suppose that servant starts
beating all the other servants
and eats and drinks and gets
drunk. 46If that happens, the
master will surely come on a day
and at a time when the servant
least expects him. That servant
will then be punished and
thrown out with the servants
who cannot be trusted.
47If servants are not ready or
willing to do what their master
wants them to do, they will be
beaten hard. 48But servants who
don't know what their master
wants them to do will not be
beaten so hard for doing wrong.
If God has been generous with
you, he will expect you to serve
him well. But if he has been more
than generous, he will expect
you to serve him even better.

Not Peace, but Trouble
(Matthew 10.34–36)

49I came to set fire to the earth,
and I surely wish it were already

12.32 **WILL YOU LET GO?** Jesus had some hard words to say about the things of this world. We are in danger of becoming too attached to our material goods. He wants us to let them go, if necessary, for the sake of doing his work.

12.42 **ALWAYS BE READY FOR THE MASTER** Jesus may return for us at any moment. Let's not be like the servants who decided their master would not be returning any time soon. Let's live each day as if it were the day Jesus is coming back to take us to be with him. It just might be. Have you been putting off sharing the good news about Jesus with someone? We might not be here tomorrow.

NOTES

on fire!* 50I am going to be put
to a hard test. And I will have
to suffer a lot of pain until it is
over. 51Do you think that I came
to bring peace to earth? No
indeed! I came to make people
choose sides. 52A family of five
will be divided, with two of them
against the other three. 53Fathers
and sons will turn against one
another, and mothers and
daughters will do the same.
Mothers-in-law and daughters-
in-law will also turn against each
other.

Knowing What to Do

(Matthew 16.2, 3; 5.25, 26)

54Jesus said to all the people:
As soon as you see a cloud
coming up in the west, you say,
"It's going to rain," and it does.
55When the south wind blows,
you say, "It's going to get hot,"
and it does. 56Are you trying to
fool someone? You can predict
the weather by looking at the
earth and sky, but you don't
really know what's going on
right now.* 57Why don't you
understand the right thing to do?
58When someone accuses you of
something, try to settle things
before you are taken to court.
If you don't, you will be dragged
before the judge. Then the judge
will hand you over to the jailer,
and you will be locked up. 59You
won't get out until you have paid
the last cent you owe.

Turn Back to God

13 About this same time Jesus
was told that Pilate had given
orders for some people from Galilee
to be killed while they were offering
sacrifices.* 2Jesus replied:
Do you think that these people
were worse sinners than
everyone else in Galilee just
because of what happened to
them? 3Not at all! But you can
be sure that if you don't turn
back to God, every one of you
will also be killed. 4What about
those eighteen people who died
when the tower in Siloam fell on
them? Do you think they were
worse than everyone else in
Jerusalem? 5Not at all! But you
can be sure that if you don't turn
back to God, every one of you
will also die.

A Story about a Fig Tree

6Jesus then told them this story:
A man had a fig tree growing
in his vineyard. One day he went
out to pick some figs, but he

12.49 **A DIVIDER OF FAMILIES** Jesus says we may be surprised by those who become our enemies because of our faith in him. Jesus wants us to have good relationships in our families, but sometimes even a believer's closest relatives will turn into enemies because of that person's faith.

12.56 **UNDERSTAND YOUR TIMES** Jesus knew his death was near. He also knew that the Jewish nation would be destroyed by invaders from Rome not many years later. God was going to punish the people for rejecting his kingdom. We live in uncertain times, too. Now is the time to find peace with God, because tomorrow might be too late.

13.1 **DEATH IS OUR PAYMENT FOR SIN** Of course, we don't like to think about death and dying. It's the most dreadful thing we face in this world. But death, however it may happen, is our fair payment for sin. When we hear about someone's death, that is when we should look into our own souls. Then we should ask God to forgive our sins and make us fit for heaven, because of what Jesus did when he died in our place, paying our sin debt himself.

NOTES

didn't find any.* 7So he said to
the gardener, "For three years
I have come looking for figs on
this tree, and I haven't found any
yet. Chop it down! Why should
it take up space?"
8The gardener answered,
"Master, leave it for another
year. I'll dig around it and put
some manure on it to make it
grow. 9Maybe it will have figs
on it next year. If it doesn't, you
can have it cut down."

Healing a Woman on the Sabbath

10One Sabbath Jesus was teaching
in a Jewish meeting place, 11and a
woman was there who had been crippled by an evil spirit for eighteen
years. She was completely bent over
and could not straighten up. 12When
Jesus saw the woman, he called her
over and said, "You are now well."
13He placed his hands on her, and
right away she stood up straight and
praised God.
14The man in charge of the meeting
place was angry because Jesus had
healed someone on the Sabbath. So
he said to the people, "Each week
has six days when we can work.
Come and be healed on one of those
days, but not on the Sabbath."*
15The Lord replied, "Are you trying
to fool someone? Won't any one of
you untie your ox or donkey and lead
it out to drink on a Sabbath? 16This
woman belongs to the family of
Abraham, but Satan has kept her
bound for eighteen years. Isn't it right
to set her free on the Sabbath?"
17Jesus' words made all his enemies
ashamed. But everyone else in the
crowd was happy about the wonderful things he was doing.

A Mustard Seed and Yeast

(Matthew 13.31–33; Mark 4.30–32)

18Jesus said, "What is God's kingdom like? What can I compare it
with? 19It is like what happens when
someone plants a mustard seed in a
garden. The seed grows as big as a
tree, and birds nest in its branches."*
20Then Jesus said, "What can I
compare God's kingdom with?
21It is like what happens when a
woman mixes yeast into three
batches of flour. Finally, all the
dough rises."

The Narrow Door

(Matthew 7.13, 14, 21–23)

22As Jesus was on his way to Jerusalem, he taught the people in the
towns and villages. 23Someone asked
him, "Lord, are only a few people
going to be saved?"

13.6 **BE A GOOD GARDENER** The fault was not in the fig tree. The gardener hadn't been doing his job. But the owner gave the gardener another chance. God doesn't like to punish us, so he is always giving us new chances to be useful to him. Are we making the best of the chances God gives us every day? Let's plan to have lots of good fruit in our lives when Jesus comes.

13.14 **GOD'S LAWS MAKE GOOD SENSE** When Jesus healed a woman on the Sabbath, the man in charge of the meeting place was angry because he thought Jesus was "working" on God's special day. The man knew something in his head about the Law of God, but he didn't understand the Law's purpose. The Sabbath was supposed to be a day for honoring God. What better way is there to honor God on his day than by doing a kind thing for someone?

13.19 **THE NEWS OF GOD'S KINGDOM SPREADS** What Jesus said about the mustard seed two thousand years ago has actually come true. The good news of the kingdom of God began as a very small thing in a very small country. But the news of that kingdom has grown into a tree which has spread all over the world. The church has gone into every nation, with amazing effects on the lives of many millions of people.

NOTES

Jesus answered:
24Do all you can to go in by
the narrow door! A lot of people
will try to get in, but will not be
able to.* 25Once the owner of the
house gets up and locks the door,
you will be left standing outside.
You will knock on the door and
say, "Sir, open the door for us!"
But the owner will answer, "I
don't know a thing about you!"
26Then you will start saying,
"We dined with you, and you
taught in our streets."
27But he will say, "I really
don't know who you are! Get
away from me, all you evil
people!"
28Then when you have been
thrown outside, you will weep
and grit your teeth because you
will see Abraham and Isaac and
all the prophets in God's
kingdom. 29People will come
from all directions and sit down
to feast in God's kingdom.
30There the ones who are now
least important will be the most
important, and those who are
now most important will be least
important.

Jesus and Herod

31At that time some Pharisees came
to Jesus and said, "You had better
get away from here! Herod[k] wants
to kill you."
32Jesus said to them:
Go tell that fox, "I am going
to force out demons and heal
people today and tomorrow, and
three days later I'll be through."
33But I am going on my way
today and tomorrow and the
next day. After all, Jerusalem is
the place where prophets are
killed.

Jesus Loves Jerusalem
(Matthew 23.37–39)

34Jerusalem, Jerusalem! Your
people have killed the prophets
and have stoned the messengers
who were sent to you. I have
often wanted to gather your
people, as a hen gathers her
chicks under her wings. But you
wouldn't let me.* 35Now your
temple will be deserted. You will
not see me again until the time
when you say,
"Blessed is the one who comes
in the name of the Lord."

Jesus Heals a Sick Man

14 One Sabbath Jesus was having
dinner in the home of an important
Pharisee, and everyone was
carefully watching Jesus.* 2All of a
sudden a man with swollen legs stood
up in front of him. 3Jesus turned and
asked the Pharisees and the teachers

[k]*Herod*: Herod Antipas, the son of Herod the Great.

13.24 **DON'T BE LEFT OUT** The door to God stands open for all who wish to go through it. Jesus himself is that door. He himself is the way to heaven. By receiving him and turning away from our selfish lives, we have eternal life. The door is narrow, and we can just squeeze through if we are willing to leave the baggage of our sins behind.

13.34 **POOR JERUSALEM** Over the centuries, the city of Jerusalem has been destroyed more than once. But the city keeps rising up again. The nation of Israel is the only ancient society that has been destroyed only to be set up again in modern times. God used the United Nations to begin restoring the land of Israel in 1948. Jesus predicted that Israel will welcome him the second time he appears, instead of rejecting him as they did the first time.

14.1 **HONORING GOD ON HIS DAY** At present the Lord's special day is Sunday, not the Sabbath (Saturday) as it was when Jesus was here. The point is the same: the Lord's Day is a day for honoring God, and we honor God when we do acts of kindness and mercy for others

NOTES

of the Law of Moses, "Is it right to heal on the Sabbath?" 4But they did not say a word.

Jesus took hold of the man. Then he healed him and sent him away. 5Afterwards, Jesus asked the people, "If your son or ox falls into a well, wouldn't you pull him out right away, even on the Sabbath?" 6There was nothing they could say.

How To Be a Guest

7Jesus saw how the guests had tried to take the best seats. So he told them:

8When you are invited to a wedding feast, don't sit in the best place. Someone more important may have been invited. 9Then the one who invited you will come and say, "Give your place to this other guest!" You will be embarrassed and will have to sit in the worst place.

10When you are invited to be a guest, go and sit in the worst place. Then the one who invited you may come and say, "My friend, take a better seat!" You will then be honored in front of all the other guests.* 11If you put yourself above others, you will be put down. But if you humble yourself, you will be honored.

12Then Jesus said to the man who had invited him:

When you give a dinner or a banquet, don't invite your friends and family and relatives and rich neighbors. If you do, they will invite you in return, and you will be paid back. 13When you give a feast, invite the poor, the crippled, the lame, and the blind. 14They cannot pay you back. But God will bless you and reward you when his people rise from death.

The Great Banquet
(Matthew 22.1–10)

15After Jesus had finished speaking, one of the guests said, "The greatest blessing of all is to be at the banquet in God's kingdom!"

16Jesus told him:

A man once gave a great banquet and invited a lot of guests. 17When the banquet was ready, he sent a servant to tell the guests, "Everything is ready! Please come."

18One guest after another started making excuses. The first one said, "I bought some land, and I've got to look it over. Please excuse me."*

19Another guest said, "I bought five teams of oxen, and I need to try them out. Please excuse me."

20Still another guest said, "I have just gotten married, and I can't be there."

21The servant told his master what happened, and the master became so angry that he said, "Go as fast as you can to every street and alley in town! Bring in everyone who is poor or crippled or blind or lame."

22When the servant returned, he said, "Master, I've done what

14.10 **JESUS INVITES US TO BE LOSERS** Being a loser doesn't seem very exciting. But it was Jesus' own way to *lose* in order to *win*. Our way is just the opposite. We all want to be winners. But Jesus puzzles us by saying we can't win by pushing other people around, or by using other people just to gain our own advantage. The real way to get ahead in God's plan is to use our own lives to help others along the path of life.

14.18 **WE CAN BE REPLACED** The invited guests were too busy to come to the banquet. All right, then—the host just sent out and brought in the most unimportant people he could find. Those guests who were first invited were probably very disappointed to find out they could be so easily replaced. If we don't accept God's kindness, he can easily find others who will.

NOTES

you told me, and there is still
plenty room for more people."
23His master then told him,
"Go out along the back roads
and fence rows and make people
come in, so that my house will
be full. 24Not one of the guests
I first invited will get even a bite
of my food!"

Being a Disciple
(Matthew 10.37, 38)

STEP LOOK INSIDE 4

25Large crowds were walking
along with Jesus, when he turned and
said:
26You cannot be my disciple,
unless you love me more than
you love your father and mother,
your wife and children, and your
brothers and sisters. You cannot
come with me unless you love
me more than you love your own
life.
27You cannot be my disciple
unless you carry your own cross
and come with me.
28Suppose one of you wants
to build a tower. What is the first
thing you will do? Won't you sit
down and figure out how much
it will cost and if you have
enough money to pay for it?*
29Otherwise, you will start
building the tower, but not be
able to finish. Then everyone
who sees what is happening will
laugh at you. 30They will say,
"You started building, but could
not finish the job."
31What will a king do if he has
only ten thousand soldiers to
defend himself against a king
who is about to attack him with
twenty thousand soldiers?
Before he goes out to battle,
won't he first sit down and
decide if he can win? 32If he
thinks he won't be able to defend
himself, he will send messengers
and ask for peace while the other
king is still a long way off. 33So
then, you cannot be my disciple
unless you give away everything
you own.

Salt and Light
(Matthew 5.13; Mark 9.50)

34Salt is good, but if it no
longer tastes like salt, how can
it be made to taste salty again?*
35It is no longer good for the soil
or even for the manure pile.
People simply throw it out. If you
have ears, pay attention!

One Sheep
(Matthew 18.12–14)

15 Tax collectors[l] and sinners
were all crowding around to
listen to Jesus. 2So the Pharisees and
the teachers of the Law of Moses
started grumbling, "This man is
friendly with sinners. He even eats
with them."
3Then Jesus told them this story:
4If any of you has a hundred
sheep, and one of them gets lost,
what will you do? Won't you
leave the ninety-nine in the field
and go look for the lost sheep

[l]*Tax collectors*: See the note at 3.12.

14.28 **"HOW MUCH WILL IT COST?"** You will usually ask this question before you buy something that might be expensive. Before you decide to follow Jesus you should also ask, "What will it cost me to be a disciple?" If you're doing it right, it will cost everything you are and all you have. But if you say "Yes" to Jesus and then try to hold back, you might end up worse off than before.

14.34 **WHAT FLAVOR IS A CHRISTIAN?** Jesus says a Christian should be "salty." He means that our lives should not be dull and lifeless, but exciting and alive. Christians have eternal life—a good reason to be joyful and encouraging to those around them. Salt was also used to preserve food. "Salty" Christians preserve others from "rotting" by showing them the good news about being saved through the Lord Jesus.

NOTES

Step 4

I will take a hard look at myself, the way I live and my moral standards.

LUKE 14.25–30

FIRST THINGS FIRST

It was going to be the greatest soapbox derby car ever built. I could already see myself flying down the hill way ahead of everyone else. My mom and dad would be on the sidelines cheering me on. They would take my picture for the paper and title it "Andy Fuller—Derby Dynamo."

In my excitement, I ran to the garage and started building my car. I built the greatest looking body, even painted racing stripes on it. What I forgot was that it had to fit the wheels, which I didn't have yet. By the time my dad got home, my great creation had turned into a great big mess. He reminded me that "if you fail to plan, you plan to fail." It's a hard lesson to learn, but dad is right on target. Let's try again.

ONE LAST THING

STEP LOOK INSIDE 4

What does it mean to be a follower of Christ? Will we have to change our habits and behavior? Will we need to reconsider some of our friends? Jesus said to consider the cost. Planning ahead is what's involved in being a fully devoted follower. We have to take a hard look at ourselves because when we decide to go with Jesus, he wants us 100 percent. That doesn't mean he expects us to have everything in order. He does expect us to love him totally, even more than we love ourselves. It is then that we can begin to build our plan for our lives because all the pieces are there.

For another "Look Inside," turn to page 371.

until you find it?* 5And when you
find it, you will be so glad that
you will put it on your shoulder
6and carry it home. Then you will
call in your friends and
neighbors and say, "Let's
celebrate! I've found my lost
sheep."
7Jesus said, "In the same way there
is more happiness in heaven because
of one sinner who turns to God than
over ninety-nine good people who
don't need to."

One Coin

8Jesus told the people another
story:
What will a woman do if she
has ten silver coins and loses one
of them? Won't she light a lamp,
sweep the floor, and look
carefully until she finds it? 9Then
she will call in her friends and
neighbors and say, "Let's
celebrate! I've found the coin I
lost."
10Jesus said, "In the same way
God's angels are happy when even
one person turns to him."

Two Sons

11Jesus also told them another
story:
Once a man had two sons.
12The younger son said to his
father, "Give me my share of the
property." So the father divided
his property between his two
sons.
13Not long after that, the
younger son packed up
everything he owned and left for
a foreign country, where he
wasted all his money in wild
living. 14He had spent
everything, when a bad famine
spread through that whole land.
Soon he had nothing to eat.
15He went to work for a man
in that country, and the man sent
him out to take care of his pigs.[m]
16He would have been glad to
eat what the pigs were eating,[n]
but no one gave him a thing.
17Finally, he came to his
senses and said, "My father's
workers have plenty to eat, and
here I am, starving to death!
18I will leave and go to my father
and say to him, 'Father, I have
sinned against God in heaven
and against you. 19I am no longer
good enough to be called your
son. Treat me like one of your
workers.' "
20The younger son got up and
started back to his father. But
when he was still a long way off,
his father saw him and felt sorry
for him. He ran to his son and
hugged and kissed him.
21The son said, "Father, I have
sinned against God in heaven
and against you. I am no longer
good enough to be called your
son."*

---

[m]*pigs*: The Jewish religion taught that pigs were not fit to eat or even to touch. A Jewish man would have felt terribly insulted if he had to feed pigs, much less eat with them. [n]*what the pigs were eating*: The Greek text has "(bean) pods," which came from a tree in Palestine. These were used to feed animals. Poor people sometimes ate them too.

15.4 **HOW VALUABLE IS ONE PERSON?** With today's growing population, individual persons seem to get lost and forgotten in the crowd. The stories about the one sheep and the one coin tell us that God knows and cares about each one of us. God doesn't just think about people in groups, but he thinks about them all *one by one*. So there is great happiness in heaven when one person comes to Jesus.

15.21 **WHO WAS THE LOST SON?** We might say that the younger son was the lost son. But wait—that lost son was *found*. At the end of the story, we aren't told what happened to the older son. The last time we saw him, he was pouting because his father loved the younger son. Let's hope that the older son did not become the lost son, *(continued)*

NOTES

Step 1

. . . I admit I cannot be successful on my own . . . I need help, daily.

LUKE 15.17

ANYTHING IS BETTER THAN THIS

I feel so cold and alone—here in my own house. No one hears me. No one cares. They say they do, but somehow it always gets back to the threats and accusations. I can't keep going on like this.

Maybe someday I'll take them up on it.
I'll run away and get out of their hair.

Anything is better than this.

A HOUSE THAT BECOMES A HOME

Nobody can make it all by themselves. We need each other. That is what being a part of a family is all about. That doesn't mean it is easy. It's not. The situation above describes what happens when attitudes within a family are not cleared up. Talking through misunderstandings and caring enough not to sweep things under the rug sometimes means tough duty for everyone involved. But the first step is to admit that we need others. That's the only way to start putting things back in place.

For another "Look Inside," turn to page 312.

22But his father said to the
servants, "Hurry and bring the
best clothes and put them on
him. Give him a ring for his
finger and sandals[o] for his feet.
23Get the best calf and prepare
it, so we can eat and celebrate.
24This son of mine was dead, but
has now come back to life. He
was lost and has now been
found." And they began to
celebrate.
25The older son had been out
in the field. But when he came
near the house, he heard the
music and dancing. 26So he
called one of the servants over
and asked, "What's going on
here?"
27The servant answered,
"Your brother has come home
safe and sound, and your father
ordered us to kill the best calf."
28The older brother got so mad
that he would not even go into
the house.
His father came out and
begged him to go in. 29But he
said to his father, "For years I
have worked for you like a slave
and have always obeyed you.
But you have never even given
me a little goat, so that I could
give a dinner for my friends.
30This other son of yours wasted
your money on bad women. And
now that he has come home, you
ordered the best calf to be killed
for a feast."
31His father replied, "My son,
you are always with me, and
everything I have is yours. 32But
we should be glad and celebrate!
Your brother was dead, but he
is now alive. He was lost and has
now been found."

A Dishonest Manager

16 Jesus said to his disciples:
A rich man once had a
manager to take care of his
business. But he was told that
his manager was wasting
money. 2So the rich man called
him in and said, "What is this I
hear about you? Tell me what
you have done! You are no
longer going to work for me."
3The manager said to himself,
"What shall I do now that my
master is going to fire me? I can't
dig ditches, and I'm ashamed to
beg. 4I know what I'll do, so that
people will welcome me into
their homes after I've lost my
job."
5Then one by one he called in
the people who were in debt to
his master. He asked the first
one, "How much do you owe my
master?"
6"A hundred barrels of olive
oil," the man answered.
So the manager said, "Take
your bill and sit down and
quickly write 'fifty'."
7The manager asked someone
else who was in debt to his
master, "How much do you
owe?"
"A thousand bushels[p] of
wheat," the man replied.
The manager said, "Take your
bill and write 'eight hundred'."
8The master praised his
dishonest manager for looking
out for himself so well. That's
how it is! The people of this
world look out for themselves
better than the people who
belong to the light.*
9My disciples, I tell you to use
wicked wealth to make friends
for yourselves. Then when it is

[o] *ring . . . sandals*: These show that the young man's father fully accepted him as his son. A ring was a sign of high position in the family. Sandals showed that he was a son instead of a slave, since slaves did not usually wear sandals. [p] *A thousand bushels*: The Greek text has "A hundred measures," and each measure is about ten or twelve bushels.

(continued) shutting himself out of his father's family. He should have joined the party, glad to see his younger brother home again. Likewise, we ought to be glad when lost people come home to Jesus.

16.8 **WHAT SHALL WE SPEND OUR LIVES FOR?** The dishonest manager spent his employer's wealth to make himself rich. We all have a certain amount of this world's goods and *(continued)*

NOTES

gone, you will be welcomed into
an eternal home. [10]Anyone who
can be trusted in little matters
can also be trusted in important
matters. But anyone who is
dishonest in little matters will be
dishonest in important matters.
[11]If you cannot be trusted with
this wicked wealth, who will
trust you with true wealth?
[12]And if you cannot be trusted
with what belongs to someone
else, who will give you
something that will be your
own? [13]You cannot be the slave
of two masters. You will like one
more than the other or be more
loyal to one than to the other.
You cannot serve God and
money.

Some Sayings of Jesus
(Matthew 11.12, 13; 5.31, 32; Mark 10.11, 12)

[14]The Pharisees really loved
money. So when they heard what Jesus said, they made fun of him.*
[15]But Jesus told them:
You are always making
yourselves look good, but God
sees what is in your heart. The
things that most people think are
important are worthless as far
as God is concerned.
[16]Until the time of John the
Baptist, people had to obey the
Law of Moses and the Books of
the Prophets.[q] But since God's
kingdom has been preached,
everyone is trying hard to get in.
[17]Heaven and earth will
disappear before the smallest
letter of the Law does.*
[18]It is a terrible sin[r] for a man
to divorce his wife and marry
another woman. It is also a
terrible sin for a man to marry
a divorced woman.

Lazarus and the Rich Man

[19]There was once a rich man
who wore expensive clothes and
every day ate the best food.
[20]But a poor beggar named
Lazarus was brought to the gate
of the rich man's house. [21]He
was happy just to eat the scraps
that fell from the rich man's
table. His body was covered with
sores, and dogs kept coming up
to lick them. [22]The poor man
died, and angels took him to the
place of honor next to
Abraham.[s]

---

[q] *the Law of Moses and the Books of the Prophets*: The Jewish Scriptures, that is, the Old Testament.
[r] *a terrible sin*: The Greek text uses a word that means the sin of being unfaithful in marriage.
[s] *the place of honor next to Abraham*: The Jewish people thought that heaven would be a banquet that God would give for them. Abraham would be the most important person there, and the guest of honor would sit next to him.

(*continued*) abilities, and these all come from God. How do we spend the wealth God gives us? Do we use the gifts of God to fatten ourselves? Or do we use them for the sake of God's heavenly kingdom?

16.14 **GOD IS NOT A MEANS TO AN END** The Pharisees really loved money. For the worst of them, that was their chief interest in life. They didn't care about pleasing God, or even about keeping the Law they were always talking about. This meant that their outward service to God was just a show by which they made themselves rich. It's horrible to think there are people who believe they can use God as a way to get wealthy.

16.17 **THE LAW MATTERS TO GOD** We shouldn't get the idea that God doesn't care about how we live, but only about how we believe. That's a false idea. Jesus made it clear that every part of the Law was important. In this passage, Jesus was aiming his words about divorce mainly at the Pharisees. The truth was that the Pharisees didn't really care about the Law, even though they were always teaching it. In fact they were breaking the Law very badly.

NOTES

The rich man also died and
was buried.* 23He went to hell[t]
and was suffering terribly. When
he looked up and saw Abraham
far off and Lazarus at his side,
24he said to Abraham, "Have
pity on me! Send Lazarus to dip
his finger in water and touch my
tongue. I'm suffering terribly in
this fire."
25Abraham answered, "My
friend, remember that while you
lived, you had everything good,
and Lazarus had everything bad.
Now he is happy, and you are
in pain. 26And besides, there is
a deep ditch between us, and no
one from either side can cross
over."
27But the rich man said,
"Abraham, then please send
Lazarus to my father's home.
28Let him warn my five brothers,
so they won't come to this
horrible place."
29Abraham answered, "Your
brothers can read what Moses
and the prophets[u] wrote. They
should pay attention to that."
30Then the rich man said, "No,
that's not enough! If only
someone from the dead would
go to them, they would listen and
turn to God."
31So Abraham said, "If they
won't pay attention to Moses and
the prophets, they won't listen
even to someone who comes
back from the dead."

Faith and Service
(Matthew 18.6, 7, 21, 22; Mark 9.42)

17 Jesus said to his disciples:
There will always be
something that causes people to
sin. But anyone who causes them
to sin is in for trouble. A person
who causes even one of my little
followers to sin 2would be better
off thrown into the ocean with
a heavy stone tied around the
neck. 3So be careful what you
do.
Correct any followers[v] of mine
who sin, and forgive the ones
who say they are sorry. 4Even
if one of them mistreats you
seven times in one day and says,
"I am sorry," you should still
forgive that person.
5The apostles said to the Lord,
"Make our faith stronger!"*
6Jesus replied:
If you had faith no bigger than
a tiny mustard seed, you could
tell this mulberry tree to pull
itself up, roots and all, and to
plant itself in the ocean. And it
would!
7If your servant comes in from
plowing or from taking care of

[t]*hell*: The Greek text has "hades," which the Jewish people often thought of as the place where the dead wait for the final judgment. [u]*Moses and the prophets*: The Jewish Scriptures, that is, the Old Testament. [v]*followers*: The Greek text has "brothers," which is often used in the New Testament for followers of Jesus.

16.22 **WHAT HAPPENS WHEN WE DIE?** Some people say death is the end of everything. But Jesus tells us that we will continue to live either in heaven or in hell. Heaven is a happy place with God, and hell is a place of great misery. Why did the rich man in this story go to hell? It wasn't because he was rich, but because he would not turn to God. Make no mistake—hell is real, and Jesus spoke of hell more than anybody else in the Bible did. We need to face the hard fact of hell, and make sure we're headed for heaven.

17.5 **MAKE OUR FAITH STRONGER** It seems that Jesus was answering the disciples' request for stronger faith when he told them the story about the servant. We really have faith when we don't think we're great just because we do what God tells us. Obeying God is only what we're supposed to do. We're great only because God loved us and forgave us as his free gift. Our good deeds are only our way of saying "thank you" to God.

NOTES

the sheep, would you say,
"Welcome! Come on in and have
something to eat"? 8No, you
wouldn't say that. You would
say, "Fix me something to eat.
Get ready to serve me, so I can
have my meal. Then later on you
can eat and drink." 9Servants
don't deserve special thanks for
doing what they are supposed to
do. 10And that's how it should
be with you. When you've done
all you should, then say, "We are
merely servants, and we have
simply done our duty."

Ten Men with Leprosy

11On his way to Jerusalem, Jesus
went along the border between Samaria and Galilee. 12As he was going
into a village, ten men with leprosy[w]
came toward him. They stood at a
distance 13and shouted, "Jesus, Master, have pity on us!"
14Jesus looked at them and said,
"Go show yourselves to the priests."[x]
On their way they were healed.
15When one of them discovered that
he was healed, he came back, shouting praises to God.* 16He bowed
down at the feet of Jesus and thanked
him. The man was from the country
of Samaria.
17Jesus asked, "Weren't ten men
healed? Where are the other nine?
18Why was this foreigner the only
one who came back to thank God?"
19Then Jesus told the man, "You may
get up and go. Your faith has made
you well."

God's Kingdom
(Matthew 24.23–28, 37–41)

20Some Pharisees asked Jesus
when God's kingdom would come.
He answered, "God's kingdom is not
something you can see.* 21There is
no use saying, 'Look! Here it is' or
'Look! There it is.' God's kingdom
is here with you."[y]
22Jesus said to his disciples:
The time will come when you
will long to see one of the days
of the Son of Man, but you will
not. 23When people say to you,
"Look there," or "Look here,"
don't go looking for him. 24The
day of the Son of Man will be
like lightning flashing across the
sky. 25But first he must suffer
terribly and be rejected by the
people of today. 26When the Son
of Man comes, things will be just
as they were when Noah lived.
27People were eating, drinking,
and getting married right up to
the day when Noah went into the
big boat. Then the flood came
and drowned everyone on earth.
28When Lot[z] lived, people
were also eating and drinking.
They were buying, selling,
planting, and building. 29But on
the very day Lot left Sodom,
fiery flames poured down from

---

[w]*leprosy*: See the note at 4.27. [x]*show yourselves to the priests*: See the note at 5.14. [y]*here with you*: Or "in your hearts." [z]*Noah . . . Lot*: When God destroyed the earth by a flood, he saved Noah and his family. And when God destroyed the cities of Sodom and Gomorrah and the evil people who lived there, he rescued Lot and his family.

17.15 **LET'S BE THANKFUL** It's always a joy to do things for thankful people. But if we're ungrateful, it isn't easy for God or humans to do kind things for us. We send the message to others that we don't appreciate kindness and we would rather just be left alone. Usually we get our wish. We just end up being alone in the world.

17.20 **WHAT IS GOD'S KINGDOM?** Jesus answered the Pharisees in a puzzling way. They couldn't see the kingdom of God because they weren't ready for the kingdom. This was plain because they didn't recognize the King himself—Jesus. If they couldn't see the King, how could they know anything about God's kingdom?

NOTES

the sky and killed everyone.
30The same will happen on the
day when the Son of Man
appears.*
31At that time no one on a
rooftop[a] should go down into the
house to get anything. No one
in a field should go back to the
house for anything. 32Remember
what happened to Lot's wife.[b]
33People who try to save their
lives will lose them, and those
who lose their lives will save
them. 34On that night two people
will be sleeping in the same bed,
but only one will be taken. The
other will be left. 35-36Two
women will be together grinding
wheat, but only one will be
taken. The other will be left.[c]
37Then Jesus' disciples spoke up,
"But where will this happen, Lord?"
Jesus said, "Where there is a
corpse, there will always be buzzards."[d]

A Widow and a Judge

18 Jesus told his disciples a story
about how they should keep on
praying and never give up:
2In a town there was once a
judge who didn't fear God or
care about people.* 3In that same
town there was a widow who
kept going to the judge and
saying, "Make sure that I get fair
treatment in court."
4For a while the judge refused
to do anything. Finally, he said
to himself, "Even though I don't
fear God or care about people,
5I will help this widow because
she keeps on bothering me. If I
don't help her, she will wear me
out."
6The Lord said:
Think about what that
crooked judge said. 7Won't God
protect his chosen ones who
pray to him day and night?
Won't he be concerned for them?
8He will surely hurry and help
them. But when the Son of Man
comes, will he find on this earth
anyone with faith?

A Pharisee and a Tax Collector

9Jesus told a story to some people
who thought they were better than
others and who looked down on
everyone else:
10Two men went into the
temple to pray.[e] One was a
Pharisee and the other a tax
collector.[f] 11The Pharisee stood

---

[a] *rooftop*: See the note at 5.19. [b] *what happened to Lot's wife*: She turned to a block of salt when she disobeyed God. [c] *will be left*: Some manuscripts add, "Two men will be in the same field, but only one will be taken. The other will be left." [d] *Where there is a corpse, there will always be buzzards*: This saying may mean that when anything important happens, people soon know about it. Or the saying may mean that whenever something bad happens, curious people gather around and stare. But the word translated "buzzard" also means "eagle" and may refer to the Roman army, which had an eagle as its symbol. [e] *into the temple to pray*: Jewish people usually prayed there early in the morning and late in the afternoon. [f] *tax collector*: See the note at 3.12.

17.30 **GOD'S KINGDOM WILL COME** King Jesus *has* come, *is* coming, and *will* come. The kingdom of God was with us when Jesus was here. The kingdom is also with us in the good news that we have today about Jesus, and among those who truly love him. And the kingdom of God will also come in a powerful and final way at a time that is still in the future, when King Jesus returns to earth.

18.2 **GOD IS LISTENING, AND HE CARES** Some people don't return our phone calls because they don't care about us. But God sometimes delays answering our prayers to teach us important lessons. God isn't a vending machine that gives us a candy bar for the right change. God is interested in what is best for us, and he has a best time for meeting our needs. God will answer our prayers when he's ready. But it's good for us to keep asking while we're waiting, because God himself is worth the time we spend talking to him.

NOTES

over by himself and prayed,[g]
"God, I thank you that I am
not greedy, dishonest, and
unfaithful in marriage like other
people. And I am really glad that
I am not like that tax collector
over there.* 12 I go without
eating[h] for two days a week, and
I give you one tenth of all I earn."
13 The tax collector stood off at
a distance and did not think he
was good enough even to look
up toward heaven. He was so
sorry for what he had done that
he pounded his chest and
prayed, "God, have pity on me!
I am such a sinner."
14 Then Jesus said, "When the two
men went home, it was the tax collector and not the Pharisee who was
pleasing to God. If you put yourself
above others, you will be put down.
But if you humble yourself, you will
be honored."

Jesus Blesses Little Children
(Matthew 19.13–15; Mark 10.13–16)

15 Some people brought their little
children for Jesus to bless. But when
his disciples saw them doing this,
they told the people to stop bothering
him.* 16 So Jesus called the children
over to him and said, "Let the children come to me! Don't try to stop
them. People who are like these children belong to God's kingdom.[i]
17 You will never get into God's kingdom unless you enter it like a child!"

A Rich and Important Man
(Matthew 19.16–30; Mark 10.17–31)

18 An important man asked Jesus,
"Good Teacher, what must I do to
have eternal life?"
19 Jesus said, "Why do you call me
good? Only God is good.* 20 You
know the commandments: 'Be faithful in marriage. Do not murder. Do
not steal. Do not tell lies about others.
Respect your father and mother.' "
21 He told Jesus, "I have obeyed all
these commandments since I was a
young man."
22 When Jesus heard this, he said,
"There is one thing you still need to
do. Go and sell everything you own!
Give the money to the poor, and you
will have riches in heaven. Then
come and be my follower." 23 When
the man heard this, he was sad, because he was very rich.
24 Jesus saw how sad the man was.
So he said, "It's terribly hard for rich
people to get into God's kingdom!
25 In fact, it's easier for a camel to
go through the eye of a needle than
for a rich person to get into God's
kingdom."
26 When the people heard this, they
asked, "How can anyone ever be
saved?"

---

[g] *stood over by himself and prayed*: Some manuscripts have "stood up and prayed to himself." [h] *without eating*: See the note at 2.37. [i] *People who are like these children belong to God's kingdom*: Or "God's kingdom belongs to people who are like these children."

18.11 **PRIDE SEPARATES US FROM GOD** The Pharisee in Jesus' story knew more about his religion than the tax collector did. The Pharisee was even a "good man" by our way of measuring goodness. But he wasn't humble enough to see himself as a needy sinner. Everybody is a sinner. So the Pharisee's pride separated him from God. But the lowly tax collector saw the truth about himself, so God accepted him.

18.15 **GOD CARES ABOUT THE SMALL** We shouldn't let ourselves get too big and important. Jesus cared about the children people brought to him. He was never too busy. He loved the honest, simple faith he saw in children, and wished people of all ages could be more like children in this way.

18.19 **ONLY GOD IS GOOD** This fits what we just saw about the Pharisee and the tax collector. As soon as we begin to think we're "good," we start to cut ourselves off from God. The important man in this passage thought he had been good all his life. But his property was too important to him, and he went away sad. God has no equals.

NOTES

27Jesus replied, "There are some things that people cannot do, but God can do anything."

28Peter said, "Remember, we left everything to be your followers!"

29Jesus answered, "You can be sure that anyone who gives up home or wife or brothers or family or children because of God's kingdom 30will be given much more in this life. And in the future world they will have eternal life."

Jesus Again Tells about His Death
(Matthew 20.17–19; Mark 10.32–34)

31Jesus took the twelve apostles aside and said:

We are now on our way to Jerusalem. Everything that the prophets wrote about the Son of Man will happen there.* 32He will be handed over to foreigners,[j] who will make fun of him, mistreat him, and spit on him. 33They will beat him and kill him, but three days later he will rise to life.

34The apostles did not understand what Jesus was talking about. They could not understand, because the meaning of what he said was hidden from them.

Jesus Heals a Blind Beggar
(Matthew 20.29–34; Mark 10.46–52)

35When Jesus was coming close to Jericho, a blind man sat begging beside the road.* 36The man heard the crowd walking by and asked what was happening. 37Some people told him that Jesus from Nazareth was passing by. 38So the blind man shouted, "Jesus, Son of David,[k] have pity on me!" 39The people who were going along with Jesus told the man to be quiet. But he shouted even louder, "Son of David, have pity on me!"

40Jesus stopped and told some people to bring the blind man over to him. When the blind man was getting near, Jesus asked, 41"What do you want me to do for you?"

"Lord, I want to see!" he answered.

42Jesus replied, "Look and you will see! Your eyes are healed because of your faith." 43Right away the man could see, and he went with Jesus and started thanking God. When the crowds saw what happened, they praised God.

Zacchaeus

19 Jesus was going through Jericho, 2where a man named Zacchaeus lived. He was in charge of collecting taxes[l] and was very rich. 3-4Jesus was heading his way, and Zacchaeus wanted to see what he was like. But Zacchaeus was a short man and could not see over the crowd. So he ran ahead and climbed up into a sycamore tree.

5When Jesus got there, he looked up and said, "Zacchaeus, hurry down! I want to stay with you today." 6Zacchaeus hurried down and gladly welcomed Jesus.*

7Everyone who saw this started grumbling, "This man Zacchaeus is

---

[j]*foreigners*: The Romans, who ruled Judea at this time. [k]*Son of David*: The Jewish people expected the Messiah to be from the family of King David, and for this reason the Messiah was often called the "Son of David." [l]*in charge of collecting taxes*: See the note at 3.12.

18.31 **JESUS PAID OUR DEBT** We miss the whole plan of God if we think Jesus came just to teach us a lot of good rules for living. Jesus came to die in our place. We owed God a very great debt because of our sins. Jesus paid that debt.

18.35 **THANK GOD** The no-longer-blind beggar went with Jesus and thanked God. These were two good things to do. When we think of what Jesus has done for us, do we walk with him? Do we thank God in a way others can see? The beggar was a good example for others: soon the crowds were praising God too.

19.6 **A MEAN MAN BECOMES KIND** Zacchaeus probably became rich by cheating people, something tax collectors were known for in those days. But Zacchaeus had a change of *(continued)*

NOTES

Step 8

ZACCHAEUS—a man who was determined to make things right with others at all costs

LUKE 19.1–10

Most of us know the story of Zacchaeus, the little man who climbed into a tree to get a better look when Jesus was passing through Jericho. Zacchaeus was determined to find out more about this man who was getting so much attention from the public. We are not sure what his motives were but we do know that he was in charge of collecting taxes. You could say he headed up the Internal Revenue Service of Jericho. Possibly Zacchaeus saw an opportunity to collect some tax money from Jesus and his disciples. A good tax collector wouldn't pass up this opportunity.

What would you do if you found out representatives of the IRS were investigating your affairs? Most of us would prefer to avoid them and give as little information as possible. Jesus did just the opposite; he decided to invite himself to Zacchaeus's house and visit with him. We don't know all that happened that day, but the story has a happy ending—Zacchaeus became a believer!

Immediately, Zacchaeus's life changed. We know this because he promised the Lord he would give half of his property to the poor and agreed to pay back four times as much money as he had stolen. A person wouldn't do this unless something dramatic had taken place. Zacchaeus was determined to set the record straight in order to clear his name. Once he did this, he was free to proclaim the name of Jesus and become an effective witness to his family, friends, and enemies.

STEP LOOK BACK 8

Determination often involves paying a price. In Zacchaeus's case the price was monetary. In our situations something different may be called for. One thing is certain—when we decide to make things right with other people in our lives, no price is too great. Determination enables us to stay on course even if others around us decide to settle for something less.

Taking a quick inventory of the character God is building in our lives through these 12 steps, do we see determination emerging in us? We probably would have quit long before now without the determination to grow and develop a closer relationship with Jesus Christ. We need to hang in there, never giving up.

Ready for Step 9?
Turn to page 31 of* InStep's *introduction.

a sinner! And Jesus is going home to eat with him."

[8]Later that day Zacchaeus stood up and said to the Lord, "I will give half of my property to the poor. And I will now pay back four times as much[m] to everyone I have ever cheated."

[9]Jesus said to Zacchaeus, "Today you and your family have been saved,[n] because you are a true son of Abraham.[o] [10]The Son of Man came to look for and to save people who are lost."

A Story about Ten Servants
(Matthew 25.14–30)

[11]The people were still listening to Jesus as he was getting close to Jerusalem. Many of them thought that God's kingdom would soon appear, [12]and Jesus told them this story:

A prince once went to a foreign country to be crowned king and then to return. [13]But before leaving, he called in ten servants and gave each of them some money. He told them, "Use this to earn more money until I get back."

[14]But the people of his country hated him, and they sent messengers to the foreign country to say, "We don't want this man to be our king."

[15]After the prince had been made king, he returned and called in his servants. He asked them how much they had earned with the money they had been given.

[16]The first servant came and said, "Sir, with the money you gave me I have earned ten times as much."

[17]"That's fine, my good servant!" the king said. "Since you have shown that you can be trusted with a small amount, you will be given ten cities to rule."

[18]The second one came and said, "Sir, with the money you gave me, I have earned five times as much."

[19]The king said, "You will be given five cities."

[20]Another servant came and said, "Sir, here is your money. I kept it safe in a handkerchief.* [21]You are a hard man, and I was afraid of you. You take what is not yours, and you harvest crops you didn't plant."

[22]"You worthless servant!" the king told him. "You have condemned yourself by what you have just said. You knew that I am a hard man, taking what is not mine and harvesting what I've not planted. [23]Why didn't you put my money in the bank? On my return, I could have had the money together with interest."

[24]Then he said to some other servants standing there, "Take the money away from him and give it to the servant who earned ten times as much."

---

[m]*pay back four times as much*: Both Jewish and Roman law said that a person must pay back four times the amount that was taken. [n]*saved*: Zacchaeus was Jewish, but it is only now that he is rescued from sin and placed under God's care. [o]*son of Abraham*: As used in this verse, the words mean that Zacchaeus is truly one of God's special people.

(*continued*) heart. He saw Jesus the Master, and he became a new man. The crowd didn't like it. They needed new hearts, too, but they couldn't stand the idea. Only people who know they're lost and need to do something about it—like Zacchaeus—can be saved.

19.20 **WHAT DOES GOD EXPECT FROM US?** Some people think it's smart to "play it safe." But God doesn't want that from us. He wants the kind of people who can be a help to his kingdom. The man who hid the money in his handkerchief had done no good for anyone—and least of all for the prince in Jesus' story. By giving ourselves and our time to carry God's blessing to others we are good servants for Jesus our King.

NOTES

25But they said, "Sir, he
already has ten times as much!"
26The king replied, "Those
who have something will be
given more. But everything will
be taken away from those who
don't have anything. 27Now
bring me the enemies who didn't
want me to be their king. Kill
them while I watch!"

Jesus Enters Jerusalem

(Matthew 21.1–11; Mark 11.1–11; John 12.12–19)

28When Jesus had finished saying
all this, he went on toward Jerusalem. 29As he was getting near to Bethphage and Bethany on the Mount of
Olives, he sent two of his disciples
on ahead. 30He told them, "Go into
the next village, where you will find
a young donkey that has never been
ridden. Untie the donkey and bring
it here. 31If anyone asks why you are
doing that, just say, 'The Lord[p] needs
it.' "
32They went off and found everything just as Jesus had said.* 33While
they were untying the donkey, its
owners asked, "Why are you doing
that?"
34They answered, "The Lord[p]
needs it."
35Then they led the donkey to Jesus. They put some of their clothes
on its back and helped Jesus get on.
36And as he rode along, the people
spread clothes on the road[q] in front
of him. 37When Jesus was starting
down the Mount of Olives, his large
crowd of disciples were happy and
praised God because of all the miracles they had seen. 38They shouted,

"Blessed is the king who comes
in the name of the Lord!
Peace in heaven
and glory to God."

39Some Pharisees in the crowd said
to Jesus, "Teacher, make your disciples stop shouting!"
40But Jesus answered, "If they
keep quiet, these stones will start
shouting."
41When Jesus came closer and
could see Jerusalem, he cried 42and
said:

It is too bad that today your
people don't know what will
bring them peace! Now it is
hidden from them. 43Jerusalem,
the time will come when your
enemies will build walls around
you to attack you. Armies will
surround you and close in on you
from every side.* 44They will
level you to the ground and kill
your people. Not one stone in
your buildings will be left on top
of another. This will happen
because you did not see that God
had come to save you.[r]

Jesus in the Temple

(Matthew 21.12–17; Mark 11.15–19; John 2.13–22)

45When Jesus entered the temple,
he started chasing out the people who

---

[p] *The Lord*: Or "The master of the donkey."
[q] *spread clothes on the road*: This was one way that the Jewish people welcomed a famous person.
[r] *that God had come to save you*: The Jewish people looked for the time when God would come and rescue them from their enemies. But when Jesus came, many of them refused to obey him.

19.32 **JESUS KNOWS** Even when he was on earth in human form, Jesus showed at times that he had knowledge about things that he had not learned in an ordinary way. It is much more so today, now that Jesus has risen from the dead and has been taken up to heaven. Jesus knows all things and all people perfectly. Not a thing can be hidden from him.

19.43 **JESUS FORETOLD THE FUTURE** Jesus exactly described the destruction of Jerusalem. Forty years after Jesus spoke these words, a Roman army under General Titus built a wall around the city. No one in Jerusalem could get out, and no food could get in. Many starved to death. The temple and other parts of the city were destroyed. If the people had accepted Jesus when they had a chance, the city could have been spared from Rome's attack.

NOTES

were selling things.* 46He told them,
"The Scriptures say, 'My house
should be a place of worship.' But
you have made it a place where robbers hide!"
47Each day Jesus kept on teaching
in the temple. So the chief priests,
the teachers of the Law of Moses,
and some other important people
tried to have him killed. 48But they
could not find a way to do it, because
everyone else was eager to listen to
him.

A Question about Jesus' Authority

(Matthew 21.23–27; Mark 11.27–33)

20 One day Jesus was teaching in
the temple and telling the good
news. So the chief priests, the teachers, and the nation's leaders 2asked
him, "What right do you have to do
these things? Who gave you this
authority?"
3Jesus replied, "I want to ask you
a question.* 4Who gave John the
right to baptize? Was it God in
heaven or merely some human
being?"
5They talked this over and said to
each other, "We can't say that God
gave John this right. Jesus will ask
us why we didn't believe John.
6And we can't say that it was merely
some human who gave John the right
to baptize. The crowd will stone us
to death, because they think John
was a prophet."
7So they told Jesus, "We don't
know who gave John the right to
baptize."
8Jesus replied, "Then I won't tell
you who gave me the right to do what
I do."

Renters of a Vineyard

(Matthew 21.33–46; Mark 12.1–12)

9Jesus told the people this story:
A man once planted a
vineyard and rented it out. Then
he left the country for a long
time. 10When it was time to
harvest the crop, he sent a
servant to ask the renters for his
share of the grapes. But they
beat up the servant and sent him
away without anything. 11So the
owner sent another servant. The
renters also beat him up. They
insulted him terribly and sent
him away without a thing. 12The
owner sent a third servant. He
was also beaten terribly and
thrown out of the vineyard.
13The owner then said to
himself, "What am I going to do?
I know what. I'll send my son,
the one I love so much. They will
surely respect him!"
14When the renters saw the
owner's son, they said to one
another, "Someday he will own
the vineyard. Let's kill him! Then
we can have it all for ourselves."
15So they threw him out of the
vineyard and killed him.
Jesus asked, "What do you think
the owner of the vineyard will do?
16I'll tell you what he will do! He
will come and kill those renters
and let someone else have his vineyard."

19.45 **WHY DID THEY WANT TO KILL JESUS?** Jesus did the most dangerous thing he could do by showing what the Jewish religious leaders were really like. For years they had gotten away with pretending to be holy men when they were actually taking bribes from merchants in the temple. It was as if Jesus threw ice water on those men. They would make him pay for his words.

20.3 **NOT MUCH HONESTY HERE** Jesus turned the Jewish leaders' question back on them. They were so concerned about their well-being that they couldn't say what was on their minds. They didn't want to risk upsetting the crowd. Maybe some of them suspected John's right to baptize was from God, but couldn't admit it to themselves. It's sad when people can't stand to be honest.

NOTES

When the people heard this, they
said, "This must never happen!"*
17But Jesus looked straight at them
and said, "Then what do the Scriptures mean when they say, 'The stone
that the builders tossed aside is now
the most important stone of all'?
18Anyone who stumbles over this
stone will get hurt, and anyone it falls
on will be smashed to pieces."
19The chief priests and the teachers
of the Law of Moses knew that Jesus
was talking about them when he was
telling this story. They wanted to arrest him right then, but they were
afraid of the people.

Paying Taxes
(Matthew 22.15–22; Mark 12.13–17)

20Jesus' enemies kept watching
him closely, because they wanted to
hand him over to the Roman governor. So they sent some men who pretended to be good. But they were really spies trying to catch Jesus saying
something wrong.* 21The spies said
to him, "Teacher, we know that you
teach the truth about what God wants
people to do. And you treat everyone
with the same respect, no matter who
they are. 22Tell us, should we pay
taxes to the Emperor or not?"
23Jesus knew that they were trying
to trick him. So he told them,
24"Show me a coin." Then he asked,
"Whose picture and name are on it?"
"The Emperor's," they answered.
25Then he told them, "Give the Emperor what belongs to him and give
God what belongs to God." 26Jesus'
enemies could not catch him saying
anything wrong there in front of the
people. They were amazed at his answer and kept quiet.

Life in the Future World
(Matthew 22.23–33; Mark 12.18–27)

27The Sadducees did not believe
that people would rise to life after
death. So some of them came to Jesus
28and said:

Teacher, Moses wrote that if
a married man dies and has no
children, his brother should
marry the widow. Their first son
would then be thought of as the
son of the dead brother.
29There were once seven
brothers. The first one married,
but died without having any
children.* 30The second one
married his brother's widow,
and he also died without having
any children. 31The same thing
happened to the third one.
Finally, all seven brothers
married that woman and died
without having any children.
32At last the woman died.
33When God raises people from
death, whose wife will this
woman be? All seven brothers
had married her.

34Jesus answered:

20.16 **WHO WILL GET THE VINEYARD?** Jesus had come to offer himself to Israel as their King. But he taught that because of Israel's coldness toward him, their special blessing would be given to other people. A lesson we can learn is that if we don't accept God's love, then he will bless other people who will appreciate him and his Son.

20.20 **HOW DECEITFUL WE CAN BE** Think of it: the spies were actually using their religion to trick Jesus. Then they would be able to have him arrested. A great prophet once said that the human heart is more deceitful than anything—so deceitful that we can even use God's word as a way to do evil. May the Lord keep us from ever being so hardhearted.

20.29 **DON'T ASK FOOLISH QUESTIONS** That's what the Sadducees were doing when they asked about the dead man's widow. The worst of it was that they even *knew* the question was foolish. But they asked it anyway, hoping to put Jesus on the spot. Later on, a famous apostle named Paul warned about asking useless questions (see 1 Timothy 6.4, 5).

NOTES

The people in this world get
married. 35But in the future
world no one who is worthy to
rise from death will either marry
36or die. They will be like the
angels and will be God's
children, because they have
been raised to life.
37In the story about the
burning bush, Moses clearly
shows that people will live again.
He said, "The Lord is the God
worshiped by Abraham, Isaac,
and Jacob."[s] 38So the Lord is not
the God of the dead, but of the
living. This means that everyone
is alive as far as God is
concerned.
39Some of the teachers of the Law
of Moses said, "Teacher, you have
given a good answer!" 40From then
on, no one dared to ask Jesus any
questions.

About David's Son
(Matthew 22.41–46; Mark 12.35–37)

41Jesus asked, "Why do people say
that the Messiah will be the son of
King David?[t]* 42In the book of
Psalms, David himself says,

'The Lord said to my Lord,
Sit at my right side[u]
43until I make your enemies
into a footstool for you.'

44David spoke of the Messiah as his
Lord, so how can the Messiah be his
son?"

Jesus and the Teachers of the Law of Moses
(Matthew 23.1–36; Mark 12.38–40; Luke 11.37–54)

45While everyone was listening to
Jesus, he said to his disciples:*
46Guard against the teachers
of the Law of Moses! They love
to walk around in long robes,
and they like to be greeted in
the market. They want the front
seats in the meeting places and
the best seats at banquets. 47But
they cheat widows out of their
homes and then pray long
prayers just to show off. These
teachers will be punished most
of all.

A Widow's Offering
(Mark 12.41–44)

21 Jesus looked up and saw some
rich people tossing their gifts
into the offering box.* 2He also saw
a poor widow putting in two pennies.
3And he said, "I tell you that this poor
woman has put in more than all the
others. 4Everyone else gave what
they didn't need. But she is very poor
and gave everything she had."

---

[s] *"The Lord is the God worshiped by Abraham, Isaac, and Jacob"*: Jesus argues that if God is worshiped by these three, they must be alive, because he is the God of the living. [t] *the son of King David*: See the note at 18.38. [u] *right side*: The place of power and honor.

20.41 **A TOUGH QUESTION** Jesus' enemies were asking "tough questions," so he tried one on them. Because Jesus is the Son of God, his ancestor David called him "my Lord." It was right there in the book of Psalms, but the enemies of Jesus didn't want to see it.

20.45 **LOVE GOD FOR HIS OWN SAKE** The "teachers of the Law of Moses" liked to be well thought of by everyone. It's not wrong to be well thought of, but these men made a career out of being popular. The truth didn't matter—as long as the teachers stayed rich and powerful. Neither was there anything wrong with the Law they taught—but they didn't *obey* it. Jesus said that these showoffs would receive more punishment. Let that be a warning to us.

21.1 **WHAT SHALL WE GIVE TO GOD?** We should never insult God by giving him what costs us nothing. God gave his very own Son for us. We owe him our very lives and all we have. As the famous hymn writer Isaac Watts put it, "Love so amazing, so divine, demands my soul, my life, my all."

NOTES

The Temple Will Be Destroyed
(Matthew 24.1, 2; Mark 13.1, 2)

5Some people were talking about the beautiful stones used to build the temple and about the gifts that had been placed in it. Jesus said,* 6"Do you see these stones? The time is coming when not one of them will be left in place. They will all be knocked down."

Warning about Trouble
(Matthew 24.3–14; Mark 13.3–13)

7Some people asked, "Teacher, when will all this happen? How can we know when these things are about to take place?"

8Jesus replied:

Don't be fooled by all those who will come and claim to be me. They will say, "I am Christ!" and "Now is the time!" But don't follow them. 9When you hear about wars and riots, don't be afraid. These things will have to happen first, but that is not the end.

10Nations will go to war against one another, and kingdoms will attack each other. 11There will be great earthquakes, and in many places people will starve to death and suffer terrible diseases. All sorts of frightening things will be seen in the sky.

12Before all this happens, you will be arrested and punished. You will be tried in the Jewish meeting places and put in jail. Because of me you will be placed on trial before kings and governors.* 13But this will be your chance to tell about your faith.

14Don't worry about what you will say to defend yourselves. 15I will give you the wisdom to know what to say. None of your enemies will be able to oppose you or to say that you are wrong. 16You will be betrayed by your own parents, brothers, family, and friends. Some of you will even be killed. 17Because of me you will be hated by everyone. 18But don't worry![v] 19You will be saved by being faithful to me.

Jerusalem Will Be Destroyed
(Matthew 24.15–21; Mark 13.14–19)

20When you see Jerusalem surrounded by soldiers, you will know that it will soon be destroyed.* 21If you are living in Judea at that time, run to the mountains. If you are in the city, leave it. And if you are out in

---

[v]*But don't worry*: The Greek text has "Not a hair of your head will be lost," which means, "There's no need to worry."

21.5 **ALL BUILDINGS PASS AWAY** We enjoy beauty of all kinds, and so we enjoy beautiful buildings. Jesus was probably sad when he announced that the beautiful temple would be destroyed—as indeed it was in the year 70. Let's not forget that even the most lasting things of this world will pass away some day. In his church Jesus is building something that will never pass away.

21.12 **BELIEVERS ARE SAVED AT LAST** Many Christians would have to go through hard times before seeing Jesus. Even those closest to them might hate them. Many of them would be killed. That was hard. Who would want to follow such a faith? Today believers still suffer for Jesus, but they come through it for three reasons: (1) Jesus suffered for us first; (2) we have his real friendship now; (3) we want to see him face to face.

21.20 **JERUSALEM WOULD BE DESTROYED** Some of the people listening to Jesus would be alive forty years later when everything he told about would happen. How did Jesus know those things in such great detail? It was because Jesus is who the Bible says he is—the Son of God from heaven. He is in charge of the past, the present, and the future.

NOTES

the country, don't go back into
the city. 22This time of
punishment is what is written
about in the Scriptures. 23It will
be an awful time for women who
are expecting babies or nursing
young children! Everywhere in
the land people will suffer
horribly and be punished.
24Some of them will be killed by
swords. Others will be carried
off to foreign countries.
Jerusalem will be overrun by
foreign nations until their time
comes to an end.

When the Son of Man Appears
(Matthew 24.29–31; Mark 13.24–27)

25Strange things will happen
to the sun, moon, and stars. The
nations on earth will be afraid
of the roaring sea and tides, and
they won't know what to do.*
26People will be so frightened
that they will faint because of
what is happening to the world.
Every power in the sky will be
shaken.[w] 27Then the Son of Man
will be seen, coming in a cloud
with great power and glory.
28When all of this starts
happening, stand up straight and
be brave. You will soon be set
free.

A Lesson from a Fig Tree
(Matthew 24.32–35; Mark 13.28–31)

29Then Jesus told them a story:
When you see a fig tree or any
other tree 30putting out leaves,
you know that summer will soon
come. 31So, when you see these
things happening, you know that
God's kingdom will soon be
here. 32You can be sure that
some of the people living today
will still be alive when all of this
takes place. 33The sky and the
earth won't last forever, but my
words will.

A Warning

34Don't spend all of your time
thinking about eating or
drinking or worrying about life.
If you do, the final day will
suddenly catch you* 35like a
trap. That day will surprise
everyone on earth. 36Watch out
and keep praying that you can
escape all that is going to happen
and that the Son of Man will be
pleased with you.
37Jesus taught in the temple each
day, and he spent each night on the
Mount of Olives.* 38Everyone got up

---

[w]*Every power in the sky will be shaken*: In ancient times people thought that the stars were spiritual powers.

21.25 **NATURE WILL BE SHAKEN** We may imagine that the sun, moon, stars, and all of nature will go on and on without end. But nothing in the material universe has to last forever. Things last only as long as their Creator keeps them all in place. Some day he will shake it all like a tree of ripe fruit, and all will come crashing down. Through it all, believers will be kept safe. Then Jesus will come, and God will make all things new.

21.34 **WE ARE NOT DEATHLESS** Are you living as if this were the day of your death? Death brings the end of all chances to get our lives in line with God. Thinking only about things like eating, drinking, jobs, houses, cars, and clothing is therefore a waste of time. It would be better to make our time spent worrying into time spent praying. Each day, each hour, may be our last on earth. Are we ready to meet God?

21.37 **WHY WAS JESUS ON THE MOUNTAIN?** Surely Jesus could have found a place to stay besides that mountain. But he needed time to be alone so he could pray to his Father, and a good place for that was on a mountain. In this way, too, Jesus is our example of how to live. We see that he spent a lot of time in public, but he also needed lots of time alone for prayer. So do we.

NOTES

early and came to the temple to hear him teach.

A Plot to Kill Jesus

(Matthew 26.1–5, 14, 16; Mark 14.1, 2, 10, 11; John 11.45–53)

22 The Feast of Thin Bread, also called Passover, was near. 2The chief priests and the teachers of the Law of Moses were looking for a way to get rid of Jesus, because they were afraid of what the people might do. 3Then Satan entered the heart of Judas Iscariot,[x] who was one of the twelve apostles.*

4Judas went to talk with the chief priests and the officers of the temple police about how he could help them arrest Jesus. 5They were very pleased and offered to pay Judas some money. 6He agreed and started looking for a good chance to betray Jesus when the crowds were not around.

Jesus Eats with His Disciples

(Matthew 26.17–25; Mark 14.12–21; John 13.21–30)

7The day had come for the Feast of Thin Bread, and it was time to kill the Passover lambs. 8So Jesus said to Peter and John, "Go and prepare the Passover meal for us to eat."

9But they asked, "Where do you want us to prepare it?"

10Jesus told them, "As you go into the city, you will meet a man carrying a jar of water.[y] Follow him into the house 11and say to the owner, 'Our teacher wants to know where he can eat the Passover meal with his disciples.' 12The owner will take you upstairs and show you a large room ready for you to use. Prepare the meal there."

13Peter and John left. They found everything just as Jesus had told them, and they prepared the Passover meal.*

The Lord's Supper

(Matthew 26.26–30; Mark 14.22–26; 1 Corinthians 11.23–25)

14When the time came for Jesus and the apostles to eat, 15he said to them, "I have very much wanted to eat this Passover meal with you before I suffer. 16I tell you that I will not eat another Passover meal until it is finally eaten in God's kingdom."

17Jesus took a cup of wine in his hands and gave thanks to God. Then he told the apostles, "Take this wine and share it with each other.* 18I tell you that I will not drink any more wine until God's kingdom comes."

19Jesus took some bread in his hands and gave thanks for it. He

---

[x] *Iscariot*: See the note at 6.16. [y] *a man carrying a jar of water*: A male slave carrying water would probably mean that the family was rich.

22.3 **LOOK OUT FOR SATAN'S WORK** Judas had allowed himself to think thoughts about Jesus that weren't true. As he turned these evil thoughts over in his mind, Satan took control of his life. We dare not imagine that Satan cannot attack us. He tries to deceive us at every turn in life. But we pray, as Jesus taught us, to be protected from "the evil one" (see the footnote at Matthew 6.13). And we will be protected.

22.13 **TIME FOR THE LAMBS TO DIE** The time to kill the Passover lambs would also be the time for Jesus, the perfect Lamb of God, to die for the sins of the world.

22.17 **WHAT DOES THE LORD'S SUPPER MEAN?** It has been said that the Lord's Supper is "the good news without words." Jesus commands us to eat and drink the supper at which we remember his death. He said, "This is my body," and, "This is my blood." The bread and the wine are not actually his body and blood, but they are a real picture of Christ's death for us. The idea is that we are to be filled with Jesus' life by his spirit working in us.

NOTES

broke the bread and handed it to his
apostles. Then he said, "This is my
body, which is given for you. Eat this
as a way of remembering me!"
20After the meal he took another
cup of wine in his hands. Then he
said, "This is my blood. It is poured
out for you, and with it God makes
his new agreement. 21The one who
will betray me is here at the table
with me! 22The Son of Man will die
in the way that has been decided for
him, but it will be terrible for the one
who betrays him!"
23Then the apostles started arguing
about who would ever do such a
thing.

An Argument about Greatness

24The apostles got into an argument about which one of them was
the greatest.* 25So Jesus told them:
Foreign kings order their
people around, and powerful
rulers call themselves
everyone's friends.[z] 26But don't
be like them. The most important
one of you should be like the
least important, and your leader
should be like a servant. 27Who
do people think is the greatest,
a person who is served or one
who serves? Isn't it the one who
is served? But I have been with
you as a servant.
28You have stayed with me in
all my troubles. 29So I will give
you the right to rule as kings,
just as my Father has given me
the right to rule as a king. 30You
will eat and drink with me in my
kingdom, and you will each sit
on a throne to judge the twelve
tribes of Israel.

Jesus' Disciples Will Be Tested
(Matthew 26.31–35; Mark 14.27–31; John 13.36–38)

31Jesus said, "Simon, listen to me!
Satan has demanded the right to test
each one of you, as a farmer does
when he separates wheat from the
husks.[a]* 32But Simon, I have prayed
that your faith will be strong. And
when you have come back to me, help
the others."
33Peter said, "Lord, I am ready to
go with you to jail and even to die
with you."
34Jesus replied, "Peter, I tell you
that before a rooster crows tomorrow
morning, you will say three times
that you don't know me."

Moneybags, Traveling Bags, and Swords

35Jesus asked his disciples, "When
I sent you out without a moneybag
or a traveling bag or sandals, did you
need anything?"
"No!" they answered.*

---

[z] *everyone's friends*: This translates a Greek word that rulers sometimes used as a title for themselves or for special friends. [a] *separates wheat from the husks*: See the note at 3.17.

22.24 **WE ARE GREAT BY SERVING** At a time like this, with Jesus about to die, the apostles argued about which of them was greatest. Jesus could see a day when they would be great in his kingdom, but for the time being they would have to be servants. We are great when we "lay down our lives" for others in service. That makes us like Jesus.

22.31 **WHY WAS SIMON TESTED?** Why are any of us tested? We take tests to see whether we can do a certain job. If we aren't tested we become weak, but testing proves how strong or weak we are. Simon Peter later discovered how weak he was when he denied Jesus. But that was good in the long run, because Simon Peter learned to trust God rather than his own ability.

22.35 **BE READY TO TRAVEL** When Jesus sent out the apostles the first time, they traveled only in Palestine. But this time Jesus was going to leave them, and they would be scattered across the whole world. So he told them to be ready for a longer journey than the first time—to take money, clothes, and even a sword.

NOTES

[36]Jesus told them, "But now, if you have a moneybag, take it with you. Also take a traveling bag, and if you don't have a sword,[b] sell some of your clothes and buy one. [37]Do this because the Scriptures say, 'He was considered a criminal.' This was written about me, and it will soon come true."

[38]The disciples said, "Lord, here are two swords!"

"Enough of that!" Jesus replied.

Jesus Prays
(Matthew 26.36–46; Mark 14.32–42)

[39]Jesus went out to the Mount of Olives, as he often did, and his disciples went with him. [40]When they got there, he told them, "Pray that you will not be tested."*

[41]Jesus walked on a little way before he kneeled down and prayed, [42]"Father, if you will, please don't make me suffer by having me drink from this cup.[c] But do what you want, and not what I want."

[43]Then an angel from heaven came to help him. [44]Jesus was in great pain and prayed so sincerely that his sweat fell to the ground like drops of blood.[d]

[45]Jesus got up from praying and went over to his disciples. They were asleep and worn out from being so sad. [46]He said to them, "Why are you asleep? Wake up and pray that you will not be tested."

Jesus Is Arrested
(Matthew 26.47–56; Mark 14.43–50; John 18.3–11)

[47]While Jesus was still speaking, a crowd came up. It was led by Judas, one of the twelve apostles. He went over to Jesus and greeted him with a kiss.[e]

[48]Jesus asked Judas, "Are you betraying the Son of Man with a kiss?"

[49]When Jesus' disciples saw what was about to happen, they asked, "Lord, should we attack them with a sword?" [50]One of the disciples even struck at the high priest's servant with his sword and cut off the servant's right ear.

[51]"Enough of that!" Jesus said. Then he touched the servant's ear and healed it.*

[52]Jesus spoke to the chief priests, the temple police, and the leaders who had come to arrest him. He said, "Why do you come out with swords and clubs and treat me like a criminal? [53]I was with you everyday in the temple, and you didn't arrest me. But this is your time, and darkness[f] is in control."

Peter Says He Does Not Know Jesus
(Matthew 26.57, 58, 67–75; Mark 14.53, 54, 66–72; John 18.12–18, 25–27)

[54]Jesus was arrested and led away to the house of the high priest, while Peter followed at a distance. [55]Some people built a fire in the middle of

---

[b]*moneybag . . . traveling bag . . . sword*: These were things that someone would take on a dangerous journey. Jesus was telling his disciples to be ready for anything that might happen. They seem to have understood what he meant (see 22.49-51). [c]*having me drink from this cup*: In the Scriptures "to drink from a cup" sometimes means to suffer. [d]*Then an angel . . . like drops of blood*: Verses 43,44 are not in some manuscripts. [e]*greeted him with a kiss*: It was the custom for people to greet each other with a kiss on the cheek. [f]*darkness*: Darkness stands for the power of the devil.

22.40 **WHY DO WE HAVE TO PRAY?** As Jesus prayed, the disciples fell asleep because they were tired. They didn't realize the danger they were in, and that Jesus would soon be arrested. If they had known these things, they would not have been able to sleep. We need to be aware—but not fearful—of the dangers we always face in the world. The answer to danger is prayer.

22.51 **JESUS HEALED THE HIGH PRIEST'S SERVANT** Not only did Jesus not fight to keep himself from being arrested, but he even healed the ear of the high priest's servant. Jesus had such love that even when he was about to be taken to his death, he had mercy on a man who was his enemy. Do we have love like that?

NOTES

Step 5

PETER—a man who discovered the importance of telling the truth regardless of the outcome

LUKE 22.54–62; ACTS 4.1–22

Telling the truth is one of the most important character qualities a person can learn. Being truthful and having integrity go hand in hand. Without truthfulness, others won't trust us, and our credibility will always be in question.

Peter was one of Jesus' disciples. In the Gospel account we find that telling the truth, the whole truth, and nothing but the truth was difficult for Peter. Yet, later on in the book of Acts we see a changed man. We can all learn from what happened in Peter's life to change him from a liar to a truth-teller.

Luke 22 records one of the lowest moments in Peter's life. After Jesus was arrested, Peter waited in a nearby courtyard with some other people. On three occasions someone accused him of being a follower of Christ, and each time he denied it and lied about being a friend of Jesus. The Bible says that just as he was doing it the third time, a rooster crowed and Jesus turned and looked at him. Peter spent the next few days in agony grieving over the reality that he had betrayed Christ.

In Acts 4 Peter gave an entirely different response when some people accused him of being a follower of Christ. After being arrested and put in jail, the next morning he came before the religious leaders who were responsible for Christ's death. This time he spoke out loud and clear and proclaimed that only in Jesus' name can anyone be saved. The officials were amazed at how brave he was. When they warned him not to teach about Jesus anymore, he said, "We cannot keep quiet about what we have seen and heard."

How did Peter change from being a liar to a truth-teller? It boils down to one fact: he was willing to admit his failure to Christ. After being forgiven, he made a commitment to himself always to speak the truth regardless of the consequences. It was a hard lesson to learn, but one that changed his life forever. History records that Peter himself was eventually put to death because he refused to deny the truth about Christ. Peter even asked to be crucified upside down because he said he was not worthy to die in the same manner as his Lord.

What changed Peter? A personal encounter with the resurrected Christ. What will it take for us to become truth-tellers? Coming face-to-face with Jesus as the Lord of our lives and being willing to admit our failures to him.

Ready for Step 6? See page 25 of* InStep's *introduction.

the courtyard and were sitting
around it. Peter sat there with them,
56and a servant girl saw him. Then
after she had looked at him carefully,
she said, "This man was with Jesus!"
57Peter said, "Woman, I don't even
know that man!"*
58A little later someone else saw
Peter and said, "You surely are one
of them!"

"No, I'm not!" Peter replied.
59About an hour later another man
insisted, "This man must have been
with Jesus. They both come from
Galilee."
60Peter replied, "I don't know what
you are talking about!" Right then,
while Peter was still speaking, a
rooster crowed.
61The Lord turned and looked at
Peter. And Peter remembered that
the Lord had said, "Before a rooster
crows tomorrow morning, you will
say three times that you don't know
me." 62Then Peter went out and cried
hard.
63The men who were guarding Jesus made fun of him and beat him.
64They put a blindfold on him and
said, "Tell us who struck you!"
65They kept on insulting Jesus in
many other ways.

Jesus Is Questioned by the Jewish Council

(Matthew 26.59–66; Mark 14.55–64; John 18.19–24)

66At daybreak the nation's leaders,
the chief priests, and the teachers of
the Law of Moses got together and
brought Jesus before their council.
67They said, "Tell us! Are you the
Messiah?"

Jesus replied, "If I said so, you
wouldn't believe me.* 68And if I asked
you a question, you wouldn't answer.
69But from now on, the Son of Man
will be seated at the right side of God
All-Powerful."
70Then they asked, "Are you the
Son of God?"[g]

Jesus answered, "You say I am!"[h]
71They replied, "Why do we need
more witnesses? He said it himself!"

Pilate Questions Jesus

(Matthew 27.1, 2, 11–14; Mark 15.1–5; John 18.28–38)

23 Everyone in the council got up
and led Jesus off to Pilate.
2They started accusing him and said,
"We caught this man trying to get
our people to riot and to stop paying
taxes to the Emperor. He also claims
that he is the Messiah, our king."*
3Pilate asked Jesus, "Are you the
king of the Jews?"

"Those are your words," Jesus
answered.
4Pilate told the chief priests and
the crowd, "I don't find him guilty
of anything."
5But they all kept on saying, "He
has been teaching and causing

---

[g]*Son of God*: This was one of the titles used for the kings of Israel. [h]*You say I am*: Or "That's what you say."

22.57 **FEAR IS A STRONG ENEMY** Peter was so afraid, he wouldn't even admit to a servant girl that he knew Jesus. We see here that fear can make cowards out of even the strongest people. Peter was sorry when he realized what he had done. It's a good thing God can forgive us when fear overcomes us and we fail him like Peter did.

22.67 **WHO WAS JESUS?** Both the Jewish council and Pilate the governor asked just about the same question. Jesus knew the words "Son of God" and "Messiah" could not mean to them what the words meant to him. So he let them answer their own question. Of course he was the Son of God. As Jesus once said, it is never right to give pearls to pigs (see Matthew 7.6).

23.2 **THE COUNCIL LIED ABOUT JESUS** Jesus certainly had not been trying to get the people to riot and stop paying taxes. He taught just the opposite. The council was accusing Jesus *(continued)*

NOTES

trouble all over Judea. He started in
Galilee and has now come all the way
here."

Jesus Is Brought before Herod

6When Pilate heard this, he asked,
"Is this man from Galilee?" 7After
Pilate learned that Jesus came from
the region ruled by Herod,[i] he sent
him to Herod, who was in Jerusalem
at that time.
8For a long time Herod had wanted
to see Jesus and was very happy because he finally had this chance. He
had heard many things about Jesus
and hoped to see him work a miracle.*
9Herod asked him a lot of questions, but Jesus did not answer.
10Then the chief priests and the
teachers of the Law of Moses stood
up and accused him of all kinds of
bad things.
11Herod and his soldiers made fun
of Jesus and insulted him. They put
a fine robe on him and sent him back
to Pilate. 12That same day Herod and
Pilate became friends, even though
they had been enemies before this.*

The Death Sentence
(Matthew 27.15–26; Mark 15.6–15; John 18.39—19.16)

13Pilate called together the chief
priests, the leaders, and the people.
14He told them, "You brought Jesus
to me and said he was a troublemaker. But I have questioned him
here in front of you, and I have not
found him guilty of anything that you
say he has done. 15Herod didn't find
him guilty either and sent him back.
This man doesn't deserve to be put
to death! 16-17I will just have him
beaten with a whip and set free."[j]
18But the whole crowd shouted,
"Kill Jesus! Give us Barabbas!"
19Now Barabbas was in jail because
he had started a riot in the city and
had murdered someone.
20Pilate wanted to set Jesus free,
so he spoke again to the crowds.
21But they kept shouting, "Nail him
to a cross! Nail him to a cross!"
22Pilate spoke to them a third time,
"But what crime has he done? I have
not found him guilty of anything for
which he should be put to death. I
will have him beaten with a whip and
set free."
23The people kept on shouting as
loud as they could for Jesus to be
put to death. 24Finally, Pilate gave
in.* 25He freed the man who was in
jail for rioting and murder, because
he was the one the crowd wanted to

[i] *Herod*: Herod Antipas, the son of Herod the Great.
[j] *set free*: Some manuscripts add, "Pilate said this, because at every Passover he was supposed to set one prisoner free for the Jewish people."

(continued) falsely. But notice that Jesus did not leap to his own defense the way most of us would. He quietly took the sins of others against him, because he knew the will of God was for him to give up his life on the cross.

23.8 **HEROD WAS CURIOUS** Curiosity is the cause of all the interest some people have in religious things. Herod was curious about miracles and wanted to see the new miracle doer. Many people, just like Herod, think it would be "fun" to see a miracle. But miracles are not for fun; they are God's works that show how he creates and saves.

23.12 **EVIL ENEMIES AGREED** Pilate was afraid of Jesus, and it seems that Herod thought Jesus was a joke. But both Pilate and Herod agreed about one thing—Jesus had to die. Evil people can agree to do wrong even if they are not friends. The world is filled with people who don't agree on many things—but they agree that they don't want God to run their lives.

23.24 **THE WORST INJUSTICE EVER** Pilate's job was to enforce Roman justice in Judea. But he knew he had to keep the Roman emperor as his friend. If he didn't, Pilate could get fired. He knew there would be trouble if he offended the Jewish leaders and got *(continued)*

NOTES

be set free. Then Pilate handed Jesus
over for them to do what they wanted
with him.

Jesus Is Nailed to a Cross
(Matthew 27.31–44; Mark 15.21–32;
John 19.17–27)

26As Jesus was being led away,
some soldiers grabbed hold of a man
from Cyrene named Simon. He was
coming in from the fields, but they
put the cross on him and made him
carry it behind Jesus.
27A large crowd was following Jesus, and in the crowd a lot of women
were crying and weeping for him.
28Jesus turned to the women and
said:

Women of Jerusalem, don't
cry for me! Cry for yourselves
and for your children.
29Someday people will say,
"Women who never had
children are really fortunate!"
30At that time everyone will say
to the mountains, "Fall on us!"
They will say to the hills, "Hide
us!" 31If this can happen when
the wood is green, what do you
think will happen when it is dry?[k]

32Two criminals were led out to be
put to death with Jesus. 33When the
soldiers came to the place called "The
Skull,"[l] they nailed Jesus to a cross.
They also nailed the two criminals
to crosses, one on each side of Jesus.
34-35Jesus said, "Father, forgive
these people! They don't know what
they're doing."[m]*

While the crowd stood there
watching Jesus, the soldiers gambled
for his clothes. The leaders insulted
him by saying, "He saved others.
Now he should save himself, if he
really is God's chosen Messiah!"
36The soldiers made fun of Jesus
and brought him some wine. 37They
said, "If you are the king of the Jews,
save yourself!"
38Above him was a sign that said,
"This is the King of the Jews."
39One of the criminals hanging
there also insulted Jesus by saying,
"Aren't you the Messiah? Save yourself and save us!"
40But the other criminal told the
first one off, "Don't you fear God?
Aren't you getting the same punishment as this man? 41We got what was
coming to us, but he didn't do anything wrong." 42Then he said to Jesus, "Remember me when you come
into power!"
43Jesus replied, "I promise that today you will be with me in paradise."[n]*

---

[k] *If this can happen when the wood is green, what do you think will happen when it is dry?*: This saying probably means, "If this can happen to an innocent person, what do you think will happen to one who is guilty?" [l] *"The Skull"*: The place was probably given this name because it was near a large rock in the shape of a human skull. [m] *Jesus said, "Father, forgive these people! They don't know what they're doing."*: These words are not in some manuscripts. [n] *paradise*: In the Greek translation of the Old Testament, this word is used for the Garden of Eden. In New Testament times it was sometimes used for the place where God's people are happy and at rest, as they wait for the final judgment.

(*continued*) them stirred up against Rome. So, even though he knew Jesus was not guilty, Pilate allowed the mob to have the Son of God nailed to a cross. The great Law of the Romans was not great this time. This was the worst day in the history of human justice.

23.34 **JESUS PRAYED FOR US** Our sins caused Jesus to be nailed to the cross. It isn't true that we would have done better than others if we had been there. But the Lord Jesus knows we don't understand how wicked we are. So he prays for us in our ignorance—"Father, forgive them." It should grieve us to think that Jesus loved us enough to pray for us even while he was dying because of our sins.

23.43 **A CRIMINAL WAS SAVED ON THE CROSS** This is a beautiful picture. Here was a criminal at the end of his wicked life. He was being put to death for his crimes. But Jesus, in his own suffering, heard the man's prayer to be saved. Notice that the man didn't (*continued*)

NOTES

The Death of Jesus
(Matthew 27.45–56; Mark 15.33–41; John 19.28–30)

44 Around noon the sky turned dark
and stayed that way until the middle
of the afternoon. 45 The sun stopped
shining, and the curtain in the temple[o] split down the middle. 46 Jesus
shouted, "Father, I put myself in your
hands!" Then he died.

47 When the Roman officer saw
what had happened, he praised God
and said, "Jesus must really have
been a good man!"

48 A crowd had gathered to see the
terrible sight. After they saw it, they
felt brokenhearted and went home.
49 All of Jesus' close friends and the
women who had come with him from
Galilee stood at a distance and
watched.*

Jesus Is Buried
(Matthew 27.57–61; Mark 15.42–47; John 19.38–42)

50-51 There was a man named Joseph, who was from Arimathea in Judea. Joseph was a good and honest
man, and he was eager for God's
kingdom to come. He was also a
member of the Jewish council, but
he did not agree with what they had
decided.

52 Joseph went to Pilate and asked
for Jesus' body. 53 He took the body
down from the cross and wrapped
it in fine cloth. Then he put it in a
tomb that had been cut out of solid
rock and had never been used.
54 It was Friday, and the Sabbath was
about to begin.[p]

55 The women who had come with
Jesus from Galilee followed Joseph
and watched how Jesus' body was
placed in the tomb. 56 Then they went
to prepare some sweet-smelling
spices for his burial. But on the Sabbath they rested, as the Law of Moses
commands.

Jesus Is Alive
(Matthew 28.1–10; Mark 16.1–8; John 20.1–10)

24 Very early on Sunday morning
the women went to the tomb,
carrying the spices that they had prepared. 2 When they found the stone
rolled away from the entrance,
3 they went in. But they did not find
the body of the Lord[q] Jesus, 4 and
they did not know what to think.

Suddenly two men in shining white
clothes stood beside them. 5 The
women were afraid and bowed to the
ground. But the men said, "Why are
you looking in the place of the dead
for someone who is alive? 6 Jesus is
not here! He has been raised from
death. Remember that while he was
still in Galilee, he told you, 7 'The Son
of Man will be handed over to sinners
who will nail him to a cross. But three
days later he will rise to life.' "
8 Then they remembered what Jesus
had said.

9-10 Mary Magdalene, Joanna,
Mary the mother of James, and some
other women were the ones who had
gone to the tomb. When they returned, they told the eleven apostles
and the others what had happened.

---

[o] *curtain in the temple*: There were two curtains in the temple. One was at the entrance, and the other separated the holy place from the most holy place that the Jewish people thought of as God's home on earth. The second curtain is probably the one which is meant. [p] *the Sabbath was about to begin*: The Sabbath begins at sunset on Friday. [q] *the Lord*: These words are not in some manuscripts.

(continued) use a lot of words—just a dying man's last prayer. Then Jesus told the man that he would be in paradise with him that very day. There is no better example of how willing Jesus is to save us from our sins.

23.49 **TRUE FRIENDS** The friends and the women who had come with Jesus from Galilee stuck by him until his death and took care of the body afterward. Their love for Jesus overcame whatever fear they might have felt. How strong is our love for Jesus? How much are we willing to stand for his sake?

NOTES

[11]The apostles thought it was all nonsense, and they would not believe.*
[12]But Peter ran to the tomb. And
when he stooped down and looked
in, he saw only the burial clothes.
Then he returned, wondering what
had happened.[r]

Jesus Appears to Two Disciples
(Mark 16.12, 13)

[13]That same day two of Jesus' disciples were going to the village of Emmaus, which was about seven miles
from Jerusalem. [14]As they were talking and thinking about what had happened, [15]Jesus came near and started
walking along beside them.* [16]But
they did not know who he was.
[17]Jesus asked them, "What were
you talking about as you walked
along?"

The two of them stood there looking sad and gloomy. [18]Then the one
named Cleopas asked Jesus, "Are
you the only person from Jerusalem
who didn't know what was happening there these last few days?"
[19]"What do you mean?" Jesus
asked.

They answered:

Those things that happened to
Jesus from Nazareth. By what
he did and said he showed that
he was a powerful prophet, who
pleased God and all the people.
[20]Then the chief priests and our
leaders had him arrested and
sentenced to die on a cross.
[21]We had hoped that he would
be the one to set Israel free! But
it has already been three days
since all this happened.
[22]Some women in our group
surprised us. They had gone to
the tomb early in the morning,
[23]but did not find the body of
Jesus. They came back, saying
that they had seen a vision of
angels who told them that he is
alive. [24]Some men from our
group went to the tomb and
found it just as the women had
said. But they didn't see Jesus
either.

[25]Then Jesus asked the two disciples, "Why can't you understand?
How can you be so slow to believe
all that the prophets said? [26]Didn't
you know that the Messiah would
have to suffer before he was given
his glory?" [27]Jesus then explained
everything written about himself in
the Scriptures, beginning with the
Law of Moses and the Books of the
Prophets.[s]
[28]When the two of them came near
the village where they were going,
Jesus seemed to be going farther.
[29]They begged him, "Stay with us!
It's already late, and the sun is going
down." So Jesus went into the house
to stay with them.

---

[r]*what had happened*: Verse 12 is not in some manuscripts. [s]*the Law of Moses and the Books of the Prophets*: The Jewish Scriptures, that is, the Old Testament.

24.11 **THEY THOUGHT IT WAS NONSENSE** Some people think that having faith was easier for people in Jesus' time than it is now. It wasn't easier at all, and here is an example. The apostles didn't believe the report that Jesus was alive, even though he had predicted more than once that he would rise again. Now that it had happened, they thought the idea was nonsense. People then were no different than people now. Faith can happen only when God makes it possible in the heart of each person.

24.15 **JESUS WALKED WITH HIS FRIENDS** Here is one of the most beautiful events in the New Testament—Jesus walking and talking with two of his disciples after he came back from death. At first they didn't recognize him. But later, as he broke bread, they remembered how he broke bread with them before. It was then that the two disciples knew who he was. Jesus still walks with us today, and we know him when we share the bread at the Lord's Supper.

NOTES

30After Jesus sat down to eat, he
took some bread. He blessed it and
broke it. Then he gave it to them.
31At once they knew who he was, but
he disappeared. 32They said to each
other, "When he talked with us along
the road and explained the Scriptures
to us, didn't it warm our hearts?"
33So they got right up and returned
to Jerusalem.

The two disciples found the eleven
apostles and the others gathered together. 34And they learned from the
group that the Lord was really alive
and had appeared to Peter. 35Then
the disciples from Emmaus told what
happened on the road and how they
knew he was the Lord when he broke
the bread.

What Jesus' Followers Must Do
(Matthew 28.16–20; Mark 16.14–18; John 20.19–23; Acts 1.6–8)

36While Jesus' disciples were talking about what had happened, Jesus
appeared to them and said, "May
God give you peace!"* 37They were
frightened and terrified because they
thought they were seeing a ghost.

38But Jesus said, "Why are you so
frightened? Why do you doubt?
39Look at my hands and my feet
and see who I am! Touch me and
find out for yourselves. Ghosts don't
have flesh and bones as you see I
have."

40After Jesus said this, he showed
them his hands and his feet. 41The
disciples were so glad and amazed
that they could not believe it. Jesus
then asked them, "Do you have
something to eat?" 42They gave him
a piece of baked fish. 43He took it
and ate it as they watched.

44Jesus said to them, "While I was
still with you, I told you that everything written about me in the Law
of Moses, the Books of the Prophets,
and in the Psalms[t] had to happen."

45Then he helped them understand
the Scriptures.* 46He told them:

> The Scriptures say that the
> Messiah must suffer, then three
> days later he will rise from
> death. 47They also say that all
> people of every nation must be
> told in my name to turn to God,
> in order to be forgiven. So
> beginning in Jerusalem, 48you
> must tell everything that has
> happened. 49I will send you the
> one my Father has promised,[u]
> but you must stay in the city until
> you are given power from
> heaven.

Jesus Returns to Heaven
(Mark 16.19, 20; Acts 1.9–11)

50Jesus led his disciples out to
Bethany, where he raised his hands
and blessed them. 51As he was doing
this, he left and was taken up to
heaven.[v] 52After his disciples had
worshiped him,[w] they returned to
Jerusalem and were very happy.
53They spent their time in the temple, praising God.

---

[t] *Psalms*: The Jewish Scriptures were made up of three parts: (1) the Law of Moses, (2) the Books of the Prophets, (3) and the Writings, which included the Psalms. Sometimes the Scriptures were just called the Law or the Law (of Moses) and the Books of the Prophets. [u] *the one my Father has promised*: Jesus means the Holy Spirit. [v] *and was taken up to heaven*: These words are not in some manuscripts. [w] *After his disciples had worshiped him*: These words are not in some manuscripts.

24.36 **JESUS AROSE IN A REAL BODY** The risen Jesus was quick to remind his disciples that he was no ghost. He was a complete person with both body and spirit. He also reminded them that his death and rising again carried out the promises of the Jewish Scriptures (the Old Testament) about him.

24.45 **JESUS WAS GOD'S ANSWER TO OUR SINS** God had a plan all along to save us from our sins. Jesus was sent to carry out that plan. He was not just a great and good teacher. Jesus was God's sacrifice for our sins—a sacrifice that we owed but could never pay.

NOTES

JOHN Tells the Good News

ABOUT THIS BOOK

Who is Jesus Christ? John answers this question in the first chapter of his Gospel. Using the words of an early Christian hymn, he calls Jesus the "Word" by which God created everything and by which he gave life to everyone (1.3,4). He shows how John the Baptist announced Jesus' coming, "Here is the Lamb of God who takes away the sin of the world" (1.29). When Philip met Jesus he knew Jesus was "the one that Moses and the Prophets wrote about" (1.45). And, in the words of Nathanael, Jesus is "the Son of God and the King of Israel" (1.49).

In John's Gospel we learn a lot about who Jesus is by observing what he said and did when he was with other people. These include a Samaritan woman who received Jesus' offer of life-giving water, a woman who had been caught in sin, his friend Lazarus who was brought back to life by Jesus, and his follower Thomas who doubted that Jesus was raised from death. Jesus also refers to himself as "I am," a phrase which translates the most holy name for God in the Hebrew Scriptures. He uses this name for himself when he makes his claim to be the life-giving bread, the light of the world, the good shepherd, and the true vine.

Jesus performs seven miracles that are more than miracles. Each of them is a "sign" that tells us something about Jesus as the Son of God. For example, by healing a lame man (5.1–8), Jesus shows that he is just like his Father, who never stops working (5.17). This sign also teaches that the Son does only what he sees his Father doing (5.19), and that like the Father "the Son gives life to anyone he wants to" (5.21).

The way John tells the story of Jesus is quite different from the other three gospels. Here, Jesus has long conversations with people about who he is and what God sent him to do. In these conversations he teaches many important things—for example, that he is the way, the truth and the life.

Why did John write? John himself tells us, "So that you will put your faith in Jesus as the Messiah and the Son of God" (20.31). How is this possible? Jesus answers that question in his words to Nicodemus:

> *God loved the people of this world so much that he gave his only* Son, *so that everyone who has faith in him will have eternal life and never die.* (3.16)

A QUICK LOOK AT THIS BOOK

1. A Hymn in Praise of the Word (1.1–18)
2. The Message of John the Baptist (1.19–34)
3. Jesus Chooses His First Disciples (1.35–51)
4. Jesus' Seven Special Miracles (2.1—12.50)
5. Jesus' Last Week: His Trial and Death (13.1—19.42)
6. Jesus Is Alive (20.1–10)
7. Jesus Appears to His Disciples (20.11—21.25)

The Word of Life

1 In the beginning was the one
who is called the Word.
The Word was with God
and was truly God.*
2 From the very beginning
the Word was with God.

3 And with this Word,
God created all things.
Nothing was made
without the Word.
Everything that was created
4 received its life from him,
and his life gave light
to everyone.
5 The light keeps shining
in the dark,
and darkness has never
put it out.[a]*
6 God sent a man named John,
7 who came to tell
about the light
and to lead all people
to have faith.
8 John wasn't that light.
He came only to tell
about the light.

9 The true light that shines
on everyone
was coming into the world.*
10 The Word was in the world,
but no one knew him,
though God had made
the world
with his Word.
11 He came into his own world,
but his own nation
did not welcome him.
12 Yet some people accepted him
and put their faith in him.
So he gave them the right
to be the children of God.
13 They were not God's children
by nature or because
of any human desires.
God himself was the one
who made them his children.

[a] *put it out*: Or "understood it."

1.1 **CHRIST CAME INTO THE WORLD** Unlike Matthew and Luke, John didn't offer any details of Jesus' birth in his Gospel. John wanted us to understand that Jesus Christ is the Word of God from heaven. And that Word is really God himself—God the Son of God the Father, who has always been and always will be.

1.5 **JESUS CHRIST IS THE TRUE LIGHT OF THE WORLD** Light chases away the darkness; darkness cannot overcome light. That is why all the darkness of evil can never put out the greatest light of all—Jesus Christ himself.

1.9 **JESUS CHRIST IS THE LIGHT OF GOD'S CHILDREN** We become God's children when we accept Jesus the Son of God as our Savior. Jesus, the light of the world, has shone on everyone, but he enters the lives of those who trust him. By faith we become members of the family of God.

NOTES

[14]The Word became
a human being
and lived here with us.
We saw his true glory,
the glory of the only Son
of the Father.
From him all the kindness
and all the truth of God
have come down to us.

[15]John spoke about him and
shouted, "This is the one I told you
would come! He is greater than I am,
because he was alive before I was
born."*

[16]Because of all that the Son is, we
have been given one blessing after
another.[b] [17]The Law was given by
Moses, but Jesus Christ brought us
undeserved kindness and truth.
[18]No one has ever seen God. The only
Son, who is truly God and is closest
to the Father, has shown us what God
is like.

John the Baptist Tells about Jesus
(Matthew 3.1–12; Mark 1.1–8; Luke 3.15–17)

[19-20]The Jewish leaders in Jerusalem sent priests and temple helpers
to ask John who he was. He told them
plainly, "I am not the Messiah."
[21]Then when they asked him if he
were Elijah, he said, "No, I am not!"
And when they asked if he were the
Prophet,[c] he also said "No!"

[22]Finally, they said, "Who are you
then? We have to give an answer to
the ones who sent us. Tell us who
you are!"

[23]John answered in the words of
the prophet Isaiah, "I am only someone shouting in the desert, 'Get the
road ready for the Lord!' "

[24]Some Pharisees had also been
sent to John. [25]They asked him,
"Why are you baptizing people, if
you are not the Messiah or Elijah or
the Prophet?"

[26]John told them, "I use water to
baptize people. But here with you is
someone you don't know. [27]Even
though I came first, I am not good
enough to untie his sandals." [28]John
said this as he was baptizing east of
the Jordan River in Bethany.[d]

The Lamb of God

[29]The next day John saw Jesus
coming toward him and said:
Here is the Lamb of God who
takes away the sin of the world!*
[30]He is the one I told you about
when I said, "Someone else will
come. He is greater than I am,
because he was alive before I
was born." [31]I didn't know who
he was. But I came to baptize
you with water, so that everyone
in Israel would see him.
[32]I was there and saw the
Spirit come down on him like a
dove from heaven. And the Spirit
stayed on him. [33]Before this I

---

[b]*one blessing after another*: Or "one blessing in place of another." [c]*the Prophet*: Many of the Jewish people expected God to send them a prophet who would be like Moses, but with even greater power. See Deuteronomy 18.15,18. [d]*Bethany*: An unknown village east of the Jordan with the same name as the village near Jerusalem.

1.15 **JOHN THE BAPTIST ANNOUNCED CHRIST'S COMING** Who was this man John? He said that he was not the Messiah, and that he had come just as the Old Testament prophet Isaiah foretold. You might say John was an announcer. Believers today also can announce the Savior to a darkened world. Jesus the true light has come. When we announce him, he shines into people's lives, and they can become new people by receiving him.

1.29 **JESUS IS THE LAMB OF GOD** Jesus has many titles, but this may seem the strangest one. In Old Testament times, God commanded a spotless lamb to be sacrificed often for the sins of the people. The people didn't understand it all then, but they were doing something that foretold the coming of the Savior. Jesus would let himself be sacrificed as the true and final offering for sins—a "spotless" lamb, without sin. That is why John used the title "Lamb of God" for Jesus.

NOTES

didn't know who he was. But the
one who sent me to baptize with
water had told me, "You will see
the Spirit come down and stay
on someone. Then you will know
that he is the one who will
baptize with the Holy Spirit."
34I saw this happen, and I tell
you that he is the Son of God.

The First Disciples of Jesus

35The next day John was there
again, and two of his followers were
with him. 36When he saw Jesus walking by, he said, "Here is the Lamb
of God!" 37John's two followers
heard him, and they went with Jesus.
38When Jesus turned and saw
them, he asked, "What do you
want?"
They answered, "Rabbi, where do
you live?" The Hebrew word "Rabbi"
means "Teacher."
39Jesus replied, "Come and see!"
It was already about four o'clock in
the afternoon when they went with
him and saw where he lived. So they
stayed on for the rest of the day.
40One of the two men who had
heard John and had gone with Jesus
was Andrew, the brother of Simon
Peter. 41The first thing Andrew did
was to find his brother and tell him,
"We have found the Messiah!" The
Hebrew word "Messiah" means the
same as the Greek word "Christ."*
42Andrew brought his brother to
Jesus. And when Jesus saw him, he
said, "Simon son of John, you will
be called Cephas." This name can be
translated as "Peter."[e]

Jesus Chooses Philip and Nathanael

43-44The next day Jesus decided to
go to Galilee. There he met Philip,
who was from Bethsaida, the hometown of Andrew and Peter. Jesus said
to Philip, "Come with me."
45Philip then found Nathanael and
said, "We have found the one that
Moses and the Prophets[f] wrote
about. He is Jesus, the son of Joseph
from Nazareth."
46Nathanael asked, "Can anything
good come from Nazareth?"
Philip answered, "Come and see."*
47When Jesus saw Nathanael
coming toward him, he said, "Here
is a true descendant of our ancestor Israel. And he is not deceitful."[g]
48"How do you know me?" Nathanael asked.
Jesus answered, "Before Philip
called you, I saw you under the fig
tree."
49Nathanael said, "Rabbi, you are
the Son of God and the King of
Israel!"
50Jesus answered, "Did you believe
me just because I said that I saw you
under the fig tree? You will see something even greater. 51I tell you for
certain that you will see heaven open

---

[e] *Peter*: The Aramaic name "Cephas" and the Greek name "Peter" each mean "rock." [f] *Moses and the Prophets*: The Jewish Scriptures, that is, the Old Testament. [g] *Israel . . . not deceitful*: Israel (meaning "a man who wrestled with God" or "a prince of God") was the name that the Lord gave to Jacob (meaning "cheater" or "deceiver"), the famous ancestor of the Jewish people.

1.41 **TELL SOMEBODY** When Andrew found Jesus and went with him, the first thing he did was tell his brother about the good news—he had found the long-awaited Messiah. His brother turned out to be the apostle Peter. We ought to be bursting to tell someone the news about what we've found in Jesus. Think of the good it will do our friend or loved one—and the good that person might do someday.

1.46 **NAZARETH OF ALL PLACES** Nathanael wasn't expecting the Messiah, the King of Israel, to come from a "hick town" like Nazareth. But it was right for Jesus to be a humble, poor person from a simple, working family. God planned it that way, so Jesus and the common people could understand each other.

NOTES

and God's angels going up and coming down on the Son of Man."[h]

Jesus at a Wedding in Cana

2 Three days later Mary, the
mother of Jesus, was at a wedding
feast in the village of Cana in Galilee.* 2Jesus and his disciples had also
been invited and were there.
3When the wine was all gone, Mary
said to Jesus, "They don't have any
more wine."
4Jesus replied, "Mother, my time
has not yet come![i] You must not tell
me what to do."
5Mary then said to the servants,
"Do whatever Jesus tells you to do."
6At the feast there were six stone
water jars that were used by the people for washing themselves in the
way that their religion said they
must. Each jar held about twenty or
thirty gallons. 7Jesus told the servants to fill them to the top with water. Then after the jars had been
filled, 8he said, "Now take some water and give it to the man in charge
of the feast."
The servants did as Jesus told
them, 9and the man in charge drank
some of the water that had now
turned into wine. He did not know
where the wine had come from, but
the servants did. He called the bridegroom over 10and said, "The best
wine is always served first. Then after the guests have had plenty, the
other wine is served. But you have
kept the best until last!"
11This was Jesus' first miracle,[j] and
he did it in the village of Cana
in Galilee. There Jesus showed his
glory, and his disciples put their faith
in him. 12After this, he went with his
mother, his brothers, and his disciples to the town of Capernaum,
where they stayed for a few days.*

Jesus in the Temple

(Matthew 21.12, 13; Mark 11.15–17; Luke 19.45, 46)

13Not long before the Jewish festival of Passover, Jesus went to Jerusalem. 14There he found people selling
cattle, sheep, and doves in the temple.
He also saw moneychangers sitting
at their tables. 15So he took some
rope and made a whip. Then he
chased everyone out of the temple,
together with their sheep and cattle.
He turned over the tables of the
moneychangers and scattered their
coins.
16Jesus said to the people who had
been selling doves, "Get those doves
out of here! Don't make my Father's
house a marketplace."
17The disciples then remembered
that the Scriptures say, "My love for
your house burns in me like a fire."

---

[h]*going up and coming down on the Son of Man*: When Jacob (see the note at verse 47) was running from his brother Esau, he had a dream in which he saw angels going up and down on a ladder from earth to heaven. See Genesis 32.22-32. [i]*my time has not yet come!*: The time when the true glory of Jesus would be seen, and he would be recognized as God's Son. See 12.23. [j]*miracle*: The Greek text has "sign." In the Gospel of John the word "sign" is used for the miracle itself and as a way of pointing to Jesus as the Son of God.

2.1 **JESUS WENT TO PARTIES** Jesus enjoyed happy gatherings of people. This may surprise us when we think about the serious work Jesus came to do. But Jesus wanted to be where he could talk to people and get them interested in the kingdom of God. He didn't preach at the wedding reception, but he added to its joy by supplying more wine. His act must have made a lasting impression on some of those who were there.

2.12 **JESUS HAD A HIGHER DUTY** After Jesus' childhood we never hear again about Joseph, Mary's husband, the man who was an earthly father to Jesus. But we continue to meet Mary, Jesus' mother, in a number of places. In this chapter we see that Mary was beginning to understand that Jesus was much more than her own Son. She would take her place among the other disciples and witnesses of his work as Savior and Lord.

NOTES

18The Jewish leaders asked Jesus,
"What miracle[j] will you work to
show us why you have done this?"
19"Destroy this temple," Jesus answered, "and in three days I will build
it again!"*
20The leaders replied, "It took
forty-six years to build this temple.
What makes you think you can rebuild it in three days?"
21But Jesus was talking about his
body as a temple. 22And when he was
raised from death, his disciples remembered what he had told them.
Then they believed the Scriptures
and the words of Jesus.

Jesus Knows What People Are Like

23In Jerusalem during Passover
many people put their faith in Jesus,
because they saw him work miracles.[j]* 24But Jesus knew what was in
their hearts, and he would not let
them have power over him. 25No one
had to tell him what people were like.
He already knew.

Jesus and Nicodemus

3 There was a man named Nicodemus who was a Pharisee and a
Jewish leader. 2One night he went
to Jesus and said, "Sir, we know that
God has sent you to teach us. You
could not work these miracles, unless
God were with you."
3Jesus replied, "I tell you for certain that you must be born from
above[k] before you can see God's
kingdom!"*
4Nicodemus asked, "How can a
grown man ever be born a second
time?"
5Jesus answered:

I tell you for certain that before
you can get into God's kingdom,
you must be born not only by
water, but by the Spirit.
6Humans give life to their
children. Yet only God's Spirit
can change you into a child of
God. 7Don't be surprised when
I say that you must be born from
above. 8Only God's Spirit gives
new life. The Spirit is like the
wind that blows wherever it
wants to. You can hear the wind,
but you don't know where it
comes from or where it is going.

9"How can this be?" Nicodemus
asked.
10Jesus replied:

---

[j]*miracle*: See the note at 2.11. [j]*miracles*: See the note at 2.11. [k]*from above*: Or "in a new way." The same Greek word is used in verses 7,31.

2.19 **JESUS PUZZLED HIS HEARERS** He said he could raise up the temple again in three days. Even if he had explained to the leaders what he meant, they wouldn't have understood. They would have been more puzzled than ever. Later they accused him of saying that he, himself, would destroy the temple (see Matthew 27.40). So we see that people of Jesus' day were just as confused by their own wickedness as people are today.

2.23 **WHAT ARE PEOPLE LIKE?** Jesus saw us as we really are, not as we like to think we are. As sinners, we don't love the things God loves, and we love ourselves too much. We are not sincere about what we say. Many people decided to "put their faith" in Jesus because they thought he would grant their selfish wishes. But they didn't want him as their Savior from sin.

3.3 **WHAT DO PEOPLE REALLY NEED?** We have just shown how Jesus sees us as we really are, not as we imagine ourselves to be. So what is needed? Jesus' talk with Nicodemus tells us our greatest need. We must be "born from above." Our old inner self must give way to a new inner self that God gives us. Then we are able to please God, because we then love the things he loves. Then we appreciate Jesus for who he really is—our Savior from heaven. We must ask God to create us all over again in this way.

NOTES

How can you be a teacher of
Israel and not know these
things? 11I tell you for certain
that we know what we are
talking about because we have
seen it ourselves. But none of
you will accept what we say.
12If you don't believe when I talk
to you about things on earth,
how can you possibly believe if
I talk to you about things in
heaven?
13No one has gone up to
heaven except the Son of Man,
who came down from there.
14And the Son of Man must be
lifted up, just as that metal snake
was lifted up by Moses in the
desert.[l]* 15Then everyone who
has faith in the Son of Man will
have eternal life.

16God loved the people of this
world so much that he gave his
only Son, so that everyone who
has faith in him will have eternal
life and never die. 17God did not
send his Son into the world to
condemn its people. He sent him
to save them! 18No one who has
faith in God's Son will be
condemned. But everyone who
does not have faith in him has
already been condemned for not
having faith in God's only Son.
19The light has come into the
world, and people who do evil
things are judged guilty because
they love the dark more than the
light.* 20People who do evil hate
the light and won't come to the
light, because it clearly shows
what they have done. 21But
everyone who lives by the truth
will come to the light, because
they want others to know that
God is really the one doing what
they do.

Jesus and John the Baptist

22Later, Jesus and his disciples
went to Judea, where he stayed with
them for a while and was baptizing
people.
23-24John had not yet been put in
jail. He was at Aenon near Salim,
where there was a lot of water, and
people were coming there for John
to baptize them.
25John's followers got into an argument with a Jewish man[m] about a
ceremony of washing.[n] 26They went
to John and said, "Rabbi, you spoke
about a man when you were with him
east of the Jordan. He is now baptizing people, and everyone is going to
him."
27John replied:
No one can do anything unless
God in heaven allows it. 28Surely
you remember how I told you
that I am not the Messiah. I am
only the one sent ahead of him.
29At a wedding the groom is
the one who gets married. The
best man is glad just to be there
and to hear the groom's voice.
That's why I am so glad. 30Jesus

---

[l]*just as that metal snake was lifted up by Moses in the desert*: When the Lord punished the people of Israel by sending snakes to bite them, he told Moses to hold a metal snake up on a pole. Everyone who looked at the snake was cured of the snake bites. See Numbers 21.4-9. [m]*a Jewish man*: Some manuscripts have "some Jewish men." [n]*about a ceremony of washing*: The Jewish people had many rules about washing themselves and their dishes, in order to make themselves fit to worship God.

3.14 **WHAT DID THE METAL SNAKE MEAN?** The metal snake that Moses made and placed on a pole stood for what Jesus would do. The people who were being bitten by snakes in the desert in Moses' time could be healed just by looking at that metal snake. By looking to Jesus who was nailed up on a cross, we can be healed from the poison of sin. In this case, it's a kind of healing that lasts forever.

3.19 **THE LIGHT SHOWS ALL** Jesus is the light that shows all the things in the world, whether they are good or evil. The people who come to the light are doing so because they love God, who sent the light. Those who don't love Jesus hate the light and would rather live in the darkness of sin.

NOTES

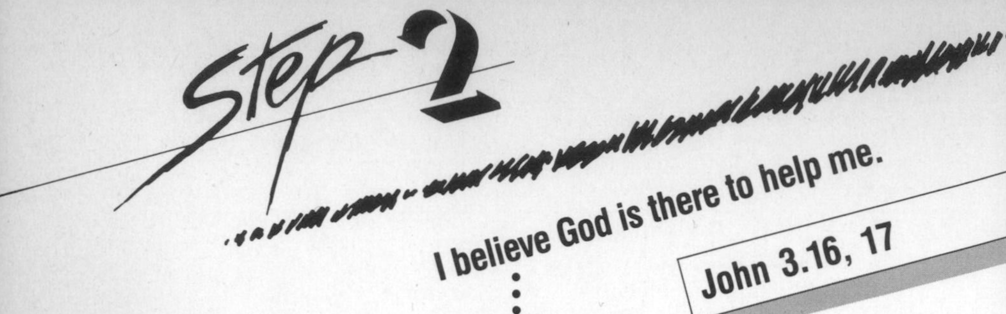

PEOPLE MATTER TO GOD

Remember the first time you ever saw one of those specials on the hungry people in Africa? I cried. Mom cried (she always does)—even Dad had tears in his eyes. Now he just sits there with the channel changer flipping right past shows like that. What's the deal?

When I first became a Christian it was the same thing. I was so thankful—so aware of what God had done. Somehow I have become desensitized or something.

JESUS LOVES THEM

The thing is—we matter to God. I mean, if we didn't, why would Jesus have come to earth in the first place? Let alone, die on the cross for our sins? We need to remember that we are important to the Lord. Our unchurched friends are too. No matter how they act or what they say, Jesus loves them.

For another "Look Inside," turn to page 567.

must become more important,
while I become less important.*

The One Who Comes from Heaven

31God's Son comes from
heaven and is above all others.
Everyone who comes from the
earth belongs to the earth and
speaks about earthly things. The
one who comes from heaven is
above all others. 32He speaks
about what he has seen and
heard, and yet no one believes
him. 33But everyone who does
believe him has shown that God
is truthful. 34The Son was sent
to speak God's message, and he
has been given the full power of
God's Spirit.

35The Father loves the Son and
has given him everything.
36Everyone who has faith in the
Son has eternal life. But no one
who rejects him will ever share
in that life, and God will be angry
with them forever.*

4 Jesus knew that the Pharisees
had heard that he was winning
and baptizing more followers than
John was. 2But Jesus' disciples were
really the ones doing the baptizing,
and not Jesus himself.

Jesus and the Samaritan Woman

3Jesus left Judea and started for
Galilee again. 4This time he had to
go through Samaria, 5and on his way
he came to the town of Sychar. It
was near the field that Jacob had long
ago given to his son Joseph. 6-8The
well that Jacob had dug was still
there, and Jesus sat down beside it
because he was tired from traveling.
It was noon, and after Jesus' disciples
had gone into town to buy some food,
a Samaritan woman came to draw
water from the well.

Jesus asked her, "Would you
please give me a drink of water?"

9"You are a Jew," she replied, "and
I am a Samaritan woman. How can
you ask me for a drink of water when
Jews and Samaritans won't have
anything to do with each other?"[o]

10Jesus answered, "You don't
know what God wants to give you,
and you don't know who is asking
you for a drink. If you did, you would
ask him for the water that gives life."*

11"Sir," the woman said, "you
don't even have a bucket, and the
well is deep. Where are you going
to get this life-giving water? 12Our
ancestor Jacob dug this well for us,
and his family and animals got water
from it. Are you greater than Jacob?"

13Jesus answered, "Everyone who
drinks this water will get thirsty
again. 14But no one who drinks the
water I give will ever be thirsty again.
The water I give is like a flowing
fountain that gives eternal life."

---

[o]*won't have anything to do with each other*: Or "won't use the same cups." The Samaritans lived in the land between Judea and Galilee. They worshiped God differently from the Jews and did not get along with them.

3.30 **PUT JESUS FIRST** John the Baptist knew who Jesus was, and John knew that Jesus had to take first place. Jesus is the Messiah, the Son of God. John thought that it was an honor just to be Christ's servant. We should learn from John that Jesus belongs in first place in our lives.

3.36 **ETERNAL LIFE RIGHT NOW** Notice that this passage says that everyone who has faith in Jesus *has* eternal life. Not *will* have, but *has*. If you have faith in Jesus, life forever with him is yours *right now*, just as surely as if you were already in heaven. That is a joyful thing to realize.

4.10 **JESUS IS LIKE LIVING WATER** In the Old Testament times of Moses the great leader of Israel, God supplied a living rock that provided water for the people in the desert. Many years later Paul the apostle said that the rock stood for Christ (1 Corinthians 10.4). Jesus told a woman that he would give her living water, and then she would have eternal life. When we come to Jesus, it is like someone dying of thirst coming to a cool spring of water. Jesus satisfies our deep need to live forever with him.

NOTES

15The woman replied, "Sir, please
give me a drink of that water! Then
I won't get thirsty and have to come
to this well again."
16Jesus told her, "Go and bring
your husband."
17-18The woman answered, "I don't
have a husband."
"That's right," Jesus replied,
"you're telling the truth. You don't
have a husband. You have already
been married five times, and the man
you are now living with is not your
husband."*
19The woman said, "Sir, I can see
that you are a prophet. 20My ancestors worshiped on this mountain,[p]
but you Jews say Jerusalem is the
only place to worship."
21Jesus said to her:
Believe me, the time is coming
when you won't worship God
either on this mountain or in
Jerusalem. 22You Samaritans
don't really know the one you
worship. But we Jews do know
the God we worship, and by
using us God will save the world.
23But a time is coming, and it is
already here! Even now the true
worshipers are being led by the
Spirit to worship the Father
according to the truth. These are
the ones the Father is seeking
to worship him. 24God is Spirit,
and those who worship God
must be led by the Spirit to
worship him according to the
truth.
25The woman said, "I know that
the Messiah will come. He is the one
we call Christ. When he comes, he
will explain everything to us."
26"I am that one," Jesus told her,
"and I am speaking to you now."
27The disciples returned about this
time and were surprised to find Jesus
talking with a woman. But none of
them asked him what he wanted or
why he was talking with her.
28The woman left her water jar and
ran back into town. She said to the
people,* 29"Come and see a man who
told me everything I have ever done!
Could he be the Messiah?" 30Every-
one in town went out to see Jesus.
31While this was happening, Jesus'
disciples were saying to him,
"Teacher, please eat something."
32But Jesus told them, "I have food
that you don't know anything about."
33His disciples started asking each
other, "Has someone brought him
something to eat?"
34Jesus said:
My food is to do what God
wants! He is the one who sent
me, and I must finish the work
that he gave me to do.* 35You

[p] *this mountain*: Mount Gerizim, near the city of Shechem.

4.17 **JESUS KNOWS AND UNDERSTANDS US** The woman at the well was living in a sinful way, and Jesus knew all about her. But he wasn't angry with her. Instead, he invited her to come and drink the water of everlasting life. The woman was surprised because she thought Jesus would condemn her. If we only knew how much Jesus loves us, we wouldn't be afraid to come to him about the things we know are wrong in our lives.

4.28 **WE CAN TELL ONLY WHAT WE KNOW ABOUT JESUS** First the people of Samaria heard *about* Jesus, then they heard him themselves. Only then were they able to tell about him. We can't tell others what we don't know personally. We must first "meet" Jesus ourselves. We can meet him because the Spirit of God reveals Jesus to our minds. Then we know him and can tell others about him and how he saved us from our sins.

4.34 **EAT THE FOOD THAT GOD GIVES** What really satisfies us? Some of us overeat because we aren't satisfied inside ourselves about life. So we try to fill our emptiness with food, or pleasures, or drugs, or other things that harm us. We can never be satisfied without God. We need to enjoy the invisible, special food that God gives to those who ask him.

NOTES

may say that there are still four
months until harvest time. But
I tell you to look, and you will
see that the fields are ripe and
ready to harvest.
36 Even now the harvest
workers are receiving their
reward by gathering a harvest
that brings eternal life. Then
everyone who planted the seed
and everyone who harvests the
crop will celebrate together.
37 So the saying proves true,
"Some plant the seed, and others
harvest the crop." 38 I am sending
you to harvest crops in fields
where others have done all the
hard work.
39 A lot of Samaritans in that town
put their faith in Jesus because the
woman had said, "This man told me
everything I have ever done."
40 They came and asked him to stay
in their town, and he stayed on for
two days.
41 Many more Samaritans put their
faith in Jesus because of what they
heard him say. 42 They told the
woman, "We no longer have faith in
Jesus just because of what you told
us. We have heard him ourselves,
and we are certain that he is the Savior of the world!"

Jesus Heals an Official's Son
(Matthew 8.5–13; Luke 7.1–10)

43-44 Jesus had said, "Prophets are
honored everywhere, except in their
own country." Then two days later
he left 45 and went to Galilee. The people there welcomed him, because
they had gone to the festival in Jerusalem and had seen everything he
had done.
46 While Jesus was in Galilee, he
returned to the village of Cana, where
he had turned the water into wine.
There was an official in Capernaum
whose son was sick. 47 And when the
man heard that Jesus had come from
Judea, he went and begged him to
keep his son from dying.
48 Jesus told the official, "You won't
have faith unless you see miracles
and wonders!"*
49 The man replied, "Lord, please
come before my son dies!"
50 Jesus then said, "Your son will
live. Go on home to him." The man
believed Jesus and started back
home.
51 Some of the official's servants
met him along the road and told him,
"Your son is better!" 52 He asked
them when the boy got better, and
they answered, "The fever left him
yesterday at one o'clock."
53 The boy's father realized that at
one o'clock the day before Jesus had
told him, "Your son will live!" So the
man and everyone in his family put
their faith in Jesus.
54 This was the second miracle[q] that
Jesus worked after he left Judea and
went to Galilee.

Jesus Heals a Sick Man

5 Later, Jesus went to Jerusalem
for another Jewish festival.[r]
2 In the city near the sheep gate was
a pool with five porches, and its name
in Hebrew was Bethzatha.[s]
3-4 Many sick, blind, lame, and crippled people were lying close to the
pool.[t]
5 Beside the pool was a man who
had been sick for thirty-eight years.

---

[q] *miracle*: See the note at 2.11. [r] *another Jewish festival*: Either the Festival of Shelters or Passover. [s] *Bethzatha*: Some manuscripts have "Bethesda" and others have "Bethsaida." [t] *pool*: Some manuscripts add, "They were waiting for the water to be stirred, because an angel from the Lord would sometimes come down and stir it. The first person to get into the pool after that would be healed."

4.48 **WHAT DO YOU PUT YOUR FAITH IN?** You've heard that "seeing is believing." This is often a sour way of saying, "I'll believe when I see it with my own eyes." But there are lots of things we believe without seeing—what science says about atoms, for example. We can be confident about putting our faith in Jesus even if he doesn't first perform a miracle. The miracle comes *after* we trust him, not before.

NOTES

6When Jesus saw the man and realized that he had been crippled for a
long time, he asked him, "Do you
want to be healed?"
7The man answered, "Lord, I don't
have anyone to put me in the pool
when the water is stirred up. I try
to get in, but someone else always
gets there first."
8Jesus told him, "Pick up your mat
and walk!" 9Right then the man was
healed. He picked up his mat and
started walking around. The day on
which this happened was a Sabbath.*
10When the Jewish leaders saw the
man carrying his mat, they said to
him, "This is the Sabbath! No one
is allowed to carry a mat on the
Sabbath."
11But he replied, "The man who
healed me told me to pick up my mat
and walk."
12They asked him, "Who is this
man that told you to pick up your
mat and walk?"* 13But he did not
know who Jesus was, and Jesus had
left because of the crowd.
14Later, Jesus met the man in the
temple and told him, "You are now
well. But don't sin anymore or something worse might happen to you."
15The man left and told the leaders
that Jesus was the one who had
healed him. 16They started making
a lot of trouble for Jesus because he
did things like this on the Sabbath.
17But Jesus said, "My Father has
never stopped working, and that is
why I keep on working." 18Now the
leaders wanted to kill Jesus for two
reasons. First, he had broken the law
of the Sabbath. But even worse, he
had said that God was his Father,
which made him equal with God.

The Son's Authority

19Jesus told the people:
I tell you for certain that the
Son cannot do anything on his
own. He can do only what he
sees the Father doing, and he
does exactly what he sees the
Father do. 20The Father loves the
Son and has shown him
everything he does. The Father
will show him even greater
things, and you will be amazed.
21Just as the Father raises the
dead and gives life, so the Son
gives life to anyone he wants to.*
22The Father doesn't judge
anyone, but he has made his Son
the judge of everyone. 23The
Father wants all people to honor
the Son as much as they honor
him. When anyone refuses to
honor the Son, that is the same
as refusing to honor the Father
who sent him. 24I tell you for
certain that everyone who hears
my message and has faith in the
one who sent me has eternal life
and will never be condemned.

5.9 **WHAT HEALED THE SICK MAN?** The pool had been there a long time, and it's still there today. But neither the water from that pool, nor any other water, had ever healed anyone. Water has no magical power. But Jesus is the Lord from heaven, God the creator in human form. Only he has authority to command us to be healed, as this man found out for himself.

5.12 **WHO IS THIS JESUS?** Jesus did miracles. But that is not the main thing that makes him great. Jesus is the everlasting Son of the everlasting Father. Just as God the Father gives life, so also God the everlasting Son gives life. It shouldn't puzzle us that the Author of life gives life when he pleases and how he pleases. He always has and always will have life for everyone who comes to him.

5.21 **WE CAN TRUST JESUS BECAUSE OF WHAT HE DOES** The world knows that Jesus was a one-of-a-kind person, that he even rose from the dead. That alone ought to lead us to trust him. But to really find out the truth about Jesus, we must come to him ourselves. He never turns anyone away. When he gives us his eternal life, then we have the proof of who Jesus really is, in our own lives.

NOTES

They have already gone from
death to life.
25I tell you for certain that the
time will come, and it is already
here, when all of the dead will
hear the voice of the Son of God.
And those who listen to it will
live! 26The Father has the power
to give life, and he has given that
same power to the Son. 27And
he has given his Son the right
to judge everyone, because he
is the Son of Man.
28Don't be surprised! The time
will come when all of the dead
will hear the voice of the Son
of Man, 29and they will come out
of their graves. Everyone who
has done good things will rise
to life, but everyone who has
done evil things will rise and be
condemned.
30I cannot do anything on my
own. The Father sent me, and
he is the one who told me how
to judge. I judge with fairness,
because I obey him, and I don't
just try to please myself.

Witnesses to Jesus

31If I speak for myself, there
is no way to prove I am telling
the truth. 32But there is someone
else who speaks for me, and I
know what he says is true.
33You sent messengers to John,
and he told them the truth.
34I don't depend on what people
say about me, but I tell you these
things so that you may be saved.
35John was a lamp that gave a
lot of light, and you were glad
to enjoy his light for a while.
36But something more
important than John speaks for
me. I mean the things that the
Father has given me to do! All
of these speak for me and say
that the Father sent me.
37The Father who sent me also
speaks for me, but you have
never heard his voice or seen
him face to face. 38You have not
believed his message, because
you refused to have faith in the
one he sent.
39You search the Scriptures,
because you think you will find
eternal life in them. The
Scriptures tell about me,* 40but
you refuse to come to me for
eternal life.
41I don't care about human
praise, 42but I do know that none
of you love God. 43I have come
with my Father's authority, and
you have not welcomed me. But
you will welcome people who
come on their own. 44How could
you possibly believe? You like
to have your friends praise you,
and you don't care about praise
that the only God can give!
45Don't think that I will be the
one to accuse you to the Father.
You have put your hope in
Moses, yet he is the very one who
will accuse you. 46Moses wrote
about me, and if you had
believed Moses, you would have
believed me.* 47But if you
don't believe what Moses wrote,
how can you believe what I say?

5.39 **THE BIBLE ITSELF CANNOT GIVE ETERNAL LIFE** The Bible is entirely the word of God. But the Bible is just "words on a page" to us until we surrender our lives to the Author of the words. The book alone can't save us from our sins any more than waving a wand can cure disease. It is God himself who gives eternal life.

5.46 **MOSES WROTE ABOUT JESUS** We must not imagine that the Bible contains two separate religions—the Old Testament religion and the New Testament religion. Someone has written that the New Testament is enclosed in the Old Testament, and the Old Testament is opened up by the New Testament. Both testaments lead us to Jesus Christ. Moses knew that the Messiah, Jesus, would come some day. Many other prophets wrote about the King who would come to Israel.

NOTES

Feeding Five Thousand
(Matthew 14.13–21; Mark 6.30–44; Luke 9.10–17)

6 Jesus crossed Lake Galilee, which was also known as Lake Tiberias. 2A large crowd had seen him work miracles to heal the sick, and those people went with him. 3-4It was almost time for the Jewish festival of Passover, and Jesus went up on a mountain with his disciples and sat down.[u]

5When Jesus saw the large crowd coming toward him, he asked Philip, "Where will we get enough food to feed all these people?" 6He said this to test Philip, since he already knew what he was going to do.

7Philip answered, "Don't you know that it would take almost a year's wages[v] just to buy only a little bread for each of these people?"

8Andrew, the brother of Simon Peter, was one of the disciples. He spoke up and said, 9"There is a boy here who has five small loaves[w] of barley bread and two fish. But what good is that with all these people?"

10The ground was covered with grass, and Jesus told his disciples to have everyone sit down. About five thousand men were in the crowd. 11Jesus took the bread in his hands and gave thanks to God. Then he passed the bread to the people, and he did the same with the fish, until everyone had plenty to eat.*

12The people ate all they wanted, and Jesus told his disciples to gather up the leftovers, so that nothing would be wasted. 13The disciples gathered them up and filled twelve large baskets with what was left over from the five barley loaves.

14After the people had seen Jesus work this miracle,[x] they began saying, "This must be the Prophet[y] who is to come into the world!" 15Jesus realized that they would try to force him to be their king. So he went up on a mountain, where he could be alone.

Jesus Walks on the Water
(Matthew 14.22–27; Mark 6.45–52)

16That evening Jesus' disciples went down to the lake. 17They got into a boat and started across for Capernaum. Later that evening Jesus had still not come to them, 18and a strong wind was making the water rough.

19When the disciples had rowed for three or four miles, they saw Jesus walking on the water. He kept coming closer to the boat, and they were terrified.* 20But he said, "I am Jesus![z] Don't be afraid!" 21The disciples wanted to take him into the boat, but suddenly the boat reached the shore where they were headed.

---

[u] *sat down*: Possibly to teach. Teachers in the ancient world, including Jewish teachers, usually sat down to teach. [v] *almost a year's wages*: The Greek text has "two hundred silver coins." Each coin was worth the average day's wages for a worker. [w] *small loaves*: These would have been flat and round or in the shape of a bun. [x] *miracle*: See the note at 2.11. [y] *the Prophet*: See the note at 1.21. [z] *I am Jesus*: The Greek text has "I am." See the note at 8.24.

6.11 **THE LORD OF CREATION FED THE CROWD** Only this miracle is told of in all four Gospels. It teaches us something important: that Jesus is the Lord of creation. He could take a few scraps of food and make enough to feed thousands. The crowd got "carried away," however, and wanted to make Jesus an earthly king. The people meant well, but they didn't fully understand who Jesus was and what he came to do, so he had to get away from them.

6.19 **FEAR OF THE SAVIOR DOESN'T MAKE SENSE** The disciples were in the middle of a storm on the lake when Jesus came walking toward them on the water. They were afraid, thinking they saw a ghost (see Matthew 14). Imagine—the disciples were afraid of Jesus, the one who could calm the winds and the waves. They weren't thinking straight in this storm. We have stormy times in our lives, too. Let's not be afraid of Jesus, the one who can lead us out of our times of trouble.

NOTES

The Bread That Gives Life

22The people who had stayed on
the east side of the lake knew that
only one boat had been there. They
also knew that Jesus had not left in
it with his disciples. But the next day
23some boats from Tiberias sailed
near the place where the crowd had
eaten the bread for which the Lord
had given thanks. 24They saw that
Jesus and his disciples had left. Then
they got into the boats and went to
Capernaum to look for Jesus. 25They
found him on the west side of the
lake and asked, "Rabbi, when did
you get here?"

26Jesus answered, "I tell you for
certain that you are not looking for
me because you saw the miracles,[a]
but because you ate all the food you
wanted. 27Don't work for food that
spoils. Work for food that gives eternal life. The Son of Man will give
you this food, because God the Father has given him the right to do
so."

28"What exactly does God want us
to do?" the people asked.

29Jesus answered, "God wants you
to have faith in the one he sent."

30They replied, "What miracle will
you work, so that we can have faith
in you? What will you do? 31For example, when our ancestors were in
the desert, they were given manna[b]
to eat. It happened just as the Scriptures say, 'God gave them bread from
heaven to eat.' "

32Jesus then told them, "I tell you
for certain that Moses was not the
one who gave you bread from
heaven. My Father is the one who
gives you the true bread from
heaven.* 33And the bread that God
gives is the one who came down from
heaven to give life to the world."

34The people said, "Lord, give us
this bread and don't ever stop!"

35Jesus replied:

I am the bread that gives life!
No one who comes to me will
ever be hungry. No one who has
faith in me will ever be thirsty.
36I have told you already that
you have seen me and still do
not have faith in me.
37Everything and everyone that
the Father has given me will
come to me, and I won't turn any
of them away.

38I didn't come from heaven
to do what I want! I came to do
what the Father wants me to do.
He sent me, 39and he wants to
make certain that none of the
ones he has given me will be lost.
Instead, he wants me to raise
them to life on the last day.[c]
40My Father wants everyone
who sees the Son to have faith
in him and to have eternal life.
Then I will raise them to life on
the last day.

41The people started grumbling because Jesus had said he was the
bread that had come down from
heaven. 42They were asking each
other, "Isn't he Jesus, the son of Joseph? Don't we know his father and
mother? How can he say that he has
come down from heaven?"*

---

[a] *miracles*: The Greek text has "signs" here and "sign" in verse 30. See the note at 2.11. [b] *manna*: When the people of Israel were wandering through the desert, the Lord gave them a special kind of food to eat. It tasted like a wafer and was called "manna," which in Hebrew means, "What is this?" [c] *the last day*: When God will judge all people.

6.32 **EAT THE BREAD THAT GIVES LIFE** You know that the bread you buy in the grocery store gives life. But that bread doesn't last. Jesus said he can give us bread that is everlasting. He himself is that bread. We feed on Jesus by taking him into our lives—not through our mouths, but through trusting him. When we do that Jesus himself becomes our very life.

6.42 **DON'T EXCUSE YOUR LACK OF TRUST** The people who were listening to Jesus found an excuse not to trust him. He was just their own fellow citizen, the son of Joseph (or so they thought). Familiarity often causes distrust. If Jesus had come from a far country, they would have listened to him just because he was new and different. Jesus (*continued*)

NOTES

THE REST IS EASY

Lord, I want to put myself in your hands—
But I'm not sure that you can help me.
I have really made a mess of it so far,
Even my best friend thinks so.

I think I have a really hard life,
It's not getting any easier this year!
At least in the eighth grade I was the oldest,
Now I'm at the bottom of the heap—again!

But I trusted you then,
So I will trust you now.
After eighth grade,
The rest is easy.

Right?

WEIGHT OF THE WORLD?

Sometimes it feels like the world is on our shoulders, doesn't it? Who needs pimples at a time like this? A new school, new classes, new teachers, and a new social order—and who is on the bottom? At times like these, we can find comfort in the knowledge that God loves us and that he really cares. So when the older kids apply the pressure, remember: one day at a time!

STEP LOOK INSIDE 3

For another "Look Inside," turn to page 320.

43Jesus told them:
Stop grumbling! 44No one can
come to me, unless the Father
who sent me makes them want
to come. But if they do come, I
will raise them to life on the last
day. 45One of the prophets wrote,
"God will teach all of them." And
so everyone who listens to the
Father and learns from him will
come to me.
46The only one who has seen
the Father is the one who has
come from him. No one else has
ever seen the Father. 47I tell you
for certain that everyone who
has faith in me has eternal life.
48I am the bread that gives life!
49Your ancestors ate manna[d] in
the desert, and later they died.
50But the bread from heaven has
come down, so that no one who
eats it will ever die. 51I am that
bread from heaven! Everyone
who eats it will live forever. My
flesh is the life-giving bread that
I give to the people of this world.
52They started arguing with each
other and asked, "How can he give
us his flesh to eat?"
53Jesus answered:
I tell you for certain that you
won't live unless you eat the
flesh and drink the blood of the
Son of Man. 54But if you do eat
my flesh and drink my blood,
you will have eternal life, and I
will raise you to life on the last
day.* 55My flesh is the true food,
and my blood is the true drink.
56If you eat my flesh and drink
my blood, you are one with me,
and I am one with you.
57The living Father sent me,
and I have life because of him.
Now everyone who eats my flesh
will live because of me. 58The
bread that comes down from
heaven is not like what your
ancestors ate. They died, but
whoever eats this bread will live
forever.
59Jesus was teaching in a Jewish
place of worship in Capernaum when
he said these things.

The Words of Eternal Life

60Many of Jesus' disciples heard
him and said, "This is too hard for
anyone to understand."
61Jesus knew that his disciples
were grumbling. So he asked, "Does
this bother you? 62What if you should
see the Son of Man go up to heaven
where he came from? 63The Spirit is
the one who gives life! Human
strength can do nothing. The words
that I have spoken to you are from
that life-giving Spirit. 64But some of
you refuse to have faith in me." Jesus
said this, because from the beginning
he knew who would have faith in
him. He also knew which one would
betray him.
65Then Jesus said, "You cannot
come to me, unless the Father makes
you want to come. That is why I have
told these things to all of you."
66Because of what Jesus said, many
of his disciples turned their backs on
him and stopped following him.
67Jesus then asked his twelve disciples if they were going to leave him.
68Simon Peter answered, "Lord,
there is no one else that we can go
to! Your words give eternal life.*

[d]*manna*: See the note at 6.31.

(*continued*) is well known among us. There are churches in every town. So many just pass Jesus off as a worn-out old story, and that is very sad.

6.54 **JESUS IS LIFE TO US** By "eat my flesh and drink my blood," Jesus was talking about having faith in him and then taking part in the Lord's Supper to show that we are united with him. The wine or grape juice stands for his blood and the bread stands for his body. When we eat and drink the Lord's Supper, we show that we are part of the church, "the body of Christ," and that we have eternal life from him.

6.68 **THERE IS NO ONE ELSE TO GO TO** Peter told the truth. Sometimes people may imagine that there are lots of religions in the world, so what's so great about Jesus? But you soon (*continued*)

NOTES

69We have faith in you, and we are
sure that you are God's Holy One."
70Jesus told his disciples, "I chose
all twelve of you, but one of you is
a demon!" 71Jesus was talking about
Judas, the son of Simon Iscariot.[e] He
would later betray Jesus, even
though he was one of the twelve
disciples.

Jesus' Brothers Don't Have Faith in Him

7 Jesus decided to leave Judea and
to start going through Galilee because the Jewish leaders wanted to
kill him. 2It was almost time for the
Festival of Shelters, 3and Jesus'
brothers said to him, "Why don't you
go to Judea? Then your disciples can
see what you are doing. 4No one does
anything in secret, if they want others to know about them. So let the
world know what you are doing!"
5Even Jesus' own brothers had not
yet become his followers.*
6Jesus answered, "My time hasn't
yet come,[f] but your time is always
here. 7The people of this world cannot hate you. They hate me, because
I tell them that they do evil things.
8Go on to the festival. My time hasn't
yet come, and I am not going."
9Jesus said this and stayed on in
Galilee.

Jesus at the Festival of Shelters

10After Jesus' brothers had gone
to the festival, he decided to go, and
he went secretly, without telling
anyone.
11During the festival the Jewish
leaders looked for Jesus and asked,
"Where is he?"* 12The crowds even
got into an argument about him.
Some were saying, "Jesus is a good
man," while others were saying, "He
is lying to everyone." 13But the people were afraid of their leaders, and
none of them talked in public about
him.
14When the festival was about half
over, Jesus stood up and started
teaching in the temple. 15The leaders
were surprised and said, "How does
this man know so much? He has
never been taught!"
16Jesus replied:
I am not teaching something
that I thought up. What I teach
comes from the one who sent
me.* 17If you really want to obey

[e]*Iscariot*: See the note at 12.4. [f]*My time hasn't yet come*: See the note at 2.4.

(*continued*) see that people who say such things haven't trusted the other religions either. They've just decided not to seek the truth at all, so they never find it. If they truly looked for the truth, they would come to Jesus, because he alone has the words that give eternal life.

7.5 **WHY DIDN'T JESUS' BROTHERS BELIEVE?** At first the brothers of Jesus turned away from him. Growing up with him may have caused them to resent or envy him. No doubt he had been the favorite son because Mary and Joseph knew about who he was. But this case ended well. After Jesus rose from death his brothers believed in him. Some of them became leaders in the early church.

7.11 **WHAT WAS THE FESTIVAL OF SHELTERS?** Many centuries before Jesus the Israelites escaped from slavery in Egypt, with Moses as their leader. Then for forty years they lived in tents (shelters) in the Sinai desert. The Festival of Shelters was held in memory of that time in Israel's history, when God freed them and kept them safe.

7.16 **JESUS DIDN'T INVENT HIS TEACHING** Jesus didn't just think up what he said. He received it from God the Father. Over the centuries many religious leaders have become famous because of teachings that were their own original work. Jesus made no such claim. He taught only what he was given in heaven. We don't need a new teaching. We need to listen to the teaching that comes from God.

NOTES

God, you will know if what I
teach comes from God or from
me. 18If I wanted to bring honor
to myself, I would speak for
myself. But I want to honor the
one who sent me. That is why I
tell the truth and not a lie.
19Didn't Moses give you the
Law? Yet none of you obey it!
So why do you want to kill me?
20The crowd replied, "You're
crazy! What makes you think someone wants to kill you?"
21Jesus answered:
I worked one miracle,[g] and it
amazed you. 22Moses
commanded you to circumcise
your sons. But it wasn't really
Moses who gave you this
command. It was your ancestors,
and even on the Sabbath you
circumcise your sons 23in order
to obey the Law of Moses. Why
are you angry with me for
making someone completely
well on the Sabbath? 24Don't
judge by appearances. Judge by
what is right.
25Some of the people from Jerusalem were saying, "Isn't this the man
they want to kill? 26Yet here he is,
speaking for everyone to hear. And
no one is arguing with him. Do you
suppose the authorities know that he
is the Messiah? 27But how could that
be? No one knows where the Messiah
will come from, but we know where
this man comes from."
28As Jesus was teaching in the temple, he shouted, "Do you really think
you know me and where I came
from? I didn't come on my own! The
one who sent me is truthful, and you
don't know him. 29But I know the one
who sent me, because I came from
him."
30Some of the people wanted to arrest Jesus right then. But no one even
laid a hand on him, because his time
had not yet come.[h] 31A lot of people
in the crowd put their faith in him
and said, "When the Messiah comes,
he surely won't perform more miracles[i] than this man has done!"

Officers Sent to Arrest Jesus

32When the Pharisees heard the
crowd arguing about Jesus, they got
together with the chief priests and
sent some temple police to arrest him.
33But Jesus told them, "I will be with
you a little while longer, and then I
will return to the one who sent me.
34You will look for me, but you won't
find me. You cannot go where I am
going."*
35The Jewish leaders asked each
other, "Where can he go to keep us
from finding him? Is he going to some
foreign country where our people
live? Is he going there to teach the
Greeks?[j] 36What did he mean by saying that we will look for him, but
won't find him? Why can't we go
where he is going?"

Streams of Life-Giving Water

37On the last and most important
day of the festival, Jesus stood up
and shouted, "If you are thirsty, come
to me and drink! 38Have faith in me,
and you will have life-giving water
flowing from deep inside you, just
as the Scriptures say." 39Jesus was
talking about the Holy Spirit, who
would be given to everyone that had
faith in him. The Spirit had not yet

---

[g] *one miracle*: The healing of the lame man (5.1-18). See the note at 2.11. [h] *his time had not yet come*: See the note at 2.4. [i] *miracles*: See the note at 2.11. [j] *Greeks*: Perhaps Gentiles or Jews who followed Greek customs.

7.34 **WHY DIDN'T THE LEADERS UNDERSTAND JESUS?** Jesus said, "You cannot go where I am going." Of course, he meant that he was going back to heaven. The leaders couldn't understand this because they were so earth-minded. They had read the Scriptures in the Old Testament about Jesus. But they were so determined to have power on earth that they cared nothing for the true Messiah from God or for the heaven he talked about.

NOTES

been given to anyone, since Jesus had not yet been given his full glory.[k]*

The People Take Sides

40When the crowd heard Jesus say this, some of them said, "He must be the Prophet!"[l] 41Others said, "He is the Messiah!" Others even said, "Can the Messiah come from Galilee? 42The Scriptures say that the Messiah will come from the family of King David. Doesn't this mean that he will be born in David's hometown of Bethlehem?" 43The people started taking sides against each other because of Jesus.* 44Some of them wanted to arrest him, but no one laid a hand on him.

The Jewish Leaders Refuse to Have Faith in Jesus

45When the temple police returned to the chief priests and Pharisees, they were asked, "Why didn't you bring Jesus here?"

46They answered, "No one has ever spoken like that man!"

47The Pharisees said to them, "Have you also been fooled? 48Not one of the chief priests or the Pharisees has faith in him. 49And these people who don't know the Law are under God's curse anyway."*

50Nicodemus was there at the time. He was the same one who had earlier come to see Jesus.[m] Nicodemus was a member of the Jewish council and said, 51"Our Law doesn't let us condemn people before we hear what they have to say. We cannot judge them before we know what they have done."

52Then they said, "Nicodemus, you must be from Galilee! Read the Scriptures, and you will find that no prophet is to come from Galilee."

A Woman Caught in Sin

8 53Everyone else went home, 1but Jesus walked out to the Mount of Olives. 2Then early the next morning he went to the temple. The people came to him, and he sat down[n] and started teaching them.

3The Pharisees and the teachers of the Law of Moses brought in a woman who had been caught in bed with a man who was not her husband. They made her stand in the middle of the crowd. 4Then they said, "Teacher, this woman was caught sleeping with a man who is not her husband. 5The Law of Moses teaches that a woman like this should be

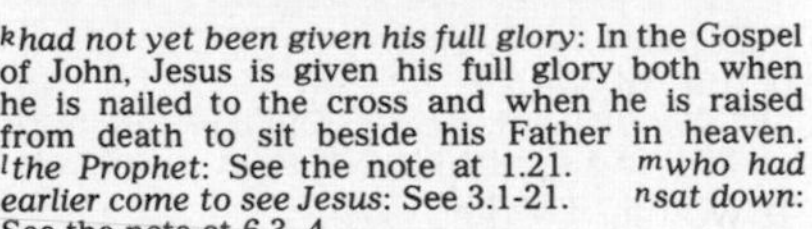

[k]*had not yet been given his full glory*: In the Gospel of John, Jesus is given his full glory both when he is nailed to the cross and when he is raised from death to sit beside his Father in heaven. [l]*the Prophet*: See the note at 1.21. [m]*who had earlier come to see Jesus*: See 3.1-21. [n]*sat down*: See the note at 6.3, 4.

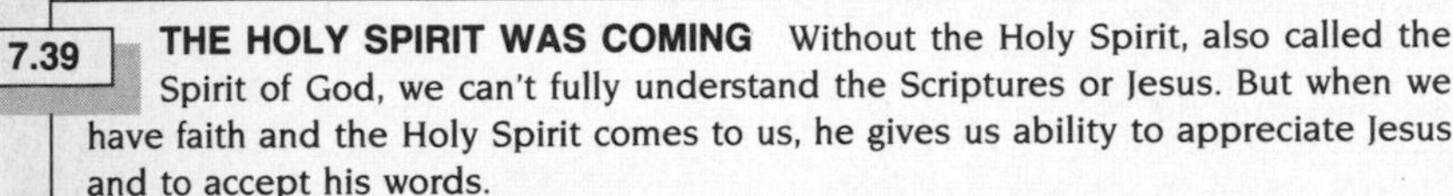

7.39 THE HOLY SPIRIT WAS COMING Without the Holy Spirit, also called the Spirit of God, we can't fully understand the Scriptures or Jesus. But when we have faith and the Holy Spirit comes to us, he gives us ability to appreciate Jesus and to accept his words.

7.43 JESUS CAUSED DIVISION Jesus promised he would be the cause of arguments. Even today people still take sides for or against Jesus. Sometimes we get tired of the endless debate and lies about him. But when Jesus comes again all of the arguments will stop forever. Which side will you be on?

7.49 BEWARE OF PRIDE The chief priests and Pharisees thought they were better than the common people. They said the common people were ignorant and didn't know the Scriptures. That may have been true. But the leaders were worse. Their sin was their pride that blinded them about Jesus. They didn't even know their Messiah when they saw him—even though they knew the Old Testament Scriptures that spoke about him.

NOTES

Step 4

A WOMAN CAUGHT IN SIN—a woman given the opportunity to start all over

JOHN 7.53—8.11

Purity comes in two ways: (1) living a sinless, perfect life or (2) allowing Christ to pay for our sins. Since Jesus was the only person ever to live a sinless life, everyone else falls into the second category.

John the Baptist was a moral and spiritual man. His entire life was lived by the book. Yet even John had sin in his life. King David was a "man after God's own heart"—but he had a man killed and took the man's wife for his own. Joseph had the right idea when he ran from Potiphar's wife when she came on to him—but even Joseph had sin in his life.

One example of how far we can fall and still be made right and pure in God's eyes is related in the story of a Woman Caught in Sin. She was caught in bed with a man who was not her husband. When the religious crowd brought her to Jesus, they were ready to kill her for what she had done. It was a common practice to stone a person who committed adultery.

STEP LOOK BACK 4

When Jesus was asked what should be done with her, he quickly pointed out that her sin was no greater than theirs. Jesus knelt down and wrote something in the sand, and then he stood up and told them, "If any of you have never sinned, then go ahead and throw the first stone at her!" Their reaction was simply to walk away. But the woman stayed long enough to hear what Jesus had to say about forgiveness and purity. In the end, she walked away with his words ringing in her ears, "You may go now, but don't sin anymore."

Did she sin again? Probably. She was human. Was it the same sin? It's doubtful. What we need to remember is that the blood of Jesus Christ provides payment and forgiveness for our past sins, our present sins, and our future sins. We are as pure before God as we were the day we were born. We need to stop doing those things that bring us down and give us a bad reputation. Some of them are dangerous.

Ready for Step 5?
See page 23 of* InStep*'s
introduction.

stoned to death! What do you say?"*
6They asked Jesus this question,
because they wanted to test him and
bring some charge against him. But
Jesus simply bent over and started
writing on the ground with his finger.
7They kept on asking Jesus about
the woman. Finally, he stood up and
said, "If any of you have never
sinned, then go ahead and throw the
first stone at her!" 8Once again he
bent over and began writing on the
ground. 9The people left one by one,
beginning with the oldest one in the
crowd. Finally, Jesus and the woman
were there alone.
10Jesus stood up and asked her,
"Where is everyone? Isn't there anyone left to accuse you?"
11"No sir," the woman answered.
Then Jesus told her, "I am not going to accuse you either. You may
go now, but don't sin anymore."[o]

Jesus Is the Light for the World

12Once again Jesus spoke to the
people. This time he said, "I am the
light for the world! Follow me, and
you won't be walking in the dark.
You will have the light that gives
life."*
13The Pharisees objected, "You are
the only one speaking for yourself,
and what you say isn't true!"
14Jesus replied:
Even if I do speak for myself,
what I say is true! I know where
I came from and where I am
going. But you don't know where
I am from or where I am going.
15You judge in the same way that
everyone else does, but I don't
judge anyone. 16If I did judge, I
would judge fairly, because I
would not be doing it alone. The
Father who sent me is here with
me. 17Your Law requires two
witnesses to prove that
something is true. 18I am one of
my witnesses, and the Father
who sent me is the other one.
19"Where is your Father?" they
asked Jesus.
"You don't know me or my Father!" Jesus answered. "If you knew
me, you would know my Father."
20Jesus said this while he was still
teaching in the place where the temple treasures were stored. But no one
arrested him, because his time had
not yet come.[p]

You Cannot Go Where I Am Going

21Jesus also told them, "I am going
away, and you will look for me. But
you cannot go where I am going, and
you will die with your sins unforgiven."
22The Jewish leaders asked, "Does
he intend to kill himself? Is that what
he means by saying we cannot go
where he is going?"
23Jesus answered, "You are from
below, but I am from above. You belong to this world, but I don't.
24That is why I said you will die with
your sins unforgiven. If you don't

---

[o]*don't sin anymore*: Verses 1-11 are not in some manuscripts. In other manuscripts these verses are placed after 7.36 or after 21.25 or after Luke 21.38, with some differences in the text. [p]*his time had not yet come*: See the note at 2.4.

8.5 **JESUS FORGIVES SINNERS** We like to feel we have good morals as long as we think we can point to someone worse than ourselves. That's how we make ourselves feel that we are good in God's eyes. That is also the way the teachers of the Law felt when they caught a woman in her sin. But Jesus saw their real attitude, and he made them understand their self-deceit. But he forgave the woman with a warning.

8.12 **WHY IS JESUS A LIGHT?** The passage about the woman caught in sin gives the answer. Jesus shows us what we are—sinners. But his light drives away the darkness of our sins. This is shown by the way he dealt with the sins of the woman. Jesus didn't come to make people feel guilty. His great work is to forgive—to take away sin and the guilt that it causes.

NOTES

have faith in me for who I am,[q] you will die, and your sins will not be forgiven."

25"Who are you?" they asked Jesus.

Jesus answered, "I am exactly who I told you at the beginning.* 26I have a lot more to say about you, especially about all the evil you have done. The one who sent me is truthful, and I tell the people of this world only what I have heard from him."

27No one understood that Jesus was talking to them about the Father.

28Jesus went on to say, "When you have lifted up the Son of Man,[r] you will know who I am. You will also know that I don't do anything on my own. I say only what my Father taught me. 29The one who sent me is with me. I always do what pleases him, and he will never leave me."

30After Jesus said this, many of the people put their faith in him.

The Truth Will Set You Free

STEP 3

31Jesus told the people who had faith in him, "If you keep on obeying what I have said, you truly are my disciples. 32You will know the truth, and the truth will set you free."*

33They answered, "We are Abraham's children! We have never been anyone's slaves. How can you say we will be set free?"

34Jesus replied:

I tell you for certain that anyone who sins is a slave of sin! 35And slaves don't stay in the family forever, though the Son will always remain in the family. 36If the Son gives you freedom, you are free! 37I know that you are from Abraham's family. Yet you want to kill me, because my message is not really in your hearts. 38I am telling you what my Father has shown me, just as you are doing what your father has taught you.

Your Father Is the Devil

39The people said to Jesus, "Abraham is our father!"

Jesus replied, "If you were Abraham's children, you would do what Abraham did. 40Instead, you want to kill me for telling you the truth that God gave me. Abraham never did anything like that. 41But you are doing exactly what your father does."

"Don't accuse us of having someone else as our father!" they said. "We just have one father, and he is God."

42Jesus answered:

If God were your Father, you would love me, because I came from God and only from him. He sent me. I did not come on my own. 43Why can't you understand what I am talking about? Can't you stand to hear what I am saying? 44Your father is the devil, and you do exactly what he wants. He has always been a murderer and a liar. There is nothing truthful about him. He speaks on his own, and everything he says is a lie. Not

---

[q]*I am*: For the Jewish people the most holy name of God is "Yahweh," which may be translated "I am." In the Gospel of John "I am" is sometimes used by Jesus to show that he is that one.
[r]*lifted up the Son of Man*: See the note at 7.39.

8.25 **WHO ARE YOU?** Jesus' words about himself were well understood by the Jewish leaders. They knew he was saying that he is the Messiah. But their hearts were cold to him. They decided they didn't want Jesus for their Messiah—because that would mean giving up their wealth and power.

8.32 **WHAT DOES IT MEAN TO BE FREE?** Over the entrance to a famous college are the words, "The truth shall make you free." But most people who go in there don't know where the words come from. The Jews didn't even remember they once had been slaves in Egypt. Jesus had come to them as the living Truth who alone sets people free from the slavery of sin.

NOTES

only is he a liar himself, but he
is also the father of all lies.*
45Everything I have told you
is true, and you still refuse to
have faith in me. 46Can any of
you accuse me of sin? If you
cannot, why won't you have
faith in me? After all, I am telling
you the truth. 47Anyone who
belongs to God will listen to his
message. But you refuse to
listen, because you don't belong
to God.

Jesus and Abraham

48The people told Jesus, "We were
right to say that you are a Samaritan[s]
and that you have a demon in you!"
49Jesus answered, "I don't have a
demon in me. I honor my Father, and
you refuse to honor me. 50I don't want
honor for myself. But there is one
who wants me to be honored, and
he is also the one who judges.
51I tell you for certain that if you obey
my words, you will never die."
52Then the people said, "Now we
are sure that you have a demon.
Abraham is dead, and so are the
prophets. How can you say that no
one who obeys your words will ever
die? 53Are you greater than our father
Abraham? He died, and so did the
prophets. Who do you think you
are?"
54Jesus replied, "If I honored myself, it would mean nothing. My Father is the one who honors me. You
claim that he is your God, 55even
though you don't really know him.
If I said I didn't know him, I would
be a liar, just like all of you. But I
know him, and I do what he says.
56Your father Abraham was really
glad to see me."
57"You are not even fifty years
old!" they said. "How could you have
seen Abraham?"
58Jesus answered, "I tell you for
certain that even before Abraham
was, I was, and I am."[t]* 59The people
picked up stones to kill Jesus, but
he hid and left the temple.

Jesus Heals a Man Born Blind

9 As Jesus walked along, he saw
a man who had been blind since
birth. 2Jesus' disciples asked,
"Teacher, why was this man born
blind? Was it because he or his parents sinned?"
3"No, it wasn't!" Jesus answered.
"But because of this, you will see God
work a miracle for him.* 4As long
as it is day, we must do what the one
who sent me wants me to do. When
night comes, no one can work.
5While I am in the world, I am the
light for the world."

---

[s] *Samaritan*: See 4.9 and the note there.
[t] *I am*: See the note at 8.24.

8.44 **WHO IS YOUR FATHER?** In one way, God is the Father of all people because he is the Creator. But sin broke the relationship. God can't be our Father again until the relationship is put back together somehow. That happens when we believe in Jesus. But until then, God will have to deny we are his children. Until we have faith, we are lost in sin, and we are the children of the devil.

8.58 **THESE WERE JESUS' MOST SHOCKING WORDS** Here Jesus tells the people that he lived—and always had lived—before Abraham, who was born some two thousand years earlier. We are glad Jesus said this when we personally know him as our Savior. But if we don't know him this way, these words don't make sense to us. They sound like something it would take a lot of nerve to say. But Jesus really is the God-Man who has lived forever.

9.3 **WHY DID JESUS HEAL THE BLIND MAN?** Jesus wanted his disciples to know he came to heal all kinds of people. The disciples thought the man was cursed with blindness because of somebody's bad deeds, and so he probably couldn't be healed. But it didn't matter what the cause of the blindness was—Jesus would heal him. Jesus also wants to open our eyes to the truth.

NOTES

6 After Jesus said this, he spit on
the ground. He made some mud and
smeared it on the man's eyes.
7 Then he said, "Go and wash off the
mud in Siloam Pool." The man went
and washed in Siloam, which means
"One Who Is Sent." When he had
washed off the mud, he could see.
8 The man's neighbors and the people who had seen him begging wondered if he really could be the same
man. 9 Some of them said he was the
same beggar, while others said he
only looked like him. But he told
them, "I am that man."
10 "Then how can you see?" they
asked.
11 He answered, "Someone named
Jesus made some mud and smeared
it on my eyes. He told me to go and
wash it off in Siloam Pool. When I
did, I could see."
12 "Where is he now?" they asked.
"I don't know," he answered.

The Pharisees Try to Find Out What Happened

13-14 The day when Jesus made the
mud and healed the man was a Sabbath. So the people took the man to
the Pharisees. 15 They asked him how
he was able to see, and he answered,
"Jesus made some mud and smeared
it on my eyes. Then after I washed
off the mud, I could see."
16 Some of the Pharisees said, "This
man Jesus does not come from God.
If he did, he would not break the law
of the Sabbath."
Others asked, "How could someone who is a sinner work such a
miracle?"[u]
Since the Pharisees could not agree
among themselves, 17 they asked the
man, "What do you say about this
one who healed your eyes?"
"He is a prophet!" the man told
them.
18 But the Jewish leaders would not
believe that the man had once been
blind. They sent for his parents
19 and asked them, "Is this the son
that you said was born blind? How
can he now see?"
20 The man's parents answered,
"We are certain that he is our son,
and we know that he was born blind.
21 But we don't know how he got his
sight or who gave it to him. Ask him!
He is old enough to speak for
himself."
22-23 The man's parents said this because they were afraid of the Jewish
leaders. The leaders had already
agreed that no one was to have anything to do with anyone who said Jesus was the Messiah.
24 The leaders called the man back
and said, "Swear by God to tell the
truth! We know that Jesus is a
sinner."
25 The man replied, "I don't know
if he is a sinner or not. All I know
is that I used to be blind, but now I
can see!"*
26 "What did he do to you?" the
Jewish leaders asked. "How did he
heal your eyes?"
27 The man answered, "I have already told you once, and you refused
to listen. Why do you want me to
tell you again? Do you also want to
become his disciples?"
28 The leaders insulted the man and
said, "You are his follower! We are
followers of Moses. 29 We are sure
that God spoke to Moses, but we
don't even know where Jesus comes
from."
30 The man replied, "How strange!
He healed my eyes, and yet you don't
know where he comes from. 31 We
know that God listens only to people
who love and obey him. God doesn't
listen to sinners. 32 And this is the first
time in history that anyone has ever
given sight to someone born blind.

---

[u] *miracle*: See the note at 2.11.

9.25 **WHAT WAS THE PHARISEES' PROBLEM?** The Pharisees knew the man could see. But they didn't want to believe what had happened. Their hatred of Jesus blinded them to the clear truth. In spite of the Pharisees' arguing, the man who was blind could see. So they took out their spite on the man who had been blind. Sin makes people unreasonable and blind in their hearts.

NOTES

33Jesus could not do anything unless
he came from God."
34The leaders told the man, "You
have been a sinner since the day you
were born! Do you think you can
teach us anything?" Then they said,
"You can never come back into any
of our meeting places!"
35When Jesus heard what had happened, he went and found the man.
Then Jesus asked, "Do you have faith
in the Son of Man?"*
36He replied, "Sir, if you will tell
me who he is, I will put my faith in
him."
37"You have already seen him," Jesus answered, "and right now he is
talking with you."
38The man said, "Lord, I put my
faith in you!" Then he worshiped
Jesus.
39Jesus told him, "I came to judge
the people of this world. I am here
to give sight to the blind and to make
blind everyone who sees."*
40When the Pharisees heard Jesus
say this, they asked, "Are we blind?"
41Jesus answered, "If you were
blind, you would not be guilty. But
now that you claim to see, you will
keep on being guilty."

A Story about Sheep

10 Jesus said:
I tell you for certain that only
thieves and robbers climb over
the fence instead of going in
through the gate to the sheep
pen. 2-3But the gatekeeper opens
the gate for the shepherd, and
he goes in through it. The sheep
know their shepherd's voice. He
calls each of them by name and
leads them out.*
4When he has led out all of his
sheep, he walks in front of them,
and they follow, because they
know his voice. 5The sheep will
not follow strangers. They don't
recognize a stranger's voice, and
they run away.
6Jesus told the people this story.
But they did not understand what he
was talking about.

Jesus Is the Good Shepherd

7Jesus said:
I tell you for certain that I am
the gate for the sheep. 8Everyone
who came before me was a thief
or a robber, and the sheep did
not listen to any of them. 9I am
the gate. All who come in
through me will be saved.
Through me they will come and
go and find pasture.
10A thief comes only to rob,
kill, and destroy. I came so that
everyone would have life, and
have it in its fullest.* 11I am the

9.35 **JESUS SHOWS US HIMSELF** The poor man didn't even know who had healed him of his blindness. Jesus hadn't demanded that the man must understand it all. Afterwards, Jesus showed himself to the man. Then the man trusted him. Jesus shows himself to us in these pages. Can we trust him too?

9.39 **DID JESUS MAKE PEOPLE BLIND?** He says he did. Jesus means he won't help people who are satisfied with themselves. Jesus came to help people who have no hope and know it. A doctor can't help dying people who say they are well, and Jesus can't help people who say they have no sin and no need of him.

10.2 **SHEEP KNOW THEIR SHEPHERD** In the land where Jesus lived—even today—shepherds call their sheep by name. Also, if you mix two flocks of sheep, and each shepherd calls to his own sheep, then each flock will go to its own shepherd. Jesus knows his people by name, and they won't follow anyone but him.

10.10 **WHO WERE THE THIEVES AND ROBBERS?** The thieves and robbers were the false shepherds, the false teachers. God wanted leaders for the people who were chosen and *(continued)*

NOTES

good shepherd, and the good
shepherd gives up his life for his
sheep. 12Hired workers are not
like the shepherd. They don't
own the sheep, and when they
see a wolf coming, they run off
and leave the sheep. Then the
wolf attacks and scatters the
flock. 13Hired workers run away
because they don't care about
the sheep.
14I am the good shepherd. I
know my sheep, and they know
me. 15Just as the Father knows
me, I know the Father, and I give
up my life for my sheep. 16I have
other sheep that are not in this
sheep pen. I must bring them
together too, when they hear
my voice. Then there will be
one flock of sheep and one
shepherd.
17The Father loves me,
because I give up my life, so that
I may receive it back again.
18No one takes my life from me.
I give it up willingly! I have the
power to give it up and the power
to receive it back again, just
as my Father commanded me to
do.
19The Jews took sides because of
what Jesus had told them. 20Many
of them said, "He has a demon in
him! He is crazy! Why listen to
him?"*
21But others said, "How could anyone with a demon in him say these
things? No one like that could give
sight to a blind person!"

Jesus Is Rejected

22That winter Jesus was in Jerusalem for the Temple Festival. 23One
day he was walking in that part of
the temple known as Solomon's
Porch,[v] 24and the people gathered all
around him. They said, "How long
are you going to keep us guessing?
If you are the Messiah, tell us
plainly!"
25Jesus answered:
I have told you, and you
refused to believe me. The things
I do by my Father's authority
show who I am. 26But since you
are not my sheep, you don't
believe me. 27My sheep know my
voice, and I know them. They
follow me, 28and I give them
eternal life, so that they will
never be lost. No one can snatch
them out of my hand.* 29My
Father gave them to me, and he
is greater than all others.[w] No
one can snatch them from his
hands, 30and I am one with the
Father.
31Once again the Jewish leaders
picked up stones in order to kill Jesus. 32But he said, "I have shown you
many good things that my Father
sent me to do. Which one are you
going to stone me for?"
33They answered, "We are not

---

[v]*Solomon's Porch*: A public place with tall columns along the east side of the temple. [w]*he is greater than all others*: Some manuscripts have "they are greater than all others."

(*continued*) guided by his own will. The leaders in Jesus' time didn't care much about the people. They were using the people to make themselves rich and important.

10.20 **THEY SAID JESUS WAS CRAZY** We could imagine people today saying Jesus was out of his mind. Some modern people think they know too much to have faith in prophets or messengers from God. In Jesus' time they didn't know about all of today's excuses for not believing. But they were like people are now—they didn't want to have faith in Jesus because their lives were not right with God.

10.28 **JESUS KEEPS HIS PEOPLE SAFE** Jesus says about his sheep (believers), "No one can snatch them out of my hand." It comforts us to know that Jesus will keep us forever when we give our lives to him. He was not just a good man. He is the Son of God, and we can never be lost if we are in his hands.

NOTES

stoning you because of any good thing you did. We are stoning you because you did a terrible thing. You are just a man, and here you are claiming to be God!"*

34Jesus replied:

In your Scriptures doesn't God say, "You are gods"? 35The Scriptures cannot be destroyed, and God spoke to those people and called them gods. 36So why do you accuse me of a terrible sin for saying that I am the Son of God? After all, it is the Father who prepared me for this work. He is also the one who sent me into the world. 37If I don't do as my Father does, you should not believe me. 38But if I do what my Father does, you should believe because of that, even if you don't have faith in me. Then you will know for certain that the Father is one with me, and I am one with the Father.

39Again they wanted to arrest Jesus. But he escaped 40and crossed the Jordan to the place where John had earlier been baptizing. While Jesus was there, 41many people came to him. They were saying, "John didn't work any miracles, but everything he said about Jesus is true."* 42A lot of those people also put their faith in Jesus.

The Death of Lazarus

11 1-2A man by the name of Lazarus was sick in the village of Bethany. He had two sisters, Mary and Martha. This was the same Mary who later poured perfume on the Lord's head and wiped his feet with her hair. 3The sisters sent a message to the Lord and told him that his good friend Lazarus was sick.

4When Jesus heard this, he said, "His sickness won't end in death. It will bring glory to God and his Son."

5Jesus loved Martha and her sister and brother. 6But he stayed where he was for two more days. 7Then he said to his disciples, "Now we'll go back to Judea."

8"Teacher," they said, "the people there want to stone you to death! Why do you want to go back?"

9Jesus answered, "Aren't there twelve hours in each day? If you walk during the day, you will have light from the sun, and you won't stumble. 10But if you walk during the night, you will stumble, because there isn't any light inside you." 11Then he told them, "Our friend Lazarus is asleep, and I am going there to wake him up."

12They replied, "Lord, if he is asleep, he will get better." 13Jesus really meant that Lazarus was dead, but they thought he was talking only about sleep.

14Then Jesus told them plainly, "Lazarus is dead! 15I am glad that I wasn't there, because now you will have a chance to put your faith in me. Let's go to him."

16Thomas, whose nickname was "Twin," said to the other disciples, "Come on. Let's go so we can die with him."*

10.33 **WHY DID THEY WANT TO STONE JESUS?** Killing people by throwing stones at them was a legal method of putting criminals to death. In the minds of the leaders Jesus was the worst kind of criminal—he had said he was God. But the Old Testament prophets also said this about him. It is hard to understand how the leaders of Jesus' day knew so little about their own Scriptures.

10.41 **MANY PEOPLE CAME TO JESUS** In spite of everything the Jewish leaders could say or do, crowds of people flocked to hear Jesus and to be healed. They had better understanding than their leaders. They could see the sense in everything Jesus said and did. But most of the leaders were blinded by jealousy and religious hate.

11.16 **OUR FAITH SOMETIMES FAILS** Jesus told his disciples that he was going to "wake up" Lazarus from death. But they didn't believe him. We talk a lot about our faith. But often (*continued*)

NOTES

Jesus Brings Lazarus to Life

17When Jesus got to Bethany, he
found that Lazarus had already been
in the tomb four days. 18Bethany was
only about two miles from Jerusalem,
19and many people had come from
the city to comfort Martha and Mary
because their brother had died.
20When Martha heard that Jesus
had arrived, she went out to meet
him, but Mary stayed in the house.
21Martha said to Jesus, "Lord, if you
had been here, my brother would not
have died. 22Yet even now I know
that God will do anything you ask."
23Jesus told her, "Your brother will
live again!"
24Martha answered, "I know that
he will be raised to life on the last
day,[x] when all the dead are raised."
25Jesus then said, "I am the one
who raises the dead to life! Everyone
who has faith in me will live, even
if they die. 26And everyone who lives
because of faith in me will never die.
Do you believe this?"*
27"Yes, Lord!" she replied. "I believe that you are Christ, the Son of
God. You are the one we hoped
would come into the world."
28After Martha said this, she went
and privately said to her sister Mary,
"The Teacher is here, and he wants
to see you." 29As soon as Mary heard
this, she got up and went out to Jesus.
30He was still outside the village
where Martha had gone to meet him.
31Many people had come to comfort
Mary, and when they saw her quickly
leave the house, they thought she was
going out to the tomb to cry. So they
followed her.
32Mary went to where Jesus was.
Then as soon as she saw him, she
kneeled at his feet and said, "Lord,
if you had been here, my brother
would not have died."
33When Jesus saw that Mary and
the people with her were crying, he
was terribly upset 34and asked,
"Where have you put his body?"
They replied, "Lord, come and you
will see."
35Jesus started crying,* 36and the
people said, "See how much he loved
Lazarus."
37Some of them said, "He gives
sight to the blind. Why couldn't he
have kept Lazarus from dying?"
38Jesus was still terribly upset. So
he went to the tomb, which was a
cave with a stone rolled against the
entrance. 39Then he told the people
to roll the stone away. But Martha
said, "Lord, you know that Lazarus
has been dead four days, and there
will be a bad smell."
40Jesus replied, "Didn't I tell you
that if you had faith, you would see
the glory of God?"
41After the stone had been rolled
aside, Jesus looked up toward
heaven and prayed, "Father, I thank
you for answering my prayer.
42I know that you always answer my
prayers. But I said this, so that the
people here would believe that you
sent me."
43When Jesus had finished praying, he shouted, "Lazarus, come
out!" 44The man who had been dead
came out. His hands and feet were
wrapped with strips of burial cloth,
and a cloth covered his face.

---

[x]*the last day*: When God will judge all people.

(*continued*) we find that our faith doesn't go very far, as the disciples' didn't in this case. The only thing that keeps us going sometimes is the fact that Jesus is always faithful toward us, even when our faith in him is weak.

11.26 **A GREAT PROMISE** There is encouragement here as Jesus says, "Everyone who lives because of faith in me will never die." If we have been at the bedside of a dying Christian, we may have seen for ourselves how true these words are. Those who trust in Jesus don't die—they go out with joy to meet him.

11.35 **WHY DID JESUS CRY?** Was Jesus crying because he had lost his friend in death? No, Jesus knew what he was going to do. But he saw the others crying, and saw how death was their great enemy. Jesus was crying for the others whom the thought of death had defeated.

NOTES

Jesus then told the people, "Untie
him and let him go."

The Plot to Kill Jesus
(Matthew 26.1–5; Mark 14.1, 2; Luke 22.1, 2)

45Many of the people who had
come to visit Mary saw the things
that Jesus did, and they put their faith
in him. 46Others went to the Pharisees and told what Jesus had done.
47Then the chief priests and the Pharisees called the council together and
said, "What should we do? This man
is working a lot of miracles.[y] 48If we
don't stop him now, everyone will put
their faith in him. Then the Romans
will come and destroy our temple and
our nation."[z]
49One of the council members was
Caiaphas, who was also high priest
that year. He spoke up and said, "You
people don't have any sense at all!
50Don't you know it is better for one
person to die for the people than for
the whole nation to be destroyed?"*
51Caiaphas did not say this on his
own. As high priest that year, he was
prophesying that Jesus would die for
the nation. 52Yet Jesus would not die
just for the Jewish nation. He would
die to bring together all of God's scattered people. 53From that day on, the
council started making plans to put
Jesus to death.
54Because of this plot against him,
Jesus stopped going around in public. He went to the town of Ephraim,
which was near the desert, and he
stayed there with his disciples.*
55It was almost time for Passover.
Many of the Jewish people who lived
out in the country had come to Jerusalem to get themselves ready[a] for
the festival. 56They looked around for
Jesus. Then when they were in the
temple, they asked each other, "You
don't think he will come here for
Passover, do you?"
57The chief priests and the Pharisees told the people to let them know
if any of them saw Jesus. That is how
they hoped to arrest him.

At Bethany
(Matthew 26.6–13; Mark 14.3–9)

12 Six days before Passover Jesus
went back to Bethany, where
he had raised Lazarus from death.
2A meal had been prepared for Jesus.
Martha was doing the serving, and
Lazarus himself was there.
3Mary took a very expensive bottle
of perfume[b] and poured it on Jesus'
feet. She wiped them with her hair,
and the sweet smell of the perfume
filled the house.
4A disciple named Judas Iscariot[c]
was there. He was the one who was
going to betray Jesus, and he asked,
5"Why wasn't this perfume sold for
three hundred silver coins and the

---

[y]*miracles*: See the note at 2.11. [z]*destroy our temple and our nation*: The Jewish leaders were afraid that Jesus would lead his followers to rebel against Rome and that the Roman army would then destroy their nation. [a]*get themselves ready*: The Jewish people had to do certain things to prepare themselves to worship God. [b]*very expensive bottle of perfume*: The Greek text has "expensive perfume made of pure spikenard," a plant used to make perfume. [c]*Iscariot*: This may mean "a man from Kerioth" (a place in Judea). But more probably it means "a man who was a liar" or "a man who was a betrayer."

11.50 **CAIAPHAS SAID A MOUTHFUL** "It is better for one person to die for the people." That was exactly what would happen. Jesus would die for his people. But the high priest said more than he understood, because he was only thinking about sacrificing Jesus to please the Romans. Notice also that Jesus died not only for the Jews but for all of God's people everywhere.

11.54 **WHY DID JESUS STAY AWAY?** Jesus was not afraid of the Jewish leaders. But he knew there was a right time for his arrest, his trial, and his death. That time would be at the Jewish Passover: the feast when a lamb was killed, when Jews remembered how they were saved from slavery in Egypt. Jesus the Lamb of God would save us by his own sacrifice from our slavery to sin and death.

NOTES

money given to the poor?" 6Judas did
not really care about the poor. He
asked this because he carried the
moneybag and sometimes would
steal from it.
7Jesus replied, "Leave her alone!
She has kept this perfume for the day
of my burial.* 8You will always have
the poor with you, but you won't always have me."

A Plot to Kill Lazarus

9A lot of people came when they
heard that Jesus was there. They also
wanted to see Lazarus, because Jesus
had raised him from death. 10So the
chief priests made plans to kill Lazarus.* 11He was the reason that many
of the Jewish people were turning
from them and putting their faith in
Jesus.

Jesus Enters Jerusalem

(Matthew 21.1–11; Mark 11.1–11; Luke 19.28–40)

12The next day a large crowd was
in Jerusalem for Passover. When
they heard that Jesus was coming for
the festival, 13they took palm
branches and went out to greet him.[d]
They shouted,

"Hooray![e]
God bless the one who comes
in the name of the Lord!
God bless the King
of Israel!"

14Jesus found a donkey and rode
on it, just as the Scriptures say,*

15"People of Jerusalem,
don't be afraid!
Your King is now coming,
and he is riding
on a donkey."

16At first, Jesus' disciples did not
understand. But after he had been
given his glory,[f] they remembered all
this. Everything had happened exactly as the Scriptures said it would.
17-18A crowd had come to meet Jesus because they had seen him call
Lazarus out of the tomb. They kept
talking about him and this miracle.[g]
19But the Pharisees said to each
other, "There is nothing that can be
done! Everyone in the world is following Jesus."

Some Greeks Want to Meet Jesus

20Some Greeks[h] had gone to Jerusalem to worship during Passover.
21Philip from Bethsaida in Galilee
was there too. So they went to him
and said, "Sir, we would like to meet

---

[d]*took palm branches and went out to greet him*: This was one way that the Jewish people welcomed a famous person. [e]*Hooray*: This translates a word that can mean "please save us." But it is most often used as a shout of praise to God. [f]*had been given his glory*: See the note at 7.39. [g]*miracle*: See the note at 2.11. [h]*Greeks*: Perhaps Gentiles who worshiped with the Jews. See the note at 7.35.

12.7 **JESUS ACCEPTED MARY'S GIFT** Maybe we think Jesus should have agreed with Judas. The money from the perfume could have been given to the poor. But it was Mary's loving act for Jesus. He always accepts our works of love, even when they don't make sense to other people. The Son of God deserves our best. Besides, Judas was only pretending. He was a thief and he didn't care what Mary did.

12.10 **TRYING TO KILL THE TRUTH** It's hard to imagine such stubbornness. The chief priests knew that Jesus had raised a man to life. But instead of believing in Jesus, they tried to kill the man. It shows how far some people will go who don't want to accept Jesus.

12.14 **THE OLD TESTAMENT HAD TOLD ABOUT THIS DAY** Jesus would ride a donkey into Jerusalem, carrying out a prophecy from the Scriptures. It is very important to see that Jesus was following the great plan of God. In ages past God had planned to send his Son to be our Savior. Prophets had been telling about this for many hundreds of years.

NOTES

Jesus."* 22Philip told Andrew. Then the two of them went to Jesus and told him.

The Son of Man Must Be Lifted Up

23Jesus said:

The time has come for the Son
of Man to be given his glory.[i]
24I tell you for certain that a grain
of wheat that falls on the ground
will never be more than one
grain unless it dies. But if it dies,
it will produce lots of wheat.
25If you love your life, you will
lose it. If you give it up in this
world, you will be given eternal
life. 26If you serve me, you must
go with me. My servants will be
with me wherever I am. If you
serve me, my Father will honor
you.

27Now I am deeply troubled,
and I don't know what to say.
But I must not ask my Father to
keep me from this time of
suffering. In fact, I came into the
world to suffer. 28So Father,
bring glory to yourself.

A voice from heaven then said, "I have already brought glory to myself, and I will do it again!" 29When the crowd heard the voice, some of them thought it was thunder. Others thought an angel had spoken to Jesus.

30Then Jesus told the crowd, "That voice spoke to help you, not me. 31This world's people are now being judged, and the ruler of this world[j] is already being thrown out! 32If I am lifted up above the earth, I will make everyone want to come to me."* 33Jesus was talking about the way he would be put to death.

34The crowd said to Jesus, "The Scriptures teach that the Messiah will live forever. How can you say that the Son of Man must be lifted up? Who is this Son of Man?"

35Jesus answered, "The light will be with you for only a little longer. Walk in the light while you can. Then you won't be caught walking blindly in the dark. 36Have faith in the light while it is with you, and you will be children of the light."

The People Refuse to Have Faith in Jesus

After Jesus had said these things, he left and went into hiding. 37He had worked a lot of miracles[k] among the people, but they were still not willing to have faith in him.* 38This happened so that what the prophet Isaiah had said would come true,

"Lord, who has believed
our message?
And who has seen
your mighty strength?"

39The people could not have faith in Jesus, because Isaiah had also said,

40"The Lord has blinded

---

[i]*be given his glory*: See the note at 7.39. [j]*world*: In the Gospel of John "world" sometimes refers to the people who live in this world and to the evil forces that control their lives. [k]*miracles*: See the note at 2.11.

12.21 **OTHER NATIONS WORSHIPED JESUS** Already we see here that the good news about Jesus was reaching the Gentile peoples. Some of them were coming to Jesus at Passover time. It was at this time that Jesus announced that he would have to suffer and die.

12.32 **JESUS WOULD BE LIFTED UP** This was another way of saying Jesus would be crucified or nailed to a cross. The crowd didn't understand that the Messiah, who is the Son of God, cannot truly die. They couldn't understand that the Messiah had to pass through death and rise again in order to give life to us.

12.37 **THE MIRACLES MADE NO DIFFERENCE** The crowds were amazed by the wonderful things Jesus did—even bringing Lazarus back from the dead. But they still did not understand or accept Jesus as their Messiah. We're all like that. We may live for Jesus one day, but the next day we may fail him. Let's pray for courage to be loyal to Jesus at all times.

NOTES

the eyes of the people,
and he has made
the people stubborn.
He did this so that they
could not see
or understand,
and so that they
would not turn to the Lord
and be healed."
41Isaiah said this, because he saw
the glory of Jesus and spoke about
him.[l] 42Even then, many of the leaders put their faith in Jesus, but they
did not tell anyone about it. The Pharisees had already given orders for
the people not to have anything to
do with anyone who had faith in Jesus. 43And besides, the leaders liked
praise from others more than they
liked praise from God.

Jesus Came to Save the World

44In a loud voice Jesus said:
Everyone who has faith in me
also has faith in the one who sent
me.* 45And everyone who has
seen me has seen the one who
sent me. 46I am the light that has
come into the world. No one who
has faith in me will stay in the
dark.
47I am not the one who will
judge those who refuse to obey
my teachings. I came to save the
people of this world, not to be
their judge. 48But everyone who
rejects me and my teachings will
be judged on the last day[m] by
what I have said. 49I don't speak
on my own. I say only what the
Father who sent me has told me
to say. 50I know that his
commands will bring eternal life.
That is why I tell you exactly
what the Father has told me.

Jesus Washes the Feet of His Disciples

13 It was before Passover, and Jesus knew that the time had
come for him to leave this world and
to return to the Father. He had always
loved his followers in this world, and
he loved them to the very end.
2Even before the evening meal
started, the devil had made Judas,
the son of Simon Iscariot,[n] decide to
betray Jesus.
3Jesus knew that he had come from
God and would go back to God. He
also knew that the Father had given
him complete power. 4So during the
meal Jesus got up, removed his outer
garment, and wrapped a towel
around his waist. 5He put some water
into a large bowl. Then he began
washing his disciples' feet and drying
them with the towel he was wearing.*
6But when he came to Simon Peter,
that disciple asked, "Lord, are you
going to wash my feet?"
7Jesus answered, "You don't really
know what I am doing, but later you
will understand."

---

[l] *he saw the glory of Jesus and spoke about him*: Or "he saw the glory of God and spoke about Jesus."
[m] *the last day*: When God will judge all people.
[n] *Iscariot*: See the note at 12.4.

12.44 **TO BELIEVE IN JESUS IS TO BELIEVE IN GOD** That's the important thing. Many people are willing to see Jesus as one of the world's great teachers. But they don't understand that our problem is not lack of teachers. There are many to tell us how we should live. What we need is someone to save us from our sins. That is why Jesus is different—he saves us from the sins that keep us away from God.

13.5 **JESUS "WASHES OUR FEET"** Jesus showed us how to be a servant. When guests came to someone's home in Jesus' time, their feet would be hot and covered with dust from the road. The host's slave (or the host if there were no slave) would wash the guests' feet. Jesus put on the clothing of a slave and did this for his disciples. He is showing us that he took the lowest place—by becoming a man and dying a shameful death—because he loves us. We also should love by serving one another.

NOTES

8"You will never wash my feet!"
Peter replied.
"If I don't wash you," Jesus told
him, "you don't really belong to me."
9Peter said, "Lord, don't wash just
my feet. Wash my hands and my
head."
10Jesus answered, "People who
have bathed and are clean all over
need to wash just their feet. And you,
my disciples, are clean, except for
one of you." 11Jesus knew who would
betray him. That is why he said, "except for one of you."
12After Jesus had washed his disciples' feet and had put his outer garment back on, he sat down again.[o]
Then he said:
Do you understand what I
have done? 13You call me your
teacher and Lord, and you
should, because that is who I am.
14And if your Lord and teacher
has washed your feet, you
should do the same for each
other. 15I have set the example,
and you should do for each other
exactly what I have done for you.
16I tell you for certain that
servants are not greater than
their master, and messengers
are not greater than the one who
sent them. 17You know these
things, and God will bless you,
if you do them.
18I am not talking about all of
you. I know the ones I have
chosen. But what the Scriptures
say must come true. And they
say, "The man who ate with me
has turned against me!" 19I am
telling you this before it all
happens. Then when it does
happen, you will believe who I
am.[p] 20I tell you for certain that
anyone who welcomes my
messengers also welcomes me,
and anyone who welcomes
me welcomes the one who sent
me.

Jesus Tells What Will Happen to Him

(Matthew 26.20–25; Mark 14.17–21; Luke 22.21–23)

21After Jesus had said these things,
he was deeply troubled and told his
disciples, "I tell you for certain that
one of you will betray me." 22They
were confused about what he meant.
And they just stared at each other.
23Jesus' favorite disciple was sitting next to him at the meal,* 24and
Simon motioned for that disciple to
find out which one Jesus meant.
25So the disciple leaned toward Jesus
and asked, "Lord, which one of us
are you talking about?"
26Jesus answered, "I will dip this
piece of bread in the sauce and give
it to the one I was talking about."
Then Jesus dipped the bread and
gave it to Judas, the son of Simon
Iscariot.[q] 27Right then Satan took
control of Judas.
Jesus said, "Judas, go quickly and
do what you have to do." 28No one
at the meal understood what Jesus
meant. 29But because Judas was in
charge of the money, some of them
thought that Jesus had told him to
buy something they needed for the
festival. Others thought that Jesus
had told him to give some money to
the poor. 30Judas took the piece of
bread and went out.
It was already night.

The New Command

31After Judas had gone, Jesus said:
Now the Son of Man will be
given glory, and he will bring
glory to God. 32Then, after God
is given glory because of him,

---

[o]*sat down again*: On special occasions the Jewish people followed the Greek and Roman custom of lying down on their left side and leaning on their left elbow, while eating with their right hand. [p]*I am*: See the note at 8.24. [q]*Iscariot*: See the note at 12.4.

13.23 **JESUS KNEW WHAT WAS GOING TO HAPPEN** Judas would sell his Master to the Jewish leaders. Jesus told this to John, the one who wrote this Gospel. But the others didn't realize what Judas was going to do. John tells us that Satan, the great spiritual enemy of God, was by that time in control of Judas' life.

NOTES

God will bring glory to him, and
God will do it very soon.
33My children, I will be with
you for a little while longer. Then
you will look for me, but you
won't find me. I tell you just as
I told the people, "You cannot
go where I am going." 34But I
am giving you a new command.
You must love each other, just
as I have loved you.* 35If you love
each other, everyone will know
that you are my disciples.

Peter's Promise

(Matthew 26.31–35; Mark 14.27–31; Luke 22.31–34)

36Simon Peter asked, "Lord, where
are you going?"
Jesus answered, "You can't go
with me now, but later on you will."
37Peter asked, "Lord, why can't I
go with you now? I would die for
you!"*
38"Would you really die for me?"
Jesus asked. "I tell you for certain
that before a rooster crows, you will
say three times that you don't even
know me."

Jesus Is the Way to the Father

14 Jesus said to his disciples,
"Don't be worried! Have faith
in God and have faith in me.[r] 2There
are many rooms in my Father's
house. I wouldn't tell you this, unless
it was true. I am going there to prepare a place for each of you.* 3After
I have done this, I will come back
and take you with me. Then we will
be together. 4You know the way to
where I am going."
5Thomas said, "Lord, we don't
even know where you are going!
How can we know the way?"
6"I am the way, the truth, and the
life!" Jesus answered. "Without me,
no one can go to the Father. 7If you
had known me, you would have
known the Father. But from now on,
you do know him, and you have seen
him."
8Philip said, "Lord, show us the Father. That is all we need."*
9Jesus replied:
Philip, I have been with you
for a long time. Don't you know
who I am? If you have seen me,
you have seen the Father. How
can you ask me to show you the
Father? 10Don't you believe that
I am one with the Father and that
the Father is one with me? What

[r]*Have faith in God and have faith in me*: Or "You have faith in God, so have faith in me."

13.34 **JESUS GIVES US A NEW COMMANDMENT** Ever since Old Testament times God has told us we should love our neighbors as we love ourselves. Jesus went further—we should love others just as Jesus loved us. He laid down his life for us. Our lives also belong to each other. People know we're Christians by the kind of love we have—the kind that says "My life is for you."

13.37 **PETER MEANT WELL** Peter really wanted to belong to Jesus, so much that he had asked Jesus to wash him from head to toe (verse 9). Peter said he would even die for Jesus. But Jesus knew that Peter's own strength would fail him. We might mean to do well, too, but in our own strength we fail Jesus again and again. But he will forgive us the way he did Peter, and then the Holy Spirit will work through us to please God.

14.2 **A PLACE FOR EACH OF US** This passage has always been a great source of comfort to believers. No matter what happens to us in this world, if we believe in Jesus, we know that he has a special place ready for each of us when we leave here. That's how much Jesus loves us and cares about us.

14.8 **WHAT DOES GOD LOOK LIKE?** Even though no one has seen what God the Father looks like, no one needs to. He sent his Son to be a human being in this world and to be seen. What does God look like? He looks like Jesus.

NOTES

I say is not said on my own. The
Father who lives in me does
these things.
11Have faith in me when I say
that the Father is one with me
and that I am one with the
Father. Or else have faith in me
simply because of the things I
do. 12I tell you for certain that
if you have faith in me, you will
do the same things that I am
doing. You will do even greater
things, now that I am going back
to the Father. 13Ask me, and I
will do whatever you ask. This
way the Son will bring honor to
the Father. 14I will do whatever
you ask me to do.

The Holy Spirit Is Promised

15Jesus said to his disciples:
If you love me, you will do as
I command. 16Then I will ask the
Father to send you the Holy
Spirit who will help[s] you and
always be with you.* 17The
Spirit will show you what is true.
The people of this world cannot
accept the Spirit, because they
don't see or know him. But you
know the Spirit, who is with you
and will keep on living in you.
18I won't leave you like
orphans. I will come back to you.
19In a little while the people of
this world won't be able to see
me, but you will see me. And
because I live, you will live.
20Then you will know that I am
one with the Father. You will
know that you are one with me,
and I am one with you. 21If you
love me, you will do what I have
said, and my Father will love
you. I will also love you and
show you what I am like.
22The other Judas, not Judas Iscariot,[t] then spoke up and asked, "Lord,
what do you mean by saying that you
will show us what you are like, but
you will not show the people of this
world?"
23Jesus replied:
If anyone loves me, they will
obey me. Then my Father will
love them, and we will come to
them and live in them. 24But
anyone who doesn't love me,
won't obey me. What they have
heard me say doesn't really
come from me, but from the
Father who sent me.
25I have told you these things
while I am still with you. 26But
the Holy Spirit will come and
help[u] you, because the Father
will send the Spirit to take my
place. The Spirit will teach you
everything and will remind you
of what I said while I was with
you.

27I give you peace, the kind of
peace that only I can give. It is
not like the peace that this world
can give. So don't be worried or
afraid.*
28You have already heard me
say that I am going and that I
will also come back to you. If
you really love me, you should
be glad that I am going back to

---

[s] *help*: The Greek word may mean "comfort," "encourage," or "defend." [t] *Iscariot*: See the note at 12.4. [u] *help*: See the note at verse 16.

14.16 **WE NEED THE HOLY SPIRIT** All the words in the Bible will not help us if we don't first have the Holy Spirit. The Holy Spirit is an invisible person—the third person in the being we call God. God the Father and God the Son send the Holy Spirit to help us understand the things God has said in the Bible, including the things Jesus said. When the Holy Spirit lives in us, it's just as if Christ himself were living in us. Then we have God with us as our friend at all times.

14.27 **WE HAVE PEACE FROM JESUS** This peace is different and greater than any other peace we can ever know. It is the peace of God. One of the apostles said this peace is greater than we can completely understand (Philippians 4.7). This is the peace we have when the Holy Spirit comes to live in us.

NOTES

Step 11

ENDURANCE—Developing inward strength by daily dependence on God

JOHN 14.15–21

LOOK BEFORE YOU LEAP

It was my turn. I took a running leap and dove deep down into the lake. But what had seemed so inviting on the surface quickly turned into a dark, frightening place. I was in deeper than I had expected to be. The weeds on the bottom wrapped around my legs, threatening to hold me under. A cramp grabbed my sides, making it painful to move. Panic set in.

I looked up and fiercely paddled my way back to the surface. My lungs were burning for air. Come on! Come on! Then there it was. Light was reaching down from the surface. The warmth urged me on. I made it . . . that time.

STEP LOOK AHEAD 11

But it taught me to pay more attention to where I jump in. Things aren't always what they seem. You can get in deeper than you planned.

CONSIDERING THE COST

It can happen before we know it. We're in over our heads. That's why we need to ask the Lord to direct our steps and help us consider the cost before we take whatever leap we face. We can be assured that if we keep looking up, God's light will help us keep our heads above the water.

For another "Look Ahead," turn to page 382.

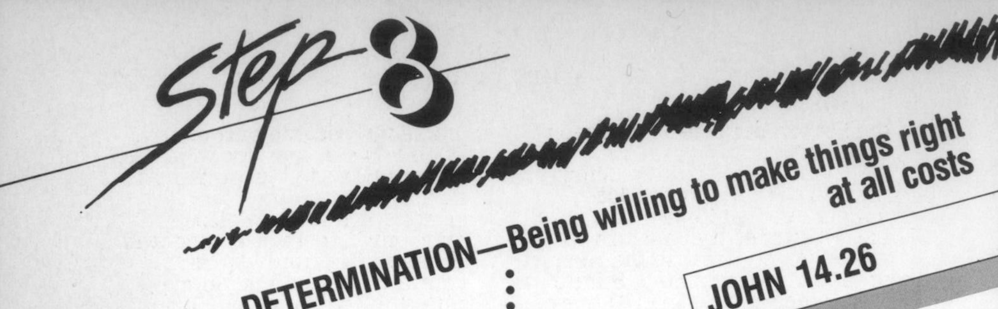

DETERMINATION—Being willing to make things right at all costs

JOHN 14.26

CREATING A SCENE

I always think the worst. I create this scene in my mind where, "I said . . . ," then, "he said . . . ," and every terrible thing you can think of happens. That way when it happens, which it usually does, I am halfway prepared.

To make a long story short, I've been dating Randy for a few months. Let's just say, we have been pretty intimate. He's everything I want in a guy—gentle, kind, and incredibly good-looking—so that made it easy to become close.

Now I'm learning that God has different plans for what I should and shouldn't be doing. Sex outside of marriage is damaging and dangerous. But how do you stop something you've already started? My feelings toward Randy haven't changed. I care for him even more now because I want things to be right with us spiritually too. At least, that's what I want. Now I have to convince Randy. I'll say, "Randy, I really care for you, but I don't think it's right that we . . . ." Then he'll say . . .

Oh! Here I go again!

THE RIGHT WORDS

It is tough to make right on things we have been doing wrong. This takes a great deal of determination. But that is what growing up is—deciding what is right for us, setting goals and heading for them. Our friends can't decide what is right or wrong for us. They are too busy taking care of themselves. Only God can help us stay focused. If we keep a running conversation going with him, he will help us say what needs to be said.

STEP LOOK AHEAD 8

For another "Look Ahead," turn to page 635.

the Father, because he is greater
than I am.
29I am telling you this before
I leave, so that when it does
happen, you will have faith in
me. 30I cannot speak with you
much longer, because the ruler
of this world is coming. But he
has no power over me. 31I obey
my Father, so that everyone in
the world might know that I love
him.
It is time for us to go now.

Jesus Is the True Vine

15 Jesus said to his disciples:
I am the true vine, and my
Father is the gardener. 2He cuts
away every branch of mine that
does not produce fruit. But he
trims clean every branch that does
produce fruit, so that it will
produce even more fruit. 3You are
already clean because of what I
have said to you.
4Stay joined to me, and I will
stay joined to you. Just as a
branch cannot produce fruit
unless it stays joined to the vine,
you cannot produce fruit unless
you stay joined to me. 5I am the
vine, and you are the branches.
If you stay joined to me, and I
stay joined to you, then you will
produce lots of fruit. But you
cannot do anything without me.*
6If you don't stay joined to me,
you will be thrown away. You
will be like dry branches that are
gathered up and burned in a fire.
7Stay joined to me and let my
teachings become part of you.
Then you can pray for whatever
you want, and your prayer will
be answered. 8When you
become fruitful disciples of
mine, my Father will be honored.
9I have loved you, just as my
Father has loved me. So make
sure that I keep on loving you.
10If you obey me, I will keep
loving you, just as my Father
keeps loving me, because I have
obeyed him.
11I have told you this to make
you as completely happy as I am.
12Now I tell you to love each
other, as I have loved you.*
13The greatest way to show love
for friends is to die for them.
14And you are my friends, if you
obey me. 15Servants don't know
what their master is doing, and
so I don't speak to you as my
servants. I speak to you as my
friends, and I have told you
everything that my Father has
told me.
16You did not choose me. I
chose you and sent you out to
produce fruit, the kind of fruit
that will last. Then my Father
will give you whatever you ask
for in my name.[v] 17So I command
you to love each other.

The World's Hatred

18If the people of this world[w]
hate you, just remember that

[v]*in my name*: Or "because you are my followers."
[w]*world*: See the note at 12.31.

15.5 **BE A BRANCH IN THE TRUE VINE** Christians know they have no life of their own. Their life comes from Jesus himself. He is like a grapevine, and we are like branches that grow out of him. Then our lives show good results, like rich grapes on the vine. But those results can only grow if we stay joined to Christ so that his life can flow through us.

15.12 **HOW MUCH DID JESUS LOVE US?** In chapter 13 of John's Gospel we saw that Jesus became a servant so we could see his love for us. But remember—Jesus is also the Son of God. It was a long way from the throne of heaven to the floor of that room where he kneeled to wash his disciples' feet. But it was a much longer way from that great throne to the cross on which the God of heaven and earth died. That's how much Jesus loved us.

NOTES

Step 2

LOYALTY—Because God is there for me, I will be there for others.

JOHN 15.12–14

MUTT AND JEFF

I was president. She was vice president. I was Peter Pan. She was Wendy. I was Batman. She was Robin. You get the picture. Carrie and I were best friends. She moved in next door when I was six. And since that time I can never remember a day, except when we were on vacation, that Carrie wasn't around. We have shared everything.

My dad calls us "Mutt and Jeff." I figured out that was because Carrie was so much bigger than I. A lot bigger. But I never noticed that until middle high when other kids started making fun of her. She was pretty big. But you don't get out much in middle high, so I was able to conceal our friendship. High school was a different story. Now there were lots of activities to join in and places to go, and to be seen with Carrie was kind of a death wish for popularity. My new friends didn't want to get to know the Carrie I knew. So what was I going to do?

STEP LOOK AHEAD 2

I figured you can know a lot of people in your life and enjoy being with them. But how could Peter get along without Wendy, and what would Batman do without Robin? There are just some teams you don't break up—like Mutt and Jeff.

DOES IT REALLY MATTER?

We have to look beyond outward appearances sometimes. What we see on the outside isn't always what we get on the inside. It takes time to get to know and appreciate people for who they really are. Good friends are worth the effort.

For another "Look Ahead," turn to page 561.

they hated me first.* 19If you belonged to the world, its people would love you. But you don't belong to the world. I have chosen you to leave the world behind, and that is why its people hate you. 20Remember how I told you that servants are not greater than their master. So if people mistreat me, they will mistreat you. If they do what I say, they will do what you say.

21People will do to you exactly what they did to me. They will do it because you belong to me, and they don't know the one who sent me. 22If I had not come and spoken to them, they would not be guilty of sin. But now they have no excuse for their sin.

23Everyone who hates me also hates my Father. 24I have done things that no one else has ever done. If they had not seen me do these things, they would not be guilty. But they did see me do these things, and they still hate me and my Father too. 25That is why the Scriptures are true when they say, "People hated me for no reason."

26I will send you the Spirit who comes from the Father and shows what is true. The Spirit will help[x] you and will tell you about me. 27Then you will also tell others about me, because you have been with me from the beginning.

16 I am telling you this to keep you from being afraid. 2You will be chased out of the Jewish meeting places. The time will come when people will kill you and think they are doing God a favor. 3They will do all these things because they don't know either the Father or me. 4I am saying this to you now, so that when the time comes, you will remember what I have said.

The Work of the Holy Spirit

I was with you at the first, and so I didn't tell you these things. 5But now I am going back to the Father who sent me, and none of you asks me where I am going.* 6You are very sad from hearing all of this. 7But I tell you that I am going to do what is best for you. That is why I am going away. The Holy Spirit cannot come to help[x] you until I leave. But after I am gone, I will send the Spirit to you.*

8The Spirit will come and show the people of this world the truth about sin and God's justice

---

[x] *help*: See the note at 14.16.

15.18 **BE READY FOR HATRED** Christians should not feel that they're being picked on because some people hate them. It has to be that way because not everybody knows and loves God. Therefore they don't understand God's people either. We ought to feel sorry for people who hate us. They're unhappy, and they need to be saved from their sins. Remember, Jesus said, "Father, forgive these people. They don't know what they're doing" (Luke 23.34).

16.5 **JESUS WAS TO RETURN TO HIS FATHER** Jesus Christ, the Son of God, did not begin his life as a baby at Bethlehem. He had been in heaven forever. He was God the Son, and God the Father was another person in the one Being the Bible calls God. God the Son became human in order to save us from our sins. Then he went back to heaven, which had been his home all along.

16.7 **WHO IS THE HOLY SPIRIT?** We have just spoken about the one God who consists of God the Father and God the Son. But there is a third person in the Being of God. That is the person the Bible calls the Holy Spirit. Jesus promised to send the Holy Spirit to be with us after Jesus went back to heaven.

NOTES

and the judgment. 9The Spirit
will show them that they are
wrong about sin, because they
didn't have faith in me. 10They
are wrong about God's justice,
because I am going to the Father,
and you won't see me again.
11And they are wrong about the
judgment, because God has
already judged the ruler of this
world.
12I have much more to say to
you, but right now it would be
more than you could understand.
13The Spirit shows what is true
and will come and guide you into
the full truth. The Spirit does not
speak on his own. He will tell
you only what he has heard from
me, and he will let you know
what is going to happen. 14The
Spirit will bring glory to me by
taking my message and telling
it to you. 15Everything that the
Father has is mine. That is why
I have said that the Spirit takes
my message and tells it to you.*

Sorrow Will Turn into Joy

16Jesus told his disciples, "You will
see me for a little while, and then
for a little while you won't see me."
17They said to each other, "What
does Jesus mean by saying that we
will see him for a little while, and
then we won't see him for a little
while? What does he mean by saying
that he is going to the Father?
18What is this 'little while' that he
is talking about? We don't know what
he means."
19Jesus knew that they had some
questions, so he said:

You are wondering what I
meant when I said that you will
see me for a little while, and then
in a little while you won't see
me. 20I tell you for certain that
you will cry and be sad, but the
world will be happy. You will be
sad, but later you will be happy.
21When a woman is about to
give birth, she is in great pain.
But after it is all over, she forgets
the pain and is happy, because
she has brought a child into the
world. 22You are now very sad.
But later I will see you, and you
will be so happy that no one will
be able to change the way you
feel.* 23When that time comes,
you won't have to ask me about
anything. I tell you for certain
that the Father will give you
whatever you ask for in my
name. 24You have not asked for
anything in this way before, but
now you must ask in my name.[y]
Then it will be given to you, so
that you will be completely
happy.
25I have used examples to
explain to you what I have been
talking about. But the time will
come when I will speak to you
plainly about the Father and will
no longer use examples like
these. 26You will ask the Father
in my name,[z] and I won't have
to ask him for you. 27God the
Father loves you because you
love me, and you believe that I
have come from him. 28I came

---

[y] *in my name . . . in my name*: Or "as my disciples . . . as my disciples." [z] *in my name*: Or "because you are my followers."

16.15 **WHAT DOES THE HOLY SPIRIT DO FOR US?** Sometimes the Holy Spirit is called the Comforter or Helper. He is the invisible presence of God who helps us to be happy in the world. He reminds us that Jesus is alive as our Savior. He also helps us to understand God's word, and he gives us the power to do things for God that will last forever.

16.22 **SOMETIMES WE ARE SAD** Jesus warned us that life would not always be "a bed of roses." Sometimes Christians are alone and mistreated in the world. But one day Jesus will come back, and all of our sadness will be gone forever. The disciples came to know what Jesus meant by this when he rose from death and proved to them that he is stronger than the grave. He overcomes all of the evil forces in the world.

NOTES

from the Father into the world,
but I am leaving the world and
returning to the Father.
29The disciples said, "Now you are
speaking plainly to us! You are not
using examples. 30At last we know
that you understand everything, and
we don't have any more questions.
Now we believe that you truly have
come from God."
31Jesus replied:
Do you really believe me?
32The time will come and is
already here when all of you will
be scattered. Each of you will go
back home and leave me by
myself. But the Father will be
with me, and I won't be alone.
33I have told you this, so that you
might have peace in your hearts
because of me. While you are in
the world, you will have to suffer.
But cheer up! I have defeated the
world.[a]

Jesus Prays

17 After Jesus had finished speaking to his disciples, he looked
up toward heaven and prayed:
Father, the time has come for
you to bring glory to your Son,
in order that he may bring glory
to you. 2And you gave him power
over all people, so that he would
give eternal life to everyone you
give him.* 3Eternal life is to
know you, the only true God, and
to know Jesus Christ, the one
you sent. 4I have brought glory
to you here on earth by doing
everything you gave me to do.
5Now, Father, give me back the
glory that I had with you before
the world was created.
6You have given me some
followers from this world, and
I have shown them what you are
like. They were yours, but you
gave them to me, and they have
obeyed you. 7They know that
you gave me everything I have.
8I told my followers what you
told me, and they accepted it.
They know that I came from you,
and they believe that you are the
one who sent me. 9I am praying
for them, but not for those who
belong to this world.[a] My
followers belong to you, and I
am praying for them.* 10All that
I have is yours, and all that you
have is mine, and they will bring
glory to me.
11Holy Father, I am no longer
in the world. I am coming to you,
but my followers are still in the
world. So keep them safe by the
power of the name that you have
given me. Then they will be one
with each other, just as you and
I are one. 12While I was with
them, I kept them safe by the
power you have given me. I
guarded them, and not one of
them was lost, except the one
who had to be lost. This
happened so that what the
Scriptures say would come true.
13Father, I am on my way to
you. But I say these things while
I am still in the world, so that
my followers will have the same
complete joy that I do. 14I have
told them your message. But the
people of this world hate them,

[a]*world*: See the note at 12.31.

17.2 **WHAT IS ETERNAL LIFE?** Usually we think of eternal life as life that goes on forever and ever. And it is. But eternal life is much more than endless time. It is a *kind* of life that is only in God. That's why Jesus says that eternal life is to know God. When we know God as he means for us to know him—when we love him—we have eternal life right now.

17.9 **JESUS PRAYED FOR BELIEVERS** Jesus says he doesn't pray for those who belong to the world. He prays for the people that his Father gave him from the world. They are the ones who really love God and obey him. You can be one of the gifts that the Father gave to his Son if only you confess your sins and ask him to accept you.

NOTES

because they don't belong to this
world, just as I don't.
15Father, I don't ask you to
take my followers out of the
world, but keep them safe from
the evil one.* 16They don't
belong to this world, and neither
do I. 17Your word is the truth.
So let this truth make them
completely yours. 18I am sending
them into the world, just as you
sent me. 19I have given myself
completely for their sake, so that
they may belong completely to
the truth.
20Father, I am not praying just
for these followers. I am also
praying for everyone else who
will have faith because of what
my followers will say about me.
21I want all of them to be one
with each other, just as I am one
with you and you are one with
me. I also want them to be one
with us. Then the people of this
world will believe that you sent
me.
22I have honored my followers
in the same way that you
honored me, in order that they
may be one with each other, just
as we are one. 23I am one with
them, and you are one with me,
so that they may become
completely one. Then this
world's people will know that
you sent me. They will know that
you love my followers as much
as you love me.
24Father, I want everyone you
have given me to be with me,
wherever I am. Then they will
see the glory that you have given
me, because you loved me before
the world was created. 25Good
Father, the people of this world
don't know you. But I know you,
and my followers know that you
sent me. 26I told them what you
are like, and I will tell them even
more. Then the love that you
have for me will become part of
them, and I will be one with
them.

Jesus Is Betrayed and Arrested
(Matthew 26.47–56; Mark 14.43–50; Luke 22.47–53)

18 When Jesus had finished praying, he and his disciples
crossed the Kidron Valley and went
into a garden.[b] 2Jesus had often met
there with his disciples, and Judas
knew where the place was.
3-5Judas had promised to betray Jesus. So he went to the garden with
some Roman soldiers and temple police, who had been sent by the chief
priests and the Pharisees. They carried torches, lanterns, and weapons.
Jesus already knew everything that
was going to happen, but he asked,
"Who are you looking for?"
They answered, "We are looking
for Jesus from Nazareth!"
Jesus told them, "I am Jesus!"[c]*

---

[b]*garden*: The Greek word is usually translated "garden," but probably referred to an olive orchard.
[c]*I am Jesus*: The Greek text has "I am." See the note at 8.24.

17.15 **HOW DOES JESUS' FATHER KEEP YOU SAFE?** God is in charge of the world, and nothing can happen to you without his permission. Even if you are put to death because you love Jesus, his Father will rescue the part of you that can never die. Most of all he will protect you from Satan, the Evil One, who is the enemy of God and the enemy of God's people.

18.3 **WHY DID JUDAS BETRAY JESUS?** Most people have "good" reasons for doing their evil deeds. Judas might have convinced himself that Jesus was the enemy of Israel. He might have thought he was doing his country good by selling out his Master to the authorities. On the other hand, some think Judas wanted to give Jesus a "push" by arranging his arrest, hoping he would defend himself more openly. Either way, Judas was on the wrong track. The devil is in the business of deceiving people as he did Judas.

NOTES

6At once they all backed away and
fell to the ground.
7Jesus again asked, "Who are you
looking for?"
"We are looking for Jesus from
Nazareth," they answered.
8This time Jesus replied, "I have
already told you that I am Jesus. If
I am the one you are looking for, let
these others go. 9Then everything
will happen, just as the Scriptures
say, 'I did not lose anyone you gave
me.' "
10Simon Peter had brought along
a sword. He now pulled it out and
struck at the servant of the high
priest. The servant's name was Mal-
chus, and Peter cut off his right ear.*
11Jesus told Peter, "Put your sword
away. I must drink from the cup[d] that
the Father has given me."

Jesus Is Brought to Annas
(Matthew 26.57, 58; Mark 14.53, 54; Luke 22.54)

12The Roman officer and his men,
together with the temple police, arrested Jesus and tied him up. 13They
took him first to Annas, who was the
father-in-law of Caiaphas, the high
priest that year.* 14This was the same
Caiaphas who had told the Jewish
leaders, "It is better if one person dies
for the people."

Peter Says He Does Not Know Jesus
(Matthew 26.69, 70; Mark 14.66–68; Luke 22.55–57)

15Simon Peter and another disciple
followed Jesus. That disciple knew
the high priest, and he followed Jesus
into the courtyard of the high priest's
house. 16Peter stayed outside near
the gate. But the other disciple came
back out and spoke to the girl at the
gate. She let Peter go in, 17but asked
him, "Aren't you one of that man's
followers?"
"No, I am not!" Peter answered.*
18It was cold, and the servants and
temple police had made a charcoal
fire. They were warming themselves
around it, when Peter went over and
stood near the fire to warm himself.

Jesus Is Questioned by the High Priest
(Matthew 26.59–66; Mark 14.55–64; Luke 22.66–71)

19The high priest questioned Jesus
about his followers and his teaching.

---

[d] *drink from the cup*: In the Scriptures a cup is sometimes used as a symbol of suffering. To "drink from the cup" is to suffer.

18.10 **PETER ATTACKED ONE OF THE OFFICERS WITH A SWORD** It was a natural thing to fight back. Peter had to learn, like the others, that God's kingdom doesn't come because we force it on others. We overcome the world by loving our enemies. This doesn't mean we stop enforcing the laws of our earthly countries. It means that God rules in this world when people let him have his way in their lives.

18.13 **WHO WAS THE HIGH PRIEST?** We have here the names of the high priest and of his father-in-law who was high priest before him. For hundreds of years the Jews had been ruled by their high priests because there was no king after 587 B.C. Even though the Herod family ruled as kings at that time, they were not lawful kings. They were placed in that position by the Romans. So Jesus was taken first to the high priest.

18.17 **WE ARE ALL COWARDS BY NATURE** We guard our earthly lives more than anything. In order not to place ourselves in danger, we often deny that we know the truth. That's what Peter did. But later, by the power of the Holy Spirit, Jesus' disciples would become bold. Over the years, untold numbers of Jesus' followers have died rather than deny their Master before cruel earthly powers. History tells us that as an older man, Peter himself was crucified for Jesus' sake.

NOTES

20But Jesus told him, "I have spoken
freely in front of everyone. And I
have always taught in our meeting
places and in the temple, where all
of our people come together. I have
not said anything in secret. 21Why
are you questioning me? Why don't
you ask the people who heard me?
They know what I have said."
22As soon as Jesus said this, one
of the temple police hit him and said,
"That's no way to talk to the high
priest!"
23Jesus answered, "If I have done
something wrong, say so. But if not,
why did you hit me?" 24Jesus was
still tied up, and Annas sent him to
Caiaphas the high priest.

Peter Again Denies that He Knows Jesus

(Matthew 26.71–75; Mark 14.69–72; Luke 22.58–62)

25While Simon Peter was standing
there warming himself, someone
asked him, "Aren't you one of Jesus'
followers?"
Again Peter denied it and said,
"No, I am not!"
26One of the high priest's servants
was there. He was a relative of the
servant whose ear Peter had cut off,
and he asked, "Didn't I see you in
the garden with that man?"
27Once more Peter denied it, and
right then a rooster crowed.

Jesus Is Tried by Pilate

(Matthew 27.1, 2, 11–14; Mark 15.1–5; Luke 23.1–5)

28It was early in the morning when
Jesus was taken from Caiaphas to
the building where the Roman governor stayed. But the Jewish crowd
waited outside. Any of them who had
gone inside would have become unclean and would not be allowed to
eat the Passover meal.[e]*
29Pilate came out and asked,
"What charges are you bringing
against this man?"
30They answered, "He is a criminal! That's why we brought him to
you."
31Pilate told them, "Take him and
judge him by your own laws."
The crowd replied, "We are not allowed to put anyone to death."
32And so what Jesus said about his
death[f] would soon come true.
33Pilate then went back inside. He
called Jesus over and asked, "Are
you the king of the Jews?"
34Jesus answered, "Are you asking
this on your own or did someone tell
you about me?"
35"You know I'm not a Jew!" Pilate
said. "Your own people and the chief
priests brought you to me. What have
you done?"
36Jesus answered, "My kingdom
does not belong to this world. If it
did, my followers would have fought
to keep the Jewish leaders from
handing me over to you. No, my kingdom does not belong to this world."
37"So you are a king," Pilate replied.
"You are saying that I am a king,"
Jesus told him. "I was born into this
world to tell about the truth. And
everyone who belongs to the truth
knows my voice."
38Pilate asked Jesus, "What is
truth?"

Jesus Is Sentenced to Death

(Matthew 27.15–31; Mark 15.6–20; Luke 23.13–25)

Pilate went back out to the Jewish
crowd and said, "I don't find this man

---

[e] *would have become unclean and would not be allowed to eat the Passover meal*: Jewish people who came in close contact with foreigners right before Passover were not allowed to eat the Passover meal.
[f] *about his death*: Jesus had said that he would die by being "lifted up," which meant that he would die on a cross. The Romans killed criminals by nailing them on a cross, but they did not let the Jews kill anyone in this way.

18.28 **THE CROWD DESERTED JESUS** The same crowd that had cheered as Jesus entered Jerusalem on a donkey was screaming for his blood. They were careful not to go into Pilate's headquarters and make themselves "unclean" according to their beliefs. But they were willing to nail the Son of God to a cross.

NOTES

guilty of anything!* 39And since I usually set a prisoner free for you at
Passover, would you like for me to
set free the king of the Jews?"
40They all shouted, "No, not him!
We want Barabbas." Now Barabbas
was a terrorist.[g]
19 Pilate gave orders for Jesus to
be beaten with a whip. 2The
soldiers made a crown out of thorn
branches and put it on Jesus. Then
they put a purple robe on him.
3They came up to him and said, "Hey,
you king of the Jews!" They also hit
him with their fists.
4Once again Pilate went out to the
crowd. This time he said, "I will have
Jesus brought out to you again. Then
you can see for yourselves that I have
not found him guilty."
5Jesus came out, wearing the
crown of thorns and the purple robe.
Pilate said, "Here is the man!"[h]
6When the chief priests and the
temple police saw him, they yelled,
"Nail him to a cross! Nail him to a
cross!"
Pilate told them, "You take him
and nail him to a cross! I don't find
him guilty of anything."*
7The crowd replied, "He claimed
to be the Son of God! Our Jewish
law says that he must be put to
death."
8When Pilate heard this, he was
terrified. 9He went back inside and
asked Jesus, "Where are you from?"
But Jesus did not answer.
10"Why won't you answer my
question?" Pilate asked. "Don't you
know that I have the power to let
you go free or to nail you to a cross?"
11Jesus replied, "If God had not
given you the power, you couldn't
do anything at all to me. But the one
who handed me over to you did something even worse."
12Then Pilate wanted to set Jesus
free. But the Jewish crowd again
yelled, "If you set this man free, you
are no friend of the Emperor! Anyone
who claims to be a king is an enemy
of the Emperor."
13When Pilate heard this, he
brought Jesus out. Then he sat down
on the judge's bench at the place
known as "The Stone Pavement." In
Aramaic this pavement is called
"Gabbatha." 14It was about noon on
the day before Passover, and Pilate
said to the crowd, "Look at your
king!"
15"Kill him! Kill him!" they yelled.
"Nail him to a cross!"
"So you want me to nail your king
to a cross?" Pilate asked.
The chief priests replied, "The Emperor is our king!" 16Then Pilate
handed Jesus over to be nailed to a
cross.

Jesus Is Nailed to a Cross

(Matthew 27.32–44; Mark 15.21–32; Luke 23.26–43)

Jesus was taken away, 17and he
carried his cross to a place known

[g]*terrorist*: Someone who stirred up trouble against the Romans in the hope of gaining freedom for the Jewish people. [h]*"Here is the man!"*: Or "Look at the man!"

18.38 **WHAT IS TRUTH?** This may be the greatest question in the Bible—perhaps even in the history of mankind. But notice that Pilate didn't wait for the answer to his question, but he went back out to listen again to the demands of Jesus' enemies. It was quite a tragedy for Pilate. Maybe he later realized the answer to his question. He had wanted to set Jesus free—but wasn't brave enough to disappoint the crowd.

19.6 **GOD'S PLAN HAPPENED** Pilate wanted to let Jesus go, but the crowd made him afraid to. So he passed the death sentence. But remember—God knew this would happen. It was his plan that Jesus would shed his blood on a cross, dying in the place of sinners. Even though this was a terrible thing, for the innocent Jesus to be killed like a criminal, God allowed it. It was why Jesus came here.

NOTES

as "The Skull."[i] In Aramaic this place
is called "Golgotha." 18There Jesus
was nailed to the cross, and on each
side of him a man was also nailed
to a cross.
19Pilate ordered the charge against
Jesus to be written on a board and
put above the cross. It read, "Jesus
of Nazareth, King of the Jews."*
20The words were written in Hebrew,
Latin, and Greek.
The place where Jesus was taken
was not far from the city, and many
of the Jewish people read the charge
against him. 21So the chief priests
went to Pilate and said, "Why did
you write that he is King of the Jews?
You should have written, 'He claimed
to be King of the Jews.' "
22But Pilate told them, "What is
written will not be changed!"
23After the soldiers had nailed Jesus to the cross, they divided up his
clothes into four parts, one for each
of them. But his outer garment was
made from a single piece of cloth,
and it did not have any seams.
24The soldiers said to each other,
"Let's not rip it apart. We'll gamble
to see who gets it." This happened
so that the Scriptures would come
true, which say,

> "They divided up my clothes
> and gambled
> for my garments."

The soldiers then did what they had
decided.
25Jesus' mother stood beside his
cross with her sister and Mary the
wife of Clopas. Mary Magdalene was
standing there too.[j] 26When Jesus
saw his mother and his favorite disciple with her, he said to his mother,
"This man is now your son."*
27Then he said to the disciple, "She
is now your mother." From then on,
that disciple took her into his own
home.

The Death of Jesus
(Matthew 27.45–56; Mark 15.33–41; Luke 23.44–49)

28Jesus knew that he had now finished his work. And in order to make
the Scriptures come true, he said, "I
am thirsty!" 29A jar of cheap wine
was there. Someone then soaked a
sponge with the wine and held it up
to Jesus' mouth on the stem of a hyssop plant. 30After Jesus drank the
wine, he said, "Everything is done!"
He bowed his head and died.*

---

[i] *"The Skull"*: The place was probably given this name because it was near a large rock in the shape of a human skull. [j] *Jesus' mother stood beside his cross with her sister and Mary the wife of Clopas. Mary Magdalene was standing there too*: The Greek text may also be understood to include only three women ("Jesus' mother stood beside the cross with her sister, Mary the mother of Clopas. Mary Magdalene was standing there too.") or merely two women ("Jesus' mother was standing there with her sister Mary of Clopas, that is Mary Magdalene."). "Of Clopas" may mean "daughter of" or "mother of."

19.19 **PILATE WROTE THE TRUTH** "Jesus of Nazareth, King of the Jews," said the sign above the head of Jesus. The priests wanted Pilate to change the wording, but he wouldn't. Jesus died not only for his friends, but even for his enemies. Pilate, too, could be saved if he would later turn to God in faith and ask to be forgiven because of the sacrifice of the crucified King. But we don't know whether Pilate ever did that.

19.26 **JESUS REMEMBERED HIS MOTHER** Even in his suffering Jesus was thinking of others. Notice that he began at home with concern for his mother. God created families, and our first duty on earth is to the people in our families. Some of us don't have families, but we can ask God to give us love for those who gave us life and for those we might bring into the world.

19.30 **"EVERYTHING IS DONE"** This is what Jesus said as he died. What did he mean? Jesus came into the world to do just what he did on the cross—to die for the very sinners who nailed him there. Let's try to understand that *our* sins also nailed Jesus to the cross. He finished the work of saving us from our sins by laying down his life for us.

NOTES

A Spear Is Stuck in Jesus' Side

31The next day would be both a Sabbath and the Passover. It was a special day for the Jewish people,[k] and they did not want the bodies to stay on the crosses during that day. So they asked Pilate to break the men's legs[l] and take their bodies down. 32The soldiers first broke the legs of the other two men who were nailed there. 33But when they came to Jesus, they saw that he was already dead, and they did not break his legs.

34One of the soldiers stuck his spear into Jesus' side, and blood and water came out. 35We know this is true, because it was told by someone who saw it happen. Now you can have faith too. 36All this happened so that the Scriptures would come true, which say, "No bone of his body will be broken" 37and, "They will see the one in whose side they stuck a spear."

Jesus Is Buried
(Matthew 27.57–61; Mark 15.42–47; Luke 23.50–56)

38Joseph from Arimathea was one of Jesus' disciples. He had kept it secret though, because he was afraid of the Jewish leaders. But now he asked Pilate to let him have Jesus' body. Pilate gave him permission, and Joseph took it down from the cross.

39Nicodemus also came with about seventy-five pounds of spices made from myrrh and aloes. This was the same Nicodemus who had visited Jesus one night.[m]* 40The two men wrapped the body in a linen cloth, together with the spices, which was how the Jewish people buried their dead. 41In the place where Jesus had been nailed to a cross, there was a garden with a tomb that had never been used. 42The tomb was nearby, and since it was the time to prepare for the Sabbath, they were in a hurry to put Jesus' body there.

Jesus Is Alive
(Matthew 28.1–10; Mark 16.1–8; Luke 24.1–12)

20 On Sunday morning while it was still dark, Mary Magdalene went to the tomb and saw that the stone had been rolled away from the entrance. 2She ran to Simon Peter and to Jesus' favorite disciple and said, "They have taken the Lord from the tomb! We don't know where they have put him."

3Peter and the other disciple started for the tomb. 4They ran side by side, until the other disciple ran faster than Peter and got there first. 5He bent over and saw the strips of linen cloth lying inside the tomb, but he did not go in.

6When Simon Peter got there, he went into the tomb and saw the strips of cloth. 7He also saw the piece of cloth that had been used to cover Jesus' face. It was rolled up and in a place by itself. 8The disciple who got there first then went into the tomb, and when he saw it, he believed. 9At that time Peter and the other disciple did not know that the Scriptures said Jesus would rise to life.* 10So the two of them went back to the other disciples.

---

[k] *a special day for the Jewish people*: Passover could be any day of the week. But according to the Gospel of John, Passover was on a Sabbath in the year that Jesus was nailed to a cross. [l] *break the men's legs*: This was the way that the Romans sometimes speeded up the death of a person who had been nailed to a cross. [m] *Nicodemus who had visited Jesus one night*: See 3.1-21.

19.39 **REMEMBER NICODEMUS?** Nicodemus, the man who had come during the night to see Jesus, came back to help Joseph from Arimathea bury the Savior's body. Nicodemus had been looking for the truth when he made his visit in the dark to question Jesus. Here it looks like Nicodemus has become a believer. Like Nicodemus, we can come to Jesus and find the new birth he offers (see John 3.3).

20.9 **THE DISCIPLES WERE NOT QUICK TO BELIEVE** Sometimes we may think it's harder to put faith in Jesus now than when he walked the earth. Perhaps we think it was just natural *(continued)*

NOTES

Step 3

JOSEPH OF ARIMATHEA—a man who showed tremendous courage and risked it all for Christ

JOHN 19.38–42; MARK 15.42–47; LUKE 23.50–56

It had been a terrible week for Joseph of Arimathea. He was a part of the religious power structure in Jerusalem, but was secretly a disciple of Jesus. The Bible says that he was afraid to go public with his faith. Perhaps he thought he could serve God by being a member of the establishment. Maybe he thought he could make a difference by working quietly on the "inside." But events leading up to Christ's arrest and trial had moved quickly. Now he was confronted with a choice: step forward and declare his loyalty to Christ, or be one of the crowd and silently do nothing. He chose to get involved by offering up his family burial plot for his Savior. When it came time to bury Jesus, he and Nicodemus brought the spices for embalming the body. They wrapped Jesus' dead body in burial clothes. Then Joseph had the stone moved to seal the tomb.

Courage shows itself even in fainthearted people. When it came time for a true test of character, hardly any of the other disciples were around. Those who had followed Christ closely were overcome with fear. But Joseph was one of two courageous followers who laid Jesus to rest, risking their future and positions of influence to take care of their crucified Savior. Did they really think it was all over? Yes! If they hadn't, they would not have gone to so much trouble for the burial and certainly would not have put so much on the line by their actions. They were simply acting out of personal loyalty to the Teacher who had opened the Scriptures to them.

STEP LOOK BACK 3

What can we learn from Joseph? Do we need a big dose of courage in order to take a stand or take the next step in life? It might mean risking our reputations in order to demonstrate our courage in following Christ. God is there to help us and to give us the strength to do what is right.

Ready for Step 4? See page 20 of* InStep's *introduction.

Jesus Appears to Mary Magdalene
(Mark 16.9–11)

11Mary Magdalene stood crying
outside the tomb. She was still weeping, when she stooped down 12and
saw two angels inside. They were
dressed in white and were sitting
where Jesus' body had been. One was
at the head and the other was at the
foot. 13The angels asked Mary, "Why
are you crying?"
She answered, "They have taken
away my Lord's body! I don't know
where they have put him."
14As soon as Mary said this, she
turned around and saw Jesus standing there. But she did not know who
he was. 15Jesus asked her, "Why are
you crying? Who are you looking
for?"
She thought he was the gardener
and said, "Sir, if you have taken his
body away, please tell me, so I can
go and get him."
16Then Jesus said to her, "Mary!"
She turned and said to him, "Rabboni." The Aramaic word "Rabboni"
means "Teacher."
17Jesus told her, "Don't hold on to
me! I have not yet gone to the Father.
But tell my disciples that I am going
to the one who is my Father and my
God, as well as your Father and your
God."* 18Mary Magdalene then went
and told the disciples that she had
seen the Lord. She also told them
what he had said to her.

Jesus Appears to His Disciples
(Matthew 28.16–20; Mark 16.14–18; Luke 24.36–49)

19The disciples were afraid of the
Jewish leaders, and on the evening
of that same Sunday they locked
themselves in a room. Suddenly, Jesus appeared in the middle of the
group. He greeted them 20and
showed them his hands and his side.
When the disciples saw the Lord,
they became very happy.*
21After Jesus had greeted them
again, he said, "I am sending you,
just as the Father has sent me."
22Then he breathed on them and said,
"Receive the Holy Spirit. 23If you forgive anyone's sins, they will be forgiven. But if you don't forgive their
sins, they will not be forgiven."

Jesus and Thomas

24Although Thomas the Twin was
one of the twelve disciples, he was
not with the others when Jesus appeared to them. 25So they told him,
"We have seen the Lord!"
But Thomas said, "First, I must see
the nail scars in his hands and touch
them with my finger. I must put my
hand where the spear went into his

(*continued*) for people of Jesus' day to be what we call "religious." But look at Mary Magdalene and the other disciples. Jesus had told them he would rise again on the third day. But they still didn't understand why his tomb was empty.

20.17 **"DON'T HOLD ON TO ME"** We learn two things from this scene outside Jesus' tomb. First, it must have been dark in the early morning of that Sunday when Mary arrived. She couldn't recognize Jesus at first. Second, he was no ghost. He had a real body which Mary could hold on to. Paul taught that some day believers too will have bodies like Jesus' body—better than the bodies we have now, but bodies that are solid and can be touched and seen (see 1 Corinthians 15).

20.20 **HE SHOWED THEM HIS WOUNDS** It would be natural to suspect that the person who came to the disciples was not the same Jesus who was nailed to a cross. But he showed them his hands and his side where the wounds of his death were. There could be no mistake. Jesus was alive, and the disciples lived and died telling others this great news for all the world.

NOTES

Step 1

THOMAS—an honest man who admitted that he did not have all of the answers

JOHN 20.24–29

Being honest about ourselves is not an easy thing to do. Some people think that devotion means that you only say what you believe—that you keep your questions to yourself. Thomas earned his nickname, "Doubting Thomas," because of his honesty. Contrary to popular belief, he had a healthy approach to his faith. He expressed his doubts out loud—not out of disrespect, but out of a heartfelt desire to know the truth at all costs.

Thomas had been a follower of Jesus throughout his ministry. As a disciple, he heard Jesus speak, saw Jesus heal people, and witnessed firsthand many of the miracles we read about in the Bible. But when Thomas was told that Jesus was alive again after he had seen him die on the cross, he needed proof. He even declared the need to put his hands on the nail-scarred hands of Jesus and touch the place where the spear had pierced his side. When Jesus appeared before the disciples again, Jesus had him do just that. Thomas touched Jesus' hand and felt his side. This was what Thomas needed to settle his doubts, and this is what Jesus was willing to allow him to do.

STEP LOOK BACK 1

By being honest about his doubts, Thomas not only discovered for himself that the resurrection of Jesus was true, but also provided an important lesson. Honesty expressed in a manner that seeks out answers to doubt and confusion will lead to solutions.

As we focus on who we really are today and on who we want to become in the years ahead, let's learn from the life of Thomas. Questions are healthy. Doubts are natural. As we come to Jesus and get to know him personally, he accepts our questions and our fears. Doubts expressed through honest questions will find their answers in the person of Christ. If we are seeking the truth about what we really believe, we can start with asking about who God is and how he revealed himself in Jesus Christ.

Ready for Step 2? See page 15 of* InStep*'s introduction.

side. I won't believe unless I do this!"*
26 A week later the disciples were
together again. This time Thomas
was with them. Jesus came in while
the doors were still locked and stood
in the middle of the group. He greeted
his disciples 27 and said to Thomas,
"Put your finger here and look at my
hands! Put your hand into my side.
Stop doubting and have faith!"
28 Thomas replied, "You are my
Lord and my God!"
29 Jesus said, "Thomas, do you have
faith because you have seen me? The
people who have faith in me without
seeing me are the ones who are really
blessed!"

Why John Wrote His Book

30 Jesus worked many other miracles[n] for his disciples, and not all of
them are written in this book.
31 But these are written so that you
will put your faith in Jesus as the
Messiah and the Son of God. If you
have faith in[o] him, you will have true
life.*

Jesus Appears to Seven Disciples

21 Jesus later appeared to his disciples along the shore of Lake
Tiberias. 2 Simon Peter, Thomas the
Twin, Nathanael from Cana in Galilee, and the two sons of Zebedee,[p]
were there, together with two other
disciples. 3 Simon Peter said, "I'm going fishing!"
The others said, "We'll go with
you." They went out in their boat.
But they didn't catch a thing that
night.
4 Early the next morning Jesus
stood on the shore, but the disciples
did not realize who he was. 5 Jesus
shouted, "Friends, have you caught
anything?"
"No!" they answered.
6 So he told them, "Let your net
down on the right side of your boat,
and you will catch some fish."
They did, and the net was so full
of fish that they could not drag it up
into the boat.*
7 Jesus' favorite disciple told Peter,
"It's the Lord!" When Simon heard
that it was the Lord, he put on the
clothes that he had taken off while
he was working. Then he jumped into
the water. 8 The boat was only about
a hundred yards from shore. So the
other disciples stayed in the boat and
dragged in the net full of fish.
9 When the disciples got out of the
boat, they saw some bread and a
charcoal fire with fish on it. 10 Jesus
told his disciples, "Bring some of the
fish you just caught." 11 Simon Peter
got back into the boat and dragged
the net to shore. In it were one hundred fifty-three large fish, but still the
net did not rip.
12 Jesus said, "Come and eat!" But
none of the disciples dared ask who
he was. They knew he was the Lord.

---

[n] *miracles*: See the note at 2.11. [o] *put your faith in . . . have faith in*: Some manuscripts have "keep on having faith in . . . keep on having faith in." [p] *the two sons of Zebedee*: James and John.

20.25 **THE DISCIPLES WERE DOUBTERS** Are you a doubter? That's natural. So were all the disciples, but especially Thomas. Of course, he was not there when Jesus appeared the first time. But even Thomas lost his doubts when he saw the Lord alive.

20.31 **JOHN'S BOOK IS FOR YOU** "So that you will put your faith in Jesus." John didn't write his book to tell us everything Jesus did. But he wrote enough to show us that faith in Jesus makes a great deal of sense. As we read John's book we are convinced that it is true.

21.6 **THE DISCIPLES CAUGHT NO FISH** There was no catch of fish at first. Then Jesus came and told the disciples what to do, and their net was full of fish. But after all, Jesus didn't need the disciples to go fishing for fish. He already had fish on the fire for breakfast. He needed the disciples to go fishing for *people*.

NOTES

[13]Jesus took the bread in his hands and gave some of it to his disciples. He did the same with the fish. [14]This was the third time that Jesus appeared to his disciples after he was raised from death.

Jesus and Peter

[15]When Jesus and his disciples had finished eating, he asked, "Simon son of John, do you love me more than the others do?"[q]

Simon Peter answered, "Yes, Lord, you know I do!"

"Then feed my lambs," Jesus said.*

[16]Jesus asked a second time, "Simon son of John, do you love me?"

Peter answered, "Yes, Lord, you know I love you!"

"Then take care of my sheep," Jesus told him.

[17]Jesus asked a third time, "Simon son of John, do you love me?"

Peter was hurt because Jesus had asked him three times if he loved him. So he told Jesus, "Lord, you know everything. You know I love you."

Jesus replied, "Feed my sheep. [18]I tell you for certain that when you were a young man, you dressed yourself and went wherever you wanted to go. But when you are old, you will hold out your hands. Then others will wrap your belt around you and lead you where you don't want to go."

[19]Jesus said this to tell how Peter would die and bring honor to God. Then he said to Peter, "Follow me!"

Jesus and His Favorite Disciple

[20]Peter turned and saw Jesus' favorite disciple following them. He was the same one who had sat next to Jesus at the meal and had asked, "Lord, who is going to betray you?" [21]When Peter saw that disciple, he asked Jesus, "Lord, what about him?"*

[22]Jesus answered, "What is it to you, if I want him to live until I return? You must follow me." [23]So the rumor spread among the other disciples that this disciple would not die. But Jesus did not say he would not die. He simply said, "What is it to you, if I want him to live until I return?"

[24]This disciple is the one who told all of this. He wrote it, and we know he is telling the truth.

[25]Jesus did many other things. If they were all written in books, I don't suppose there would be room enough in the whole world for all the books.

---

[q]*more than the others do?*: Or "more than you love these things?"

21.15 **DO YOU LOVE JESUS?** Like Peter, we may be ashamed to say, "Yes, Lord, you know I do." Peter had denied the Lord three times. Three times Peter was asked to confess that he loved Jesus. Sometimes we feel that we fail our Lord—and we're right. But he keeps calling us back to the important question—"Do you honestly love me?" What is your answer?

21.21 **WHAT ABOUT JOHN?** There is envy even among those who put their faith in Jesus. Peter envied John. Peter always thought he should be first, but he probably felt guilty here because he had denied the Lord—and John had not. Jesus simply told Peter that John's work was John's business, not Peter's. Peter was to follow Jesus. And so must we all. (History says that John was the only disciple who died of old age, when he was about a hundred years old. All of the other apostles were put to death for their preaching.)

NOTES

Step 12

Because God is changing my life through following these steps, I will tell others about them and daily practice what I have learned.

JOHN 21.15–19

LOVE THAT SHOWS

"I love you more than anyone else in the world. You give me a reason for living. When I'm with you I don't have to pretend to be someone I'm not. You mean everything to me. But listen . . . while I think you're great, not everyone else does, so maybe we'd better not be seen together. And don't be disappointed if I never mention your name to anyone. It doesn't mean I think any less of you. I promise I'll make it up to you when we are in private. It's going to take a while for people to get used to our being together. We're kind of an unlikely pair. You do understand, don't you?"

STEP LOOK INSIDE 12

It doesn't make much sense does it? When we love someone, we aren't embarrassed to be seen with them or to talk about them. In fact, declaring our love in front of others makes it more official. That's what going steady or being engaged is all about.

TELLING OTHERS

Jesus was saying the same thing to Peter when he told him, "If you love me, you will feed my sheep." That means, "If you love me, you will want to tell others about our love so they may have this same love in their lives too." Let your love for Jesus be seen and heard.

For another "Look Inside," turn to page 417.

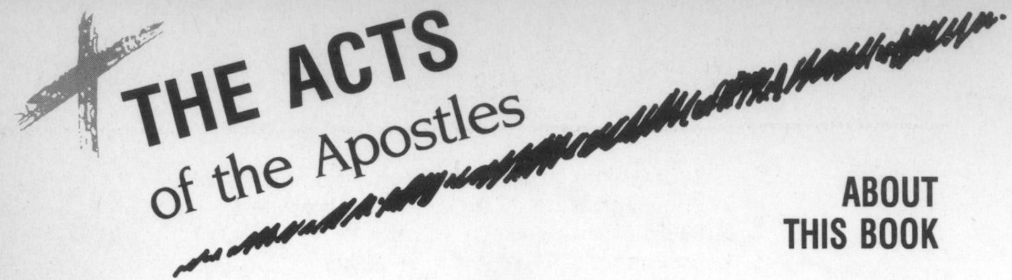

ABOUT THIS BOOK

This is the second book written by Luke. His first one is commonly known as the Gospel of Luke. In it he told "all that Jesus did and taught from the very first until he was taken up to heaven" (1.1,2). In this book Luke continues the story by describing some of the struggles the disciples faced as they tried to obey the command of Jesus: "You will tell everyone about me in Jerusalem, in all Judea, in Samaria, and everywhere in the world" (1.8).

So many different countries are mentioned in Acts that the book may seem to have been written only to tell about the spread of the Christian message. But that is only part of the story. After Jesus was taken up to heaven, one of the big problems for his followers was deciding who could belong to God's people. And since Jesus and his first followers were Jews, it was only natural for many of them to think that his message was only for Jews. But in Acts the Spirit is always present to show that Jesus came to save both Jews and Gentiles, and that God wants followers from every nation and race to be part of his people.

The first conflict between Christians and Jews took place when some of the Jewish religious leaders rejected the message about Jesus (4.1–31; 7.1–59). But the most serious problems for the early church happened because the disciples at first failed to understand that anyone could become a follower of Jesus without first becoming a Jew. This began to change when Philip dared to take the message to the Samaritans (8.7–25), and when Peter went to the home of Cornelius, a captain in the Roman army (10.1–48).

Finally, Peter reported to the church in Jerusalem (11.1–18) and a meeting was held there (15.3–35) to discuss the question of who could become followers of Christ. Before the meeting was over, everyone agreed that the Spirit of God was leading them to reach out to Gentiles as well as Jews with the good news of Jesus.

The one who did the most for the spread of the faith was a man named Paul, and much of the book tells about his preaching among the Gentiles. Finally, he took the message to Rome, the world's most important city at that time (28.16–31). One of Luke's main reasons for writing was to show that nothing could keep the Christian message from spreading everywhere:

> *For two years Paul stayed in a rented house and welcomed everyone who came to see him. He bravely preached about God's kingdom and taught about the Lord Jesus Christ, and no one tried to stop him.* (28.30,31)

A QUICK LOOK AT THIS BOOK

1 Theophilus, I first wrote to you[a]
about all that Jesus did and
taught from the very first* 2until he
was taken up to heaven. But before
he was taken up, he gave orders to
the apostles he had chosen with the
help of the Holy Spirit.
3For forty days after Jesus had suffered and died, he proved in many
ways that he had been raised from
death. He appeared to his apostles
and spoke to them about God's kingdom. 4While he was still with them,
he said:

Don't leave Jerusalem yet.
Wait here for the Father to give
you the Holy Spirit, just as I told
you he has promised to do.
5John baptized with water, but
in a few days you will be
baptized with the Holy Spirit.

Jesus Is Taken to Heaven

6While the apostles were still with
Jesus, they asked him, "Lord, are you
now going to give Israel its own king
again?"[b]
7Jesus said to them, "You don't
need to know the time of those events
that only the Father controls. 8But
the Holy Spirit will come upon you
and give you power. Then you will
tell everyone about me in Jerusalem,
in all Judea, in Samaria, and everywhere in the world." 9After Jesus had
said this and while they were watching, he was taken up into a cloud.
They could not see him,* 10but as he
went up, they kept looking up into
the sky.
Suddenly two men dressed in white
clothes were standing there beside
them. 11They said, "Why are you men
from Galilee standing here and looking up into the sky? Jesus has been
taken to heaven. But he will come

[a] *I first wrote to you*: The Gospel of Luke. [b] *are you now going to give Israel its own king again?*: Or "Are you now going to rule Israel as its king?"

1.1 **THEOPHILUS HONORED AGAIN** Acts continues the history Luke began in his Gospel. Like Luke's Gospel, the book of Acts is addressed to his friend, Theophilus. The name means "lover of God." He may have been an important Gentile citizen of that time. As an educated Gentile himself, Luke wanted to present to his people the message of Christ in a complete and accurate way.

1.9 **JESUS RETURNED TO HEAVEN** Again in Acts, Luke reviews this happening that he also covered at the end of his Gospel. Jesus' return to heaven was an important final event in his earthly life. The presence of Christ before God now stands as a guarantee that his saving work for us on earth cannot be canceled. Jesus is our representative in heaven.

NOTES

back in the same way that you have seen him go."*

Someone to Take the Place of Judas

12-13The Mount of Olives was about half a mile from Jerusalem. The apostles who had gone there were Peter, John, James, Andrew, Philip, Thomas, Bartholomew, Matthew, James the son of Alphaeus, Simon, known as the Eager One,[c] and Judas the son of James.

After the apostles returned to the city, they went upstairs to the room where they had been staying.

14The apostles often met together and prayed with a single purpose in mind.[d] The women and Mary the mother of Jesus would meet with them, and so would his brothers.*
15One day there were about a hundred and twenty of the Lord's followers meeting together, and Peter stood up to speak to them. 16-17He said:

My friends, long ago by the power of the Holy Spirit, David said something about Judas, and what he said has now happened. Judas was one of us and had worked with us, but he brought the mob to arrest Jesus. 18Then Judas bought some land with the money he was given for doing that evil thing. He fell headfirst into the field. His body burst open, and all his insides came out. 19When the people of Jerusalem found out about this, they called the place Akeldama, which in the local language means "Field of Blood."

20In the book of Psalms David said,

"Leave his house empty,
and don't let anyone
live there."

It also says,

"Let someone else
have his job."

21-22So we need someone else to help us tell others that Jesus has been raised from death. He must also be one of the men who was with us from the very beginning. He must have been with us from the time the Lord Jesus was baptized by John until the day he was taken to heaven.*

23Two men were suggested: One of them was Joseph Barsabbas, known as Justus, and the other was Matthias. 24Then they all prayed, "Lord, you know what everyone is like! Show us the one you have chosen 25to be an apostle and to serve

---

[c]*known as the Eager One*: The Greek text has "Canaanean," which probably comes from a Hebrew word meaning "zealous" (see Luke 6.15). "Zealot" was the name later given to the members of a Jewish group which resisted and fought against the Romans.
[d]*met together and prayed with a single purpose in mind*: Or "met together in a special place for prayer."

1.11 **JESUS WILL COME BACK TO EARTH** Jesus didn't die and rise from death only so we could go to heaven. He will return again and set up his rule on earth. A new day is coming, long foretold by the ancient prophets. Then this present world system will pass away, and Christ himself will govern a new world of righteousness.

1.14 **THE LORD'S FOLLOWERS MET FOR PRAYER** Right away after Jesus was taken to heaven, his followers began meeting together for prayer. It is important for the Lord's followers to pray together. That's how we get wisdom and guidance from God. Remember what Jesus said (Matthew 18.20): "Whenever two or three of you come together in my name, I am there with you."

1.21 **SEEKING THE RIGHT REPLACEMENT** Jesus' followers needed to replace Judas Iscariot with someone who could tell about Jesus as a witness who had been with him. Today we have the New Testament as an accurate witness to Jesus. At that time it was very important for someone who was preaching to be able to say, "I was there and I saw it with my own eyes."

NOTES

in place of Judas, who got what he
deserved." 26 They drew names, and
Matthias was chosen to join the
group of the eleven apostles.

The Coming of the Holy Spirit

2 On the day of Pentecost[e] all the
Lord's followers were together in
one place. 2 Suddenly there was a
noise from heaven like the sound of
a mighty wind! It filled the house
where they were meeting. 3 Then they
saw what looked like fiery tongues
moving in all directions, and a tongue
came and settled on each person
there. 4 The Holy Spirit took control
of everyone, and they began speaking whatever languages the Spirit let
them speak.

5 Many religious Jews from every
country in the world were living in
Jerusalem. 6 And when they heard
this noise, a crowd gathered. But they
were surprised, because they were
hearing everything in their own languages. 7 They were excited and
amazed, and said:

Don't all these who are
speaking come from Galilee?
8 Then why do we hear them
speaking our very own
languages? 9 Some of us are from
Parthia, Media, and Elam.
Others are from Mesopotamia,
Judea, Cappadocia, Pontus,
Asia, 10 Phrygia, Pamphylia,
Egypt, parts of Libya near
Cyrene, Rome, 11-12 Crete, and
Arabia. Some of us were born
Jews, and others of us have
chosen to be Jews. Yet we all
hear them using our own
languages to tell the wonderful
things God has done.

Everyone was excited and confused. Some of them even kept asking each other, "What does all this
mean?"*

13 Others made fun of the Lord's followers and said, "They are drunk."

Peter Speaks to the Crowd

14 Peter stood with the eleven apostles and spoke in a loud and clear
voice to the crowd:

Friends and everyone else
living in Jerusalem, listen
carefully to what I have to say!
15 You are wrong to think that
these people are drunk. After all,
it is only nine o'clock in the
morning. 16 But this is what God
had the prophet Joel say,

17 "When the last days come,
I will give my Spirit
to everyone.
Your sons and daughters
will prophesy.
Your young men
will see visions,
and your old men
will have dreams.*
18 In those days I will give
my Spirit to my servants,
both men and women,
and they will prophesy.

19 I will work miracles
in the sky above

---

[e] *Pentecost*: A Jewish festival that came fifty days after Passover and celebrated the wheat harvest. Jews later celebrated Pentecost as the time when they were given the Law of Moses.

2.12 **"WHAT DOES ALL THIS MEAN?"** This was the question people asked when the Holy Spirit of God came. Jesus had returned to heaven. But he had promised that he and his Father would send the Holy Spirit to be the constant Helper and Companion of believers on earth. The Holy Spirit makes Jesus real to us and gives us power to live for God.

2.17 **PETER TOLD THE HISTORY OF GOD'S PROMISE** The coming of the Holy Spirit, who is God himself, was a planned event that had been talked about for centuries. The prophets had predicted years before about this great happening, which was like the great birthday of Christianity. On this day, it was clear that God's word would be spread in a powerful way, because the Holy Spirit would give power to the preaching of that word.

NOTES

and wonders
on the earth below.
There will be blood and fire
and clouds of smoke.
20The sun will turn dark,
and the moon
will be as red as blood
before the great
and wonderful day
of the Lord appears.

21Then the Lord
will save everyone
who asks for his help."
22Now, listen to what I have
to say about Jesus from
Nazareth. God proved that he
sent Jesus to you by having him
work miracles, wonders, and
signs. All of you know this.
23God had already planned and
decided that Jesus would be
handed over to you. So you took
him and had evil men put him
to death on a cross. 24But God
set him free from death and
raised him to life. Death could
not hold him in its power. 25What
David said are really the words
of Jesus,
"I always see the Lord
near me,
and I will not be afraid
with him at my right side.*
26Because of this,
my heart will be glad,
my words will be joyful,
and I will live in hope.
27The Lord won't leave me
in the grave.
I am his holy one,
and he won't let
my body decay.
28He has shown me
the path to life,
and he makes me glad
by being near me."
29My friends, it is right for me
to speak to you about our
ancestor David. He died and was
buried, and his tomb is still here.
30But David was a prophet, and
he knew that God had made a
promise he would not break. He
had told David that someone
from his own family would
someday be king.
31David knew this would
happen, and so he told us that
Christ would be raised to life. He
said that God would not leave
him in the grave or let his body
decay. 32All of us can tell you
that God has raised Jesus to life!
33Jesus was taken up to sit at
the right side[f] of God, and he was
given the Holy Spirit, just as the
Father had promised. Jesus is
also the one who has given the
Spirit to us, and that is what you
are now seeing and hearing.
34David didn't go up to heaven.
So he wasn't talking about
himself when he said, "The Lord
told my Lord to sit at his right
side, 35until he made my Lord's
enemies into a footstool for
him." 36Everyone in Israel
should then know for certain
that God has made Jesus both
Lord and Christ, even though
you put him to death on a cross.
37When the people heard this, they
were very upset. They asked Peter
and the other apostles, "Friends,
what shall we do?"
38Peter said, "Turn back to God!
Be baptized in the name of Jesus
Christ, so that your sins will be forgiven. Then you will be given the
Holy Spirit.* 39This promise is for you

[f]*right side*: The place of honor and power.

2.25 **KING DAVID HAD TOLD ABOUT CHRIST** David was a great king of the Jews who lived a thousand years before Jesus was born. In fact, David was a great ancestor of Jesus. It's exciting to see how David knew that his great descendant, Jesus, would rise from death a thousand years later. David knew this because God showed it to him.

2.38 **WHY DID PETER PREACH?** Was Peter just trying to amaze the crowd? No, Peter told the people that Christ had died and risen to save them from their sins. So he taught *(continued)*

NOTES

and your children. It is for everyone
our Lord God will choose, no matter
where they live."
40Peter told them many other
things as well. Then he said, "I beg
you to save yourselves from what will
happen to all these evil people."
41On that day about three thousand
believed his message and were baptized. 42They spent their time learning from the apostles, and they were
like family to each other. They also
broke bread[g] and prayed together.

Life among the Lord's Followers

43Everyone was amazed by the
many miracles and wonders that the
apostles worked. 44All the Lord's followers often met together, and they
shared everything they had.* 45They
would sell their property and possessions and give the money to whoever
needed it. 46Day after day they met
together in the temple. They broke
bread[g] together in different homes
and shared their food happily and
freely, 47while praising God. Everyone liked them, and each day the
Lord added to their group others who
were being saved.

Peter and John Heal a Lame Man

3 The time of prayer[h] was about
three o'clock in the afternoon,
and Peter and John were going into
the temple. 2A man who had been
born lame was being carried to the
temple door. Each day he was placed
beside this door, known as the Beautiful Gate. He sat there and begged
from the people who were going in.
3The man saw Peter and John en-
tering the temple, and he asked them
for money. 4But they looked straight
at him and said, "Look up at us!"
5The man stared at them and
thought he was going to get something. 6But Peter said, "I don't have
any silver or gold! But I will give you
what I do have. In the name of Jesus
Christ from Nazareth, get up and
start walking." 7Peter then took him
by the right hand and helped him up.
At once the man's feet and ankles
became strong,* 8and he jumped up
and started walking. He went with
Peter and John into the temple, walking and jumping and praising God.
9Everyone saw him walking around
and praising God. 10They knew that
he was the beggar who had been lying beside the Beautiful Gate, and
they were completely surprised.
They could not imagine what had
happened to the man.

Peter Speaks in the Temple

11While the man kept holding on
to Peter and John, the whole crowd
ran to them in amazement at the
place known as Solomon's Porch.[i]

---

[g]*broke bread*: They ate together and celebrated the Lord's Supper. [h]*The time of prayer*: Many of the Jewish people prayed in their homes at regular times each day (see Daniel 6.11), and on special occasions they prayed in the temple. [i]*Solomon's Porch*: A public place with tall columns along the east side of the temple.

(*continued*) them to turn back to God, and their sins would be forgiven. Then they too would receive the Holy Spirit. This is the reason for all Christian preaching and witnessing: to get listeners to answer with faith toward God.

2.44 **HOW SHOULD CHRISTIANS BEHAVE?** Notice how the Holy Spirit changed the lives of those who believed Peter's preaching. Luke tells us they were eager to learn about God, and they treated each other like family members. They shared their money and food, and they were a happy people. This is the kind of behavior that spreads the good news about Jesus by *showing* as well as by talking.

3.7 **JESUS' WORKS CONTINUE** Jesus didn't stop working because he had gone up to heaven. By the Holy Spirit he continued his work on earth through the apostles, like Peter. So we shouldn't be surprised at Peter's command to the lame man. Peter believed that Jesus still lived, and that Jesus would heal the man.

NOTES

12Peter saw that a crowd had gathered, and he said:

Friends, why are you
surprised at what has happened?
Why are you staring at us? Do
you think we have some power
of our own? Do you think we
were able to make this man walk
because we are so religious?*
13The God that Abraham, Isaac,
Jacob, and our other ancestors
worshiped has brought honor to
his Servant[j] Jesus. He is the one
you betrayed. You turned
against him when he was being
tried by Pilate, even though
Pilate wanted to set him free.

14You rejected Jesus, who was
holy and good. You asked for a
murderer to be set free, 15and
you killed the one who leads
people to life. But God raised him
from death, and all of us can tell
you what he has done. 16You see
this man, and you know him. He
put his faith in the name of Jesus
and was made strong. Faith in
Jesus made this man completely
well while everyone was
watching.

17My friends, I am sure that
you and your leaders didn't
know what you were doing.
18But God had his prophets tell
that his Messiah would suffer,
and now he has kept that
promise. 19So turn to God! Give
up your sins, and you will be
forgiven. 20Then that time will
come when the Lord will give
you fresh strength. He will send
you Jesus, his chosen Messiah.
21But Jesus must stay in heaven
until God makes all things new,
just as his holy prophets
promised long ago.*

22Moses said, "The Lord your
God will choose one of your own
people to be a prophet, just as
he chose me. Listen to
everything he tells you. 23No one
who disobeys that prophet will
be one of God's people any
longer."

24Samuel and all the other
prophets who came later also
spoke about what is now
happening. 25You are really the
ones God told his prophets to
speak to. And you were given
the promise that God made to
your ancestors. He said to
Abraham, "All nations on earth
will be blessed because of
someone from your family."
26God sent his chosen Son[k] to
you first, because God wanted
to bless you and make each one
of you turn away from your sins.

Peter and John Are Brought in Front of the Council

4 The apostles were still talking to
the people, when some priests,
the captain of the temple guard, and
some Sadducees arrived. 2These men
were angry because the apostles
were teaching the people that the
dead would be raised from death, just
as Jesus had been raised from death.

[j]*Servant*: Or "Son." [k]*Son*: Or "Servant."

3.12 **WHAT IS THE GOOD NEWS?** Peter gave us an example of preaching the good news about Jesus as he spoke in the temple. He explained to his hearers that Jesus was not just a good man who simply came and helped them with their problems, and then died like other men. Jesus was the one foretold by the prophets and great leaders that people knew from reading the Old Testament: he was the Messiah, who would save his people from their sins.

3.21 **IT'S NOT OVER YET** We must see that the coming of Jesus was in the great plan of God from eternal ages past. The coming of Jesus will also make a great difference for the eternal future. Jesus is the King of heaven who will bring his everlasting kingdom to a new world. He is raising up a new people, his church, by their faith in him. They will serve someday in his kingdom.

NOTES

3By now it was already late in the
afternoon, and they arrested Peter
and John and put them in jail for the
night.* 4But a lot of people who had
heard the message believed it. So by
now there were about five thousand
followers of the Lord.
5The next morning the leaders, the
elders, and the teachers of the Law
of Moses met in Jerusalem. 6The high
priest Annas was there, as well as
Caiaphas, John, Alexander, and
other members of the high priest's
family. 7They brought in Peter and
John and made them stand in the
middle while they questioned them.
They asked, "By what power and in
whose name have you done this?"
8Peter was filled with the Holy
Spirit and told the nation's leaders
and the elders:*

9You are questioning us today
about a kind deed in which a
crippled man was healed. 10But
there is something we must tell
you and everyone else in Israel.
This man is standing here
completely well because of the
power of Jesus Christ from
Nazareth. You put Jesus to death
on a cross, but God raised him
to life. 11He is the stone that you
builders thought was worthless,
and now he is the most important
stone of all. 12Only Jesus has the
power to save! His name is the
only one in all the world that can
save anyone.

13The officials were amazed to see
how brave Peter and John were, and
they knew that these two apostles
were only ordinary men and not well
educated. The officials were certain
that these men had been with Jesus.
14But they could not deny what had
happened. The man who had been
healed was standing there with the
apostles.
15The officials commanded them to
leave the council room. Then the officials said to each other, 16"What can
we do with these men? Everyone in
Jerusalem knows about this miracle,
and we cannot say it didn't happen.
17But to keep this thing from spreading, we will warn them never again
to speak to anyone about the name
of Jesus." 18So they called the two
apostles back in and told them that
they must never, for any reason,
teach anything about the name of
Jesus.*
19Peter and John answered, "Do
you think God wants us to obey you
or to obey him? 20We cannot keep
quiet about what we have seen and
heard."
21-22The officials could not find any

4.3 **CHRISTIANS ARE OFTEN MISTREATED** It doesn't take a negative attitude to realize that Christians often suffer unjustly. Even some news items by non-Christian reporters have noted this fact. The wonder is that the mistreatment happens even though there is no true reason for being unkind to Christians. But sometimes people just feel threatened because Christians are different. Such people sometimes strike out against what they don't understand.

4.8 **HOW DO CHRISTIANS ANSWER THEIR ACCUSERS?** The Holy Spirit helped Peter with his answer, and the same Holy Spirit helps us. Peter reminded his accusers that they were angry because he did a kind deed. That should have caused them shame. But then Peter told them straight out that they had crucified the Son of God, who is now alive and saves people from their sins. Again, Peter showed his hearers that they would have to decide about Jesus.

4.18 **THE TRUTH STOPS EVIL** Those who arrested Peter and John were confused and didn't know what to do. Peter had stopped them in their tracks when he reminded them that he had only done a kind deed. So the officials just ordered the apostles to be quiet and let them go. (Of course, there would be no way to keep them quiet.) In the end, we'll never be sorry for being bold about Jesus.

NOTES

reason to punish Peter and John. So they threatened them and let them go. The man who was healed by this miracle was more than forty years old, and everyone was praising God for what had happened.

Peter and Others Pray for Courage

23As soon as Peter and John had been set free, they went back and told the others everything that the chief priests and the leaders had said to them. 24When the rest of the Lord's followers heard this, they prayed together and said:

Master, you created heaven and earth, the sea, and everything in them.* 25And by the Holy Spirit you spoke to our ancestor David. He was your servant, and you told him to say:

"Why are all the Gentiles
so furious?
Why do people
make foolish plans?
26The kings of earth
prepare for war,
and the rulers
join together
against the Lord
and his Messiah."

27Here in Jerusalem, Herod[l] and Pontius Pilate got together with the Gentiles and the people of Israel. Then they turned against your holy Servant[m] Jesus, your chosen Messiah. 28They did what you in your power and wisdom had already decided would happen.

29Lord, listen to their threats! We are your servants. So make us brave enough to speak your message. 30Show your mighty power, as we heal people and work miracles and wonders in the name of your holy Servant[m] Jesus.

31After they had prayed, the meeting place shook. They were all filled with the Holy Spirit and bravely spoke God's message.

Sharing Possessions

32The group of followers all felt the same way about everything. None of them claimed that their belongings were their own, and they shared everything they had with each other.*
33In a powerful way the apostles told everyone that the Lord Jesus was now alive. God greatly blessed his followers,[n] 34and no one went in need of anything. Everyone who owned land or houses would sell them and bring the money 35to the apostles. Then they would give the money to anyone who needed it.
36-37Joseph was one of the followers who had sold a piece of property and brought the money to the apostles. He was a Levite from Cyprus, and the apostles called him Barnabas, which means, "one who encourages others."

Peter Condemns Ananias and Sapphira

5 Ananias and his wife Sapphira also sold a piece of property.
2But they agreed to cheat and keep

---

[l]*Herod*: Herod Antipas, the son of Herod the Great. [m]*Servant*: See the note at 3.13. [n]*God greatly blessed his followers*: Or "Everyone highly respected his followers."

4.24 **PRAYER IS THE KEY** When Peter and John were freed they didn't start preaching again right away. They and the other Christians met to pray. Prayer brings power for serving God. God answered the believers' prayers by giving them power to witness for Jesus. He will also give us power (for his glory) when we seek him first.

4.32 **CHRISTIANS ARE WILLING SHARERS** Was this combining of property some sort of communism? Not really. The Christians were not forced to give up their property. They were sharing it with each other willingly. They were putting their property together because of their faith in Christ, and they could decide for themselves whether to do so.

NOTES

some of the money for themselves.
So when Ananias took the rest of
the money to the apostles, 3Peter
said, "Why has Satan made you keep
back some of the money from the
sale of the property? Why have you
lied to the Holy Spirit? 4The property
was yours before you sold it, and
even after you sold it, the money was
still yours. What made you do such
a thing? You didn't lie to people. You
lied to God!"*
5As soon as Ananias heard this, he
dropped dead, and everyone who
heard about it was frightened.
6Some young men came in and
wrapped up his body. Then they took
it out and buried it.
7Three hours later Sapphira came
in, but she did not know what had
happened to her husband. 8Peter
asked her, "Tell me, did you sell the
property for this amount?"
"Yes," she answered, "that's the
amount."
9Then Peter said, "Why did the two
of you agree to test the Lord's Spirit?
The men who buried Ananias are by
the door, and they will carry you
out!" 10At once she fell at Peter's feet
and died.
When the young men came back
in, they found Sapphira lying there
dead. So they carried her out and buried her beside her husband. 11All the
church members were afraid, and so
was everyone else who heard what
had happened.

Peter's Unusual Power

12The apostles worked many miracles and wonders among the people.
All of the Lord's followers often met
in the part of the temple known as
Solomon's Porch.[o] 13No one outside
their group dared join them, even
though everyone liked them very
much.
14Many men and women started
having faith in the Lord. 15Then sick
people were brought out to the road
and placed on cots and mats. It was
hoped that Peter would walk by, and
his shadow would fall on them and
heal them.* 16A lot of people living
in the towns near Jerusalem brought
those who were sick or troubled by
evil spirits, and they were all healed.

The Jewish Leaders Make Trouble for the Apostles

17The high priest and all the other
Sadducees who were with him became jealous. 18They arrested the
apostles and put them in the city jail.
19But that night an angel from the
Lord opened the doors of the jail and
led the apostles out. The angel said,
20"Go to the temple and tell the people everything about this new life."
21So they went into the temple before
sunrise and started teaching.
The high priest and his men called
together their council, which included all of Israel's leaders. Then
they ordered the apostles to be
brought to them from the jail.
22The servants who were sent to the
jail did not find the apostles. They
returned and said, 23"We found the
jail locked tight and the guards standing at the doors. But when we opened

[o]*Solomon's Porch*: See the note at 3.11.

5.4 **TELL GOD THE TRUTH** Wealthy people among the Christians sold land and gave the money to the apostles so they could help the poor. But two people described in this chapter, Ananias and Sapphira, were only putting on a show of being kind. Their fate is a warning to us about trying to deceive God. Sooner or later, lying results in punishment.

5.15 **TRUE DIVINE HEALING HONORS GOD** Sadly, some people have falsely pretended to be great miracle healers. God wants to heal us when he can be honored by the work, but not to bring wealth or honor to a human celebrity. Peter was able to heal because of the power of the Holy Spirit in him. But those who thought it was Peter's shadow that had the power to heal them had the wrong idea.

NOTES

the doors and went in, we didn't find
anyone there." 24The captain of the
temple guard and the chief priests
listened to their report, but they did
not know what to think about it.
25Just then someone came in and
said, "Right now those men you put
in jail are in the temple, teaching the
people!" 26The captain of the temple
police went with some of his servants
and brought the apostles back. But
they did not use force. They were
afraid that the people might start
throwing stones at them.
27When the apostles were brought
before the council, the high priest
said to them,* 28"We told you plainly
not to teach in the name of Jesus.
But look what you have done! You
have been teaching all over Jerusalem, and you are trying to blame us
for his death."
29Peter and the apostles replied:

We don't obey people. We
obey God. 30You killed Jesus by
nailing him to a cross. But the
God our ancestors worshiped
raised him to life 31and made him
our Leader and Savior. Then
God gave him a place at his right
side,[p] so that the people of Israel
would turn back to him and be
forgiven. 32We are here to tell
you about all this, and so is the
Holy Spirit, who is God's gift to
everyone who obeys God.

33When the council members
heard this, they became so angry that
they wanted to kill the apostles.
34But one of them was the Pharisee
Gamaliel, a highly respected teacher.
He ordered the apostles to be taken
out of the room for a little while.
35Then he said to the council:

Men of Israel, be careful what
you do with these two men.
36Not long ago Theudas claimed
to be someone important, and
about four hundred men joined
him. But he was killed. All his
followers were scattered, and
that was the end of that.
37Later, when the people of
our nation were being counted,
Judas from Galilee showed up.
A lot of people followed him, but
he was killed, and all his
followers were scattered.
38So I advise you to stay away
from these men. Leave them
alone. If what they are planning
is something of their own doing,
it will fail.* 39But if God is behind
it, you cannot stop it anyway,
unless you want to fight against
God.

The council members agreed with
what he said, 40and they called the
apostles back in. They had them
beaten with a whip and warned them
not to speak in the name of Jesus.
Then they let them go.
41The apostles left the council and
were happy, because God had considered them worthy to suffer for the
sake of Jesus. 42Every day they spent
time in the temple and in one home
after another. They never stopped
teaching and telling the good news
that Jesus is the Messiah.

Seven Leaders for the Church

6 A lot of people were now becoming followers of the Lord. But

[p]*right side*: See the note at 2.33.

5.27 **WHAT WAS WRONG WITH THE LEADERS?** The apostles were released from prison by a miracle, and they were teaching in the temple. But the temple leaders were jealous. Why? They too might have enjoyed the good things the apostles were preaching about. But the leaders refused, because they loved their important place in society more than they loved God. These were unhappy people.

5.38 **YOU CAN'T HAVE IT BOTH WAYS** Poor Gamaliel—he was afraid to see the apostles killed, but he also wanted to please the temple leaders. We don't read that Gamaliel objected to the whipping of the apostles. He hoped to keep peace with God and with an evil society as well. That's a sad spot to be in, but it's the spot Gamaliel chose for himself.

NOTES

some of the ones who spoke Greek started complaining about the ones who spoke Aramaic. They complained that the Greek-speaking widows were not given their share when the food supplies were handed out each day.*

2The twelve apostles called the whole group of followers together and said, "We should not give up preaching God's message in order to serve at tables.[q] 3My friends, choose seven men who are respected and wise and filled with God's Spirit. We will put them in charge of these things. 4We can spend our time praying and serving God by preaching."*

5This suggestion pleased everyone, and they began by choosing Stephen. He had great faith and was filled with the Holy Spirit. Then they chose Philip, Prochorus, Nicanor, Timon, Parmenas, and also Nicolaus, who worshiped with the Jewish people[r] in Antioch. 6These men were brought to the apostles. Then the apostles prayed and placed their hands on the men to show that they had been chosen to do this work. 7God's message spread, and many more people in Jerusalem became followers. Even a large number of priests put their faith in the Lord.

Stephen Is Arrested

8God gave Stephen the power to work great miracles and wonders among the people.* 9But some Jews from Cyrene and Alexandria were members of a group who called themselves "Free Men."[s] They started arguing with Stephen. Some others from Cilicia and Asia also argued with him. 10But they were no match for Stephen, who spoke with the great wisdom that the Spirit gave him. 11So they talked some men into saying, "We heard Stephen say terrible things against Moses and God!"

12They turned the people and their leaders and the teachers of the Law of Moses against Stephen. Then they all grabbed Stephen and dragged him in front of the council.

13Some men agreed to tell lies about Stephen, and they said, "This man keeps on saying terrible things about this holy temple and the Law of Moses. 14We have heard him claim that Jesus from Nazareth will destroy this place and change the customs that Moses gave us." 15Then all the council members stared at Stephen. They saw that his face looked like the face of an angel.

---

[q] *to serve at tables*: This may mean either that they were in charge of handing out food to the widows or that they were in charge of the money, since the Greek word "table" may also mean "bank." [r] *worshiped with the Jewish people*: This translates the Greek word "proselyte" that means a Gentile who had accepted the Jewish religion. [s] *"Free Men"*: A group of Jewish men who had once been slaves, but had been freed.

6.1 **WE ARE ONE FAMILY OF GOD** Some Jews had been living for a long time among Gentiles. So these Jews took on Greek language and ways. Other Jews had been living in Palestine. So their language and ways were different from the Greek-speaking Jews. That caused a division among the Christians. In that division we see the beginning of cracks in the happy Christian unity we saw in Acts 2.

6.4 **GOD NEEDS DIFFERENT KINDS OF WORKERS** The apostles were burdened with preaching the good news. But somebody had to care for the needy. So they appointed special helpers for that work. Some think this was the beginning of the work of *deacons*. The word "deacon" comes from a Greek word meaning servant. Many churches still have deacons today.

6.8 **WHAT WAS STEPHEN'S WORK?** Stephen was one of the chosen servants, but his work wasn't only collecting and caring for the poor. Stephen was able to work miracles. He also was a power-filled debater. Not only that, but he preached a mighty sermon, as we shall see. The Christ who has gone to heaven gives power to his servants.

NOTES

Stephen's Speech

7 The high priest asked Stephen,
"Are they telling the truth about
you?"
2Stephen answered:
Friends, listen to me. Our
glorious God appeared to our
ancestor Abraham while he was
still in Mesopotamia, before he
had moved to Haran.* 3God told
him, "Leave your country and
your relatives and go to a land
that I will show you." 4Then
Abraham left the land of the
Chaldeans and settled in Haran.
After his father died, Abraham
came and settled in this land
where you now live. 5God didn't
give him any part of it, not even
a square foot. But God did
promise to give it to him and his
family forever, even though
Abraham didn't have any
children. 6God said that
Abraham's descendants would
live for a while in a foreign land.
There they would be slaves and
would be mistreated four
hundred years. 7But he also said,
"I will punish the nation that
makes them slaves. Then later
they will come and worship me
in this place."
8God said to Abraham, "Every
son in each family must be
circumcised to show that you
have kept your agreement with
me." So when Isaac was eight
days old, Abraham circumcised
him. Later, Isaac circumcised his
son Jacob, and Jacob
circumcised his twelve sons.
9 These men were our ancestors.
Joseph was also one of our
famous ancestors. His brothers
were jealous of him and sold him
as a slave to be taken to Egypt.
But God was with him* 10and
rescued him from all his
troubles. God made him so wise
that the Egyptian king Pharaoh
thought highly of him. Pharaoh
even made Joseph governor over
Egypt and put him in charge of
everything he owned.
11Everywhere in Egypt and
Canaan the grain crops failed.
There was terrible suffering, and
our ancestors could not find
enough to eat. 12But when Jacob
heard that there was grain in
Egypt, he sent our ancestors
there for the first time. 13It was
on their second trip that Joseph
told his brothers who he was,
and Pharaoh learned about
Joseph's family.
14Joseph sent for his father
and his relatives. In all, there
were seventy-five of them. 15His
father went to Egypt and died
there, just as our ancestors did.
16Later their bodies were taken
back to Shechem and placed in
the tomb that Abraham had
bought from the sons of Hamor.
17Finally, the time came for
God to do what he had promised
Abraham. By then the number
of our people in Egypt had
greatly increased. 18Another
king was ruling Egypt, and he
didn't know anything about
Joseph. 19He tricked our
ancestors and was cruel to them.

7.2 **STEPHEN TOLD ABOUT ABRAHAM** Abraham was the great ancestor of the Jews who lived two thousand years before Christ. Stephen reminded his listeners of God's promise that Abraham would be the father of a great people. Because Abraham believed God, he was called the father of the faithful. His name means "father of many people."

7.9 **STEPHEN TOLD ABOUT JOSEPH** Joseph was another great man in Jewish history. He was a great-grandson of Abraham, and he became a great leader in Egypt. Because of his position of power and influence, Joseph was used by God to save his people the Israelites from starvation. We see from this that God can see our needs years in advance, and is able to provide answers.

NOTES

He even made them leave their
babies outside, so they would die.

20During this time Moses was
born. He was a very beautiful
child, and for three months his
parents took care of him in their
home.* 21Then when they were
forced to leave him outside, the
king's daughter found him and
raised him as her own son.
22Moses was given the best
education in Egypt. He was a
strong man and a powerful
speaker.
23When Moses was forty years
old, he wanted to help the
Israelites because they were his
own people. 24One day he saw
an Egyptian mistreating one of
them. So he rescued the man and
killed the Egyptian. 25Moses
thought the rest of his people
would realize that God was
going to use him to set them free.
But they didn't understand.
26The next day Moses saw two
of his own people fighting, and
he tried to make them stop. He
said, "Men, you are both
Israelites. Why are you so cruel
to each other?"
27But the man who had started
the fight pushed Moses aside and
asked, "Who made you our ruler
and judge? 28Are you going to
kill me, just as you killed that
Egyptian yesterday?" 29When
Moses heard this, he ran away
to live in the country of Midian.
His two sons were born there.
30Forty years later, an angel
appeared to Moses from a
burning bush in the desert near
Mount Sinai. 31Moses was
surprised by what he saw. He
went closer to get a better look,
and the Lord said, 32"I am the
God who was worshiped by your
ancestors, Abraham, Isaac, and
Jacob." Moses started shaking
all over and didn't dare to look
at the bush.
33The Lord said to him, "Take
off your sandals. The place
where you are standing is holy.
34With my own eyes I have seen
the suffering of my people in
Egypt. I have heard their groans
and have come down to rescue
them. Now I am sending you
back to Egypt."
35This was the same Moses
that the people rejected by
saying, "Who made you our
leader and judge?" God's angel
had spoken to Moses from the
bush. And God had even sent the
angel to help Moses rescue the
people and be their leader.
36In Egypt and at the Red Sea
and in the desert, Moses rescued
the people by working miracles
and wonders for forty years.
37Moses is the one who told the
people of Israel, "God will
choose one of your people to be
a prophet, just as he chose me."
38Moses brought our people
together in the desert, and the
angel spoke to him on Mount
Sinai. There he was given these
life-giving words to pass on to
us. 39But our ancestors refused
to obey Moses. They rejected
him and wanted to go back to
Egypt.*

7.20 **STEPHEN TOLD ABOUT MOSES** Moses was the Jews' great lawgiver who lived about fifteen hundred years before Christ. Moses was God's man to lead the Jews out of Egypt after four hundred years of slavery. Then Moses was given the Ten Commandments and all the other laws that the Jews lived by. Moses was like Jesus, who leads us out of the slavery of sin.

7.39 **PEOPLE WOULDN'T LET GOD BLESS THEM** God himself had given Moses his Law on Mount Sinai, but the people kept rebelling. All through Israel's history, the people kept turning from God in spite of the many ways he had shown his love to them. Right up to the day Stephen spoke, most of the Jewish people and their leaders were refusing to see what God had done for them. That's "human nature," not wanting to trust God and live for him.

NOTES

Step 2

MOSES—a man who listened to, was led by, and had lasting loyalty to God

ACTS 7.20–39

Moses is one of the greatest men who ever lived. In the story of his life, we see a man who believed God and was willing to follow him at all costs. He gave up the comforts of his life in the courts of Egypt, and God used him to lead an entire nation out of slavery and into a life of freedom. Moses depended daily on God for guidance during the forty years that the people of Israel wandered through the desert. Even though he was not permitted to cross over into the promised land with his people, Moses remained loyal to the end. His ability to lead was the result of his being willing to listen to and obey God even when he was uncertain of the outcome.

The cornerstone of Moses' character was that he placed loyalty to God over self-image. He refused to compromise his moral convictions in order to avoid being ridiculed by his peers. Moses set high standards for himself and the people he led, and he worked hard to keep his people on track. If he could speak to us now, Moses would tell us that it is not easy to stand alone and speak out for what is right. And even doing so doesn't mean we won't make mistakes sometimes. In the end, though, listening to God and trusting him for guidance is well worth the effort.

What will it take for us to be like Moses, and successfully devoted followers of Christ? We need to be willing to listen to God, depend upon his leadership, and even when we aren't sure of the outcome, remain loyal to him.

STEP LOOK BACK 2

Ready for Step 3? See page 17 of **InStep's** *introduction.*

40The people said to Aaron,
"Make some gods to lead us!
Moses led us out of Egypt, but
we don't know what's happened
to him now." 41Then they made
an idol in the shape of a calf.
They offered sacrifices to the
idol and were pleased with what
they had done.
42God turned his back on his
people and left them. Then they
worshiped the stars in the sky,
just as it says in the Book of the
Prophets, "People of Israel, you
didn't offer sacrifices and
offerings to me during those
forty years in the desert.
43Instead, you carried the tent
where the god Molech is
worshiped, and you took along
the star of your god Rephan. You
made those idols and worshiped
them. So now I will have you
carried off beyond Babylonia."
44The tent where our ancestors
worshiped God was with them
in the desert. This was the same
tent that God had commanded
Moses to make. And it was made
like the model that Moses had
seen. 45Later it was given to our
ancestors, and they took it with
them when they went with
Joshua. They carried the tent
along as they took over the land
from those people that God had
chased out for them. Our
ancestors used this tent until the
time of King David.46 He pleased
God and asked him if he could
build a house of worship for the
people[t] of Israel. 47And it was
finally King Solomon who built
a house for God.[u]
48But the Most High God does
not live in houses made by
humans. It is just as the prophet
said, when he spoke for the Lord,
49"Heaven is my throne,
and the earth
is my footstool.
What kind of house
will you build for me?
In what place will I rest?
50 I have made everything."
51You stubborn and
hardheaded people! You are
always fighting against the Holy
Spirit, just as your ancestors did.
52Is there one prophet that your
ancestors didn't mistreat? They
killed the prophets who told
about the coming of the One
Who Obeys God.[v] And now you
have turned against him and
killed him. 53Angels gave you
God's Law, but you still don't
obey it.

Stephen Is Stoned to Death

54When the council members
heard Stephen's speech, they were
angry and furious.* 55But Stephen
was filled with the Holy Spirit. He
looked toward heaven, where he saw
our glorious God and Jesus standing
at his right side.[w] 56Then Stephen
said, "I see heaven open and the Son
of Man standing at the right side of
God!"
57The council members shouted
and covered their ears. At once they
all attacked Stephen 58and dragged
him out of the city. Then they started
throwing stones at him. The men who
had brought charges against him put
their coats at the feet of a young man
named Saul.[x]
59As Stephen was being stoned to
death, he called out, "Lord Jesus,
please welcome me!" 60He kneeled

---

[t]*the people*: Some manuscripts have "God." [u]*God*: Or "the people." [v]*One Who Obeys God*: That is, Jesus. [w]*standing at his right side*: The "right side" is the place of honor and power. "Standing" may mean that Jesus is welcoming Stephen (see verse 59). [x]*Saul*: Better known as Paul, who became a famous follower of Jesus.

7.54 **WHY WAS STEPHEN MURDERED?** Stephen's speech proved to his hearers that they had been disobedient to God. This made them feel guilty and angry. So the mob killed Stephen. Even today some people will get angry when they are told they have rejected God's message. They like to feel that their sins are their own business. But we owe our very lives to God, and he expects us to do his will.

NOTES

down and shouted, "Lord, don't
blame them for what they have
done." Then he died.
8 1-2Saul approved the stoning of
Stephen. Some faithful followers
of the Lord buried Stephen and
mourned very much for him.

Saul Makes Trouble for the Church

At that time the church in Jerusalem suffered terribly. All of the Lord's
followers, except the apostles, were
scattered everywhere in Judea and
Samaria.* 3Saul started making a lot
of trouble for the church. He went
from house to house, arresting men
and women and putting them in jail.

The Good News Is Preached in Samaria

4The Lord's followers who had
been scattered went from place to
place, telling the good news. 5Philip
went to the town of Samaria and told
the people about Christ.* 6They
crowded around Philip because they
were eager to hear what he was saying and to see him work miracles.
7Many people with evil spirits were
healed, and the spirits went out of
them with a shout. A lot of crippled
and lame people were also healed.
8Everyone in that city was very glad
because of what was happening.
9For some time a man named Simon had lived in the city of Samaria
and had amazed the people. He practiced witchcraft and claimed to be
somebody great. 10Everyone, rich
and poor, crowded around him. They
said, "This man is the power of God
called 'The Great Power.' "
11For a long time Simon had used
witchcraft to amaze the people, and
they kept crowding around him.*
12But when they believed what Philip
was saying about God's kingdom and
about the name of Jesus Christ, they
were all baptized. 13Even Simon believed and was baptized. He stayed
close to Philip, because he marveled
at all the miracles and wonders.
14When the apostles in Jerusalem
heard that some people in Samaria
had accepted God's message, they
sent Peter and John. 15When the two
apostles arrived, they prayed that the
people would be given the Holy
Spirit. 16Before this, the Holy Spirit
had not been given to anyone in Samaria though some of them had been
baptized in the name of the Lord Jesus. 17Peter and John then placed
their hands on everyone who had
faith in the Lord, and they were given
the Holy Spirit.
18Simon noticed that the Spirit was
given only when the apostles placed
their hands on the people. So he
brought money 19and said to Peter
and John, "Let me have this power
too! Then anyone I place my hands

8.1 **WHO WAS SAUL?** We are going to read much more about this young man Saul. He was a leading Pharisee, a smart student and teacher of the Law. (Later, his name would be changed to Paul after he became a Christian.) At first Saul was the greatest single enemy of Christ, so his later faith in Christ would be a great miracle and a source of wonder to those in the church. We will see by this that no one is so awful that they are beyond being saved.

8.5 **WHO WAS PHILIP?** Philip was one of the men we met in chapter 6 who were appointed to help the poor. Stephen was also one of those men. But we see that Philip, like Stephen, was also used by God as a great preacher of the good news about the Lord Jesus.

8.11 **WHO WAS SIMON?** Don't confuse this man with the apostle, Simon Peter. The Simon we meet here practiced witchcraft. We would say today that he practiced the occult. You could imagine someone like that today being called "The Great Power" (verse 10). Such practices come from the devil. Simon tried to "buy his way in," thinking he could get the power of the Holy Spirit with money. Peter scolded him for such foolishness.

NOTES

on will also be given the Holy Spirit."
20Peter said to him, "You and your
money will both end up in hell if you
think you can buy God's gift! 21You
don't have any part in this, and God
sees that your heart is not right.
22Get rid of these evil thoughts and
ask God to forgive you. 23I can see
that you are jealous and bound by
your evil ways."
24Simon said, "Please pray to the
Lord, so that what you said won't
happen to me."
25After Peter and John had
preached about the Lord, they returned to Jerusalem. On their way
they told the good news in many villages of Samaria.

Philip and an Ethiopian Official

26The Lord's angel said to Philip,
"Go south[y] along the desert road that
leads from Jerusalem to Gaza."[z]
27So Philip left.
An important Ethiopian official
happened to be going along that road
in his chariot. He was the chief treasurer for Candace, the Queen of Ethiopia. The official had gone to Jerusalem to worship* 28and was now on
his way home. He was sitting in his
chariot, reading the book of the
prophet Isaiah.
29The Spirit told Philip to catch up
with the chariot. 30Philip ran up close
and heard the man reading aloud
from the book of Isaiah. Philip asked
him, "Do you understand what you
are reading?"
31The official answered, "How can
I understand unless someone helps
me?" He then invited Philip to come
up and sit beside him.
32The man was reading the passage
that said,

"He was led like a sheep
on its way to be killed.
He was silent as a lamb,
whose wool
is being cut off,
and he did not say
a word.
33He was treated like a nobody
and did not receive
a fair trial.
How can he have children,
if his life
is snatched away?"

34The official said to Philip, "Tell
me, was the prophet talking about
himself or about someone else?"
35So Philip began at this place in the
Scriptures and explained the good
news about Jesus.
36-37As they were going along the
road, they came to a place where
there was some water. The official
said, "Look! Here is some water.
Why can't I be baptized?"[a]* 38He ordered the chariot to stop. Then they
both went down into the water, and
Philip baptized him.
39After they had come out of the
water, the Lord's Spirit took Philip
away. The official never saw him
again, but he was very happy as he
went on his way.
40Philip later appeared in Azotus.
He went from town to town, all the

---

[y]*Go south*: Or "About noon go." [z]*the desert road that leads from Jerusalem to Gaza*: Or "the road that leads from Jerusalem to Gaza in the desert." [a]*Why can't I be baptized*: Some manuscripts add, "Philip replied, 'You can, if you believe with all your heart.' "The official answered, 'I believe that Jesus Christ is the Son of God.' "

8.27 **PHILIP EXPLAINED ABOUT JESUS** The man Philip met was from Ethiopia, a country in Africa. The man was reading in a place in the Old Testament that tells how Jesus would die for our sins. But the man from Ethiopia didn't know who the Old Testament prophet was talking about. So Philip told the man about Jesus. We must use every chance we get to explain Jesus to people.

8.37 **"WHY CAN'T I BE BAPTIZED?"** As soon as the official believed in Jesus, he wanted to be baptized as Jesus taught. That's the sign of an obedient heart. Sometimes when people decide to have faith in Jesus, they are embarrassed about being baptized. Surely this official wasn't embarrassed—he couldn't wait.

NOTES

way to Caesarea, telling people about
Jesus.

Saul Becomes a Follower of the Lord

(Acts 22.6–16; 26.12–18)

9 Saul kept on threatening to kill
the Lord's followers. He even
went to the high priest 2and asked
for letters to the Jewish leaders in
Damascus. He did this because he
wanted to arrest and take to Jerusalem any man or woman who had accepted the Lord's Way.[b] 3When Saul
had almost reached Damascus, a
bright light from heaven suddenly
flashed around him. 4He fell to the
ground and heard a voice that said,
"Saul! Saul! Why are you so cruel
to me?"
5"Who are you?" Saul asked.
"I am Jesus," the Lord answered.
"I am the one you are so cruel to.*
6Now get up and go into the city,
where you will be told what to do."
7The men with Saul stood there
speechless. They had heard the voice,
but they had not seen anyone.
8Saul got up from the ground, and
when he opened his eyes, he could
not see a thing. Someone then led
him by the hand to Damascus,
9and for three days he was blind and
did not eat or drink.
10A follower named Ananias lived
in Damascus, and the Lord spoke to
him in a vision. Ananias answered,
"Lord, here I am."
11The Lord said to him, "Get up
and go to the house of Judas on
Straight Street. When you get there,
you will find a man named Saul from
the city of Tarsus. Saul is praying,
12and he has seen a vision. He saw
a man named Ananias coming to him
and putting his hands on him, so that
he could see again."
13Ananias replied, "Lord, a lot of
people have told me about the terrible things this man has done to your
followers in Jerusalem. 14Now the
chief priests have given him the
power to come here and arrest anyone who worships in your name."
15The Lord said to Ananias, "Go!
I have chosen him to tell foreigners,
kings, and the people of Israel about
me. 16I will show him how much he
must suffer for worshiping in my
name."
17Ananias left and went into the
house where Saul was staying. Ananias placed his hands on him and
said, "Saul, the Lord Jesus has sent
me. He is the same one who appeared
to you along the road. He wants you
to be able to see and to be filled with
the Holy Spirit."*
18Suddenly something like fish
scales fell from Saul's eyes, and he
could see. He got up and was baptized. 19Then he ate and felt much
better.

Saul Preaches in Damascus

For several days Saul stayed with
the Lord's followers in Damascus.
20Soon he went to the Jewish meeting
places and started telling people that

---

[b]*accepted the Lord's Way*: In the book of Acts, this means to become a follower of the Lord Jesus.

9.5 **SAUL MET HIS MASTER** Saul the Pharisee was very eager to destroy the followers of Jesus. But Saul got a surprise. Jesus was alive from the dead, and he met Saul who was on his way to arrest the Christians in Damascus. The risen Christ changed Saul's mind, and he became the most powerful apostle of all. As Paul, he would write thirteen books of the New Testament. Not even the worst enemy of the Lord Jesus can resist him when he is ready to work in that person's life.

9.17 **SAUL RECEIVED HIS SIGHT** Saul had been blinded by the bright appearance of the risen Savior. Then Saul was filled with the Holy Spirit and he got back his sight. When the Holy Spirit fills our lives, we too receive new sight. As Jesus said, when you are born from above, you can see (or understand) the kingdom of God (John 3.3).

NOTES

Jesus is the Son of God.* 21Everyone
who heard Saul was amazed and
said, "Isn't this the man who caused
so much trouble for those people in
Jerusalem who worship in the name
of Jesus? Didn't he come here to arrest them and take them to the chief
priests?"
22Saul preached with such power
that he completely confused the Jewish people in Damascus, as he tried
to show them that Jesus is the
Messiah.
23Later some of them made plans
to kill Saul, 24but he found out about
it. He learned that they were guarding the gates of the city day and night
in order to kill him. 25Then one night
his followers let him down over the
city wall in a large basket.*

Saul in Jerusalem

26When Saul arrived in Jerusalem,
he tried to join the followers. But they
were all afraid of him, because they
did not believe he was a true follower.
27Then Barnabas helped him by taking him to the apostles. He explained
how on the road to Damascus, Saul
had seen the Lord and how the Lord
had spoken to Saul. Barnabas also
said that when Saul was in Damascus, he had spoken bravely in the
name of Jesus.
28Saul moved about freely with the
followers in Jerusalem and told everyone about the Lord. 29He was always arguing with the Jews who
spoke Greek, and so they tried to kill
him. 30But the followers found out
about this and took Saul to Caesarea.
From there they sent him to the city
of Tarsus.
31The church in Judea, Galilee, and
Samaria now had a time of peace and
kept on worshiping the Lord. The
church became stronger, as the Holy
Spirit encouraged it and helped it
grow.

Peter Heals Aeneas

32While Peter was traveling from
place to place, he visited the Lord's
followers who lived in the town of
Lydda. 33There he met a man named
Aeneas, who for eight years had been
sick in bed and could not move.
34Peter said to Aeneas, "Jesus Christ
has healed you! Get up and make up
your bed."[c] Right away he stood up.*
35Many people in the towns of
Lydda and Sharon saw Aeneas and
became followers of the Lord.

Peter Brings Dorcas Back to Life

36In Joppa there was a follower
named Tabitha. Her Greek name was

---

[c]*and make up your bed*: Or "and fix something to eat."

9.20 **SAUL TOLD ABOUT JESUS RIGHT AWAY** Saul, the former Pharisee, couldn't wait to tell people about Jesus. At first the Christians were surprised at Saul because he had persecuted them. They thought maybe this was some sort of trick. But Saul was filled with the Holy Spirit and had to share about it. When Jesus changes our lives, we want to bring others to know him, too.

9.25 **GOD MADE A WAY OF ESCAPE** Poor Saul was faced with a trap at Damascus. The gates were being watched so he could be arrested when he tried to leave. But the Christians in the city "used their heads" and let Saul down over the wall in a basket. When enemies of Christ tried to kill Saul in Jerusalem, he went back to Tarsus where he grew up. God had a plan for Saul, and would not let anyone else prevent it from being carried out. God has a plan for every person who believes in him, and he provides for us in dangerous times.

9.34 **JESUS CONTINUES HIS WORK** Notice that Peter didn't say *he* healed Aeneas. He said Jesus did. Remember, Jesus is not a dead hero; he is a living Savior. We are his body in the world today. Like Peter, all believers are in a position to do the work of Jesus. Are you a worker for the living Lord?

NOTES

Dorcas, which means "deer." She
was always doing good things for
people and had given much to the
poor. 37But she got sick and died, and
her body was washed and placed in
an upstairs room. 38Joppa was not
far from Lydda, and the followers
heard that Peter was there. They sent
two men to say to him, "Please come
with us as quickly as you can!"
39Right away Peter went with them.

The men took Peter upstairs into
the room. Many widows were there
crying. They showed him the coats
and clothes that Dorcas had made
while she was still alive.

40After Peter had sent everyone out
of the room, he kneeled down and
prayed. Then he turned to the body
of Dorcas and said, "Tabitha, get
up!" The woman opened her eyes,
and when she saw Peter, she sat up.*
41He took her by the hand and helped
her to her feet.

Peter called in the widows and the
other followers and showed them
that Dorcas had been raised from
death. 42Everyone in Joppa heard
what had happened, and many of
them put their faith in the Lord.
43Peter stayed on for a while in Joppa
in the house of a man named Simon,
who made leather.

Peter and Cornelius

10 In Caesarea there was a man
named Cornelius, who was the
captain of a group of soldiers called
"The Italian Unit." 2Cornelius was
a very religious man. He worshiped
God, and so did everyone else who
lived in his house. He had given a
lot of money to the poor and was always praying to God.

3One afternoon at about three
o'clock,[d] Cornelius had a vision. He
saw an angel from God coming to
him and calling him by name.*
4Cornelius was surprised and stared
at the angel. Then he asked, "What
is this all about?"

The angel answered, "God has
heard your prayers and knows about
your gifts to the poor. 5Now send
some men to Joppa for a man named
Simon Peter. 6He is visiting with Simon the leather maker, who lives in
a house near the sea." 7After saying
this, the angel left.

Cornelius called in two of his servants and one of his soldiers who
worshiped God. 8He explained everything to them and sent them off to
Joppa.

9The next day about noon these
men were coming near to Joppa. Peter went up on the roof[e] of the house
to pray 10and became very hungry.
While the food was being prepared,
he fell sound asleep and had a vision.
11He saw heaven open, and something came down like a huge sheet
held up by its four corners. 12In it
were all kinds of animals, snakes,
and birds. 13A voice said to him,
"Peter, get up! Kill these and eat
them."

14But Peter said, "Lord, I can't do
that! I've never eaten anything that
is unclean and not fit to eat."[f]

15The voice spoke to him again,

---

[d]*at about three o'clock*: Probably while he was praying. See 3.1 and the note there. [e]*roof*: In Palestine the houses usually had a flat roof. Stairs on the outside led up to the roof, which was made of beams and boards covered with packed earth. [f]*unclean and not fit to eat*: The Law of Moses taught that some foods were not fit to eat.

9.40 **COULD PETER RAISE PEOPLE FROM DEATH?** If he were here, Peter would tell us he could do nothing except what Jesus did through him, including the raising up of Dorcas. We ought to think and pray constantly about how our Lord would wish to use us in his continuing work. Jesus Christ can do great things by his power working through us.

10.3 **GOD CAME TO A ROMAN SOLDIER** God is in the business of saving all kinds of people, not only Jewish fishermen like Peter. Cornelius was an officer in the Roman army, and the Lord wanted to save him. The Gentile, non-Jewish world was being brought into the church. Cornelius was the beginning of this work.

NOTES

"When God says that something can
be used for food, don't say it isn't
fit to eat."
16This happened three times before
the sheet was suddenly taken back
to heaven.
17Peter was still wondering what
all of this meant, when the men sent
by Cornelius came and stood at the
gate. They had found their way to
Simon's house 18and were asking if
Simon Peter was staying there.
19While Peter was still thinking
about the vision, the Holy Spirit said
to him, "Three[g] men are here looking for you. 20Hurry down and go
with them. Don't worry, I sent
them."
21Peter went down and said to the
men, "I am the one you are looking
for. Why have you come?"
22They answered, "Captain Cornelius sent us. He is a good man and
worships God. All the Jewish people
like him. One of God's holy angels
told Cornelius to send for you, so he
could hear what you have to say."*
23Peter invited them to spend the
night.
The next morning Peter and some
of the Lord's followers in Joppa left
with the men who had come from
Cornelius. 24The next day they all arrived in Caesarea where Cornelius
was waiting for them. He had also
invited his relatives and close
friends.
25When Peter arrived, Cornelius
greeted him. Then he kneeled at Peter's feet and started worshiping him.
26But Peter took hold of him and said,
"Stand up! I am nothing more than
a human."
27As Peter entered the house, he
was still talking with Cornelius.
Many people were there, 28and Peter
said to them, "You know that we
Jews are not allowed to have anything to do with other people. But
God has shown me that he doesn't
think anyone is unclean or unfit.* 29I agreed to come here, but
I want to know why you sent for
me."
30Cornelius answered:

Four days ago at about three
o'clock in the afternoon I was
praying at home. Suddenly a
man in bright clothes stood in
front of me. 31He said,
"Cornelius, God has heard your
prayers, and he knows about
your gifts to the poor. 32Now
send to Joppa for Simon Peter.
He is visiting in the home of
Simon the leather maker, who
lives near the sea."
33I sent for you right away, and
you have been good enough to
come. All of us are here in the
presence of the Lord God, so that
we can hear what he has to say.

34Peter then said:

Now I am certain that God
treats all people alike. 35God is
pleased with everyone who
worships him and does right, no
matter what nation they come

---

[g] *Three*: Some manuscripts have "two;" one manuscript has "some."

10.22 **CORNELIUS WAS A TRUE FOLLOWER OF GOD** Even before Peter came to him, Cornelius had worshiped God. The Jews had earlier spread all over the Roman Empire and had taken the Old Testament with them. Through the Jews many Gentiles became what were called "God-fearers." They didn't know about Jesus yet, but they worshiped God according to all they knew from the Old Testament.

10.28 **WHY DID THE JEWS HAVE SUCH STRICT RULES?** Under the Law that God gave them, Jews were not allowed to eat with Gentiles or have them as friends. This was God's way of keeping his people pure until Jesus came. If the Jews had not obeyed these rules they would have been mixed in with the Gentiles, and they would no longer have been a separate race for Jesus the Son of David to be born as the Scriptures predicted.

NOTES

from.* 36This is the same
message that God gave to the
people of Israel, when he sent
Jesus Christ, the Lord of all, to
offer peace to them.
37You surely know what
happened[h] everywhere in Judea.
It all began in Galilee after John
had told everyone to be baptized.
38God gave the Holy Spirit and
power to Jesus from Nazareth.
He was with Jesus, as he went
around doing good and healing
everyone who was under the
power of the devil. 39We all saw
what Jesus did both in Israel and
in the city of Jerusalem.
Jesus was put to death on a
cross. 40But three days later, God
raised him to life and let him be
seen. 41Not everyone saw him.
He was seen only by us, who ate
and drank with him after he was
raised from death. We were the
ones God chose to tell others
about him.
42God told us to announce
clearly to the people that Jesus
is the one he has chosen to judge
the living and the dead. 43Every
one of the prophets has said that
all who have faith in Jesus will
have their sins forgiven in his
name.

44While Peter was still speaking,
the Holy Spirit took control of everyone who was listening.* 45Some Jewish followers of the Lord had come
with Peter, and they were surprised
that the Holy Spirit had been given
to Gentiles. 46Now they were hearing
Gentiles speaking unknown languages and praising God.

Peter said, 47"These Gentiles have
been given the Holy Spirit, just as
we have! I am certain that no one
would dare stop us from baptizing
them." 48Peter ordered them to be
baptized in the name of Jesus Christ,
and they asked him to stay on for a
few days.

Peter Reports to the Church in Jerusalem

11 The apostles and the followers
in Judea heard that Gentiles
had accepted God's message. 2So
when Peter came to Jerusalem, some
of the Jewish leaders started arguing
with him. They wanted Gentile followers to be circumcised, and
3they said, "You stayed in the homes
of Gentiles, and you even ate with
them!"

4Then Peter told them exactly what
had happened:*

5I was in the town of Joppa
and was praying when I fell
sound asleep and had a vision.
I saw heaven open, and
something like a huge sheet held
by its four corners came down
to me. 6When I looked in it, I

---

[h]*what happened*: Or "the message that went."

10.35 **PETER CHANGED HIS MIND ABOUT GENTILES** At first Peter imagined that the Messiah had come only for the Jews. God had to shake Peter up about this opinion. Even from Old Testament times, God's prophets had been telling about his great plan to bless the Gentile nations. This began to happen in a big way at this point. The result is that today the church includes not only Jews but Gentiles too, mostly Gentiles.

10.44 **THE HOLY SPIRIT MADE THE DIFFERENCE** Until Peter came and preached the good news about Jesus to Cornelius, all the Gentile God-fearers had was the Law and the Old Testament. Peter said the old differences between Jews and Gentiles don't matter anymore. The Holy Spirit came into the lives of Cornelius and the other Gentiles. The Jewish Christians could see that they were all one family of God along with the Gentile believers.

11.4 **THE CHURCH BELIEVED PETER** Peter told the church at Jerusalem all that had happened to the Gentile believers. He shared the whole exciting story with the Christians at (*continued*)

NOTES

saw animals, wild beasts,
snakes, and birds. 7I heard a
voice saying to me, "Peter, get
up! Kill these and eat them."
8But I said, "Lord, I can't do
that! I've never taken a bite of
anything that is unclean and not
fit to eat."[i]
9The voice from heaven spoke
to me again, "When God says
that something can be used for
food, don't say it isn't fit to eat."
10This happened three times
before it was all taken back into
heaven.
11Suddenly three men from
Caesarea stood in front of the
house where I was staying.
12The Holy Spirit told me to go
with them and not to worry.
Then six of the Lord's followers
went with me to the home of a
man 13who told us that an angel
had appeared to him. The angel
had ordered him to send to Joppa
for someone named Simon
Peter. 14Then Peter would tell
him how he and everyone in his
house could be saved.
15After I started speaking, the
Holy Spirit was given to them,
just as the Spirit had been given
to us at the beginning. 16I
remembered that the Lord had
said, "John baptized with water,
but you will be baptized with the
Holy Spirit." 17God gave those
Gentiles the same gift that he
gave us when we put our faith
in the Lord Jesus Christ. So how
could I have gone against God?
18When the Jewish leaders heard
Peter say this, they stopped arguing
and started praising God. They said,
"God has now let Gentiles turn to
him, and he has given life to them!"

The Church in Antioch

19Some of the Lord's followers had
been scattered because of the terrible
trouble that started when Stephen
was killed. They went as far as Phoenicia, Cyprus, and Antioch, but they
told the message only to the Jews.*
20Some of the followers from Cyprus and Cyrene went to Antioch and
started telling Gentiles[j] the good
news about the Lord Jesus. 21The
Lord's power was with them, and
many people turned to the Lord and
put their faith in him. 22News of what
was happening reached the church
in Jerusalem. Then they sent Barnabas to Antioch.*
23When Barnabas got there and
saw what God had been kind enough

---

[i] *unclean and not fit to eat*: See the note at 10.14.
[j] *Gentiles*: This translates a Greek word that may mean "people who speak Greek" or "people who live as Greeks do." Here the word seems to mean "people who are not Jews." Some manuscripts have "Greeks," which also seems to mean "people who are not Jews."

(*continued*) Jerusalem. Peter was not starting a new Gentile religion. The truths believed by Cornelius and the Gentiles had to be the same as those that were given to the Jewish Christians. No group of Christians is an item unto itself. We believers are all one family in God's eyes.

11.19 **TROUBLE SPREADS THE GOOD NEWS** It had been a sad day for the Christians in Jerusalem when Stephen was put to death (see chapter 7). But God used this tragedy to spread the good news. Many Christians decided to leave Jerusalem and go up to live in Antioch, which was then a city in the country of Syria. There the Christians told the people of Syria about Christ, and many of them became Christians. Today, too, God often uses the bad times in our lives to bring about good.

11.22 **WHO WAS BARNABAS?** His name means "son of comfort," and he was a great comfort to Christians everywhere. When he saw how the Christians at Antioch believed, he could see that God was doing the same work there as he did in Jerusalem. We can all be "sons of comfort" by encouraging our brothers and sisters in Christ about the great work God is doing through them wherever they might be.

NOTES

to do for them, he was very glad. So
he begged them to remain faithful
to the Lord with all their hearts.
24 Barnabas was a good man of great
faith, and he was filled with the Holy
Spirit. Many more people turned to
the Lord.
25 Barnabas went to Tarsus to look
for Saul. 26 He found Saul and
brought him to Antioch, where they
met with the church for a whole year
and taught many of its people. There
in Antioch the Lord's followers were
first called Christians.*
27 During this time some prophets
from Jerusalem came to Antioch.
28 One of them was Agabus. Then
with the help of the Spirit, he told
that there would be a terrible famine
everywhere in the world. And it happened when Claudius was Emperor.[k]
29 The followers in Antioch decided
to send whatever help they could to
the followers in Judea. 30 So they had
Barnabas and Saul take their gifts
to the church leaders in Jerusalem.

Herod Causes Trouble for the Church

12 At that time King Herod[l]
caused terrible suffering for
some members of the church. 2 He ordered soldiers to cut off the head of
James, the brother of John.* 3 When
Herod saw that this pleased the Jewish people, he had Peter arrested during the Feast of Thin Bread. 4 He put
Peter in jail and ordered four squads
of soldiers to guard him. Herod
planned to put him on trial in public
after the feast.
5 While Peter was being kept in jail,
the church never stopped praying to
God for him.

Peter Is Rescued

6 The night before Peter was to be
put on trial, he was asleep and bound
by two chains. A soldier was guarding him on each side, and two other
soldiers were guarding the entrance
to the jail. 7 Suddenly an angel from
the Lord appeared, and light flashed
around in the cell. The angel poked
Peter in the side and woke him up.
Then he said, "Quick! Get up!"
The chains fell off his hands,*

[k] *when Claudius was Emperor*: A.D. 41-54.
[l] *Herod*: Herod Agrippa I, the grandson of Herod the Great.

11.26 **SAUL WAS ACCEPTED AT ANTIOCH** You will remember that Saul (Paul) had gone back to Tarsus to live. This city was in an area called Cilicia, not far from Antioch. Some time later, Barnabas got Saul and brought him to Antioch, which was by then the headquarters of the Christian church. The leaders at Antioch accepted Saul as a Christian worker, and he was sent with Barnabas to help in Jerusalem. We see how Saul had to "bide his time" before God was ready to use him. It must have taken patience, but Saul was able to prepare during his time of waiting. Sometimes God has us wait like that. Are we patient? Do we make good use of the time?

12.2 **CHRISTIANS ARE NOT ALWAYS TOLERATED** King Herod Agrippa killed the apostle James, brother of the John who wrote John's Gospel, and jailed other church leaders. He figured it would make him popular. We may wonder why Christians, a peace-loving people, are often hated by the world. The reason is that the world doesn't love God and therefore doesn't love God's people either. Evil can't stand good.

12.7 **HOW WAS PETER RESCUED?** To answer this question we must believe that God is able and willing to do what he did for Peter. A person who did not believe in God would be very puzzled by this. That person would have to explain Peter's escape in some other way. Non-believers have to explain a lot of things. It makes more sense to let God have the credit for what he has done.

NOTES

8and the angel said, "Get dressed and put on your sandals." Peter did what he was told. Then the angel said, "Now put on your coat and follow me." 9Peter left with the angel, but he thought everything was only a dream. 10They went past the two groups of soldiers, and when they came to the iron gate to the city, it opened by itself. They went out and were going along the street, when all at once the angel disappeared.

11Peter now realized what had happened, and he said, "I am certain that the Lord sent his angel to rescue me from Herod and from everything the Jewish leaders planned to do to me." 12Then Peter went to the house of Mary the mother of John whose other name was Mark. Many of the Lord's followers had come together there and were praying.

13Peter knocked on the gate, and a servant named Rhoda came to the door. 14When she heard Peter's voice, she was too excited to open the gate. She ran back into the house and said that Peter was standing there.*

15Everyone told her, "You are crazy!" But she kept saying that it was Peter. Then they said, "It must be his angel."[m] 16But Peter kept on knocking, until finally they opened the gate. They saw him and were completely amazed.

17Peter motioned for them to keep quiet. Then he told how the Lord had led him out of jail. He also said, "Tell James and the others what has happened." After that, he left and went somewhere else.

18The next morning the soldiers who had been on guard were terribly worried and wondered what had happened to Peter. 19Herod ordered his own soldiers to search for him, but they could not find him. Then he questioned the guards and had them put to death. After this, Herod left Judea to stay in Caesarea for a while.

Herod Dies

20Herod and the people of Tyre and Sidon were very angry with each other. But their country got its food supply from the region that he ruled. So a group of them went to see Blastus, who was one of Herod's high officials. They convinced Blastus that they wanted to make peace between their cities and Herod,* 21and a day was set for them to meet with him.

Herod came dressed in his royal robes. He sat down on his throne and made a speech. 22The people shouted, "You speak more like a god than a man!" 23At once an angel from the Lord struck him down because he took the honor that belonged to God. Later, Herod was eaten by worms and died.

24God's message kept spreading. 25And after Barnabas and Saul had done the work they were sent to do, they went back to Jerusalem[n] with John, whose other name was Mark.

Barnabas and Saul Are Chosen and Sent

13 The church at Antioch had several prophets and teachers. They were Barnabas, Simeon, also

---

[m] *his angel*: Probably meaning "his guardian angel."
[n] *went back to Jerusalem*: Some manuscripts have "left Jerusalem," and others have "went to Antioch."

12.14 **RHODA WASN'T CRAZY** The Christians were praying at the home of John Mark, author of Mark's Gospel. They were probably praying for Peter's release from prison. But when it happened, they didn't believe it. They thought Rhoda was crazy because she said Peter was at the door. Many times Christians are that way today—we have faith enough to pray, but not enough faith to expect an answer.

12.20 **HUMAN POWER COMES TO AN END** Herod Agrippa, who is the first Herod we read of in the book of Acts, was a cruel and brutal man. He was like the two Herods before him, written about in the Gospels. This Herod killed the soldiers who had guarded Peter before his escape. Then he pretended to be equal with God. But his power ended when he died of a terrible disease. Proud human power comes to a bad end.

NOTES

called Niger, Lucius from Cyrene, Manaen, who was Herod's[o] close friend, and Saul. 2While they were worshiping the Lord and going without eating,[p] the Holy Spirit told them, "Appoint Barnabas and Saul to do the work for which I have chosen them."* 3Everyone prayed and went without eating for a while longer. Next, they placed their hands on Barnabas and Saul to show that they had been appointed to do this work. Then everyone sent them on their way.

Barnabas and Saul in Cyprus

4After Barnabas and Saul had been sent by the Holy Spirit, they went to Seleucia. From there they sailed to the island of Cyprus. 5They arrived at Salamis and began to preach God's message in the Jewish meeting places. They also had John[q] as a helper.

6They went all the way to the city of Paphos on the other end of the island, where they met a Jewish man named Bar-Jesus. He practiced witchcraft and was a false prophet. 7He also worked for Sergius Paulus, who was very smart and was the governor of the island. Sergius Paulus wanted to hear God's message, and he sent for Barnabas and Saul. 8But Bar-Jesus, whose other name was Elymas, was against them. He even tried to keep the governor from having faith in the Lord.

9Then Saul, better known as Paul, was filled with the Holy Spirit. He looked straight at Elymas* 10and said, "You son of the devil! You are a liar, a crook, and an enemy of everything that is right. When will you stop speaking against the true ways of the Lord? 11The Lord is going to punish you by making you completely blind for a while."

Suddenly the man's eyes were covered by a dark mist, and he went around trying to get someone to lead him by the hand. 12When the governor saw what had happened, he was amazed at this teaching about the Lord. So he put his faith in the Lord.

Paul and Barnabas in Antioch of Pisidia

13Paul and the others left Paphos and sailed to Perga in Pamphylia. But John[q] left them and went back to Jerusalem. 14The rest of them went on from Perga to Antioch in Pisidia. Then on the Sabbath they went to the Jewish meeting place and sat down.*

---

[o] *Herod's*: Herod Antipas, the son of Herod the Great. [p] *going without eating*: The Jews often went without eating as a way of showing how much they loved God. This is also called "fasting." [q] *John*: Whose other name was Mark (12.12,25).

13.2 **GOD CHOSE HIS SERVANTS** Notice that the church at Antioch didn't decide to send Barnabas and Saul. God himself made the decision, while the people prayed and fasted (went without eating). The people were fasting not for health reasons or to punish themselves, but so they could concentrate more on praying. Meals take a lot of attention, and there are times when not having meals is helpful.

13.9 **INTRODUCING: PAUL** We see Saul and Barnabas going out as missionaries from Antioch to the lands that lay before them to the west. At this point we notice that Saul's name has been changed to Paul. Sometimes Christians changed their names as a way of reminding themselves that they were new people who were "born again." Saul means "asked for," and Paul means "little," which may tell us that Paul was sort of small physically. Or maybe it was Paul's way of being humble instead of proud like the old Saul.

13.14 **THE TRAVELING GOOD NEWS** Until this time, the good news about Jesus had been heard only in Israel and Syria. Then Cyprus heard it. Then Paul and Barnabas brought the good news to the regions of Pamphylia and Pisidia in Turkey. (In those days part of Turkey was called "Asia." Turkey is just a tiny part of the huge continent we call Asia today.)

NOTES

15After the reading of the Law and the Prophets,[r] the leaders sent someone over to tell Paul and Barnabas, "Friends, if you have anything to say that will help the people, please say it."

16Paul got up. He motioned with his hand and said:

People of Israel, and everyone else who worships God, listen! 17The God of Israel chose our ancestors, and he let our people prosper while they were living in Egypt. Then with his mighty power he led them out, 18and for about forty years he took care of[s] them in the desert. 19He destroyed seven nations in the land of Canaan and gave their land to our people. 20All this happened in about 450 years.

Then God gave our people judges until the time of the prophet Samuel, 21but the people demanded a king. So for forty years God gave them King Saul, the son of Kish from the tribe of Benjamin. 22Later, God removed Saul and let David rule in his place. God said about him, "David the son of Jesse is the kind of person who pleases me most! He does everything I want him to do."

23God promised that someone from David's family would come to save the people of Israel, and Jesus is that one.* 24But before Jesus came, John was telling everyone in Israel to turn back to God and be baptized. 25Then, when John's work was almost done, he said, "Who do you people think I am? Do you think I am the Promised One? He will come later, and I am not good enough to untie his sandals."

26Now listen, you descendants of Abraham! Pay attention, all of you Gentiles who are here to worship God! Listen to this message about how to be saved, because it is for everyone. 27The people of Jerusalem and their leaders didn't realize who Jesus was. And they didn't understand the words of the prophets that they read each Sabbath. So they condemned Jesus just as the prophets had said.

28-29They did exactly what the Scriptures said they would. Even though they couldn't find any reason to put Jesus to death, they still asked Pilate to have him killed.

After Jesus had been put to death, he was taken down from the cross[t] and put in a tomb. 30But God raised him from death! 31Then for many days Jesus appeared to his followers who had gone with him from Galilee to Jerusalem. Now they are telling our people about him.

32God made a promise to our ancestors. And we are here to tell you the good news 33that he has kept this promise to us. It is just as the second Psalm says about Jesus,

"You are my son because today
I have become your Father."*

34God raised Jesus from death

---

[r]*the Law and the Prophets*: The Jewish Scriptures, that is, the Old Testament. [s]*took care of*: Some manuscripts have "put up with." [t]*cross*: This translates a Greek word that means "wood," "pole," or "tree."

13.23 **PAUL PREACHED ABOUT THE SON OF DAVID** In Pisidia there was another town called Antioch (not to be confused with the town of the same name in Syria). Paul and Barnabas stayed in this Antioch many days, and Paul preached a great sermon. He showed how God's old promise to save both Jews and Gentiles was fulfilled in the work of Jesus Christ the Lord, the Son of David. Many people in Antioch believed the good news and came back the following week to hear more.

13.33 **THE JEWISH SCRIPTURES POINT TO JESUS** As we saw earlier in the preaching of Peter and Stephen, and as we see in Paul's speech here, the early Christians were very clear *(continued)*

NOTES

and will never let his body decay.
It is just as God said,
"I will make to you
the same holy promise
that I made to David."
35And in another psalm it says,
"God will never let the body of
his Holy One decay."
36When David was alive, he
obeyed God. Then after he died,
he was buried in the family
grave, and his body decayed.
37But God raised Jesus from
death, and his body did not
decay.
38My friends, the message is
that Jesus can forgive your sins!
The Law of Moses could not set
you free from all your sins.
39But everyone who has faith in
Jesus is set free. 40Make sure that
what the prophets have said
doesn't happen to you. They
said,
41"Look, you people
who make fun of God!
Be amazed
and disappear.
I will do something today
that you won't believe,
even if someone
tells you about it!"
42As Paul and Barnabas were leaving the meeting, the people begged
them to say more about these same
things on the next Sabbath. 43After
the service, many Jews and a lot of
Gentiles who worshiped God went
with them. Paul and Barnabas
begged them all to remain faithful
to God, who had been so kind to
them.
44The next Sabbath almost everyone in town came to hear the message
about the Lord.[u] 45When the Jewish
people saw the crowds, they were
very jealous. They insulted Paul and
spoke against everything he said.
46But Paul and Barnabas bravely
said:
We had to tell God's message
to you before we told it to anyone
else. But you rejected the
message! This proves that you
don't deserve eternal life. Now
we are going to the Gentiles.*
47The Lord has given us this
command,
"I have placed you here
as a light
for the Gentiles.
You are to take
the saving power of God
to people everywhere
on earth."
48This message made the Gentiles
glad, and they praised what they had
heard about the Lord.[u] Everyone
who had been chosen for eternal life
then put their faith in the Lord.
49The message about the Lord
spread all over that region. 50But the
Jewish leaders went to some of the
important men in the town and to
some respected women who were religious. They turned them against
Paul and Barnabas and started making trouble for them. They even
chased them out of that part of the
country.
51Paul and Barnabas shook the
dust from that place off their feet[v]
and went on to the city of Iconium.
52But the Lord's followers in Anti-

[u]*the Lord*: Some manuscripts have "God."
[v]*shook the dust from that place off their feet*: This was a way of showing rejection.

(*continued*) that the news about Jesus was not a new thing. The history of Israel, as told in the Scriptures, had been leading up to him for centuries. A Jew who believed the word of God should have believed in the Messiah whom God predicted he would send.

13.46 **JEWS REJECTED THE MESSAGE AND GENTILES ACCEPTED IT** Here is an amazing thing. The Jews had been the ones who gave us the promise of the coming Messiah. But now that he had come, most Jews rejected him. On the other hand, the Gentiles had been outsiders to what God had done for the Jews. But here it is Gentiles we see welcoming the good news. God is always reaching out to people who will listen to his word.

NOTES

och were very happy and were filled with the Holy Spirit.

Paul and Barnabas in Iconium

14 Paul and Barnabas spoke in the Jewish meeting place in Iconium, just as they had done at Antioch, and many Jews and Gentiles[w] put their faith in the Lord.* [2]But the Jews who did not have faith in him made the other Gentiles angry and turned them against the Lord's followers.

[3]Paul and Barnabas stayed there for a while, having faith in the Lord and bravely speaking his message. The Lord gave them the power to work miracles and wonders, and he showed that their message about his great kindness was true.

[4]The people of Iconium did not know what to think. Some of them believed the Jewish group, and others believed the apostles. [5]Finally, some Gentiles and Jews, together with their leaders, decided to make trouble for Paul and Barnabas and to kill them by throwing stones at them.

[6-7]But when the two apostles found out what was happening, they escaped to the region of Lycaonia. They preached the good news there in the towns of Lystra and Derbe and in the nearby countryside.

Paul and Barnabas in Lystra

[8]In Lystra there was a man who had been born with crippled feet and had never been able to walk. [9]The man was listening to Paul speak, when Paul saw that he had faith in Jesus and could be healed. So he looked straight at the man [10]and shouted, "Stand up!" The man jumped up and started walking around.

[11]When the crowd saw what Paul had done, they yelled out in the language of Lycaonia, "The gods have turned into humans and have come down to us!"* [12]They gave Barnabas the name Zeus, and they gave Paul the name Hermes,[x] because he did the talking.

[13]The temple of Zeus was near the entrance to the city. Its priest and the crowds wanted to offer a sacrifice to Barnabas and Paul. So the priest brought some bulls and flowers to the city gates. [14]When the two apostles found out about this, they tore their clothes in horror and ran to the crowd, shouting:

> [15]Why are you doing this? We are humans just like you. Please give up all this foolishness. Turn to the living God, who made the sky, the earth, the sea, and everything in them. [16]In times past, God let each nation go its own way. [17]But he showed that he was there by the good things he did. God sends rain from heaven and makes your crops

---

[w]*Gentiles*: The Greek text has "Greeks," which probably means people who were not Jews. But it may mean Gentiles who worshiped with the Jews.
[x]*Hermes*: The Greeks thought of Hermes as the messenger of the other gods, especially of Zeus, their chief god.

14.1 **THE APOSTLES KEPT MOVING** Paul and Barnabas didn't wait around to be killed in Antioch. The believers there would carry on the work. But the apostles went on to the next city, Iconium. There they preached the good news again, and again some believed. But others wanted to kill the apostles. Christians must realize that everybody is not on God's side. The good news will please some and anger others.

14.11 **CAN PEOPLE BE GODS?** Of course people cannot be gods, only children of the one true God. The people of Lystra wanted to believe that Barnabas and Paul were gods. The two apostles "tore their clothes"—a Jewish way of expressing grief—and pleaded with the people not to worship them. One basic problem humans have is that they want to "hero worship" other humans. But God said, "You shall have no other gods."

NOTES

grow. He gives food to you and
makes your hearts glad.
18Even after Paul and Barnabas
had said all this, they could hardly
keep the people from offering a sacrifice to them.
19Some Jewish leaders from Antioch and Iconium came and turned
the crowds against Paul. They hit him
with stones and dragged him out of
the city, thinking he was dead.*
20But when the Lord's followers
gathered around Paul, he stood
up and went back into the city. The
next day he and Barnabas went to
Derbe.

Paul and Barnabas Return to Antioch in Syria

21Paul and Barnabas preached the
good news in Derbe and won some
people to the Lord. Then they went
back to Lystra, Iconium, and Antioch
in Pisidia.* 22They encouraged the
followers and begged them to remain
faithful. They told them, "We have
to suffer a lot before we can get into
God's kingdom." 23Paul and Barnabas chose some of those who had
faith in the Lord to be leaders for
each of the churches. Then they went
without eating[y] and prayed that the
Lord would take good care of these
leaders.
24Paul and Barnabas went on
through Pisidia to Pamphylia,
25where they preached in the town
of Perga. Then they went down to
Attalia 26and sailed to Antioch in
Syria. It was there that they had been
placed in God's care for the work
they had now completed.[z]
27After arriving in Antioch, they
called the church together. They told
the people what God had helped
them do and how he had made it possible for the Gentiles to believe.
28Then they stayed there with the followers for a long time.
15 Some people came from Judea
and started teaching the Lord's
followers that they could not be
saved, unless they were circumcised
as Moses had taught. 2This caused
trouble, and Paul and Barnabas argued with them about this teaching.
So it was decided to send Paul and
Barnabas and a few others to Jerusalem to discuss this problem with the
apostles and the church leaders.

The Church Leaders Meet in Jerusalem

3The men who were sent by the
church went through Phoenicia and
Samaria and told how the Gentiles
had turned to God. This news made
the Lord's followers very happy.
4When the men arrived in Jerusalem,
they were welcomed by all the
church, including the apostles and
the leaders. They told them everything that God had helped them do.
5But some Pharisees had become followers of the Lord. They stood up
and said, "Gentiles who have faith
in the Lord must be circumcised and
told to obey the Law of Moses."
6The apostles and church leaders
met to discuss this problem about

[y]*went without eating*: See the note at 13.2.
[z]*the work they had now completed*: See 13.1-3.

14.19 **WHY DID THEY WANT TO KILL PAUL?** It's not easy to explain human spite—resentment of something new, jealousy, fear of what we don't understand. All of these things cause people to act the way they did toward Paul. Christians are not fanatics—we have no need to strike out in anger against our enemies. God takes care of us and defends us. God defended Paul, too.

14.21 **PAUL AND BARNABAS RETRACED THEIR STEPS** The two apostles went back through the towns they had visited. This gave them a chance to see people there who had believed in Jesus. That's a good policy: to "follow up" on the people with whom we have shared the good news, to make sure they are growing well in their faith.

NOTES

Gentiles.* 7They had talked it over
for a long time, when Peter got up
and said:

My friends, you know that God
decided long ago to let me be
the one from your group to
preach the good news to the
Gentiles. God did this so that
they would hear and obey him.
8He knows what is in everyone's
heart. And he showed that he
had chosen the Gentiles, when
he gave them the Holy Spirit, just
as he had given his Spirit to us.
9God treated them in the same
way that he treated us. They put
their faith in him, and he made
their hearts pure.

10Now why are you trying to
make God angry by placing a
heavy burden on these
followers? This burden was too
heavy for us or our ancestors.
11But our Lord Jesus was kind
to us Jews, and we are saved by
faith in him, just as the Gentiles
are.

12Everyone kept quiet and listened
as Barnabas and Paul told how God
had given them the power to work
a lot of miracles and wonders for the
Gentiles.

13After they had finished speaking,
James[a] said:

My friends, listen to me!*
14Simon Peter[b] has told how God
first came to the Gentiles and
made some of them his own
people. 15This agrees with what
the prophets wrote,

16"I, the Lord, will return
and rebuild
David's fallen house.
I will build it from its ruins
and set it up again.
17Then other nations
will turn to me
and be my chosen ones.
I, the Lord, say this.
18 I promised it long ago."

19And so, my friends, I don't
think we should place burdens
on the Gentiles who are turning
to God. 20We should simply
write and tell them not to eat
anything that has been offered
to idols. They should be told not
to eat the meat of any animal
that has been strangled or that
still has blood in it. They must
also not commit any terrible
sexual sins.[c]

21We must remember that the
Law of Moses has been preached
in city after city for many years,
and every Sabbath it is read
when we Jews meet.

A Letter to Gentiles Who Had Faith in the Lord

22The apostles, the leaders, and all
the church members decided to send
some men to Antioch along with Paul
and Barnabas. They chose Silas and
Judas Barsabbas,[d] who were two

---

[a]*James*: The Lord's brother. [b]*Simon Peter*: The Greek text has "Simeon," which is another form of the name "Simon." The apostle Peter is meant. [c]*not commit any terrible sexual sins*: This probably refers to the laws about the wrong kind of marriages that are forbidden in Leviticus 18.6-18 or to some serious sexual sin. [d]*Judas Barsabbas*: He may have been a brother of Joseph Barsabbas (see 1.23), but the name "Barsabbas" was often used by the Jewish people.

15.6 **WHAT WAS THE MEETING ABOUT?** Paul and Barnabas had just finished the first great Christian missionary journey to the Gentiles. While they were gone, some of the Jewish Christians were upset because Paul and Barnabas didn't make Gentile Christians obey the strict Jewish laws. So the Christian leaders met in Jerusalem to decide what to do.

15.13 **WHAT WAS DECIDED AT THE JERUSALEM MEETING?** Peter made it clear that both Jews and Gentiles are saved through faith in Jesus, and not by following Jewish customs. Gentile Christians should not have been asked to live exactly like the Jews. James, the leader at Jerusalem, agreed and said that the Gentiles must obey laws having to do with morality and offerings to idols, but not the special Jewish religious customs.

NOTES

leaders of the Lord's followers.
23They wrote a letter that said:

We apostles and leaders send friendly greetings to all of you Gentiles who are followers of the Lord in Antioch, Syria, and Cilicia.*

24We have heard that some
people from here have terribly
upset you by what they said. But
we did not send them! 25So we
met together and decided to
choose some men and to send
them to you along with our good
friends Barnabas and Paul.
26These men have risked their
lives for our Lord Jesus Christ.
27We are also sending Judas and
Silas, who will tell you in person
the same things that we are
writing.

28The Holy Spirit has shown
us that we should not place any
extra burden on you. 29But you
should not eat anything offered
to idols. You should not eat any
meat that still has the blood in
it or any meat of any animal that
has been strangled. You must
also not commit any terrible
sexual sins. If you follow these
instructions, you will do well.

We send our best wishes.

30The four men left Jerusalem and
went to Antioch. Then they called all
the church members together and
gave them the letter. 31When the letter was read, it made everyone glad
and gave them lots of encouragement. 32Judas and Silas were prophets, and they spoke a long time, encouraging and helping the Lord's
followers.

33The men from Jerusalem stayed
on in Antioch for a while. And when
they left to return to the ones who
had sent them, the followers wished
them well. 34-35But Silas, Paul, and
Barnabas stayed on in Antioch,
where they and many others taught
and preached about the Lord.[e]

Paul and Barnabas Go Their Separate Ways

36Sometime later Paul said to Barnabas, "Let's go back and visit the
Lord's followers in all the cities
where we preached his message.
Then we will know how they are doing." 37Barnabas wanted to take
along John, whose other name was
Mark.* 38But Paul did not want to,
because Mark had left them in Pamphylia and had stopped working with
them.

39Paul and Barnabas argued, then
each of them went his own way. Barnabas took Mark and sailed to Cyprus, 40but Paul took Silas and left
after the followers had placed them
in God's care. 41They traveled
through Syria and Cilicia, encouraging the churches.

---

[e]Verse 34, which says that Silas decided to stay on in Antioch, is not in some manuscripts.

15.23 **HOW BAD WAS THE "GENTILE PROBLEM"?** Many things were not yet clear about the new faith. Just how did God expect the Gentile Christians to live? This question caused bad feeling against Paul, because some Jewish Christians thought he was too easy on the Gentiles. Some accused him of being a false apostle because he didn't make the Gentiles keep the Jewish customs. The letter from Jerusalem helped to calm the Jewish believers, but that was not the end of arguments in the church. Groups of Christians continue to make trouble about issues that aren't very important in God's eyes.

15.37 **CHRISTIANS SOMETIMES DISAGREE** You sometimes have to be tough-minded to be an effective Christian. We see this in the argument between Paul and Barnabas about John Mark. This young man was Barnabas' nephew, and he had left the apostles on their first trip. So Paul said "No" to John on the second trip. But later in life Paul praised John Mark as a useful young friend in the Lord (see 2 Timothy 4.11).

NOTES

Timothy Works with Paul and Silas

16 Paul and Silas went back to
Derbe and Lystra, where there
was a follower named Timothy. His
mother was also a follower. She was
Jewish, and his father was Greek.*
2The Lord's followers in Lystra and
Iconium said good things about
Timothy, 3and Paul wanted him to
go with them. But Paul first had him
circumcised, because all the Jewish
people around there knew that Timothy's father was Greek.[f]
4As Paul and the others went from
city to city, they told the followers
what the apostles and leaders in Jerusalem had decided, and they urged
them to follow these instructions.
5The churches became stronger in
their faith, and each day more people
put their faith in the Lord.

Paul's Vision in Troas

6Paul and his friends went through
Phrygia and Galatia, but the Holy
Spirit would not let them preach in
Asia.* 7After they arrived in Mysia,
they tried to go into Bithynia, but the
Spirit of Jesus would not let them.
8So they went on through Mysia until
they came to Troas.
9During the night, Paul had a vision
of someone from Macedonia who
was standing there and begging him,
"Come over to Macedonia and help
us!" 10After Paul had seen the vision,
we began looking for a way to go
to Macedonia. We were sure that God
had called us to preach the good news
there.*

Lydia Becomes a Follower of the Lord

11We sailed from Troas and went
straight to Samothrace. The next day
we arrived in Neapolis. 12From there
we went to Philippi, which is a Roman colony in the first district of
Macedonia.[g]
We spent several days in Philippi.
13Then on the Sabbath we went outside the city gate to a place by the
river, where we thought there would
be a Jewish meeting place for prayer.
We sat down and talked with the
women who came. 14One of them was
Lydia, who was from the city of Thyatira and sold expensive purple cloth.
She was a worshiper of the Lord God,
and he made her willing to accept
what Paul was saying.* 15Then after

---

[f] *had him circumcised . . . Timothy's father was Greek*: Timothy would not have been acceptable to the Jews unless he had been circumcised, and Greeks did not circumcise their sons. [g] *in the first district of Macedonia*: Some manuscripts have "and the leading city of Macedonia."

16.1 **A YOUNG HELPER TAKEN ON** We will hear more about this young man. Paul wrote two letters to him, 1 and 2 Timothy. Notice that Paul wasn't totally against the Jewish practice of circumcision. By granting circumcision to Timothy, Paul avoided a useless quarrel with the Jews, many of whom would have welcomed such an excuse to reject the message Paul was bringing.

16.6 **PAUL CALLED TO EUROPE** Up to this point, the good news had gone only as far west as Asia Minor (present-day Turkey). Paul's dream told him that God was about to send the good news further westward to Europe. So Paul set out for Macedonia in northern Greece.

16.10 **LUKE WAS AN EYEWITNESS** The last few chapters have been mostly about Paul, Barnabas, and then Silas. So far the author has used the "they" pronoun. Here the writer begins to use the word "we," which shows he had just joined the group. Luke, the author of Acts, accompanied Paul, Silas, and Timothy on their journey into Greece.

16.14 **A GREAT CHRISTIAN LADY** Lydia was a wealthy merchant. As a leader in her community she must have had great influence for the Christian faith. We are impressed by her kindness to the apostles. Kind hearts and kind deeds make the good news hard to resist.

NOTES

she and her family were baptized, she
kept on begging us, "If you think I
really do have faith in the Lord, come
stay in my home." Finally, we accepted her invitation.

Paul and Silas Are Put in Jail

16One day on our way to the place
of prayer, we were met by a slave
girl. She had a spirit in her that gave
her the power to tell the future. By
doing this she made a lot of money
for her owners. 17The girl followed
Paul and the rest of us and kept yelling, "These men are servants of the
Most High God! They are telling you
how to be saved."
18This went on for several days. Finally, Paul got so upset that he turned
and said to the spirit, "In the name
of Jesus Christ, I order you to leave
this girl alone!" At once the evil spirit
left her.*
19When the girl's owners realized
that they had lost all chances for
making more money, they grabbed
Paul and Silas and dragged them into
court. 20They told the officials,
"These Jews are upsetting our city!
21They are telling us to do things we
Romans are not allowed to do."
22The crowd joined in the attack
on Paul and Silas. Then the officials
tore the clothes off the two men and
ordered them to be beaten with a
whip. 23After they had been badly
beaten, they were put in jail, and the
jailer was told to guard them carefully.* 24The jailer did as he was told.
He put them deep inside the jail and
chained their feet to heavy blocks of
wood.
25About midnight Paul and Silas
were praying and singing praises to
God, while the other prisoners listened. 26Suddenly a strong earthquake shook the jail to its foundations. The doors opened, and the
chains fell from all the prisoners.*
27When the jailer woke up and saw
that the doors were open, he thought
that the prisoners had escaped. He
pulled out his sword and was about
to kill himself. 28But Paul shouted,
"Don't harm yourself! No one has
escaped."
29The jailer asked for a torch and
went into the jail. He was shaking
all over as he kneeled down in front
of Paul and Silas. 30After he had led
them out of the jail, he asked, "What
must I do to be saved?"
31They replied, "Have faith in the
Lord Jesus and you will be saved!
This is also true for everyone who
lives in your home."*
32Then Paul and Silas told him and

16.18 **EVIL TAKES MANY FORMS** Here was a young female slave who was inspired by Satan to say all the right things in the wrong way. She told everybody in a loud voice what the apostles were doing. But people were being scared off by this loud-mouthed young woman. So Paul drove out the evil spirit that was causing her behavior.

16.23 **SATAN NEVER GIVES UP** The slave girl was free, but this made Satan's servants angry at Paul and Silas. The men who owned her had made money from her fortune telling. Now they had lost their income from her. So they got even with the apostles by having them thrown in jail. Don't be surprised if everything seems to go wrong in your life just when you have done a great work for God.

16.26 **OUR BAD TIMES CAN BE GOD'S GOOD TIMES** God uses the hard times in our lives to make good things happen. Many people would have given up hope, but Paul and Silas were singing in jail. Then God acted, and they were free.

16.31 **A JAILER CAME TO CHRIST** This is one of the great missionary passages in the New Testament. "What must I do to be saved?" has its answer: "Have faith in the Lord Jesus." This is the answer to everyone who has been defeated in life. The jailer trusted in Jesus. Then he and his family were saved. There must have been quite a celebration at that jailer's home.

NOTES

everyone else in his house about the Lord. 33While it was still night, the jailer took them to a place where he could wash their cuts and bruises. Then he and everyone in his home were baptized. 34They were very glad that they had put their faith in God. After this, the jailer took Paul and Silas to his home and gave them something to eat.

35The next morning the officials sent some police with orders for the jailer to let Paul and Silas go. 36The jailer told Paul, "The officials have ordered me to set you free. Now you can leave in peace."

37But Paul told the police, "We are Roman citizens,[h] and the Roman officials had us beaten in public without giving us a trial. They threw us into jail. Now do they think they can secretly send us away? No, they cannot! They will have to come here themselves and let us out."

38When the police told the officials that Paul and Silas were Roman citizens, the officials were afraid. 39So they came and apologized. They led them out of the jail and asked them to please leave town. 40But Paul and Silas went straight to the home of Lydia, where they saw the Lord's followers and encouraged them. Then they left.

Trouble in Thessalonica

17 After Paul and his friends had traveled through Amphipolis and Apollonia, they went on to Thessalonica. A Jewish meeting place was in that city. 2So as usual, Paul went there to worship, and on three Sabbaths he spoke to the people. He used the Scriptures* 3to show them that the Messiah had to suffer, but that he would rise from death. Paul also told them that Jesus is the Messiah he was preaching about. 4Some of the Jews believed what Paul had said, and they became followers with Paul and Silas. Some Gentiles[i] and many important women also believed the message.

5The Jewish leaders were jealous and got some worthless bums who hung around the marketplace to start a riot in the city. They wanted to drag Paul and Silas out to the mob, and so they went straight to Jason's home. 6But when they did not find them there, they dragged out Jason and some of the Lord's followers. They took them to the city authorities and shouted, "Paul and Silas have been upsetting things everywhere. Now they have come here,* 7and Jason has welcomed them into his home. All of them break the laws of the Roman Emperor by claiming that someone named Jesus is king."

8The officials and all the people were upset when they heard this. 9So they made Jason and the other followers pay bail before they would let them go.

People in Berea Welcome the Message

10That same night the Lord's followers sent Paul and Silas on to

---

[h] *Roman citizens*: Only a small number of the people living in the Roman Empire were citizens, and they had special rights and privileges. [i] *Gentiles*: See the note at 14.1.

17.2 **MORE STRUGGLE** Others besides the local Jewish leaders were allowed to speak at meeting places on the Sabbath. So Paul was able to use the meeting places wherever he went, to preach the good news about the Messiah for whom the Jews had been waiting. But the authorities at Thessalonica were jealous of Paul's success, so they caused a riot. Then Paul and Silas were arrested again.

17.6 **DOES THE GOOD NEWS BRING PEACE?** We've heard it said that the good news about Jesus brings peace, and so the Bible says. But what about Paul and Silas? It seems that trouble followed them everywhere. We *do* have peace within, but Jesus said that the message about him would cause trouble with those who do not know him (see John 16.2, 3).

NOTES

Berea, and after they arrived, they
went to the Jewish meeting place.
11The people in Berea were much
nicer than those in Thessalonica, and
they gladly accepted the message.
Day after day they studied the Scriptures to see if these things were true.*
12Many of them put their faith in the
Lord, including some important
Greek women and several men.
13When the Jewish leaders in Thessalonica heard that Paul had been
preaching God's message in Berea,
they went there and caused trouble
by turning the crowds against Paul.
14Right away the followers sent
Paul down to the coast, but Silas and
Timothy stayed in Thessalonica.
15Some men went with Paul as far
as Athens. They returned with instructions for Silas and Timothy to
join him as soon as possible.

Paul in Athens

16While Paul was waiting in Athens, he was upset to see all the idols
in the city. 17He went to the Jewish
meeting place to speak to the Jews
and to anyone who worshiped with
them. Day after day he also spoke
to everyone he met in the market.
18Some of them were Epicureans[j]
and some were Stoics,[k] and they
started arguing with him.

People were asking, "What is this
know-it-all trying to say?"

Some even said, "Paul must be
preaching about foreign gods! That's
what he means when he talks about
Jesus and about people rising from
death."[l]

19They brought Paul before a council called the Areopagus, and said,
"Tell us what your new teaching is
all about. 20We have heard you say
some strange things, and we want
to know what it means."

21More than anything else the
people of Athens and the foreigners
living there loved to hear and to talk
about anything new.* 22So Paul stood
up in front of the council and said:

People of Athens, I see that
you are very religious. 23As I was
going through your city and
looking at the things you
worship, I found an altar with
the words, "To an Unknown
God." You worship this God, but
you don't really know him. So I
want to tell you about him.
24This God made the world and
everything in it. He is Lord of
heaven and earth, and he doesn't
live in temples built by human
hands. 25He doesn't need help
from anyone. He gives life,
breath, and everything else to all
people. 26From one person God
made all nations who live on
earth, and he decided when and
where every nation would be.
27God has done all this, so that
we will look for him and reach
out and find him. He is not far
from any of us, 28and he gives

---

[j]*Epicureans*: People who followed the teaching of a man named Epicurus, who taught that happiness should be the main goal in life. [k]*Stoics*: Followers of a man named Zeno, who taught that people should learn self-control and be guided by their consciences. [l]*people rising from death*: Or "a goddess named 'Rising from Death.'"

17.11 **SOMETIMES WE ARE ENCOURAGED** Paul and Silas were welcomed at Berea. The people at the Jewish meeting place were eager to hear and read about Jesus the Messiah. Then many put their trust in Christ. But once again there was trouble—the Jewish leaders followed the apostles to Berea and made life hard for them.

17.21 **"WISDOM" AT ATHENS** Athens was the cultural center of the world in Paul's day. Here the great leaders in human wisdom had taught for years—men like Socrates, Plato, and Aristotle. The people of Athens were very proud of their great thinkers. But the good news sounded like nonsense to most of the citizens. The idea of a risen Savior seemed impossible to them—as it does to many wise heads today.

NOTES

us the power to live, to move,
and to be who we are. "We are
his children," just as some of
your poets have said.*
29Since we are God's children,
we must not think that he is like
an idol made out of gold or silver
or stone. He is not like anything
that humans have thought up
and made. 30In the past God
forgave all this because people
did not know what they were
doing. But now he says that
everyone everywhere must turn
to him. 31He has set a day when
he will judge all the world's
people with fairness. And he has
chosen the man Jesus to do the
judging for him. God has given
proof of this to all of us by raising
Jesus from death.
32As soon as the people heard Paul
say that a man had been raised from
death, some of them started laughing. Others said, "We'll hear you talk
about this some other time." 33When
Paul left the council meeting, 34some
of the men put their faith in the Lord
and went with Paul. One of them was
a council member named Dionysius.
A woman named Damaris and several others also put their faith in the
Lord.

Paul in Corinth

18 Paul left Athens and went to
Corinth,* 2where he met
Aquila, a Jewish man from Pontus.
Not long before this, Aquila had
come from Italy with his wife Priscilla, because Emperor Claudius had
ordered all the Jewish people to leave
Rome.[m] Paul went to see Aquila and
Priscilla 3and found out that they
were tent makers. Paul was a tent
maker too. So he stayed with them,
and they worked together.
4Every Sabbath Paul went to the
Jewish meeting place. He spoke to
Jews and Gentiles[n] and tried to win
them over. 5But after Silas and Timothy came from Macedonia, he spent
all his time preaching to the Jews
about Jesus the Messiah. 6Finally,
they turned against him and insulted
him. So he shook the dust from his
clothes[o] and told them, "Whatever
happens to you will be your own
fault! I am not to blame. From now
on I am going to preach to the
Gentiles."
7Paul then moved into the house
of a man named Titius Justus, who
worshiped God and lived next door
to the Jewish meeting place. 8Crispus
was the leader of the meeting place.
He and everyone in his family put
their faith in the Lord. Many others
in Corinth also heard the message,
and all the people who had faith in
the Lord were baptized.
9One night Paul had a vision, and
in it the Lord said, "Don't be afraid

---

[m]*Emperor Claudius had ordered all the Jewish people to leave Rome*: Probably A.D. 49, though it may have been A.D. 41. [n]*Gentiles*: Here the word is "Greeks." But see the note at 14.1. [o]*shook the dust from his clothes*: This means the same as shaking dust from the feet. See the note at 13.51.

17.28 **PAUL'S LEARNING** Paul had been more than just a Jewish teacher who knew only the Scriptures, as good as that would have been. He had grown up in Tarsus of Cilicia, second only to Athens for its learning. A great university and brilliant teachers were there. So Paul knew the wisdom of the Greeks, and he was able to speak to them about their beliefs. But most Athenians were not interested in Paul's message. They were satisfied with themselves.

18.1 **CORINTH NEEDED THE NEWS** Corinth was an important city near the southern tip of Greece. Paul spent about eighteen months there preaching and setting up a Christian church. He had more success in Corinth than at Athens, even though Corinth was a very immoral city. But the most undesirable people in the world are often the people God is seeking. Corinth is where Paul met Aquila and Priscilla, a couple who helped him very much in his ministry.

NOTES

to keep on preaching. Don't stop!*
10I am with you, and you won't be
harmed. Many people in this city belong to me." 11Paul stayed on in
Corinth for a year and a half, teaching God's message to the people.

12While Gallio was governor of
Achaia, some of the Jewish leaders got together and grabbed Paul. They brought him into court 13and said,
"This man is trying to make our people worship God in a way that is against our Law!"

14Even before Paul could speak,
Gallio said, "If you were charging this man with a crime or some other wrong, I would have to listen to you.
15But since this concerns only words, names, and your own law, you will have to take care of it. I refuse to judge such matters." 16Then he sent
them all out of the court. 17The crowd
grabbed Sosthenes, the Jewish leader, and beat him up in front of the court. But none of this mattered to Gallio.

Paul Returns to Antioch in Syria

18After Paul had stayed for a while
with the Lord's followers in Corinth, he told them good-by and sailed on to Syria with Aquila and Priscilla. But before he left, he had his head shaved[p] at Cenchreae because he had made a promise to God.*
19The three of them arrived in
Ephesus, where Paul left Priscilla and Aquila. He then went into the Jewish meeting place to talk with the people there. 20They asked him to
stay longer, but he refused. 21He told
them good-by and said, "If God lets me, I will come back."

22Paul sailed to Caesarea, where
he greeted the church. Then he went on to Antioch. 23After staying there
for a while, he left and visited several places in Galatia and Phrygia. He helped all the followers there to become stronger in their faith.*

Apollos in Ephesus

24A Jewish man named Apollos
came to Ephesus. Apollos had been born in the city of Alexandria. He was a very good speaker and knew a lot about the Scriptures. 25He also
knew much about the Lord's Way,[q] and he spoke about it with great excitement. What he taught about Jesus was right, but all he knew was John's message about baptism.

26Apollos started speaking bravely
in the Jewish meeting place. But when Priscilla and Aquila heard him, they took him to their home and

[p] *he had his head shaved*: Paul had promised to be a "Nazarite" for a while. This meant that for the time of the promise, he could not cut his hair or drink wine. When the time was over, he would have to cut his hair and offer a sacrifice to God.
[q] *the Lord's Way*: See the note at 9.2.

18.9 **THE LORD PROTECTS US** Just as elsewhere, the Jewish leaders at Corinth rejected the good news about Christ. So Paul began preaching to the Gentiles. But surprisingly, Justus and the leader of the Jewish meeting place accepted Paul's message. Then, however, some of the community's leading Jews had Paul arrested. But see how God caused the Roman governor to let Paul go. The Lord is in charge of our lives, and harm cannot come to us without his permission.

18.18 **THE END OF PAUL'S SECOND MISSION** This is the second time Paul had gone out from Antioch in Syria, the Christian headquarters, to preach the good news to the Gentiles of the Western world. On this second trip Paul had gone beyond Asia Minor to Macedonia and Greece. He returned to Antioch by way of Ephesus.

18.23 **THE BEGINNING OF PAUL'S THIRD JOURNEY** This was Paul's last real missionary trip. He went back to Asia Minor and there visited the Roman provinces of Galatia and Phrygia. He had been there before and had started new churches. Now Paul was encouraging these young churches. He cared deeply about the people he had led to faith in Jesus.

NOTES

helped him understand God's Way
even better.*
27 Apollos decided to travel through
Achaia. So the Lord's followers
wrote letters and encouraged the followers there to welcome him. After
Apollos arrived in Achaia, he was a
great help to everyone who had put
their faith in the Lord Jesus because
of God's kindness. 28 He got into
fierce arguments with the Jewish
people, and in public he used the
Scriptures to prove that Jesus is the
Messiah.

Paul in Ephesus

19 While Apollos was in Corinth,
Paul traveled across the hill
country to Ephesus, where he met
some of the Lord's followers.*
2 He asked them, "When you put your
faith in Jesus, were you given the
Holy Spirit?"
"No!" they answered. "We have
never even heard of the Holy Spirit."
3 "Then why were you baptized?"
Paul asked.
They answered, "Because of what
John taught."[r]
4 Paul replied, "John baptized people so that they would turn to God.
But he also told them that someone
else was coming, and that they
should put their faith in him. Jesus
is the one that John was talking
about." 5 After the people heard Paul
say this, they were baptized in the
name of the Lord Jesus. 6 Then Paul
placed his hands on them. The Holy
Spirit was given to them, and they
spoke unknown languages and
prophesied. 7 There were about
twelve men in this group.
8 For three months Paul went to the
Jewish meeting place and talked
bravely with the Jewish people about
God's kingdom. He tried to win them
over, 9 but some of them were stubborn and refused to believe. In front
of everyone they said terrible things
about God's Way. Paul left and took
the followers with him to the lecture
hall of Tyrannus. He spoke there every day 10 for two years, until every
Jew and Gentile[s] in Asia had heard
the Lord's message.

The Sons of Sceva

11 God gave Paul the power to work
great miracles. 12 People even took
handkerchiefs and aprons that had
touched Paul's body, and they carried them to everyone who was sick.
All of the sick people were healed,
and the evil spirits went out.
13 Some Jewish men started going
around trying to force out evil spirits
by using the name of the Lord Jesus.
They said to the spirits, "Come out
in the name of that same Jesus that
Paul preaches about!"*
14 Seven sons of a Jewish high

---

[r] *Then why were you baptized? . . . Because of what John taught*: Or "In whose name were you baptized? . . . We were baptized in John's name."
[s] *Gentile(s)*: The text has "Greek(s)" (see the note at 14.1).

18.26 **WE HAVE TO GROW UP IN OUR CHRISTIAN FAITH** Apollos seems to have been a bright young man. But he had a lot to learn. He can be thankful that Paul's friends, Priscilla and Aquila, were on hand to help Apollos understand the full meaning of the good news. We are all on our way to God's eternal city, and we need one another's help along the road. Like Apollos, let's be good learners as we go.

19.1 **EPHESUS REACHED FOR CHRIST** Ephesus was an important Roman city on the western coast of Asia Minor. There again Paul was opposed by many of the Jews. But he stayed in Ephesus for about three years, preaching and teaching. To really reach people for Jesus, the church should be a place where Christians are taught the word of God in detail.

19.13 **FAKES REALLY EXIST** Loving everybody doesn't mean accepting everybody's teaching. We have to know the difference between truth and falsehood. There are people who go *(continued)*

NOTES

priest named Sceva were doing this,
15when an evil spirit said to them,
"I know Jesus! And I have heard
about Paul. But who are you?"
16Then the man with the evil spirit
jumped on them and beat them up.
They ran out of the house, naked and
bruised.
17All the Jews and Gentiles[s] in
Ephesus heard about this. They were
so frightened that they praised the
name of the Lord Jesus. 18Many who
were followers now started telling
everyone about the evil things they
had been doing. 19Some who had
been practicing witchcraft even
brought their books and burned them
in public. These books were worth
about fifty thousand silver coins.
20So the Lord's message spread and
became even more powerful.

The Riot in Ephesus

21After all of this had happened,
Paul decided[t] to visit Macedonia and
Achaia on his way to Jerusalem. Paul
had said, "From there I will go on
to Rome." 22So he sent his two helpers, Timothy and Erastus, to Macedonia. But he stayed on in Asia for a
while.
23At that time there was serious
trouble because of the Lord's Way.[u]*
24A silversmith named Demetrius
had a business that made silver models of the temple of the goddess Artemis. Those who worked for him
earned a lot of money. 25Demetrius
brought together everyone who was
in the same business and said:

Friends, you know that we
make a good living at this. 26But
you have surely seen and heard
how this man Paul is upsetting
a lot of people, not only in
Ephesus, but almost everywhere
in Asia. He claims that the gods
we humans make are not really
gods at all. 27Everyone will start
saying terrible things about our
business. They will stop
respecting the temple of the
goddess Artemis, who is
worshiped in Asia and all over
the world. Our great goddess will
be forgotten!

28When the workers heard this,
they got angry and started shouting,
"Great is Artemis, the goddess of the
Ephesians!" 29Soon the whole city
was in a riot, and some men grabbed
Gaius and Aristarchus, who had
come from Macedonia with Paul.
Then everyone in the crowd rushed
to the place where the town meetings
were held.
30Paul wanted to go out and speak
to the people, but the Lord's followers
would not let him. 31A few of the local
officials were friendly to Paul, and
they sent someone to warn him not
to go.
32Some of the people in the meeting
were shouting one thing, and others
were shouting something else. Everyone was completely confused,
and most of them did not even know
why they were there.
33Several of the Jewish leaders
pushed a man named Alexander to
the front of the crowd and started
telling him what to say. He motioned
with his hand and tried to explain
what was going on. 34But when the
crowd saw that he was Jewish, they
all shouted for two hours, "Great is

---

[s] *Gentile(s)*: The text has "Greek(s)" (see the note at 14.1). [t] *Paul decided*: Or "Paul was led by the Holy Spirit." [u] *the Lord's Way*: See the note at 9.2.

(*continued*) around offering themselves as messengers of truth, but like the sons of Sceva they are really out for personal power. False teachers are often showy and self-important. Many times just common sense will track down a fake. And the Bible is always the test of truth.

19.23 **A RIOT ABOUT IDOLS** Many Ephesians worshiped a statue named Artemis, which people claimed fell from heaven. Paul's message about the one true God hurt the business of metalworkers who made idols, so they started a riot. Paul's message was brave, clear, and direct. It left no doubt that the idol dealers were not in keeping with God's truth.

NOTES

Artemis, the goddess of the Ephesians!"
35Finally, a town official made the
crowd be quiet. Then he said:

People of Ephesus, who in the
world does not know that our
city is the center for worshiping
the great goddess Artemis? Who
does not know that her image
which fell from heaven is right
here?* 36No one can deny this,
and so you should calm down
and not do anything foolish.
37You have brought men in here
who have not robbed temples or
spoken against our goddess.

38If Demetrius and his workers
have a case against these men,
we have courts and judges. Let
them take their complaints
there. 39But if you want to do
more than that, the matter will
have to be brought before the
city council. 40We could easily
be accused of starting a riot
today. There is no excuse for it!
We cannot even give a reason
for this uproar.

41After saying this, he told the people to leave.

Paul Goes Through Macedonia and Greece

20 When the riot was over, Paul
sent for the followers and encouraged them. He then told them
good-by and left for Macedonia.
2As he traveled from place to place,
he encouraged the followers with
many messages. Finally, he went to
Greece[v] 3and stayed there for three
months.

Paul was about to sail to Syria. But
some of the Jewish leaders plotted
against him, so he decided to return
by way of Macedonia. 4With him
were Sopater, son of Pyrrhus from
Berea, and Aristarchus and Secun-
dus from Thessalonica. Gaius from
Derbe was also with him, and so were
Timothy and the two Asians, Tychicus and Trophimus. 5They went on
ahead to Troas and waited for us
there. 6After the Feast of Thin Bread,
we sailed from Philippi. Five days
later we met them in Troas and
stayed there for a week.*

Paul's Last Visit to Troas

7On the first day of the week[w] we
met to worship and to break bread
together.[x] Paul spoke to the people
until midnight because he was leaving the next morning. 8In the upstairs
room where we were meeting, there
were a lot of lamps. 9A young man
by the name of Eutychus was sitting
on a window sill. While Paul was
speaking, the young man got very
sleepy. Finally, he went to sleep and
fell three floors all the way down to
the ground. When they picked him
up, he was dead.*

---

[v]*Greece*: Probably Corinth. [w]*On the first day of the week*: Since the Jewish day began at sunset, the meeting would have begun in the evening. [x]*break bread together*: See the note at 2.42.

19.35 **THE TRUTH WINS IN THE END** There is still a lot of common sense in the world, and the town official had lots of it. We don't know what his personal faith was, but he had the ability to see right and wrong, and he soon cooled the rioters down. God has people everywhere who will not let lies go unchecked. Let's be thankful for all kinds of helpers along the way.

20.6 **THE FEAST OF THIN BREAD** About 3,500 years ago, God led the ancient Jews out of slavery in Egypt. This was called "the Passover," which was celebrated in the early spring. The "feast of thin bread" was celebrated for seven days after Passover started. "Thin bread" means bread that is not mixed with leaven, or yeast, to make the bread rise. This feast was the way the Jews remembered that they had no time to wait for bread to rise when they were escaping from Egypt.

20.9 **STAY AWAKE** Eutychus (pronounced YOU-ti-kus) must not have been very excited by Paul's preaching. Paul himself said he was not a great speaker. Let's be attentive to God's *(continued)*

NOTES

10Paul went down and bent over Eutychus. He took him in his arms and said, "Don't worry! He's alive."
11After Paul had gone back upstairs, he broke bread, and ate with us. He then spoke until dawn and left.
12Then the followers took the young man home alive and were very happy.

The Voyage from Troas to Miletus

13Paul decided to travel by land to Assos. The rest of us went on ahead by ship, and we were to take him aboard there.
14When he met us in Assos, he came aboard, and we sailed on to Mitylene.
15The next day we came to a place near Chios, and the following day we reached Samos. The day after that we sailed to Miletus.*
16Paul had decided to sail on past Ephesus, because he did not want to spend too much time in Asia. He was in a hurry and wanted to be in Jerusalem in time for Pentecost.[y]

Paul Says Good-by to the Church Leaders of Ephesus

17From Miletus Paul sent a message for the church leaders at Ephesus to come and meet with him.
18When they got there, he said:

You know everything I did during the time I was with you when I first came to Asia.
19Some of the Jews plotted against me and caused me a lot of sorrow and trouble. But I served the Lord and was humble.
20When I preached in public or taught in your homes, I didn't hold back from telling anything that would help you.
21I told Jews and Gentiles to turn to God and have faith in our Lord Jesus.

22I don't know what will happen to me in Jerusalem, but I must obey God's Spirit and go there.
23In every city that I visit, the Holy Spirit tells me I will be put in jail and will be in trouble in Jerusalem.
24But I don't care what happens to me, as long as I finish the work that the Lord Jesus gave me to do. And that work is to tell the good news about God's great kindness.*

25I have gone from place to place, preaching to you about God's kingdom, but now I know that none of you will ever see me again.
26I tell you today that I am no longer responsible for any of you!
27I have told you everything that God wants you to know.
28Look after yourselves and everyone the Holy Spirit has placed in your care. Be like shepherds to God's church. It is the flock that he bought with the blood of his own Son.[z]

29I know that after I am gone, others will come like fierce wolves to attack you.
30Some of your own people will tell lies to win over the Lord's followers.
31Be on your guard! Remember how day and night for three years I kept warning you with tears in my eyes.

---

[y] *in time for Pentecost*: The Jewish people liked to be in Jerusalem for this festival. See the note at 2.1.
[z] *the blood of his own Son*: Or "his own blood."

(*continued*) word at all times, even if we have to force ourselves to stay awake. Preachers may not always be fascinating, but the truth is always important.

20.15 **BEING A CHRISTIAN IS WORK** Christians don't just sit around reading the Bible and praying, as necessary as these activities are. There is also work to do for God, and sometimes the work is hard. Paul's travels were hard work, but it was worth it in order to get the good news about Jesus to people.

20.24 **A CHRISTIAN UNDERSTANDS THE REAL WORLD** Paul didn't kid himself. He knew that the world was against his message. But he was prepared to obey God because he also knew the good news would win in the long run. Christians must look beyond the present to the future—and the goal of helping people to know Jesus as Savior.

NOTES

32 I now place you in God's
care. Remember the message
about his great kindness! This
message can help you and give
you what belongs to you as
God's people. 33 I have never
wanted anyone's money or
clothes. 34 You know how I have
worked with my own hands to
make a living for myself and my
friends.* 35 By everything I did,
I showed how you should work
to help everyone who is weak.
Remember that our Lord Jesus
said, "More blessings come from
giving than from receiving."
36 After Paul had finished speaking,
he kneeled down with all of them and
prayed. 37 Everyone cried and hugged
and kissed him. 38 They were especially sad because Paul had told
them, "You will never see me again."
Then they went with him to the
ship.

Paul Goes to Jerusalem

21 After saying good-by, we
sailed straight to Cos. The next
day we reached Rhodes and from
there sailed on to Patara. 2 We found
a ship going to Phoenicia, so we got
on board and sailed off.
3 We came within sight of Cyprus
and then sailed south of it on to the
port of Tyre in Syria. The ship was
going to unload its cargo there.
4 We looked up the Lord's followers
and stayed with them for a week. The
Holy Spirit had told them to warn
Paul not to go on to Jerusalem.
5 But when the week was over, we
started on our way again. All the
men, together with their wives and
children, walked with us from the
town to the seashore. We kneeled on
the beach and prayed.* 6 Then after
saying good-by to each other, we got
into the ship, and they went back
home.
7 We sailed from Tyre to Ptolemais,
where we greeted the followers and
stayed with them for a day. 8 The next
day we went to Caesarea and stayed
with Philip, the preacher. He was one
of the seven men who helped the
apostles, 9 and he had four unmarried[a] daughters who prophesied.
10 We had been in Caesarea for several days, when the prophet Agabus
came to us from Judea. 11 He took
Paul's belt, and with it he tied up his
own hands and feet. Then he told us,
"The Holy Spirit says that some of
the Jewish leaders in Jerusalem will
tie up the man who owns this belt.
They will also hand him over to the
Gentiles." 12 After Agabus said this,
we and the followers living there
begged Paul not to go to Jerusalem.
13 But Paul answered, "Why are
you crying and breaking my heart?
I am not only willing to be put in
jail for the Lord Jesus. I am even willing to die for him in Jerusalem!"*

[a] *unmarried*: Or "virgin."

20.34 **CHRISTIANS ARE NOT FREELOADERS** A freeloader is able to work, but lives by the work of others. Paul was willing to work with his own hands to make a living. Whatever your calling may be in the world, be sure you aren't just loafing. Be sure you are producing something that will give glory to God and be of real benefit to mankind.

21.5 **A CHRISTIAN LIVES IN HOPE** We might wonder what kept Paul going. He couldn't see, as we do, the centuries ahead when his work would have such great results. But he lived and worked in the confidence that God's way must win at last. As we trust God to help us, we also have Paul's confidence that our work for God will not be useless.

21.13 **WAS PAUL A FANATIC?** Paul was willing to die for Christ—and eventually he did. The term "fanatic" is usually a way of describing an overexcited or overzealous person. So we ask the question, was Paul an overzealous fanatic? No. The difference here is that Christ is truly worth dying for.

NOTES

14Since we could not get Paul to
change his mind, we gave up and
said, "Lord, please make us willing
to do what you want."
15Then we got ready to go to Jerusalem. 16Some of the followers from
Caesarea went with us and took us
to stay in the home of Mnason. He
was from Cyprus and had been a follower from the beginning.

Paul Visits James

17When we arrived in Jerusalem,
the Lord's followers gladly welcomed us. 18Paul went with us to see
James[b] the next day, and all the
church leaders were present.*
19Paul greeted them and told how
God had used him to help the Gentiles. 20Everyone who heard this
praised God and said to Paul:

> My friend, you can see how
> many tens of thousands of the
> Jewish people have become
> followers! And all of them are
> eager to obey the Law of Moses.
> 21But they have been told that
> you are teaching those who live
> among the Gentiles to disobey
> this Law. They claim that you
> are telling them not to
> circumcise their sons or to follow
> Jewish customs.
> 22What should we do now that
> our people have heard that you
> are here? 23Please do what we
> ask, because four of our men
> have made special promises to
> God. 24Join with them and
> prepare yourself for the
> ceremony that goes with the
> promises. Pay the cost for their
> heads to be shaved. Then
> everyone will learn that the
> reports about you are not true.
> They will know that you do obey
> the Law of Moses.
> 25Some while ago we told the
> Gentile followers what we think
> they should do. We instructed
> them not to eat anything offered
> to idols. They were told not to
> eat any meat with blood still in
> it or the meat of an animal that
> has been strangled. They were
> also told not to commit any
> terrible sexual sins.[c]

26The next day Paul took the four
men with him and got himself ready
at the same time they did. Then he
went into the temple and told when
the final ceremony would take place
and when an offering would be made
for each of them.

Paul Is Arrested

27When the period of seven days
for the ceremony was almost over,
some of the Jewish people from Asia
saw Paul in the temple. They got a
large crowd together and started attacking him. 28They were shouting,
"Friends, help us! This man goes
around everywhere, saying bad
things about our nation and about
the Law of Moses and about this temple. He has even brought shame to
this holy temple by bringing in Gentiles." 29Some of them thought that
Paul had brought Trophimus from
Ephesus into the temple, because
they had seen them together in the
city.
30The whole city was in an uproar,
and the people turned into a mob.
They grabbed Paul and dragged him
out of the temple. Then suddenly the
doors were shut.* 31The people were

[b] *James*: The Lord's brother. [c] *not to commit any terrible sexual sins*: See the note at 15.20.

21.18 **JAMES** We see that Paul visited "James" in Jerusalem. We saw this James earlier in Acts 15, when he made a speech stating the decision of the council at Jerusalem. This James was a leader of the Jerusalem church. He was also a younger brother of Jesus. James came to believe in Jesus after his brother rose from death. (This is not the James written about in Acts 12.2, who was the brother of John the apostle.)

21.30 **DON'T LET YOUR FAITH BECOME BIGOTRY** The Jews at Jerusalem had a great heritage. God had given them great promises. But they turned bitter because Jewish Christians had (*continued*)

NOTES

about to kill Paul when the Roman army commander heard that all Jerusalem was starting to riot. 32So he quickly took some soldiers and officers and ran to where the crowd had gathered.

As soon as the mob saw the commander and soldiers, they stopped beating Paul. 33The army commander went over and arrested him and had him bound with two chains. Then he tried to find out who Paul was and what he had done. 34Part of the crowd shouted one thing, and part of them shouted something else. But they were making so much noise that the commander could not find out a thing. Then he ordered Paul to be taken into the fortress.* 35As they reached the steps, the crowd became so wild that the soldiers had to lift Paul up and carry him. 36The crowd followed and kept shouting, "Kill him! Kill him!"

Paul Speaks to the Crowd

37When Paul was about to be taken into the fortress, he asked the commander, "Can I say something to you?"

"How do you know Greek?" the commander asked. 38"Aren't you that Egyptian who started a riot not long ago and led four thousand terrorists into the desert?"

39"No!" Paul replied. "I am a Jew from Tarsus, an important city in Cilicia. Please let me speak to the crowd."

40The commander told him he could speak, so Paul stood on the steps and motioned to the people. When they were quiet, he spoke to them in Aramaic:

22 "My friends and leaders of our nation, listen as I explain what happened!" 2When the crowd heard Paul speak to them in Aramaic, they became even quieter. Then Paul said:

3I am a Jew, born and raised in the city of Tarsus in Cilicia. I was a student of Gamaliel and was taught to follow every single law of our ancestors. In fact, I was just as eager to obey God as any of you are today.*

4I made trouble for everyone who followed the Lord's Way,[d] and I even had some of them killed. I had others arrested and put in jail. I didn't care if they were men or women. 5The high priest and all the council members can tell you that this is true. They even gave me letters to the Jewish leaders in Damascus, so that I could arrest people there and bring them to Jerusalem to be punished.

6One day about noon I was getting close to Damascus, when a bright light from heaven suddenly flashed around. 7I fell to the ground and heard a voice asking me, "Saul, Saul, why are you so cruel to me?"

---

[d]*followed the Lord's Way*: See the note at 9.2.

(*continued*) been associating with Gentiles. Many Jews wanted to put a stop to this and have Paul killed. It was an act of bigotry—wanting to harm someone for religious reasons. We ought to learn from this ugly scene and avoid bigotry in our own hearts.

21.34 **THANK GOD FOR GOOD GOVERNMENT** No human government is perfect, but God expects us to obey the just laws of our government. If it had not been for the Roman commander, the Jews would have murdered Paul. It's pretty sad that a pagan government was more merciful than God's chosen people were at that time.

22.3 **DO YOU HAVE A STORY TO TELL?** Christians should be ready to tell others about how they came to Christ. Not all of us will have a dramatic message like Paul's, but it will be a good story if it's real. Maybe you found Christ as a child at home—or maybe in a prison—but it's always a great story regardless.

NOTES

[8]"Who are you?" I answered.
The Lord replied, "I am Jesus
from Nazareth! I am the one you
are so cruel to." [9]The men who
were traveling with me saw the
light, but did not hear the voice.
[10]I asked, "Lord, what do you
want me to do?"

Then he told me, "Get up and
go to Damascus. When you get
there, you will be told what to
do." [11]The light had been so
bright that I couldn't see. And
the other men had to lead me
by the hand to Damascus.
[12]In that city there was a man
named Ananias, who faithfully
obeyed the Law of Moses and
was well liked by all the Jewish
people living there. [13]He came
to me and said, "Saul, my friend,
you can now see again!"

At once I could see. [14]Then
Ananias told me, "The God that
our ancestors worshiped has
chosen you to know what he
wants done. He has chosen you
to see the One Who Obeys God[e]
and to hear his voice. [15]You must
tell everyone what you have seen
and heard. [16]What are you
waiting for? Get up! Be baptized,
and wash away your sins by
praying to the Lord."
[17]After this I returned to
Jerusalem and went to the
temple to pray. There I had a
vision [18]of the Lord who said to
me, "Hurry and leave Jerusalem!
The people will not listen to what
you say about me."
[19]I replied, "Lord, they know
that in many of our meeting
places I arrested and beat people
who had faith in you. [20]Stephen
was killed because he spoke for
you, and I stood there and
cheered them on. I even guarded
the clothes of the men who
murdered him."
[21]But the Lord told me to go,
and he promised to send me far
away to the Gentiles.
[22]The crowd listened until Paul
said this. Then they started shouting,
"Get rid of this man! He doesn't deserve to live."* [23]They kept shouting.
They waved their clothes around and
threw dust into the air.

Paul and the Roman Army Commander

[24]The Roman commander ordered
Paul to be taken into the fortress and
beaten with a whip. He did this to
find out why the people were screaming at Paul.
[25]While the soldiers were tying
Paul up to be beaten, he asked the
officer standing there, "Is it legal to
beat a Roman citizen before he has
been tried in court?"
[26]When the officer heard this, he
went to the commander and said,
"What are you doing? This man is
a Roman citizen!"
[27]The commander went to Paul and
asked, "Tell me, are you a Roman
citizen?"

"Yes," Paul answered.
[28]The commander then said, "I
paid a lot of money to become a Roman citizen."[f]

But Paul replied, "I was born a Roman citizen."
[29]The men who were about to beat
and question Paul quickly backed off.
And the commander himself was
frightened when he realized that he
had put a Roman citizen in chains.

Paul Is Tried by the Council

[30]The next day the commander
wanted to know the real reason why

---

[e]*One Who Obeys God*: That is, Jesus. [f]*Roman citizen*: See the note at 16.37.

22.22 **PAUL "HIT A NERVE"** The crowd was willing to listen to Paul's detailed story of how he came to know the Lord Jesus—until Paul "hit a nerve" by mentioning that he would take the good news to the Gentiles too. The Jerusalem crowd would not believe that God's blessings could go outside of Israel. Sadly, even today people still have such wrong attitudes about race, language, or place of birth.

NOTES

the Jewish leaders had brought
charges against Paul. So he had
Paul's chains removed, and he ordered the chief priests and the whole
council to meet. Then he had Paul
led in and made him stand in front
of them.

23 Paul looked straight at the
council members and said,
"My friends, to this day I have served
God with a clear conscience!"*
2Then Ananias the high priest ordered the men standing beside Paul
to hit him on the mouth. 3Paul turned
to the high priest and said, "You
whitewashed wall![g] God will hit you.
You sit there to judge me by the Law
of Moses. But at the same time you
order men to break the Law by hit-
ting me."
4The men standing beside Paul
asked, "Don't you know you are insulting God's high priest?"
5Paul replied, "Oh! I didn't know
he was the high priest. The Scriptures
do tell us not to speak evil about a
leader of our people."
6When Paul saw that some of the
council members were Sadducees
and others were Pharisees, he
shouted, "My friends, I am a Pharisee
and the son of a Pharisee. I am on
trial simply because I believe that the
dead will be raised to life."
7As soon as Paul said this, the Pharisees and the Sadducees got into a
big argument, and the council members started taking sides. 8The Sadducees do not believe in angels or
spirits or that the dead will rise to
life. But the Pharisees believe in all
of these, 9and so there was a lot of
shouting. Some of the teachers of the
Law of Moses were Pharisees. Finally, they became angry and said,
"We don't find anything wrong with
this man. Maybe a spirit or an angel
really did speak to him."
10The argument became fierce, and
the commander was afraid that Paul
would be pulled apart. So he ordered
the soldiers to go in and rescue Paul.
Then they took him back into the
fortress.
11That night the Lord stood beside
Paul and said, "Don't worry! Just as
you have told others about me in Jerusalem, you must also tell about me
in Rome."*

A Plot to Kill Paul

12-13The next morning more than
forty Jewish men got together and
vowed that they would not eat or
drink anything until they had killed
Paul. 14Then some of them went to
the chief priests and the nation's
leaders and said, "We have promised
God that we would not eat a thing
until we have killed Paul. 15You and
everyone in the council must go to
the commander and pretend that you
want to find out more about the
charges against Paul. Ask for him to
be brought before your court. Meanwhile, we will be waiting to kill him
before he gets there."
16When Paul's nephew heard
about the plot, he went to the fortress
and told Paul about it. 17So Paul said
to one of the army officers, "Take
this young man to the commander.
He has something to tell him."
18The officer took the young man
to the commander and said, "The

[g]*whitewashed wall*: Someone who pretends to be good, but really isn't.

23.1 **IT PAYS TO BE WISE** Paul finally had to stand before the council. Quickly he turned the tables by showing that it was the high priest who was the lawbreaker. Then he got the Pharisees and Sadducees into an argument between themselves. So the Roman commander had to take Paul safely away from danger. Paul had used his wits very well, and we should too.

23.11 **GOD IS NEAR US IN TROUBLE** After the uproar between the Pharisees and Sadducees, the Lord visited Paul and promised to be with him. In the darkest night of your trouble God will comfort you, too. The Lord is not a faraway God, but a God who is always near, a God who makes himself known to us when we need him.

NOTES

prisoner named Paul asked me to bring this young man to you, because he has something to tell you."

19The commander took the young man aside and asked him in private, "What do you want to tell me?"

20He answered, "Some men are planning to ask you to bring Paul down to the Jewish council tomorrow. They will claim that they want to find out more about him. 21But please don't do what they say. More than forty men are going to attack Paul. They have made a vow not to eat or drink anything until they have killed him. Even now they are waiting to hear what you decide."

22The commander sent the young man away after saying to him, "Don't let anyone know that you told me this."

Paul Is Sent to Felix the Governor

23The commander called in two of his officers and told them, "By nine o'clock tonight have two hundred soldiers ready to go to Caesarea. Take along seventy men on horseback and two hundred foot soldiers with spears.* 24Get a horse ready for Paul and make sure that he gets safely through to Felix the governor."

25The commander wrote a letter that said:

> 26Greetings from Claudius Lysias to the Honorable Governor Felix:
>
> 27Some Jews grabbed this man and were about to kill him. But when I found out that he was a Roman citizen, I took some soldiers and rescued him.* 28I wanted to find out what they had against him. So I brought him before their council 29and learned that the charges concern only their Jewish laws. This man is not guilty of anything for which he should die or even be put in jail.
>
> 30As soon as I learned that there was a plot against him, I sent him to you and told their leaders to bring charges against him in your court.

31The soldiers obeyed the commander's orders, and that same night they took Paul to the city of Antipatris. 32The next day the foot soldiers returned to the fortress and let the soldiers on horseback take him the rest of the way. 33When they came to Caesarea, they gave the letter to the governor and handed Paul over to him.

34The governor read the letter. Then he asked Paul and found out that he was from Cilicia. 35The governor said, "I will listen to your case as soon as the people come to bring their charges against you." After saying this, he gave orders for Paul to be kept as a prisoner in Herod's palace.[h]

Paul Is Accused in the Court of Felix

24 Five days later Ananias the high priest, together with the Jewish leaders and a lawyer named Tertullus, went to the governor to present their case against Paul.

---

[h] *Herod's palace*: The palace built by Herod the Great and used by the Roman governors of Palestine.

23.23 **A CONTINUING STRUGGLE** The Jews were not satisfied that Paul was arrested, but they wanted to murder him. So they plotted against him. Once again, God had a way to save Paul from his enemies. Even the Romans seemed to be sympathetic to Paul. So the commander sent Paul to the governor's city under heavy guard.

23.27 **USE THE TOOLS YOU HAVE** Paul was not wealthy, and he didn't have a lot of friends in the Roman world. Many people wanted him dead. But Paul was a Roman citizen. It's almost funny at times how Paul was able to use his rights as a citizen to escape harm. Eventually he even got a free sea trip to Rome. Don't be afraid to use every good tool you have to get God's work done.

NOTES

2So Paul was called in, and Tertullus
stated the case against him:[i]

Honorable Felix, you have
brought our people a long period
of peace, and because of your
concern our nation is much
better off. 3All of us are always
grateful for what you have done.
4I don't want to bother you, but
please be patient with us and
listen to me for just a few
minutes.

5This man has been found to
be a real pest and troublemaker
for Jews all over the world. He
is also a leader of a group called
Nazarenes.* 6-8When he tried to
disgrace the temple, we arrested
him.[j] If you question him, you
will find out for yourself that all
our charges are true.

9The Jewish crowd spoke up and
agreed with what Tertullus had said.

Paul Defends Himself

10The governor motioned for Paul
to speak, and he began:

I know that you have judged
the people of our nation for
many years, and I am glad to
defend myself in your court.

11It was no more than twelve
days ago that I went to worship
in Jerusalem. You can find this
out easily enough. 12Never once
did the Jews find me arguing
with anyone in the temple. I
didn't cause trouble in the
Jewish meeting places or in the
city itself. 13There is no way that
they can prove these charges
that they are now bringing
against me.

14I admit that the Jewish
leaders think that the Lord's
Way[k] which I follow is based on
wrong beliefs. But I still worship
the same God that my ancestors
worshiped. And I believe
everything written in the Law of
Moses and in the Prophets.[l]
15I am just as sure as these
people are that God will raise
from death everyone who is
good or evil. 16And because I am
sure, I try my best to have a clear
conscience in whatever I do for
God or for people.*

17After being away for several
years, I returned here to bring
gifts for the poor people of my
nation and to offer sacrifices.
18This is what I was doing when
I was found going through a
ceremony in the temple. I was
not with a crowd, and there was
no uproar.

19Some Jews from Asia were
there at that time, and if they
have anything to say against me,
they should be here now. 20Or
ask the ones who are here. They
can tell you that they didn't find
me guilty of anything when I was
tried by their own council. 21The
only charge they can bring
against me is what I shouted out
in court, when I said, "I am on
trial today because I believe that

---

[i]*Paul was called in, and Tertullus stated the case against him*: Or "Tertullus was called in and stated the case against Paul." [j]*we arrested him*: Some manuscripts add, "We wanted to judge him by our own laws. But Lysias the commander took him away from us by force. Then Lysias ordered us to bring our charges against this man in your court." [k]*the Lord's Way*: See the note at 9.2. [l]*Law of Moses . . . the Prophets*: The Jewish Scriptures, that is, the Old Testament.

24.5 **WAS PAUL A PEST?** No doubt the Jews thought Paul was a pest, and his preaching greatly irritated them. This was probably a tough burden for Paul to carry—to be hated so by his own people. But he had to make the choice between the friendship of his people and the friendship of God. Every Christian has to make this choice at some time.

24.16 **GOD'S PEACE GIVES US CLEAR MINDS** Paul knew he had done no wrong—to God or to his people. But he was accused of disturbing the peace. All the same, Paul had God's peace, as always when he testified for Christ. So Paul was able to show that the charges against him were nonsense. When we have peace with God we can think straight.

NOTES

the dead will be raised to life!"

22Felix knew a lot about the Lord's Way.[m] But he brought the trial to an end and said, "I will make my decision after Lysias the commander arrives." 23He then ordered the army officer to keep Paul under guard, but not to lock him up or to stop his friends from helping him.

Paul Is Kept Under Guard

24Several days later Felix and his wife Drusilla, who was Jewish, went to the place where Paul was kept under guard. They sent for Paul and listened while he spoke to them about having faith in Christ Jesus. 25But Felix was frightened when Paul started talking to them about doing right, about self-control, and about the coming judgment. So he said to Paul, "That's enough for now. You may go. But when I have time I will send for you." 26After this, Felix often sent for Paul and talked with him, because he hoped that Paul would offer him a bribe.*

27Two years later Porcius Festus became governor in place of Felix. But since Felix wanted to do the Jewish leaders a favor, he kept Paul in jail.

Paul Asks To Be Tried by the Roman Emperor

25 Three days after Festus had become governor, he went from Caesarea to Jerusalem. 2There the chief priests and the Jewish leaders told him about their charges against Paul. They also asked Festus 3if he would be willing to bring Paul to Jerusalem. They begged him to do this because they were planning to attack and kill Paul on the way. 4But Festus told them, "Paul will be kept in Caesarea, and I am soon going there myself. 5If he has done anything wrong, let your leaders go with me and bring charges against him there."

6Festus stayed in Jerusalem for eight or ten more days before going to Caesarea. Then the next day he took his place as judge and had Paul brought into court. 7As soon as Paul came in, the Jewish leaders from Jerusalem crowded around him and said he was guilty of many serious crimes. But they could not prove anything. 8Then Paul spoke in his own defense, "I have not broken the Law of my people. And I have not done anything against either the temple or the Emperor."

9Festus wanted to please the Jewish leaders. So he asked Paul, "Are you willing to go to Jerusalem and be tried by me on these charges?"

10Paul replied, "I am on trial in the Emperor's court, and that's where I should be tried. You know very well that I have not done anything to harm the Jewish nation.* 11If I had done something deserving death, I would not ask to escape the death penalty. But I am not guilty of any of these crimes, and no one has the right to hand me over to these Jews. I now ask to be tried by the Emperor himself."

12After Festus had talked this over with members of his council, he told Paul, "You have asked to be tried by the Emperor, and to the Emperor you will go!"

---

[m] *the Lord's Way*: See the note at 9.2.

24.26 **FELIX WANTED A BRIBE** Even today in many countries, you can hardly get civil servants to do anything for you unless you bribe them. Paul ran into this problem with Felix. Paul probably had no money and would not have bribed Felix if he had. So he stayed in jail for two years.

25.10 **PAUL'S APPEAL TO ROME** Whatever we think of the ancient Romans, they were famous for their system of laws. We see an example of this in Paul's appeal to Rome. He couldn't get a fair trial in Palestine because the Jews hated him so much. But the law allowed Paul, a citizen of Rome, to be taken there for trial. So the governor had to let Paul take a sea trip to Rome to be tried.

NOTES

Paul Speaks to Agrippa and Bernice

13A few days later King Agrippa
and Bernice came to Caesarea to visit
Festus.* 14They had been there for
several days, when Festus told the
king about the charges against Paul.
He said:

Felix left a man here in jail,
15and when I went to Jerusalem,
the chief priests and the Jewish
leaders came and asked me to
find him guilty. 16I told them that
it is not the Roman custom to
hand a man over to people who
are bringing charges against
him. He must first have the
chance to meet them face to face
and to defend himself against
their charges.

17So when they came here
with me, I wasted no time. On
the very next day I took my place
on the judge's bench and ordered
him to be brought in. 18But when
the men stood up to make their
charges against him, they did not
accuse him of any of the crimes
that I thought they would.
19Instead, they argued with him
about some of their Jewish
beliefs and about a dead man
named Jesus, who Paul said was
alive.

20Since I did not know how to
find out the truth about all this,
I asked Paul if he would be
willing to go to Jerusalem and
be put on trial there. 21But Paul
asked to be kept in jail until the
Emperor could decide his case.
So I ordered him to be kept here
until I could send him to the
Emperor.

22Then Agrippa said to Festus, "I
would also like to hear what this man
has to say."

Festus answered, "You can hear
him tomorrow."

23The next day Agrippa and Bernice made a big show as they came
into the meeting room. High ranking
army officers and leading citizens of
the town were also there. Festus then
ordered Paul to be brought in*
24and said:

King Agrippa and other
guests, look at this man! Every
Jew from Jerusalem and
Caesarea has come to me,
demanding for him to be put to
death. 25I have not found him
guilty of any crime deserving
death. But because he has asked
to be judged by the Emperor, I
have decided to send him to
Rome.

26I have to write some facts
about this man to the Emperor.
So I have brought him before all
of you, but especially before you,
King Agrippa. After we have
talked about his case, I will then
have something to write. 27It
makes no sense to send a
prisoner to the Emperor without
stating the charges against him.

Paul's Defense before Agrippa

26 Agrippa told Paul, "You may
now speak for yourself."
Paul stretched out his hand and said:

2King Agrippa, I am glad for
this chance to defend myself
before you today on all these
charges that my own people

25.13 **ANOTHER KING AGRIPPA** This was King Agrippa the Second, the son of the King Agrippa who had put James the apostle to death (Acts 12). Agrippa the Second was less than thirty years old at the time of the events in Acts 25. Years later, he returned to Rome after Jerusalem was destroyed, and he died in the year 100.

25.23 **FIRST-CENTURY POLITICS** Quite a show was put on here in Caesarea at this "summit conference" between the Roman governor and King Agrippa. Paul was brought out and questioned, but we get the impression that this was mostly for the sake of political relations between Festus and Agrippa, not because of a desire to do Paul justice. But God used it just the same.

NOTES

have brought against me.* 3You
know a lot about our Jewish
customs and the beliefs that
divide us. So I ask you to listen
patiently to me.
4-5All the Jews have known me
since I was a child. They know
what kind of life I have lived in
my own country and in
Jerusalem. If they were willing,
they could tell you that I was a
Pharisee, a member of a group
that is more strict than any other.
6Now I am on trial because I
believe the promise that God
made to our people long ago.
7Day and night our twelve
tribes have earnestly served
God, waiting for his promised
blessings. King Agrippa,
because of this hope, the Jewish
leaders have brought charges
against me. 8Why should any of
you doubt that God raises the
dead to life?
9I once thought that I should
do everything I could to oppose
Jesus from Nazareth. 10I did this
first in Jerusalem, and with the
authority of the chief priests I
put many of God's people in jail.
I even voted for them to be killed.
11I often had them punished in
our meeting places, and I tried
to make them give up their faith.
In fact, I was so angry with them,
that I went looking for them in
foreign cities.
12King Agrippa, one day I was
on my way to Damascus with the
authority and permission of the
chief priests. 13About noon I saw
a light brighter than the sun. It
flashed from heaven on me and
on everyone traveling with me.
14We all fell to the ground. Then
I heard a voice say to me in
Aramaic, "Saul, Saul, why are
you so cruel to me? It's foolish
to fight against me!"
15"Who are you?" I asked.
Then the Lord answered, "I
am Jesus! I am the one you are
so cruel to. 16Now stand up. I
have appeared to you, because
I have chosen you to be my
servant. You are to tell others
what you have learned about me
and what I will show you later."
17The Lord also said, "I will
protect you from the Jews and
from the Gentiles that I am
sending you to. 18I want you to
open their eyes, so that they will
turn from darkness to light and
from the power of Satan to God.
Then their sins will be forgiven,
and by faith in me they will
become part of God's holy
people."
19King Agrippa, I obeyed this
vision from heaven. 20First I
preached to the people in
Damascus, and then I went to
Jerusalem and all over Judea.
Finally, I went to the Gentiles
and said, "Stop sinning and turn
to God! Then prove what you
have done by the way you live."
21That is why the Jews
grabbed me in the temple and
tried to kill me. 22But all this time
God has helped me, and I have
preached both to the rich and to
the poor. I have told them only
what the prophets and Moses
said would happen. 23I told them
how the Messiah would suffer
and be the first to be raised from
death, so that he could bring
light to his own people and to
the Gentiles.
24Before Paul finished defending
himself, Festus shouted, "Paul,
you're crazy! Too much learning has
driven you out of your mind."

26.2 **KING AGRIPPA HEARD THE GOOD NEWS** Once again Paul seized the chance to tell how he became a Christian. Governor Festus and King Agrippa were much upset by what they heard. It seems as though Agrippa would almost have been willing to be a Christian if only he had more time to think about it. So far as we know, however, Agrippa never turned to Christ. As Paul would later write, God has not called many mighty men. But he does call some. God seeks all kinds of people.

NOTES

25But Paul replied, "Honorable Festus, I am not crazy. What I am saying is true, and it makes sense. 26None of these things happened off in a corner somewhere. I am sure that King Agrippa knows what I am talking about. That's why I can speak so plainly to him."

27Then Paul said to Agrippa, "Do you believe what the prophets said? I know you do."

28Agrippa asked Paul, "In such a short time do you think you can talk me into being a Christian?"

29Paul answered, "Whether it takes a short time or a long time, I wish you and everyone else who hears me today would become just like me! Except, of course, for these chains."

30Then King Agrippa, Governor Festus, Bernice, and everyone who was with them got up. 31But before they left, they said, "This man is not guilty of anything. He doesn't deserve to die or to be put in jail."

32Agrippa told Festus, "Paul could have been set free, if he had not asked to be tried by the Roman Emperor."*

Paul Is Taken to Rome

27 When it was time for us to sail to Rome, Captain Julius from the Emperor's special troops was put in charge of Paul and the other prisoners. 2We went aboard a ship from Adramyttium that was about to sail to some ports along the coast of Asia. Aristarchus from Thessalonica in Macedonia sailed on the ship with us.

3The next day we came to shore at Sidon. Captain Julius was very kind to Paul. He even let him visit his friends, so they could give him whatever he needed. 4When we left Sidon, the winds were blowing against us, and we sailed close to the island of Cyprus to be safe from the wind. 5Then we sailed south of Cilicia and Pamphylia until we came to the port of Myra in Lycia. 6There the army captain found a ship from Alexandria that was going to Italy. So he ordered us to board that ship.

7We sailed along slowly for several days and had a hard time reaching Cnidus. The wind would not let us go any farther in that direction, so we sailed past Cape Salmone, where the island of Crete would protect us from the wind. 8We went slowly along the coast and finally reached a place called Fair Havens, not far from the town of Lasea.

9By now we had already lost a lot of time, and sailing was no longer safe. In fact, even the Day of Atonement[n] was past. 10Then Paul spoke to the crew of the ship, "Men, listen to me! If we sail now, our ship and its cargo will be badly damaged, and many lives will be lost."* 11But Julius listened to the captain of the ship and its owner, rather than to Paul.

12The harbor at Fair Havens was not a good place to spend the winter. Because of this, almost everyone agreed that we should at least try to sail along the coast of Crete as far as Phoenix. It had a harbor that

---

[n]*Day of Atonement*: This Jewish festival took place near the end of September. The sailing season was dangerous after the middle of September, and it was stopped completely between the middle of November and the middle of March.

26.32 **PAUL COULD HAVE BEEN FREE** Think of that—Paul chose to go to Rome, although he could have been set free at his trial before Agrippa. Why did Paul do this? Jesus had called Paul to go to the Gentiles, and this trip to Rome was Paul's big chance to carry out his work. All things were working together to get Paul to Rome where he would continue his ministry for several years.

27.10 **PAUL TOOK CHARGE** A Roman army captain was in charge of Paul's ship to Rome. Sailing across the Mediterranean Sea, Paul warned the captain that there would be rough weather if they set out from the island of Crete after the middle of April. But he didn't listen to Paul. During the storm that followed, the crew and passengers were saved only when they took Paul's advice.

NOTES

opened toward the southwest and
northwest,[o] and we could spend the
winter there.

The Storm at Sea

13When a gentle wind from the
south started blowing, the men
thought it was a good time to do what
they had planned. So they pulled up
the anchor, and we sailed along the
coast of Crete. 14But soon a strong
wind called "The Northeaster" blew
against us from the island. 15The
wind struck the ship, and we could
not sail against it. So we let the wind
carry the ship.

16We went along the island of
Cauda on the side that was protected
from the wind. We had a hard time
holding the lifeboat in place, 17but
finally we got it where it belonged.
Then the sailors wrapped ropes
around the ship to hold it together.
They lowered the sail and let the ship
drift along, because they were afraid
it might hit the sandbanks in the gulf
of Syrtis.

18The storm was so fierce that the
next day they threw some of the
ship's cargo overboard. 19Then on
the third day, with their bare hands
they threw overboard some of the
ship's gear. 20For several days we
could not see either the sun or the
stars. A strong wind kept blowing,
and we finally gave up all hope of
being saved.

21Since none of us had eaten anything for a long time, Paul stood up
and told the men:

> You should have listened to
> me! If you had stayed on in
> Crete, you would not have had
> this damage and loss. 22But now
> I beg you to cheer up, because
> you will be safe. Only the ship
> will be lost.
>
> 23I belong to God, and I
> worship him. Last night he sent
> an angel 24to tell me, "Paul, don't
> be afraid! You will stand trial
> before the Emperor. And
> because of you, God will save
> the lives of everyone on the
> ship." 25Cheer up! I am sure that
> God will do exactly what he
> promised. 26But we will first be
> shipwrecked on some island.

27For fourteen days and nights we
had been blown around over the
Mediterranean Sea. But about midnight the sailors realized that we
were getting near land. 28They measured and found that the water was
about one hundred and twenty feet
deep. A little later they measured
again and found it was only about
ninety feet. 29The sailors were afraid
that we might hit some rocks, and
they let down four anchors from the
back of the ship. Then they prayed
for daylight.

30The sailors wanted to escape
from the ship. So they lowered the
lifeboat into the water, pretending
that they were letting down an anchor from the front of the ship.
31But Paul said to Captain Julius and
the soldiers, "If the sailors don't stay
on the ship, you won't have any
chance to save your lives." 32The soldiers then cut the ropes that held the
lifeboat and let it fall into the sea.

33Just before daylight Paul begged
the people to eat something. He told
them, "For fourteen days you have
been so worried that you haven't
eaten a thing. 34I beg you to eat something. Your lives depend on it. Do
this and not one of you will be hurt."

35After Paul had said this, he took
a piece of bread and gave thanks to
God. Then in front of everyone, he
broke the bread and ate some.*
36They all felt encouraged, and each
of them ate something. 37There were

---

[o]*southwest and northwest*: Or "northeast and southeast."

27.35 **A WITNESS FOR JESUS** Even as they were being tossed around on the waves, Paul took advantage of an opportunity to witness about his faith. As he took bread in his hands and broke it, he gave thanks to God. The other people on the ship were encouraged and got their appetites back. Paul the prisoner was Paul the leader, by the power of the Holy Spirit.

NOTES

276 people on the ship, 38and after
everyone had eaten, they threw the
cargo of wheat into the sea to make
the ship lighter.

The Shipwreck

39Morning came, and the ship's
crew saw a coast that they did not
recognize. But they did see a cove
with a beach. So they decided to try
to run the ship aground on the beach.
40They cut the anchors loose and let
them sink into the sea. At the same
time they untied the ropes that were
holding the rudders. Next, they
raised the sail at the front of the ship
and let the wind carry the ship toward the beach. 41But it ran aground
on a sandbank. The front of the ship
stuck firmly in the sand, and the rear
was being smashed by the force of
the waves.
42The soldiers decided to kill the
prisoners to keep them from swimming away and escaping. 43But Captain Julius wanted to save Paul's life,
and he did not let the soldiers do what
they had planned. Instead, he ordered everyone who could swim to
dive into the water and head for
shore. 44Then he told the others to
hold on to planks of wood or parts
of the ship. At last, everyone safely
reached shore.

On the Island of Malta

28 When we came ashore, we
learned that the island was
called Malta.* 2The local people were
very friendly, and they welcomed us
by building a fire, because it was
rainy and cold.
3After Paul had gathered some
wood and had put it on the fire, the
heat caused a snake to crawl out, and
it bit him on the hand. 4When the
local people saw the snake hanging
from Paul's hand, they said to each
other, "This man must be a murderer!
He didn't drown in the sea, but the
goddess of justice will kill him
anyway."
5Paul shook the snake off into the
fire and was not harmed. 6The people
kept thinking that Paul would either
swell up or suddenly drop dead. They
watched him for a long time, and
when nothing happened to him, they
changed their minds and said, "This
man is a god."
7The governor of the island was
named Publius, and he owned some
of the land around there. Publius was
very friendly and welcomed us into
his home for three days. 8His father
was in bed, sick with fever and stomach trouble, and Paul went to visit
him. Paul healed the man by praying
and placing his hands on him.
9After this happened, everyone on
the island brought their sick people
to Paul, and they were all healed.
10The people were very respectful to
us, and when we sailed, they gave
us everything we needed.

From Malta to Rome

11Three months later we sailed in
a ship that had been docked at Malta
for the winter. The ship was from Alexandria in Egypt and was known
as "The Twin Gods."[p]* 12We arrived

---

[p]*known as "The Twin Gods"*: Or "carried on its bow a wooden carving of the Twin Gods." These gods were Castor and Pollux, two of the favorite gods among sailors.

28.1 **PAUL CONTINUED HIS WORK** The island of Malta, in the central Mediterranean Sea, is a military base today. In Paul's time it was a Roman colony. While Paul was there he wonderfully survived a snake bite, just as Jesus had promised in Mark 16.18. Paul also healed the governor's sick father. Wherever Paul went, he used his time to spread the good news about Christ.

28.11 **PAUL WENT ON TO ROME** Notice that Luke, the author of the book of Acts, had been with the group since they left Palestine (see in chapter 27 the many times the word "we" appears). Arriving at Italy, Paul and his companions traveled to Rome by the Appian Way, a road still used today.

NOTES

in Syracuse and stayed for three
days. 13From there we sailed to Rhe-
gium. The next day a south wind
began to blow, and two days later
we arrived in Puteoli. 14There we
found some of the Lord's followers,
who begged us to stay with them.
A week later we left for the city of
Rome.

15Some of the followers in Rome
heard about us and came to meet us
at the Market of Appius and at the
Three Inns. When Paul saw them,
he thanked God and was encouraged.

Paul in Rome

16We arrived in Rome, and Paul
was allowed to live in a house by
himself with a soldier to guard
him.

17Three days after we got there,
Paul called together some of the Jewish leaders and said:

> My friends, I have never done
> anything to hurt our people, and
> I have never gone against the
> customs of our ancestors. But in
> Jerusalem I was handed over as
> a prisoner to the Romans. 18They
> looked into the charges against
> me and wanted to release me.
> They found that I had not done
> anything deserving death.
> 19The Jewish leaders disagreed,
> so I asked to be tried by the
> Emperor.
>
> But I don't have anything to
> say against my own nation.
> 20I am bound by these chains
> because of what we people of
> Israel hope for. That's why I
> have called you here to talk
> about this hope of ours.

21The Jewish leaders replied, "No
one from Judea has written us a letter
about you. And not one of them has
come here to report on you or to
say anything against you. 22But we
would like to hear what you have
to say. We understand that people
everywhere are against this new
group."

23They agreed on a time to meet
with Paul, and many of them came
to his house. From early morning until late in the afternoon, Paul talked
to them about God's kingdom. He
used the Law of Moses and the Books
of the Prophets[q] to try to win them
over to Jesus.

24Some of the Jewish leaders
agreed with what Paul said, but others did not. 25Since they could not
agree among themselves, they
started leaving. But Paul said, "The
Holy Spirit said the right thing when
he sent Isaiah the prophet* 26to tell
our ancestors,

'Go to these people
  and tell them:
You will listen and listen,
  but never understand.
You will look and look,
  but never see.
27All of you
  have stubborn hearts.
Your ears are stopped up,
  and your eyes are covered.
You cannot see or hear
  or understand.
If you could,
you would turn to me,
  and I would heal you.' "

28-29Paul said, "You may be sure
that God wants to save the Gentiles!
And they will listen."[r]

---

[q] *Law of Moses and the Books of the Prophets*: The Jewish Bible, that is, the Old Testament.
[r] *And they will listen*: Some manuscripts add, "After Paul said this, the people left, but they got into a fierce argument among themselves."

28.25 **PAUL MET WITH THE JEWS AT ROME** Again Paul defended his ministry before the Jewish people living at Rome. But once again many of the Jewish leaders were against Paul. So he had to continue his ministry to the Gentiles. We have to realize that everybody in the world will not agree with the good news. But God calls us to share that news as Paul did, with everyone who will hear.

NOTES

30For two years Paul stayed in a
rented house and welcomed everyone who came to see him.* 31He
bravely preached about God's kingdom and taught about the Lord Jesus
Christ, and no one tried to stop him.

28.30 **PAUL RENTED HIS OWN HOUSE** Fortunately, Paul did not have to go to prison while he awaited trial at Rome. He had his own rented home, and he seems to have been guarded by one soldier. There he enjoyed much freedom, and for two years was able to teach those who came to his house. After that he was probably released for a time and may have traveled as far as Spain. But he was arrested again and executed during Emperor Nero's reign, in about the year 67. (See Paul's Second Letter to Timothy, written just before the apostle's death.)

NOTES

Paul's Letter TO THE CHURCH IN ROME

ABOUT THIS LETTER

Paul wrote this letter to introduce himself and his message to the church at Rome. He had never been to this important city, although he knew the names of many Christians there and hoped to visit them soon (15.22—16.21). Paul tells them that he is an apostle, chosen to preach the good news (1.1). And the message he proclaims "is God's powerful way of saving all people who have faith, whether they are Jews or Gentiles" (1.16).

Paul reminds his readers, "All of us have sinned and fallen short of God's glory" (3.23). But how can we be made acceptable to God? This is the main question that Paul answers in this letter. He begins by showing how everyone has failed to do what God requires. The Jews have not obeyed the Law of Moses, and the Gentiles have refused even to think about God, although God has spoken to them in many different ways (1.18—3.20).

> *Now we see how God does make us acceptable to him . . . God treats everyone alike. He accepts people only because they have faith in Jesus Christ . . . God treats us better than we deserve. And because of Jesus Christ, he freely accepts us and sets us free from our sins.* (3.21, 22, 24)

> *God gave Jesus to die for our sins, and he raised him to life, so that we would be made acceptable to God.* (4.25)

A QUICK LOOK AT THIS LETTER

1. Paul and His Message of Good News (1.1–17)
2. Everyone Is Guilty (1.18—3.20)
3. God's Way of Accepting People (3.21—4.25)
4. A New Life for God's People (5.1—8.39)
5. What about the People of Israel? (9.1—11.36)
6. How to Live the New Life of Love (12.1—15.13)
7. Paul's Plans and Personal Greetings (15.14—16.27)

1 From Paul, a servant of Christ
Jesus.
God chose me to be an apostle, and
he appointed me to preach the good
news* 2that he promised long ago by
what his prophets said in the holy
Scriptures. 3-4This good news is
about his Son, our Lord Jesus Christ!
As a human, he was from the family
of David. But the Holy Spirit[a] proved
that Jesus is the powerful Son of
God,[b] because he was raised from
death.*
5Jesus was kind to me and chose
me to be an apostle,[c] so that people
of all nations would obey and have
faith. 6You are some of those people
chosen by Jesus Christ.*
7This letter is to all of you in Rome.
God loves you and has chosen you
to be his very own people.
I pray that God our Father and our
Lord Jesus Christ will be kind to you
and will bless you with peace!

A Prayer of Thanks

8First, I thank God in the name of
Jesus Christ for all of you. I do this
because people everywhere in the
world are talking about your faith.
9God has seen how I never stop praying for you, while I serve him with
all my heart and tell the good news
about his Son.*
10In all my prayers, I ask God to
make it possible for me to visit you.
11I want to see you and share with
you the same blessings that God's
Spirit has given me. Then you will
grow stronger in your faith. 12What
I am saying is that we can encourage
each other by the faith that is ours.
13My friends, I want you to know
that I have often planned to come
for a visit. But something has always
kept me from doing it. I want to win
followers to Christ in Rome, as I have
done in many other places. 14-15It
doesn't matter if people are civilized
and educated or if they are uncivilized and uneducated. I must tell the
good news to everyone. That's why
I am eager to visit all of you in Rome.*

---

[a] *the Holy Spirit*: Or "his own spirit of holiness." [b] *proved that Jesus is the powerful Son of God*: Or "proved in a powerful way that Jesus is the Son of God." [c] *Jesus was kind to me and chose me to be an apostle*: Or "Jesus was kind to us and chose us to be his apostles."

1.1 **PAUL WAS A SERVANT** Paul had a greater ministry than all the other apostles put together. But still he called himself a servant. Paul obeyed the command of Jesus that the chief among his apostles should be the servant of all (Luke 22.26).

1.4 **PAUL'S NEWS IS ABOUT A RISEN SAVIOR** Paul had something both old and new to tell about. By rising from the grave, the long-promised Christ completed the eternal plan to save believers. This proved that Jesus is the Son of God, who could die for our sins. He is a living Savior.

1.6 **JESUS CHOOSES BELIEVERS** It insults human pride to think that Jesus chooses us, instead of our choosing him. Some day we will understand better what Paul writes here and in other places about that. For now, let's be humble enough to accept the idea that God has had us in mind for a very long time.

1.9 **LET'S PRAY FOR ONE ANOTHER** Paul prayed a lot, and so should we. God sees to it that our prayers for one another make a difference. Often the best thing we can do is pray for the needs of others, especially for things that we can't help ourselves. Only God can convince people that they need Christ. Our words alone won't do it, but prayer makes a difference.

1.14 **THE GOOD NEWS IS FOR ALL KINDS OF PEOPLE** The news about Jesus is not only for the "civilized and educated," but for the "uncivilized and uneducated." The good news is for people regardless of their importance in the world. We must be careful not to make the good news hard for people to understand. Even small children should be able to come to Jesus and be saved.

NOTES

The Power of the Good News

16 I am proud of the good news! It
is God's powerful way of saving all
people who have faith, whether they
are Jews or Gentiles. 17 The good
news tells how God accepts everyone
who has faith, but only those who
have faith.[d] It is just as the Scriptures
say, "The people God accepts because of their faith will live."[e]*

Everyone Is Guilty

18 From heaven God shows how angry he is with all the wicked and evil
things that sinful people do to crush
the truth. 19 They know everything
that can be known about God, because God has shown it all to them.
20 God's eternal power and character
cannot be seen. But from the beginning of creation, God has shown
what these are like by all he has
made. That's why those people don't
have any excuse. 21 They know about
God, but they don't honor him or
even thank him. Their thoughts are
useless, and their stupid minds are
in the dark. 22 They claim to be wise,
but they are fools. 23 They don't worship the glorious and eternal God.
Instead, they worship idols that are
made to look like humans who cannot live forever, and like birds, animals, and reptiles.
24 So God let these people go their
own way. They did what they wanted
to do, and their filthy thoughts made
them do shameful things with their
bodies. 25 They gave up the truth
about God for a lie, and they worshiped God's creation instead of God,
who will be praised forever. Amen.
26 God let them follow their own evil
desires. Women no longer wanted to
have sex in a natural way, and they
did things with each other that were
not natural. 27 Men behaved in the
same way. They stopped wanting to
have sex with women and had strong
desires for sex with other men. They
did shameful things with each other,
and what has happened to them is
punishment for their foolish deeds.
28 Since these people refused even
to think about God, he let their useless minds rule over them. That's why
they do all sorts of indecent things.*
29 They are evil, wicked, and greedy,
as well as mean in every possible
way. They want what others have,
and they murder, argue, cheat, and
are hard to get along with. They gossip, 30 say cruel things about others,
and hate God. They are proud, conceited, and boastful, always thinking
up new ways to do evil.
These people don't respect their
parents. 31 They are stupid, unreli-
able, and don't have any love or pity
for others. 32 They know God has said
that anyone who acts this way deserves to die. But they keep on doing
evil things, and they even encourage
others to do them.

God's Judgment Is Fair

2 Some of you accuse others of doing wrong. But there is no excuse
for what you do. When you judge others, you condemn yourselves, be-

---

[d]*but only those who have faith*: Or "and faith is all that matters." [e]*The people God accepts because of their faith will live*: Or "The people God accepts will live because of their faith."

1.17 **FAITH IS THE KEY** Faith is trusting what God has said about his Son. Faith says, "I accept Jesus as my Savior and I ask him to take away my sins." When we have this kind of faith, Paul writes that we "will live." For the first time, we realize what real living is like—when God breathes his own life into us. Without faith, we live a life of sin, rebellion, and death.

1.28 **WHAT HAPPENS WHEN WE REJECT GOD** When we reject God, everything else goes wrong, too. Paul lists the things that happen in our lives when we turn our backs on God. The picture of human behavior that Paul paints is an ugly one indeed. The tragedy is that it is all so needless. God calls us back from this "wrong turn" to enjoy friendship with him.

NOTES

cause you are guilty of doing the very
same things.* 2We know that God is
right to judge everyone who behaves
in this way. 3Do you really think God
won't punish you, when you behave
exactly like the people you accuse?
4You surely don't think much of
God's wonderful goodness or of his
patience and willingness to put up
with you. Don't you know that the
reason God is good to you is because
he wants you to turn to him?

5But you are stubborn and refuse
to turn to God. So you are making
things even worse for yourselves on
that day when he will show how angry he is and will judge the world
with fairness. 6God will reward each
of us for what we have done. 7He
will give eternal life to everyone who
has patiently done what is good in
the hope of receiving glory, honor,
and life that lasts forever. 8But he
will show how angry and furious he
can be with every selfish person who
rejects the truth and wants to do evil.
9All who are wicked will be punished
with trouble and suffering. It doesn't
matter if they are Jews or Gentiles.
10But all who do right will be rewarded with glory, honor, and peace,
whether they are Jews or Gentiles.
11God doesn't have any favorites!

12Those people who don't know
about God's Law will still be punished for what they do wrong. And
the Law will be used to judge everyone who knows what it says.*
13God accepts those who obey his
Law, but not those who simply hear
it.

14Some people naturally obey the
Law's commands, even though they
don't have the Law. 15This proves
that the conscience is like a law written in the human heart. And it will
show whether we are forgiven or
condemned, 16when God has Jesus
Christ judge everyone's secret
thoughts, just as my message says.

The Jews and the Law

17Some of you call yourselves
Jews. You trust in the Law and take
pride in God.* 18By reading the Scriptures you learn how God wants you
to behave, and you discover what is
right. 19You are sure that you are a
guide for the blind and a light for
all who are in the dark. 20And since
there is knowledge and truth in God's
Law, you think you can instruct fools
and teach young people.

21But how can you teach others
when you refuse to learn? You
preach that it is wrong to steal. But
do you steal? 22You say people
should be faithful in marriage. But
are you faithful? You hate idols, yet
you rob their temples. 23You take
pride in the Law, but you disobey
the Law and bring shame to God.
24It is just as the Scriptures tell us,

2.1 **BE CAREFUL ABOUT JUDGING** We might make judgments correctly about others, but if God decided to find fault with us, we would be in bad shape. There's a saying: when you point your finger at someone, you have three more pointing back at you. Meaning: when you make judgments, remember that you too are a sinner.

2.12 **HOW GOD JUDGES** God judges by his Law. If God judges us according to what we deserve, then there is no hope for any of us. But read on—God offers another way for us to be accepted by him. Everyone has sinned, and the Law can only condemn us. But God has made it possible for us to come back to him and have our sins forgiven.

2.17 **THE JEWS WERE AN EXAMPLE OF DISOBEDIENCE** The Jews had the Scriptures and they knew the Law. They even became very proud of these facts. But they were really no better than other people. They too failed to keep God's Law. There is a danger that people can imagine that they are good just because they *know* what they should do. But they don't *do* what they should, so their knowledge does them no good.

NOTES

"You have made foreigners say insulting things about God."
25Being circumcised is worthwhile,
if you obey the Law. But if you don't
obey the Law, you are no better off
than people who are not circumcised.* 26In fact, if they obey the Law,
they are as good as anyone who is
circumcised. 27So everyone who
obeys the Law, but has never been
circumcised, will condemn you. Even
though you are circumcised and have
the Law, you still don't obey its
teachings.
28Just because you live like a Jew
and are circumcised does not make
you a real Jew. 29To be a real Jew
you must obey the Law. True circumcision is something that happens
deep in your heart, not something
done to your body. And besides, you
should want praise from God and not
from humans.

3 What good is it to be a Jew? What
good is it to be circumcised?
2It is good in a lot of ways! First of
all, God's messages were spoken to
the Jews. 3It is true that some Jews
did not believe the message. But does
this mean that God cannot be trusted,
just because they did not have faith?*
4No, indeed! God tells the truth, even
if everyone else is a liar. The Scriptures say about God,

"Your words
will be proven true,
and in court
you will win your case."

5If our evil deeds show how right
God is, then what can we say? Is it
wrong for God to become angry and
punish us? What a foolish thing to
ask. 6But the answer is, "No." Otherwise, how could God judge the
world? 7Since your lies bring great
honor to God by showing how truthful he is, you may ask why God still
says you are a sinner. 8You might
as well say, "Let's do something evil,
so that something good will come of
it!" Some people even claim that we
are saying this. But God is fair and
will judge them as well.

No One Is Good

9What does all this mean? Does it
mean that we Jews are better off[f]
than the Gentiles? No, it doesn't!
Jews, as well as Gentiles, are ruled
by sin, just as I have said. 10The Scriptures tell us,

"No one is acceptable to God!*
11Not one of them understands
or even searches for God.
12They have all turned away
and are worthless.
There is not one person
who does right.
13Their words are like
an open pit,

[f] *better off*: Or "worse off."

2.25 **MERE RELIGION CAN'T COVER OUR SINS** The Jews had many religious ceremonies. But God couldn't accept their religious ceremonies without obedient lives. Today's Christians might count too much on ceremonies, too. Sometimes children enjoy playing church, but it's sad when grownups "play church" and aren't living and worshiping in a way that pleases God.

3.3 **OUR DISOBEDIENCE DOESN'T MEAN GOD IS WRONG TOO** Today, too, people blame their unhappiness and even their sins on God. It is our own actions that make us miserable. God always can be trusted to do right, to tell us the truth about himself and ourselves. It makes sense to listen to God and not be fooled by lies.

3.10 **ALL OF US ARE SINNERS** Paul has been writing these hard things about us to show that we are all disobedient and that no one is excused. When we come before God, we have to admit the truth of all that Paul has written. This makes us feel very bad, because we know that it's no good to blame God or others for the way we are. Each of us falls short of what God rightly expects of people made in his image.

NOTES

and their tongues are good
only for telling lies.
Each word is as deadly
as the fangs of a snake,
14 and they say nothing
but bitter curses.
15 These people quickly
become violent.
16 Wherever they go,
they leave ruin
and destruction.
17 They don't know how
to live in peace.
18 They don't even fear God."

19 We know that everything in the
Law was written for those who are
under its power. The Law says these
things to stop anyone from making
excuses and to let God show that the
whole world is guilty. 20 God does not
accept people simply because they
obey the Law. No, indeed! All the
Law does is to point out our sin.

God's Way of Accepting People

21 Now we see how God does make
us acceptable to him. The Law and
the Prophets[g] tell how we become
acceptable, and it isn't by obeying
the Law of Moses.* 22 God treats everyone alike. He accepts people only
because they have faith in Jesus
Christ. 23 All of us have sinned and
fallen short of God's glory. 24 But God
treats us much better than we deserve.[h] And because of Jesus Christ,
he freely accepts us and sets us free
from our sins. 25-26 God sent Christ to
be our sacrifice. Christ offered
his life's blood, so that by faith in
him we could come to God. And
God did this to show that in the
past he was right to be patient and
forgive sinners. This also shows
that God is right when he accepts people who have faith in Jesus.*

27 What is left for us to brag about?
Not a thing! Is it because we obeyed
some law? No! It is because of faith.
28 We see that people are acceptable
to God because they have faith, and
not because they obey the Law.
29 Does God belong only to the Jews?
Isn't he also the God of the Gentiles?
Yes, he is! 30 There is only one God,
and he accepts Gentiles as well as
Jews, simply because of their faith.
31 Do we destroy the Law by our faith?
Not at all! We make it even more
powerful.*

---

[g] *The Law and the Prophets*: The Jewish Scriptures, that is, the Old Testament. [h] *treats us much better than we deserve:* The Greek word *charis*, traditionally rendered "grace," is translated here and other places in the CEV to express the overwhelming kindness of God.

3.21 **CHRIST IS THE ANSWER** There's good news: God has provided the way of escape from the penalty of his Law. It's the way his Son Jesus provided by paying our debt, by dying on the cross in our place. There Jesus accepted all of God's judgment for our sins. When we receive Jesus as our sin-bearer, then God says we are "declared not guilty."

3.25 **SOMEONE TOOK YOUR PLACE** Imagine you have committed a bad crime. You are in court, and the judge is about to sentence you. Then he stops, and he calls someone from the back of the courtroom. It's the judge's own son. Speaking to you, the judge says, "You deserve to die for your crime, but my son has asked to die in your place. I have decided to let my very own son die for you." That is what Jesus did for you.

3.31 **DOES GOD DESTROY HIS LAW?** Through Jesus, God has made his Law work better than ever. Jesus carried the load of our sins as he hung on the cross. Now God gives us, as a free gift, the goodness of Jesus. He paid all that we owed. Now we belong to God forever, and we love to please the one who saved us.

NOTES

The Example of Abraham

4 Well then, what can we say about
our ancestor Abraham?* 2If he
became acceptable to God because
of what he did, then he would have
something to brag about. But he
would never be able to brag about
it to God. 3The Scriptures say, "God
accepted Abraham because Abraham had faith in him."
4Money paid to workers isn't a gift.
It is something they earn by working.
5But you cannot make God accept
you because of something you do.
God accepts sinners only because
they have faith in him. 6In the Scriptures David talks about the blessings
that come to people who are acceptable to God, even though they don't
do anything to deserve these blessings. David says,
7"God blesses people
whose sins are forgiven
and whose evil deeds
are forgotten.*
8The Lord blesses people
whose sins are erased
from his book."
9Are these blessings meant for circumcised people or for those who are
not circumcised? Well, the Scriptures
say that God accepted Abraham because Abraham had faith in him.
10But when did this happen? Was it
before or after Abraham was circumcised? Of course, it was before.
11Abraham let himself be circumcised to show that he had been accepted because of his faith even before he was circumcised. This makes
Abraham the father of all who are
acceptable to God because of their
faith, even though they are not circumcised. 12This also makes Abraham the father of everyone who is
circumcised and has faith in God, as
Abraham did before he was circumcised.*

The Promise Is for All Who Have Faith

13God promised Abraham and his
descendants that he would give them
the world. This promise was not
made because Abraham had obeyed
the Law, but because his faith in God
made him acceptable. 14If Abraham
and his descendants were given this
promise because they had obeyed the
Law, then faith would mean nothing,
and the promise would be worthless.
15God becomes angry when his law
is broken. But where there isn't a
Law, it cannot be broken. 16Every-
thing depends on having faith in God,
so that God can keep his promise because he is kind. This promise is not
only for Abraham's descendants who
have the Law. It is for all who are
Abraham's descendants because
they have faith, just as he did. Abraham is the ancestor of us all. 17The
Scriptures say that Abraham would
become the ancestor of many nations. This promise was made to
Abraham because he had faith in
God, who raises the dead to life and
creates new things.
18God promised Abraham a lot of
descendants. And when it all seemed
hopeless, Abraham still had faith in
God and became the ancestor of
many nations. 19Abraham's faith
never became weak, not even when

4.1 **YOU CAN'T EARN GOD'S FORGIVENESS** Abraham is an example of God's free gift. We can't pay to be saved, but God himself could bless us as a gift. The gift wasn't really free, however. Jesus paid the price with his own blood. Like Abraham, we are accepted by God because of our faith.

4.7 **KING DAVID KNEW ABOUT JESUS** David sang in his Psalms about what Jesus would do. He said that God can wipe out our sins as though they never happened. Think about it—God is able to forget that we ever sinned against him.

4.12 **WHAT CIRCUMCISION WAS FOR** Hospitals today often circumcise baby boys, Jew and Gentile, for health reasons. In Bible times, circumcision was for Jews only—a sign of membership in the family of God. But *faith* was the really important thing. Paul points out that Abraham had to be a believer in God before he was circumcised.

NOTES

he was nearly a hundred years old.
He knew that he was almost dead
and that his wife Sarah could not
have children. 20But Abraham never
doubted or questioned God's promise. His faith made him strong, and
he gave all the credit to God.
21Abraham was certain that God
could do what he had promised.
22So God accepted him, 23just as we
read in the Scriptures. But these
words were not written only for
Abraham. 24They were written for us,
since we will also be accepted because of our faith in God, who raised
our Lord Jesus to life.* 25God gave
Jesus to die for our sins, and he raised
him to life, so that we would be made
acceptable to God.

What It Means To Be Acceptable to God

5 By faith we have been made acceptable to God. And now, because of our Lord Jesus Christ, we
live at peace[l] with God.* 2Christ has
also introduced us[j] to God's undeserved kindness on which we take
our stand. So we are happy, as we
look forward to sharing in the glory
of God. 3But that's not all! We gladly
suffer,[k] because we know that suffering helps us to endure. 4And endurance builds character, which gives
us a hope 5that will never disappoint

us. All of this happens because God
has given us the Holy Spirit, who fills
our hearts with his love.*
6Christ died for us at a time when
we were helpless and sinful. 7No one
is really willing to die for an honest
person, though someone might be
willing to die for a truly good person.
8But God showed how much he loved
us by having Christ die for us, even
though we were sinful.
9But there is more! Now that God
has accepted us because Christ sacrificed his life's blood, we will also be
kept safe from God's anger. 10Even
when we were God's enemies, he
made peace with us, because his Son
died for us. Yet something even
greater than friendship is ours. Now
that we are at peace with God, we
will be saved by his Son's life.*
11And in addition to everything else,
we are happy because God sent our
Lord Jesus Christ to make peace with
us.

Adam and Christ

12Adam sinned, and that sin
brought death into the world. Now
everyone has sinned, and so everyone must die. 13Sin was in the world

[l]*we live at peace*: Some manuscripts have "let us live at peace." [j]*introduced us*: Some manuscripts add "by faith." [k]*We gladly suffer*: Or "Let us gladly suffer."

4.24 **GOD PROMISES ETERNAL LIFE TO ALL BELIEVERS** Not only to Abraham and the Jews, but to all people, God offers to save those who trust God as Abraham did. This promise is as old as Abraham himself, because God promised him that his blessing would come to all nations. That includes you and me.

5.1 **GOD CAN BE TRUSTED** The first thing God wants us to do is have faith in him. If we're sick and go to a doctor, but don't have faith in his or her ability, we might as well stay home. Neither will God help us if we don't trust him.

5.5 **THE HOLY SPIRIT HELPS US** At one time our future was uncertain, but not any more. Even though people may reject us, we have the promise of God's friendship forever. We know this because God's Holy Spirit now lives in us and assures us that God loves us.

5.10 **NOW NOTHING SEPARATES US FROM GOD** Only our own refusal to accept his kindness can separate us from God. Imagine you have long owed a lot of money to someone—so much you could never pay it. But then a rich friend pays off your debt for you. That is what Jesus did when he paid for your sins. So now you may be at peace with God.

NOTES

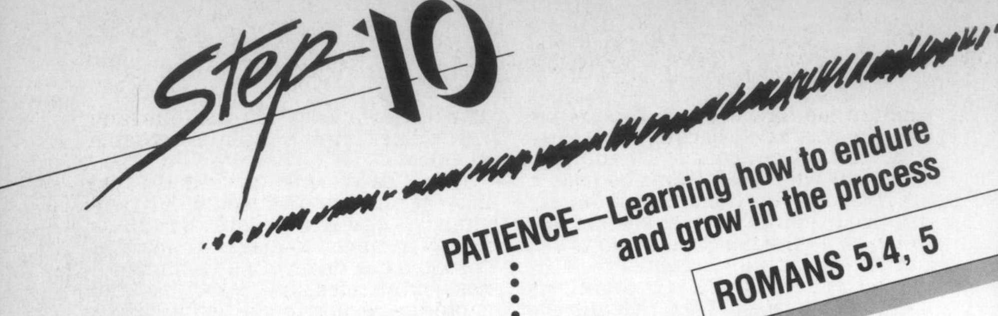

PATIENCE—Learning how to endure and grow in the process

ROMANS 5.4, 5

BE PATIENT

According to Hebrew folklore, Abraham was sitting outside his tent one night when he noticed a weary, old man approaching. Abraham rushed out to meet him and invited him into his tent. He washed the old man's feet and offered him something to eat.

Without saying a blessing or a thank you, the old man started eating. So Abraham asked, "Don't you worship God?" The old traveler replied, "I worship fire only and reverence no other god." When Abraham heard this, he became angry, grabbed the old man by the shoulders and threw him out of his tent and into the cold night air.

When the old man had walked off into the night, God paid a visit to his friend Abraham and asked about the stranger. "I threw him out because he did not worship you," Abraham replied. God answered, "I have been patient with him for eighty years, even though he dishonors me. Couldn't you have endured him one night?" Suddenly Abraham realized how wrong he had been.

Do we have problems with patience—especially when it comes to people who don't believe, act, dress, or smell the way we do? It's natural. But when we allow God to continue the process of change in our lives, we suddenly become more tolerant, more forgiving, and a little less judgmental.

STEP LOOK AHEAD 10

Patience enables us to take a hard look at our lives and to admit when we have wrong attitudes and actions. In Romans 5.4, 5 Paul wrote, "And endurance builds character, which gives us a hope that will never disappoint us. All of this happens because God has given us the Holy Spirit, who fills our hearts with his love." Our reputations will soar to new heights as we allow God to teach us patience and as we remain willing to admit when we are wrong.

For another "Look Ahead," turn to page 413.

before the Law came. But no record
of sin was kept, because there was
no Law. 14Yet death still had power
over all who lived from the time of
Adam to the time of Moses. This happened, though not everyone disobeyed a direct command from God,
as Adam did.
In some ways Adam is like Christ
who came later. 15But the gift that
God was kind enough to give was
very different from Adam's sin. That
one sin brought death to many others. Yet in an even greater way, Jesus
Christ alone brought God's gift of
kindness to many people.
16There is a lot of difference between Adam's sin and God's gift.
That one sin led to punishment. But
God's gift made it possible for us to
be acceptable to him, even though
we have sinned many times.* 17Death
ruled like a king because Adam had
sinned. But that cannot compare with
what Jesus Christ has done. God has
been so kind to us, and he has accepted us because of Jesus. And so
we will live and rule like kings.
18Everyone was going to be punished because Adam sinned. But because of the good thing that Christ
has done, God accepts us and gives
us the gift of life. 19Adam disobeyed
God and caused many others to be
sinners. But Jesus obeyed him and
will make many people acceptable
to God.
20The Law came, so that the full
power of sin could be seen. Yet where
sin was powerful, God's kindness
was even more powerful.* 21Sin ruled
by means of death. But God's kindness now rules, and God has accepted us because of Jesus Christ our
Lord. This means that we will have
eternal life.

Dead to Sin but Alive because of Christ

6 What should we say? Should we
keep on sinning, so that God's
kindness will show up even better?*
2No, we should not! If we are dead
to sin, how can we go on sinning?
3Don't you know that all who share
in Christ Jesus by being baptized also
share in his death? 4When we were
baptized, we died and were buried
with Christ. We were baptized, so
that we would live a new life, as
Christ was raised to life by the glory
of God the Father.

5If we shared in Jesus' death by
being baptized, we will surely be
raised to life with him. 6We know
that the persons we used to be were
nailed to the cross with Jesus. This

5.16 **WE ARE SINFUL CHILDREN OF ADAM** We are all children of our very first ancestor, Adam, who passed on his sinful nature to us. Sin caused death. But God has made a way to help us. Jesus undid the harm that Adam did by bringing sin into the world. By sending Jesus to die in our place God passed on Jesus' godly nature to all who accept him.

5.20 **WHAT GOOD DID THE LAW DO?** If God had not given us his Law, we would not clearly know how great our disobedience is. That was the Law's purpose—to show us our need to be saved from our sins. We must not think that God gave us his Law because we can be saved by keeping it. We can't. But by his kindness God has given the gift of his Son, Jesus. When Jesus died and rose again from death he made it possible for us to have our sins forgiven and to have life forever with him.

6.1 **WHAT DO WE DO ABOUT OUR SINS?** We should not go on sinning just because God has forgiven us. If God has forgiven us, we will hate our sins. But we can't stop sinning by ourselves. If Christ lives in us then we have a new life from him because he rose from death. But he also put our sins to death when he died on the cross. So we claim his death as death for our sins. Our old selves are dead, and we are now new people because Christ lives in us.

NOTES

was done, so that our sinful bodies
would no longer be the slaves of sin.
7We know that sin does not have
power over dead people.*
8As surely as we died with Christ,
we believe we will also live with him.
9We know that death no longer has
any power over Christ. He died and
was raised to life, never again to die.
10When Christ died, he died for sin
once and for all. But now he is alive,
and he lives only for God. 11In the
same way, you must think of yourselves as dead to the power of sin.
But Christ Jesus has given life to you,
and you live for God.

12Don't let sin rule your body. After
all, your body is bound to die, so don't
obey its desires* 13or let any part of
it become a slave of evil. Give yourselves to God, as people who have
been raised from death to life. Make
every part of your body a slave that
pleases God. 14Don't let sin keep ruling your lives. You are ruled by God's
kindness and not by the Law.

Slaves Who Do What Pleases God

15What does all this mean? Does
it mean we are free to sin, because
we are ruled by God's kindness and
not by the Law? Certainly not!
16Don't you know that you are slaves
of anyone you obey? You can be
slaves of sin and die, or you can be
obedient slaves of God and be acceptable to him. 17You used to be slaves
of sin. But I thank God that with all
your heart you obeyed the teaching
you received from me. 18Now you are
set free from sin and are slaves who
please God.*
19I am using these everyday examples, because in some ways you are
still weak. You used to let the different parts of your body be slaves of
your evil thoughts. But now you must
make every part of your body serve
God, so that you will belong completely to him.
20When you were slaves of sin, you
didn't have to please God. 21But what
good did you receive from the things
you did? All you have to show for
them is your shame, and they lead
to death. 22Now you have been set
free from sin, and you are God's
slaves. This will make you holy and
will lead you to eternal life.* 23Sin
pays off with death. But God's gift
is eternal life given by Jesus Christ
our Lord.

An Example from Marriage

7 My friends, you surely understand enough about law to know
that laws only have power over people who are alive. 2For example, the

6.7 **DEAD TO SIN** When we really put our faith in Christ, we feel so close to him that it is as if we have experienced his death and new life. We are dead to sin and alive with Christ. He helps us live in a new way—his way—a way that leaves no room for sin.

6.12 **SIN WORKS THROUGH OUR BODIES** God created our bodies very good. But since Adam's time, our bodies have become the means by which sin works. We live in physical bodies, and our actions are carried out by our bodies. But Christ's death for us means that our bodies don't have to live for sin anymore.

6.18 **THE LAW IS NOT OUR MASTER** When we live in sin, we live in fear, because the Law reminds us of how sinful we are. But that fear caused by the Law only makes us sin more and more. When God gives us the new life of Jesus, his Son, then we don't fear the Law anymore. We want to obey God because we love him, not because we're afraid.

6.22 **WE AREN'T FREE TO SIN** A criminal who has been in prison is set free. What does he do then? Does he go back to his old ways of crime? Not if he's smart. He has learned that crime doesn't pay. The Christian is like a criminal who has been set free by Christ. Now the Christian sees that obeying God is the true way of happiness and everlasting life.

NOTES

Step 6

JOYFULNESS—Enjoying the inward results of right living

ROMANS 6.12–14

"NO!"

I said "no." I can't believe it! I mean, I'm glad I said it, but I still can't believe it. When you've waited as long as I have just to have a date and then Mr. Wonderful happens along and tells you he thinks you are terrific and wouldn't you . . .

Am I stupid or what? I've read about it in magazines. I've listened to other girls talk about it and finally when I have my big chance to do it—I say "no"! It's not that I didn't want to say "yes." My mind was screaming, "Go for it! This may be your last chance!" But somewhere in my heart I knew I'd rather be known as someone who had a good reputation than as someone who just had a good time.

SAYING "YES" TO GOD

A deep sense of joy always follows when we say "no" to temptation. Being tempted is not a sin—even Jesus was tempted. The Holy Spirit is always there for us!

STEP LOOK AHEAD 6

For another "Look Ahead," turn to page 381.

Law says that a man's wife must remain his wife as long as he lives. But
once her husband is dead, she is free*
[3]to marry someone else. However, if
she goes off with another man while
her husband is still alive, she is said
to be unfaithful.
[4]That is how it is with you, my
friends. You are now part of the body
of Christ and are dead to the power
of the Law. You are free to belong
to Christ, who was raised to life so
that we could serve God. [5]When we
thought only of ourselves, the Law
made us have sinful desires. It made
every part of our bodies into slaves
who are doomed to die.* [6]But the Law
no longer rules over us. We are like
dead people, and it cannot have any
power over us. Now we can serve
God in a new way by obeying his
Spirit, and not in the old way by obeying the written Law.

The Battle with Sin

[7]Does this mean that the Law is
sinful? Certainly not! But if it had
not been for the Law, I would not
have known what sin is really like.
For example, I would not have known
what it means to want something that
belongs to someone else, unless the
Law had told me not to do that.
[8]It was sin that used this command
as a way of making me have all kinds
of desires. But without the Law, sin
is dead.
[9]Before I knew about the Law, I
was alive. But as soon as I heard that
command, sin came to life, [10]and I
died. The very command that was
supposed to bring life to me, instead
brought death. [11]Sin used this command to trick me, and because of it
I died. [12]Still, the Law and its commands are holy and correct and
good.*
[13]Am I saying that something good
caused my death? Certainly not! It
was sin that killed me by using something good. Now we can see how terrible and evil sin really is. [14]We know
that the Law is spiritual. But I am
merely a human, and I have been sold
as a slave to sin. [15]In fact, I don't
understand why I act the way I do.
I don't do what I know is right. I do
the things I hate. [16]Although I don't
do what I know is right, I agree that
the Law is good. [17]So I am not the
one doing these evil things. The sin
that lives in me is what does them.
[18]I know that my selfish desires
won't let me do anything that is good.
Even when I want to do right, I cannot.* [19]Instead of doing what I know

7.2 **MARRIAGE IS FOR LIFE** Many marriages fail because people don't realize at the start that marriage is for life. Paul uses marriage to show that we were once "married" to the Law. But we died with Jesus when he died on the cross. Now we are free from the old Law and we are "married" to Christ in his risen life. Marriage to Christ in this way is a happy marriage that lasts forever.

7.5 **HOW THE LAW WORKS** Do you remember when someone told you when you were small, "Don't do that, or you'll be punished," but the command only made you want to do that thing even more? That is the way sin works through the Law. Sin becomes worse because without being saved, sinners want to disobey what is right.

7.12 **THE LAW IS GOOD** What Paul writes about the Law may lead someone to think the Law is an evil thing. Not so. Our sinful nature uses the Law to make us sin worse. Until we receive Christ into our lives we continue to live in wickedness. When Jesus comes in, our love of sin passes away, and we come to love goodness.

7.18 **CHRISTIANS ARE IN A NEW WAR WITH SIN** Before Jesus becomes real to us as our Savior, our sins don't upset us very much. Then Jesus comes into our lives, so our old slavery to sin and its misery can be broken. But if we don't ask Jesus for his help, sin still tempts us and makes us unhappy. We can win when Jesus fights our war for us against sin.

NOTES

is right, I do wrong. 20And so, if I
don't do what I know is right, I am
no longer the one doing these evil
things. The sin that lives in me is what
does them.
21The Law has shown me that
something in me keeps me from doing what I know is right. 22With my
whole heart I agree with the Law of
God. 23But in every part of me I discover something fighting against my
mind, and it makes me a prisoner
of sin that controls everything I do.
24What a miserable person I am. Who
will rescue me from this body that
is doomed to die? 25Thank God! Jesus
Christ will rescue me.[l]
So with my mind I serve the Law
of God, although my selfish desires
make me serve the law of sin.

Living by the Power of God's Spirit

8 If you belong to Christ Jesus, you
won't be punished.* 2The Holy
Spirit will give you life that comes
from Christ Jesus and will set you[m]
free from sin and death. 3The Law
of Moses cannot do this, because our
selfish desires make the Law weak.
But God set you free when he sent
his own Son to be like us sinners and
to be a sacrifice for our sin. God used
Christ's body to condemn sin.
4He did this, so that we would do
what the Law commands by obeying the Spirit instead of our own desires.*
5People who are ruled by their desires think only of themselves. Everyone who is ruled by the Holy Spirit
thinks about spiritual things. 6If our
minds are ruled by our desires, we
will die. But if our minds are ruled
by the Spirit, we will have life and
peace. 7Our desires fight against God,
because they do not and cannot obey
God's laws. 8If we follow our desires,
we cannot please God.*

9You are no longer ruled by your
desires, but by God's Spirit, who lives
in you. People who don't have the
Spirit of Christ in them don't belong
to him. 10But Christ lives in you. So
you are alive because God has accepted you, even though your bodies
must die because of your sins.
11Yet God raised Jesus to life! God's
Spirit now lives in you, and he will
raise you to life by his Spirit.*
12My dear friends, we must not live
to satisfy our desires. 13If you do, you
will die. But you will live, if by the
help of God's Spirit you say "No"
to your desires. 14Only those people
who are led by God's Spirit are his

---

[l] *me*: Or "us." [m] *you*: Some manuscripts have "me."

8.1 **JESUS TOOK OUR PUNISHMENT** Why did sin have to be punished? Why couldn't God just let everyone into heaven, sins and all? But how would you like to live in a heaven where sinful people keep getting worse and worse forever and ever? That's why Jesus, the Son of God, let himself be punished for our sins. Then God could take away our sins and let us live with him forever.

8.4 **BE RULED BY THE HOLY SPIRIT** When we are ruled by God's Spirit, we love thoughts of God and goodness. This is a wonderful way to live, because we are then free from the desires that were killing us, even when we didn't know they were.

8.8 **DON'T GIVE IN TO ALL YOUR DESIRES** Think of the diseases and unhappiness that result from giving our bodies everything they want. We ought to feed our new spiritual nature on the things of the Holy Spirit. Then we will grow in our ability to love and enjoy God. This is exactly what we were created to do.

8.11 **BELIEVERS WILL HAVE NEW BODIES SOMEDAY** When a seed is planted, it seems to die, but it grows up into a beautiful new plant. When Jesus died for us, he was buried, but he rose again in a more wonderful body. Believers in Jesus will have wonderful bodies like his when they rise from death.

NOTES

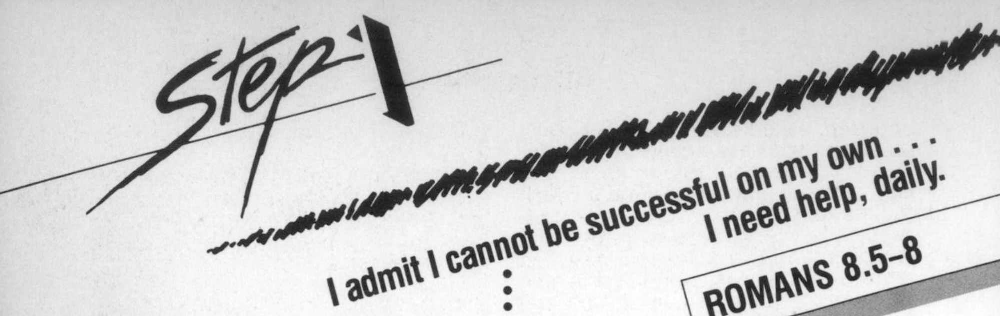

DEAR DIARY

"**D**ear Diary,
Eric took his ring back today. He said he thought we should date other people. There isn't anyone else I want to go out with. Eric is everything I wanted.

Mom says someday I'll be able to look back and laugh. But today all I can do is cry . . .

I just hurt.

I love him.

I hate him.

No, I don't know what to think.

What do I do now?"

REACHING OUT

When we lose something that is very special, it is natural to feel hurt. Tears are a sign of admitting our need. Grieving can lead to an emotional release. The danger lies in getting stuck with resentment. We will either continue in our hurts or move toward being helped. Reaching out to God allows his Spirit to provide peace in the midst of pain. God desires to take our pain, help us work through the grief, and allow us to move on with life.

For another "Look Inside," turn to page 369.

children. 15God's Spirit doesn't make us slaves who are afraid of him. Instead, we become his children and call him our Father.[n] 16God's Spirit makes us sure that we are his children. 17His Spirit lets us know that together with Christ we will be given what God has promised. We will also share in the glory of Christ, because we have suffered with him.

A Wonderful Future for God's People

18I am sure that what we are suffering now cannot compare with the glory that will be shown to us. 19In fact, all creation is eagerly waiting for God to show who his children are. 20Meanwhile, creation is confused, but not because it wants to be confused. God made it this way in the hope 21that creation would be set free from decay and would share in the glorious freedom of his children. 22We know that all creation is still groaning and is in pain, like a woman about to give birth.*

23The Spirit makes us sure about what we will be in the future. But now we groan silently, while we wait for God to show that we are his children.[o] This means that our bodies will also be set free. 24And this hope is what saves us. But if we already have what we hope for, there is no need to keep on hoping. 25However, we hope for something we have not yet seen, and we patiently wait for it.

26In certain ways we are weak, but the Spirit is here to help us. For example, when we don't know what to pray for, the Spirit prays for us in ways that cannot be put into words.* 27All of our thoughts are known to God. He can understand what is in the mind of the Spirit, as the Spirit prays for God's people. 28We know that God is always at work for the good of everyone who loves him.[p] They are the ones God has chosen for his purpose, 29and he has always known who his chosen ones would be. He had decided to let them become like his own Son, so that his Son would be the first of many children. 30God then accepted the people he had already decided to choose, and he has shared his glory with them.*

God's Love

31What can we say about all this? If God is on our side, can anyone be

---

[n] *our Father*: The Greek text uses the Aramaic word "Abba" (meaning "father"), which shows the close relation between the children and their father. [o] *to show that we are his children*: These words are not in some manuscripts. The translation of the remainder of the verse would then read, "while we wait for God to set our bodies free." [p] *God is always at work for the good of everyone who loves him*: Or "All things work for the good of everyone who loves God" or "God's Spirit always works for the good of everyone who loves God."

8.22 **WHY DOES GOD'S CREATION SUFFER?** God has a plan to save his creation from the bad effects of sin. Now, our world is full of decay, unhappiness, and pain. But as a woman feels some pain when she is about to give birth to a baby, so too does the world feel pain now while it awaits the birth of a new and wonderful creation from God.

8.26 **THE HOLY SPIRIT PRAYS FOR US** We may sometimes pray for things that aren't really good for us, or we might not know what to pray for. But the Holy Spirit steps in and prays for us. Then, more and more, we find ourselves praying for the things that will please God. And God is always arranging everything for our good—if we love him.

8.30 **GOD KNOWS HIS CHILDREN** Here is a great mystery, but it's not so strange if you think about it. God has always known who his people would be. He has been planning a whole new human race with Jesus as the head instead of Adam. Whoever wants to be in God's family can be a member by accepting Jesus.

NOTES

against us? 32God did not keep back
his own Son, but he gave him for us.
If God did this, won't he freely give
us everything else? 33If God says his
chosen ones are acceptable to him,
can anyone bring charges against
them? 34Or can anyone condemn
them? No indeed! Christ died and
was raised to life, and now he is at
God's right side,[q] speaking to him
for us. 35Can anything separate us
from the love of Christ? Can trouble,
suffering, and hard times, or hunger
and nakedness, or danger and death?
36It is exactly as the Scriptures say,

"For you we face death
all day long.
We are like sheep
on their way
to the butcher."

37In everything we have won more
than a victory because of Christ who
loves us. 38I am sure that nothing can
separate us from God's love—not life
or death, not angels or spirits, not
the present or the future,* 39and not
powers above or powers below.
Nothing in all creation can separate
us from God's love for us in Christ
Jesus our Lord!

God's Choice of Israel

9 I am a follower of Christ, and the
Holy Spirit is a witness to my conscience. So I tell the truth and I am
not lying when I say 2my heart is broken and I am in great sorrow.
3I would gladly be placed under
God's curse and be separated from
Christ for the good of my own Jewish
people.* 4They are the descendants
of Israel, and they are also God's chosen people. God showed them his
glory. He made agreements with
them and gave them his Law. The
temple is theirs and so are the promises that God made to them. 5They
have those famous ancestors, who
were also the ancestors of Jesus
Christ. I pray that God, who rules
over all, will be praised forever![r]
Amen.

6It cannot be said that God broke
his promise. After all, not all of the
people of Israel are the true people
of God. 7-8In fact, when God made
the promise to Abraham, he meant
only Abraham's descendants by his
son Isaac. God was talking only
about Isaac when he promised
9Sarah, "At this time next year I will
return, and you will already have a
son."

10Don't forget what happened to
the twin sons of Isaac and Rebecca.
11-12Even before they were born or
had done anything good or bad, the
Lord told Rebecca that her older son
would serve the younger one. The
Lord said this to show that he makes
his own choices and that it was not
because of anything either of them
had done. 13That's why the Scriptures say that the Lord liked Jacob
more than Esau.

14Are we saying that God is unfair?

---

[q]*right side*: The place of power and honor.
[r]*Christ. I pray that God, who rules over all, will be praised forever*: Or "Christ, who rules over all. I pray that God will be praised forever" or "Christ. And I pray that Christ, who is God and rules over all, will be praised forever."

8.38 **IS GOD ON OUR SIDE?** Whether God is on our side depends on whether *we* are on *God's* side. If we are, nothing can stop us from doing and being all that God would like us to be. No one can accuse us or condemn us. God has accepted us. Nothing in heaven or earth or hell can separate us from Jesus. That's the greatest news in the world.

9.3 **PAUL LOVED HIS PEOPLE MORE THAN HIMSELF** Most people seem to be interested in themselves. That's why we are sometimes called the "me" generation. It comes as a shock to us to find a truly unselfish person. This was Paul. He even said he would rather go to hell himself than see his people lost in sin. We should think about Paul's kind of love.

NOTES

Certainly not!* 15The Lord told Moses that he has pity and mercy on
anyone he wants to. 16Everything
then depends on God's mercy and
not on what people want or do.
17In the Scriptures the Lord says to
Pharaoh, "I let you become king, so
that I could show you my power and
be praised by all people on earth."
18Everything depends on what God
decides to do, and he can either have
pity on people or make them
stubborn.

God's Anger and Mercy

19Someone may ask, "How can
God blame us, if he makes us behave
in the way he wants us to?" 20But,
my friend, I ask, "Who do you think
you are to question God? Does the
clay have the right to ask the potter
why he shaped it the way he did?
21Doesn't a potter have the right to
make a fancy bowl and a plain bowl
out of the same lump of clay?"

22God wanted to show his anger
and reveal his power against everyone who deserved to be destroyed.
But instead, he patiently put up with
them. 23He did this by showing how
glorious he is when he has pity on
the people he has chosen to share
in his glory.* 24Whether Jews or Gentiles, we are those chosen ones,
25just as the Lord says in the book
of Hosea,

"Although they are not
my people,
I will make them my people.
I will treat with love
those nations
that have never been loved.
26Once they were told,
'You are not my people.'
But in that very place
they will be called
children of the living God."

27And this is what the prophet
Isaiah said about the people of Israel,

"The people of Israel
are as many
as the grains of sand
along the beach.
But only a few who are left
will be saved.
28The Lord will be quick
and sure to do on earth
what he has warned
he will do."

29Isaiah also said,

"If the Lord All-Powerful
had not spared some
of our descendants,
we would have been destroyed
like the cities of Sodom
and Gomorrah."[s]

Israel and the Good News

30What does all of this mean? It
means that the Gentiles were not trying to be acceptable to God, but they
found that he would accept them if
they had faith.* 31It also means that

---

[s] *Sodom and Gomorrah*: During the time of Abraham the Lord destroyed these two cities because their people were so sinful.

9.14 **GOD IS NOT UNFAIR** If God had been a human being he would be unfair for choosing some and not others. He has mercy on some, and not on others. But God is not a selfish man, and he has perfect reasons for the decisions he makes, even if we can't understand his reasons. An infant doesn't understand its parent either. But if we love God, we trust him to do everything as it should be done. Then we don't ask foolish questions, like the man Paul describes in verse 19.

9.23 **WHY DID GOD CHOOSE SOME PEOPLE?** God's mercy was the reason he chose to save some. He could have let us all go to hell, but in his kindness he decided to send his Son to die for people. Then, whoever really wanted to could be saved by choosing Christ. Which are you choosing today: your own way, or God's way? That choice tells the story of your future.

9.30 **DON'T STUMBLE OVER JESUS** God opened a way for all to be saved, by faith. He also put a stone in front of those who would try to earn their way into heaven. All without faith would stumble over that stone, which is Jesus.

NOTES

the people of Israel were not acceptable to God. And why not? It was
because they were trying[t] to be
acceptable by obeying the Law
32instead of by having faith in God.
The people of Israel fell over the
stone that makes people stumble,
33just as God says in the Scriptures,

"Look! I am placing in Zion
a stone to make people
stumble and fall.
But those who have faith
in that one will never
be disappointed."

10 Dear friends, my greatest wish
and my prayer to God is for
the people of Israel to be saved.
2I know they love God, but they don't
understand 3what makes people acceptable to him. So they refuse to
trust God, and they try to be acceptable by obeying the Law.* 4But Christ
makes the Law no longer necessary[u]
for those who become acceptable to
God by faith.

Anyone Can Be Saved

5Moses said that a person could become acceptable to God by obeying
the Law. He did this when he wrote,
"If you want to live, you must do all
that the Law commands."

6But people whose faith makes
them acceptable to God will never
ask, "Who will go up to heaven to
bring Christ down?" 7Neither will
they ask, "Who will go down into
the world of the dead to raise him
to life?"

8All who are acceptable because
of their faith simply say, "The message is as near as your mouth or your
heart." And this is the same message
we preach about faith. 9So you will
be saved, if you honestly say, "Jesus
is Lord," and if you believe with all
your heart that God raised him from
death.* 10God will accept you and
save you, if you truly believe this and
tell it to others.

11The Scriptures say that no one
who has faith will be disappointed,
12no matter if that person is a Jew
or a Gentile. There is only one Lord,
and he is generous to everyone who
asks for his help. 13All who call out
to the Lord will be saved.

14But how can people ask the Lord
to save them, if they have never had
faith in him? How can they hear
about him unless someone tells
them? 15And how can anyone tell
them without being sent by the Lord?
The Scriptures say it is a beautiful
sight to see even the feet of someone
coming to preach the good news.*
16Yet not everyone has believed the
message. For example, the prophet
Isaiah asked, "Lord, has anyone believed what we said?"

17No one can have faith without
hearing the message about Christ.
18But am I saying that the people of
Israel did not hear? No, I am not!
The Scriptures say,

"The message was told
everywhere on earth.

[t]*because they were trying*: Or "while they were trying" or "even though they were trying." [u]*But Christ makes the Law no longer necessary*: Or "But Christ gives the full meaning to the Law."

10.3 **FAITH GETS US ACCEPTED** The Law is for knowing what God expects, but it can't make people good. The Law helps people realize they are sinners. Trying to be accepted by keeping the Law is a "dead-end street." God accepts people by faith in his Son Jesus.

10.9 **JUST ASK GOD TO SAVE YOU** Do you want to be saved? You don't have to know everything the religious experts know. You only have to know that God is waiting for you to come back to him. Then you will be safe forever with him. Everyone is saved who asks God for forgiveness because of Jesus who died and rose again.

10.15 **BEAUTIFUL FEET** Here is a strange but good expression. God wants us to carry this good news about how to be saved all over the world, and many are doing this. The nations can't believe in Jesus if our feet don't carry the good news. Such feet are beautiful feet indeed.

NOTES

It was announced
all over the world."*
19 Did the people of Israel understand
or not? Moses answered this question
when he told that the Lord had said,
"I will make Israel jealous
of people
who are a nation
of nobodies.
I will make them angry
at people
who don't understand
a thing."
20 Isaiah was fearless enough to tell
that the Lord had said,
"I was found by people
who were not looking
for me.
I appeared to the ones
who were not asking
about me."
21 And Isaiah said about the people
of Israel,
"All day long the Lord
has reached out
to people who are stubborn
and refuse to obey."*

God Has Not Rejected His People

11 Am I saying that God has
turned his back on his people?
Certainly not! I am one of the people
of Israel, and I myself am a descendant of Abraham from the tribe of
Benjamin. 2 God did not turn his back
on his chosen people. Don't you remember reading in the Scriptures
how Elijah complained to God about
the people of Israel?* 3 He said, "Lord,
they killed your prophets and destroyed your altars. I am the only one
left, and now they want to kill me."
4 But the Lord told Elijah, "I still
have seven thousand followers who
have not worshiped Baal." 5 It is the
same way now. God was kind to the
people of Israel, and so a few of them
are still his followers. 6 This happened
because of God's undeserved kindness and not because of anything
they have done. It could not have
happened except for God's kindness.
7 This means that only a chosen few
of the people of Israel found what
all of them were searching for. And
the rest of them were stubborn,
8 just as the Scriptures say,
"God made them so stupid
that their eyes are blind,
and their ears
are still deaf."
9 Then David said,
"Turn their meals
into bait for a trap,
so that they will stumble
and be given
what they deserve.
10 Blindfold their eyes!
Don't let them see.
Bend their backs
beneath a burden
that will never be lifted."

Gentiles Will Be Saved

11 Do I mean that the people of Israel fell, never to get up again? Cer-

10.18 **THE GOOD NEWS COMES TO THE GENTILES** The Jews heard the good news first, but many of them refused to put their faith in Jesus. So God continued with his plan. He used some of the Jewish believers to carry the good news to the people of other nations, and a great many of them trusted in Christ as their Savior.

10.21 **GOD HAS NO SPOILED CHILDREN** The Jews became spoiled because they thought God cared only about them. They even hated other nations, whom they treated as outsiders. God soon corrected that idea. He sent his word to the Gentiles, and many of them have believed the good news.

11.2 **GOD KEEPS HIS PROMISES** At first it may seem that God has forgotten Israel because of their sins. But he hasn't. God used the Jews as a channel to reach the Gentiles with the good news. But the Gentiles must remember how much they owe the Jews for the message they have received. The Lord also will remember his chosen people, the Jews, when he brings them back into his kingdom.

NOTES

tainly not! Their failure made it possible for the Gentiles to be saved, and
this will make the people of Israel
jealous. 12 But if the rest of the world's
people were helped so much by Israel's sin and loss, they will be helped
even more by Israel's full return.

13 I am now speaking to you Gentiles, and as long as I am an apostle
to you, I will take pride in my work.
14 I hope in this way to make some
of my own people jealous enough to
be saved. 15 When Israel rejected
God,[v] the rest of the people in the
world were able to turn to him. So
when God makes friends with Israel,
it will be like bringing the dead back
to life. 16 If part of a batch of dough
is made holy by being offered to God,
then all of the dough is holy. If the
roots of a tree are holy, the rest of
the tree is holy too.

17 You Gentiles are like branches
of a wild olive tree that were made
to be part of a cultivated olive tree.
You have taken the place of some
branches that were cut away from
it. And because of this, you enjoy the
blessings that come from being part
of that cultivated tree.* 18 But don't
think you are better than the
branches that were cut away. Just
remember that you are not supporting the roots of that tree. Its roots
are supporting you.

19 Maybe you think those branches
were cut away, so that you could be
put in their place. 20 That's true
enough. But they were cut away because they did not have faith, and
you are where you are because you
do have faith. So don't be proud, but
be afraid. 21 If God cut away those
natural branches, couldn't he do the
same to you?

22 Now you see both how kind and
how hard God can be. He was hard
on those who fell, but he was kind
to you. And he will keep on being
kind to you, if you keep on trusting
in his kindness. Otherwise, you will
be cut away too.

23 If those other branches will start
having faith, they will be made a part
of that tree again. God has the power
to put them back. 24 After all, it was
not natural for branches to be cut
from a wild olive tree and to be made
part of a cultivated olive tree. So it
is much more likely that God will join
the natural branches back to the cultivated olive tree.

The People of Israel Will Be Brought Back

25 My friends, I don't want you Gentiles to be too proud of yourselves.
So I will explain the mystery of what
has happened to the people of Israel.
Some of them have become stubborn,
and they will stay like that until the
complete number of you Gentiles has
come in.* 26 In this way all of Israel
will be saved, as the Scriptures say,

"From Zion someone will come
to rescue us.
Then Jacob's descendants
will stop being evil.
27 This is what the Lord
has promised to do
when he forgives
their sins."

---

[v] *When Israel rejected God:* Or "When Israel was rejected."

11.17 **WE ARE LIKE BRANCHES IN A TREE** We can't be proud about being Christians. All that we are and have comes from God. Not only that, but we're like small branches in a bigger tree that God has planted. Abraham, the father of the Jews, was the original root of the tree. The early branches were the Jews. But Gentile believers are only the later branches put onto God's tree.

11.25 **WATCH OUT FOR PRIDE** We must be careful about being proud. God can save anyone he wishes. He has chosen to save all who have faith in Jesus, whether they are Jews or Gentiles. When we consider people who have not accepted Jesus, we should be humble, not proud. God has the right to save or not save anyone. It is his mercy, not our "smart move," that does the saving.

NOTES

28The people of Israel are treated as God's enemies, so that the good news can come to you Gentiles. But they are still the chosen ones, and God loves them because of their famous ancestors. 29God does not take back the gifts he has given or forget about the people he has chosen.

30At one time you Gentiles rejected God. But now Israel has rejected God, and you have been shown mercy. 31And because of the mercy shown to you, they will also be shown mercy. 32All people have disobeyed God, and that's why he treats them as prisoners. But he does this, so that he can have mercy on all of them.

33Who can measure the wealth and wisdom and knowledge of God? Who can understand his decisions or explain what he does?*

34"Has anyone known
the thoughts of the Lord
or given him advice?
35Has anyone loaned
something to the Lord
that must be repaid?"

36Everything comes from the Lord. All things were made because of him and will return to him. Praise the Lord forever! Amen.

Christ Brings New Life

12 Dear friends, God is good. So I beg you to offer your bodies to him as a living sacrifice, pure and pleasing. That's the most sensible way to serve God.* 2Don't be like the people of this world, but let God change the way you think. Then you will know how to do everything that is good and pleasing to him.

3I realize how kind God has been to me, and so I tell each of you not to think you are better than you really are. Use good sense and measure yourself by the amount of faith God has given you. 4A body is made up of many parts, and each of them has its own use. 5That's how it is with us. There are many of us, but we each are part of the body of Christ, as well as part of one another.

6God has also given each of us different gifts to use. If we can prophesy, we should do it according to the amount of faith we have.* 7If we can serve others, we should serve. If we can teach, we should teach. 8If we can encourage others, we should encourage them. If we can give, we should be generous. If we are leaders, we should do our best. If we are good to others, we should do it cheerfully.

Rules for Christian Living

9Be sincere in your love for others. Hate everything that is evil and hold tight to everything that is good.*

11.33 **WE CAN'T FIGURE OUT GOD'S WAYS** Our goal in life is to obey God, not to understand all that he is doing. We know that he does everything right and he does everything well. God is the Creator and Owner of all that we can and cannot see. All that we have comes from him. We just have to trust him for the things we can't understand.

12.1 **WHAT YOU CAN GIVE TO GOD** Since God owns everything anyway, you can't give him anything he doesn't already possess. But you can willingly give back your life to him as an act of thanksgiving. Jesus died for you, so surely you can live for him. Then let God change your mind. When you think God's thoughts your life will be happy, because you will then want to please God.

12.6 **DO YOUR JOB** God has given us different jobs to do. We honor God and we reach our goals by doing well whatever he gives us to do in the world. What do you think God wants you to do for him?

12.9 **LOVE IS THE GREAT ANSWER** If we have the love of God in our hearts, then we will do all things in a way that pleases him. We can't do wrong to anyone if we are controlled by love. And we should have a special love for other believers, our brothers and sisters in the Lord.

NOTES

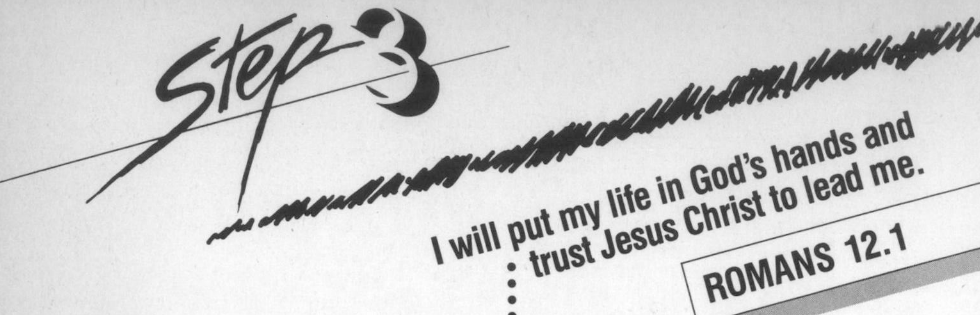

LIVING SACRIFICES

The Old Testament talks a lot about sacrifices. Not much of that goes on today, right? The apostle Paul wrote to the first church in Rome, telling its people to offer their bodies as a "living sacrifice." Sounds weird.

But what it means is that we give all of ourselves to God when we promise to follow and trust him. Some of us give our schedules—we promise that we will go to church from now on. Some of us promise our money—that we will start sharing part of what we have with God and the church, and quit being so selfish.

Others of us tell God that we will give him any part of life that is out of control, but cling to the parts we think are under control. "God, you can have this or that, but not what is most important."

GETTING HONEST

The Bible says here that God will have none of that. He wants all of each of us. He wants our minds, our wills, and our emotions. Have we ever made that kind of promise to God?

For another "Look Inside," turn to page 554.

10Love each other as brothers and
sisters and honor others more than
you do yourself. 11Never give up. Eagerly follow the Holy Spirit and serve
the Lord. 12Let your hope make you
glad. Be patient in time of trouble
and never stop praying.* 13Take care
of God's needy people and welcome
strangers into your home.
14Ask God to bless everyone who
mistreats you. Ask him to bless them
and not to curse them. 15When others
are happy, be happy with them, and
when they are sad, be sad. 16Be
friendly with everyone. Don't be
proud and feel that you are smarter
than others. Make friends with ordinary people.[w] 17Don't mistreat someone who has mistreated you. But try
to earn the respect of others, 18and
do your best to live at peace with
everyone.

19Dear friends, don't try to get
even. Let God take revenge. In the
Scriptures the Lord says,

"I am the one to take revenge
and pay them back."*

20The Scriptures also say,

"If your enemies are hungry,
give them something to eat.
And if they are thirsty,
give them something
to drink.
This will be the same
as piling burning coals
on their heads."

21Don't let evil defeat you, but defeat
evil with good.

Obey Rulers

13 Obey the rulers who have authority over you. Only God can
give authority to anyone, and he puts
these rulers in their places of power.*
2People who oppose the authorities
are opposing what God has done, and
they will be punished. 3Rulers are a
threat to evil people, not to good people. There is no need to be afraid of
the authorities. Just do right, and
they will praise you for it. 4After all,
they are God's servants, and it is their
duty to help you.

If you do something wrong, you
ought to be afraid, because these rulers have the right to punish you. They
are God's servants who punish criminals to show how angry God is.*
5But you should obey the rulers because you know it is the right thing

[w] *Make friends with ordinary people*: Or "Do ordinary jobs."

12.12 **WHERE HOPE COMES FROM** Hope looks for the best even when things are going wrong. And hope comes from having a healthy trust in God. We don't always understand what God plans to do, but we know he does everything just as it should be done. Then we are glad and have hope.

12.19 **HOW DO YOU TREAT ENEMIES?** You can't trust those who do you wrong, but hating them isn't the answer either. Feelings of hate destroy the hater more than the hated person. People who have a hateful spirit are actually ruining their health and taking years off their lives. It's better to be kind to our enemies as God was kind to us.

13.1 **HUMAN GOVERNMENT IS PART OF GOD'S PLAN** We shouldn't imagine that because we're Christians we don't have to obey laws. Some people in history have imagined that, and they have done a lot of harm to God's work in the world. Of course we can't obey laws that really cause us to disobey God. But in general, Christians are good citizens who pay their taxes and do what the law says.

13.4 **EARTHLY RULERS ARE ALSO GOD'S SERVANTS** Rulers may not always mean to serve God, but God sees to it that they do. They carry out God's plan whether they wish to or not. So you don't need to be afraid of authorities, even cruel ones. God will take care of us just the same.

NOTES

to do, and not just because of God's
anger.
6You must also pay your taxes. The
authorities are God's servants, and
it is their duty to take care of these
matters. 7Pay all that you owe,
whether it is taxes and fees or respect
and honor.

Love

8Let love be your only debt! If you
love others, you have done all that
the Law demands.* 9In the Law there
are many commands, such as, "Be
faithful in marriage. Do not murder.
Do not steal. Do not want what belongs to others." But all of these are
summed up in the command that
says, "Love others as much as you
love yourself." 10No one who loves
others will harm them. So love is all
that the Law demands.

The Day When Christ Returns

11You know what sort of times we
live in, and so you should live properly. It is time to wake up. You know
that the day when we will be saved
is nearer now than when we first put
our faith in the Lord. 12Night is almost over, and day will soon appear.
We must stop behaving as people do
in the dark and be ready to live in
the light.* 13So behave properly, as
people do in the day. Don't go to wild
parties or get drunk or be vulgar or
indecent. Don't quarrel or be jealous.
14Let the Lord Jesus Christ be as near
to you as the clothes you wear. Then
you won't try to satisfy your selfish
desires.

Don't Criticize Others

14 Welcome all the Lord's followers, even those whose faith is
weak. Don't criticize them for having
beliefs that are different from yours.*
2Some think it is all right to eat anything, while those whose faith is
weak will eat only vegetables.
3But you should not criticize others
for eating or for not eating. After all,
God welcomes everyone. 4What right
do you have to criticize someone
else's servants? Only their Lord can
decide if they are doing right, and
the Lord will make sure that they do
right.
5Some of the Lord's followers think
one day is more important than another. Others think all days are the
same. But each of you should make
up your own mind. 6Any followers
who count one day more important
than another day do it to honor their
Lord. And any followers who eat
meat give thanks to God, just like
the ones who don't eat meat.
7Whether we live or die, it must
be for God, rather than for ourselves.* 8Whether we live or die, it

13.8 **LOVE PROVES ITSELF TO BE RIGHT** Jesus summed up the Law of God by commanding us to love one another. Just as Paul says, when we love others we do them no wrong. But we do them a lot of good. The good news about Jesus would spread all over the world if Christians loved one another completely.

13.12 **JESUS IS COMING SOON** Even in Paul's day the times were so evil that it seemed the Lord must come very soon. We live in days like that too. This world is passing away. Since we know the Lord is surely coming, we should spend our lives in ways that honor Christ and bless others.

14.1 **WE'RE ALL DIFFERENT** There are no two people alike. So we can't very well expect everybody to live like ourselves in every way. If we aren't careful, we can get into the habit of finding fault with little things that don't really matter. Of course, sin is always wrong, but when it comes to mere customs, let's give people room to be themselves.

14.7 **WHY DO WE LIVE?** It's important to know why we live. We quickly come to the end of our earthly lives, and we shouldn't waste the time God has given us. We won't get to live this life again. We want to be able to say, "I spent my time trying to honor God."

NOTES

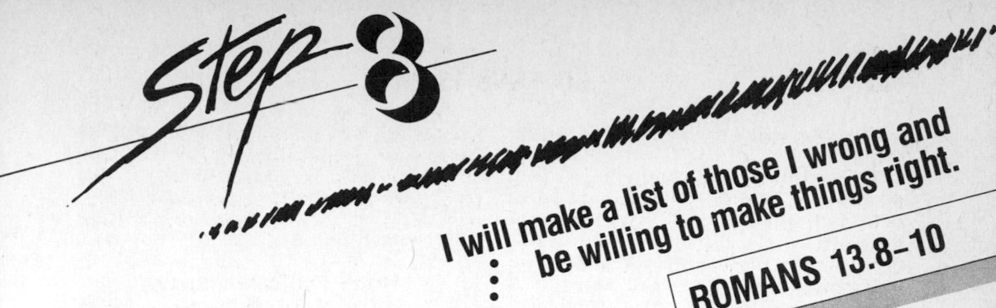

I will make a list of those I wrong and be willing to make things right.

ROMANS 13.8–10

SNEAKING OUT

Sometimes parents do some really stupid things, like grounding Christy because she failed her Earth Science test. Earth Science, *please!* Since when does knowing the components of soil have anything to do with life? Now, going to Eric Taylor's party on Saturday night, that has everything to do with living life to the fullest—my life that is.

Christy didn't really want to do it, but I wasn't about to show up without my girlfriend, so I talked her into sneaking out. I said she owed it to me if she really loved me. Being together is what going steady means. After her folks went to bed, Christy climbed out her bedroom window. I was waiting for her around the corner. I was laughing so hard about how easy it was to get away that I didn't see the STOP sign. When the other car hit the passenger door, Christy was thrown out the front windshield.

Christy lived through it, but her face is permanently scarred. I didn't get hurt at all, physically. But every single day I think about how I hurt Christy and her family and all the pain my actions caused them. I have tried every way I know to get rid of the guilt and the shame—partying, drinking, new friends. But so far I haven't been able to block out these feelings. They are always there.

STEP LOOK INSIDE 8

DEEP SCARS

We can never run away from guilt and shame. They are feelings in our lives that have to be dealt with, sometimes over and over again. We begin to deal with such feelings by making things right with those who have been affected by our behavior. But this can be very hard to do. Speaking openly and honestly with those we have hurt is a risk. They may reject us or become angry. When Christ entered our lives, he gave us a helper named the Holy Spirit. It is the Holy Spirit who will give us the power to do what is right by asking for forgiveness. He will guide us at the right time and in a way that reaches out to those we have hurt.

For another "Look Inside," turn to page 411.

must be for the Lord. Alive or dead,
we still belong to the Lord. 9This is
because Christ died and rose to life,
so that he would be the Lord of the
dead and of the living. 10Why do you
criticize other followers of the Lord?
Why do you look down on them? The
day is coming when God will judge
all of us.* 11In the Scriptures God
says,

"I swear by my very life
that everyone will kneel down
and praise my name!"

12And so, each of us must give an
account to God for what we do.

Don't Cause Problems for Others

13We must stop judging others. We
must also make up our minds not to
upset anyone's faith.* 14The Lord
Jesus has made it clear to me that
God considers all foods fit to eat. But
if you think some foods are unfit to
eat, then for you they are not fit.
15If you are hurting others by the
foods you eat, you are not guided by
love. Don't let your appetite destroy
someone Christ died for. 16Don't let
your right to eat bring shame to
Christ. 17God's kingdom is not about
eating and drinking. It is about pleasing God, about living in peace, and
about true happiness. All this comes
from the Holy Spirit. 18If you serve
Christ in this way, you will please
God and be respected by people.
19We should try[x] to live at peace and
help each other have a strong faith.
20Don't let your appetite destroy
what God has done. All foods are fit
to eat, but it is wrong to cause problems for others by what you eat.
21It is best not to eat meat or drink
wine or do anything else that causes
problems for other followers of the
Lord. 22What you believe about these
things should be kept between you
and God. You are fortunate, if your
actions don't make you have doubts.*
23But if you do have doubts about
what you eat, you are going against
your beliefs. And you know that is
wrong, because anything you do
against your beliefs is sin.

Please Others and Not Yourself

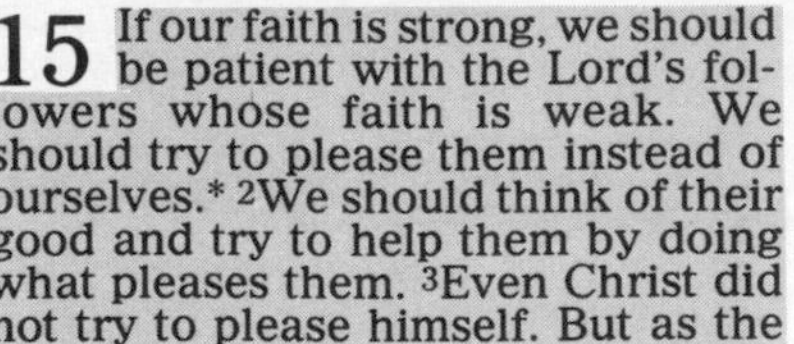

15 If our faith is strong, we should
be patient with the Lord's followers whose faith is weak. We
should try to please them instead of
ourselves.* 2We should think of their
good and try to help them by doing
what pleases them. 3Even Christ did
not try to please himself. But as the
Scriptures say, "The people who in-

[x] *We should try*: Some manuscripts have "We try."

14.10 GOD WILL JUDGE EVERYONE We may have to judge others' abilities to decide what they are fit to do, but we can't decide what God thinks about people. He is the only judge of that. We may be surprised to find out that some people we turn away from now are people God will one day accept.

14.13 CONSIDER OTHERS' FEELINGS We might feel free to do certain things that another believer doesn't feel free to do. If so, we should not wave our freedom in the other believer's face. It might hurt that believer's conscience. Out of love, we sometimes need to choose not to use our freedom right in front of such a person.

14.22 IF IN DOUBT, DON'T If we doubt whether something is right or wrong, that makes it wrong for us. We ought to have a clear conscience. Better to *know* we're not sinning than to have to *hope* we aren't.

15.1 THE IMPORTANCE OF PATIENCE When you have friends who fall into sin, what do you do? Do you make sure they feel as guilty as they should? Or do you try to help them through their failure and show them you still love them? Patience doesn't quickly give up on people. Also, you sometimes might have to be patient with people who judge *you* harshly.

NOTES

Step 9

I will make things right with people I wrong, except when to do so would hurt them or others.

ROMANS 15.1–6

A SITTING DUCK

Our actions, whether good or bad, have had an impact on the people around us. Before we got things straight with God, it's likely most of our relationships with others were pretty one-sided—whatever worked out best for us. That probably means we have some apologies to make.

Living at peace with others is our goal now. We have made peace with God and we're now working on forgiving ourselves, but until we make peace with people we have offended, we are sitting ducks.

STEP LOOK INSIDE 9

It works like this. More than likely, it was an out-of-balance relationship that led to our bad attitudes in the first place. That's why when we keep walls between ourselves and the people we have wronged or who have wronged us, then we are allowing those old attitudes to take root in us.

A MOVING TARGET

We owe it to ourselves and to those who care about us to make things right and keep them that way. Besides, when we are moving toward God and away from our past, we are more likely to be in the right place, doing the right thing. We need to take off the masks and tear down the walls. It is worth it!

For another "Look Inside," turn to page 398.

sulted you also insulted me." 4And
the Scriptures were written to teach
and encourage us by giving us hope.
5God is the one who makes us patient
and cheerful. I pray that he will help
you live at peace with each other,
as you follow Christ. 6Then all of you
together will praise God, the Father
of our Lord Jesus Christ.

The Good News Is for Jews and Gentiles

7Honor God by accepting each
other, as Christ has accepted you.*
8I tell you that Christ came as a servant of the Jews to show that God
has kept the promises he made to
their famous ancestors. Christ also
came, 9so that the Gentiles would
praise God for being kind to them.
It is just as the Scriptures say,

"I will tell the nations
about you,
and I will sing praises
to your name."

10The Scriptures also say to the
Gentiles, "Come and celebrate with
God's people."
11Again the Scriptures say,

"Praise the Lord,
all you Gentiles.
All you nations, come
and worship him."

12Isaiah says,

"Someone from David's family
will come to power.
He will rule the nations,
and they will put their hope
in him."

13I pray that God, who gives hope,
will bless you with complete happiness and peace because of your faith.
And may the power of the Holy Spirit
fill you with hope.

Paul's Work as a Missionary

14My friends, I am sure that you
are very good and that you have all
the knowledge you need to teach
each other.* 15But I have spoken to
you plainly and have tried to remind
you of some things. God was so kind
to me! 16He chose me to be a servant
of Christ Jesus for the Gentiles and
to do the work of a priest in the service of his good news. God did this
so that the Holy Spirit could make
the Gentiles into a holy offering,
pleasing to him.
17Because of Christ Jesus, I can
take pride in my service for God.
18In fact, all I will talk about is how
Christ let me speak and work, so that
the Gentiles would obey him.
19Indeed, I will tell how Christ
worked miracles and wonders by the
power of the Holy Spirit. I have
preached the good news about him
all the way from Jerusalem to Illyri-
cum. 20But I have always tried to
preach where people have never
heard about Christ. I am like a
builder who doesn't build on anyone
else's foundation. 21It is just as the
Scriptures say,

"All who have not
been told about him
will see him,
and those who have not
heard about him
will understand."

15.7 **ACCEPT EACH OTHER** In Paul's day, the problem was between Jews and Gentiles. In our time the problem is often between Christians with different beliefs. We must all try hard to learn the truth. But we have to be patient with differences and accept one another until we get to heaven. Let's not quarrel about words and teachings that no one understands perfectly.

15.14 **WHAT IS A MISSIONARY?** A missionary is not just someone who carries the good news across the sea. We should do that, too. But a missionary is a Christian who always tries, as Paul did, to share the news about Jesus with all who have never heard or understood why Jesus came. Every Christian is called by God to be a missionary like that.

NOTES

Paul's Plan to Visit Rome

22My work has always kept me from coming to see you.* 23Now there is nothing left for me to do in this part of the world, and for years I have wanted to visit you. 24So I plan to stop off on my way to Spain. Then after a short, but refreshing, visit with you, I hope you will quickly send me on.

25-26I am now on my way to Jerusalem to deliver the money that the Lord's followers in Macedonia and Achaia collected for God's needy people.* 27This is something they really wanted to do. But sharing their money with the Jews was also like paying back a debt, because the Jews had already shared their spiritual blessings with the Gentiles. 28After I have safely delivered this money, I will visit you and then go on to Spain. 29And when I do arrive in Rome, I know it will be with the full blessings of Christ.

30My friends, by the power of the Lord Jesus Christ and by the love that comes from the Holy Spirit, I beg you to pray sincerely with me and for me.* 31Pray that God will protect me from the unbelievers in Judea, and that his people in Jerusalem will be pleased with what I am doing. 32Ask God to let me come to you and have a pleasant and refreshing visit. 33I pray that God, who gives peace, will be with all of you. Amen.

Personal Greetings

16 I have good things to say about Phoebe, who is a leader in the church at Cenchreae.* 2Welcome her in a way that is proper for someone who has faith in the Lord and is one of God's own people. Help her in any way you can. After all, she has proved to be a respected leader for many others, including me.

3Give my greetings to Priscilla and Aquila. They have not only served Christ Jesus together with me, 4but they have even risked their lives for me. I am grateful for them and so are all the Gentile churches. 5Greet the church that meets in their home.

Greet my dear friend Epaenetus, who was the first person in Asia to have faith in Christ.

15.22 **HOW DID THE CHURCH AT ROME GET STARTED?** Notice that Paul hadn't been to Rome yet. So he is writing in his letter to a church that existed before he made the journey we read about at the end of the book of Acts. It may be that the Roman church was started by Roman Jews who were present at the Day of Pentecost told about in Acts 2.

15.26 **CHRISTIANS HELP ONE ANOTHER** Paul was carrying a gift from the Greeks to the believing Jews in Jerusalem. The Jewish Christians at Jerusalem were unable to earn a living because the other Jews rejected them. Here is a beautiful early example of the care Christians have for one another. Where there is true Christianity there is kindness.

15.30 **PRAYER HELPS** Paul asked the Roman Christians to pray for his safety in Judea, where he was going. We know from the book of Acts that Paul had a hard time in Judea with unbelieving Jews. But God saved Paul from those who wanted to kill him there. God answers our prayers, but not always in the way we might expect.

16.1 **PAUL HAD MANY TO GREET** Rome was a crossroads that became home to many people who had been born elsewhere, a lot like New York City and Los Angeles are today. Some people would live in Rome for a while and then move on. Paul must have known many Roman Christians, even though he had never set foot there, and there were many he wanted to greet.

NOTES

6 Greet Mary, who has worked so hard for you.

7 Greet my relatives[y] Andronicus and Junias, who were in jail with me. They are highly respected by the apostles and were followers of Christ before I was.

8 Greet Ampliatus, my dear friend whose faith is in the Lord.

9 Greet Urbanus, who serves Christ along with us.

Greet my dear friend Stachys.

10 Greet Apelles, a faithful servant of Christ.

Greet Aristobulus and his family.

11 Greet Herodion, who is a relative[y] of mine.

Greet Narcissus and the others in his family, who have faith in the Lord.

12 Greet Tryphaena and Tryphosa, who work hard for the Lord.

Greet my dear friend Persis. She also works hard for the Lord.

13 Greet Rufus, that special servant of the Lord, and greet his mother, who has been like a mother to me.

14 Greet Asyncritus, Phlegon, Hermes, Patrobas, and Hermas, as well as our friends who are with them.

15 Greet Philologus, Julia, Nereus and his sister, and Olympas, and all of God's people who are with them.

16 Be sure to give each other a warm greeting.

All of Christ's churches greet you.

17 My friends, I beg you to watch out for anyone who causes trouble and divides the church by refusing to do what all of you were taught. Stay away from them!* 18 They want to serve themselves and not Christ the Lord. Their flattery and fancy talk fool people who don't know any better. 19 I am glad that everyone knows how well you obey the Lord. But still, I want you to understand what is good and not have anything to do with evil. 20 Then God, who gives peace, will soon crush Satan under your feet. I pray that our Lord Jesus will be kind to you.

21 Timothy, who works with me, sends his greetings, and so do my relatives,[y] Lucius, Jason, and Sosipater.

22 I, Tertius, also send my greetings. I am a follower of the Lord, and I wrote this letter.[z]

23-24 Gaius welcomes me and the whole church into his home, and he sends his greetings.

Erastus, the city treasurer, and our dear friend Quartus send their greetings too.[a]

Paul's Closing Prayer

25 Praise God! He can make you strong by means of my good news, which is the message about[b] Jesus Christ. For ages and ages this message was kept secret,* 26 but now at last it has been told. The eternal God commanded his prophets to write about the good news, so that all nations would obey and have faith. 27 And now, because of Jesus Christ, we can praise the only wise God forever! Amen.[c]

---

[y] *relative*(s): Or "Jewish friend(s)." [z] *I wrote this letter*: Paul probably dictated this letter to Tertius. [a] *send their greetings, too*: Some manuscripts add, "I pray that our Lord Jesus Christ will always be kind to you. Amen." [b] *about*: Or "from." [c] *Amen*: Some manuscripts have verses 25-27 after 14.23. Others have the verses here and after 14.23, and one manuscript has them after 15.33.

16.17 **WATCH OUT FOR TROUBLEMAKERS** Paul had taught the Roman Christians what they should believe and how they should live. But he wanted them to watch out for people who cause arguments and divide the church. Sadly, there are some like that today. Such troublemakers often deceive with smooth words and pretend to be something they really are not. We must follow God's word in all things.

16.25 **PAUL'S PRAYER WAS ANSWERED** Through the years Paul's great letter to the Romans has been a bright, guiding light to Christians. Those who hear their Master's voice through Paul's good words have been strengthened and kept in their faith. Only the good news about Jesus can save us from sin and give us eternal life with God.

NOTES

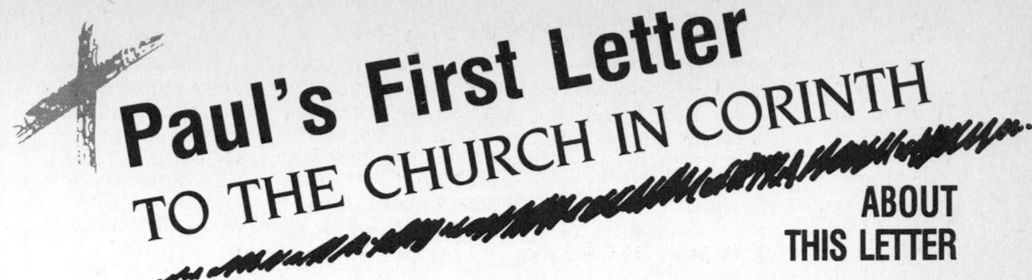

Paul's First Letter TO THE CHURCH IN CORINTH

ABOUT THIS LETTER

Although this letter is called the First Letter to the Corinthians, it is not really the first one that Paul wrote to this church. We know this because he mentions in this letter that he had written one before (5.9). The Christians in Corinth had also written to him (7.1), and part of First Corinthians contains Paul's answers to questions they had asked.

Corinth is a large port city in southern Greece. Paul began his work there in a Jewish meeting place, but he had to move next door to the home of a Gentile who had become a follower of Jesus (Acts 18.1–17). Most of the followers in Corinth were poor people (1 Corinthians 1.26–29), though some of them were wealthy (1 Corinthians 11.18–21), and one was even the city treasurer (Romans 16.23). While he was in Corinth, Paul worked as a tentmaker to earn a living (Acts 18.3; 1 Corinthians 4.12; 9.1–18).

Paul was especially concerned about the way the Corinthian Christians were always arguing and dividing themselves into groups (1.10—4.21) and about the way they treated one another (5.1—6.20). These are two of Paul's main concerns as he writes this letter. But he also wants to answer the questions they asked him about marriage (7.1–40) and food offered to idols (8.1–13). Paul encourages them to worship God the right way (10.1—14.40) and to be firm in their belief that God has given them victory over death (15.1–58).

Love, Paul tells them, is even more important than faith or hope. All of the problems in the church could be solved, if all the members would love one another, as Christians should:

Love is kind and patient,
never jealous, boastful,
proud, or rude.
Love rejoices in the truth,
but not in evil.
Love is always supportive,
loyal, hopeful,
and trusting.
Love never fails!
(13.4,5*a*,6–8)

A QUICK LOOK AT THIS LETTER

1 From Paul, chosen by God to be an apostle of Christ Jesus, and from Sosthenes, who is also a follower.

[2]To God's church in Corinth. Christ Jesus chose you to be his very own people, and you worship in his name, as we and all others do who call him Lord.

[3]My prayer is that God our Father and the Lord Jesus Christ will be kind to you and will bless you with peace!

[4]I never stop thanking my God for being kind enough to give you Christ Jesus,* [5]who helps you speak and understand so well. [6]Now you are certain that everything we told you about our Lord Christ Jesus is true. [7]You are not missing out on any blessings, as you wait for him to return. [8]And until the day Christ does return, he will keep you completely innocent. [9]God can be trusted, and he chose you to be partners with his Son, our Lord Jesus Christ.

Taking Sides

[10]My dear friends, as a follower of our Lord Jesus Christ, I beg you to get along with each other. Don't take sides. Always try to agree in what you think.* [11]Several people from Chloe's family[a] have already reported to me that you keep arguing with each other. [12]They have said that some of you claim to follow me, while others claim to follow Apollos or Peter[b] or Christ.

[13]Has Christ been divided up? Was I nailed to a cross for you? Were you baptized in my name? [14]I thank God[c] that I didn't baptize any of you except Crispus and Gaius. [15]Not one of you can say that you were baptized in my name. [16]I did baptize the family[d] of Stephanas, but I don't remember if I baptized anyone else. [17]Christ did not send me to baptize. He sent me to tell the good news without using big words that would make the cross of Christ lose its power.

---

[a]*family*: Family members and possibly slaves and others who may have lived in the house. [b]*Peter*: The Greek text has "Cephas," which is an Aramaic name meaning "rock." Peter is the Greek name with the same meaning. [c]*I thank God*: Some manuscripts have "I thank my God." [d]*family*: See the note at 1.11.

1.4 **PAUL WAS A GOOD THANKER** Paul never stopped thanking God for giving Jesus to believers. We probably don't thank God as much as we should. Notice also how quickly Paul mentioned the return of the Lord Jesus. Do we expect Jesus as strongly today? We should. He could return at any time.

1.10 **CHRISTIANS ARE ONE FAMILY** How easy it is to take our eyes off Jesus and become followers of some other leader. We revere the earthly teachers God sends to us, especially those who lead us to believe in Christ. But our true leader is Jesus himself. There ought to be no division in the family of God. We are the earthly body of Christ, and he is the head of that body.

NOTES

Christ Is God's Power and Wisdom

18The message about the cross
doesn't make any sense to lost people. But for those of us who are being
saved, it is God's power at work.*
19As God says in the Scriptures,

"I will destroy the wisdom
of all who claim
to be wise.
I will confuse those
who think they know
so much."

20What happened to those wise
people? What happened to those experts in the Scriptures? What happened to the ones who think they
have all the answers? Didn't God
show that the wisdom of this world
is foolish? 21God was wise and decided not to let the people of this
world use their wisdom to learn
about him.

Instead, God chose to save only
those who believe the foolish message we preach. 22Jews ask for miracles, and Greeks want something that
sounds wise. 23But we preach that
Christ was nailed to a cross. Most
Jews have problems with this, and
most Gentiles think it is foolish.
24Our message is God's power and
wisdom for the Jews and the Greeks
that he has chosen. 25Even when God
is foolish, he is wiser than everyone
else, and even when God is weak,
he is stronger than everyone else.

26My dear friends, remember what
you were when God chose you. The
people of this world didn't think that
many of you were wise. Only a few
of you were in places of power, and
not many of you came from important families.* 27But God chose the
foolish things of this world to put the
wise to shame. He chose the weak
things of this world to put the powerful to shame.

28What the world thinks is worthless, useless, and nothing at all is
what God has used to destroy what
the world considers important.
29God did all this to keep anyone
from bragging to him. 30You are
God's children. He sent Christ Jesus
to save us and to make us wise, acceptable, and holy. 31So if you want
to brag, do what the Scriptures say
and brag about the Lord.

Telling about Christ and the Cross

2 Friends, when I came and told
you the mystery[e] that God had
shared with us, I didn't use big words
or try to sound wise. 2In fact, while
I was with you, I made up my mind
to speak only about Jesus Christ, who
had been nailed to a cross.*

3At first, I was weak and trembling

---

[e] *mystery*: Some manuscripts have "testimony."

1.18 **GOD'S FOOLISHNESS IS WISDOM** Paul didn't mean that God can really be foolish. Paul uses that language to show that the greatest human wisdom counts for nothing compared to God's simplest thoughts. Paul's remarks take away any pride we may have about how smart we are. What we must do is learn God's wisdom by thinking his thoughts. But God's thoughts are shown by the preaching of Christ nailed to the cross, which most people think is foolishness.

1.26 **SEE HOW GOD CHOSE** Paul writes that God mainly chose humble, ordinary people to be believers, usually not the "VIP's." We should remember that when we share the good news today. All types of people are important in God's eyes, but especially the ones who are the least in the eyes of the world.

2.2 **CHRISTIANS HAVE ONE MESSAGE** The ancient Greeks were proud of their great schools of wisdom. Paul put all of that to shame by saying that God's wisdom is Christ nailed to the cross, not great human thoughts. Scholars often spend a lot of time, in today's places of learning, guessing about the meaning of life. God has told us life's meaning by sending his Son to die for our sins. That is the great wisdom of God that makes life worthwhile.

NOTES

with fear. 4When I talked with you
or preached, I didn't try to prove anything by sounding wise. I simply let
God's Spirit show his power. 5That
way you would have faith because
of God's power and not because of
human wisdom.
6We do use wisdom when speaking
to people who are mature in their
faith. But it is not the wisdom of this
world or of its rulers, who will soon
disappear. 7We speak of God's hidden and mysterious wisdom that God
decided to use for our glory long before the world began. 8The rulers of
this world didn't know anything
about this wisdom. If they had known
about it, they would not have nailed
the glorious Lord to a cross. 9But it
is just as the Scriptures say,

"What God has planned
for people who love him
is more than eyes have seen
or ears have heard.
It has never even
entered our minds!"

10God's Spirit has shown you
everything. His Spirit finds out everything, even what is deep in the mind
of God.* 11You are the only one who
knows what is in your own mind, and
God's Spirit is the only one who
knows what is in God's mind.
12But God has given us his Spirit.
That's why we don't think the same
way that the people of this world
think. That's also why we can recognize the blessings that God has given
us.
13Every word we speak was taught
to us by God's Spirit, not by human
wisdom. And this same Spirit helps
us teach spiritual things to spiritual
people.[f] 14That's why only someone
who has God's Spirit can understand
spiritual blessings. Anyone who does
not have God's Spirit thinks these
blessings are foolish. 15People who
are guided by the Spirit can make
all kinds of judgments, but they cannot be judged by others. 16The Scriptures ask,

"Has anyone ever known
the thoughts of the Lord
or given him advice?"

But we understand what Christ is
thinking.[g]

Working Together for God

3 My friends, you are acting like
the people of this world. That's
why I could not speak to you as spiritual people. You are like babies as
far as your faith in Christ is concerned.* 2So I had to treat you like
babies and feed you milk. You could
not take solid food, and you still cannot, 3because you are not yet spiritual. You are jealous and argue with
each other. This proves that you are
not spiritual and that you are acting
like the people of this world.
4Some of you say that you follow
me, and others claim to follow Apollos. Isn't that how ordinary people
behave? 5Apollos and I are merely
servants who helped you to have
faith. It was the Lord who made it
all happen. 6I planted the seeds, Apollos watered them, but God made
them sprout and grow.* 7What mat-

---

[f] *teach spiritual things to spiritual people*: Or "compare spiritual things with spiritual things."
[g] *we understand what Christ is thinking*: Or "we think as Christ does."

2.10 **GOD'S SPIRIT OUR TEACHER** This is an important thing the Holy Spirit does for believers: he reveals the mind of God. It was the Spirit who inspired the writers of this letter and other Scriptures. And the same Spirit shows us God's truth as we read. God's wisdom is a wonderful treasure, ready to be revealed to us if we are open to the Holy Spirit.

3.1 **GROW UP** Have you ever been told to grow up? This is what Paul says to us when we argue about small things that don't matter. Truly grown-up Christians have learned to be at peace with God and with those around them. Otherwise they're still babies.

3.6 **PLANTERS AND WATERERS** Sometimes one Christian will "plant the seed" of the good news, but another will "water," and then it is God who makes it grow. When we share the (*continued*)

NOTES

ters is not those who planted or watered, but God who made the plants
grow. 8The one who plants is just as
important as the one who waters.
Each one will be paid for what they
do. 9Apollos and I work together for
God, and you are God's garden and
God's building.

Only One Foundation

10God was kind and let me become
an expert builder. I laid a foundation
on which others have built. But we
must each be careful how we build,*
11because Christ is the only foundation. 12-13Whatever we build on that
foundation will be tested by fire on
the day of judgment. Then everyone
will find out if we have used gold,
silver, and precious stones, or wood,
hay, and straw. 14We will be rewarded if our building is left standing. 15But if it is destroyed by the fire,
we will lose everything. Yet we ourselves will be saved, like someone
escaping from flames.
16All of you surely know that you
are God's temple and that his Spirit
lives in you. 17Together you are God's
holy temple, and God will destroy
anyone who destroys his temple.
18Don't fool yourselves! If any of
you think you are wise in the things
of this world, you will have to become
foolish before you can be truly wise.
19This is because God considers the
wisdom of this world to be foolish.
It is just as the Scriptures say, "God
catches the wise when they try to
outsmart him." 20The Scriptures also
say, "The Lord knows that the plans
made by wise people are useless."
21-22So stop bragging about what
anyone has done. Paul and Apollos
and Peter[h] all belong to you. In fact,
everything is yours, including the
world, life, death, the present, and
the future. Everything belongs to
you, 23and you belong to Christ, and
Christ belongs to God.

The Work of the Apostles

4 Think of us as servants of Christ
who have been given the work
of explaining God's mysterious
ways. 2And since our first duty is to
be faithful to the one we work for,
3it doesn't matter to me if I am judged
by you or even by a court of law. In
fact, I don't judge myself. 4I don't
know of anything against me, but
that doesn't prove that I am right.
The Lord is my judge.* 5So don't
judge anyone until the Lord comes.
He will show what is hidden in the
dark and what is in everyone's heart.
Then God will be the one who praises
each of us.

6Friends, I have used Apollos and
myself as examples to teach you the
meaning of the saying, "Follow the
rules." I want you to stop saying that
one of us is better than the other.
7What is so special about you? What

[h]*Peter*: See the note at 1.12.

(*continued*) message about Jesus, we should not always expect to see results right away. There is sometimes a lot more watering and growing that still has to happen. It might look like somebody is rejecting the message. But God and other Christians can help your seed grow.

3.10 **BUILD ON A GOOD FOUNDATION** The secret of a building that lasts is its foundation. If we want to build a good life, we must build our lives on Jesus. Paul isn't against our being wise if Christ is the foundation of our wisdom. But we can't know any more about God than what he shows us in his word. Wisdom is what makes us able to use God's word to live well.

4.4 **OUR JUDGE IS GOD** We can look at this two ways. First, since God is our judge, we do what we ought to do for him, without trying to please all of the human "judges" who are looking on. Second, we ought to remember always that God is indeed the judge of all we think, say, and do. So we must always honor him and his word.

NOTES

do you have that you were not given?
And if it was given to you, how can
you brag? 8Are you already satisfied?
Are you now rich? Have you become
kings while we are still nobodies? I
wish you were kings. Then we could
have a share in your kingdom.
9It seems to me that God has put
us apostles in the worst possible
place. We are like prisoners on their
way to death. Angels and the people
of this world just laugh at us.
10Because of Christ we are thought
of as fools, but Christ has made you
wise. We are weak and hated, but
you are powerful and respected.
11Even today we go hungry and
thirsty and don't have anything to
wear except rags. We are mistreated
and don't have a place to live.*
12We work hard with our own hands,
and when people abuse us, we wish
them well. When we suffer, we are
patient. 13When someone curses us,
we answer with kind words. Until
now we are thought of as nothing
more than the trash and garbage of
this world.
14I am not writing to embarrass
you. I want to help you, just as parents help their own dear children.
15Ten thousand people may teach
you about Christ, but I am your only
father. You became my children
when I told you about Christ Jesus,
16and I want you to be like me.
17That's why I sent Timothy to you.
I love him like a son, and he is a faithful servant of the Lord. Timothy will
tell you what I do to follow Christ
and how it agrees with what I always
teach about Christ in every church.
18Some of you think I am not coming for a visit, and so you are bragging. 19But if the Lord lets me come,
I will soon be there. Then I will find
out if the ones who are doing all this
bragging really have any power.
20God's kingdom is not just a lot of
words. It is power. 21What do you
want me to do when I arrive? Do you
want me to be hard on you or to be
kind and gentle?

Immoral Followers

5 I have heard terrible things about
some of you. In fact, you are behaving worse than the Gentiles. A
man is even sleeping with his own
stepmother.[l]* 2You are proud, when
you ought to feel bad enough to chase
away anyone who acts like that.
3-4I am with you only in my
thoughts. But in the name of our Lord
Jesus I have already judged this man,
as though I were with you in person.
So when you meet together and the
power of the Lord Jesus is with you,
I will be there too. 5You must then
hand that man over to Satan. His
body will be destroyed, but his spirit
will be saved when the Lord Jesus
returns.
6Stop being proud! Don't you know
how a little yeast can spread through
the whole batch of dough? 7Get rid
of the old yeast! Then you will be
like fresh bread made without yeast,
and that is what you are. Our Passover lamb is Christ, who has already
been sacrificed. 8So don't celebrate
the festival by being evil and sinful,
which is like serving bread made
with yeast. Be pure and truthful and

---

[l]*is even sleeping with his own stepmother*: Or "has even married his own stepmother."

4.11 **RICHES DON'T COUNT WITH GOD** Jesus wasn't a rich man, and neither was Paul. In fact Paul said he had nothing to wear but rags. If we want to be leaders for Christ, let's not set our minds on being wealthy. If we do, we may forget Christ in our pursuit of riches. The desire to be rich is like quicksand: you can be swallowed by the very thing you hoped would hold you up.

5.1 **A CHRISTIAN CAN'T BE IMMORAL** Make no mistake about it—oil and water can't mix, and Christ and immoral living can't mix. Either the immoral practice must go, or you will be in danger of losing the friendship of Christ. Too often we hear of foolish people who thought they could be Christians and follow the devil too. That's hopeless.

NOTES

celebrate by using bread made without yeast.

9In my other letter[j] I told you not to have anything to do with immoral people. 10But I wasn't talking about the people of this world. You would have to leave this world to get away from everyone who is immoral or greedy or who cheats or worships idols. 11I was talking about your own people who are immoral or greedy or worship idols or curse others or get drunk or cheat. Don't even eat with them! 12Why should I judge outsiders? Aren't we supposed to judge only church members? 13God judges everyone else. The Scriptures say, "Chase away any of your own people who are evil."

Taking Each Other to Court

6 When one of you has a complaint against another, do you take your complaint to a court of sinners? Or do you take it to God's people?* 2Don't you know that God's people will judge the world? And if you are going to judge the world, can't you settle small problems? 3Don't you know that we will judge angels? And if that is so, we can surely judge everyday matters. 4Why do you take everyday complaints to judges who are not respected by the church? 5I say this to your shame. Aren't any of you wise enough to act as a judge between one follower and another? 6Why should one of you take another to be tried by unbelievers?

7When one of you takes another to court, all of you lose. It would be better to let yourselves be cheated and robbed. 8But instead, you cheat and rob other followers.

9Don't you know that evil people won't have a share in the blessings of God's kingdom? Don't fool yourselves! No one who is immoral or worships idols or is unfaithful in marriage or is a pervert or behaves like a homosexual 10will share in God's kingdom. Neither will any thief or greedy person or drunkard or anyone who curses and cheats others. 11Some of you used to be like that. But now the name of our Lord Jesus Christ and the power of God's Spirit have washed you and made you holy and acceptable to God.

Honor God with Your Body

12Some of you say, "We can do anything we want to." But I tell you that not everything is good for us. So I refuse to let anything have power over me.* 13You also say, "Food is meant for our bodies, and our bodies are meant for food." But I tell you that God will destroy them both. We are not supposed to do indecent things with our bodies. We are to use them for the Lord who is in charge of our bodies. 14God will raise us from death by the same power that he used when he raised our Lord to life.

15Don't you know that your bodies are part of the body of Christ? Is it right for me to join part of the body of Christ to an immoral woman? No,

[j] *other letter*: An unknown letter that Paul wrote to the Christians at Corinth before he wrote this one.

6.1 **LET CHRISTIANS ACT LIKE BROTHERS AND SISTERS** Christians should be able to settle their own differences. If we can't agree in private, then we can always ask wiser brothers and sisters in Christ to help us with our disagreements. Our goal is not to get the best of one another, but to honor our Savior. And we should not mind losing if we are "dead with Christ."

6.12 **OUR BODIES ARE CHRIST'S PROPERTY** We belong to Jesus, who paid for us with his blood. The Holy Spirit lives inside us, and we are parts of the body of Christ, the church. So we should treat our bodies as the holy things they are, keeping them pure for Jesus' sake. This is especially important to remember in these days of widespread drug abuse and sexual sin.

NOTES

it isn't! 16Don't you know that a man
who does that becomes part of her
body? The Scriptures say, "The two
of them will be like one person."
17But anyone who is joined to the
Lord is one in spirit with him.

18Don't be immoral in matters of
sex. That is a sin against your own
body in a way that no other sin is.
19Surely you know that your body
is a temple where the Holy Spirit
lives. The Spirit is in you and is a
gift from God. You are no longer your
own. 20God paid a great price for you.
So use your body to honor God.

Questions about Marriage

7 Now I will answer the questions
that you asked in your letter. You
asked, "Is it best for people not to
marry?"[k]* 2Well, having your own
husband or wife should keep you
from doing something immoral.
3Husbands and wives should be fair
with each other about having sex.
4A wife belongs to her husband instead of to herself, and a husband
belongs to his wife instead of to himself. 5So don't refuse sex to each
other, unless you agree not to have
sex for a little while, in order to spend
time in prayer. Then Satan won't be
able to tempt you because of your
lack of self-control. 6In my opinion
that is what should be done, though
I don't know of anything the Lord
said about this matter. 7I wish that
all of you were like me, but God has
given different gifts to each of us.

8Here is my advice for people who
have never been married and for widows. You should stay single, just as
I am. 9But if you don't have enough
self-control, then go ahead and get
married. After all, it is better to marry
than to burn with desire.[l]

10I instruct married couples to stay
together, and this is exactly what the
Lord himself taught. A wife who
leaves her husband 11should either
stay single or go back to her husband.
And a husband should not leave his
wife.

12I don't know of anything else the
Lord said about marriage. All I can
do is to give you my own advice. If
your wife is not a follower of the
Lord, but is willing to stay with you,
don't divorce her. 13If your husband
is not a follower, but is willing to stay
with you, don't divorce him. 14Your
husband or wife who is not a follower
is made holy by having you as a mate.
This also makes your children holy
and keeps them from being unclean
in God's sight.

15If your husband or wife is not a
follower of the Lord and decides to
divorce you, then you should agree
to it. You are no longer bound to that
person. After all, God chose you and
wants you to live at peace. 16And besides, how do you know if you will
be able to save your husband or wife
who is not a follower?

Obeying the Lord at All Times

17In every church I tell the people
to stay as they were when the Lord
Jesus chose them and God called
them to be his own. Now I say the
same thing to you.* 18If you are already circumcised, don't try to
change it. If you are not circumcised,

---

[k]*people not to marry*: Or "married couples not to have sex." [l]*with desire*: Or "in the flames of hell."

7.1 **BE LOYAL TO THE ONE YOU MARRY** If we say we're Christians, and we say we love one another, but we don't love our wives or husbands, then where is the love? Loving your neighbor, as Jesus said, certainly must mean loving the one closest to you—your husband or your wife. For love's sake and for Christ's, we ought to learn to give and take in marriage. Not forgiving and carrying each other's burdens leads to misery and ruin.

7.17 **SEND DOWN YOUR ROOTS** It is said that tumbleweeds never send down roots—which means they never amount to anything. Christians need to appreciate the places where God *(continued)*

NOTES

Step 4

PURITY—Obeying God with my moral choices

1 CORINTHIANS 6.18–20

LOOKING GOOD

She looks terrific, and she's coming on to me like there is no tomorrow! But for the first time in my life there is a tomorrow, and it's looking good. I don't need this extra baggage to carry around. Now I know it's not right to use people. God created our bodies for more than just a five-minute good time. Besides, if she really understood what she is doing and how she is selling herself short, she would quit.

Maybe I can steer things in a different direction and let her know how important she is, and not just because she has the best looking legs at school. Those legs! Help me, Lord, you know it's hard to kick old habits!

STEP LOOK AHEAD 4

HELPING YOURSELF

It's kind of neat. When we control our thoughts and actions, we not only help ourselves, but we help other people as well. Particularly in the area of sex, since as they say, "It takes two to tango"! We should encourage our friends to build good relationships. Taking time to work at them is worth it.

For another "Look Ahead," turn to page 423.

don't get circumcised. 19Being circumcised or uncircumcised is not really what matters. The important
thing is to obey God's commands.
20So don't try to change what you
were when God chose you. 21Are you
a slave? Don't let that bother you.
But if you can win your freedom, you
should. 22When the Lord chooses
slaves, they become his free people.
And when he chooses free people,
they become slaves of Christ. 23God
paid a great price for you. So don't
become slaves of anyone else.
24Stay what you were when God
chose you.

Unmarried People

25I don't know of anything that the
Lord said about widows or people
who have never been married.[m] But
I will tell you what I think. And you
can trust me, because the Lord has
treated me with kindness. 26We are
now going through hard times, and
I think it is best for you to stay as
you are. 27If you are married, stay
married. If you are not married, don't
try to get married.* 28It isn't wrong
to marry, even if you have never been
married before. But those who marry
will have a lot of trouble, and I want
to protect you from that.
29My friends, what I mean is that
the Lord will soon come,[n] and it won't
matter if you are married or not.
30It will be all the same if you are
crying or laughing, or if you are buying or are completely broke. 31It
won't make any difference how much
good you are getting from this world
or how much you like it. This world
as we know it is now passing away.
32I want all of you to be free from
worry. An unmarried man worries
about how to please the Lord.
33But a married man has more worries. He must worry about the things
of this world, because he wants to
please his wife. 34So he is pulled in
two directions. Unmarried women
and women who have never been
married[o] worry only about pleasing
the Lord, and they keep their bodies
and minds pure. But a married
woman worries about the things of
this world, because she wants to
please her husband. 35What I am saying is for your own good. I want to
help you to live right and to love the
Lord above all else.
36But suppose you are engaged to
someone old enough to be married,
and you want her so much that all
you can think about is getting married. Then go ahead and marry.[p]
There is nothing wrong with that.
37But it is better to have self-control
and to make up your mind not to
marry. 38It is perfectly all right to
marry, but it is better not to get married at all.
39A wife should stay married to her
husband until he dies. Then she is
free to marry again, but only to a
man who is a follower of the Lord.
40However, I think I am obeying

---

[m] *people who have never been married*: Or "virgins."
[n] *the Lord will soon come*: Or "there's not much time left" or "the time for decision comes quickly."
[o] *women who have never been married*: Or "virgins."
[p] *But suppose you are engaged . . . go ahead and marry*: Verses 36-38 may also be translated: 36"If you feel that you are not treating your grown daughter right by keeping her from getting married, then let her marry. You won't be doing anything wrong. 37But it is better to have self-control and make up your mind not to let your daughter get married. 38It is all right for you to let her marry. But it is better if you don't let her marry at all."

(*continued*) plants them. Let's not always be looking for a new church, or a new job, or a new home. God sometimes might be leading a person someplace else, but every Christian should be thankful for the place God has given, and use it to grow strong as Christ's servant.

7.27 **MARRIAGE ISN'T THE GOAL OF LIFE** Too many young people rush into marriage without counting what it will cost them. Then the marriage often ends in ruin. It's far better not to marry at all than to make a marriage that can't be happy. Marriage may cost more self-sacrifice for your husband's or wife's sake than you plan on giving. Think it over seriously.

NOTES

God's Spirit when I say she would
be happier to stay single.

Food Offered to Idols

8 In your letter you asked me about
food offered to idols. All of us
know something about this subject.
But knowledge makes us proud of
ourselves, while love makes us helpful to others.* 2In fact, people who

think they know so much don't know
anything at all. 3But God has no
doubts about who loves him.
4Even though food is offered to
idols, we know that none of the idols
in this world are alive. After all, there
is only one God. 5Many things in
heaven and on earth are called gods
and lords, but none of them really
are gods or lords. 6We have only one
God, and he is the Father. He created
everything, and we live for him. Jesus
Christ is our only Lord. Everything
was made by him, and by him life
was given to us.
7Not everyone knows these things.
In fact, many people have grown up
with the belief that idols have life in
them. So when they eat meat offered
to idols, they are bothered by a weak
conscience. 8But food doesn't bring
us any closer to God. We are no
worse off if we don't eat, and we are
no better off if we do.
9Don't cause problems for someone with a weak conscience, just because you have the right to eat anything.* 10You know all this, and so
it doesn't bother you to eat in the
temple of an idol. But suppose a person with a weak conscience sees you
and decides to eat food that has been
offered to idols. 11Then what you
know has destroyed someone Christ
died for. 12When you sin by hurting
a follower with a weak conscience,
you sin against Christ. 13So if I hurt
one of the Lord's followers by what
I eat, I will never eat meat as long
as I live.

The Rights of an Apostle

9 I am free. I am an apostle. I have
seen the Lord Jesus and have led
you to have faith in him. 2Others may
think that I am not an apostle, but
you are proof that I am an apostle
to you.
3When people question me, I tell
them 4that Barnabas and I have the
right to our food and drink. 5We each
have the right to marry one of the
Lord's followers and to take her
along with us, just as the other apostles and the Lord's brothers and
Peter[q] do. 6Are we the only ones who
have to support ourselves by working
at another job? 7Do soldiers pay their
own salaries? Don't people who raise
grapes eat some of what they grow?
Don't shepherds get milk from their
own goats?*
8-9I am not saying this on my own
authority. The Law of Moses tells us
not to muzzle an ox when it is grind-

[q] *Peter*: See the note at 1.12.

8.1 **TRUTH IS WHAT COUNTS** Christians in Corinth were concerned about eating food that might have been offered to some false idol in a temple. But Paul advised them not to worry about things they couldn't know for sure. After all, an idol is a false god, not a real one. A lesson for us here is that we should keep our eyes on the true God, and not worry so much about unknown dangers.

8.9 **BE WILLING TO LOSE YOUR RIGHTS** "Getting my rights" is too important to many people. When we have Christ, we don't need to go around demanding our rights. This is especially true if using our right to do something means someone else will be offended by it. In a case like that, we should think about the other person's feelings more than our own rights.

9.7 **SUPPORTING THE LORD'S WORK** A good worker doing good work deserves good pay. This is especially true of those who preach the good news and work to help churches. But all too often, Christians give pastors and other religious workers low pay, as if they *(continued)*

NOTES

ing grain. But was God concerned only about an ox? [10]No, he wasn't! He was talking about us. This was written in the Scriptures so that all who plow and all who grind the grain will look forward to sharing in the harvest.

[11]When we told the message to you, it was like planting spiritual seed. So we have the right to accept material things as our harvest from you. [12]If others have the right to do this, we have an even greater right. But we haven't used this right of ours. We are willing to put up with anything to keep from causing trouble for the message about Christ.

[13]Don't you know that people who work in the temple make their living from what is brought to the temple? Don't you know that a person who serves at the altar is given part of what is offered? [14]In the same way, the Lord wants everyone who preaches the good news to make a living from preaching this message.

[15]But I have never used these privileges of mine, and I am not writing this because I want to start now. I would rather die than have someone rob me of the right to take pride in this. [16]I don't have any reason to brag about preaching the good news. Preaching is something God told me to do, and if I don't do it, I am doomed. [17]If I preach because I want to, I will be paid. But even if I don't want to, it is still something that God has sent me to do. [18]What pay am I given? It is the chance to preach the good news free of charge and not to use the privileges that are mine because I am a preacher.

[19]I am not anyone's slave. But I have become a slave to everyone, so that I can win as many people as possible.* [20]When I am with the Jews, I live like a Jew to win Jews. They are ruled by the Law of Moses, and I am not. But I live by the Law to win them. [21]And when I am with people who are not ruled by the Law, I forget about the Law to win them. Of course, I never really forget about the law of God. In fact, I am ruled by the law of Christ. [22]When I am with people whose faith is weak, I live as they do to win them. I do everything I can to win everyone I possibly can. [23]I do all this for the good news, because I want to share in its blessings.

A Race and a Fight

[24]You know that many runners enter a race, and only one of them wins the prize. So run to win!* [25]Athletes work hard to win a crown that cannot last, but we do it for a crown that will last forever. [26]I don't run without a goal. And I don't box by beating my fists in the air. [27]I keep my body under control and make it my slave, so I won't lose out after telling the good news to others.

(*continued*) weren't doing anything very important. Pastors certainly don't need to be rich, but let's not keep them poor while we live well. God is not honored by that.

9.19 **DO WHAT IT TAKES TO WIN PEOPLE TO CHRIST** Missionaries need to live among the people they hope to bring to Jesus. This means taking on their customs, as much as someone can without sinning. Paul was willing to live like a Jew or like a Gentile. He would do whatever he was called to do for spreading the good news. Let's not be so "set in our ways" that we can't give up our personal desires in order to attract people to Jesus.

9.24 **WE NEED SELF-CONTROL** Professional athletes need to go without many luxuries if they're going to make the team. Keeping weight down and muscles toned requires work and discipline. The Christian is like such an athlete. We have decided to follow Jesus, and we're glad to leave behind the things that hold us back from spreading the good news about him. Can you play the game of life for Jesus?

NOTES

Don't Worship Idols

10 Friends, I want to remind you
that all of our ancestors walked
under the cloud and went through
the sea. 2This was like being baptized
and becoming followers of Moses.
3All of them also ate the same spiritual food 4and drank the same spiritual drink, which flowed from the
spiritual rock that followed them.
That rock was Christ. 5But most of
them did not please God. So they
died, and their bodies were scattered
all over the desert.
6What happened to them is a warning to keep us from wanting to do
the same evil things.* 7They worshiped idols, just as the Scriptures
say, "The people sat down to eat and
drink. Then they got up to dance
around." So don't worship idols.
8Some of those people did shameful
things, and in a single day about
twenty-three thousand of them died.
Don't do shameful things as they did.
9And don't try to test Christ,[r] as some
of them did and were later bitten by
poisonous snakes. 10Don't even
grumble, as some of them did and
were killed by the destroying angel.
11These things happened to them as
a warning to us. All this was written
in the Scriptures to teach us who live
in these last days.

12Even if you think you can stand
up to temptation, be careful not to
fall. 13You are tempted in the same
way that everyone else is tempted.
But God can be trusted not to let you
be tempted too much, and he will
show you how to escape from your
temptations.
14My friends, you must keep away
from idols. 15I am speaking to you
as people who have enough sense to
know what I am talking about.
16When we drink from the cup that
we ask God to bless, isn't that sharing
in the blood of Christ? When we eat
the bread that we break, isn't that
sharing in the body of Christ?
17By sharing in the same loaf of
bread, we become one body, even
though there are many of us.
18Aren't the people of Israel sharing in the worship when they gather
around the altar and eat the sacrifices
offered there? 19Am I saying that either the idols or the food sacrificed
to them is anything at all? 20No, I
am not! That food is really sacrificed
to demons and not to God. I don't
want you to have anything to do with
demons. 21You cannot drink from the
cup of demons and still drink from
the Lord's cup. You cannot eat at the
table of demons and still eat at
the Lord's table. 22We would make
the Lord jealous if we did that. And
we are not stronger than the Lord.

Always Honor God

23Some of you say, "We can do
whatever we want to!" But I tell you
that not everything we do is good or
helpful.* 24We should think about
others and not about ourselves.
25However, when you buy meat in
the market, go ahead and eat it. Keep
your conscience clear by not asking
where the meat came from. 26The
Scriptures say, "The earth and everything in it belong to the Lord."

[r]*Christ*: Some manuscripts have "the Lord."

10.6 **DO WE WORSHIP IDOLS?** We usually don't make statues of stone or wood and pray to them. But an idol is really anything besides God that comes first in our lives. An idol can be a career, a loved one, or something as trivial as a new car. God said, "You shall have no gods other than me." It only makes sense that God our Creator should be first in all of our thoughts.

10.23 **CHRISTIANS ARE FREE, BUT . . .** Believers are not living under the Jewish system of laws. The law that really governs Christians is the law of love. But love doesn't allow us to live in a way that dishonors God. The difference between right and wrong is always the same. Love means, too, that we should do without things that may set a bad example for other people, even though those things don't hurt us personally.

NOTES

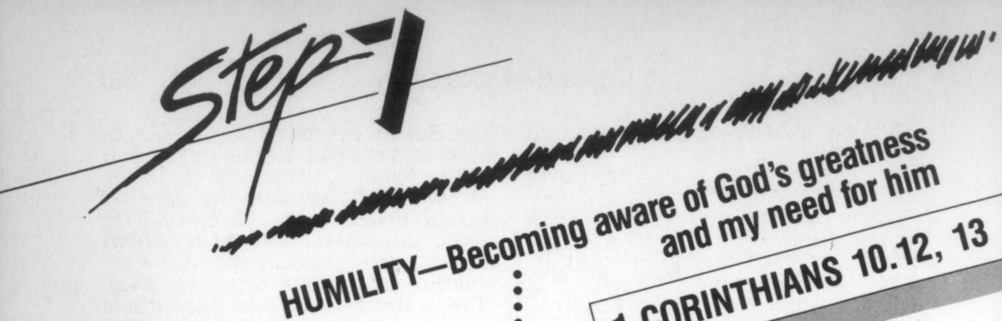

KICK THE HABIT

9:00 A.M.
This is it. This is the day I stop smoking. It's a nasty, dirty habit and I don't need it in my life.

10:00 A.M.
Piece of cake. I've got this thing licked. I'm halfway into the morning, and I don't even want a cigarette. I knew I could do it!

12:00 NOON
Okay, so maybe I'm eating a little more than usual. I need something in my mouth. It's going to be all right.

12:30 P.M.
Where are those matches?

HELP IS ON THE WAY

There are just some things in life we can't handle by ourselves. Unfortunately, we or someone we know has already found that out the hard way. Relying on God to help us through the rough times is our best defense.

We don't have to make it alone. The last thing Jesus said before he left this earth was, "I will be with you always." He will help us kick the habit.

STEP 7 LOOK AHEAD

For another "Look Ahead," turn to page 361.

27If an unbeliever invites you to
dinner, and you want to go, then go.
Eat whatever you are served. Don't
cause a problem for someone's conscience by asking where the food
came from. 28-29But if you are told
that it has been sacrificed to idols,
don't cause a problem by eating it.
I don't mean a problem for yourself,
but for the one who told you. Why
should my freedom be limited by
someone else's conscience? 30If I give
thanks for what I eat, why should
anyone accuse me of doing wrong?
31When you eat or drink or do anything else, always do it to honor God.
32Don't cause problems for Jews or
Greeks or anyone else who belongs
to God's church. 33I always try to
please others instead of myself, in
the hope that many of them will be
11 saved. 1You must follow my
example, as I follow the example of Christ.*

Rules for Worship

2I am proud of you, because you
always remember me and obey the
teachings I gave you. 3Now I want
you to know that Christ is the head
over all men, and a man is the
head over a woman. But God is the
head over Christ. 4This means that
any man who prays or prophesies
with something on his head brings
shame to his head.
5But any woman who prays or
prophesies without something on her
head brings shame to her head. In
fact, she may as well shave her head.[s]
6A woman should wear something
on her head. It is a disgrace for a
woman to shave her head or cut her
hair. But if she refuses to wear something on her head, let her cut off her
hair.
7Men were created to be like God
and to bring honor to God. This
means that a man should not wear
anything on his head. Women were
created to bring honor to men.
8It was the woman who was made
from a man, and not the man who
was made from a woman. 9He was
not created for her. She was created
for him. 10And so, because of this,
and also because of the angels, a
woman ought to wear something on
her head. This will show that she is
under someone's authority.
11As far as the Lord is concerned,
men and women need each other.
12It is true that the first woman came
from a man, but all other men have
been given birth by women. Yet God
is the one who created everything.
13Ask yourselves if it is proper for a
woman to pray without something
on her head. 14Isn't it unnatural and
disgraceful for men to have long
hair? 15But long hair is a beautiful
way for a woman to cover her head.
16This is how things are done in all
of God's churches,[t] and that's why
none of you should argue about what
I have said.

Rules for the Lord's Supper

17Your worship services do you
more harm than good. I am certainly
not going to praise you for this.*

---

[s] *she may as well shave her head*: A woman's hair was a mark of beauty, and it was shameful for a woman to cut her hair short or to shave her head, so that she looked like a man. [t] *This is how things are done in all of God's churches*: Or "There is no set rule for this in any of God's churches."

11.1 **BE NATURAL** Paul writes here about customs of worship and personal grooming. Although it seems that some of these matters are minor, there is an important idea here: we should honor the social customs of others. If we break them just to prove we're superior, that's pride, which is a sin. We should not try to be "one up" on somebody else. In our life together our goal is not to force our opinions on people, but to accept each other's wishes as much as we can.

11.17 **PROPER BEHAVIOR AT WORSHIP** How awful it is when people sin even while they meet together for worship. We should honor God with our thoughts, words, and actions at all times, but especially when we meet to worship him. To truly worship God, we need to have him on the throne, not ourselves.

NOTES

18I am told that you can't get along
with each other when you worship,
and I am sure that some of what I
have heard is true. 19You are bound
to argue with each other, but it is
easy to see which of you have God's
approval.

20When you meet together, you
don't really celebrate the Lord's Supper. 21You even start eating before
everyone gets to the meeting, and
some of you go hungry, while others
get drunk. 22Don't you have homes
where you can eat and drink? Do you
hate God's church? Do you want to
embarrass people who don't have
anything? What can I say to you? I
certainly cannot praise you.

The Lord's Supper
(Matthew 26.26–29; Mark 14.22–25; Luke 22.14–20)

23I have already told you what the
Lord Jesus did on the night he was
betrayed. And it came from the Lord
himself.

He took some bread in his
hands.* 24Then after he had
given thanks, he broke it and
said, "This is my body, which
is given for you. Eat this and
remember me."

25After the meal, Jesus took a
cup of wine in his hands and
said, "This is my blood, and with
it God makes his new agreement
with you. Drink this and
remember me."

26The Lord meant that when you
eat this bread and drink from this
cup, you tell about his death until he
comes.

27But if you eat the bread and drink
the wine in a way that is not worthy
of the Lord, you sin against his body
and blood. 28That's why you must ex-
amine the way you eat and drink.
29If you fail to understand that you
are the body of the Lord, you will
condemn yourselves by the way you
eat and drink. 30That's why many of
you are sick and weak and why a
lot of others have died. 31If we carefully judge ourselves, we won't be
punished. 32But when the Lord
judges and punishes us, he does it
to keep us from being condemned
with the rest of the world.

33My dear friends, you should wait
until everyone gets there before you
start eating. 34If you really are hungry, you can eat at home. Then you
won't condemn yourselves when you
meet together.

After I arrive, I will instruct you
about the other matters.

Spiritual Gifts

12 My friends, you asked me
about spiritual gifts.* 2I want
you to remember that before you became followers of the Lord, you were
led in all the wrong ways by idols
that cannot even talk. 3Now I want
you to know that if you are led by
God's Spirit, you will say that Jesus
is Lord, and you will never curse
Jesus.

4There are different kinds of spiritual gifts, but they all come from the
same Spirit. 5There are different
ways to serve the same Lord, 6and
we can each do different things. Yet
the same God works in all of us and
helps us in everything we do.

7The Spirit has given each of us
a special way of serving others.
8Some of us can speak with wisdom,
while others can speak with knowledge, but these gifts come from the

11.23 **WE LOVE THE LORD'S SUPPER** The Lord's Supper is the special time when we remember our Savior's death as a Christian group. Because Jesus died for our sins, we owe him our very lives. Remembering the Lord in this way draws us closer to him and reminds us of what his death means to us.

12.1 **GOD GIVES US GIFTS FOR SERVICE** The Holy Spirit gives at least one spiritual gift to each believer. The gift is not for showing off, but it is for serving in a way that builds up God's church. It's important that each of us is not just a watcher of how others use their gifts. But each must find out his or her gift and use it as God commands.

NOTES

same Spirit. 9To others the Spirit
has given great faith or the power
to heal the sick 10or the power to
work mighty miracles. Some of us
are prophets, and some of us recognize when God's Spirit is present.[u]
Others can speak different kinds of
languages, and still others can tell
what these languages mean. 11But it
is the Spirit who does all this and
decides which gifts to give to each
of us.

One Body with Many Parts

12The body of Christ has many different parts, just as any other body
does.* 13Some of us are Jews, and
others are Gentiles. Some of us are
slaves, and others are free. But God's
Spirit baptized each of us and made
us part of the body of Christ. Now
we each drink from that same Spirit.[v]
14Our bodies don't have just one
part. They have many parts. 15Sup-
pose a foot says, "I'm not a hand,
and so I'm not part of the body."
Wouldn't the foot still belong to the
body? 16Or suppose an ear says,
"I'm not an eye, and so I'm not part
of the body." Wouldn't the ear still
belong to the body? 17If our bodies
were only an eye, we couldn't hear a
thing. And if they were only an ear,
we couldn't smell a thing. 18But God
has put all parts of our body together
in the way that he decided is best.
19A body is not really a body, unless there is more than one part.
20It takes many parts to make a single
body. 21That's why the eyes cannot
say they don't need the hands. That's
also why the head cannot say it
doesn't need the feet. 22In fact, we
cannot get along without the parts
of the body that seem to be the weakest. 23We take special care to dress
up some parts of our bodies. We are
modest about our personal parts,
24but we don't have to be modest
about other parts.

God put our bodies together in such
a way that even the parts that seem
the least important are valuable.
25He did this to make all parts of the
body work together smoothly, with
each part caring about the others.
26If one part of our body hurts, we
hurt all over. If one part of our body
is honored, the whole body will be
happy.
27Together you are the body of
Christ. Each one of you is part of his
body.* 28First, God chose some people to be apostles and prophets and
teachers for the church. But he also
chose some to work miracles or heal
the sick or help others or be leaders
or speak different kinds of languages. 29Not everyone is an apostle.
Not everyone is a prophet. Not everyone is a teacher. Not everyone can
work miracles. 30Not everyone can
heal the sick. Not everyone can speak
different kinds of languages. Not
everyone can tell what these languages mean. 31I want you to desire
the best gifts.[w] So I will show you a
much better way.

---

[u]*and some of us . . . present:* Or "and some of us recognize the difference between God's Spirit and other spirits." [v]*Some of us are Jews . . . that same Spirit:* Verse 13 may also be translated, "God's Spirit is inside each of us, and all around us as well. So it doesn't matter that some of us are Jews and others are Gentiles and that some are slaves and others are free. Together we are one body." [w]*I want you to desire the best gifts:* Or "You desire the best gifts."

12.12 **BE A WORKING PART OF CHRIST'S BODY** Jesus leaves us on earth to be his presence in the world. In a real sense, we all are parts of the present earthly body of Jesus. That's awesome, isn't it? Think of how necessary it is for you to do your part in the body. If you don't, then the body is crippled. Pray that God will help you every day to be what he wants you to be in the world.

12.27 **DIFFERENT PEOPLE, DIFFERENT PARTS** Imagine what it would be like if an actor in a play started saying lines that were not his, but another actor's. The play would be a mess. Likewise, not all people in the church have all of the gifts God has given. We ought to know the place where God wants us, and do our best for him there.

NOTES

Love

13 What if I could speak
all languages of humans
and of angels?
If I did not love others,
I would be nothing more
than a noisy gong
or a clanging cymbal.*
2 What if I could prophesy
and understand all secrets
and all knowledge?
And what if I had faith
that moved mountains?
I would be nothing,
unless I loved others.
3 What if I gave away all
that I owned
and let myself
be burned alive?[x]
I would gain nothing,
unless I loved others.

4 Love is kind and patient,
never jealous, boastful,
proud, or 5 rude.
Love isn't selfish
or quick tempered.
It doesn't keep a record
of wrongs that others do.
6 Love rejoices in the truth,
but not in evil.
7 Love is always supportive,
loyal, hopeful,
and trusting.
8 Love never fails!

Everyone who prophesies
will stop,
and unknown languages
will no longer
be spoken.
All that we know
will be forgotten.
9 We don't know everything,
and our prophecies
are not complete.*
10 But what is perfect
will someday appear,
and what is not perfect
will then disappear.

11 When we were children,
we thought and reasoned
as children do.
But when we grew up,
we quit our childish ways.
12 Now all we can see of God
is like a cloudy picture
in a mirror.
Later we will see him
face to face.
We don't know everything,
but then we will,
just as God completely
understands us.
13 For now there are faith,
hope, and love.
But of these three,
the greatest is love.

Speaking Unknown Languages and Prophesying

14 Love should be your guide. Be
eager to have the gifts that
come from the Holy Spirit, especially
the gift of prophecy. 2 If you speak
languages that others don't know,
God will understand what you are
saying, though no one else will know
what you mean. You will be talking
about mysteries that only the Spirit

---

[x] *and let myself be burned alive*: Some manuscripts have "so that I could brag."

13.1 **THE GREATEST GIFT** When Paul got through describing spiritual gifts, he wanted to show that one gift is greater than all others. That gift is love. As you read carefully the way this love works, ask yourself, "Am I like that?" We would all be ashamed to know how far short of real love we come at times. But God will help us. Our love should be for the world, especially for other believers, and particularly for those with whom we live closest.

13.9 **SOMEDAY WE'LL HAVE THE ANSWERS** In this world God has revealed a lot to us, but there is still a lot that we just don't understand. But when God takes us to himself someday, the rest of what there is to know will become very clear to us. What a time that will be, as God opens up the treasures of his knowledge to us.

NOTES

understands. 3But when you prophesy, you will be understood, and others will be helped. They will be encouraged and made to feel better.

4By speaking languages that others don't know, you help only yourself. But by prophesying you help everyone in the church.* 5I am glad for you to speak unknown languages, although I had rather for you to prophesy. In fact, prophesying does much more good than speaking unknown languages, unless someone can help the church by explaining what you mean.

6My friends, what good would it do, if I came and spoke unknown languages to you and didn't explain what I meant? How would I help you, unless I told you what God had shown me or gave you some knowledge or prophecy or teaching? 7If all musical instruments sounded alike, how would you know the difference between a flute and a harp? 8If a bugle call isn't clear, how would you know to get ready for battle?

9That's how it is when you speak unknown languages. If no one can understand what you are talking about, you will only be talking to the wind. 10There are many different languages in this world, and all of them make sense. 11But if I don't understand the language that someone is using, we will be like foreigners to each other. 12If you really want spiritual gifts, choose the ones that will be most helpful to the church.

13When we speak languages that others don't know, we should pray for the power to explain what we mean. 14For example, if I use an unknown language in my prayers, my spirit prays but my mind is useless. 15Then what should I do? There are times when I should pray with my spirit, and times when I should pray with my mind. Sometimes I should sing with my spirit, and at other times I should sing with my mind.

16Suppose some strangers are in your worship service, when you are praising God with your spirit. If they don't understand you, how will they know to say, "Amen"? 17You may be worshiping God in a wonderful way, but no one else will be helped. 18I thank God that I speak unknown languages more than any of you. 19But words that make sense can help the church. That's why in church I had rather speak five words that make sense than to speak ten thousand words in a language that others don't know.

20My friends, stop thinking like children. Think like mature people and be as innocent as tiny babies.* 21In the Scriptures the Lord says,

"I will use strangers
who speak
unknown languages
to talk to my people.
They will speak to them
in foreign languages,
but still my people
won't listen to me."

22Languages that others don't know may mean something to unbelievers, but not to the Lord's followers. Prophecy, on the other hand, is for followers, not for unbelievers. 23Suppose everyone in your worship service started speaking unknown languages, and some outsiders or some unbelievers come in. Won't they think you are crazy? 24But suppose all of you are prophesying when those unbelievers and outsiders come in. They will realize that they are sinners, and they will want to

14.4 **ALWAYS TRY TO MAKE GOOD SENSE** Let's be sure we speak of God's saving work in ways that make sense to those around us. Just because people have the ability to speak strange languages and puzzle others, that doesn't mean they're doing something wonderful and good. Prophecy is useful, writes Paul, because it is a message that makes good sense to everybody.

14.20 **BE BOTH YOUNG AND OLD** Paul's advice to the church at Corinth was for them to be both young and old. Christians should be innocent as little children, honest and trusting. But we should have the maturity of adults, behaving ourselves and not being selfish.

NOTES

change their ways because of what
you are saying. 25They will tell what
is hidden in their hearts. Then they
will kneel down and say to God, "We
are certain that you are with these
people."

Worship Must Be Orderly

26My friends, when you meet to
worship, you must do everything for
the good of everyone there. That's
how it should be when someone sings
or teaches or tells what God has said
or speaks an unknown language or
explains what the language means.*
27No more than two or three of you
should speak unknown languages
during the meeting. You must take
turns, and someone should always
be there to explain what you mean.
28If no one can explain, you must
keep silent in church and speak only
to yourself and to God.
29Two or three persons may
prophesy, and everyone else must listen carefully. 30If someone sitting
there receives a message from God,
the speaker must stop and let the
other person speak. 31Let only one
person speak at a time, then all of
you will learn something and be encouraged. 32A prophet should be willing to stop and let someone else
speak. 33God wants everything to be
done peacefully and in order.
When God's people meet in church,
34the women must not be allowed to
speak. They must keep quiet and listen, as the Law of Moses teaches.
35If there is something they want to
know, they can ask their husbands
when they get home. It is disgraceful
for women to speak in church.
36God's message did not start with
you people, and you are not the only
ones it has reached.
37If you think of yourself as a
prophet or a spiritual person, you will
know that I am writing only what
the Lord has commanded. 38So don't
pay attention to anyone who ignores
what I am writing. 39My friends, be
eager to prophesy and don't stop anyone from speaking languages that
others don't know. 40But do everything properly and in order.

Christ Was Raised to Life

15 My friends, I want you to remember the message that I
preached and that you believed and
trusted. 2You will be saved by this
message, if you hold firmly to it. But
if you don't, your faith was all for
nothing.
3I told you the most important part
of the message, and you believed it.
That part is:
Christ died for our sins,
as the Scriptures say.*
4He was buried,
and three days later
he was raised to life,
as the Scriptures say.
5Christ appeared to Peter,[y]
then to the twelve.
6After this, he appeared
to more than five hundred
other followers.
Most of them are still alive,
but some have died.
7He also appeared to James,
and then to all
of the apostles.
8Finally, he appeared to me, even

[y]*Peter*: See the note at 1.12.

14.26 **A CHURCH MEETING ISN'T A RIOT** It seems that some of the meetings at Corinth were almost riots. Everybody was talking at once, and there was a lot of noise and confusion. It takes self-control to be a good listener, so others can have a turn at speaking. God is the One we want to hear from, not our noisy selves.

15.3 **WHAT THE GOOD NEWS IS** The good news is that Jesus didn't stay in his tomb. He rose up again on the third day, and he is alive now. If he lives in you by the Holy Spirit, you will be able to do his work now. Then other people will believe the good news about Jesus and live forever with him. Because he lives, we will live too.

NOTES

though I am like someone who was
born at the wrong time.[z]
9I am the least important of all the
apostles. In fact, I caused so much
trouble for God's church that I don't
even deserve to be called an apostle.
10But God was kind! He made me
what I am, and his kindness was not
wasted. I worked much harder than
any of the other apostles, although
it was really God's kindness at work
and not me. 11But it doesn't matter
if I preached or if they preached. All
of you believed the message just the
same.

God's People Will Be Raised to Life

12If we preach that Christ was
raised from death, how can some of
you say that the dead will not be
raised to life? 13If they won't be raised
to life, Christ himself was not raised
to life. 14And if Christ was not raised
to life, our message is worthless, and
so is your faith.* 15If the dead won't
be raised to life, we have told lies
about God by saying that he raised
Christ to life, when he really did not.
16So if the dead won't be raised to
life, Christ was not raised to life.
17Unless Christ was raised to life,
your faith is useless, and you are still
living in your sins. 18And those people who died after putting their faith
in him are completely lost. 19If our
hope in Christ is good only for this
life, we are worse off than anyone
else.
20But Christ has been raised to life!
And he makes us certain that others
will also be raised to life. 21Just as
we will die because of Adam, we will
be raised to life because of Christ.
22Adam brought death to all of us,
and Christ will bring life to all of us.
23But we must each wait our turn.
Christ was the first to be raised to
life, and his people will be raised to
life when he returns. 24Then after
Christ has destroyed all powers and
forces, the end will come, and he will
give the kingdom to God the Father.
25Christ will rule until he puts all
his enemies under his power,*
26and the last enemy he destroys will
be death. 27When the Scriptures say
that he will put everything under his
power, they don't include God. It was
God who put everything under the
power of Christ. 28After everything
is under the power of God's Son, he
will put himself under the power of
God, who put everything under his
Son's power. Then God will mean
everything to everyone.
29If the dead are not going to be
raised to life, what will people do who
are being baptized for them? Why
are they being baptized for those
dead people? 30And why do we always risk our lives 31and face death
every day? The pride that I have in
you because of Christ Jesus our Lord
is what makes me say this. 32What
do you think I gained by fighting wild
animals in Ephesus? If the dead are
not raised to life,

"Let's eat and drink.
Tomorrow we die."

33Don't fool yourselves. Bad friends
will destroy you. 34Be sensible and
stop sinning. You should be embar-

---

[z]*who was born at the wrong time*: The meaning of these words in Greek is not clear.

15.14 **THE RISEN CHRIST** What Paul's whole message rests on is the fact that Jesus Christ was raised to life. Without a risen Christ, the good news could not help anyone. A dead Savior whose bones lie cold in a grave somewhere could not save anyone from sin. But praise God—the grave is empty. Jesus Christ is alive.

15.25 **CHRIST WILL REIGN OVER ALL** When Jesus came the first time, he mostly acted like a servant. He wanted us not to be afraid of him, but to trust him. And he needed to die to save us. But some day he will return, and then we will see what a great King he really is. No other king could ever be like him. He shall reign forever and ever. That will be a glad forever indeed.

NOTES

rassed that some people still don't
know about God.

What Our Bodies Will Be Like

35 Some of you have asked, "How
will the dead be raised to life? What
kind of bodies will they have?"*
36 Don't be foolish. A seed must die
before it can sprout from the ground.
37 Wheat seeds and all other seeds
look different from the sprouts that
come up. 38 This is because God gives
everything the kind of body he wants
it to have. 39 People, animals, birds,
and fish are each made of flesh, but
none of them are alike. 40 Everything
in the heavens has a body, and so
does everything on earth. But each
one is very different from all the others. 41 The sun is not like the moon,
the moon is not like the stars, and
each star is different.

42 That's how it will be when our
bodies are raised to life. These bodies
will die, but the bodies that are raised
will live forever. 43 These ugly and
weak bodies will become beautiful
and strong. 44 As surely as there are
physical bodies, there are spiritual
bodies. And our physical bodies will
be changed into spiritual bodies.

45 The first man was named Adam,
and the Scriptures tell us that he was
a living person. But Jesus, who may
be called the last Adam, is a life-
giving spirit. 46 We see that the one
with a spiritual body did not come
first. He came after the one who had
a physical body. 47 The first man was
made from the dust of the earth, but
the second man came from heaven.
48 Everyone on earth has a body like
the body of the one who was made
from the dust of the earth. And everyone in heaven has a body like the
body of the one who came from
heaven. 49 Just as we are like the one
who was made out of earth, we will
be like the one who came from
heaven.

50 My friends, I want you to know
that our bodies of flesh and blood
will decay. This means that they cannot share in God's kingdom, which
lasts forever. 51 I will explain a mystery to you. Not every one of us will
die, but we will all be changed.*
52 It will happen suddenly, quicker
than the blink of an eye. At the sound
of the last trumpet the dead will be
raised. We will all be changed, so that
we will never die again. 53 Our dead
and decaying bodies will be changed
into bodies that won't die or decay.
54 The bodies we now have are weak
and can die. But they will be changed
into bodies that are eternal. Then the
Scriptures will come true,

"Death has lost the battle!
55 Where is its victory?
Where is its sting?"

56 Sin is what gives death its sting,
and the Law is the power behind sin.
57 But thank God for letting our Lord
Jesus Christ give us the victory!

58 My dear friends, stand firm and
don't be shaken. Always keep busy
working for the Lord. You know
that everything you do for him is
worthwhile.*

15.35 **HOW WILL WE LIVE AGAIN?** Jesus said that he came to give us life—a new kind of life, the life of God himself. When we have that life of God, we don't really die. If our bodies die before Jesus returns, we know that someday we will be raised to life with bodies that can never die. This is the kind of life God planned for us before sin came into the world and caused death.

15.51 **CHRIST WILL RETURN SUDDENLY** When Jesus returns, his living followers will be changed in that moment, and believers who have died will be raised. All weakness, sickness, and death that we have grown used to will be no more. We shall be new people with new and different bodies that experience only health, strength, and happiness. Believers who had died will be reunited with those they left behind, never to be separated again.

15.58 **WHAT WE DO FOR GOD WILL NEVER BE LOST** Paul elsewhere describes work done for God as gold, silver, and precious stones (see 1 Corinthians 3.12). Anything not done for God *(continued)*

NOTES

A Collection for God's People

16 When you collect money for
God's people, I want you to do
exactly what I told the churches in
Galatia to do. 2That is, each Sunday
each of you must put aside part of
what you have earned. If you do this,
you won't have to take up a collection
when I come. 3Choose some followers to take the money to Jerusalem.
I will send them on with the money
and with letters which show that you
approve of them. 4If you think I
should go along, they can go with
me.

Paul's Travel Plans

5After I have gone through Macedonia, I hope to see you* 6and visit
with you for a while. I may even stay
all winter, so that you can help me
on my way to wherever I will be going
next. 7If the Lord lets me, I would
rather come later for a longer visit
than to stop off now for only a short
visit. 8I will stay in Ephesus until Pentecost, 9because there is a wonderful
opportunity for me to do some work
here. But there are also many people
who are against me.

10When Timothy arrives, give him
a friendly welcome. He is doing the
Lord's work, just as I am. 11Don't let
anyone mistreat him. I am looking
for him to return to me together with
the other followers. So when he
leaves, send him off with your
blessings.

12I have tried hard to get our friend
Apollos to visit you with the other
followers. He doesn't want to come
just now, but he will come when he
can.

Personal Concerns and Greetings

13Keep alert. Be firm in your faith.
Stay brave and strong.* 14Show love
in everything you do.

15You know that Stephanas and his
family were the first in Achaia to
have faith in the Lord. They have
done all they can for God's people.
My friends, I ask you 16to obey leaders like them and to do the same for
all others who work hard with you.

17I was glad to see Stephanas and
Fortunatus and Achaicus. Having
them here was like having you.
18They made me feel much better,
just as they made you feel better. You
should appreciate people like them.

19Greetings from the churches in
Asia.

Aquila and Priscilla, together with
the church that meets in their house,
send greetings in the name of the
Lord.

20All of the Lord's followers send
their greetings.

Give each other a warm greeting.

21I am signing this letter myself:
PAUL.

22I pray that God will put a curse
on everyone who does not love the
Lord. And may the Lord come soon.

23I pray that the Lord Jesus will
be kind to you.

24I love everyone who belongs to
Christ Jesus. Amen.

(*continued*) will not last. That is a great privilege. We can work with God to do things that last forever. The people we win to Christ, and even the little things we do, like giving a cool drink of water for Christ, will be treasured forever by God.

16.5 **CHRISTIANS ARE FRIENDLY** Notice this other side of Paul's character. Usually we think of him as being concerned only about high matters, perhaps even severe at times. But Paul's real personality was tender and friendly. He enjoyed the friendship of God's people. This is a model for us. A stand-offish Christian just doesn't make sense.

16.13 **STRENGTH PLUS LOVE** Paul's advice here for Christians is to be firm, brave, and strong, *and* always to show love. That's quite a combination—to be tough and tender at the same time. But that's what it means to be like Jesus.

NOTES

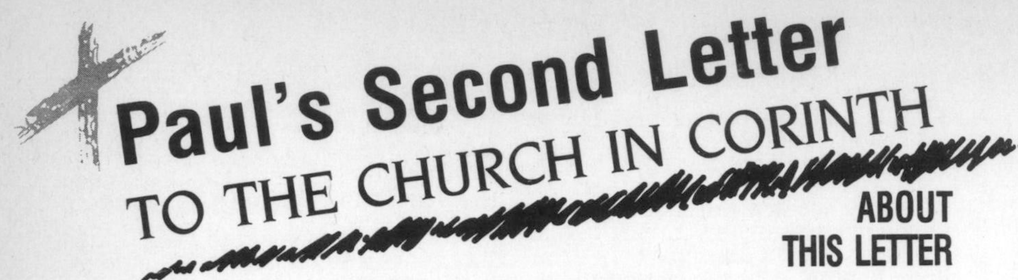

Paul's Second Letter TO THE CHURCH IN CORINTH

ABOUT THIS LETTER

In the beginning of this letter Paul answers the concerns of the Christians in Corinth who accused him of not living up to his promise to visit them. Paul had changed his mind for a good reason. He had stayed away from Corinth so that he would not seem to be too hard and demanding (1.23). He also wanted to see if they would follow his instructions about forgiving and comforting people who had sinned (2.5–11).

Paul reminds the Corinthians that God is generous and wants them to be just as generous in their giving to help God's people in Jerusalem and Judea (8.1—9.15).

Paul is a servant of God's new agreement (3.1–17). He is faithful in trying to bring people to God, even if it means terrible suffering for himself (4.1—6.13; 10.1—12.10). And what has God done to make it possible for us to come to him?

> *God has done it all! He sent Christ to make peace between himself and us, and he has given us the work of making peace between himself and others. What we mean is that God was in Christ, offering peace and forgiveness to the people of this world. And he has given us the work of sharing his message about peace.* (5.18,19)

A QUICK LOOK AT THIS LETTER

1. Paul Gives Thanks to God (1.1–11)
2. The Work of an Apostle for God's People (1.12—2.17)
3. Guided by the Love of Christ (3.1—7.16)
4. Gifts for the Poor (8.1—9.15)
5. Paul Is a True Apostle (10.1—13.10)
6. Final Greetings (13.11–13)

1 From Paul, chosen by God to be
an apostle of Jesus Christ, and
from Timothy, who is also a follower.
To God's church in Corinth and to
all of God's people in Achaia.
2I pray that God our Father and
the Lord Jesus Christ will be kind
to you and will bless you with peace!

Paul Gives Thanks

3Praise God, the Father of our Lord
Jesus Christ! The Father is a merciful
God, who always gives us comfort.
4He comforts us when we are in trouble, so that we can share that same
comfort with others in trouble.
5We share in the terrible sufferings
of Christ, but also in the wonderful
comfort he gives.* 6We suffer in the
hope that you will be comforted and
saved. And because we are comforted, you will also be comforted,
as you patiently endure suffering like
ours. 7You never disappoint us. You
suffered as much as we did, and we
know that you will be comforted as
we were.
8My friends, I want you to know
what a hard time we had in Asia.
Our sufferings were so horrible and
so unbearable that death seemed certain. 9In fact, we felt sure that we
were going to die. But this made us
stop trusting in ourselves and start
trusting God, who raises the dead to
life. 10God saved us from the threat
of death,[a] and we are sure that he
will do it again and again. 11Please
help us by praying for us. Then many
people will give thanks for the blessings we receive in answer to all these
prayers.

Paul's Change of Plans

12We can be proud of our clear conscience. We have always lived honestly and sincerely, especially when
we were with you. And we were
guided by God's kindness instead of
by the wisdom of this world. 13I am
not writing anything you cannot read
and understand. I hope you will understand it completely, 14just as you
already partly understand us. Then
when our Lord Jesus returns, you can
be as proud of us as we are of you.
15I was so sure of your pride in us
that I had planned to visit you first
of all. In this way you would have
the blessing of two visits from me.
16Once on my way to Macedonia and
again on my return from there. Then
you could send me on to Judea.
17Do you think I couldn't make up
my mind about what to do? Or do I
seem like someone who says "Yes"
or "No" simply to please others?
18God can be trusted, and so can I,
when I say that our answer to you
has always been "Yes" and never
"No." 19This is because Jesus Christ
the Son of God is always "Yes" and
never "No." And he is the one that
Silas,[b] Timothy, and I told you
about.*
20Christ says "Yes" to all of God's
promises. That's why we have Christ
to say "Amen"[c] for us to the glory
of God. 21And so God makes it possi-

[a] *the threat of death*: Some manuscripts have "many threats of death." [b] *Silas*: The Greek text has "Silvanus," which is another form of the name Silas. [c] *Amen*: The word "amen" is used here with the meaning of "yes."

1.5 **SUFFERING SHOULD HELP US** No one wants to suffer. But living in the world brings some suffering to everyone. For Christians, suffering is a means of drawing us into closer friendship with God. When we suffer, we remember that Jesus himself suffered for us. The Holy Spirit helps us even to be thankful for suffering. Times of suffering are times when God comes nearest to us and comforts us with his presence.

1.19 **JESUS SAYS "YES"** This means that the Corinthians enjoyed the good things God promised to those who love his only Son. If we love Jesus as many of the Corinthians did, then God is saying "yes" to us, too. We say "yes" to God's offer to save us because of Jesus and his death on the cross. Then we have God's "yes" in reply. He has accepted us, and he will never leave us.

NOTES

ble for you and us to stand firmly
together with Christ. God is also the
one who chose us 22and put his Spirit
in our hearts to show that we belong
only to him.
23God is my witness that I stayed
away from Corinth, just to keep from
being hard on you. 24We are not
bosses who tell you what to believe.
We are working with you to make
you glad, because your faith is
strong.

2 I have decided not to make my
next visit with you so painful.
2If I make you feel bad, who would
be left to cheer me up, except the
people I had made to feel bad?
3The reason I want to be happy is
to make you happy. I wrote as I did
because I didn't want to visit you and
be made to feel bad, when you should
make me feel happy. 4At the time I
wrote, I was suffering terribly. My
eyes were full of tears, and my heart
was broken. But I didn't want to
make you feel bad. I only wanted to
let you know how much I cared for
you.

Forgiveness

5I don't want to be hard on you.
But if one of you has made someone
feel bad, I am not really the one who
has been made to feel bad. Some of
you are the ones. 6Most of you have
already pointed out the wrong that
person did, and that is punishment
enough for what was done.
7When people sin, you should forgive and comfort them, so they won't
give up in despair.* 8You should
make them sure of your love for
them.
9I also wrote because I wanted to
test you and find out if you would
follow my instructions. 10I will forgive anyone you forgive. Yes, for
your sake and with Christ as my witness, I have forgiven whatever
needed to be forgiven. 11I have done
this to keep Satan from getting the
better of us. We all know what goes
on in his mind.
12When I went to Troas to preach
the good news about Christ, I found
that the Lord had already prepared
the way. 13But I was worried when
I didn't find my friend Titus there.
So I left the other followers and went
on to Macedonia.

14I am grateful that God always
makes it possible for Christ to lead
us to victory. God also helps us
spread the knowledge about Christ
everywhere, and this knowledge is
like the smell of perfume.* 15-16In
fact, God thinks of us as a perfume
that brings Christ to everyone. For
people who are being saved, this perfume has a sweet smell and leads
them to a better life. But for people
who are lost, it has a bad smell and
leads them to a horrible death.
No one really has what it takes to
do this work. 17A lot of people try
to get rich from preaching God's message. But we are God's sincere messengers, and by the power of Christ
we speak our message with God as
our witness.

God's New Agreement

3 Are we once again bragging
about ourselves? Do we need letters to you or from you to tell others about us? Some people do need

2.7 **MERCY IS BETTER THAN PUNISHMENT** Being like Jesus means wanting to forgive instead of blame. It means wanting to bring back sinners instead of punishing them and sending them away. This is the way we should act toward people in our churches who have sinned. We should do all we can to get them to turn from their sins and come back.

2.14 **DOES THE GOOD NEWS SMELL SWEET TO YOU?** This is an unusual statement. But it's a good way of saying that the news about Jesus really comes as happy, good news to many people. But, strangely, to others it comes as bad news. This "bad smell" is how the news about Jesus seems to people who don't want their lives to change. The news only makes them uncomfortable.

NOTES

Step 9

COMPASSION—Considering how our actions may create reactions in others

2 CORINTHIANS 2.5–8

HALF A CHANCE

I want to say, "It's all your fault I'm in this mess!" If you and Dad hadn't split up, you would be home when I need you. I got in with the wrong crowd because they were the only ones there for me."

It is so much easier to place the blame for my mistakes on someone else. Of course, my parents are responsible for a lot of what I've been through, but, ultimately, a seventeen-year-old should know better. I did. Even though they got a divorce from each other, they didn't divorce me. They made sure I knew the difference between right and wrong. I just got mad at them for breaking up my home and decided to make their lives as miserable as they have made mine.

STEP 9 LOOK AHEAD

I understand now that we have to make our own happiness. We decide inside whether we are going to be losers or winners. Circumstances don't determine that; they just make it easier or harder to get there. That is why I decided to back off putting the guilt trip on my mom. I know she is doing the best she can to love me. I need to give her half a chance.

A TEAM EFFORT

No one can go it alone. God doesn't expect us to. But sometimes the team that God put us on doesn't work well together. The children of a broken home probably have a lot of reasons to point a finger and place the blame, but what good would it do? We need to be careful when we are tempted to attack the team members in our lives. We can make a difference by helping them through our encouragement and love.

For another "Look Ahead," turn to page 476.

letters that tell about them. 2But you are our letter, and you are in our[d] hearts for everyone to read and understand. 3You are like a letter written by Christ and delivered by us. But you are not written with pen and ink or on tablets made of stone. You are written in our hearts by the Spirit of the living God.

4We are sure about all this. Christ makes us sure in the very presence of God. 5We don't have the right to claim that we have done anything on our own. God gives us what it takes to do all that we do. 6He makes us worthy to be the servants of his new agreement that comes from the Holy Spirit and not from a written Law. After all, the Law brings death, but the Spirit brings life.*

7The Law of Moses brought only the promise of death, even though it was carved on stones and given in a wonderful way. Still the Law made Moses' face shine so brightly that the people of Israel could not look at it, even though it was a fading glory. 8So won't the agreement that the Spirit brings to us be even more wonderful? 9If something that brings the death sentence is glorious, won't something that makes us acceptable to God be even more glorious? 10In fact, the new agreement is so wonderful that the Law is no longer glorious at all. 11The Law was given with a glory that faded away. But the glory of the new agreement is much greater, because it will never fade away.

12This wonderful hope makes us feel like speaking freely. 13We are not like Moses. His face was shining, but he covered it to keep the people of Israel from seeing the brightness fade away. 14The people were stubborn, and something still keeps them from seeing the truth when the Law is read. Only Christ can take away the covering that keeps them from seeing.*

15When the Law of Moses is read, the people of Israel have their minds covered over 16with a covering that is removed only for those who turn to the Lord. 17The Lord and the Spirit are one and the same, and the Lord's Spirit sets us free. 18So our faces are not covered. They show the bright glory of the Lord, as the Lord's Spirit makes us more and more like our glorious Lord.

Treasure in Clay Jars

4 God has been kind enough to trust us with this work. That's why we never give up. 2We don't do shameful things that must be kept secret. And we don't try to fool anyone or twist God's message around. God is our witness that we speak only the truth, so others will be sure that we can be trusted. 3If there is anything hidden about our message, it is hidden only to someone who is lost.

4The god who rules this world has blinded the minds of unbelievers. They cannot see the light, which is the good news about our glorious Christ, who shows what God is like. 5We are not preaching about ourselves. Our message is that Jesus Christ is Lord. He also sent us to be your servants. 6The Scriptures say,

---

[d]*our*: Some manuscripts have "your."

3.6 **JESUS BRINGS LIFE** The Old Testament was a part of God's plan that has passed away. The Law that it proclaimed was a good Law that brought death to those who refused to obey it. But the New Testament grows out of the Old Testament. Jesus Christ was the One promised by the Old Testament prophets. Jesus doesn't bring death, but life everlasting by the Holy Spirit.

3.14 **CHRIST REMOVES THE COVERING** Sometimes people can hear about the good news again and again, and they don't accept it. It's like their understanding is hidden under a covering. That's what sin does—it keeps people from seeing God's truth. But Jesus Christ can remove the covering, so even the worst sinner can see the truth. Do you know someone whose mind is still "covered"? Pray that Christ will take the covering away.

NOTES

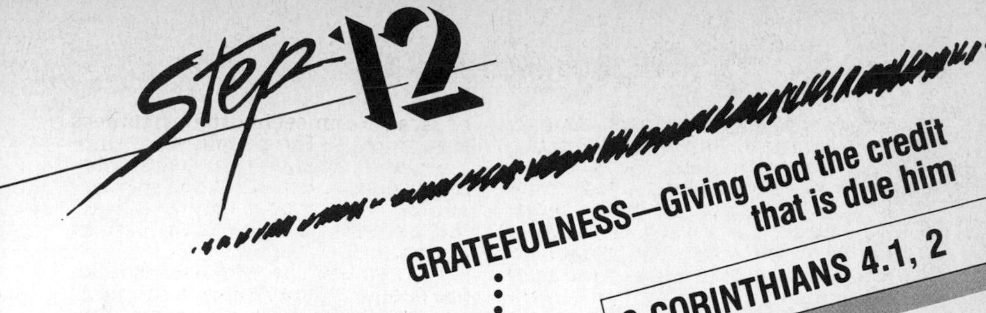

2 CORINTHIANS 4.1, 2

ADMIRATION SOCIETY

It is so hard not to be able to fix his problems like I did when he was little. He's almost a grown man now so I can't play "Mommy" in his life anymore. I can be his mother who loves him and supports him, but I can't make it right when he does wrong. He has to account for his own actions.

That has been a really hard lesson for Eric, but he's coming around. Just yesterday I was so proud of him when he controlled his temper with his dad. They don't always see eye-to-eye, and Eric's outbursts have only made things worse. But this time he just sat there quietly. I don't know if he was listening, but he wasn't yelling. It worked too. His dad backed off when he saw Eric wasn't going to start the "leave me alone, it's my life" routine again. I know it's not easy for him but he's working at changing. I admire that.

STEP LOOK AHEAD 12

MAKE A DIFFERENCE

It's amazing that when we begin to change, other people change as well. We may not always get a positive reaction, but people will take notice. For some, it will take time to see if we are sincere. That is why it is so important to put into practice all we have learned about letting go and letting God work in and through our lives. Hang in there! We will make a difference.

For another "Look Ahead," turn to page 640.

"God commanded light to shine in
the dark." Now God is shining in our
hearts to let you know that his glory
is seen in Jesus Christ.

7We are like clay jars in which this
treasure is stored. The real power
comes from God and not from us.*
8We often suffer, but we are never
crushed. Even when we don't know
what to do, we never give up. 9In
times of trouble, God is with us, and
when we are knocked down, we get
up again. 10-11We face death every
day because of Jesus. Our bodies
show what his death was like, so that
his life can also be seen in us.
12This means that death is working
in us, but life is working in you.

13In the Scriptures it says, "I spoke
because I had faith." We have that
same kind of faith. So we speak
14because we know that God raised
Jesus Christ to life. And just as God
raised Jesus, he will also raise us to
life. Then he will bring us into his
presence together with you. 15All of
this has been done for you, so that
more and more people will know how
kind God is and will praise and honor
him.

Faith in the Lord

16We never give up. Our bodies are
gradually dying, but we ourselves are
being made stronger each day.
17These little troubles are getting us
ready for an eternal glory that will
make all our troubles seem like nothing. 18Things that are seen don't last
forever, but things that are not seen
are eternal. That's why we keep our
minds on the things that cannot be
seen.

5 Our bodies are like tents that we
live in here on earth. But when
these tents are destroyed, we know
that God will give each of us a place
to live. These homes will not be buildings that someone has made, but they
are in heaven and will last forever.*
2While we are here on earth, we sigh
because we want to live in that heavenly home. 3We want to put it on like
clothes and not be naked.

4These tents we now live in are like
a heavy burden, and we groan. But
we don't do this just because we want
to leave these bodies that will die.
It is because we want to change them
for bodies that will never die. 5God
is the one who makes all of this possible. He has given us his Spirit to make
us certain that he will do it. 6So always be cheerful!

As long as we are in these bodies,
we are away from the Lord. 7But we
live by faith, not by what we see.
8We should be cheerful, because we
would rather leave these bodies and
be at home with the Lord. 9But
whether we are at home with the
Lord or away from him, we still try
our best to please him. 10After all,
Christ will judge each of us for the
good or the bad that we do while living in these bodies.*

4.7 **CHRIST LIVES IN CHRISTIANS** When we are "born from above" (John 3.3), Jesus really comes to live inside us. We're new people after we're born again. In one way we remain the same persons we were, but in another way we're changed to be like Jesus. We can stand whatever trouble the world might send our way, not because of our strength, but on account of the strength of the Son of God, who was crucified and rose again.

5.1 **OUR BODIES ARE LIKE TENTS** A tent is a place to live in for just a short time. Likewise, we live for a short time in our bodies. Sometimes our bodies give us trouble. But we are happy as we realize what a great and everlasting treasure we carry inside ourselves since God made us new people. The old life that we lived for the body is passing away. We will live forever the new life that we live for God.

5.10 **HOW CHRIST WILL JUDGE CHRISTIANS** When Paul writes that Christ will judge us according to the good we have done in our bodies, we should not confuse this judgment with *(continued)*

NOTES

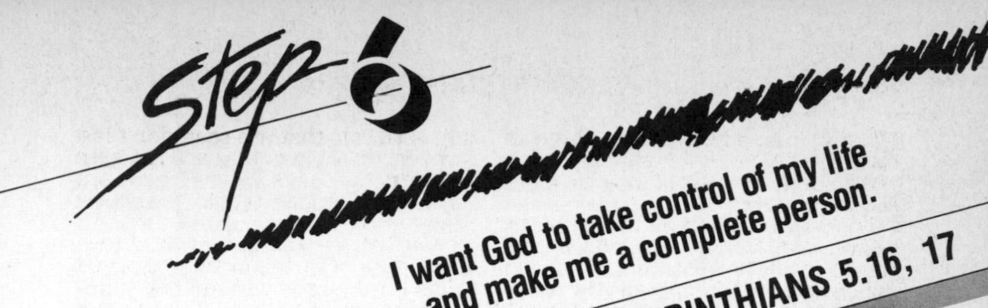

PAID IN FULL

To Whom It May Concern:

Please disregard the invoice you received on October 18 concerning past-due payments of $310.00. Our updated records indicate that your account is paid in full.

Signed,
The Management

A long time ago, way back in the Garden of Eden, past-due accounts began. It was because of something called sin. Every person was getting deeper and deeper in debt to God. That is, until Jesus came.

GOD TAKES CARE OF IT

Jesus died on the cross to pay our debt. That means as followers of Christ, no matter what we have done in the past—the mistakes we have made, our bad decisions, hateful actions, whatever sins we have run up—the Bible promises that when God takes out our ledger sheets, there is a big stamp across the middle that reads ACCOUNT PAID IN FULL.

For another "Look Inside," turn to page 425.

Bringing People to God

11We know what it means to respect the Lord, and we encourage everyone to turn to him. God himself knows what we are like, and I hope you also know what kind of people we are. 12We are not trying once more to brag about ourselves. But we want you to be proud of us, when you are with those who are not sincere and brag about what others think of them.

13If we seem out of our minds, it is between God and us. But if we are in our right minds, it is for your good. 14We are ruled by Christ's love for us. We are certain that if one person died for everyone else, then all of us have died. 15And Christ did die for all of us. He died so we would no longer live for ourselves, but for the one who died and was raised to life for us.

16We are careful not to judge people by what they seem to be, though we once judged Christ in that way. 17Anyone who belongs to Christ is a new person. The past is forgotten, and everything is new.

18God has done it all! He sent Christ to make peace between himself and us, and he has given us the work of making peace between himself and others.

19What we mean is that God was in Christ, offering peace and forgiveness to the people of this world. And he has given us the work of sharing his message about peace. 20We were sent to speak for Christ, and God is begging you to listen to our message. We speak for Christ and sincerely ask you to make peace with God. 21Christ never sinned! But God treated him as a sinner, so that Christ could make us acceptable to God.*

6 We work together with God, and we beg you to make good use of God's kindness to you. 2In the Scriptures God says,

"When the time came,
I listened to you,
and when you needed help,
I came to save you."

That time has come. This is the day for you to be saved.*

3We don't want anyone to find fault with our work, and so we try hard not to cause problems. 4But in everything and in every way we show that we truly are God's servants. We have always been patient, though we have had a lot of trouble, suffering, and hard times. 5We have been beaten, put in jail, and hurt in riots. We have worked hard and have gone without sleep or food. 6But we have kept ourselves pure and have been understanding, patient, and kind. The Holy Spirit has been with us, and our love has been real. 7We have spoken the truth, and God's power has worked in us. In all our struggles we have said and done only what is right.

8Whether we were honored or dishonored or praised or cursed, we always told the truth about ourselves. But some people said we did not. 9We are unknown to others, but well known to you. We seem to be dying, and yet we are still alive. We have been punished, but never killed,

(*continued*) being saved. We are saved by having faith in Jesus Christ, who suffered in our place on the cross, died, and then rose again. When Christ judges the good we have done, he will be judging believers who are already saved. This judgment determines the *rewards* each saved person will receive.

5.21 **JESUS TOOK THE PLACE OF SINNERS** Not only did God treat Jesus as a sinner, but as he hung there on the cross, Jesus actually took upon himself the punishment for all of our sins. Our sin became his to carry, and his goodness became ours.

6.2 **TODAY IS THE DAY** Paul was writing to a church, but it could be that some of the people there still needed to put their trust in Jesus and be saved. There is no time like the present. Who can be sure that they will have more time to "play games" with God? Death could come at any time, and so could the Lord's return.

NOTES

Step 1

HUMILITY—Becoming aware of God's greatness and my need for him

2 CORINTHIANS 5.18

TAKING TIME

It's going to take time. I haven't liked myself for so long. I have to get used to the idea that there is someone great inside of me. No one ever told me that before. People liked me "if" or "when." There always seemed to be a condition. This unconditional love stuff is strange. I have to admit, it does feel different. No, it feels good. I can't put myself down like I used to. Now it's like I'm insulting God. Believe it or not, he likes me just the way I am—short, fat, and ugly. Oops, there I go again! "Sorry, Lord."

REPAIRING THE DAMAGE

When we have spent most of our lives disliking ourselves, we have to expect it will take time to repair our broken images. But God is committed to us. He knows how very special we are, and he wants to convince us of it.

For another "Look Ahead," turn to page 606.

10 and we are always happy, even in
times of suffering. Although we are
poor, we have made many people
rich. And though we own nothing,
everything is ours.
11 Friends in Corinth, we are telling
the truth when we say that there is
room in our hearts for you. 12 We are
not holding back on our love for you,
but you are holding back on your love
for us. 13 I speak to you as I would
speak to my own children. Please
make room in your hearts for us.

The Temple of the Living God

14 Stay away from people who are
not followers of the Lord! Can someone who is good get along with someone who is evil? Are light and darkness the same?* 15 Is Christ a friend
of Satan?[e] Can people who follow the
Lord have anything in common with
those who don't? 16 Do idols belong
in the temple of God? We are the temple of the living God, as God himself
says,

"I will live with these people
  and walk among them.
I will be their God,
  and they will be my people."

17 The Lord also says,

"Leave them and stay away!
Don't touch anything
  that is not clean.
Then I will welcome you
18 and be your Father.
You will be my sons
  and my daughters,
as surely as I am God,
  the all-powerful."

7 My friends, God has made us
these promises. So we should stay
away from everything that keeps our
bodies and spirits from being clean.
We should honor God and try to be
completely like him.*

The Church Makes Paul Happy

2 Make a place for us in your hearts!
We haven't mistreated anyone or
hurt anyone. We haven't cheated
anyone. 3 I am not saying this to be
hard on you. But, as I have said before, you will always be in our
thoughts, whether we live or die.
4 I trust you completely.[f] I am always
proud of you, and I am greatly encouraged. In all my trouble I am still
very happy.
5 After we came to Macedonia, we
didn't have any chance to rest. We
were faced with all kinds of problems. We were troubled by enemies
and troubled by fears. 6 But God
cheers up people in need, and that
is what he did when he sent Titus
to us. 7 Of course, we were glad to
see Titus, but what really made us
glad is the way you cheered him up.
He told how sorry you were and how
concerned you were about me. And
this made me even happier.
8 I don't feel bad anymore, even
though my letter[g] hurt your feelings.
I did feel bad at first, but I don't now.

---

[e] *Satan*: The Greek text has "Beliar," which is another form of the Hebrew word "Belial," meaning "wicked" or "useless." The Jewish people sometimes used this as a name for Satan. [f] *I trust you completely*: Or "I have always spoken the truth to you" or "I can speak freely to you." [g] *my letter*: There is no copy of this letter that Paul wrote to the church at Corinth.

6.14 **GOOD AND EVIL DON'T MIX** Believers are still in the world, and there is evil all around. Many of the unsaved people we know and live with daily care little for God. Many of them may be living very sinful lives. God doesn't expect us to avoid such people entirely, but someone else's sinful lifestyle can have a bad effect on a believer. When we have a choice, we should seek the company of other believers and help build each other up in faith.

7.1 **CHRISTIANS FLOCK WITH CHRISTIANS** People who are alike attract one another. Christians will want to enjoy the friendship of other Christians. We should, of course, be kind and helpful to non-Christians, but often we will find that their lifestyles are sinful and destructive. It's easy to be influenced badly by them. We should choose our friends carefully because in time we become like them.

NOTES

I know that the letter hurt you for a while.* 9Now I am happy, but not because I hurt your feelings. It is because God used your hurt feelings to make you turn back to him, and none of you were harmed by us. 10When God makes you feel sorry enough to turn to him and be saved, you don't have anything to feel bad about. But when this world makes you feel sorry, it can cause your death.

11Just look what God has done by making you feel sorry! You sincerely want to prove that you are innocent. You are angry. You are shocked. You are eager to see that justice is done. You have proved that you were completely right in this matter. 12When I wrote you, it wasn't to accuse the one who was wrong or to take up for the one who was hurt. I wrote, so that God would show you how much you do care for us. 13And we were greatly encouraged.

Although we were encouraged, we felt even better when we saw how happy Titus was, because you had shown that he had nothing to worry about. 14We had told him how much we thought of you, and you did not disappoint us. Just as we have always told you the truth, so everything we told him about you has also proved to be true. 15Titus loves all of you very much, especially when he remembers how you obeyed him and how you trembled with fear when you welcomed him. 16It makes me really glad to know that I can depend on you.

Generous Giving

8 My friends, we want you to know that the churches in Macedonia[h] have shown others how kind God is. 2Although they were going through hard times and were very poor, they were glad to give generously.* 3They gave as much as they could afford and even more, simply because they wanted to. 4They even asked and begged us to let them have the joy of giving their money for God's people. 5And they did more than we had hoped. They gave themselves first to the Lord and then to us, just as God wanted them to do.

6Titus was the one who got you started doing this good thing, so we begged him to have you finish what you had begun. 7You do everything better than anyone else. You have stronger faith. You speak better and know more. You are eager to give, and you love us better.[i] Now you must give more generously than anyone else.

8I am not ordering you to do this. I am simply testing how real your love is by comparing it with the concern that others have shown. 9You know that our Lord Jesus Christ was kind enough to give up all his riches and become poor, so that you could become rich.

---

[h]*churches in Macedonia*: The churches that Paul had started in Philippi and Thessalonica. The church in Berea is probably also meant. [i]*you love us better*: Some manuscripts have "we love you better."

7.8 **CHURCHES SOMETIMES HAVE PROBLEMS** We see Paul's deep concern for the church at Corinth. He had written an earlier letter to them that hurt their feelings. It could be a lost letter, but some wonder if it may have been 1 Corinthians. That letter had blamed them for tolerating serious sin in the church (1 Corinthians 5.1–5). Let us be thankful for faithful leaders who will kindly but firmly correct us when we fall into sin.

8.2 **WE SHOULD GIVE TO GOD'S WORK** The Macedonians gave gladly to the apostles to support them in their ministry. Our love for God is shown by how much we give of ourselves and our goods to his work. Giving for the spread of the Christian faith is a necessary and joyful habit. We can't take our money to heaven, but we can send it ahead to God by giving to his work now.

NOTES

10A year ago you were the first ones
to give, and you gave because you
wanted to. So listen to my advice.
11I think you should finish what you
started. If you give according to what
you have, you will prove that you are
as eager to give as you were to think
about giving.* 12It doesn't matter how
much you have. What matters is how
much you are willing to give from
what you have.

13I am not trying to make life easier
for others by making life harder for
you. But it is only fair 14for you to
share with them when you have so
much, and they have so little. Later,
when they have more than enough,
and you are in need, they can share
with you. Then everyone will have
a fair share, 15just as the Scriptures
say,

> "Those who gathered
> too much
> had nothing left.
> Those who gathered
> only a little
> had all they needed."

Titus and His Friends

16I am grateful that God made Titus
care as much about you as we do.*
17When we begged Titus to visit you,
he said he would. He wanted to because he cared so much for you.
18With Titus we are also sending one
of the Lord's followers who is well
known in every church for spreading
the good news. 19The churches chose
this follower to travel with us while
we carry this gift that will bring
praise to the Lord and show how
much we hope to help. 20We don't
want anyone to find fault with the
way we handle your generous gift.
21But we want to do what pleases the
Lord and what people think is right.

22We are also sending someone
else with Titus and the other follower. We approve of this man. In
fact, he has already shown us many
times that he wants to help. And now
he wants to help even more than ever,
because he trusts you so much.
23Titus is my partner, who works
with me to serve you. The other two
followers are sent by the churches,
and they bring honor to Christ.
24Treat them in such a way that the
churches will see your love and will
know why we bragged about you.

The Money for God's People

9 I don't need to write you about
the money you plan to give for
God's people. 2I know how eager you
are to give. And I have proudly told
the Lord's followers in Macedonia
that you people in Achaia have been
ready for a whole year. Now your
desire to give has made them want
to give.* 3That's why I am sending
Titus and the two others to you. I
want you to be ready, just as I promised. This will prove that we were
not wrong to brag about you.

4Some followers from Macedonia

NOTES

8.11 **FINISH WHAT YOU STARTED** It's good to give, but it's important to *keep* giving. Sometimes Christians will get generous and give a one-time gift to a ministry. But how would you like to live on a series of uncertain, one-time gifts? God is steady in his giving to us, so we too should be steady in our giving to his work.

8.16 **HELP FROM TITUS** Titus was a young Greek disciple of Paul, the son of Gentile parents. When Titus was converted, Paul took him to Jerusalem where some Jews demanded that Titus must be circumcised according to their Law. But Paul refused (Galatians 2.1–5). As we read here, Titus helped Paul with the problems of the church at Corinth in southern Greece. The last we hear about Titus is during his faithful ministry on the island of Crete, where Paul sent him a letter (see Paul's Letter to Titus).

9.2 **BE AN EAGER GIVER** The Corinthians were eager to give, and Paul even boasted about their giving. Maybe he was also trying to tease them a little by comparing them to the (*continued*)

may come with me, and I want them
to find that you have the money
ready. If you don't, I would be embarrassed for trusting you to do this. But
you would be embarrassed even
more. 5So I have decided to ask Titus
and the others to spend some time
with you before I arrive. This way
they can arrange to collect the money
you have promised. Then you will
have the chance to give because you
want to, and not because you feel
forced to.

6Remember this saying,

"A few seeds make
a small harvest,
but a lot of seeds make
a big harvest."

STEP 11

7Each of you must make up your
own mind about how much to give.
But don't feel sorry that you must
give and don't feel that you are forced
to give. God loves people who love
to give. 8God can bless you with
everything you need, and you will always have more than enough to do
all kinds of good things for others.
9The Scriptures say,

"God freely gives his gifts
to the poor,
and always does right."

10God gives seed to farmers and provides everyone with food. He will increase what you have, so that you
can give even more to those in need.*
11You will be blessed in every way,
and you will be able to keep on being
generous. Then many people will
thank God when we deliver your gift.
12What you are doing is much more
than a service that supplies God's
people with what they need. It is
something that will make many others thank God. 13The way in which
you have proved yourselves by this
service will bring honor and praise
to God. You believed the message
about Christ, and you obeyed it by
sharing generously with God's people and with everyone else. 14Now
they are praying for you and want
to see you, because God used you
to bless them so very much. 15Thank
God for his gift that is too wonderful
for words!

Paul Defends His Work for Christ

10 Do you think I am a coward
when I am with you and brave
when I am far away? Well, I ask you
to listen, because Christ himself was
humble and gentle. 2Some people
have said that we act like the people
of this world. So when I arrive, I expect I will have to be firm and forceful
in what I say to them. Please don't
make me treat you that way. 3We live
in this world, but we don't act like
its people 4or fight our battles with
the weapons of this world. Instead,
we use God's power that can destroy
fortresses. We destroy arguments*
5and every bit of pride that keeps
anyone from knowing God. We capture people's thoughts and make
them obey Christ. 6And when you
completely obey him, we will punish
anyone who refuses to obey.

7You judge by appearances.[j] If any

---

[j] *You judge by appearances*: Or "Take a close look at yourselves."

(*continued*) church at Macedonia in northern Greece. In Paul's time Christians were very eager to have a part in spreading the good news about Jesus, who had brought them so much happiness. They were strongly aware of how they had been saved from death.

9.10 **GOD GIVES SO WE CAN** Paul writes that God gives to us so we can give to others. This does not mean that giving a little will get us a lot from God, making us rich. It means that God gives an extra blessing so we can "pass it on."

10.4 **FACE YOUR OPPONENTS** Enemies test the Christian's strength, because a Christian may not use harsh language or force to convince people. But, like Paul, we have to be able to present our case for Christ in a clear, convincing, and brave way. Why should Christians be cowards? We're children of the mighty God. So let's arm ourselves with the knowledge we need to fight all ignorance.

NOTES

of you think you are the only ones
who belong to Christ, then think
again. We belong to Christ as much
as you do. 8Maybe I brag a little too
much about the authority that the
Lord gave me to help you and not
to hurt you. Yet I am not embarrassed
to brag. 9And I am not trying to scare
you with my letters. 10Some of you
are saying, "Paul's letters are harsh
and powerful. But in person, he is a
weakling and has nothing worth saying."* 11Those people had better understand that when I am with you, I
will do exactly what I say in my
letters.

12We won't dare compare ourselves with those who think so much
of themselves. But they are foolish
to compare themselves with themselves. 13We won't brag about something we don't have a right to brag
about. We will only brag about the
work that God has sent us to do, and
you are part of that work. 14We are
not bragging more than we should.
After all, we did bring the message
about Christ to you.

15We don't brag about what others
have done, as if we had done those
things ourselves. But I hope that as
you become stronger in your faith,
we will be able to reach many more
of the people around you.[k] That has
always been our goal. 16Then we will
be able to preach the good news in
other lands where we cannot take
credit for work someone else has already done. 17The Scriptures say, "If
you want to brag, then brag about
the Lord." 18You may brag about
yourself, but the only approval that
counts is the Lord's approval.

Paul and the False Apostles

11 Please put up with a little of
my foolishness.* 2I am as concerned about you as God is. You were
like a virgin bride I had chosen only
for Christ. 3But now I fear that you
will be tricked, just as Eve was
tricked by that lying snake. I am
afraid that you might stop thinking
about Christ in an honest and sincere
way. 4We told you about Jesus, and
you received the Holy Spirit and accepted our message. But you let some
people tell you about another Jesus.
Now you are ready to receive another
spirit and accept a different message.
5I think I am as good as any of those
super apostles. 6I may not speak as
well as they do, but I know as much.
And this has already been made perfectly clear to you.

7Was it wrong for me to lower myself and honor you by preaching
God's message free of charge?
8I robbed other churches by taking
money from them to serve you.
9Even when I was in need, I still didn't
bother you. In fact, some of the Lord's
followers from Macedonia brought
me what I needed. I have not been
a burden to you in the past, and I
will never be a burden. 10As surely
as I speak the truth about Christ, no

---

[k]*we will be able to reach many more of the people around you*: Or "you will praise us even more because of our work among you."

10.10 **THE PROBLEM AT CORINTH** The Greeks, including those at Corinth, were used to hearing powerful speakers who often had a commanding appearance. Paul was not a good speaker, and he seems to have been thin and short. He may also have been badly scarred by beatings and stonings he had received. Many of the people at Corinth looked down on Paul and were embarrassed to have him speak at their church. But Paul soon straightened them out.

11.1 **SOME COMEDY HELPS OUR WITNESS** We don't have to be angry or "dead serious" with those who speak against us. Paul was able to joke about people's low opinion of him. It's as if he were saying, "Go ahead, call me a fool, but listen now to my foolishness." That must have made them blush with shame. Paul's critics in Corinth didn't really hate him—they just didn't know what to make of this little man who didn't look like much.

NOTES

one in Achaia can stop me from bragging about this. 11And it isn't because I don't love you. God himself knows how much I do love you.

12I plan to go on doing just what I have always done. Then those people won't be able to brag about doing the same things we are doing. 13Anyway, they are no more than false apostles and dishonest workers. They only pretend to be apostles of Christ. 14And it is no wonder. Even Satan tries to make himself look like an angel of light.* 15So why does it seem strange for Satan's servants to pretend to do what is right? Someday they will get exactly what they deserve.

Paul's Sufferings for Christ

16I don't want any of you to think that I am a fool. But if you do, then let me be a fool and brag a little. 17When I do all this bragging, I do it as a fool and not for the Lord. 18Yet if others want to brag about what they have done, so will I. 19And since you are so smart, you will gladly put up with a fool. 20In fact, you let people make slaves of you and cheat you and steal from you. Why, you even let them strut around and slap you in the face. 21I am ashamed to say that we are too weak to behave in such a way.

If they can brag, so can I, but it is a foolish thing to do. 22Are they Hebrews? So am I. Are they Jews? So am I. Are they from the family of Abraham? Well, so am I.* 23Are they servants of Christ? I am a fool to talk this way, but I serve him better than they do. I have worked harder and have been put in jail more times. I have been beaten with whips more and have been in danger of death more often.

24Five times the Jews gave me thirty-nine lashes with a whip. 25Three times the Romans beat me with a big stick, and once my enemies stoned me. I have been shipwrecked three times, and I even had to spend a night and a day in the sea. 26During my many travels, I have been in danger from rivers, robbers, Jews, and foreigners. My life has been in danger in cities, in deserts, at sea, and with people who only pretended to be the Lord's followers.

27I have worked and struggled and spent many sleepless nights. I have gone hungry and thirsty and often had nothing to eat. I have been cold from not having enough clothes to keep me warm. 28Besides everything else, each day I am burdened down, worrying about all the churches. 29When others are weak, I am weak too. When others are tricked into sin, I get angry.[l]

30If I have to brag, I will brag about how weak I am. 31God, the Father of our Lord Jesus, knows I am not lying. And God is to be praised forever! 32The governor of Damascus at the time of King Aretas had the city gates guarded, so that he could capture me. 33But I escaped by being let down in a basket through a window in the city wall.

---

[l]*When others are tricked into sin, I get angry*: Or "When others stumble into sin, I hurt for them."

11.14 **STICK WITH THE PURE GOOD NEWS** The Corinthians had been listening to false teachers who made the good news complicated. The teachers had said that Gentiles had to obey Jewish religious customs. Being saved by faith in God's mercy through the sacrifice of Jesus is a simple idea, which people often like to make harder than it has to be.

11.22 **GET TO KNOW PAUL** Here was a humble-looking man that Christ had called to preach to the Gentiles. He had been cruelly beaten, stoned, left for dead, and even shipwrecked. He had marks in his body that probably embarrassed the Corinthians. They called him a fool. So Paul just uses their own language. Paul is "the fool" who preached the good news about Jesus to them for nothing. That must have made them ashamed.

NOTES

Visions from the Lord

12 I have to brag. There is nothing to be gained by it, but I must brag about the visions and other things that the Lord has shown me.* 2I know about one of Christ's followers who was taken up into the third heaven fourteen years ago. I don't know if the man was still in his body when it happened, but God surely knows.

3As I said, only God really knows if this man was in his body at the time. 4But he was taken up into paradise,[m] where he heard things that are too wonderful to tell. 5I will brag about that man, but not about myself, except to say how weak I am.

6Yet even if I did brag, I would not be foolish. I would simply be speaking the truth. But I will try not to say too much. That way, none of you will think more highly of me than you should because of what you have seen me do and say. 7Of course, I am now referring to the wonderful things I saw. One of Satan's angels was sent to make me suffer terribly, so that I would not feel too proud.[n]

8Three times I begged the Lord to make this suffering go away. 9But he replied, "My kindness is all you need. My power is strongest when you are weak." So if Christ keeps giving me his power, I will gladly brag about how weak I am. 10Yes, I am glad to be weak or insulted or mistreated or to have troubles and sufferings, if it is for Christ. Because when I am weak, I am strong.

Paul's Concern for the Lord's Followers at Corinth

11I have been making a fool of myself. But you forced me to do it, when you should have been speaking up for me. I may be nothing at all, but I am as good as those super apostles. 12When I was with you, I was patient and worked all the powerful miracles and signs and wonders of a true apostle. 13You missed out on only one blessing that the other churches received. That is, you didn't have to support me. Forgive me for doing you wrong.

14I am planning to visit you for the third time. But I still won't make a burden of myself. What I really want is you, and not what you have. Children are not supposed to save up for their parents, but parents are supposed to take care of their children. 15So I will gladly give all that I have and all that I am. Will you love me less for loving you too much? 16You agree that I was not a burden to you. Maybe that's because I was trying to catch you off guard and trick you. 17Were you cheated by any of those I sent to you? 18I urged Titus to visit you, and I sent another follower with him. But Titus didn't cheat you, and we felt and behaved the same way he did.

19Have you been thinking all along that we have been defending ourselves to you? Actually, we have been speaking to God as followers of Christ. But, my friends, we did it all for your good.

20I am afraid that when I come, we won't be pleased with each other. I fear that some of you may be arguing or jealous or angry or selfish or gossiping or insulting each other. I even fear that you may be proud and

---

[m] *paradise*: In the Greek translation of the Old Testament, this word is used for the Garden of Eden. In New Testament times it was sometimes used for the place where God's people are happy and at rest, as they wait for the final judgment. [n] *Of course . . . too proud*: Or "Because of the wonderful things that I saw, one of Satan's angels was sent to make me suffer terribly, so that I would not feel too proud."

12.1 **GOD'S KINDNESS IS ENOUGH FOR US** Paul had seen many wonderful things, but the best of all was that God's kindness was Paul's continual support. We aren't great or strong because of what we have seen or what we know. Our greatness and strength come directly from God himself. He keeps us going when we fail and even when our friends fail. Jesus said, "I will never leave you."

NOTES

Step 1

I admit I cannot be successful on my own . . . I need help, daily.

2 CORINTHIANS 12.8–10

BODYBUILDING

His junior high football coach once told him that he was too small, too skinny, and too slow. "You'll never make it," he said.

So he started a daily routine that included push-ups, sit-ups, and running. With the encouragement of his mother and the challenge of proving the coach wrong, "You'll never make it" went on to star in high school and then in college. In fact, he won the Heisman Trophy as the best college football player in the United States. After college he became an All-Pro running back with Dallas and Minnesota. Do you know his name? Here's a hint: he played college football for the University of Georgia and participated in the Winter Olympics on the U.S. bobsled team. You're right, it was Herschel Walker.

GROWING STRONG

Bodybuilding takes work. In order to make a muscle stronger, you must first work it to a point of fatigue—actually make it weaker in order to make it strong eventually. The resistance that comes with weight training or exercise helps to develop the part of the body that gets used.

The Christian life offers a similar paradox. When we are at our weakest point, God comes through. He is always ready to prove himself. As we face tests and learn to trust God to see us through them, we grow spiritually and learn to trust him more. Are we trusting God today? We can't make it on our own. We need our Christian family for support and encouragement.

STEP 1 LOOK INSIDE

For another "Look Inside," turn to page 725.

acting like a mob.* 21I am afraid God will make me ashamed when I visit you again. I will feel like crying because many of you have never given up your old sins. You are still doing things that are immoral, indecent, and shameful.

Final Warnings and Greetings

13 I am on my way to visit you for the third time. And as the Scriptures say, "Any charges must be proved true by at least two or three witnesses." 2During my second visit I warned you that I would punish you and anyone else who doesn't stop sinning. I am far away from you now, but I give you the same warning. 3This should prove to you that I am speaking for Christ. When he corrects you, he won't be weak. He will be powerful! 4Although he was weak when he was nailed to the cross, he now lives by the power of God. We are weak, just as Christ was. But you will see that we will live by the power of God, just as Christ does.

STEP LOOK INSIDE 4

5Test yourselves and find out if you really are true to your faith. If you pass the test, you will discover that Christ is living in you. But if Christ isn't living in you, you have failed.* 6I hope you will discover that we have not failed. 7We pray that you will stop doing evil things. We don't pray like this to make ourselves look good, but to get you to do right, even if we are failures.

8All we can do is to follow the truth and not fight against it. 9Even though we are weak, we are glad that you are strong, and we pray that you will do even better. 10I am writing these things to you before I arrive. This way I won't have to be hard on you when I use the authority that the Lord has given me. I was given this authority, so that I could help you and not destroy you.*

11Good-by, my friends. Do better and pay attention to what I have said. Try to get along and live peacefully with each other.

Now I pray that God, who gives love and peace, will be with you. 12Give each other a warm greeting. All of God's people send their greetings.

13I pray that the Lord Jesus Christ will bless you and be kind to you! May God bless you with his love, and may the Holy Spirit join all your hearts together.

12.20 **WHAT ABOUT THE CHURCH AT CORINTH?** The church had grown. But Corinth was one of the most wicked cities in the world of that time. The people who came into the church had a lot of sins to leave behind, but some people seem to have brought their sins with them. That's why Paul had to speak to them so sharply. They needed to wake up and live like Christians.

13.5 **LET'S KNOW OURSELVES** Many of the Corinthians were proud. They thought their love of human wisdom was enough for them. Who needed a Paul to tell them what to believe? We, like they, need to know if Christ can really live in us with an attitude like that. Surely he can't. Saying we're Christians doesn't make it true; living like Christians proves we are.

13.10 **GOD DOESN'T IGNORE SIN** Paul wanted the Corinthians to realize that God does not ignore sin. Paul was God's appointed agent. He warned them that he was not really weak or foolish. He would come personally, in the power of Christ. Then the church would have to get back in line with God's will.

NOTES

Step 4

I will take a hard look at myself, the way I live and my moral standards.

2 CORINTHIANS 13.5–7

POP QUIZ

"Class, put away your books, and get out a piece of paper. We are going to have a pop quiz."

These words strike horror in the hearts of the unprepared student. All the "I meant to study, but . . ." good intentions don't mean much. It is on the line now, what we know or don't know. Have we been preparing and keeping up with the class material? Or, have we been putting it off and getting further and further behind?

For a Christian, life isn't on the pass-fail grading system. Once we put our lives in God's hands and trust Christ to lead us, the Bible promises that in the end we will pass the test. We are promised eternal life in heaven and an abundant life now. The best way to make good on our commitment to Christ is every now and then to give ourselves a spiritual "pop quiz."

STEP LOOK INSIDE 4

CHECKING OURSELVES OUT

Are we living a life of good morals? Is there any behavior pattern that makes us ashamed? Do our attitudes, conduct, and moral standards measure up to Christ's example in the Bible? Just as at school, we can't always be expected to get everything right in the Christian walk. God doesn't expect us to either. That is why 1 John 1.9 tells us, "If we confess our sins to God, he can always be trusted to forgive us and take our sins away." It is good to know that in God's classroom we are guaranteed an *A* for effort.

For another "Look Inside," turn to page 392.

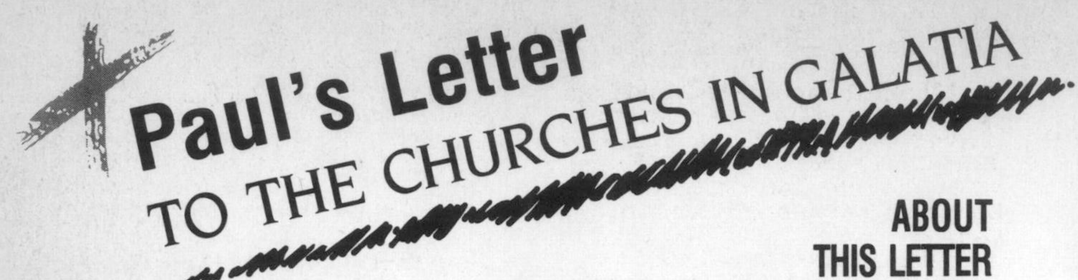

Paul's Letter TO THE CHURCHES IN GALATIA

ABOUT THIS LETTER

From the very beginning of this letter to the churches in the region of Galatia (in central Asia Minor), Paul makes two things clear to his readers: he is a true apostle, and his message is the only true message (1.1–10). These statements were very important, because some people claimed that Paul was a false apostle with a false message.

Paul was indeed a true apostle, and his mission to the Gentiles was given to him by the Lord and approved by the apostles in Jerusalem (1.18—2.10). Paul had even corrected the apostle Peter, when he had stopped eating with Gentile followers who were not obeying the Law of Moses (2.1–18).

Faith is the only way to be saved. Paul insists that this was true already for Abraham, who had received God's promise by faith. And Paul leaves no doubt about what his own faith means to him:

> I *have been nailed to the cross with Christ.* I *have died, but Christ lives in me. And* I *now live by faith in the Son of God, who loved me and gave his life for me.*
>
> (2.19*b*,20)

A QUICK LOOK AT THIS LETTER

1. A True Apostle and the True Message (1.1–10)
2. God Chose Paul To Be an Apostle (1.11–24)
3. Paul Defends His Message (2.1–21)
4. Faith Is the Only Way To Be Saved (3.1—4.31)
5. Guided by the Spirit and Love (5.1—6.10)
6. Final Warnings (6.11–18)

1 1-2From the apostle Paul and from
all the Lord's followers with me.
I was chosen to be an apostle by
Jesus Christ and by God the Father,
who raised him from death. No mere
human chose or appointed me to this
work.
To the churches in Galatia.*
3I pray that God the Father and our
Lord Jesus Christ will be kind to you
and will bless you with peace!
4Christ obeyed God our Father and
gave himself as a sacrifice for our
sins to rescue us from this evil world.
5God will be given glory forever and
ever. Amen.

The Only True Message

6I am shocked that you have so
quickly turned from God, who chose
you because of his kindness.[a] You
have believed another message,*
7when there is really only one true
message. But some people are causing you trouble and want to make
you turn away from the good news
about Christ. 8I pray that God will
punish anyone who preaches anything different from our message to
you! It doesn't matter if that person
is one of us or an angel from heaven.
9I have said it before, and I will say
it again. I hope God will punish anyone who preaches anything different
from what you have already believed.
10I am not trying to please people.
I want to please God. Do you think
I am trying to please people? If I were
doing that, I would not be a servant
of Christ.

How Paul Became an Apostle

11My friends, I want you to know
that no one made up the message I
preach. 12It was not given or taught
to me by some mere human. My message came directly from Jesus Christ
when he appeared to me.
13You know how I used to live as
a Jew. I was cruel to God's church
and even tried to destroy it. 14I was
a much better Jew than anyone else
my own age, and I obeyed every law
that our ancestors had given us.
15But even before I was born, God
had chosen me. He was kind and had
decided 16to show me his Son, so that
I would announce his message to the
Gentiles. I didn't talk this over with
anyone. 17I didn't say a word, not
even to the men in Jerusalem who
were apostles before I was. Instead,
I went at once to Arabia, and afterwards I returned to Damascus.*
18Three years later I went to visit

---

[a]*his kindness*: Some manuscripts have "the kindness of Christ."

1.2 **WHAT MAKES A CHRISTIAN LEADER?** Does education fit us for Christian service? Not necessarily. Many people have taken training courses but have failed as Christian leaders. Does having the desire to serve as a leader prove that someone has been called to do so? We surely need to desire to work for the Lord. But desire alone doesn't make us able. God proves who his servants are by the way he uses them in his work. Paul was such a God-chosen servant.

1.6 **TURNING ASIDE** Paul had to keep an eye on the churches he helped to start. He would move on only to discover later that the believers he left behind were listening to false teachers. The new believers had to be shown again and again that sinners are saved by God's mercy, not by good works.

1.17 **GOD PREPARES HIS SERVANTS** Sometimes God takes many years to get his servants ready to work for him. Such was the case with Moses in the Old Testament. God also took his time preparing Paul. Be sure that, if God is going to use you in a special way, it will take more than overnight. Some lessons can be learned only by living with God day by day through all of the "ins and outs" of life.

NOTES

Peter[b] in Jerusalem and stayed with
him for fifteen days. 19The only other
apostle I saw was James, the Lord's
brother. 20And in the presence of God
I swear I am telling the truth.
21Later, I went to the regions of
Syria and Cilicia. 22But no one who
belonged to Christ's churches in Judea had ever seen me in person.
23They had only heard that the one
who had been cruel to them was now
preaching the message that he had
once tried to destroy. 24And because
of me, they praised God.
2 Fourteen years later I went to Jerusalem with Barnabas. I also
took along Titus. 2But I went there
because God had told me to go, and
I explained the good news that I had
been preaching to the Gentiles. Then
I met privately with the ones who
seemed to be the most important
leaders. I wanted to make sure that
all my work in the past and my future
work would not be for nothing.
3Titus went to Jerusalem with me.
He was a Greek, but still he was not
forced to be circumcised. 4We went
there because of those who pretended to be followers and had
sneaked in among us as spies. They
had come to take away the freedom
that Christ Jesus had given us, and
they were trying to make us their
slaves.* 5But we wanted you to have
the true message. That's why we
didn't give in to them, not even for
a second.
6Some of them were supposed to
be important leaders, but I didn't care
who they were. God doesn't have any
favorites! None of these so-called
special leaders added anything to my
message. 7They realized that God
had sent me with the good news for
Gentiles, and that he had sent Peter
with the same message for Jews.
8God, who had sent Peter on a mission to the Jews, was now using me
to preach to the Gentiles.
9James, Peter,[b] and John realized
that God had given me the message
about his kindness. And these men
are supposed to be the pillars of the
church. They even gave Barnabas
and me a friendly handshake. This
was to show that we would work with
Gentiles and that they would work
with Jews. 10They only asked us to
remember the poor, and that was
something I had always been eager
to do.

Paul Corrects Peter at Antioch

11When Peter came to Antioch, I
told him face-to-face that he was
wrong.* 12He used to eat with Gentile
followers of the Lord, until James
sent some Jewish followers. Peter
was afraid of the Jews and soon
stopped eating with Gentiles. 13He
and the other Jews hid their true feelings so well that even Barnabas was
fooled. 14But when I saw that they
were not really obeying the truth that
is in the good news, I corrected Peter
and said:

> Peter, you are a Jew, but you
> live like a Gentile. So how can
> you force Gentiles to live like
> Jews?

---

[b]*Peter*: The Greek text has "Cephas," which is an Aramaic name meaning "rock." Peter is the Greek name with the same meaning.

2.4 **SNEAKING IN LIKE SPIES** Paul did not flatter the false teachers. They were sneaking in like spies, he said, trying to get people who had been saved by faith to put themselves back under the Law. Paul's hard words show how serious the charge was: lives were at stake. The false teachers were getting people to depend on good deeds, which could never save them.

2.11 **PETER WAS WISHY-WASHY** A wishy-washy Christian isn't very convincing. Peter had tried before to be on two sides at the same time, when he said he didn't know Jesus (Matthew 26.69–75). It may be a good thing sometimes just to be quiet and say nothing. But it is never a good thing to live a double life—acting like a Christian sometimes, but pretending not to be one when it suits those around us.

NOTES

15We are Jews by birth and are
not sinners like Gentiles. 16But
we know that God accepts only
those who have faith in Jesus
Christ. No one can please God
by simply obeying the Law. So
we put our faith in Christ Jesus,
and God accepted us because of
our faith.
17When we Jews started
looking for a way to please God,
we discovered that we are
sinners too. Does this mean that
Christ is the one who makes us
sinners? No, it doesn't! 18But if
I tear down something and then
build it again, I prove that I was
wrong at first. 19It was the Law
itself that killed me and freed me
from its power, so that I could
live for God.
I have been nailed to the cross
with Christ. 20I have died, but
Christ lives in me. And I now
live by faith in the Son of God,
who loved me and gave his life
for me. 21I don't turn my back
on God's kindness. If we can be
acceptable to God by obeying
the Law, it was useless for Christ
to die.

Faith Is the Only Way

3 You stupid Galatians! I told you
exactly how Jesus Christ was
nailed to a cross. Has someone now
put an evil spell on you? 2I want to
know only one thing. How were you
given God's Spirit? Was it by obeying
the Law of Moses or by hearing about
Christ and having faith in him?
3How can you be so stupid? Do you
think that by yourself you can complete what God's Spirit started in
you?* 4Have you gone through all of
this for nothing? Is it all really for
nothing? 5God gives you his Spirit
and works miracles in you. But does
he do this because you obey the Law
of Moses or because you have heard
about Christ and have faith in him?
6The Scriptures say that God accepted Abraham because Abraham
had faith. 7And so, you should understand that everyone who has faith
is a child of Abraham.[c] 8Long ago the
Scriptures said that God would accept the Gentiles because of their
faith. That's why God told Abraham
the good news that all nations would
be blessed because of him. 9This
means that everyone who has faith
will share in the blessings that were
given to Abraham because of his
faith.

10Anyone who tries to please God
by obeying the Law is under a curse.
The Scriptures say, "Everyone who
doesn't obey everything in the Law
is under a curse." 11No one can please
God by obeying the Law. The Scriptures also say, "The people God accepts because of their faith will
live."[d]
12The Law is not based on faith.
It promises life only to people who
obey its commands. 13But Christ rescued us from the Law's curse, when
he became a curse in our place. This
is because the Scriptures say that
anyone who is nailed to a tree is under a curse. 14And because of what
Jesus Christ has done, the blessing
that was promised to Abraham was
taken to the Gentiles. This happened
so that by faith we would be given
the promised Holy Spirit.

The Law and the Promise

15My friends, I will use an everyday
example to explain what I mean.
Once someone agrees to something,
no one else can change or cancel the

---

[c] *a child of Abraham*: God chose Abraham, and so it was believed that anyone who was a child of Abraham was also a child of God. See the note at 3.29.
[d] *The people God accepts because of their faith will live*: Or "The people God accepts will live because of their faith."

3.3 **ADD NOTHING TO THE MESSAGE** Being saved is God's gift that we receive by faith. Jesus alone earned that gift for us by being nailed to the cross. It's good to learn Bible history, and it is also necessary to honor God in our daily lives. But nothing we do or learn will add anything to what Jesus alone could do—and did do—to save sinners.

NOTES

agreement.[e] 16That is how it is with
the promises that God made to Abraham and his descendant.[f] The promises were not made to many descendants, but only to one, and that one
is Christ. 17What I am saying is that
the Law cannot change or cancel
God's promise that was made 430
years before the Law was given.
18If we have to obey the Law in order
to receive God's blessings, those
blessings don't really come to us because of God's promise. But God was
kind to Abraham and made him a
promise.

19What is the use of the Law? It
was given later to show that we sin.
But it was only supposed to last until
the coming of that descendant[g] who
was given the promise. In fact, angels
gave the Law to Moses, and he gave
it to the people.* 20There is only one
God, and the Law did not come directly from him.

Slaves and Children

21Does the Law disagree with
God's promises? No, it doesn't! If any
law could give life to us, we could
become acceptable to God by obeying that law. 22But the Scriptures say
that sin controls everyone, so that
God's promises will be for anyone
who has faith in Jesus Christ.

23The Law controlled us and kept
us under its power until the time
came when we would have faith.
24In fact, the Law was our teacher.
It was supposed to teach us until we
had faith and were acceptable to God.
25But once a person has learned to
have faith, there is no more need to
have the Law as a teacher.

26All of you are God's children because of your faith in Christ Jesus.*
27And when you were baptized, it
was as though you had put on Christ
in the same way you put on new
clothes. 28Faith in Christ Jesus is
what makes each of you equal with
each other, whether you are a Jew
or a Greek, a slave or a free person, a man or a woman. 29So if you
belong to Christ, you are now
part of Abraham's family,[h] and
you will be given what God has
4 promised. 1Children who are under age are no better off than
slaves, even though everything their
parents own will someday be theirs.
2This is because children are placed
in the care of guardians and teachers
until the time their parents have set.
3That is how it was with us. We were
like children ruled by the powers of
this world.

4But when the time was right, God
sent his Son, and a woman gave birth
to him. His Son obeyed the Law,
5so he could set us free from the Law,
and we could become God's children.
6Now that we are his children, God
has sent the Spirit of his Son into
our hearts. And his Spirit tells us that

---

[e] *Once someone . . . cancel the agreement*: Or "Once a person makes out a will, no one can change or cancel it." [f] *descendant*: The Greek text has "seed," which may mean one or many descendants. In this verse Paul says it means Christ. [g] *that descendant*: Jesus. [h] *you are now part of Abraham's family*: Paul tells the Galatians that faith in Jesus Christ is what makes someone a true child of Abraham and of God. See the note at 3.7.

3.19 **WHAT GOOD IS THE LAW?** The Law of God, described in the Old Testament, shows people everywhere how much we all need God to save us, because no one can keep the Law and never break it. No one can honestly look at the Law and say, "I deserve eternal life." The Law's purpose is to bring people to faith. It is a "teacher," showing us how holy God is and how much we need his Son Jesus to save us.

3.26 **CHRISTIANS ARE FREE FROM THE CURSE OF THE LAW** The curse of the Law is that it rightly condemned us for our sins. But now the Judge himself has paid the debt of obedience we owed him. So we are no longer under that curse. As true children of God, not slaves, we love to do the things that please our heavenly Father because we are born again and have a new nature.

NOTES

God is our Father.* 7You are no
longer slaves. You are God's children, and you will be given what he
has promised.

Paul's Concern for the Galatians

8Before you knew God, you were
slaves of gods that are not real.
9But now you know God, or better
still, God knows you. How can you
turn back and become the slaves of
those weak and pitiful powers?[i]
10You even celebrate certain days,
months, seasons, and years. 11I am
afraid I have wasted my time working with you.

12My friends, I beg you to be like
me, just as I once tried to be like you.
You didn't mistreat me 13when I first
preached to you. No you didn't, even
though you knew I had come there
because I was sick. 14My illness must
have caused you some trouble, but
you didn't hate me or turn me away
because of it. You welcomed me as
though I were one of God's angels
or even Christ Jesus himself.
15Where is that good feeling now? I
am sure that if it had been possible,
you would have taken out your own
eyes and given them to me. 16Am I
now your enemy, just because I told
you the truth?

17Those people may be paying you
a lot of attention, but it isn't for your
good. They only want to keep you
away from me, so you will pay them
a lot of attention. 18It is always good
to give your attention to something
worthwhile, even when I am not with
you. 19My children, I am in terrible
pain until Christ may be seen living
in you. 20I wish I were with you now.
Then I would not have to talk this
way. You really have me puzzled.

Hagar and Sarah

21Some of you would like to be under the rule of the Law of Moses. But
do you know what the Law says?
22In the Scriptures we learn that
Abraham had two sons. The mother
of one of them was a slave, while
the mother of the other one had always been free.* 23The son of the
slave woman was born in the usual
way. But the son of the free woman
was born because of God's promise.

24All of this has another meaning
as well. Each of the two women
stands for one of the agreements God
made with his people. Hagar, the
slave woman, stands for the agreement that was made at Mount Sinai.
Everyone born into her family is a
slave. 25Hagar also stands for Mount
Sinai in Arabia[j] and for the present
city of Jerusalem. She[k] and her children are slaves.

26But our mother is the city of Jerusalem in heaven above, and she isn't
a slave. 27The Scriptures say about
her,

"You have never had children,
  but now you can be glad.
You have never given birth,
  but now you can shout.
Once you had no children,

[i] *powers*: Spirits were thought to control human lives and were believed to be connected with the movements of the stars. [j] *Hagar also stands for Mount Sinai in Arabia*: Some manuscripts have "Sinai is a mountain in Arabia." This sentence would then be translated: "Sinai is a mountain in Arabia, and Hagar stands for the present city of Jerusalem." [k] *She*: "Hagar" or "Jerusalem."

4.6 **HOW WE KNOW WE ARE GOD'S CHILDREN** Saying we are God's children doesn't make it true. But we now act like God's children. Without the fear we used to have, we now love to obey the commandments of God. Even more than that, we know we are God's children because the Holy Spirit—God himself—now lives within us. The Holy Spirit makes us know we belong to God.

4.22 **BE BORN OF THE RIGHT "MOTHER"** The truth is, we can't do anything at all to make ourselves Christians. We must be born all over again—this time by the Holy Spirit. Then we will have a whole new outlook on what pleases God. By faith we are born of the "free mother" (the heavenly Jerusalem), not of the "slave mother" (the Law).

NOTES

but now you will have
more children than a woman
who has been married
for a long time."

28My friends, you were born because of this promise, just as Isaac was. 29But the child who was born in the natural way made trouble for the child who was born because of the Spirit. The same thing is happening today. 30The Scriptures say, "Get rid of the slave woman and her son! He won't be given anything. The son of the free woman will receive everything." 31My friends, we are children of the free woman and not of the slave.

Christ Gives Freedom

5 Christ has set us free! This means we are really free. Now hold on to your freedom and don't ever become slaves of the Law again.*

2I, Paul, promise you that Christ won't do you any good if you get circumcised. 3If you do, you must obey the whole Law. 4And if you try to please God by obeying the Law, you have cut yourself off from Christ and his kindness. 5But the Spirit makes us sure that God will accept us because of our faith in Christ. 6If you are a follower of Christ Jesus, it makes no difference whether you are circumcised or not. All that matters is your faith that makes you love others.

7You were doing so well until someone made you turn from the truth. 8And that person was certainly not sent by the one who chose you. 9A little yeast can change a whole batch of dough, 10but you belong to the Lord. That makes me certain that you will do what I say, instead of what someone else tells you to do. Whoever is causing trouble for you will be punished.

11My friends, if I still preach that people need to be circumcised, why am I in so much trouble? The message about the cross would no longer be a problem, if I told people to be circumcised. 12I wish that everyone who is upsetting you would not only get circumcised, but would cut off much more!

13My friends, you were chosen to be free. So don't use your freedom as an excuse to do anything you want. Use it as an opportunity to serve each other with love. 14All that the Law says can be summed up in the command to love others as much as you love yourself. 15But if you keep attacking each other like wild animals, you had better watch out or you will destroy yourselves.

God's Spirit and Our Own Desires

16If you are guided by the Spirit, you won't obey your selfish desires.* 17The Spirit and your desires are enemies of each other. They are always fighting each other and keeping you from doing what you feel you should. 18But if you obey the Spirit, the Law of Moses has no control over you.

19People's desires make them give in to immoral ways, filthy thoughts, and shameful deeds. 20They worship idols, practice witchcraft, hate others, and are hard to get along with. People become jealous, angry,

5.1 **RULES CANNOT FREE US** Paul was talking about the rituals the Jews were required to do daily and at other times, such as circumcising boys soon after birth. The Jewish religion had gotten tangled up in a set of rules. The Jews could never keep them all, and rules could never save them from their sins anyway. Only God could save them. But they let their religious rituals take the place of God. That was wrong.

5.16 **GOD'S SPIRIT BRINGS LIFE** The life we were living before the Holy Spirit came to live in us was a sad and dying kind of life. Now that he lives in us, our desires are changed. We no longer wish to do the things that were killing us and dragging us down to hell. This is the kind of life that everybody needs. Then there would be no more hatred, jealousy, or other kinds of sin in the world.

NOTES

Step 11

I will pray to God on a regular basis, asking him to direct me and give me the power to live for him.

GALATIANS 5.16–18

THE CONSTANT BATTLE

"I'm really trying. I want to do what is right, but it's so easy to go back to my old way of life. Even though I was miserable and I guess I really hated myself, at least I was comfortable. I know what is expected of me. Just when I think I'm doing things right—*bam*—something in my past comes back to get me again. It's like I'm fighting a constant battle."

If we are experiencing the frustration of the old versus the new in our lives, we can be encouraged. It means we really are getting the hang of things! Our desires are changing. We want things to be different.

The Bible says the ways of the world (old life) and the ways of the Lord (new life), will always work against each other. It is a constant battle. So, how do we ever win?

STEP LOOK INSIDE 11

KEEP IN TOUCH WITH HEADQUARTERS

We have to stay in touch with the Commanding General. The Lord gave us the Holy Spirit to help us fight these battles. Prayer is our greatest weapon. We need to learn how to use it.

For another "Look Inside," turn to page 403.

and selfish. They not only argue and
cause trouble, but they are 21envious.
They get drunk, carry on at wild parties, and do other evil things as well.
I told you before, and I am telling
you again: No one who does these
things will share in the blessings of
God's kingdom.
22God's Spirit makes us loving,
happy, peaceful, patient, kind, good,
faithful, 23gentle, and self-controlled.
There is no law against behaving in
any of these ways. 24And because we
belong to Christ, we have killed our
selfish feelings and desires. 25God's
Spirit has given us life, and so we
should follow the Spirit. 26But don't
be conceited or make others jealous
by claiming to be better than they
are.

Help Each Other

6 My friends, you are spiritual. So
if someone is trapped in sin, you
should gently lead that person back
to the right path. But watch out, and
don't be tempted yourself.* 2You
obey the law of Christ when you offer
each other a helping hand.
3If you think you are better than
others, when you really aren't, you
are wrong. 4Do your own work well,
and then you will have something to
be proud of. But don't compare yourself with others. 5We each must carry
our own load.
6Share every good thing you have
with anyone who teaches you what
God has said.
7You cannot fool God, so don't
make a fool of yourself! You will harvest what you plant. 8If you follow
your selfish desires, you will harvest
destruction, but if you follow the
Spirit, you will harvest eternal life.
9Don't get tired of helping others.
You will be rewarded when the time
is right, if you don't give up. 10We
should help people whenever we can,
especially if they are followers of the
Lord.

Final Warnings

11You can see what big letters I
make when I write with my own
hand.*
12Those people who are telling you
to get circumcised are only trying to
show how important they are. And
they don't want to get into trouble
for preaching about the cross of
Christ. 13They are circumcised, but
they don't obey the Law of Moses.
All they want is to brag about having
you circumcised. 14But I will never
brag about anything except the cross
of our Lord Jesus Christ. Because
of his cross, the world is dead as
far as I am concerned, and I am
dead as far as the world is concerned.
15It doesn't matter if you are circumcised or not. All that matters is
that you are a new person.*

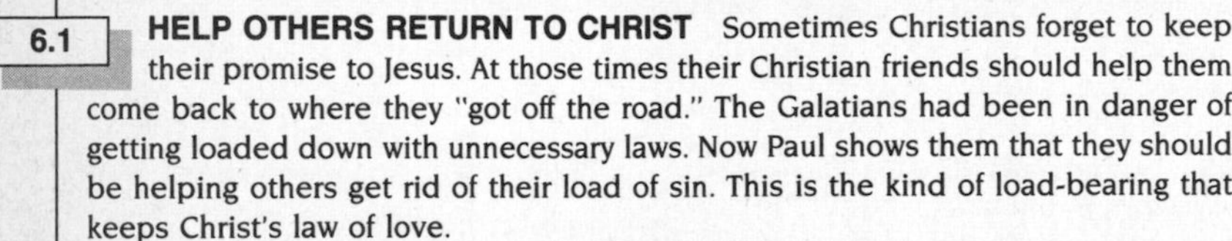

6.1 **HELP OTHERS RETURN TO CHRIST** Sometimes Christians forget to keep their promise to Jesus. At those times their Christian friends should help them come back to where they "got off the road." The Galatians had been in danger of getting loaded down with unnecessary laws. Now Paul shows them that they should be helping others get rid of their load of sin. This is the kind of load-bearing that keeps Christ's law of love.

6.11 **WE KNOW THIS IS A LETTER FROM PAUL** Paul proved this letter was from him by pointing out the "big letters" which he used to write his words. Many people believe Paul had eyesight problems, so he had to write in large handwriting. Eyeglasses had not yet been invented in Paul's time.

6.15 **BE A NEW CREATION OF GOD** Being created over again by God is what Paul means by becoming a "new person." That is the main point of his letter. Not marks made on our bodies like circumcision, but a completely new person is God's great answer to our needs. Jesus' answer to Nicodemus is still true: "You must be born from above" (John 3.7).

NOTES

JOYFULNESS—Enjoying the inward results of right living

GALATIANS 6.7, 8

THOSE CHEATING EYES

It's too bad they don't have a course in cheating. It's the one subject I would ace! People think you are stupid if you cheat. You don't know the answers because you aren't smart. It seems to me you are pretty smart if you know how to get the right answers and never have to study.

I guess I should say that's how it "seemed" to me. Things are different now. Making my decision to accept Jesus Christ has changed my attitude about a lot of things. Now I like myself and want to be different. That means I want to do the best for me. I don't just want to know the right answers to pass a test. I want to consider the kind of questions that will make me a better person. I have to admit, I'm a lot happier inside now. I don't have to worry if the teacher is looking at me or what will happen if I get caught. That's why it's eyes straight ahead now. Nothing up my sleeve or on the bottom of my shoe. And it's paying off. Yesterday Melissa Wright asked me since I knew so much about history, would I be able to help her study for next week's exam. Yes!!

A GOOD HARVEST

There is a great principle in the Bible that says, "You reap what you sow." It's great, that is, if we are planting good things in our life. Sowing the good seed of smart choices will insure that somewhere along the line we are going to get good things back. That's a promise from God himself!

For another "Look Ahead," turn to page 509.

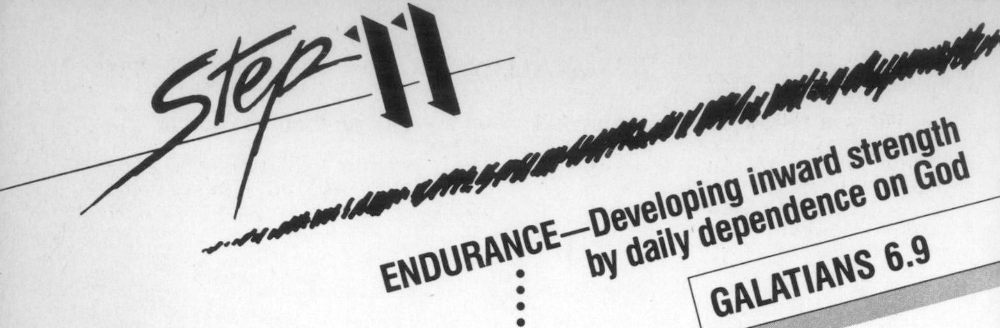

POWER RESERVES

The instructions on a camcorder say that for best results you should let the battery pack run down completely before you recharge it. Do you know why? This actually increases the endurance of the battery and makes it more efficient for the long term. Using up all the power the battery has to offer before recharging it increases its capacity for a longer-lasting charge!

Hard choices, tough times, and emotional struggles build endurance. When our reserves are on "Empty," time spent being recharged by prayer will increase our capacity to endure and live a consistent life serving God and others. Today we may be in one of those "draining" times. It may seem as if we are at the end of our power reserve. We should pray for strength! There are big pluses when we do.

Renewed strength comes from the power of the Holy Spirit. As we pray and ask God to direct us, he gives us the power to live for him. We develop deep spiritual reserves so that when we lack the energy to go on, God takes over. The results are lasting.

Galatians 6.9 speaks to this: "Don't get tired of helping others. You will be rewarded when the time is right, if you don't give up." This means that God is watching over us and that not only will he give us the strength, but he will reward us when we do the right thing, day after day, night after night. It's a promise.

STEP LOOK AHEAD 11

For another "Look Ahead," turn to page 491.

16If you follow this rule, you will
belong to God's true people. God will
treat you with kindness and will bless
you with peace.
17On my own body are scars that
prove I belong to Christ Jesus. So I
don't want anyone to bother me
anymore.
18My friends, I pray that the Lord
Jesus Christ will be kind to you!
Amen.

Paul's Letter TO THE CHURCH IN EPHESUS

ABOUT THIS LETTER

"Praise the God and Father of our Lord Jesus Christ for the spiritual blessings that Christ has brought us from heaven!" (1.3). Paul begins his letter to the Christians in Ephesus with a powerful reminder of the main theme of his message. Christ died on the cross to set us free (1.7,8). But God raised Christ from death, and he now sits at God's right side in heaven, where he rules over this world. And he will rule over the future world as well (1.20,21).

Christ brought Jews and Gentiles together by "breaking down the wall of hatred" that separated them (2.14) and he united them all as part of that holy temple where God's Spirit lives (2.22). This was according to God's eternal plan (3.11).

There is only one Lord, one Spirit of God, and one God, who is the Father of all people (4.4,5). This means that Christians must let the Spirit keep their hearts united, so they can live at peace with each other (4.3). The idea of all Christians being one with Christ is so central to this letter that it occurs twenty times. There is one faith and one baptism by which believers become one body.

Ephesus was a port city on the western shore of Asia Minor (modern-day Turkey). In Paul's time this was the fourth largest city in the Roman empire. It was also an ancient center of nature religion where the goddess Artemis was widely worshiped (Acts 19).

Paul lets the Ephesians know that much is expected of people who are called to a new life (4.17—5.20). Followers of the Lord are God's dear children, and they must do as God does (5.1). They used to live in the dark, but they must now live in the light and make their light shine (5.8,9).

Paul then teaches husbands and wives, children and parents, and slaves and masters how to live as Christians (5.21—6.9).

Paul never forgets how kind God is:

> *God was merciful! We were dead because of our sins, but God loved us so much that he made us alive with Christ, and God's kindness is what saves you.* (2.4–5)
>
> *You were saved by faith in God, who treats us much better than we deserve. This is God's gift to you, and not anything you have done on your own.* (2.8)

A QUICK LOOK AT THIS LETTER

1. Greetings (1.1,2)
2. Christ Brings Spiritual Blessings (1.3—3.21)
3. A New Life in Unity with Christ (4.1—6.20)
4. Final Greetings (6.21–24)

1 From Paul, chosen by God to be an apostle of Christ Jesus.

To God's people who live in Ephesus and[a] are faithful followers of Christ Jesus.

2I pray that God our Father and our Lord Jesus Christ will be kind to you and will bless you with peace!

Christ Brings Spiritual Blessings

3Praise the God and Father of our Lord Jesus Christ for the spiritual blessings that Christ has brought us from heaven!* 4Before the world was created, God had Christ choose us to live with him and to be his holy and innocent and loving people. 5God was kind[b] and decided that Christ would choose us to be God's own adopted children. 6God was very kind to us because of the Son he dearly loves, and so we should praise God.

7-8Christ sacrificed his life's blood to set us free, which means that our sins are now forgiven. Christ did this because God was so kind to us. God has great wisdom and understanding, 9and by what Christ has done, God has shown us his own mysterious ways. 10Then when the time is right, God will do all that he has planned, and Christ will bring together everything in heaven and on earth.

11God always does what he plans, and that's why he had Christ choose us.* 12He did this so that we Jews would bring honor to him and be the first ones to have hope because of him. 13Christ also brought you the truth, which is the good news about how you can be saved. You put your faith in Christ and were given the promised Holy Spirit to show that you belong to God. 14The Spirit also makes us sure that we will be given what God has stored up for his people. Then we will be set free, and God will be honored and praised.

Paul's Prayer

15I have heard about your faith in the Lord Jesus and your love for all of God's people. 16So I never stop being grateful for you, as I mention you in my prayers. 17I ask the glorious

[a]*live in Ephesus and*: Some manuscripts do not have these words. [b]*holy and innocent and loving people. 5God was kind*: Or "holy and innocent people. God was loving 5and kind."

1.3 JESUS STANDS FOR US IN HEAVEN Jesus not only brought us blessings from heaven. He is now standing for us in heaven. We enjoy spiritual blessings now because Jesus is in heaven before us. He has given us the Holy Spirit so that we can have some of heaven on earth right now. That's how we know that there is even more and better to come when we join Jesus in the place he has prepared for us.

1.11 GOD CHOSE US Jesus once reminded his disciples that they had not chosen him, but he chose them (John 15.16). So also he chose each of us who believe, long ago before he created the world. God chose us to believe *and* to be holy and innocent and loving. In that way we would show others in the world how good God is in all his ways. So Christians have a great privilege and a great duty to be like Jesus in the world.

NOTES

Father and God of our Lord Jesus
Christ to give you his Spirit. The
Spirit will make you wise and let you
understand what it means to know
God. 18My prayer is that light will
flood your hearts and that you will
understand the hope that was given
to you when God chose you. Then
you will discover the glorious blessings that will be yours together with
all of God's people.
19I want you to know about the
great and mighty power that God has
for us followers. It is the same wonderful power he used* 20when he
raised Christ from death and let him
sit at his right side[c] in heaven.
21There Christ rules over all forces,
authorities, powers, and rulers. He
rules over all beings in this world and
will rule in the future world as well.
22God has put all things under the
power of Christ, and for the good of
the church he has made him the head
of everything. 23The church is
Christ's body and is filled with Christ
who completely fills everything.[d]

From Death to Life

2 In the past you were dead because
you sinned and fought against
God. 2You followed the ways of this
world and obeyed the devil. He rules
the world, and his spirit has power
over everyone who does not obey
God. 3Once we were also ruled by
the selfish desires of our bodies and
minds. We had made God angry, and
we were going to be punished.
4-5But God was merciful! We were
dead because of our sins, but God
loved us so much that he made us
alive with Christ, and God's kindness
is what saves you.* 6God raised us
from death to life with Christ Jesus,
and he has given us a place beside
Christ in heaven above. 7God did this
so that in the future world he could
show how truly good and kind he is
to us because of what Christ Jesus
has done. 8You were saved by faith

in God, who treats us much better
than we deserve.[e] This is God's gift
to you, and not anything you have
done on your own. 9It isn't something
you have earned, so there is nothing
you can brag about. 10God planned
for us to do good things and to live
as he has always wanted us to live.
That's why he sent Christ to make
us what we are.

United by Christ

11Don't forget that you are Gentiles. In fact, you used to be called
"uncircumcised" by Jews, who take
pride in being circumcised. 12At that
time you did not know about Christ.
You were foreigners to the people
of Israel, and you had no part in the
promises that God had made to them.
You were living in this world without
hope and without God, 13and you
were far from God. But Christ offered
his life's blood as a sacrifice and
brought you near to God.
14Christ has made peace between

---

[c]*right side*: The place of power and honor. [d]*and is filled with Christ who completely fills everything*: Or "which completely fills Christ and fully completes his work." [e]*treats us much better than we deserve*: The Greek word *charis*, traditionally rendered "grace," is translated here and other places in the CEV to express the overwhelming kindness of God.

1.19 **WHAT MAKES US FOLLOWERS OF JESUS?** We follow the Lord not simply by our own decision, but by the power of God himself. Paul says that is the same power that raised Jesus from death. We were dead as far as knowing God was concerned. But God "raised us up" to the new life of knowing him, and he used the same power that he used to raise Christ from death.

2.4 **DON'T BE A WALKING DEAD PERSON** When we don't know God, that's a way of being "dead," even though we're still walking around. But when Christ rose from death, he made it possible for us to live in the same way that he lives—by enjoying the very life of God. By faith we realize that we were dead before Christ came to live in us, but now we're really alive.

NOTES

Jews and Gentiles, and he has united us by breaking down the wall of hatred that separated us. Christ gave his own body* 15to destroy the Law of Moses with all its rules and commands. He even brought Jews and Gentiles together as though we were only one person, when he united us in peace. 16On the cross Christ did away with our hatred for each other. He also made peace[f] between us and God by uniting Jews and Gentiles in one body. 17Christ came and preached peace to you Gentiles, who were far from God, and peace to us Jews, who were near to God. 18And because of Christ, all of us can come to the Father by the same Spirit.

19You Gentiles are no longer strangers and foreigners. You are citizens with everyone else who belongs to the family of God. 20You are like a building with the apostles and prophets as the foundation and with Christ as the most important stone. 21Christ is the one who holds the building together and makes it grow into a holy temple for the Lord. 22And you are part of that building Christ has built as a place for God's own Spirit to live.

Paul's Mission to the Gentiles

3 Christ Jesus made me his prisoner, so that I could help you Gentiles. 2You have surely heard about God's kindness in choosing me to help you.* 3In fact, this letter tells you a little about how God has shown me his mysterious ways. 4As you read the letter, you will also find out how well I really do understand the mystery about Christ. 5No one knew about this mystery until God's Spirit told it to his holy apostles and prophets. 6And the mystery is this: Because of Christ Jesus, the good news has given the Gentiles a share in the promises that God gave to the Jews. God has also let the Gentiles be part of the same body.

7God treated me with kindness. His power worked in me, and it became my job to spread the good news. 8I am the least important of all God's people. But God was kind and chose me to tell the Gentiles that because of Christ there are blessings that cannot be measured. 9God, who created everything, wanted me to help everyone understand the mysterious plan that had always been hidden in his mind. 10Then God would use the church to show the powers and authorities above that he has many different kinds of wisdom.

11God did this according to his eternal plan. And he was able to do what he had planned because of all that Christ Jesus our Lord had done. 12Christ now gives us courage and confidence, so that we can come to God by faith. 13That's why you should not be discouraged when I suffer for you. After all, it will bring honor to you.

Christ's Love for Us

14I kneel in prayer to the Father. 15All beings in heaven and on earth

---

[f]*He also made peace*: Or "The cross also made peace."

2.14 **GENTILES HAVE BEEN BROUGHT INTO GOD'S FAMILY** For centuries the Jews enjoyed the friendship of God. They believed him and were his true followers except when they disobeyed, which was often. But now God has also brought Gentiles into that family. Gentiles and Jews now share by faith in the results of the saving work of Jesus Christ. This is what God promised Abraham, the great father of the Jews, two thousand years before Christ was born, saying, "Through you all the families of the earth will be blessed."

3.2 **GOD CHOSE PAUL TO BRING THE GOOD NEWS** Paul had been an enemy of Christ and his followers. But then one day Jesus appeared to Paul (see Acts 9) when he was still called Saul. Then God gave to Paul a new understanding about why Jesus came. After that time when he met Jesus, Paul became a great missionary to the Gentile world.

NOTES

receive their life from him.[g] 16God
is wonderful and glorious. I pray that
his Spirit will make you become
strong followers 17and that Christ
will live in your hearts because of
your faith. Stand firm and be deeply
rooted in his love. 18I pray that you
and all of God's people will understand what is called wide or long or
high or deep.[h] 19I want you to know
all about Christ's love, although it is
too wonderful to be measured. Then
your lives will be filled with all that
God is.*

20-21I pray that Christ Jesus and the
church will forever bring praise to
God. His power at work in us can
do far more than we dare ask or
imagine. Amen.

Unity with Christ

4 As a prisoner of the Lord, I beg
you to live in a way that is worthy
of the people God has chosen to be
his own.* 2Always be humble and
gentle. Patiently put up with each
other and love each other. 3Try your
best to let God's Spirit keep your
hearts united. Do this by living at
peace. 4All of you are part of the same
body. There is only one Spirit of God,
just as you were given one hope when
you were chosen to be God's people.
5We have only one Lord, one faith,
and one baptism. 6There is one God
who is the Father of all people. Not
only is God above all others, but he
works by using all of us, and he lives
in all of us.

7Christ has generously divided out
his gifts to us. 8As the Scriptures say,

"When he went up
to the highest place,
he led away many prisoners
and gave gifts
to people."

9When it says, "he went up," it
means that Christ had been deep in
the earth. 10This also means that the
one who went deep into the earth is
the same one who went into the highest heaven, so that he would fill the
whole universe.

11Christ chose some of us to be
apostles, prophets, missionaries,
pastors, and teachers, 12so that his
people would learn to serve and his
body would grow strong. 13This will
continue until we are united by our
faith and by our understanding of the
Son of God. Then we will be mature,
just as Christ is, and we will be completely like him.[i]

14We must stop acting like children. We must not let deceitful people trick us by their false teachings,
which are like winds that toss us
around from place to place. 15Love
should always make us tell the truth.
Then we will grow in every way and
be more like Christ, the head*
16of the body. Christ holds it together
and makes all of its parts work perfectly, as it grows and becomes
strong because of love.

---

[g] *receive their life from him*: Or "know who they really are because of him." [h] *what is called wide or long or high or deep*: This may refer to the heavenly Jerusalem or to God's love or wisdom or to the meaning of the cross. [i] *and we will be completely like him*: Or "and he is completely perfect."

3.19 **CHRIST'S LOVE IS GREAT** Paul says you can't measure the love Jesus has for us. We know when ordinary people love us, and we're comforted by that. But when we know Christ's love, we never have to feel unloved again. His love goes on and on, and we're never alone. People cheat themselves of the greatest of all gifts when they fail to accept the love of Jesus.

4.1 **PAUL WROTE WITH A METHOD** If you look carefully you'll see that Paul teaches in Ephesians 1 through 3 mainly about what we should believe, and in chapters 4 through 6 about how we should live. This will help you as you study this great little book. Right Christian believing leads to right Christian living.

4.15 **WE ARE GROWING UP IN CHRIST** Jesus is our head, our leader, and he has given us different gifts and abilities to serve him. The reason for these differences is so that we may help one another grow spiritually and become mature, until we are truly like Christ.

NOTES

I will admit to God, to myself, and to someone I trust what I do wrong.

EPHESIANS 4.14–16

BUYING A LIE

"**W**ho is going to know?"

"**Y**ou owe it to me; we've been dating for two months."

"**W**e love each other, and that makes it right."

"**T**ry it just once. If you don't like it, forget it."

"**E**veryone is doing it."

There is nothing more persuasive than a lying tongue. And it usually speaks in people who have impressed us, and we find ourselves trying to impress them. Somewhere in the back of our minds we know we shouldn't do what they are asking, but at the time their opinion matters more than ours, so we buy the lie. Then we know what happens next. Either we get caught and pay the price right off the bat, or we get sucked in and the one-time lie becomes a lifestyle. Even if no one ever finds out, we still have to live with the guilt.

STEP 5 LOOK INSIDE

JUST ADMIT IT

It is very important to admit it when we have done wrong. When we face the mistakes of our past and deal with them, we break the chains of lying that have kept our life bound up. John 8.32 tells us that the "truth will set [us] free." That verse is talking about the truth of God's Word, but it can also apply to the truth of our words.

For another "Look Inside," turn to page 394.

"DON'T FORGET WHAT YOU'RE MADE OF"

In his book, *Integrity,* Ted Engstrom tells this story: "For coach Cleveland Stroud and the Bulldogs of Rockdale County High School (Conyers, Georgia), it was their championship season: 21 wins and 5 losses on the way to the Georgia boys' basketball tournament which culminated in a dramatic come-from-behind victory in the state finals."

But now the new glass trophy case outside the high school gymnasium is bare. The Georgia High School Association took away Rockdale County's championship after school officials said that a player who was scholastically ineligible had played 45 seconds in the first game of the post-season tournament.

"'We didn't know he was ineligible at the time; we didn't know it until a few weeks ago,' Coach Stroud said. 'Some people have said we should have just kept quiet about it, that it was just 45 seconds and the player wasn't an impact player. But you've got to do what's honest and right and what the rules say. I told my team that people forget the scores of basketball games; they don't ever forget what you're made of.'"

STEP LOOK AHEAD 5

"We are part of the same body. Stop lying and start telling each other the truth" (Ephesians 4.25). Being a truth-teller is an absolute must for a growing believer in Jesus Christ. Jesus set the example when he was being falsely accused in front of the high priest. "I am," he said, when asked if he were the Christ. The price he paid for telling the truth led to his death on the cross. It was the price he was willing to pay for our lies.

For another "Look Ahead," turn to page 453.

The Old Life and the New Life

17As a follower of the Lord, I order
you to stop living like stupid, godless
people. 18Their minds are in the dark,
and they are stubborn and ignorant
and have missed out on the life that
comes from God. They no longer
have any feelings about what is right,
19and they are so greedy that they
do all kinds of indecent things.
20-21But that isn't what you were
taught about Jesus Christ. He is the
truth, and you heard about him and
learned about him. 22You were told
that your foolish desires will destroy
you and that you must give up your
old way of life with all its bad habits.
23Let the Spirit change your way of
thinking* 24and make you into a new
person. You were created to be like
God, and so you must please him and
be truly holy.

Rules for the New Life

25We are part of the same body.
Stop lying and start telling each other
the truth. 26Don't get so angry that
you sin. Don't go to bed angry
27and don't give the devil a chance.
28If you are a thief, quit stealing.
Be honest and work hard, so you will
have something to give to people in
need.
29Stop all your dirty talk. Say the
right thing at the right time and help
others by what you say.
30Don't make God's Spirit sad. The
Spirit makes you sure that someday
you will be free from your sins.
31Stop being bitter and angry and
mad at others. Don't yell at one another or curse each other or ever be
rude. 32Instead, be kind and merciful,
and forgive others, just as God forgave you because of Christ.

5 Do as God does. After all, you
are his dear children. 2Let love
be your guide. Christ loved us[j] and
offered his life for us as a sacrifice
that pleases God.

3You are God's people, so don't let
it be said that any of you are immoral
or indecent or greedy. 4Don't use
dirty or foolish or filthy words. Instead, say how thankful you are.
5Being greedy, indecent, or immoral
is just another way of worshiping
idols. You can be sure that people
who behave in this way will never
be part of the kingdom that belongs
to Christ and to God.

Living as People of Light

6Don't let anyone trick you with
foolish talk. God punishes everyone
who disobeys him and says[k] foolish
things.* 7So don't have anything to
do with anyone like that.

8You used to be like people living
in the dark, but now you are people
of the light because you belong to
the Lord. So act like people of the
light 9and make your light shine. Be
good and honest and truthful, 10as
you try to please the Lord. 11Don't
take part in doing those worthless
things that are done in the dark. Instead, show how wrong they are.
12It is disgusting even to talk about
what is done in the dark. 13But the
light will show what these things are

---

[j] *us*: Some manuscripts have "you." [k] *says*: Or "does."

4.23 **LET THE SPIRIT CHANGE YOUR MIND** Because we are born into this sinful world, our thinking about God and our lives is twisted by sin. But Christ gives us a new mind, a new understanding, when we are born anew by the Holy Spirit (John 3.3). We must allow the Holy Spirit to keep on changing our minds as long as we live. As our minds change, so do our lives.

5.6 **HOW YOU TALK IS IMPORTANT** By "foolish talk" Paul means talk that is not decent. If we are Christians, we have the light of Christ living and shining in us. This should keep us from speaking in a way that brings disgrace on Christ. Filthy talk reveals a filthy mind. This can't be the mind of Christ who lives in the Christian.

NOTES

Step 4

I will take a hard look at myself, the way I live and my moral standards.

EPHESIANS 5.3–5

WORDS SPEAK LOUDER THAN ACTIONS

She was one of the most beautiful girls I had ever seen. When she walked in a room, heads turned automatically. There was pretty, and then there was Lauren—that is, until she opened her mouth. What came out of those perfect lips would embarrass guys in a locker room, if you know what I mean. In her case, beauty really was only skin-deep. After five minutes with Lauren, you quit looking at her beautiful eyes because all you could hear were the filthy words coming from her mouth.

STRONG WORDS

Words are very powerful. They can build up or tear down, not only other people but also our own reputations. Are we known as people who speak wisely, or do we use words that abuse and confuse? The Bible says that what comes out of our mouths is a real indication of what is in our hearts. If our relationships with Christ are real, then what comes out of our mouths should also be real.

For another "Look Inside," turn to page 474.

really like. 14Light shows up everything,[l] just as the Scriptures say,

"Wake up from your sleep
and rise from death.
Then Christ will shine
on you."

15Act like people with good sense
and not like fools. 16These are evil
times, so make every minute count.
17Don't be stupid. Instead, find out
what the Lord wants you to do.
18Don't destroy yourself by getting
drunk, but let the Spirit fill your life.
19When you meet together, sing
psalms, hymns, and spiritual songs,
as you praise the Lord with all your
heart. 20Always use the name of the
Lord Jesus Christ to thank God the
Father for everything.

Wives and Husbands

21Honor Christ and put others first.
22A wife should put her husband first,
as she does the Lord.* 23A husband
is the head of his wife, as Christ is
the head and the Savior of the
church, which is his own body.
24Wives should always put their husbands first, as the church puts Christ
first.

25A husband should love his wife
as much as Christ loved the church
and gave his life for it. 26He made
the church holy by the power of his
word, and he made it pure by washing it with water. 27Christ did this,
so that he would have a glorious and
holy church, without faults or spots
or wrinkles or any other flaws.

28In the same way, a husband
should love his wife as much as he
loves himself. A husband who loves
his wife shows that he loves himself.
29None of us hate our own bodies.
We provide for them and take good
care of them, just as Christ does for
the church, 30because we are each
part of his body. 31As the Scriptures
say, "A man leaves his father and
mother to get married, and he becomes like one person with his wife."
32This is a great mystery, but I understand it to mean Christ and his
church. 33So each husband should
love his wife as much as he loves
himself, and each wife should respect
her husband.

Children and Parents

6 Children, you belong to the Lord,
and you do the right thing when
you obey your parents. The first commandment with a promise says,*
2"Obey your father and your mother,
3and you will have a long and happy
life."

4Parents, don't be hard on your
children. Raise them properly. Teach
them and instruct them about the
Lord.

Slaves and Masters

5Slaves, you must obey your
earthly masters. Show them great respect and be as loyal to them as you

---

[l]*Light shows up everything*: Or "Everything that is seen in the light becomes light itself."

5.22 **WHO WILL BE FIRST?** In our times there is a lot of unhappiness between husbands and wives because either one or both don't follow God's plan for the home. The desire to be "one up" on someone else doesn't come from what God's word tells us. What Paul says about the home is clear. But let us be sure that our love, our desire to serve each other, is sincere. One party should not be doing all the loving and serving. "Love your neighbor" surely must also mean to love the person closest to you.

6.1 **THE FAMILY TEACHES LIFE** Children are wise to obey their parents. Later in life they will realize how important this was for them. Living in harmony with others begins by living in harmony with our families.

NOTES

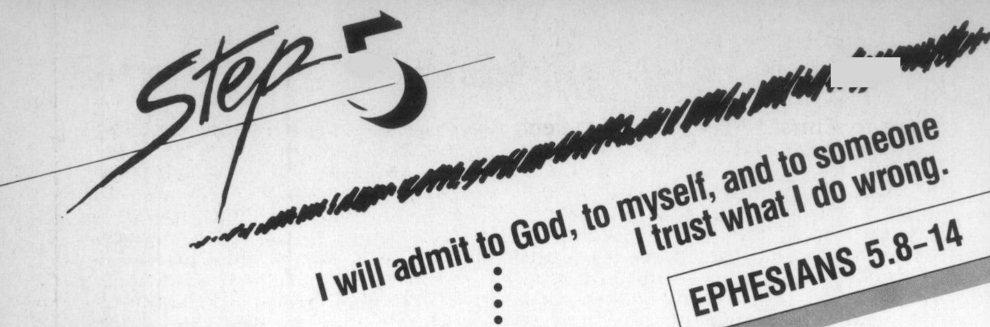

DARK TO LIGHT

We have all experienced fumbling in the dark for a light switch. But if we want to know true darkness, the place to go is a cave. When we put out our lamps in a cave, it is totally black. There are no shadows or images to guide our way. We can't even see our hands in front of our faces. And it is a darkness that we don't quickly recover from either. Once we come out of the cave, it takes a long time for our eyes to adjust to the light. We have to go slowly, a little at a time, for our eyes to focus properly.

A PERIOD OF ADJUSTMENT

A life lived in darkness requires a period of adjustment to the light. Once we are exposed to the truth of God's Word, it is usually a slow process of adjusting to the changes needed in our lives. We have to take it one day at a time, one step at a time, until our spiritual eyes adjust to the light and we can see more of Jesus.

For another "Look Inside," turn to page 481.

are to Christ.* 6Try to please them
at all times, and not just when you
think they are watching. You are
slaves of Christ, so with your whole
heart you must do what God wants
you to do. 7Gladly serve your masters, as though they were the Lord
himself, and not simply people.
8You know that you will be rewarded
for any good things you do, whether
you are slaves or free.
9Slave owners, you must treat your
slaves with this same respect. Don't
threaten them. They have the same
Master in heaven that you do, and
he doesn't have any favorites.

The Fight against Evil

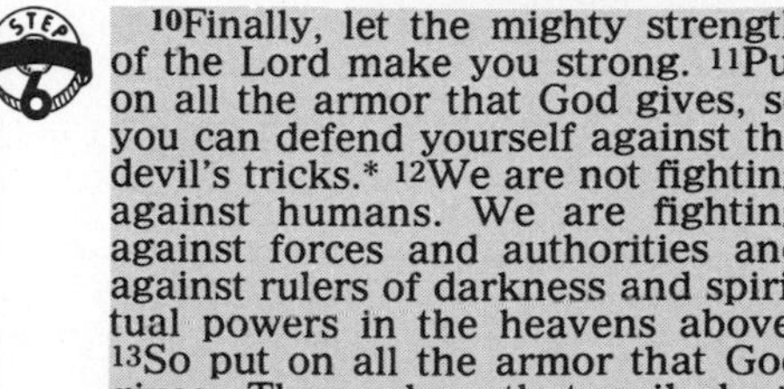
10Finally, let the mighty strength
of the Lord make you strong. 11Put
on all the armor that God gives, so
you can defend yourself against the
devil's tricks.* 12We are not fighting
against humans. We are fighting
against forces and authorities and
against rulers of darkness and spiritual powers in the heavens above.
13So put on all the armor that God
gives. Then when that evil day[m]
comes, you will be able to defend
yourself. And when the battle is over,
you will still be standing firm.
14Be ready! Let the truth be like a
belt around your waist, and let God's
justice protect you like armor.
15Your desire to tell the good news
about peace should be like shoes on
your feet. 16Let your faith be like a
shield, and you will be able to stop
all the flaming arrows of the evil one.
17Let God's saving power be like a
helmet, and for a sword use God's
message that comes from the Spirit.
18Never stop praying, especially
for others. Always pray by the power
of the Spirit. Stay alert and keep
praying for God's people. 19Pray that
I will be given the message to speak
and that I may fearlessly explain the
mystery about the good news.
20I was sent to do this work, and
that's the reason I am in jail. So pray
that I will be brave and will speak
as I should.*

Final Greetings

21-22I want you to know how I am
getting along and what I am doing.
That's why I am sending Tychicus
to you. He is a dear friend, as well
as a faithful servant of the Lord. He
will tell you how I am doing, and he
will cheer you up.
23I pray that God the Father and
the Lord Jesus Christ will give peace,
love, and faith to every follower!
24May God be kind to everyone who
keeps on loving our Lord Jesus
Christ.

---

[m] *that evil day*: Either the present (see 5.16) or "the day of death" or "the day of judgment."

6.5 **BE A GOOD CHRISTIAN WORKER** We don't have slaves today. But Paul's advice still holds, because just about everybody has to work for somebody else. Christian employees should see the wisdom in Paul's directions about serving. This is Christian love at work in the real world.

6.11 **GOD SUPPLIES OUR WEAPONS** The Christian life is like a war. Our enemy Satan wants to attack us, both from outside and from inside ourselves. Let's think about every weapon and piece of armor that Paul writes about. Then let's pray that we will learn to use each piece well, for the glory of God, as we come up against our daily trials.

6.20 **PAUL THE MIGHTY PRISONER** Even though Paul had been put in jail for his beliefs, he had strength and wisdom from God, and stayed cheerful and positive about what he was going through. He did some of his greatest writing in chains. Let's remember Paul as our example when we suffer in this life.

NOTES

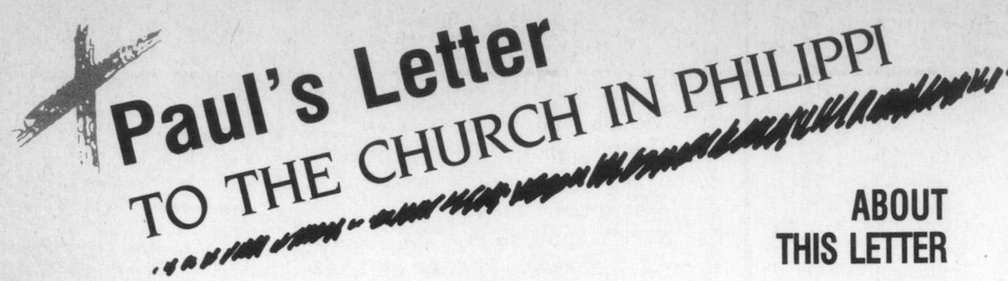

Paul's Letter TO THE CHURCH IN PHILIPPI

ABOUT THIS LETTER

Paul wrote this letter from jail (1.7) to thank the Lord's followers at Philippi for helping him with their gifts and prayers (1.5; 4.10–19). He hopes to be set free, so that he can continue preaching the good news (3.17–19). But he knows that he might be put to death (1.21; 2.17; 3.10).

The city of Philippi is in the part of northern Greece known as Macedonia. It was at Philippi that Paul had entered Europe for the first time, and there he preached the good news and began a church (Acts 16). He now warns the Christians at Philippi that they may have to suffer, just as Christ suffered and Paul is now suffering. If this happens, the Philippians should count it a blessing that comes from having faith in Christ (1.28–30).

There were problems in the church at Philippi, because some of the members claimed that people must obey the law of Moses, or they could not be saved. But Paul has no patience with such members and warns the church, "Watch out for those people who behave like dogs!" (3.2–11). This letter is also filled with joy. Even in jail, Paul is happy because he has discovered how to make the best of a bad situation and because he remembers all the kindness shown to him by the people in the church at Philippi.

Paul reminds them that God's people are to live in harmony (2.2; 4.2,3) and to think the same way that Christ Jesus did:

Christ was truly God.
But he did not try to remain
equal with God.
He gave up everything
and became a slave,
when he became
like one of us. (2.6,7)

A QUICK LOOK AT THIS LETTER

1. Greetings and a Prayer (1.1–11)
2. What Life Means to Paul (1.12–30)
3. Christ's Example of True Humility (2.1–18)
4. News about Paul's Friends (2.19–30)
5. Being Acceptable to God (3.1—4.9)
6. Paul Thanks the Philippians (4.10–20)
7. Final Greetings (4.21–23)

1 From Paul and Timothy, servants
of Christ Jesus.
To all of God's people who belong
to Christ Jesus at Philippi and to all
of your church officials and officers.[a]
2I pray that God our Father and
the Lord Jesus Christ will be kind
to you and will bless you with peace!

Paul's Prayer for the Church in Philippi

3Every time I think of you, I thank
my God.* 4And whenever I mention
you in my prayers, it makes me
happy. 5This is because you have
taken part with me in spreading the
good news from the first day you
heard about it. 6God is the one who
began this good work in you, and I
am certain that he won't stop before
it is complete on the day that Christ
Jesus returns.
7You have a special place in my
heart. So it is only natural for me
to feel the way I do. All of you have
helped in the work that God has
given me, as I defend the good news
and tell about it here in jail. 8God
himself knows how much I want to
see you. He knows that I care for you
in the same way that Christ Jesus
does.

9I pray that your love will keep on
growing and that you will fully know
and understand 10how to make the
right choices. Then you will still be
pure and innocent when Christ returns. And until that day,* 11Jesus
Christ will keep you busy doing good
deeds that bring glory and praise to
God.

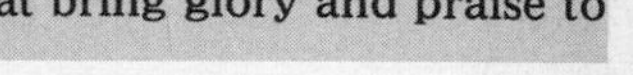

What Life Means to Paul

12My dear friends, I want you to
know that what has happened to me
has helped to spread the good news.
13The Roman guards and all the
others know that I am here in jail
because I serve Christ. 14Now most
of the Lord's followers have become
brave and are fearlessly telling the
message.[b]
15Some are preaching about Christ
because they are jealous and envious
of us. Others are preaching because

---

[a]*church officials and officers*: Or "bishops and deacons." [b]*the message*: Some manuscripts have "the Lord's message," and others have "God's message."

1.3 **A BEAUTIFUL WAY TO THINK** Paul thanked God every time he remembered one of Christ's people. Giving thanks for one another is a good way never to think thoughts of envy or resentment about our Christian brothers and sisters. We have many good memories of the love and kindness of such friends. God is pleased when we give thanks for each one that is so well remembered.

1.10 **GOD WILL FINISH HIS WORK IN US** God didn't plan to save us and draw us into his friendship just so he could turn around and throw us away. No—he will complete his good work in us when Jesus comes back to earth. In the meantime, God is doing that work daily—molding and shaping us to be like his Son.

NOTES

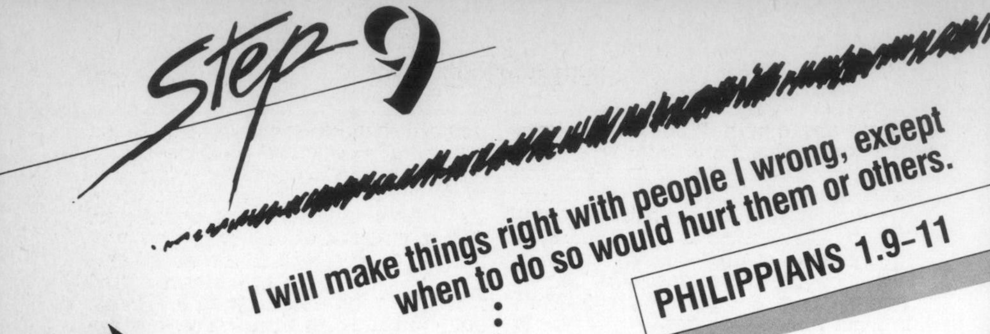

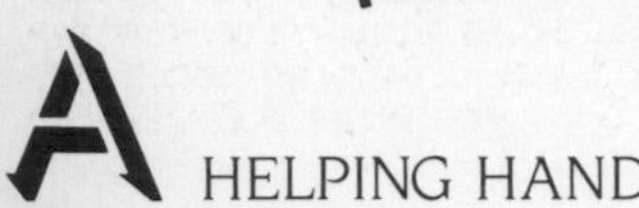

A HELPING HAND

I can remember when, as a kid, I took a piece of candy from a food store. When I got in the car, my dad spotted it. After a stern lecture on stealing, he told me I would have to go back into the store and return the candy. I can remember saying, "But Dad, what will I say?"

He rehearsed the words of apology with me, and then, taking my hand, he walked me back to the scene of the crime.

GOING BACK

There may be times when we want to make things right with someone but we just don't know what to say. We need to remember that God's Spirit is with us now and will help us find the right words. God will speak through us to others. We don't have to go "back into the store" by ourselves. Our Heavenly Father will walk with us.

For another "Look Inside," turn to page 507.

they want to help. 16They love Christ
and know that I am here to defend
the good news about him. 17But the
ones who are jealous of us are not
sincere. They just want to cause trouble for me while I am in jail. 18But
that doesn't matter. All that matters
is that people are telling about Christ,
whether they are sincere or not. That
is what makes me glad.

I will keep on being glad, 19because
I know that your prayers and the help
that comes from the Spirit of Christ
Jesus will keep me safe. 20I honestly
expect and hope that I will never do
anything to be ashamed of. Whether
I live or die, I always want to be as
brave as I am now and bring honor
to Christ.

21If I live, it will be for Christ, and
if I die, I will gain even more.*
22I don't know what to choose. I could
keep on living and doing something
useful. 23It is a hard choice to make.
I want to die and be with Christ, because that would be much better.
24-25But I know that all of you still
need me. That's why I am sure I will
stay on to help you grow and be
happy in your faith. 26Then, when I
visit you again, you will have good
reason to take great pride in Christ
Jesus because of me.[c]

27Above all else, you must live in
a way that brings honor to the good
news about Christ. Then, whether I
visit you or not, I will hear that all
of you think alike. I will know that
you are working together and that
you are struggling side by side to get
others to believe the good news.

28Be brave when you face your enemies. Your courage will show them
that they are going to be destroyed,
and it will show you that you will
be saved. God will make all of this
happen,* 29and he has blessed you.
Not only do you have faith in Christ,
but you suffer for him. 30You saw me
suffer, and you still hear about my
troubles. Now you must suffer in the
same way.

True Humility

2 Christ encourages you, and his
love comforts you. God's Spirit
unites you, and you are concerned
for others. 2Now make me completely happy! Live in harmony by
showing love for each other. Be
united in what you think, as if you
were only one person. 3Don't be jealous or proud, but be humble and consider others more important than
yourselves. 4Care about them as
much as you care about yourselves
5and think the same way that Christ
Jesus did:[d]

6Christ was truly God.
But he did not try to remain[e]
equal with God.*

---

[c]*take great pride in Christ Jesus because of me*: Or "take great pride in me because of Christ Jesus." [d]*think the same way that Christ Jesus did*: Or "think the way you should because you belong to Christ Jesus." [e]*remain*: Or "become."

1.21 **WHAT IS YOUR GOAL IN LIFE?** Paul said he lived his life for Christ, and we can easily believe it. The letters to the Ephesians, the Philippians, the Colossians, and Philemon were probably written when Paul was a prisoner in Rome (see Acts 28). But notice Paul's Christlike and generous spirit. When we're set free from selfishness, it's not hard to be cheerful.

1.28 **COURAGE SAYS A LOT** The believer's courage does two things. First, it shows enemies that they are defeated, even though they might seem to be winning. And it shows the believer that God is in control, and that he saves the soul. No one can truly hurt the believer who has such courage from God.

2.6 **JESUS IS OUR EXAMPLE** Jesus didn't insist on being treated as God—even though he had a right to. He left his royal glory behind to become a servant to people on earth. So what is our "claim to fame"? When we understand what Jesus did to save us from our sins, how can we feel important? The King of glory himself became a man to seek lost people. That ought to make us humble.

NOTES

7He gave up everything[f]
and became a slave,
when he became
like one of us.

8Christ was humble.
He obeyed God and even died
on a cross.
9Then God gave Christ
the highest place
and honored his name
above all others.

10So at the name of Jesus
everyone will bow down,
those in heaven, on earth,
and under the earth.
11And to the glory
of God the Father
everyone will openly agree,
"Jesus Christ is Lord!"

Lights in the World

12My dear friends, you always
obeyed when I was with you. Now
that I am away, you should obey even
more. So work with fear and trembling to discover what it really means
to be saved. 13God is working in you
to make you willing to obey him.*

14Do everything without grumbling or arguing. 15Then you will be
the pure and innocent children of
God. You live among people who are
crooked and evil, but you must not
do anything that they can say is
wrong. Try to shine as lights among
the people of this world, 16as you hold
firmly to[g] the message that gives life.
Then on the day when Christ returns,
I can take pride in you. I can also
know that my work and efforts were
not useless.
17Your faith in the Lord and your
service are like a sacrifice offered to
him. And my own blood may have
to be poured out with the sacrifice.[h]
If this happens, I will be glad and
rejoice with you. 18In the same way,
you should be glad and rejoice with
me.

Timothy and Epaphroditus

19I want to be encouraged by news
about you. So I hope the Lord Jesus
will soon let me send Timothy to you.
20I don't have anyone else who cares
about you as much as he does.
21The others think only about what
interests them and not about what
concerns Christ Jesus.* 22But you
know what kind of person Timothy
is. He has worked with me like a son
in spreading the good news. 23I hope
to send him to you, as soon as I find
out what is going to happen to me.
24I feel sure that the Lord will also
let me come soon.
25I think I ought to send my dear
friend Epaphroditus back to you. He
is a follower and a worker and a soldier of the Lord, just as I am. You
sent him to look after me, 26but now
he is eager to see you. He is worried,
because you heard he was sick.
27In fact, he was very sick and almost
died. But God was kind to him, and
also to me, and he kept me from being
burdened down with sorrow.
28Now I am more eager than ever
to send Epaphroditus back again.

---

[f] *He gave up everything*: Greek, "He emptied himself." [g] *hold firmly to*: Or "offer them." [h] *my own blood may have to be poured out with the sacrifice*: Offerings of water or wine were sometimes poured out when animals were sacrificed on the altar.

2.13 **WE AREN'T ALONE** We aren't in a do-it-yourself improvement program. "God is working in you," says Paul. This makes us happy as we realize that we are, after all, God's own workmanship. It is God who is shaping and molding us into the kind of people he wants us to be. Sunshine and rain, good times and hard times, are God's ways of completing his great plan for us.

2.21 **BE JESUS-MINDED** Paul praises Timothy for thinking first about what concerns Jesus. Life is a lot simpler and happier for people who are "Jesus-minded," who aren't struggling for the sake of their own interests, but who are looking out for his.

NOTES

Step 10

I need to continue looking inside—admitting when I am wrong.

PHILIPPIANS 2.14–16

SKELETONS IN THE CLOSET

The headlines read "Maxwell's Past Ends His Future." The most qualified candidate wasn't elected because of indiscretions in his past. Reporters discovered he used drugs in college and had been involved in extra-marital affairs.

We could argue that actions of our past should have nothing to do with our ability to perform now, but they do. That is why it is so important to go to those people we have offended or disappointed and ask them to forgive us. Then we can try, with God's help, to live lives that can't be used against us.

TELL GOD FIRST

The Lord wants to hear about what is going on inside us before the news reaches the outside world. He is there to help us deal with the anger, resentment, and temptation that, if not stopped, may someday result in more skeletons in our closets.

For another "Look Inside," turn to page 472.

You will be glad to see him, and I
won't have to worry any longer.
29Be sure to give him a cheerful welcome, just as people who serve the
Lord deserve. 30He almost died working for Christ, and he risked his own
life to do for me what you could not.

Being Acceptable to God

3 Finally, my dear friends, be glad
that you belong to the Lord. It
doesn't bother me to write the same
things to you that I have written
before. In fact, it is for your own
good.
2Watch out for those people who
behave like dogs! They are evil and
want to do more than just circumcise
you. 3But we are the ones who are
truly circumcised, because we worship by the power of God's Spirit[i]
and take pride in Christ Jesus. We
don't brag about what we have done,
4although I could. Others may brag
about themselves, but I have more
reason to brag than anyone else.
5I was circumcised when I was eight
days old,[j] and I am from the nation
of Israel and the tribe of Benjamin.
I am a true Hebrew. As a Pharisee,
I strictly obeyed the Law of Moses.
6And I was so eager that I even made
trouble for the church. I did everything the Law demands in order to
please God.
7But Christ has shown me that
what I once thought was valuable is
worthless.* 8Nothing is as wonderful
as knowing Christ Jesus my Lord. I
have given up everything else and
count it all as garbage. All I want is
Christ 9and to know that I belong to
him. I could not make myself acceptable to God by obeying the Law of
Moses. God accepted me simply because of my faith in Christ. 10All I
want is to know Christ and the power
that raised him to life. I want to suffer
and die as he did, 11so that somehow
I also may be raised to life.

Running toward the Goal

12I have not yet reached my goal,
and I am not perfect. But Christ has
taken hold of me. So I keep on running and struggling to take hold of
the prize.* 13My friends, I don't feel
that I have already arrived. But I forget what is behind, and I struggle for
what is ahead. 14I run toward the
goal, so that I can win the prize of
being called to heaven. This is the
prize that God offers because of what
Christ Jesus has done. 15All of us who
are mature should think in this same
way. And if any of you think differently, God will make it clear to you.
16But we must keep going in the direction that we are now headed.
17My friends, I want you to follow
my example and learn from others
who closely follow the example we
set for you. 18I often warned you that
many people are living as enemies
of the cross of Christ. And now with
tears in my eyes, I warn you again
19that they are headed for hell!
They worship their stomachs and
brag about the disgusting things

---

[i] *by the power of God's Spirit*: Or "sincerely."
[j] *when I was eight days old*: Jewish boys are circumcised eight days after birth.

3.7 **WHAT REALLY COUNTS** Paul had once been the "golden boy" of the Pharisees. He was smart, had lots of energy, and did all of the things that a good Pharisee ought to do. But that was all garbage to Paul once he learned the really important thing—knowing Jesus. How about you? Is there garbage in your life that needs to be taken away?

3.12 **PAUL THE RUNNER** Paul knew he didn't have to earn forgiveness. But to know Christ better was his goal in life, so he compared himself to a runner. Jesus is worth running for, stretching every nerve and every muscle to "take hold of" the One who is more desirable than all earthly prizes.

NOTES

Step 11

I will pray to God on a regular basis, asking him to direct me and give me the power to live for him.

PHILIPPIANS 3.12–16

PRESS ON

When I first decided to run in the road race, it seemed like a great idea. How far can 10K be anyway? I'm in pretty good shape. I'm young and healthy. I figured if those old guys could do it, so could I.

Two kilometers to go! It might as well be 2,000! I'm going to die, right here in front of everyone. What am I saying? I can't stop now; even the old guys are still running.

Press on. That is God's word to us today. We may have thoughts of giving up and dropping out, but we tried that already. We took the easy way out until we realized we were losing the race. So we decided to run a new course.

STEP LOOK INSIDE 11

FINISHING STRONG

There may be days when it seems like we aren't making any headway and we want to quit. That's when it's time to stop and pray. God will get us back on track and help us finish the race.

For another "Look Inside," turn to page 590.

All they can think about are the
things of this world.*
20But we are citizens of heaven and
are eagerly waiting for our Savior
to come from there. Our Lord Jesus
Christ 21has power over everything,
and he will make these poor bodies
of ours like his own glorious body.

4 Dear friends, I love you and long
to see you. Please keep on being
faithful to the Lord. You are my pride
and joy.

Paul Encourages the Lord's Followers

2Euodia and Syntyche, you belong
to the Lord, so I beg you to stop arguing with each other. 3And, my true
partner,[k] I ask you to help them.
These women have worked together
with me and with Clement and with
the others in spreading the good
news. Their names are now written
in the book of life.[l]

4Always be glad because of the
Lord! I will say it again: Be glad.
5Always be gentle with others. The
Lord will soon be here.* 6Don't worry
about anything, but pray about
everything. With thankful hearts offer up your prayers and requests to
God. 7Then, because you belong to
Christ Jesus, God will bless you with
peace that no one can completely understand. And this peace will control
the way you think and feel.
8Finally, my friends, keep your
minds on whatever is true, pure,
right, holy, friendly, and proper.
Don't ever stop thinking about what
is truly worthwhile and worthy of
praise. 9You know the teachings I
gave you, and you know what you
heard me say and saw me do. So follow my example. And God, who gives
peace, will be with you.

Paul Gives Thanks for the Gifts He Was Given

10The Lord has made me very
grateful that at last you have thought
about me once again. Actually, you
were thinking about me all along, but
you didn't have any chance to show
it. 11I am not complaining about having too little. I have learned to be satisfied with[m] whatever I have.* 12I
know what it is to be poor or to have
plenty, and I have lived under all
kinds of conditions. I know what it
means to be full or to be hungry, to
have too much or too little. 13Christ
gives me the strength to face anything.
14It was good of you to help me
when I was having such a hard time.

---

[k] *partner*: Or "Syzygus," a person's name. [l] *the book of life*: A book in which the names of God's people are written. [m] *be satisfied with*: Or "get by on."

3.19 **WHAT IS YOUR REAL TREASURE?** Paul was depressed because some who had claimed to be followers of Jesus turned out to be traitors later on. We all see this amazing thing from time to time—people who seemed to have it all, but threw Christ away for a few earthly pleasures that would soon pass away.

4.5 **JESUS WILL RETURN SOON** Paul was expecting Jesus to return in his own time, and so should we. It is right to expect Jesus at any time. The years seem long to us, but with God a thousand years are like a moment. That is why Jesus commands us to "watch" (Matthew 24.42). His return is just as likely today as it will be any other day.

4.11 **ARE YOU SATISFIED?** Can Christians usually be satisfied? Yes, they can. We don't expect to be satisfied with what this world has to offer. If our needs are met, we consider ourselves well off. Some people without Christ may have more than they can ever use, but they're never satisfied because they still dream of finding what they want in this world. They never seem to find it. They just keep working and seeking more and more, but happiness is always just out of reach.

NOTES

15My friends at Philippi, you remember what it was like when I started preaching the good news in Macedonia.[n] After I left there, you were the only church that became my partner by giving blessings and by receiving them in return. 16Even when I was in Thessalonica, you helped me more than once. 17I am not trying to get something from you, but I want you to receive the blessings that come from giving.

18I have been paid back everything, and with interest. I am completely satisfied with the gifts that you had Epaphroditus bring me. They are like a sweet-smelling offering or like the right kind of sacrifice that pleases God.* 19I pray that God will take care of all your needs with the wonderful blessings that come from Christ Jesus! 20May God our Father be praised forever and ever. Amen.

Final Greetings

21Give my greetings to all who are God's people because of Christ Jesus.

The Lord's followers here with me send you their greetings.

22All of God's people send their greetings, especially those in the service of the Emperor.

23I pray that our Lord Jesus Christ will be kind to you and will bless your life!

---

[n] *when I started preaching the good news in Macedonia*: Paul is talking about his first visit to Philippi. See Acts 16.12-40.

4.18 **GIVING TO OTHERS IS GIVING TO GOD** When we give things to others, we are giving an offering to God. Paul says we are blessed by God for being generous, but our main reason should always be our love toward God, and our desire to serve him by giving to those who are in need.

NOTES

Paul's Letter TO THE CHURCH IN COLOSSAE

ABOUT THIS LETTER

Colossae was an important city in western Asia Minor, about 100 miles east of the port city of Ephesus. Paul had never been to Colossae, but he was pleased to learn that the Christians there were strong in their faith (1.3–7; 2.6,7). They had heard the good news from a man named Epaphras who had lived there (1.7; 4.12,13), but was in jail with Paul (Philemon 23) at the time that Paul wrote this letter (1.14; 4.3,10,18).

Many of the church members in Colossae were Gentiles (1.27), and some of them were influenced by strange religious ideas and practices (2.16–23). They thought that to obey God fully they must give up certain physical desires and worship angels and other spiritual powers. But Paul wanted them to know that Christ was with God in heaven, ruling over all powers in the universe (3.1). And so, their worship should be directed to Christ.

Paul quotes a beautiful hymn that explains who Christ is:

Christ is exactly like God,
who cannot be seen.
He is the first-born Son,
superior to all creation.
God himself was pleased
to live fully in his Son.
And God was pleased
for him to make peace
by sacrificing his blood
on the cross.
(1.15,19,20*a*)

A QUICK LOOK AT THIS LETTER

1. Greetings (1.1,2)
2. A Prayer of Thanks (1.3–8)
3. The Person and Work of Christ (1.9—2.19)
4. New Life with Christ (2.20—4.6)
5. Final Greetings (4.7–18)

1 From Paul, chosen by God to be
an apostle of Christ Jesus, and
from Timothy, who is also a follower.
2To God's people who live in Colossae and are faithful followers of
Christ.
I pray that God our Father will be
kind to you and will bless you with
peace!

A Prayer of Thanks

3Each time we pray for you, we
thank God, the Father of our Lord
Jesus Christ. 4We have heard of your
faith in Christ and of your love for
all of God's people, 5because what
you hope for is kept safe for you in
heaven. You first heard about this
hope when you believed the true message, which is the good news.
6The good news is spreading all
over the world with great success.
It has spread in that same way among
you, ever since the first day you
learned the truth about God's kindness 7from our good friend Epaphras.
He works together with us for Christ
and is a faithful worker for you.[a]
8He is also the one who told us about
the love that God's Spirit has given
you.

The Person and Work of Christ

STEP 12 9We have not stopped praying for
you since the first day we heard about
you. In fact, we always pray that God
will show you everything he wants
you to do and that you may have all
the wisdom and understanding that
his Spirit gives.* 10Then you will live
a life that honors the Lord, and you
will always please him by doing good
deeds. You will come to know God
even better. 11His glorious power will
make you patient and strong enough
to endure anything, and you will be
truly happy.
12I pray that you will be grateful
to God for letting you[a] have part in
what he has promised his people in
the kingdom of light. 13God rescued
us from the dark power of Satan and
brought us into the kingdom of his
dear Son, 14who forgives our sins and
sets us free.

15Christ is exactly like God,
who cannot be seen.
He is the first-born Son,
superior to all creation.
16Everything was created
by him,
everything in heaven
and on earth,
everything seen and unseen,
including all forces
and powers,
and all rulers
and authorities.
All things were created
by God's Son,
and everything was made
for him.*

17God's Son was before all else,
and by him everything
is held together.
18He is the head of his body,
which is the church.
He is the very beginning,
the first to be raised
from death,

---

[a]*you*: Some manuscripts have "us."

1.9 **PAUL LOVED HIS PEOPLE** This is one of the letters Paul wrote when he was a prisoner in Rome. Even as a prisoner Paul's main thoughts were about the people he had won to Christ. Paul was an apostle, but he was also the model pastor. He was careful to teach young Christians the truth, and he also cared for their spiritual well-being.

1.16 **ALL THINGS BELONG TO CHRIST** Jesus is no longer merely the humble servant he was when he was on earth. Even before he was born in Bethlehem, Jesus was always the everlasting Son of God who created everything. So we all belong to Christ by the fact that we are his creations. All things that we enjoy in the world are provided by him. He holds everything together. So it makes sense to surrender our lives to Jesus.

NOTES

so that he would be
above all others.

19God himself was pleased
to live fully in his Son.
20And God was pleased
for him to make peace
by sacrificing his blood
on the cross,
so that all beings in heaven
and on earth
would be brought back
to God.

21You used to be far from God.
Your thoughts made you his enemies,
and you did evil things. 22But his Son
became a human and died. So God
made peace with you, and now he
lets you stand in his presence as people who are holy and faultless and
innocent. 23But you must stay deeply
rooted and firm in your faith. You
must not give up the hope you received when you heard the good
news. It was preached to everyone
on earth, and I myself have become
a servant of this message.

Paul's Service to the Church

24I am glad that I can suffer for
you. I am pleased also that in my own
body I can continue[b] the suffering
of Christ for his body, the church.
25God's plan was to make me a servant of his church and to send me
to preach his complete message to
you. 26For ages and ages this message was kept secret from everyone,
but now it has been explained to
God's people. 27God did this because
he wanted you Gentiles to understand his wonderful and glorious
mystery. And the mystery is that
Christ lives in you, and he is your
hope of sharing in God's glory.*

28We announce the message about
Christ, and we use all our wisdom
to warn and teach everyone, so that
all of Christ's followers will grow and
become mature. 29That's why I work
so hard and use all the mighty power
he gives me.

2 I want you to know what a struggle I am going through for you,
for God's people at Laodicea, and for
all of those followers who have never
met me. 2I do it to encourage them.
Then as their hearts are joined together in love, they will be wonderfully blessed with complete understanding. And they will truly know
Christ. Not only is he the key to God's
mystery, 3but all wisdom and knowledge are hidden away in him.
4I tell you these things to keep you
from being fooled by fancy talk.*
5Even though I am not with you, I
keep thinking about you. I am glad
to know that you are living as you
should and that your faith in Christ
is strong.

Christ Brings Real Life

6You have accepted Christ Jesus
as your Lord. Now keep on following
him. 7Plant your roots in Christ and
let him be the foundation for your
life. Be strong in your faith, just as
you were taught. And be grateful.
8Don't let anyone fool you by using
senseless arguments. These arguments may sound wise, but they are
only human teachings. They come
from the powers of this world[c] and
not from Christ.

---

[b]*continue*: Or "complete." [c]*powers of this world*: Spirits and unseen forces were thought to control human lives and were believed to be connected with the movements of the stars.

1.27 **JESUS WILL LIVE IN YOU** Paul calls this a "mystery." It's something that is revealed to us, that we never could have figured out on our own. The whole purpose of becoming a Christian is so that the Son of God himself may dwell in us forever. This is what really makes us sons and daughters of God.

2.4 **DON'T BE FOOLED** Paul warns us about false teaching. In his day false teachers were claiming to have special knowledge about spiritual things. There are still such false teachers around today, as a look through many bookstores will quickly show. We are not saved by superior knowledge, but by Christ himself who gives us eternal life.

NOTES

PLAYING ON A NEW TEAM

Several years ago, professional baseball's all-star centerfielder, Brett Butler, decided to leave the San Francisco Giants as a free agent and sign with the Los Angeles Dodgers, cross-state rivals. When Butler returned to San Francisco for the first time as a Los Angeles Dodger, Giants fans greeted him with a mixture of boos and cheers.

The sporadic cheers turned to loud boos, however, when Butler hugged Los Angeles manager Tommy Lasorda. "It turned a page in my career," said Butler. "I'm an L.A. Dodger now; I'm not a Giant. That just kind of solidified it. I wanted them to know, I'm a Dodger."

When people come to Christ, it takes courage to go public in front of old friends and classmates. Colossians 3.1, 2 says, "You have been raised to life with Christ. Now set your heart on what is in heaven, where Christ rules at God's right side. Think about what is up there, not about what is here on earth."

As Christians, we are playing for a new team. The crowd that matters is the one looking down from heaven. That doesn't mean that our old friends should be cast aside. But it does mean that our acceptance is assured in another group—so we don't have to say and do the popular things to gain acceptance by the crowd.

Courage takes a long look at life and asks, "What am I here for? What is going to be important ten or twenty years from now?" In fact, if we can get above it all and think in terms of what matters for eternity, we can get a better idea of what is really important today.

We don't have to be afraid. God is there, and he is aware of the decisions we need to make, the choices that will face us this week. We can trust Christ to lead us!

For another "Look Ahead," turn to page 458.

9God lives fully in Christ. 10And you are fully grown because you belong to Christ, who is over every power and authority. 11Christ has also taken away your selfish desires, just as circumcision removes flesh from the body. 12And when you were baptized, it was the same as being buried with Christ. Then you were raised to life because you had faith in the power of God, who raised Christ from death.* 13You were dead, because you were sinful and were not God's people. But God let Christ make you[d] alive, when he forgave all our sins.

14God wiped out all the charges that were against us for disobeying the Law of Moses. He took them away and nailed them to the cross. 15There Christ defeated all powers and forces. He let the whole world see them being led away as prisoners when he celebrated his victory.

16Don't let anyone tell you what you must eat or drink. Don't let them say that you must celebrate the New Moon festival, the Sabbath, or any other festival. 17These things are only a shadow of what was to come. But Christ is real!

18Don't be cheated by people who make a show of acting humble and who worship angels.[e] They brag about seeing visions. But it is all nonsense, because their minds are filled with selfish desires. 19They are no longer part of Christ, who is the head of the whole body. Christ gives the body its strength, and he uses its joints and muscles to hold it together, as it grows by the power of God.

Christ Brings New Life

20You died with Christ. Now the forces of the universe[f] don't have any power over you. Why do you live as if you had to obey such rules as,* 21"Don't handle this. Don't taste that. Don't touch this."? 22After these things are used, they are no longer good for anything. So why be bothered with all the rules that humans have made up? 23Obeying these rules may seem to be the smart thing to do. They appear to make you love God more and to be very humble and to have control over your body. But they don't really have any power over our desires.

3 You have been raised to life with Christ. Now set your heart on what is in heaven, where Christ rules at God's right side.[g] 2Think about what is up there, not about what is here on earth.* 3You died, which means that your life is hidden with Christ, who sits beside God. 4Christ gives meaning to your[h] life, and when he appears, you will also appear with him in glory.

5Don't be controlled by your body. Kill every desire for the wrong kind of sex. Don't be immoral or indecent or have evil thoughts. Don't be greedy, which is the same as worshiping idols. 6God is angry with people who disobey him by doing these

---

[d] *you*: Some manuscripts have "us." [e] *worship angels*: Or "worship with angels (in visions of heaven)." [f] *forces of the universe*: See the note at 2.8. [g] *right side*: The place of power and honor. [h] *your*: Some manuscripts have "our."

2.12 **DYING WITH CHRIST** Different churches have different ways of baptizing. Whatever the method, Paul shows here that being under water in baptism is a picture of being dead and buried with Christ. Then, just as Christ rose again, we are with him in new life as we live for God by the power he gives us.

2.20 **CHRIST IS OUR LIFE** Christians are people who have died—in the sense that our disobedient nature was nailed to the cross with Christ. Our true life now comes from Christ who lives in us. We can't make ourselves holy merely by obeying rules. Only Jesus living in us makes it possible for us to live as God's people.

3.2 **WHERE ARE YOUR THOUGHTS?** The best way to get rid of evil thoughts is to replace them with good thoughts. We do this by concentrating on the things of heaven where Christ is. When we do that, there is no room left for evil desires that eat away at our happiness.

NOTES

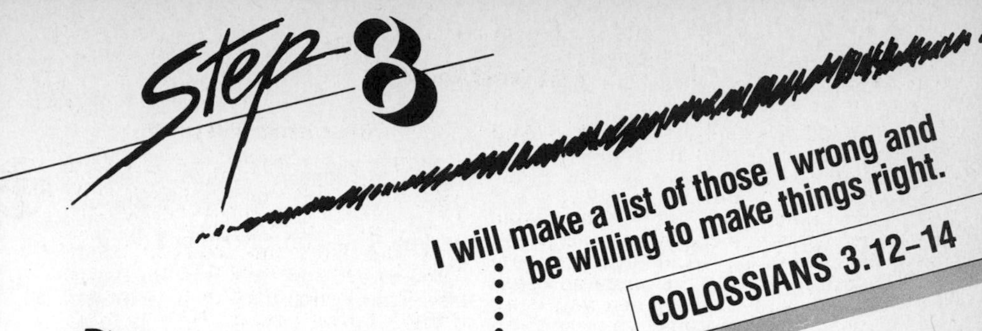

RUDE AWAKENINGS

"Just because I'm related to you doesn't mean I have to like you."

That pretty much sums up life with my older brother. He didn't have to like me, but he did have to put up with me. We had our good days, and we had our bad days, but no matter how it went we were brothers and a permanent part of each other's lives.

That is why going away to college and living with different people was such a rude awakening for me. My roommates didn't have to like me, and I didn't have to like them. There were no memories or family ties holding us together. So I learned early in the roommate game that if you want to keep peace you have to be willing to admit when you are wrong and look for a way to work things out.

KEEP IT CLEAN

STEP 8 LOOK INSIDE

People will always disappoint us if we don't give them room to make a few mistakes. After all, nobody is perfect, except Jesus. He was the One who said loving other people is the greatest thing we can do. We were made to live in peace. Arguing and fighting lead to bitter attitudes that eventually will eat us up. That is why it is important to keep a clean slate with people. Asking their forgiveness and making peace with people we have wronged is essential to having peace inside.

For another "Look Inside," turn to page 707.

things.[i] 7And that is exactly what you
did, when you lived among people
who behaved in this way. 8But now
you must stop doing such things. You
must quit being angry, hateful, and
evil. You must no longer say insulting
or cruel things about others. 9And
stop lying to each other. You have
given up your old way of life with
all its habits.
10Each of you is now a new person.
You are becoming more and more
like your Creator, and you will understand him better.* 11It doesn't matter
if you are a Greek or a Jew, or if
you are circumcised or not. You may
even be a barbarian or a Scythian,[j]
and you may be a slave or a free person. Yet Christ is all that matters,
and he lives in all of us.
12God loves you and has chosen
you as his own special people. So be
gentle, kind, humble, meek, and patient. 13Put up with each other, and
forgive anyone who does you wrong,
just as Christ has forgiven you.
14Love is more important than anything else. It is what ties everything
completely together.

15Each one of you is part of the
body of Christ, and you were chosen
to live together in peace. So let the
peace that comes from Christ control
your thoughts. And be grateful.*
16Let the message about Christ completely fill your lives, while you use
all your wisdom to teach and instruct
each other. With thankful hearts,
sing psalms, hymns, and spiritual
songs to God. 17Whatever you say
or do should be done in the name
of the Lord Jesus, as you give thanks
to God the Father because of him.

Some Rules for Christian Living

18A wife must put her husband
first. This is her duty as a follower
of the Lord.
19A husband must love his wife and
not abuse her.
20Children must always obey their
parents. This pleases the Lord.
21Parents, don't be hard on your
children. If you are, they might give
up.
22Slaves, you must always obey
your earthly masters. Try to please
them at all times, and not just when
you think they are watching. Honor
the Lord and serve your masters with
your whole heart.* 23Do your work
willingly, as though you were serving
the Lord himself, and not just your
earthly master. 24In fact, the Lord
Christ is the one you are really serving, and you know that he will reward
you. 25But Christ has no favorites!
He will punish evil people, just as
they deserve.
4 Slave owners, be fair and honest
with your slaves. Don't forget

---

[i] *with people who disobey him by doing these things*: Some manuscripts do not have these words.
[j] *a barbarian or a Scythian*: Barbarians were people who could not speak Greek and would be in the lower class of society. Scythians were people who were known for their cruelty.

3.10 **CHRISTIANS ARE NEW PEOPLE** We know that Christ has made us new by the things we now love. We used to love things that hurt us and other people. We lived in jealousy and hatred. Now our hearts are being filled with love for others. We are becoming more like God every day in our attitudes and lifestyles.

3.15 **PEACE IS IN CONTROL** Christians can live together in peace. If Jesus has won the battle against sin, and we are with him in his death and new life, we can stop struggling through life. We can have the peace that God gives and be thankful for what he has done.

3.22 **BE HONEST WORKERS** We don't have slaves nowadays. But we do make agreements to serve someone for so much time every day and for so much money. Christian workers should be known for being cheerful and useful, not dishonest. Likewise, Christian employers also honor Christ by treating their employees well and not taking advantage of them.

NOTES

Step 10

PATIENCE—Learning how to endure and grow in the process

COLOSSIANS 3.15–17

GUILTY BY ASSOCIATION

"Massey, Ferguson, and Taylor . . . I have had enough! I want you down in my office in five minutes. Bring your books with you! You're on your way out of here!"

Massey, Ferguson, and Taylor? I didn't do anything! In fact, I told those guys it was stupid and they were going to get caught and kicked out. It doesn't matter what I do; they still associate me with those losers. It's not fair! They aren't going to listen to me. I'm going to be put on detention!

What do I expect? That's how it's going to be if I keep hanging around these guys. We *have* done some pretty obnoxious things in the past. It's probably time to make new friends, at least until Eddie and Brian grow up. Guess that will have to wait until Thursday though. Chances are, I won't be here tomorrow.

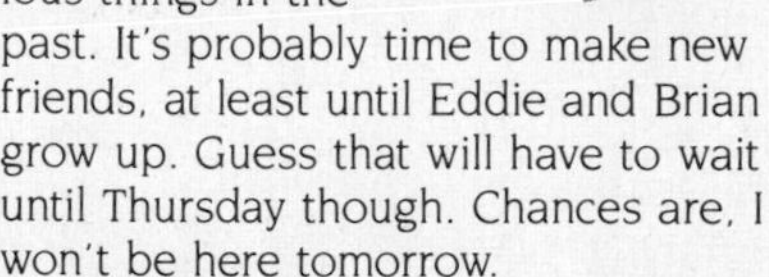

PAST MISTAKES

It's going to take time for people to see that we have changed. We need to be patient with them. It may not be fair, but all they have to go on is the way we have acted in the past. They haven't experienced enough of the "new and improved us" yet to change their opinions. Maybe we need to get away from the ways of our old lifestyles long enough so they can.

Let's ask God to help us when it seems we are going two steps back for every one step forward. He will guide us in moving ahead.

For another "Look Ahead," turn to page 486.

that you have a Master in heaven.
2Never give up praying. And when
you pray, keep alert and be thankful.
3Be sure to pray that God will make
a way for us to spread his message
and explain the mystery about
Christ, even though I am in jail for
doing this. 4Please pray that I will
make the message as clear as
possible.*

STEP 12

5When you are with unbelievers,
always make good use of the time.
6Be pleasant and hold their interest
when you speak the message. Choose
your words carefully and be ready
to give answers to anyone who asks
questions.

Final Greetings

7Tychicus is the dear friend, who
faithfully works and serves the Lord
with us, and he will give you the news
about me. 8I am sending him to cheer
you up by telling you how we are
getting along. 9Onesimus, that dear
and faithful follower from your own
group, is coming with him. The two
of them will tell you everything that
has happened here.
10Aristarchus is in jail with me. He
sends greetings to you, and so does
Mark, the cousin of Barnabas. You
have already been told to welcome
Mark, if he visits you. 11Jesus, who
is known as Justus, sends his greetings. These three men are the only
Jewish followers who have worked
with me for the kingdom of God.
They have given me much comfort.
12Your own Epaphras, who serves
Christ Jesus, sends his greetings. He
always prays hard that you may fully
know what the Lord wants you to
do and that you may do it completely.
13I have seen how much trouble he
has gone through for you and for the
followers in Laodicea and Hierapolis.
14Our dear doctor Luke sends you
his greetings, and so does Demas.*
15Give my greetings to the followers at Laodicea, especially to Nym-
pha and the church that meets in her
home.
16After this letter has been read to
your people, be sure to have it read
in the church at Laodicea. And you
should read the letter that I have sent
to them.[k]
17Remind Archippus to do the
work that the Lord has given him
to do.
18I am signing this letter myself:
PAUL.

Don't forget that I am in jail.

I pray that God will be kind to you.

---

[k]*the letter that I have sent to them*: This is the only mention of the letter to the church at Laodicea.

4.4 **BE AN EFFECTIVE WITNESS** An effective witness of Jesus Christ is friendly to those around him or her. Also, it's important that our hearers understand what we say. If we are confused in our own thoughts, we will confuse others and our message will not be clear. We need to think carefully about how we can best share Christ with others.

4.14 **REMEMBER DEMAS** In his final greetings Paul mentions several of his old friends, some of whom should be familiar to you by now, such as Mark and Luke. But he also sends good wishes from Demas. Later, Paul has to say that Demas deserted him (2 Timothy 4.10). Decide right now never to be a Demas.

NOTES

Paul's First Letter TO THE CHURCH IN THESSALONICA

ABOUT THIS LETTER

Paul started the church in Thessalonica (2.13,14), while working hard to support himself (2.9). In this important city of northern Greece, many of the followers had worshiped idols before becoming Christians (1.9). But they were faithful to the Lord, and because of them the Lord's message had spread everywhere in that region (1.8). This letter may have been the first one that Paul wrote, and maybe even the first of all the New Testament writings.

Some people in Thessalonica began to oppose Paul, and he had to escape to Athens. But he sent his young friend Timothy to find out how the Christians were doing (3.1–5). When Timothy returned, he gave Paul good reports of their faith and love (3.6–10).

The church itself had problems. Some of its members had quit working, since they thought that the Lord would soon return (4.11,12). Others were worried because relatives and friends had already died before Christ's return. So Paul tried to explain to them more clearly what would happen when the Lord returns (4.13–15), and then told them how they should live in the meanwhile (5.1–11).

Paul's final instructions are well worth remembering:

Always be joyful and never stop praying. Whatever happens, keep thanking God because of Jesus Christ. This is what God wants you to do. (5.16–18)

A QUICK LOOK AT THIS LETTER

1. Greetings (1.1–3)
2. The Thessalonians' Faith and Example (1.4—3.13)
3. A Life That Pleases God (4.1–12)
4. What to Expect When the Lord Returns (4.13—5.11)
5. Final Instructions and Greetings (5.12–28)

1 From Paul, Silas,[a] and Timothy.
To the church in Thessalonica,
the people of God the Father and of
the Lord Jesus Christ.
I pray that God will be kind to you
and will bless you with peace!
2We thank God for you and always
mention you in our prayers. Each
time we pray,* 3we tell God our Father about your faith and loving work
and about your firm hope in our Lord
Jesus Christ.

The Thessalonians' Faith and Example

4My dear friends, God loves you,
and we know he has chosen you to
be his people. 5When we told you the
good news, it was with the power and
assurance that come from the Holy
Spirit, and not simply with words.
You knew what kind of people we
were and how we helped you.
6So, when you accepted the message,
you followed our example and the
example of the Lord. You suffered,
but the Holy Spirit made you glad.

7You became an example for all
the Lord's followers in Macedonia
and Achaia.* 8And because of you,
the Lord's message has spread everywhere in those regions. Now the
news of your faith in God is known
all over the world, and we don't have
to say a thing about it. 9Everyone is
talking about how you welcomed us
and how you turned away from idols
to serve the true and living God.
10They also tell how you are waiting
for his Son Jesus to come from
heaven. God raised him from death,
and on the day of judgment Jesus
will save us from God's anger.

Paul's Work in Thessalonica

2 My friends, you know that our
time with you was not wasted.
2As you remember, we had been mistreated and insulted at Philippi. But
God gave us the courage to tell you
the good news about him, even
though many people caused us trouble. 3We didn't have any hidden motives when we won you over, and we
didn't try to fool or trick anyone.
4God was pleased to trust us with his
message. We didn't speak to please
people, but to please God who knows
our motives.
5You also know that we didn't try
to flatter anyone. God himself knows
that what we did was not a cover-
up for greed. 6We were not trying
to get you or anyone else to praise
us. 7But as apostles, we could have
demanded help from you. After all,
Christ is the one who sent us. We
chose to be like children or like a
mother[b] nursing her baby. 8We cared
so much for you, and you became
so dear to us, that we were willing
to give our lives for you when we
gave you God's message.*
9My dear friends, you surely
haven't forgotten our hard work and

---

[a]*Silas*: The Greek text has "Silvanus," which is another form of the name Silas. [b]*like children or like a mother*: Some manuscripts have "as gentle as a mother."

1.2 **THE CHRISTIAN'S FIRST WORK** Paul didn't rush out to preach the good news, but he first reminds us that he prayed for his people and his hearers. That's a good example. We can't do anything for God unless God himself works with us and in the hearts of our hearers. So the first thing to do is to lift up to God the whole matter of our work and the people we are trying to reach.

1.7 **EXAMPLE IS THE BEST TEACHER** The Thessalonian people showed by their lifestyles that they loved Jesus Christ. Even a quiet Christian reminds people of Jesus. What we are should shout so loudly that people should hardly need to hear what we say. People may not know Jesus themselves, but if they see him in your life they will want to know him.

2.8 **WHAT IS TRUE LOVE?** Is love a warm feeling for others? It may well be so, but love is much more than a feeling. Notice how Paul and his friends gave themselves for the (*continued*)

NOTES

Step 12

Because God is changing my life through following these steps, I will tell others about them and daily practice what I have learned.

1 THESSALONIANS 1.7–10

EVERYONE IS WATCHING

It was ten years past high school when I received the letter. My best friend was confirming what I already knew. I was the brunt of many comments and jokes because I had decided not to drink and do drugs or be involved in the heavy partying of high school. My friends really didn't dislike me. It was just that I led a lifestyle different from theirs. I had a purpose, and it wasn't just to have a good time. I had decided to turn my life around and give God a chance to make something out of it. From the abuse I took, I didn't think my friends understood. But now my best friend was writing to tell me that underneath all the jokes and ridicule there was an element of respect.

"We really looked up to you and wanted you to hang in there. Thanks for doing it."

Maybe we have experienced friends laughing behind our backs because we have allowed God to change our lives. But we can believe that, deep down, many of them respect us, and they are watching. They want to see how we handle ourselves. What do we do when the pressure is on? Can we say no? Is this new life for real?

STEP 12 LOOK INSIDE

MAKING A DIFFERENCE

What we do now not only makes a difference in our lives, but in the lives of those around us. We can share the greatest news we have ever heard, the "Good News," by hanging in there every day and living as Christian examples. Maybe someday others will thank us for it.

For another "Look Inside," turn to page 489.

hardships. You remember how night
and day we struggled to make a living, so that we could tell you God's
message without being a burden to
anyone. 10Both you and God are witnesses that we were pure and honest
and innocent in our dealings with
you followers of the Lord. 11You
also know we did everything for
you that parents would do for their
own children. 12We begged, encouraged, and urged each of you to
live in a way that would honor
God. He is the one who chose you
to share in his own kingdom and
glory.
13We always thank God that you
believed the message we preached.
It came from him, and it is not something made up by humans. You accepted it as God's message, and now
he is working in you. 14My friends,
you did just like God's churches in
Judea and like the other followers
of Christ Jesus there. And so, you
were mistreated by your own people,
in the same way they were mistreated
by the Jewish people.*
15Those Jews killed the Lord Jesus
and the prophets, and they even
chased us away. God doesn't like
what they do and neither does anyone else. 16They keep us from speaking his message to the Gentiles and
from leading them to be saved. The
Jews have always gone too far
with their sins. Now God has finally become angry and will punish
them.

Paul Wants to Visit the Church Again

17My friends, we were kept from
coming to you for a while, but we
never stopped thinking about you.
We were eager to see you and tried
our best to visit you in person.
18We really wanted to come. I myself
tried several times, but Satan always
stopped us. 19After all, when the Lord
Jesus appears, who else but you will
give us hope and joy and be like a
glorious crown for us? 20You alone
are our glory and joy!
3 Finally, we couldn't stand it any
longer. We decided to stay in Athens by ourselves 2and send our friend
Timothy to you. He works with us
as God's servant and preaches the
good news about Christ. We wanted
him to make you strong in your faith
and to encourage you. 3We didn't
want any of you to be discouraged
by all these troubles. You knew we
would have to suffer,* 4because when
we were with you, we told you this
would happen. And we did suffer, as
you well know. 5At last, when I could
not wait any longer, I sent Timothy
to find out about your faith. I hoped
that Satan had not tempted you and
made all our work useless.
6Timothy has come back from his
visit with you and has told us about
your faith and love. He also said that
you always have happy memories of
us and that you want to see us as
much as we want to see you.

(*continued*) good of others. "We were willing to give our lives for you," he said. And Paul finally did give his life at Rome. Christians are those who have made up their minds that their lives belong to God—to be kept or lost for *him*.

2.14 **IT'S HARD TO HAVE ENEMIES** Paul's enemies were people of his own national and religious background—the Jews. Think of how hard this must have been for someone who loved his country as Paul did. Sometimes you may have to suffer mistreatment by those you love the most. That is hard to bear. But remember, that was the path Jesus followed also, and he will help you to follow him with peace in your heart.

3.3 **DON'T LET TROUBLE DISCOURAGE YOU** Trouble didn't discourage Paul. It was just what he expected. Everybody who lives in the world has trouble sooner or later. If we have listened to God's word, we know trouble is coming. But we're not discouraged, because we know God is in charge of our lives at all times.

NOTES

7My friends, even though we have
a lot of trouble and suffering, your
faith makes us feel better about you.
8Your strong faith in the Lord is like
a breath of new life. 9How can we
possibly thank God enough for all
the happiness you have brought us?*
10Day and night we sincerely pray
that we will see you again and help
you to have an even stronger faith.
11We pray that God the Father and
our Lord Jesus Christ will let us visit
you. 12May the Lord make your love
for each other and for everyone else
grow by leaps and bounds. That's
how our love for you has grown.
13And when our Lord comes with all
of his people, I pray that he will make
your hearts pure and innocent in the
sight of God the Father.

A Life That Pleases God

4 Finally, my dear friends, since
you belong to the Lord Jesus, we
beg and urge you to live as we taught
you. Then you will please God. You
are already living that way, but try
even harder.* 2Remember the instructions we gave you as followers
of the Lord Jesus. 3God wants you
to be holy, so don't be immoral in
matters of sex. 4Respect and honor
your wife.[c] 5Don't be a slave of your
desires or live like people who don't
know God. 6You must not cheat any
of the Lord's followers in matters of
sex.[d] Remember, we warned you that
he punishes everyone who does such
things. 7God didn't choose you to be
filthy, but to be pure. 8So if you don't
obey these rules, you are not really
disobeying us. You are disobeying
God, who gives you his Holy Spirit.
9We don't have to write you about
the need to love each other. God has
taught you to do this, 10and you already have shown your love for all
of his people in Macedonia. But, my
dear friends, we ask you to do even
more. 11Try your best to live quietly,
to mind your own business, and to
work hard, just as we taught you to
do. 12Then you will be respected by
people who are not followers of the
Lord, and you won't have to depend
on anyone.

The Lord's Coming

13My friends, we want you to understand how it will be for those followers who have already died. Then
you won't grieve over them and be
like people who don't have any hope.
14We believe that Jesus died and was
raised to life. We also believe that
when God brings Jesus back again,
he will bring with him all who had
faith in Jesus before they died.*
15Our Lord Jesus told us that when
he comes, we won't go up to meet
him ahead of his followers who have
already died.
16With a loud command and with

[c]*your wife*: Or "your body." [d]*in matters of sex*: Or "in business."

3.9 **ENCOURAGE YOUR LEADERS** If you belong to a local church (as Christians should), you have a pastor. Perhaps you have elders and deacons too. Do you know that sometimes leaders get lonely? But your faithfulness in your Christian life and duty will encourage them. Leaders are human. They need love and support, perhaps even more than others. Don't be shy about saying a kind word or doing a kind deed for your God-given church leaders. Their work can be a heavy burden, and it's good to let them know they're appreciated.

4.1 **DARE TO BE DIFFERENT** A world where all was the same color or all was flat wouldn't be very exciting. Christians should be exciting people because they're different in good ways. They're free from habits that make them get sick and die early. They enjoy living because they know Christ, the author of life. They're true friends of God and of those in need of his love.

4.14 **CHRIST'S RETURN FOR HIS CHURCH** Jesus could come back at any time. It's the moment we eagerly look forward to. When Jesus returns he will give glorious new bodies to all of (*continued*)

NOTES

the shout of the chief angel and a
blast of God's trumpet, the Lord will
return from heaven. Then those who
had faith in Christ before they died
will be raised to life. 17Next, all of
us who are still alive will be taken
up into the clouds together with them
to meet the Lord in the sky. From
that time on we will all be with the
Lord forever. 18Encourage each other
with these words.

5 I don't need to write you about
the time or date when all this will
happen.* 2You surely know that the
Lord's return[e] will be as a thief coming at night. 3People will think they
are safe and secure. But destruction
will suddenly strike them like the
pains of a woman about to give birth.
And they won't escape.

4My dear friends, you don't live in
darkness, and so that day won't surprise you like a thief. 5All of you belong to the light and live in the day.
We don't live in the night or belong
to the dark. 6Others may sleep, but
we should stay awake and be alert.
7People sleep during the night, and
some even get drunk. 8But we belong
to the day. So we must stay sober
and let our faith and love be like a
suit of armor. Our firm hope that we
will be saved is our helmet.

9God does not intend to punish us,
but to have our Lord Jesus Christ
save us. 10Christ died for us, so that
we could live with him, whether we
are alive or dead when he comes.
11That's why you must encourage
and help each other, just as you are
already doing.

Final Instructions and Greetings

12My friends, we ask you to be
thoughtful of your leaders who work
hard and tell you how to live for the
Lord. 13Show them great respect and
love because of their work. Try to
get along with each other.* 14My
friends, we beg you to warn anyone
who is not living right. Encourage
anyone who feels left out, help all
who are weak, and be patient with
everyone. 15Don't be hateful to people, just because they are hateful to
you. Rather, be good to each other
and to everyone else.

16Always be joyful 17and never
stop praying. 18Whatever happens,
keep thanking God because of Jesus
Christ. This is what God wants you
to do.

19Don't turn away God's Spirit 20or
ignore prophecies. 21Put everything
to the test. Accept what is good 22and
don't have anything to do with evil.

23I pray that God, who gives peace,
will make you completely holy. And
may your spirit, soul, and body be
kept healthy and faultless until our
Lord Jesus Christ returns. 24The one
who chose you can be trusted, and
he will do this.

25Friends, please pray for us.

26Give all the Lord's followers a
warm greeting.

27In the name of the Lord I beg you
to read this letter to all his followers.

28I pray that our Lord Jesus Christ
will be kind to you!

---

[e] *the Lord's return*: The Greek text has "the day of the Lord."

(*continued*) those who have believed in him and have died. The believers who are still alive will join them, also in new bodies, and there will be a great heavenly reunion for God's church. Then we will be with him forever. You'll be there, won't you?

5.1 **WHEN WILL CHRIST COME?** Paul tells us that Christ's coming will be very sudden and so take many by surprise—like a thief who breaks down the door. But Paul also says that Christians should be so alert that Christ's coming does not surprise them. They will be waiting with great expectation. Let's be filled with joy as we look forward to that great event.

5.13 **TRY TO GET ALONG** Getting along isn't always easy. Sometimes even believers "rub each other the wrong way." That's when our Christian character must show. If we have been loved by Christ himself, we can afford to accept insults and love people just the same. What do we have to lose but our tempers?

NOTES

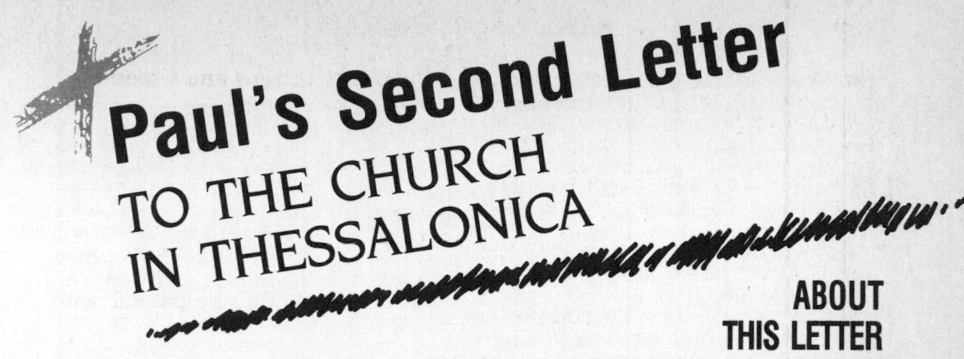

Paul's Second Letter TO THE CHURCH IN THESSALONICA

ABOUT THIS LETTER

In this letter to the believers in Thessalonica, Paul begins by thanking God that their faith and love keep growing all the time (1.3). They were going through a lot of troubles, but Paul insists that this is God's way of testing their faith, not a way of punishing them (1.4,5).

Someone in Thessalonica claimed to have a letter from Paul, saying that the Lord had already returned (2.2). But Paul warns the church not to be fooled! The Lord will not return until after the "wicked one" has appeared (2.3).

Paul also warns against laziness (3.6–10), and he tells the church to guard against any followers who refuse to obey what he has written in this letter.

The letter closes with a prayer:

I pray that the Lord, who gives peace, will keep blessing you with peace no matter where you are. May the Lord be with all of you. (3.16)

A QUICK LOOK AT THIS LETTER

1. Greetings (1.1,2)
2. The Lord's Return Will Bring Justice (1.3–12)
3. The Lord Has Not Returned Yet (2.1–12)
4. Be Faithful (2.13–17)
5. Pray and Work (3.1–15)
6. A Final Prayer (3.16–18)

1 From Paul, Silas,[a] and Timothy.
To the church in Thessalonica,
the people of God our Father and of
the Lord Jesus Christ.
2I pray that God our Father and
the Lord Jesus Christ will be kind
to you and will bless you with peace!

When Christ Returns

3My dear friends, we always have
good reason to thank God for you,
because your faith in God and your
love for each other keep growing all
the time.* 4That's why we brag about
you to all of God's churches. We tell
them how patient you are and how
you keep on having faith, even
though you are going through a lot
of trouble and suffering.
5All of this shows that God judges
fairly and that he is making you fit
to share in his kingdom for which
you are suffering. 6It is only right for
God to punish everyone who is causing you trouble, 7but he will give you
relief from your troubles. He will do
the same for us, when the Lord Jesus
comes from heaven with his powerful
angels 8and with a flaming fire.
Our Lord Jesus will punish anyone
who doesn't know God and won't
obey his message. 9Their punishment
will be eternal destruction, and they
will be kept far from the presence
of our Lord and his glorious strength.
10This will happen on that day when
the Lord returns to be praised and
honored by all who have faith in him
and belong to him. This includes you,
because you believed what we said.
11God chose you, and we keep
praying that God will make you worthy of being his people. We pray for
God's power to help you do all the
good things that you hope to do and
that your faith makes you want to
do.* 12Then, because God and our
Lord Jesus Christ are so kind, you
will bring honor to the name of our
Lord Jesus, and he will bring honor
to you.

The Lord's Return

2 When our Lord Jesus returns, we
will be gathered up to meet him.
So I ask you, my friends, 2not to be
easily upset or disturbed by people
who claim that the Lord[b] has already
come. They may say that they heard
this directly from the Holy Spirit, or
from someone else, or even that they
read it in one of our letters. 3But don't
be fooled! People will rebel against
God. Then before the Lord returns,
the wicked[c] one who is doomed to
be destroyed will appear.* 4He will
brag and oppose everything that is
holy or sacred. He will even sit in
God's temple and claim to be God.
5Don't you remember that I told you
this while I was still with you?
6You already know what is holding
this wicked one back until it is time

[a]*Silas*: The Greek text has "Silvanus," which is another form of the name Silas. [b]*Lord*: The Greek text has "day of the Lord." [c]*wicked*: Some manuscripts have "sinful."

1.3 **FAITH AND LOVE GROW** Anything that lives grows. We're dying if we're not growing. That's true about faith and love, too. Our muscles are strengthened by exercise. So our faith grows by testing, and our love grows by practice.

1.11 **GOD MAKES US WHAT HE WANTS** God chose us, and so we have a great desire to become like Jesus. By God's power we will reach this goal. From God come both the desire and the ability to be what God plans for us. So we can be comforted as we know we will not fail to be worthy of being called Christians. But this is only because of God's power at work in us.

2.3 **THERE WILL BE AN "ANTICHRIST"** John later writes about Antichrist in his letters. Paul calls him "the wicked one." So the world is warned and can expect that a wicked leader will arise to lead all the forces of evil on the earth. Then many will be fooled by the false miracles of Satan. It will be a terrible time in history, but God will take his church out of harm's way.

NOTES

Step 4

PURITY—Obeying God with my moral choices

2 THESSALONIANS 2.16, 17

THE GREAT UMPIRE

Umpires and referees are the judge and jury when it comes to sports. Once when baseball umpire, Babe Pinelli, called "the Babe" (Babe Ruth) out on strikes, Ruth vigorously protested, "There's 40,000 people here who know that last one was a ball, tomato head."

Pinelli replied, "Maybe so, but mine is the only opinion that counts."

As Christians we must always keep in mind that in the end, only one opinion counts: that of the Umpire of all humans affairs—our Heavenly Father.

STEP LOOK AHEAD 4

We need to remember that no matter how many are doing it, no matter if the President and the entire Congress and Senate agree that safe sex is okay—the Supreme Leader says it's not right if it occurs outside of marriage. That standard is not designed to restrict us, but to protect us.

The apostle Peter wrote, "Do your best to improve your faith. You can do this by adding goodness, understanding, self-control, patience, devotion to God, concern for others, and love. If you keep growing in this way, it will show that what you know about our Lord Jesus Christ has made your lives useful and meaningful" (2 Peter 1.5–8).

For another "Look Ahead," turn to page 693.

for him to come. 7His mysterious
power is already at work, but someone is holding him back. And the
wicked one won't appear until that
someone is out of the way. 8Then he
will appear, but the Lord Jesus will
kill him simply by breathing on him.
He will be completely destroyed by
the Lord's glorious return.
9When the wicked one appears, Satan will pretend to work all kinds of
miracles, wonders, and signs. 10Lost
people will be fooled by his evil
deeds. They could be saved, but they
will refuse to love the truth and accept it. 11So God will make sure that
they are fooled into believing a lie.
12All of them will be punished, because they would rather do evil than
believe the truth.

Be Faithful

13My friends, the Lord loves you,
and it is only natural for us to thank
God for you. God chose you to be
the first ones to be saved.[d] His Spirit
made you holy, and you put your
faith in the truth.* 14God used our
preaching as his way of inviting you
to share in the glory of our Lord Jesus
Christ. 15My friends, that's why you
must remain faithful and follow
closely what we taught you in person
and by our letters.

16God our Father loves us. He is
kind and has given us eternal comfort
and a wonderful hope. We pray that
our Lord Jesus Christ and God our
Father 17will encourage you and help
you always to do and say the right
thing.

Pray for Us

3 Finally, our friends, please pray
for us. This will help the message
about the Lord to spread quickly, and
others will respect it, just as you do.*
2Pray that we may be kept safe from
worthless and evil people. After all,
not everyone has faith. 3But the Lord
can be trusted to make you strong
and protect you from harm. 4He has
made us sure that you are obeying
what we taught you and that you will
keep on obeying. 5I pray that the Lord
will guide you to be as loving as God
and patient as Christ.

Warnings against Laziness

6My dear friends, in the name of[e]
the Lord Jesus, I beg you not to have
anything to do with any of your people who loaf around and refuse to
obey the instructions we gave you.*

---

[d]*God chose you to be the first ones to be saved*: Some manuscripts have "From the beginning God chose you to be saved." [e]*in the name of*: Or "as a follower of."

2.13 **THE EARLY CHRISTIANS ARE OUR MODELS** Paul writes that God chose the Thessalonians first. They and many other early believers were the "pioneers" to show the way Christians should think and live. They remained faithful and became our examples. They are gone now, of course, and we don't know any of them personally. But we're thankful to them for showing us the way Christians should walk with God.

3.1 **PRAYER MAKES A DIFFERENCE** God spreads the good news because we pray. If we don't pray, the good news will still go forward, but probably not where we are. God wants followers who care enough about his work to be continually speaking to him about it. He is pleased by prayer for his honor and glory.

3.6 **CHRISTIANS ARE NOT LOAFERS** It looks like some of the Thessalonians spent so much time looking for Christ's coming that they had even quit work. But they had the wrong idea. Christians must keep on with whatever God gives them to do until Christ comes. We don't know the day and the hour of Jesus' return, and we must set a good example by not being a burden to others. In fact, if we don't work, other Christians should avoid us. Jesus said, "My father works until now, and I work." So must you and I.

NOTES

Step 6

I want God to take control of my life and make me a complete person.

2 THESSALONIANS 3.3–5

THE EYES OF LOVE

Holmes looks up at me with his big, brown, basset hound eyes. I like what they see—somebody great!

In Holmes's eyes it doesn't matter what I look like, how well I do in my classes, or if I make a few mistakes. He thinks I am great. I guess it is because I am the one he trusts the most. For ten years I have been feeding him, brushing him, and taking him for long walks . . . all the things he loves. He counts on me to take care of him, and I count on him to keep seeing the good in me.

You have heard the phrase, "the best of both worlds." That is how it is with God. Like a much-loved pet, we can depend on our Master to love and protect us because we belong to him.

STEP LOOK INSIDE 6

GOD SEES POTENTIAL

God has promised to meet all our needs and to complete the incomplete parts in our lives. We also receive from the Lord unconditional admiration and affection. When he looks at us, his love goes beyond the outward appearance and directly to our hearts where he sees great potential. We can count on the Lord to care for us and believe that because of Jesus we are great too.

For another "Look Inside," turn to page 455.

7You surely know that you should
follow our example. We didn't waste
our time loafing, 8and we didn't accept food from anyone without paying for it. We didn't want to be a burden to any of you, so night and day
we worked as hard as we could.

9We had the right not to work, but
we wanted to set an example for you.
10We also gave you the rule that if
you don't work, you don't eat.
11Now we learn that some of you just
loaf around and won't do any work,
except the work of a busybody.
12So, for the sake of our Lord Jesus
Christ, we ask and beg these people
to settle down and start working for
a living. 13Dear friends, you must
never become tired of doing right.

14Be on your guard against any followers who refuse to obey what we
have written in this letter. Put them
to shame by not having anything to
do with them. 15Don't consider them
your enemies, but speak kindly to
them as you would to any other
follower.

Final Prayer

16I pray that the Lord, who gives
peace, will keep blessing you with
peace no matter where you are. May
the Lord be with all of you.

17I always sign my letters as I am
now doing: PAUL.

18I pray that our Lord Jesus Christ
will be kind to all of you.

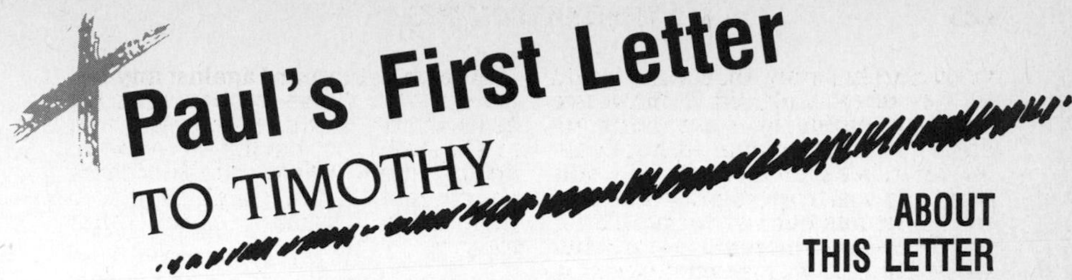

Paul's First Letter TO TIMOTHY

ABOUT THIS LETTER

Timothy traveled and worked with Paul (Romans 16.21; 1 Corinthians 16.10; Philippians 2.19), and because of their shared faith, Timothy was like a son to Paul (1.2). Timothy became one of Paul's most faithful co-workers, and Paul mentions Timothy in five of his letters.

Although this letter is addressed to Timothy personally, it actually addresses many of the concerns Paul had with the life of the entire church. Guidelines are given for choosing church officials (3.1–7), officers (3.8–13), and leaders (5.17–20).

Christians are to pray for everyone and to remember:

There is only one God,
and Christ Jesus
is the only one
who can bring us
to God.
(2.5)

A QUICK LOOK AT THIS LETTER

1. Greetings (1.1,2)
2. Instructions for Church Life (1.3—3.13)
3. The Mystery of Our Religion (3.14—4.5)
4. Paul's Advice to Timothy (4.6—6.21)

1 From Paul.
God our Savior and Christ Jesus
commanded me to be an apostle of
Christ Jesus, who gives us hope.
[2]Timothy, because of our faith, you
are like a son to me. I pray that God
our Father and our Lord Jesus Christ
will be kind and merciful to you. May
they bless you with peace!

Warning against False Teaching

[3]When I was leaving for Macedonia, I asked you to stay on in Ephesus
and warn certain people there to stop
spreading their false teachings.*
[4]You needed to warn them to stop
wasting their time on senseless
stories and endless lists of ancestors.
Such things only cause arguments.
They don't help anyone to do God's
work that can only be done by faith.
[5]You must teach people to have
genuine love, as well as a good conscience and true faith. [6]There are
some who have given up these for
nothing but empty talk. [7]They want
to be teachers of the Law of Moses.
But they don't know what they are
talking about, even though they think
they do.
[8]We know that the Law is good,
if it is used in the right way. [9]We
also understand that it was not given
to control people who please God,
but to control lawbreakers, criminals, godless people, and sinners. It
is for wicked and evil people, and
for murderers, who would even kill
their own parents. [10]The Law was
written for people who are sexual
perverts or who live as homosexuals
or are kidnappers or liars or won't
tell the truth in court. It is for anything else that opposes the correct
teaching [11]of the good news that the
glorious and wonderful God has
given me.

Being Thankful for God's Kindness

[12]I thank Christ Jesus our Lord. He
gives me the strength for my work
because he knew that he could trust
me. [13]I used to say terrible and insulting things about him, and I was cruel.
But he had mercy on me because I
didn't know what I was doing, and
I had not yet put my faith in him.
[14]Christ Jesus our Lord was very
kind to me. He has greatly blessed
my life with faith and love just like
his own.
[15]"Christ Jesus came into the world
to save sinners." This saying is true,
and it can be trusted. I was the worst
sinner of all!* [16]But since I was worse
than anyone else, God had mercy on
me and let me be an example of the
endless patience of Christ Jesus. He
did this so that others would put their
faith in Christ and have eternal life.
[17]I pray that honor and glory will always be given to the only God, who
lives forever and is the invisible and
eternal King! Amen.
[18]Timothy, my son, the instructions
I am giving you are based on what
some prophets[a] once said about you.
If you follow these instructions, you
will fight like a good soldier. [19]You
will be faithful and have a clear conscience. Some people have made a
mess of their faith because they
didn't listen to their consciences.
[20]Two of them are Hymenaeus and
Alexander. I have given these men

---

[a]*prophets*: Probably the Christian prophets referred to in 4.14.

1.3 **TIMOTHY BECAME A PASTOR** Pastoring was the job Paul gave to Timothy at Ephesus. Before, Timothy had traveled with Paul as a missionary. In this letter Paul tells Timothy how to carry on his work of teaching as the pastor at Ephesus. His job was to warn and guide people into the truth.

1.15 **PAUL WAS THE WORST OF SINNERS** There were probably lots of people who sinned more kinds of sin than Paul. But Paul called himself the worst of sinners to show what kind of sin God hates the most. Paul had been a self-righteous, stubborn, proud Pharisee. Such people are hard to convince of their sins. A brokenhearted mess of a sinner is usually easier to reach with the good news than a "respectable," unsaved churchgoer.

NOTES

over to the power of Satan, so they
will learn not to oppose God.

How to Pray

2 First of all, I ask you to pray for
everyone. Ask God to help and
bless them all, and tell God how
thankful you are for each of them.
2Pray for kings and others in power,
so that we may live quiet and peaceful lives as we worship and honor
God.* 3This kind of prayer is good,
and it pleases God our Savior.
4God wants everyone to be saved and
to know the whole truth, which is,

5There is only one God,
and Christ Jesus
is the only one
who can bring us
to God.
Jesus was truly human,
and he gave himself
to rescue all of us.*
6God showed us this
at the right time.

7This is why God chose me to be a
preacher and an apostle of the good
news. I am telling the truth. I am not
lying. God sent me to teach the Gentiles about faith and truth.
8I want everyone everywhere to lift
innocent hands toward heaven and
pray, without being angry or arguing
with each other.
9I would like for women to wear
modest and sensible clothes. They
should not have fancy hairdos, or
wear expensive clothes, or put on
jewelry made of gold or pearls.
10Women who claim to love God
should do helpful things for others,*
11and they should learn by being
quiet and paying attention. 12They
should be silent and not be allowed
to teach or to tell men what to do.
13After all, Adam was created before
Eve, 14and the man Adam was not
the one who was fooled. It was the
woman Eve who was completely
fooled and sinned. 15But women will
be saved by having children,[b] if they
stay faithful, loving, holy, and modest.

Church Officials

3 It is true that[c] anyone who desires
to be a church official[d] wants to
be something worthwhile.* 2That's

---

[b]*saved by having children*: Or "brought safely through childbirth" or "saved by the birth of a child" (that is, by the birth of Jesus) or "saved by being good mothers." [c]*It is true that*: These words may be taken with 2.15. If so, that verse would be translated: "It is true that women will be saved . . . holy, and modest." And 3.1 would be translated, "Anyone who desires . . . something worthwhile." [d]*church official*: Or "bishop."

2.2 **PRAY FOR YOUR GOVERNMENT** Paul mentions kings "and others in power." The government's decisions often affect the church of God and the peace of society in general. So we should pray, as Paul suggests, that officials will not do anything that will make our lives and our work harder. The government of this world will pass away, but God's kingdom is forever.

2.5 **CHRISTIANS BELIEVE WHAT GOD SAYS** There is plenty of teaching all through the Bible, but Paul tells us what we must mainly believe: There is one God, and he sent Jesus his Son to become a man so he could save us from our sins. This is the basic Christian faith. We will be saved if we truly believe in what Jesus did for us.

2.10 **SERVICE IS THE MAIN THING** Some women put a lot of effort into making sure they are the center of attention. Paul writes that the main goal of a woman should be to help others humbly, not to be admired for physical beauty. There's truth in this for men, too.

3.1 **LEADERS MUST BE EXAMPLES** People can't see God, but they can see their pastors and other church leaders. These officers of the church must live in a way that helps people understand what God himself is like. If leaders aren't examples of how a Christian lives, who is? Pastors, teachers, and other leaders must practice what they preach.

NOTES

why officials must have a good reputation and be married only once.[e]
They must be self-controlled, sensible, well-behaved, friendly to strangers, and able to teach. 3They must
not be heavy drinkers or troublemakers. Instead, they must be kind
and gentle and not love money.

4Church officials must be in control
of their own families, and they must
see that their children are obedient
and always respectful. 5If they don't
know how to control their own families, how can they look after God's
people?

6They must not be new followers
of the Lord. If they are, they might
become proud and be doomed along
with the devil. 7Finally, they must be
well-respected by people who are
not followers. Then they won't be
trapped and disgraced by the devil.

Church Officers

8Church officers[f] should be serious. They must not be liars, heavy
drinkers, or greedy for money.
9And they must have a clear conscience and hold firmly to what God
has shown us about our faith.
10They must first prove themselves.
Then if no one has anything against
them, they can serve as officers.

11Women[g] must also be serious.
They must not gossip or be heavy
drinkers, and they must be faithful
in everything they do.

12Church officers must be married
only once.[h] They must be in full control of their children and everyone
else in their home. 13Those who serve
well as officers will earn a good reputation and will be highly respected
for their faith in Christ Jesus.

The Mystery of Our Religion

14I hope to visit you soon. But I
am writing these instructions,
15so that if I am delayed, you will
know how everyone who belongs to
God's family ought to behave. After
all, the church of the living God is
the strong foundation of truth.*

16Here is the great mystery of our
religion:

Christ[i] came as a human.
The Spirit proved
  that he pleased God,
and he was seen by angels.

Christ was preached
  to the nations.
People in this world
  put their faith in him,
and he was taken up to glory.

People Will Turn from Their Faith

4 God's Spirit clearly says that in
the last days many people will
turn from their faith. They will be
fooled by evil spirits and by teachings
that come from demons.* 2They will
also be fooled by the false claims of
liars whose consciences have lost all
feeling. These liars 3will forbid peo-

---

[e]*married only once*: Or "the husbands of only one wife" or "faithful in marriage." [f]*church officers*: Or "deacons." [g]*Women*: Either church officers or the wives of church officers. [h]*married only once*: See the note at 3.2. [i]*Christ*: The Greek text has "he," probably meaning "Christ." Some manuscripts have "God."

3.15 **HOW SHOULD WE BEHAVE?** Christianity isn't just what we believe, it is also a special way of living. We aren't expected to figure out this way of living by ourselves. But God has given us his word to show us how to act at all times. We don't have to guess. We should study the Scriptures so we won't fall into lifestyles that hurt us and hurt God's plans for us.

4.1 **BE FAITHFUL** Paul warns Timothy of coming times when "many people will turn from their faith." Why? Because they're fooled into thinking that what they can have from the world is better than what they can have from God. Let's keep our eyes on things that matter. This world will pass away, but our souls will live forever. Our decision now will determine how we will spend eternity. Only God can satisfy our deepest longings.

NOTES

ple to marry or to eat certain foods.
But God created these foods to be
eaten with thankful hearts by his
followers who know the truth.
[4]Everything God created is good.
And if you give thanks, you may eat
anything. [5]What God has said and
your prayer will make it fit to eat.

Paul's Advice to Timothy

[6]If you teach these things to other
followers, you will be a good servant
of Christ Jesus. You will show that
you have grown up on the teachings
about our faith and on the good instructions you have obeyed. [7]Don't
have anything to do with worthless,
senseless stories. Work hard to be
truly religious. [8-9]As the saying goes,

"Exercise is good
for your body,
but religion helps you
in every way.
It promises life
now and forever."

These words are worthwhile and
should not be forgotten.* [10]We have
put our hope in the living God, who
is the Savior of everyone, but especially of those who have faith. That's
why we work and struggle so hard.[j]

[11]Teach these things and tell everyone to do what you say. [12]Don't let
anyone make fun of you, just because
you are young. Set an example for
other followers by what you say and
do, as well as by your love, faith, and
purity.

[13]Until I arrive, be sure to keep on
reading the Scriptures in worship,
and don't stop preaching and teaching. [14]Use the gift you were given
when the prophets spoke and the
group of church leaders[k] blessed you
by placing their hands on you.
[15]Remember these things and think
about them, so everyone can see how
well you are doing. [16]Be careful about
the way you live and about what you
teach. Keep on doing this, and you
will save not only yourself, but the
people who hear you.

How to Act toward Others

5 Don't correct an older man. Encourage him, as you would your
own father. Treat younger men as
you would your own brother, [2]and
treat older women as you would your
own mother. Show the same respect
to younger women that you would
to your sister.

[3]Take care of any widow who is
really in need. [4]But if a widow has
children or grandchildren, they
should learn to serve God by taking
care of her, as she once took care
of them. This is what God wants them
to do. [5]A widow who is really in need
is one who does not have any relatives. She has faith in God, and she
keeps praying to him night and day,
asking for his help.

[6]A widow who thinks only about
having a good time is already dead,
even though she is still alive.*

[7]Tell all of this to everyone, so they
will do the right thing. [8]People who
don't take care of their relatives, and
especially their own families, have
given up their faith. They are worse
than someone who doesn't have faith
in the Lord.

[9]For a widow to be put on the list

---

[j]*struggle so hard*: Some manuscripts have "are treated so badly." [k]*group of church leaders*: Or "group of elders" or "group of presbyters" or "group of priests." This translates one Greek word, and it is related to the one used in 5.17,19.

4.8 **PUT FIRST THINGS FIRST** It makes sense to keep your body fit. Then you will feel more like living and doing things for the Lord. But it is even more important to exercise your *spiritual* life—that's the part of you that lives forever. Bible reading, prayer, and friendship with other Christians will promote the health of your soul.

5.6 **LOVE MEANS RESPECT** Love isn't just a feeling. Love is respect that expresses itself by treating others the way we like to be treated. But people who have no self-respect, like the widows Paul wrote about, need to be corrected. Their lifestyle leads only to ruin.

NOTES

Step 11

TIMOTHY—a young man who learned endurance and became strong through daily dependence

1 TIMOTHY 4.6–16

Did you know that Timothy was a teenager when he met Paul? He grew up in a Christian home and showed leadership potential early in his life. Because of his obedience to Christ as a teen and the spiritual gifts God had equipped him with, he was given the responsibility of leading and caring for one of the first Christian congregations. Quite a responsibility for a young man, but it is clear how he did it.

Timothy was willing to put his priorities in place while he was young. He probably participated in many different activities in school and had fun with his friends, but that wasn't all he did. He also took time to develop his spiritual life. Timothy made sure that a personal relationship with Jesus Christ was the driving force in his life. This prepared him early for a position of leadership. You can be sure that he faced some intense peer pressure to go along with the crowd, but he stood strong and was not willing to compromise his convictions. He chose to spend some quality time with a wise man like Paul and learn from him how to live a successful life.

Paul told Timothy in his personal letter to him, "Don't let anyone make fun of you, just because you are young." Age has little to do with potential. We don't have to wait until we grow up to make positive and powerful contributions as Christians. What matters is that we know and understand what God wants and that we faithfully do what he says. We can be sure that we will also have to face some peer pressure from those who don't want to live for Christ. Proverbs 13.20 is good advice: "Wise friends make you wise, but you hurt yourself by going around with fools." Do our friends help or hinder our personal and spiritual growth?

In life, the main thing is to keep the main thing the main thing. The "main thing" is to develop a daily dependence on God and let him produce in us the character quality of inner strength and endurance. We have committed to stay the course and do the right thing even though we may face some persecution or peer pressure. While we are young, we can make a difference for Christ by keeping the main thing the main thing.

Ready for Step 12?
Turn to page 39 of* InStep's *introduction.

of widows, she must be at least sixty years old, and she must have been married only once.[l] 10She must also be well-known for doing all sorts of good things, such as raising children, giving food to strangers, welcoming God's people into her home,[m] helping people in need, and always making herself useful.

11Don't put young widows on the list. They may later have a strong desire to get married. Then they will turn away from Christ 12and become guilty of breaking their promise to him. 13Besides, they will become lazy and get into the habit of going from house to house. Next, they will start gossiping and become busybodies, talking about things that are none of their business.

14I would prefer that young widows get married, have children, and look after their families. Then the enemy won't have any reason to say insulting things about us. 15Look what's already happened to some of the young widows! They have turned away to follow Satan.

16If a woman who is a follower has any widows in her family, she[n] should help them. This will keep the church from having that burden, and then the church can help widows who are really in need.*

Church Leaders

17Church leaders[o] who do their job well deserve to be paid[p] twice as much, especially if they work hard at preaching and teaching. 18It is just as the Scriptures say, "Don't muzzle an ox when you are using it to grind grain." You also know the saying, "Workers are worth their pay."

19Don't listen to any charge against a church leader, unless at least two or three people bring the same charges.* 20But if any of the leaders should keep on sinning, they must be corrected in front of the whole group, as a warning to everyone else.

21In the presence of God and Christ Jesus and their chosen angels, I order you to follow my instructions! Be fair with everyone, and don't have any favorites.

22Don't be too quick to accept people into the service of the Lord[q] by placing your hands on them.

Don't sin because others do, but stay close to God.

23Stop drinking only water. Take a little wine to help your stomach trouble and the other illnesses you always have.

24Some people get caught in their sins right away, even before the time of judgment. But other people's sins don't show up until later. 25It is the same with good deeds. Some are easily seen, but none of them can be hidden.

6 If you are a slave, you should respect and honor your owner. This will keep people from saying bad things about God and about our

---

[l]*married only once*: Or "the wife of only one husband" or "faithful in marriage." [m]*welcoming God's people into her home*: The Greek text has "washing the feet of God's people." In New Testament times most people either went barefoot or wore sandals, and a host would often wash the feet of special guests. [n]*woman . . . she*: Some manuscripts have "man . . . he," and others have "man or woman . . . that person." [o]*leaders*: Or "elders" or "presbyters" or "priests." [p]*paid*: Or "honored" or "respected." [q]*to accept people into the service of the Lord*: Or "to forgive people."

5.16 **LOVE BEGINS AT HOME** It's a cheap kind of love that pretends to care about a lost world but won't look after one's own family. When Jesus taught us to love our "neighbors" he had in mind those we live closest to. They should benefit most from our caring, and then they too will be able to love others. Love comes from being loved. We love because God first loved us.

5.19 **LEADERS DESERVE FAIRNESS** Here is advice that "cuts both ways." A good leader deserves generous pay. But a leader who sins is to be tried fairly, and then corrected publicly if guilty of repeated sin. Leaders get much honor or much dishonor, depending on their behavior.

NOTES

teaching. 2If any of you slaves have
owners who are followers, you
should show them respect. After
all, they are also followers of Christ,
and he loves them. So you should
serve and help them the best you
can.

False Teaching and True Wealth

These are the things you must
teach and tell the people to do.
3Anyone who teaches something different disagrees with the correct and
godly teaching of our Lord Jesus
Christ. 4Those people who disagree
are proud of themselves, but they
don't really know a thing. Their
minds are sick, and they like to argue
over words. They cause jealousy, disagreements, unkind words, evil sus-
picions, 5and nasty quarrels. They
have wicked minds and have missed
out on the truth.

These people think religion is supposed to make you rich. 6And religion
does make your life rich, by making
you content with what you have.*
7We didn't bring anything into this
world, and we won't[r] take anything
with us when we leave. 8So we should
be satisfied just to have food and
clothes. 9People who want to be rich
fall into all sorts of temptations and
traps. They are caught by foolish and
harmful desires that drag them down
and destroy them. 10The love of
money causes all kinds of trouble.
Some people want money so much
that they have given up their faith
and caused themselves a lot of
pain.

Fighting a Good Fight for the Faith

11Timothy, you belong to God, so
keep away from all these evil things.
Try your best to please God and to
be like him. Be faithful, loving, dependable, and gentle. 12Fight a good
fight for the faith and claim eternal
life. God offered it to you when you
clearly told about your faith, while
so many people listened. 13Now I ask
you to make a promise. Make it in
the presence of God, who gives life
to all, and in the presence of Jesus
Christ, who openly told Pontius Pilate about his faith.* 14Promise to
obey completely and fully all that you
have been told until our Lord Jesus
Christ returns.

15The glorious God
  is the only Ruler,
  the King of kings
  and Lord of lords.
At the time that God
  has already decided,
he will send Jesus Christ
  back again.

16Only God lives forever!
And he lives in light
  that no one can come near.
No human has ever seen God
  or ever can see him.
God will be honored,
and his power
  will last forever. Amen.

17Warn the rich people of this
world not to be proud or to trust in
wealth that is easily lost. Tell them
to have faith in God, who is rich and

---

[r]*we won't*: Some manuscripts have "we surely won't."

6.6 **BE CONTENT WITH WHAT YOU HAVE** People who are discontented have missed the most important kind of wealth: God himself. No matter what our circumstances, we never have a right to complain. God will provide enough for our needs if we will only trust him. But complaining leads to bitterness, and bitterness makes us unable to enjoy any good that comes to us.

6.13 **MAKE YOUR PROMISE TO GOD** We shouldn't make promises we can't keep. But it makes good sense to promise God that we'll be faithful to him always. Let that promise to God be the greatest event of your life. Let it be the time at which you can look back and say "That's when I told God I would spend my whole life for him." Otherwise you may just drift along and not live for God at all.

NOTES

blesses us with everything we need
to enjoy life.* 18Instruct them to do
as many good deeds as they can and
to help everyone. Remind the rich to
be generous and share what they
have. 19This will lay a solid foundation for the future, so that they will
know what true life is like.

20Timothy, guard what God has
placed in your care! Don't pay any
attention to that godless and stupid
talk that sounds smart but really
isn't. 21Some people have even lost
their faith by believing this talk.

I pray that the Lord will be kind to all of you!

6.17 **SHARE THE WEALTH** Some people are gifted by God with the ability to become wealthy. When God does this, he means that such people should use their plenty for him. Any earthly project costs money. That includes the Christian project of spreading the good news. That is the great opportunity for wealthy people to do their part for Christ.

NOTES

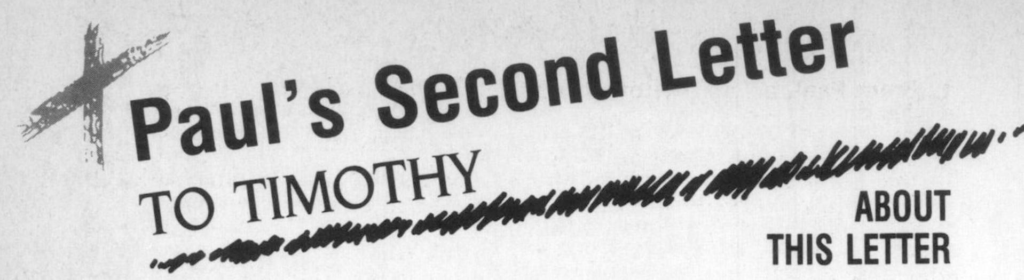

Paul's Second Letter TO TIMOTHY

ABOUT THIS LETTER

In his second letter to Timothy Paul is more personal than in his first one. Timothy is like a "dear child" to Paul, and Paul always mentions him in his prayers (1.2,3) because he wants Timothy to be a "good soldier" of Christ Jesus and to learn to endure suffering (2.1,3). Paul mentions Timothy's mother and grandmother by name in this letter and reminds Timothy how he had placed his hands on him as a special sign that the Spirit was guiding his work.

Some who claimed to be followers of the Lord had already been trapped by the devil, and Paul warns Timothy to run from those temptations that often catch young people (2.20–26; 3.1–9). He tells Timothy to keep preaching God's message, even if it is not the popular thing to do (4.2). He should also beware of false teachers.

Paul knows that he will soon die for his faith, but he will be rewarded for his faithfulness (4.6–8), and he reminds Timothy of the true message:

If we died with Christ,
we will live with him.
If we don't give up,
we will rule with him.
(2.11,12*a*)

A QUICK LOOK AT THIS LETTER

1. Greetings and Prayer for Timothy (1.1,2)
2. Do Not Be Ashamed of the Lord (1.3–18)
3. How To Be a Good Soldier of Christ (2.1–26)
4. What People Will Be Like in the Last Days (3.1–9)
5. Keep Being Faithful (3.10—4.8)
6. Personal Instructions and Final Greetings (4.9–22)

1 From Paul, an apostle of Christ Jesus.

God himself chose me to be an apostle, and he gave me the promised life that Jesus Christ makes possible.

2Timothy, you are like a dear child to me. I pray that God our Father and our Lord Christ Jesus will be kind and merciful to you and will bless you with peace!

Do Not Be Ashamed of the Lord

3Night and day I mention you in my prayers. I am always grateful for you, as I pray to the God my ancestors and I have served with a clear conscience. 4I remember how you cried, and I want to see you, because that will make me truly happy. 5I also remember the genuine faith of your mother Eunice. Your grandmother Lois had the same sort of faith, and I am sure that you have it as well.* 6So I ask you to make full use of the gift that God gave you when I placed my hands on you.[a] Use it well. 7God's Spirit[b] does not make cowards out of us. The Spirit gives us power, love, and self-control.

8Don't be ashamed to speak for our Lord. And don't be ashamed of me, just because I am in jail for serving him. Use the power that comes from God and join with me in suffering for telling the good news.

9God saved us and chose us
to be his holy people.
We did nothing
to deserve this,
but God planned it
because he is so kind.
Even before time began
God planned for Christ Jesus
to show kindness to us.*

10Now Christ Jesus has come
to show us the kindness
of God.
Christ our Savior
defeated death
and brought us
the good news.
It shines like a light
and offers life
that never ends.

11My work is to be a preacher, an apostle, and a teacher.[c] 12That's why I suffer. But I am not ashamed! I know the one I have faith in, and I am sure that he can guard until the last day what he has trusted me with.[d] 13Now follow the example of the correct teaching I gave you, and let the faith and love of Christ Jesus be your model. 14You have been trusted with a wonderful treasure. Guard it with the help of the Holy Spirit, who lives within you.

15You know that everyone in Asia has turned against me, especially Phygelus and Hermogenes.

16I pray that the Lord will be kind to the family of Onesiphorus. He often cheered me up and was not ashamed of me when I was put in jail. 17Then after he arrived in Rome,

---

[a]*when I placed my hands on you*: Church leaders placed their hands on people who were being appointed to preach or teach. See 1 Timothy 4.14. [b]*God's Spirit*: Or "God." [c]*teacher*: Some manuscripts add "of the Gentiles." [d]*what he has trusted me with*: Or "what I have trusted him with."

1.5 **GOOD PARENTS ARE A GREAT TREASURE** Timothy's mother and grandmother had been great women of faith. They had taught Timothy the Scriptures, and when he got older their example and teaching paid off in Timothy's life. Parents make the biggest difference in the way their children turn out. They can influence where their children spend eternity. Godly mothers and fathers are the best teachers about Jesus.

1.9 **TEACH YOURSELF TO SING TO GOD** This is one of the little poems or songs that were probably sung by Christians in the days of Paul and Timothy. Their songs didn't have rhyme and rhythm like modern songs. But they expressed great and beautiful thoughts about God. Such songs meant a lot for the faith of the people then. God wants us to sing to him now, too.

NOTES

he searched everywhere until he
found me. 18I pray that the Lord Jesus
will ask God to show mercy to Onesiphorus on the day of judgment.
You know how much he helped me
in Ephesus.

A Good Soldier of Christ Jesus

2 Timothy, my child, Christ Jesus
is kind, and you must let him
make you strong. 2You have often
heard me teach. Now I want you to
tell these same things to followers
who can be trusted to tell others.
3As a good soldier of Christ Jesus
you must endure your share of suffering.* 4Soldiers on duty don't work
at outside jobs. They try only to
please their commanding officer.
5No one wins an athletic contest without obeying the rules. 6And farmers
who work hard are the first to eat
what grows in their field. 7If you keep
in mind what I have told you, the
Lord will help you understand completely.
8Keep your mind on Jesus Christ!
He was from the family of David and
was raised from death, just as my
good news says. 9And because of this
message, I am locked up in jail and
treated like a criminal. But God's
good news isn't locked in jail,
10and so I am willing to put up with
anything. Then God's special people
will be saved. They will be given eternal glory because they belong to
Christ Jesus. 11Here is a true message:

"If we died with Christ,
we will live with him.
12If we don't give up,
we will rule with him.
If we deny
that we know him,
he will deny
that he knows us.
13If we are not faithful,
he will still be faithful.
Christ cannot deny
who he is."

An Approved Worker

14Don't let anyone forget these
things. And with God[e] as your witness, you must warn them not to argue about words. These arguments
don't help anyone. In fact, they ruin
everyone who listens to them.
15Do your best to win God's approval
as a worker who does not need to
be ashamed and who teaches only
the true message.
16Keep away from worthless and
useless talk. It only leads people farther away from God.* 17That sort of
talk is like a sore that won't heal.
And Hymenaeus and Philetus have
been talking this way 18by teaching
that the dead have already been
raised to life. This is far from the
truth, and it is destroying the faith
of some people.
19But the foundation that God has
laid is solid. On it is written, "The
Lord knows who his people are. So
everyone who worships the Lord
must turn away from evil."
20In a large house some dishes are
made of gold or silver, while others
are made of wood or clay. Some of
these are special, and others are not.

[e]*God*: Some manuscripts have "the Lord," and others have "Christ."

2.3 **BE A GOOD SOLDIER OF CHRIST** Being a Christian is no easy life. We have to live in a world that is no friend to Christ. This calls for careful living. A well-known Christian of the 1700's named John Wesley was called a "Methodist" because he and his friends set up a careful method for living a godly life. We, too, can be good soldiers for Christ by making sure we're "in shape" with a life of prayer, study, and useful Christian service.

2.16 **LET'S AVOID SILLY ARGUMENTS** Some people talk as if their faith depended on winning arguments about things that don't really matter. There are things worth speaking up for, and even dying for, but a lot of debates about religion are useless. They often get people more mixed up than they were before they started arguing.

NOTES

21That's also how it is with people. The ones who stop doing evil and make themselves pure will become special. Their lives will be holy and pleasing to their Master, and they will be able to do all kinds of good deeds.

22Run from temptations that capture young people. Always do the right thing. Be faithful, loving, and easy to get along with. Worship with people whose hearts are pure.*
23Stay away from stupid and senseless arguments. These only lead to trouble, 24and God's servants must not be troublemakers. They must be kind to everyone, and they must be good teachers and very patient.

25Be humble when you correct people who oppose you. Maybe God will lead them to turn to him and learn the truth. 26They have been trapped by the devil, and he makes them obey him, but God may help them escape.

What People Will Be Like in the Last Days

3 You can be certain that in the last days there will be some very hard
times.* 2People will love only themselves and money. They will be proud, stuck-up, rude, and disobedient to their parents. They will also
be ungrateful, godless, 3heartless, and hateful. Their words will be cruel, and they will have no self-control or pity. These people will hate
everything that is good. 4They will be sneaky, reckless, and puffed up with pride. Instead of loving God,
they will love pleasure. 5Even though they will make a show of being religious, their religion won't be real. Don't have anything to do with such people.

6Some men fool whole families, just to get power over those women, who are slaves of sin and are controlled by all sorts of desires. 7These women always want to learn something new, but they never can discover the truth. 8Just as Jannes and
Jambres[f] opposed Moses, these people are enemies of the truth. Their minds are sick, and their faith isn't
real. 9But they won't get very far with their foolishness. Soon everyone will know the truth about them, just as Jannes and Jambres were found out.

Paul's Last Instructions to Timothy

10Timothy, you know what I teach and how I live. You know what I want to do and what I believe. You have seen how patient and loving I am, and how in the past I put up with
11trouble and suffering in the cities of Antioch, Iconium, and Lystra. Yet the Lord rescued me from all those
terrible troubles. 12Anyone who belongs to Christ Jesus and wants to live right will have trouble from others. 13But evil people who pretend to be what they are not will become worse than ever, as they fool others and are fooled themselves.

---

[f]*Jannes and Jambres*: These names are not found in the Old Testament. But many believe these were the names of the two Egyptian magicians who opposed Moses when he wanted to lead the people of Israel out of Egypt. See Exodus 7.11,22.

2.22 **RUN FROM TEMPTATIONS** Some Christians think they can "play with fire" and not get burned. Paul writes that we should run when we see temptation. We shouldn't assume that we are so strong that we can't be drawn away from godly living. Believers should strengthen and encourage each other to live for Jesus.

3.1 **BE AWARE OF EVIL PEOPLE** In these days we see a lot of what Paul writes about here concerning the "last days." It would be nice if the world were a sweet place, but it isn't. Paul reminds us that there are a lot of mean and deceitful people in the world. We must be careful to keep our own hearts pure and keep a sharp eye out for the kinds of people Paul describes in this passage. We can get hurt spiritually if we're not careful.

NOTES

14 Keep on being faithful to what
you were taught and to what you believed. After all, you know who
taught you these things.* 15 Since
childhood, you have known the Holy
Scriptures that are able to make you
wise enough to have faith in Christ
Jesus and be saved. 16 Everything in
the Scriptures is God's Word. All of
it is useful for teaching and helping
people and for correcting them and
showing them how to live. 17 The
Scriptures train God's servants to do
all kinds of good deeds.

4 When Christ Jesus comes as king,
he will be the judge of everyone,
whether they are living or dead. So
with God and Christ as witnesses, I
command you 2 to preach God's message. Do it willingly, even if it is not
the popular thing to do. You must
correct people and point out their
sins. But also cheer them up, and
when you instruct them, always be
patient.* 3 The time is coming when
people won't listen to good teaching.
Instead, they will look for teachers
who will please them by telling them
only what they are itching to hear.
4 They will turn from the truth and
eagerly listen to senseless stories.
5 But you must stay calm and be willing to suffer. You must work hard
to tell the good news and to do your
job well.
6 Now the time has come for me
to die. My life is like a drink offering[g]
being poured out on the altar.
7 I have fought well. I have finished
the race, and I have been faithful.*
8 So a crown will be given to me for
pleasing the Lord. He judges fairly,
and on the day of judgment he will
give a crown to me and to everyone
else who wants him to appear with
power.

Personal Instructions

9 Come to see me as soon as you
can. 10 Demas loves the things of this
world so much that he left me and
went to Thessalonica. Crescens has
gone to Galatia, and Titus has gone
to Dalmatia. 11 Only Luke has stayed
with me.
Mark can be very helpful to me,
so please find him and bring him with
you.* 12 I sent Tychicus to Ephesus.
13 When you come, bring the coat
I left at Troas with Carpus. Don't

---

[g] *drink offering*: Water or wine was sometimes poured out as an offering when an animal sacrifice was made.

3.14 **TEACH THE CHILDREN** Here Paul writes that Timothy has known the Scriptures since childhood. Christians who have grown up on God's word often have more wisdom to draw from than those who have not. The greatest good we can do for our young people is to teach them God's word, then show by our lives that we love that word.

4.2 **LET'S BE FIRM BUT CHEERFUL** This was Paul's last known letter before his execution in Rome. Because of the evils he describes in chapter 3, it's important for all of us to see the needs around us. Sometimes our brothers and sisters in Christ need to be warned. At the same time, let's be cheerful and trust God for a good outcome.

4.7 **ARE YOU READY TO DIE?** Paul was ready to give up his life here on earth. Let's make up our minds to live every day so that we can say with Paul, "I have fought well." God will help us to get past the things in our lives that hold us back from serving him. Fear is one thing that keeps us back: fear of death, embarrassment, hunger, and other trials. Let's remember Paul the prisoner at such times.

4.11 **BE READY TO STAND ALONE** Maybe you've heard that "one with God is a majority." That's a true statement. Paul was finally deserted by his friends. But when he was left *(continued)*

NOTES

Step 10

PAUL—a servant who learned patience through his trials and remained faithful until the end

2 TIMOTHY 4.9–18

Paul was a type "A" personality. Type "A" as in action; full speed, flat out. He was a "lead, follow, or get out of the way" kind of guy. So why would he be the role model for patience?

God developed patience in Paul the old-fashioned way: he allowed frustration, failure, and even physical illness to teach him. All of this transformed Paul into a prominent and powerful leader for Christ.

From Paul's first encounter with the Lord on the Damascus Road, he did nothing in moderation. He didn't take only one mission trip; he took four. He didn't drop his profession (tentmaking) when he became a missionary; he did both.

STEP LOOK BACK 10

Much of the New Testament was written by Paul or about him. Yet at the end of his life, we see a picture of a simple, contented, and patient man who was ready to pass on the mission of carrying the message of Christ to others.

He enjoyed the company of close friends: "Come to me as soon as you can . . . Only Luke has stayed with me" (verses 9 and 11). He had few needs: "Bring the coat I left at Troas with Carpus" (verse 13). He was more relaxed and had time to read: "Don't forget to bring the scrolls, especially the ones made of leather" (verse 13).

We can read into it all that Paul was willing to leave the world-changing business to the men he had trained over years of faithful service. With failing eyesight and a shaky hand, Paul wrote his final words, demonstrating his confidence that his task has been completed.

Paul patiently groomed young men, such as John Mark and Timothy, to pass on the gospel of Jesus Christ. We are part of that chain to carry on the Great Commission. We, too, must be patient, first of all with ourselves. God isn't finished with us yet. We can be sure he will be faithful to us, so we should be faithful to him.

Ready for Step 11?
Turn to page 36 of **InStep's** *introduction.*

forget to bring the scrolls, especially
the ones made of leather.[h]
14Alexander, the metalworker, has
hurt me in many ways. But the Lord
will pay him back for what he has
done. 15Alexander opposes what we
preach. You had better watch out for
him.
16When I was first put on trial, no
one helped me. In fact, everyone deserted me. I hope it won't be held
against them. 17But the Lord stood
beside me. He gave me the strength
to tell his full message, so that all
Gentiles would hear it. And I was
kept safe from hungry lions. 18The
Lord will always keep me from being
harmed by evil, and he will bring me
safely into his heavenly kingdom.
Praise him forever and ever! Amen.

Final Greetings

19Give my greetings to Priscilla
and Aquila and to the family of Onesiphorus.
20Erastus stayed at Corinth.
Trophimus was sick, when I left
him at Miletus.
21Do your best to come before
winter.
Eubulus, Pudens, Linus, and Clau-
dia send you their greetings, and so
do the rest of the Lord's followers.
22I pray that the Lord will bless
your life and will be kind to you.

---

[h] *the ones made of leather*: A scroll was a kind of rolled up book, and it could be made out of paper (called "papyrus") or leather (that is, animal skin) or even copper.

(continued) alone—that's when he knew best what a friend God is. There is a proverb by Solomon in the Old Testament: "There is a friend who sticks closer than a brother." That friend is Jesus, the Son of God who became a man. With him we are never really alone.

NOTES

Paul's Letter TO TITUS

ABOUT THIS LETTER

Paul mentions Titus several times in his letters as someone who worked with him in Asia Minor and Greece (2 Corinthians 2.13; 7.6,13; 8.6,16,23; 12.18; Galatians 2.3). He is told by Paul to appoint church leaders and officials in Crete.

Paul instructs Titus to make sure that church leaders and officials have good reputations (1.5–9) and that all of the Lord's followers keep themselves pure and avoid arguments (1.10—2.9).

Paul includes special instructions for the different groups within the church in Crete. He reminds Titus that a new way of life is possible because of what God has done by sending Jesus Christ: God has saved them, washed them by the power of the Holy Spirit, and given them a fresh start and the hope of eternal life.

Paul also tells how we are saved:

God our Savior showed us
how good and kind he is.
He saved us because
of his mercy,
and not because
of any good things
that we have done.
(3.4,5)

A QUICK LOOK AT THIS LETTER

1. Greetings and a Prayer for Titus (1.1–4)
2. Instructions for Church Officials (1.5–16)
3. Instructions for Church People (2.1—3.11)
4. Personal Advice and Final Greetings (3.12–15)

1 From Paul, a servant of God and
an apostle of Jesus Christ.
I encourage God's own people to
have more faith and to understand
the truth about religion.* 2Then they
will have the hope of eternal life that
God promised long ago. And God
never tells a lie! 3So, at the proper
time, God our Savior gave this message and told me to announce what
he had said.
4Titus, because of our faith, you are
like a son to me. I pray that God our
Father and Christ Jesus our Savior
will be kind to you and will bless you
with peace!

What Titus Was to Do in Crete

5I left you in Crete to do what had
been left undone and to appoint leaders[a] for the churches in each town.
As I told you, 6they must have a good
reputation and be married only
once.[b] Their children must be followers of the Lord and not have a
reputation for being wild and disobedient.
7Church officials[c] are in charge of
God's work, and so they must also
have a good reputation. They must
not be bossy, quick-tempered, heavy
drinkers, bullies, or dishonest in
business.* 8Instead, they must be
friendly to strangers and enjoy doing
good things. They must also be sensible, fair, pure, and self-controlled.
9They must stick to the true message
they were taught, so that their good
teaching can help others and correct
everyone who opposes it.
10There are many who don't respect authority, and they fool others
by talking nonsense. This is especially true of some Jewish followers.
11But you must make them be quiet.
They are after money, and they upset
whole families by teaching what they
should not. 12It is like one of their
own prophets once said,

"The people of Crete
always tell lies.
They are greedy and lazy
like wild animals."

13That surely is a true saying. And
you should be hard on such people,
so you can help them grow stronger
in their faith. 14Don't pay any attention to any of those senseless Jewish
stories and human commands. These
are made up by people who won't
obey the truth.
15Everything is pure for someone
whose heart is pure. But nothing is
pure for an unbeliever with a dirty
mind. That person's mind and conscience are destroyed.* 16Such people claim to know God, but their actions prove that they really don't.

---

[a]*leaders*: Or "elders" or "presbyters" or "priests." [b]*married only once*: Or "the husband of only one wife" or "faithful in marriage." [c]*Church officials*: Or "Bishops."

1.1 LEARN THE TRUTH Jesus said, "The truth will make you free" (John 8.32). That's what Paul is writing here. Our minds have to be changed so that we can appreciate what God wants to teach us. Then we will be made free from everything that keeps us from enjoying all the good things that the Lord wants us to have. Those good things are summed up in the words "eternal life."

1.7 GOOD LEADERS Here is more of the same advice Paul gave to Timothy, about what a good church official is. This was very important information, which Paul didn't mind writing again to Titus. The success or failure of a church often depends on who is leading it. Pastors and other leaders need our prayers.

1.15 KEEP YOUR HEART PURE Everything looks dirty when we look through a dirty window. A heart that is not pure sees evil in things that are not evil. Some people in Paul's day, and in later times, believed that evil comes from having anything to do with the material world. But it isn't the material world that is evil. Sinful people make the world evil by the bad ways they use the good things God made.

NOTES

They are disgusting. They won't obey God, and they are too worthless to do anything good.

Instructions for Different Groups of People

2 Titus, you must teach only what is correct. 2 Tell the older men to have self-control and to be serious and sensible. Their faith, love, and patience must never fail.

3 Tell the older women to behave as those who love the Lord should. They must not gossip about others or be slaves of wine. They must teach what is proper, 4 so the younger women will be loving wives and mothers. 5 Each of the younger women must be sensible and kind, as well as a good homemaker, who puts her own husband first. Then no one can say insulting things about God's message.

6 Tell the young men to have self-control in everything.

7 Always set a good example for others. Be sincere and serious when you teach.* 8 Use clean language that no one can criticize. Do this, and your enemies will be too ashamed to say anything against you.

9 Tell slaves always to please their owners by obeying them in everything. Slaves must not talk back to their owners 10 or steal from them. They must be completely honest and trustworthy. Then everyone will show great respect for what is taught about God our Savior.

God's Kindness and the New Life

11 God has shown us how kind he is by coming to save all people. 12 He taught us to give up our wicked ways and our worldly desires and to live decent and honest lives in this world. 13 We are filled with hope, as we wait for the glorious return of our great God and Savior Jesus Christ.[d]* 14 He gave himself to rescue us from everything that is evil and to make our hearts pure. He wanted us to be his own people and to be eager to do right.

15 Teach these things, as you use your full authority to encourage and correct people. Make sure you earn everyone's respect.

Doing Helpful Things

3 Remind your people to obey the rulers and authorities and not to be rebellious. They must always be ready to do something helpful 2 and not say cruel things or argue. They should be gentle and kind to everyone.* 3 We used to be stupid,

---

[d] *the glorious return of our great God and Savior Jesus Christ*: Or "the glorious return of our great God and our Savior Jesus Christ" or "the return of Jesus Christ, who is the glory of our great God and Savior."

2.7 **BE AN EXAMPLE** The best arguments for Christianity are not found in textbooks. The most convincing argument is the life of a Christian. If we talk well but live badly, we only disgrace the name of Jesus. But if we show our love for him by a life of constant goodwill, kindness, and joy, no one can argue with that.

2.13 **ARE YOU WAITING FOR JESUS?** Political leaders sometimes speak of bringing about a "new world order." Everyone would like to see peace among the nations. But Christians know this great new order will come fully only when Jesus returns to earth to establish his kingdom. In all of our activity for God, let the coming of Jesus be our great desire and inspiration.

3.2 **CHRISTIANS ARE GENTLE** Before we were saved we may have been bad-tempered, stubborn, and hostile toward authority. This was because we thought we could save ourselves and our possessions by demanding our personal rights. But this world is dying, and we have no possessions that are really worth fighting about. Christians can afford to be gentle because their treasure is in heaven.

NOTES

disobedient, and foolish, as well as
slaves of all sorts of desires and pleasures. We were evil and jealous.
Everyone hated us, and we hated
everyone.

4God our Savior showed us
how good and kind he is.
5He saved us because
of his mercy,
and not because
of any good things
that we have done.

God washed us by the power
of the Holy Spirit.
He gave us new birth
and a fresh beginning.
6God sent Jesus Christ
our Savior
to give us his Spirit.*

7Jesus treated us much better
than we deserved.
He made us acceptable to God
and gave us the hope
of eternal life.

8This message is certainly true.
These teachings are useful and
helpful for everyone. I want you to
insist that the people follow them, so
that all who have faith in God will
be sure to do good deeds. 9But don't
have anything to do with stupid arguments about ancestors. And stay
away from disagreements and quarrels about the Jewish Law. Such arguments are useless and senseless.
10Warn troublemakers once or
twice. Then don't have anything else
to do with them. 11You know that
their minds are twisted, and their
own sins show how guilty they are.

Personal Instructions and Greetings

12I plan to send Artemas or Tychicus to you. After they arrive, please
try your best to meet me at Nicopolis.
I have decided to spend the winter
there.
13When Zenas the lawyer and
Apollos get ready to leave, help them
as much as you can, so they won't
have need of anything.
14Our people should learn to spend
their time doing something useful
and worthwhile.*
15Greetings to you from everyone
here. Greet all of our friends who
share in our faith.
I pray that the Lord will be kind
to all of you!

3.6 **GOD IS OUR EXAMPLE** God is love, and he proves it by what he does. He saved us from our sins and their result, death, by sending his dear Son to die in our place. If God could do this for us, then we have no excuse for not being like him. Our lives ought to copy his love.

3.14 **CHRISTIANS ARE PRACTICAL** Being a Christian doesn't mean having our heads in the clouds. We have two countries—earth and heaven. But we prove we are solid citizens of both countries by the way we do the job that is ours to do right now. God has left us here for a reason: to bless those around us and to share the news about his Son.

NOTES

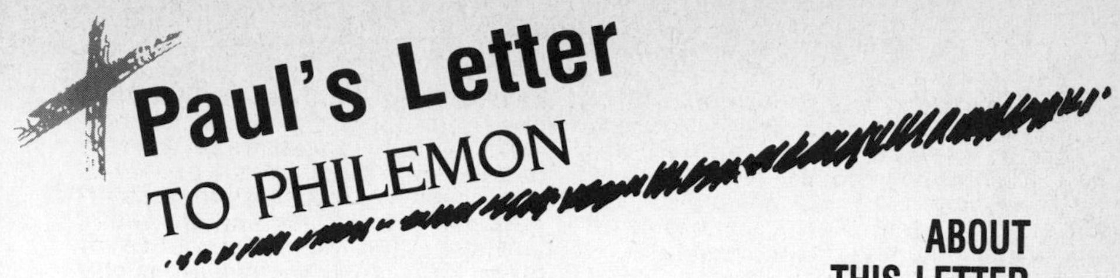

Paul's Letter TO PHILEMON

ABOUT THIS LETTER

Philemon was a wealthy man who owned slaves and who used his large house for church meetings (2). He probably lived in Colossae, since Paul's letter to the Colossians mentions Onesimus, a slave of Philemon, and Archippus (Colossians 4.9,17).

Paul is writing from jail on behalf of Onesimus, a run-away slave owned by Philemon. Onesimus had become a follower of the Lord and a valuable friend to Paul, and Paul is writing to encourage Philemon to accept Onesimus also as a friend and follower of the Lord.

This letter is an excellent example of the art of letter-writing in the Roman world, and it is the most personal of all Paul's letters. The way the letter is written suggests that Paul and Philemon were close friends.

A QUICK LOOK AT THIS LETTER

1. Greetings to Philemon (1–3)
2. Paul Speaks to Philemon about Onesimus (4–22)
3. Final Greetings and a Prayer (23–25)

1From Paul, who is in jail for serving Christ Jesus, and from Timothy,
who is like a brother because of our
faith.

Philemon, you have worked with
us and are very dear to us. This letter
is to you 2and to the church that
meets in your home. It is also to our
dear friend Apphia and to Archippus,
who serves the Lord as we do.

3I pray that God our Father and
our Lord Jesus Christ will be kind
to you and will bless you with peace!

Philemon's Love and Faith

4Philemon, each time I mention
you in my prayers, I thank God.
5I hear about your faith in our Lord
Jesus and about your love for all of
God's people. 6As you share your
faith with others, I pray that they may

come to know all the blessings Christ
has given us. 7My friend, your love
has made me happy and has greatly
encouraged me. It has also cheered
the hearts of God's people.*

Paul Speaks to Philemon about Onesimus

8Christ gives me the courage to tell
you what to do. 9But I would rather
ask you to do it because of love, since
I am a messenger[a] in jail for Christ.
10So I beg you to help Onesimus,[b]
who has been like a son to me here
in jail. 11Before this, he was useless
to you, but now he is useful to you
and me.
12Sending Onesimus to you has
made me very sad. 13I would like to
keep him here with me, where he
could take your place in helping me
spread the good news while I am a
prisoner. 14But I won't do anything
unless you agree to it first. I want
your act of kindness to come from
your heart, and not be something you
feel forced to do.
15Perhaps Onesimus was taken
from you for a little while so that you
could have him back for good,
16but not as a slave. Onesimus is
much more than a slave. To me he
is a dear friend, but to you he is even
more, both as a person and as a follower of the Lord.
17If you consider me a friend because of Christ, then welcome Onesimus as you would welcome me.
18If he has cheated you or owes you
anything, charge it to my account.*
19With my own hand I write: I, PAUL,
WILL PAY YOU BACK. But don't
forget that you owe me your life.
20My dear friend, I pray that the Lord
will make you useful to me and that,
as a follower of Christ, you will cheer
me up.
21I am sure you will do all I have
asked, and even more. 22Please get
a room ready for me. I hope your
prayers will be answered, and I can
visit you.
23Epaphras is also here in jail for
being a follower of Christ Jesus. He
sends his greetings, 24and so do
Mark, Aristarchus, Demas, and
Luke, who work together with me.
25I pray that the Lord Jesus Christ
will be with you!

---

[a] *a messenger*: Or "an old man." [b] *Onesimus*: In Greek this name means "useful."

NOTES

7 LET'S CARE ABOUT INDIVIDUALS It's easy to say, "I love everybody." But we prove our love by the way we treat individual people. Paul had a large ministry. But, even in prison, he wrote this whole letter about one poor slave. It's a beautiful personal letter from Paul to his friend, Philemon. This letter brings us close to Paul the man, where we can see what he was really like.

18 CARRY THE BURDENS OF OTHERS Paul didn't just write a kind letter about Onesimus. He was even willing to pay that young slave's debts. It didn't seem to bother Paul at all that he was in prison where he had very little, and he might never see Philemon again. Still he was willing to make this promise. More than most people, Paul was free from selfishness. It seems that his kindness was boundless.

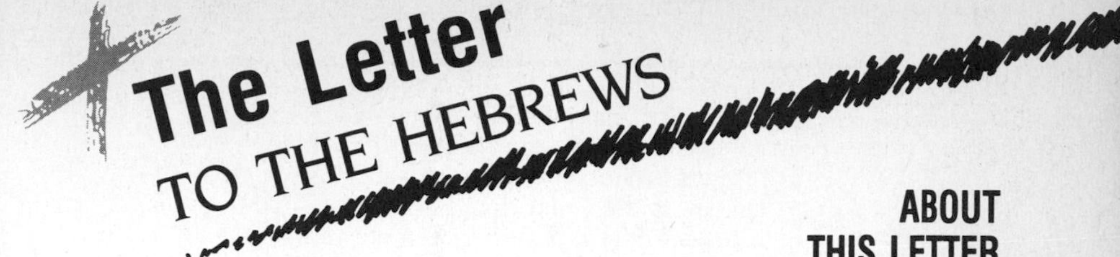

The Letter TO THE HEBREWS

ABOUT THIS LETTER

Many religious people in the first century after Jesus' birth, both Jews and Gentiles, had questions about the religion of the early Christians. They were looking for evidence that this new faith was genuine. Jews had the miracle of crossing the Red Sea and the agreement made with God at Mount Sinai to support their faith. But what miracles did Christians have? Jews had beautiful worship ceremonies and a high priest who offered sacrifices in the temple so that the people would be forgiven. But what did Christians have? How could this new Christian faith, centered in Jesus, offer forgiveness of sins and friendship with God?

The letter to the Hebrews was written to answer exactly these kinds of questions. In it the author tells the readers how important Jesus really is. He is greater than any of God's angels (1.5–14), greater than any prophet, and greater even than Moses and Joshua (2.1—4.14). Jesus is the perfect high priest because he never sinned, and by offering his own life he has made the perfect sacrifice for sin once for all time (9.23—10.18). By his death and return from death he has opened the way for all people to come to God (4.14—5.10; 7.1—8.13).

This letter has much to say about the importance of faith. The writer points out that what Jesus offers comes only by faith. And this faith makes his followers sure of what they hope for and gives them proof of things that cannot be seen. The writer praises God's faithful people of the past (11.1–40) and encourages those who follow Jesus now to keep their eyes on him as they run the race (12.1–3).

What does it mean to have a high priest like Jesus?

> *Jesus understands every weakness of ours, because he was tempted in every way that we are. But he did not sin! So whenever we are in need, we should come bravely before the throne of our merciful God. There we will be treated with undeserved kindness, and we will find help.* (4.15,16)

A QUICK LOOK AT THIS LETTER

1. The Greatness of God's Son (1.1–4)
2. Jesus Is Greater than Angels (1.5—2.18)
3. Jesus Is Greater than Moses and Joshua (3.1—4.13)
4. Jesus Is the Great High Priest (4.14—7.28)
5. Jesus Brings a Better Agreement (8.1—9.22)
6. Jesus' Sacrifice Is Once and for All (9.23—10.31)
7. Some of God's People Who Had Great Faith (11.1–40)
8. Follow the Example of Jesus (12.1—13.19)
9. Final Prayers and Greetings (13.20–25)

1 Long ago in many ways and at
many times God's prophets spoke
his message to our ancestors. 2But
now at last God sent his Son to bring
his message to us. God created the
universe by his Son, and everything
will someday belong to the Son.
3God's Son has all the brightness of
God's own glory and is like him in
every way. By his own mighty word
he holds the universe together.

After the Son had washed away
our sins, he sat down at the right side[a]
of the glorious God in heaven.*
4He had become much greater than
the angels, and the name he was
given is far greater than any of
theirs.

God's Son Is Greater than Angels

5God has never said
to any of the angels,
"You are my Son,
because today
I have become your Father!"
Neither has God said
to any of them,
"I will be his Father,
and he will be my Son!"
6When God brings his first-born
Son[b] into the world, he commands
all of his angels to worship him.
7And when God speaks about the
angels, he says,
"I change my angels into wind
and my servants
into flaming fire."

8But God says about his Son,
"You are God,
and you will rule
as King forever!
Your[c] royal power
brings about justice.
9You loved justice
and hated evil,
and so I, your God,
have chosen you.
I appointed you
and made you happier
than any of your friends."

10The Scriptures also say,
"Lord, in the beginning
you were the one

[a]*right side*: The place of honor and power. [b]*first-born Son*: The first son born into a family had certain privileges that the other children did not have. In 12.23 "first-born" refers to God's special people. [c]*Your*: Some manuscripts have "His."

1.3 **JESUS EARNED HIS GLORY** We know that Jesus came from heaven where he shared equally the glory of his Father. And yet we can say that Jesus earned his glory. Jesus put himself in the position of a servant who had to do a certain work in order to return to heaven. That work was his earthly obedience, his suffering, and his death for our sins. Jesus was again raised to glory after he finished his work.

NOTES

who laid the foundation
of the earth
and created the heavens.*
11They will all disappear
and wear out like clothes,
but you will last forever.
12You will roll them up
like a robe
and change them
like a garment.
But you are always the same,
and you will live forever."
13God never said to any
of the angels,
"Sit at my right side
until I make your enemies
into a footstool for you!"
14Angels are merely spirits sent to
serve people who are going to be
saved.

This Great Way of Being Saved

2 We must give our full attention
to what we were told, so that we
won't drift away. 2The message spoken by angels proved to be true, and
all who disobeyed or rejected it were
punished as they deserved. 3So if we
refuse this great way of being saved,
how can we hope to escape? The Lord
himself was the first to tell about it,
and people who heard the message
proved to us that it was true. 4God
himself showed that his message was
true by working all kinds of powerful
miracles and wonders. He also gave
his Holy Spirit to anyone he chose
to.

The One Who Leads Us To Be Saved

5We know that God did not put the
future world under the power of angels. 6Somewhere in the Scriptures
someone says to God,
"What makes you care
about us humans?
Why are you concerned
for weaklings such as we?
7You made us lower
than the angels
for a while.
Yet you have crowned us
with glory and honor.[d]
8And you have put everything
under our power!"
God has put everything under our
power and has not left anything out
of our power. But we still don't see
it all under our power.* 9What we
do see is Jesus, who for a little while
was made lower than the angels. Because of God's kindness, Jesus died
for everyone. And now that Jesus has
suffered and died, he is crowned with
glory and honor!
10Everything belongs to God, and
all things were created by his power.
So God did the right thing when he
made Jesus perfect by suffering, as
Jesus led many of God's children to
be saved and to share in his glory.
11Jesus and the people he makes holy
all belong to the same family. That
is why he is not ashamed to call them
his brothers and sisters. 12He even
said to God,
"I will tell them your name
and sing your praises
when they come together
to worship."
13He also said,
"I will trust God."

---

[d]*and honor*: Some manuscripts add "and you have placed us in charge of all you created."

1.10 **CHRIST CREATED ALL THINGS** Let's not forget that the man Jesus, whom we met in Matthew, Mark, Luke, and John, was hiding his real nature within a body of flesh. But all that time he was still the Son of God, the very One who brought the universe into being. We should adore Jesus even more when we realize how much he humbled himself to become a man with flesh and blood like ours.

2.8 **THE POWER GOD GIVES US** Has God really given us his mighty power? Yes, he has, through Jesus our great representative. Through Jesus we have power over sin and creation. We have not yet fully realized or understood this power. But one day believers actually shall reign as kings on the earth (see Revelation 1.6). So now we see what great honors Christ our King has bought for us at the price of his own life.

NOTES

Then he said,
"Here I am with the children
God has given me."
STEP 2
14We are people of flesh and blood.
That is why Jesus became one of us.
He died to destroy the devil, who had
power over death.* 15But he also died
to rescue all of us who live each day
in fear of dying. 16Jesus clearly did
not come to help angels, but he did
come to help Abraham's descendants. 17He had to be one of us, so
that he could serve God as our merciful and faithful high priest and sacrifice himself for the forgiveness of our
sins. 18And now that Jesus has suffered and was tempted, he can help
anyone else who is tempted.

Jesus Is Greater than Moses

3 My friends, God has chosen you
to be his holy people. So think
about Jesus, the one we call our apostle and high priest! 2Jesus was faithful to God, who appointed him, just
as Moses was faithful in serving all
of[e] God's people. 3But Jesus deserves
more honor than Moses, just as the
builder of a house deserves more
honor than the house. 4Of course,
every house is built by someone, and
God is really the one who built
everything.
5Moses was a faithful servant and
told all of God's people what would
be said in the future.* 6But Christ is
the Son in charge of God's people.
And we are those people, if we keep
on being brave and don't lose hope.

A Rest for God's People

7It is just as the Holy Spirit says,
"If you hear God's voice today,
8 don't be stubborn!
Don't rebel like those people
who were tested
in the desert.
9-10For forty years your ancestors
tested God and saw
the things he did.

"Then God got tired of them
and said,
'You people never
show good sense,
and you don't understand
what I want you to do.'
11God became angry
and told the people,
'You will never enter
my place of rest!' "
12My friends, watch out! Don't let
evil thoughts or doubts make any of
you turn from the living God. 13You
must encourage one another each
day. And you must keep on while
there is still a time that can be called
"today." If you don't, then sin may
fool some of you and make you stubborn. 14We were sure about Christ
when we first became his people. So
let's hold tightly to our faith until the
end. 15The Scriptures say,
"If you hear his voice today,
don't be stubborn
like those who rebelled."*

---

[e] *all of*: Some manuscripts do not have these words.

2.14 **JESUS DESTROYED SATAN'S POWER** The devil, Satan, had power over death, and therefore death was our great enemy. But Jesus broke Satan's power by carrying the weight of our sins on the cross, and then rising up from death. Now he has given us as a gift the life he was raised with. Satan can't frighten us with death anymore. Jesus said, "I have the keys to death."

3.5 **WHY JESUS IS GREATER THAN MOSES** Moses was God's ancient lawgiver who told his people of God's commandments. But Moses couldn't give anyone power over the sinfulness that breaks the commandments. Christ, the Lord who gave Moses the Law, is also the One who came and obeyed that Law for us. Then he died to pay for our sins against his Law. So Jesus did what Moses never could have done.

3.15 **OBEDIENCE TO GOD** In Old Testament times God tested his people's obedience with many rules. They resisted God by not following him. But even following rules doesn't (*continued*)

NOTES

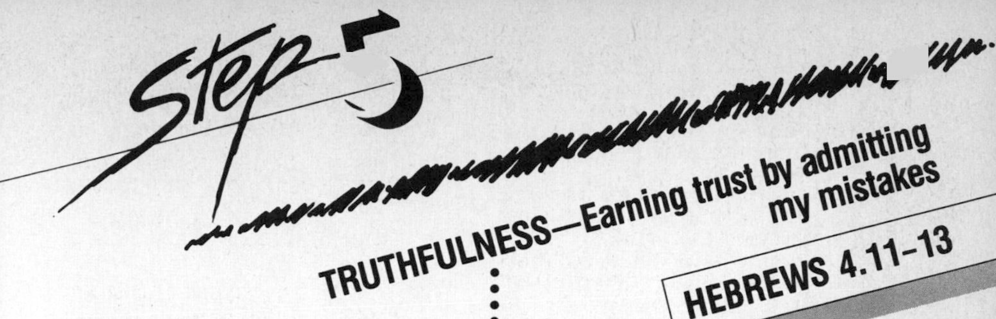

ROSES

My dad has these real pretty rose bushes on the side of the house. They are big and full and look great to me. But every spring he cuts them way back until they are just ugly little stubs sticking out. It's weird. When I asked him why he does that, he said, "You have to get rid of the old. Beautiful roses can only bloom through new growth."

ADMITTING MISTAKES

It wouldn't be too farfetched to look at our lives as beautiful roses. God sees us that way. And as roses have to be pruned back to grow, so do we. By admitting our mistakes and being honest about our past, we are doing what is right for our future. At the time, we may feel kind of ugly, like a stub sticking out, but if we hang in there, we will turn out to be terrific!

For another "Look Ahead," turn to page 723.

16Who were those people that
heard God's voice and rebelled?
Weren't they the same ones that
came out of Egypt with Moses?
17Who were the people that made
God angry for forty years? Weren't
they the ones that sinned and died
in the desert? 18And who did God say
would never enter his place of rest?
Weren't they the ones that disobeyed
him? 19We see that those people did
not enter the place of rest because
they did not have faith.

4 The promise to enter the place
of rest is still good, and we must
take care that none of you miss out.
2We have heard the message, just as
they did. But they failed to believe
what they heard, and the message
did not do them any good. 3Only people who have faith will enter the place
of rest. It is just as the Scriptures say,

"God became angry
and told the people,
'You will never enter
my place of rest!' "

God said this, even though everything has been ready from the time
of creation.* 4In fact, somewhere the
Scriptures say that God rested on the
Sabbath. 5We also read that he later
said, "You people will never enter
my place of rest!" 6This means that
the promise to enter is still good, because those who first heard about it
disobeyed and did not enter. 7Much
later God told David to make the
promise again, just as I have already
said,

"If you hear his voice today,
don't be stubborn!"

8If Joshua had really given the people rest, there would not be any need
for God to talk about another day
of rest. 9But God has promised us a
Sabbath when we will rest, even
though it has not yet come. 10On that
day God's people will rest from their
work, just as God rested from his
work.

11We should do our best to enter
that place of rest, so that none of us
will disobey and miss going there,
as they did. 12What God has said is
not only alive and active! It is sharper
than any double-edged sword. His
word can cut through our spirits and
souls and through our joints and mar-
row, until it discovers the desires and
thoughts of our hearts. 13Nothing is
hidden from God! He sees through
everything, and we will have to tell
him the truth.

Jesus Is the Great High Priest

14We have a great high priest, who
has gone into heaven, and he is Jesus
the Son of God. That is why we must
hold on to what we have said about
him.* 15Jesus understands every
weakness of ours, because he was
tempted in every way that we are.
But he did not sin! 16So whenever
we are in need, we should come
bravely before the throne of our merciful God. There we will be treated
with undeserved kindness, and we
will find help.

(continued) change hearts. Real obedience is accepting God's plan to save us by what Jesus did for us. It's obedience when we honestly give ourselves to him. Then our hearts are made new, and pleasing God becomes a joy.

4.3 **WHAT IS THE REST THAT GOD GIVES?** When we're always working by our own strength to please God, obeying then disobeying, there is no rest for us. But when we have given ourselves to God, then we have rest in him. Rest is knowing we're safely in his everlasting care. Then one day we will enter into his presence, and all of our weariness will pass away. Then we will rest, even though we will still be busy serving God.

4.14 **CHRIST OUR GREAT HIGH PRIEST** In Old Testament times the high priest was the spiritual leader of the people. He was the only one who could appear before God once a year to make an offering for the people's sins. The high priest was a picture of the great high priest of the New Testament, Jesus Christ. Instead of the animals that priests sacrificed in the Old Testament, Jesus gave a perfect sacrifice for sins: himself.

NOTES

Step 6

I want God to take control of my life and make me a complete person.

HEBREWS 4.14–16

PICKING UP THE TAB

When you are a freshman in college you might be rich in academics, but you are usually very poor in finances. That was certainly true in my case.

In between classes, when I could afford it, I would treat myself to lunch at the Student Union. A sandwich and drink had to stay within my budget. One day the waitress brought a big bowl of soup and a salad with my order. I told her it must be for someone else. I couldn't afford all that food. She told me it was for me. Apparently, a lady who comes to the restaurant often had seen how little I had been eating. She thought I should have a complete meal, so she ordered the extra food—her treat. What was really unbelievable was that she intended to do so every time I visited the restaurant.

STEP LOOK INSIDE 6

MEETING NEEDS

God knew we would be spiritually incomplete because of the sin in our lives. That is why he sent Jesus to this earth—to make sure we could become complete in him. He understands where we are weak. He knows what is missing in our lives. And with great love and kindness Jesus is ready to meet these needs. The best part is that his wonderful gift is God's treat. Jesus has already paid the price.

For another "Look Inside," turn to page 556.

5 Every high priest is appointed to
help others by offering gifts and
sacrifices to God because of their
sins. 2A high priest has weaknesses
of his own, and he feels sorry for foolish and sinful people. 3That is why
he must offer sacrifices for his own
sins and for the sins of others.
4But no one can have the honor of
being a high priest simply by wanting
to be one. Only God can choose a
priest, and God is the one who chose
Aaron.

5That is how it was with Christ.
He became a high priest, but not just
because he wanted the honor of being one. It was God who told him,

"You are my Son,
because today
I have become your Father!"

6In another place, God says,

"You are a priest forever
just like Melchizedek."[f]*

7God had the power to save Jesus
from death. And while Jesus was on
earth, he begged God with loud crying and tears to save him. He truly
worshiped God, and God listened to
his prayers. 8Jesus is God's own Son,
but still he had to suffer before he
could learn what it really means to
obey God. 9Suffering made Jesus perfect, and now he can save forever
all who obey him.* 10This is because
God chose him to be a high priest
like Melchizedek.

Warning against Turning Away

11Much more could be said about
this subject. But it is hard to explain,
and all of you are slow to understand.
12By now you should have been
teachers, but once again you need
to be taught the simplest things about
what God has said. You need milk
instead of solid food. 13People who
live on milk are like babies who don't
really know what is right. 14Solid
food is for mature people who have
been trained to know right from
wrong.

6 We must try to become mature
and start thinking about more
than just the basic things we were
taught about Christ. We shouldn't
need to keep talking about why we
ought to turn from deeds that bring
death and why we ought to have faith
in God. 2And we shouldn't need to
keep teaching about baptisms[g] or
about the laying on of hands[h] or
about people being raised from death
and the future judgment. 3Let's grow
up, if God is willing.

4-6But what about people who turn
away after they have already seen
the light and have received the gift
from heaven and have shared in the
Holy Spirit? What about those who
turn away after they have received
the good message of God and the

---

[f]*Melchizedek*: When Melchizedek is mentioned in the Old Testament, he is described as a priest who lived before Aaron. Nothing is said about his ancestors or his death (see 7.3 and Genesis 14.17-20).
[g]*baptisms*: Or "ceremonies of washing."
[h]*laying on of hands*: This was a ceremony in which church leaders and others put their hands on people to show that those people were chosen to do some special kind of work.

5.6 **WHO WAS MELCHIZEDEK?** The Old Testament tells about a meeting of Abraham (the great ancestor of the Hebrew people) with a mysterious high priest called Melchizedek. We're told that Abraham offered a tenth of what he had to God in an act of worship before this strange person, whom we never see or hear from again. This high priest pointed ahead to the coming of Christ. Melchizedek means the "king who brings justice" (see chapter 7).

5.9 **JESUS WAS MADE COMPLETE BY SUFFERING** Think of that: even the Son of God himself had something he had to do to be all that God meant him to be. When we read that "suffering made Jesus perfect," of course it doesn't mean that Jesus was ever sinful. "Perfect" here means "complete." Jesus could not complete his work that saves us without perfectly obeying his heavenly Father and suffering for our sins. In this way Jesus became complete or perfect as our Savior.

NOTES

powers of the future world? There
is no way to bring them back. What
they are doing is the same as nailing
the Son of God to a cross and insulting him in public!*
7A field is useful to farmers, if there
is enough rain to make good crops
grow. In fact, God will bless that field.
8But land that produces only thorn
bushes is worthless. It is likely to fall
under God's curse, and in the end it
will be set on fire.
9My friends, we are talking this
way. But we are sure that you are
doing those really good things that
people do when they are being saved.
10God is always fair. He will remember how you helped his people in the
past and how you are still helping
them. You belong to God, and he
won't forget the love you have shown
his people. 11We wish that each of
you would always be eager to show
how strong and lasting your hope really is. 12Then you would never be
lazy. You would be following the example of those who had faith and
were patient until God kept his promise to them.

God's Promise Is Sure

13No one is greater than God. So
he made a promise in his own name
when he said to Abraham, 14"I, the
Lord, will bless you with many descendants!"* 15Then after Abraham
had been very patient, he was given
what God had promised. 16When
anyone wants to settle an argument,
they make a vow by using the name
of someone or something greater
than themselves. 17So when God
wanted to prove for certain that his
promise to his people could not be
broken, he made a vow. 18God cannot
tell lies! And so his promises and
vows are two things that can never
be changed.

We have run to God for safety. Now
his promises should greatly encourage us to take hold of the hope that
is right in front of us. 19This hope is
like a firm and steady anchor for our
souls. In fact, hope reaches behind
the curtain[i] and into the most holy
place. 20Jesus has gone there ahead
of us, and he is our high priest forever, just like Melchizedek.[j]

The Priestly Family of Melchizedek

7 Melchizedek was both king of Salem and priest of God Most High.
He was the one who went out and
gave Abraham his blessing, when
Abraham returned from killing the
kings.* 2Then Abraham gave him a
tenth of everything he had.
The meaning of the name Melchizedek is "King Who Brings Justice."

---

[i] *behind the curtain*: In the tent that was used for worship, a curtain separated the "holy place" from the "most holy place," which only the high priest could enter. [j] *Melchizedek*: See the note at 5.6.

6.4 **CHRISTIANS CONTINUE TO THE END** Real Christians never give up. If they do give up and go back to their old ways, then they prove that they don't love Christ at all. Their hearts are harder than ever before, and they almost never come back to Christ. So let's not have ideas that we can take Jesus or leave him depending on what suits us. If we take Jesus, it must be for real and it must be forever.

6.14 **GOD GAVE ABRAHAM A GREAT FAMILY** The "many descendants" God promised Abraham in the Old Testament includes all those who put their faith in Jesus now. This was a very solemn promise that God made to Abraham. We can see this promise of God as an anchor that rests on our Savior's love and can never be moved.

7.1 **JUST WHO WAS THIS KING?** We have seen in chapter 5 that the name of Melchizedek means the "the king who brings justice." Now we see that he was also the king of Salem. Salem was an ancient name for Jerusalem. Jerusalem means "city of peace," (*continued*)

NOTES

TAKE A LOOK

It was the hardest thing I have ever had to do in my life. But because I was able to say, "Help me, I am an alcoholic," I now have a life. It had gotten to where my days consisted of dragging myself out of bed or off the floor just in time to clean up enough to be back out boozing by the afternoon.

When I went to school, I was just going through the motions. Nothing and nobody meant anything to me. All that mattered was where I was going to get the next drink. Until I met Jill.

She knew I was into drinking but she liked me anyway. When she invited me to her church, I decided to go, because I trusted Jill.

It didn't happen right away, but to make a long story short, I found out that God liked me anyway too. That's why I'm determined to put the booze away now and take a look at myself. Maybe I'll like what I see.

TAKING THE STEP

Trusting someone else takes courage. Particularly, when we have been burned by people before. But we can trust God to bring new people into our lives—people who will love and support us.

For another "Look Ahead," turn to page 484.

But since Salem means "peace," he
is also "King Who Brings Peace."
3We are not told that he had a father
or mother or ancestors or beginning
or end. He is like the Son of God and
will be a priest forever.[k]
4Notice how great Melchizedek is!
Our famous ancestor Abraham gave
him a tenth of what he had taken
from his enemies. 5The Law teaches
that even Abraham's descendants
must give a tenth of what they possess. And they are to give this to their
own relatives, who are the descendants of Levi and are priests.
6Although Melchizedek was not a
descendant of Levi, Abraham gave
him a tenth of what he had. Then
Melchizedek blessed Abraham, who
had been given God's promise.
7Everyone agrees that a person who
gives a blessing is greater than the
one who receives the blessing.
8Priests are given a tenth of what
people earn. But all priests die, except Melchizedek, and the Scriptures
teach that he is alive. 9Levi's descendants are now the ones who receive
a tenth from people. We could even
say that when Abraham gave Melchizedek a tenth, Levi also gave him
a tenth. 10This is because Levi was
born later into the family of Abraham, who gave a tenth to Melchizedek.
11Even though the Law of Moses
says that the priests must be descendants of Levi, those priests cannot
make anyone perfect. So there needs
to be a priest like Melchizedek, rather
than one from the priestly family of
Aaron.[l] 12And when the rules for se-
lecting a priest are changed, the Law
must also be changed.
13The person we are talking about
is our Lord, who came from a tribe
that had never had anyone to serve
as a priest at the altar. 14Everyone
knows he came from the tribe of Judah, and Moses never said that
priests would come from that tribe.
15All of this becomes clearer, when
someone who is like Melchizedek is
appointed to be a priest. 16That person was not appointed because of his
ancestors, but because his life can
never end. 17The Scriptures say
about him,

"You are a priest forever,
just like Melchizedek."*

18In this way a weak and useless command was put aside, 19because the
Law cannot make anything perfect.
At the same time, we are given a
much better hope, and it can bring
us close to God.
20-21God himself made a promise
when this priest was appointed. But
he did not make a promise like this
when the other priests were appointed. The promise he made is,

"I, the Lord, promise that you
will be a priest forever!
And I will never
change my mind!"

22This means that Jesus guarantees
us a better agreement with God.
23There have been a lot of other
priests, and all of them have died.
24But Jesus will never die, and so he
will be a priest forever! 25He is forever able to save[m] the people he leads
to God, because he always lives to
speak to God for them.
26Jesus is the high priest we need.

---

[k] *will be a priest forever*: See the note at 5.6.
[l] *descendants of Levi . . . from the priestly family of Aaron*: Levi was the ancestor of the tribe from which priests and their helpers (called "Levites") were chosen. Aaron was the first high priest.
[m] *forever able to save*: Or "able to save forever."

(*continued*) while Salem means simply "peace." So Melchizedek was both the king of justice and peace, as well as being that mysterious priest who visited Abraham, the great ancestor of the Jews. Melchizedek points toward Jesus, our true and everlasting King of justice and peace.

7.17 **JESUS IS A PRIEST FOREVER** Whoever Melchizedek was, he was indeed like Jesus who would come two thousand years later. So God calls his Son "a priest forever, just like Melchizedek." As our priest, Jesus stands for us in heaven. There he presents his own body as our true and only sacrifice for sins.

NOTES

He is holy and innocent and faultless,
and not at all like us sinners. Jesus
is honored above all beings in
heaven, 27and he is better than any
other high priest. Jesus does not need
to offer sacrifices each day for his
own sins and then for the sins of the
people. He offered a sacrifice once
for all, when he gave himself.*
28The Law appoints priests who have
weaknesses. But God's promise,
which came later than the Law, appoints his Son. And he is the perfect
high priest forever.

A Better Promise

8 What I mean is that we have a
high priest who sits at the right
side[n] of God's great throne in heaven.
2He also serves as the priest in the
most holy place[o] inside the real tent
there in heaven. This tent of worship
was set up by the Lord, not by
humans.*
3Since all priests must offer gifts
and sacrifices, Christ also needed to
have something to offer. 4If he were
here on earth, he would not be a
priest at all, because here the Law
appoints other priests to offer sacrifices. 5But the tent where they serve
is just a copy and a shadow of the
real one in heaven. Before Moses
made the tent, he was told, "Be sure
to make it exactly like the pattern
you were shown on the mountain!"
6Now Christ has been appointed to
serve as a priest in a much better
way, and he has given us much assurance of a better agreement.
7If the first agreement with God
had been all right, there would not
have been any need for another one.
8But the Lord found fault with it and
said,

"I tell you the time will come,
when I will make
a new agreement
with the people of Israel
and the people of Judah.*
9It won't be like the agreement
that I made
with their ancestors,
when I took them by the hand
and led them out of Egypt.
They broke their agreement
with me,
and I stopped caring
about them!

10"But now I tell the people
of Israel
this is my new agreement:
'The time will come
when I, the Lord,
will write my laws
on their minds and hearts.
I will be their God,
and they will be
my people.

[n] *right side*: See the note at 1.3. [o] *most holy place*: See the note at 6.19.

7.27 **ONE TRUE SACRIFICE** Because Jesus is the Son of God, his own death on the cross was all the sacrifice any believer would ever need. Killing animals on an altar was just a sign to point to Jesus. We don't have to do that now.

8.2 **THE TENT IN HEAVEN** In Old Testament times, before a stone temple was built, God commanded Moses to raise a tent where the sacrifices for sin were made. A tent was used because, at that time, the people were wandering in the desert. In that tent there was a special section called the most holy place. The high priest went there once a year to make a special offering for the people's sins. But now Christ himself is our high priest forever in heaven, and his own crucified but living body is the real payment for our sins.

8.8 **GOD MAKES A NEW AGREEMENT** The Old Testament prophet Jeremiah described this new agreement that would cancel the old agreement. Now the Law of God would be in our minds and hearts, not on stone or any other material. Only Jesus himself, the Son of God, was able to be the sacrifice to pay for our sins. This was something neither we nor anyone else could do. Because of Jesus, we can have friendship with God.

NOTES

11Not one of them
will have to teach another
to know me, their Lord.'

"All of them will know me,
no matter who they are.
12I will treat them
with kindness,
even though they
are wicked.
I will surely forget
their sins."

13When the Lord talks about a new agreement, he means that the first one is out of date. And anything that is old and useless will soon disappear.

The Tent in Heaven

9 The first promise that was made
included rules for worship and a
tent for worship here on earth.
2The first part of the tent was called
the holy place, and a lampstand, a table, and the sacred loaves of bread were kept there.*

3Behind the curtain was the most
holy place. 4The gold altar that was
used for burning incense was in this holy place. The gold-covered sacred chest was also there, and inside it were three things. First, there was a gold jar filled with manna.[p] Then there was Aaron's walking stick that sprouted.[q] Finally, there were the flat stones with the Ten Commandments
written on them. 5On top of the chest
were the glorious creatures with wings[r] opened out above the place of mercy.[s]

Now is not the time to go into detail
about these things. 6But this is how
everything was when the priests went each day into the first part of
the tent to do their duties. 7However,
only the high priest could go into the second part of the tent, and he went in only once a year. Each time he carried blood to offer for his sins and for any sins that the people had committed without meaning to.

8All of this is the Holy Spirit's way of saying that no one could enter the most holy place while the tent was
still the place of worship. 9This also
has a meaning for today. It shows that we cannot make our consciences clear by offering gifts and sacrifices.
10These rules are merely about such things as eating and drinking and ceremonies for washing ourselves. And rules about physical things will last only until the time comes to change them for something better.

11Christ came as the high priest of the good things that are now here.[t] He also went into a much better tent that was not made by humans and that does not belong to this world.
12Then Christ went once for all into the most holy place and freed us from sin forever. He did this by offering his own blood instead of the blood of goats and bulls.

13According to the Jewish religion, those people who become unclean are not fit to worship God. Yet they will be considered clean, if they are

---

[p]*manna*: When the people of Israel were wandering through the desert, the Lord provided them with food that could be made into thin wafers. This food was called manna, which in Hebrew means "What is it?" [q]*Aaron's walking stick that sprouted*: According to Numbers 17.1-11, Aaron's walking stick sprouted and produced almonds to show that the Lord was pleased with him and Moses. [r]*glorious creatures with wings*: Two of these creatures (called "cherubim" in Hebrew and Greek) with outspread wings were on top of the sacred chest and were symbols of God's throne. [s]*place of mercy*: The lid of the sacred chest, which was thought to be God's throne on earth. [t]*that are now here*: Some manuscripts have "that were coming."

9.2 **THE THINGS IN THE TENT** In the part of the tent called "the holy place" there were three main things: the lampstand, which stands for the light-giving presence of God's Spirit; the gold altar of incense, which was a symbol of the prayers of the people rising up to heaven; and the table of bread, which meant God was the life of his people. Then "the most holy place," behind a heavy curtain, contained a gold-covered chest that contained God's Law. Now, all of these things have been replaced by Jesus Christ himself.

NOTES

sprinkled with the blood of goats and bulls and with the ashes of a sacrificed calf. 14But Christ was sinless, and he offered himself as an eternal and spiritual sacrifice to God. That's why his blood is much more powerful and makes our[u] consciences clear. Now we can serve the living God and no longer do things that lead to death.

15Christ died to rescue those who had sinned and broken the old agreement. Now he brings his chosen ones a new agreement with its guarantee of God's eternal blessings!* 16In fact, making an agreement of this kind is like writing a will. This is because the one who makes the will must die before it is of any use. 17In other words, a will does not go into effect as long as the one who made it is still alive.

18Blood was also used[v] to put the first agreement into effect. 19Moses told the people all that the Law said they must do. Then he used red wool and a hyssop plant to sprinkle the people and the book of the Law with the blood of bulls and goats[w] and with water. 20He told the people, "With this blood God makes his agreement with you." 21Moses also sprinkled blood on the tent and on everything else that was used in worship. 22The Law says that almost everything must be sprinkled with blood, and no sins can be forgiven unless blood is offered.*

Christ's Great Sacrifice

23These things are only copies of what is in heaven, and so they had to be made holy by these ceremonies. But the real things in heaven must be made holy by something better. 24This is why Christ did not go into a tent that had been made by humans and was only a copy of the real one. Instead, he went into heaven and is now there with God to help us.

25Christ did not have to offer himself many times. He was not like a high priest who goes into the most holy place each year to offer the blood of an animal. 26If he had offered himself every year, he would have suffered many times since the creation of the world. But instead, near the end of time he offered himself once and for all, so that he could be a sacrifice that does away with sin.

27We die only once, and then we are judged. 28So Christ died only once to take away the sins of many people. But when he comes again, it will not be to take away sin. He will come to save everyone who is waiting for him.

10 The Law of Moses is like a shadow of the good things to come. This shadow is not the good things themselves, because it cannot free people from sin by the sacrifices that are offered year after year. 2If there were worshipers who already have their sins washed away and their consciences made clear, there would not be any need to go on offering sacrifices. 3-4But the blood of bulls and goats cannot take

---

[u] *our*: Some manuscripts have "your," and others have "their." [v] *Blood was also used*: Or "There also had to be a death." [w] *blood of bulls and goats*: Some manuscripts do not have "and goats."

9.15 **WHY DID SOMEONE NEED TO DIE?** It's helpful to look at it this way: We are made immune to certain diseases by serums made from the dead remains of those diseases. Like a disease, sin causes the death of sinners. So you might say someone had to die in a way that would "kill the disease of sin" and make us immune to it. The death of animals couldn't do this. It took the death of the sinless Son of God to destroy sin and to overcome death.

9.22 **BLOOD IS NEEDED** Blood stands for life. Our natural bodies couldn't live without blood in our veins. When Jesus' blood was shed on the cross, it stood for the new life we could have by believing in him and his perfect sacrifice for us.

NOTES

away sins. It only reminds people of
their sins from one year to the next.
5When Christ came into the world,
he said to God,
"Sacrifices and offerings
are not what you want,
but you have given me
my body.*
6No, you are not pleased
with animal sacrifices
and offerings for sin."

7Then Christ said,
"And so, my God,
I have come to do
what you want,
as the Scriptures say."
8The Law teaches that offerings
and sacrifices must be made because
of sin. But why did Christ mention
these things and say that God did not
want them? 9Well, it was to do away
with offerings and sacrifices and to
replace them. That is what he meant
by saying to God, "I have come to
do what you want." 10So we are made
holy because Christ obeyed God and
offered himself once for all.
11The priests do their work each
day, and they keep on offering sacrifices that can never take away sins.
12But Christ offered himself as a sacrifice that is good forever. Now he
is sitting at God's right side,[x] 13and
he will stay there until his enemies
are put under his power. 14By his one
sacrifice he has forever set free from
sin the people he brings to God.
15The Holy Spirit also speaks of
this by telling us that the Lord said,
16"When the time comes,
I will make an agreement
with them.
I will write my laws
on their minds and hearts.
17Then I will forget
about their sins
and no longer remember
their evil deeds."
18When sins are forgiven, there is
no more need to offer sacrifices.

Encouragement and Warning

19My friends, the blood of Jesus
gives us courage to enter the most
holy place* 20by a new way that leads
to life! And this way takes us through
the curtain that is Christ himself.
21We have a great high priest who
is in charge of God's house. 22So let's
come near to God with pure hearts
and a confidence that comes from
having faith. Let's keep our hearts
pure, our consciences free from evil,
and our bodies washed with clean
water. 23We must hold tightly to the
hope that we say is ours. After all,
we can trust the one who made the
agreement with us. 24We should keep
on encouraging each other to be
thoughtful and to do helpful things.
25Some people have gotten out of the
habit of meeting for worship, but we
must not do that. We should keep
on encouraging each other, especially since you know that the day of
the Lord's coming is getting closer.
26No sacrifices can be made for
people who decide to sin after they
find out about the truth. 27They are
God's enemies, and all they can look
forward to is a terrible judgment and

---

[x]*right side*: See the note at 1.3.

10.5 **WE NEEDED ONE SACRIFICE FOR SIN** In Old Testament times, sacrifices were made every day. There were also special times of sacrifice, festivals held once a year. By making sacrifices the people were able to see the horrible cost of sin. But the sacrifices were also signs that pointed ahead to Jesus Christ. His one death paid the whole price of sin for believers forever. His death made the Old Testament sacrifices unnecessary.

10.19 **WE CAN ENTER THE MOST HOLY PLACE** In Old Testament times the people could not come directly before God. The high priest alone could do this only once a year. But now, Jesus himself is our high priest. When Jesus died, the curtain that hid the most holy place was opened (see Matthew 27.51). Now we can all come into God's presence.

NOTES

a furious fire. 28If two or more witnesses accused someone of breaking
the Law of Moses, that person could
be put to death. 29But it is much worse
to dishonor God's Son and to disgrace the blood of the promise that
made us holy. And it is just as bad
to insult the Holy Spirit, who shows
us mercy. 30We know that God has
said he will punish and take revenge.
We also know that the Scriptures
say the Lord will judge his people.
31It is a terrible thing to fall into the
hands of the living God!

32Don't forget all the hard times
you went through when you first received the light. 33Sometimes you
were abused and mistreated in public, and at other times you shared in
the sufferings of others. 34You were
kind to people in jail. And you gladly
let your possessions be taken away,
because you knew you had something better, something that would
last forever.

35Keep on being brave! It will bring
you great rewards.* 36Learn to be
patient, so that you will please God
and be given what he has promised.
37As the Scriptures say,

"God is coming soon!
It won't be very long.
38The people God accepts
will live because
of their faith.[y]
But he is not pleased
with anyone
who turns back."

39We are not like those people who
turn back and get destroyed. We will
keep on having faith until we are
saved.

The Great Faith of God's People

11 Faith makes us sure of what
we hope for and gives us proof
of what we cannot see.* 2It was their
faith that made our ancestors pleasing to God.

3Because of our faith, we know that
the world was made at God's command. We also know that what can
be seen was made out of what cannot
be seen.*

4Because Abel had faith, he offered
God a better sacrifice than Cain did.
God was pleased with him and his
gift, and even though Abel is now
dead, his faith still speaks for him.

5Enoch had faith and did not die.
He pleased God, and God took him
up to heaven. That's why his body
was never found. 6But without faith
no one can please God. We must believe that God is real and that he rewards everyone who searches for
him.

7Because Noah had faith, he was
warned about something that had not
yet happened. He obeyed and built
a boat that saved him and his family.
In this way the people of the world
were judged, and Noah was given the
blessings that come to everyone who
pleases God.

8Abraham had faith and obeyed
God. He was told to go to the land
that God had said would be his, and
he left for a country he had never
seen. 9Because Abraham had faith,
he lived as a stranger in the promised

---

[y] *The people God accepts will live because of their faith*: Or "The people God accepts because of their faith will live."

10.35 **BE BRAVE** Let's not turn back, but be brave. There is only one sacrifice for sin. That is the sacrifice made by Jesus. If we turn back from him, we have no hope. God loves his Son, so we must understand how serious it is to reject Jesus after we have promised to follow him.

11.1 **FAITH IS PROOF** Seeing is believing, but only if we dare to believe what we see. We believe in God because the Holy Spirit makes us able to know him. That is the way faith works, by trusting what God has promised.

11.3 **WHERE DID OUR WORLD COME FROM?** Some people like to think that the world just happened without any cause. It takes a lot of nerve to believe that. We know that there is a cause for everything that happens around us. Why should the world be any different? It makes sense to believe that the world was brought into being by a very powerful God.

NOTES

land. He lived there in a tent, and
so did Isaac and Jacob, who were
later given the same promise.
10Abraham did this, because he was
waiting for the eternal city that God
had planned and built.
11Even when Sarah was too old to
have children, she had faith that God
would do what he had promised, and
she had a son. 12Her husband Abraham was almost dead, but he became
the ancestor of many people. In fact,
there are as many of them as there
are stars in the sky or grains of sand
along the beach.
13Every one of those people died.
But they still had faith, even though
they had not received what they had
been promised. They were glad just
to see these things from far away,
and they agreed that they were only
strangers and foreigners on this
earth.* 14When people talk this way,
it is clear that they are looking for
a place to call their own. 15If they
had been talking about the land
where they had once lived, they could
have gone back at any time. 16But
they were looking forward to a better
home in heaven. That's why God was
not ashamed for them to call him
their God. He even built a city for
them.
17-18Abraham had been promised
that Isaac, his only son,[z] would continue his family. But when Abraham
was tested, he had faith and was willing to sacrifice Isaac, 19because he
was sure that God could raise people
to life. This was just like getting Isaac
back from death.
20Isaac had faith, and he promised
blessings to Jacob and Esau. 21Later,
when Jacob was about to die, he
leaned on his walking stick and worshiped. Then because of his faith he
blessed each of Joseph's sons.
22And right before Joseph died, he
had faith that God would lead the
people of Israel out of Egypt. So he
told them to take his bones with
them.
23Because Moses' parents had
faith, they kept him hidden until he
was three months old. They saw that
he was a beautiful child, and they
were not afraid to disobey the king's
orders.[a] 24Then after Moses grew up,
his faith made him refuse to be called
Pharaoh's grandson. 25He chose to
be mistreated with God's people instead of having the good time that
sin could bring for a little while.
26Moses knew that the treasures of
Egypt were not as wonderful as what
he would receive from suffering for
the Messiah,[b] and he looked forward
to his reward.*
27Because of his faith, Moses left
Egypt. Moses had seen the invisible
God and was not afraid of the king's
anger. 28His faith also made him celebrate Passover. He sprinkled the
blood of animals on the first-born

[z]*his only son*: Although Abraham had a son by a slave woman, his son Isaac was considered his only son, because he was born as a result of God's promise to Abraham. [a]*the king's orders*: The king of Egypt ordered all Israelite baby boys to be left outside of their homes, so they would die or be killed. [b]*the Messiah*: Or "Christ."

11.13 **"THEY STILL HAD FAITH"** This chapter includes a great "hall of fame" of faithful men and women who lived during Old Testament times. It's a very exciting story. You should read about these lives in a translation of the Old Testament. See how these believing people overcame very difficult challenges just by continuing to trust God. Sometimes they died without ever seeing all of what they had been promised, but their faith stood firm.

11.26 **GOD'S REWARD FOR HIS PEOPLE WAS SURE** God promised the people of the Old Testament that a Savior would come and die for their sins. But they never lived to see it. Abraham, Isaac, and Jacob were to be the ancestors of the Messiah. Moses would point to him. But it would take years and years to happen—with many troubles and heartaches along the way. But in Jesus we have seen the fulfillment of God's great promise. So we have no excuse for not trusting him.

NOTES

sons of the people of Israel, so that
they would not be killed by the destroying angel.
29Because of their faith, the people
walked through the Red Sea on dry
land. But when the Egyptians tried
to do it, they were drowned.
30God's people had faith, and when
they had walked around the city of
Jericho for seven days, its walls fell
down.
31Rahab had been an immoral
woman, but she had faith and welcomed the spies. So she was not
killed with the people who disobeyed.
32What else can I say? There is not
enough time to tell about Gideon,
Barak, Samson, Jephthah, David,
Samuel, and the prophets. 33Their
faith helped them conquer kingdoms,
and because they did right, God made
promises to them. They closed the
jaws of lions 34and put out raging
fires and escaped from the swords
of their enemies. Although they were
weak, they were given the strength
and power to chase foreign armies
away.
35Some women received their
loved ones back from death. Many
of these people were tortured, but
they refused to be released. They
were sure that they would get a better
reward when the dead are raised to
life.* 36Others were made fun of and
beaten with whips, and some were
chained in jail. 37Still others were
stoned to death or sawed in two[c] or
killed with swords. Some had nothing but sheep skins or goat skins to
wear. They were poor, mistreated,
and tortured. 38The world did not deserve these good people, who had to
wander in deserts and on mountains
and had to live in caves and holes
in the ground.
39All of them pleased God because
of their faith! But still they died without being given what had been promised. 40This was because God had
something better in store for us. And
he did not want them to reach the
goal of their faith without us.

A Large Crowd of Witnesses

12 Such a large crowd of witnesses is all around us! So we
must get rid of everything that slows
us down, especially the sin that just
won't let go. And we must be determined to run the race that is ahead
of us.* 2We must keep our eyes on
Jesus, who leads us and makes our
faith complete. He endured the
shame of being nailed to a cross, because he knew that later on he would
be glad he did. Now he is seated at
the right side[d] of God's throne!
3So keep your mind on Jesus, who
put up with many insults from sinners. Then you won't get discouraged
and give up.
4None of you have yet been hurt[e]
in your battle against sin. 5But you
have forgotten that the Scriptures
say to God's children,
"When the Lord punishes you,
don't make light of it,
and when he corrects you,
don't be discouraged.
6The Lord corrects the people
he loves
and disciplines those
he calls his own."

---

[c]*sawed in two*: Some manuscripts have "tested" or "tempted." [d]*right side*: See the note at 1.3. [e]*hurt*: Or "killed."

11.35 **SUFFERING MAY COME** Many who have loved God over the years have been treated very badly, even tortured. We are no better than they. We also might be called upon to suffer for Jesus. But God has never forgotten his brave believers, and he will remember us too.

12.1 **RUN YOUR RACE FOR CHRIST** A Christian is like a runner. Athletes can't follow a lifestyle of sin. Their strength would give out, their muscles would get soft, and their health would fail. Runners can't carry any extra weight in a race, because it would slow them down. Christians, too, must live so that they aren't weakened or slowed down by sin.

NOTES

7Be patient when you are being
corrected! This is how God treats his
children. Don't all parents correct
their children? 8God corrects all of
his children, and if he doesn't correct
you, then you don't really belong to
him. 9Our earthly fathers correct us,
and we still respect them. Isn't it even
better to be given true life by letting
our spiritual Father correct us?
10Our human fathers correct us for
a short time, and they do it as they
think best. But God corrects us for
our own good, because he wants us
to be holy, as he is.* 11It is never fun
to be corrected. In fact, at the time
it is always painful. But if we learn
to obey by being corrected, we will
do right and live at peace.
12Now stand up straight! Stop your
knees from shaking 13and walk a
straight path. Then lame people will
be healed, instead of getting worse.

Warning against Turning from God

14Try to live at peace with everyone! Live a clean life. If you don't,
you will never see the Lord. 15Make
sure that no one misses out on God's
kindness. Don't let anyone become
bitter and cause trouble for the rest
of you. 16Watch out for immoral and
ungodly people like Esau, who sold
his future blessing[f] for only one meal.
17You know how he later wanted it
back. But there was nothing he could
do to change things, even though he
begged his father and cried.
18You have not come to a place like
Mount Sinai[g] that can be seen and
touched. There is no flaming fire or
dark cloud or storm 19or trumpet
sound. The people of Israel heard a
voice speak. But they begged it to
stop, 20because they could not obey
its commands. They were even told
to kill any animal that touched the
mountain. 21The sight was so frightening that Moses said he shook with
fear.
22You have now come to Mount
Zion and to the heavenly Jerusalem.
This is the city of the living God,
where thousands and thousands of
angels have come to celebrate.*
23Here you will find all of God's dearest children,[h] whose names are written in heaven. And you will find God
himself, who judges everyone. Here
also are the spirits of those good people who have been made perfect.
24And Jesus is here! He is the one
who makes God's new agreement
with us, and his sprinkled blood says
much better things than the blood of
Abel.[i]
25Make sure that you obey the one
who speaks to you. The people of Israel did not escape, when they refused to obey the one who spoke to
them at Mount Sinai. Do you think
you can possibly escape, if you refuse
to obey the one who speaks to you
from heaven? 26When God spoke the
first time, his voice shook only the
earth. This time he has promised to
shake the earth once again, and
heaven too.
27The words "once again" mean
that these created things will some-

---

[f]*sold his future blessing*: As the first-born son, Esau had certain privileges that were known as a "birthright." [g]*a place like Mount Sinai*: The Greek text has "a place," but the writer is referring to the time that the Lord spoke to the people of Israel from Mount Sinai (Exodus 19.16-25). [h]*all of God's dearest children*: The Greek text has "the gathering of the first-born children." See the note at 1.6. [i]*blood of Abel*: Cain and Abel were the two sons of Adam and Eve. Cain murdered Abel (Genesis 4.1-16).

12.10 **WE NEED TO BE CORRECTED** Only the foolish say they never make mistakes and never need to be corrected. As parents correct children when they are wrong, God corrects us, too, as a loving father. We should be glad he does. If he didn't, we would hurt ourselves badly.

12.22 **THE HEAVENLY CITY LASTS FOREVER** All around us we see proof daily that everything in this world passes away. It must pass away if God's plan is to be carried out. It's important for this present world to disappear at last so that the everlasting world of God can take its place.

NOTES

day be shaken and removed. Then
what cannot be shaken will last.
28We should be grateful that we were
given a kingdom that cannot be
shaken. And in this kingdom we
please God by worshiping him and
by showing him great honor and respect. 29Our God is like a destructive
fire!

Service That Pleases God

13 Keep being concerned about
each other as the Lord's followers should.
2Be sure to welcome strangers into
your home. By doing this, some people have welcomed angels as guests,
without even knowing it.*
3Remember the Lord's people who
are in jail and be concerned for them.
Don't forget those who are suffering,
but imagine that you are there with
them.
4Have respect for marriage. Always be faithful to your partner, because God will punish anyone who
is immoral or unfaithful in marriage.
5Don't fall in love with money. Be
satisfied with what you have. The
Lord has promised that he will not
leave us or desert us.* 6That should
make you feel like saying,

"The Lord helps me!
Why should I be afraid
of what people can do
to me?"

7Don't forget about your leaders
who taught you God's message. Remember what kind of lives they lived
and try to have faith like theirs.
8Jesus Christ never changes! He is
the same yesterday, today, and forever.* 9Don't be fooled by any kind
of strange teachings. It is better to
receive strength from God's kindness
than to depend on certain foods. After all, these foods don't really help
the people who eat them. 10But we
have an altar where even the priests
who serve in the place of worship
have no right to eat.
11After the high priest offers the
blood of animals as a sin offering,
the bodies of those animals are
burned outside the camp. 12Jesus
himself suffered outside the city gate,
so that his blood would make people
holy. 13That's why we should go outside the camp to Jesus and share in
his disgrace. 14On this earth we don't
have a city that lasts forever, but we
are waiting for such a city.
15Our sacrifice is to keep offering
praise to God in the name of Jesus.
16But don't forget to help others and
to share your possessions with them.
This too is like offering a sacrifice
that pleases God.
17Obey your leaders and do what
they say. They are watching over
you, and they must answer to God.
So don't make them sad as they do
their work. Make them happy. Otherwise, they won't be able to help you
at all.*

13.2 **CHRISTIANS CARE ABOUT EVERYONE** Whether they are friends or strangers, all people are God's creations for whom Christ died. We owe all people our love and care even if we don't know them.

13.5 **CHRISTIANS ARE SATISFIED PEOPLE** Believers aren't looking for more than they need, and they know God will supply what they must have. So they don't worry about money. Some of us need to pray for God to help us with our complaining attitude.

13.8 **JESUS IS ALWAYS THE SAME** As we read about his life in Matthew, Mark, Luke, and John, we should know that Jesus is still with us today. He said, "I will never leave you." As we pray, let us ask the Holy Spirit to help us realize that Jesus is always at our side. He grieves when we sin, and he wants to help us in all our troubles.

13.17 **WE NEED EARTHLY LEADERS** We wouldn't get far without leadership. That's why God gives us pastors, teachers, and others to guide and advise us about our Christian life. If *(continued)*

NOTES

18Pray for us. Our consciences are clear, and we always try to live right. 19I especially want you to pray that I can visit you again soon.

Final Prayers and Greetings

20God gives peace, and he raised our Lord Jesus Christ from death. Now Jesus is like a Great Shepherd whose blood was used to make God's eternal agreement with his flock.[j] 21I pray that God will make you ready to obey him and that you will always be eager to do right. May Jesus help you do what pleases God. To Jesus Christ be glory forever and ever! Amen.*

22My friends, I have written only a short letter to encourage you, and I beg you to pay close attention to what I have said.

23By now you surely must know that our friend Timothy is out of jail. If he gets here in time, I will bring him with me when I come to visit you.

24Please give my greetings to your leaders and to the rest of the Lord's people.

His followers from Italy send you their greetings.

25I pray that God will be kind to all of you![k]

---

[j]*whose blood was used to make God's eternal agreement with his flock*: See 9.18-22. [k]*to all of you!*: Some manuscripts add "Amen."

(*continued*) we don't listen to the earthly leaders God gives us, then we probably won't obey God either. Just like earthly families, we need the spiritual family and the leaders of the church.

13.21 **FAITH IS EAGER TO DO RIGHT** To please God, we are eager to do right. We do right not so we can earn our way into heaven, but because we love God. We know Jesus has saved us, and we are grateful, so we want God to be happy. Saving faith is what makes believers so eager to please.

NOTES

ABOUT THIS LETTER

This is a good example of a general letter, because it is addressed to Christians scattered throughout the Roman empire. Though written as a letter, it is more like a short book of instructions for daily living.

For James faith means action! In fact, the entire book is a series of examples that show faith in action in wise and practical ways.

His advice was clear and to the point: If you are poor, don't despair! Don't give up when your faith is being tested. Don't get angry quickly. Don't favor the rich over the poor. Do good things for others. Control your tongue and desires. Surrender to God and rely on his wisdom. Resist the devil. Don't brag about what you are going to do. If you are rich, use your money to help the poor. Be patient and kind, and pray for those who need God's help.

A QUICK LOOK AT THIS LETTER

1 From James, a servant of God and
of our Lord Jesus Christ. Greetings to the twelve tribes scattered all
over the world.[a]*

Faith and Wisdom

2My friends, be glad, even if you
have a lot of trouble. 3You know that
you learn to endure by having your
faith tested. 4But you must learn to
endure everything, so that you will
be completely mature and not lack-
ing in anything.

5If any of you need wisdom, you
should ask God, and it will be given
to you. God is generous and won't
correct you for asking. 6But when
you ask for something, you must
have faith and not doubt. Anyone
who doubts is like an ocean wave
tossed around in a storm. 7-8If you
are that kind of person, you can't
make up your mind, and you surely
can't be trusted. So don't expect the
Lord to give you anything at all.

Poor People and Rich People

9Any of God's people who are poor
should be glad that he thinks so
highly of them.* 10But any who are
rich should be glad when God makes
them humble. Rich people will disappear like wild flowers 11scorched by
the burning heat of the sun. The flowers lose their blossoms, and their
beauty is destroyed. That is how the
rich will disappear, as they go about
their business.

Trials and Temptations

12God will bless you, if you don't
give up when your faith is being
tested. He will reward you with a glorious life,[b] just as he rewards everyone who loves him.

13Don't blame God when you are
tempted! God cannot be tempted by
evil, and he doesn't use evil to tempt
others. 14We are tempted by our own
desires that drag us off and trap us.
15Our desires make us sin, and when
sin is finished with us, it leaves us
dead.

16Don't be fooled, my dear friends.
17Every good and perfect gift comes
down from the Father who created
all the lights in the heavens. He is
always the same and never makes
dark shadows by changing. 18He
wanted us to be his own special people,[c] and so he sent the true message
to give us new birth.

Hearing and Obeying

19My dear friends, you should be
quick to listen and slow to speak or

---

[a]*twelve tribes scattered all over the world*: James is saying that the Lord's followers are like the tribes of Israel that were scattered everywhere by their enemies. [b]*a glorious life*: The Greek text has "the crown of life." In ancient times an athlete who had won a contest was rewarded with a crown of flowers as a sign of victory. [c]*his own special people*: The Greek text has "the first of his creatures." The Law of Moses taught that the firstborn of all animals and the first part of the harvest were special and belonged to the Lord.

1.1 **WHO WAS JAMES?** This is the James we met personally in Acts 15. Matthew mentions him in his Gospel, chapter 13, verse 35. So the author of this letter is probably the half-brother of Jesus. James was the son of Joseph and Mary; but Jesus is the Son of God, born of Mary. Notice how James calls himself "a servant of God, and our Lord Jesus Christ." He humbly refuses to claim his family tie to Jesus.

1.9 **IT'S OKAY TO BE POOR** Being poor isn't punishment. Jesus was a poor young man who grew up working with his hands. Not having a lot of riches helps us to keep our eyes on the things of God. The fewer possessions Christians have, the more they depend on the Lord. The rich are tempted to trust their wealth and the power it gives them over others. But "you can't take it with you."

NOTES

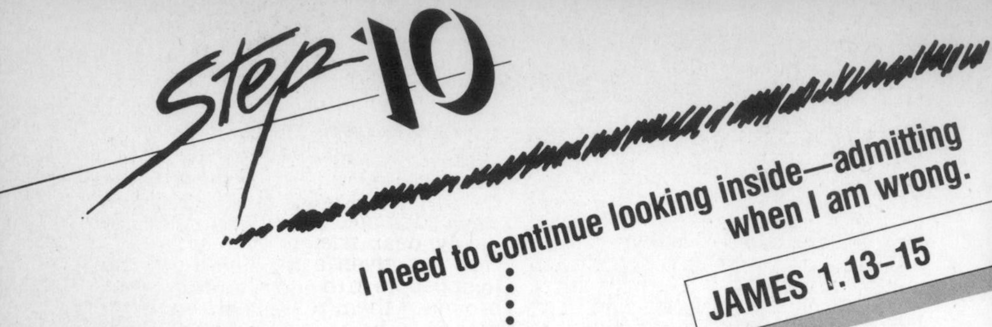

SETTING A TRAP

Ted Bundy, a convicted serial killer, once confessed that his perverted desire for abusive sex began when he was a teenager. He described hiding out in his bedroom to read pornography. From there his desire grew for physical contact, and the horror story of years of brutality and abuse began. We must be careful what we put in our minds. We could very likely to be setting a trap of destruction, thinking for ourselves.

Whatever it is that consumes us—feelings of inadequacy, pornography, drugs, sex, overeating, pride—we have to respect their dangerous power. We were not able to handle their effects on our lives before, and we can't now. Dabbling in things that have messed us up before is even more treacherous the second time around. We have more to lose now because we know what it is like to get straight with God and feel good about ourselves.

STAYING FREE

STEP LOOK INSIDE 10

It is time to get our focus back on God. We need to admit that we are struggling and ask God to help us avoid getting caught in the trap of our old dependencies.

For another "Look Inside," turn to page 499.

to get angry.* 20If you are angry, you cannot do any of the good things that God wants done. 21You must stop doing anything immoral or evil. Instead be humble and accept the message that is planted in you to save you.

22Obey God's message! Don't fool yourselves by just listening to it. 23If you hear the message and don't obey it, you are like people who stare at themselves in a mirror 24and forget what they look like as soon as they leave. 25But you must never stop looking at the perfect law that sets you free. God will bless you in everything you do, if you listen and obey, and don't just hear and forget.*

26If you think you are being religious, but can't control your tongue, you are fooling yourself, and everything you do is useless. 27Religion that pleases God the Father must be pure and spotless. You must help needy orphans and widows and not let this world make you evil.

Warning against Having Favorites

2 My friends, if you have faith in our glorious Lord Jesus Christ, you won't treat some people better than others. 2Suppose a rich person wearing fancy clothes and a gold ring comes to one of your meetings. And suppose a poor person dressed in worn-out clothes also comes. 3You must not give the best seat to the one in fancy clothes and tell the one who is poor to stand at the side or sit on the floor. 4That is the same as saying that some people are better than others, and you would be acting like a crooked judge.

5My dear friends, pay attention. God has given a lot of faith to the poor people in this world. He has also promised them a share in his kingdom that he will give to everyone who loves him. 6You mistreat the poor. But isn't it the rich who boss you around and drag you off to court? 7Aren't they the ones who make fun of your Lord?

8You will do all right, if you obey the most important law[d] in the Scriptures. It is the law that commands us to love others as much as we love ourselves.* 9But if you treat some people better than others, you have done wrong, and the Scriptures teach that you have sinned.

10If you obey every law except one, you are still guilty of breaking them all. 11The same God who told us to be faithful in marriage also told us not to murder. So even if you are faithful in marriage, but murder someone, you still have broken God's Law.

12Speak and act like people who will be judged by the law that sets

---

[d] *most important law*: The Greek text has "royal law," meaning the one given by the king (that is, God).

1.19 **ARE YOU LISTENING?** Solomon wrote in one of his wise sayings that even fools are considered wise if they don't talk much. Or, as you may have heard, "Better to be quiet and be thought a fool, than to open your mouth and remove all doubt." These are strong words but good advice.

1.25 **SHOW AND TELL** Although much talking about religion may deceive others and ourselves, only *doing* impresses God. In his book *The Pilgrim's Progress,* John Bunyan describes a man he calls Talkative. The man bored his listeners with great talk, then came to a bad end because talking was all he could do. We ought to be able to *show* the truth as well as we tell it.

2.8 **WHAT DOES GOD EXPECT?** God doesn't expect the impossible, but love does a lot. We show true love when we are kind to people who may not be able to pay us back. Our love is really working when we care about those closest to us, such as family members. But if we say we're Christians and don't even care about our wives and husbands, then we aren't telling the truth about ourselves.

NOTES

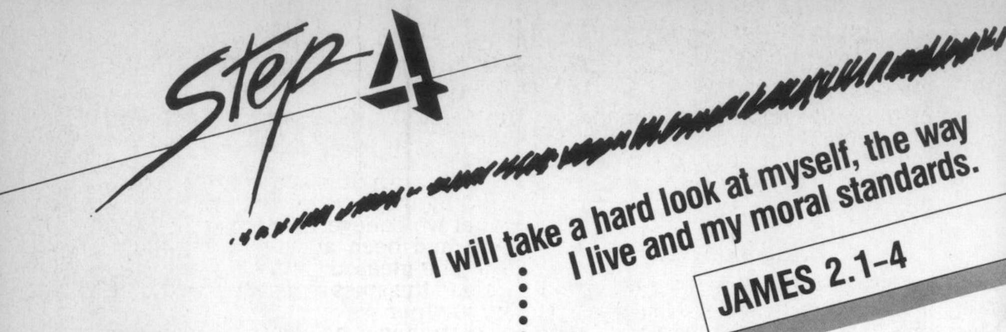

OUT OF FOCUS

"Can you believe what Marianne has on today? You don't wear those shoes with that kind of outfit. And her hair . . . please! I wore mine like that when I was in elementary school! If she wants friends so bad, why doesn't she try looking a little more normal? Everyone has problems on the inside, so why create more for yourself on the outside? How could she be happy looking like that?"

It's funny how we decide whether or not we like someone almost before we talk to them. We size them up by their outward appearance and figure that must be what they are like on the inside. If you look good, you probably are good. If you look bad, well, you get the idea. But sometimes the shoe is on the other foot in life . . . people judge us without knowing us.

GOD'S POINT OF VIEW

The Bible spends a lot of time talking about how God sees people. Looks don't matter, how smart or rich we are doesn't matter, all the outside stuff isn't that important to God. He is interested in what is in our hearts and our thoughts. Our character matters more to God than our qualifications.

Let's think about our relationships. Do we judge people from the outside, never giving them a chance to show us who they really are? Or worse yet, are we among those who feel rejected by others? We have already decided what they will think about us, and we work hard to make that image come true? The chips we carry are so big that no one has the chance to see the real us.

When we get things in focus, we begin to see, from inside out, the good things in other people so they can begin to see them in us too.

For another "Look Inside," turn to page 705.

us free. 13Do this, because on the day
of judgment there will be no pity for
those who have not had pity on others. But even in judgment, God is
merciful![e]

Faith and Works

14My friends, what good is it to say
you have faith, when you don't do
anything to show that you really do
have faith? Can that kind of faith save
you? 15If you know someone who
doesn't have any clothes or food,*
16you shouldn't just say, "I hope all
goes well for you. I hope you will
be warm and have plenty to eat."
What good is it to say this, unless
you do something to help? 17Faith
that doesn't lead us to do good deeds
is all alone and dead!

18Suppose someone disagrees and
says, "It is possible to have faith without doing kind deeds."

I would answer, "Prove that you
have faith without doing kind deeds,
and I will prove that I have faith by
doing them." 19You surely believe
there is only one God. That's fine.
Even demons believe this, and it
makes them shake with fear.

20Does some stupid person want
proof that faith without deeds is useless? 21Well, our ancestor Abraham
pleased God by putting his son Isaac
on the altar to sacrifice him. 22Now
you see how Abraham's faith and
deeds worked together. He proved
that his faith was real by what he
did.* 23This is what the Scriptures
mean by saying, "Abraham had faith
in God, and God was pleased with
him." That's how Abraham became
God's friend.

24You can now see that we please
God by what we do and not only by
what we believe. 25For example, Rahab had been an immoral woman.
But she pleased God when she welcomed the spies and sent them home
by another way.

26Anyone who doesn't breathe is
dead, and faith that doesn't do anything is just as dead!

The Tongue

3 My friends, we should not all try
to become teachers. In fact, teachers will be judged more strictly than
others. 2All of us do many wrong
things. But if you can control your
tongue, you are mature and able to
control your whole body.

3By putting a bit into the mouth
of a horse, we can turn the horse in
different directions. 4It takes strong
winds to move a large sailing ship,
but the captain uses only a small rud-
der to make it go in any direction.
5Our tongues are small too, and yet
they brag about big things.

It takes only a spark to start a forest
fire! 6The tongue is like a spark. It
is an evil power that dirties the rest
of the body and sets a person's entire
life on fire with flames that come
from hell itself.* 7All kinds of

[e] *But even in judgment, God is merciful!*: Or "So be merciful, and you will be shown mercy on the day of judgment."

2.15 **GOOD DEEDS ARE IMPORTANT** Christian faith is not just an "other-worldly" thing. Believers cannot just close their eyes to the needs and suffering of others. Our love toward God must also be love toward others, which shows itself in real acts of kindness.

2.22 **REAL FAITH WORKS** Paul told us in his letter to the Romans that God accepted Abraham because he had faith. That's true. But a living faith doesn't exist all by itself, just as an acorn doesn't exist forever by itself. The acorn either becomes an oak tree, or else it dies. Abraham had faith in God and he acted on that faith. You can see people's faith by the things they do. Like the acorn, faith dies if it doesn't work. But real faith always works.

3.6 **WHERE DO WE GO WRONG?** The tongue causes a lot of mischief for such a small muscle. The tongue's bad words begin with bad thoughts. But if we check those thoughts before *(continued)*

NOTES

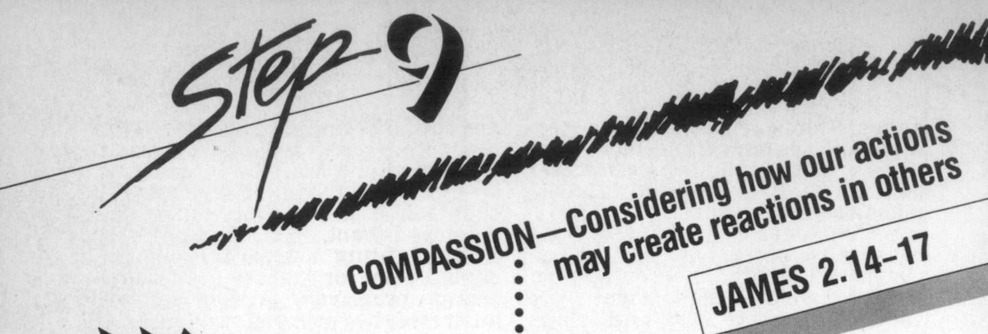

COMPASSION—Considering how our actions may create reactions in others

JAMES 2.14–17

WE HAVE THEM SURROUNDED

A few years ago, the *Times-Reporter* of New Philadelphia, Ohio, reported a celebration that was held at a New Orleans municipal pool. Over two hundred guests gathered, half of whom were certified lifeguards, to celebrate the first summer in memory that no one had drowned in any of the city's many swimming pools.

As the party was breaking up, to their horror they saw a fully clothed body at the bottom of the deep end of the pool. The lifeguards tried their best to revive Jerome Moody, but the thirty-one-year-old man was dead. He had drowned surrounded by a group of lifeguards celebrating their successful season.

It is acceptable to celebrate when we are willing to make things right with those we have wronged. However, compassion compels us to consider how our efforts may affect other people. It can be tragic when we focus on trying to make things right in our life and neglect the negative impact our actions may have on others. Something can appear so right and at the same time pull others under.

Compassion can be summarized in this verse, "If we have all we need and see one of our own people in need, we must have pity on that person, or else we cannot say we love God" (1 John 3.17).

To take a "Look Back" at a man who exhibited compassion, turn to page 145.

animals, birds, reptiles, and sea creatures can be tamed and have been tamed. 8But our tongues get out of control. They are restless and evil, and always spreading deadly poison.

9-10My dear friends, with our tongues we speak both praises and curses. We praise our Lord and Father, and we curse people who were created to be like God, and this is not right. 11Can clean water and dirty water both flow from the same spring? 12Can a fig tree produce olives or a grapevine produce figs? Does fresh water come from a well full of salt water?

Wisdom from Above

13Are any of you wise or sensible? Then show it by living right and by being humble and wise in everything you do.* 14But if your heart is full of bitter jealousy and selfishness, don't brag or lie to cover up the truth. 15That kind of wisdom doesn't come from above. It is earthly and selfish and comes from the devil himself. 16Whenever people are jealous or selfish, they cause trouble and do all sorts of cruel things. 17But the wisdom that comes from above leads us to be pure, friendly, gentle, sensible, kind, helpful, genuine, and sincere. 18When peacemakers plant seeds of peace, they will harvest justice.

Friendship with the World

4 Why do you fight and argue with each other? Isn't it because you are full of selfish desires that fight to control your body? 2You want something you don't have, and you will do anything to get it. You will even kill! But you still cannot get what you want, and you won't get it by fighting and arguing. You should pray for it. 3Yet even when you do pray, your prayers are not answered, because you pray just for selfish reasons.

4You people aren't faithful to God! Don't you know that if you love the world, you are God's enemies? And if you decide to be a friend of the world, you make yourself an enemy of God.* 5Do you doubt the Scriptures that say, "God truly cares about the Spirit he has put in us"?[f] 6In fact, God treats us with even greater kindness, just as the Scriptures say,

"God opposes everyone
who is proud,
but he is kind to everyone
who is humble."

7Surrender to God! Resist the devil, and he will run from you. 8Come near to God, and he will come near to you. Clean up your lives, you sinners. Purify your hearts, you people who can't make up your mind. 9Be sad and sorry and weep. Stop laughing and start crying. Be gloomy instead of glad. 10Be humble in the Lord's presence, and he will honor you.

---

[f]*God truly cares about the Spirit he has put in us*: The meaning of the Greek text is unclear, and other translations are possible, such as, "The Spirit that God put in us truly cares."

(*continued*) they become words, then the wrong words don't come out. Notice that bad words are often the beginning of bad actions. Before we speak let's ask, "Does this remark honor God, and will it really help those who hear me?"

3.13 **WHAT IS WISDOM?** Wisdom isn't just the ability to amaze people with our clever talk. Wisdom reflects God's own life at work in us. This wisdom results in actions that bring peace and happiness to those around us. That which gives glory to God and love to others is truly wise.

4.4 **ARE YOU "A FRIEND OF THE WORLD"?** James surely doesn't want us to think we shouldn't be friendly. If a Christian is anything, he is certainly a friend. But James is speaking about being friendly to the ways of the evil world system which people have made. Christians should want to avoid and discourage everything that is evil in the world.

NOTES

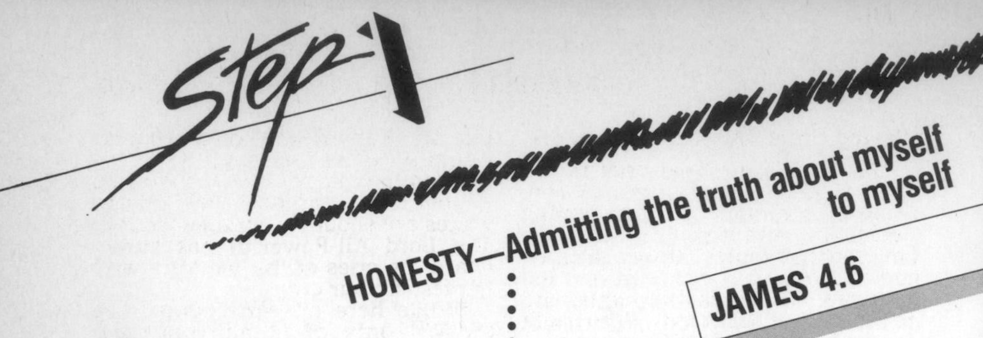

ON MY OWN

I don't like being told what to do. It makes me feel like I'm not in control of my life. It's like being a child again. My parents have rules. The school has rules. Even my so-called friends want to decide what is right or wrong for me. So I tuned out. Who needs them anyway? I want to live my life for me!

What a mistake! Now I see I wasn't being controlled by other people, but by my own selfishness. It determined my relationships, my actions, and my attitudes. Pretty soon all I had left was me. I discovered that wasn't enough. I do need others.

GOD REALLY CARES

God didn't create me to make it alone. I need his love. When I let go and receive his love, I find it works out pretty good. God has something in common with me. He thinks a lot of me too!

For another "Look Ahead," turn to page 631.

Saying Cruel Things about Others

11My friends, don't say cruel things
about others! If you do, or if you condemn others, you are condemning
God's Law. And if you condemn the
Law, you put yourself above the Law
and refuse to obey either it 12or God
who gave it. God is our judge, and
he can save or destroy us. What right
do you have to condemn anyone?

Warning against Bragging

13You should know better than to
say, "Today or tomorrow we'll go to
the city. We'll do business there for
a year and make a lot of money!"*
14What do you know about tomorrow? How can you be so sure about
your life? It is nothing more than mist
that appears for only a little while
before it disappears. 15You should
say, "If the Lord lets us live, we will
do these things." 16Yet you are stupid
enough to brag, and it is wrong to
be so proud. 17If you don't do what
you know is right, you have sinned.

Warning to the Rich

5 You rich people should cry and
weep! Terrible things are going
to happen to you.* 2Your treasures
have already rotted, and moths have
eaten your clothes. 3Your money has
rusted, and the rust will be evidence
against you, as it burns your body
like fire. Yet you keep on storing up
wealth in these last days. 4You refused to pay the people who worked
in your fields, and now their unpaid
wages are shouting out against you.
The Lord All-Powerful has surely
heard the cries of the workers who
harvested your crops.
5While here on earth, you have
thought only of filling your own
stomachs and having a good time.
But now you are like fat cattle on
their way to be butchered. 6You have
condemned and murdered innocent
people, who couldn't even fight back.

Be Patient and Kind

7My friends, be patient until the
Lord returns. Think of farmers who
wait patiently for the spring and summer rains to make their valuable
crops grow.* 8Be patient like those
farmers and don't give up. The Lord
will soon be here! 9Don't grumble
about each other or you will be
judged, and the judge is right outside
the door.
10My friends, follow the example
of the prophets who spoke for the
Lord. They were patient, even when
they had to suffer. 11In fact, we praise
the ones who endured the most. You
remember how patient Job was and
how the Lord finally helped him. The
Lord did this because he is so merciful and kind.

4.13 **PUT YOUR LIFE IN GOD'S HANDS** We're asking for disappointment and misery when we imagine we can control our futures. Only God is in charge of what is to be. We do well to make wise plans, but let's give those plans to God and let him decide what is best. We may plan our way, but God actually directs our steps.

5.1 **WE MUST ACCOUNT FOR OUR WEALTH** God has entrusted some of us with more money than others. That means he expects us to use our wealth for his glory and the good of others. If we hoard our money, and even cheat people out of what we owe them, that is a very bad sign about our relationship with God. He sees our greed, and religion can't cover it up.

5.7 **PATIENTLY WAIT FOR JESUS** The Lord will return, maybe in our own lifetimes, and we should wait patiently for him. But that waiting shouldn't be a *do-nothing* kind of waiting, but a *do-something* kind. The farmer who waits for the rain to make things grow is not just sitting around. There is a lot of work to be done daily. Let's get busy. Jesus has left us much with which to occupy ourselves until he comes.

NOTES

12My friends, above all else, don't
take an oath. You must not swear
by heaven or by earth or by anything
else. "Yes" or "No" is all you need
to say. If you say anything more, you
will be condemned.
13If you are having trouble, you
should pray. And if you are feeling
good, you should sing praises.
14If you are sick, ask the church leaders[g] to come and pray for you. Ask
them to put olive oil[h] on you in the
name of the Lord. 15If you have faith
when you pray for sick people, they
will get well. The Lord will heal them,
and if they have sinned, he will forgive them.

16If you have sinned, you should
tell each other what you have done.
Then you can pray for one another
and be healed. The prayer of an innocent person is powerful, and it can
help a lot.* 17Elijah was just as human
as we are, and for three and a half
years his prayers kept the rain from
falling. 18But when he did pray for
rain, it fell from the skies and made
the crops grow.
19My friends, if any followers have
wandered away from the truth, you
should try to lead them back. 20If
you turn sinners from the wrong way,
you will save them from death, and
many of their sins will be forgiven.

---

[g]*church leaders*: Or "elders" or "presbyters" or "priests." [h]*olive oil*: The Jewish people used olive oil for healing.

5.16 **PRAYER WORKS** We should pray for the needs of our brothers and sisters in Christ. If anyone is sick or has a problem with sin, they should share their need for healing. Then Christians can join together in prayer. God has promised to hear our prayers and honor them according to his love and wisdom.

NOTES

Step 5

I will admit to God, to myself, and to someone I trust what I do wrong.

JAMES 5.16

KEEPING SHORT ACCOUNTS

One brick at a time. That's how the house next door was being built. The bricklayers would pick up a brick, spread mortar across it like buttering a sandwich, and then edge it into place next to the others. Brick after brick, row after row, and pretty soon a wall had been built.

That is how it is in our lives. We let anger, resentment, guilt, fears, lies, wrong actions—the negatives—build up in our lives. Then when we don't deal with them, little by little, one mistake at a time, a wall goes up. Maybe it's between us and our parents, teachers, or friends. Worse yet, it could be a wall between us and God.

STEP LOOK INSIDE 5

MAKING IT RIGHT

Keeping short accounts with problems simply means we make right any wrong before it has time to settle in. If we don't, it's like building the house: the mortar hardens. Instead of adjusting one brick, the whole wall has to be broken down to make it right. When we let someone we trust know what is happening in our lives, when we are up-front and honest, then we are working toward building a life that is solid and strong.

For another "Look Inside," turn to page 502.

PETER'S FIRST LETTER

ABOUT THIS LETTER

In this letter Peter has much to say about suffering. He shows how it can be a way of serving the Lord, of sharing the faith, and of being tested. The letter was written to Christians scattered all over the northern part of Asia Minor. In this part of the Roman empire many Christians had already suffered unfair treatment from people who did not believe in Jesus. And they could expect to suffer even more.

Peter was quick to offer encouragement. His letter reminds the readers that some of the Lord's followers may have to go through times of hard testing. But this should make them glad, Peter declares, because it will strengthen their faith and bring them honor on the day when Jesus Christ returns (1.6,7).

Peter reminds them that Christ suffered here on earth, and when his followers suffer for doing right they are sharing his sufferings (2.18–25; 4.12–17). In fact, Christians should expect to suffer for their faith (3.8—4.19).

But because of who God is and because of what God has done by raising Jesus Christ from death, Christians can have hope in the future. Just as Christ suffered before he received honor from God, so will Christians be tested by suffering before they receive honor when the Lord returns. Peter uses poetic language to remind his readers of what Christ has done:

Christ died once for our sins.
An innocent person died
for those who are guilty.
Christ did this
to bring you to God,
when his body
was put to death
and his spirit
was made alive.
(3.18)

A QUICK LOOK AT THIS LETTER

1. Greetings and Prayer (1.1,2)
2. A Real Reason for Hope (1.3–12)
3. Living as God's Holy People (1.13—2.17)
4. The Example of Christ's Suffering (2.18–25)
5. Being a Christian and Suffering (3.1—4.19)
6. Advice for Church Leaders (5.1–11)
7. Final Greetings (5.12–14)

1 From Peter, an apostle of Jesus
Christ.
To God's people who are scattered
like foreigners in Pontus, Galatia,
Cappadocia, Asia, and Bithynia.
2God the Father decided to choose
you as his people, and his Spirit has
made you holy. You have obeyed Jesus Christ and are sprinkled with his
blood.[a]
I pray that God will be kind to you
and will keep on giving you peace!*

A Real Reason for Hope

3Praise God, the Father of our Lord
Jesus Christ. God is so good, and by
raising Jesus from death, he has
given us new life and a hope that lives
on. 4God has something stored up for
you in heaven, where it will never
decay or be ruined or disappear.
5You have faith in God, whose
power will protect you until the last
day.[b] Then he will save you, just as
he has always planned to do. 6On that
day you will be glad, even if you have
to go through many hard trials for
a while. 7Your faith will be like gold
that has been tested in a fire. And
these trials will prove that your faith
is worth much more than gold that
can be destroyed. They will show that
you will be given praise and honor
and glory when Jesus Christ returns.
8You have never seen Jesus, and
you don't see him now. But still you
love him and have faith in him, and
no words can tell how glad and
happy* 9you are to be saved. That's
why you have faith.
10Some prophets told how kind
God would be to you, and they
searched hard to find out more about
the way you would be saved. 11The
Spirit of Christ was in them and was
telling them how Christ would suffer
and would then be given great honor.
So they searched to find out exactly
who Christ would be and when this
would happen. 12But they were told
that they were serving you and not
themselves. They preached to you by
the power of the Holy Spirit, who was
sent from heaven. And their message
was only for you, even though angels
would like to know more about it.

Chosen to Live a Holy Life

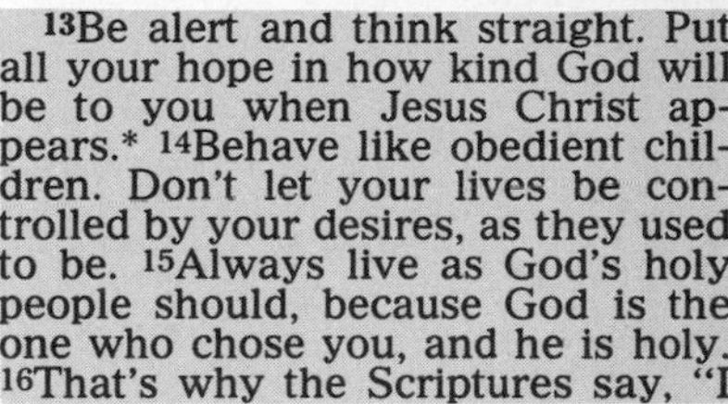

13Be alert and think straight. Put
all your hope in how kind God will
be to you when Jesus Christ appears.* 14Behave like obedient children. Don't let your lives be controlled by your desires, as they used
to be. 15Always live as God's holy
people should, because God is the
one who chose you, and he is holy.
16That's why the Scriptures say, "I

---

[a]*sprinkled with his blood*: According to Exodus 24.3-8 the people of Israel were sprinkled with the blood of cows to show they would keep their agreement with God. Peter says that it is the blood of Jesus that seals the agreement between God and his people. See Hebrews 9.18-21. [b]*the last day*: When God will judge all people.

1.2 **CHRISTIANS ARE CHOSEN** It's good to know that God has chosen every person who has faith in him. We did not force ourselves on God, but he selected each believer personally. Surely God will never forget any of us. We are his by his own will.

1.8 **WE LOVE A SAVIOR WE HAVE NEVER SEEN** We have never looked on the face of Jesus. In fact the Bible says very little about what he looked like on earth. Yet we can know Jesus even better than we know anyone else. Jesus is alive, and he is as close to us as it is possible to be.

1.13 **THINKING STRAIGHT** Before we were saved our thoughts were crooked. For one thing, we were always "cutting corners" to get away from God and to avoid confessing our sins. We tried to cover up by satisfying ourselves with a lifestyle that would only lead to ruin. But we started to think straight when we began seeing ourselves from God's point of view. We started thinking God's thoughts, according to his way of looking at things.

NOTES

IT'S OKAY

I will probably never have a date again! When Richard gets finished telling everyone about our date, it will be hands off. I can already hear the "nun" jokes. I am doomed to spend the rest of my life at home, but that's okay. Even if I have to play games with my parents on Friday nights until I'm 40, I can do that. I would rather like myself than be another notch on Rich Wallace's belt. I did what was right. I know I did. Well, I might as well go downstairs and get out the game.

"**L**isa, it's the phone. Richard Wallace wants to know if you are busy tonight."

SETTING LIMITS

It takes courage to set limits. Making right choices and standing up for what God says about morals is not an easy thing to do. Sometimes we risk relationships that are important to us. But we can trust God. He knows what and *who* is best for us.

To take a "Look Back" at a man who showed tremendous courage and risked it all for Christ, turn to page 234.

am the holy God, and you must be
holy too."
17You say that God is your Father,
but God does not have favorites! He
judges all people by what they do.
So you must honor God while you
live as strangers here on earth.
18You were rescued[c] from the useless
way of life that you learned from your
ancestors. But you know that you
were not rescued by such things as
silver or gold that don't last forever.
19You were rescued by the precious
blood of Christ, that spotless and innocent lamb. 20Christ was chosen
even before the world was created,
but because of you, he did not come
until these last days. 21And when he
did come, it was to lead you to have
faith in God, who raised him from
death and honored him in a glorious
way. That's why you have put your
faith and hope in God.
22You obeyed the truth,[d] and your
souls were made pure. Now you sincerely love each other. But you must
keep on loving with all your heart.
23Do this because God has given you
new birth by his message that lives
on forever. 24The Scriptures say,

"Humans wither like grass,
and their glory fades
like wild flowers.
Grass dries up,
and flowers fall
to the ground.*
25But what the Lord has said
will stand forever."

Our good news to you is what the
Lord has said.

A Living Stone and a Holy Nation

2 Stop being hateful! Quit trying to
fool people, and start being sincere. Don't be jealous or say cruel
things about others. 2Be like new-
born babies who are thirsty for the
pure spiritual milk that will help you
grow and be saved. 3You have already found out how good the Lord
really is.
4Come to Jesus Christ. He is the
living stone that people have rejected, but which God has chosen and
highly honored.* 5And now you are
living stones that are being used to
build a spiritual house. You are also
a group of holy priests, and with the
help of Jesus Christ you will offer
sacrifices that please God. 6It is just
as God says in the Scriptures,

"Look! I am placing in Zion
a choice and precious
cornerstone.
No one who has faith
in that one
will be disappointed."

7You are followers of the Lord, and
that stone is precious to you. But it
isn't precious to those who refuse to
follow him. They are the builders
who tossed aside the stone that
turned out to be the most important
one of all. 8They disobeyed the message and stumbled and fell over that
stone, because they were doomed.
9But you are God's chosen and special people. You are a group of royal
priests and a holy nation. God has
brought you out of darkness into his
marvelous light. Now you must tell
all the wonderful things that he has
done. The Scriptures say,

10"Once you were nobody.
Now you are God's people.
At one time no one
had pity on you.

---

[c] *rescued*: The Greek word often, though not always, means payment of a price to free a slave or prisoner.
[d] *You obeyed the truth*: Some manuscripts add "by the power of the Spirit."

1.24 **GOD'S WORD NEVER FAILS** Today's hot news is tomorrow's waste paper, but the word of God is just as fresh today as the day it was written down. The Bible stands forever, inspired by God himself, telling us the truth about the past, the present, and the future.

2.4 **BE A LIVING STONE** God doesn't live in buildings of brick and stone. But God is building a great living house to dwell in. That house is made up of people who love Christ and have built their lives on him. Christ is the living foundation of that great house of God. He wants to live in us forever.

NOTES

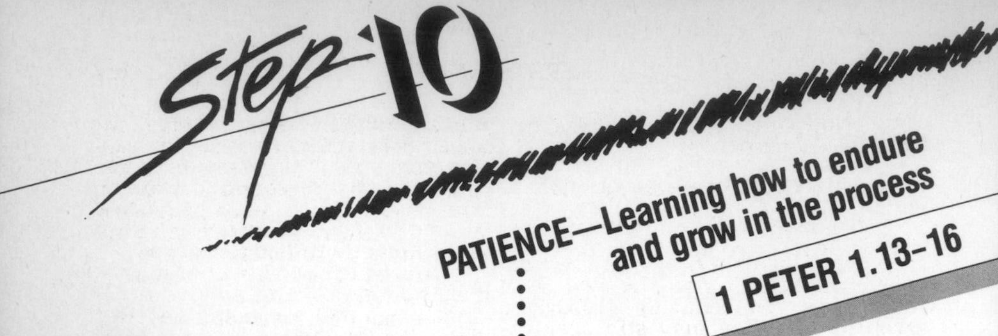

DISAPPOINTMENTS

We started out early so we could catch the sun coming up over the edge of the mountain. Hiking in the dim morning light is difficult, but the view was going to be worth it.

I had been looking forward to this weekend. It would be the first one since school started that I didn't have to work. We packed up the night before and drove three hours to reach the trail that leads to Abram's Peak.

I was the first one awake. My buddies and I had had this planned for a long time. I wasn't about to miss one minute of it. It was slow going in the dark, but if we timed it right, we expected to reach the Peak just as the sun rose. Just over this hill and . . . fog! It was so thick you could hardly see two feet in front of you. There wouldn't be a view of anything but the back of your hand that morning. What a disappointment!

STEP LOOK AHEAD 10

PRESS ON

Do we feel that way sometimes? We have everything planned and are headed for some peak in life when unexpectedly the fog rolls in and keeps us from being able to see. What was so clear is muddied by poor judgment, misunderstandings with others, or a step back to old ways of doing things. We think, "Lord, we were going to get it so right this time, but we blew it again." You know what? God knows we will take steps back in life. That's why he promised not only to go before us, but to follow behind when we need help getting back on track.

Keep pressing on! The view of our lives lived God's way is worth seeing.

To take a "Look Back" at a servant who learned through his trials and remained faithful until the end, turn to page 441.

Now God has treated you
with kindness.

Live as God's Servants Should

11Dear friends, you are foreigners
and strangers on this earth. So I beg
you not to surrender to those desires
that fight against you. 12Always let
others see you behaving properly,
even though they may still accuse
you of doing wrong. Then on the day
of judgment they will honor God by
telling the good things they saw you
do.

13The Lord wants you to obey all
human authorities, especially the
Emperor, who rules over everyone.*
14You must also obey governors, because they are sent by the Emperor
to punish criminals and to praise
good citizens. 15God wants you to silence stupid and ignorant people by
doing right. 16You are free, but still
you are God's servants, and you must
not use your freedom as an excuse
for doing wrong. 17Respect everyone
and show special love for God's people. Honor God and respect the
Emperor.

The Example of Christ's Suffering

18Servants, you must obey your
masters and always show respect to
them. Do this, not only to those who
are kind and thoughtful, but also to
those who are cruel. 19God will bless
you, even if others treat you unfairly
for being loyal to him.* 20You don't
gain anything by being punished for
some wrong you have done. But God
will bless you, if you have to suffer
for doing something good. 21After all,
God chose you to suffer as you follow
in the footsteps of Christ, who set
an example by suffering for you.

22Christ did not sin
or ever tell a lie.
23Although he was abused,
he never tried to get even.
And when he suffered,
he made no threats.
Instead, he had faith in God,
who judges fairly.
24Christ carried the burden
of our sins.
He was nailed to the cross,
so that we would stop sinning
and start living right.
By his cuts and bruises
you are healed.
25You had wandered away
like sheep.
Now you have returned
to the one
who is your shepherd
and protector.

Wives and Husbands

3 If you are a wife, you must put
your husband first. Even if he opposes our message, you will win him
over by what you do. No one else
will have to say anything to him,*
2because he will see how you honor
God and live a pure life. 3Don't depend on things like fancy hairdos or

2.13 **LET'S BE LAW-ABIDING CITIZENS** Christians have less at stake in this world than others. Our main citizenship is in the kingdom of God. Yet Christians should be known as people who obey the laws of the land they live in. Many people who don't know Jesus are always in trouble with the law. But we will give ourselves and Christ a good name by our law-abiding lifestyle.

2.19 **LIFE ISN'T ALWAYS FAIR** If we're not careful, we may resent being treated badly in the world. That very resentment can hurt our souls. The world isn't always fair, but it wasn't fair to Jesus when it nailed him to a cross. The world is just "doing its thing" when it is being unfair to Christians. The world is not neutral—people either love Christ or they hate him. That means they must either love or hate Christ's people too.

3.1 **WHO WILL BE FIRST?** In these days there is a lot of quiet quarreling, and some not so quiet, about who will be given first place in society and in the home. That conflict is one way *(continued)*

NOTES

gold jewelry or expensive clothes to
make you look beautiful. 4Be beautiful in your heart by being gentle and
quiet. This kind of beauty will last,
and God considers it very special.
5Long ago those women who worshiped God and put their hope in
him made themselves beautiful by
putting their husbands first. 6For example, Sarah obeyed Abraham and
called him her master. You are her
true children, if you do right and
don't let anything frighten you.
7If you are a husband, you should
be thoughtful of your wife. Treat her
with honor, because she is not as
strong as you are, and she shares
with you in the gift of life. Then nothing will stand in the way of your
prayers.

Suffering for Doing Right

8Finally, all of you should agree
and have concern and love for each
other. You should also be kind and
humble. 9Don't be hateful and insult
people just because they are hateful
and insult you. Instead, treat everyone with kindness. You are God's
chosen ones, and he will bless you.
The Scriptures say,*

10"Do you really love life?
Do you want to be happy?
Then stop saying cruel things
and quit telling lies.
11Give up your evil ways
and do right,
as you find and follow
the road that leads
to peace.
12The Lord watches over
everyone who obeys him,
and he listens
to their prayers.
But he opposes everyone
who does evil."

13Can anyone really harm you for
being eager to do good deeds?
14Even if you have to suffer for doing
good things, God will bless you. So
stop being afraid and don't worry
about what people might do. 15Honor
Christ and let him be the Lord of your
life.

Always be ready to give an answer
when someone asks you about your
hope.* 16Give a kind and respectful
answer and keep your conscience
clear. This way you will make people
ashamed for saying bad things about
your good conduct as a follower of
Christ. 17You are better off to obey
God and suffer for doing right than
to suffer for doing wrong.

18Christ died once for our sins.
An innocent person died
for those who are guilty.
Christ did this
to bring you to God,
when his body
was put to death
and his spirit
was made alive.

19Christ then preached to the spirits that were being kept in prison.
20They had disobeyed God while
Noah was building the boat, but God
had been patient with them. Eight
people went into that boat and were
brought safely through the flood.
21Those flood waters were like

(continued) in which Satan can destroy our happiness. It's good that as Christians we don't have to worry about being first and "getting ours" in this world.

3.9 **CHRISTIANS CAN BE POLITE** Sometimes people who believe in Christ are a little rude the way they witness for him. As the saying goes, "you catch more flies with honey than with vinegar." It's nice to be important, but it's more important to be nice. Courtesy costs nothing, and it goes a long way toward gaining attention for the good news about Jesus.

3.15 **BE READY TO ANSWER** We shouldn't be trying to start a debate wherever we go—but we ought to be ready to answer questions. It's sad when Christians can't explain what Jesus has done for us. We need to be able to tell the good news about Jesus to another person any time we're called on to do so.

NOTES

Step 12

Because God is changing my life through following these steps, I will tell others about them and daily practice what I have learned.

1 PETER 3.15–17

SPEAK UP!

"**N**o? You don't want a drink? What gives? I can't believe this. Hey everyone! I have an announcement to make. Our friend and all-around good buddy, Jeff Candler, has lost it! He has just turned down the first drink of his life. The only thing I can figure is that he's having brain surgery tomorrow and isn't supposed to have anything to eat or drink. We knew sooner or later they'd get you for that lobotomy, Jeff!"

We can be sure it's going to happen. People will notice the changes God's been making in our lives, and we will get one of two reactions. They will encourage us, or they will ridicule us. Either way, God's Word says we should see their reactions as opportunities to tell others how God can make a difference in their lives. We probably think that's a lot easier said than done.

STEP LOOK INSIDE 12

SOMETHING TO SAY

But what has been easy? With God's help, we have worked hard to recover from the negative dependencies in our lives; and with his help, we will continue to make it. We have something to say now that others need to hear—so we should speak up!

For another "Look Inside," turn to page 495.

baptism that now saves you. But baptism is more than just washing your body. It means turning to God with a clear conscience, because Jesus Christ was raised from death. 22Christ is now in heaven, where he sits at the right side[e] of God. All angels, authorities, and powers are under his control.

Being Faithful to God

4 Christ suffered here on earth. Now you must be ready to suffer as he did, because suffering shows that you have stopped sinning.* 2It means you have turned from your own desires and want to obey God for the rest of your life. 3You have already lived long enough like people who don't know God. You were immoral and followed your evil desires. You went around drinking and partying and carrying on. In fact, you even worshiped disgusting idols. 4Now your former friends wonder why you have stopped running around with them, and they curse you for it. 5But they will have to answer to God, who judges the living and the dead. 6The good news has even been preached to the dead,[f] so that after they have been judged for what they have done in this life, their spirits will live with God.

7Everything will soon come to an end. So be serious and be sensible enough to pray.

8Most important of all, you must sincerely love each other, because love wipes away many sins.

9Welcome people into your home and don't grumble about it.

10Each of you has been blessed with one of God's many wonderful gifts to be used in the service of others. So use your gift well.* 11If you have the gift of speaking, preach God's message. If you have the gift of helping others, do it with the strength that God supplies. Everything should be done in a way that will bring honor to God because of Jesus Christ, who is glorious and powerful forever. Amen.

Suffering for Being a Christian

12Dear friends, don't be surprised or shocked that you are going through testing that is like walking through fire. 13Be glad for the chance to suffer as Christ suffered. It will prepare you for even greater happiness when he makes his glorious return.

14Count it a blessing when you suffer for being a Christian. This shows that God's glorious Spirit is with you.* 15But you deserve to suffer if you are a murderer, a thief, a crook,

---

[e] *right side*: The place of honor and power.
[f] *the dead*: Either people who died after becoming followers of Christ or the people of Noah's day (3.19).

4.1 **FORMER FRIENDS** Christians need to be ready to suffer for the sake of Jesus. Here's a warning: our enemies might be people we once counted as friends. Sometimes unsaved people are bitter when a friend turns to Jesus. They might not feel comfortable around the saved person. They might not be happy to know they are sinners who need Jesus too. But keep praying—many of them get saved later.

4.10 **WHAT IS YOUR GIFT?** Peter repeats what Paul also says about Christian gifts. Note that Peter says these gifts are for serving others. When you use your gift from God, then people are blessed and God is honored in the world. How do you serve others with your gifts?

4.14 **SUFFER FOR A GOOD REASON** Again we see that life isn't always fair. Christians often suffer for their goodness. The godless world is jealous of our happiness in Christ. But be sure you're not suffering because of faults in your behavior. A pure Christian life of love and kindness produces a clear conscience that can help us bear much trouble.

NOTES

Step 11

ENDURANCE—Developing inward strength by daily dependence on God

1 PETER 4.10, 11

GETTING IT TOGETHER

She picked up her jacket and walked off, just like that. I don't know what got into her. The coach is always riding us. But this time she took it personally and started ranting and raving that she was the best player and if it weren't for her there wouldn't be a team. Then she called the coach several choice names and left the court.

I'll admit the pressure can get to you. There are times I feel the same way. I want to throw in the towel and quit too. But I made a commitment to ten other people when I joined this team. We decided to work together and do the best we could to win. And the only way to do that is to get our act together and keep it that way.

QUITTING POINTS

We will face quitting points in our lives. But when we crash through them, God gives us the strength to endure. Anyone can quit. We begin to mature when we hang in there.

To take a "Look Back" at a young man who learned endurance and became strong through daily dependence, turn to page 432.

or a busybody. 16Don't be ashamed
to suffer for being a Christian. Praise
God that you belong to him. 17God
has already begun judging his own
people. And if his judgment begins
with us, imagine how terrible it will
be for those who refuse to obey his
message. The Scriptures say,

18"If good people barely escape,
what will happen to sinners
and to others
who don't respect God?"

19If you suffer for obeying God, you
must have complete faith in your
faithful Creator and keep on doing
right.

Helping Christian Leaders

5 Church leaders,[g] I am writing to
encourage you. I too am a leader,
as well as a witness to Christ's suffering, and I will share in his glory when
it is shown to us.*

2Just as shepherds watch over their
sheep, you must watch over everyone
God has placed in your care. Do it
willingly in order to please God, and
not simply because you think you
must. Let it be something you want
to do, instead of something you do
merely to make money. 3Don't be
bossy to those people who are in your
care, but set an example for them.
4Then when Christ the Chief Shepherd returns, you will be given a
crown that will never lose its glory.

5All of you young people should
obey your elders. In fact, everyone
should be humble toward everyone
else. The Scriptures say,

"God opposes proud people,
but he helps everyone
who is humble."

6Be humble in the presence of
God's mighty power, and he will
honor you when the time comes.
7God cares for you, so turn all your
worries over to him.

8Be on your guard and stay awake.
Your enemy, the devil, is like a roaring lion, sneaking around to find
someone to attack. 9But you must resist the devil and stay strong in your
faith. You know that all over the
world the Lord's followers are suffering just as you are. 10But God shows
kindness to everyone. That's why he
had Christ Jesus choose you to share
in his eternal glory. You will suffer
for a while, but God will make you
complete, steady, strong, and firm.*
11God will be in control forever!
Amen.

Final Greetings

12Silvanus helped me write this
short letter, and I consider him a
faithful follower of the Lord. I wanted
to encourage you and tell you how
kind God really is, so that you will
keep on having faith in him.

13Greetings from the Lord's followers in Babylon.[h] They are God's chosen ones.

Mark, who is like a son to me, sends
his greetings too.

14Give each other a warm greeting.
I pray that God will give peace to
everyone who belongs to Christ.[i]

---

[g] *Church leaders*: Or "Elders" or "Presbyters" or "Priests." [h] *Babylon*: This may be a secret name for the city of Rome. [i] Christ: Some manuscripts add "Amen."

5.1 **WHERE HAS GOD PLACED YOU?** Are you a mechanic, a student, or perhaps a teacher? Let those around you know it is your greatest pleasure to be doing what God has assigned to you. Are you a young person? Use this time of your life to learn from others who have gone before you. God looks for people who are serious and sincere workers for him.

5.10 **GOD CARES FOR YOU** If you can remember at all times that *God cares*, life will not discourage you. The Lord is in charge of your life, and he knows about everything that comes your way. The key to happiness in this world is *trust*. You'll see that God always makes a way through every problem, even if the way is sometimes hard to see or a long time in coming.

NOTES

PETER'S SECOND LETTER

ABOUT THIS LETTER

The writer of this letter wants the readers to know that Christians must live in a way that pleases God (1.3) and hold firmly to the truth they were given (1.12).

He warns them that false prophets and teachers had entered the Christian community and were trying to lead the Lord's followers away from the truth. But they will be punished for their evil deeds (2.1–22). When false teachers are at work, Christians must stick to their faith and be examples for others of right living. They must have understanding, self-control and patience, and they should show love for God and all people.

The readers must never forget that the Lord's return is certain, no matter what others may say (3.1–18):

> *Don't forget that for the Lord one day is the same as a thousand years, and a thousand years is the same as one day. The Lord isn't slow about keeping his promises, as some people think he is. In fact, God is patient, because he wants everyone to turn from sin and no one to be lost.* (3.8,9)

A QUICK LOOK AT THIS LETTER

1. Greetings and Prayer (1.1,2)
2. How the Lord's Followers Should Live (1.3–15)
3. The Glory of Christ (1.16–21)
4. False Prophets and Teachers (2.1–22)
5. The Lord's Return Is Certain (3.1–18)

1 From Simon Peter, a servant and
an apostle of Jesus Christ. To
everyone who shares with us in the
privilege of believing that our God
and Savior Jesus Christ will do what
is just and fair.[a]
2I pray that God will be kind to
you and will let you live in perfect
peace! May you keep learning more
and more about God and our Lord
Jesus.

[a] *To everyone who . . . just and fair*: Or "To everyone whose faith in the justice and fairness of our God and Savior Jesus Christ is as precious as our own faith."

Living as the Lord's Followers Should

3We have everything we need to live a life that pleases God. It was all given to us by God's own power, when we learned that he had invited us to share in his wonderful goodness. 4God made great and marvelous promises, so that his nature would become part of us. Then we could escape our evil desires and the corrupt influences of this world.*

5Do your best to improve your faith. You can do this by adding goodness, understanding, 6self-control, patience, devotion to God, 7concern for others, and love. 8If you keep growing in this way, it will show that what you know about our Lord Jesus Christ has made your lives useful and meaningful. 9But if you don't grow, you are like someone who is nearsighted or blind, and you have forgotten that your past sins are forgiven.

10My friends, you must do all you can to show that God has really chosen and selected you. If you keep on doing this, you won't stumble and fall. 11Then our Lord and Savior Jesus Christ will give you a glorious welcome into his kingdom that will last forever.

12You are holding firmly to the truth that you were given. But I am still going to remind you of these things. 13In fact, I think I should keep on reminding you until I leave this body. 14And our Lord Jesus Christ has already told me that I will soon leave it behind. 15That is why I am doing my best to make sure that each of you remembers all of this after I am gone.

The Message about the Glory of Christ

16When we told you about the power and the return of our Lord Jesus Christ, we were not telling clever stories that someone had made up. But with our own eyes we saw his true greatness. 17God, our great and wonderful Father, truly honored him by saying, "This is my own dear Son, and I am pleased with him." 18We were there with Jesus on the holy mountain and heard this voice speak from heaven.

19All of this makes us even more certain that what the prophets said is true. So you should pay close attention to their message, as you would to a lamp shining in some dark place. You must keep on paying attention until daylight comes and the morning star rises in your hearts.* 20But you need to realize that no one alone can understand any of the prophecies in the Scriptures. 21The prophets did not think these things up on their own, but they were guided by the Spirit of God.

False Prophets and Teachers

2 Sometimes false prophets spoke to the people of Israel. False teachers will also sneak in and speak harmful lies to you. But these teachers don't really belong to the Master who paid a great price for them, and they will quickly destroy themselves. 2Many people will follow their evil

1.4 **GOD HIMSELF LIVES IN US** Some religions are just a set of ideas. But Christians aren't merely religious people who hold certain opinions about God that they can't be sure about. God himself comes to live in us. We know him by personal experience. Because God reveals himself to us by the Holy Spirit in us, we are changed more and more to be like him.

1.19 **FOLLOW THE LIGHT** Peter tells us the word of God is like a lamp in a dark place. The dark place is the world we now live in. We need that light because of the confusing messages we hear in the darkened world. God's word is the true message and the true light that leads us to the dawn of God's coming day. Then the darkness will pass away, and God's light of truth will remain.

NOTES

Step 12

Because God is changing my life through following these steps, I will tell others about them and daily practice what I have learned.

2 PETER 1.5–9

STAY FOCUSED

When we are traveling, my dad is famous for pulling off at every scenic outlook, good or bad. I will admit though, this time the view was incredible. That is until my klutzy sister tripped over a rock and came blasting into me, knocking my glasses off. So much for the beautiful scenery. All I could make out then were green and brown shades. Everything was out of focus.

When our behavior is determined by other people or artificial agents, we walk around unable to see life for ourselves. Our perspective of who we are and where we are headed is out of focus. But once we realize who God is and begin to see what he wants to see in our lives, it is like putting our glasses on. It all becomes clear again.

TAKING OUR EYES OFF OURSELVES

There will still be times when we get knocked around in the world and our "spiritual glasses" will get cracked. They may even fall off. This is when we have to retrace our steps and carefully put things back into perspective. Once we get things straight, we should take our eyes off ourselves and start to see how God wants to love other people through us. It's the best way to stay focused.

STEP LOOK INSIDE 12

For another "Look Inside," turn to page 637.

ways and cause others to tell lies
about the true way. 3They will be
greedy and cheat you with smooth
talk. But long ago God decided to
punish them, and God does not sleep.
4God did not have pity on the angels that sinned. He had them tied
up and thrown into the dark pits of
hell until the time of judgment.
5And during Noah's time God did not
have pity on the ungodly people of
the world. He destroyed them with
a flood, though he did save eight people, including Noah, who preached
the truth.
6God punished the cities of Sodom
and Gomorrah[b] by burning them to
ashes, and this is a warning to anyone else who wants to sin.*
7-8Lot lived right and was greatly
troubled by the terrible way those
wicked people were living. He was
a good man, and day after day he
suffered because of the evil things
he saw and heard. So the Lord rescued him. 9This shows that the Lord
knows how to rescue godly people
from their sufferings and to punish
evil people while they wait for the
day of judgment.
10The Lord is especially hard on
people who disobey him and don't
think of anything except their own
filthy desires. They are reckless and
proud and are not afraid of cursing
the glorious beings in heaven.
11Although angels are more powerful
than these evil beings,[c] even the angels don't dare to accuse them to the
Lord.
12These people are no better than
senseless animals that live by their
feelings and are born to be caught
and killed. They speak evil of things
they don't know anything about. But
their own corrupt deeds will destroy
them. 13They have done evil, and they
will be rewarded with evil.
They think it is fun to have wild
parties during the day. They are immoral, and the meals they eat with
you are spoiled by the shameful and
selfish way they carry on.[d] 14All they
think about is having sex with someone else's husband or wife. There is
no end to their wicked deeds. They
trick people who are easily fooled,
and their minds are filled with greedy
thoughts. But they are headed for
trouble!
15They have left the true road and
have gone down the wrong path by
following the example of the prophet
Balaam. He was the son of Beor and
loved what he got from being a
crook.* 16But a donkey corrected him
for this evil deed. It spoke to him with
a human voice and made him stop
his foolishness.
17These people are like dried up
water holes and clouds blown by a
windstorm. The darkest part of hell
is waiting for them. 18They brag out

---

[b]*Sodom and Gomorrah*: During the time of Abraham the Lord destroyed these cities because the people there were so evil. See Genesis 19.24. [c]*evil beings*: or "evil teachers." [d]*and the meals they eat with you are spoiled by the shameful and selfish way they carry on*: Some manuscripts have "and the meals they eat with you are spoiled by the shameful way they carry on during your feasts of Christian love."

2.6 **GOD DOESN'T TOLERATE EVIL** Some misguided people would like us to think their evil lifestyles are merely "different" and not evil at all. But even common sense shows that their so-called different lifestyles, including sexual immorality, cause great unhappiness and ruin people's lives. God destroyed the two cities of Sodom and Gomorrah (told of in the Old Testament book of Genesis) to show how much he hates sin.

2.15 **A SPEAKING DONKEY** Balaam was a strange prophet (see the book of Numbers in the Old Testament). The enemies of Israel offered him money to preach against the people of God. When Balaam seemed to go along with the plan, his own donkey told him off. It was funny but sad that the Lord had to use a dumb animal to speak God's word to a foolish prophet. Balaam is a warning to us that giving in to evil will hurt us in the end.

NOTES

loud about their stupid nonsense.
And by being vulgar and crude, they
trap people who have barely escaped
from living the wrong kind of life.
19They promise freedom to everyone.
But they are merely slaves of filthy
living, because people are slaves of
whatever controls them.

20When they learned about our
Lord and Savior Jesus Christ, they
escaped from the filthy things of this
world. But they are again caught up
and controlled by these filthy things,
and now they are in worse shape than
they were at first. 21They would have
been better off if they had never
known about the right way. Even after they knew what was right, they
turned their backs on the holy commandments that they were given.
22What happened to them is just like
the true saying,

"A dog will come back
to lick up its own vomit.
A pig that has been washed
will roll in the mud."

The Lord Will Return

3 My dear friends, this is the second
letter I have written to encourage
you to do some honest thinking. I
don't want you to forget 2what God's
prophets said would happen. You
must never forget what the holy
prophets taught in the past. And you
must remember what the apostles
told you our Lord and Savior has
commanded us to do.

3But first you must realize that in
the last days some people won't think
about anything except their own selfish desires. They will make fun of
you 4and say, "Didn't your Lord
promise to come back? Yet the first
leaders have already died, and the
world hasn't changed a bit."

5They will say this because they
want to forget that long ago the heavens and the earth were made by
God's command. The earth came out
of water and was made from water.*
6Later it was destroyed by the waters
of a mighty flood. 7But God has commanded the present heavens and
earth to remain until the day of judgment. Then they will be set on fire,
and ungodly people will be destroyed.

8Dear friends, don't forget that for
the Lord one day is the same as a
thousand years, and a thousand
years is the same as one day.*
9The Lord isn't slow about keeping
his promises, as some people think
he is. In fact, God is patient, because
he wants everyone to turn from sin
and no one to be lost.

10The day of the Lord's return will
surprise us like a thief. The heavens
will disappear with a loud noise, and
the heat will melt the whole universe.[e] Then the earth and everything on it will be seen for what they
are.[f]

11Everything will be destroyed. So
you should serve and honor God by
the way you live. 12You should look
forward to the day when God judges
everyone, and you should try to make

---

[e] *the whole universe*: Probably the sun, moon, and stars, or the elements that everything in the universe is made of. [f] *will be seen for what they are*: Some manuscripts have "will go up in flames."

3.5 **GOD HAS WARNED THE WORLD** Imagine Noah building his ship as he looked for the great flood that God had promised. Think of how Noah's neighbors would have laughed at him: "When is it going to rain, Noah?" But Noah just went on building. We know that God is going to judge the world. The tragedy is that many don't take God seriously.

3.8 **GOD HAS LOTS OF TIME** A thousand or even a million years are no time at all to God. In God's eternity time doesn't matter. He has forever to do what he plans. Therefore, we do well not to be anxious about God's timetable. But we ought to live each day as if it were our last. When all is said and done, we will be with God, and he will deal with what people have done or not done in this present age.

NOTES

it come soon.[g] On that day the heavens will be destroyed by fire, and
everything else will melt in the heat.
13But God has promised us a new
heaven and a new earth, where justice will rule. We are really looking
forward to that!*
14My friends, while you are waiting, you should make certain that the
Lord finds you pure, spotless, and living at peace. 15Don't forget that the
Lord is patient because he wants people to be saved. This is also what our
dear friend Paul said when he wrote
you with the wisdom that God had
given him. 16Paul talks about these
same things in all his letters, but part
of what he says is hard to understand.
Some ignorant and unsteady people
even destroy themselves by twisting
what he said. They do the same thing
with other Scriptures too.*
17My dear friends, you have been
warned ahead of time! So don't let
the errors of evil people lead you
down the wrong path and make you
lose your balance. 18Let the kindness
and the understanding that come
from our Lord and Savior Jesus
Christ help you to keep on growing.
Praise Jesus now and forever!
Amen.[h]

---

[g]*and you should try to make it come soon*: Or "and you should eagerly desire for that day to come."
[h]*Amen*: Some manuscripts do not have "Amen."

3.13 **WHAT WILL GOD'S WORLD BE LIKE?** The Lord has promised a new heaven and a new earth after the present world has passed away. Peter writes that justice will rule there. Also there will be no more sorrow, or pain, or sickness, or death. But we will live with God himself, and we will be his people. The question is, are you God's person right now?

3.16 **DON'T TWIST THE SCRIPTURES** Some things in God's word are not as easy to understand as others. The important thing is to believe and obey what we do understand. As time goes by, the rest will become clear. Let the Holy Spirit reveal the truth to you as you compare one passage with another. But beware of "reading into" the Bible your own opinions.

NOTES

Step 10

I need to continue looking inside—admitting when I am wrong.

2 PETER 3.17, 18

A BAD MIX

Not being a great scientist or anything, how was I supposed to know that certain chemicals don't mix well together? I always depended on my lab partner, Mr. Total Egghead, to know what we were doing. Obviously, he was absent the day of the "great explosion." They say I was lucky I didn't burn my face off.

We all know people who just aren't good for us. Together we are a bad mix. Intentionally or unintentionally the chemistry between us is explosive. Before we know it, we are doing things we don't want to do and falling back into an old lifestyle that just doesn't work.

GOOD ADVICE

We need to take a daily inventory of our lives, which includes thinking about our friends. Do they encourage us positively or do they lead us down wrong paths? Before we get burned again, let's review God's formula for successful living.

STEP LOOK INSIDE 10

For another "Look Inside," turn to page 703.

JOHN'S FIRST LETTER

ABOUT THIS LETTER

John wants Christian believers to know that when we confess our sins to God, he will forgive us and take them away (1.9).

The true test of faith is love for each other (3.11–24). Because God is love, his people must be like him (4.1–21). For a complete victory over sin, we must not only love others, but we must believe that Jesus, the Son of God, is truly Christ, and that his death for us was real (5.1–12).

Remember:

The Word that gives life
was from the beginning,
and this is the one
our message is about.
(1.1)

A QUICK LOOK AT THIS LETTER

1 The Word that gives life
was from the beginning,
and this is the one
our message is about.
Our ears have heard,
our own eyes have seen,
and our hands touched
this Word.*

1.1 **JOHN SAW AND TOUCHED JESUS** Jesus' disciples saw and touched him when he came back from death, as the four Gospels tell us. John was not writing here about something he had only heard about. He had seen and touched Jesus, whom John calls "the Word" (see also John 1.1). We ourselves have not yet been able to see and touch the risen Lord Jesus, but we have the statements of honest witnesses who have.

NOTES

2The one who gives life appeared! We saw it happen, and we are witnesses to what we have seen. Now we are telling you about this eternal life that was with the Father and appeared to us. 3We are telling you what we have seen and heard, so that you may share in this life with us. And we share in it with the Father and with his Son Jesus Christ.* 4We are writing to tell you these things, because this makes us[a] truly happy.

God Is Light

5Jesus told us that God is light and doesn't have any darkness in him. Now we are telling you.

6If we say that we share in life with God and keep on living in the dark, we are lying and are not living by the truth. 7But if we live in the light, as God does, we share in life with each other. And the blood of his Son Jesus washes all our sins away.* 8If we say that we have not sinned, we are fooling ourselves, and the truth is not in our hearts. 9But if we confess our sins to God, he can always be trusted to forgive us and take our sins away.

10If we say that we have not sinned, we make God a liar, and his message is not in our hearts.[b]

Christ Helps Us

2 My children, I am writing this so that you will not sin. But if you do sin, Jesus Christ always does the right thing, and he will speak to the Father for us.* 2Christ is the sacrifice that takes away our sins and the sins of all the world's people.

3When we obey God, we are sure that we know him. 4But if we claim to know him and don't obey him, we are lying and the truth is not in our hearts. 5We truly love God only when we obey him as we should, and then we know that we belong to him. 6If we say we are his, we must follow the example of Christ.

The New Commandment

7My dear friends, I am not writing to give you a new commandment. It is the same one you were first given, and it is the message you heard. 8But it really is a new commandment, and you know its true meaning, just as Christ does. You can see the

---

[a]*us*: Some manuscripts have "you." [b]*and his message is not in our hearts*: Or "because we have not accepted his message."

1.3 **JESUS SHARES ETERNAL LIFE WITH US** John describes the risen Jesus as the one who has eternal life. Jesus had overcome death and was alive forever with a glory that must have been wonderful to see. But remember, Jesus is now able to give us eternal life too. We believe in him and are saved, and the Holy Spirit dwells in us. Believers have eternal life straight from God himself.

1.7 **LET'S LIVE IN GOD'S LIGHT** Living in constant darkness would be a gloomy existence. In fact, we would die very soon, because we need light to live. John tells us to live in God's own light. To live in God's light is to have life that lasts forever and can't fade away. God's light is the truth that sets us free from our sins.

2.1 **JESUS PRAYS FOR US** If we truly love the Lord Jesus, we also hate our sins. But we still sin at times. When that happens, it's important not to try to hide or forget our sins. We should bring them to Jesus, and he will ask his Father to forgive us. The best thing is to love Jesus so much, and to be so filled with the Holy Spirit, that sin will not control our thoughts and actions.

NOTES

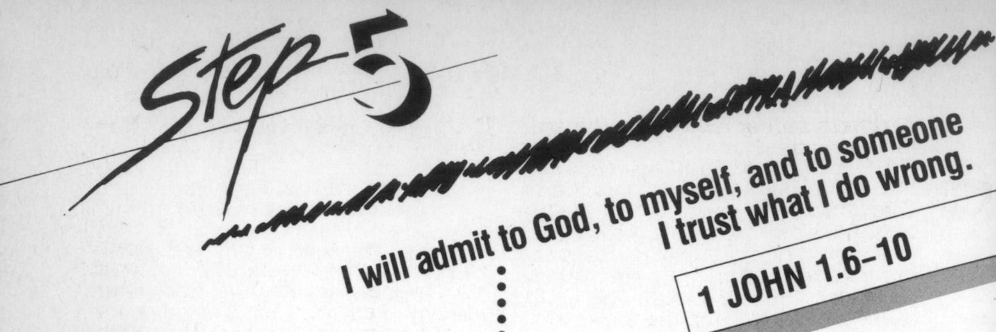

GOING BAREFOOT

One of the best things about summer is taking our shoes off and going barefoot. At first, it is little rough because our feet have yet to become hardened. But, in a short time, they become callused, and we can walk or run without feeling discomfort.

Our hearts are a lot like our feet. The longer we continue living a lie and deceiving other people, the more hardened our hearts become. One lie leads to another. One wrong action leads to others. The thing that once thrilled and satisfied doesn't anymore, so we try something else. All the while our hearts are becoming more callused until we aren't able to hear God anymore.

WALKING WITH GOD

It's time to stop and put our shoes back on. We need to ask ourselves, "Am I living a lie? Can I hear or see what is right anymore? Has my attitude gotten hard and callous?" We need to admit to God and to ourselves that we want a tender heart again. We need to decide that we are willing to give up the false freedom we felt while running barefoot and wild for the real freedom found walking in God's steps.

For another "Look Inside," turn to page 612.

darkness fading away and the true
light already shining.*
9If we claim to be in the light and
hate someone, we are still in the dark.
10But if we love others, we are in the
light, and we don't cause problems
for them.[c] 11If we hate others, we are
living and walking in the dark. We
don't know where we are going, because we can't see in the dark.

12Children, I am writing you,
because your sins
have been forgiven
in the name of Christ.
13Parents, I am writing you,
because you have known
the one who was there
from the beginning.
Young people,
I am writing you,
because you have defeated
the evil one.
14Children, I am writing you,
because you have known
the Father.
Parents, I am writing you,
because you have known
the one who was there
from the beginning.
Young people,
I am writing you,
because you are strong.
God's message is firm
in your hearts,
and you have defeated
the evil one.

15Don't love the world or anything
that belongs to the world. If you love
the world, you cannot love the Father. 16Our foolish pride comes from
this world, and so do our selfish desires and our desire to have everything we see. None of this comes from
the Father. 17The world and the desires it causes are disappearing. But
if we obey God, we will live forever.

The Enemy of Christ

18Children, this is the last hour.
You heard that the enemy of Christ
would appear at this time, and many
of Christ's enemies have already appeared. So we know that the last hour
is here.* 19These people came from
our own group, yet they were not part
of us. If they had been part of us,
they would have stayed with us. But
they left, which proves that they did
not belong to our group.
20Christ, the Holy One,[d] has
blessed[e] you, and now all of you
understand.[f] 21I did not need to write
you about the truth, since you already know it. You also know that
liars do not belong to the truth.
22And a liar is anyone who says that
Jesus isn't truly Christ. Anyone who
says this is an enemy of Christ and
rejects both the Father and the Son.
23If we reject the Son, we reject the
Father. But if we say that we accept
the Son, we have the Father. 24Keep
thinking about the message you first
heard, and you will always be one

---

[c] *and we don't cause problems for them*: Or "and we can see anything that might make us fall." [d] *Christ, the Holy One*: The Greek text has "the Holy One" which may refer either to Christ or to God the Father. [e] *blessed*: This translates a word which means "to pour olive oil on (someone's head)." In Old Testament times it was the custom to pour olive oil on a person's head when that person was chosen to be a priest or a king. Here the meaning is not clear. It may refer to the ceremony of pouring olive oil on the followers of the Lord right before they were baptized or it may refer to the gift of the Holy Spirit which they were given at baptism (see verse 27). [f] *now all of you understand*: Some manuscripts have "you understand all things."

2.8 **THE TRUE LIGHT IS SHINING** It was a dark time before Jesus came. People had very little hope for the future. But now that Jesus has come, we can have great hope and joy. Jesus has opened heaven's doors. Now eternal life and light come streaming toward us, and the darkness is past.

2.18 **CHRIST'S ENEMY IS COMING** Sometimes this person is called "the man of sin" or "the Antichrist." John also calls him "the beast" in Revelation 17.11. He will some day arise in the world to defy God's authority, and he will torment God's people. But in the end he will be destroyed (Revelation 20.10).

NOTES

in your heart with the Son and with the Father. 25The Son[g] has promised us[h] eternal life.

26I am writing to warn you about those people who are misleading you. 27But Christ has blessed you with the Holy Spirit.[i] Now the Spirit stays in you, and you don't need any teachers. The Spirit is truthful and teaches you everything. So stay one in your heart with Christ, just as the Spirit has taught you to do.*

Children of God

28Children, stay one in your hearts with Christ. Then when he returns, we will have confidence and won't have to hide in shame. 29You know that Christ always does right and that everyone who does right is a child of God.

3 Think how much the Father loves us. He loves us so much that he lets us be called his children, as we truly are. But since the people of this world did not know who Christ[j] is, they don't know who we are. 2My dear friends, we are already God's children, though what we will be has not yet been seen. But we do know that when Christ returns, we will be like him, because we will see him as he truly is.* 3This hope makes us keep ourselves holy, just as Christ[k] is holy.

4Everyone who sins breaks God's law, because sin is the same as breaking God's law. 5You know that Christ came to take away sins. He isn't sinful, 6and people who stay one in their hearts with him won't keep on sinning. If they do keep on sinning, they don't know Christ, and they have never seen him.

7Children, don't be fooled. Anyone who does right is good, just like Christ himself. 8Anyone who keeps on sinning belongs to the devil. He has sinned from the beginning, but the Son of God came to destroy all that he has done. 9God's children cannot keep on being sinful. His life-giving power[l] lives in them and makes them his children, so that they cannot keep on sinning.* 10You can tell God's children from the devil's children, because those who belong to the devil refuse to do right or to love each other.

Love Each Other

11From the beginning you were told that we must love each other.

---

[g] *The Son*: The Greek text has "he" and may refer to God the Father. [h] *us*: Some manuscripts have "you." [i] *Christ has blessed you with the Holy Spirit*: The Greek text has "You received a pouring on of olive oil from him" (see verse 20). The "pouring on of olive oil" is here taken to refer to the gift of the Holy Spirit, and "he" may refer either to Christ or to the Father. [j] *Christ*: The Greek text has "he" and may refer to God. [k] *Christ*: The Greek text has "that one" and may refer to God. [l] *His life-giving power*: The Greek text has "his seed."

2.27 **THE HOLY SPIRIT TEACHES US** We are never alone. The Holy Spirit is the real presence of God who dwells in us when we have put our trust in Jesus. That same Spirit continually comforts us, reminding us that we will belong to Christ forever. The Holy Spirit also speaks God's truth to us as we read the Scriptures.

3.2 **WE WILL BE LIKE JESUS** Have you watched a leafless tree in the springtime? It looks dry and dead. Then the branches begin to send out buds, and we begin to hope that the tree will live again. One morning we get up, and there the tree is covered with beautiful leaves. It's all new. One day we, too, will wake up in God's morning, and we will bloom with new life from above.

3.9 **WHEN BELIEVERS SIN** Believers do not keep living in sin. Does this mean that we are not saved any more if we sin? No, we are still saved, and God will forgive us when we ask him. But for those who have faith, sin is no longer a way of life. When we sin, we feel bad, and we can't wait to get things right with God again. That includes asking forgiveness from someone we might have hurt.

NOTES

Step 7

I need God to remove my shortcomings.

1 JOHN 3.4–6

THREE STRIKES AND YOU'RE OUT

She called from the police station, crying hysterically and rambling incoherently. Finally I was able to get her to calm down and explain: she had been arrested for stealing a girl's purse.

"It was a joke; I was going to give it back," she told me.

I consoled her and told her that because it was a first offense the police would probably reprimand her and send her home. Then she confessed it wasn't her first offense; she had been caught shoplifting two times before. What could I say? Three strikes and you're out.

The girl in this story wound up going to a juvenile detention center for several months. It wasn't a good experience. The Bible tells us the sentence for sin is even greater—separation from God forever.

STEP 7 LOOK INSIDE

SOMEONE HAS TO PAY

Because of his great love for you, God sent Jesus to pay the price for your sin. There is only one requirement—that we believe it and allow Christ who is now in us to be in control of us.

For another "Look Inside," turn to page 575.

12Don't be like Cain, who belonged
to the devil and murdered his own
brother. Why did he murder him? He
did it because his brother was good,
and he was evil. 13My friends, don't
be surprised if the people of this
world hate you. 14Our love for each
other proves that we have gone from
death to life. But if you don't love
each other, you are still under the
power of death.

15If you hate each other, you are
murderers, and we know that murderers do not have eternal life.
16We know what love is because Jesus gave his life for us. That's why
we must give our lives for each other.
17If we have all we need and see one
of our own people in need, we must
have pity on that person, or else we
cannot say we love God. 18Children,
you show love for others by truly
helping them, and not merely by talking about it.

19When we love others, we know
that we belong to the truth, and we
feel at ease in the presence of God.*
20But even if we don't feel at ease,
God is greater than our feelings, and
he knows everything. 21Dear friends,
if we feel at ease in the presence of
God, we will have the courage to
come near to him. 22He will give us
whatever we ask, because we obey
him and do what pleases him.
23God wants us to have faith in his
Son Jesus Christ and to love each
other. This is also what Jesus taught
us to do. 24If we obey God's commandments, we will stay one in our
hearts with him, and he will stay one
with us. The Spirit that he has given
us is proof that we are one with him.

God Is Love

4 Dear friends, don't believe everyone who claims to have the Spirit
of God. Test them all to find out if
they really do come from God. Many
false prophets have already gone out
into the world, 2and you can know
which ones come from God. His
Spirit says that Jesus Christ had a
truly human body. 3But when someone does not say this about Jesus,
you know that person has a spirit
that does not come from God and is
the enemy of Christ. You knew that
this enemy was coming into the
world and now is already here.*

4Children, you belong to God, and
you have defeated these enemies.
God's Spirit[m] is in you and is more
powerful than the one that is in the
world. 5These enemies belong to this
world, and the world listens to them,
because they speak its language.
6We belong to God, and everyone
who knows God will listen to us. But
the people who don't know God
won't listen to us. That's how we can
tell the Spirit that speaks the truth
from the one that tells lies.

7My dear friends, we must love
each other. Love comes from God,
and when we love each other, it
shows that we have been given new
life. We are now God's children, and
we know him. 8God is love, and anyone who doesn't love others has
never known him. 9God showed his
love for us when he sent his only Son
into the world to give us life. 10Real

---

[m]*God's Spirit*: The Greek text has "he" and may refer to the Spirit or to God or to Jesus.

3.19 **THE IMPORTANCE OF LOVE** Joy, peace, and patience are kinds of goodness too. But love is the kind of goodness that gives life. Hatred brings about death. Love is shown by the way we care. Even plants and animals live well when we care for them. But most of all, people need love, or their lives aren't worth living. God's love brings life, and believers share God's love with others.

4.3 **REMEMBER WHO JESUS IS** After Jesus went back to heaven, some people in New Testament times were saying that Jesus was really like a ghost that had no body. They said this because they wrongly believed that any physical body always has to be evil. Their opinion seemed very religious to them, but Jesus could not have died for our sins unless he had a body that could die.

NOTES

Step 9

I will make things right with people I wrong, except when to do so would hurt them or others.

1 JOHN 3.15–18

I'M SORRY

Several years ago a movie had a famous line in it that said, "Love means never having to say you're sorry." While it was touching and brought audiences to tears, it just wasn't the truth. When we really care for people and have done them wrong, we must say we are sorry, not only to restore our relationship, but for our own well-being. Forgiveness is healing.

There may be times when the words "I'm sorry" just aren't enough. We may also have to show the offended parties that we want to make things right.

BELIEVE IT

These Bible verses also bring to mind another familiar saying, "Actions speak louder than words." It's a line that may not bring tears, but we *can* believe it's the truth.

For another "Look Inside," turn to page 670.

love is not our love for God, but his
love for us. God sent his Son to be
the sacrifice by which our sins are
forgiven. 11Dear friends, since God
loved us this much, we must love
each other.*

12No one has ever seen God. But
if we love each other, God lives in
us, and his love is truly in our hearts.

STEP LOOK AHEAD 6

13God has given us his Spirit. That
is how we know that we are one with
him, just as he is one with us.
14God sent his Son to be the Savior
of the world. We saw his Son and
are now telling others about him.
15God stays one with everyone who
openly says that Jesus is the Son of
God. That's how we stay one with
God 16and are sure that God loves us.

God is love. If we keep on loving
others, we will stay one in our hearts
with God, and he will stay one with
us. 17If we truly love others and live
as Christ did in this world, we won't
be worried about the day of judgment. 18A real love for others will
chase those worries away. The
thought of being punished is what
makes us afraid. It shows that we
have not really learned to love.

19We love because God loved us
first. 20But if we say we love God and
don't love each other, we are liars.
We cannot see God. So how can we
love God, if we don't love the people
we can see? 21The two commandments that God has given us are:
"Love God and love each other!"

Victory over the World

STEP 11

5 If we believe that Jesus is truly
Christ, we are God's children.
Everyone who loves the Father will
also love his children.* 2If we love
and obey God, we know that we will
love his children. 3We show our love
for God by obeying his commandments, and they are not hard to
follow.

4Every child of God can defeat the
world, and our faith is what gives
us this victory. 5No one can defeat
the world without having faith in Jesus as the Son of God.

Who Jesus Is

6Water and blood came out from
the side of Jesus Christ. It was not
just water, but water and blood.[n] The
Spirit tells about this, because the
Spirit is truthful. 7In fact, there are
three who tell about it. 8They are the
Spirit, the water, and the blood, and
they all agree.

9We believe what people tell us.
But we can trust what God says even
more, and God is the one who has
spoken about his Son. 10If we have
faith in God's Son, we have believed
what God has said. But if we don't
believe what God has said about his
Son, it is the same as calling God a
liar. 11God has also said that he gave
us eternal life and that this life comes
to us from his Son. 12And so, if we
have God's Son, we have this life.

---

[n] *Water and blood came out from the side of Jesus Christ. It was not just water, but water and blood*: See John 19.34. It is also possible to translate, "Jesus Christ came by the water of baptism and by the blood of his death! He was not only baptized, but he bled and died." The purpose of the verse is to tell that Jesus was truly human and that he really died.

4.11 **HOW DOES TRUE LOVE HAPPEN?** One of the greatest things about God is love, and all love flows from him. When you meet people who are full of hate, it is because they have never known or accepted love for themselves. When God's love is poured into us, then our response is to love him and to love others.

5.1 **WHY WE LOVE GOD** We are not naturally loving people—we are born sinners. But God loves us first, and then we are able to love him. God loved us by creating us. Then God gave his Son to die for us and save us from our sinful selves. His love gives us eternal life, which sin cannot destroy. It's sad that there are still so many people who fear God and wish he didn't exist. God loves the world and wants everyone to come back to him.

NOTES

Step 6

JOYFULNESS—Enjoying the inward results of right living

1 JOHN 4.13–18

REJECTED

My greatest fear was being rejected—sitting alone in the lunchroom; showing up at a game by myself; standing at the bus stop with no one talking to me. That's why the drinking and drug route seemed the best way to go. It gave me something in common with some other people. I was selling myself short though. Now I see that the problem wasn't that other people might not like me. It was that I didn't like myself. I didn't have enough confidence in myself to be likable.

STEP LOOK AHEAD 6

ABIDING LOVE

Then I learned that God loves me all the time. I'm walking around loved. Regardless of how I look or how I rank in the popularity polls for the day, God thinks I'm terrific. The Bible calls it "staying" in love. Whatever . . . it works for me. I still don't like to sit by myself, but when it happens, I picture Jesus sitting across from me, giving me a little pep talk. It helps me to relax. God really does love me.

To take a "Look Back" at a man who had a heart for God that resulted in a joy-filled life with God, turn to page 565.

But if we don't have the Son, we don't
have this life.*

Knowing about Eternal Life

13All of you have faith in the Son
of God, and I have written to let you
know that you have eternal life.
14We are certain that God will hear
our prayers when we ask for what
pleases him. 15And if we know that
God listens when we pray, we are
sure that our prayers have already
been answered.
16Suppose you see one of our people commit a sin that is not a deadly
sin. You can pray, and that person
will be given eternal life. But the sin
must not be one that is deadly.
17Everything that is wrong is sin, but
not all sins are deadly.
18We are sure that God's children
do not keep on sinning. God's own
Son protects them, and the devil cannot harm them.
19We are certain that we come from
God and that the rest of the world
is under the power of the devil.*
20We know that Jesus Christ the
Son of God has come and has shown
us the true God. And because of Jesus, we now belong to the true God
who gives eternal life.
21Children, you must stay away
from idols.

NOTES

5.12 **THE SON IS THE DIFFERENCE** Having eternal life or not having it depends on what we believe about Jesus. Some people say they believe in God, but they try to make Jesus into a "great teacher" instead of God's Son. It doesn't work that way. We are saved by believing that Jesus is the Son of God who died and rose again, who alone has the authority to forgive sins. Rejecting him is not only foolish, it's deadly.

5.19 **UNDER THE DEVIL'S POWER** In this age, we live in a world over which the devil has power. It won't always be that way. Jesus will return and claim the earth for himself. But for now, the devil has power, and we can see the results all around us.

JOHN'S SECOND LETTER

ABOUT THIS LETTER

John writes again about the importance of love in a Christian's life. He points out that truth and love must go together. We must also believe that Christ was truly human, and we must love each other.

A QUICK LOOK AT THIS LETTER

1. Greetings and Prayer (1–3)
2. Truth and Love (4–11)
3. Final Greetings (12,13)

1From the church leader.[a]
To a very special woman and her
children.[b] I truly love all of you, and
so does everyone else who knows the
truth.* 2We love you because the
truth is now in our hearts, and it will
be there forever.
3I pray that God the Father and Jesus Christ his Son will be kind and
merciful to us! May they give us
peace and truth and love.

Truth and Love

4I was very glad to learn that some
of your children are obeying the
truth, as the Father told us to do.
5Dear friend, I am not writing to tell
you and your children to do something you have not done before. I am
writing to tell you to love each other,
which is the first thing you were told
to do. 6Love means that we do what
God tells us. And from the beginning,
he told you to love him.

[a]*church leader*: Or "elder" or "presbyter" or "priest." [b]*very special woman and her children*: A group of the Lord's followers who met together for worship. "The children of your . . . sister" (verse 13) is another group of followers. "Very special" (here and verse 13) probably means "chosen (by the Lord)."

1 **WHO WAS THIS "SPECIAL WOMAN"?** It could be that the "woman" was really a congregation of God's people in a certain area. So it would be John's loving way of speaking to the church. Notice that he says, "Some of your children are obeying the truth." All in that church might not have been living faithfully. They might not have been doing as God commanded.

NOTES

[7]Many liars have gone out into the
world. These deceitful liars are saying that Jesus Christ did not have a
truly human body. But they are liars
and the enemies of Christ.* [8]So be
sure not to lose what we[c] have
worked for. If you do, you won't be
given your full reward. [9]Don't keep
changing what you were taught
about Christ, or else God will no
longer be with you. But if you hold
firmly to what you were taught, both
the Father and the Son will be with
you. [10]If people won't agree to this
teaching, don't welcome them into
your home or even greet them.
[11]Greeting them is the same as taking
part in their evil deeds.

Final Greetings

[12]I have much more to tell you, but
I don't want to write it with pen and
ink. I want to come and talk to you
in person, because that will make us[d]
really happy.
[13]Greetings from the children of
your very special sister.[e]

---

[c]*we*: Some manuscripts have "you." [d]*us*: Some manuscripts have "you." [e]*sister*: See the note at verse 1.

7 **THE BIG LIE** As in his first letter, John writes against the false teaching that said that although Jesus came, he didn't have a real body. That was the devil's clever way of attacking the good news that Jesus died for our sins. A spirit without a body wouldn't be able to die.

NOTES

JOHN'S THIRD LETTER

ABOUT THIS LETTER

In this letter the writer reminds Christian readers that they should help support those who go to other parts of the world to tell others about the Lord. The letter is written to an important church member named Gaius, who had been very helpful to Christians who traveled around and preached the good news.

A QUICK LOOK AT THIS LETTER

1From the church leader.[a]
To my dear friend Gaius.
I love you because we follow the
truth, 2dear friend, and I pray that
all goes well for you. I hope that you
are as strong in body, as I know you
are in spirit. 3It makes me very happy
when the Lord's followers come by
and speak openly of how you obey
the truth.* 4Nothing brings me
greater happiness than to hear that
my children[b] are obeying the truth.

Working Together

5Dear friend, you have always been
faithful in helping other followers of
the Lord, even the ones you didn't
know before. 6They have told the
church about your love. They say you
were good enough to welcome them
and to send them on their mission
in a way that God's servants deserve.
7When they left to tell others about
the Lord, they decided not to accept
help from anyone who was not a follower. 8We must support people like
them, so that we can take part in what
they are doing to spread the truth.

---

[a]*church leader*: Or "elder" or "presbyter" or "priest." [b]*children*: Probably persons that the leader had led to be followers of the Lord.

ONE WELL SPOKEN OF Gaius had a valuable treasure called a good reputation. People told of his obedience to God's truth. It's good to be known for loving God and doing his will. It's not that we want glory for ourselves, but for the Lord Jesus and what he has done.

NOTES

9 I wrote to the church. But Diotrephes likes to be the number-one
leader, and he won't pay any attention to us.* 10 So if I come, I will remind him of how he has been attacking us with gossip. Not only has he
been doing this, but he refuses to welcome any of the Lord's followers who
come by. And when other church
members want to welcome them, he
puts them out of the church.
11 Dear friend, don't copy the evil
deeds of others! Follow the example
of people who do kind deeds. They
are God's children, but those who are
always doing evil have never seen
God.
12 Everyone speaks well of Demetrius, and so does the true message
that he teaches. I also speak well of
him, and you know what I say is
true.*

Final Greetings

13 I have much more to say to you,
but I don't want to write it with pen
and ink. 14 I hope to see you soon,
and then we can talk in person.
15 I pray that God will bless you
with peace!
Your friends send their greetings.
Please give a personal greeting to
each of our friends.

9 **THERE IS ONLY ONE "NUMBER ONE"** God is number one. Poor Diotrephes (pronounced dye-AH-tra-fees) thought his purpose in life was to get ahead of everyone else. You meet a lot of people like this. Often they just get discouraged and quit. The main thing is to remember who God is, and that we are his servants. God doesn't need more bosses, he needs more workers.

12 **BE A DEMETRIUS** Pronounce his name de-MEE-tree-us. You can just imagine how different he was from Diotrephes. Demetrius loved the truth, and he was everybody's friend. People knew they could trust him to show them the path of life and help solve their problems. He was a good and faithful teacher.

NOTES

Jude has much to say about false teachers. They are evil! God will punish them, and Christians should not follow their teaching or imitate the way they live.

Jude ends with a beautiful prayer-like blessing:

> *Offer praise to God our Savior because of our Lord Jesus Christ! Only God can keep you from falling and make you pure and joyful in his glorious presence. Before time began and now and forevermore, God is worthy of glory, honor, power, and authority. Amen.* (24–25)

A QUICK LOOK AT THIS LETTER

1. Greetings (1,2)
2. Defending the Faith against False Teachers (3–23)
3. Final Prayer (24,25)

1From Jude, a servant of Jesus
Christ and the brother of James.
To all who are chosen and loved by God the Father and are kept safe by Jesus Christ.
2I pray that God will greatly bless
you with kindness, peace, and love!

False Teachers

3My dear friends, I really wanted
to write you about God's saving power at work in our lives. But instead, I must write and ask you to defend the faith that God has once
for all given to his people. 4Some god-
less people have sneaked in among us and are saying, "God is kind, and so it is all right to be immoral." They even deny that we must obey Jesus Christ as our only Master and Lord. But long ago the Scriptures warned that these godless people were doomed.*

KNOW GOD'S ENEMIES Jude describes in great detail the enemies of the truth. They live loose lives and they disobey Christ. They laugh at authority. They let their desires run their lives. You can see how believers must be different from the crowd. Our lives should reflect the beauty of Jesus, so others in this sinful world might also be saved.

NOTES

5Don't forget what happened to
those people the Lord rescued from
Egypt. Some of them did not have
faith, and he later destroyed them.
6You also know about the angels[a]
who didn't do their work and left
their proper places. God chained
them with everlasting chains and is
now keeping them in dark pits until
the great day of judgment. 7We
should also be warned by what happened to the cities of Sodom and Gomorrah[b] and the nearby towns. Their
people became immoral and did all
sorts of sexual sins. Then God made
an example of them and punished
them with eternal fire.

8The people I am talking about are
behaving just like those dreamers
who destroyed their own bodies.
They reject all authority and insult
angels. 9Even Michael, the chief angel, didn't dare to insult the devil,
when the two of them were arguing
about the body of Moses.[c] All Michael said was, "The Lord will punish
you!"

10But these people insult powers
they don't know anything about.
They are like senseless animals that
end up getting destroyed, because
they live only by their feelings.
11Now they are in for real trouble.
They have followed Cain's example[d]
and have made the same mistake that
Balaam[e] did by caring only for
money. They have also rebelled
against God, just as Korah did.[f] Because of all this, they will be destroyed.

12These people are filthy minded,
and because of their shameful and
selfish actions they spoil the meals
you eat together. They are like clouds
blown along by the wind, but never
bringing any rain. They are like leafless trees, uprooted and dead, and
unable to produce fruit. 13Their
shameful deeds show up like foam
on wild ocean waves. They are like
wandering stars forever doomed to
the darkest pits of hell.

14Enoch was the seventh person after Adam, and he was talking about
these people when he said:

> Look! The Lord is coming with
> thousands and thousands of holy
> angels 15to judge everyone. He
> will punish all those ungodly
> people for all the evil things they
> have done. The Lord will surely
> punish those ungodly sinners for
> every evil thing they have ever
> said about him.

16These people grumble and complain and live by their own selfish
desires. They brag about themselves
and flatter others to get what they
want.*

More Warnings

17My dear friends, remember the
warning you were given by the apostles of our Lord Jesus Christ. 18They
told you that near the end of time,
selfish and godless people would
start making fun of God. 19And now
these people are already making you
turn against each other. They think
only about this life, and they don't
have God's Spirit.

20Dear friends, keep building on
the foundation of your most holy
faith, as the Holy Spirit helps you

---

[a] *angels*: This may refer to the angels who liked the women on earth so much that they came down and married them (Genesis 6.2). [b] *Sodom and Gomorrah*: During the time of Abraham the Lord destroyed these cities because the people there were so evil. [c] *Michael . . . the body of Moses*: This refers to what was said in an ancient Jewish book about Moses. [d] *Cain's example*: Cain murdered his brother Abel. [e] *Balaam*: According to the biblical account, Balaam refused to curse the people of Israel for profit (Numbers 22.18; 24.13), though he led them to be unfaithful to the Lord (Numbers 25.1-3; 31.16). But by New Testament times, some Jewish teachers taught that Balaam was greedy and did accept money to curse them. [f] *just as Korah did*: Together with Dathan and Abiram, Korah led a rebellion against Moses and Aaron (Numbers 16.1-35; 26.9, 10).

16 **STUCK IN THIS WORLD** Jude writes that while God's enemies care little for God, they care a great deal about this world and its things. Their whole life seems devoted to pleasure. They flatter and "wheel and deal" to get what they want, and they are miserable when they don't get it. Of course, they are never satisfied. How sad. If these people had Jesus they would have everything that is really valuable.

NOTES

to pray. [21]And keep in step with God's love, as you wait for our Lord Jesus Christ to show how kind he is by giving you eternal life. [22]Be helpful to[g] all who may have doubts. [23]Rescue any who need to be saved, as you would rescue someone from a fire. Then with fear in your own hearts, have mercy on everyone who needs it. But hate even the clothes of those who have been made dirty by their filthy deeds.

Final Prayer

[24-25]Offer praise to God our Savior because of our Lord Jesus Christ! Only God can keep you from falling and make you pure and joyful in his glorious presence. Before time began and now and forevermore, God is worthy of glory, honor, power, and authority. Amen.*

---

[g]*Be helpful to*: Some manuscripts have "Correct."

24 **A GOOD PRAYER TO LEARN** Jude's prayer contains the great truths of our faith. God is our Savior by his Son, our Lord Jesus Christ. He keeps us from falling back into our sinful ways and brings us at last to himself. This is the eternal God, and he deserves all glory, honor, power, and authority. He should be the very center of our lives.

NOTES

REVELATION

ABOUT THIS BOOK

This book tells what John had seen in a vision about God's message and about what Jesus Christ had said and done (1.2). The message has three main parts: (1) There are evil forces at work in the world, and Christians may have to suffer and die; (2) Jesus is Lord, and he will conquer all people and powers who oppose God; and (3) God has wonderful rewards in store for his faithful people, who remain faithful to him, especially for those who lose their lives in his service.

This was a powerful message of hope for those early Christians who had to suffer or die for their faith. In this book they learned that, in spite of the cruel power of the Roman empire, the Lamb of God would win the final victory. And this gave them the courage to be faithful.

Because this book is so full of visions that use ideas and word pictures from the Old Testament, it was like a book with secret messages for the early Christians. The book could be passed around and be understood by Christians, but an official of the Roman empire would not be able to understand it. For example, when the fall of Babylon is described (chapter 18), the early Christians knew that this pointed to the fall of the Roman empire. This knowledge gave them hope.

At the beginning of this book there are seven letters to seven churches. These letters show what different groups of the Lord's followers will do in times of persecution (2.1—3.22).

The author uses many powerful images to describe God's power and judgment. The vision of God's throne (4.1–11) and of the scroll and the Lamb (5.1–14) show that God and Christ are in control of all human and supernatural events. Opening seven seals (6.1—8.5), blowing the seven trumpets (8.6—11.19), and emptying the seven bowls (16.1–21) are among the visions that show God's fierce judgment on the world.

After the suffering has ended, God's faithful people will receive the greatest blessing of all:

> *God's home is now with his people. He will live with them, and they will be his own. Yes, God will make his home among his people. He will wipe all tears from their eyes, and there will be no more death, suffering, crying, or pain. These things of the past are gone forever.* (21.3,4)

A QUICK LOOK AT THIS BOOK

1. A Prophecy from John (1.1–8)
2. A Vision of the Living Lord (1.9–20)
3. Letters to the Seven Churches (2.1—3.22)
4. A Vision of Worship in Heaven (4.1–11)
5. A Scroll with Seven Seals (5.1—6.17)
6. Worship in Front of God's Throne (7.1–17)
7. Seven Trumpets (8.1—11.19)
8. A Dragon and Two Beasts (12.1—13.18)
9. Visions of God's Judgment and Protection (14.1—15.8)
10. Seven Bowls of God's Anger (16.1–21)
11. God's Enemies Are Defeated (17.1—20.10)
12. The Final Judgment (20.11–15)
13. A New Heaven and a New Earth (21.1–8)
14. New Jerusalem (21.9—22.5)
15. Christ Will Soon Return (22.6–21)

1 This is what God showed to Jesus
Christ, so that he could tell his
servants what must happen soon.
Christ then sent his angel with the
message to his servant John. 2And
John told everything that he had seen
about God's message and about what
Jesus Christ had said and done.
3God will bless everyone who
reads this prophecy to others,[a] and
he will bless everyone who hears and
obeys it. The time is almost here.*
4From John to the seven churches
in Asia.[b]

I pray that you
will be blessed
with kindness and peace
from God, who is and was
and is coming.
May you receive
kindness and peace
from the seven spirits
before the throne of God.
5May kindness and peace
be yours
from Jesus Christ,
the faithful witness.

Jesus was the first
to conquer death,
and he is the ruler
of all earthly kings.
Christ loves us,
and by his blood
he set us free
from our sins.
6He lets us rule as kings
and serve God his Father
as priests.
To him be glory and power
forever and ever! Amen.
7Look! He is coming
with the clouds.
Everyone will see him,

---

[a]*who reads this prophecy to others*: A public reading, in a worship service. [b]Asia: The section 1.4—3.22 is in the form of a letter. Asia was in the eastern part of the Roman empire and is present day Turkey.

1.3 **YOU REALLY OUGHT TO READ THIS BOOK** You won't understand all of this amazing book, but you will get a look behind the scenes at God's great plans for the future. This reading will be a happy experience if you are trusting in Jesus and watching for his return. John writes, "The time is almost here." The time until Jesus comes could be very short. We ought to pay attention to what God has to say about the last days of the society we live in.

NOTES

even the ones who stuck
a sword through him.
All people on earth
will weep because of him.
Yes, it will happen! Amen.
8The Lord God says, "I am Alpha
and Omega,[c] the one who is and
was and is coming. I am God All-
Powerful!"*

A Vision of the Risen Lord

9I am John, a follower together
with all of you. We all suffer because
Jesus is our king, but he gives us the
strength to endure. I was sent to Patmos Island,[d] because I had preached
God's message and had told about
Jesus. 10On the Lord's day[e] the Spirit
took control of me, and behind me I
heard a loud voice that sounded like
a trumpet. 11The voice said, "Write
in a book what you see. Then send
it to the seven churches in Ephesus,
Smyrna, Pergamum, Thyatira, Sardis, Philadelphia, and Laodicea."[f]
12When I turned to see who was
speaking to me, I saw seven gold
lampstands. 13There with the lampstands was someone who seemed to
be the Son of Man.[g] He was wearing
a robe that reached down to his feet,
and a gold cloth was wrapped around
his chest. 14His head and his hair
were white as wool or snow, and his
eyes looked like flames of fire.*
15His feet were glowing like bronze
being heated in a furnace, and his
voice sounded like the roar of a
waterfall. 16He held seven stars in his
right hand, and a sharp double-edged
sword was coming from his mouth.
His face was shining as bright as the
sun at noon.
17When I saw him, I fell at his feet
like a dead person. But he put his
right hand on me and said:
Don't be afraid! I am the first,
the last,* 18and the living one. I
died, but now I am alive
forevermore, and I have the keys
to death and the world of the
dead.[h] 19Write what you have
seen and what is and what will
happen after these things. 20I
will explain the mystery of the
seven stars that you saw at my
right side and the seven gold
lampstands. The seven stars are
the angels[i] of the seven

---

[c]*Alpha and Omega*: The first and last letters of the Greek alphabet, which sometimes mean "first" and "last." [d]*Patmos Island*: A small island where prisoners were sometimes kept by the Romans. [e]*Lord's day*: Sunday, the day when Jesus was raised from death, and when many Christians worship. [f]*Ephesus . . . Laodicea*: Ephesus was in the center with the six other cities forming a half-circle around it. [g]*Son of Man*: That is, Jesus. [h]*keys to death and the world of the dead*: That is, power over death and the world of the dead. [i]*angels*: Perhaps guardian angels that represent the churches, or they may be church leaders or messengers sent to the churches.

1.8 **GOD IS ETERNAL** These words, a way of saying "the beginning and the end" in Greek, tell us that the Lord Jesus Christ was the One who brought in the beginning of time and will bring about the end of time. In fact Christ himself is God the Creator of time (see Colossians 1.16). Humans should remember that all of history is in God's hands. He started it and he will end it when he is ready.

1.14 **JESUS SHOWED HIS REAL GLORY** In this book we see Jesus Christ as he really is. During his short time on earth the Son of God humbled himself as a servant and went about doing good. Then he died like a criminal on a cross. But he rose from death and is now back where he came from, in heaven. John got to see the Lord Jesus in his real glory.

1.17 **"DON'T BE AFRAID"** These are the comforting words that the risen Savior spoke to John. It's no wonder John was afraid. He had to struggle to describe what he saw and heard. This surely was a different view of Jesus than John ever had before. Now we, too, can be unafraid as we realize that all nature and our own lives are in the hands of a great Savior.

NOTES

churches, and the lampstands
are the seven churches.

The Letter to Ephesus

2 This is what you must write to
the angel of the church in Ephesus:

I am the one who holds the
seven stars in my right hand, and
I walk among the seven gold
lampstands. Listen to what I
say.*

2I know everything you have
done, including your hard work
and how you have endured. I
know you won't put up with
anyone who is evil. When some
people pretended to be apostles,
you tested them and found out
that they were liars. 3You have
endured and gone through hard
times because of me, and you
have not given up.

4But I do have something
against you! And it is this: You
don't have as much love as you
used to. 5Think about where you
have fallen from, and then turn
back and do as you did at first.
If you don't turn back, I will
come and take away your
lampstand. 6But there is one
thing you are doing right. You
hate what the Nicolaitans[j] are
doing, and so do I.*

7If you have ears, listen to
what the Spirit says to the
churches. I will let everyone who
wins the victory eat from the life-
giving tree in God's wonderful
garden.

The Letter to Smyrna

8This is what you must write to the
angel of the church in Smyrna:

I am the first and the last. I
died, but now I am alive! Listen
to what I say.*

9I know how much you suffer
and how poor you are, but you
are rich. I also know the cruel
things being said about you by
people who claim to be Jews. But
they are not really Jews. They
are a group that belongs to
Satan.

10Don't worry about what you
will suffer. The devil will throw
some of you into jail, and you
will be tested and made to suffer
for ten days. But if you are
faithful until you die, I will
reward you with a glorious life.[k]

11If you have ears, listen to
what the Spirit says to the
churches. Whoever wins the
victory will not be hurt by the
second death.[l]

---

[j] *Nicolaitans*: Nothing else is known about these people, though it is possible that they claimed to be followers of Nicolaus from Antioch (Acts 6.5). [k] *a glorious life*: The Greek text has "a crown of life." In ancient times an athlete who had won a contest was rewarded with a crown of flowers as a sign of victory. [l] *second death*: The first death is physical death, and the "second death" is eternal death.

2.1 **LET'S KEEP OUR LOVE WARM** The Christians at Ephesus had let their love grow cold. Ephesus had been John's home church, and it is interesting that the first of seven letters is sent there. They had kept their faith, but they had not continued to be excited about Jesus. Loving Christ is not just having correct ideas about him. Our service for him proves our faith is sincere.

2.6 **BE A CHRISTIAN ALL THROUGH** As suggested in the footnote, it is believed there was a group at Ephesus who followed a certain Nicolaus. Some think he may have been a false teacher who led people to believe they could lead an immoral life and still be true Christians. It is a mistake to imagine we can say we are Christians and live like the worst members of our society.

2.8 **RUN FOR THE PRIZE** This is what Jesus told the Christians at Smyrna. They had suffered much. But their Lord promised them a life after death that would be glorious if they would just be faithful to him. The second death he refers to is to be thrown into the lake of fire (see chapter 20, verse 15).

NOTES

The Letter to Pergamum

12This is what you must write to
the angel of the church in Pergamum:
I am the one who has the sharp double-edged sword! Listen to what I say.
13I know that you live where Satan has his throne.[m] But you have kept true to my name. Right there where Satan lives, my faithful witness Antipas[n] was taken from you and put to death. Even then you did not give up your faith in me.
14I do have a few things against you. Some of you are following the teaching of Balaam.[o] Long ago he told Balak to teach the people of Israel to eat food that had been offered to idols and to be immoral.
15Now some of you are following
the teaching of the Nicolaitans.[p]
16Turn back! If you don't, I will come quickly and fight against these people. And my words will cut like a sword.
17If you have ears, listen to what the Spirit says to the churches. To everyone who wins the victory, I will give some of the hidden food.[q] I will also give each one a white stone[r] with a new name[s] written on it. No one will know that name except the one who is given the stone.*

The Letter to Thyatira

18This is what you must write to
the angel of the church in Thyatira:
I am the Son of God! My eyes are like flames of fire, and my feet are like bronze. Listen to what I say.
19I know everything about you, including your love, your faith, your service, and how you have endured. I know that you are doing more now than you
have ever done before. 20But I
still have something against you because of that woman Jezebel.[t] She calls herself a prophet, and you let her teach and mislead my servants to do immoral things and to eat food offered to idols.*
21I gave her a chance to turn from her sins, but she did not want to stop doing these immoral things.
22I am going to strike down

---

[m] *where Satan has his throne*: The meaning is uncertain, but it may refer to the city as a center of pagan worship or of Emperor worship. [n] *Antipas*: Nothing else is known about this man, who is mentioned only here in the New Testament. [o] *Balaam*: According to Numbers 22—24, Balaam refused to disobey the Lord. But in other books of the Old Testament, he is spoken of as evil (Deuteronomy 23.4,5; Joshua 13.22; 24.9,10; Nehemiah 13.2). [p] *Nicolaitans*: See the note at verse 6. [q] *hidden food*: When the people of Israel were going through the desert, the Lord provided a special food for them. Some of this was placed in a jar and stored in the sacred chest (Exodus 16). According to later Jewish teaching, the prophet Jeremiah rescued the sacred chest when the temple was destroyed by the Babylonians. He hid the chest in a cave, where it would stay until God came to save his people. [r] *white stone*: The meaning of this is uncertain, though it may be the same as a ticket that lets a person into God's banquet where the "hidden food" is eaten. Or it may be a symbol of victory. [s] *a new name*: Either the name of Christ or God or the name of the follower who is given the stone. [t] *Jezebel*: Nothing else is known about her. This may have been her real name or a name that was given to her because she was like Queen Jezebel, who opposed the Lord (1 Kings 19.1,2; 21.1-26).

2.17 **EAT THE HIDDEN FOOD** The footnote tells you where this idea comes from. Also, Jesus called himself the "bread that gives life" (see John 6.35). He is the one whose life we need to feed on every day. He is the true bread who came down from heaven and gave his life to us. When we feed on Christ through his word and the Holy Spirit, we have real nourishment.

2.20 **WATCH OUT FOR JEZEBELS** The people at Thyatira were listening to a woman called Jezebel who was leading them into immoral living. Today, there are a lot of "Jezebels" in and out of the church. We are easily misled by tempting voices on television, in movies, and in other places. We hear the message that sin is fun, that it's not so bad. That's a lie. Don't let Jezebels lead you away from the Lord Jesus.

NOTES

Jezebel. Everyone who does
these immoral things with her
will also be punished, if they
don't stop. 23 I will even kill her
followers.[u] Then all the churches
will see that I know everyone's
thoughts and feelings. I will treat
each of you as you deserve.
24 Some of you in Thyatira
don't follow Jezebel's teaching.
You don't know anything about
what her followers call the "deep
secrets of Satan." So I won't
burden you down with any other
commands. 25 But until I come,
you must hold firmly to the
teaching you have.
26 I will give power over the
nations to everyone who wins
the victory and keeps on obeying
me until the end. 27-28 I will give
each of them the same power
that my Father has given me.
They will rule the nations with
an iron rod and smash those
nations to pieces like clay pots.
I will also give them the morning
star.[v]
29 If you have ears, listen to
what the Spirit says to the
churches.*

The Letter to Sardis

3 This is what you must write to
the angel of the church in Sardis:
I have the seven spirits of God
and the seven stars. Listen to
what I say.
I know what you are doing.
Everyone may think you are
alive, but you are dead. 2 Wake
up! You have only a little
strength left, and it is almost
gone. So try to become stronger.
I have found that you are not
completely obeying God.*
3 Remember the teaching that
you were given and that you
heard. Hold firmly to it and turn
from your sins. If you don't wake
up, I will come when you least
expect it, just as a thief does.
4 A few of you in Sardis have
not dirtied your clothes with sin.
You will walk with me in white
clothes, because you are worthy.
5 Everyone who wins the victory
will wear white clothes. Their
names will not be erased from
the book of life,[w] and I will tell
my Father and his angels that
they are my followers.
6 If you have ears, listen to
what the Spirit says to the
churches.

The Letter to Philadelphia

7 This is what you must write to the
angel of the church in Philadelphia:
I am the one who is holy and
true, and I have the keys that
belonged to David.[x] When I
open a door, no one can close
it. And when I close a door, no
one can open it. Listen to what
I say.
8 I know everything you have
done. And I have placed before
you an open door that no one
can close. You were not very
strong, but you obeyed my
message and did not deny that

---

[u] *her followers*: Or "her children." [v] *the morning star*: Probably thought of as the star that signals the end of night and the beginning of day. In 22.16 Christ is called the "morning star." [w] *book of life*: The book in which the names of God's people are written. [x] *the keys that belonged to David*: The keys stand for authority over David's kingdom.

2.29 **LISTEN TO THE SPIRIT** All seven of Jesus' letters to the churches contain the command to "listen to the Spirit." There are so many voices in the world that it is easy to tune out the Holy Spirit. That is why you should read the word of God every day to hear what the Spirit is saying.

3.2 **LET'S BE LIVING CHRISTIANS** That's what Jesus said to the people at Sardis. We can go around talking a good religion, but Christ may not be living in us. Words don't make us Christians. We may fool a lot of people, but God sees what we are inside. If Christ truly lives in us, we are truly clean.

NOTES

you are my followers.[y]* 9Now
you will see what I will do with
those people who belong to
Satan's group. They claim to be
Jews, but they are liars. I will
make them come and kneel
down at your feet. Then they will
know that I love you.
10You obeyed my message and
endured. So I will protect you
from the time of testing that
everyone in all the world must
go through. 11I am coming soon.
So hold firmly to what you have,
and no one will take away the
crown that you will be given as
your reward.
12Everyone who wins the
victory will be made into a pillar
in the temple of my God, and
they will stay there forever. I will
write on each of them the name
of my God and the name of his
city. It is the new Jerusalem that
my God will send down from
heaven. I will also write on them
my own new name.
13If you have ears, listen to
what the Spirit says to the
churches.

The Letter to Laodicea

14This is what you must write to
the angel of the church in Laodicea:
I am the one called Amen![z] I
am the faithful and true witness
and the source[a] of God's
creation. Listen to what I say.
15I know everything you have
done, and you are not cold or
hot. I wish you were either one
or the other. 16But since you are
lukewarm and neither cold nor
hot, I will spit you out of my
mouth.* 17You claim to be rich
and successful and to have
everything you need. But you
don't know how bad off you are.
You are pitiful, poor, blind, and
naked.
18Buy your gold from me. It
has been refined in a fire, and
it will make you rich. Buy white
clothes from me. Wear them and
you can cover up your shameful
nakedness. Buy medicine for
your eyes, so that you will be
able to see.
19I correct and punish
everyone I love. So make up your
minds to turn away from your
sins. 20Listen! I am standing and
knocking at your door. If you
hear my voice and open the door,
I will come in and we will eat
together.* 21Everyone who wins
the victory will sit with me on
my throne, just as I won the
victory and sat with my Father
on his throne.
22If you have ears, listen to
what the Spirit says to the
churches.

[y]*did not deny that you are my followers*: Or "did not say evil things about me." [z]*Amen*: Meaning "Trustworthy." [a]*source*: Or "beginning."

3.8 WE HAVE AN OPEN DOOR The open door is Jesus (John 10.7). He has eternal life. No one can close the door that he has opened, and all we have to do is walk through that door. This means that we accept Jesus as the only Savior, who opens the way to a satisfying life, and then finally the way to heaven with him.

3.16 A LUKEWARM DRINK IS UNPLEASANT It's better not to be baked at all than to be half-baked. A lukewarm or halfhearted Christian may be fooled into thinking everything is okay. But Jesus doesn't want halfway followers. What joy can there be in a half faith that wants to be half saved and half lost? That's a two-faced, dishonest way to live.

3.20 JESUS IS KNOCKING AT YOUR DOOR God's Son wants to come in and be your friend forever. Eating a meal together is a beautiful picture of friendship. But you must open the door of your life, and say, "Come in, Jesus. Be my honored guest and the Lord of my life."

NOTES

Worship in Heaven

4 After this, I looked and saw a door that opened into heaven. Then the voice that had spoken to me at first and that sounded like a trumpet said, "Come up here! I will show you what must happen next."* 2Right then the Spirit took control of me, and there in heaven I saw a throne and someone sitting on it. 3The one who was sitting there sparkled like precious stones of jasper[b] and carnelian.[c] A rainbow that looked like an emerald[d] surrounded the throne.

4Twenty-four other thrones were in a circle around that throne. And on each of these thrones there was an elder dressed in white clothes and wearing a gold crown. 5Flashes of lightning and roars of thunder came out from the throne in the center of the circle. Seven torches, which are the seven spirits of God, were burning in front of the throne. 6Also in front of the throne was something that looked like a glass sea, clear as crystal.

Around the throne in the center were four living creatures covered front and back with eyes.* 7The first creature was like a lion, the second one was like a bull, the third one had the face of a human, and the fourth was like a flying eagle. 8Each of the four living creatures had six wings, and their bodies were covered with eyes. Day and night they never stopped singing,

"Holy, holy, holy is the Lord,
the all-powerful God,
who was and is
and is coming!"

9The living creatures kept praising, honoring, and thanking the one who sits on the throne and who lives forever and ever.* 10At the same time the twenty-four elders kneeled down before the one sitting on the throne. And as they worshiped the one who lives forever, they placed their crowns in front of the throne and said,

11"Our Lord and God,
you are worthy
to receive glory,
honor, and power.
You created all things,
and by your decision they are
and were created."

The Scroll and the Lamb

5 In the right hand of the one sitting on the throne I saw a scroll[e] that

---

[b]*jasper*: Usually green or clear. [c]*carnelian*: Usually deep-red or reddish-white. [d]*emerald*: A precious stone, usually green. [e]*scroll*: A roll of paper or special leather used for writing on. Sometimes a scroll would be sealed on the outside with one or more pieces of wax.

4.1 **JOHN WENT UP TO HEAVEN** Up to here, John had been writing about things seen and heard on earth. Here we see him taken up to heaven itself, where he saw a great throne. Because of the rainbow, like a veil surrounding the throne, John couldn't see clearly the One sitting there. But we know that this is a vision of God. As we read John's words we share in the beauty of what he saw.

4.6 **WE CAN COME ONLY SO NEAR** John was separated from the throne by a sea. We are separated from God by his majesty. We can't grasp all that is God because we are creations of the infinite Creator. But we see his glory in Christ who is God the Son. It is more than enough for us that we have the friendship of Jesus.

4.9 **HEAVENLY BEINGS WORSHIP GOD** We have never seen these beings that John describes in God's throne room. They seem superior to God's other creations. Yet they never cease to worship God. Do you think our worship on earth should in many ways be like their worship? If we know God as he really is, how can we not worship him continually?

NOTES

had writing on the inside and on the
outside. And it was sealed in seven
places.* 2I saw a mighty angel ask
with a loud voice, "Who is worthy
to open the scroll and break its
seals?" 3No one in heaven or on earth
or under the earth was able to open
the scroll or see inside it.
4I cried hard because no one was
found worthy to open the book or
see inside it. 5Then one of the elders
said to me, "Stop crying and look!
The one who is called both the 'Lion
from the Tribe of Judah'[f] and 'King
David's Great Descendant'[g] has won
the victory. He will open the book
and its seven seals."*
6Then I looked and saw a Lamb
standing in the center of the throne
that was surrounded by the four living creatures and the elders. The
Lamb looked as if it had once been
killed. It had seven horns and seven
eyes, which are the seven spirits[h] of
God, sent out to all the earth.
7The Lamb went over and took the
scroll from the right hand of the one
who sat on the throne. 8After he had
taken it, the four living creatures and
the twenty-four elders kneeled down
before him. Each of them had a harp
and a gold bowl full of incense,[i]
which are the prayers of God's people. 9Then they sang a new song,
"You are worthy
to receive the scroll
and open its seals,
because you were killed.
And with your own blood
you bought for God
people from every tribe,
language, nation, and race.*
10You let them become kings
and serve God as priests,
and they will rule on earth."
11As I looked, I heard the voices
of a lot of angels around the throne
and the voices of the living creatures
and of the elders. There were millions
and millions of them, 12and they were
saying in a loud voice,
"The Lamb who was killed
is worthy to receive power,
riches, wisdom, strength,
honor, glory, and praise."
13Then I heard all beings in heaven
and on the earth and under the earth
and in the sea offer praise. Together,
all of them were saying,
"Praise, honor, glory,
and strength
forever and ever

---

[f] *'Lion from the Tribe of Judah'*: In Genesis 49.9 the tribe of Judah is called a young lion, and King David was from Judah. [g] *'King David's Great Descendant'*: The Greek text has "the root of David" which is a title for the Messiah based on Isaiah 11.1,10. [h] *the seven spirits*: Some manuscripts have "the spirits." [i] *incense*: A material that produces a sweet smell when burned. Sometimes it is a symbol for the prayers of God's people.

5.1 **THE SCROLL OF FUTURE HISTORY** We shall see that the scroll unfolds the events that are to come. It is God's history book written beforehand. We get comfort from knowing that the story of mankind is not just "a happening." God himself is the grand director of the drama of the ages. All things are under the control of God, who created time itself. Good must win over evil.

5.5 **THE LION OF JUDAH** A picture of the lion, which stood for the ancient tribe of Judah in Israel, was on King David's banner. The lion spoken of here is David's very great Grandson, the Lord Jesus Christ himself. But he is also called "the Lamb." This is the word that John the Baptist used for Jesus (John 1.29). It tells us a lot about Jesus that he is called both Lion and Lamb. He is both strong and gentle.

5.9 **THE LAMB CAN OPEN THE SCROLL** Of course—Jesus, the Lamb of God, is able to open the scroll and unlock the meaning of time and history. He died to free the world from sin's slavery, and he is able to unfold before our eyes that work of setting free. Jesus has the key that unlocks all secrets. Time has meaning only as it points to God's eternal plan for the ages.

NOTES

to the one who sits
on the throne
and to the Lamb!"
14The four living creatures said
"Amen," while the elders kneeled
down and worshiped.

Opening the Seven Seals

6 At the same time that I saw the
Lamb open the first of the seven
seals, I heard one of the four living
creatures shout with a voice like
thunder. It said, "Come out!"*
2Then I saw a white horse. Its rider
carried a bow and was given a crown.
He had already won some victories,
and he went out to win more.
3When the Lamb opened the second seal, I heard the second living
creature say, "Come out!" 4Then another horse came out. It was fiery
red. And its rider was given the
power to take away all peace from
the earth, so that people would
slaughter one another. He was also
given a big sword.
5When the Lamb opened the third
seal, I heard the third living creature
say, "Come out!" Then I saw a black
horse, and its rider had a balance
scale in one hand. 6I heard what
sounded like a voice from somewhere among the four living creatures. It said, "A quart of wheat will
cost you a whole day's wages! Three
quarts of barley will cost you a day's
wages too. But don't ruin the olive
oil or the wine."
7When the Lamb opened the fourth
seal, I heard the voice of the fourth
living creature say, "Come out!"
8Then I saw a pale green horse. Its
rider was named Death, and Death's
Kingdom followed behind. They
were given power over one fourth of
the earth, and they could kill its people with swords, famines, diseases,
and wild animals.
9When the Lamb opened the fifth
seal, I saw under the altar the souls
of everyone who had been killed for
speaking God's message and telling
about their faith.* 10They shouted,
"Master, you are holy and faithful!
How long will it be before you judge
and punish the people of this earth
who killed us?"
11Then each of those who had been
killed was given a white robe and
told to rest for a little while. They
had to wait until the complete number of the Lord's other servants and
followers would be killed.
12When I saw the Lamb open the
sixth seal, I looked and saw a great
earthquake. The sun turned as dark
as sackcloth,[j] and the moon became
as red as blood. 13The stars in the
sky fell to earth, just like figs shaken
loose by a windstorm. 14Then the sky
was rolled up like a scroll,[k] and all
mountains and islands were moved
from their places.
15The kings of the earth, its famous
people, and its military leaders hid
in caves or behind rocks on the
mountains. They hid there together
with the rich and the powerful and

---

[j] *sackcloth*: A rough, dark-colored cloth made from goat or camel hair and used to make grain sacks. It was worn in times of trouble or sorrow.
[k] *scroll*: See the note at 5.1.

6.1 **DEATH IS THE STORY OF LIFE** The first four seals opened by Christ reveal a time of death, warfare, and destruction. As the years go by, wars are only more mammoth and deadly, as millions of people can be destroyed in a few moments. The Prince of Peace alone can bring an end to war. Until then, death of all kinds is continually present to remind the world that sin still carries a high price (Romans 6.23).

6.9 **THE WORLD KILLS GOD'S MESSENGERS** God's people are not silent. They are his witnesses. But when we witness for God, the world is often hostile to that witness. The witnesses are often put to death, especially in parts of the world where the good news about Jesus is very unwelcome. But the Lord knows when you suffer for him, and his judgment is coming to a world that rejects him and his messengers.

NOTES

with all the slaves and free people.
16Then they shouted to the mountains and the rocks, "Fall on us! Hide
us from the one who sits on the
throne and from the anger of the
Lamb.* 17That terrible day has come!
God and the Lamb will show their
anger, and who can face it?"

The 144,000 Are Marked for God

7 1-2After this I saw four angels.
Each one was standing on one of
the earth's four corners. The angels
held back the four winds, so that no
wind would blow on the earth or on
the sea or on any tree. These angels
had also been given the power to
harm the earth and the sea. Then I
saw another angel come up from
where the sun rises in the east, and
he was ready to put the mark of the
living God on people. He shouted to
the four angels, 3"Don't harm the
earth or the sea or any tree! Wait
until I have marked the foreheads of
the servants of our God."
4Then I heard how many people
had been marked on the forehead.
There were one hundred forty-four
thousand, and they came from every
tribe of Israel:*
5 12,000 from the tribe
of Judah,
12,000 from the tribe
of Reuben,
12,000 from the tribe
of Gad,
6 12,000 from the tribe
of Asher,
12,000 from the tribe
of Naphtali,
12,000 from the tribe
of Manasseh,
7 12,000 from the tribe
of Simeon,
12,000 from the tribe
of Levi,
12,000 from the tribe
of Issachar,
8 12,000 from the tribe
of Zebulun,
12,000 from the tribe
of Joseph, and
12,000 from the tribe
of Benjamin.

People from Every Nation

9After this, I saw a large crowd with
more people than could be counted.
They were from every race, tribe, nation, and language, and they stood
before the throne and before the
Lamb. They wore white robes and
held palm branches in their hands,*
10as they shouted,
"Our God, who sits
upon the throne,
has the power
to save his people,
and so does the Lamb."

6.16 **GOD WILL JUDGE THE WORLD** Expect tremendous things to happen as God gets ready to judge the world. The order of nature will be disturbed. As unsaved people, great and small, begin to realize what is happening to them, they will cry out in horror in the presence of God's justice. Those who have not known God as Savior will know him as their Judge.

7.4 **ISRAEL HAS NOT BEEN FORGOTTEN** When you are reading the Old Testament you will see, over and over, that God made some very special promises to ancient Israel. Many faithful Israelites will be saved from the time of trouble to come. In God's new order, the believing nation of Israel will receive her promised blessings. At that time, Israel will no longer be the victim of wars and the hatred of the nations that surround her.

7.9 **COUNTLESS SAVED PEOPLE** John saw a crowd in heaven so large that no one could count them, from every nation on earth. Such a thing could happen because of men and women who carried the good news about Jesus to every place in the world. Blessed are those who have gone to faraway places to share the news about Jesus with every tribe and race.

NOTES

11The angels who stood around the
throne kneeled in front of it with their
faces to the ground. The elders and
the four living creatures kneeled
there with them. Then they all worshiped God 12and said,

"Amen! Praise, glory, wisdom,
thanks, honor, power,
and strength belong to our God
forever and ever! Amen!"

13One of the elders asked me, "Do
you know who these people are that
are dressed in white robes? Do you
know where they come from?"*
14"Sir," I answered, "you must
know."

Then he told me:

"These are the ones
who have gone through
the great suffering.
They have washed their robes
in the blood of the Lamb
and have made them white.
15And so they stand
before the throne of God
and worship him in his temple
day and night.
The one who sits on the throne
will spread his tent
over them.
16They will never hunger
or thirst again,
and they won't be troubled
by the sun
or any scorching heat.
17The Lamb in the center
of the throne
will be their shepherd.
He will lead them to streams
of life-giving water,
and God will wipe all tears
from their eyes."*

The Seventh Seal Is Opened

8 When the Lamb opened the seventh seal, there was silence in
heaven for about half an hour.
2I noticed that the seven angels who
stood before God were each given a
trumpet.
3Another angel, who had a gold
container for incense,[l] came and
stood at the altar. This one was given
a lot of incense to offer with the
prayers of God's people on the gold
altar in front of the throne.* 4Then
the smoke of the incense, together
with the prayers of God's people,
went up to God from the hand of the
angel.
5After this, the angel filled the incense container with fire from the altar and threw it on the earth. Thunder
roared, lightning flashed, and the
earth shook.

---

[l]*incense*: See the note at 5.8.

7.13 **GOD'S PEOPLE SUFFER** The crowd John saw in heaven was made up of those who suffered on earth because they loved Christ more than the wickedness of the world. Even today we see that sin divides people, so that those who don't love Christ usually resent people who do. God is healing the world through the suffering of his Son—and his people are sometimes called on to share in that suffering.

7.17 **THE LAMB WHO IS ALSO A SHEPHERD** Jesus is "the Lamb" we have seen before in this book, and now the elder says that the Lamb is also a "Shepherd." David the King called the Lord his Shepherd a thousand years before John wrote this book (see Psalm 23). We are the "sheep" that Jesus tends and cares for now and forever, in fields where flowers never fade.

8.3 **PRAYER IS A SWEET AROMA** Sometimes prayer seems hard for us, but the sincere prayers of his people please God very much. The fact that we personally take time to spend with God shows that we genuinely love him. Just as a father enjoys quiet talks with his children, so much more God loves the time we spend speaking with him about our joys, concerns, and troubles.

NOTES

The Trumpets

6 The seven angels now got ready
to blow their trumpets.
7 When the first angel blew his
trumpet, hail and fire mixed with
blood were thrown down on the
earth. A third of the earth, a third
of the trees, and a third of all green
plants were burned.*
8 When the second angel blew his
trumpet, something like a great fiery
mountain was thrown into the sea.
A third of the sea turned to blood,
9 a third of the living creatures in the
sea died, and a third of the ships was
destroyed.
10 When the third angel blew his
trumpet, a great star fell from
heaven. It was burning like a torch,
and it fell on a third of the rivers and
on a third of the springs of water.
11 The name of the star was Bitter,
and a third of the water turned bitter.
Many people died because the water
was so bitter.
12 When the fourth angel blew his
trumpet, a third of the sun, a third
of the moon, and a third of the stars
were struck. They each lost a third
of their light. So during a third of
the day there was no light, and a third
of the night was also without light.
13 Then I looked and saw a lone eagle flying across the sky. It was
shouting, "Trouble, trouble, trouble
to everyone who lives on earth! The
other three angels are now going to
blow their trumpets."

9 When the fifth angel blew his
trumpet, I saw a star[m] fall from
the sky to earth. It was given the key
to the tunnel that leads down to the
deep pit.* 2 As it opened the tunnel,
smoke poured out like the smoke of
a great furnace. The sun and the air
turned dark because of the smoke.
3 Locusts came out of the smoke and
covered the earth. They were given
the same power that scorpions have.
4 The locusts were told not to harm
the grass on the earth or any plant
or any tree. They were to punish only
those people who did not have God's
mark on their foreheads. 5 The locusts
were allowed to make them suffer
for five months, but not to kill them.
The suffering they caused was like
the sting of a scorpion. 6 In those days
people will want to die, but they will
not be able to. They will hope for
death, but it will escape from them.
7 These locusts looked like horses
ready for battle. On their heads they
wore something like gold crowns,
and they had human faces. 8 Their
hair was like a woman's long hair,
and their teeth were like those of a
lion. 9 On their chests they wore armor made of iron. Their wings roared
like an army of horse-drawn chariots
rushing into battle. 10 Their tails were
like a scorpion's tail with a stinger
that had the power to hurt someone
for five months. 11 Their king was the
angel in charge of the deep pit. In
Hebrew his name was Abaddon, and
in Greek it was Apollyon.[n]
12 The first horrible thing has now
happened! But wait. Two more horrible things will happen soon.
13 Then the sixth angel blew his
trumpet. I heard a voice speak from
the four corners of the gold altar that

---

[m] *star*: In the ancient world, stars were often thought of as living beings, such as angels. [n] *Abaddon . . . Apollyon*: The Hebrew word "Abaddon" and the Greek word "Apollyon" each mean "destruction."

8.7 **HARD TIMES ARE COMING** World history is a story of small amounts of peace followed by great trouble. It is dangerous to think that such trouble just "happens." By allowing trouble, God warns the world that it loves the wrong things. This passage shows that the last round of trouble will be the worst ever by far. Yet people still turn their backs on God.

9.1 **THE DEEP PIT WILL SEND FORTH EVIL** This passage, with its references to the deep pit, locusts, and the angel of destruction, reminds us that Satan and his demons are quite real and able to do much harm. Even though Jesus has won the victory over sin and death, we still ought to take the devil very seriously.

NOTES

stands in the presence of God.
14The voice spoke to this angel and
said, "Release the four angels who
are tied up beside the great Euphrates River." 15The four angels had
been prepared for this very hour and
day and month and year. Now they
were set free to kill a third of all
people.
16By listening, I could tell there
were more than two hundred million
of these war horses.* 17In my vision
their riders wore fiery-red, dark-blue,
and yellow armor on their chests. The
heads of the horses looked like lions,
with fire and smoke and sulphur
coming out of their mouths. 18One
third of all people were killed by the
three terrible troubles caused by the
fire, the smoke, and the sulphur.
19The horses had powerful mouths,
and their tails were like poisonous
snakes that bite and hurt.
20The people who lived through
these terrible troubles did not turn
away from the idols they had made,
and they did not stop worshiping demons. They kept on worshiping idols
that were made of gold, silver,
bronze, stone, and wood. Not one of
these idols could see, hear, or walk.
21No one stopped murdering or practicing witchcraft or being immoral or
stealing.

The Angel and the Little Scroll

10 I saw another powerful angel
come down from heaven. This
one was covered with a cloud, and
a rainbow was over his head. His face
was like the sun, his legs were like
columns of fire,* 2and with his hand
he held a little scroll[o] that had been
unrolled. He stood there with his
right foot on the sea and his left foot
on the land. 3Then he shouted with
a voice that sounded like a growling
lion. Thunder roared seven times.
4After the thunder stopped, I was
about to write what it had said. But
a voice from heaven shouted, "Keep
it secret! Don't write these things."
5The angel I had seen standing on
the sea and the land then held his
right hand up toward heaven.
6He made a promise in the name of
God who lives forever and who created heaven, earth, the sea, and every
living creature. The angel said, "You
won't have to wait any longer.
7God told his secret plans to his servants the prophets, and it will all happen by the time the seventh angel
sounds his trumpet."
8Once again the voice from heaven
spoke to me. It said, "Go and take
the open scroll from the hand of the
angel standing on the sea and the
land."
9When I went over to ask the angel
for the little scroll, the angel said,
"Take the scroll and eat it! Your
stomach will turn sour, but the taste
in your mouth will be as sweet as

[o]*scroll*: See the note at 5.1.

9.16 **SUFFERING COMES UP FROM HELL** We have read and heard about the horrible suffering in wars that have taken place in our own lifetime. We are reminded that there seems to be no limit to the ugly ways ungodly people can torment their neighbors. Right up until the time of the Lord's return to judge the world, mankind will suffer from terrible wars. Force cannot change human nature, but people can be changed if only they will turn to Jesus.

10.1 **ANGELS ARE GOD'S AGENTS** We meet these personalities all through the Bible. The word "angel" comes from a Greek word meaning "messenger." So an angel is a messenger of God. Angels are God's spiritual agents who announce his plans and serve him as he wishes. The angel in John's vision announces that all the plans God told the ancient prophets would soon be carried out. Count on it: every promise God has made will come true.

NOTES

honey."* 10I took the little scroll from
the hand of the angel and ate it. The
taste was as sweet as honey, but my
stomach turned sour.
11Then some voices said, "Keep on
telling what will happen to the people
of many nations, races, and languages, and also to kings."*

The Two Witnesses

11 An angel gave me a measuring stick and said:

Measure around God's temple.
Be sure to include the altar and
everyone worshiping there.
2But don't measure the
courtyard outside the temple
building. Leave it out. It has been
given to those people who don't
know God, and they will trample
all over the holy city for forty-two months. 3My two witnesses
will wear sackcloth,[p] while I let
them preach for one thousand
two hundred sixty days.

4These two witnesses are the two
olive trees and the two lampstands
that stand in the presence of the Lord
who rules the earth. 5Any enemy who
tries to harm them will be destroyed
by the fire that comes out of their
mouths. 6They have the power to lock
up the sky and to keep rain from falling while they are prophesying. And
whenever they want to, they can turn
water to blood and cause all kinds
of terrible troubles on earth.

7After the two witnesses have finished preaching God's message, the
beast that lives in the deep pit will
come up and fight against them. It
will win the battle and kill them.*
8Their bodies will be left lying in the
streets of the same great city where
their Lord was nailed to a cross. And
that city is spiritually like the city
of Sodom or the country of Egypt.
9For three and a half days the people of every nation, tribe, language,
and race will stare at the bodies of
these two witnesses and refuse to let
them be buried. 10Everyone on earth
will celebrate and be happy. They
will give gifts to each other, because
of what happened to the two prophets
who caused them so much trouble.
11But three and a half days later, God
will breathe life into their bodies.
They will stand up, and everyone
who sees them will be terrified.
12The witnesses then heard a loud
voice from heaven, saying, "Come up
here." And while their enemies were
watching, they were taken up to
heaven in a cloud. 13At that same moment there was a terrible earthquake
that destroyed a tenth of the city.
Seven thousand people were killed,
and the rest were frightened and
praised the God who rules in heaven.
14The second horrible thing has

---

[p]*sackcloth*: See the note at 6.12.

10.9 **GOD'S PLAN IS JUDGMENT** That's why the scroll John ate was bitter after it entered his stomach. God's word may be pleasant to read at first, and it has sweet comfort for those who are saved by faith. Yet the carrying out of that word will be very unpleasant for those who don't love the true God but love their own sinful ways instead.

10.11 **"KEEP ON TELLING"** Our job is to be faithful in telling people about God's plans for the future. Then some of them will believe us and be saved from the great judgment to come. Some will not want to hear us, but we must warn them.

11.7 **CAN PEOPLE BE SO BLIND?** Here John tells beforehand how God's two witnesses will be treated. Yet it seems that nobody will care that the witnesses are murdered. The people of the world are strangely careless about the terrible things they have done. But as godless ways increase, so does ignorance of God's warnings. We see such ignorance every day, even though more people than ever can read and hear the word of God.

NOTES

now happened! But the third one will be here soon.

The Seventh Trumpet

15At the sound of the seventh trumpet, loud voices were heard in heaven. They said,

"Now the kingdoms
of this world
belong to our Lord
and to his Chosen One!
And he will rule
forever and ever!"*

16Then the twenty-four elders, who were seated on thrones in God's presence, kneeled down and worshiped him. 17They said,

"Lord God All-Powerful,
you are and you were,
and we thank you.
You used your great power
and started ruling.
18When the nations got angry,
you became angry too!
Now the time has come
for the dead
to be judged.
It is time for you to reward
your servants the prophets
and all of your people
who honor your name,
no matter who they are.
It is time to destroy everyone
who has destroyed
the earth."

19The door to God's temple in heaven was then opened, and the sacred chest[q] could be seen inside the temple. I saw lightning and heard roars of thunder. The earth trembled and huge hailstones fell to the ground.*

The Woman and the Dragon

12 Something important appeared in the sky. It was a woman whose clothes were the sun. The moon was under her feet, and a crown made of twelve stars was on her head. 2She was about to give birth, and she was crying because of the great pain.

3Something else appeared in the sky. It was a huge red dragon with seven heads and ten horns, and a crown on each of its seven heads.
4With its tail, it dragged a third of the stars from the sky and threw them down to the earth. Then the dragon turned toward the woman, because it wanted to eat her child as soon as it was born.

5The woman gave birth to a son, who would rule all nations with an iron rod. The boy was snatched away. He was taken to God and placed on his throne.* 6The woman ran into the desert to a place that

[q]*sacred chest*: In Old Testament times the sacred chest was kept in the tent used for worship. It was the symbol of God's presence with his people and also of his agreement with them.

11.15 **GOD'S KINGDOM IS NEAR** The seventh trumpet announces the coming of Christ to rule the world. We need this comfort as we read about God's frightening judgments. As one of the Psalms says, "At night we may cry, but when morning comes we will celebrate." At the end of the dark night of sin and its trouble comes the dawn of the Son of God's wonderful reign.

11.19 **THE SACRED CHEST IN HEAVEN** The footnote tells what this chest was. Now we see that God has never forgotten his ancient agreement. The happiness promised in the agreement God made with his people was based on the keeping of the God-given Law, the Ten Commandments, a copy of which was put in the sacred chest. Christ himself kept that Law by living a sinless life and dying for us on the cross.

12.5 **GOD SAVES HIS SON** In John's vision of the dragon we see the birth of Jesus all over again (see Matthew 1 and 2 with Luke 1 and 2). Satan, who is called "the dragon," began trying to destroy the Christ child as soon as he was born. But we know the rest. *(continued)*

NOTES

God had prepared for her. There she
would be taken care of for one thousand two hundred sixty days.

Michael Fights the Dragon

7A war broke out in heaven. Michael and his angels were fighting
against the dragon and its angels.
8But the dragon lost the battle. It and
its angels were forced out of their
places in heaven 9and were thrown
down to the earth. Yes, that old snake
and his angels were thrown out of
heaven! That snake, who fools everyone on earth, is known as the devil
and Satan. 10Then I heard a voice
from heaven shout,

"Our God has shown
his saving power,
and his kingdom has come!
God's own Chosen One
has shown his authority.
Satan accused our people
in the presence of God
day and night.
Now he has been thrown out!

11Our people defeated Satan
because of the blood[r]
of the Lamb
and the message of God.
They were willing
to give up their lives.

12The heavens should rejoice,
together with everyone
who lives there.
But pity the earth
and the sea,
because the devil
was thrown down
to the earth.
He knows his time is short,
and he is very angry."

13When the dragon realized that it
had been thrown down to the earth,
it tried to make trouble for the
woman who had given birth to a son.*
14But the woman was given two
wings like those of a huge eagle, so
that she could fly into the desert.
There she would escape from the
snake and be taken care of for a time,
two times, and half a time.
15The snake then spit out water like
a river to sweep the woman away.
16But the earth helped her and swallowed the water that had come from
the dragon's mouth. 17This made the
dragon terribly angry with the
woman. So it started a war against
the rest of her children. They are the
people who obey God and are faithful
to what Jesus did and taught. 18The
dragon[s] stood on the beach beside
the sea.

The Two Beasts

13 I looked and saw a beast coming up from the sea. This one
had ten horns and seven heads, and
a crown was on each of its ten horns.
On each of its heads were names that
were an insult to God.* 2The beast

[r]*blood*: Or "death." [s]*The dragon*: The text has "he," and some manuscripts have "I."

(*continued*) Jesus was killed and buried but rose again, and then he returned to heaven. So Satan could not destroy God's plan to save us. The woman is more than just the mother of Jesus. She stands for God's people Israel, whom he protects until Satan is finally defeated forever.

12.13 **SATAN IS ON EARTH** Satan doesn't live in hell, as some wrongly think. He is a spiritual being who was thrown out of heaven and lives in this world. Although he knows he can't win his war against the Lord, his insane desire is to destroy the Lord's people. If we are careful to listen to God's word, we know that Satan's cause is hopeless.

13.1 **ANTICHRIST** The beast is "Antichrist," which means what the word says, a spirit opposed to Christ, or here, a particular person who opposes Christ in the last years before his return. Antichrist will even pretend to be a savior for the world. He will be very attractive, and many will follow his leadership. John writes about this person in his first letter (1 John 2.3). Paul also writes about him in 2 Thessalonians 2.

NOTES

that I saw had the body of a leopard,
the feet of a bear, and the mouth of
a lion. The dragon handed over its
own power and throne and great
authority to this beast. 3One of its
heads seemed to have been fatally
wounded, but now it was well. Everyone on earth marveled at this beast,
4and they worshiped the dragon who
had given its authority to the beast.
They also worshiped the beast and
said, "No one is like this beast! No
one can fight against it."
5The beast was allowed to brag and
claim to be God, and for forty-two
months it was allowed to rule.
6The beast cursed God, and it cursed
the name of God. It even cursed the
place where God lives, as well as
everyone who lives in heaven with
God. 7It was allowed to fight against
God's people and defeat them. It was
also given authority over the people
of every tribe, nation, language, and
race. 8The beast was worshiped by
everyone whose name was not written before the time of creation in the
book of the Lamb who was killed.[t]
9If you have ears,
then listen!
10If you are doomed
to be captured,
you will be captured.
If you are doomed
to be killed by a sword,
you will be killed
by a sword.
This means that God's people must
learn to endure and be faithful!
11I now saw another beast. This
one came out of the ground. It had
two horns like a lamb, but spoke like
a dragon.* 12It worked for the beast
whose fatal wound had been healed.
And it used all its authority to force
the earth and all its people to worship
that beast. 13It worked mighty miracles, and while people watched, it
even made fire come down from the
sky.
14This second beast fooled people
on earth by working miracles for the
first one. Then it talked them into
making an idol in the form of the
beast that did not die after being
wounded by a sword. 15It was allowed to put breath into the idol, so
that it could speak. Everyone who
refused to worship the idol of the
beast was put to death. 16All people
were forced to put a mark on their
right hand or forehead. Whether they
were powerful or weak, rich or poor,
free people or slaves, 17they all had
to have this mark, or else they could
not buy or sell anything. This mark
stood for the name of the beast and
for the number of its name.
18You need wisdom to understand
the number of the beast! But if you
are smart enough, you can figure this
out. Its number is six hundred sixty-
six, and it stands for a person.

The Lamb and His 144,000 Followers

14 I looked and saw the Lamb
standing on Mount Zion![u] With
him were a hundred forty-four thousand, who had his name and his Father's name written on their foreheads.* 2Then I heard a sound from
heaven that was like a roaring flood

[t]*not written . . . was killed*: Or "not written in the book of the Lamb who was killed before the time of creation." [u]*Mount Zion*: Another name for Jerusalem.

13.11 **THE SECOND BEAST** John writes of another beast who appears and works for the first one. He does miracles and gets people to worship the first beast as if he were God. False religion will be this second beast's specialty. Many people will actually adore Antichrist as if he were God.

14.1 **PRAISE FOR THE PROMISE-KEEPING GOD** We met this crowd of 144,000 before, in chapter 7. There we were told they represent the saved from the nation of Israel at this time. Once again we are reminded of the wonderful goodness of God who always keeps his promises. Israel was his first love, and he promised their ancestors, such as Abraham, that he would be their protector forever. The 144,000 will sing a new song to their Savior. Even now, we too should have a song of love to Christ in our hearts.

NOTES

or loud thunder or even like the music
of harps. 3And a new song was being
sung in front of God's throne and in
front of the four living creatures and
the elders. No one could learn that
song, except the one hundred forty-
four thousand who had been rescued
from the earth. 4All of these are pure
virgins, and they follow the Lamb
wherever he leads. They have been
rescued to be presented to God and
the Lamb as the most precious people[v] on earth. 5They never tell lies,
and they are innocent.

The Messages of the Three Angels

6I saw another angel. This one was
flying across the sky and had the
eternal good news to announce to the
people of every race, tribe, language,
and nation on earth. 7The angel
shouted, "Worship and honor God!
The time has come for him to judge
everyone. Kneel down before the one
who created heaven and earth, the
oceans, and every stream."
8A second angel followed and said,
"The great city of Babylon has fallen!
This is the city that made all nations
drunk and immoral. Now God is angry, and Babylon has fallen."
9Finally, a third angel came and
shouted:

> Here is what will happen if you
> worship the beast and the idol
> and have the mark of the beast
> on your hand or forehead.*
> 10You will have to drink the wine
> that God gives to everyone who
> makes him angry. You will feel
> his mighty anger, and you will
> be tortured with fire and burning
> sulphur, while the holy angels
> and the Lamb look on.
> 11If you worship the beast and
> the idol and accept the mark of
> its name, you will be tortured
> day and night. The smoke from
> your torture will go up forever
> and ever, and you will never be
> able to rest.

12God's people must learn to endure. They must also obey his commands and have faith in Jesus.
13Then I heard a voice from heaven
say, "Put this in writing. From now
on, the Lord will bless everyone who
has faith in him when they die."
The Spirit answered, "Yes, they
will rest from their hard work, and
they will be rewarded for what they
have done."*

The Earth Is Harvested

14I looked and saw a bright cloud,
and someone who seemed to be the
Son of Man[w] was sitting on the cloud.
He wore a gold crown on his head
and held a sharp sickle[x] in his hand.
15An angel came out of the temple
and shouted, "Start cutting with your
sickle! Harvest season is here, and
all crops on earth are ripe." 16The
one on the cloud swung his sickle
and harvested the crops.

---

[v] *the most precious people*: The Greek text has "the first people." The Law of Moses taught that the first-born of all animals and the first part of the harvest were special and belonged to the Lord. [w] *Son of Man*: See the note at 1.13. [x] *sickle*: A knife with a long curved blade, used to cut grain and other crops.

14.9 **WHAT DO YOU LIVE FOR?** What you worship is what you live for. If you live for the satisfaction of your body and all that this world has to offer, that is what you worship—and the result will be very ugly indeed. It is part of what the angel calls worshiping "the beast and the idol." If you serve the devil you get back all that the devil gives—hatred, heartache, and sorrow. False worship pays bitter wages.

14.13 **THE LORD WILL BE YOUR SHEPHERD** Have you ever watched the restful scene of a flock of sheep in a pasture? This is, in a way, a picture of the peace that waits for God's people beyond death. Those who die with faith in the Lord have the comfort of knowing that he will take them into his eternal fields where there will be no more dying, or sorrow, or pain. We will be with our great Shepherd forever.

NOTES

17Another angel with a sharp sickle
then came out of the temple. 18After
this, an angel with power over fire
came from the altar and shouted to
the angel who had the sickle. He said,
"All grapes on earth are ripe! Harvest
them with your sharp sickle."*
19The angel swung his sickle on earth
and cut off its grapes. He threw them
into a pit[y] where they were stomped
on as a sign of God's anger. 20The
pit was outside the city, and when
the grapes were mashed, blood
flowed out. The blood turned into a
river that was about two hundred
miles long and almost deep enough
to cover a horse.

The Last of the Terrible Troubles

15 After this, I looked at the sky
and saw something else that
was strange and important. Seven
angels were bringing the last seven
terrible troubles. When these are
ended, God will no longer be angry.
2Then I saw something that looked
like a glass sea mixed with fire, and
people were standing on it. They
were the ones who had defeated the
beast and the idol and the number
that tells the name of the beast. God
had given them harps, 3and they were
singing the song that his servant Moses and the Lamb had sung. They
were singing,

"Lord God All-Powerful,
you have done great
and marvelous things.
You are the ruler
of all nations,
and you do what is
right and fair.*
4Lord, who does not honor
and praise your name?
You alone are holy,
and all nations will come
and worship you,
because you have shown
that you judge
with fairness."

5After this, I noticed something
else in heaven. The sacred tent used
for a temple was open. 6And the
seven angels who were bringing the
terrible troubles were coming out of
it. They were dressed in robes of pure
white linen and wore belts made of
pure gold. 7One of the four living
creatures gave each of the seven angels a bowl made of gold. These
bowls were filled with the anger of
God who lives forever and ever.
8The temple quickly filled with
smoke from the glory and power of
God. No one could enter it until the
seven angels had finished pouring
out the seven last troubles.

The Bowls of God's Anger

16 From the temple I heard a voice
shout to the seven angels, "Go
and empty the seven bowls of God's
anger on the earth."*

[y]*pit*: It was the custom to put grapes in a pit (called a wine press) and stomp on them to make juice that would later turn to wine.

14.18 **THIS HARVEST WILL BE AWFUL** When the grapes are ripe, the owner of the vineyard harvests them. Likewise, the world will come to a time when it is "ripe and ready for harvesting." But this will not be a joyful harvest—it will be a sad one with much suffering. God will finally deal with the evil world that has refused to accept his Son.

15.3 **THERE WILL BE SINGING IN HEAVEN** Before the bowls of God's anger are poured out, there will be worship in heaven. Listen to the beautiful words of the song. Consider all of the glorious things the choir will sing about God. He is "All-Powerful," the "ruler of all nations," and he does "what is right and fair." Don't listen to people who belittle the Lord. Because he is God, he always does what is right.

16.1 **WHAT ARE THESE SEVEN BOWLS?** Beginning in chapter 5 we saw Christ the Lamb begin to open the seven seals of the future. This scene ends with the sounding of the *(continued)*

NOTES

2 The first angel emptied his bowl
on the earth. At once ugly and painful
sores broke out on everyone who had
the mark of the beast and worshiped
the idol.
3 The second angel emptied his
bowl on the sea. Right away the sea
turned into blood like that of a dead
person, and every living thing in the
sea died.
4 The third angel emptied his bowl
into the rivers and streams. At once
they turned to blood. 5 Then I heard
the angel, who has power over water,
say,

"You have always been,
and you always will be
the holy God.
You had the right
to judge in this way.
6 They poured out the blood[z]
of your people
and your prophets.
So you gave them blood
to drink, as they deserve!"
7 After this, I heard
the altar shout,
"Yes, Lord God All-Powerful,
your judgments are honest
and fair."

8 The fourth angel emptied his bowl
on the sun, and it began to scorch
people like fire. 9 Everyone was
scorched by its great heat, and all
of them cursed the name of God who
had power over these terrible troubles. But no one turned to God and
praised him.
10 The fifth angel emptied his bowl
on the throne of the beast. At once
darkness covered its kingdom, and
its people began biting their tongues
in pain. 11 And because of their painful sores, they cursed the God who
rules in heaven. But still they did not
stop doing evil things.
12 The sixth angel emptied his bowl
on the great Euphrates River, and it
completely dried up to make a road
for the kings from the east. 13 An evil
spirit that looked like a frog came
out of the mouth of the dragon. One
also came out of the mouth of the
beast, and another out of the mouth
of the false prophet. 14 These evil spirits had the power to work miracles.
They went to every king on earth,
to bring them together for a war
against God All-Powerful. But that
will be the day of God's great victory.
15 Remember that Christ says,
"When I come, it will surprise you
like a thief! But God will bless you,
if you are awake and ready. Then
you won't have to walk around naked
and be ashamed."
16 Those armies came together in
a place that in Hebrew is called
Armagedon.[a]*
17 As soon as the seventh angel
emptied his bowl in the air, a loud
voice from the throne in the temple
shouted, "It's done!" 18 There were
flashes of lightning, roars of thunder,
and the worst earthquake in all history. 19 The great city of Babylon split
into three parts, and the cities of
other nations fell. So God made Babylon drink from the wine cup that
was filled with his anger. 20 Every island ran away, and the mountains
disappeared. 21 Hailstones, weighing

---

[z] *They poured out the blood*: A way of saying, "They murdered." [a] *Armagedon*: The Hebrew form of the name would be "Har Megeddo," meaning "Hill of Megeddo," where many battles were fought in ancient times (see Judges 5.19; 2 Kings 23.29,30).

(*continued*) seven trumpets in chapters 8 through 11. (The seven trumpets are included in the seventh seal.) Now we read the conclusion of this review of future history. In this chapter the seven bowls picture the judgments of God at the end of this age. The number "seven" throughout Scripture often suggests completeness. The age of sin and sorrow will be completed, and then Jesus will return to rule.

16.16 **ARMAGEDON** At the end of this great time of trouble, the armies of the world will gather one last time to try to defeat the Lord. They will come together to fight at a place called Armagedon. But they will not be able to overcome the All-Powerful God. It looks foolish that they could try such a thing. But there are people now who fight God every day.

NOTES

about a hundred pounds each, fell from the sky on people. Finally, the people cursed God, because the hail was so terrible.*

The Immoral Woman and the Beast

17 One of the seven angels who had emptied the bowls came over and said to me, "Come on! I will show you how God will punish that shameless and immoral woman who sits on many oceans.*
2Every king on earth has slept with her, and her shameless ways are like wine that has made everyone on earth drunk."
3With the help of the Spirit, the angel took me into the desert, where I saw a woman sitting on a red beast. The beast was covered with names that were an insult to God, and it had seven heads and ten horns.
4The woman was dressed in purple and scarlet robes, and she wore jewelry made of gold, precious stones, and pearls. In her hand she held a gold cup filled with the filthy and nasty things she had done.
5On her forehead a mysterious name was written:

I AM THE GREAT CITY
OF BABYLON,
THE MOTHER
OF EVERY IMMORAL
AND FILTHY THING ON EARTH.*

6I could tell that the woman was drunk on the blood of God's people who had given their lives for Jesus. This surprising sight amazed me,
7and the angel said:

Why are you so amazed? I will explain the mystery about this woman and about the beast she is sitting on, with its seven heads and ten horns.
8The beast you saw is one that used to be and no longer is. It will come back from the deep pit, but only to be destroyed. Everyone on earth whose names were not written in the book of life[b] before the time of creation will be amazed. They will see this beast that used to be and no longer is, but will be once more.

9Anyone with wisdom can figure this out. The seven heads that the woman is sitting on stand for seven hills. These heads are also seven kings.
10Five of the kings are dead. One is ruling now, and the other one has not yet come. But when he does, he will rule for only a little while.

11You also saw a beast that used to be and no longer is. That beast is one of the seven kings

[b]*book of life*: The book in which the names of God's people are written.

16.21 **SOME PEOPLE NEVER CHANGE** John Milton's great poem, *Paradise Lost*, quotes Satan as saying, "Better to reign in hell than serve in heaven." In spite of the judgments that will happen before Christ comes again, people will curse God. All that God can do will make no difference to them. God even sent his Son into the world to die for sinners. Then he waited many centuries for people to believe in him. But right up to the end, there will be people who would rather die than turn from their sins.

17.1 **EVIL LIKES TO LOOK GOOD** The immoral woman in John's vision doesn't want to look ugly. Even prostitutes like to "look nice." That's their trap. The immoral woman here is trapping a lot of people too. While trying to look like the beautiful "bride of Christ" in chapter 21, she is really a deceiver and "drunk on the blood of God's people." But in the end the very world powers that she serves will destroy her.

17.5 **FILTHY, ROTTEN BABYLON** Babylon was an ancient city that contained all forms of evil. It was destroyed years ago, never to be built again. The name is a way of speaking of the world's immorality. A system of evil exists around the world, which God will finally destroy.

NOTES

who will return as the eighth
king, but only to be destroyed.
12The ten horns that you saw
are ten more kings, who have
not yet come into power, and
they will rule with the beast for
only a short time.* 13They all
think alike and will give their
power and authority to the beast.
14These kings will go to war
against the Lamb. But he will
defeat them, because he is Lord
over all lords and King over all
kings. His followers are chosen
and special and faithful.
15The oceans that you saw the
immoral woman sitting on are
crowds of people from all races
and languages. 16The ten horns
and the beast will start hating
the shameless woman. They will
strip off her clothes and leave
her naked. Then they will eat her
flesh and throw the rest of her
body into a fire. 17God is the one
who made these kings all think
alike and decide to give their
power to the beast. And they will
do this until what God has said
comes true.
18The woman you saw is the
great city that rules over all
kings on earth.

The Fall of Babylon

18 I saw another angel come from
heaven. This one had great
power, and the earth was bright because of his glory. 2The angel
shouted,

"Fallen! Powerful Babylon
has fallen
and is now the home
of demons.
It is the den
of every filthy spirit
and of all unclean birds,
and every dirty
and hated animal.
3Babylon's evil
and immoral wine
has made all nations drunk.
Every king on earth
has slept with her,
and every merchant on earth
is rich because of
her evil desires."

4Then I heard another voice
from heaven shout,
"My people, you must escape
from Babylon.
Don't take part in her sins
and share her punishment.*
5Her sins are piled
as high as heaven.
God has remembered the evil
she has done.
6Treat her as she
has treated others.
Make her pay double
for what she has done.
Make her drink twice as much
of what she mixed
for others.
7That woman honored herself
with a life of luxury.
Reward her now
with suffering and pain.

"Deep in her heart
Babylon said,
'I am the queen!
Never will I be a widow
or know what it means
to be sad.'
8And so, in a single day
she will suffer the pain
of sorrow, hunger,
and death.

17.12 **EVIL ALLIES** The ten horns stand for ten nations that will follow the beast. Notice how they will turn on the immoral woman. There's a saying that "there is no honor among thieves." Those who band together to do evil cannot even trust each other.

18.4 **GET OUT OF BABYLON** Living in the world has always been hard for those who love Christ, because the world's ways are not God's ways. For now there is no escape from living in the world, except death. Until the Lord comes back to change everything, he warns those who love him to avoid bad lifestyles and evil cooperation with the sinful world.

NOTES

Fire will destroy
her dead body,
because her judge
is the powerful Lord God."
9Every king on earth who slept
with her and shared in her luxury
will mourn. They will weep, when
they see the smoke from that fire.
10Her sufferings will frighten them,
and they will stand at a distance and
say,
"Pity that great
and powerful city!
Pity Babylon!
In a single hour
her judgment has come."*
11Every merchant on earth will
mourn, because there is no one to
buy their goods. 12There won't be
anyone to buy their gold, silver, jewels, pearls, fine linen, purple cloth,
silk, scarlet cloth, sweet-smelling
wood, fancy carvings of ivory and
wood, as well as things made of
bronze, iron, or marble. 13No one will
buy their cinnamon, spices, incense,
myrrh, frankincense,[c] wine, olive oil,
fine flour, wheat, cattle, sheep,
horses, chariots, slaves, and other
humans.
14Babylon, the things
your heart desired
have all escaped
from you.
Every luxury
and all your glory
will be lost forever.
You will never
get them back.
15The merchants had become rich
because of her. But when they saw
her sufferings, they were terrified.
They stood at a distance, crying and
mourning. 16Then they shouted,
"Pity the great city
of Babylon!
She dressed in fine linen
and wore purple
and scarlet cloth.
She had jewelry
made of gold
and precious stones
and pearls.
17Yet in a single hour
her riches disappeared."
Every ship captain and passenger
and sailor stood at a distance, together with everyone who does business by traveling on the sea. 18When
they saw the smoke from her fire,
they shouted, "This was the greatest
city ever!"
19They cried loudly, and in their
sorrow they threw dust on their
heads, as they said,
"Pity the great city
of Babylon!
Everyone who sailed the seas
became rich
from her treasures.
But in a single hour
the city was destroyed.*
20The heavens should be happy
with God's people
and apostles and prophets.
God has punished her
for them."
21A powerful angel then picked up
a huge stone and threw it into the
sea. The angel said,
"This is how the great city
of Babylon

[c]*myrrh, frankincense*: Myrrh was a valuable sweet-smelling powder often used in perfume. Frankincense was a valuable powder that was burned to make a sweet smell.

18.10 **THE WORLD LOVES BABYLON** "Pity that great and powerful city." The center of the world's wickedness in John's time was the city of Rome. Now the evils are more modern, and are spread all over the so-called "civilized world." Those evils have also gotten into the very church of God. Many people accept religion if it will just agree to bless their evil doings.

18.19 **WHAT DO YOU VALUE IN LIFE?** Notice that people will mourn when the world system called "Babylon" falls. It's easy to imagine that material goods are what life is really all about. The mistake here is our failure to realize that the world's little joys pass away at last. If we set our hearts on them, we end up losers when they're gone. Those "things" are just an empty, false god.

NOTES

will be thrown down,
never to rise again.
22The music of harps and singers
and of flutes and trumpets
will no longer be heard.
No workers will ever
set up shop in that city,
and the sound
of grinding grain
will be silenced forever.
23Lamps will no longer shine
anywhere in Babylon,
and couples will never again
say wedding vows there.
Her merchants ruled
the earth,
and by her witchcraft
she fooled all nations.
24On the streets of Babylon
is found the blood
of God's people
and of his prophets,
and everyone else."*

19 After this, I heard what
sounded like a lot of voices in
heaven, and they were shouting,
"Praise the Lord!
To our God belongs
the glorious power to save,*
2because his judgments
are honest and fair.
That filthy, immoral woman
ruined the earth
with shameful deeds.
But God has judged her
and made her pay
the price for murdering
his servants."

3Then the crowd shouted,
"Praise the Lord!
Smoke will never stop rising
from her burning body."
4After this, the twenty-four elders
and the four living creatures all
kneeled before the throne of God and
worshiped him. They said, "Amen!
Praise the Lord!"

The Marriage Supper of the Lamb

5From the throne a voice said,
"If you worship
and fear our God,
give praise to him,
no matter who you are."
6Then I heard what seemed to be
a large crowd that sounded like a
roaring flood and loud thunder all
mixed together. They were saying,
"Praise the Lord!
Our Lord God All-Powerful
now rules as king.
7So we will be glad and happy
and give him praise.
The wedding day of the Lamb
is here,
and his bride is ready.*
8She will be given
a wedding dress
made of pure
and shining linen.
This linen stands
for the good things
God's people have done."
9Then the angel told me, "Put this
in writing. God will bless everyone
who is invited to the wedding feast
of the Lamb." The angel also said,
"These things that God has said are
true."
10I kneeled at the feet of the angel

18.24 **CHRISTIANS PAY A PRICE** Of course, if you don't crave the joys of this world, the world will be glad to see that you don't get them. They say "the race is to the swift." You may have to make a clever deal now and then if you're going to get a big share of the world's goods. But is it worth it?

19.1 **THERE WILL BE JOY IN HEAVEN** All who love God will be glad to see the vicious system described above destroyed. Right now, dishonesty and immorality seem to be the rule. The world is mean to you if you don't join the crowd and become part of the system. But this system will pass away, and then we will be glad when we see our Lord win his victory.

19.7 **A ROYAL WEDDING** The world has seen some royal weddings, but none to match this. The King Jesus, the Lamb of God, will be the royal bridegroom, and those who have been saved will be the bride, clothed in a gown that stands for the goodness that comes from him.

NOTES

and began to worship him. But the
angel said, "Don't do that! I am a
servant, just like you and everyone
else who tells about Jesus. Don't worship anyone but God. Everyone who
tells about Jesus does it by the power
of the Spirit."

The Rider on the White Horse

11I looked and saw that heaven was
open, and a white horse was there.
Its rider was called Faithful and True,
and he is always fair when he judges
or goes to war. 12He had eyes like
flames of fire, and he was wearing
a lot of crowns. His name was written
on him, but he was the only one who
knew what the name meant.
13The rider wore a robe that was
covered with[d] blood, and he was
known as "The Word of God."*
14He was followed by armies from
heaven, which rode on horses and
were dressed in pure white linen.
15From his mouth a sharp sword went
out to attack the nations. He will rule
them with an iron rod and will show
the fierce anger of God All-Powerful
by stomping the grapes in the pit
where wine is made. 16On the part
of the robe that covered his thigh was
written, "KING OF KINGS AND
LORD OF LORDS."
17I then saw an angel standing on
the sun, and he shouted to all the
birds flying in the sky, "Come and
join in God's great feast! 18You can
eat the flesh of kings, rulers, leaders,
horses, riders, free people, slaves, important people, and everyone else."
19I also saw the beast and all kings
of the earth come together. They
fought against the rider on the white
horse and against his army. 20But the
beast was captured and so was the
false prophet. This is the same
prophet who had worked miracles
for the beast, so that he could fool
everyone who had the mark of the
beast and worshiped the idol. The
beast and the false prophet were
thrown alive into a lake of burning
sulphur. 21But the rest of their army
was killed by the sword that came
from the mouth of the rider on the
horse. Then birds stuffed themselves
on the dead bodies.

The Thousand Years

20 I saw an angel come down from
heaven, carrying the key to the
deep pit and a big chain. 2He chained
the dragon for a thousand years. It
is that old snake, who is also known
as the devil and Satan. 3Then the angel threw the dragon into the pit. He
locked and sealed it, so that a thousand years would go by before the
dragon could fool the nations again.
But after that, it would have to be
set free for a little while.
4I saw thrones, and sitting on those
thrones were the ones who had been
given the right to judge. I also saw
the souls of the people who had their
heads cut off because they had told
about Jesus and preached God's message. They were the same ones who
had not worshiped the beast or the
idol, and they had refused to let its
mark be put on their hands or foreheads. They will come to life and rule
with Christ for a thousand years.*

[d]*covered with*: Some manuscripts have "sprinkled with."

19.13 **CHRIST THE KING WILL MAKE WAR** Jesus Christ will ride against the beast and his armies in a tremendous battle. There can be only one certain outcome of this great war of the ages. Christ is the King of kings. His enemies will realize that they never really had a chance against his authority.

20.4 **CHRIST WILL REIGN ON EARTH** The ones who loved Jesus and suffered for him will be raised up from death by his power, and will reign with him when he wins his victory. That was always the right outcome of the conflict between God and Satan, between good and evil. It was never possible that the hopeless dreams of the devil and his followers could come true. While evil seems to run the world we are sometimes discouraged, but in God's time we will see Jesus reign in mighty power.

NOTES

5-6These people are the first to be
raised to life, and they are especially
blessed and holy. The second death[e]
has no power over them. They will
be priests for God and Christ and will
rule with them for a thousand years.
No other dead people were raised
to life until a thousand years later.

Satan Is Defeated

7At the end of the thousand years,
Satan will be set free. 8He will fool
the countries of Gog and Magog,
which are at the far ends of the earth,
and their people will follow him into
battle. They will have as many followers as there are grains of sand
along the beach, 9and they will march
all the way across the earth. They
will surround the camp of God's people and the city that his people love.
But fire will come down from heaven
and destroy the whole army. 10Then
the devil who fooled them will be
thrown into the lake of fire and burning sulphur. He will be there with
the beast and the false prophet, and
they will be in pain day and night
forever and ever.*

The Judgment at the Great White Throne

11I saw a great white throne with
someone sitting on it. Earth and
heaven tried to run away, but there
was no place for them to go. 12I also
saw all the dead people standing in
front of that throne. Every one of
them was there, no matter who they
had once been. Several books were
opened, and then the book of life[f]
was opened. The dead were judged
by what those books said they had
done.
13The sea gave up the dead people
who were in it, and death and its
kingdom also gave up their dead.
Then everyone was judged by what
they had done. 14Afterwards, death
and its kingdom were thrown into
the lake of fire. This is the second
death.[g] 15Anyone whose name was
not written in the book of life was
thrown into the lake of fire.

The New Heaven and the New Earth

21 I saw a new heaven and a new
earth. The first heaven and the
first earth had disappeared, and so
had the sea.* 2Then I saw New Jerusalem, that holy city, coming down
from God in heaven. It was like a
bride dressed in her wedding gown
and ready to meet her husband.
3I heard a loud voice shout from
the throne:

> God's home is now with his
> people. He will live with them,
> and they will be his own. Yes,
> God will make his home among
> his people. 4He will wipe all tears
> from their eyes, and there will
> be no more death, suffering,
> crying, or pain. These things of
> the past are gone forever.

5Then the one sitting on the throne
said:

---

[e] *second death*: The first death is physical death, and the "second death" is eternal death. [f] *book of life*: See the note at 3.5. [g] *second death*: See the note at verse 6.

20.10 **GOD WILL PUNISH EVIL** It is an unpleasant subject. Nevertheless, the warnings are clear that everlasting punishment in hell, the "lake of fire," awaits Satan, his antichrist, and their willing followers. Evil is not something people follow blindly, and they have been warned that evil cannot exist along with God's eternal goodness. So they will have the evil they chose, along with evil's natural and tragic results.

21.1 **GOD'S EVERLASTING ORDER WILL ARRIVE** Time itself will pass away, and eternity will begin. The old order will fall away like a worn-out suit of clothes. The tree that was bare and dry will burst forth with healthy leaves and fruit. The kingdom of God will come. Good people have long dreamed and spoken of a "new order," but God always had this in mind. God himself will live with his people.

NOTES

I am making everything new.
Write down what I have said. My
words are true and can be
trusted. 6Everything is finished!
I am Alpha and Omega,[h] the
beginning and the end. I will
freely give water from the life-
giving fountain to everyone who
is thirsty. 7All who win the
victory will be given these
blessings. I will be their God, and
they will be my people.
8But I will tell you what will
happen to cowards and to
everyone who is unfaithful or
dirty-minded or who murders or
is sexually immoral or uses
witchcraft or worships idols or
tells lies. They will be thrown
into that lake of fire and burning
sulphur. This is the second
death.[i]

The New Jerusalem

9I saw one of the seven angels who
had the bowls filled with the seven
last terrible troubles. The angel came
to me and said, "Come on! I will show
you the one who will be the bride
and wife of the Lamb." 10Then with
the help of the Spirit, he took me to
the top of a very high mountain.
There he showed me the holy city
of Jerusalem coming down from God
in heaven.*
11The glory of God made the city
bright. It was dazzling and crystal
clear like a precious jasper[j] stone.
12The city had a high and thick wall
with twelve gates, and each one of
them was guarded by an angel. On
each of the gates was written the
name of one of the twelve tribes of
Israel. 13Three of these gates were
on the east, three were on the north,
three more were on the south, and
the other three were on the west.
14The city was built on twelve foundation stones. On each of the stones
was written the name of one of the
Lamb's twelve apostles.
15The angel who spoke to me had
a gold measuring stick to measure
the city and its gates and its walls.
16The city was shaped like a cube,
because it was just as high as it was
wide. When the angel measured the
city, it was about fifteen hundred
miles high and fifteen hundred miles
wide. 17Then the angel measured the
wall, and by our measurements it was
about two hundred sixteen feet high.
18The wall was built of jasper, and
the city was made of pure gold, clear
as crystal. 19Each of the twelve foundations was a precious stone. The
first was jasper, the second was sapphire, the third was agate, the fourth
was emerald, 20the fifth was onyx,
the sixth was carnelian, the seventh
was chrysolite, the eighth was beryl,
the ninth was topaz, the tenth was
chrysoprase, the eleventh was jacinth, and the twelfth was amethyst.
21Each of the twelve gates was a solid
pearl. The streets of the city were
made of pure gold, clear as crystal.
22I did not see a temple there. The
Lord God All-Powerful and the Lamb
were its temple. 23And the city did
not need the sun or the moon. The
glory of God was shining on it, and
the Lamb was its light.
24Nations will walk by the light of
that city, and kings will bring their

---

[h]*Alpha and Omega*: See the note at 1.8. [i]*second death*: See the note at 20.6. [j]*jasper*: The precious and semi-precious stones mentioned in verses 19,20 are of different colors. *Jasper* is usually green or clear; *sapphire* is blue; *agate* has circles of brown and white; *emerald* is green; *onyx* has different bands of color; *carnelian* is deep-red or reddish-white; *chrysolite* is olive-green; *beryl* is green or bluish-green; *topaz* is yellow; *chrysoprase* is apple-green; *jacinth* is reddish-orange; and *amethyst* is deep purple.

21.10 **THERE WILL BE A NEW CITY OF GOD** A great Christian named Augustine long ago wrote a book called *The City of God*. Believers have always tried to picture what God's new Jerusalem will be like. Old Jerusalem was a poor shadow of the city God plans for the future. Look at the size of it (verse 16). An Old Testament prophet tells us that the name of the city will be "The Lord Is There." God himself will be the beauty and glory of his eternal city.

NOTES

riches there. 25Its gates are always
open during the day, and night never
comes. 26The glorious treasures of
nations will be brought into the city.
27But nothing unworthy will be allowed to enter. No one who is dirty-
minded or who tells lies will be there.
Only those whose names are written
in the Lamb's book of life[k] will be
in the city.*

22 The angel showed me a river
that was crystal clear, and its
waters gave life. The river came from
the throne where God and the Lamb
were seated. 2Then it flowed down
the middle of the city's main street.
On each side of the river are trees[l]
that grow a different kind of fruit
each month of the year. The fruit
gives life, and the leaves are used as
medicine to heal the nations.
3God's curse will no longer be on
the people of that city. He and the
Lamb will be seated there on their
thrones, and its people will worship
God 4and will see him face to face.
God's name will be written on the
foreheads of the people. 5Never again
will night appear, and no one who
lives there will ever need a lamp or
the sun. The Lord God will be their
light, and they will rule forever.

The Coming of Christ

6Then I was told:
These words are true and can
be trusted. The Lord God
controls the spirits of his
prophets, and he is the one who
sent his angel to show his
servants what must happen right
away. 7Remember, I am coming
soon! God will bless everyone
who pays attention to what this
book tells about the future.*
8My name is John, and I am the
one who heard and saw these things.
Then after I had heard and seen all
this, I kneeled down and began to
worship at the feet of the angel who
had shown it to me.
9But the angel said,
Don't do that! I am a servant,
just like you. I am the same as
a follower or a prophet or
anyone else who obeys what is
written in this book. God is the
one you should worship.
10Don't keep the prophecies in
this book a secret. These things
will happen soon.
11Evil people will keep on
being evil, and everyone who is
dirty-minded will still be dirty-
minded. But good people will
keep on doing right, and God's
people will always be holy.
12Then I was told:
I am coming soon! And when
I come, I will reward everyone
for what they have done. 13I am
Alpha and Omega,[m] the first and
the last, the beginning and the
end.
14God will bless all who have
washed their robes. They will
each have the right to eat fruit

---

[k] *book of life*: A book in which the names of God's people are written. [l] *trees*: The Greek has "tree," which is used in a collective sense of trees on both sides of the heavenly river. [m] *Alpha and Omega*: See the note at 1.8.

21.27 **WHO WILL LIVE IN THE CITY?** "The bride," the ones who love Jesus and are saved by him, whose names are in the book of life, will live in God's city. But even now, if you love Jesus, he will come to live in you. Have you given your life to Jesus? It's the only reasonable thing to do with your life. God made you for himself. So you can be happy only when you have given your life to him.

22.7 **WHEN WILL JESUS COME?** The child asks, "When will Daddy come home?" The answer is usually, "Soon." So the child waits, at times a little impatiently. But when the father returns the child forgets all about the waiting. The return of Jesus for his church is like that. He is coming "soon," but that includes some waiting—how long, we cannot say. The main thing is to watch and live in a way that will make us glad to see Jesus when he appears.

NOTES

from the tree that gives life, and
they can enter the gates of the
city. 15But outside the city will
be dogs, witches, immoral
people, murderers, idol
worshipers, and everyone who
loves to tell lies and do wrong.
16I am Jesus! And I am the one
who sent my angel to tell all of
you these things for the
churches. I am David's Great
Descendant,[n] and I am also the
bright morning star.[o]
17The Spirit and the bride say,
"Come!"

Everyone who hears this[p] should say, "Come!"

If you are thirsty, come! If you want life-giving water, come and take it. It's free!

18Here is my warning for everyone
who hears the prophecies in this
book:

If you add anything to them,
God will make you suffer all the
terrible troubles written in this
book.* 19If you take anything
away from these prophecies,
God will not let you have part
in the life-giving tree and in the
holy city described in this book.
20The one who has spoken these
things says, "I am coming soon!"

So, Lord Jesus, please come soon!
21I pray that the Lord Jesus will
be kind to all of you.

---

[n]*David's Great Descendant*: See the note at 5.5. [o]*the bright morning star*: Probably thought of as the brightest star. See 2.27,28. [p]*who hears this*: The reading of the book of Revelation in a service of worship.

22.18 **BE HONEST WITH GOD'S WORD** Some people might like to cut out or add to some of the things John wrote down in Revelation. Yes, there are some very shocking words in this book. But a Christian believes that God himself gave John these visions, just as surely as God gave us the rest of the Bible. By what God has spoken, we can know what he promises and what he expects. So let's pay serious attention to all that God says in his word, the Bible.

NOTES

Psalms
Proverbs

PSALMS

ABOUT THIS BOOK

The book of Psalms is the longest book in the Bible. Psalms are poems that can either be sung as songs or spoken as prayers by individuals or groups. There are 150 psalms in this book, and many of them list King David as their author. They were collected over a long period of time and became a very important part of the worship of the people of Israel.

Some of the psalms tell the music leader what instruments should be used and what tunes should be followed. For example, look at Psalm 4 and Psalm 45.

Many of the Bible's main ideas are echoed in the Psalms: praise, thankfulness, faith, hope, sorrow for sin, God's loyalty and help. And at the heart of all the psalms there is a deep trust in God. The writers of the psalms always express their true feelings, whether they are praising God for his blessings or complaining in times of trouble.

In ancient Israel the psalms were used in several different ways: (1) to praise God, as in Psalm 105; (2) to express sorrow, as in Psalm 13; (3) to teach, as in Psalm 1; (4) to honor Israel's king and pray for fairness in his rule, as in Psalm 72; (5) to tell of God's power over all creation, as in Psalm 47; (6) to show love for Jerusalem, as in Psalm 46; and (7) to celebrate festivals, as in Psalm 121. Of course, many of the psalms could be used for more than one purpose.

Jesus used the psalms when he preached and taught, and they were often quoted by the writers of the New Testament. The earliest Christians also used the psalms in worship, teaching, and telling others the good news about what God has done through Jesus Christ. A verse from Psalm 118, for example, is directly referred to six times in the New Testament:

The stone that the builders
tossed aside
has now become
the most important stone.
(118.22)

A QUICK LOOK AT THIS BOOK

The Book of Psalms is divided into five sections or "books." Most of the psalms in Books I and II were written by David, while many in Book III were written by either Asaph or the people of Korah. Psalms 120—134 are all "celebration psalms." The five sections of the Book of Psalms are:

1. Book I (1—41)
2. Book II (42—72)
3. Book III (73—89)
4. Book IV (90—106)
5. Book V (107—150)

BOOK I (Psalms 1–41)

Psalm 1

The Way to Happiness

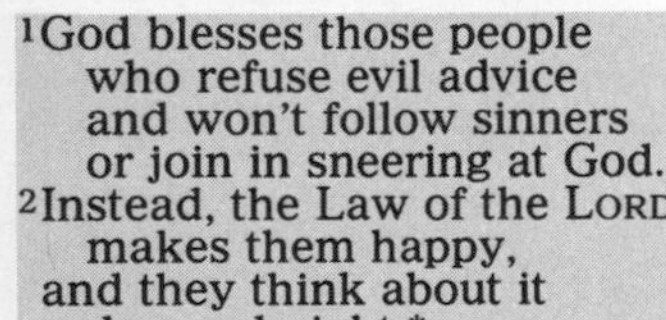

1God blesses those people
who refuse evil advice
and won't follow sinners
or join in sneering at God.
2Instead, the Law of the LORD
makes them happy,
and they think about it
day and night.*

3They are like trees
growing beside a stream,
trees that produce
fruit in season
and always have leaves.
Those people succeed
in everything they do.

4That isn't true of those
who are evil,
because they are like straw
blown by the wind.
5Sinners won't have an excuse
on the day of judgment,
and they won't have a place
with the people of God.

6The LORD protects everyone
who follows him,
but the wicked follow a road
that leads to ruin.

Psalm 2

The Lord's Chosen King

1Why do the nations plot,[a]
and why do their people
make useless plans?[b]
2The kings of this earth
have all joined together
to turn against the LORD
and his chosen one.
3They say, "Let's cut the ropes
and set ourselves free!"

4In heaven the LORD laughs
as he sits on his throne,
making fun of the nations.
5The LORD becomes furious
and threatens them.
His anger terrifies them
as he says,
6"I've put my king on Zion,
my sacred hill."

---

[a] *Why . . . plot?*: Or "Why are the nations restless?"
[b] *make useless plans*: Or "grumble uselessly."

1.2 **WHO ARE THE HAPPY PEOPLE?** The truly happy people are the people God blesses. In fact, to be "blessed" can mean to be happy. We destroy a delicate instrument when we use it in the wrong way. Likewise, when we use our lives in a way God did not intend, we hurt ourselves—even permanently. But when we think a lot about God's plan for us, then we will live as he intended us to do. That's the secret of very great happiness.

NOTES

7I will tell the promise
that the LORD made to me:
"You are my son, because today
I have become your father.*
8Ask me for the nations,
and every nation on earth
will belong to you.
9You will smash them
with an iron rod
and shatter them
like dishes of clay."

10Be smart, all you rulers,
and pay close attention.
11Serve and honor the LORD,
be glad and tremble.
12Show respect to his son
because if you don't,
the LORD might become furious
and suddenly destroy you.[c]
But he blesses and protects
everyone who runs to him.

Psalm 3

[*Written by David when he was running from his son Absalom.*]

An Early Morning Prayer

1I have a lot of enemies, LORD.
Many fight against 2me and say,
"God won't rescue you!"

3But you are my shield,
and you give me victory
and great honor.*
4I pray to you, and you answer
from your sacred hill.

5I sleep and wake up refreshed
because you, LORD,
protect me.

6Ten thousand enemies attack
from every side,
but I am not afraid.

7Come and save me, LORD God!
Break my enemies' jaws
and shatter their teeth,
8because you protect
and bless your people.

Psalm 4

[*A psalm by David for the music leader. Use stringed instruments.*]

An Evening Prayer

1You are my God and protector.
Please answer my prayer.
I was in terrible distress,
but you set me free.
Now have pity and listen
as I pray.

2How long will you people
refuse to respect me?[d]
You love foolish things,
and you run after
what is worthless.[e]

3The LORD has chosen
everyone who is faithful
to be his very own,[f]
and he answers my prayers.
4But each of you
had better tremble
and turn from your sins.

---

[c]*Serve . . . you*: One possible meaning for the difficult Hebrew text of verses 11, 12. [d]*me*: Or "my God." [e]*foolish . . . worthless*: This may refer to idols and false gods. [f]*has chosen . . . very own*: Some Hebrew manuscripts have "work miracles for his faithful people."

2.7 **WHO IS GOD'S SON?** This psalm may refer first of all to King David or his son Solomon. But sometimes the writers of psalms were also looking far into the future. So we have the amazing fact that this psalm is mentioned more than any other in the New Testament, where it is said to speak of Jesus Christ, the great Son of God.

3.3 **GOD PROTECTS US FROM DANGER** Everybody has seen pictures of soldiers of early times. They nearly always carried a shield to defend themselves against enemy arrows and sword thrusts. David speaks here of a full-length shield that protected his whole body from such attacks. So he compares God to a shield like that. Even when we sleep God protects us from many dangers that we may not even be aware of (verses 5 and 6). God is the invisible presence who constantly stands guard to save us from ruin.

NOTES

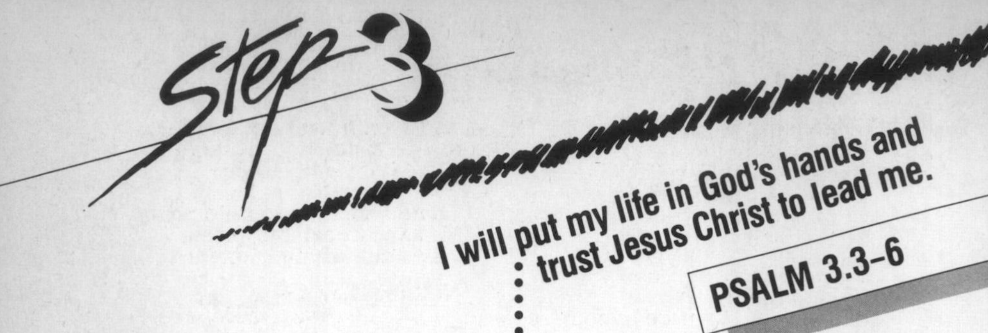

GOD IS THERE

"If there is a God, where is he? Why has he let me get into such a mess?"

We are starting to realize God has been there all the time for us, but we never saw him. We looked in for a while, thinking we could make it on our own, but that didn't work. Then we looked out, depending on other people and/or destructive addictions to make things happen, but that certainly didn't work. Now, like King David discovered, we are finally looking up and seeing that God really is there for us. We don't have to be afraid of the "enemies [who] attack from every side."

JUST LOOK UP

God loves us and offers us his protection. He is there just for us. King David learned that he could count on God when things looked bad—when he was outnumbered and completely surrounded by his enemies. We can too. All we have to do is look up!

For another "Look Inside," turn to page 687.

Silently search your heart
as you lie in bed.*
5 Offer the proper sacrifices
and trust the LORD.

6 There are some who ask,
"Who will be good to us?"
Let your kindness, LORD,
shine brightly on us.
7 You brought me more happiness
than a rich harvest
of grain and grapes.
8 I can lie down
and sleep soundly
because you, LORD,
will keep me safe.

Psalm 5

[*A psalm by David for the music leader. Use flutes.*]

A Prayer for Help

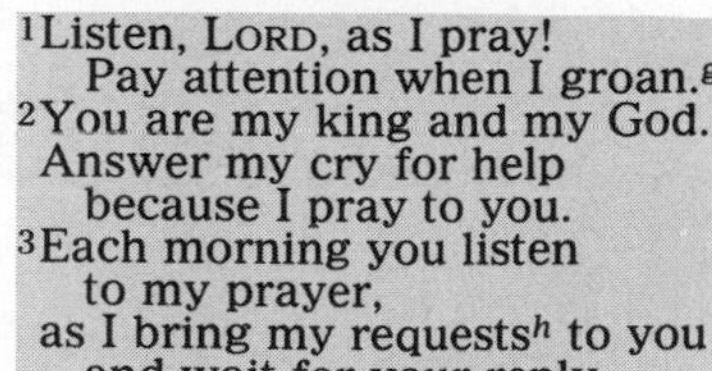

1 Listen, LORD, as I pray!
Pay attention when I groan.[g]
2 You are my king and my God.
Answer my cry for help
because I pray to you.
3 Each morning you listen
to my prayer,
as I bring my requests[h] to you
and wait for your reply.

4 You are not the kind of God
who is pleased with evil.
Sinners can't stay with you.
5 No one who boasts can stand
in your presence, LORD,
and you hate evil people.
6 You destroy every liar,
and you despise violence
and deceit.

7 Because of your great mercy,
I come to your house, LORD,
and I am filled with wonder
as I bow down to worship
at your holy temple.*
8 You do what is right,
and I ask you to guide me.
Make your teaching clear
because of my enemies.

9 Nothing they say is true!
They just want to destroy.
Their words are deceitful
like a hidden pit,
and their tongues are good
only for telling lies.
10 Punish them, God,
and let their own plans
bring their downfall.
Get rid of them!
They keep committing crimes
and turning against you.

11 Let all who run to you
for protection
always sing joyful songs.
Provide shelter for those
who truly love you
and let them rejoice.
12 Our LORD, you bless those
who live right,
and you shield them
with your kindness.

Psalm 6

[*A psalm by David for the music leader. Use stringed instruments.*[i]]

A Prayer in Time of Trouble

1 Don't punish me, LORD,
or even correct me

---

[g] *when I groan*: Or "to my thoughts" or "to my words." [h] *requests*: Or "sacrifices." [i] *instruments*: The Hebrew text adds "according to the sheminith," which may refer to a musical instrument with eight strings.

4.4 **WHAT'S WRONG WITH SIN?** Sometimes people joke about sin. They think the word is old-fashioned and that only superstitious people worry about their sins. But time has shown that sin is a true evil that wrecks people's lives. Sin is anything that is unnatural—that is, against the way God planned for us. David wisely advised thinking about that in quiet times.

5.7 **WHAT IS WORSHIP, REALLY?** David said he went to God's house because he was thankful for God's "great mercy." Thanksgiving is the beginning of real worship. But also, along with our gratitude, is a great sense of wonder and adoration in the presence of the great Creator who is beyond our understanding.

NOTES

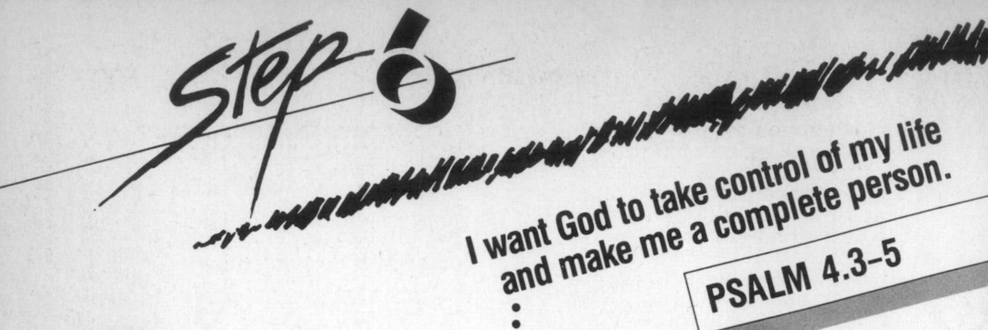

TOSSING AND TURNING

"There's no way they'll let me!"

"Have you asked yet?"

"I don't have to; I already know what they will say: No."

"Maybe they won't . . . just try."

"Would you let me if you were them? I don't exactly have the greatest track record. They'll bring up all the times I've screwed up when they "trusted me." Then they will look at me and say, 'When you grow up, then we will trust you. You have to prove yourself first.'

"Sounds like you have heard that speech before."

MIDNIGHT CONVERSATIONS

We know this conversation or one like it. We have them with ourselves as we are tossing back and forth on our pillows trying desperately to go to sleep. We rehearse "what I'll say" . . . "What they'll say" over and over again. The Bible says these midnight conversations with ourselves are very important. It is the only time we can let our guard down and be completely honest because no one is listening, except the Lord. But with God there are no harsh looks or hurtful accusations—just love.

STEP 6 LOOK INSIDE

For another "Look Inside," turn to page 582.

when you are angry!
2Have pity on me and heal
my feeble body.
My bones tremble with fear,
3and I am in deep distress.
How long will it be?

4Turn and come to my rescue.
Show your wonderful love
and save me, LORD.
5If I die, I cannot praise you
or even remember you.
6My groaning has worn me out.
At night my bed and pillow
are soaked with tears.
7Sorrow has made my eyes dim,
and my sight has failed
because of my enemies.

8You, LORD, heard my crying,
and those hateful people
had better leave me alone.
9You have answered my prayer
and my plea for mercy.*
10My enemies will be ashamed
and terrified,
as they quickly run away
in complete disgrace.

Psalm 7

[*Written by David.*[j] *He sang this to the* LORD *because of Cush from the tribe of Benjamin.*]

The LORD Always Does Right

1You, LORD God,
are my protector.
Rescue me and keep me safe
from all who chase me.
2Or else they will rip me apart
like lions attacking a victim,
and no one will save me.

3I am innocent, LORD God!
4I have not betrayed a friend
or had pity on an enemy[k]
who attacks for no reason.
5If I have done any of this,
then let my enemies
chase and capture me.
Let them stomp me to death
and leave me in the dirt.

6Get angry, LORD God!
Do something!
Attack my furious enemies.
See that justice is done.
7Make the nations come to you,
as you sit on your throne[l]
above them all.

8Our LORD, judge the nations!
Judge me and show that I
am honest and innocent.
9You know every heart and mind,
and you always do right.
Now make violent people stop,
but protect all of us
who obey you.*

10You, God, are my shield,
the protector of everyone
whose heart is right.

[j] *Written by David*: The Hebrew text has "a shiggaion by David," which may refer to a psalm of mourning. [k] *had pity on an enemy*: Or "failed to have pity on an enemy." [l] *sit . . . throne*: Or "return to your place."

6.9 **PRAYER MAKES A DIFFERENCE** David knew his prayer was heard even before God gave him what he asked. Prayer isn't just saying words without thinking about them. When we pray, and really mean what we ask, we will also know that God is listening, and we will know he cares. Then, even before we see the results of our prayers, we have the deep knowledge that God is going to take care of everything.

7.9 **GOD KNOWS ALL ABOUT US** When we were small, many of us used to hear about the "bogey man," a ghostlike being who was always watching us. The bad part of it was that the bogey man was someone who was always waiting to do us harm. The "bogey man" was a bad idea. Only the good and great God knows all about us, and he always waits to do us good. We don't need to be afraid of the all-knowing God.

NOTES

11 You see that justice is done,
and each day
you take revenge.
12 Whenever your enemies refuse
to change their ways,
you sharpen your sword
and string your bow.
13 Your deadly arrows are ready
with flaming tips.

14 An evil person is like a woman
about to give birth
to a hateful, deceitful,
and rebellious child.
15 Such people dig a deep hole,
then fall in it themselves.
16 The trouble they cause
comes back on them,
and their heads are crushed
by their own evil deeds.

17 I will praise you, LORD!
You always do right.
I will sing about you,
the LORD Most High.

Psalm 8

[*A psalm by David for the music leader.*[m]]

The Wonderful Name of the LORD

1 Our LORD and Ruler,
your name is wonderful
everywhere on earth!
You let your glory be seen[n]
in the heavens above.
2 With praises from children
and from tiny infants,
you have built a fortress.
It makes your enemies silent,
and all who turn against you
are left speechless.

3 I often think of the heavens
your hands have made,
and of the moon and stars
you put in place.
4 Then I ask, "Why do you care
about us humans?
Why are you concerned
for us weaklings?"
5 You made us a little lower
than you yourself,[o]
and you have crowned us
with glory and honor.

6 You let us rule everything
your hands have made.
And you put all of it
under our power—
7 the sheep and the cattle,
and every wild animal,
8 the birds in the sky,
the fish in the sea,
and all ocean creatures.

9 Our LORD and Ruler,
your name is wonderful
everywhere on earth!*

Psalm 9

[*A psalm by David for the music leader. To the tune "The Death of the Son."*]

Sing Praises to the LORD

1 I will praise you, LORD,
with all my heart
and tell about the wonders
you have worked.
2 God Most High, I will rejoice;
I will celebrate and sing
because of you.

3 When my enemies face you,
they run away and stumble
and are destroyed.
4 You take your seat as judge,

---

[m] *leader*: The Hebrew text adds "according to the gittith," which may refer to either a musical instrument or a tune. [n] *You . . . seen*: Or "I will worship your glory." [o] *you yourself*: Or "the angels" or "the beings in heaven."

8.9 **SEE GOD IN ALL CREATION** God wants us to know and enjoy him. That's why he hasn't hidden himself from us, but he has put his personal stamp on everything and everyone he has made. True, we don't see God walking around the way we see ourselves. God himself cannot be seen that way because he is an invisible Spirit who is above and beyond all that he created. But for those who have eyes to see, God truly is everywhere.

NOTES

and your fair decisions prove
that I was in the right.
5 You warn the nations
and destroy evil people;
you wipe out their names
forever and ever.
6 Our enemies are destroyed
completely for all time.
Their cities are torn down,
and they will never
be remembered again.

7 You rule forever, LORD,
and you are on your throne,
ready for judgment.
8 You judge the world fairly
and treat all nations
with justice.
9 The poor can run to you
because you are a fortress
in times of trouble.
10 Everyone who honors your name
can trust you,
because you are faithful
to all who depend on you.*

11 You rule from Zion, LORD,
and we sing about you
to let the nations know
everything you have done.
12 You did not forget
to punish the guilty
or listen to the cries
of those in need.

13 Please have mercy, LORD!
My enemies mistreat me.
Keep me from the gates
that lead to death,
14 and I will sing about you
at the gate to Zion.
I will be happy there
because you rescued me.

15 Our LORD, the nations fell
into their own pits,
and their feet were caught
in their own traps.
16 You showed what you are like,
and you made certain
that justice is done,
but evil people are trapped
by their own evil deeds.
17 The wicked will go down
to the world of the dead
to be with those nations
that forgot about you.

18 The poor and the homeless
won't always be forgotten
and without hope.

19 Do something, LORD!
Don't let the nations win.
Make them stand trial
in your court of law.
20 Make the nations afraid
and let them all discover
just how weak they are.

Psalm 10

A Prayer for Help

1 Why are you far away, LORD?
Why do you hide yourself
when I am in trouble?
2 Proud and brutal people
hunt down the poor.
But let them get caught
by their own evil plans!

3 The wicked brag about
their deepest desires.
Those greedy people hate
and curse you, LORD.
4 The wicked are too proud
to turn to you
or even think about you.
5 They are always successful,
though they can't understand
your teachings,
and they keep sneering
at their enemies.

6 In their hearts they say,
"Nothing can hurt us!

9.10 **GOD IS ALWAYS FAITHFUL** Is there anyone we can always trust? We'll be disappointed if we think we can always trust people. The truth is that all of us fail one another sometimes. So we shouldn't expect too much of others. But God is *always* faithful; he *never* breaks his promises; he will do *everything* he has said he will do. When we trust God, then we don't need to trust others about things that matter most to us. God takes care of us at all times.

NOTES

We'll always be happy
and free from trouble."*
7They curse and tell lies,
and all they talk about
is how to be cruel
or how to do wrong.

8They hide outside villages,
waiting to strike and murder
some innocent victim.
9They are hungry lions
hiding in the bushes,
hoping to catch
some helpless passerby.
They trap the poor in nets
and drag them away.
10They crouch down and wait
to grab a victim.
11They say, "God can't see!
He's got on a blindfold."

12Do something, LORD God,
and use your powerful arm
to help those in need.
13The wicked don't respect you.
In their hearts they say,
"God won't punish us!"

14But you see the trouble
and the distress,
and you will do something.
The poor can count on you,
and so can orphans.
15Now break the arms
of all merciless people.
Punish them for doing wrong
and make them stop.

16Our LORD, you will always rule,
but nations will vanish
from the earth.

17You listen to the longings
of those who suffer.
You offer them hope,
and you pay attention
to their cries for help.
18You defend orphans
and everyone else in need,
so that no one on earth
can terrify others again.

Psalm 11

[*A psalm by David for the music leader.*]

Trusting the LORD

1The LORD is my fortress!
Don't say to me,
"Escape like a bird
to the mountains!"
2You tell me, "Watch out!
Those evil people have put
their arrows on their bows,
and they are standing
in the shadows,
aiming at good people.
3What can an honest person do
when everything crumbles?"

4The LORD is sitting
in his sacred temple
on his throne in heaven.
He knows everything we do
because he sees us all.
5The LORD tests honest people,
but despises those
who are cruel
and love violence.
6He will send fiery coals[p]
and flaming sulphur
down on the wicked,
and they will drink nothing
but a scorching wind.

7The LORD always does right
and wants justice done.
Everyone who does right
will see his face.

Psalm 12

[*A psalm by David for the music leader.*[q]]

A Prayer for Help

1Please help me, LORD!
All who were faithful

[p]*fiery coals*: Or "trouble, fire." [q]*leader*: The Hebrew text adds "according to the sheminith," which may be a musical instrument with eight strings.

10.6 **TRUST ONLY IN GOD** We can always safely trust God to guide our steps. But it's very dangerous to trust in our own cleverness to carry us through life. No one is so smart that he's not going to make a mistake sometimes, and one mistake can ruin everything we've built. We need to realize how limited we are. Then we'll discuss all our plans with God, who knows our way from beginning to end.

NOTES

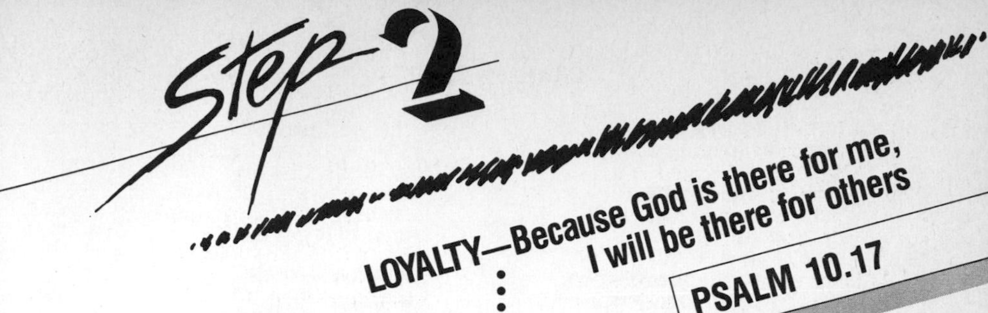

SEE PAST THE WORDS

He said he hates me and wants me to leave. Then he said a lot of other things, but these are the only ones fit to print. It's hard to stand there and listen to a friend destroy your character. Before, I would have defended myself and yelled back. But now I know it's not really me he's attacking; it's himself.

Life has been hard for him. His parents split when he was ten. Half the time he has no idea where his dad is or what he is doing. When he finally shows up, he's drunk. His older brother left when he was sixteen. Now it's just him and his mom. She tries hard, but she can't always be there for him. That's where I fit in—his friend. That may be kind of hard to believe with all the insults he's hurling at me. But I've learned to see past the words and try to understand what he's really saying. I'll leave for a while because he needs some time to himself. But I'll come back. I'm his friend.

FRIENDS FOREVER

Hanging in there with our friends is an expression of loyalty. They may make bad choices, say the wrong thing—or as in this case—be going through a tough time. God rewards loyalty with lifelong friendships. And sometimes with "forever friends," when they come to Christ because of who we are in their lives.

For another "Look Ahead," turn to page 709.

and all who were loyal
have disappeared.
2Everyone tells lies,
and no one is sincere.
3Won't you chop off
all flattering tongues
that brag so loudly?
4They say to themselves,
"We are great speakers.
No one else has a chance."

5But you, LORD, tell them,
"I will do something!
The poor are mistreated
and helpless people moan.
I'll rescue all who suffer."

6Our LORD, you are true
to your promises,
and your word is like silver
heated seven times
in a fiery furnace.[r]
7You will protect us
and always keep us safe
from those people.
8But all who are wicked
will keep on strutting,
while everyone praises
their shameless deeds.[s]*

Psalm 13

[*A psalm by David for the music leader.*]

A Prayer for the LORD's Help

1How much longer, LORD,
will you forget about me?
Will it be forever?
How long will you hide?
2How long must I be confused
and miserable all day?
How long will my enemies
keep beating me down?

3Please listen, LORD God,
and answer my prayers.
Make my eyes sparkle again,
or else I will fall
into the sleep of death.
4My enemies will say,
"Now we've won!"
They will be greatly pleased
when I am defeated.

5I trust your love,
and I feel like celebrating
because you rescued me.
6You have been good to me, LORD,
and I will sing about you.*

Psalm 14

[*A psalm by David for the music leader.*]

No One Can Ignore the LORD

1Only a fool would say,
"There is no God!"

[r] *in a fiery furnace*: The Hebrew text has "in a furnace to the ground," which may describe part of a process for refining silver in Old Testament times.
[s] *while . . . deeds*: One possible meaning for the difficult Hebrew text.

12.8 **SOMETIMES WICKED PEOPLE PROSPER** We're often in a hurry to see people paid back for their deeds. We want good people to be rewarded, and we want the wicked punished—right away. But God waits patiently. He has a right time for everything, and it usually isn't our time! Evil people seem to have it all their own way, but God's time for judgment will come. In the meantime he waits to see if some of them will still change their minds, because judgment is a last resort. God is more patient than we are.

13.6 **LET'S SING OFTEN TO GOD** God has been good to us—more than we deserve—and that's good reason for singing to him and about him. Music was created for praising the great Author of creation. The greatest music ever written has been composed to praise God. Yes, let's make a habit of having a song in our hearts and on our lips because of God's goodness to us. People who are praising God are happy people.

NOTES

People like that are worthless;
they are heartless and cruel
and never do right.

2From heaven the LORD
looks down to see
if anyone is wise enough
to search for him.*
3But all of them are corrupt;
no one does right.

4Won't you evil people learn?
You refuse to pray,
and you gobble down
the LORD's people.
5But you will be frightened,
because God is on the side
of every good person.
6You may spoil the plans
of the poor,
but the LORD protects them.

7I long for someone from Zion
to come and save Israel!
Our LORD, when you bless
your people again,
Jacob's family will be glad,
and Israel will celebrate.

Psalm 15

[*A psalm by David.*]

Who May Worship the LORD?

1Who may stay in God's temple
or live on the holy mountain
of the LORD?*

2Only those who obey God
and do as they should.
They speak the truth
3 and don't spread gossip;
they treat others fairly
and don't say cruel things.

4They hate worthless people
but show respect for all
who worship the LORD.
And they keep their promises,
no matter what the cost.
5They lend their money
without charging interest,
and they don't take bribes
to hurt the innocent.

Those who do these things
will always stand firm.

Psalm 16

[*A special psalm by David.*]

The Best Choice

1Protect me, LORD God!
I run to you for safety,
2and I have said,
"Only you are my Lord!
Every good thing I have
is a gift from you."

3Your people are wonderful,
and they make me happy,[t]
4but worshipers of other gods
will have much sorrow.[u]

[t] *Your people . . . happy*: Or "I was happy worshiping gods I thought were powerful." [u] *but . . . sorrow*: One possible meaning for the difficult Hebrew text.

14.2 **ARE WE LOOKING FOR GOD?** Wise people do. They know that the beautiful heavens and earth didn't just "happen." Someone has made all these things—from the vast galaxies to the tiniest earth creatures. If we're looking for God, we won't have to search very far. He is seen right away in all his masterworks of creation. Though God is so great, he is a friend to all who love him.

15.1 **GOD'S TEMPLE IS EVERYWHERE** In old time, many people thought God lived only in a special building—his temple. Then, as time passed, it became clear that this idea was inadequate, that the infinite God could be contained in such a small space! All creation is God's temple, and his worshipers are those who love him and his works. In a marvelous way, the limitless God can also actually live in people like that. God loves to show himself in the beautiful lives of those who enjoy pleasing him.

NOTES

I refuse to offer sacrifices
of blood to those gods
or worship in their name.

5You, LORD, are all I want!
You are my choice,
and you keep me safe.
6You make my life pleasant,
and my future is bright.

7I praise you, LORD,
for being my guide.
Even in the darkest night,
your teachings fill my mind.
8I will always look to you,
as you stand beside me
and protect me from fear.
9With all my heart,
I will celebrate,
and I can safely rest.

10I am your chosen one.
You won't leave me in the grave
or let my body decay.*
11You have shown me
the path to life,
and you make me glad
by being near to me.
Sitting at your right side,[v]
I will always be joyful.

Psalm 17

[*A prayer by David.*]

The Prayer of an Innocent Person

1I am innocent, LORD!
Won't you listen as I pray
and beg for help?
I am honest!
Please hear my prayer.
2Only you can say
that I am innocent,
because only your eyes
can see the truth.

3You know my heart,
and even during the night
you have tested me
and found me innocent.
I have made up my mind
never to tell a lie.
4I don't do like others.
I obey your teachings
and am not cruel.
5I have followed you,
without ever stumbling.

6I pray to you, God,
because you will help me.
Listen and answer my prayer!
7 Show your wonderful love.
Your mighty arm protects those
who run to you for safety
from their enemies.
8Protect me as you would
your very own eyes;
hide me in the shadow
of your wings.

9Don't let my brutal enemies
attack from all sides
and kill me.
10They refuse to show mercy,
and they keep bragging.

11They have caught up with me!
My enemies are everywhere,
eagerly hoping to smear me
in the dirt.
12They are like hungry lions
hunting for food,
or like young lions
hiding in ambush.

13Do something, LORD!
Attack and defeat them.
Take your sword and save me
from those evil people.
14Use your powerful arm
and rescue me
from the hands of mere humans
whose world won't last.[w]

You provide food
for those you love.
Their children have plenty,

---

[v]*right side*: The place of power and honor.
[w]*last*: One possible meaning for the difficult Hebrew text of verse 14.

16.10 **WHO IS THE CHOSEN ONE?** In the New Testament these words are applied to the Lord Jesus. God, his Father, didn't leave him in the grave, but raised him up again from death. This is the greatest of all good news. Because Jesus lives, we will live with him too. He shows us the path of life that leads to heaven, where we will be at his side forever. Jesus also walks beside us now as our best Friend.

NOTES

DAVID—a man who had a heart for God that resulted in a joy-filled life with God

PSALM 16.10, 11

King David's life can be divided into four periods. First, there was his life as a young shepherd boy who faithfully tended his father's sheep. Next, David wrote psalms, which he sang in King Saul's palace. The third period of David's life might be labeled "On the Run," as he fled from a king who was jealous of his success. The fourth major period was David's reign as king of Israel. Throughout his life there were ups and downs, successes and failures, but there always seemed to be a song in David's heart.

"Joyfulness" literally means having a "glad heart." The Bible says that David, with all his strengths and weaknesses, was "a man after God's own heart." He had a heart that was full of joy because he was willing to allow God to control him and make him a complete person.

David was shaken by circumstances, such as King Saul's distrust and jealousy, but he remained joyful. David was saddened when God showed him the awfulness of his sin with Bathsheba and his guilt in Uriah's death, but his heart was still hungry for God's heart. He wept and mourned over the death of his little baby, but he didn't blame God. His response was to remain faithful and worship God regardless of the circumstances.

Joyfulness often gets confused with happiness. They are very different. Happiness is an outward emotion related to "right happenings." Joyfulness is an inner state resulting from a "right relationship." Happiness puts a smile on our faces whiie joy puts a song in our hearts. Joyfulness is the link between our spirit and God's Spirit. King David had it; how about us?

Joyfulness is one character quality we are born again with. No matter what happens in our lives, regardless of who or what disappoints us, our relationship with God is always secure. Even if circumstances blow up in our faces, letting Christ control us means a joy-filled song will reside inside us. Join in and sing!

Ready for Step 7?
Turn to page 27 of* InStep's *introduction.

and their grandchildren
will have more than enough.

15 I am innocent, LORD,
and I will see your face!
When I awake, all I want
is to see you as you are.*

Psalm 18

[For the music leader. A psalm by David, the LORD's servant. David sang this to the LORD after the LORD had rescued him from his enemies, but especially from Saul.]

David's Song of Thanks

1 I love you, LORD God,
and you make me strong.*
2 You are my mighty rock,[x]
my fortress, my protector,
the rock where I am safe,
my shield, my powerful weapon,[y]
and my place of shelter.

3 I praise you, LORD!
I prayed, and you rescued me
from my enemies.
4 Death had wrapped
its ropes around me,
and I was almost swallowed
by its flooding waters.

5 Ropes from the world
of the dead
had coiled around me,
and death had set a trap
in my path.
6 I was in terrible trouble
when I called out to you,
but from your temple
you heard me
and answered my prayer.

7 The earth shook and shivered,
and the mountains trembled
down to their roots.
You were angry
8 and breathed out smoke.
Scorching heat and fiery flames
spewed from your mouth.

9 You opened the heavens
like curtains,
and you came down
with storm clouds
under your feet.
10 You rode on the backs
of flying creatures
and swooped down
with the wind as wings.
11 Darkness was your robe;
thunderclouds filled the sky,
hiding you from sight.
12 Hailstones and fiery coals
lit up the sky
in front of you.

13 LORD Most High, your voice
thundered from the heavens,
as hailstones and fiery coals
poured down like rain.
14 You scattered your enemies
with arrows of lightning.
15 You roared at the sea,
and its deepest channels
could be seen.
You snorted,
and the earth shook
to its foundations.

---

[x] *mighty rock*: The Hebrew text has "rock," which is sometimes used in poetry to compare the Lord to a mountain where his people can run for protection from their enemies. [y] *my powerful weapon*: The Hebrew text has "the horn," which refers to the horn of a bull, one of the most powerful animals in ancient Palestine.

17.15 **WE WILL SEE THE LORD** Those who know God love that One they have never seen with their eyes. Yet we know him so well, it is almost as if we actually do see him who is invisible. This is what faith really is. But one day—the greatest of all days—the mists will vanish. Then the bright sun of our souls will beam brightly on us, and we will see God as he is! Let's live always looking forward to that glad morning when faith will become sight.

18.1 **GOD MAKES US STRONG** By ourselves we are weak, and by God's standards we last only a few days. But he is not the God of weak people. When we love him, he makes us strong—strong enough to live, enjoy, and honor him forever. We are no longer afraid of either life or death when God makes us strong. Each day is a chance to do great things for him. Then we can look death in the face and say, "Christ has ruined your power!"

NOTES

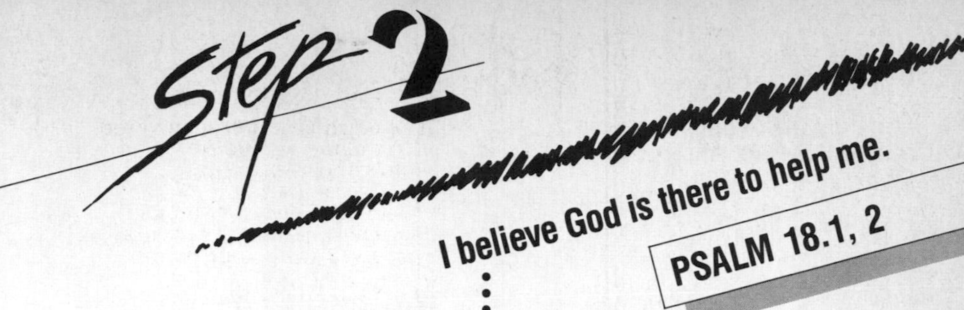

THE CROSSROAD

"Quit worrying and do what feels good."

"This stuff will help you make it through the day. Trust me."

"Tune things out. Life is a bummer. Forget them."

Which way do we go when we come to a crossroad in life? Do we keep on believing the false promises of others? Do we turn to our addictions and dependencies? We found out the hard way that they don't work for us anymore. They may get us through the day but they leave tomorrow looking hopeless.

TURNING THE CORNER

How do we turn the corner of life? We turn toward God. We find that he wants to help build us up, not tear us down. He wants to walk with us into your tomorrows and give us hope. But it's up to us. Which way are we going to turn?

For another "Look Inside," turn to page 584.

16 You reached down from heaven,
and you lifted me
from deep in the ocean.
17 You rescued me from enemies,
who were hateful
and too powerful for me.
18 On the day disaster struck,
they came and attacked,
but you defended me.
19 When I was fenced in,
you freed and rescued me
because you love me.

20 You are good to me, LORD,
because I do right,
and you reward me
because I am innocent.
21 I do what you want
and never turn to do evil.
22 I keep your laws in mind
and never look away
from your teachings.
23 I obey you completely
and guard against sin.
24 You have been good to me
because I do right;
you have rewarded me
for being innocent
by your standards.

25 You are always loyal
to your loyal people,
and you are faithful
to the faithful.
26 With all who are sincere,
you are sincere,
but you treat the unfaithful
as their deeds deserve.

27 You rescue the humble,
but you put down all
who are proud.

28 You, the LORD God,
keep my lamp burning
and turn darkness to light.
29 You help me defeat armies
and capture cities.

30 Your way is perfect, LORD,
and your word is correct.
You are a shield for those
who run to you for help.
31 You alone are God!
Only you are a mighty rock.[z]
32 You give me strength
and guide me right.
33 You make my feet run as fast
as those of a deer,
and you help me stand
on the mountains.

34 You teach my hands to fight
and my arms to use
a bow of bronze.
35 You alone are my shield.
Your right hand supports me,
and by coming to help me,
you have made me famous.
36 You clear the way for me,
and now I won't stumble.

37 I kept chasing my enemies,
until I caught them
and destroyed them.
38 I stuck my sword
through my enemies,
and they were crushed
under my feet.
39 You helped me win victories,
and you forced my attackers
to fall victim to me.

40 You made my enemies run,
and I killed them.
41 They cried out for help,
but no one saved them;
they called out to you,
but there was no answer.
42 I ground them to dust
blown by the wind,
and I poured them out
like mud in the streets.

43 You rescued me
from stubborn people,
and you made me the leader
of foreign nations,
who are now my slaves.
44 They obey and come crawling.
45 They have lost all courage,
and from their fortresses,
they come trembling.

46 You are the living LORD!
I will praise you.
You are a mighty rock.[z]
I will honor you
for keeping me safe.*

---

[z] *mighty rock*: See the note at verse 2.

18.46 **WE PRAISE A LIVING GOD** Strange as it may seem, some people don't think of God as a living person. They imagine God is simply a "force" of nature that has no love or (*continued*)

NOTES

47 You took revenge for me,
and you put nations
in my power.
48 You protected me
from violent enemies
and made me much greater
than all of them.

49 I will praise you, LORD,
and I will honor you
among the nations.
50 You give glorious victories
to your chosen king.
Your faithful love for David
and for his descendants
will never end.

Psalm 19

[*A psalm by David for the music leader.*]

The Wonders of God and the Goodness of His Law

1 The heavens keep telling
the wonders of God,
and the skies declare
what he has done.
2 Each day informs
the following day;
each night announces
to the next.
3 They don't speak a word,
and there is never
the sound of a voice.
4 Yet their message reaches
all the earth,
and it travels
around the world.

In the heavens a tent
is set up for the sun.
5 It rises like a bridegroom
and gets ready like a hero
eager to run a race.
6 It travels all the way
across the sky.
Nothing hides from its heat.

7 The Law of the LORD is perfect;
it gives us new life.
His teachings last forever,
and they give wisdom
to ordinary people.*
8 The LORD's instruction is right;
it makes our hearts glad.
His commands shine brightly,
and they give us light.

9 Worshiping the LORD is sacred;
he will always be worshiped.
All of his decisions
are correct and fair.
10 They are worth more
than the finest gold
and are sweeter than honey
from a honeycomb.

11 By your teachings, Lord,
I am warned;
by obeying them,
I am greatly rewarded.
12 None of us know our faults.
Forgive me when I sin
without knowing it.
13 Don't let me do wrong
on purpose, Lord,
or let sin have control
over my life.
Then I will be innocent,
and not guilty
of some terrible fault.

14 Let my words and my thoughts
be pleasing to you, LORD,

(*continued*) personal concern for the world. But David knew God as the "living LORD." He compared God to a mighty rock whose strength protected David from all who would hurt him. We should think of our living Lord in that way. He is strong and makes us strong for every battle of life.

19.7 **GOD'S LAW IS PERFECT** David here refers to God's word as God's Law. Why is that Law perfect? God's word tells us the exact truth about ourselves. It doesn't come natural for us to obey God. But God's law of life gives us a new life so that we now can do things that please him. God will put his law of life inside us if we really want to live to please him. Along with that gift comes a bonus of peace and joy that we never dreamed possible!

NOTES

because you are my mighty rock[a]
and my protector.

Psalm 20

[*A psalm by David for the music leader.*]

A Prayer for Victory

1I pray that the LORD
will listen when you
are in trouble,
and that the God of Jacob
will keep you safe.
2May the LORD send help
from his temple
and come to your rescue
from Mount Zion.
3May he remember your gifts
and be pleased
with what you bring.

4May God do what you want most
and let all go well for you.
5Then you will win victories,
and we will celebrate,
while raising our banners
in the name of our God.
May the LORD answer
all of your prayers!

6I am certain, LORD,
that you will help
your chosen king.
You will answer my prayers
from your holy place
in heaven,
and you will save me
with your mighty arm.

7Some people trust the power
of chariots or horses,
but we trust you, LORD God.*
8Others will stumble and fall,
but we will be strong
and stand firm.

9Give the king victory, LORD,
and answer our prayers.[b]

Psalm 21

[*A psalm by David for the music leader.*]

Thanking the LORD for Victory

1Our LORD, your mighty power
makes the king glad,
and he celebrates victories
that you have given him.
2You did what he wanted most
and never told him "No."
3You truly blessed the king,
and you placed on him
a crown of finest gold.
4He asked to live a long time,
and you promised him life
that never ends.

5The king is highly honored.
You have let him win victories
that have made him famous.
6You have given him blessings
that will last forever,
and you have made him glad
by being so near to him.
7LORD Most High,
the king trusts you,
and your kindness
keeps him from defeat.

8With your mighty arm, LORD,
you will strike down all
of your hateful enemies.
9They will be destroyed by fire
once you are here,
and because of your anger,
flames will swallow them.
10You will wipe their families
from the earth,
and they will disappear.
11All their plans to harm you
will come to nothing.

---

[a]*mighty rock*: The Hebrew text has "rock," which is sometimes used in poetry to compare the Lord to a mountain where his people can run for protection from their enemies. [b]*victory . . . prayers*: Or "victory. He (God or the king) answers us."

20.7 **WHAT DO WE TRUST?** These days David would say that some people trust in guns, tanks, and planes. In his own time horses and chariots were the machinery of war. We ought to know better than to think that God's kingdom will come because of human military power. Yes, David was a man of war, and he knew that armies are necessary. But David also knew that only God himself must win the great battle for right and truth. It makes sense to trust in God just as David did.

NOTES

12 You will make them run away
by shooting your arrows
at their faces.

13 Show your strength, LORD,
so that we may sing
and praise your power.

Psalm 22

[*A psalm by David for the music leader. To the tune "A Deer at Dawn."*]

Suffering and Praise

1 My God, my God, why have you
deserted me?
Why are you so far away?
Won't you listen to my groans
and come to my rescue?*
2 I cry out day and night,
but you don't answer,
and I can never rest.

3 Yet you are the holy God,
ruling from your throne
and praised by Israel.
4 Our ancestors trusted you,
and you rescued them.
5 When they cried out for help,
you saved them,
and you did not let them down
when they depended on you.

6 But I am merely a worm,
far less than human,
and I am hated and rejected
by people everywhere.
7 Everyone who sees me
makes fun and sneers.
They shake their heads,
8 and say, "Trust the LORD!
If you are his favorite,
let him protect you
and keep you safe."

9 You, LORD, brought me
safely through birth,
and you protected me
when I was a baby
at my mother's breast.
10 From the day I was born,
I have been in your care,
and from the time of my birth,
you have been my God.

11 Don't stay far off
when I am in trouble
with no one to help me.
12 Enemies are all around
like a herd of wild bulls.
Powerful bulls from Bashan[c]
are everywhere.
13 My enemies are like lions
roaring and attacking
with jaws open wide.

14 I have no more strength
than a few drops of water.
All my bones are out of joint;
my heart is like melted wax.
15 My strength has dried up
like a broken clay pot,
and my tongue sticks
to the roof of my mouth.
You, God, have left me
to die in the dirt.

16 Brutal people surround me
like a pack of dogs,
and my enemies have tied up[d]
my hands and my feet.
17 I can count all my bones,
and my enemies just stare
and sneer at me.
18 They took my clothes
and gambled for them.

19 Don't stay far away, LORD!
My strength comes from you,
so hurry and help.

---

[c] *Bashan*: A land east of the Jordan River, where there were pastures suitable for raising fine cattle.
[d] *and my . . . up*: One possible meaning for the difficult Hebrew text.

22.1 **JESUS WAS DESERTED** In the New Testament this psalm is said to refer to the suffering of Jesus the Son of God. David wrote about Jesus on the cross a thousand years before Jesus actually hung there. The New Testament doesn't tell us much about Jesus' prayers and thoughts on the cross, and so this psalm tells us more about his feelings than we find anywhere else. Most of all, Jesus even felt deserted by God his Father. This was the darkest moment of life.

NOTES

20 Rescue me from enemy swords
and save me from those dogs.
21 Don't let lions eat me.

You rescued me from the horns
of wild bulls,
22 and when your people meet,
I will praise you, LORD.

23 All who worship the LORD,
now praise him!
You belong to Jacob's family
and to the people of Israel,
so fear and honor the LORD!
24 The LORD doesn't hate
or despise the helpless
in all of their troubles.
When I cried out, he listened
and did not turn away.

25 When your people meet,
you will fill my heart
with your praises, LORD,
and everyone will see me
keep my promises to you.
26 The poor will eat and be full,
and all who worship you
will be thankful
and live in hope.

27 Everyone on this earth
will remember you, LORD.
People all over the world
will turn and worship you,
28 because you are in control,
the ruler of all nations.

29 All who are rich
and have more than enough
will bow down to you, Lord.
Even those who are dying
and almost in the grave
will come and bow down.
30 In the future, everyone
will worship and learn
about you, our Lord.
31 People not yet born
will be told,
"The Lord has saved us!"*

Psalm 23

[*A psalm by David.*]

The Good Shepherd

1 You, LORD, are my shepherd.
I will never be in need.*
2 You let me rest in fields
of green grass.
You lead me to streams
of peaceful water,
3 and you refresh my life.

You are true to your name,
and you lead me
along the right paths.
4 I may walk through valleys
as dark as death,
but I won't be afraid.
You are with me,
and your shepherd's rod[e]
makes me feel safe.

5 You treat me to a feast,
while my enemies watch.

[e] *shepherd's rod*: The Hebrew text mentions two objects carried by the shepherd: a club to defend against wild animals and a long pole to guide and control the sheep.

22.31 **JESUS SAVED US** The very name "Jesus" means "The Lord Saves." That's what Jesus the Son of God came to do and why he had to suffer on the cross—to pay for our sins. Then God would look at us as if we had never sinned. It was as if we were now as pure as Jesus. That was a terrible price for the Son of God to pay, but he did it willingly because he loved us and wanted us to enjoy heaven with him. Let us thank God for his amazing gift.

23.1 **THE LORD IS OUR SHEPHERD** God often pictured himself as the shepherd of those who love and follow him. Some of the most common paintings of Jesus show him leading a flock of sheep and carrying a lamb. Yes, he even said, "I am the good shepherd." Unlike other animals, sheep are easily confused and separated from their flocks. Then the shepherd goes out to find them. In the same way Jesus comes looking for us when we become separated from him in the world.

NOTES

You honor me as your guest,
and you fill my cup
until it overflows.
6 Your kindness and love
will always be with me
each day of my life,
and I will live forever
in your house, LORD.

Psalm 24

[*A psalm by David.*]

Who Can Enter the LORD's Temple?

1 The earth and everything on it
belong to the LORD.
The world and its people
belong to him.
2 The LORD placed it all
on the oceans and rivers.

3 Who may climb the LORD's hill[f]
or stand in his holy temple?*
4 Only those who do right
for the right reasons,
and don't worship idols
or tell lies under oath.
5 The LORD God, who saves them,
will bless and reward them,
6 because they worship and serve
the God of Jacob.[g]
7 Open the ancient gates,
so that the glorious king
may come in.

8 Who is this glorious king?
He is our LORD, a strong
and mighty warrior.

9 Open the ancient gates,
so that the glorious king
may come in.

10 Who is this glorious king?
He is our LORD,
the All-Powerful!

Psalm 25

[*By David.*]

A Prayer for Guidance and Help

1 I offer you my heart, LORD God,*
2 and I trust you.
Don't make me ashamed
or let enemies defeat me.
3 Don't disappoint any
of your worshipers,
but disappoint all
deceitful liars.
4 Show me your paths
and teach me to follow;
5 guide me by your truth
and instruct me.
You keep me safe,
and I always trust you.

6 Please, LORD, remember,
you have always
been patient and kind.
7 Forget each wrong I did
when I was young.
Show how truly kind you are
and remember me.
8 You are honest and merciful,
and you teach sinners
how to follow your path.

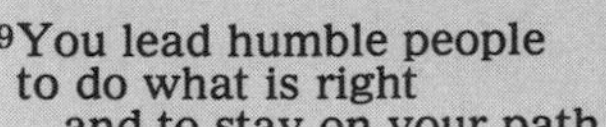

9 You lead humble people
to do what is right
and to stay on your path.

---

[f] *the LORD's hill*: The hill in Jerusalem where the temple was built. [g] *worship . . . Jacob*: Two ancient versions; Hebrew "worship God and serve the descendants of Jacob."

24.3 **WE CAN LIVE WITH GOD** David speaks about climbing God's hill. Of course, the temple, or place of worship, in David's time was built on a hill. But this hill of God is a picture of high heaven where God dwells in a special way. We may climb up that hill of heaven some day and live there with God if our hearts and lives please him while we live on earth.

25.1 **GIVE GOD YOUR HEART** To give your heart to God means to give him your whole life. This is the real gift we owe to God. After all, he gave us life, so our lives belong to him. But God waits for us to come to him with thanksgiving for his love and his gift of saving us from our sins. Giving your life to God is like putting your life savings in a bank that never goes broke. Only with God is your life completely safe.

NOTES

10 In everything you do,
you are kind and faithful
to everyone who keeps
our agreement with you.

11 Be true to your name, LORD,
by forgiving each one
of my terrible sins.
12 You will show the right path
to all who worship you.
13 They will have plenty,
and then their children
will receive the land.

14 Our LORD, you are the friend
of your worshipers,
and you make an agreement
with all of us.
15 I always look to you,
because you rescue me
from every trap.

16 I am lonely and troubled.
Show that you care
and have pity on me.
17 My awful worries keep growing.
Rescue me from sadness.
18 See my troubles and misery
and forgive my sins.

19 Look at all my enemies!
See how much they hate me.
20 I come to you for shelter.
Protect me, keep me safe,
and don't disappoint me.
21 I obey you with all my heart,
and I trust you, knowing
that you will save me.

22 Our God, please save Israel
from all of its troubles.

Psalm 26

[*By David.*]

The Prayer of an Innocent Person

1 Show that I am right, LORD!
I stay true to myself,
and I have trusted you
without doubting.
2 Test my thoughts and find out
what I am like.
3 I never forget your kindness,
and I am always faithful
to you.[h]
4 I don't spend my time
with worthless liars
5 or go with evil crowds.

6 I wash my hands, LORD,
to show my innocence,
and I worship at your altar,
7 while gratefully singing
about your wonders.
8 I love the temple
where you live, and where
your glory shines.
9 Don't sweep me away,
as you do sinners.
Don't punish me with death
as you do those people
who are brutal
10 or full of meanness
or who bribe others.
11 I stay true to myself.
Be kind and rescue me.

12 Now I stand on solid ground!
And when your people meet,
I will praise you, LORD.*

Psalm 27

[*By David.*]

A Prayer of Praise

1 You, LORD, are the light
that keeps me safe.
I am not afraid of anyone.
You protect me,
and I have no fears.
2 Brutal people may attack
and try to kill me,
but they will stumble.
Fierce enemies may attack,
but they will fall.

---

[h] *I am . . . to you*: Or "I trust your faithfulness."

26.12 **WHERE CAN WE STAND?** David stood on solid ground, and so can we. Jesus Christ is our solid rock (see Luke 6.47–48). Our present world will pass away, and the powers of nature will fail. But "Jesus Christ never changes! He is the same yesterday, today, and forever" (Hebrews 13.8). Be sure your feet are planted firmly on that solid ground that can never give way.

NOTES

Step 7

I need God to remove my shortcomings.

PSALM 25.6–10

THE COACH KNOWS

I can't tell you how many baskets I have scored in my lifetime. It must be in the hundreds by now. So you would think when I walked up to the free throw line with the chance either to win or lose the play-off game, I would have confidence. But the truth is, I was scared to death. The other team called for a time-out so my fear could develop into full-blown panic. It worked. I had time to think about every free throw I've ever missed. "You're going to blow it" kept going over and over in my mind. My hands may have been prepared to win but my mind was completely defeated. What a loser!

STEP 7 LOOK INSIDE

That's when coach came over. I told him I was feeling the pressure. He put his hands on my shoulder and said, "Remember what I taught you. Picture the ball going in the basket, and tune out any distraction. You won't miss. Trust me, I know." He knew.

TRUST ME

God knows everything about us because he made us. He knows our strengths and our weaknesses. He knows when we do well and when we blow it. Mistakes don't take the Lord by surprise. In great patience and love he says, "Let's talk about it. Are you scared, discouraged, or really disappointed in yourself? Remember what I taught you. I have a wonderful plan for your life and I have had it since before you were born. Picture yourself the way I see you and tune out Satan's distractions. You won't miss. Trust me, I know.

For another "Look Inside," turn to page 676.

3 Armies may surround me,
but I won't be afraid;
war may break out,
but I will trust you.

4 I ask only one thing, LORD:
Let me live in your house
every day of my life
to see how wonderful you are
and to pray in your temple.*

5 In times of trouble,
you will protect me.
You will hide me in your tent
and keep me safe
on top of a mighty rock.[i]
6 You will let me defeat
all of my enemies.
Then I will celebrate,
as I enter your tent
with animal sacrifices
and songs of praise.

7 Please listen when I pray!
Have pity. Answer my prayer.
8 My heart tells me to pray.
I am eager to see your face,
9 so don't hide from me.
I am your servant,
and you have helped me.
Don't turn from me in anger.
You alone keep me safe.
Don't reject or desert me.
10 Even if my father and mother
should desert me,
you will take care of me.*

11 Teach me to follow, LORD,
and lead me on the right path
because of my enemies.
12 Don't let them do to me
what they want.
People tell lies about me
and make terrible threats,
13 but I know I will live
to see how kind you are.

14 Trust the LORD!
Be brave and strong
and trust the LORD.

Psalm 28

[*By David.*]

A Prayer for Help

1 Only you, LORD,
are a mighty rock![i]
Don't refuse to help me
when I pray.
If you don't answer me,
I will soon be dead.
2 Please listen to my prayer
and my cry for help,
as I lift my hands
toward your holy temple.

3 Don't drag me away, LORD,
with those cruel people,
who speak kind words,
while planning trouble.
4 Treat them as they deserve!
Punish them for their sins.
5 They don't pay any attention
to your wonderful deeds.
Now you will destroy them
and leave them in ruin.

6 I praise you, LORD,
for answering my prayers.

---

[i] *mighty rock*: The Hebrew text has "rock," which is sometimes used in poetry to compare the Lord to a mountain where his people can run for protection from their enemies.

27.4 **WHAT IS YOUR GREATEST WISH?** The greatest thing some people might hope for is to win millions of dollars in a lottery. That would solve a lot of problems—for a while. But life is short, and all the money in the world can't change that fact. David had a true sense of value—to enjoy being with God forever. Does anything come close to that enjoyment? No, because we were created to live with God. Nothing else can satisfy us.

27.10 **GOD CARES FOR US** Who would care more about us than our fathers and mothers? Sadly, we hear more and more about parents deserting their babies—or killing them! Isn't it wonderful to know that even if our family and loved ones forget us, still God will be there with open arms to comfort us and care for our needs. Whatever happens, we will always be safe in God's hands.

NOTES

7You are my strong shield,
and I trust you completely.
You have helped me,
and I will celebrate
and thank you in song.

8You give strength
to your people, LORD,
and you save and protect
your chosen ones.
9Come save us and bless us.
Be our shepherd and always
carry us in your arms.

Psalm 29

[*A psalm by David.*]

The Voice of the LORD in a Storm

1All of you angels[j] in heaven,
honor the glory and power
of the LORD!
2Honor the wonderful name
of the LORD,
and worship the LORD
most holy and glorious.[k]

3The voice of the LORD
echoes over the oceans.
The glorious LORD God
thunders above the roar
of the raging seas,
4and his voice is mighty
and marvelous.
5The voice of the LORD
destroys the cedar trees;
the LORD shatters cedars
on Mount Lebanon.
6God makes Mount Lebanon
skip like a calf
and Mount Hermon
jump like a wild ox.

7The voice of the LORD
makes lightning flash
8 and the desert tremble.
And because of the LORD,
the desert near Kadesh
shivers and shakes.

9The voice of the LORD
makes deer give birth
before their time.[l]
Forests are stripped of leaves,
and the temple is filled
with shouts of praise.

10The LORD rules on his throne,
king of the flood[m] forever.*
11Pray that our LORD
will make us strong
and give us peace.

Psalm 30

[*A psalm by David for the dedication of the temple.*]

A Prayer of Thanks

1I will praise you, LORD!
You saved me from the grave
and kept my enemies
from celebrating my death.
2I prayed to you, LORD God,
and you healed me,
3saving me from death
and the grave.

4Your faithful people, LORD,
will praise you with songs
and honor your holy name.
5Your anger lasts a little while,
but your kindness lasts
for a lifetime.
At night we may cry,
but when morning comes
we will celebrate.

6I was carefree and thought,
"I'll never be shaken!"
7You, LORD, were my friend,

---

[j]*angels*: Or "supernatural beings" or "gods." [k]*most . . . glorious*: Or "in his holy place" or "and wear your glorious clothes." [l]*makes . . . time*: Or "twists the oak trees around." [m]*king of the flood*: In ancient times the people of Israel believed that a mighty ocean surrounded all of creation, and that God could release the water to flood the earth.

29.10 **GOD RULES OVER ALL** Sometimes we may think that God is in heaven and that he is in charge of everything there, though it seems that people run all the business of this world. But, in fact, God is equally everywhere, and he is in charge of all that happens in this and all other worlds. Yes, we choose and decide what we will do. But behind the scenes is God, the engineer of the universe, guiding all events and directing history toward his certain goal. Yes, all nature moves at God's command.

NOTES

and you made me as strong
as a mighty mountain.
But when you hid your face,
I was crushed.*

8I prayed to you, LORD,
and in my prayer I said,
9"What good will it do you
if I am in the grave?
Once I have turned to dust,
how can I praise you
or tell how loyal you are?
10 Have pity, LORD! Help!"

11You have turned my sorrow
into joyful dancing.
No longer am I sad
and wearing sackcloth.[n]
12I thank you from my heart,
and I will never stop
singing your praises,
my LORD and my God.

Psalm 31

[*A psalm by David for the music leader.*]

A Prayer for Protection

1I come to you, LORD,
for protection.
Don't let me be ashamed.
Do as you have promised
and rescue me.
2Listen to my prayer
and hurry to save me.
Be my mighty rock[o]
and the fortress
where I am safe.

3You, LORD God,
are my mighty rock
and my fortress.
Lead me and guide me,
so that your name
will be honored.*
4Protect me from hidden traps
and keep me safe.
5You are faithful,
and I trust you
because you rescued me.

6I hate the worshipers
of worthless idols,
but I trust you, LORD.
7I celebrate and shout
because you are kind.
You saw all my suffering,
and you cared for me.
8You kept me from the hands
of my enemies,
and you set me free.

9Have pity, LORD!
I am hurting and almost blind.
My whole body aches.
10I have known only sorrow
all my life long, and I suffer
year after year.
I am weak from sin,
and my bones are limp.

11My enemies insult me.
Neighbors are even worse,
and I disgust my friends.
People meet me on the street,
and they turn and run.
12I am completely forgotten
like someone dead.
I am merely a broken dish.

---

[n]*sackcloth*: A rough, dark-colored cloth made from goat or camel hair and used to make grain sacks. It was worn in times of trouble or sorrow.
[o]*mighty rock*: The Hebrew text has "rock," which is sometimes used in poetry to compare the Lord to a mountain where his people can run for protection from their enemies.

30.7 **GOD IS A FRIEND** Like ourselves, God has many sides to his nature. Is he Creator? Yes. Is he King of the universe? Yes. Is he Judge of all? Yes. God is all these things. Yet God also waits to be our wise and sympathizing friend. But friendship has to work two ways. God can only be our friend if we want him and invite him to be. To have a friend you have to be friendly yourself.

31.3 **GOD IS A PROTECTOR** Many of us have heard the stirring hymn by Martin Luther, "A Mighty Fortress Is Our God." David was the one who first described God as a fortress. Of course, God isn't made of stone and concrete like a real fortress, but he is like a fortress because we are safe in his care. God never fails us when we depend on him for safe-keeping and protection.

NOTES

13 I hear the crowds whisper,
"Everyone is afraid!"
They are plotting and scheming
to murder me.

14 But I trust you, LORD,
and I claim you as my God.*
15 My life is in your hands.
Save me from enemies
who hunt me down.*
16 Smile on me, your servant.
Have pity and rescue me.

17 I pray only to you.
Don't disappoint me.
Disappoint my cruel enemies
until they lie silent
in their graves.
18 Silence those proud liars!
Make them stop bragging
and insulting your people.

19 You are wonderful,
and while everyone watches,
you store up blessings for all
who honor and trust you.
20 You are their shelter
from harmful plots,
and you are their protection
from vicious gossip.

21 I will praise you, LORD,
for showing great kindness
when I was like a city
under attack.

22 I was terrified and thought,
"They've chased me
far away from you!"
But you answered my prayer
when I shouted for help.

23 All who belong to the LORD,
show how you love him.
The LORD protects the faithful,
but he severely punishes
everyone who is proud.
24 All who trust the LORD,
be cheerful and strong.

Psalm 32

[*A special psalm by David.*]

The Joy of Forgiveness

1 Our God, you bless everyone
whose sins you forgive
and wipe away.
2 You bless them by saying,
"You told me your sins,
without trying to hide them,
and now I forgive you."*

3 Before I confessed my sins,
my bones felt limp,
and I groaned all day long.
4 Night and day your hand
weighed heavily on me,
and my strength was gone
as in the summer heat.

31.14 **TRUST IS THE IMPORTANT THING** David had his faults. In fact, at one time he sinned very seriously. But he kept his faith in God. David's trust in God carried him through the bad times and the good. We need to learn from David never to give up, no matter how black everything looks. God is still in charge of all that troubles us, and he knows how to lead us out of our problems. Yes, "keeping the faith" both on the sunny days and the stormy days is the key that unlocks all doors to happiness.

31.15 **OUR LIVES ARE IN GOD'S HANDS** Nothing can happen to us that God does not permit. We aren't likely to panic easily when we truly realize that fact. God planned every step of our lives. If we've trusted and loved him, we can be sure that everything will turn out for our good in the end. A person with that kind of faith will always be calm and can't be destroyed by bad luck or enemies.

32.2 **TELL GOD ABOUT YOUR SINS** Yes, God already knows all about us. But until we admit we're wrong, neither God nor anyone else can help us. If we're satisfied to go on as if everything is fine, when it really isn't, we'll only sink deeper into our sins. David knew that by bitter experience. But when we turn and face God with the truth about ourselves, he forgives us at once, and our sins will be gone.

NOTES

5 So I confessed my sins
and told them all to you.
I said, "I'll tell the LORD
each one of my sins."
Then you forgave me
and took away my guilt.

6 We worship you, Lord,
and we should always pray
whenever we find out
that we have sinned.[p]
Then we won't be swept away
by a raging flood.
7 You are my hiding place!
You protect me from trouble,
and you put songs in my heart
because you have saved me.

8 You said to me,
"I will point out the road
that you should follow.
I will be your teacher
and watch over you.
9 Don't be stupid
like horses and mules
that must be led with ropes
to make them obey."

10 All kinds of troubles
will strike the wicked,
but your kindness shields those
who trust you, LORD.
11 And so your good people
should celebrate and shout.

Psalm 33

Sing Praises to the LORD

1 You are the LORD's people.
Obey him and celebrate!
He deserves your praise.
2 Praise the LORD with harps!
Use harps with ten strings
to make music for him.
3 Sing a new song. Shout!
Play beautiful music.
4 The LORD is truthful;
he can be trusted.*
5 He loves justice and fairness,
and he is kind to everyone
everywhere on earth.

6 The LORD made the heavens
and everything in them
by his word.
7 He scooped up the ocean
and stored the water.
8 Everyone in this world
should worship and honor
the LORD!
9 As soon as he spoke
the world was created;
at his command,
the earth was formed.

10 The LORD destroys the plans
and spoils the schemes
of the nations.
11 But what the LORD has planned
will stand forever.
His thoughts never change.
12 The LORD blesses each nation
that worships only him.
He blesses his chosen ones.
13 The LORD looks at the world
14 from his throne in heaven,
and he watches us all.
15 The LORD gave us each a mind,
and nothing we do
can be hidden from him.

16 Mighty armies alone
cannot win wars for a king;
great strength by itself
cannot keep a soldier safe.
17 In war the strength of a horse
cannot be trusted
to take you to safety.
18 But the LORD watches over
all who honor him
and trust his kindness.

[p] *whenever . . . sinned*: Hebrew "at a time of finding only."

33.4 **WE CAN COUNT ON GOD** All of us are liars to some extent. But just think of it—God is perfectly truthful at all times. He has never said or done anything that is not according to the way things actually are. Often that fact about God makes us uncomfortable. We'd rather not know the truth sometimes. But God's truthfulness is always best, even when it hurts. And God always mixes the truth with love, because God *is* love even in his sternness.

NOTES

[19]He protects them from death
and starvation.

[20]We depend on you, LORD,
to help and protect us.
[21]You make our hearts glad
because we trust you,
the only God.
[22]Be kind and bless us!
We depend on you.

Psalm 34

[*Written by David when he pretended to be crazy in front of Abimelech, so that Abimelech would send him away, and David could leave.*]

Honor the LORD

[1]I will always praise the LORD.
[2]With all my heart,
I will praise the LORD.
Let all who are helpless,
listen and be glad.
[3]Honor the LORD with me!
Celebrate his great name.

[4]I asked the LORD for help,
and he saved me
from all my fears.
[5]Keep your eyes on the LORD!
You will shine like the sun
and never blush with shame.
[6]I was a nobody, but I prayed,
and the LORD saved me
from all my troubles.

[7]If you honor the LORD,
his angel will protect you.
[8]Discover for yourself
that the LORD is kind.
Come to him for protection,
and you will be glad.

[9]Honor the LORD!
You are his special people.
No one who honors the LORD
will ever be in need.*
[10]Young lions[q] may go hungry
or even starve,
but if you trust the LORD,
you will never miss out
on anything good.

[11]Come, my children, listen
as I teach you
to respect the LORD.
[12]Do you want to live
and enjoy a long life?
[13]Then don't say cruel things
and don't tell lies.
[14]Do good instead of evil
and try to live at peace.

[15]If you obey the LORD,
he will watch over you
and answer your prayers.
[16]But God despises evil people,
and he will wipe them all
from the earth,
till they are forgotten.
[17]When his people pray for help,
he listens and rescues them
from their troubles.

[18]The LORD is there to rescue
all who are discouraged
and have given up hope.

[19]The LORD's people
may suffer a lot,
but he will always
bring them safely through.
[20]Not one of their bones
will ever be broken.

[21]Wicked people are killed
by their own evil deeds,
and if you hate God's people
you will be punished.

---

[q] *Young lions*: In the Psalms wild animals often stand for God's enemies.

34.9 **SUFFERING IS PART OF LIVING** Even God's own people suffer—sometimes more than others. But they have a secret. God stands beside them, comforts them, and holds them up in all their pains. They may even be put to death just because they love him. In New Testament times, Jesus later promised a grieving lady that those who believe in him never really die. They only go to be with him forever. David also says elsewhere that crying may last for a night, but celebration comes in the morning (see 30.5).

NOTES

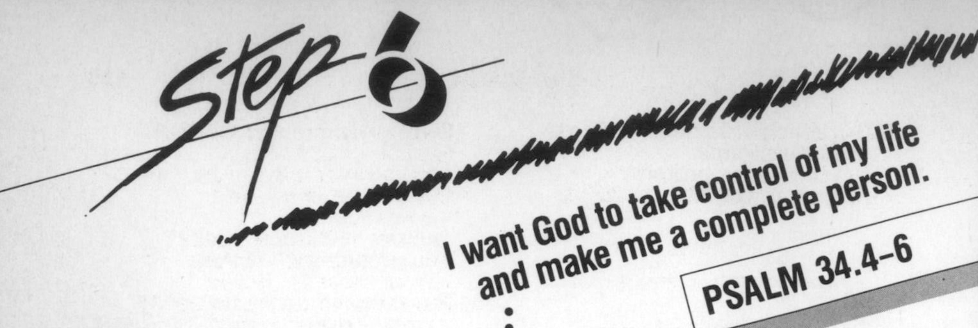

KEEP LOOKING UP

She was shivering with cold, her lips beginning to turn blue. The rescue attempts were proving futile. She had fallen into the icy water. In the panic of the situation most parents would have become hysterical, but her father calmly repeated over and over again, "Just keep your eyes on Daddy, Sweetheart. It's going to be all right."

Inch by inch he crept out closer to her until at last he grabbed her arm and slowly pulled her to safety. Until the moment she buried her head in his shoulder, she never took her eyes off him.

Regardless of the deep waters we fall into, our Heavenly Father reaches out to us, telling us, "Hold on and keep your eyes on me. It's going to be all right."

STEP LOOK INSIDE 6

IT'S GOING TO BE ALL RIGHT

Just like that little girl, when we focus on the hope of our rescue and stop looking at the hopelessness of the situation, we find safety. The Lord has promised to save us from our fears and the things that trouble us. We just have to keep looking up.

To take a "Look Ahead," turn to page 309.

22 The LORD saves the lives
of his servants.
Run to him for protection,
and you won't be punished.

Psalm 35

[*A psalm by David.*]

A Prayer for Protection from Enemies

1 Fight my enemies, LORD!
Attack my attackers!
2 Shield me and help me.
3 Aim your spear at everyone
who hunts me down,
but promise to save me.

4 Let all who want to kill me
be disappointed
and disgraced.
Chase away and confuse
all who plan to harm me.
5 Send your angel after them
and let them be like straw
in the wind.
6 Make them run in the dark
on a slippery road,
as your angel chases them.
7 I did them no harm,
but they hid a net
to trap me,
and they dug a deep pit
to catch and kill me.
8 Surprise them with disaster!
Trap them in their own nets
and let them fall and rot
in the pits they have dug.

9 I will celebrate and be joyful
because you, LORD,
have saved me.*
10 Every bone in my body
will shout:
"No one is like the LORD!"
You protect the helpless
from those in power;
you save the poor and needy
from those who hurt them.

11 Liars accuse me of crimes
I know nothing about.
12 They repay evil for good,
and I feel all alone.
13 When they were sick,
I wore sackcloth[r]
and went without food.[s]
I truly prayed for them,[t]*
14 as I would for a friend
or a relative.
I was in sorrow and mourned,
as I would for my mother.

15 I have stumbled,
and worthless liars
I don't even know
surround me and sneer.
16 Worthless people make fun[u]
and never stop laughing.
17 But all you do is watch!

---

[r]*sackcloth*: A rough, dark-colored cloth made from goat or camel hair and used to make grain sacks. It was worn in times of trouble or sorrow. [s]*went without food*: People sometimes went without food (called "fasting") to show sorrow. [t]*I . . . them*: Or "My prayer wasn't answered, but I prayed." [u]*Worthless . . . fun*: One possible meaning for the difficult Hebrew text.

35.9 **ARE YOU A JOYFUL BELIEVER?** David was. He could see God's power at work in saving him and other helpless people, and this made David very glad. Do we stop to think of all the ways in which God has saved us from great troubles? He is reaching out to people all the time, pleading with them to accept his friendship and his power to save them. It's always a beautiful thing to see someone turn to God and call him "Friend."

35.13 **DO WE LOVE OUR ENEMIES?** That seems impossible sometimes. A writer in the New Testament says that the love of God is poured out in the hearts of his people. It's impossible not to love—even your enemies—when you've been loved by God. David was hounded all his life by those who hated him, but here we see him sincerely sorry for them and praying for them. That's a miracle—a true wonder that God worked in David's life. God performs that same wonder today. Sometimes we ourselves are surprised that God makes us able to love our enemies.

NOTES

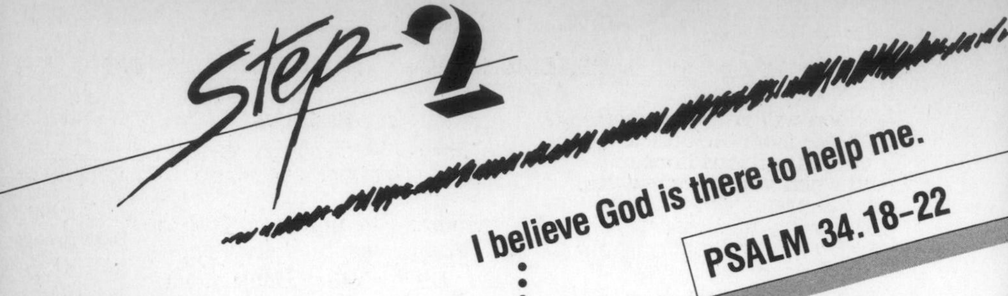

SAFE PLACES

Do you have a safe place? A place where you can go and be alone, a place where your little brother or sister can't bother you. This is the place where you do most of your "serious" thinking and dreaming. The place the real you lives!

God has prepared a place like that for us. It's called *his will*.

When we are doing what God wants us to do, we are safe. When we are going where God wants us to go, we are safe. When we are being what God wants us to be, we are safe. By safe, we mean that we are in the right place at the right time, and we are being the right person there. Nothing can harm us as long as we are safe in his will.

WHERE TO FIND GOD'S WILL

God's will is something that is hard to recognize at first. But do we really know where to look? It all starts with trusting God to lead and direct us. Contrary to what many people think, God's will is not what we do for him; it is who we are becoming as a result of trusting in him.

STEP LOOK INSIDE 2

To take a "Look Ahead," turn to page 224.

When will you do something?
Save me from the attack
of those vicious lions.
18 And when your people meet,
I will praise you
and thank you, Lord,
in front of them all.

19 Don't let my brutal enemies
be glad because of me.
They hate me for no reason.
Don't let them wink
behind my back.
20 They say hurtful things,
and they lie to people
who want to live in peace.
21 They are quick to accuse me.
They say, "You did it!
We saw you ourselves."

22 You see everything, LORD!
Please don't keep silent
or stay so far away.
23 Fight to defend me, Lord God,
24 and prove that I am right
by your standards.
Don't let them laugh at me
25 or say to each other,
"Now we've got what we want!
We'll gobble him down!"

26 Disappoint and confuse
all who are glad
to see me in trouble,
but disgrace and embarrass
my proud enemies who say to me,
"You are nothing!"

27 Let all who want me to win
be happy and joyful.
From now on let them say,
"The LORD is wonderful!
God is glad when all goes well
for his servant."
28 Then I will shout all day,
"Praise the LORD God!
He did what was right."

Psalm 36

[For the music leader by David, the Lord's servant.]

Human Sin and God's Goodness

1 Sinners don't respect God;
sin is all they think about.
2 They like themselves too much
to hate their own sins
or even to see them.*
3 They tell deceitful lies,
and they don't have the sense
to live right.
4 Those people stay awake,
thinking up mischief,
and they follow the wrong road,
refusing to turn from sin.

5 Your love is faithful, LORD,
and even the clouds in the sky
can depend on you.
6 Your decisions are always fair.
They are firm like mountains,
deep like the sea,
and all people and animals
are under your care.

7 Your love is a treasure,
and everyone finds shelter
in the shadow of your wings.
8 You give your guests a feast
in your house,
and you serve a tasty drink
that flows like a river.
9 The life-giving fountain
belongs to you,
and your light gives light
to each of us.

10 Our LORD, keep showing love
to everyone who knows you,
and use your power to save all
whose thoughts please you.
11 Don't let those proud
and merciless people
kick me around
or chase me away.

36.2 **SELF-LOVE IS OUR WORST ENEMY** People who love themselves so much they never see anything wrong in themselves are in a sad condition. Unfortunately, they often see plenty of faults in others. Sooner or later, such people meet up with the awful truth. They meet the enemy, and the enemy is themselves! We need to be continually asking God to save us from such self-love and all the pride that goes along with that attitude. Pride leads to destruction.

NOTES

[12]Look at those wicked people!
They are knocked down,
never to get up again.

Psalm 37

[*By David.*]

Trust the LORD

[1]Don't be annoyed by anyone
who does wrong,
and don't envy them.*
[2]They will soon disappear
like grass without rain.

[3]Trust the LORD and live right!
The land will be yours,
and you will be safe.
[4]Do what the LORD wants,
and he will give you
your heart's desire.

[5]Let the LORD lead you
and trust him to help.
[6]Then it will be as clear
as the noonday sun
that you were right.

[7]Be patient and trust the LORD.
Don't let it bother you
when all goes well for those
who do sinful things.
[8]Don't be angry or furious.
Anger can lead to sin.
[9]All sinners will disappear,
but if you trust the LORD,
the land will be yours.

[10]Sinners will soon disappear,
never to be found,
[11]but the poor will take the land
and enjoy a big harvest.

[12]Merciless people make plots
against good people
and snarl like animals,
[13]but the Lord laughs and knows
their time is coming soon.
[14]The wicked kill with swords
and shoot arrows to murder
the poor and the needy
and all who do right.
[15]But they will be killed
by their own swords,
and their arrows
will be broken.

[16]It is better to live right
and be poor
than to be sinful and rich.
[17]The wicked will lose all
of their power,
but the LORD gives strength
to everyone who is good.

[18]Those who obey the LORD
are daily in his care,
and what he has given them
will be theirs forever.
[19]They won't be in trouble
when times are bad,
and they will have plenty
when food is scarce.

[20]Wicked people are enemies
of the LORD
and will vanish like smoke
from a field on fire.

[21]An evil person borrows
and never pays back;
a good person is generous
and never stops giving.
[22]Everyone the LORD blesses
will receive the land;
everyone the LORD curses
will be destroyed.

[23]If you do what the LORD wants,
he will make certain
each step you take is sure.
[24]The LORD will hold your hand,
and if you stumble,
you still won't fall.

[25]As long as I can remember,
good people have never
been left helpless,
and their children have never
gone begging for food.

37.1 **ANGER DOESN'T CHANGE THE WORLD** Getting angry at people who do evil things won't make them any different. In fact, anger only hurts ourselves. It's bad for health. Let's decide we're going to keep calm when wrong seems to have the upper hand. God is still in charge, and we can afford to leave wrongdoers in his hands. God knows how and when to settle his accounts with evil in the world.

NOTES

26They gladly give and lend,
and their children
turn out good.

27If you stop sinning
and start doing right,
you will keep living
and be secure forever.
28The LORD loves justice,
and he won't ever desert
his faithful people.
He always protects them,
but destroys the children
of the wicked.
29God's people will own the land
and live here forever.

30Words of wisdom come
when good people speak
for justice.
31They remember God's teachings,
and they never take
a wrong step.

32The wicked try to trap
and kill good people,
33but the LORD is on their side,
and he will defend them
when they are on trial.

34Trust the LORD and follow him.
He will give you the land,
and you will see
the wicked destroyed.

35I have seen brutal people
abuse others and grow strong
like trees in rich soil.[v]
36Suddenly they disappeared!
I looked, but they were gone
and no longer there.

37Think of the bright future
waiting for all the families
of honest and innocent
and peace-loving people.
38But not a trace will be left
of the wicked
or their families.

39The LORD protects his people,
and they can come to him
in times of trouble.*
40The LORD helps them
and saves them from the wicked
because they run to him.

Psalm 38

[*A psalm by David to be used when an offering is made.*]

A Prayer in Times of Trouble

1When you are angry, LORD,
please don't punish me
or even correct me.
2You shot me with your arrows,
and you struck me
with your hand.

3My body hurts all over
because of your anger.
Even my bones are in pain,
and my sins 4are so heavy
that I am crushed.

5Because of my foolishness,
I am covered with sores
that stink and spread.
6My body is twisted and bent,
and I groan all day long.
7Fever has my back in flames,
and I hurt all over.
8I am worn out and weak,
moaning and in distress.

9You, Lord, know every one
of my deepest desires,
and my noisy groans
are no secret to you.
10My heart is beating fast.
I feel weak all over,
and my eyes are red.

---

[v]*like . . . soil*: One possible meaning for the difficult Hebrew text.

37.39 **GOD WILL TAKE CARE OF YOU** We should never feel alone in the world, because God is always there to take care of us. Of course, we can't tell God what he must do to solve our problems. His wisdom is perfect, and he *always* does what is best for us. Again and again God shows that he knows all about our troubles, and, like a caring father, he works to make everything right in the end. Sometimes there are long days and nights of waiting, but the secret is to put our lives in his loving hands every morning—and leave the rest to him.

NOTES

11 Because of my sickness,
no friends or neighbors
will come near me.
12 All who want me dead
set traps to catch me,
and those who want
to harm and destroy me
plan and plot all day.

13 I am not able to hear
or speak a word;
14 I am completely deaf
and can't make a sound.

15 I trust you, LORD God,
and you will do something.
16 I said, "Don't let them laugh
or brag because I slip."

17 I am about to collapse
from constant pain.
18 I told you my sins,
and I am sorry for them.
19 Many deadly and powerful
enemies hate me,
20 and they repay evil for good
because I try to do right.

21 You are the LORD God!
Stay nearby
and don't desert me.*
22 You are the one who saves me.
Please hurry and help.

Psalm 39

[*A psalm by David for Jeduthun, the music leader.*]

A Prayer for Forgiveness

1 I told myself, "I'll be careful
not to sin by what I say,
and I'll muzzle my mouth
when evil people are near."
2 I kept completely silent,
but it did no good,[w]
and I hurt even worse.

3 I felt a fire burning inside,
and the more I thought,
the more it burned,
until at last I said:
4 "Please, LORD,
show me my future.
Will I soon be gone?
5 You made my life short,
so brief that the time
means nothing to you.

"Human life is but a breath,*
6 and it disappears
like a shadow.
Our struggles are senseless;
we store up more and more,
without ever knowing
who will get it all.

7 "What am I waiting for?
I depend on you, Lord!
8 Save me from my sins.
Don't let fools sneer at me.
9 You treated me like this,
and I kept silent,
not saying a word.

10 "Won't you stop punishing me?
You have worn me down.
11 You punish us severely
because of our sins.
Like a moth, you destroy
what we treasure most.
We are as frail as a breath.

[w] *but . . . good*: One possible meaning for the difficult Hebrew text.

38.21 **GOD IS ALWAYS NEAR** David knew, no matter how great his suffering, that God would not desert him. His prayer is a good one to remember. David recognized that God was the almighty Lord, and he could call on him at any time to "stay nearby." God would always be there for David. God will always be there for you too, if you will only trust him as your best Friend.

39.5 **EARTHLY LIFE IS SHORT** It is a mistake to imagine our time here will go on and on without end. One day it will all stop for each of us. Remembering this makes us think about what is really important. Storing up wealth is foolish because we soon leave it. What really matters is eternity and where we will spend those endless days to come. Let's store up works that God will keep in his treasure house forever.

NOTES

[12]"Listen, LORD, to my prayer!
My eyes are flooded with tears,
as I pray to you.
I am merely a stranger
visiting in your home
as my ancestors did.
[13]Stop being angry with me
and let me smile again
before I am dead and gone."

Psalm 40

[*A psalm by David for the music leader.*]

A Prayer for Help

[1]I patiently waited, LORD,
for you to hear my prayer.
You listened* [2]and pulled me
from a lonely pit
full of mud and mire.
You let me stand on a rock
with my feet firm,
[3]and you gave me a new song,
a song of praise to you.
Many will see this,
and they will honor and trust
you, the LORD God.

[4]You bless all of those
who trust you, LORD,
and refuse to worship idols
or follow false gods.
[5]You, LORD God, have done
many wonderful things,
and you have planned
marvelous things for us.
No one is like you!
I would never be able to tell
all you have done.

[6]Sacrifices and offerings
are not what please you;
gifts and payment for sin
are not what you demand.
But you made me willing
to listen and obey.
[7]And so, I said, "I am here
to do what is written
about me in the book,
where it says,*
[8]'I enjoy pleasing you.
Your Law is in my heart.' "

[9]When your people worshiped,
you know I told them,
"Our LORD always helps!"
[10]When all your people met,
I did not keep silent.
I said, "Our LORD is kind.
He is faithful and caring,
and he saves us."

[11]You, LORD, never fail
to have pity on me;
your love and faithfulness
always keep me secure.

[12]I have more troubles
than I can count.
My sins are all around me,
and I can't find my way.
My sins outnumber
the hairs on my head,
and I feel weak.
[13]Please show that you care
and come to my rescue.
Hurry and help me!

[14]Disappoint and confuse
all who want me dead;
turn away and disgrace
all who want to hurt me.

40.1 **WAIT FOR GOD'S ANSWER** Wait patiently. God's answer will come, but it doesn't always come right away. As God works in our lives, he asks us two questions: 1) Are we willing to let him have his way? 2) Do we really trust him to do what we ask—and even more than we ask? If so, then we need to be patient in waiting for his perfect answer. We will experience great joy as we see how wise God is in making our way for us.

40.7 **GOD'S WAY IS BEST** In the New Testament the words of this verse are applied to Jesus and his willing obedience in going to the cross for us. So death on the cross was written about long before in God's book. David, a thousand years before Jesus was born, made this prediction about Jesus and the cross. Let us pray to be like Jesus—willing to go wherever God leads us in life.

NOTES

Step 11

I will pray to God on a regular basis, asking him to direct me and give me the power to live for him.

PSALM 40.1–5

CHECKING OUT

This is tough. I want a drink. It makes me feel better. Who am I kidding? I don't drink so that I will feel better; I drink so that I won't have to feel at all. I won't hear my parents arguing. I won't have to deal with school. I can just check out for awhile. That works until you realize you have to check back in sometime. I have decided that will be now. I want to be able to handle life sober. I can't just depend on a liquor bottle. Little by little, it gets sucked away—just like my life. Lord, I put my life in your control. I need your help now to leave it there.

STEP LOOK INSIDE 11

Over and over the Bible records Jesus saying, "Come to me," "Seek me," "Find me"—"I will meet your need, if you just ask."

LOOKING UP

Once we may have depended on outside things to satisfy our need for love. Things like security, self-worth, and peace. Now God wants to do that for us. So why not let him? Let's pray about our desires, our frustrations, our temptations. God promises to meet our needs, and that's a promise worth checking out.

For another "Look Inside," turn to page 663.

15 Embarrass and shame
all of those who say,
"Just look at you now!"
16 Our LORD, let your worshipers
rejoice and be glad.
They love you for saving them,
so let them always say,
"The LORD is wonderful!"

17 I am poor and needy,
but, LORD God,
you care about me,
and you come to my rescue.
Please hurry and help.

Psalm 41

[*A psalm by David for the music leader.*]

A Prayer in Time of Sickness

1 You, LORD God, bless everyone
who cares for the poor,
and you rescue those people
in times of trouble.
2 You protect them
and keep them alive.
You make them happy here
in this land,
and you don't hand them over
to their enemies.
3 You always heal them
and restore their strength
when they are sick.
4 I prayed, "Have pity, LORD!
Heal me, though I have sinned
against you."
5 My vicious enemies ask me,
"When will you die
and be forgotten?"
6 When visitors come,
all they ever bring
are worthless words,
and when they leave,
they spread gossip.

7 My enemies whisper about me.
They think the worst,
8 and they say,
"You have some fatal disease!
You'll never get well."
9 My most trusted friend
has turned against me,
though he ate at my table.*

10 Have pity, LORD! Heal me,
so I can pay them back.
11 Then my enemies
won't defeat me,
and I will know
that you really care.
12 You have helped me
because I am innocent,
and you will always
be close to my side.

13 You, the LORD God of Israel,
will be praised forever!
Amen and amen.

BOOK II
(Psalms 42–72)

Psalm 42

[*A special psalm for the people of Korah and for the music leader.*]

Longing for God

1 As a deer gets thirsty
for streams of water,
I truly am thirsty
for you, my God.
2 In my heart, I am thirsty
for you, the living God.
When will I see your face?
3 Day and night my tears
are my only food,
as everyone keeps asking,
"Where is your God?"

4 Sorrow floods my heart,
when I remember
leading the worshipers
to your house.[x]

---

[x] *leading . . . house*: One possible meaning for the difficult Hebrew text.

41.9

ONLY ONE FRIEND NEVER FAILS David was sad because his best friend had turned against him. Has that ever happened to you? Sometimes those we love and trust most become traitors at last. Even Jesus knew this bitter experience. All of his closest friends deserted him when he was arrested. So let's not feel sorry for ourselves. God is an unchanging friend who never fails those who count on him.

NOTES

I can still hear them shout
their joyful praises.
5Why am I discouraged?
Why am I restless?
I trust you!
And I will praise you again
because you help me,
6 and you are my God.

I am deeply discouraged
as I think about you
from where the Jordan begins
at Mount Hermon
and from Mount Mizar.[y]
7Your vicious waves
have swept over me
like an angry ocean
or a roaring waterfall.

8Every day, you are kind,
and at night
you give me a song
as my prayer to you,
the living LORD God.

9You are my mighty rock.[z]
Why have you forgotten me?
Why must enemies mistreat me
and make me sad?
10Even my bones are in pain,
while all day long
my enemies sneer and ask,
"Where is your God?"

11Why am I discouraged?
Why am I restless?
I trust you!
And I will praise you again
because you help me,
and you are my God.*

Psalm 43

A Prayer in Times of Trouble

1Show that I am right, God!
Defend me against everyone
who doesn't know you;
rescue me from each
of those deceitful liars.
2I run to you
for protection.
Why have you turned me away?
Why must enemies mistreat me
and make me sad?

3Send your light and your truth
to guide me.
Let them lead me to your house
on your sacred mountain.*
4Then I will worship
at your altar because you
make me joyful.
You are my God,
and I will praise you.
Yes, I will praise you
as I play my harp.

5Why am I discouraged?
Why am I restless?
I trust you!
And I will praise you again
because you help me,
and you are my God.

---

[y]*Mount Mizar*: The location is not known.
[z]*mighty rock*: The Hebrew text has "rock," which is sometimes used in poetry to compare the Lord to a mountain where his people can run for protection from their enemies.

42.11 **EVERYONE GETS DISCOURAGED SOMETIMES** How is it possible that someone of great faith can be discouraged? Great faith also calls for great actions, and we can't always see any good coming from what we do. Then we're discouraged. But God knows the self-satisfied person is a proud person, and he won't work with proud people. Our discouragements drive us to pray because we know that no good can come from our works unless God helps us.

43.3 **WE NEED LIGHT TO SEE TRUTH** An important person once asked Jesus, "What is truth?" But the man didn't expect an answer, and he didn't get one. The truth is what agrees with God's mind and purpose. Jesus said that the truth makes us free. There is no scarcity of the truth, but there isn't much understanding of it. Understanding of the truth comes from the light that God gives to those who value the truth more than anything else.

NOTES

Psalm 44

[*A special psalm for the people of Korah and for the music leader.*]

A Prayer for Help

1 Our God, our ancestors told us
what wonders you worked
and we listened carefully.
2 You chased off the nations
by causing them trouble
with your powerful arm.
Then you let our ancestors
take over their land.
3 Their strength and weapons
were not what won the land
and gave them victory!
You loved them and fought
with your powerful arm
and your shining glory.

4 You are my God and King,
and you give victory[a]
to the people of Jacob.
5 By your great power,
we knocked our enemies down
and stomped on them.
6 I don't depend on my arrows
or my sword to save me.
7 But you saved us
from our hateful enemies,
and you put them to shame.
8 We boast about you, our God,
and we are always grateful.

9 But now you have rejected us;
you don't lead us into battle,
and we look foolish.*
10 You made us retreat,
and our enemies have taken
everything we own.
11 You let us be slaughtered
like sheep,
and you scattered us
among the nations.
12 You sold your people
for little or nothing,
and you earned no profit.
13 You made us look foolish
to our neighbors,
and people who live nearby
insult us and sneer.
14 Foreigners joke about us
and shake their heads.
15 I am embarrassed every day,
and I blush with shame.
16 But others mock and sneer,
as they watch my enemies
take revenge on me.

17 All of this has happened to us,
though we didn't forget you
or break our agreement.
18 We always kept you in mind
and followed your teaching.
19 But you crushed us,
and you covered us
with deepest darkness
where wild animals live.

20 We did not forget you
or lift our hands in prayer
to foreign gods.
21 You would have known it
because you discover
every secret thought.
22 We face death all day for you.
We are like sheep on their way
to be slaughtered.

23 Wake up! Do something, Lord!
Why are you sleeping?
Don't desert us forever.
24 Why do you keep looking away?
Don't forget our sufferings
and all of our troubles.
25 We are flat on the ground,
holding on to the dust.
26 Do something! Help us!
Show how kind you are
and come to our rescue.

---

[a] *and . . . victory*: One ancient version; Hebrew "please give victory."

44.9 **SOMETIMES OUR FAITH FAILS** We're only pretending if we say we never doubt God's faithfulness. Sometimes everything seems to go wrong with us. Like the writer of this psalm, right away we may accuse God of failing us—as if he owed it to us that we should win all the time. God never promised that. Disappointments in life come to all. But God has promised to come through for us in the end. And he always does.

NOTES

Psalm 45

[*A special psalm for the people of Korah and for the music leader. To the tune "Lilies." A love song.*]

For a Royal Wedding

1 My thoughts are filled
with beautiful words
for the king,
and I will use my voice
as a writer would use
pen and ink.

2 No one is as handsome as you!
Your words are always kind.
That is why God
will always bless you.
3 Mighty king, glorious ruler,
strap on your sword
4 and ride out in splendor!
Win victories for truth
and mercy and justice.
Do fearsome things
with your powerful arm.
5 Send your sharp arrows
through enemy hearts
and make all nations fall
at your feet.

6 You are God, and you will rule
forever as king.[b]
Your royal power
brings about justice.*
7 You love justice and hate evil.
And so, your God chose you
and made you happier
than any of your friends.
8 The sweet aroma of the spices
myrrh, aloes, and cassia,
covers your royal robes.
You enjoy the music of harps
in palaces decorated
with ivory.
9 Daughters of kings are here,
and your bride stands
at your right side,
wearing a wedding gown
trimmed with pure gold.[c]

10 Bride of the king,
listen carefully to me.
Forget your own people
and your father's family.
11 The king is your husband,
so do what he desires.
12 All of the richest people
from the city of Tyre
will try to influence you
13 with precious treasures.

Your bride, my king,
has inward beauty,[d]
and her wedding gown is woven
with threads of gold.
14 Wearing the finest garments,
she is brought to you,
followed by her young friends,
the bridesmaids.
15 Everyone is excited,
as they follow you
to the royal palace.

16 Your sons and your grandsons
will also be kings
as your ancestors were.
You will make them the rulers
everywhere on earth.

17 I will make your name famous
from now on,
and you will be praised
forever and ever.

Psalm 46

[*A special song for the people of Korah and for the music leader.*]

God Is Our Mighty Fortress

1 God is our mighty fortress,
always ready to help
in times of trouble.

[b] *You . . . king*: Or "God has made you king, and you will rule forever." [c] *trimmed with pure gold*: Hebrew has "with gold from Ophir," which may have been in Africa or India. Gold from there was considered the very best. [d] *has inward beauty*: Or "is dressed in her room."

45.6 **GOD IS THE EVERLASTING KING** One of the greatest problems in the world is the problem of good government. All human governments fail to bring real justice to the earth. We can understand that when we realize that people, including governments, are far from perfect. No, it is only God who can bring real justice. Until we serve and worship him in the right way we will continue to suffer from human injustice.

NOTES

2And so, we won't be afraid!
Let the earth tremble
and the mountains tumble
into the deepest sea.
3Let the ocean roar and foam,
and its raging waves shake
the mountains.

4A river and its streams
bring joy to the city,
which is the sacred home
of God Most High.*
5God is in that city,
and it won't be shaken.
He will help it at dawn.

6Nations rage! Kingdoms fall!
But at the voice of God
the earth itself melts.
7The LORD All-Powerful
is with us.
The God of Jacob
is our fortress.

8Come! See the fearsome things
the LORD has done on earth.
9God brings wars to an end
all over the world.
He breaks the arrows,
shatters the spears,
and burns the shields.[e]
10Our God says, "Calm down,
and learn that I am God!
All nations on earth
will honor me."

11The LORD All-Powerful
is with us.
The God of Jacob
is our fortress.

Psalm 47

[*A psalm for the people of Korah and for the music leader.*]

God Rules the Nations

1All of you nations,
clap your hands and shout
joyful praises to God.
2The LORD Most High is fearsome,
the ruler of all the earth.
3God has put every nation
under our power,
4and he chose for us the land
that was the pride of Jacob,
his favorite.

5God goes up to his throne,
as people shout
and trumpets blast.
6Sing praises to God our King,
7the ruler of all the earth!
Praise God with songs.

8God rules the nations
from his sacred throne.*
9Their leaders come together
and are now the people
of Abraham's God.
All rulers on earth
surrender their weapons,
and God is greatly praised!

---

[e]*shields*: Or "chariots."

46.4 **WHAT IS THE RIVER OF GOD?** The book of Revelation in the New Testament also speaks of a river that runs through the eternal city of God (see Revelation 22.1, 2). Drinking from that water of life we will never die. Didn't Jesus say that whoever drinks of the water that he gives receives everlasting life? See John 4.13, 14. Let us pray daily that God will lead us to his river of life even now. That river is really the life that flows from God, bubbling up inside us with joy that never ends.

47.8 **PRAISE GOD THE KING** Present earthly governments and rulers will come to an end. But God will rule over his new world forever as King, and he will be praised and honored by all people. That world seems far away now, when evil often seems to be winning. But in that coming age these times will pass away. All sorrow and all suffering will be forgotten, and God's beautiful works everywhere will cause us to sing and shout his praise.

NOTES

Psalm 48

[*A song and a psalm for the people of Korah.*]

The City of God

1The LORD God is wonderful!
He deserves all praise
in the city where he lives.
His holy mountain,
2beautiful and majestic,
brings joy to all on earth.
Mount Zion, truly sacred,
is home for the Great King.
3God is there to defend it
and has proved to be
its protector.

4Kings joined forces
to attack the city,
5but when they saw it,
they were terrified
and ran away.
6They trembled all over
like women giving birth
7or like seagoing ships[f]
wrecked by eastern winds.
8We had heard about it,
and now we have seen it
in the city of our God,
the LORD All-Powerful.
This is the city that God
will let stand forever.

9Our God, here in your temple
we think about your love.
10You are famous and praised
everywhere on earth,
as you win victories
with your powerful arm.
11Mount Zion will celebrate,
and all Judah will be glad,
because you bring justice.

12Let's walk around Zion
and count its towers.*
13We will see its strong walls
and visit each fortress.
Then you can say
to future generations,
14"Our God is like this forever
and will always[g] guide us."

Psalm 49

[*A psalm for the people of Korah and for the music leader.*]

Don't Depend on Wealth

1Everyone on this earth,
now listen to what I say!
2Listen, no matter who you are,
rich or poor.
3I speak words of wisdom,
and my thoughts make sense.
4I have in mind a mystery
that I will explain
while playing my harp.

5Why should I be afraid
in times of trouble,
when I am surrounded
by vicious enemies?
6They trust in their riches
and brag about
all of their wealth.
7You cannot buy back your life
or pay off God!
8It costs far too much
to buy back your life.
You can never pay God enough
9to stay alive forever
and safe from death.*

10We see that wise people die,
and so do stupid fools.

---

[f]*seagoing ships*: The Hebrew text has "ships of Tarshish," which probably means large, seagoing ships. [g]*always*: One possible meaning for the difficult Hebrew text.

48.12 **WHAT IS GOD'S CITY LIKE?** All through the Bible, and especially in the book of Revelation, we read glowing descriptions of the city of God. We must remember that the beautiful description in the Psalms and in the Revelation were the best pictures of heaven that human words could paint. But the true beauty of God's coming city is beyond language. Just try to imagine a world in which sin and all its ugly effects are completely absent! Only perfect goodness, peace, joy, and love will remain.

49.9 **GOD'S SAVING WORK IS FREE** We're used to paying for everything we get in this life. But salvation from sin and death costs us nothing. God pays the full price. It was to pay (*continued*)

NOTES

Then their money is left
for someone else.
11The grave[h] will be their home
forever and ever,
although they once had land
of their own.
12Our human glory disappears,
and, like animals, we die.

13Here is what happens to fools
and to those who trust
the words of fools:
14They are like sheep
with death as their shepherd,
leading them to the grave.[i]
In the morning God's people
will walk all over them,
as their bodies lie rotting
in their home, the grave.
15But God will rescue me
from the power of death.

16Don't let it bother you
when others get rich
and live in luxury.
17Soon they will die
and all of their wealth
will be left behind.

18We humans are praised
when we do well,
and all of us are glad
to be alive.
19But we each will go down
to our ancestors,
never again to see
the light of day.
20Our human glory disappears,
and, like animals, we die.

Psalm 50

[*A psalm by Asaph.*]

What Pleases God

1From east to west,
the powerful LORD God
has been calling together
everyone on earth.
2God shines brightly from Zion,
the most beautiful city.

3Our God approaches,
but not silently;
a flaming fire comes first,
and a storm surrounds him.
4God comes to judge his people.
He shouts to the heavens
and to the earth,
5"Call my followers together!
They offered me a sacrifice,
and we made an agreement."

6The heavens announce,
"God is the judge,
and he is always honest."

7My people, I am God!
Israel, I am your God.
Listen to my charges
against you.
8Although you offer sacrifices
and always bring gifts,
9I won't accept your offerings
of bulls and goats.

10Every animal in the forest
belongs to me,
and so do the cattle
on a thousand hills.
11I know all the birds
in the mountains,
and every wild creature
is in my care.

12If I were hungry,
I wouldn't tell you,
because I own the world
and everything in it.
13I don't eat the meat of bulls
or drink the blood of goats.
14I am God Most High!
The only sacrifice I want
is for you to be thankful
and to keep your word.
15Pray to me in time of trouble.
I will rescue you,
and you will honor me.

16But to the wicked I say:
"You don't have the right
to mention my laws or claim
to keep our agreement!

[h] *The grave*: Some ancient versions; Hebrew "Their inward thoughts." [i] *as their . . . grave*: One possible meaning for the difficult Hebrew text.

(*continued*) that price that Jesus died, that whoever trusts him will have the life of God that lasts forever. We want to live for God once we've received this wonderful new life that never ends. This is the way we thank him for his gift.

NOTES

17 You refused correction
and rejected my commands.
18 You made friends
with every crook you met,
and you liked people who break
their wedding vows.
19 You talked only about violence
and told nothing but lies;
20 you sat around gossiping,
ruining the reputation
of your own relatives."

21 When you did all of this,
I didn't say a word,
and you thought,
"God is just like us!"
But now I will accuse you.
22 You have ignored me!
So pay close attention
or I will tear you apart,
and no one can help you.

23 The sacrifice that honors me
is a thankful heart.
Obey me,[j] and I, your God,
will show my power to save.*

Psalm 51

[*For the music leader. A psalm by David when the prophet Nathan came to him after David had been with Bathsheba.*]

A Prayer for Forgiveness

1 You are kind, God!
Please have pity on me.
You are always merciful!
Please wipe away my sins.
2 Wash me clean from all
of my sin and guilt.
3 I know about my sins,
and I cannot forget
my terrible guilt.*

4 You are really the one
I have sinned against;
I have disobeyed you
and have done wrong.
So it is right and fair for you
to correct and punish me.

5 I have sinned and done wrong
since the day I was born.
6 But you want complete honesty,
so teach me true wisdom.
7 Wash me with hyssop[k]
until I am clean
and whiter than snow.
8 Let me be happy and joyful!
You crushed my bones,
now let them celebrate.

9 Turn your eyes from my sin
and cover my guilt.
10 Create pure thoughts in me
and make me faithful again.
11 Don't chase me away from you
or take your Holy Spirit
away from me.

12 Make me as happy as you did
when you saved me;
make me want to obey!
13 I will teach sinners your Law,
and they will return to you.
14 Keep me from any deadly sin.
Only you can save me!
Then I will shout and sing
about your power to save.

---

[j] *Obey me*: One possible meaning for the difficult Hebrew text. [k] *hyssop*: A small bush with bunches of small, white flowers. It was sometimes used as a symbol for making a person clean from sin.

50.23 **DON'T PLAY GAMES WITH GOD** In this psalm God says he doesn't want just the outward acts of worship. God wants our sincere love that is expressed in deeds of thanksgiving for his great salvation. We may fool ourselves, but we can't fool God. Wholehearted living for God is the proof of the words we sing and speak.

51.3 **WHAT IS CONFESSION OF SIN?** People of faith don't try to hide the truth about themselves from God. It's the common fashion to downplay the ugly reality of our sins. But even if we haven't actually done the things David did, our sinful thoughts are just as hateful to the holy God. To know and worship him truly, we must also know this truth about ourselves.

NOTES

15Help me to speak,
and I will praise you, Lord.
16Offerings and sacrifices
are not what you want.
17The way to please you
is to feel sorrow
deep in our hearts.
This is the kind of sacrifice
you won't refuse.

18Please be willing, Lord,
to help the city of Zion
and to rebuild its walls.
19Then you will be pleased
with the proper sacrifices,
and we will offer bulls
on your altar once again.

Psalm 52

[A special psalm by David for the music leader. He wrote this when Doeg from Edom went to Saul and said, "David has gone to Ahimelech's house."]

God Is in Control

1You people may be strong
and brag about your sins,
but God can be trusted
day after day.
2You plan brutal crimes,
and your lying words cut
like a sharp razor.
3You would rather do evil
than good, and tell lies
than speak the truth.
4You love to say cruel things,
and your words are a trap.
5God will destroy you forever!
He will grab you and drag you
from your homes.
You will be uprooted
and left to die.
6When good people see
this fearsome sight,
they will laugh and say,
7 "Just look at them now!
Instead of trusting God,
they trusted their wealth
and their cruelty."

8But I am like an olive tree
growing in God's house,
and I can count on his love
forever and ever.*
9I will always thank God
for what he has done;
I will praise his good name
when his people meet.

Psalm 53

[A special psalm by David for the music leader. To the tune "Mahalath."[l]]

No One Can Ignore God

1Only a fool would say,
"There is no God!"
People like that are worthless!
They are heartless and cruel
and never do right.*

2From heaven God
looks down to see

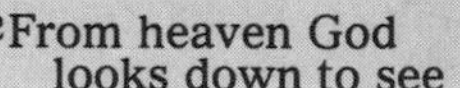

[l] *"Mahalath"*: Or "For flutes," one possible meaning for the difficult Hebrew text.

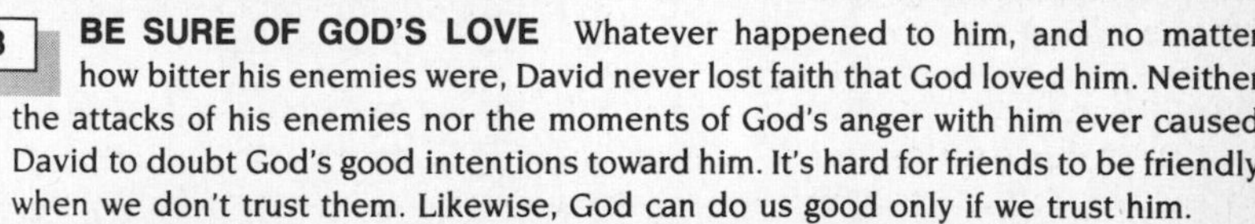

52.8 **BE SURE OF GOD'S LOVE** Whatever happened to him, and no matter how bitter his enemies were, David never lost faith that God loved him. Neither the attacks of his enemies nor the moments of God's anger with him ever caused David to doubt God's good intentions toward him. It's hard for friends to be friendly when we don't trust them. Likewise, God can do us good only if we trust him.

53.1 **GOD EXISTS** There have always been a lot of wise fools going around saying God does not exist. They deny the proof all around them that only the almighty God could have designed and made the universe in all of its amazing order. So they cheat themselves and make themselves poor in understanding their world by their hostile unbelief. Such an attitude is not a mere innocent difference of opinion. Such people are rebelling against the true Governor of the universe, and so they deprive themselves of the joy of his friendship. They "never do right," says David, because they really do everything only to please themselves.

NOTES

if anyone is wise enough
to search for him.
3But all of them
are crooked and corrupt.
Not one of them does right.

4Won't you lawbreakers learn?
You refuse to pray
and you gobble down
the people of God.
5But you will be terrified
worse than ever before.
God will scatter the bones
of his enemies,
and you will be ashamed
when God rejects you.

6I long for someone from Zion
to come and save Israel!
Our God, when you bless
your people again,
Jacob's family will be glad,
and Israel will celebrate.

Psalm 54

[*For the music leader. Use with stringed instruments. A special psalm that David wrote when the people of Ziph went to Saul and said, "David is hiding here with us."*]

Trusting God in Times of Trouble

1Save me, God, by your power
and prove that I am right.
2Listen to my prayer
and hear what I say.
3Cruel strangers have attacked
and want me dead.
Not one of them cares
about you.

4You will help me, Lord God,
and keep me from falling;
5you will punish my enemies
for their evil deeds.
Be my faithful friend
and destroy them.

6I will bring a gift
and offer a sacrifice
to you, LORD.
I will praise your name
because you are good.
7You have rescued me
from all of my troubles,
and my own eyes have seen
my enemies fall.*

Psalm 55

[*A special psalm by David for the music leader. Use with stringed instruments.*]

Betrayed by a Friend

1Listen, God, to my prayer!
Don't reject my request.
2Please listen and help me.
My thoughts are troubled,
and I keep groaning
3because my loud enemies
shout and attack.
They treat me terribly
and hold angry grudges.
4My heart is racing fast,
and I am afraid of dying.
5I am trembling with fear,
completely terrified.

6I wish I had wings
like a dove,
so I could fly far away
and be at peace.*
7I would go and live
in some distant desert.
8I would quickly find shelter
from howling winds
and raging storms.

9Confuse my enemies, Lord!
Upset their plans.

54.7 **GOD SAVES US FROM TROUBLE** Elsewhere David says that God's people will have many troubles, but the Lord saves them from them all. We mustn't be surprised that we have sorrow in our lives as time goes by. No one can avoid trouble. Jesus said that the sunshine and the rain fall on both good and wicked people alike. So let's not be discouraged by setbacks and misfortunes. If we will only wait a little while, we'll see how they pass away like the spring rain clouds.

55.6 **LET'S MEET OUR PROBLEMS HEAD-ON** Like all of us, David sometimes wished he could escape from his troubles. That's a natural reaction to everyday problems that seem to (*continued*)

NOTES

Cruelty and violence
are all I see in the city,
10and they are like guards
on patrol day and night.
The city is full of trouble,
evil, 11and corruption.
Troublemakers and liars
freely roam the streets.

12My enemies are not the ones
who sneer and make fun.
I could put up with that
or even hide from them.
13But it was my closest friend,
the one I trusted most.
14We enjoyed being together,
and we went with others
to your house, our God.

15All who hate me are controlled
by the power of evil.
Sentence them to death
and send them down alive
to the world of the dead.

16I ask for your help, LORD God,
and you will keep me safe.
17Morning, noon, and night
you hear my concerns
and my complaints.
18I am attacked from all sides,
but you will rescue me
unharmed by the battle.
19You have always ruled,
and you will hear me.
You will defeat my enemies
because they won't turn
and worship you.

20My friend turned against me
and broke his promise.
21His words were smoother
than butter, and softer
than olive oil.
But hatred filled his heart,
and he was ready to attack
with a sword.

22Our LORD, we belong to you.
We tell you what worries us,
and you won't let us fall.
23But what about those people
who are cruel and brutal?
You will throw them down
into the deepest pit
long before their time.
I trust you, LORD!

Psalm 56

[*For the music leader. To the tune "A Silent Dove in the Distance."*[m] *A special psalm by David when the Philistines captured him in Gath.*]

A Prayer of Trust in God

1-2Have pity, God Most High!
My enemies chase me all day.
Many of them are pursuing
and attacking me,
3but even when I am afraid,
I keep on trusting you.
4I praise your promises!
I trust you and am not afraid.
No one can harm me.

5Enemies spend the whole day
finding fault with me;
all they think about
is how to do me harm.
6They attack from ambush,
watching my every step
and hoping to kill me.
7They won't get away[n]
with these crimes, God,
because when you get angry,
you destroy people.

8You have kept record
of my days of wandering.
You have stored my tears
in your bottle
and counted each of them.

9When I pray, LORD God,
my enemies will retreat,
because I know for certain
that you are with me.
10I praise your promises!

---

[m]*A Silent . . . Distance*: One possible meaning for the difficult Hebrew text. [n]*They . . . away*: One possible meaning for the difficult Hebrew text.

(*continued*) grind us up. But David really knew that reaction was not the answer. We have to look trouble in the eye, and with one eye on God we attack each test head-on. Otherwise our problems have a way of adding up to a big, discouraging mountain that gets much harder to climb each day.

NOTES

11I trust you and am not afraid.
No one can harm me.

12I will keep my promises
to you, my God,
and bring you gifts.*
13You protected me from death
and kept me from stumbling,
so that I would please you
and follow the light
that leads to life.

Psalm 57

[*For the music leader. To the tune "Don't Destroy."*[o] *A special psalm by David when he was in the cave while running from Saul.*]

Praise and Trust in Times of Trouble

1God Most High, have pity on me!
Have mercy. I run to you
for safety.
In the shadow of your wings,
I seek protection
till danger dies down.
2I pray to you, my protector.
3You will send help from heaven
and save me,
but you will bring trouble
on my attackers.
You are faithful,
and you can be trusted.

4I live among lions,
who gobble down people!
They have spears and arrows
instead of teeth,
and they have sharp swords
instead of tongues.

5May you, my God, be honored
above the heavens;
may your glory be seen
everywhere on earth.*

6Enemies set traps for my feet
and struck me down.
They dug a pit in my path,
but fell in it themselves.
7I am faithful to you,
and you can trust me.
I will sing and play music
for you, my God.
8I feel wide awake!
I will wake up my harp
and wake up the sun.
9I will praise you, Lord,
for everyone to hear,
and I will sing hymns to you
in every nation.
10Your love reaches higher
than the heavens;
your loyalty extends
beyond the clouds.

11May you, my God, be honored
above the heavens;
may your glory be seen
everywhere on earth.

[o]*Don't Destroy*: One possible meaning for the difficult Hebrew text.

56.12 **LET'S KEEP OUR PROMISES TO GOD** We need to make a good start if we're going to arrive where we want to go in life. But everybody knows that just "starting" isn't enough. We have to keep on going. We usually start by making promises to God. We promise him our lives and our loyalty forever. But as time goes by, the way gets hard, or just plain dull, and we may begin to wish for a different road than we started out on. At such times, we need to remember our promises. Let's never have to admit we were so weak we couldn't keep our pledge to God. In good times and bad times, let's keep our word.

57.5 **GOD DESERVES TO BE HONORED** To honor someone means several things. Included in such honor are respect, reverence, and, where God is concerned—obedience. We are rightly commanded to honor our parents and those in civic and spiritual authority. Make no mistake—where there is no honor, neither is there any love, because honor is basic to real love. That means we consider those we love in all our actions that affect them. We also protect and defend their good name. Such respect for loved ones begins with honor for the God who created them in his likeness. He, above all, deserves and ought to be honored.

NOTES

Psalm 58

[*A special psalm by David for the music leader. To the tune "Don't Destroy."*[p]]

A Prayer When All Goes Wrong

1Do you mighty people[q] talk
only to oppose justice?[r]
Don't you ever judge fairly?
2You are always planning evil,
and you are brutal.
3You have done wrong and lied
from the day you were born.
4Your words spread poison
like the bite of a cobra
5that refuses to listen
to the snake charmer.

6My enemies are as fierce
as lions, LORD God!
Shatter their teeth.
Snatch out their fangs.
7Make them disappear
like leaking water,
and make their arrows miss.
8Let them dry up like snails
or be like a child that dies
before seeing the sun.
9Wipe them out quicker
than a pot can be heated
by setting thorns on fire.[s]

10Good people will be glad
when they see the wicked
getting what they deserve,
and they will wash their feet
in their enemies' blood.
11Everyone will say, "It's true!
Good people are rewarded.
God does rule the earth
with justice."*

Psalm 59

[*For the music leader. To the tune "Don't Destroy."*[t] *A special psalm by David when Saul had David's house watched so that he could kill him.*]

A Prayer for Protection

1Save me, God! Protect me
from enemy attacks!
2Keep me safe from brutal people
who want to kill me.

3Merciless enemies, LORD,
are hiding and plotting,
hoping to kill me.
I have not hurt them
in any way at all.
4But they are ready to attack.
Do something! Help me!
Look at what's happening.
5LORD God All-Powerful,
you are the God of Israel.
Punish the other nations
and don't pity those terrible
and rebellious people.

6My enemies return at evening,
growling like dogs
roaming the city.
7They curse and their words
cut like swords,
as they say to themselves,
"No one can hear us!"

8You, LORD, laugh at them
and sneer at the nations.
9You are my mighty fortress,
and I depend on you.
10You love me and will let me
see my enemies defeated.
11Don't kill them,
or everyone may forget!
Just use your mighty power
to make them tremble
and fall.

You are a shield
for your people.
12My enemies are liars!
So let them be trapped
by their boastful lies.
13Get angry and destroy them.
Leave them in ruin.
Then all the nations will know
that you rule in Israel.

---

[p]*Don't Destroy*: One possible meaning for the difficult Hebrew text. [q]*mighty people*: Or "mighty rulers" or "mighty gods." [r]*Do . . . justice*: One possible meaning for the difficult Hebrew text. [s]*Wipe. . . fire*: One possible meaning for the difficult Hebrew text. [t]*Don't Destroy*: One possible meaning for the difficult Hebrew text.

58.11 **GOD RULES WITH JUSTICE** Sometimes it's hard to believe there's justice anywhere. Human laws often seem to protect criminals more than their innocent victims. That's no *(continued)*

NOTES

14 Those liars return at evening,
growling like dogs
roaming the city.
15 They search for scraps of food,
and they snarl
until they are stuffed.*

16 But I will sing about
your strength, my God,
and I will celebrate
because of your love.
You are my fortress,
my place of protection
in times of trouble.
17 I will sing your praises!
You are my mighty fortress,
and you love me.

Psalm 60

[*For the music leader. To the tune "Lily of the Promise." A special psalm by David for teaching. He wrote it during his wars with Aram-naharaim and Aram-zobah,*[u] *when Joab came back and killed twelve thousand Edomites*[v] *in Salt Valley.*]

You Can Depend on God

1 You, God, are angry with us!
We are rejected and crushed.
Make us strong again!
2 You made the earth shake
and split wide open;
now heal its wounds
and stop its trembling.
3 You brought hard times
on your people,
and you gave us wine
that made us stagger.

4 You gave a signal to those
who worship you,
so they could escape
from enemy arrows.[w]
5 Answer our prayers!
Use your powerful arm
and give us victory.
Then the people you love
will be safe.

6 Our God, you solemnly promised,
"I would gladly divide up
the city of Shechem
and give away Succoth Valley
piece by piece.*
7 The lands of Gilead
and Manasseh are mine.
Ephraim is my war helmet,
and Judah is the symbol
of my royal power.
8 Moab is merely my washbasin.
Edom belongs to me,
and I shout in triumph
over the Philistines."

9 Our God, who will bring me
to the fortress,
or lead me to Edom?

---

[u]*wars . . . Aram-zobah*: See 2 Samuel 8.3-8, 10.16-18; 1 Chronicles 18.3-11, 19.6-19. [v]*killed . . . Edomites*: See 2 Samuel 8.13; 1 Chronicles 18.12. [w]*so . . . arrows*: Some ancient versions and one possible meaning for the difficult Hebrew text.

(*continued*) exaggeration! But with such thoughts we're in danger of becoming discouraged. Let's not be too upset by these conditions. We have plenty of reason to believe that God is still on the throne, and his justice will win out in the end. The rise and fall of many world empires of the past is a token of the infallible fact that God's justice will be done after all.

59.15 **KEEP ON SINGING** No matter how vicious David's enemies were or how much they threatened his life, David could remember to sing. He sang about God, about his strength, and about his love. These psalms are a collection of those very songs. David is our example. Because of God's great love and care, we, too, can sing.

60.6 **KEEP ON PRAYING** David had little relief from the pressures of life. Are you living in a "pressure cooker"? This psalm shows you the answer: Don't stop praying. Even in the struggles and tensions of everyday living, keep on praying through it all. You will receive strength from your continual conversation with God. More than that, he will give you success in your struggles.

NOTES

10 Have you rejected us
and deserted our armies?
11 Help us defeat our enemies!
No one else can rescue us.
12 You will give us victory
and crush our enemies.

Psalm 61

[*A psalm by David for the music leader. Use with stringed instruments.*]

Under the Protection of God

1 Please listen, God,
and answer my prayer!
2 I feel hopeless,
and I cry out to you
from a faraway land.

Lead me to the mighty rock[x]
high above me.
3 You are a strong tower,
where I am safe
from my enemies.*

4 Let me live with you forever
and find protection
under your wings, my God.
5 You heard my promises,
and you have blessed me,
just as you bless everyone
who worships you.

6 Let the king have a long
and healthy life.
7 May he always rule
with you, God, at his side;
may your love and loyalty
watch over him.

8 I will sing your praises
forever and will always
keep my promises.

Psalm 62

[*A psalm by David for Jeduthun, the music leader.*]

God Is Powerful and Kind

1 Only God can save me,
and I calmly wait for[y] him.
2 God alone is the mighty rock[z]
that keeps me safe
and the fortress
where I am secure.

3 I feel like a shaky fence
or a sagging wall.
How long will all of you
attack and assault me?
4 You want to bring me down
from my place of honor.
You love to tell lies,
and when your words are kind,
hatred hides in your heart.

5 Only God gives inward peace,
and I depend on him.
6 God alone is the mighty rock
that keeps me safe,
and he is the fortress
where I feel secure.
7 God saves me and honors me.
He is that mighty rock
where I find safety.

8 Trust God, my friends,
and always tell him
each one of your concerns.
God is our place of safety.

9 We humans are only a breath;
none of us are truly great.

---

[x]*mighty rock*: The Hebrew text has "rock," which is sometimes used in poetry to compare the Lord to a mountain where his people can run for safety from their enemies. [y]*calmly wait for*: Or "am at peace with." [z]*mighty rock*: The Hebrew text has "rock," which is sometimes used in poetry to compare the Lord to a mountain where his people can run for safety.

61.3 **GOD IS A HIDING PLACE** Corrie Ten Boom, survivor of a Nazi extermination camp in World War II, wrote a book, *The Hiding Place*, that has also become a movie. Corrie's "hiding place," her "strong tower," her "mighty rock" was God himself. Learn to hide away in God from the raging storms of life. Deep within each of us is a little temple, a quiet place where we can be alone with God and know we are safe. Make a habit of spending all your spare moments in that quiet place with God. There you will find peace that no one can take from you.

NOTES

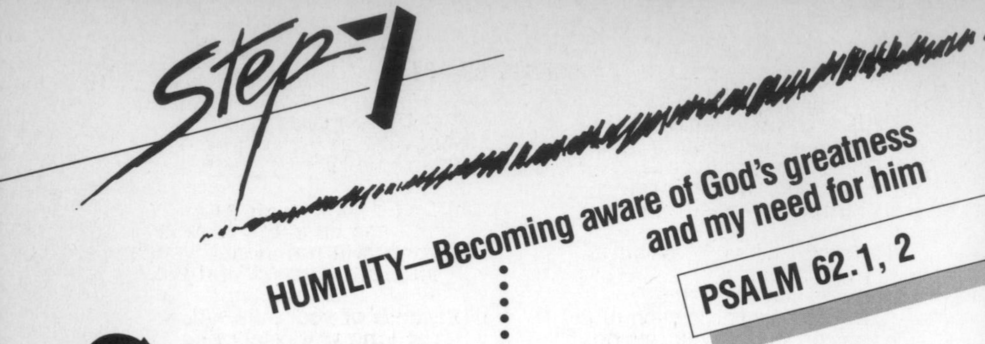

GOD IS THERE FOR YOU

During World War II, a father in London, England, was running from a building that had been struck by a bomb. As he ran, he held his small son by the hand. When they reached an enormous shell hole in the front yard, the father jumped into the hole and held up his arms for his son to follow.

Terrified, yet hearing his father's voice telling him to jump, the boy replied, "I can't see you!" The father, looking up against the sky tinted red by the burning buildings, called to the silhouette of his son, "But I can see you. Jump!" The boy jumped, because he trusted his father.

When we consider whether God will be there for us, it is not because we can see him, but because we can be certain that we are seen by him. We won't know all the answers, but we are known by the One who does.

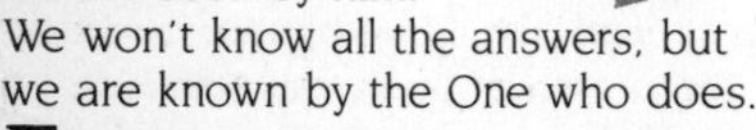

Faith is seeing what God sees and acting upon it. We can jump into the arms of our Heavenly Father because we know that he will be there to catch us. This leap of faith is based on what we know in our minds about God's character and what we sense in our emotions about his love and care for us. It will always be a battle of our emotions and our will as we stand looking out into the blackness of the unknown. It takes a willingness to humble ourselves and jump into God's mighty hand in order to become all that God wants us to become. We will find that the leaps get easier as we get to know God better. He is always there to catch us!

Trusting God will build our faith and remove our shortcomings. Here's a great verse for today: "Faith makes us sure of what we hope for and gives us proof of what we cannot see" (Hebrews 11.1).

To take a "Look Back" at a woman whose greatness is measured by a humble spirit toward God and others, turn to page 116.

All of us together weigh less
than a puff of air.
10 Don't trust in violence
or depend on dishonesty
or rely on great wealth.

11 I heard God say two things:
"I am powerful,*
12 and I am very kind."
The Lord rewards each of us
according to what we do.

Psalm 63

[A psalm by David when he was in the desert of Judah.]

God's Love Means More than Life

1 You are my God. I worship you.
In my heart, I long for you,
as I would long for a stream
in a scorching desert.

2 I have seen your power
and your glory
in the place of worship.
3 Your love means more
than life to me,
and I praise you.
4 As long as I live,
I will pray to you.
5 I will sing joyful praises
and be filled with excitement
like a guest at a banquet.

6 I think about you
before I go to sleep,
and my thoughts turn to you
during the night.*
7 You have helped me,
and I sing happy songs
in the shadow of your wings.
8 I stay close to you,
and your powerful arm
supports me.

9 All who want to kill me
will end up in the ground.
10 Swords will run them through,
and wild dogs will eat them.

11 Because of you, our God,
the king will celebrate
with your faithful followers,
but liars will be silent.

Psalm 64

[A psalm by David for the music leader.]

Celebrate because of the Lord

1 Listen to my concerns, God,
and protect me
from my terrible enemies.
2 Keep me safe from secret plots
of corrupt and evil gangs.
3 Their words cut like swords,
and their cruel remarks
sting like sharp arrows.
4 They fearlessly ambush
and shoot innocent people.

5 They are determined to do evil,
and they tell themselves,
"Let's set traps!
No one can see us."[a]
6 They make evil plans and say,
"We'll commit a perfect crime.
No one knows our thoughts."[b]

---

[a] *us*: One ancient version; Hebrew "them."
[b] *thoughts*: One possible meaning for the difficult Hebrew text of verse 6.

62.11 **GOD IS BOTH POWERFUL AND KIND** Some folks think God must be a tyrant because he is so powerful. But the all-powerful God is also infinitely kind. This is a wonderful thing—that unlimited strength should be combined with great gentleness. We see this fact clearly in the person of Jesus, the God-Man, who had the power to command the storm, but could also speak peace to a troubled soul.

63.6 **MAY GOD BE YOUR LAST THOUGHT** Two times are ideal for speaking with God—early morning and late night. These are the quiet times of our lives, the hours when our deepest thoughts are clear, and there is little interruption. So let's learn to seek God late and early. God then whispers to us wonderful things that the noisy business of the day drowns out. During such minutes, and even hours, God speaks to our deepest needs.

NOTES

7 But God will shoot his arrows
and quickly wound them.
8 They will be destroyed
by their own words,
and everyone who sees them
will tremble with fear.[c]
9 They will be afraid and say,
"Look at what God has done
and keep it all in mind."

10 May the LORD bless his people
with peace and happiness
and let them celebrate.*

Psalm 65

[*A psalm by David and a song for the music leader.*]

God Answers Prayer

1 Our God, you deserve[d] praise
in Zion, where we keep
our promises to you.
2 Everyone will come to you
because you answer prayer.
3 Our terrible sins get us down,
but you forgive us.
4 You bless your chosen ones,
and you invite them
to live near you
in your temple.
We will enjoy your house,
the sacred temple.

5 Our God, you save us,
and your fearsome deeds answer
our prayers for justice!
You give hope to people
everywhere on earth,
even those across the sea.
6 You are strong,
and your mighty power
put the mountains in place.
7 You silence the roaring waves
and the noisy shouts
of the nations.
8 People far away marvel
at your fearsome deeds,
and all who live under the sun
celebrate and sing
because of you.
9 You take care of the earth
and send rain to help the soil
grow all kinds of crops.
Your rivers never run dry,
and you prepare the earth
to produce much grain.
10 You water all of its fields
and level the lumpy ground.
You send showers of rain
to soften the soil
and help the plants sprout.
11 Wherever your footsteps
touch the earth,
a rich harvest is gathered.
12 Desert pastures blossom,
and mountains celebrate.
13 Meadows are filled
with sheep and goats;
valleys overflow with grain
and echo with joyful songs.

Psalm 66

[*A song and a psalm for the music leader.*]

Shout Praises to God

1 Tell everyone on this earth
to shout praises to God!
2 Sing about his glorious name.
Honor him with praises.
3 Say to God, "Everything you do
is fearsome,
and your mighty power makes
your enemies come crawling.
4 You are worshiped by everyone!
We all sing praises to you."

5 Come and see the fearsome things
our God has done!
6 When God made the sea dry up,
our people walked across,
and because of him,
we celebrated there.
7 His mighty power rules forever,
and nothing the nations do
can be hidden from him.
So don't turn against God.

---

[c] *tremble with fear*: Or "turn and run." [d] *deserve*: One possible meaning for the difficult Hebrew text.

64.10 **WORSHIP GOD WITH GLADNESS** God's people have great reason to be glad. He has saved them from their sins and given them eternal life. So a joyful lifestyle becomes those who love God. Joy is the second quality, after love, that should be seen most in us. Our everyday life can be a worship service, as we spread happiness up to the maximum.

NOTES

8All of you people,
come praise our God!
Let his praises be heard.
9God protects us from death
and keeps us steady.

10Our God, you tested us,
just as silver is tested.
11You trapped us in a net
and gave us heavy burdens.
12You sent war chariots
to crush our skulls.
We traveled through fire
and through floods,
but you brought us
to a land of plenty.

13I will bring sacrifices
into your house, my God,
and I will do what I promised
14 when I was in trouble.
15I will sacrifice my best sheep
and offer bulls and goats
on your altar.

16All who worship God,
come here and listen;
I will tell you everything
God has done for me.
17I prayed to the Lord,
and I praised him.
18If my thoughts had been sinful,
he would have refused
to hear me.
19But God did listen
and answered my prayer.
20Let's praise God!
He listened when I prayed,
and he is always kind.*

Psalm 67

[*A psalm and a song for the music leader. Use with stringed instruments.*]

Tell the Nations to Praise God

1Our God, be kind and bless us!
Be pleased and smile.
2Then everyone on earth
will learn to follow you,
and all nations will see
your power to save us.*

3Make everyone praise you
and shout your praises.
4Let the nations celebrate
with joyful songs,
because you judge fairly
and guide all nations.
5Make everyone praise you
and shout your praises.

6Our God has blessed the earth
with a wonderful harvest!
7Pray for his blessings
to continue
and for everyone on earth
to worship our God.

Psalm 68

[*A psalm and a song by David for the music leader.*]

God Will Win the Battle

1Do something, God!
Scatter your hateful enemies.
Make them turn and run.

66.20 **PRAYER MAKES A DIFFERENCE** Sometimes we don't pray because we think God doesn't hear us or that he doesn't care about what he hears. So we make do with our own feeble efforts to change our circumstances. Very often the results are disappointing. Let's give prayer the chance it deserves. *God is*! He has promised to listen to us, and millions agree that he does. He makes a difference in our lives because we pray.

67.2 **SEEING IS BELIEVING** In a very real way people can see our faith. They see our faith because of the way it works in our lives. If we only talk and don't give our lives over to God, then others find it hard to trust in God. Yes, God himself is seen in what we do. God's people ought to be unusual in the simple but God-like way they do the most ordinary things—the way they speak, the way they work, and the kindness they just naturally show.

NOTES

2Scatter them like smoke!
When you come near,
make them melt
like wax in a fire.
3But let your people be happy
and celebrate because of you.

4Our God, you are the one
who rides on the clouds,
and we praise you.
Your name is the LORD,
and we celebrate
as we worship you.

5Our God, from your sacred home
you take care of orphans
and protect widows.
6You find families
for those who are lonely.
You set prisoners free
and let them prosper,[e]
but all who rebel will live
in a scorching desert.

7You set your people free,
and you led them
through the desert.
8God of Israel,
the earth trembled,
and rain poured down.
You alone are the God
who rules from Mount Sinai.
9When your land was thirsty,
you sent showers
to refresh it.
10Your people settled there,
and you were generous
to everyone in need.

11You gave the command,
and a chorus of women told
what had happened:
12"Kings and their armies
retreated and ran,
and everything they left
is now being divided.
13And for those who stayed back
to guard the sheep,
there are metal doves
with silver-coated wings
and shiny gold feathers."

14God All-Powerful, you scattered
the kings like snow falling
on Mount Zalmon.[f]

15Our LORD and our God,
Bashan is a mighty mountain
covered with peaks.
16Why is it jealous of Zion,
the mountain you chose
as your home forever?

17When you, LORD God, appeared
to your people[g] at Sinai,
you came with thousands
of mighty chariots.
18When you climbed
the high mountain,
you took prisoners with you
and were given gifts.
Your enemies didn't want you
to live there,
but they gave you gifts.

19We praise you, Lord God!
You treat us with kindness
day after day,
and you rescue us.
20You always protect us
and save us from death.

21Our Lord and our God,
your terrible enemies
are ready for war,[h]
but you will crush
their skulls.
22You promised to bring them
from Bashan
and from the deepest sea.
23Then we could stomp
on their blood,
and our dogs could chew
on their bones.

24We have seen crowds marching
to your place of worship,
our God and King.
25The singers come first,
and then the musicians,
surrounded by young women
playing tambourines.
26They come shouting,
"People of Israel,
praise the LORD God!"
27The small tribe of Benjamin
leads the way,
followed by the leaders
from Judah.
Then come the leaders
from Zebulun and Naphtali.

28Our God, show your strength!
Show us once again.

---

[e] *and let them prosper*: Or "and give them a song." [f] *Mount Zalmon*: The location of this mountain is not known. [g] *to your people*: Or "in all your holiness" or "in your holy place." [h] *are ready for war*: The Hebrew text has "have long hair," which probably refers to the ancient custom of wearing long hair on special occasions, such as a "holy war."

29 Then kings will bring gifts
to your temple
in Jerusalem.[i]

30 Punish that animal
that lives in the swamp![j]
Punish that nation
whose leaders and people
are like wild bulls.
Make them come crawling
with gifts of silver.
Scatter those nations
that enjoy making war.[k]
31 Force the Egyptians to bring
gifts of bronze;
make the Ethiopians[l] hurry
to offer presents.[m]

32 Now sing praises to God!
Every kingdom on earth,
sing to the Lord!*
33 Praise the one who rides
across the ancient skies;
listen as he speaks
with a mighty voice.

34 Tell about God's power!
He is honored in Israel,
and he rules the skies.
35 The God of Israel is fearsome
in his temple,
and he makes us strong.
Let's praise our God!

Psalm 69

[*By David for the music leader. To the tune "Lilies."*]

God Can Be Trusted

1 Save me, God!
I am about to drown.*
2 I am sinking deep in the mud,
and my feet are slipping.
I am about to be swept under
by a mighty flood.
3 I am worn out from crying,
and my throat is dry.
I have waited for you
till my eyes are blurred.

4 There are more people
who hate me for no reason
than there are hairs
on my head.
Many terrible enemies
want to destroy me, God.
Am I supposed to give back
something I didn't steal?
5 You know my foolish sins.
Not one is hidden from you.

6 LORD God All-Powerful,
ruler of Israel,
don't let me embarrass anyone
who trusts and worships you.
7 It is for your sake alone
that I am insulted
and blush with shame.
8 I am like a stranger
to my relatives
and like a foreigner
to my own family.

9 My love for your house
burns in me like a fire,

---

[i] *Our God . . . Jerusalem*: One possible meaning for the difficult Hebrew text of verses 28, 29. [j] *animal . . . swamp*: Probably Egypt. [k] *war*: One possible meaning for the difficult Hebrew text of verse 30. [l] *the Ethiopians*: The Hebrew text has "the people of Cush," which was a region south of Egypt that included parts of the present countries of Ethiopia and Sudan. [m] *presents*: One possible meaning for the difficult Hebrew text of verse 31.

68.32 **WILL THE NATIONS SING TO GOD?** In the Old Testament "the nations" were all those people who were not part of Israel. Often they are called "Gentiles." Today the nations are all people who haven't yet heard about Jesus Christ. It is our job to tell all nations about him and his great salvation. That was Jesus' last command to us. When we obey him, people from "every kingdom on earth" will praise God, not only in this world, but in endless ages to come.

69.1 **ARE YOU DROWNING?** Perhaps these words have found you in a time of deep trouble. Financial ruin is near; a marriage is breaking up; there's bad news from the doctor. Many, many people today are drowning in sorrow, starvation, and fear. These words are written to you, whoever you are, so that you may know there's someone to turn to—God. He can help, and he *will* if only you ask him sincerely.

NOTES

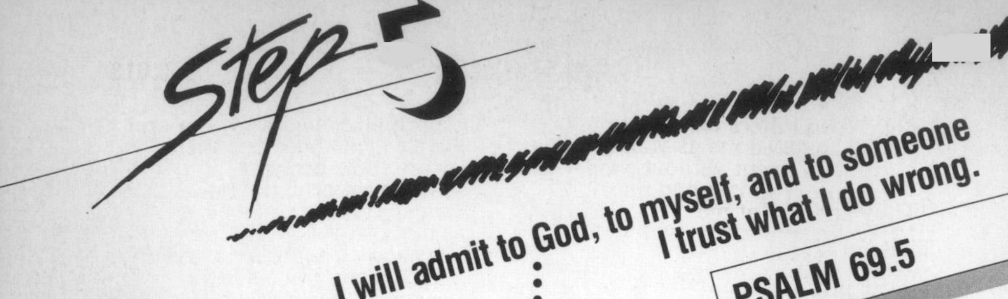

EYES IN THE BACK OF THEIR HEADS

"Don't lie to me. I know what you have been doing."

It can get pretty frustrating when even our best attempts at deception fail. How do parents usually know?

The truth is, parents really don't have eyes in the back of their heads. What they do have is a working knowledge about us. Whether we like it or not, our parents are experts on us. This is because they have been observing our character and behavior for a long time and can predict how we will act or react in a given situation. With this information, our parents do their best to raise us.

CONFESSION IS THE KEY

In an even greater way, God knows us. Not only from observing our outward behavior, but, as the Bible states, God knows our every thought and intention of heart. When we admit our mistakes in life and agree with what God already knows, then healing can begin. Confession is the key to closing the door on the past so we can open the door to a bright and happy future.

To take a "Look Ahead," turn to page 390.

and when others insulted you,
they insulted me as well.*
10 I cried and went without food,[n]
but they still insulted me.
11 They sneered at me
for wearing sackcloth[o]
to show my sorrow.
12 Rulers and judges gossip
about me,
and drunkards make up songs
to mock me.

13 But I pray to you, LORD.
So when the time is right,
answer me and help me
with your wonderful love.
14 Don't let me sink in the mud,
but save me from my enemies
and from the deep water.
15 Don't let me be
swept away by a flood
or drowned in the ocean
or swallowed by death.

16 Answer me, LORD!
You are kind and good.
Pay attention to me!
You are truly merciful.
17 Don't turn away from me.
I am your servant,
and I am in trouble.
Please hurry and help!
18 Come and save me
from my enemies.

19 You know how I am insulted,
mocked, and disgraced;
you know every one
of my enemies.
20 I am crushed by insults,
and I feel sick.
I had hoped for mercy and pity,
but there was none.
21 Enemies poisoned my food,
and when I was thirsty,
they gave me vinegar.

22 Make their table a trap
for them and their friends.
23 Blind them with darkness
and make them tremble.
24 Show them how angry you are!
Be furious and catch them.
25 Destroy their camp
and don't let anyone live
in their tents.

26 They cause trouble for people
you already punished;
their gossip hurts those
you have wounded.
27 Make them guiltier than ever
and don't forgive them.
28 Wipe their names from the book
of the living;
remove them from the list
of the innocent.
29 I am mistreated and in pain.
Protect me, God,
and keep me safe!

30 I will praise the LORD God
with a song
and a thankful heart.
31 This will please the LORD
better than offering an ox
or a full-grown bull.
32 When those in need see this,
they will be happy,
and the LORD's worshipers
will be encouraged.
33 The LORD will listen
when the homeless cry out,
and he will never forget
his people in prison.

34 Heaven and earth
will praise our God,
and so will the oceans
and everything in them.
35 God will rescue Jerusalem,
and he will rebuild
the towns of Judah.
His people will live there
on their own land,

[n] *went without food*: People sometimes went without food (called "fasting") to show sorrow. [o] *sackcloth*: A rough, dark-colored cloth made from goat or camel hair and used to make grain sacks. It was worn in times of trouble or sorrow.

69.9 **DO WE LOVE GOD'S HOUSE?** God's house isn't really a building, although his people usually meet in a building. God's house is his kingdom that he is building with men and boys, women and girls, to be his prized possession forever. In the New Testament the words of this verse are applied to Jesus, who loved God's house so much that he died for it. They who love God will also love his people—God's house, God's family.

NOTES

36 and when the time comes,
their children will inherit
the land.
Then everyone who loves God
will also settle there.

Psalm 70

[*By David for the music leader. To be used when an offering is made.*]

God Is Wonderful

1 Save me, LORD God!
Hurry and help.
2 Disappoint and confuse
all who want to kill me.
Turn away and disgrace
all who want to hurt me.
3 Embarrass and shame those
who say, "We told you so!"

4 Let your worshipers celebrate
and be glad because of you.
They love your saving power,
so let them always say,
"God is wonderful!"
5 I am poor and needy,
but you, the LORD God,
care about me.

You are the one who saves me.
Please hurry and help!*

Psalm 71

A Prayer for God's Protection

STEP 2

1 I run to you, LORD,
for protection.
Don't disappoint me.
2 You do what is right,
so come to my rescue.
Listen to my prayer
and keep me safe.
3 Be my mighty rock,[p] the place
where I can always run
for protection.
Save me by your command!
You are my mighty rock
and my fortress.

4 Come and save me, LORD God,
from vicious and cruel
and brutal enemies!
5 I depend on you,
and I have trusted you
since I was young.*
6 I have relied on you[q]
from the day I was born.
You brought me safely
through birth,
and I always praise you.

7 Many people think of me
as something evil.
But you are my mighty protector,
8 and I praise and honor you
all day long.
9 Don't throw me aside
when I am old;
don't desert me
when my strength is gone.

---

[p]*mighty rock*: The Hebrew has "rock," which is sometimes used in poetry to compare the Lord to a mountain where his people can run for protection from their enemies. [q]*I . . . you*: One possible meaning for the difficult Hebrew text.

70.5 **GOD CARES ABOUT THE POOR** All through the Bible we read of God's care for people who are in want, and he commands us to care for them, too. There are different ways to be poor. Many are poor in material needs. Both they and others are poor in spirit. They have little to live for, and often no one seems to care. Many times they take their own lives or die of starvation. We have to get the news out to such people that someone does care about them—God cares. And we must show that he does by our own generosity. Some people only need someone to talk to, and that's the least we can spare.

71.5 **TRUST GOD WHEN YOU'RE YOUNG** It's hard to change after we're grown up. But when we're young—that's the time to break new trails for ourselves. God's path is the right path. His way is the best. Then, as you grow, you'll realize more and more what a privilege it is to belong to Jesus the Lord. That's the way to avoid a lot of heartache—and also a wrecked life. His way is the path to happiness forever.

NOTES

10My enemies are plotting
because they want me dead.
11They say, "Now we'll catch you!
God has deserted you,
and no one can save you."
12Come closer, God!
Please hurry and help.
13Embarrass and destroy
all who want me dead;
disgrace and confuse
all who want to hurt me.
14I will never give up hope
or stop praising you.
15All day long I will tell
the wonderful things you do
to save your people.
But you have done much more
than I could possibly know.
16I will praise you, LORD God,
for your mighty deeds
and your power to save.

17You have taught me
since I was a child,
and I never stop telling about
your marvelous deeds.
18Don't leave me when I am old
and my hair turns gray.
Let me tell future generations
about your mighty power.*
19Your deeds of kindness
are known in the heavens.
No one is like you!

20You made me suffer a lot,
but you will bring me
back from this deep pit
and give me new life.
21You will make me truly great
and take my sorrow away.

22I will praise you, God,
the Holy One of Israel.
You are faithful.
I will play the harp
and sing your praises.
23You have rescued me!
I will celebrate and shout,
singing praises to you
with all my heart.
24All day long I will announce
your power to save.
I will tell how you disgraced
and disappointed those
who wanted to hurt me.

Psalm 72

[*By Solomon.*]

A Prayer for God to Guide and Help the King

1Please help the king
to be honest and fair
just like you, our God.
2Let him be honest and fair
with all your people,
especially the poor.
3Let peace and justice rule
every mountain and hill.
4Let the king defend the poor,
rescue the homeless, and crush
everyone who hurts them.
5Let the king live[r] forever
like the sun and the moon.
6Let him be as helpful as rain
that refreshes the meadows
and the ground.
7Let the king be fair
with everyone,
and let there be peace
until the moon
falls from the sky.

8Let his kingdom reach
from sea to sea,
from the Euphrates River
across all the earth.*

---

[r]*Let the king live*: One ancient version; Hebrew "Let them worship you."

71.18 **WE, TOO, CAN TELL ABOUT GOD'S POWER** Since he was a child the writer of this song had been telling people about God's great works. Now that he was old and grayheaded, he still looked forward to telling "future generations" about God's power. He could do this through the music he had created (verse 22). We, too, can tell about the wonderful power God has shown in our own lives.

72.8 **JESUS WILL REIGN OVER ALL** Here is another of those great psalms that describe the future reign of Christ when he will set up his kingdom forever. Of course, Solomon (*continued*)

NOTES

9 Force the desert tribes
to accept his rule,
and make his enemies
crawl in the dirt.
10 Force the rulers of Tarshish[s]
and of the islands
to pay taxes to him.
Make the kings of Sheba
and of Seba[t] bring gifts.
11 Make other rulers bow down
and all nations serve him.

12 Do this because the king
rescues the homeless
when they cry out,
and he helps everyone
who is poor and in need.
13 The king has pity
on the weak and the helpless
and protects those in need.
14 He cares when they hurt,
and he saves them from cruel
and violent deaths.

15 Long live the king!
Give him gold from Sheba.
Always pray for the king
and praise him each day.
16 Let cities overflow with food
and hills be covered with grain,
just like Mount Lebanon.
Let the people in the cities
prosper like wild flowers.
17 May the glory of the king
shine brightly forever
like the sun in the sky.
Let him make nations prosper
and learn to praise him.

18 LORD God of Israel,
we praise you.
Only you can work miracles.
19 We will always praise
your glorious name.
Let your glory be seen
everywhere on earth.
Amen and amen.

20 This ends the prayers
of David, the son of Jesse.

BOOK III
(Psalms 73–89)

Psalm 73

[*A psalm by Asaph.*]

God Is Good

1 God is truly good to Israel,[u]
especially to everyone
with a pure heart.
2 But I almost stumbled and fell,
3 because it made me jealous
to see proud and evil people
and to watch them prosper.
4 They never have to suffer;[v]
they stay healthy,
5 and they don't have troubles
like everyone else.

6 Their pride is like a necklace,
and they commit sin more often
than they dress themselves.
7 Their eyes poke out with fat,
and their minds are flooded
with foolish thoughts.
8 They sneer and say cruel things,
and because of their pride,
they make violent threats.
9 They dare to speak against God
and to order others around.

10 God will bring his people back,
and they will drink the water
he so freely gives.[w]*

---

[s] *Tarshish*: The exact location of this city is not known. [t] *Sheba . . . Seba*: Sheba may have been a place in what is now southwest Arabia, and Seba may have been in southern Arabia. [u] *to Israel*: Or "to those who do right." [v] *They . . . suffer*: Or "They die a painless death." [w] *gives*: One possible meaning for the difficult Hebrew text of verse 10.

(*continued*) originally wrote the psalm about himself. He may not have realized that God had an even greater King in mind. Isn't it wonderful how God controlled the minds and pens of his early writers! They spoke more than they understood about God's plans. Christ's everlasting kingdom will reach "from sea to sea."

73.10 **JESUS GIVES THE WATER OF LIFE** Jesus said that whoever believes in him will never thirst. Even the woman who first heard these words didn't understand right away what he (*continued*)

NOTES

11Only evil people would say,
"God Most High cannot
know everything!"
12Yet all goes well for them,
and they live in peace.
13What good did it do me
to keep my thoughts pure
and refuse to do wrong?
14I am sick all day,
and I am punished
each morning.
15If I had said evil things,
I would not have been loyal
to your people.

16It was hard for me
to understand all this!
17Then I went to your temple,
and there I understood
what will happen
to my enemies.
18You will make them stumble,
never to get up again.
19They will be terrified,
suddenly swept away
and no longer there.
20They will disappear, Lord,
despised like a bad dream
the morning after.

21Once I was bitter
and brokenhearted.
22I was stupid and ignorant,
and I treated you
as a wild animal would.
23But I never really left you,
and you hold my right hand.
24Your advice has been my guide,
and later you will welcome me
in glory.[x]
25In heaven I have only you,
and on this earth
you are all I want.
26My body and mind may fail,
but you are my strength
and my choice forever.

27Powerful LORD God,
all who stay far from you
will be lost,
and you will destroy those
who are unfaithful.
28It is good for me
to be near you.
I choose you as my protector,
and I will tell about
your wonderful deeds.

Psalm 74

[*A special psalm by Asaph.*]

A Prayer for the Nation in Times of Trouble

1Our God, why have you
completely rejected us?
Why are you so angry
with the ones you care for?
2Remember the people
you rescued long ago,
the tribe you chose
to be your very own.
Think of Mount Zion,
your home;
3walk over to the temple
left in ruins forever
by those who hate us.

4Your enemies roared like lions
in your holy temple,
and they have placed
their banners there.
5It looks like a forest
chopped to pieces.[y]
6They used axes and hatchets
to smash the carvings.
7They burned down your temple
and badly disgraced it.
8They said to themselves,
"We'll crush them!"
Then they burned every one
of your meeting places
all over the country.
9There are no more miracles
and no more prophets.
Who knows how long
it will be like this?

---

[x]*in glory*: Or "with honor." [y]*pieces*: One meaning for the difficult Hebrew text of verse 5.

(*continued*) meant. For he spoke of "living water" that doesn't come out of wells or fountains. Cool water revives and refreshes us. So the life of Jesus refreshes us always. He pours himself into us, and that sweet water of life keeps flowing in us forever.

NOTES

10 Our God, how much longer
will our enemies sneer?
Won't they ever stop
insulting you?
11 Why don't you punish them?
Why are you holding back?

12 Our God and King,
you have ruled
since ancient times;
you have won victories
everywhere on this earth.*
13 By your power you made a path
through the sea,
and you smashed the heads
of sea monsters.
14 You crushed the heads
of the monster Leviathan,[z]
then fed him to wild creatures
in the desert.
15 You opened the ground
for streams and springs
and dried up mighty rivers.
16 You rule the day and the night,
and you put the moon
and the sun in place.
17 You made summer and winter
and gave them to the earth.[a]

18 Remember your enemies, LORD!
They foolishly sneer
and won't respect you.
19 You treat us like pet doves,
but they mistreat us.
Don't keep forgetting us
and letting us be fed
to those wild animals.
20 Remember the agreement
you made with us.
Violent enemies are hiding
in every dark corner
of the earth.
21 Don't disappoint those in need
or make them turn from you,
but help the poor and homeless
to shout your praises.
22 Do something, God!
Defend yourself.
Remember how those fools
sneer at you all day long.
23 Don't forget the loud shouts
of your enemies.

Psalm 75

[A psalm and a song by Asaph for the music leader. To the tune "Don't Destroy."[b]]

Praise God for All He Has Done

1 Our God, we thank you
for being so near to us!
Everyone celebrates
your wonderful deeds.*

2 You have set a time
to judge with fairness.
3 The earth trembles,
and its people shake;
you alone keep
its foundations firm.
4 You tell every bragger,
"Stop bragging!"
And to the wicked you say,
"Don't boast of your power!
5 Stop bragging! Quit telling me
how great you are."

---

[z] *Leviathan*: God's victory over this monster sometimes stands for his power over all creation and sometimes for his defeat of Egypt. [a] *gave . . . earth*: Or "made boundaries for the earth." [b] *Don't Destroy*: One possible meaning for the difficult Hebrew text.

74.12 **GOD IS ETERNAL** We need to think about this word "eternal." We hear it from time to time, but we also need to understand it. Of course, to be eternal means to have no beginning and no ending. So there has never been a time, and there never will be a time, when God does not exist. But eternal life is also a life of completeness and perfection. God shares his eternal life with those who love him.

75.1 **GOD IS NEAR** Often people think of God as a being who is far away. And he is. But God is also very near to all of us. As God, he has no limits, but he is everywhere at all times. Sometimes we may not "feel" God's nearness because we aren't paying attention to him. When we ignore someone, after a while it's as if that person doesn't even exist anymore. In the same way, we also "tune out" God—because we don't want to think about him. But he really is very near, and he wants us to know and enjoy him.

NOTES

6 Our LORD and our God,
victory doesn't come
from the east or the west
or from the desert.
7 You are the one who judges.
You can take away power
and give it to others.
8 You hold in your hand
a cup filled with wine,[c]
strong and foaming.
You will pour out some
for every sinful person
on this earth,
and they will have to drink
until it is gone.
9 But I will always tell about
you, the God of Jacob,
and I will sing your praise.

10 Our Lord, you will destroy
the power of evil people,
but you will give strength
to those who are good.

Psalm 76

[*A song and a psalm for the music leader. Use stringed instruments.*]

God Always Wins

1 You, our God,
are famous in Judah
and honored in Israel.
2 Your home is on Mount Zion
in the city of peace.
3 There you destroyed
fiery arrows, shields, swords,
and all the other weapons.

4 You are more glorious than
the eternal mountains.[d]*
5 Brave warriors were robbed
of what they had taken,
and now they lie dead,
unable to lift an arm.
6 God of Jacob, when you roar,
enemy chariots and horses
drop dead in their tracks.
7 Our God, you are fearsome,
and no one can oppose you
when you are angry.
8 From heaven you announced
your decisions as judge!
And all who live on this earth
were terrified and silent
9 when you took over as judge,
ready to rescue
everyone in need.
10 Even the most angry people
will praise you
when you are furious.[e]

11 Everyone, make your promises
to the LORD your God
and do what you promise.
The LORD is fearsome,
and all of his servants
should bring him gifts.
12 God destroys the courage
of rulers and kings
and makes cowards of them.

Psalm 77

[*A psalm by Asaph for Jeduthun, the music leader.*]

In Times of Trouble God Is with His People

1 I pray to you, Lord God,
and I beg you to listen.
2 In days filled with trouble,
I search for you.
And at night I tirelessly
lift my hands in prayer,
refusing comfort.
3 When I think of you,
I feel restless and weak.

4 Because of you, Lord God,
I can't sleep.

---

[c] *a cup . . . wine*: In the Old Testament "a cup filled with wine" sometimes stands for God's anger.
[d] *the eternal mountains*: One ancient version; Hebrew "the mountains of victims (of wild animals)."
[e] *furious*: One possible meaning for the difficult Hebrew text of verse 10.

76.4 **EVEN THE MOUNTAINS WILL PASS AWAY** This verse says the mountains are eternal. Actually, the word "eternal" is used here to give us an idea of the great age of the mountains. But, in fact, even the mountains will finally melt away. Nothing in the world that is seen lasts forever. And how short our own lives are when compared to the mountains!

NOTES

I am restless
and can't even talk.
5I think of times gone by,
of those years long ago.*
6Each night my mind
is flooded with questions:f
7"Have you rejected me forever?
Won't you be kind again?
8Is this the end of your love
and your promises?
9Have you forgotten
how to have pity?
Do you refuse to show mercy
because of your anger?"
10Then I said, "God Most High,
what hurts me most
is that you no longer help us
with your mighty arm."

11Our LORD, I will remember
the things you have done,
your miracles of long ago.
12I will think about each one
of your mighty deeds.
13Everything you do is right,
and no other god
compares with you.
14You alone work miracles,
and you have let nations
see your mighty power.
15With your own arm you rescued
your people, the descendants
of Jacob and Joseph.

16The ocean looked at you, God,
and it trembled deep down
with fear.
17Water flowed from the clouds.
Thunder was heard above
as your arrows of lightning
flashed about.
18Your thunder roared
like chariot wheels.
The world was made bright
by lightning,
and all the earth trembled.

19You walked through the water
of the mighty sea,
but your footprints
were never seen.
20You guided your people
like a flock of sheep,
and you chose Moses and Aaron
to be their leaders.

Psalm 78

[*A special psalm by Asaph.*]

What God Has Done for His People

1My friends, I beg you
to listen as I teach.
2I will give instruction
and explain the mystery
of what happened long ago.
3These are things we learned
from our ancestors,*
4and we will tell them
to the next generation.
We won't keep secret
the glorious deeds
and the mighty miracles
of the LORD.

---

f*my mind . . . questions*: One ancient version; Hebrew "I remember my music."

77.5 **MEMORY IS A GREAT TEACHER** Asaph, the songwriter, was thinking of "years long ago." Remembering the past teaches us to appreciate God's faithfulness in bringing us through many difficulties. We are then able to realize we didn't "do it all ourselves." God's hand has brought us to our present place. Memory is also good for people who have missed life's opportunities. It's never too late to start over with God. He fills our empty lives with his promises of better things to come.

78.3 **LET'S LEARN FROM THE PAST** History seems like a dull subject when we're in school. We'd rather be out playing football or going to a party. Do we ever think about the hard work of the good people of the past who made it possible for us to enjoy such good things? That's part of the meaning of history. But history is also known as "his-story"—God's marvelous plan of the ages by which he brings about his eternal kingdom. If we're going to appreciate God's plans for the future, we have to be thankful for the past also—"things we learned from our ancestors."

NOTES

5God gave his Law
to Jacob's descendants,
the people of Israel.
And he told our ancestors
to teach their children,
6so that each new generation
would know his Law
and tell it to the next.
7Then they would trust God
and obey his teachings,
without forgetting anything
God had done.
8They would be different
from their ancestors,
who were stubborn, rebellious,
and unfaithful to God.

9The warriors from Ephraim
were armed with arrows,
but they ran away
when the battle began.
10They broke their agreement
with God,
and they turned their backs
on his teaching.
11They forgot all he had done,
even the mighty miracles
12he did for their ancestors
near Zoan[g] in Egypt.

13God made a path in the sea
and piled up the water
as he led them across.
14He guided them during the day
with a cloud,
and each night he led them
with a flaming fire.
15God made water flow
from rocks he split open
in the desert,
and his people drank freely,
as though from a lake.
16He made streams gush out
like rivers from rocks.

17But in the desert,
the people of God Most High
kept sinning and rebelling.
18They stubbornly tested God
and demanded from him
what they wanted to eat.
19They challenged God by saying,
"Can God provide food
out here in the desert?
20It's true God struck the rock
and water gushed out
like a river,
but can he give his people
bread and meat?"

21When the LORD heard this,
he was angry and furious
with Jacob's descendants,
the people of Israel.
22They had refused to trust him,
and they had doubted
his saving power.

23But God gave a command
to the clouds,
and he opened the doors
in the skies.
24From heaven he sent grain
that they called manna.[h]
25He gave them more than enough,
and each one of them ate
this special food.

26God's mighty power
brought a strong wind
from the southeast,
27and it brought birds
that covered the ground,
like sand on the beach.
28Then God made the birds fall
in the camp of his people
near their tents.

29God gave his people
all they wanted,
and each of them ate
until they were full.
30But before they had swallowed
the last bite,
31God became angry and killed
the strongest and best
from the families of Israel.

32But the rest kept on sinning
and would not trust
God's miracles.
33So he cut their lives short
and made them terrified.
34After he killed some of them,
the others turned to him
with all their hearts.
35They remembered God
Most High,
the mighty rock[i]
that kept them safe.
36But they tried to flatter God,
and they told him lies;

---

[g]*Zoan*: A city in the eastern part of the Nile Delta. [h]*manna*: When the people of Israel were wandering through the desert, the Lord gave them a special kind of food to eat. It tasted like a wafer and was called "manna," which in Hebrew means, "What is this?" [i]*mighty rock*: The Hebrew text has "rock," which is sometimes used in poetry to compare the Lord to a mountain where his people can run for protection from their enemies.

37they were unfaithful
and broke their promises.

38Yet God was kind.
He kept forgiving their sins
and didn't destroy them.
He often became angry,
but never lost his temper.*
39God remembered that they
were made of flesh
and were like a wind
that blows once
and then dies down.

40While they were in the desert,
they often rebelled
and made God sad.
41They kept testing him
and caused terrible pain
for the Holy One of Israel.
42They forgot about his power
and how he had rescued them
from their enemies.
43God showed them all kinds
of wonderful miracles
near Zoan[j] in Egypt.
44He turned the rivers of Egypt
into blood,
and no one could drink
from the streams.
45He sent swarms of flies
to pester the Egyptians,
and he sent frogs
to cause them trouble.

46God let worms and grasshoppers
eat their crops.
47He destroyed their grapevines
and their fig trees
with hail and floods.[k]
48Then he killed their cattle
with hail
and their other animals
with lightning.

49God was so angry and furious
that he went into a rage
and caused them great trouble
by sending swarms
of destroying angels.
50God gave in to his anger
and slaughtered them
in a terrible way.
51He killed the first-born son
of each Egyptian family.

52Then God led his people
out of Egypt
and guided them in the desert
like a flock of sheep.
53He led them safely along,
and they were not afraid,
but their enemies drowned
in the sea.

54God brought his people
to the sacred mountain
that he had taken
by his own power.
55He made nations run
from the tribes of Israel,
and he let the tribes
take over their land.

56But the people tested
God Most High,
and they refused
to obey his laws.
57They were as unfaithful
as their ancestors,
and they were as crooked
as a twisted arrow.
58God demanded all their love,
but they made him angry
by worshiping idols.

59So God became furious
and completely rejected
the people of Israel.
60Then he deserted his home
at Shiloh, where he lived
here on earth.
61He let enemies capture
the sacred chest[l]
and let them dishonor him.

---

[j]*Zoan*: See the note at verse 12. [k]*floods*: Or "frost." [l]*sacred chest*: The Hebrew text has "his power," which refers to the sacred chest. In Psalm 132.8 it is called "powerful."

78.38 **GOD IS PATIENT** One of the things our study of history teaches us is God's great patience with us. No one can honestly look at the past doings of people and say, "Aren't we a great and wonderful people!" No, the human race keeps on failing, generation after generation. But God doesn't destroy nations right away. He always waits for many years and pleads with them to return and obey his laws.

NOTES

62 God took out his anger
on his chosen ones
and let them be killed
by enemy swords.
63 Fire destroyed the young men,
and the young women were left
with no one to marry.
64 Priests died violent deaths,
but their widows
were not allowed to mourn.

65 Finally the Lord woke up,
and he shouted
like a drunken soldier.
66 God scattered his enemies
and made them ashamed
forever.

67 Then the Lord decided
not to make his home
with Joseph's descendants
in Ephraim.[m]
68 Instead he chose the tribe
of Judah,
and he chose Mount Zion,
the place he loves.
69 There he built his temple
as lofty as the mountains
and as solid as the earth
that he had made
to last forever.

70 The Lord God chose David
to be his servant and took him
from tending sheep
71 and from caring for lambs.
Then God made him the leader
of Israel, his own nation.
72 David treated the people fairly
and guided them with wisdom.

Psalm 79

[*A psalm by Asaph.*]

Have Pity on Jerusalem

1 Our God, foreign nations
have taken your land,
disgraced your temple,
and left Jerusalem in ruins.
2 They have fed the bodies
of your servants
to flesh-eating birds;
your loyal people are food
for savage animals.
3 All Jerusalem is covered
with their blood,
and there is no one left
to bury them.
4 Every nation around us
sneers and makes fun.

5 Our LORD, will you keep on
being angry?
Will your angry feelings
keep flaming up like fire?
6 Get angry with those nations
that don't know you
and won't worship you!
7 They have gobbled down
Jacob's descendants
and left the land in ruins.

8 Don't make us pay for the sins
of our ancestors.
Have pity and come quickly!
We are completely helpless.
9 Our God, you keep us safe.
Now help us! Rescue us.
Forgive our sins
and bring honor to yourself.

10 Why should nations ask us,
"Where is your God?"
Let us and the other nations
see you take revenge
for your servants who died
a violent death.

11 Listen to the prisoners groan!
Let your mighty power save all
who are sentenced to die.
12 Each of those nations sneered
at you, our Lord.
Now let others sneer at them,
seven times as much.*

---

[m] *with . . . Ephraim*: Ephraim was Joseph's youngest son. One of the twelve tribes was named after him, and sometimes the northern kingdom of Israel was also known as Ephraim. The town of Shiloh was in the territory of Ephraim, but the place where God was worshiped was moved from there to Zion (Jerusalem) in the territory of Judah.

79.12 **LET'S BE THANKFUL** Unthankful people are unhappy people. They always feel shortchanged in life, and they show their feelings to those around them. Thankful people are just the opposite. They count their blessings and remember all the good things that have *(continued)*

NOTES

13 Then we, your people,
will always thank you.
We are like sheep
with you as our shepherd,
and all generations
will hear us praise you.

Psalm 80

[*A psalm by Asaph for the music leader. To the tune "Lilies of the Agreement."*]

Help Our Nation

1 Shepherd of Israel, you lead
the descendants of Joseph,
and you sit on your throne
above the winged creatures.[n]
Listen to our prayer
and let your light shine
2 for the tribes of Ephraim,
Benjamin, and Manasseh.
Save us by your power.

3 Our God, make us strong again!
Smile on us and save us.

4 LORD God All-Powerful,
how much longer
will the prayers of your people
make you angry?
5 You gave us tears for food,
and you made us drink them
by the bowlful.
6 Because of you,
our enemies who live nearby
laugh and joke about us.
7 But if you smile on us,
we will be saved.

8 We were like a grapevine
you brought out of Egypt.
You chased other nations away
and planted us here.
9 Then you cleared the ground,
and we put our roots deep,
spreading over the land.
10 Shade from this vine covered
the mountains.
Its branches climbed
the mighty cedars
11 and stretched to the sea;
its new growth reached
to the river.[o]

12 Our Lord, why have you
torn down the wall
from around the vineyard?
You let everyone who walks by
pick the grapes.
13 Now the vine is gobbled down
by pigs from the forest
and other wild animals.

14 God All-Powerful,
please do something!
Look down from heaven
and see what's happening
to this vine.
15 With your own hands
you planted its roots,
and you raised it
as your very own.

16 Enemies chopped the vine down
and set it on fire.
Now show your anger
and destroy them.
17 But help the one who sits
at your right side,[p]
the one you raised
to be your own.
18 Then we will never turn away.
Put new life into us,
and we will worship you.*

19 LORD God All-Powerful,
make us strong again!
Smile on us and save us.

---

[n] *winged creatures*: Two winged creatures made of gold were on the top of the sacred chest and were symbols of the Lord's throne on earth. See Exodus 25.18. [o] *the sea . . . the river*: The Mediterranean Sea and the Euphrates River were part of the ideal boundaries for Israel. [p] *right side*: The place of honor and power.

(*continued*) happened to them. They realize that what little or great good they have in the world comes from the hand of a kind God. Their thankfulness shows, and such people are easy to love.

80.18 **THE NEW LIFE GOD GIVES MAKES US ABLE TO WORSHIP HIM** It helps us to know the One who is at the center of worship. God is invisible, but he is the greatest of all reality. Before we can worship, he must pour his life into us so that we can love and honor him for who he is.

NOTES

Psalm 81

[By Asaph for the music leader.[q]*]*

God Makes Us Strong

1Be happy and shout to God
who makes us strong!
Shout praises to the God
of Jacob.
2Sing as you play tambourines
and the lovely sounding
stringed instruments.
3Sound the trumpets and start
the New Moon Festival.[r]
We must also celebrate
when the moon is full.
4This is the law in Israel,
and it was given to us
by the God of Jacob.
5The descendants of Joseph
were told to obey it,
when God led them out
from the land of Egypt.

In a language unknown to me,
I heard someone say:
6"I lifted the burden
from your shoulder
and took the heavy basket
from your hands.
7When you were in trouble,
I rescued you,
and from the thunderclouds,
I answered your prayers.
Later I tested you
at Meribah Spring.[s]*

8"Listen, my people,
while I, the Lord,
correct you!
Israel, if you would only
pay attention to me!
9Don't worship foreign gods
or bow down to gods
you know nothing about.
10I am the LORD your God.
I rescued you from Egypt.
Just ask, and I will give you
whatever you need.

11"But, my people, Israel,
you refused to listen,
and you would have nothing
to do with me!
12So I let you be stubborn
and keep on following
your own advice.

13"My people, Israel,
if only you would listen
and do as I say!
14I, the LORD, would quickly
defeat your enemies
with my mighty power.
15Everyone who hates me
would come crawling,
and that would be the end
of them.
16But I would feed you
with the finest bread
and with the best honey[t]
until you were full."

Psalm 82

[A psalm by Asaph.]

Please Do Something, God!

1When all of the other gods[u]
have come together,

---

[q]*leader*: The Hebrew text adds "according to the gittith," which may have been either a musical instrument or a tune. [r]*New Moon Festival*: Celebrated on the first day of each new moon, which was the beginning of the month. But this may refer to either the New Year celebration or the Harvest Festival. "The moon is full" suggests a festival in the middle of the month. [s]*Meribah Spring*: When the people of Israel complained to Moses about the need for water, God commanded Moses to strike a rock with his walking stick, and water came out. The place was then named Massah ("test") and Meribah ("argument"). [t]*the best honey*: The Hebrew text has "honey from rocks," referring to honey taken from beehives in holes or cracks in large rocks. [u]*the other gods*: This probably refers to the gods of the nations that God defeated, but it could refer to God's servants (angels) in heaven or to the gods of the nations that God has defeated or even to human rulers.

81.7 **REMEMBER GOD'S KINDNESS** Many of us can remember times when we were in trouble, and—just in time—God saved us out of that trouble. God delights in being kind to people who are burdened. Jesus takes our heavy loads and gives us a lighter one. He said, "This burden is light" (Matthew 11.30). The road to heaven is a happy one, and no load we carry for Jesus is too much.

NOTES

the Lord God judges them
and says:
2"How long will you
keep judging unfairly
and favoring evil people?
3Be fair to the poor
and to orphans.
Defend the helpless
and everyone in need.
4Rescue the weak and homeless
from the powerful hands
of heartless people.

5"None of you know
or understand a thing.
You live in darkness,
while the foundations
of the earth tremble.[v]

6"I, the Most High God, say
that all of you are gods[w]
and also my own children.
7But you will die,
just like everyone else,
including powerful rulers."

8Do something, God!
Judge the nations of the earth;
they belong to you.

Psalm 83

[*A song and a psalm by Asaph.*]

God Rules All the Earth

1Our God, don't just sit there,
silently doing nothing!
2Your hateful enemies
are turning against you
and rebelling.
3They are sly, and they plot
against those you treasure.
4They say, "Let's wipe out
the nation of Israel
and make sure that no one
remembers its name!"

5All of them fully agree
in their plans against you,
and among them are
6Edom and the Ishmaelites;
Moab and the Hagrites;
7Gebal, Ammon, and Amalek;
Philistia and Phoenicia.[x]
8Even Assyria has joined forces
with Moab and Ammon.[y]

9Our Lord, punish all of them
as you punished Midian.
Destroy them, as you destroyed
Sisera and Jabin
at Kishon Creek 10near Endor,
and let their bodies rot.
11Treat their leaders as you did
Oreb and Zeeb,
Zebah and Zalmunna.
12All of them said, "We'll take
God's valuable land!"

13Our God, scatter them around
like dust in a whirlwind.
14Just as flames destroy forests
on the mountains,
15pursue and terrify them
with storms of your own.
16Make them blush with shame,
until they turn and worship
you, our LORD.
17Let them be forever ashamed
and confused.
Let them die in disgrace.
18Make them realize that you
are the LORD Most High,
the only ruler of earth!*

Psalm 84

[*For the music leader.[z] A psalm for the people of Korah.*]

The Joy of Worship

1LORD God All-Powerful,
your temple is so lovely!

---

[v]*foundations . . . tremble*: In ancient times it was believed that the earth was flat and supported by columns. [w]*all of you are gods*: See the note at verse 1. [x]*Phoenicia*: The Hebrew text has "Tyre," the main city in Phoenicia. [y]*Moab and Ammon*: The Hebrew text has "the descendants of Lot," whose older daughter was the mother of the Moabites and whose younger daughter was the mother of the Ammonites (see Genesis 19.30-38). [z]*leader*: The Hebrew text adds "according to the gittith," which may refer either to a musical instrument or to a tune. The exact meaning of the words is not known.

83.18 **GOD IS IN CHARGE OF EVERYTHING** There is no peace like the peace that comes from knowing that God is in complete control of this and any other worlds he created. (*continued*)

NOTES

[2]Deep in my heart I long
for your temple,
and with all that I am
I sing joyful songs to you.

[3]LORD God All-Powerful,
my King and my God,
sparrows find a home
near your altars;
swallows build nests there
to raise their young.

[4]You bless everyone
who lives in your house,
and they sing your praises.
[5]You bless all who depend
on you for their strength
and all who deeply desire
to visit your temple.
[6]When they reach Dry Valley,[a]
springs start flowing,
and the autumn rain fills it
with pools of water.[b]
[7]Your people grow stronger,
and you, the God of gods,
will be seen in Zion.

[8]LORD God All-Powerful,
the God of Jacob,
please answer my prayer!
[9]You are the shield
that protects your people,
and I am your chosen one.
Won't you smile on me?

[10]One day in your temple
is better than a thousand
anywhere else.
I would rather serve
in your house,
than live in the homes
of the wicked.*

[11]Our LORD and our God,
you are like the sun
and also like a shield.
You treat us with kindness
and with honor,
never denying any good thing
to those who live right.

[12]LORD God All-Powerful,
you bless everyone
who trusts you.

Psalm 85

[A psalm by the people of Korah for the music leader.]

A Prayer for Peace

[1]Our LORD, you have blessed
your land
and made all go well
for Jacob's descendants.
[2]You have forgiven the sin
and taken away the guilt
of your people.
[3]Your fierce anger is no longer
aimed at us.

[4]Our LORD and our God,
you save us!
Please bring us back home
and don't be angry.
[5]Will you always be angry
with us and our families?
[6]Won't you give us fresh life
and let your people be glad
because of you?*

---

[a]*Dry Valley*: Or "Balsam Tree Valley." The exact location is not known. [b]*and . . . water*: One possible meaning for the difficult Hebrew text.

(continued) Because this is true, we can believe that right will win out in the struggle of evil against goodness. So the songwriter's prayer will be answered: God will show to everyone that he is in charge of his universe.

84.10 **LIVE IN GOD'S HOUSE** We can't very well live in a church, but just the same we can live in God's true "house." God's house is wherever God is, and to live with God is to live in his house. Wherever we've been living up until now, let's from now on decide to live where God is. There we can enjoy his beauty and learn from him all the days of our lives.

85.6 **GOD GIVES NEW LIFE** Every day God wants to give us fresh life. Peter the apostle says in the New Testament that God causes us to share in his very own nature (see 2 Peter *(continued)*

NOTES

[7]Show us your love
and save us!

[8]I will listen to you, LORD God,
because you promise peace
to those who are faithful
and no longer foolish.
[9]You are ready to rescue
everyone who worships you,
so that you will live with us
in all of your glory.

[10]Love and loyalty
will come together;
goodness and peace
will unite.
[11]Loyalty will sprout
from the ground;
justice will look down
from the sky above.

[12]Our LORD, you will bless us;
our land will produce
wonderful crops.
[13]Justice will march in front,
making a path
for you to follow.

Psalm 86

[*A prayer by David.*]

A Prayer for Help

[1]Please listen, LORD,
and answer my prayer!
I am poor and helpless.
[2]Protect me and save me
because you are my God.
I am your faithful servant,
and I trust you.
[3]Be kind to me!
I pray to you all day.
[4]Make my heart glad!
I serve you,
and my prayer is sincere.
[5]You willingly forgive,
and your love is always there
for those who pray to you.
[6]Please listen, LORD!
Answer my prayer for help.
[7]When I am in trouble, I pray,
knowing you will listen.

[8]No other gods are like you;
only you work miracles.
[9]You created each nation,
and they will all bow down
to worship and honor you.
[10]You perform great wonders
because you alone are God.

[11]Teach me to follow you,
and I will obey your truth.
Always keep me faithful.*
[12]With all my heart I thank you;
I praise you, LORD God.
[13]Your love for me is so great
that you protected me
from death and the grave.

[14]Proud and violent enemies,
who don't care about you,
have ganged up to attack
and kill me.
[15]But you, the Lord God,
are kind and merciful.
You don't easily get angry,
and your love
can always be trusted.
[16]I serve you, LORD,
and I am the child
of one of your servants.
Look on me with kindness.
Make me strong and save me.
[17]Show that you approve of me!

(*continued*) 1.4). That's an almost shocking thing: God pours his very life into us every day. Just as we eat our daily meals, so we feed on God's invisible nature. Jesus also says, "I am the bread that gives life! No one who comes to me will ever be hungry" (John 6.35).

86.11 **GOD KEEPS US FAITHFUL** David knew that he couldn't be faithful just by trying. God says elsewhere that he himself will always be faithful (see Psalm 89.33). So our faithfulness always depends on his help every moment of our lives. This is a good thing to remember. It's one of God's rules that he doesn't help smug, self-confident people. He does stand by those who trust him for everything—even for their own faith.

NOTES

Then my hateful enemies
will feel like fools,
because you have helped
and comforted me.

Psalm 87

[*A psalm and a song by the people of Korah.*]

The Glory of Mount Zion

1 Zion was built by the LORD
on the holy mountain,
2 and he loves that city
more than any other place
in all of Israel.
3 Zion, you are the city of God,
and wonderful things
are told about you.*

4 Egypt,[c] Babylonia, Philistia,
Phoenicia,[d] and Ethiopia[e]
are some of those nations
that know you,
and their people all say,
"I was born in Zion."

5 God Most High will strengthen
the city of Zion.
Then everyone will say,
"We were born here too."
6 The LORD will make a list
of his people,
and all who were born here
will be included.

7 All who sing or dance will say,
"I too am from Zion."

Psalm 88

[*A song and a psalm by the people of Korah for the music leader. To the tune Mahalath Leannoth.*[f] *A special psalm by Heman the Ezrahite.*]

A Prayer When You Can't Find the Way

1 You keep me safe, LORD God.
So when I pray at night,*
2 please listen carefully
to each of my concerns.

3 I am deeply troubled
and close to death;
4 I am as good as dead
and completely helpless.
5 I am no better off
than those in the grave,
those you have forgotten
and no longer help.

6 You have put me in the deepest
and darkest grave;
7 your anger rolls over me
like ocean waves.
8 You have made my friends turn
in horror from me.
I am a prisoner
who cannot escape,

[c] *Egypt*: The Hebrew text has "Rahab," the name of a monster that stands for Egypt (see Isaiah 30.7). [d] *Phoenicia*: The Hebrew text has "Tyre," the main city in Phoenicia. [e] *Ethiopia*: The Hebrew text has "Cush," which was a region south of Egypt that included parts of the present countries of Ethiopia and Sudan. [f] *To . . . Leannoth*: Or "For the flutes," one possible meaning for the difficult Hebrew text.

87.3 **WHERE IS THE CITY OF GOD?** In Old Testament times Jerusalem was a very special city because the temple was there. But God meant that city and that temple to be small models or pictures of where he really lives. We have seen before that God's "temple" (or worship place) is now wherever God is. So, too, God's city is wherever his people are living obediently for him. One day his eternal city will fill the whole universe, and everyone will serve him there.

88.1 **GOD KEEPS US SAFE** In this psalm the songwriter wrote about his troubles. Even so, he knew his life was safe in God's hands. We can't expect life to be easy all the time either. Living in the world brings its share of trouble to everyone. But let's keep in mind that God doesn't mean to hurt us. As exercise strengthens the body, so trouble strengthens our faith—if we continue to trust in God's safe-keeping in spite of everything that disturbs us.

NOTES

9and I am almost blind
because of my sorrow.

Each day I lift my hands
in prayer to you, LORD.
10Do you work miracles
for the dead?
Do they stand up
and praise you?
11Are your love and loyalty
announced in the world
of the dead?
12Do they know of your miracles
or your saving power
in the dark world below
where all is forgotten?

13Each morning I pray
to you, LORD.
14Why do you reject me?
Why do you turn from me?
15Ever since I was a child,
I have been sick
and close to death.
You have terrified me
and made me helpless.[g]

16Your anger is like a flood!
And I am shattered
by your furious attacks
17that strike each day
and from every side.
18My friends and neighbors
have turned against me
because of you,
and now darkness
is my only companion.

Psalm 89

[*A special psalm by Ethan the Ezrahite.*]

The LORD's Agreement with David

1Our LORD, I will sing
of your love forever.
Everyone yet to be born
will hear me praise
your faithfulness.
2I will tell them, "God's love
can always be trusted,
and his faithfulness lasts
as long as the heavens."

3You said, "David, my servant,
is my chosen one,
and this is the agreement
I made with him:
4David, one of your descendants
will always be king."

5Our LORD, let the heavens
now praise your miracles,
and let all of your angels
praise your faithfulness.

6None who live in the heavens
can compare with you.
7You are the most fearsome
of all who live in heaven;
all the others fear
and greatly honor you.
8You are LORD God All-Powerful!
No one is as loving
and faithful as you are.
9You rule the roaring sea
and calm its waves.
10You crushed the monster Rahab,[h]
and with your powerful arm
you scattered your enemies.
11The heavens and the earth
belong to you.
And so does the world
with all its people
because you created them
12 and everything else.[i]

Mount Tabor and Mount Hermon
gladly praise you.
13You are strong and mighty!
14Your kingdom is ruled
by justice and fairness
with love and faithfulness
leading the way.

15Our LORD, you bless those
who join in the festival
and walk in the brightness
of your presence.
16We are happy all day
because of you,
and your saving power
brings honor to us.
17Your own glorious power
makes us strong,
and because of your kindness,
our strength increases.
18Our LORD and our king,
the Holy One of Israel,
you are truly our shield.

19In a vision, you once said
to your faithful followers:

---

[g]*and made me helpless*: One possible meaning for the difficult Hebrew text. [h]*Rahab*: Many people in the ancient world thought that the world was controlled by this sea monster that the Lord destroyed at the time of creation (see Isaiah 51.9). [i]*and everything else*: The Hebrew text has "Zaphon and Yamin," which may either be the names of mountains or refer to the directions "north and south," with the meaning "everything from north to south."

"LISTEN UP!"

I never stayed around long enough to listen. It's not that I didn't think my parents had something to say; it's just that I didn't want to hear it. I know I'm not exactly what they planned for in a son. What difference does it make anyway? They got perfect in my brother Sean. So why don't they get off my back? One out of two isn't so bad.

I don't know, maybe they are right. I am pretty smart. I could get better grades. I don't want to be the "black sheep" forever. Inside, I want my parents to be proud of me. I'd like to be a good son.

But can I change? Is it too late? Maybe I'm ready to listen.

GROWING STRONGER

There are lots of tough questions in life. Especially when we are deciding who we are and who we want to be. Finding the answer doesn't have to be a continuous struggle of trial and error. Sometimes it does pay to listen.

For another "Look Ahead," turn to page 711.

"I have helped a mighty hero.
I chose him from my people
and made him famous.
20 David, my servant, is the one
I chose to be king,
21 and I will always be there
to help and strengthen him.

22 "No enemy will outsmart David,
and he won't be defeated
by any hateful people.
23 I will strike down and crush
his troublesome enemies.
24 He will always be able
to depend on my love,
and I will make him strong
with my own power.
25 I will let him rule the lands
across the rivers and seas.
26 He will say to me,
'You are my Father
and my God,
as well as the mighty rock[j]
where I am safe.'

27 "I have chosen David
as my first-born son,
and he will be the ruler
of all kings on earth.
28 My love for him will last,
and my agreement with him
will never be broken.*

29 "One of David's descendants
will always be king,
and his family will rule
until the sky disappears.
30 Suppose some of his children
should reject my Law
and refuse my instructions.
31 Or suppose they should disobey
all of my teachings.
32 Then I will correct
and punish them
because of their sins.
33 But I will always love David
and faithfully keep all
of my promises to him.

34 "I won't break my agreement
or go back on my word.
35 I have sworn once and for all
by my own holy name,
and I won't lie to David.
36 His family will always rule.
I will let his kingdom last
as long as the sun 37 and moon
appear in the sky."

38 You are now angry, God,
and you have turned your back
on your chosen king.
39 You broke off your agreement
with your servant, the king,
and you completely destroyed
his kingdom.
40 The walls of his city
have been broken through,
and every fortress
now lies in ruin.
41 All who pass by
take what they want,
and nations everywhere
joke about the king.

42 You made his enemies powerful
and let them celebrate.
43 But you forced him to retreat
because you did not fight
on his side.
44 You took his crown[k]
and threw his throne
in the dirt.
45 You made an old man of him
and put him to shame.

46 How much longer, LORD?
Will you hide forever?
How long will your anger
keep burning like fire?

---

[j] *mighty rock*: The Hebrew text has "rock," which is sometimes used in poetry to compare the Lord to a mountain where his people can run for safety.
[k] *You took . . . crown*: One possible meaning for the difficult Hebrew text.

89.28 **GOD IS A PROMISE-KEEPER** God's friendship with us is based on his ancient promise. Just as he promised to be David's friend forever, God has also promised to be the friend of all who trust and love him as David did. That is perhaps the most important thing to remember about God—he keeps all his promises forever. Knowing that fact keeps us steady and brave in the world.

NOTES

47Remember, life is short![l]
Why did you empty our lives
of all meaning?
48No one can escape the power
of death and the grave.

49Our Lord, where is the love
you have always shown
and that you promised
so faithfully to David?
50Remember your servants, Lord!
People make jokes about us,
and I suffer many insults.*
51I am your chosen one,
but your enemies chase
and make fun of me.

52Our LORD, we praise you
forever. Amen and amen.

BOOK IV
(Psalms 90–106)

Psalm 90

[*A prayer by Moses, the man of God.*]

God Is Eternal

1Our Lord, in all generations
you have been our home.
2You have always been God—
long before the birth
of the mountains,
even before you created
the earth and the world.

3At your command we die
and turn back to dust,
4but a thousand years
mean nothing to you!
They are merely a day gone by
or a few hours in the night.

5You bring our lives to an end
just like a dream.
We are merely tender grass
6 that sprouts and grows
in the morning,
but dries up by evening.
7Your furious anger frightens
and destroys us,
8and you know all of our sins,
even those we do in secret.

9Your anger is a burden
each day we live,
then life ends like a sigh.
10We can expect seventy years,
or maybe eighty,
if we are healthy,
but even our best years
bring trouble and sorrow.
Suddenly our time is up,
and we disappear.
11No one knows the full power
of your furious anger,
but it is as great as the fear
that we owe to you.
12Teach us to use wisely
all the time we have.*

13Help us, LORD! Don't wait!
Pity your servants.
14When morning comes,
let your love satisfy
all our needs.
Then we can celebrate

[l]*Remember . . . short*: One possible meaning for the difficult Hebrew text.

89.50 **EVERYBODY FAILS SOMETIMES** We shouldn't be surprised by our weaknesses. The Bible shows that temporary failure of faith happens to the most faithful of God's people. Even the disciples of Jesus found out how weak they were when they all ran away after he was arrested. Sometimes ungodly people make jokes about us. What else did we expect? Are we more special than Jesus? Although he never failed, even he was discouraged sometimes.

90.12 **ASK GOD FOR WISDOM** This great psalm by Moses reminds us that God is time-less, but we are beings of time who pass away like the grass and the flowers. What, then, should be our greatest aim and prayer? Solomon said it was wisdom. And Moses agreed. All other good things will flow from the divine gift of wisdom—things like love, happiness, peacefulness, gentleness, self-control. Such qualities result from the wisdom that comes down from heaven.

NOTES

and be glad for what time
we have left.
15 Make us happy for as long
as you caused us trouble
and sorrow.
16 Do wonderful things for us,
your servants,
and show your mighty power
to our children.
17 Our Lord and our God,
treat us with kindness
and let all go well for us.
Please let all go well!

Psalm 91

The LORD Is My Fortress

1 Live under the protection
of God Most High
and stay in the shadow
of God All-Powerful.
2 Then you will say to the LORD,
"You are my fortress,
my place of safety;
you are my God,
and I trust you."*

3 The Lord will keep you safe
from secret traps
and deadly diseases.
4 He will spread his wings
over you
and keep you secure.
His faithfulness is like
a shield or a city wall.[m]

5 You won't need to worry
about dangers at night
or arrows during the day.
6 And you won't fear diseases
that strike in the dark
or sudden disaster at noon.

7 You will not be harmed,
though thousands fall
all around you.
8 And with your own eyes
you will see the punishment
of the wicked.
9 The LORD Most High
is your fortress.
Run to him for safety,
10 and no terrible disasters
will strike you
or your home.

11 God will command his angels
to protect you
wherever you go.
12 They will carry you
in their arms,
and you won't hurt your feet
on the stones.
13 You will overpower
the strongest lions
and the most deadly snakes.

14 The Lord says, "If you love me
and truly know who I am,
I will rescue you
and keep you safe.
15 When you are in trouble,
call out to me.
I will answer and be there
to protect and honor you.
16 You will live a long life
and see my saving power."

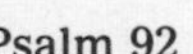

Psalm 92

[*A psalm and a song for the Sabbath.*]

Sing Praises to the LORD

1 It is wonderful to be grateful
and to sing your praises,
LORD Most High!
2 It is wonderful each morning
to tell about your love
and at night to announce
how faithful you are.

---

[m] *city wall*: One possible meaning for a difficult Hebrew word; it may possibly mean some kind of shield or weapon.

91.2 **GOD IS OUR REAL SECURITY** Everyone wants to be secure and to feel secure. We hear a lot today about the problems that insecurity brings. People are looking desperately for a place of safety in the world. Security means different things to different people. To some it is having a good home. To others it means having a lot of money. This psalm tells us where to find the greatest security of all. God is like a fortress for us that nothing can break through.

NOTES

Step 8

DETERMINATION—Being willing to make things right at all costs

PSALM 91.14–16

FLAPS DOWN

On a flight from Portland, Maine, to Boston, Massachusetts, pilot Henry Dempsey heard a strange sound near the rear of the small aircraft. He turned the controls over to his co-pilot and went to check it out.

As he reached the tail section, the plane hit an air pocket, and Dempsey was tossed against the rear door. He quickly discovered the source of the noise. The rear door had not been latched properly, and it flew open and Dempsey flew out!

The co-pilot, seeing the red light that indicated an open door, radioed to the nearest airport. He reported the pilot had fallen out of the plane and requested an emergency landing.

STEP LOOK AHEAD 8

After the plane landed, they found Henry Dempsey, holding on to the outdoor ladder! Somehow, when the door opened he had caught the ladder and had held on for ten minutes flying 200 M.P.H. at an altitude of 4,000 feet. While landing, he kept his head above the runway—only twelve inches away. He was determined to hang on, and his life depended on it.

When things get turbulent in our lives, it will take determination to hang on—to be willing to make things right with others. At times, we may not feel like it, but after all, what choice do we have?

As people committed to growing in our faith, we should take this verse of Scripture to heart: "I have fought well. I have finished the race, and I have been faithful. So a crown will be given to me for pleasing the Lord. He judges fairly, and on the day of judgment he will give a crown to me and to everyone else who wants him to appear with power" (2 Timothy 4.7, 8).

Hanging on at all costs is sometimes what it takes. When we think that one more disappointment will do us in; when friends let us down; when parents fail to understand—these are times we need to hang tough in our faith and keep relationships open and honest.

Maturity comes when we have survived a few falls and escaped disaster. Bumps build character. Turbulence usually makes us even more determined to do the right thing in God's eyes.

To take a "Look Back" at a man who was determined to make things right with others at all costs, turn to page 167.

3 I enjoy praising your name
to the music of harps,
4 because everything you do
makes me happy,
and I sing joyful songs.

5 You do great things, LORD.
Your thoughts are too deep*
6 for an ignorant fool
to know or understand.
7 Though the wicked sprout
and spread like grass,
they will be pulled up
by their roots.
8 But you will rule
over all of us forever,
9 and your hateful enemies
will be scattered
and then destroyed.

10 You have given me
the strength of a wild ox,
and you have chosen me
to be your very own.
11 My eyes have seen,
and my ears have heard
the doom and destruction
of my terrible enemies.

12 Good people will prosper
like palm trees,
and they will grow strong
like the cedars of Lebanon.
13 They will take root
in your house, LORD God,
and they will do well.
14 They will be like trees
that stay healthy and fruitful,
even when they are old.
15 And they will say about you,
"The LORD always does right!
God is our mighty rock."[n]

Psalm 93

The LORD Is King

1 Our LORD, you are King!
Majesty and power
are your royal robes.
You put the world in place,
and it will never be moved.
2 You have always ruled,
and you are eternal.

3 The ocean is roaring, LORD!
The sea is pounding hard.
4 Its mighty waves are majestic,
but you are more majestic,
and you rule over all.
5 Your decisions are firm,
and your temple will always
be beautiful and holy.*

Psalm 94

The LORD Punishes the Guilty

1 LORD God, you punish
the guilty.
Show what you are like
and punish them now.
2 You judge the earth.
Come and help us!
Pay back those proud people
for what they have done.
3 How long will the wicked
celebrate and be glad?

4 All of those cruel people
strut and boast,

[n] *mighty rock*: The Hebrew text has "rock," which is sometimes used in poetry to compare the Lord to a mountain where his people can run to him for safety from their enemies.

92.5 **HOW MUCH DO WE KNOW?** Great value is placed on knowledge. We need to know a great many things to live effectively in our world. But how much do we really know? God knows all things, and compared to him we know very little. But realizing that fact affects us in two ways: 1) we can never be proud of our little knowledge; 2) we can be calm in the assurance that God understands us and all things completely.

93.5 **GOD NEVER MAKES A MISTAKE** That's why his decisions are "firm"—he never has to change his mind. We're constantly changing our opinions, and in many ways that's a good thing. But the messes we sometimes make of matters happen because we make the wrong choices in the first place. God never has to do that. His plans, his choices, his decisions are always correct. So we owe thanks to him for all the good we enjoy in life.

NOTES

Step 12

Because God is changing my life through following these steps, I will tell others about them and daily practice what I have learned.

PSALM 92.1–4

MAKING IT THROUGH THE NIGHT

Have you ever looked forward to something yet dreaded it at the same time? That is how the night has always been for me. It was my favorite time because I could party and get away from the daily grind. But it was also the worst time because eventually I had to try and go to sleep. Unless I was wiped out on drugs or booze, falling asleep was torture. My conscience would beat away at me—accusing me, condemning me.

But I have learned that God is bigger than my conscience. He has forgiven me, so I can forgive myself. Satan wants me to believe that I can never fix all the broken parts in my life. But that is a lie. With God's help, I have come a long way.

TELLING OUR FRIENDS

That is what we want to tell our friends—God is faithful. He is there for us when we struggle with things in our past, and he wants to help us face the future. And when we lie down and close our eyes, we can peacefully fall asleep because we know he is with us—all through the night.

STEP LOOK INSIDE 12

To take a "Look Ahead," turn to page 69.

[5]and they crush and wound
your chosen nation, LORD.
[6]They murder widows,
foreigners, and orphans.
[7]Then they say,
"The LORD God of Jacob
doesn't see or know."

[8]Can't you fools see?
Won't you ever learn?
[9]God gave us ears and eyes!
Can't he hear and see?
[10]God instructs the nations
and gives knowledge to us all.
Won't he also correct us?
[11]The LORD knows how useless
our plans really are.

[12]Our LORD, you bless everyone
that you instruct and teach
by using your Law.
[13]You give them rest
from their troubles,
until a pit can be dug
for the wicked.
[14]You won't turn your back
on your chosen nation.
[15]Justice and fairness
will go hand in hand,
and all who do right
will follow along.

[16]Who will stand up for me
against those cruel people?
[17]If you had not helped me, LORD,
I would soon have gone
to the land of silence.[o]
[18]When I felt my feet slipping,
you came with your love
and kept me steady.
[19]And when I was burdened
with worries,
you comforted me
and made me feel secure.*
[20]But you are opposed
to dishonest lawmakers
[21]who gang up to murder
innocent victims.

[22]You, LORD God, are my fortress,
that mighty rock[p]
where I am safe.
[23]You will pay back my enemies,
and you will wipe them out
for the evil they did.

Psalm 95

Worship and Obey the LORD

[1]Sing joyful songs to the LORD!
Praise the mighty rock[p]
where we are safe.
[2]Come to worship him
with thankful hearts
and songs of praise.

[3]The LORD is the greatest God,
king over all other gods.
[4]He holds the deepest part
of the earth in his hands,
and the mountain peaks
belong to him.
[5]The ocean is the Lord's
because he made it,
and with his own hands
he formed the dry land.

[6]Bow down and worship
the LORD our Creator!
[7]The LORD is our God,
and we are his people,
the sheep he takes care of
in his own pasture.

Listen to God's voice today!
[8]Don't be stubborn and rebel
as your ancestors did

[o]*land of silence*: The grave or the world of the dead.
[p]*mighty rock*: The Hebrew text has "rock," which is sometimes used in poetry to compare the Lord to a mountain where his people can run for safety.

94.19 **GOD COMFORTS TROUBLED PEOPLE** There are many lonely, troubled people all around us. They reach out for someone to comfort them, and very often they're disappointed. We human beings are not always good at comforting others. If only we can show hurting people that there is a God who knows the answers to their worries! We must be living signposts that show others how to find comfort in God.

NOTES

at Meribah and Massah[q]
out in the desert.
9-10For forty years
they tested God and saw
the things he did.
Then God got tired of them
and said,
"You never show good sense,
and you don't understand
what I want you to do."*
11In his anger, God told them,
"You people will never enter
my place of rest."

Psalm 96

Sing a NewSong to the LORD

1Sing a new song to the LORD!
Everyone on this earth,
sing praises to the LORD,
2 sing and praise his name.

Day after day announce,
"The LORD has saved us!"
3Tell every nation on earth,
"The LORD is wonderful
and does marvelous things!
4The LORD is great and deserves
our greatest praise!
He is the only God
worthy of our worship.
5Other nations worship idols,
but the LORD created
the heavens.
6Give honor and praise
to the LORD,
whose power and beauty
fill his holy temple."

7Tell everyone of every nation,
"Praise the glorious power
of the LORD.
8He is wonderful! Praise him
and bring an offering
into his temple.
9Everyone on earth, now tremble
and worship the LORD,
majestic and holy."

10Announce to the nations,
"The LORD is King!
The world stands firm,
never to be shaken,
and he will judge its people
with fairness."

11Tell the heavens and the earth
to be glad and celebrate!
Command the ocean to roar
with all of its creatures
12and the fields to rejoice
with all of their crops.
Then every tree in the forest
will sing joyful songs
13 to the LORD.
He is coming to judge
all people on earth
with fairness and truth.

Psalm 97

The LORD Brings Justice

1The LORD is King!
Tell the earth to celebrate
and all islands to shout.*
2Dark clouds surround him,

---

[q]*Meribah and Massah*: When the people of Israel complained to Moses about the need for water, God commanded Moses to strike a rock with his walking stick, and water came out. The place was then named Massah ("test") and Meribah ("argument").

95.9 **GOD GETS TIRED OF SOME PEOPLE** Why? Because they don't listen and just keep on going in their same old ways. Living things grow and develop. Dying things shrink and decay. God is like a gardener who looks for plants that grow tall and strong and produce seed for other plants to grow. We're like those plants. But if we don't grow, develop, and show others the way to knowing him, he gets tired of us. And don't we know what becomes of useless plants in a garden?

97.1 **GOOD GOVERNMENT IS COMING** In our own time, as always, people are suffering under unjust and indifferent rulers. We hear of many misdeeds in high office. And we, the governed, often have reason to feel betrayed by those we elect. But God has the answer. He will do away with all dishonest rulers, and he will establish his own government forever. Everyone will see the glory of his government.

NOTES

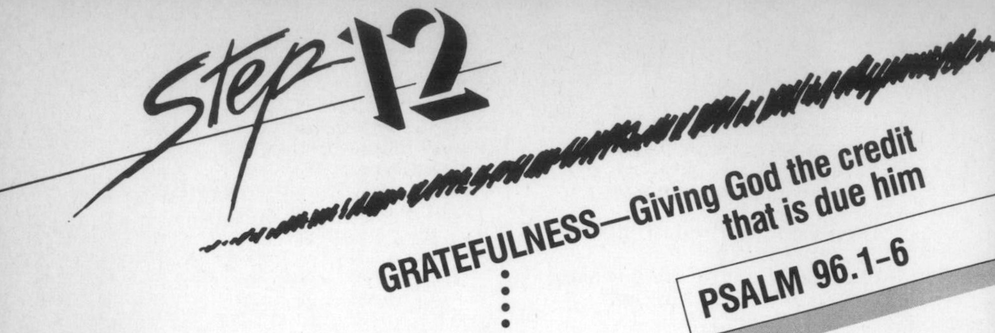

CHIP ON THE SHOULDER

"He's got a chip on his shoulder."

Have you ever heard that expression? It means you live your life with a negative attitude. Kind of like a voice inside your head that tells you everyone is out to get you. Don't trust anyone. Don't express your feelings. Put up a wall between you and others so no one can hurt you.

It's all a lie. I have discovered that there are people in my life who genuinely care about me. It's okay to accept their love. It is safe. God is in control of my life now, and he is teaching me how to trust and be trustworthy with others.

The chip on my shoulder got much too heavy. God's been helping me lighten that load.

THE BUDDY SYSTEM

What a relief to be able to let down our defenses and relax. There are people in our lives with whom we can share both disappointments and accomplishments. God made us to need other people and other people to need us. That's what friends are for.

To take a "Look Back" at a man who showed his gratitude to God by telling others about the good news of Jesus Christ, turn to page 97.

and his throne is supported
by justice and fairness.
3Fire leaps from his throne,
destroying his enemies,
4and his lightning is so bright
that the earth sees it
and trembles.
5Mountains melt away like wax
in the presence of the LORD
of all the earth.

6The heavens announce,
"The LORD brings justice!"
Everyone sees God's glory.
7Those who brag about
the useless idols they worship
are terribly ashamed,
and all the false gods
bow down to the LORD.

8When the people of Zion
and of the towns of Judah
hear that God brings justice,
they will celebrate.
9The LORD rules the whole earth,
and he is more glorious
than all the false gods.

10Love the LORD
and hate evil!
God protects his loyal people
and rescues them
from violence.
11If you obey and do right,
a light will show you the way
and fill you with happiness.
12You are the LORD's people!
So celebrate and praise
the only God.

Psalm 98

The LORD Works Miracles

1Sing a new song to the LORD!
He has worked miracles,
and with his own powerful arm,
he has won the victory.*
2The LORD has shown the nations
that he has the power to save
and to bring justice.
3God has been faithful
in his love for Israel,
and his saving power is seen
everywhere on earth.

4Tell everyone on this earth
to sing happy songs
in praise of the LORD.
5Make music for him on harps.
Play beautiful melodies!
6Sound the trumpets and horns
and celebrate with joyful songs
for our LORD and King!

7Command the ocean to roar
with all of its creatures,
and the earth to shout
with all of its people.
8Order the rivers
to clap their hands,
and all of the hills
to sing together.
9Let them worship the LORD!
He is coming to judge
everyone on the earth,
and he will be honest
and fair.

Psalm 99

Our LORD Is King

1Our LORD, you are king!
You rule from your throne
above the winged creatures,[r]
as people tremble
and the earth shakes.

---

[r]*winged creatures*: Two winged creatures made of gold were on the top of the sacred chest and were symbols of the LORD's throne on earth. See Exodus 25.18.

98.1 **GOD WORKS MIRACLES** We live in an age of doubt. We are not only doubters of God but also doubters of ourselves. We don't see miracles because we don't expect them. The same was true in Bible times. But God rules the universe, and he makes everything move according to his wishes. He delights in working miracles to save his people from sin and sin's effects. Jesus the Son of God was himself a walking miracle. Let's keep our minds and hearts open to what God can do for us and in us.

NOTES

2 You are praised in Zion,
and you control all nations.
3 Only you are God!
And your power alone,
so great and fearsome,
is worthy of praise.
4 You are our mighty King,[s]
a lover of fairness,
who sees that justice is done
everywhere in Israel.
5 Our LORD and our God,
we praise you
and kneel down to worship you,
the God of holiness!

6 Moses and Aaron were two
of your priests.
Samuel was also one of those
who prayed in your name,
and you, our LORD,
answered their prayers.
7 You spoke to them
from a thick cloud,
and they obeyed your laws.

8 Our LORD and our God,
you answered their prayers
and forgave their sins,
but when they did wrong,
you punished them.*
9 We praise you, LORD God,
and we worship you
at your sacred mountain.
Only you are God!

Psalm 100

[*A psalm of praise.*]

The LORD Is God

1 Shout praises to the LORD,
everyone on this earth.
2 Be joyful and sing
as you come in
to worship the LORD!

3 You know the LORD is God!
He created us,
and we belong to him;
we are his people,
the sheep in his pasture.

4 Be thankful and praise the LORD
as you enter his temple.
5 The LORD is good!
His love and faithfulness
will last forever.*

Psalm 101

[*A psalm by David.*]

A King and His Promises

1 I will sing to you, LORD!
I will celebrate your kindness
and your justice.
2 Please help me learn
to do the right thing,
and I will be honest and fair
in my own kingdom.*

[s] *You . . . King*: One possible meaning for the difficult Hebrew text.

99.8 **SIN MUST BE PUNISHED** Yes, God forgives sin. But also, to get our attention, he has to punish us when we continue in our self-destroying ways. Wouldn't we rather be corrected by a good God than pay the natural price that sin brings in the end? So let's pray that God will rightly discipline us when we are doing wrong. Right discipline is good medicine.

100.5 **THE LORD IS GOOD** Does this seem like an obvious truth? Of course everybody knows that God is supposed to be good. But quite often we only recognize his goodness when he agrees with us—which he doesn't always do. When God disagrees with some choice we've made, we treat him like an enemy. We'd rather not have him around if he isn't going to please us. But God is always good, and we're smart to admit that fact.

101.2 **GOD, HELP US TO BE GOOD!** Here is a good prayer. When we find out we're on the wrong side of God, as we saw in the last psalm, the answer is to ask him to make us right. God isn't waiting to trap us in our sins; he wants to help us, but we need to ask his help. Because he is gentle, God doesn't often intrude on our privacy. But he does care greatly about our needs.

NOTES

3I refuse to be corrupt
or to take part
in anything crooked,
4and I won't be dishonest
or deceitful.

5Anyone who spreads gossip
will be silenced,
and no one who is conceited
will be my friend.

6I will find trustworthy people
to serve as my advisers,
and only an honest person
will serve as an official.

7No one who cheats or lies
will have a position
in my royal court.
8Each morning I will silence
any lawbreakers I find
in the countryside
or in the city of the LORD.

Psalm 102

[*A prayer for someone who hurts and needs to ask the* LORD *for help.*]

A Prayer in Time of Trouble

1I pray to you, LORD!
Please listen.
2Don't hide from me
in my time of trouble.
Pay attention to my prayer
and quickly give an answer.

3My days disappear like smoke,
and my bones are burning
as though in a furnace.*
4I am wasting away like grass,
and my appetite is gone.
5My groaning never stops,
and my bones can be seen
through my skin.
6I am like a lonely owl
in the desert
7or a restless sparrow
alone on a roof.

8My enemies insult me all day,
and they use my name
for a curse word.
9Instead of food,
I have ashes to eat
and tears to drink,
10because you are furious
and have thrown me aside.
11My life fades like a shadow
at the end of day
and withers like grass.

12Our LORD, you are king forever
and will always be famous.
13You will show pity to Zion
because the time has come.
14We, your servants,
love each stone in the city,
and we are sad to see them
lying in the dirt.

15Our LORD, the nations
will honor you,
and all kings on earth
will praise your glory.
16You will rebuild
the city of Zion.
Your glory will be seen,
17and the prayers of the homeless
will be answered.

18Future generations must also
praise the LORD,
so write this for them:
19"From his holy temple,
the LORD looked down
at the earth.
20He listened to the groans
of prisoners,
and he rescued everyone
who was doomed to die."

21All Jerusalem should praise
you, our LORD,
22when people from every nation
meet to worship you.

23I should still be strong,
but you, LORD, have made
an old person of me.

102.3 **OUR PAINS ARE NATURAL** When we're young and full of energy, being hurt is a strange thing that happens when we fall or cut our finger. But later in life it may seem that there are more days of pain than freedom from it. Someone has said that God whispers to us in our joys, but he shouts to us in our suffering. Times of pain and sickness are times for talking to God in special ways. As we get close to him, the pain doesn't seem important anymore.

NOTES

24 You will live forever!
Years mean nothing to you.
Don't cut my life in half!

25 In the beginning, LORD,
you laid the earth's foundation
and created the heavens.
26 They will all disappear
and wear out like clothes.
You change them,
as you would a coat,
but you last forever.
27 You are always the same.
Years cannot change you.
28 Every generation of those
who serve you
will live in your presence.

Psalm 103

[*By David.*]

The LORD's Wonderful Love

1 With all my heart
I praise the LORD,
and with all that I am
I praise his holy name!
2 With all my heart
I praise the LORD!
I will never forget
how kind he has been.

3 The LORD forgives our sins,
heals us when we are sick,
4 and protects us from death.
His kindness and love
are a crown on our heads.
5 Each day that we live,[t]
he provides for our needs
and gives us the strength
of a young eagle.

6 For all who are mistreated,
the LORD brings justice.
7 He taught his Law to Moses
and showed all Israel
what he could do.

8 The LORD is merciful!
He is kind and patient,
and his love never fails.*
9 The LORD won't always be angry
and point out our sins;
10 he doesn't punish us
as our sins deserve.

11 How great is God's love for all
who worship him?
Greater than the distance
between heaven and earth!
12 How far has the LORD taken
our sins from us?
Farther than the distance
from east to west!

13 Just as parents are kind
to their children,
the LORD is kind
to all who worship him,
14 because he knows
we are made of dust.
15 We humans are like grass
or wild flowers
that quickly bloom.
16 But a scorching wind blows,
and they quickly wither
to be forever forgotten.

17 The LORD is always kind
to those who worship him,
and he keeps his promises
to their descendants
18 who faithfully obey him.

19 God has set up his kingdom
in heaven, and he rules
the whole creation.
20 All of you mighty angels,
who obey God's commands,
come and praise your LORD!
21 All of you thousands
who serve and obey God,
come and praise your LORD!
22 All of God's creation
and all that he rules,
come and praise your LORD!
With all my heart
I praise the LORD!

---

[t] *Each . . . live*: One possible meaning for the difficult Hebrew text.

103.8 **GOD'S LOVE NEVER FAILS** That's the main thing to remember when things don't seem to go our way. Our luck goes up and down, but God remains the same toward us. If he lets us go through dark times, it's only to draw us closer to himself—where we belong! Let's pray not to complain about our circumstances. If we can believe in his love during the dark days, think of how we will praise him in the sunny days!

NOTES

Psalm 104

The LORD Takes Care of His Creation

1 I praise you, LORD God,
with all my heart.
You are glorious and majestic,
dressed in royal robes*
2 and surrounded by light.
You spread out the sky
like a tent,
3 and you built your home
over the mighty ocean.
The clouds are your chariot
with the wind as its wings.
4 The winds are your messengers,
and flames of fire
are your servants.

5 You built foundations
for the earth, and it
will never be shaken.
6 You covered the earth
with the ocean that rose
above the mountains.
7 Then your voice thundered!
And the water flowed
8 down the mountains
and through the valleys
to the place you prepared.
9 Now you have set boundaries,
so that the water will never
flood the earth again.

10 You provide streams of water
in the hills and valleys,
11 so that the donkeys
and other wild animals
can satisfy their thirst.
12 Birds build their nests nearby
and sing in the trees.
13 From your home above
you send rain on the hills
and water the earth.
14 You let the earth produce
grass for cattle,
plants for our food,
15 wine to cheer us up,
olive oil for our skin,
and grain for our health.

16 Our LORD, your trees
always have water,
and so do the cedars
you planted in Lebanon.
17 Birds nest in those trees,
and storks make their home
in the fir trees.
18 Wild goats find a home
in the tall mountains,
and small animals can hide
between the rocks.

19 You created the moon
to tell us the seasons.
The sun knows when to set,
20 and you made the darkness,
so the animals in the forest
could come out at night.
21 Lions roar as they hunt
for the food you provide.
22 But when morning comes,
they return to their dens,
23 then we go out to work
until the end of day.

24 Our LORD, by your wisdom
you made so many things;
the whole earth is covered
with your living creatures.*
25 But what about the ocean
so big and wide?
It is alive with creatures,
large and small.

104.1 **PRAISING GOD IS OUR REASON FOR BEING** Of course, praise is not only the words we utter and sing to God. Real praise is to use our whole being, in all our activities, to bring the honor to God that he deserves. Why does God need our praise? He doesn't! But praising him with all that we are we find meaning in our lives that is found in no other way. God made us for himself.

104.24 **GOD MADE ALL THINGS** For many people this is too simple. How could any single being, or any god, create everything we see around us, and much more? The tragedy is that such people have not known God as he really is. Their "god" is too small. When we know God in a true way, it becomes clear that none of the things we see and enjoy—even ourselves—could have existed without him.

NOTES

26 And there are the ships,
as well as Leviathan,[u]
the monster you created
to splash in the sea.

27 All of these depend on you
to provide them with food,
28 and you feed each one
with your own hand,
until they are full.
29 But when you turn away,
they are terrified;
when you end their life,
they die and rot.
30 You created all of them
by your Spirit,
and you give new life
to the earth.

31 Our LORD, we pray
that your glory
will last forever
and that you will be pleased
with what you have done.
32 You look at the earth,
and it trembles.
You touch the mountains,
and smoke goes up.
33 As long as I live,
I will sing and praise you,
the LORD God.
34 I hope my thoughts
will please you,
because you are the one
who makes me glad.

35 Destroy all wicked sinners
from the earth
once and for all.
With all my heart
I praise you, LORD!
I praise you!

Psalm 105

The LORD Can Be Trusted

STEP 12

1 Praise the LORD
and pray in his name!
Tell everyone
what he has done.
2 Sing praises to the LORD!
Tell about his miracles.
3 Celebrate and worship
his holy name
with all your heart.

4 Trust the LORD
and his mighty power.
5 Remember his miracles
and all his wonders
and his fair decisions.
6 You belong to the family
of Abraham, his servant;
you are his chosen ones,
the descendants of Jacob.*

7 The LORD is our God,
bringing justice
everywhere on earth.
8 He will never forget
his agreement or his promises,
not in thousands of years.
9-10 God made an eternal promise
to Abraham, Isaac, and Jacob,
11 when he said, "I'll give you
the land of Canaan."

12 At the time there were
only a few of us,
and we were homeless.
13 We wandered from nation
to nation, from one country
to another.
14 God did not let anyone
mistreat our people.
Instead he protected us
by punishing rulers
15 and telling them,
"Don't touch my chosen leaders
or harm my prophets!"

16 God kept crops from growing
until food was scarce
everywhere in the land.

---

[u] *Leviathan*: God's victory over this monster sometimes stands for his power over all creation and sometimes for his defeat of Egypt.

105.6 **WHAT IS THE FAMILY OF ABRAHAM?** Usually we think of the descendants of Abraham as the Hebrew people. But Abraham's family is really bigger. The New Testament later says that those who have faith like Abraham's are his real descendants. Abraham's "spiritual" family is made up of everyone who trusts God to save him or her from sin so that they enjoy the very life of God himself forever.

NOTES

17But he had already sent Joseph,
sold as a slave into Egypt,
18with chains of iron
around his legs and neck.

19Joseph remained a slave
until his own words
had come true,
and the LORD had finished
testing him.
20Then the King of Egypt
set Joseph free
21and put him in charge
of everything he owned.
22Joseph was in command
of the officials,
and he taught the leaders
how to use wisdom.

23Jacob and his family
came and settled in Egypt
as foreigners.
24They were the LORD's people,
so he let them grow stronger
than their enemies.
25They served the LORD,
and he made the Egyptians plan
hateful things against them.
26God sent his servant Moses.
He also chose and sent Aaron
27 to his people in Egypt,
and they worked miracles
and wonders there.
28Moses and Aaron obeyed God,
and he sent darkness
to cover Egypt.
29God turned their rivers
into streams of blood,
and the fish all died.
30Frogs were everywhere,
even in the royal palace.
31When God gave the command,
flies and gnats
swarmed all around.

32In place of rain,
God sent hailstones
and flashes of lightning.
33He destroyed their grapevines
and their fig trees,
and he made splinters
of all the other trees.
34God gave the command,
and more grasshoppers came
than could be counted.
35They ate every green plant
and all the crops that grew
in the land of Egypt.
36Then God took the life
of every first-born son.
37When God led Israel from Egypt,
they took silver and gold,
and no one was left behind.
38The Egyptians were afraid
and gladly let them go.
39God hid them under a cloud
and guided them by fire
during the night.

40When they asked for food,
he sent more birds
than they could eat.
41God even split open a rock,
and streams of water
gushed into the desert.
42God never forgot
his sacred promise
to his servant Abraham.

43When the Lord rescued
his chosen people from Egypt,
they celebrated with songs.
44The Lord gave them the land
and everything else
the nations had worked for.
45He did this so that his people
would obey all of his laws.
Shout praises to the LORD!

Psalm 106

A Nation Asks for Forgiveness

1We will celebrate
and praise you, LORD!
You are good to us,
and your love never fails.
2No one can praise you enough
for all of the mighty things
you have done.
3You bless those people
who are honest and fair
in everything they do.

4Remember me, LORD,
when you show kindness
by saving your people.
5Let me prosper with the rest
of your chosen ones,
as they celebrate with pride
because they belong to you.

6We and our ancestors
have sinned terribly.
7When they were in Egypt,
they paid no attention
to your marvelous deeds
or your wonderful love.
And they turned against you
at the Red Sea.[v]

[v]*Red Sea*: Or "Sea of Reeds."

8But you were true to your name,
and you rescued them to prove
how mighty you are.
9You said to the Red Sea,[v]
"Dry up!"
Then you led your people across
on land as dry as a desert.
10-11You saved all of them
and drowned every one
of their enemies.
12Then your people trusted you
and sang your praises.

13But they soon forgot
what you had done
and rejected your advice.*
14They became greedy for food
and tested you there
in the desert.
15So you gave them
what they wanted,
but later you destroyed them
with a horrible disease.

16Everyone in camp was jealous
of Moses and of Aaron,
your chosen priest.
17Dathan and Abiram rebelled,
and the earth opened up
and swallowed them.
18Then fire broke out
and destroyed all
of their followers.

19At Horeb your people
made and worshiped the statue
20 of a bull, instead of you,
their glorious God.
21You worked powerful miracles
to save them from Egypt,
but they forgot about you
22and the fearsome things
you did at the Red Sea.[v]
23You were angry and started
to destroy them,
but Moses, your chosen leader,
begged you not to do it.

24They would not trust
you, LORD,
and they did not like
the promised land.
25They would not obey you,
and they grumbled
in their tents.
26So you threatened them
by saying, "I'll kill you
out here in the desert!
27I'll scatter your children
everywhere in the world."

28Your people became followers
of a god named Baal Peor,
and they ate sacrifices
offered to the dead.[w]
29They did such terrible things
that you punished them
with a deadly disease.
30But Phinehas[x] helped them,
and the sickness stopped.
31Now he will always
be highly honored.

32-33At Meribah Spring[y]
they turned against you
and made you furious.
Then Moses got into trouble
for speaking in anger.

34Our LORD, they disobeyed you
by refusing to destroy
the nations.
35Instead they were friendly
with those foreigners
and followed their customs.
36Then they fell into the trap
of worshiping idols.
37They sacrificed their sons
and their daughters to demons
38 and to the gods of Canaan.

---

[v] *Red Sea*: Or "Sea of Reeds." [w] *the dead*: Or "lifeless idols." [x] *Phinehas*: The grandson of Aaron, who put two people to death and kept the Lord from being angry with the rest of his people (see Numbers 25.1-13). [y] *Meribah Spring*: When the people of Israel complained to Moses about the need for water, God commanded Moses to strike a rock with his walking stick, and water came out. The place was then named Meribah ("argument").

106.13 **KEEP ON TRUSTING GOD** This verse is a sad reminder that many people forget how they began with God. Once, they trusted him completely. God was everything to them. Then, as time went by, other interests crowded out that simple trust in God. New things came to share a place with him in their worship. Then the peace and joy they knew were gone. Let's learn from those who are described in this psalm.

NOTES

Then they poured out the blood
of these innocent children
and made the land filthy.
39By doing such gruesome things,
they also became filthy.

40Finally, LORD, you were angry
and terribly disgusted
with your people.
41So you put them in the power
of nations that hated them.
42They were mistreated and abused
by their enemies,
43but you saved them
time after time.
They were determined to rebel,
and their sins caused
their downfall.

44You answered their prayers
when they were in trouble.
45You kept your agreement
and were so merciful
46that their enemies
had pity on them.

47Save us, LORD God!
Bring us back
from among the nations.
Let us celebrate and shout
in praise of your holy name.*

48LORD God of Israel,
you deserve to be praised
forever and ever.
Let everyone say, "Amen!
Shout praises to the LORD!"

BOOK V
(Psalms 107–150)

Psalm 107

The LORD Is Good to His People

1Shout praises to the LORD!
He is good to us,
and his love never fails.
2Everyone the LORD has rescued
from trouble
should praise him,
3everyone he has brought
from the east and the west,
the north and the south.[z]

4Some of you were lost
in the scorching desert,
far from a town.
5You were hungry and thirsty
and about to give up.
6You were in serious trouble,
but you prayed to the LORD,
and he rescued you.
7Right away he brought you
to a town.
8You should praise the LORD
for his love
and for the wonderful things
he does for all of us.
9To everyone who is thirsty,
he gives something to drink;
to everyone who is hungry,
he gives good things to eat.

10Some of you were prisoners
suffering in deepest darkness
and bound by chains,
11because you had rebelled
against God Most High
and refused his advice.
12You were worn out
from working like slaves,
and no one came to help.
13You were in serious trouble,
but you prayed to the LORD,
and he rescued you.
14He brought you out
of the deepest darkness
and broke your chains.

15You should praise the LORD
for his love
and for the wonderful things
he does for all of us.
16He breaks down bronze gates
and shatters iron locks.

17Some of you had foolishly
committed a lot of sins
and were in terrible pain.

[z]*south*: The Hebrew text has "sea," probably referring to the Mediterranean Sea.

106.47 **GOD HEARS SINCERE PRAYERS** The writer of this psalm did the right thing. When he saw how far the people had fallen, he cried out to God for forgiveness. He knew that he and they needed to be restored to their former life with God. The next verse shows that this man's prayer was answered. God always hears the prayers of those who admit they're wrong.

NOTES

18The very thought of food
was disgusting to you,
and you were almost dead.
19You were in serious trouble,
but you prayed to the LORD,
and he rescued you.
20By the power of his own word,
he healed you and saved you
from destruction.

21You should praise the LORD
for his love
and for the wonderful things
he does for all of us.
22You should celebrate
by offering sacrifices
and singing joyful songs
to tell what he has done.

23Some of you made a living
by sailing the mighty sea,
24and you saw the miracles
the LORD performed there.
25At his command a storm arose,
and waves covered the sea.*
26You were tossed to the sky
and to the ocean depths,
until things looked so bad
that you lost your courage.
27You staggered like drunkards
and gave up all hope.
28You were in serious trouble,
but you prayed to the LORD,
and he rescued you.
29He made the storm stop
and the sea be quiet.
30You were happy because of this,
and he brought you to the port
where you wanted to go.

31You should praise the LORD
for his love
and for the wonderful things
he does for all of us.
32Honor the LORD
when you and your leaders
meet to worship.

33-34If you start doing wrong,
the LORD will turn rivers
into deserts,
flowing streams
into scorched land,
and fruitful fields
into beds of salt.

35But the LORD can also turn
deserts into lakes
and scorched land
into flowing streams.*
36If you are hungry,
you can settle there
and build a town.
37You can plant fields
and vineyards that produce
a good harvest.
38The LORD will bless you
with many children
and with herds of cattle.

39Sometimes you may be crushed
by troubles and sorrows,
until only a few of you
are left to survive.
40But the LORD will take revenge
on those who conquer you,
and he will make them wander
across desert sands.
41When you are suffering
and in need,
he will come to your rescue,
and your families will grow
as fast as a herd of sheep.
42You will see this because
you obey the LORD,
but everyone who is wicked
will be silenced.

43Be wise! Remember this
and think about the kindness
of the LORD.

107.25 **GOD IS IN THE STORMS OF LIFE** Being caught in a sea storm is a very frightening experience. Green mountains of water threaten to destroy you every moment. The storms of hardship, sickness, and other troubles can be just as terrifying. But let's learn to see God in all of our storms. Then, although the winds of trouble howl around us, we will grow calm within ourselves. His presence brings peace.

107.35 **GOD GIVES JOY FOR SORROW** The deserts and scorched land remind us of the hard places we've all been in sometimes. There seemed to be no relief from the difficulty we may have brought upon ourselves. So we turned away from our foolish thoughts and let God have control of our lives. Then springtime seemed to burst forth all around us again.

NOTES

Psalm 108

[*A song and a psalm by David.*]

With God on Our Side

1Our God, I am faithful to you
with all my heart,
and you can trust me.
I will sing
and play music for you
with all that I am.
2I will start playing my harps
before the sun rises.
3I will praise you, LORD,
for everyone to hear;
I will sing hymns to you
in every nation.*
4Your love reaches higher
than the heavens,
and your loyalty extends
beyond the clouds.

5Our God, may you be honored
above the heavens;
may your glory be seen
everywhere on earth.
6Answer my prayers
and use your powerful arm
to give us victory.
Then the people you love
will be safe.

7Our God, from your holy place
you made this promise:
"I will gladly divide up
the city of Shechem
and give away Succoth Valley
piece by piece.
8The lands of Gilead
and Manasseh are mine.
Ephraim is my war helmet,
and Judah is my symbol
of royal power.
9Moab is merely my washbasin,
and Edom belongs to me.
I shout with victory
over the Philistines."
10Our God, who will bring me
to the fortress
or lead me to Edom?
11Have you rejected us?
You don't lead our armies.
12Help us defeat our enemies!
No one else can rescue us.
13You are the one
who gives us victory
and crushes our enemies.

Psalm 109

[*A psalm by David for the music leader.*]

A Prayer for the LORD's Help

1I praise you, God!
Don't keep silent.
2Destructive and deceitful lies
are told about me,
3and hateful things are said
for no reason.
4I had pity and prayed[a]
for my enemies,
but their words to me
were harsh and cruel.
5For being friendly and kind,
they paid me back
with meanness and hatred.
6My enemies said,
"Find some worthless fools
to accuse him of a crime.
7Try him and find him guilty!
Consider his prayers a lie.
8Cut his life short
and let someone else
have his job.
9Make orphans of his children
and a widow of his wife;
10make his children beg for food
and live in the slums.

---

[a]*and prayed*: One possible meaning for the difficult Hebrew text.

108.3 **PRAISE GOD EVERYWHERE** David was not satisfied to keep his faith to himself. He wanted to sing God's song "in every nation." We don't hear of missions in the Old Testament very much, but here we read that David saw the need to make God known everywhere. Are we as eager as David to spread the good news of salvation? We ought to be even more urgent to tell the world around us about Jesus because it was the last thing he commanded us to do (see Matthew 28.18–20).

NOTES

11"Let the people he owes
take everything he owns.
Give it all to strangers.
12Don't let anyone be kind to him
or have pity on the children
he leaves behind.
13Bring an end to his family,
and from now on let him be
a forgotten man.

14"Don't let the LORD forgive
the sins of his parents
and his ancestors.
15Don't let the LORD forget
the sins of his family,
or let anyone remember
his family ever lived.
16He was so cruel to the poor,
homeless, and discouraged
that they died young.

17"He cursed others.
Now place a curse on him!
He never wished others well.
Wish only trouble for him!
18He cursed others more often
than he dressed himself.
Let his curses strike him deep,
just as water and olive oil
soak through to our bones.
19Let his curses surround him,
just like the clothes
he wears each day."

20Those are the cruel things
my enemies wish for me.
Let it all happen to them!
21Be true to your name, LORD God!
Show your great kindness
and rescue me.

22I am poor and helpless,
and I have lost all hope.
23I am fading away
like an evening shadow;
I am tossed aside
like a crawling insect.
24I have gone without eating,[b]
until my knees are weak,
and my body is bony.
25When my enemies see me,
they say cruel things
and shake their heads.

26Please help me, LORD God!
Come and save me
because of your love.
27Let others know that you alone
have saved me.
28I don't care if they curse me,
as long as you bless me.
You will make my enemies fail
when they attack,
and you will make me glad
to be your servant.
29You will cover them with shame,
just as their bodies
are covered with clothes.

30I will sing your praises
and thank you, LORD,
when your people meet.
31You help everyone in need,
and you defend them
when they are on trial.

Psalm 110

[*A psalm by David.*]

The LORD Gives Victory

1The LORD said to my Lord,
"Sit at my right side,[c]
until I make your enemies
into a footstool for you."*

2The LORD will let your power
reach out from Zion,
and you will rule
over your enemies.
3Your glorious power
will be seen on the day
you begin to rule.
You will wear the sacred robes

---

[b] *without eating*: People sometimes went without eating (often called "fasting") to show their sorrow.
[c] *right side*: The place of power and honor.

110.1 **DAVID SINGS ABOUT JESUS** Notice there are two "Lords" here. The first "Lord" is God the Father. The second is the Father's eternal Son, Jesus Christ. The Father is telling Jesus, the Son, to sit beside him until a coming time when all who hate the Son on earth are overcome. Now Jesus is seated in heaven with his Father until the Day of Judgment, when all things will be made new.

NOTES

and shine like the morning sun
in all of your strength.[d]
4The LORD has made a promise
that will never be broken:
"You will be a priest forever,
just like Melchizedek."

5My Lord is at your right side,
and when he gets angry
he will crush
the other kings.
6He will judge the nations
and crack their skulls,
leaving piles of dead bodies
all over the earth.
7He will drink from any stream
that he chooses, while winning
victory after victory.[e]

Psalm 111

Praise the LORD for All He Has Done

1Shout praises to the LORD!
With all my heart
I will thank the LORD
when his people meet.
2The LORD has done
many wonderful things!
Everyone who is pleased
with God's marvelous deeds
will keep them in mind.
3Everything the LORD does
is glorious and majestic,
and his power to bring justice
will never end.

4The LORD God is famous
for his wonderful deeds,
and he is kind and merciful.
5He gives food to his worshipers
and always keeps his agreement
with them.
6He has shown his mighty power
to his people
and has given them the lands
of other nations.

7God is always honest and fair,
and his laws can be trusted.*
8They are true and right
and will stand forever.
9God rescued his people,
and he will never break
his agreement with them.
He is fearsome and holy.

10Respect and obey the LORD!
This is the first step
to wisdom and good sense.[f]
God will always be respected.

Psalm 112

God Blesses His Worshipers

1Shout praises to the LORD!
The LORD blesses everyone
who worships him and gladly
obeys his teachings.
2Their descendants will have
great power in the land,
because the LORD blesses
all who do right.
3They will get rich and prosper
and will always be remembered
for their fairness.
4They will be so kind
and merciful and good,
that they will be a light
in the dark for others
who do the right thing.

5Life will go well for those
who freely lend
and are honest in business.*
6They won't ever be troubled,
and the kind things they do
will never be forgotten.

---

[d] *You will . . . strength*: One possible meaning for the difficult Hebrew text. [e] *while . . . victory*: Or "God will give him victory after victory." [f] *This . . . sense*: Or "This is what wisdom and good sense are all about."

111.7 **WE CAN TRUST GOD TO BE FAIR** Sometimes we act as if God's laws are unfair or too hard. Actually, they do us a lot of good when we obey them. In the New Testament John the apostle says God's commandments "are not hard to follow" (1 John 5.3). All the troubles we have in this world originally come from breaking God's laws. But there is happiness when they are obeyed.

112.5 **HONESTY PAYS** Trace the lives of honest people, and you'll find they're respected nearly everywhere. Of course, dishonest people envy their success. Honest people are usually *(continued)*

NOTES

7Bad news won't bother them;
they have decided
to trust the LORD.
8They are dependable
and not afraid,
and they will live to see
their enemies defeated.
9They will always be remembered
and greatly praised,
because they were kind
and freely gave to the poor.
10When evil people see this,
they angrily bite their tongues
and disappear.
They will never get
what they really want.

Psalm 113

The LORD Helps People in Need

1Shout praises to the LORD!
Everyone who serves him,
come and praise his name.

2Let the name of the LORD
be praised now and forever.
3From dawn until sunset
the name of the LORD
deserves to be praised.
4The LORD is far above
all of the nations;
he is more glorious
than the heavens.*

5No one can compare
with the LORD our God.
His throne is high above,
6and he looks down to see
the heavens and the earth.
7God lifts the poor and needy
from dust and ashes,
8and he lets them take part
in ruling his people.
9When a wife has no children,
he blesses her with some,
and she is happy.
Shout praises to the LORD!

Psalm 114

The LORD Works Wonders

1God brought his people
out of Egypt, that land
with a strange language.*
2He made Judah his holy place
and ruled over Israel.

3When the sea looked at God,
it ran away,
and the Jordan River
flowed upstream.
4The mountains and the hills
skipped around like goats.

5Ask the sea why it ran away
or ask the Jordan
why it flowed upstream.
6Ask the mountains and the hills
why they skipped like goats!

7Earth, you will tremble,
when the Lord God of Jacob
comes near,

(*continued*) generous, and they are loved by many. It's easy to get trapped into thinking dishonest shortcuts will pay off in fat bank accounts. But such actions are soon found out. Just watch and see: even if such people don't go to jail they lose in the end.

113.4 **GOD IS GREATER THAN NATURE** The world above and around us is so beautiful that many people even worship nature. They believe that God and nature are the same thing—that "God" consists of everything they can see. That's why we call them *pantheists*, meaning "all is God." But God is greater than all creation. It's ungrateful to worship nature instead of its Creator.

114.1 **GOD RESCUES HIS PEOPLE** The story of the Exodus is even more wonderful when we realize that it tells of a real happening. The rescue of God's people from Egypt is also a great example of the way God remembers to save his people of all time. Like the Hebrews of old, we may wait long to experience the deliverance that God has planned for us. But, just as surely, that day will come when our difficulties will also be a distant memory.

NOTES

8because he turns solid rock
into flowing streams
and pools of water.

Psalm 115

The LORD Deserves to Be Praised

1We don't deserve praise!
The LORD alone deserves
all of the praise,
because of his love
and faithfulness.
2Why should the nations ask,
"Where is your God?"*

3Our God is in the heavens,
doing as he chooses.
4The idols of the nations
are made of silver and gold.
5They have a mouth and eyes,
but they can't speak or see.
6Their ears can't hear,
and their noses can't smell.
7Their hands have no feeling,
their legs don't move,
and they can't make a sound.
8Everyone who made the idols
and all who trust them
are just as helpless
as those useless gods.

9People of Israel,
you must trust the LORD
to help and protect you.
10Family of Aaron the priest,
you must trust the LORD
to help and protect you.
11All of you worship the LORD,
so you must trust him
to help and protect you.
12The LORD will not forget
to give us his blessing;
he will bless all of Israel
and the family of Aaron.
13All who worship the LORD,
no matter who they are,
will receive his blessing.

14I pray that the LORD
will let your family
and your descendants
always grow strong.
15May the LORD who created
the heavens and the earth
give you his blessing.

16The LORD has kept the heavens
for himself,
but he has given the earth
to us humans.
17The dead are silent
and cannot praise the LORD,
18but we will praise him
now and forevermore.
Shout praises to the LORD!

Psalm 116

When the LORD Saves You from Death

1I love you, LORD!
You answered my prayers.
2You paid attention to me,
and so I will pray to you
as long as I live.
3Death attacked from all sides,
and I was captured
by its painful chains.
But when I was really hurting,
4I prayed and said, "LORD,
please don't let me die!"*

115.2 WHERE IS YOUR GOD? This is a sarcastic question that people asked the Jews long ago. "You're in so much trouble. Why doesn't your God help you?" The gods of the other people were made of stone and metal, and they could be seen. But Israel's God (and ours) is invisible. He is known only by those who love him. The sneers of others should not disturb our peace. Our God lives, and he will always act just in time to save us.

116.4 GOD PROVES HIS LOVE The one who wrote this song had been near death, but God healed him, and he lived. Of course, the man did die later on, but God proved his love by saving him from an early death. Even though our bodies finally grow old and wear out, still there is something eternal about us. In fact, Jesus promised us we would never really die if we trusted him. God's love for us never ends.

NOTES

5You are kind, LORD,
so good and merciful.
6You protect ordinary people,
and when I was helpless,
you saved me
7and treated me so kindly
that I don't need
to worry anymore.

8You, LORD, have saved
my life from death,
my eyes from tears,
my feet from stumbling.
9Now I will walk at your side
in this land of the living.
10I was faithful to you
when I was suffering,
11though in my confusion I said,
"I can't trust anyone!"

12What must I give you, LORD,
for being so good to me?
13I will pour out an offering
of wine to you,
and I will pray in your name
because you
have saved me.
14I will keep my promise to you
when your people meet.
15You are deeply concerned
when one of your loyal people
faces death.

16I worship you, LORD,
just as my mother did,
and you have rescued me
from the chains of death.
17I will offer you a sacrifice
to show how grateful I am,
and I will pray.
18I will keep my promise to you
when your people
19gather at your temple
in Jerusalem.
Shout praises to the LORD!

Psalm 117

Come Praise the LORD

1All of you nations,
come praise the LORD!
Let everyone praise him.*
2His love for us is wonderful,
his faithfulness never ends.
Shout praises to the LORD!

Psalm 118

The LORD Is Always Merciful

1Tell the LORD
how thankful you are,
because he is kind
and always merciful.

2Let Israel shout,
"God is always merciful!"
3Let the family of Aaron
the priest shout,
"God is always merciful!"
4Let every true worshiper
of the LORD shout,
"God is always merciful!"

5When I was really hurting,
I prayed to the LORD.
He answered my prayer,
and took my worries away.
6The LORD is on my side,
and I am not afraid
of what others can do to me.
7With the LORD on my side,
I will defeat all
of my hateful enemies.
8It is better to trust the LORD
for protection
than to trust anyone else,
9 including strong leaders.
10Nations surrounded me,
but I got rid of them
by the power of the LORD.
11They attacked from all sides,
but I got rid of them
by the power of the LORD.
12They swarmed around like bees,
but by the power of the LORD,
I got rid of them
and their fiery sting.
13Their attacks were so fierce
that I nearly fell,
but the LORD helped me.

117.1 **GOD CALLS TO THE NATIONS** Here again we have the missionary call in the Old Testament. The "nations" were invited to know and praise the Lord who revealed himself to the Jews. The great lesson here is that God has always cared about all peoples of the world—not just one nation. He wants us to reach out in kindness to people of all colors and races, because all are created in his likeness.

NOTES

14My power and my strength
come from the LORD,
and he has saved me.

15From the tents of God's people
come shouts of victory:
"The LORD is powerful!
16With his mighty arm
the LORD wins victories!
The LORD is powerful!"

17And so my life is safe,
and I will live to tell
what the LORD has done.
18He punished me terribly,
but he did not let death
lay its hands on me.
19Open the gates of justice!
I will enter and tell the LORD
how thankful I am.

20Here is the gate of the LORD!
Everyone who does right
may enter this gate.

21I praise the LORD
for answering my prayers
and saving me.
22The stone that the builders
tossed aside
has now become
the most important stone.

23The LORD has done this,
and it is amazing to us.
24This day belongs to the LORD!
Let's celebrate
and be glad today.
25We'll ask the LORD to save us!
We'll sincerely ask the LORD
to let us win.

26God bless the one who comes
in the name of the LORD!
We praise you from here
in the house of the LORD.

27The LORD is our God,
and he has given us light!
Start the celebration!
March with palm branches
all the way to the altar.[g]

28The LORD is my God!
I will praise him and tell him
how thankful I am.

29Tell the LORD
how thankful you are,
because he is kind
and always merciful.

Psalm 119

In Praise of the Law of the LORD

1Our LORD, you bless everyone
who lives right
and obeys your Law.
2You bless all of those
who follow your commands
from deep in their hearts
3and who never do wrong
or turn from you.
4You have ordered us always
to obey your teachings;
5I don't ever want to stray
from your laws.
6Thinking about your commands
will keep me from doing
some foolish thing.*
7I will do right and praise you
by learning to respect
your perfect laws.
8I will obey all of them!
Don't turn your back on me.

9Young people can live
a clean life
by obeying your word.
10I worship you
with all my heart.
Don't let me walk away
from your commands.
11I treasure your word
above all else;

[g]*Start . . . altar*: One possible meaning for the difficult Hebrew text.

119.6 **GOOD DEEDS COME FROM GOOD THOUGHTS** Solomon said that a person is what he or she thinks. Jesus said that what we do comes from what is inside us. A good tree bears good fruit. What do we spend time thinking about? Most of us could admit that many of our thoughts are a waste of time and even self-destroying. Let's spend time thinking God's thoughts after him.

NOTES

it keeps me from sinning
against you.
12I praise you, LORD!
Teach me your laws.
13With my own mouth,
I tell others the laws
that you have spoken.
14Obeying your instructions
brings as much happiness
as being rich.
15I will study your teachings
and follow your footsteps.
16I will take pleasure
in your laws
and remember your words.

17Treat me with kindness, Lord,
so that I may live
and do what you say.
18Open my mind
and let me discover
the wonders of your Law.
19I live here as a stranger.
Don't keep me from knowing
your commands.
20What I want most of all
and at all times
is to honor your laws.
21You punish those boastful,
worthless nobodies who turn
from your commands.
22Don't let them sneer
and insult me
for following you.
23I keep thinking about
your teachings, Lord,
even if rulers plot
against me.
24Your laws are my greatest joy!
I follow their advice.

25I am at the point of death.
Let your teachings
breathe new life into me.
26When I told you my troubles,
you answered my prayers.
Now teach me your laws.
27Help me to understand
your teachings,
and I will think about
your marvelous deeds.
28I am overcome with sorrow.
Encourage me,
as you have promised to do.
29Keep me from being deceitful,
and be kind enough
to teach me your Law.
30I am determined to be faithful
and to respect your laws.
31I follow your rules, LORD.
Don't let me be ashamed.
32I am eager to learn all
that you want me to do;
help me to understand
more and more.

33Point out your rules to me,
and I won't disobey
even one of them.
34Help me to understand your Law;
I promise to obey it
with all my heart.*
35Direct me by your commands!
I love to do what you say.
36Make me want to obey you,
rather than to be rich.
37Take away my foolish desires,
and let me find life
by walking with you.
38I am your servant!
Do for me what you promised
to those who worship you.
39Your wonderful teachings
protect me from the insults
that I hate so much.

40I long for your teachings.
Be true to yourself
and let me live.*

41Show me your love
and save me, LORD,
as you have promised.
42Then I will have an answer

119.34 **PRAY TO UNDERSTAND** It's a very good thing to memorize God's Word. But it's far better to understand what we read and memorize. Sometimes we think that the Scriptures are too hard for us. But we aren't alone! God has promised to be our teacher. As we read and memorize, let's always ask God to show us the meaning of what he says. Then ask him to show us how the teaching fits into our own lives.

119.40 **HAVE AN APPETITE FOR GOD'S WORD** This songwriter had a deep desire for God's teachings. One of the signs of good health is a good appetite. It is also a sign of being on *(continued)*

NOTES

for everyone who insults me
for trusting your word.
43 I rely on your laws!
Don't take away my chance
to speak your truth.
44 I will keep obeying your Law
forever and ever.
45 I have gained perfect freedom
by following your teachings,
46 and I trust them so much
that I tell them to kings.
47 I love your commands!
They bring me happiness.
48 I love and respect them
and will keep them in mind.

49 Don't forget your promise
to me, your servant.
I depend on it.
50 When I am hurting,
I find comfort in your promise
that leads to life.
51 Conceited people sneer at me,
but I obey your Law.
52 I find true comfort, LORD,
because your laws have stood
the test of time.
53 I get furious when evil people
turn against your Law.
54 No matter where I am,
your teachings
fill me with songs.
55 Even in the night
I think about you, LORD,
and I obey your Law.
56 You have blessed me
because I have always followed
your teachings.

57 You, LORD, are my choice,
and I will obey you.
58 With all my heart
I beg you to be kind to me,
just as you have promised.
59 I pay careful attention
as you lead me,
and I follow closely.
60 As soon as you command,
I do what you say.
61 Evil people may set a trap,
but I obey your Law.
62 Your laws are so fair
that I wake up and praise you
in the middle of the night.
63 I choose as my friends
everyone who worships you
and follows your teachings.
64 Our LORD, your love is seen
all over the world.
Teach me your laws.

65 I am your servant, LORD,
and you have kept your promise
to treat me with kindness.
66 Give me wisdom and good sense.
I trust your commands.
67 Once you corrected me
for not obeying you,
but now I obey.
68 You are kindhearted,
and you do good things,
so teach me your laws.
69 My reputation is being ruined
by conceited liars,
but with all my heart
I follow your teachings.
70 Those liars have no sense,
but I find happiness
in your Law.
71 When you corrected me,
it did me good
because it taught me
to study your laws.
72 I would rather obey you
than to have a thousand pieces
of silver and gold.

73 You created me
and put me together.
Make me wise enough to learn
what you have commanded.*
74 Your worshipers will see me,
and they will be glad
that I trust your word.

(*continued*) friendly terms with God that we love his Word. If we like someone, we enjoy his or her company. If we love God, we also love to enjoy him and all the things he says in the Scriptures. How much does your Bible mean to you?

119.73 **GOD GIVES US ABILITY TO LEARN** God, who made us, understands very well how our minds work. He knows how to give us an appreciation for his words. When soldiers first tried to arrest Jesus, they only reported that no one ever spoke as he did. We, (*continued*)

NOTES

75 Your decisions are correct,
and you were right
to punish me.
76 I serve you, LORD.
Comfort me with your love,
just as you have promised.
77 I love to obey your Law!
Have mercy and let me live.
78 Put down those proud people
who hurt me with their lies,
because I have chosen
to study your teachings.
79 Let your worshipers come to me,
so they will learn
to obey your rules.
80 Let me truly respect your laws,
so I won't be ashamed.

81 I long for you to rescue me!
Your word is my only hope.
82 I am worn out from waiting
for you to keep your word.
When will you have mercy?
83 My life is wasting away
like a dried-up wineskin,[h]
but I have not forgotten
your teachings.
84 I am your servant!
How long must I suffer?
When will you punish
those troublemakers?
85 Those proud people reject
your teachings,
and they dig pits
for me to fall in.
86 Your laws can be trusted!
Protect me from cruel liars.
87 They have almost killed me,
but I have been faithful
to your teachings.
88 Show that you love me
and let me live,
so that I may obey all
of your commands.

89 Our LORD, you are eternal!
Your word will last as long
as the heavens.[i]
90 You remain faithful
in every generation,
and the earth you created
will keep standing firm.
91 All things are your servants,
and the laws you made
are still in effect today.
92 If I had not found happiness
in obeying your Law,
I would have died in misery.
93 I won't ever forget
your teachings,
because you give me new life
by following them.
94 I belong to you,
and I have respected your laws,
so keep me safe.
95 Brutal enemies are waiting
to ambush and destroy me,
but I obey your rules.
96 Nothing is completely perfect,
except your teachings.

97 I deeply love your Law!
I think about it all day.
98 Your laws never leave my mind,
and they make me much wiser
than my enemies.
99 Thinking about your teachings
gives me better understanding
than my teachers,
100 and obeying your laws
makes me wiser than those
who have lived a long time.*
101 I obey your word

[h]*wineskin*: The Hebrew text has "a wineskin in the smoke." In ancient times bags were made from animal skins to hold wine, but when the bags dried up they cracked and could no longer be used.
[i]*Our . . . heavens*: Or "Our LORD, your word is eternal. It will last as long as the heavens."

(*continued*) too, can come to the place where we see that the Bible is not just a lot of strange stories. It is God's love letter in which he speaks personally to those who are seeking him. Let's ask God for understanding. He will give it.

119.100 **JUST HOW WISE ARE YOU?** Some people say they have had twenty-five years' experience, when they really should say they have had only one year's experience twenty-five times! Often very young people do show more wisdom than those who have lived a long time. Wisdom doesn't come just by living. Wisdom is a gift of God that can come early or late—or that may not come at all!

NOTES

instead of following a way
that leads to trouble.
102 You have been my teacher,
and I won't reject
your instructions.
103 Your teachings are sweeter
than honey.
104 They give me understanding
and make me hate all lies.

105 Your word is a lamp
that gives light
wherever I walk.
106 Your laws are fair,
and I have given my word
to respect them all.
107 I am in terrible pain!
Save me, LORD,
as you said you would.
108 Accept my offerings of praise
and teach me your laws.
109 I never forget your teachings,
although my life is always
in danger.
110 Some merciless people
are trying to trap me,
but I never turn my back
on your teachings.
111 They will always be
my most prized possession
and my source of joy.
112 I have made up my mind
to obey your laws forever,
no matter what.

113 I hate anyone
whose loyalty is divided,
but I love your Law.
114 You are my place of safety
and my shield.
Your word is my only hope.
115 All of you worthless people,
get away from me!
I am determined to obey
the commands of my God.

116 Be true to your word, LORD.
Keep me alive and strong;
don't let me be ashamed
because of my hope.
117 Keep me safe and secure,
so that I will always
respect your laws.
118 You reject all deceitful liars
because they refuse
your teachings.
119 As far as you are concerned,
all evil people are[j] garbage,
and so I follow your rules.
120 I tremble all over
when I think of you
and the way you judge.

121 I did what was fair and right!
Don't hand me over to those
who want to mistreat me.
122 Take good care of me,
your servant,
and don't let me be harmed
by those conceited people.
123 My eyes are weary from waiting
to see you keep your promise
to come and save me.
124 Show your love for me,
your servant,
and teach me your laws.
125 I serve you,
so let me understand
your teachings.
126 Do something, LORD!
They have broken your Law.
127 Your laws mean more to me
than the finest gold.
128 I follow all of your commands,[k]
but I hate anyone
who leads me astray.

129 Your teachings are wonderful,
and I respect them all.
130 Understanding your word
brings light to the minds
of ordinary people.
131 I honestly want to know
everything you teach.
132 Think about me and be kind,
just as you are to everyone
who loves your name.
133 Keep your promise
and don't let me stumble
or let sin control my life.
134 Protect me from abuse,
so I can obey your laws.
135 Smile on me, your servant,
and teach me your laws.
136 When anyone disobeys you,
my eyes overflow with tears.

137 Our LORD, you always do right,
and your decisions are fair.
138 All of your teachings are true
and trustworthy.
139 It upsets me greatly
when my enemies neglect
your teachings.

---

[j] *As far as . . . are*: A few Hebrew manuscripts and ancient versions. Most Hebrew manuscripts have "You get rid of evil people as if they were."
[k] *I . . . commands*: One possible meaning for the difficult Hebrew text.

140 Your word to me, your servant,
is like pure gold;
I treasure what you say.
141 Everyone calls me a nobody,
but I remember your laws.
142 You will always do right,
and your teachings are true.
143 I am in deep distress,
but I love your teachings.
144 Your rules are always fair.
Help me to understand them
and live.

145 I pray to you, LORD!
Please answer me.
I promise to obey your laws.
146 I beg you to save me,
so I can follow your rules.
147 Even before sunrise,
I pray for your help,
and I put my hope
in what you have said.
148 I lie awake at night,
thinking of your promises.
149 Show that you love me, LORD,
and answer my prayer.
Please do the right thing
and save my life.
150 People who disobey your Law
have made evil plans
and want to hurt me,
151 but you are with me,
and all of your commands
can be trusted.
152 From studying your laws,
I found out long ago
that you made them
to last forever.

153 I have not forgotten your Law!
Look at the trouble I am in,
and rescue me.
154 Be my defender and protector!
Keep your promise
and save my life.
155 Evil people won't obey you,
and so they have no hope
of being saved.
156 You are merciful, LORD!
Please do the right thing
and save my life.
157 I have a lot of brutal enemies,
but still I never turn
from your laws.
158 All of those unfaithful people
who refuse to obey you
are disgusting to me.
159 Remember how I love your laws,
and show your love for me
by keeping me safe.
160 All you say can be trusted;
your teachings are true
and will last forever.

161 Rulers are cruel to me
for no reason.
But with all my heart
I respect your words,
162 because they bring happiness
like treasures taken in war.
163 I can't stand liars,
but I love your Law.
164 I praise you seven times a day
because your laws are fair.
165 You give peace of mind
to all who love your Law.
Nothing can make them fall.
166 You are my only hope
for being saved, LORD,
and I do all you command.
167 I love and obey your laws
with all my heart.
168 You know everything I do.
You know I respect every law
you have given.

169 Please, LORD, hear my prayer
and give me the understanding
that comes from your word.
170 Listen to my concerns
and keep me safe,
just as you have promised.
171 If you will teach me your laws,
I will praise you 172 and sing
about your promise,
because all of your teachings
are what they ought to be.
173 Be ready to protect me
because I have chosen
to obey your laws.
174 I am waiting for you
to save me, LORD.
Your Law makes me happy.*

119.174 **DOES GOD'S WORD MAKE YOU HAPPY?** We're missing the greatest joy of life if we find the Scriptures boring. Contained in the Bible's pages is the greatest news ever heard. And there are so many individual stories about people who discovered that great *(continued)*

NOTES

Step 11

I will pray to God on a regular basis, asking him to direct me and give me the power to live for him.

PSALM 119.140–144

STICKS AND STONES

"**Y**ou are worthless."
"**W**hen you turn 18 you're out of here!"
"**I** knew you would never amount to anything."
"**I** wish you were never born!"
"**C**an't you do anything right?"
"**S**ticks and stones may break my bones, but words will never hurt me." Did you ever say that as a child? It seemed to work then, and we could even believe it. But now we realize it is a lie. The truth is, as a verse in the Bible says, words cut deeper than a sword. They are painful, cutting deep into the soul.

STEP LOOK INSIDE 11

We have made a decision to turn our lives around. We want to speak the truth instead of lies. We want to depend on God instead of alcohol, drugs, bad friends, or whatever has been pulling us down. We are ready to follow the rules instead of breaking them. We are ready, but it's going to take a while before those around us will understand. Trust is something we have to earn.

HANG IN THERE

It takes time to rebuild character. That is why it is so important to stay in touch with the Lord. We are going to need his help to hang in there when stones of criticism are thrown at us. He will give us strength to react in his love and power until, little by little, others lay their weapons down.

To take a "Look Ahead," turn to page 221.

175 Keep me alive,
so I can praise you,
and let me find help
in your teachings.
176 I am your servant,
but I have wandered away
like a lost sheep.
Please come after me,
because I have not forgotten
your teachings.

Psalm 120

[*A song for worship.*]

A Prayer for the LORD's Help

1 When I am in trouble, I pray,
2 "Come and save me, LORD,
from deceitful liars!"

3 What punishment is fitting
for you deceitful liars?
4 Your reward should be
sharp and flaming arrows!

5 But I must live as a foreigner
among the people of Meshech
and in the tents of Kedar.[l]*
6 I have spent too much time
living among people
who hate peace.
7 I am in favor of peace,
but when I speak of it,
all they want is war.

Psalm 121

[*A song for worship.*]

The LORD Will Protect His People

1 I look to the hills!
Where will I find help?*
2 It will come from the LORD,
who created the heavens
and the earth.

3 The LORD is your protector,
and he won't go to sleep
or let you stumble.
4 The protector of Israel
doesn't doze
or ever get drowsy.

5 The LORD is your protector,
there at your right side
to shade you from the sun.
6 You won't be harmed
by the sun during the day
or by the moon[m] at night.

7 The LORD will protect you
and keep you safe
from all dangers.

---

[l] *Meshech . . . Kedar*: Meshech was a country near the Black Sea, and Kedar was a tribe of the Syrian desert. [m] *harmed . . . sun . . . moon*: In ancient times people saw the harmful effects of the rays of the sun, and they thought that certain illnesses (especially mental disorders) were also caused by the rays of the moon.

(*continued*) news. God wants to give us his best, and he did so when he gave his son Jesus to die for our sins. Jesus came back to life and now lives to make those who love him the happiest people in the world.

120.5 **WE'RE OFTEN STRANGERS IN THE WORLD** This songwriter was lonely in a world that didn't want him. It has always been that way with God's people. They're the salt of the earth, but they're unwelcome in a society that doesn't know their God. Even Jesus was treated like an outsider by his own people. But we're glad when we know why we're outsiders. We're a different people because we've been made citizens of God's kingdom that will last forever. So we enjoy the things of that kingdom.

121.1 **DOES HELP COME FROM NATURE?** The hills and mountains are very inspiring, so it's not strange that we can sit and gaze at them for hours with great longing in our hearts. But sooner or later we should realize that, lovely as they are, the mountains are only earth and rocks. There is no lasting help from nature. It is the God who made nature that we must look up to. The one who cares for the hills, the trees, and the animals cares even more for us, and he is pleased when we turn to him.

NOTES

8The LORD will protect you
now and always
wherever you go.

Psalm 122

[*A song by David for worship.*]

A Song of Praise

1It made me glad
to hear them say,
"Let's go to the house
of the LORD!"
2Jerusalem, we are standing
inside your gates.

3Jerusalem, what a strong
and beautiful city you are!*
4Every tribe of the LORD
obeys him and comes to you
to praise his name.
5David's royal throne is here
where justice rules.

6Jerusalem, we pray
that you will have peace,
and that all will go well
for those who love you.
7May there be peace
inside your city walls
and in your palaces.
8Because of my friends
and my relatives,
I will pray for peace.
9And because of the house
of the LORD our God,
I will work for your good.

Psalm 123

[*A song for worship.*]

A Prayer for Mercy

1Our LORD and our God,
I turn my eyes to you,
on your throne in heaven.*
2Servants look to their master,
but we will look to you,
until you have mercy on us.

3Please have mercy, LORD!
We have been insulted
more than we can stand,
4and we can't take more abuse
from those proud,
conceited people.

Psalm 124

[*A song by David for worship.*]

Thanking the LORD for Victory

1The LORD was on our side!
Let everyone in Israel say:
2 "The LORD was on our side!
Otherwise, the enemy attack
3would have killed us all,
because it was furious.
4We would have been swept away
in a violent flood
5 of high and roaring waves."

6Let's praise the LORD!
He protected us from enemies

122.3 **THE CITY OF GOD LASTS FOREVER** The Old Testament contains a lot of "word pictures" of unseen realities, like the kingdom of God. David was ruler over Jerusalem, the beloved city, for forty years. Eventually the city was destroyed by enemies, although it still exists today. But it is not the "Eternal City." No earthly city is really eternal. The eternal city is where God dwells and the place from which he will reign forever.

123.1 **WHERE IS GOD'S THRONE?** The songwriter turned his eyes to God's throne in heaven. All we can say about heaven's location right now is that it is where God is. But God's throne, or place of his government, can also be in our own lives. And if he rules over us, then we can be a little bit of heaven ourselves. Do we bring heaven near to others, and do they see something of heaven about us? This is how it ought to be with you and me.

NOTES

who were like wild animals,*
7and we escaped like birds
from a hunter's torn net.

8The LORD made heaven and earth,
and he is the one
who sends us help.

Psalm 125

[*A song for worship.*]

The LORD's People Are Safe

1Everyone who trusts the LORD
is like Mount Zion
that cannot be shaken
and will stand forever.*
2Just as Jerusalem is protected
by mountains on every side,
the LORD protects his people
by holding them in his arms
now and forever.
3He won't let the wicked
rule his people
or lead them to do wrong.
4Let's ask the LORD to be kind
to everyone who is good
and completely obeys him.

5When the LORD punishes
the wicked,
he will punish everyone else
who lives a crooked life.
Pray for peace in Israel!

Psalm 126

[*A song for worship.*]

Celebrating the Harvest

1It seemed like a dream
when the LORD brought us back
to the city of Zion.[n]
2We celebrated with laughter
and joyful songs.
In foreign nations it was said,
"The LORD has worked miracles
for his people."
3And so we celebrated
because the LORD had indeed
worked miracles for us.

4Our LORD, we ask you to bless
our people again,
and let us be like streams
in the southern desert.*
5We cried as we went out
to plant our seeds.
Now let us celebrate
as we bring in the crops.
6We cried on the way
to plant our seeds,
but we will celebrate and shout
as we bring in the crops.

---

[n]*brought . . . Zion*: Or "made the city of Zion prosperous again."

124.6 **GOD PROTECTS US FROM ENEMIES** Time and again, God has saved various peoples from destruction by unscrupulous enemies. He is always defending the right—so long as his honor is upheld. We must not be careless with the blessings that have come to us because of the faithfulness of our forefathers. We must be faithful as well.

125.1 **ARE YOU LIKE A MOUNTAIN?** Mountains are pretty unshakable. Are we easily "shook up" by mishaps and annoyances? If so, then we're not very mountainlike, are we? Perhaps that fact tells us something about how well or how poorly our faith is working. The wind blows straw around, but it can't move mountains. Let's ask God to help us begin anew to trust him about everything. Then we won't be so shaken up any more.

126.4 **LET'S MAKE THE WORLD BEAUTIFUL** There are so many ugly things that happen in our world. We need to think of ways to make the world around us lovely. Some folks do this by planting flowers. But we can also plant the flowers of happiness in the life of everyone we meet. Then we will be like fresh streams that make flowers grow even in the desert. And when we bring happiness to others, we also bring happiness to ourselves.

NOTES

Psalm 127

[*A song by Solomon for worship.*]

Only the LORD Can Bless a Home

1Without the help of the LORD
it is useless to build a home
or to guard a city.
2It is useless to get up early
and stay up late
in order to earn a living.
God takes care of his own,
even while they sleep.[o]*

3Children are a blessing
and a gift from the LORD.
4Having a lot of children
to take care of you
in your old age
is like a warrior
with a lot of arrows.
5The more you have,
the better off you will be,
because they will protect you
when your enemies attack
with arguments.

Psalm 128

[*A song for worship.*]

The LORD Rewards His Faithful People

1The LORD will bless you
if you respect him
and obey his laws.*
2Your fields will produce,
and you will be happy
and all will go well.
3Your wife will be as fruitful
as a grapevine,
and just as an olive tree
is rich with olives,
your home will be rich
with healthy children.
4That is how the LORD will bless
everyone who respects him.

5I pray that the LORD
will bless you from Zion
and let Jerusalem prosper
as long as you live.
6May you live long enough
to see your grandchildren.
Let's pray for peace
in Israel!

Psalm 129

[*A song for worship.*]

A Prayer for Protection

1Since the time I was young,
enemies have often attacked!
Let everyone in Israel say:
2"Since the time I was young,
enemies have often attacked!
But they have not defeated me,*

[o]*God . . . sleep*: One possible meaning for the difficult Hebrew text.

127.2 **SPEND YOUR LIFE WISELY** For some people, getting and having things seems to be their only reason for living, and they work very hard to own a lot of property. But they're often disappointed after spending the best part of their lives working to own material things. Somehow they just feel dried up inside. They're unable to enjoy real beauty, and they find they can't love. But God can still touch such people and give them hearts that can love again.

128.1 **IT PAYS TO HONOR GOD'S LAWS** Of course, we can honor God's laws only when we respect him. Parents need to win the respect of their children if they want their children to obey them. God knows this, and he has done much to gain our respect. It is enough that he has made us, but he has done ever so much more—loving us, protecting us, and caring for our needs. Now we owe him our respect, and when we obey his laws we will be happy always.

129.2 **IS THE WORLD AGAINST YOU?** Sometimes we feel the world is against us even when it isn't. The fact is, we may be worrying about ourselves too much. But whether people are (*continued*)

NOTES

3 though my back is like a field
that has just been plowed."

4 The LORD always does right,
and he has set me free
from the ropes
of those cruel people.
5 I pray that all who hate
the city of Zion
will be made ashamed
and forced to turn and run.
6 May they be like grass
on the flat roof of a house,
grass that dries up
as soon as it sprouts.
7 Don't let them be like wheat
gathered in bundles.
8 And don't let anyone
who passes by say to them,
"The LORD bless you!
I give you my blessing
in the name of the LORD."

Psalm 130

[*A song for worship.*]

Trusting the LORD in Times of Trouble

1 From a sea of troubles
I call out to you, LORD.
2 Won't you please listen
as I beg for mercy?

3 If you kept record of our sins,
no one could last long.
4 But you forgive us,
and so we will worship you.

5 With all my heart,
I am waiting, LORD, for you!
I trust your promises.*
6 I wait for you more eagerly
than a soldier on guard duty
waits for the dawn.
Yes, I wait more eagerly
than a soldier on guard duty
waits for the dawn.

7 Israel, trust the LORD!
He is always merciful,
and he has the power
to save you.
8 Israel, the LORD will save you
from all of your sins.

Psalm 131

[*A song by David for worship.*]

Trust the LORD!

1 I am not conceited, LORD,
and I don't waste my time
on impossible schemes.*
2 But I have learned to feel safe
and satisfied,
just like a young child
on its mother's lap.

3 People of Israel,
you must trust the LORD
now and forever.

(*continued*) really against us, or we're just being thin-skinned, God is the One who makes everything right for us. When we turn our eyes upon Jesus, all of these thoughts about ourselves melt away. It doesn't matter who is against us, or who is for us, when God is on our side.

130.5 **DO YOU WAIT FOR GOD?** Perhaps you'll say, "I didn't know God was late." No, he never is, but sometimes we're early! God has his own times for doing things, and it does no good to be impatient with him. Like the songwriter here, let us eagerly wait for God to do all the beautiful things he plans to do in our lives.

131.1 **THINK ABOUT WHAT'S TRUE** Some people have too high an opinion of themselves. Others put themselves down. How do we keep from falling into these two traps? By not thinking about ourselves too much at all! But let's think about how good God is to us and how safe we are in his care. Then it will be easier to live our lives in useful ways. There are many lonely and unhappy people in the world. They need us at our best so they, too, can see the way to being happy through God's love.

NOTES

Psalm 132

[*A song for worship.*]

The LORD Is Always with His People

1Our LORD, don't forget David
and how he suffered.
2Mighty God of Jacob,
remember how he promised:
3"I won't go home
or crawl into bed
4 or close my eyelids,
5until I find a home for you,
the mighty LORD God
of Jacob."

6When we were in Ephrathah,
we heard that the sacred chest
was somewhere near Jaar.
7Then we said, "Let's go
to the throne of the LORD
and worship at his feet."

8Come to your new home, LORD,
you and the sacred chest
with all of its power.
9Let victory be like robes
for the priests;
let your faithful people
celebrate and shout.
10David is your chosen one,
so don't reject him.
11You made a solemn promise
to David, when you said,
"I, the LORD, promise
that someone in your family
will always be king.
12If they keep our agreement
and follow my teachings,
then someone in your family
will rule forever."
13You have gladly chosen Zion
as your home, our LORD.*
14You said, "This is my home!
I will live here forever.
15I will bless Zion with food,
and even the poor will eat
until they are full.
16Victory will be like robes
for the priests,
and its faithful people
will celebrate and shout.
17I will give mighty power
to the kingdom of David.
Each one of my chosen kings
will shine like a lamp
18 and wear a sparkling crown.
But I will disgrace
their enemies."

Psalm 133

[*A song for worship.*]

Living Together in Peace

1It is truly wonderful
when relatives live together
in peace.*
2It is as beautiful as olive oil
poured on Aaron's head[p]
and running down his beard
and the collar of his robe.
3It is like the dew
from Mount Hermon,
falling on Zion's mountains
where the LORD has promised
to bless his people
with life forevermore.

---

[p] *head*: Olive oil was poured on Aaron's head to show that God had chosen him to be the high priest.

132.13 **WHERE IS ZION?** On the earth's map, Zion is where the Old Testament temple used to be. A Moslem mosque is there now. One day the temple may be built there again. But there is also an eternal Zion that never changes. It is where God's everlasting throne is. There God will satisfy his people with the food of heaven forever. Are you looking forward to living in that endless Zion with God?

133.1 **CAN THERE BE PEACE?** The world has lived so long without peace that we have almost given up hope for real peace. All the same, God has promised future peace that will never end. That peace has already been bought and paid for by the very blood and death of Jesus the Savior. His dying was the guarantee that hate would one day come to an end and he would reign in our hearts forever.

NOTES

Step 9

I will make things right with people I wrong, except when to do so would hurt them or others.

PSALM 133.1–3

HOME SWEET HOME

It may be hard to remember when kind words were spoken in our homes. It seems every time we are around, chaos ensues, and, before we know it, World War III is under way. For a long time we may have thought it was our parents' problem. They just didn't understand us. They pressured us to be what we could never be. They didn't respect us or our privacy. They wouldn't let us grow up. The only solution was to leave. So we did. Maybe not by running away, but we left all the same. We turned to anyone or anything in an attempt to find happiness. But it was never there.

STEP 9 LOOK INSIDE

MAKING PEACE

We know now that happiness starts inside us. The first step is to get right in our relationship with God and learn to love and forgive ourselves. After that, it's time to take this message of peace back home.

For another "Look Inside," turn to page 700.

Psalm 134

[*A song for worship.*]

Praising the LORD at Night

1Everyone who serves the LORD,
come and offer praises.
Everyone who has gathered
in his temple tonight,
2lift your hands in prayer
toward his holy place
and praise the LORD.*

3The LORD is the Creator
of heaven and earth,
and I pray that the LORD
will bless you from Zion.

Psalm 135

In Praise of the LORD's Kindness

1Shout praises to the LORD!
You are his servants,
so praise his name.
2All who serve in the temple
of the LORD our God,
3 come and shout praises.
Praise the name of the LORD!
He is kind and good.
4He chose the family of Jacob
and the people of Israel
for his very own.

5The LORD is much greater
than any other god.
6He does as he chooses
in heaven and on earth
and deep in the sea.
7The LORD makes the clouds rise
from far across the earth,
and he makes lightning
to go with the rain.
Then from his secret place
he sends out the wind.

8The LORD killed the first-born
of people and animals
in the land of Egypt.
9God used miracles and wonders
to fight the king of Egypt
and all of his officials.
10He destroyed many nations
and killed powerful kings,
11including King Sihon
of the Amorites
and King Og of Bashan.
He conquered every kingdom
in the land of Canaan
12and gave their property
to his people Israel.

13The name of the LORD
will be remembered forever,
and he will be famous
for all time to come.
14The LORD will bring justice
and show mercy to all
who serve him.

15Idols of silver and gold
are made and worshiped
in other nations.
16They have a mouth and eyes,
but they can't speak or see.
17They are completely deaf,
and they can't breathe.
18Everyone who makes idols
and all who trust them
will end up as helpless
as their idols.*

134.2 **GOD IS IN THE HOLY PLACE** In the Old Testament temple there were two "holy places"—the Holy Place and the Most Holy Place. The Most Holy Place was behind a thick curtain where God was present. When Jesus was later crucified, that curtain was torn open by God to show that we all could now come into his Most Holy Place in heaven. But heaven is not really far away, and we can come in there every time we pray.

135.18 **IDOLS ARE USELESS** Most of us wouldn't kneel before a real idol—a statue of wood, stone, or metal. But many foolishly worship things just as hopeless—things such as money, big homes, cars, or other material goods. Mostly, the temptation is to think of ourselves in a way that we should think about God. So we become our own idols. Let's adore our Creator instead. That is the worship that really makes our lives rich because God honors those who honor him.

NOTES

19 Everyone in Israel,
come praise the LORD!
All the family of Aaron
20 and all the tribe of Levi,[q]
come praise the LORD!
All of his worshipers,
come praise the LORD.
21 Praise the LORD from Zion!
He lives here in Jerusalem.
Shout praises to the LORD!

Psalm 136

God's Love Never Fails

1 Praise the LORD! He is good.
God's love never fails.
2 Praise the God of all gods.
God's love never fails.
3 Praise the Lord of lords.
God's love never fails.*

4 Only God works great miracles.[r]
God's love never fails.
5 With wisdom he made the sky.
God's love never fails.
6 The Lord stretched the earth
over the ocean.
God's love never fails.
7 He made the bright lights
in the sky.
God's love never fails.
8 He lets the sun rule each day.
God's love never fails.
9 He lets the moon and the stars
rule each night.
God's love never fails.

10 God struck down the first-born
in every Egyptian family.
God's love never fails.
11 He rescued Israel from Egypt.
God's love never fails.
12 God used his great strength
and his powerful arm.
God's love never fails.
13 He split the Red Sea[s] apart.
God's love never fails.
14 The Lord brought Israel safely
through the sea.
God's love never fails.
15 He destroyed the Egyptian king
and his army there.
God's love never fails.
16 The Lord led his people
through the desert.
God's love never fails.

17 Our God defeated mighty kings.
God's love never fails.
18 And he killed famous kings.
God's love never fails.
19 One of them was Sihon,
king of the Amorites.
God's love never fails.
20 Another was King Og of Bashan.
God's love never fails.
21 God took away their land.
God's love never fails.
22 He gave their land to Israel,
the people who serve him.
God's love never fails.

23 God saw the trouble we were in.
God's love never fails.
24 He rescued us from our enemies.
God's love never fails.
25 He gives food to all who live.
God's love never fails.

26 Praise God in heaven!
God's love never fails.

Psalm 137

A Prayer for Revenge

1 Beside the rivers of Babylon
we thought about Jerusalem,

---

[q] *Aaron . . . Levi*: Aaron was from the tribe of Levi, and all priests were from his family. The temple helpers, singers, and musicians were also from the tribe of Levi. [r] *great miracles*: One Hebrew manuscript and one ancient version have "miracles." [s] *Red Sea*: Or "Sea of Reeds."

136.3 **GOD'S LOVE IS FOREVER** Sad to say, human love can be a very temporary thing. Even an animal's love for its owner is often more faithful than our love for one another. But there is one kind of love that never quits. It is God's love for those who trust him—and even for those who don't. To those who do trust God, he proves his love over and over. And he often surprises those who never trusted him by being kind to them in ways they can never forget. Then they love God because he first loved them.

NOTES

and we sat down and cried.
2We hung our small harps
on the willow[t] trees.
3Our enemies had brought us here
as their prisoners,
and now they wanted us to sing
and entertain them.
They insulted us and shouted,
"Sing about Zion!"

4Here in a foreign land,
how can we sing
about the LORD?*
5Jerusalem, if I forget you,
let my right hand go limp.
6Let my tongue stick
to the roof of my mouth,
if I don't think about you
above all else.

7Our LORD, punish the Edomites!
Because the day Jerusalem fell,
they shouted,
"Completely destroy the city!
Tear down every building!"

8Babylon, you are doomed!
I pray the Lord's blessings
on anyone who punishes you
for what you did to us.
9May the Lord bless everyone
who beats your children
against the rocks!

Psalm 138

[*By David.*]

Praise the LORD with All Your Heart

STEP 12

1With all my heart
I praise you, LORD.
In the presence of angels[u]
I sing your praises.
2I worship at your holy temple
and praise you for your love
and your faithfulness.
You were true to your word
and made yourself more famous
than ever before.[v]
3When I asked for your help,
you answered my prayer
and gave me courage.[w]

4All kings on this earth
have heard your promises, LORD,
and they will praise you.
5You are so famous
that they will sing about
the things you have done.
6Though you are above us all,
you care for humble people,
and you keep a close watch
on everyone who is proud.

7I am surrounded by trouble,
but you protect me
against my angry enemies.
With your own powerful arm
you keep me safe.*

8You, LORD, will always
treat me with kindness.
Your love never fails.

---

[t] *willow*: Or "poplar." [u] *angels*: Or "gods" or "supernatural beings" who worship and serve God in heaven or "rulers" or "leaders." [v] *You were . . . before*: One possible meaning for the difficult Hebrew text. [w] *and gave me courage*: One possible meaning for the difficult Hebrew text.

137.4 **CAN WE SING ABOUT THE LORD?** If we're honest, it's hard sometimes to sing our thanks and praise to God. Like the Jews in this psalm, we are "outsiders" in this world, and heaven too often seems far away. But God can give us *inner* sight to see all the things he has planned for those who love him. Then we aren't sad anymore, and we begin to sing again.

138.7 **ARE YOU IN TROUBLE?** So is everyone else—yes, even God's people. But the thing that makes us different is the same thing David wrote about in this verse. He said that God protected him. Likewise, we aren't alone with trouble when God walks beside us, and he will stay with us if we ask him to.

NOTES

You have made us what we are.
Don't give up on us now![x]

Psalm 139

[*A psalm by David for the music leader.*]

The LORD Is Always Near

1 You have looked deep
into my heart, LORD,
and you know all about me.
2 You know when I am resting
or when I am working,
and from heaven
you discover my thoughts.

3 You notice everything I do
and everywhere I go.
4 Before I even speak a word,
you know what I will say,
5 and with your powerful arm
you protect me
from every side.
6 I can't understand all of this!
Such wonderful knowledge
is far above me.

7 Where could I go to escape
from your Spirit
or from your sight?
8 If I were to climb up
to the highest heavens,
you would be there.
If I were to dig down
to the world of the dead
you would also be there.

9 Suppose I had wings
like the dawning day
and flew across the ocean.
10 Even then your powerful arm
would guide and protect me.
11 Or suppose I said, "I'll hide
in the dark until night comes
to cover me over."
12 But you see in the dark
because daylight and dark
are all the same to you.

13 You are the one
who put me together
inside my mother's body,
14 and I praise you because of
the wonderful way
you created me.
Everything you do is marvelous!
Of this I have no doubt.

15 Nothing about me
is hidden from you!
I was secretly woven together
deep in the earth below,
16 but with your own eyes you saw
my body being formed.
Even before I was born,
you had written in your book
everything I would do.

17 Your thoughts are far beyond
my understanding,
much more than I
could ever imagine.
18 I try to count your thoughts,
but they outnumber the grains
of sand on the beach.
And when I awake,
I will find you nearby.

19 How I wish that you would kill
all cruel and heartless people
and protect me from them!
20 They are always rebelling
and speaking evil of you.[y]
21 You know I hate anyone
who hates you, LORD,
and refuses to obey.
22 They are my enemies too,
and I truly hate them.

23 Look deep into my heart, God,
and find out everything
I am thinking.
24 Don't let me follow evil ways,
but lead me in the way
that time has proven true.

Psalm 140

[*A psalm by David for the music leader.*]

A Prayer for the LORD's Help

1 Rescue me from cruel
and violent enemies, LORD!
2 They think up evil plans
and always cause trouble.
3 Their words bite deep

---

[x] *You have . . . now*: Or "Please don't desert your people." [y] *you*: One possible meaning for the difficult Hebrew text of verse 20.

like the poisonous fangs
of a snake.*

4 Protect me, LORD, from cruel
and brutal enemies,
who want to destroy me.
5 Those proud people have hidden
traps and nets
to catch me as I walk.

6 You, LORD, are my God!
Please listen to my prayer.
7 You have the power to save me,
and you keep me safe
in every battle.

8 Don't let the wicked succeed
in doing what they want,
or else they might never
stop planning evil.
9 They have me surrounded,
but make them the victims
of their own vicious lies.[z]
10 Dump flaming coals on them
and throw them into pits
where they can't climb out.
11 Chase those cruel liars away!
Let trouble hunt them down.

12 Our LORD, I know that you
defend the homeless
and see that the poor
are given justice.
13 Your people will praise you
and will live with you
because they do right.

Psalm 141

[*A psalm by David.*]

A Prayer for the LORD's Protection

1 I pray to you, LORD!
Please listen when I pray
and hurry to help me.
2 Think of my prayer
as sweet-smelling incense,
and think of my lifted hands
as an evening sacrifice.

3 Help me to guard my words
whenever I say something.*
4 Don't let me want to do evil
or waste my time doing wrong
with wicked people.
Don't let me even taste
the good things they offer.

5 Let your faithful people
correct and punish me.
My prayers condemn the deeds
of those who do wrong,
so don't let me be friends
with any of them.
6 Everyone will admit
that I was right
when their rulers are thrown
down a rocky cliff,
7 and their bones lie scattered
like broken rocks
on top of a grave.[a]

8 You are my LORD and God,
and I look to you for safety.
Don't let me be harmed.
9 Protect me from the traps
of those violent people,
10 and make them fall
into their own traps
while you help me escape.

---

[z] *or else . . . lies*: One possible meaning for the difficult Hebrew text. [a] *Let . . . grave*: One possible meaning for the difficult Hebrew text of verses 5-7.

140.3 **SHARP WORDS CAN HURT** King David had feelings, and he was hurt when his enemies said harsh things about him. He compared their words to the bite of a poisonous snake. But David knew the cure for that kind of snakebite. He could curl up like a child in God's arms and find comfort. God was David's friend, and God will be just as much a friend to any of us who ask him.

141.3 **PRAY FOR RIGHT SPEECH** Many of us have foot-in-mouth disease. We keep saying the wrong things at the wrong times. We need to pray that God will guard our speech and help us not to say things that are unwise or even hurtful. We need to train ourselves to think as God wants us to about all that happens around us. Then we'll also speak in ways God would have us to speak.

NOTES

GUARDRAILS

The rain was coming down so hard I couldn't see out the window. The fog and darkness of the night made driving even more hazardous. It didn't help that this was new territory for me. Of course, having had my license less than a year, everywhere I went was new territory. I slowed down to what I thought was a safe speed, but it wasn't enough. As I rounded the turn, my car started to skid. I sat there totally helpless as it spun out of control. When the car finally stopped, it was resting up against the guardrails. If they hadn't been there, my short life of 16 years would have been over. Next time I'll slow down even more.

Slowing down and considering the consequences of our actions and words is the best way to live life at a safe speed. Looking back at our lives may reveal many things we would do differently. At times we wish we could go back and start over again. Is that really possible?

FORGIVE AND FORGET

The Lord has promised to forgive and forget our past mistakes if we are open and honest with him and ourselves. We might daily put up "spiritual guardrails" by asking the Lord to help us say and do the right things. A little more thinking before acting.

The world has many quick solutions to offer. We have to be careful to guard our minds so we don't wind up out of control.

For another "Look Inside," turn to page 688.

Psalm 142

[*A special psalm and a prayer by David when he was in the cave.*]

A Prayer for Help

1I pray to you, LORD.
I beg for mercy.
2I tell you all of my worries
and my troubles,*
3and whenever I feel low,
you are there to guide me.

A trap has been hidden
along my pathway.
4Even if you look,
you won't see anyone
who cares enough
to walk beside me.
There is no place to hide,
and no one who really cares.

5I pray to you, LORD!
You are my place of safety,
and you are my choice
in the land of the living.
Please answer my prayer.
I am completely helpless.

6Help! They are chasing me,
and they are too strong.
7Rescue me from this prison,
so I can praise your name.
And when your people notice
your wonderful kindness to me,
they will rush to my side.

Psalm 143

[*A psalm by David.*]

A Prayer in Time of Danger

1Listen, LORD, as I pray!
You are faithful and honest
and will answer my prayer.
2I am your servant.
Don't try me in your court,
because no one is innocent
by your standards.*
3My enemies are chasing me,
crushing me in the ground.
I am in total darkness,
like someone long dead.
4I have given up all hope,
and I feel numb all over.

5I remember to think about
the many things you did
in years gone by.
6Then I lift my hands in prayer,
because my soul is a desert,
thirsty for water from you.

7Please hurry, LORD,
and answer my prayer.
I feel hopeless.
Don't turn away
and leave me here to die.
8Each morning let me learn
more about your love
because I trust you.
I come to you in prayer,
asking for your guidance.

9Please rescue me
from my enemies, LORD!
I come to you for safety.[b]
10You are my God. Show me
what you want me to do,
and let your gentle Spirit
lead me in the right path.

11Be true to your name, LORD,
and keep my life safe.
Use your saving power
to protect me from trouble.
12I am your servant.
Show how much you love me
by destroying my enemies.

[b]*I . . . safety*: Or "You are my hiding place."

142.2 **TALK TO GOD ABOUT PROBLEMS** There's no need to keep our troubles to ourselves. God is listening, and he wants to hear from us. He also has the ability to change things for us. He brings us through those problems in the end.

143.2 **GOD'S STANDARDS ARE VERY HIGH** In fact, we can't measure up to God's standards. But we can all throw ourselves on God's mercy and find forgiveness there. There's no room for people who believe in their own goodness. God only laughs at that, because Jesus said truly that only God is good. It keeps us in the right attitude to remember that God's free forgiveness is all we have. Jesus paid for that by dying on the cross.

NOTES

Psalm 144

[*By David.*]

A Prayer for the Nation

1I praise you, LORD!
You are my mighty rock,[c]
and you teach me
how to fight my battles.
2You are my friend,
and you are my fortress
where I am safe.
You are my shield,
and you made me the ruler
of our people.[d]

3Why do we humans
mean anything
to you, our LORD?
Why do you care about us?
4We disappear like a breath;
we last no longer
than a faint shadow.

5Open the heavens like a curtain
and come down, LORD.
Touch the mountains
and make them send up smoke.
6Use your lightning as arrows
to scatter my enemies
and make them run away.
7Reach down from heaven
and set me free.
Save me from the mighty flood
8of those lying foreigners
who can't tell the truth.

9In praise of you, our God,
I will sing a new song,
while playing my harp.
10By your power, kings win wars,
and your servant David is saved
from deadly swords.
11Won't you keep me safe
from those lying foreigners
who can't tell the truth?
12Let's pray that our young sons
will grow like strong plants
and that our daughters
will be as lovely as columns
in the corner of a palace.
13May our barns be filled
with all kinds of crops.
May our fields be covered
with sheep by the thousands,
14and every cow have calves.[e]
Don't let our city be captured
or any of us be taken away,
and don't let cries of sorrow
be heard in our streets.

15Our LORD and our God,
you give these blessings
to all who worship you.*

Psalm 145

[*By David for praise.*]

The LORD Is Kind and Merciful

1I will praise you,
my God and King,
and always honor your name.
2I will praise you each day
and always honor your name.
3You are wonderful, LORD,
and you deserve all praise,
because you are much greater
than anyone can understand.

4Each generation will announce
to the next your wonderful
and powerful deeds.*

[c]*mighty rock*: The Hebrew text has "rock," which is sometimes used in poetry to compare the Lord to a mountain where his people can run for protection from their enemies. [d]*of our people*: Some Hebrew manuscripts and ancient versions have "of the nations." [e]*have calves*: Or "grow fat."

144.15 **BE FAITHFUL** The blessings David just wrote about came to his people as long as they were faithful. But the people were taken away by enemies when they forgot God. It's true that God will walk beside us and care for us as long as we walk with him and care about the things that he cares about. So friendship with God works two ways, just like any other friendship. Both friends must keep their promises. God always will. Now what about us?

145.4 **THE STORY GOES ON** We know God today because the generations before us passed along the good news of God's love. This was God's way of keeping his message alive. We owe a great debt to God. But we also owe a debt to all those generations before us who were faithful in handing down God's words of life. Let's follow their example and give the good news of salvation to our children.

NOTES

5 I will keep thinking about
your marvelous glory
and your mighty miracles.[f]
6 Everyone will talk about
your fearsome deeds,
and I will tell all nations
how great you are.
7 They will celebrate and sing
about your matchless mercy
and your power to save.

8 You are merciful, LORD!
You are kind and patient
and always loving.
9 You are good to everyone,
and you take care
of all your creation.

10 All creation will thank you,
and your loyal people
will praise you.
11 They will tell about
your marvelous kingdom
and your power.
12 Then everyone will know about
the mighty things you do
and your glorious kingdom.
13 Your kingdom will never end,
and you will rule forever.

Our LORD, you keep your word
and do everything you say.[g]
14 When someone stumbles or falls,
you give a helping hand.
15 Everyone depends on you,
and when the time is right,
you provide them with food.
16 By your own hand you satisfy
the desires of all who live.

17 Our LORD, everything you do
is kind and thoughtful,
18 and you are near to everyone
whose prayers are sincere.
19 You satisfy the desires
of all your worshipers,
and you come to save them
when they ask for help.
20 You take care of everyone
who loves you,
but you destroy the wicked.

21 I will praise you, LORD,
and everyone will respect
your holy name forever.

Psalm 146

Shout Praises to the LORD

1 Shout praises to the LORD!
With all that I am,
I will shout his praises.
2 I will sing and praise
the LORD God
for as long as I live.

3 You can't depend on anyone,
not even a great leader.*
4 Once they die and are buried,
that will be the end
of all their plans.

5 The LORD God of Jacob blesses
everyone who trusts him
and depends on him.
6 God made heaven and earth;
he created the sea
and everything else.
God always keeps his word.
7 He gives justice to the poor
and food to the hungry.

The LORD sets prisoners free
8 and heals blind eyes.
He gives a helping hand
to everyone who falls.
The LORD loves good people
9 and looks after strangers.
He defends the rights
of orphans and widows,
but destroys the wicked.

10 The LORD God of Zion
will rule forever!
Shout praises to the LORD!

---

[f] *and . . . miracles*: One Hebrew manuscript and two ancient versions have "as others tell about your mighty miracles." [g] *Our . . . say*: These words are found in one Hebrew manuscript and two ancient versions.

146.3 **PUT YOUR TRUST IN THE RIGHT PLACE** We admire great leaders, and they often deserve our praise. But remember, they're only human. They forget, they fail, and they die. But God never forgets his promises, and he never dies. He always does what he says he will do.

NOTES

Psalm 147

Sing and Praise the LORD

1Shout praises to the LORD!
Our God is kind,
and it is right and good
to sing praises to him.
2The LORD rebuilds Jerusalem
and brings the people of Israel
back home again.*
3He renews our hopes
and heals our bodies.
4He decided how many stars
there would be in the sky
and gave each one a name.
5Our LORD is great and powerful!
He understands everything.
6The LORD helps the poor,
but he smears the wicked
in the dirt.

7Celebrate and sing!
Play your harps
for the LORD our God.
8He fills the sky with clouds
and sends rain to the earth,
so that the hills
will be green with grass.
9He provides food for cattle
and for the young ravens,
when they cry out.
10The LORD does not care about
the strength of horses
or powerful armies.
11The LORD is pleased only
with those who worship him
and trust his love.

12Everyone in Jerusalem,
come and praise
the LORD your God!
13He makes your city gates strong
and blesses your people
by giving them children.
14God lets you live in peace,
and he gives you
the very best wheat.
15As soon as God speaks,
the earth obeys.
16He covers the ground with snow
like a blanket of wool,
and he scatters frost
like ashes on the ground.
17God sends down hailstones
like chips of rocks.
Who can stand the cold?
18At his command the ice melts,
the wind blows,
and streams begin to flow.

19God gave his laws and teachings
to the descendants of Jacob,
the nation of Israel.
20But he has not given his laws
to any other nation.
Shout praises to the LORD!

Psalm 148

Come Praise the LORD

1Shout praises to the LORD!
Shout the LORD's praises
in the highest heavens.
2All of you angels,
and all who serve him above,
come and offer praise.

3Sun and moon,
and all of you bright stars,
come and offer praise.*
4Highest heavens, and the water
above the highest heavens,[h]
come and offer praise.

---

[h]*the water . . . heavens*: It was believed that the earth and the heavens were surrounded by water.

147.2 **IT'S GOOD TO BE HOME** Have you ever said this after a long trip? Nearly everyone has. And how often we give thanks to God for our safe return and the return of our loved ones after a day at work or school! God has a home for us that will last forever. Jesus has gone to make our place ready. Do you sometimes think of that wonderful home that we'll never have to leave again?

148.3 **ALL NATURE PRAISES GOD** Nature isn't just an "it" or a dead thing. Nature is the living creation of God that unveils his glory everywhere. The beauty of nature is the way nature praises God. Trees and flowers, animals, birds, the song of the wind, the blue sky, the stars, the sea and all its creatures display the glory of God. Shall we who are made in God's likeness do less than these? Praise the Lord!

NOTES

5 Let all things praise
the name of the LORD,
because they were created
at his command.
6 He made them to last forever,
and nothing can change
what he has done.[l]

7-8 All creatures on earth,
you obey his commands,
so come praise the LORD!

Sea monsters and the deep sea,
fire and hail, snow and frost,
and every stormy wind,
come praise the LORD!

9 All mountains and hills,
fruit trees and cedars,
10 every wild and tame animal,
all reptiles and birds,
come praise the LORD!
11 Every king and every ruler,
all nations on earth,
12 every man and every woman,
young people and old,
come praise the LORD!

13 All creation, come praise
the name of the LORD.
Praise his name alone.
The glory of God is greater
than heaven and earth.

14 Like a bull with mighty horns,
the LORD protects
his faithful nation Israel,
because they belong to him.
Shout praises to the LORD!

Psalm 149

A New Song of Praise

1 Shout praises to the LORD!
Sing him a new song of praise
when his loyal people meet.
2 People of Israel, rejoice
because of your Creator.
People of Zion, celebrate
because of your King.
3 Praise his name by dancing
and playing music on harps
and tambourines.*
4 The LORD is pleased
with his people,
and he gives victory
to those who are humble.
5 All of you faithful people,
praise our glorious Lord!
Celebrate and worship.
6 Praise God with songs
on your lips
and a sword in your hand.
7 Take revenge and punish
the nations.
8 Put chains of iron
on their kings and rulers.
9 Punish them as they deserve;
this is the privilege
of God's faithful people.
Shout praises to the LORD!

Psalm 150

The LORD Is Good to His People

1 Shout praises to the LORD!
Praise God in his temple.
Praise him in heaven,
his mighty fortress.*
2 Praise our God!
His deeds are wonderful,
too marvelous to describe.

3 Praise God with trumpets
and all kinds of harps.

---

[l] *nothing . . . done*: Or "his laws will never change."

149.3 **PRAISE GOD WITH JOY** Sometimes we may have to grieve, but more often it is right to praise God with joy. We are not hopeless people, but we have received many rich blessings from God's hand. A long face and tears are not the right answer to the goodness of God and his kindness. Let's tune our lives to express our overflowing happiness in God's family.

150.1 **GOD IS PRAISED IN HEAVEN** There we will see clearly what was invisible here. We will see the Lord in his beauty. Then how powerfully the orchestra of heaven will play, and the (*continued*)

NOTES

4Praise him with tambourines
and dancing,
with stringed instruments
and woodwinds.
5Praise God with cymbals,
with clashing cymbals.
6Let every living creature
praise the LORD.
Shout praises to the LORD!

(continued) thunder of the great choir will be overpowering. Doesn't that scene make us want to praise God with everything we are and have? Halfhearted praise is an insult! Let our very lives be a continual song, worshiping God.

NOTES

PROVERBS

ABOUT THIS BOOK

The book of Proverbs is a collection of sayings that were used in ancient Israel to teach God's people how to live right. For the most part, these sayings go back to Solomon, but others are traced back to Agur (30.1) and King Lemuel (31.1).

Like the psalms, all the proverbs are written in poetic form. A typical proverb takes the form of a short verse in which the first half states the theme and the second half echoes it. What makes the Bible's proverbs so popular is that they make such powerful statements with very few words. This makes them easy to memorize and apply to daily life.

One of the main teachings in Proverbs is that all wisdom is a gift from God. This wisdom supplies practical advice for everyday living, in the home, in society, in politics, at school and at work. The Book of Proverbs also teaches the importance of fairness, humility, loyalty and concern for the poor and needy.

Because most proverbs are so brief, and make their point in one verse, many are often not connected to those around them. In some parts of the book, however, a common theme can be found. How not to be a fool is the theme of chapter 26.1–12, for example. In chapters 8—9, Wisdom is pictured as a woman who advises people to turn from their foolish ways and to live wisely.

A QUICK LOOK AT THIS BOOK

1. Introduction: How Proverbs Can Be Used (1.1–7)
2. Parental Advice on the Importance of Seeking Wisdom and Not Being Foolish (1.8—7.27)
3. In Praise of Wisdom (8.1–35)
4. Wisdom's Feast (9.1–18)
5. Solomon's Wise Sayings (10.1—24.34)
6. More of Solomon's Wise Sayings (25.1—29.27)
7. The Sayings of Agur (30.1–33)
8. What King Lemuel's Mother Taught Him (31.1–31)

How Proverbs Can Be Used

1 These are the proverbs
of King Solomon of Israel,
the son of David.
2 Proverbs will teach you
wisdom and self-control
and how to understand
sayings with deep meanings.
3 You will learn what is right
and honest and fair.
4 From these, an ordinary person
can learn to be smart,
and young people can gain
knowledge and good sense.

5 If you are already wise,
you will become even wiser.
And if you are smart,
you will learn to understand
6 proverbs and sayings,
as well as words of wisdom
and all kinds of riddles.
7 Respect and obey the LORD!
This is the beginning
of knowledge.[a]
Only a fool rejects wisdom
and good advice.

Warnings against Bad Friends

8 My child, obey the teachings
of your parents,
9 and wear their teachings
as you would a lovely hat
or a pretty necklace.
10 Don't be tempted by sinners
or listen 11 when they say,
"Come on! Let's gang up
and kill somebody,
just for the fun of it!
12 They're well and healthy now,
but we'll finish them off
once and for all.
13 We'll take their valuables
and fill our homes
with stolen goods.
14 If you join our gang,
you'll get your share."
15 Don't follow anyone like that
or do what they do.
16 They are in a big hurry
to commit some crime,
perhaps even murder.
17 They are like a bird
that sees the bait,
but ignores the trap.[b]
18 They gang up to murder someone,
but they are the victims.
19 The wealth you get from crime
robs you of your life.

Wisdom Speaks

20 Wisdom[c] shouts in the streets
wherever crowds gather.*
21 She shouts in the market places
and near the city gates
as she says to the people,
22 "How much longer
will you enjoy
being stupid fools?
Won't you ever stop sneering
and laughing at knowledge?
23 Listen as I correct you
and tell you what I think.
24 You completely ignored me
and refused to listen;
25 you rejected my advice
and paid no attention
when I warned you.

26-27 "So when you are struck
by some terrible disaster,
or when trouble and distress
surround you like a whirlwind,
I will laugh and make fun.
28 You will ask for my help,
but I won't listen;

[a] *the beginning of knowledge*: Or "what knowledge is all about." [b] *They are . . . trap*: Or "Be like a bird that won't go for the bait, if it sees the trap." [c] *Wisdom*: In the book of Proverbs the word "wisdom" is sometimes used when talking about a supernatural being who was with God at the time of creation.

1.20 **WISDOM IS NO SECRET** You can find it everywhere—if you're really looking. We don't become wise for living because we don't learn from what can be seen all around. What makes the ant prosperous? It works hard all day. Do we want to be prosperous in spiritual and material goods? Wisdom for daily life comes from watching, careful doing, and using our time well.

NOTES

you will search,
but you won't find me.
29No, you would not learn,
and you refused
to respect the LORD.
30You rejected my advice
and paid no attention
when I warned you.

31"Now you will eat the fruit
of what you have done,
until you are stuffed full
with your own schemes.
32Sin and self-satisfaction
bring destruction and death
to stupid fools.
33But if you listen to me,
you will be safe and secure
without fear of disaster."

Wisdom and Bad Friends

2 My child, you must follow
and treasure my teachings
and my instructions.
2Keep in tune with wisdom
and think what it means
to have common sense.
3Beg as loud as you can
for good common sense.
4Search for wisdom
as you would search for silver
or hidden treasure.
5Then you will understand
what it means to respect
and to know the LORD God.

6All wisdom comes from the LORD,
and so do common sense
and understanding.
7God gives helpful advice[d]
to everyone who obeys him
and protects all of those
who live as they should.
8God sees that justice is done,
and he watches over everyone
who is faithful to him.
9With wisdom you will learn
what is right
and honest and fair.
10Wisdom will control your mind,
and you will be pleased
with knowledge.
11Sound judgment and good sense
will watch over you.
12Wisdom will protect you
from evil schemes
and from those liars*
13who turned from doing good
to live in the darkness.
14Most of all they enjoy
being mean and deceitful.
15They are dishonest themselves,
and all they do is crooked.

Wisdom and Sexual Purity

16Wisdom will protect you
from the smooth talk
of a sinful woman,
17who breaks her wedding vows
and leaves the man she married
when she was young.
18The road to her house leads
down to the dark world
of the dead.
19Visit her, and you will never
find the road to life again.

STEP 4

20Follow the example
of good people
and live an honest life.
21If you are honest and innocent,
you will keep your land;
22if you do wrong
and can never be trusted,
you will be rooted out.

STEP 10

Trust God

3 My child, remember
my teachings and instructions
and obey them completely.
2They will help you live
a long and prosperous life.
3Let love and loyalty

[d]*helpful advice*: Or "wisdom."

2.12 **WISDOM SAVES US FROM DISHONEST PEOPLE** Have you seen in newscasts how many simple people have been tricked by shysters? It isn't enough to be innocent. We must realize the need to be careful in a world where there are many dishonest people. We're responsible to God for the goods he allows us to have, and we must not be easy targets for crooks.

NOTES

always show like a necklace,
and write them in your mind.
4God and people will like you
and consider you a success.

5With all your heart
you must trust the LORD
and not your own judgment.*
6Always let him lead you,
and he will clear the road
for you to follow.
7Don't ever think that you
are wise enough,
but respect the LORD
and stay away from evil.
8This will make you healthy,
and you will feel strong.
9Honor the LORD by giving him
your money and the first part
of all your crops.
10Then you will have
more grain and grapes
than you will ever need.

11My child, don't turn away
or become bitter
when the LORD corrects you.
12The LORD corrects
everyone he loves,
just as parents correct
their favorite child.

The Value of Wisdom

13God blesses everyone
who has wisdom
and common sense.
14Wisdom is worth more
than silver;
it makes you much richer
than gold.
15Wisdom is more valuable
than precious jewels;
nothing you want
compares with her.

16In her right hand
Wisdom holds a long life,
and in her left hand
are wealth and honor.
17Wisdom makes life pleasant
and leads us safely along.
18Wisdom is a life-giving tree,
the source of happiness
for all who hold on to her.

19By his wisdom and knowledge
the LORD created
heaven and earth.
20By his understanding
he let the ocean break loose
and clouds release the rain.
21My child, use common sense
and sound judgment!
Always keep them in mind.
22They will help you to live
a long and beautiful life.
23You will walk safely
and never stumble;
24you will rest without a worry
and sleep soundly.
25So don't be afraid
of sudden disasters
or storms that strike
those who are evil.
26You can be sure that the LORD
will protect you from harm.

27Do all you can for everyone
who deserves your help.
28Don't tell your neighbor
to come back tomorrow,
if you can help today.
29Don't try to be mean
to neighbors who trust you.
30Don't argue just to be arguing,
when you haven't been hurt.
31Don't be jealous
of cruel people
or follow their example.

32The LORD doesn't like
anyone who is dishonest,
but he lets good people
be his friends.
33He places a curse on the home
of everyone who is evil,
but he blesses the home
of every good person.

3.5 **GOD CAN BE TRUSTED COMPLETELY** We have to use good judgment every day, but our own judgment, by itself, will often fail. The only safe course is to consult God about everything we do. The more we do that, the less trouble we get into, because God knows how to steer us around the danger spots that we don't even see. Yes, that practice of "asking God first" will save us a lot of grief.

NOTES

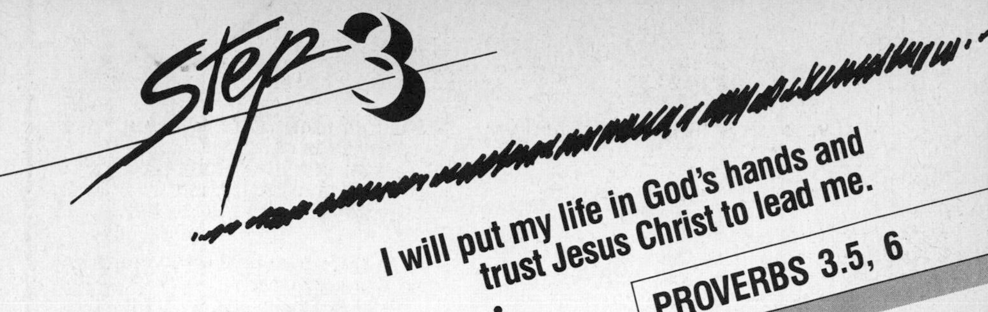

ME, MYSELF, AND I

"I don't need anyone. It's my life!"

We may not have put it in those words, but the thought is the same. For some reason we had been looking to ourselves to make it through life. Unfortunately, we quickly came to the end of ourselves. Then we began to fill the gaps with drugs, or booze, or destructive relationships to try and make things right. We quickly came to the end of those too.

AN OPEN HEART

These verses say that we weren't made to be totally responsible for our own lives. While God gave us minds to reason and understand, He also gave us hearts that would be open to his direction and guidance. Look at it this way, maybe we've tried everything we could think of. Maybe now it's time to follow our hearts.

To take a "Look Ahead," turn to page 409.

Step 7

I need God to remove my shortcomings.

PROVERBS 3.11, 12

PLAY BY THE RULES

"You knew the rules, and you broke them; now you pay the consequences. That's how it works. We have rules in this house because we love you; and whether you like it or not, you are going to have to learn to follow them."

"They make rules because they love me. That doesn't sound right. If they loved me they would trust me."

It does seem kind of strange—love versus rules. Maybe that is because we are looking at it all wrong. God's Word will help us see it differently: it says, love equals rules. Rules protect us and steer us in the right direction. They give a standard to live up to. Trust comes by showing we can keep the rules. It also comes by paying the consequences and learning from our mistakes.

BECAUSE GOD LOVES US

Asking the Lord to remove our shortcomings is a way of admitting we are ready to play by the rules. We are tired of bucking the system. We realize that God, out of his great love, has set up rules for us to live by. These rules are for our protection and benefit.

STEP 7 LOOK INSIDE

To take a "Look Ahead," turn to page 342.

34The LORD sneers at those
who sneer at him,
but he is kind to everyone
who is humble.
35You will be praised
if you are wise,
but you will be disgraced
if you are a stubborn fool.

Advice to Young People

4 My child, listen closely
to my teachings
and learn common sense.
2My advice is useful,
so don't turn away.
3When I was still very young
and my mother's favorite child,
my father 4said to me:
"If you follow my teachings
and keep them in mind,
you will live.
5Be wise and learn good sense;
remember my teachings
and do what I say.

6If you love Wisdom
and don't reject her,
she will watch over you.
7The best thing about Wisdom
is Wisdom herself;
good sense is more important
than anything else.
8If you value Wisdom
and hold tightly to her,
great honors will be yours.
9It will be like wearing
a glorious crown
of beautiful flowers.

The Right Way and the Wrong Way

10My child, if you listen
and obey my teachings,
you will live a long time.*
11I have shown you the way
that makes sense;
I have guided you
along the right path.
12Your road won't be blocked,
and you won't stumble
when you run.
13Hold firmly to my teaching
and never let go.
It will mean life for you.
14Don't follow the bad example
of cruel and evil people.
15Turn aside and keep going.
Stay away from them.
16They can't sleep or rest
until they do wrong or harm
some innocent victim.
17Their food and drink
are violence and cruelty.

18The lifestyle of good people
is like sunlight at dawn
that keeps getting brighter
until broad daylight.
19The lifestyle of the wicked
is like total darkness,
and they will never know
what makes them stumble.

20My child, listen carefully
to everything I say.
21Don't forget a single word,
but think about it all.
22Knowing these teachings
will mean true life
and good health for you.
23Carefully guard your thoughts
because they are the source
of true life.
24Never tell lies or be deceitful
in what you say.
25Keep looking straight ahead,
without turning aside.
26Know where you are headed,
and you will stay
on solid ground.
27Don't make a mistake by turning
to the right or the left.

Be Faithful to Your Wife

5 My son, if you listen closely
to my wisdom
and good sense,
2you will have sound judgment,

4.10 **WISDOM BRINGS LONG LIFE** Another way of saying this might be, "Wise people stay out of trouble." As a rule, wisdom will lead us to live in ways that are healthy and safe. Wise people don't drive their cars over the speed limit, and they don't take drugs and other things that destroy their bodies. They avoid the diseases that careless-living people get. Yes, they live longer and happier lives because they are wise.

NOTES

and you will always know
the right thing to say.
3The words of an immoral woman
may be as sweet as honey
and as smooth as olive oil.
4But all that you really get
from being with her
is bitter poison and pain.
5If you follow her,
she will lead you down
to the world of the dead.*
6She has missed the path
that leads to life
and doesn't even know it.

7My son, listen to me
and do everything I say.
8Stay away from a bad woman!
Don't even go near the door
of her house.
9You will lose your self-respect
and end up in debt
to some cruel person
for the rest of your life.
10Strangers will get your money
and everything else
you have worked for.
11When it's all over,
your body will waste away,
as you groan 12and shout,
"I hated advice and correction!
13I paid no attention
to my teachers,
14and now I am disgraced
in front of everyone."

15You should be faithful
to your wife,
just as you take water
from your own well.[e]
16And don't be like a stream
from which just any woman
may take a drink.
17Save yourself for your wife
and don't have sex
with other women.
18Be happy with the wife
you married
when you were young.
19She is beautiful and graceful,
just like a deer;
you should be attracted to her
and stay deeply in love.

20Don't go crazy over a woman
who is unfaithful
to her own husband!
21The LORD sees everything,
and he watches us closely.
22Sinners are trapped and caught
by their own evil deeds.
23They get lost and die
because of their foolishness
and lack of self-control.

Don't Be Foolish

6 My child, suppose you agree
to pay the debt of someone
who cannot repay a loan.
2Then you are trapped
by your own words,
3and you are now in the power
of someone else.
Here is what you should do:
Go and beg for permission
to call off the agreement.
4Do this before you fall asleep
or even get sleepy.
5Save yourself, just as a deer
or a bird tries to escape
from a hunter.

6You lazy people can learn
by watching an anthill.
7Ants don't have leaders,
8but they store up food
during harvest season.
9How long will you lie there
doing nothing at all?
When are you going to get up
and stop sleeping?
10Sleep a little. Doze a little.
Fold your hands
and twiddle your thumbs.

---

[e]*own well*: In biblical times water was scarce and wells were carefully guarded.

5.5 **IMMORALITY COSTS TOO MUCH** Are we free to do everything we please? Yes, if we're willing to pay the price. But we soon find out that the price of the immoral use of our bodies is too high. We pay for immoral living by becoming unable to experience true love for anyone. Disease and lonely death are the final costs. Read this chapter carefully, and take every word to heart. Here is a real signpost to lasting happiness.

NOTES

11 Suddenly, everything is gone,
as though it had been taken
by an armed robber.

12 Worthless liars go around
13 winking and giving signals
to deceive others.
14 They are always thinking up
something cruel and evil,
and they stir up trouble.
15 But they will be struck
by sudden disaster
and left without a hope.

16 There are six or seven
kinds of people
the LORD doesn't like:
17 Those who are too proud
or tell lies or murder,
18 those who make evil plans
or are quick to do wrong,
19 those who tell lies in court
or stir up trouble
in a family.

20 Obey the teaching
of your parents—
21 always keep it in mind
and never forget it.
22 Their teaching will guide you
when you walk,
protect you when you sleep,
and talk to you
when you are awake.

23 The Law of the Lord is a lamp,
and its teachings
shine brightly.
Correction and self-control
will lead you through life.*
24 They will protect you
from the flattering words
of someone else's wife.[f]
25 Don't let yourself be attracted
by the charm and lovely eyes
of someone like that.
26 A woman who sells her love
can be bought for as little
as the price of a meal.
But making love
to another man's wife
will cost you everything.
27 If you carry burning coals,
you burn your clothes;
28 if you step on hot coals,
you burn your feet.
29 And if you go to bed
with another man's wife,
you pay the price.

30 We don't put up with thieves,
not even[g] with one who steals
for something to eat.
31 And thieves who get caught
must pay back
seven times what was stolen
and lose everything.
32 But if you go to bed
with another man's wife,
you will destroy yourself
by your own stupidity.
33 You will be beaten
and forever disgraced,
34 because a jealous husband
can be furious and merciless
when he takes revenge.
35 He won't let you pay him off,
no matter what you offer.

The Foolishness of Unfaithfulness

7 My son, pay close attention
and don't forget
what I tell you to do.
2 Obey me, and you will live!
Let my instructions be
your greatest treasure.
3 Keep them at your fingertips
and write them
in your mind.
4 Let wisdom be your sister

---

[f] *someone else's wife*: Or "an evil woman."
[g] *not even*: Or "except."

6.23 **GOD'S WORD LIGHTS OUR WAY** It's very hard to walk in the dark in a strange place. We really can't tell where we're going. This world is a strange place, too, when we don't have a safe guide. Sometimes it's hard to know the right way from the wrong way. But God shows us in his Word how to live our lives, step by step. As we follow his lead we can't make a wrong move, even when we don't know for sure where our path is taking us next. The important thing is, we'll end up in God's city forever.

NOTES

and make common sense
your closest friend.*
5 They will protect you
from the flattering words
of someone else's wife.

6 From the window of my house,
I once happened to see
7 some foolish young men.
8-9 It was late in the evening,
sometime after dark.
One of these young men
turned the corner
and was walking by the house
of an unfaithful wife.
10 She was dressed fancy
like a woman of the street
with only one thing in mind.
11 She was one of those women
who are loud and restless
and never stay at home,
12 who walk street after street,
waiting to trap a man.

13 She grabbed him and kissed him,
and with no sense of shame,
she said:
14 "I had to offer a sacrifice,
and there is enough meat
left over for a feast.
15 So I came looking for you,
and here you are!
16 The sheets on my bed
are bright-colored cloth
from Egypt.
17 And I have covered it
with perfume made of myrrh,
aloes, and cinnamon.

18 "Let's go there
and make love all night.
19 My husband is traveling,
and he's far away.
20 He took a lot of money along,
and he won't be back home
before the middle
of the month."

21 And so, she tricked him
with all of her sweet talk
and her flattery.
22 Right away he followed her
like an ox on the way
to be slaughtered,
or like a fool on the way
to be punished[h]
23 and killed with arrows.
He was no more than a bird
rushing into a trap,
without knowing
it would cost him his life.

24 My son, pay close attention
to what I have said.
25 Don't even think about
that kind of woman
or let yourself be misled
by someone like her.
26 Such a woman has caused
the downfall and destruction
of a lot of men.
27 Her house is a one-way street
leading straight down
to the world of the dead.

In Praise of Wisdom

8 With great understanding,
Wisdom[i] is calling out
2 as she stands at the crossroads
and on every hill.
3 She stands by the city gate
where everyone enters the city,
and she shouts:
4 "I am calling out
to each one of you!
5 Good sense and sound judgment
can be yours.
6 Listen, because what I say
is worthwhile and right.
7 I always speak the truth
and refuse to tell a lie.
8 Every word I speak is honest,
not one is misleading
or deceptive.

9 "If you have understanding,
you will see that my words
are just what you need.

---

[h] *a fool . . . punished*: One possible meaning for the difficult Hebrew text. [i] *Wisdom*: In the book of Proverbs "wisdom" is sometimes used of a supernatural being who was with God at the time of creation.

7.4 **GOOD SENSE IS THE MAIN THING** Good sense isn't common, but it's there for those who realize its worth. So let's aim at good, straight thinking about how we live our lives. Foolish, wrong living leads to misery in the end. But the wise use of our time leads to a full life of happiness.

NOTES

TRASH THE TRASH

I never realized what was happening. At first it was just a joke with me and the guys. We'd get out the magazines, talk dirty, and pretend we knew what was going on in the pictures. But soon a stupid pastime was becoming an obsession. It was all I could think about. I couldn't wait to get home from school and look at the magazines. Of course, I had to hide them from my mom. That should have been my first clue that I was off base.

Now I understand what was going on. I was filling my mind and my heart with garbage. It was wrong to think I could handle this without getting dirty. I came across a saying, "Garbage in, garbage out." Before it leads to something else, I decided I better clean up my act and trash the trash.

KEEPING CLEAN

Wherever we are someone is usually pulling us to lower our moral standards. If it's not television and movies, it's our friends. Sex is not bad. God made it for our pleasure. But when it comes outside of marriage or starts to consume our thoughts, it is unhealthy. Let's take charge of our moral choices and "trash the trash."

To take a "Look Back" at a woman who was given the opportunity to start all over, turn to page 205.

10 Let instruction and knowledge
mean more to you than silver
or the finest gold.
11 Wisdom is worth much more
than precious jewels
or anything else you desire."

Wisdom Speaks

12 I am Wisdom[j]—Common Sense
is my closest friend;
I possess knowledge
and sound judgment.
13 If you respect the LORD,
you will hate evil.
I hate pride and conceit
and deceitful lies.
14 I am strong, and I offer
sensible advice
and sound judgment.
15 By my power kings govern,
and rulers make laws
that are fair.
16 Every honest leader rules
with help from me.

17 I love everyone who loves me,
and I will be found by all
who honestly search.
18 I can make you rich and famous,
important and successful.
19 What you receive from me
is more valuable
than even the finest gold
or the purest silver.
20 I always do what is right,
21 and I give great riches
to everyone who loves me.

22 From the beginning,
I was with the LORD.[k]
I was there before he began*
23 to create the earth.
At the very first,
the LORD gave life to[l] me.
24 When I was born,
there were no oceans
or springs of water.
25 My birth was before
mountains were formed
or hills were put in place.
26 It happened long before God
had made the earth
or any of its fields
or even the dust.

27 I was there when the LORD
put the heavens in place
and stretched the sky
over the surface of the sea.
28 I was with him when he placed
the clouds in the sky
and created the springs
that fill the ocean.
29 I was there when he set
boundaries for the sea
to make it obey him,
and when he laid foundations
to support the earth.

30 I was right beside the LORD,
helping him plan and build.[m]
I made him happy each day,
and I was happy at his side.
31 I was pleased with his world
and pleased with its people.

32 Pay attention, my children!
Follow my advice,
and you will be happy.
33 Listen carefully
to my instructions,
and you will be wise.

34 Come to my home each day
and listen to me.
You will find happiness.
35 By finding me, you find life,
and the LORD will be pleased
with you.
36 But if you don't find me,
you hurt only yourself,
and if you hate me,
you are in love with death.

---

[j] *Wisdom*: See the note at 8.1. [k] *From the beginning . . . with the LORD*: Or "In the very beginning, the LORD created me." [l] *gave life to*: Or "formed." [m] *helping . . . build*: Or "like his own child."

8.22 **WHAT IS WISDOM?** To be wise is not just the ability to say clever things. Wisdom is what makes us able to live above the blind feelings that drive us to hurt others and ourselves. By wisdom we learn to live and act in ways that build up rather than destroy. Wisdom stops at the danger signals along life's way. In the New Testament Jesus is called the Wisdom of God (see Luke 11.49). So we have wisdom when Christ lives in us.

NOTES

Wisdom Gives a Feast

9 Wisdom has built her house
with its seven columns.
2 She has prepared the meat
and set out the wine.
Her feast is ready.

3 She has sent her servant women
to announce her invitation
from the highest hills.
4 "Everyone who is ignorant
or foolish is invited!
5 All of you are welcome
to my meat and wine.
6 If you want to live,
give up your foolishness
and let understanding
guide your steps."

True Wisdom

7 Correct a worthless bragger,
and all you will get
are insults and injuries.
8 Any bragger you correct
will only hate you.
But if you correct someone
who has common sense,
you will be loved.
9 If you have good sense,
instruction will help you
to have even better sense.
And if you live right,
education will help you
to know even more.

10 Respect and obey the LORD!
This is the beginning
of wisdom.[n]
To have understanding,
you must know the Holy God.*
11 I am Wisdom. If you follow me,
you will live a long time.
12 Good sense is good for you,
but if you brag,
you hurt yourself.

A Foolish Invitation

13 Stupidity[o] is reckless,
senseless, and foolish.
14 She sits in front of her house
and on the highest hills
in the town.
15 She shouts to everyone
who passes by,
16 "If you are stupid,
come on inside!"
And to every fool she says,
17 "Stolen water tastes best,
and the food you eat in secret
tastes best of all."
18 None who listen to Stupidity
understand that her guests
are as good as dead.

Solomon's Wise Sayings

10 Here are some proverbs
of Solomon:
Children with good sense
make their parents happy,
but foolish children
make them sad.
2 What you gain by doing evil
won't help you at all,
but being good[p]
can save you from death.

3 If you obey the LORD,
you won't go hungry;
if you are wicked,
God won't let you have
what you want.
4 Laziness leads to poverty;
hard work makes you rich.
5 At harvest season
it's smart to work hard,
but stupid to sleep.

6 Everyone praises good people,
but evil hides behind
the words of the wicked.
7 Good people are remembered
long after they are gone,
but the wicked
are soon forgotten.

---

[n] *the beginning of wisdom*: Or "what wisdom is all about." [o] *Stupidity*: Or "A foolish woman." [p] *good*: Or "generous."

9.10 **HOW DOES WISDOM BEGIN?** We begin to be wise when we begin to see God as he really is. God is the Author of all that is true. In fact, God himself is Truth, and he is Wisdom in person. Wisdom and truth, then, are much more than the way we think about things. To be wise is to think as God wants us to think, so wisdom must begin with the right attitude toward God—loving and honoring him above everything else.

NOTES

8If you have good sense,
you will listen and obey;
if all you do is talk,
you will destroy yourself.
9You will be safe,
if you always do right,
but you will get caught,
if you are dishonest.
10Deceit causes trouble,
and foolish talk
will bring you to ruin.[q]
11The words of good people
are a source of life,
but evil hides behind
the words of the wicked.

12Hatred stirs up trouble;
love overlooks the wrongs
that others do.*
13If you have good sense,
it will show when you speak.
But if you are stupid,
you will be beaten
with a stick.
14If you have good sense,
you will learn all you can,
but foolish talk
will soon destroy you.

15Great wealth can be a fortress,
but poverty
is no protection at all.
16If you live right,
the reward is a good life;
if you are evil,
all you have is sin.

17Accept correction,
and you will find life;
reject correction,
and you will miss the road.
18You can hide your hatred
by telling lies,
but you are a fool
to spread lies.
19You will say the wrong thing
if you talk too much—
so be sensible and watch
what you say.
20The words of a good person
are like pure silver,
but the thoughts
of an evil person
are almost worthless.
21Many are helped
by useful instruction,
but fools are killed
by their own stupidity.

22When the LORD blesses you
with riches,
you have nothing to regret.[r]
23Fools enjoy doing wrong,
but anyone with good sense
enjoys acting wisely.
24What evil people dread most
will happen to them,
but good people will get
what they want most.
25Those crooks will disappear
when a storm strikes,
but God will keep safe
all who obey him.
26Having a lazy person on the job
is like a mouth full of vinegar
or smoke in your eyes.

27If you respect the LORD,
you will live longer;
if you keep doing wrong,
your life will be cut short.
28If you obey the Lord,
you will be happy,
but there is no future
for the wicked.
29The LORD protects everyone
who lives right,
but he destroys anyone
who does wrong.
30Good people will stand firm,
but the wicked
will lose their land.
31Honest people speak sensibly,
but deceitful liars
will be silenced.

32If you obey the Lord,

[q]*and foolish . . . ruin*: One ancient version has "but you can help people by correcting them."
[r]*When . . . regret*: Or "No matter how hard you work, your riches really come from the Lord."

10.12 **LOVE DOESN'T FIND FAULT** It's easy to go around looking for the failings of others. We may think that doing so makes us better people than those we find fault with. But fault-finding only shows how small our hearts are. Love looks for the best in others, and it benefits the one who loves as much as the one who is loved. Love makes us live at peace with those around us, and serving others becomes a great joy.

NOTES

you will always know
the right thing to say.
But no one will trust you
if you tell lies.

Watch What You Say and Do

11 The LORD hates anyone
who cheats,
but he likes everyone
who is honest.
2 Too much pride
can put you to shame.
It's wiser to be humble.
3 If you do the right thing,
honesty will be your guide.
But if you are crooked,
you will be trapped
by your own dishonesty.

4 When God is angry,
money won't help you.
Obeying God is the only way
to be saved from death.
5 If you are truly good,
you will do right;
if you are wicked,
you will be destroyed
by your own sin.
6 Honesty can keep you safe,
but if you can't be trusted,
you trap yourself.
7 When the wicked die,
their hopes die with them.
8 Trouble goes right past
the LORD's people
and strikes the wicked.

9 Dishonest people use gossip
to destroy their neighbors;
good people are protected
by their own good sense.
10 When honest people prosper
and the wicked disappear,
the whole city celebrates.
11 When God blesses his people,
their city prospers,
but deceitful liars
can destroy a city.

12 It's stupid to say bad things
about your neighbors.
If you are sensible,
you will keep quiet.*
13 A gossip tells everything,
but a true friend
will keep a secret.
14 A city without wise leaders
will end up in ruin;
a city with many wise leaders
will be kept safe.

15 It's a dangerous thing
to guarantee payment
for someone's debts.
Don't do it!
16 A gracious woman
will be respected,
but a man must work hard
to get rich.[s]
17 Kindness is rewarded—
but if you are cruel,
you hurt yourself.
18 Meanness gets you nowhere,
but goodness is rewarded.
19 Always do the right thing,
and you will live;
keep on doing wrong,
and you will die.

20 The LORD hates sneaky people,
but he likes everyone
who lives right.
21 You can be sure of this:
All crooks will be punished,
but God's people won't.
22 A beautiful woman
who acts foolishly
is like a gold ring
on the snout of a pig.
23 Good people want what is best,
but troublemakers
hope to stir up trouble.[t]

24 Sometimes you can become rich
by being generous
or poor by being greedy.
25 Generosity will be rewarded:
Give a cup of water,

---

[s] *but . . . rich*: Or "a ruthless man will only get rich."
[t] *Good people . . . trouble*: Or "Good people do what is best, but troublemakers just stir up trouble."

11.12 **USE YOUR SPEECH TO HELP OTHERS** How easy it is to speak words that make others look bad! It's a sin we easily fall into. But we can ask God to give us minds and hearts that want the best for people around us. Then our words will bless and encourage and bring peace to those we live and work among.

NOTES

and you will receive
a cup of water in return.
26 Charge too much for grain,
and you will be cursed;
sell it at a fair price,
and you will be praised.
27 Try hard to do right,
and you will win friends;
go looking for trouble,
and you will find it.
28 Trust in your wealth,
and you will be a failure,
but God's people will prosper
like healthy plants.

29 Fools who cause trouble
in the family
won't inherit a thing.
They will end up as slaves
of someone with good sense.
30 Live right, and you will eat
from the life-giving tree.
And if you act wisely,
others will follow.[u]
31 If good people are rewarded[v]
here on this earth,
all who are cruel and mean
will surely be punished.

You Can't Hide behind Evil

STEP 7

12 To accept correction is wise,
to reject it is stupid.
2 The LORD likes everyone
who lives right,
but he punishes everyone
who makes evil plans.
3 Sin cannot offer security!
But if you live right,
you will be as secure
as a tree with deep roots.
4 A helpful wife is a jewel
for her husband,
but a shameless wife
will make his bones rot.

5 Good people have kind thoughts,
but you should never trust
the advice of someone evil.
6 Bad advice is a deadly trap,
but good advice
is like a shield.
7 Once the wicked are defeated,
they are gone forever,
but no one who obeys God
will ever be thrown down.
8 Good sense is worthy of praise,
but stupidity is a curse.
9 It's better to be ordinary
and have only one servant[w]
than to think you are somebody
and starve to death.
10 Good people are kind
to their animals,
but a mean person is cruel.

11 Hard working farmers have more
than enough food;
daydreamers are nothing more
than stupid fools.*
12 An evil person tries to hide
behind evil;[x]
good people are like trees
with deep roots.
13 We trap ourselves
by telling lies,
but we stay out of trouble
by living right.
14 We are rewarded or punished
for what we say and do.
15 Fools think they know
what is best,
but a sensible person
listens to advice.

16 Losing your temper is foolish;
ignoring an insult is smart.
17 An honest person
tells the truth in court,
but a dishonest person
tells nothing but lies.

---

[u] *act . . . follow*: Hebrew; one ancient version "but violence leads to death." [v] *rewarded*: Or "punished." [w] *It's . . . servant*: Or "It is better just to have an ordinary job." [x] *An evil . . . evil*: Or "Evil people love what they get from being evil."

12.11 **THERE'S NO SUBSTITUTE FOR HARD WORK** We praise faith a lot because it is the first thing God asks us to have if he is going to be our friend. But faith can't take the place of a day's honest work in the service of God and others. In fact, a person who has real faith in God is also the person you'll find working the hardest. People of faith are happy when they are pleasing God and helping others. So their work is a happy activity, not grudging drudgery.

NOTES

18 Sharp words cut like a sword,
but words of wisdom heal.
19 Truth will last forever;
lies are soon found out.
20 An evil mind is deceitful,
but gentle thoughts
bring happiness.
21 Good people never have trouble,
but troublemakers
have more than enough.
22 The LORD hates every liar,
but he is the friend of all
who can be trusted.
23 Be sensible and don't tell
everything you know—
only fools spread
foolishness everywhere.

24 Work hard, and you
will be a leader;
be lazy, and you
will end up a slave.
25 Worry is a heavy burden,
but a kind word
always brings cheer.
26 You are better off to do right,
than to lose your way
by doing wrong.[y]
27 Anyone too lazy to cook
will starve,
but a hard worker
is a valuable treasure.[z]
28 Follow the road to life,
and you won't be bothered
by death.

Wise Friends Make You Wise

13 Children with good sense
accept correction
from their parents,
but stubborn children
ignore it completely.
2 You will be well rewarded
for saying something kind,
but all some people think about
is how to be cruel and mean.
3 Keep what you know to yourself,
and you will be safe;
talk too much,
and you are done for.
4 No matter how much you want,
laziness won't help a bit,
but hard work will reward you
with more than enough.
5 A good person hates deceit,
but those who are evil
cause shame and disgrace.
6 Live right, and you are safe!
But sin will destroy you.
7 Some who have nothing
may pretend to be rich,
and some who have everything
may pretend to be poor.
8 The rich may have
to pay a ransom,
but the poor don't have
that problem.
9 The lamp of a good person
keeps on shining;
the lamp of an evil person
soon goes out.
10 Too much pride causes trouble.
Be sensible and take advice.

11 Money wrongly gotten
will disappear bit by bit;
money earned little by little
will grow and grow.
12 Not getting what you want
can make you feel sick,
but a wish that comes true
is a life-giving tree.
13 If you reject God's teaching,
you will pay the price;
if you obey his commands,
you will be rewarded.

14 Sensible instruction
is a life-giving fountain
that helps you escape
all deadly traps.
15 Sound judgment is praised,
but people without good sense
are on the way to disaster.[a]
16 If you have good sense,
you will act sensibly,
but fools act like fools.
17 Whoever delivers your message
can make things better
or worse for you.

18 All who refuse correction
will be poor and disgraced;
all who accept correction
will be praised.
19 It's a good feeling
to get what you want,
but only a stupid fool
hates to turn from evil.
20 Wise friends make you wise,
but you hurt yourself

---

[y] *wrong*: One possible meaning for the difficult Hebrew text of verse 26. [z] *but . . . treasure*: One possible meaning for the difficult Hebrew text. [a] *people . . . disaster*: One possible meaning for the difficult Hebrew text.

Step 9

I will make things right with people I wrong, except when to do so would hurt them or others.

PROVERBS 12.18–20

SPRING BREAK

Spring Break—the students' way to recover! You drop what you are doing, throw a few clothes in a bag, and head for the sunshine. Once you lie down on the sandy beach and the sun begins to warm you, you slowly feel the layers of winter disappear. With the sea breeze gently blowing and the cloudless sky above, you know things are going to be all right. In a matter of a few minutes, you can feel a deep sigh of relief well up inside—what a great way to spend a week!

Forgiveness is a lot like spring break. When we make things right with the people we have wronged, we take off layers of hatred, anger, and resentment. Honesty replaces lies. Gentleness replaces anger. There is new hope in our lives, and we know things are going to be all right.

STEP LOOK INSIDE 9

GETTING A LIFE

We need to determine not to spend another day, another week, walking around with guilt and bad feelings. That is no way to spend life! We need to make things right with those who have been wronged! Starting with the little things, we can work our way up to any major ones.

To take a "Look Ahead," turn to page 129.

by going around with fools.*
21 You are in for trouble
if you sin,
but you will be rewarded
if you live right.
22 If you obey God,
you will have something
to leave your grandchildren.
If you don't obey God,
those who live right
will get what you leave.

23 Even when the land of the poor
produces good crops,
they get cheated
out of what they grow.[b]
24 If you love your children,
you will correct them;
if you don't love them,
you won't correct them.
25 If you live right,
you will have plenty to eat;
if you don't live right,
you will go away empty.

Wisdom Makes Good Sense

14 A woman's family
is held together
by her wisdom,
but it can be destroyed
by her foolishness.
2 By living right, you show
that you respect the LORD;
by being deceitful, you show
that you despise him.
3 Proud fools are punished
for their stupid talk,
but sensible talk
can save your life.
4 Without the help of an ox
there can be no crop,
but with a strong ox
a big crop is possible.
5 An honest witness
tells the truth;
a dishonest witness
tells nothing but lies.

6 Make fun of wisdom,
and you will never find it.
But if you have understanding,
knowledge comes easily.
7 Stay away from fools,
or you won't learn a thing.
8 Wise people have enough sense
to find their way,
but stupid fools get lost.
9 Fools don't care
if they are wrong,[c]
but God is pleased
when people do right.

10 No one else can really know
how sad or happy you are.
11 The tent of a good person
stands longer than the house
of someone evil.
12 You may think you are
on the right road
and still end up dead.
13 Sorrow may hide
behind laughter,
and happiness may end
in sorrow.
14 You harvest what you plant,
whether good or bad.*

---

[b] *grow*: One possible meaning for the difficult Hebrew text of verse 23. [c] *Fools . . . wrong*: One possible meaning for the difficult Hebrew text.

13.20 **WHO ARE YOUR FRIENDS?** We need friends, and we ought to be friends to others. Friends help us through the hard places of life, and if they're wise they'll straighten us out when we're wrong. But unwise and false friends lead us down the wrong paths. Let's make friends of people who have proved they can solve the problems of living in the world. Their wisdom will rub off on us and will help to make us stronger so that we can be better friends to them and to others.

14.14 **OUR DEEDS CATCH UP TO US** Perhaps you've heard the bitter saying: "What goes around comes around!" That's another way of saying what this verse says. If we're planting deeds of kindness everywhere we go, good things will come back to us. Sad to say, it works the other way, too. If we continually bring unhappiness to those around us, we will find out that our cruelty has not been forgotten. One day the whole load of unkindness will fall back on us.

NOTES

15 Don't be stupid
and believe all you hear;
be smart and know
where you are headed.
16 Only a stupid fool
is never cautious—
so be extra careful
and stay out of trouble.
17 Fools have quick tempers,
and no one likes you
if you can't be trusted.
18 Stupidity leads to foolishness;
be smart and learn.

19 The wicked will come crawling
to those who obey God.
20 You have no friends
if you are poor,
but you have lots of friends
if you are rich.
21 It's wrong to hate others,
but God blesses everyone
who is kind to the poor.
22 It's a mistake
to make evil plans,
but you will have loyal friends
if you want to do right.
23 Hard work is worthwhile,
but empty talk
will make you poor.
24 Wisdom can make you rich,
but foolishness leads
to more foolishness.
25 An honest witness
can save your life,
but liars can't be trusted.

26 If you respect the LORD,
you and your children
have a strong fortress
27 and a life-giving fountain
that keeps you safe
from deadly traps.

28 Rulers of powerful nations
are held in honor;
rulers of weak nations
are nothing at all.
29 It's smart to be patient,
but it's stupid
to lose your temper.
30 It's healthy to be content,
but envy can eat you up.
31 If you mistreat the poor,
you insult your Creator;
if you are kind to them,
you show him respect.
32 In times of trouble
the wicked are destroyed,
but even at death
the innocent have faith.[d]

33 Wisdom is found in the minds
of people with good sense,
but fools don't know it.[e]
34 Doing right brings honor
to a nation,
but sin brings disgrace.
35 Kings reward servants
who act wisely,
but they punish those
who act foolishly.

The LORD Sees Everything

15 A kind answer
soothes angry feelings,
but harsh words
stir them up.*
2 Words of wisdom
come from the wise,
but fools speak foolishness.

3 The LORD sees everything,
whether good or bad.
4 Kind words are good medicine,
but deceitful words
can really hurt.
5 Don't be a fool

[d] *but even . . . faith*: One meaning for the difficult Hebrew text. Some ancient versions have "but good people trust their innocence." [e] *but . . . it*: One possible meaning for the difficult Hebrew text. Some ancient versions have "but not in the mind of a fool."

15.1 **WORDS ARE POWERFUL** Talking is easy, and too often we aren't careful about what we say. Nations have been built and destroyed by words. Lives can be made richer or they can be ruined by the words spoken to them. Having happy relationships with those around us depends very much on what we say and how we say it. We need to learn to think before we speak, rather than to speak before we think.

NOTES

Step 10

I need to continue looking inside—admitting when I am wrong.

PROVERBS 15.18–21

SILENCE IS GOLDEN

"I can't stand it when you just stand there and don't say anything!"

"What do you want me to say?"

"I want you to say you hate me."

"Why do you want me to say that?"

"Because I hate me."

So many times unspoken words can bring out the truth more than all the badgering and yelling ever could. Silence has a way of breaking down walls that go up at the first sound of anger. Do we lose our tempers? Do we rant and rave and end up regretting half of the things we've said? Senseless words are a good way to destroy our image with other people as well as with ourselves.

TAKE IT BACK

Do we need to take back some words today? Something we said to someone you really care about? Progress usually can be made, but remember—three steps forward, two steps back. We need to do the right thing and keep looking our actions from God's point of view.

STEP LOOK INSIDE 10

For another "Look Inside," turn to page 719.

and disobey your parents.
Be smart! Accept correction.
6 Good people become wealthy,
but those who are evil
will lose what they have.
7 Words of wisdom
make good sense;
the thoughts of a fool
make no sense at all.

8 The LORD is disgusted
by gifts from the wicked,
but it makes him happy
when his people pray.
9 The LORD is disgusted
with all who do wrong,
but he loves everyone
who does right.
10 If you turn from the right way,
you will be punished;
if you refuse correction,
you will die.

11 If the LORD can see everything
in the world of the dead,
he can see in our hearts.
12 Those who sneer at others
don't like to be corrected,
and they won't ask help
from someone with sense.
13 Happiness makes you smile;
sorrow can crush you.
14 Anyone with good sense
is eager to learn more,
but fools are hungry
for foolishness.

15 The poor have a hard life,
but being content is as good
as an endless feast.
16 It's better to obey the LORD
and have only a little,
than to be very rich
and terribly confused.
17 A simple meal with love
is better than a feast
where there is hatred.

18 Losing your temper
causes a lot of trouble,
but staying calm
settles arguments.
19 Being lazy is like walking
in a thorn patch,
but everyone who does right
walks on a smooth road.
20 Children with good sense
make their parents happy,
but foolish children
are hateful to them.
21 Stupidity brings happiness
to senseless fools,
but everyone with good sense
follows the straight path.

22 Without good advice
everything goes wrong—
it takes careful planning
for things to go right.
23 Giving the right answer
at the right time
makes everyone happy.
24 All who are wise follow a road
that leads upward to life
and away from death.

25 The LORD destroys the homes
of those who are proud,
but he protects the property
of widows.
26 The LORD hates evil thoughts,
but kind words please him.
27 Being greedy causes trouble
for your family,
but you protect yourself
by refusing bribes.
28 Good people think
before they answer,
but the wicked speak evil
without ever thinking.

29 The LORD never even hears
the prayers of the wicked,
but he answers the prayers
of all who obey him.
30 A friendly smile
makes you happy,
and good news
makes you feel strong.
31 Healthy correction is good,
and if you accept it,
you will be wise.

32 You hurt only yourself
by rejecting instruction,
but it makes good sense
to accept it.
33 Showing respect to the LORD
will make you wise,
and being humble
will bring honor to you.

The LORD Has the Final Word

16 We humans make plans,
but the LORD
has the final word.
2 We may think we know
what is right,
but the LORD is the judge
of our motives.

Step 4

I will take a hard look at myself, the way I live and my moral standards.

PROVERBS 15.31–33

FOURTH QUARTER FOUL-UP

First down: The coach sends in the play to run the ball. The quarterback calls an audible for a pass pattern. The play is broken up.

Second down: The coach sends in the play to run the ball. Once again the quarterback calls an audible for a pass pattern. The ball is intercepted and taken in for a touchdown.

Final Score: 20–14.

It certainly wasn't the intention of this high school quarterback to lose the game, but that is exactly what he did. He thought he knew what was right. The first time, in his inexperience, he didn't realize that the opposing team expected the pass and had dropped back in position to cover it. That left the middle wide open for a run—it was the coach's call.

STEP LOOK INSIDE 4

A MATTER OF TRUST

We all make mistakes, even with the best intentions. But it is when we continue to make the same mistakes over and over that we can expect to lose. That is why at times we have to stop and take a hard look at our lives—where we are headed. Are things happening downfield that we aren't paying attention to? Are we getting ready to make the same mistake twice? Let's try sharing our plans with the Lord. Just like in the football game, we can trust that our coach really does know what is best.

To take a "Look Ahead," turn to page 337.

3 Share your plans with the LORD,
and you will succeed.

4 The LORD has a reason
for everything he does,
and he lets evil people live
only to be punished.
5 The LORD doesn't like
anyone who is conceited—
you can be sure
they will be punished.
6 If we truly love God,
our sins will be forgiven;
if we show him respect,
we will keep away from sin.
STEP 9
7 When we please the LORD,
even our enemies
make friends with us.
8 It's better to be honest
and poor
than to be dishonest
and rich.

STEP 3
9 We make our own plans,
but the LORD decides
where we will go.*
10 Rulers speak with authority
and are never wrong.
11 The LORD doesn't like it
when we cheat in business.
12 Justice makes rulers powerful.
They should hate evil
13 and like honesty and truth.
14 An angry ruler
can put you to death.
So be wise!
Don't make one angry.
15 When a ruler is happy
and pleased with you,
it's like refreshing rain,
and you will live.

16 It's much better to be wise
and sensible
than to be rich.
17 God's people avoid evil ways,
and they protect themselves
by watching where they go.
18 Too much pride
will destroy you.
19 You are better off
to be humble and poor
than to get rich
from what you take by force.
20 If you know what you're doing,[f]
you will prosper.
God blesses everyone
who trusts him.
21 Good judgment proves
that you are wise,
and if you speak kindly,
you can teach others.
22 Good sense is a fountain
that gives life,
but fools are punished
by their foolishness.
23 You can persuade others
if you are wise
and speak sensibly.

24 Kind words are like honey—
they cheer you up
and make you feel strong.
25 Sometimes what seems right
is really a road to death.
26 The hungrier you are,
the harder you work.
27 Worthless people plan trouble.
Even their words burn
like a flaming fire.
28 Gossip is no good!
It causes hard feelings
and comes between friends.

29 Don't trust violent people.
They will mislead you
to do the wrong thing.
30 When someone winks
or grins behind your back,
trouble is on the way.
31 Gray hair is a glorious crown
worn by those
who have lived right.
32 Controlling your temper
is better than being a hero
who captures a city.

---

[f] *know what . . . doing*: Or "do what you're taught."

16.9

GOD KNOWS THE BEST WAY It's comforting to know we can put our plans in the hands of God. Then we know that all will be well. Where we're wrong, God will change our plans and lead us in the right way after all. Then we'll be glad and say, "God had a better idea." Let's make a constant habit of asking God about everything we plan. How much happier our lives will be as he smooths the path before us!

NOTES

Step 8

I will make a list of those I wrong and be willing to make things right.

PROVERBS 17.9, 10

LET GO

"I really like her, but she is smothering me. If I don't call as soon as I get home from dropping her off, she thinks I've stopped at another girl's house. If she ever starts crying, I always have to reassure her that there isn't anyone else. I'm not sure how long I can live with this."

"Why can't I trust him? I know he's not seeing anybody else. How could he? I make sure I'm with him all the time. But still, I've caught him talking to Beth more than once. And she is so pretty. I've got to do something to keep him. Maybe if he thought I would kill myself . . ."

Perhaps we need people because they fill the empty places in our lives. We want security, but we hold on too hard. Insecurity and distrust are usually caused by an unhealthy relationship in our past. So much of who we are, how we think, and what we do is related to how others have treated us. If we don't have an example of trust and love in our lives, it is very hard to be secure with others. Healing has to take place in our emotional and spiritual world.

STEP LOOK INSIDE 8

IT IS NEVER EASY

It is critical that we forgive those in our past who have hurt us and then that we apologize for the way we have let this past pattern smother people in our present. Asking forgiveness is never easy to do, but if we are willing, God will make a way for us to try.

To take a "Look Ahead," turn to page 13.

33 We make our own decisions,
but the LORD alone
determines what happens.

Our Thoughts Are Tested by the LORD

17 A dry crust of bread eaten
in peace and quiet
is better than a feast eaten
where everyone argues.*
2 A hard-working slave
will be placed in charge
of a no-good child,
and that slave will be given
the same inheritance
that each child receives.
3 Silver and gold are tested
by flames of fire;
our thoughts are tested
by the LORD.
4 Troublemakers listen
to troublemakers,
and liars listen to liars.
5 By insulting the poor,
you insult your Creator.
You will be punished
if you make fun
of someone in trouble.
6 Grandparents are proud
of their grandchildren,
and children should be proud
of their parents.

7 It sounds strange for a fool
to talk sensibly,
but it's even worse
for a ruler to tell lies.
8 A bribe works miracles
like a magic charm
that brings good luck.

9 You will keep your friends
if you forgive them,
but you will lose your friends
if you keep talking about
what they did wrong.
10 A sensible person
accepts correction,
but you can't beat sense
into a fool.

11 Cruel people want to rebel,
and so vicious attackers
will be sent against them.
12 A bear robbed of her cubs
is far less dangerous
than a stubborn fool.
13 You will always have trouble
if you are mean to those
who are good to you.
14 The start of an argument
is like a water leak—
so stop it before
real trouble breaks out.
15 The LORD doesn't like those
who defend the guilty
or condemn the innocent.
16 Why should fools have money
for an education
when they refuse to learn?

17 A friend is always a friend,
and relatives are born
to share our troubles.

18 It's stupid to guarantee
someone else's loan.
19 The wicked and the proud
love trouble and keep begging
to be hurt.
20 Dishonesty does you no good,
and telling lies
will get you in trouble.
21 It's never pleasant
to be the parent of a fool
and have nothing but pain.
22 If you are cheerful,
you feel good;
if you are sad,
you hurt all over.

23 Crooks accept secret bribes
to keep justice
from being done.
24 Anyone with wisdom knows
what makes good sense,
but fools can never
make up their minds.
25 Foolish children bring sorrow
to their father
and pain to their mother.

17.1 **MONEY ISN'T EVERYTHING** Rich people generally are no happier than people who have little. Even wealth brings its own problems—How much will our money be taxed? Is there anyone we can trust to manage our money? Being wealthy is great if we can also have peace of mind. But having peace of mind is more important than having money.

NOTES

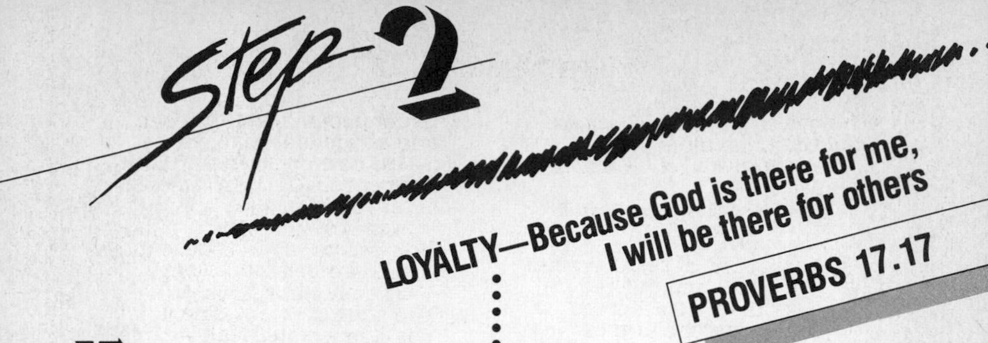

THROUGH TOUGH TIMES

In the December 31, 1989 *Chicago Tribune*, the editors printed their choices for photos of the decade. One of them, by Michael Fryer, captured a grim-faced fireman and paramedic carrying a victim away from the scene.

The fire had at first seemed routine. But then the firefighters discovered the bodies of a mother and five children huddled in the kitchen of an apartment.

Fryer said the firefighters had determined, "She could have escaped with two or three of her children but couldn't decide who to pick. She chose to wait with all of them for the firefighters to arrive. All of them died of smoke inhalation."

There are times when you just don't leave the ones you love. In the tough times, you hang in there. When the tide goes out, you stay with the boat. When your plane is headed down, you don't parachute to safety and let the crew take it alone. Who knows, the firefighters may get there in time *next* time. And if they don't?

Proverbs 17.17 says, "A friend is always a friend, and relatives are born to share our troubles."

To take a "Look Back" at a man who listened to, was led by, and had lasting loyalty to God, turn to page 254.

26 It isn't fair
to punish the innocent
and those who do right.
27 It makes a lot of sense
to be a person of few words
and to stay calm.
28 Even fools seem smart
when they are quiet.

It's Wrong to Favor the Guilty

18 It's selfish and stupid
to think only of yourself
and to sneer at people
who have sense.[g]
2 Fools have no desire to learn;
they would much rather
give their own opinion.
3 Wrongdoing leads to shame
and disgrace.
4 Words of wisdom
are a stream that flows
from a deep fountain.
5 It's wrong to favor the guilty
and keep the innocent
from getting justice.

6 Foolish talk will get you
into a lot of trouble.
7 Saying foolish things
is like setting a trap
to destroy yourself.
8 There's nothing so delicious
as the taste of gossip!
It melts in your mouth.
9 Being lazy is no different
from being a troublemaker.

10 The LORD is a mighty tower
where his people can run
for safety—
11 the rich think their money
is a wall of protection.

12 Pride leads to destruction;
humility leads to honor.
13 It's stupid and embarrassing
to give an answer
before you listen.
14 Being cheerful helps
when we are sick,
but nothing helps
when we give up.
15 Everyone with good sense
wants to learn.*
16 A gift will get you in
to see anyone.
17 You may think you have won
your case in court,
until your opponent speaks.
18 Drawing straws is one way
to settle a difficult case.
19 Making up with a friend
you have offended[h]
is harder than breaking
through a city wall.

20 Make your words good—
you will be glad you did.
21 Words can bring death or life!
Talk too much, and you will eat
everything you say.
22 A man's greatest treasure
is his wife—
she is a gift from the LORD.
23 The poor must beg for help,
but the rich can give
a harsh reply.
24 Some friends don't help,[i]
but a true friend is closer
than your own family.

It's Wise To Be Patient

19 It's better to be poor
and live right
than to be a stupid liar.

[g]*sense*: One possible meaning for the difficult Hebrew text of verse 1. [h]*Making . . . offended*: One possible meaning for the difficult Hebrew text. [i]*Some . . . help*: One possible meaning for the difficult Hebrew text.

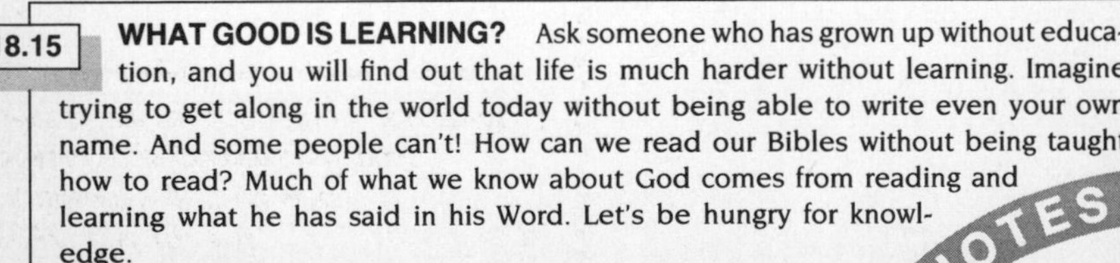

18.15 **WHAT GOOD IS LEARNING?** Ask someone who has grown up without education, and you will find out that life is much harder without learning. Imagine trying to get along in the world today without being able to write even your own name. And some people can't! How can we read our Bibles without being taught how to read? Much of what we know about God comes from reading and learning what he has said in his Word. Let's be hungry for knowledge.

NOTES

Step 1

HONESTY—Admitting the truth about myself to myself

PROVERBS 18.12

HARD OF HEARING

I admit it. The hardest person to talk to is me. I'm the one who has the attitude in this house. I have accused my parents of being impossible. You know those lines, "You don't listen to my side. You only hear what you want to hear." But if the truth were known, I didn't want to listen or admit the truth about me. After all, who wants to take an honest look at themselves? It's not an easy thing to do. In fact, admitting the truth about myself to myself was the hardest thing I have ever had to do. I'm talking about a real no "if's" or "but's"—just the "what is" kind of session. One where I didn't blame anyone else. Even though it was hard and I didn't like what I saw inside me, I'm glad I did it.

STEP 1 LOOK AHEAD

WORTH THE EFFORT

Now that the truth is out, I am starting to deal with it. There are times that I beat up on myself, but I'm learning that everyone has a long way to go, nobody does it perfectly, and I can hang in there because God knows I'm trying.

To take a "Look Back" at an honest man who admitted he didn't have all of the answers, turn to page 236.

2 Willingness and stupidity
don't go well together.
If you are too eager,
you will miss the road.
3 We are ruined
by our own stupidity,
though we blame the LORD.

4 The rich have many friends;
the poor have none.
5 Dishonest witnesses and liars
won't escape punishment.
6 Everyone tries to be friends
of those who can help them.
7 If you are poor,
your own relatives reject you,
and your friends are worse.
When you really need them,
they are not there.[j]

8 Do yourself a favor
by having good sense—
you will be glad you did.
9 Dishonest witnesses and liars
will be destroyed.
10 It isn't right for a fool
to live in luxury
or for a slave to rule
in place of a king.
11 It's wise to be patient
and show what you are like
by forgiving others.
12 An angry king roars
like a lion,
but when a king is pleased,
it's like dew on the crops.

13 A foolish son brings disgrace
to his father.
A nagging wife goes on and on
like the drip, drip, drip
of the rain.
14 You may inherit all you own
from your parents,
but a sensible wife
is a gift from the LORD.
15 If you are lazy
and sleep your time away,
you will starve.

16 Obey the Lord's teachings
and you will live—
disobey and you will die.
17 Caring for the poor
is lending to the LORD,
and you will be well repaid.

18 Correct your children
before it's too late;
if you don't punish them,
you are destroying them.
19 People with bad tempers
are always in trouble,
and they need help
over and over again.[k]*
20 Pay attention to advice
and accept correction,
so you can live sensibly.

21 We may make a lot of plans,
but the LORD will do
what he has decided.

22 What matters most is loyalty.
It's better to be poor
than to be a liar.

23 Showing respect to the LORD
brings true life—
if you do it, you can relax
without fear of danger.

24 Some people are too lazy
to lift a hand
to feed themselves.
25 Stupid fools learn good sense
by seeing others punished;
a sensible person learns
by being corrected.
26 Children who bring disgrace
rob their father
and chase their mother away.

---

[j] *When . . . there*: One possible meaning for the difficult Hebrew text. [k] *and they . . . again*: One possible meaning for the difficult Hebrew text.

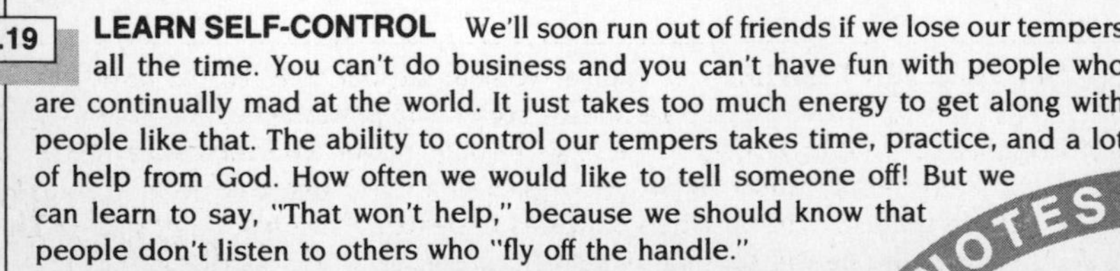

19.19 **LEARN SELF-CONTROL** We'll soon run out of friends if we lose our tempers all the time. You can't do business and you can't have fun with people who are continually mad at the world. It just takes too much energy to get along with people like that. The ability to control our tempers takes time, practice, and a lot of help from God. How often we would like to tell someone off! But we can learn to say, "That won't help," because we should know that people don't listen to others who "fly off the handle."

27If you stop learning,
you will forget
what you already know.
28A lying witness makes fun
of the court system,
and criminals think crime
is really delicious.
29Every stupid fool
is just waiting
to be punished.

Words of Wisdom Are Better than Gold

20 It isn't smart to get drunk!
Drinking makes a fool of you
and leads to fights.
2An angry ruler
is like a roaring lion—
make either one angry,
and you are dead.
3It makes you look good
when you avoid a fight—
only fools love to quarrel.
4If you are too lazy to plow,
don't expect a harvest.
5Someone's thoughts may be
as deep as the ocean,
but if you are smart,
you will discover them.

6There are many who say,
"You can trust me!"
But can they be trusted?
7Good people live right,
and God blesses the children
who follow their example.
8When rulers decide cases,
they weigh the evidence.
9Can any of us really say,
"My thoughts are pure,
and my sins are gone"?

10Two things the LORD hates
are dishonest scales
and dishonest measures.
11The good or bad
that children do
shows what they are like.
12Hearing and seeing
are gifts from the LORD.
13If you sleep all the time,
you will starve;
if you get up and work,
you will have enough food.
14Everyone likes to brag
about getting a bargain.
15Sensible words are better
than gold or jewels.

16You deserve to lose your coat
if you loan it to someone
to guarantee payment
for the debt of a stranger.
17The food you get by cheating
may taste delicious,
but it turns to gravel.
18Be sure you have sound advice
before making plans
or starting a war.
19Stay away from gossips—
they tell everything.
20Children who curse their parents
will go to the land of darkness
long before their time.

21Getting rich quick[l]
may turn out to be a curse.
22Don't try to get even.
Trust the LORD,
and he will help you.*

23The LORD hates dishonest scales
and dishonest weights.
So don't cheat!
24How can we know
what will happen to us
when the LORD alone decides?
25Don't fall into the trap
of making promises to God
before you think!
26A wise ruler severely punishes
every criminal.
27Our inner thoughts are a lamp
from the LORD,
and they search our hearts.

[l]*quick*: Or "the wrong way."

20.22 **REVENGE ISN'T SWEET** Of course, we hear the opposite all the time. But it just isn't so. When we pay back somebody's wrong against us, we feel ugly inside ourselves. That makes sense because we only prove to ourselves that we're no better than the one who hurt us. Here again is a place where we can safely put the whole matter in God's hands. God settles all scores, and we can be sure he will do what is right for everyone.

NOTES

28 Rulers are protected
by God's mercy and loyalty,
but[m] they must be merciful
for their kingdoms to last.
29 Young people take pride
in their strength,
but the gray hairs of wisdom
are even more beautiful.
30 A severe beating can knock all
of the evil out of you!

The LORD Is in Charge

21 The LORD controls rulers,
just as he determines
the course of rivers.*
2 We may think we are doing
the right thing,
but the LORD always knows
what is in our hearts.
3 Doing what is right and fair
pleases the LORD
more than an offering.
4 Evil people are proud
and arrogant,
but sin is the only crop
they produce.[n]
5 If you plan and work hard,
you will have plenty;
if you get in a hurry,
you will end up poor.

6 Cheating to get rich
is a foolish dream
and no less than suicide.[o]
7 You destroy yourself
by being cruel and violent
and refusing to live right.
8 All crooks are liars,
but anyone who is innocent
will do right.
9 It's better to stay outside
on the roof of your house
than to live inside
with a nagging wife.
10 Evil people want to do wrong,
even to their friends.
11 An ignorant fool learns
by seeing others punished;
a sensible person learns
by being instructed.

12 God is always fair!
He knows what the wicked do
and will punish them.
13 If you won't help the poor,
don't expect to be heard
when you cry out for help.
14 A secret bribe will save you
from someone's fierce anger.
15 When justice is done,
good citizens are glad
and crooks are terrified.
16 If you stop using good sense,
you will find yourself
in the grave.
17 Heavy drinkers and others
who live only for pleasure
will lose all they have.

18 God's people will escape,
but all who are wicked
will pay the price.
19 It's better out in the desert
than at home with a nagging,
complaining wife.
20 Be sensible and store up
precious treasures—
don't waste them
like a fool.
21 If you try to be kind and good,
you will be blessed with life
and goodness and honor.
22 One wise person can defeat
a city full of soldiers
and capture their fortress.

23 Watching what you say
can save you
a lot of trouble.
24 If you are proud and conceited,
everyone will say,
"You're a snob!"

---

[m] *by God's mercy . . . but*: Or "by their mercy . . . and." [n] *but sin . . . produce*: Or "but sin is the only light they ever follow." [o] *and . . . suicide*: One possible meaning for the difficult Hebrew text.

21.1 **GOD RUNS THE GOVERNMENT** Does this surprise you? We usually think we ourselves control our governments. And it does seem as though we spend a lot of money and effort to elect people that we expect to do the things we want done. Yet, even governments, with all their pretended power, are really God's instruments to bring about his grand purposes in history.

NOTES

25-26If you want too much
and are too lazy to work,
it could be fatal.
But people who obey God
are always generous.

27The Lord despises the offerings
of wicked people
with evil motives.
28If you tell lies in court,
you are done for;
only a reliable witness
can do the job.
29Wicked people bluff their way,
but God's people think
before they take a step.

30No matter how much you know
or what plans you make,
you can't defeat the LORD.
31Even if your army has horses
ready for battle,
the LORD will always win.

The Value of a Good Reputation

22 A good reputation and respect
are worth much more
than silver and gold.
2The rich and the poor
are all created
by the LORD.
3When you see trouble coming,
don't be stupid
and walk right into it—
be smart and hide.

4Respect and serve the LORD!
Your reward will be wealth,
a long life, and honor.
5Crooks walk down a road
full of thorny traps.
Stay away from there!
6Teach your children
right from wrong,
and when they are grown
they will still do right.*
7The poor are ruled by the rich,
and those who borrow
are slaves of moneylenders.
8Troublemakers get in trouble,
and their terrible anger
will get them nowhere.

9The LORD blesses everyone
who freely gives food
to the poor.
10Arguments and fights
will come to an end,
if you chase away those
who insult others.
11The king is the friend of all
who are sincere
and speak with kindness.

12The LORD watches over everyone
who shows good sense,
but he frustrates the plans
of deceitful liars.
13Don't be so lazy that you say,
"If I go to work,
a lion will eat me!"
14The words of a bad woman
are like a deep pit;
if you make the LORD angry,
you will fall right in.
15All children are foolish,
but firm correction
will make them change.
16Cheat the poor to make profit
or give gifts to the rich—
either way you lose.

Thirty Wise Sayings

17Here are some sayings
of people with wisdom,
so listen carefully
as I teach.
18You will be glad
that you know these sayings
and can recite them.
19I am teaching them today,
so that you
may trust the LORD.
20I have written thirty sayings
filled with sound advice.
21You can trust them completely

22.6 **GOOD TRAINING IS IMPORTANT** It's amazing how many young people do grow up to be fine and good people without much home training. But it's mainly true that there is little hope for most people who don't learn God's plan for living when they're young. A tree usually grows up the way it was bent when it was just a young shoot in the ground. People also usually grow up with the teaching they saw and heard in their childhood.

NOTES

to give you the right words
for those in charge of you.

– 1 –

22 Don't take advantage
of the poor
or cheat them in court.
23 The LORD is their defender,
and what you do to them,
he will do to you.

– 2 –

24 Don't make friends with anyone
who has a bad temper.
25 You might turn out like them
and get caught in a trap.

– 3 –

26 Don't guarantee to pay
someone else's debt.
27 If you don't have the money,
you might lose your bed.

– 4 –

28 Don't move a boundary marker [p]
set up by your ancestors.

– 5 –

29 If you do your job well,
you will work for a ruler
and never be a slave.

– 6 –

23 When you are invited
to eat with a king,
use your best manners.
2 Don't go and stuff yourself!
That would be just the same
as cutting your throat.
3 Don't be greedy for all
of that fancy food!
It may not be so tasty.

– 7 –

4 Give up trying so hard
to get rich.
5 Your money flies away
before you know it,
just like an eagle
suddenly taking off.*

– 8 –

6 Don't accept an invitation
to eat a selfish person's food,
no matter how good it is.
7 People like that take note
of how much you eat.[q]
They say, "Take all you want!"
But they don't mean it.
8 Each bite will come back up,
and all your kind words
will be wasted.

– 9 –

9 Don't talk to fools—
they will just make fun.

– 10 –

10 Don't move a boundary marker [r]
or take the land
that belongs to orphans.
11 God All-Powerful is there
to defend them against you.

– 11 –

12 Listen to instruction
and do your best to learn.

– 12 –

13 Don't fail to correct
your children.
You won't kill them
by being firm,
14 and it may even
save their lives.

– 13 –

15 My children,
if you show good sense,
I will be happy,

---

[p] *marker*: In ancient Israel boundary lines were sacred because all property was a gift from the Lord. See Deuteronomy 19.14. [q] *People . . . eat*: One possible meaning for the difficult Hebrew text. [r] *marker*: See the note at 22.28.

23.5 **MONEY HAS ITS OWN VALUE** We need money to buy and sell in a world of material goods. Yes, money is necessary, but it can be valued too highly. If we live only to gather physical wealth, then we won't be able to enjoy anything that money can't buy. We can't buy love, and we can't buy God's approval. So we need to use our energy for finding and gaining things that can never die, or we end up really poor.

NOTES

16and if you are truthful,
I will really be glad.

– 14 –

17Don't be jealous of sinners,
but always honor the LORD.
18Then you will truly have hope
for the future.

– 15 –

19Listen to me, my children!
Be wise and have enough sense
to follow the right path.
20Don't be a heavy drinker
or stuff yourself with food.
21It will make you feel drowsy,
and you will end up poor
with only rags to wear.

– 16 –

22Pay attention to your father,
and don't neglect your mother
when she grows old.
23Invest in truth and wisdom,
discipline and good sense,
and don't part with them.

24Make your father truly happy
by living right and showing
sound judgment.
25Make your parents proud,
especially your mother.

– 17 –

26My son, pay close attention,
and gladly follow
my example.
27Bad women and unfaithful wives
are like a deep pit—
28they are waiting to attack you
like a gang of robbers
with victim after victim.

– 18 –

29Who is always in trouble?
Who argues and fights?
Who has cuts and bruises?
Whose eyes are red?
30Everyone who stays up late,
having just one more drink.
31Don't even look
at that colorful stuff
bubbling up in the glass!
It goes down so easily,
32but later it bites
like a poisonous snake.
33You will see weird things,
and your mind
will play tricks on you.
34You will feel tossed about
like someone trying to sleep
on a ship in a storm.
35You will be bruised all over,
without even remembering
how it all happened.
And you will lie awake asking,
"When will morning come,
so I can drink some more?"

– 19 –

24 Don't be jealous of crooks
or want to be their friends.
2All they think about
and talk about
is violence and cruelty.

– 20 –

3Use wisdom and understanding
to establish your home;
4let good sense fill the rooms
with priceless treasures.

– 21 –

5Wisdom brings strength,
and knowledge gives power.
6Battles are won
by listening to advice
and making a lot of plans.

– 22 –

7Wisdom is too much for fools!
Their advice is no good.

– 23 –

8No one but troublemakers
think up trouble.
9Everyone hates senseless fools
who think up ways to sin.

– 24 –

10Don't give up and be helpless
in times of trouble.

– 25 –

11Don't fail to rescue those
who are doomed to die.
12Don't say, "I didn't know it!"
God can read your mind.
He watches each of us
and knows our thoughts.
And God will pay us back
for what we do.

– 26 –

13Honey is good for you,
my children,
and it tastes sweet.
14Wisdom is like honey
for your life—
if you find it,
your future is bright.

– 27 –

15Don't be a cruel person
who attacks good people
and hurts their families.
16Even if good people
fall seven times,
they will get back up.
But when trouble strikes
the wicked,
that's the end of them.

– 28 –

17Don't be happy
to see your enemies trip
and fall down.
18The LORD will find out
and be unhappy.
Then he will stop
being angry with them.

– 29 –

19Don't let evil people
worry you
or make you jealous.
20They will soon be gone
like the flame of a lamp
that burns out.

– 30 –

21My children, you must respect
the LORD and the king,
and you must not make friends
with anyone who rebels
against either of them.
22Who knows what sudden disaster
the LORD or a ruler
might bring?

More Sayings That Make Good Sense

23Here are some more sayings
that make good sense:
When you judge,
you must be fair.
24If you let the guilty
go free,
people of all nations
will hate and curse you.
25But if you punish the guilty,
things will go well for you,
and you will prosper.
26Giving an honest answer
is a sign
of true friendship.
27Get your fields ready
and plant your crops
before starting a home.
28Don't accuse anyone
who isn't guilty.
Don't ever tell a lie
29or say to someone,
"I'll get even with you!"

30I once walked by the field
and the vineyard
of a lazy fool.
31Thorns and weeds
were everywhere,
and the stone wall
had fallen down.
32When I saw this,
it taught me a lesson:
33Sleep a little. Doze a little.
Fold your hands
and twiddle your thumbs.
34Suddenly poverty hits you
and everything is gone!

More of Solomon's Wise Sayings

25 Here are more
of Solomon's proverbs.
They were copied by the officials
of King Hezekiah of Judah.
2God is praised
for being mysterious;
rulers are praised
for explaining mysteries.
3Who can fully understand
the thoughts of a ruler?
They reach beyond the sky
and go deep in the earth.

4Silver must be purified
before it can be used
to make something of value.
5Evil people must be removed
before anyone can rule
with justice.

6Don't try to seem important
in the court of a ruler.
7It's better for the ruler
to give you a high position
than for you to be embarrassed
in front of royal officials.
Be sure you are right
8 before you sue someone,
or you might lose your case
and be embarrassed.

9When you and someone else
can't get along,
don't gossip about it.[s]

---

[s]*When . . . it*: Or "Settle a problem privately between you and your neighbor and don't involve others."

Step 10

I need to continue looking inside—admitting when I am wrong.

PROVERBS 24.16

THE GOOD GUY

It was a clean shot with enough power to knock him off his horse. Lying face down in the dirt, the hero seemed to be finished. But when they turned him over to see if he was dead, he fired at them point-blank. Then, standing up, he got back on his horse and rode off into the sunset.

Watching old movies, we know the scenario—the good guy may be down but he is never out. That's how it is with Christians. The Bible says you can't keep a good guy down. When we go to the Lord and admit that we have fallen, he promises to pick us up and send us back out ready to take on the world.

STEP LOOK INSIDE 10

DUST YOURSELF OFF

Have we fallen down again? Instead of getting discouraged with our mouths, our attitudes, or our relapses, we need to start over. We need to get up, brush off the dust, and get on with life. We can continue to make great progress!

To take a "Look Ahead," turn to page 306.

10 Others will find out,
and your reputation
will then be ruined.

11 The right word
at the right time
is like precious gold
set in silver.
12 Listening to good advice
is worth much more
than jewelry made of gold.
13 A messenger you can trust
is just as refreshing
as cool water in summer.
14 Broken promises
are worse than rain clouds
that don't bring rain.
15 Patience and gentle talk
can convince a ruler
and overcome any problem.

16 Eating too much honey
can make you sick.

17 Don't visit friends too often,
or they will get tired of it
and start hating you.
18 Telling lies about friends
is like attacking them
with clubs and swords
and sharp arrows.
19 A friend you can't trust
in times of trouble
is like having a toothache
or a sore foot.
20 Singing to someone
in deep sorrow
is like pouring vinegar
in an open cut.[t]

21 If your enemies are hungry,
give them something to eat.
And if they are thirsty,
give them something
to drink.*
22 This will be the same
as piling burning coals
on their heads.
And the LORD
will reward you.
23 As surely as rain blows in
from the north,
anger is caused
by cruel words.
24 It's better to stay outside
on the roof of your house
than to live inside
with a nagging wife.

25 Good news from far away
refreshes like cold water
when you are thirsty.
26 When a good person gives in
to the wicked,
it's like dumping garbage
in a stream of clear water.
27 Don't eat too much honey
or always want praise.[u]

28 Losing self-control
leaves you as helpless
as a city without a wall.

Don't Be a Fool

26 Expecting snow in summer
and rain in the dry season
makes more sense
than honoring a fool.
2 A curse you don't deserve
will take wings and fly away
like a sparrow or a swallow.
3 Horses and donkeys
must be beaten and bridled—
and so must fools.
4 Don't make a fool of yourself
by answering a fool.*

---

[t] *cut*: One possible meaning for the difficult Hebrew text of verse 20. [u] *or . . . praise*: One possible meaning for the difficult Hebrew text.

25.21 **BE KIND TO ENEMIES** Hundreds of years after these words were written, the apostle Paul quoted them in Romans 12.20. They are words that never really grow old. Our usual reaction is to strike back at our enemies with more unkindness. That's not only wrong in God's sight, it has bad results, too. It only makes the forces of hatred burn hotter; then both sides in the argument lose, and the world becomes that much harder to live in as a result. The world needs a kind face and a gentle word to remind people that God's way is the best way.

26.4 **EVERY REMARK DOESN'T CALL FOR AN ANSWER** It's often clear when someone says a dumb thing. Sometimes the words are meant to be an insult. We only make matters worse by thinking we have to answer back. Yes, some things are better left alone *(continued)*

NOTES

5 But if you answer any fools,
show how foolish they are,
so they won't feel smart.

6 Sending a message by a fool
is like chopping off your foot
and drinking poison.
7 A fool with words of wisdom
is like an athlete
with legs that can't move.[v]
8 Are you going to honor a fool?
Why not shoot a slingshot
with the rock tied tight?
9 A thornbush waved around
in the hand of a drunkard
is no worse than a proverb
in the mouth of a fool.

10 It's no smarter to shoot arrows
at every passerby
than it is to hire a bunch
of worthless nobodies.[w]
11 Dogs return to eat their vomit,
just as fools repeat
their foolishness.
12 There is more hope for a fool
than for someone who says,
"I'm really smart!"

13 Don't be lazy and keep saying,
"There's a lion outside!"
14 A door turns on its hinges,
but a lazy person
just turns over in bed.
15 Some of us are so lazy
that we won't lift a hand
to feed ourselves.
16 A lazy person says,
"I am smarter
than everyone else."

17 It's better to take hold
of a mad dog by the ears
than to take part
in someone else's argument.

18 It's no crazier to shoot
sharp and flaming arrows
19 than to cheat someone and say,
"I was only fooling!"

20 Where there is no fuel
a fire goes out;
where there is no gossip
arguments come to an end.
21 Troublemakers start trouble,
just as sparks and fuel
start a fire.
22 There is nothing so delicious
as the taste of gossip!
It melts in your mouth.

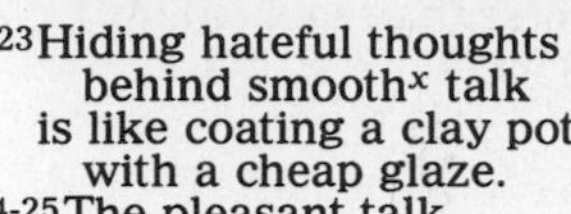

23 Hiding hateful thoughts
behind smooth[x] talk
is like coating a clay pot
with a cheap glaze.
24-25 The pleasant talk
of an enemy
hides more evil plans
than can be counted—
so don't believe a word!
26 Everyone will see through
those evil plans.
27 If you dig a pit,
you will fall in;
if you start a stone rolling,
it will roll back on you.
28 Watch out for anyone
who tells lies and flatters—
they are out to get you.

Don't Brag about Tomorrow

27 Don't brag about tomorrow!
Each day brings
its own surprises.*

---

[v] *with . . . move*: One possible meaning for the difficult Hebrew text. [w] *nobodies*: One possible meaning for the difficult Hebrew text of verse 10. [x] *smooth*: One ancient version; Hebrew "hateful."

(*continued*) without our comment. Then it will often become clear how foolish the remark was to begin with. Silence is an excellent teacher because it gives people time to think about what they have said.

27.1 **TOMORROW IS IN GOD'S HANDS** We have to make plans. If we don't, our lives will be a mess. We need to think ahead so that we know how to finish the work we began in previous days. But we can never be absolutely certain about the future. Today could be all the future we're going to have in this world. At the end of our road of life stands God, and none of us knows for sure how long or short that road will be. Knowing this also makes us aware of how important it is to live today's moments carefully.

NOTES

2 Don't brag about yourself—
let others praise you.
3 Stones and sand are heavy,
but trouble caused by a fool
is a much heavier load.
4 An angry person is dangerous,
but a jealous person
is even worse.

5 A truly good friend
will openly correct you.
6 You can trust a friend
who corrects you,
but kisses from an enemy
are nothing but lies.
7 If you have had enough to eat,
honey doesn't taste good,
but if you are really hungry,
you will eat anything.

8 When you are far from home,
you feel like a bird
without a nest.
9 The sweet smell of incense
can make you feel good,
but true friendship
is better still.[y]
10 Don't desert an old friend
of your family
or visit your relatives
when you are in trouble.
A friend nearby is better
than relatives far away.

11 My child, show good sense!
Then I will be happy
and able to answer anyone
who criticizes me.
12 Be cautious and hide
when you see danger—
don't be stupid and walk
right into trouble.
13 Don't loan money to a stranger
unless you are given something
to guarantee payment.
14 A loud greeting
early in the morning
is the same as a curse.
15 The steady dripping of rain
and the nagging of a wife
are one and the same.
16 It's easier to catch the wind
or hold olive oil in your hand
than to stop a nagging wife.

17 Just as iron sharpens iron,
friends sharpen the minds
of each other.
18 Take care of a tree,
and you will eat its fruit;
look after your master,
and you will be praised.
19 You see your face in a mirror
and your thoughts
in the minds of others.
20 Death and the grave
are never satisfied,
and neither are we.
21 Gold and silver are tested
in a red-hot furnace,
but we are tested by praise.
22 No matter how hard
you beat a fool,
you can't pound out
the foolishness.

23 You should take good care
of your sheep and goats,
24 because wealth and honor
don't last forever.
25 After the hay is cut
and the new growth appears
and the harvest is over,
26 you can sell lambs and goats
to buy clothes and land.
27 From the milk of the goats,
you can make enough cheese
to feed your family
and all your servants.

The Law of God Makes Sense

28 Wicked people run away
when no one chases them,
but those who live right
are as brave as lions.
2 In time of civil war
there are many leaders,
but a sensible leader
restores law and order.[z]
3 When someone poor takes over
and mistreats the poor,
it's like a heavy rain
destroying the crops.

4 Lawbreakers praise criminals,
but law-abiding citizens
always oppose them.
5 Criminals don't know
what justice means,
but all who respect the LORD
understand it completely.
6 It's better to be poor
and live right,
than to be rich
and dishonest.

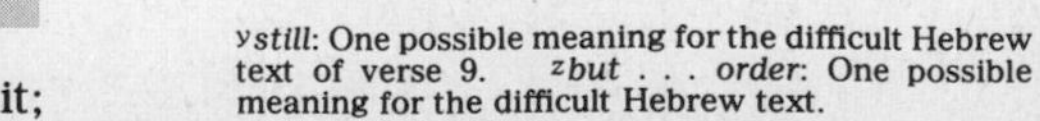
[y] *still*: One possible meaning for the difficult Hebrew text of verse 9. [z] *but . . . order*: One possible meaning for the difficult Hebrew text.

INTERNAL CONTROL

Control Tower: This is the Internal Control Tower to Adam Loyd's conscience. Over . . .

Adam Loyd: Can't you see I'm busy? What is it this time?

Control Tower: The cargo you are carrying must be unloaded on Runway B, as in "Be honest." You are currently headed for Runway A, as in "I am going to tell another lie." Get back on course. You are headed for disaster! Over . . .

Adam Loyd: I can't tell my folks I got kicked off the team for cheating! They'll hit the roof, especially my dad!

Control Tower: Mr. Loyd, you are on the wrong course. I repeat, the wrong course. Correct your position immediately or a crash is unavoidable. Over . . .

Adam Loyd: Okay! Okay! I'll tell the truth if you will tune out and leave me alone.

Control Tower: Radar indicates your conscience has brought you back on course. Disaster has been averted. Move ahead. This is the Internal Control Tower. Over and out . . .

TUNING OUT

One of the benefits of giving God control is that he sends the Holy Spirit to help keep us on track, to keep us under control. The Holy Spirit, often speaking through our consciences, will influence us to do what is right before we make a mistake. It pays to tune in.

To take a "Look Back" at a man who discovered the importance of telling the truth regardless of the outcome, turn to page 178.

7It makes good sense
to obey the Law of God,
but you disgrace your parents
if you make friends
with worthless nobodies.
8If you make money by charging
high interest rates,
you will lose it all to someone
who cares for the poor.
9God cannot stand the prayers
of anyone who disobeys
his Law.*
10By leading good people to sin,
you dig a pit for yourself,
but all who live right
will have a bright future.

11The rich think highly
of themselves,
but anyone poor and sensible
sees right through them.
12When an honest person wins,
it's time to celebrate;
when crooks are in control,
it's best to hide.

13If you don't confess your sins,
you will be a failure.
But God will be merciful
if you confess your sins
and give them up.
14The LORD blesses everyone
who is afraid to do evil,
but if you are cruel,
you will end up in trouble.

15A ruler who mistreats the poor
is like a roaring lion
or a bear hunting for food.
16A heartless leader is a fool,
but anyone who refuses
to get rich by cheating others
will live a long time.
17Don't give help to murderers!
Make them stay on the run
for as long as they live.[a]

18Honesty will keep you safe,
but everyone who is crooked
will suddenly fall.

19Work hard, and you will have
a lot of food;
waste time, and you will have
a lot of trouble.

20God blesses his loyal people,
but punishes all who want
to get rich quick.
21It isn't right to be unfair,
but some people can be bribed
with only a piece of bread.
22Don't be selfish
and eager to get rich—
you will end up worse off
than you can imagine.

23Honest correction
is appreciated
more than flattery.

24If you cheat your parents
and don't think it's wrong,
you are a common thief.
25Selfish people cause trouble,
but you will live a full life
if you trust the LORD.
26Only fools would trust
what they alone think,
but if you live by wisdom,
you will do all right.

27Giving to the poor
will keep you from poverty,
but if you close your eyes
to their needs,
everyone will curse you.
28When crooks are in control,
everyone tries to hide,
but when they lose power,
good people are everywhere.

Use Good Sense

29 If you keep being stubborn
after many warnings,

[a]live: One possible meaning for the difficult Hebrew text of verse 17.

28.9 **WORDS DON'T IMPRESS GOD** Jesus said that some people in his time loved to be heard making long prayers. But he also said their unloving works proved their prayers were just idle words. Let's be careful not to pretend to be something we aren't. Everyone needs to be honest with God, because God will always be honest with us, and that can be a very rude awakening.

NOTES

Step 1

I admit I cannot be successful on my own . . . I need help, daily.

PROVERBS 28.26

WISE UP

"Everyone does it."
"I'm just a normal teenager."
"It's my life."
"Don't worry about me."
"You're going to ruin my life."
"I'm old enough to make my own decisions."
"Stop treating me like a baby!"
"Don't get so uptight. Lighten up."
"I'm not hurting anybody."
"What do you expect from me?"

To say—or even think—things like this is normal. We all think we can handle things on our own, but nobody is smart enough to make it all alone. We are just not put together that way. The Bible says that one's heart is not to be trusted. That is why we need to bounce big decisions off people we know and trust. Parents can help. Teachers can help too. But the best place to start is with the Lord and his Word.

A WORD TO THE WISE

He who trusts in his own heart is a fool. Whoever walks wisely will be delivered.

To take a "Look Ahead," turn to page 478.

you will suddenly discover
you have gone too far.
2 When justice rules a nation,
everyone is glad;
when injustice rules,
everyone groans.
3 If you love wisdom
your parents will be glad,
but chasing after bad women
will cost you everything.
4 An honest ruler
makes the nation strong;
a ruler who takes bribes
will bring it to ruin.

5 Flattery is nothing less
than setting a trap.
6 Your sins will catch you,
but everyone who lives right
will sing and celebrate.
7 The wicked don't care
about the rights of the poor,
but good people do.
8 Sneering at others is a spark
that sets a city on fire;
using good sense can put out
the flames of anger.

9 Be wise and don't sue a fool.
You won't get satisfaction,
because all the fool will do
is sneer and shout.
10 A murderer hates everyone
who is honest
and lives right.[b]
11 Don't be a fool
and quickly lose your temper—
be sensible and patient.

12 A ruler who listens to lies
will have corrupt officials.
13 The poor and all who abuse them
must each depend on God
for light.
14 Kings who are fair to the poor
will rule forever.

15 Correct your children,
and they will be wise;
children out of control
disgrace their mothers.
16 Crime increases
when crooks are in power,
but law-abiding citizens
will see them fall.
17 If you correct your children,
they will bring you peace
and happiness.

18 Without guidance from God
law and order disappear,
but God blesses everyone
who obeys his Law.*
19 Even when servants are smart,
it takes more than words
to make them obey.
20 There is more hope for a fool
than for someone who speaks
without thinking.
21 Slaves that you treat kindly
from their childhood
will cause you sorrow.[c]
22 A person with a quick temper
stirs up arguments
and commits a lot of sins.

23 Too much pride brings disgrace;
humility leads to honor.
24 If you take part in a crime
you are your worst enemy,
because even under oath
you can't tell the truth.
25 Don't fall into the trap
of being a coward—
trust the LORD,
and you will be safe.
26 Many try to make friends
with a ruler,

---

[b] *and lives right*: Or "and those who live right are friends of honest people." [c] *will . . . sorrow*: One possible meaning for the difficult Hebrew text.

29.18

WITHOUT GOD THERE IS NO LAW Is crime increasing in our land? Nea everyone would agree it is. At the same time are people looking to God for guidance of their lives? No, it is clear that there is widespread disrespect for God, for his name, and for his laws. When people look no higher than themselves for guidance, they are like people of water trying to climb out of the water on ladders of water. Without God we have no truth to stand on.

NOTES

but justice comes
from the LORD.
27 Good people and criminals
can't stand each other.

The Sayings of Agur

30 These are the sayings
and the message
of Agur son of Jakeh.
Someone cries out to God,
"I am completely worn out!
How can I last?[d]
2 I am far too stupid
to be considered human.
3 I never was wise,
and I don't understand
what God is like.

4 Has anyone gone up to heaven
and come back down?
Has anyone grabbed hold
of the wind?
Has anyone wrapped up the sea
or marked out boundaries
for the earth?
If you know of any
who have done such things,
then tell me their names
and their children's names.

5 Everything God says is true—
and it's a shield for all
who come to him for safety.
6 Don't change what God has said!
He will correct you and show
that you are a liar.

7 There are two things, Lord,
I want you to do for me
before I die:
8 Make me absolutely honest
and don't let me be too poor
or too rich.
Give me just what I need.
9 If I have too much to eat,
I might forget about you;
if I don't have enough,
I might steal
and disgrace your name.

10 Don't tell a slave owner
something bad about one
of the slaves.
That slave will curse you,
and you will be in trouble.

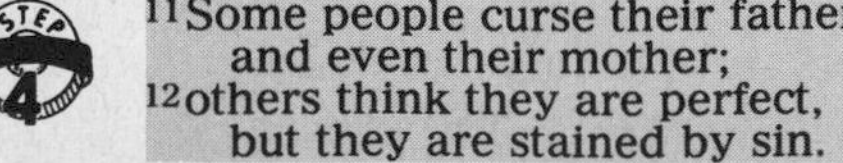

11 Some people curse their father
and even their mother;
12 others think they are perfect,
but they are stained by sin.
13 Some people are stuck-up
and act like snobs;
14 others are so greedy
that they gobble down
the poor and homeless.

15 Greed[e] has twins,
each named "Give me!"
There are three or four things
that are never satisfied:
16 The world of the dead
and a childless wife,
the thirsty earth
and a flaming fire.

17 Don't make fun of your father
or disobey your mother—
crows will peck out your eyes,
and buzzards will eat
the rest of you.

18 There are three or four things
I cannot understand:
19 How eagles fly so high
or snakes crawl on rocks,
how ships sail the ocean
or people fall in love.

20 An unfaithful wife says,
"Sleeping with another man
is as natural as eating."

21 There are three or four things
that make the earth tremble
and are unbearable:
22 A slave who becomes king,
a fool who eats too much,
23 a hateful woman
who finds a husband,
and a slave who takes the place
of the woman who owns her.

24 On this earth four things
are small but very wise:
25 Ants, who seem to be feeble,
but store up food
all summer long;
26 badgers, who seem to be weak,
but live among the rocks;
27 locusts, who have no king,
but march like an army;
28 lizards,[f] which can be caught
in your hand,
but sneak into palaces.

---

[d] *last*: One possible meaning for the difficult Hebrew text of verse 1. [e] *Greed*: Or "A leech." [f] *lizards*: Or "spiders."

29 Three or four creatures
really strut around:
30 Those fearless lions
who rule the jungle,
31 those proud roosters,
those mountain goats,
and those rulers
who have no enemies.[g]

32 If you are foolishly bragging
or planning something evil,
then stop it now!
33 If you churn milk
you get butter;
if you pound on your nose,
you get blood—
and if you stay angry,
you get in trouble.

What King Lemuel's Mother Taught Him

31 These are the sayings
that King Lemuel of Massa
was taught by his mother.
2 My son Lemuel, you were born
in answer to my prayers,
so listen carefully.
3 Don't waste your life
chasing after women!
This has ruined many kings.

4 Kings and leaders
should not get drunk
or even want to drink.
5 Drinking makes you forget
your responsibilities,
and you mistreat the poor.
6 Beer and wine are only
for the dying or for those
who have lost all hope.
7 Let them drink and forget
how poor and miserable
they feel.
8 But you must defend
those who are helpless
and have no hope.
9 Be fair and give justice
to the poor and homeless.

In Praise of a Good Wife

10 A truly good wife
is the most precious treasure
a man can find!*
11 Her husband depends on her,
and she never
lets him down.
12 She is good to him
every day of her life,
13 and with her own hands
she gladly makes clothes.

14 She is like a sailing ship
that brings food
from across the sea.
15 She gets up before daylight
to prepare food for her family
and for her servants.[h]
16 She knows how to buy land
and how to plant a vineyard,
17 and she always works hard.
18 She knows when to buy or sell,
and she stays busy
until late at night.
19 She spins her own cloth,
20 and she helps the poor
and the needy.
21 Her family has warm clothing,
and so she doesn't worry
when it snows.
22 She does her own sewing,
and everything she wears
is beautiful.

---

[g] *enemies*: One possible meaning for the difficult Hebrew text of verse 31. [h] *and . . . servants*: Or "and to tell her servants what to do."

31.10

MAKE A GOOD MARRIAGE Too many people rush into marriage without stopping to think what it will mean: having the close company of that person for a lifetime! That can be a great blessing or a dreadful curse. It's a beautiful thing to have a spouse who is constantly faithful and loving, and there are such people. But to have a good marriage partner, you must first be a good partner yourself. Marriage means giving as well as taking. If we're selfish and ungiving, we'll be disappointed and brokenhearted at last. But if we're always thinking of how to make our husband or wife happy, then we ourselves will be happy too.

NOTES

23Her husband is a well-known
and respected leader
in the city.
24She makes clothes to sell
to the shop owners.
25She is strong and graceful,[i]
as well as cheerful
about the future.
26Her words are sensible,
and her advice
is thoughtful.
27She takes good care
of her family
and is never lazy.
28Her children praise her,
and with great pride
her husband says,
29"There are many good women,
but you are the best!"

30Charm can be deceiving,
and beauty fades away,
but a woman
who honors the LORD
deserves to be praised.
31Show her respect—
praise her in public
for what she has done.

---

[i]*She . . . graceful*: Or "The clothes she makes are attractive and of good quality."

Word List

Aaron The brother of Moses. Only he and his descendants were to serve as priests and offer sacrifices for the people of Israel.

Abel The second son of Adam and Eve and the younger brother of Cain, who killed him, after God accepted Abel's offering and refused Cain's.

Abijah A descendant of Aaron. King David divided the priests into twenty-four groups, and Abijah was head of the eighth group.

Abraham The husband of Sarah and the father of Isaac. God promised Abraham that he would be a blessing to everyone on earth, because Abraham had faith in him.

Adam The first man and the husband of Eve.

Agrippa (1) Herod Agrippa was king of Judea A.D. 41–44 and mistreated Christians (Acts 12.1–5). (2) Agrippa II was the son of Herod Agrippa and ruled Judea A.D. 44–53. He and his sister Bernice listened to Paul defend himself (Acts 25.13–26,32).

aloes A sweet-smelling spice that was mixed with myrrh and used as a perfume.

amen A Hebrew word used after a prayer or a blessing and meaning, "Let it be that way."

ancestor Someone born one or more generations earlier in a family line, such as a grandparent or great-grandparent.

angel A supernatural being who tells God's messages or protects God's people.

Antipas The father of Herod the Great and ruler of Judea 55–43 B.C. He was also known as Antipater.

apostle A person chosen by Christ to take his message to others.

Aramaic A language closely related to Hebrew. It was spoken by many Jews including Jesus during New Testament times.

Asia A Roman province in what is today western Turkey.

Augustus This is the title meaning "honored" that the Romans gave to Octavian when he began ruling the Roman world in 27 B.C. He was Emperor when Jesus was born (Luke 2.1).

barley A grain something like wheat and used to make bread.

Cain The first son of Adam and Eve and the brother of Abel.

Christ A Greek word meaning "the Chosen One" and used to translate the Hebrew word "Messiah." It is used in the New Testament both as a title and a name for Jesus.

circumcise To cut off the foreskin from the male organ. This is done for Jewish boys as part of a religious ceremony eight days after they are born to show that they belong to God's people. God's command to Abraham (Genesis 17.9–14) was to circumcise all males on the eighth day. Jesus' circumcision on the eighth day is reported in Luke 2.21.

citizen A person who is given special rights and privileges by a nation or state. In return, a citizen was expected to be loyal to that nation or state.

commandments God's rules for his people to live by.

council A leading group of Jewish men who were allowed by the Roman government to meet and make certain decisions for their people.

cumin A plant with small seeds used for seasoning food.

David The most famous ancestor of the Jewish people and the most powerful king Israel ever had. They hoped that one of his descendants would always be their king.

Day of Atonement The one day each year (the tenth day after the Jewish new year's day in the fall) when the high priest went into the most holy part of the temple and sprinkled some of the blood of a sacrificed bull on the sacred chest. This was done so that the people's sins would be forgiven. This holy day is called Yom Kippur in Hebrew.

demons and **evil spirits** Supernatural beings that do harmful things to people and sometimes cause them to do bad things. In the New Testament they are sometimes called "unclean spirits," because people under their power were thought to be unclean and unfit to worship God.

descendant Someone born one or more generations later in a family line, such as a grandchild or great-grandchild.

devil The chief of the demons and evil spirits, also known as "Satan."

disciple Someone who was a follower of Jesus and learned from him.

elders Men whose age and wisdom made them respected leaders.

Elijah A prophet who spoke for God in the ninth century B.C. Many Jews in later centuries thought Elijah would return to get things ready for the coming of the Lord.

Emperor The ruler who lived in the city of Rome and governed all the land around the Mediterranean Sea.

Epicureans People who followed the teachings of a man named Epicurus, who taught that happiness should be a person's main goal in life.

eternal life Life that is the gift of God and never ends.

evil spirits See "demons."

exile The time in Jewish history (597–539 B.C.) when the Babylonians took away most of the people of Jerusalem and Judah as prisoners of war and made them live in Babylonia.

Feast of Thin Bread The days after Passover when Jews eat a kind of thin, flat bread made without yeast to remember how God freed the people of Israel from slavery in Egypt and gave them a fresh start.

Felix The Roman governor of Judea A.D. 52–60, who listened to Paul speak and kept him in jail.

Festival of Shelters This festival celebrates the period of forty years when the people of Israel walked through the desert and lived in small shelters. This happy celebration takes place each year in connection with the fall harvest season. Its name in Hebrew is Sukkoth.

Festus The Roman governor after Felix, who sent Paul to stand trial in Rome.

Gentile Someone who is not a Jew.

God's kingdom God's rule over people, both in this life and in the next.

God's Law God's rules for his people to live by. They are found in the Old Testament, especially in the first five books.

God's tent The tent where the people of Israel worshiped God before the temple was built.

Greek The language in which the New Testament was written.

Hagar A personal servant of Sarah, the wife of Abraham. When Sarah could not have any children, she followed the ancient custom of letting her husband have a child by Hagar, her servant woman. The boy's name was Ishmael.

Hebrew The language used by the people of Israel and for the writing of most of the Old Testament.

Hermes The Greek god of skillful speaking and the messenger of the other Greek gods.

Herod (1) Herod the Great was the king of all Palestine 37–4 B.C. He ruled Judea at the time Jesus was born. (2) Herod Antipas was the son of Herod the Great and the ruler of Galilee 4 B.C.–A.D. 39, during the time of John the Baptist and Jesus. (3) Herod Agrippa I, the grandson of Herod the Great, ruled Palestine A.D. 41–44.

high priest See "priest."

Holy One A name for the Savior that God had promised to send. See "Savior."

incense A material that makes a sweet smell when burned and is used in the worship of God.

Isaac The son of Abraham and Sarah and the father of Esau and Jacob. Abraham, Isaac, and Jacob are three of the most famous ancestors of the Jewish people.

Isaiah A prophet from Jerusalem, who lived during the eighth century B.C. He served as a prophet during the rule of four different kings of Judah, between the years 740–700 B.C.

Jacob The son of Isaac and Rebecca. He is better known by the name Israel, which God gave to him. See "Isaac."

judges Leaders chosen by the Lord for the people of Israel after the time of Joshua and before the time of the kings.

Law and the Prophets The sacred writings of the Jews in Jesus' day (the first two of the three sections of the Old Testament).

Law of Moses and **Law of the Lord** Usually refers to the first five books of the Old Testament, but sometimes to the entire Old Testament.

Levite A member of the tribe of Levi, from which priests were chosen. Men from this tribe who were not priests helped with the work in the temple.

Messiah A Hebrew word meaning "the Chosen One." See "Christ."

mint A garden plant used for seasoning and medicine.

Moses The leader of the people of Israel when God rescued them from Egypt.

myrrh A valuable sweet-smelling powder used in perfume.

Nazarenes A name that was sometimes used for the followers of Jesus, who came from the small town of Nazareth.

Noah When God destroyed the world by a flood, Noah and his family were kept safe in a big boat that God had told him to build.

paradise The place where God's people go when they die, often understood as another name for heaven.

Passover A day each year in the spring when Jews celebrate the time God rescued them from slavery in Egypt.

Pentecost A Jewish festival fifty days after Passover to celebrate the wheat harvest.

Pharisees A large group of Jews who thought they could best serve God by strictly obeying the laws of the Old Testament as well as their own teachings.

pit or **deep pit** The place of punishment for demons and evil spirits.

priest A man who led the worship in the temple and offered sacrifices. Some of the more important priests were called "chief priests," and the most important priest was called the "high priest."

Promised One A title for the Savior that God promised to send. See "Savior."

prophesy See "prophet."

prophet Someone who speaks God's message and tells what will happen in the future. To speak as a prophet is thus to "prophesy."

rue A garden plant used for seasoning and medicine.

Sabbath The seventh day of the week when Jews worship and do not work, in obedience to the commandment.

Sadducees A small and powerful group of Jews who were closely connected with the high priests and who accepted only the first five books of the Old Testament as their Bible. They also did not believe in life after death.

Samaria A district between Judea and Galilee. The people of Samaria, called Samaritans, worshiped God differently from the Jews and did not get along with them.

Sarah The wife of Abraham and the mother of Isaac. When she was very old, God promised her that she would have a son.

Satan See "devil."

save To rescue people from the power of evil, to give them new life, and to place them under God's care. See "Savior."

Savior The one who rescues people from the power of evil, gives them new life, and places them under God's care. See "save."

Scriptures The sacred writings known as the Old Testament. These were first written in Hebrew and Aramaic, then translated into Greek about two centuries before the birth of Jesus. This Greek translation, known as the Septuagint, was used both by Jews and Christians in the first century.

Son of Man A name often used by Jesus to refer to himself. It is also found in the book of Daniel and refers to the one to whom God has given the power to rule.

Stoics Followers of a man named Zeno, who believed that nature was controlled by the gods and who taught that people should learn self-control.

taxes and **tax collectors** Special fees collected by rulers, usually part of the value of a citizen's crops, property, or income. There were also market taxes to be paid, and customs taxes were collected at ports and border crossings. The wealthy Zacchaeus (Luke 19.1–10) was a tax collector who collected taxes at a border crossing near Jericho. Jews hired by the Roman government to collect taxes from other Jews were hated by their own people.

temple A building used as a place of worship. The Jewish temple was in Jerusalem.

Temple Festival In 165 B.C. the Jewish people recaptured the Jerusalem temple from their enemies and made it fit for worship again. They celebrate this event in December of each year by a festival which they call "dedication" (Hanukkah). In the New Testament it is mentioned only in John 10.22.

Theophilus The name means "someone God loves" and is found only in Luke 1.3 and Acts 1.1. Nothing else is known about him.

Way In the book of Acts the Christian religion is sometimes called "the Way" or "the Way of the Lord" or "God's Way."

Zeus The chief god of the Greeks.